THE OXFORD HANDBOOK OF

THE SOCIOLOGY OF DISABILITY

THE OXFORD HANDBOOK OF

THE SOCIOLOGY OF DISABILITY

Edited by

ROBYN LEWIS BROWN,
MICHELLE MAROTO,

and

DAVID PETTINICCHIO

OXFORD
UNIVERSITY PRESS

OXFORD
UNIVERSITY PRESS

Oxford University Press is a department of the University of Oxford. It furthers
the University's objective of excellence in research, scholarship, and education
by publishing worldwide. Oxford is a registered trade mark of Oxford University
Press in the UK and certain other countries.

Published in the United States of America by Oxford University Press
198 Madison Avenue, New York, NY 10016, United States of America.

© Oxford University Press 2023

Library of Congress Cataloging-in-Publication Data
Names: Brown, Robyn Lewis, editor. | Maroto, Michelle, editor. |
Pettinicchio, David, editor.
Title: The Oxford handbook of the sociology of disability / edited by Robyn
Lewis Brown, Michelle Maroto and David Pettinicchio.
Description: New York, NY : Oxford University Press, [2023] |
Series: Oxford handbooks series | Includes bibliographical references and index. |
Identifiers: LCCN 2022053496 (print) | LCCN 2022053497 (ebook) |
ISBN 9780190093167 (hardback) | ISBN 9780190093174 (online resource) |
ISBN 9780190093198 (epub)
Subjects: LCSH: Sociology of disability. | People with disabilities—Social conditions.
Classification: LCC HV1568 .O95 2023 (print) | LCC HV1568 (ebook) |
DDC 362.4—dc23/eng/20221108
LC record available at https://lccn.loc.gov/2022053496
LC ebook record available at https://lccn.loc.gov/2022053497

DOI: 10.1093/oxfordhb/9780190093167.001.0001

Printed by Integrated Books International, United States of America

Contents

SECTION II: EXPERIENCING DISABILITY ACROSS THE LIFE COURSE

SECTION III: DISABILITY, POLITICS, AND THE LAW

About the Editors

Robyn Lewis Brown is a quantitative sociologist who specializes in the study of stigma and discrimination among women and people with disabilities. She has also written extensively about differential responses to collective trauma or macro-level stressors including those associated with the Great Recession, the 9/11 attacks, and, more recently, the COVID-19 pandemic. She has published more than 50 articles and chapters on these topics and is currently supported by a Switzer Fellowship from NIDILRR. She is an Associate Professor of Sociology at the University of Kentucky, where she also serves as Director of the Health, Society, and Populations Program. Her work has been featured in international and US-centric media outlets.

Michelle Maroto is an Associate Professor of Sociology at the University of Alberta. Her research interests include social stratification, gender and family, race and ethnicity, labor and credit markets, and disability studies. Her recent projects address the many dimensions of wealth inequality, the complicated dynamics behind social class in Canada, and economic outcomes for people with different types of disabilities during the pandemic.

David Pettinicchio is an Associate Professor of Sociology and affiliated faculty in the Munk School of Global Affairs and Public Policy at the University of Toronto. His research lies at the intersection of politics and inequality, with a focus on disability as a global axis of exclusion and marginalization. He published his book, *Politics of Empowerment*, with Stanford University Press and recently edited Volume 28 of *Research in Political Sociology* (Emerald). He has published in numerous peer-reviewed journals, and his work has also been featured in popular publications including the *Washington Post*, *USA Today*, the *Huffington Post*, the *Globe and Mail*, and the *Toronto Star*.

LIST OF CONTRIBUTORS

Meryl Alper, Associate Professor, Department of Communication Studies, Northeastern University

Barbara M. Altman, Disability Statistics Consultant, Retired, National Center for Health Statistics

Aizan Sofia Amin, Senior Lecturer, Centre for Research in Psychology and Human Well-being, Faculty of Social Sciences and Humanities, University of Kebangsaan Malaysia

Fabricio E. Balcazar, Professor, Disability and Human Development, University of Illinois at Chicago

Anthony R. Bardo, Assistant Professor, Department of Sociology, University of Kentucky

Sharon N. Barnartt, Professor Emerita, Department of Sociology, Gallaudet University

Evan Batty, Research Project Manager, Department of Sociology, University of Kentucky

Jennifer D. Brooks, Research Associate, Yang-Tan Institute on Employment and Disability, Cornell University

Susanne M. Bruyère, Professor and Academic Director, Yang-Tan Institute on Employment and Disability, Industrial and Labor Relations School, Cornell University

Anne Bryden, Associate Professor, MetroHealth Center for Rehabilitation Research, Department of Physical Medicine and Rehabilitation, Case Western Reserve University School of Medicine

Allison C. Carey, Professor of Sociology, Chair of the Department of Sociology and Anthropology, Director of the Master of Science in Organizational Development and Leadership, Department of Sociology and Anthropology, Shippensburg University

Vera Chouinard, Professor, School of Earth Environment and Society, McMaster University

Sabrina Cordon, Indiana University–Purdue University

Patrick W. Corrigan, Distinguished Professor, Department of Psychology, Illinois Institute of Technology

Heather Dillaway, Professor of Sociology and Dean of the College of Arts and Sciences, Illinois State University

Justine E. Egner, Customer/Product Development Partner, Innovation, Edge - Gundersen Health System

Marta Elliott, Professor, Department of Sociology, University of Nevada, Reno

April D. Fernandes, Assistant Professor, Department of Sociology and Anthropology, North Carolina State University

Jordan Foster, Sessional Instructor, Department of Sociology, University of Toronto

Heather Fritz, Associate Professor and Founding Director, School of Occupational Therapy, Pacific Northwest University of Health Sciences

Brian Gran, Professor of Sociology, Law, and Applied Social Sciences, Case Western Reserve University

Shaun Grech, Director of The Critical Institute, Fellow at Manchester Metropolitan University, Christian Blind Mission and University of Cape Town

Stacy Hewitt, Specialist Teacher and Assessor, Inclusive Support, Oxford Brookes University

Bill Hughes, Professor, Department of Sociology, Glasgow Caledonian University

Patrick Kermit, Professor, Department of Mental Health, Norwegian University of Science and Technology (NTNU) and NTNU Social Research

Douglas L. Kruse, Distinguished Professor, School of Management and Labor Relations, Rutgers University

Victoria Kurdyla, Assistant Professor, Department of Sociology and Criminal Justice, University of North Carolina at Pembroke

Scott D. Landes, Associate Professor, Department of Sociology, Syracuse University

Kenzie Latham-Mintus, Associate Professor, Department of Sociology, Indiana University–Purdue University Indianapolis

Andrew S. London, Associate Dean and Professor, Maxwell School of Citizenship and Public Affairs Dean's Office and Department of Sociology, Syracuse University

Catherine Lysack, Professor, Department of Health Care Sciences, Wayne State University

Brianna Marzolf, Resident, Family Medicine, University of Michigan

Alymamah Mashrah, Strategic Partnerships & Medicaid, Michigan Public Health Institute

Laura Mauldin, Associate Professor, Women's, Gender and Sexuality Studies and Human Development and Family Sciences, University of Connecticut

Terje Olsen, Research Director, Fafo Institute for Labour and Social Research, Norway

Nomi Ostrander, Associate Professor, Department of Social Work, University of Minnesota-Duluth

Paula Campos Pinto, Associate Professor and Coordinator of the Disability and Human Rights Observatory, School of Social and Political Sciences, University of Lisboa

Kate Prendella, Doctoral Candidate, Department of Media Studies, School of Communication and Information, Rutgers University

Michael Prince, Landsdowne Professor of Social Policy, Human and Social Development, University of Victoria

Norma Ramirez, Student, University of Illinois of Chicago

Jordan C. Reuter, Doctoral Candidate, Interdisciplinary Social Psychology Ph.D. Program, University of Nevada, Reno

Matthew Saleh, Senior Research Associate and Lecturer, Industrial and Labor Relations School, Cornell University

Lisa Schur, Professor, Department of Labor Studies and Employment Relations, Rutgers University

Richard Scotch, Professor of Sociology and Public Policy and Political Economy, School of Economic, Political, and Policy Sciences, University of Texas at Dallas

Tom Shakespeare, Professor of Disability Research, Department of Population Health, London School of Hygiene and Tropical Medicine

Carrie Shandra, Associate Professor of Sociology, State University of New York at Stony Brook

Lindsay Sheehan, Assistant Professor, Department of Psychology, Illinois Institute of Psychology

Dara Shifrer, Associate Professor, Department of Sociology, Portland State University

Kim Shuey, Professor, Department of Sociology, The University of Western Ontario

J. Dalton Stevens, Doctoral Candidate, Department of Sociology, Syracuse University

Justin D. Strong, Doctoral Candidate, Department of Criminology, Law and Society, University of California-Irvine

Kara Sutton, Lecturer, Department of Sociology, Southern Methodist University

Bryan L. Sykes, Associate Professor, Department of Criminology, Law and Society, University of California-Irvine

Wassim Tarraf, Associate Professor, Department Occupational Therapy, Wayne State University

Sally Tomlinson, Emeritus Professor of Education, Goldsmiths, University of London and Honorary Research Fellow, Department of Education, University of Oxford

Minerva Rivas Velarde, Team Leader and Director of the Europe and Central Asia of the Disability Data Initiative Hub, Department of Radiology and Medical Informatics and iEH2 – Institute for Ethics, History, and the Humanities, University of Geneva

Ashley Vowels, Doctoral Candidate, Department of Sociology, University of Kentucky

Nicholas Watson, Chair of Disability Research, School of Social and Political Sciences, University of Glasgow

Andrea Willson, Associate Professor, Department of Sociology, The University of Western Ontario

Janet M. Wilmoth, Professor and Chair, Department of Sociology, Syracuse University

INTRODUCTION

CHAPTER 1

....

INTRODUCTION

A New Direction in the Sociology of Disability

....

ROBYN LEWIS BROWN, MICHELLE MAROTO, AND
DAVID PETTINICCHIO

INTRODUCTION

....

THE *Oxford Handbook of the Sociology of Disability* brings together, for the first time, the wide range and depth of sociological theory and research on disability. This uniquely sociological perspective—presented by a variety of experts on intersecting social, economic, political, and cultural dimensions of disability—complements the field of disability studies and other disability scholarship. Across disciplinary and geographic boundaries, the editors and authors share a commitment to raising awareness about the concerns and experiences of people with disabilities, who compose a diverse group that includes at least 15% of the world population. But, we also have in common our appreciation of the institutional practices, social policies, and cultural norms that shape and are shaped by lived experience.

A key objective of this handbook was to bring disability further into the discipline of sociology. Doing so allowed contributors to address central sociological questions about the links between individuals, structures, and cultures, and the ways in which societies are organized, and to provide critical insights on continuity and change in social structures. All of this is at the heart of a *sociology of disability*.

Disability studies continues to challenge sociology to explore disability as a structural and cultural axis of inequality, drawing links with other axes, including gender. In turn, because the discipline of sociology is especially well suited in providing useful theoretical frameworks and a host of empirical tools, it extends social scientific insight on how inequality is (re)produced. But while these mutually beneficial relationships abound, they remain underexplored. Sociologists continue to ignore disability across its subspecialties, but perhaps most troubling is disability's absence in studies of stratification, inequality, and discrimination. As a result, the dialogue between disability studies and sociology is not as rich as it could be. This may not be all of sociology's fault, nor is it especially unique to this area of study, but it is an underdeveloped area in which theoretical and methodological attention could lead to lasting social change.

Sociology is a large and constantly evolving discipline that, like the education system more generally, has been shaped by the very institutions it seeks to understand. Although sociology is well poised—perhaps more so than any other discipline—to use knowledge to transform itself and the world around it, the discipline is often stifled by constraints promoting the status quo. One consequence is that scholars working at the margins who potentially could inject new ideas into extant fields risk marginalization themselves. This handbook, therefore, seeks to provide an inroad for new sociologists of disability, those who want to challenge the discipline of sociology and are looking for a path forward.

While acknowledging the growth of disability studies, we sought to address disability-related research questions through a distinctly sociological lens that still speaks to perspectives and traditions across different fields, as these in turn intersect or connect with sociological insights. The 38 chapters in this handbook, organized into three major sections, provide an assessment of where we have been, where we are now, and where we must go with research on and in the sociology of disability.

Section 1: Understanding, Theorizing, and Measuring Disability

Divided into three parts, Section 1 of the handbook focuses on understanding, theorizing, and measuring disability. As many authors indicate, this is not a simple task. The history of a sociology of disability is rife with misunderstandings and poor theorizing, often driven by individualist and medical models that emphasize deficits and deviance. Although the social model of disability has drastically improved upon these understandings of disability, it also comes with limitations, necessitating a stronger model that incorporates the body and impairment. Chapters in Part 1 of the handbook address these issues, while orienting readers to key themes woven throughout the rest of the volume.

In Chapter 2, Shakespeare and Watson begin the handbook with the question, "What are the roles of impairment and disablement in the lives of disabled people and the construction of the disability experience?" In addressing this question, they highlight the complexity of disability while promoting a model built on critical realism. Although disability must be brought into conversations about stratification and discussed in conjunction with other status characteristics like race, class, and gender, it is also unique.

The next chapter furthers this conversation and centers the question, "How has disability been conceptualized and discussed in sociology?" The answer, unfortunately, is that disability has often been overlooked and misunderstood within sociology. As Mauldin highlights in Chapter 3, disability has primarily been located in subareas of medical sociology and the body and embodiment, and within feminist sociological scholarship. As a result, broader sociology has failed to understand the social category of disability and the processes of ableism. Mauldin ends with a powerful call to sociologists to make disability a central axis of inequality.

In Chapter 4, Chouinard outlines how feminists have worked to challenge common understandings of disability by recognizing increasing diversity in bodies and minds, considering how multiple social relations of power and oppression are implicated in disabled people's lives, and emphasizing the importance of a global geographic context. Throughout this chapter, Chouinard also makes sure to describe the production of impairment, disability, and ableness as enmeshed in the dynamics of neoliberal global capitalism, implicating the continued emphasis on profit-making and politics of austerity in this process.

In Chapter 5, Hughes provides a historical perspective that captures dimensions of ableism in the pursuit of power. Grounding his argument within themes of power and control, Hughes takes readers on a journey from the slave societies of ancient Greece and Rome, which engaged in eugenic practices aimed at eliminating or abusing people with disabilities, through the colonialist projects of the late 19th and early 20th centuries, where racist and ableist ideologies were used to justify the exploitation of lands, resources, and bodies, including the enslavement of people around the world.

The final two chapters in this introductory section focus on defining, operationalizing, and measuring disability. Measurement is shaped by and shapes our understanding of disability. It includes measurement of disability itself and the larger environment. In Chapter 6, Latham-Mintus and Cordon directly address the relationship between disability and the environment using a place-based approach. They review various hybrid models that link the health and social dimensions of disability. They also examine measurement in relation to the physical and built environment and the social environment, discussing the relationship between impairment and environmental context—between individual and society—which is central to sociological definitions and measurement of disability.

In Chapter 7, Barnartt and Altman address how disability is defined, conceptualized, and measured. Throughout, they emphasize that measurement has consequences for how we understand different groups and divisions, which shapes the distribution of resources and policy. Their analysis of changing definitions of disability across US censuses from 1830 to 1900 reveals flaws in how disability has been understood and recorded, and adds weight to their discussion of current measurement challenges.

Part 2 broadens the scope of research in sociology of disability to address global perspectives on disability—an often-overlooked dimension of scholarship in both sociology and disability studies. Although global perspectives are weaved throughout the different sections of the handbook, Part 2 brings three key chapters together to emphasize critical perspectives, gender, and human rights in relation to the Global South. We use the term "Global South" to refer to both power-based and geographical distinctions.

As Grech describes, "Global South" delineates "power, resource, and epistemological differentials, which though not localized, embrace a substantial portion of the world living in a scenario of profound geopolitical asymmetries, poverty, and isolation confronting deeply entrenched centers of concentrated wealth and power accumulated historically and perpetuated in times of coloniality."

In Chapter 8, Grech calls out researchers and the international development sector for their roles in simplifying understandings of disability and the Global South, framing disabled people as vulnerable, limiting their agency, and viewing their bodies as a place for intervention. Grech ends the chapter by discussing a decolonizing approach to disability and development, what he refers to as a critical global disability studies (CGDS). In Chapter 9, Amin conducts an intersectional analysis of the healthcare experiences of disabled women in the Global South. Amin focuses on Malaysian women with disabilities' lived experiences to demonstrate how multiple dimensions, including access to modern medicine and cultural beliefs, affect their experiences in healthcare settings and increase their vulnerability to sexual abuse by both traditional healers and physicians.

Wrapping up this part of the handbook in Chapter 10, Campos Pinto reviews the central international frameworks that guide disability and human rights. She grounds her analysis around the adoption of the UN Convention on the Rights of Persons with Disabilities (UN-CRPD) in 2006 and describes a human rights model that asserts "the inherent dignity of all persons with disabilities, regardless the complexity of their needs and impairments," while also valuing impairment as part of human diversity. This model complements the social model for disability and provides a framework for understanding policy and the struggles that surround it. This model is not without its limitations. Like many frameworks developed by researchers in the Global North, the human rights model reproduces colonialist views, relies on northern conceptions of disability that accentuate the disability/impairment divide, often depicts disabled people in the Global South as victims in need of rescue, and over-emphasizes an individualist conception of rights.

The final part of this section focuses on representation. Representation in media whether it be television shows, online and social media, or appearance-based industries like fashion and beauty often functions to normalize and legitimize inequality. In the first chapter of this section, Prendella and Alper keenly note that inequality in media is about much more than access to technology and also arises in the under- and misrepresentation of disability. They examine the daily encounters people with disabilities have with media, how their experiences with media are shaped by disability, and the detrimental consequences of limited deficit-based portrayals of disability in mass media. In Chapter 12, Foster continues the important discussion of representation with a focus on fashion. Due to its wide circulation and role in both challenging and reinforcing appearance norms, fashion media presents "an ideal vehicle through which to assess mainstream norms and widely shared cultural ideals." Foster's analysis of two years of *Teen Vogue* editorials demonstrates both progress and limitations for disability in fashion. Bringing together this part of the handbook, Carey then emphasizes aspects of *belonging* in Chapter 13, discussing "how exclusion is enacted via informal social patterns and formal policy" in relation to legal rights, culture, and the accordance of moral values, power as a relational concept, and access to valued roles, opportunities, and social capital.

These four areas are linked where, if meaningful change is to occur, each must be addressed. For instance, although there may be progress in securing legal rights for people with intellectual disabilities in many national contexts, the presence of formal rights does not necessarily guarantee their legitimacy, enactment, or enforcement. These require inclusion and acceptance in cultural settings as well as political, economic, and interpersonal empowerment. Most importantly, Carey reminds us that "While moral value, rights, and power are key ingredients, belonging is perhaps most fundamentally centered on the degree to which we enjoy meaningful and fulfilling relationships."

SECTION 2: EXPERIENCING DISABILITY ACROSS THE LIFE COURSE

Section 2, *Experiencing Disability across the Life Course*, presents not a single perspective but rather a combination of perspectives interested in the synergistic effects of individual biography, societal contexts, and historic change. The common theme across the chapters in this section concerns the dynamic processes linking individuals, institutions, and structures. Variations on this theme provide insight into the issues most salient to contemporary disability scholars and sociologists more generally.

In Part 4, we are oriented to a long view of individual biography in three chapters applying life course theories to the study of disability. Each of these chapters addresses the important interplay between individual experience and historic time and place. In Chapter 14, Stevens discusses how the historic moment we occupy shapes cultural norms and guidelines for family care work. Expanding on this theme, Stevens further explores how our capacity for care fluctuates across our own life course. Dillaway and colleagues in Chapter 15 present research findings from their study on the impact of acquired disabilities for intimacy and motherhood. They emphasize the need to consider *when* individuals encounter disabilities in understanding what it means to be a mother with a disability. In Chapter 16, Bardo and Vowels examine how people with disabilities of different age cohorts across different historic periods have experienced the transition to adulthood. Deconstructing current understanding of the transition to adulthood based on educational advancement and entry into the paid labor force, they bring into focus the institutional transitions that have marked this life stage transition over time.

The institutions of education and employment are given further consideration in the next two parts of the handbook. Part 5 broadens our focus from the individual or micro-level to the institutional or meso/macro-level, and it challenges us to consider how educational policies and practices related to disability are also products of time and place.

In Chapter 17, Shifrer provides a comprehensive assessment of how educational policies affect every stage of education from kindergarten through grade twelve and into higher education. Balcazar and Ramirez in Chapter 18 expand on this theme by considering institutional barriers and supports associated with federal vocational rehabilitation transition programs in the United States. In Chapter 19, Tomlinson and Hewitt then address the varying ability or willingness of educational institutions to adapt to the needs of people with disabilities in a global context.

Shifting our attention to the sphere of work and occupations, Part 6 maintains an institutional focus while introducing an understanding of institutions as agents through which structural inequalities are reproduced. Maroto and Pettinicchio in Chapter 20 expand upon this perspective, describing paths through which ableism, as a structural form of disadvantage, is distilled into relational forms of inequality. Work precarity reflects one intermediary path through which ableism impacts the employment outcomes of people with disabilities, as Schur and Kruse in Chapter 21 illustrate. In Chapter 22, London, Wilmoth, and Landes consider an alternative to the expected path from employment disadvantage to personal disadvantage by discussing the unique array of institutional resources available to US veterans with service-connected disability and the exception they grant from poverty for this segment of the disabled population. Shuey and Wilson in Chapter 23 then consider in greater detail the implications of cumulative employment disadvantage for the lifelong earning potential and financial stability of people with disabilities.

Part 7 further grapples with the individual and interpersonal impacts of ableism. This has been the focus of the majority of research on ableism. Yet, as Brown and Batty outline in Chapter 24, the experiences of people with non-physical disabilities and multiple impairment conditions are not well documented, and this diminishes the practical relevance of research on ableism. To this point, study findings presented by Elliott and Reuter in Chapter 25 demonstrate how workplace accommodations developed for people with physical disabilities are comparably fraught with obstacles for working professionals with bipolar disorder and major depression. Sheehan and Corrigan in Chapter 26 then describe unique processes which discourage people with psychological disabilities from seeking out mental health services and the kinds of research agendas that are needed to address them.

SECTION 3: DISABILITY, POLITICS, AND THE LAW

In the broad field of social science, sociological inquiry has always been best poised to uncover how interactions between individuals and institutions account for the reproduction of inequality and the creation and durability of domination, subjugation, and marginalization. In Part 3 of the handbook, *Disability, Policy, and the Law,* chapters investigate the reproduction of inequality through the interaction of people with disabilities with the law, policy, and related institutions and systems. They also examine how social and political participation empowers people with disabilities to shape attitudes, beliefs, policies, and practices, helping to mitigate inequalities and social marginalization.

With many countries seeking to address social, political, and economic inequalities experienced by disabled people, understanding policy developments in a global context has become even more important. Doing so requires considering how disability is defined (i.e., through a social welfare framework, human rights framework, and other administrative, programmatic, regulatory, and judicial definitions). It also involves making sense of the intersection of different policy frameworks and how these successfully and unsuccessfully provide key public goods to disabled citizens.

In Part 9, chapters take a global approach to addressing policy developments, programmatic failures, and the experiences of disabled people in negotiating their rights and social services with their governments. In Chapter 30, Bruyère and Saleh focus on cross-national similarities in disability policy development in the interrelationship between rights and service provision. Importantly, they consider how policy mechanisms worldwide continue to perpetuate a stigmatizing and patronizing picture of people with disabilities. Within this global convergence of disability policy frameworks, Sykes and Strong (Chapter 31) remind us that nation-states remain instrumental in addressing disability-based inequalities. They show how variation in disability rates are tied to three axes of inequality: health metrics, disability policy, and democratic ideals.

Chapters in this section place a spotlight on how government interventions alleviate or exacerbate inequality. In Chapter 32, Gran and Bryden specifically ask whether and how human rights policy frames are useful tools in producing positive outcomes for people with disabilities. Here, the authors situate the international push for a global disability human rights framework with their actual implementation (or lack thereof) by individual nations. Within this context, they consider the role of rights-based movements and activism as these interact with international and national efforts to remove obstacles to social, political, and economic inclusion.

In keeping with Section Three's theme, Part 10 directly investigates the interaction of people with disabilities with the criminal justice system. Chapters consider contact with these systems both in terms of disabled victims and offenders. The interaction of disabled offenders with the criminal justice system remains a relatively understudied and unfocused subfield in sociology and criminology but limited work shows disproportionate experiences with discrimination and violence as well as sentencing disparities.

Drawing from the broad tradition of social control and punishment, Fernandes and Kurdyla in Chapter 33 look at the lived experiences of people with disabilities within the criminal justice system. They take an intersectional approach to illustrate how the interaction of disability, race, sexual identity, age, and gender with criminal justice challenges existing narratives of punishment, correction, and incarceration. Ostrander too in Chapter 34 draws from an intersectional frame of race and disability linking the growth of the disabled prison population to the War on Drugs to shed light on violence in carceral settings. This growth is tied to the inadequacy among correctional institutions to deal with the specific circumstances of disabled inmates who also face more violence and manipulation from other inmates and guards. Carrying forward the theme of attitudinal and institutionally based reproductions of inequality, Kermit and Olsen (Chapter 35) examine legal protections and experiences of deaf people with the Norwegian criminal justice system. The authors show how specific programmatic and organizational changes lead to positive outcomes by strengthening the rights of disabled inmates and ensuring justice is carried out fairly.

To conclude the handbook, the final set of chapters address the numerous ways in which programs, advocacy, volunteerism, and activism encourage the social and political participation of disabled citizens and document the consequences of citizen participation on social, political, and economic outcomes. For instance, disability rights movements and advocacy worldwide have played a critical role in disseminating, entrenching, and embedding a disability and human rights paradigm in various spheres of life. In Chapter 36, Prince provides an account of the dynamic relationship between policy change and changes in styles of advocacy. This is especially important as multitargeted activism interacts with different jurisdictional spaces and has varied goals and objectives when it comes to promoting inclusion and participation of disabled people. As Shandra notes in Chapter 37, participation is a key component of activism and advocacy but is nonetheless an amorphous concept. Shandra's chapter discusses the challenges in measuring social participation and the importance of doing so to address continued obstacles to integration in different social contexts. Finally, in the concluding chapter, Chapter 38, Scotch and Sutton focus on the strategies of movement activism in the United States and elsewhere, as well as the structure and organization of disability mobilization. Their chapter traces the origins of disability social movements and their impact on policy and culture.

CONCLUSION

Throughout the chapters, a narrative of intersectional oppression emerges, addressing how ableism, racism, sexism, heterosexism, classism, and other institutions are linked and support stratification. This narrative begins with the front cover, adorned with a pile of broken masks that were part of a larger piece of performance art by disabled artist, Danielle Caswell. Masks, for many of us, embody the aspects of identity we choose to present to the world around us and the "armor" we wear to protect our sense of self. Since the start of the pandemic, masks have also come to symbolize things we may not wish to share. They represent care and compassion for those around us and a basic support for public health, but they can also show that we have a health condition, feel vulnerable, or are afraid. As Caswell describes, masks are inflexible and isolating. Whether masking reflects self-enhancement or self-protection, then, it commits us to a version of reality that is both our own version of reality and limited reality. Broken masks signify a more genuine understanding of the world and our place in it—unguarded, but with the potential to work together in solidarity.

However, broken masks also symbolize the inflexible demands of a society not made for or by disabled people in which we are exposed and without the luxury of protections. This theme continues through chapters that review important theoretical frameworks of disability in Section 1, outline experiences of disability throughout the life course in Section 2, and address disability at the intersections of policy, politics, and the legal system in Section 3. Although the focus of the handbook is to situate specifically disability and ableism within the sociology of inequality, it also extends beyond disability by demonstrating links between different social categories and the geographic, historical, institutional, and cultural spaces they occupy.

This diversity of perspectives is a reminder that a bigger picture exists. In turn, we can both appreciate the complexities of the current moment and think beyond our immediate concerns. Many if not all of the themes, issue areas, and research streams covered by this handbook were affected by the COVID-19 global pandemic. At the same time, it is also important to showcase, as the handbook does, persisting and longstanding areas of concern and inquiry that, while impacted by crisis, will continue, as they have before the pandemic, to generate important scholarship. We would be remiss if we did not acknowledge this fact, and the hard work and efforts of our contributors during these difficult times. We are grateful for each and every contribution to this handbook.

DEFINING, MEASURING, AND UNDERSTANDING DISABILITY

PART I

Understanding, Theorizing, and Studying Disability

CHAPTER 2

....

FRAMEWORKS, MODELS, THEORIES, AND EXPERIENCES FOR UNDERSTANDING DISABILITY

....

TOM SHAKESPEARE AND NICHOLAS WATSON

INTRODUCTION

....

THE social sciences are confronted with both an intellectual and practical task of improving how we study disability, especially if we are to develop theoretical and methodological approaches that are fully representative of the disability experience, in all its diversity. We suggest that applied social science must be able to provide both an understanding of what life is like for disabled people and, at the same time, a pathway for the provision of better services and the removal of the barriers and practices that serve to exclude disabled people. We need to be able to provide data and arguments that can be applied in reforming approaches to disability in the social, cultural, and political realms. The COVID-19 pandemic has made clear how urgent this reform is (Shakespeare et al., 2022).

We frame our arguments drawing on empirical research from three separate studies to answer the key question that has dogged disability research and disability studies since its first inception, namely, what are the roles of impairment and disablement in the lives of disabled people and the construction of the disability experience? Traditionally, the discipline of disability studies has focused on the barriers disabled people face, leaving the subjective and personal experience of impairment to the discipline of medical sociology. This paper builds on and develops our earlier work (Shakespeare & Watson, 2001a, 2010; Shakespeare, 2013) where we have sought to create a more nuanced approach that bridges this divide.

We are not the first to attempt this. Carol Thomas (1999, 2007), for example, combined her earlier empirical work in medical sociology with female cancer patients and carers, and with terminally ill cancer patients, with data drawn from interviews with disabled people and theoretical contributions to disability studies, to create what she called a more relational, albeit still materialist, account. She called for the development of a sociology of disablism, with a focus on barriers, plus a sociology of impairment and impairment effects, arguing that the two have to work together, but are separate entities (Thomas, 2007). However, as we have argued previously, it is not easy to present impairment and disability as dichotomous experiences or fields of study (Watson 2012). There is no clear divide between the private, personal experience of impairment and the public, social experience of disability. This separation, while core to materialist disability studies (Shakespeare, 2013) is neither helpful nor useful.

Recognizing this is particularly important if we are to try and improve both our understanding of what it is like to live with a long-term condition and to improve opportunities for people with impairments to flourish and promote their well-being. At the outset, there is perhaps a need to reflect on why this divide exists and to try and link the two. The chapter therefore begins with a brief description of the background to the divide, focusing on the emergence of disability studies in the 1980s and 1990s. We then turn to the response of medical sociology. The next section presents some data from three studies led by ourselves, which demonstrate why the current divide cannot be sustained empirically. We also draw on other research pointing in the same direction as our own. We end the chapter by proposing a framework for social researchers to come together, incorporating ideas from critical realism and the work of Roy Bhaskar as well as the ideas of Amartya Sen and Martha Nussbaum and the capabilities approach.

Our claim is that there is a continuum between the private, personal experiences and the public, social experiences of disablement. This process of disablement is dynamic and bi-directional. Austerity and other processes can affect the personal experience of ill-health (Ryan, 2019). Ill-health has an impact on capacity to work and participate, regardless of environmental barriers or settings (Abberley, 1996). Disability is the result of the interaction between physical- or mental-health conditions, individual psychology, and environmental and social factors, which include culture. It is a dynamic, scalar, multi-factorial experience, which can be very different for different people with the same impairment in the same setting, let alone the billions of disabled people around the world. These differences could be the result of impairment/illness, gender, class, ethnicity, environment, personality, upbringing, social and political barriers, or even luck.

BACKGROUND TO THE SPLIT

The emergence of disability studies as an academic discipline, in the United Kingdom at least, can be linked to the publication of the *Fundamental Principles of Disablement* by the Union of the Physically Impaired Against Segregation (UPIAS) in 1976. UPIAS were part of a growing number of groups of disabled people in the 1970s who, like many other disenfranchised movements, were driven by a dissatisfaction with their prolonged and continued exclusion from the benefits of growth that had marked the post-war years. They objected to the growing inequality of their experience compared to their nondisabled peers. The *Fundamental Principles* was developed in the course of a polemic against the Disability Alliance, which they saw as being dominated by non-disabled academics such as Peter Townsend. This early engagement with academia together with the Tavistock research at Le Court Cheshire Home published as *A Life Apart* (Miller & Gwynne, 1972), explains some of the animosity between disability studies, the disabled people's movement, and medical sociology (Watson 2019).

UPIAS were brought together by Paul Hunt, a resident in the Le Court Cheshire Home, and Vic Finkelstein, an emigree from apartheid South Africa (Campbell & Oliver, 1996). They sought to change the way that people looked at the problem of disability and to politicize it. UPIAS built on and developed ideas on disability that had emerged in the post war period to provide an alternative perspective to define the social problems faced by disabled people, and importantly their origins and their solution. The *Fundamental Principles* was the origin of the dualism that comprises what Oliver (1983) later termed the "social model of disability"—impairment versus disability. Impairment was defined as "lacking part of or all of a limb, or having a defective limb, organism or mechanism of the body" and disability as "the disadvantage or restriction of activity caused by contemporary organisation which takes no or little account of people who have physical impairments and thus excludes them from the mainstream of social activities."

Finkelstein and Hunt almost certainly came up with the social model, but Michael Oliver took these ideas and formalized them (1983, 1990). He re-created disability as a problem of social justice, locating the origins of disablement within the state, and in particular state-led capitalism and the mode of production. The promise afforded by the welfare state was not being achieved because the way it was delivered was seen as restricting individual autonomy: it was failing to deliver the liberation that was promised. For Oliver, Finkelstein, Abberley, Barnes, and other early disability studies scholars, special schools, care homes, rehabilitation units, hospitals, segregated workshops, and other services all served to disadvantage and to segregate disabled people. They benefitted non-disabled professionals more than they did the purported beneficiaries. These structures formed part of the oppressive regimes that excluded disabled people on the grounds that they were not able to work as fast or produce the equivalent of their nondisabled peers. Other key developments included the emergence of the emancipatory research paradigm facilitating a politics of the possible by confronting social oppression at whatever levels it occurred (Oliver, 1992).

The social model of disability was key part of the development of disability politics, especially in the United Kingdom (Shakespeare & Watson, 2001b). Vic Finkelstein took social model thinking and promoted it vigorously at the Singapore World Congress of Disabled People's International (Driedger, 1989). By locating disability as the outcome of the way that society treats and deals with people who have an impairment, the focus shifted from an individual analysis to the social, economic, and cultural factors that create the problem. The new disability politics that emerged alongside the social model called for changes at the level of meaning and culture attached to disability, as well as changes in the way that professionals, caregivers, and others interacted with disabled people, demanding structural changes at the macro level. While initially developed in the United Kingdom, the influence of the social model extended far beyond and, largely thanks to activism within *Rehabilitation International*, eventually influenced a worldwide movement (Driedger, 1989). Across the globe the social model became key to the explanation of disability (Charlton, 1998).

The picture in the United States is somewhat different. Unlike the rest of the world, the disabled peoples' movement in the United States never really fully endorsed the social model of disability (Burke & Barnes, 2018a). Heavily influenced by other civil rights movements, it broadly followed what Hahn has termed the "minority group model", which sees "attitudinal discrimination as the principal problem facing disabled persons" (1996, p. 41). While early disability activists in the United States emphasized the role of barriers in constraining the lives of disabled people, rather than locating their origin in medicalization and capitalism, as the social model does, stigmatizing attitudes were seen as the chief causative factor. As a result, the United States has taken a much more individualistic approach, emphasizing identity and identification and the use of lawsuits to punish individual acts of discrimination (Burke & Barnes, 2018b). It lacks the structural and materialist focus of the social model.

The academic study of disability in the United States has also followed a different trajectory from that found in the United Kingdom and in the Nordic countries. In the United Kingdom, disability studies grew out of the social sciences, particularly sociology and social policy, but in the United States, it is more likely to be located in the arts and humanities (Vehmas & Watson, 2014). Disability studies in North America has been much more eclectic and multi-disciplinary in its approach and has drawn heavily on, and drawn links with, other identity-based, rights-influenced approaches, especially critical race, feminist, and queer theory. There has as a consequence been much more emphasis on the cultural production of disability.

There was a real sense of optimism within the social model, a fact that is often overlooked. Rather than focus on how awful life was as a disabled person, the focus shifted to how things could be changed and how life could be improved. It is what Levitas (2013) might describe as a utopic model, providing an approach through which the negatives in human experience can be removed. It offered a way of thinking about disability in an holistic way, linking and integrating the economic, social, cultural, and environmental process that disable people with impairments. Finkelstein (1988) even posited such a utopia in an article in which he imagined a community where everything was accessible, and disability disappeared. The social model marked a sea change in the way disability was represented; spend any time with organizations of disabled people, and you will soon meet people who will claim that their lives were turned around by the social model of disability. In relocating the problem of disability away from the individual and toward the wider social structure, the social model enabled people to feel better about themselves. Simple, direct, and effective, it is a really powerful and life-affirming model, it is a charismatic idea, what Hasler described as "our one big idea" (1993).

It is important to acknowledge the impact of this model, not just in United Kingdom but around the world. The last quarter of the 20th century saw radical changes for disabled people, at least in the Global North. In the United Kingdom, for example, the disabled people's movement used the concept of the social model in their campaigns against barriers and for the establishment of antidiscrimination legislation (Barnes, 1991), which culminated in the passing of the Disability Discrimination Act (1995), later incorporated into the 2010 Single Equality Act. Disability is now accepted as a protected characteristic, alongside gender, ethnicity, sexuality, among others. The closure of long-stay hospitals and other segregated settings and the normative assumptions around the rights of disabled people to participation and toward inclusion, all achieved as a result of the actions of the disabled people's movement, are a good thing. More than that actually, they are a triumph: they mark a turning point in human history, and should be celebrated as such.

The social model of disability, or at least a barriers-focused approach, is, in policy terms, the dominant model of disability. Thanks to the structural influence of the social model, the World Health Organization changed their own categorization of disability, creating the International Classification of Functioning, Disability and Health (WHO 2001), in which environmental factors are key. In fact, the social model forms the basis of definitions across a range of different settings, from the local right up to the national and the transnational, informing policy development in the European Union, and the World Trade Organization. At the United Nations, it underpins the Convention on the Rights of Persons with Disabilities (2006). Although it might not have completely changed practices, the social model has played a significant part in altering the discourse that surrounds disability, not just in the Global North, but internationally and multinationally and at the highest levels (WHO, 2011). Not a bad impact for a group of disgruntled residents from a care home.

The influence also extends well beyond disability, the demands for co-production, personalization, and personal budgets, asset-based approaches once so radical and part of the disabled people's movement's demand for inclusion, are now mainstreamed and are part of the public-service reform agenda (Christie, 2011), although their origin and the debt owed to the Disabled People's Movement are rarely discussed or acknowledged. It is also true that much of the original radical element of the calls have been diluted.

The success, however, in transforming the way that policy portrays the problem of disability has not resulted in the institutional change that was hoped for. Cases such as Winterbourne View (Flynne & Citerella, 2013), the death of Connor Sparrowhawk (Ryan, 2017) and other similar outrages still occur far too often. Further, despite over 20 years of anti-discrimination legislation in the United Kingdom, disabled people are still far more likely than their non-disabled peers to be living in poverty. A recent report for the Social Metrics Commission found that 48% of people who live in poverty in the

United Kingdom are either disabled themselves or live in a family where someone is disabled (2019). Inequalities in work still persist and the disability employment gap is larger than for any other protected characteristic (DWP, 2015). Disabled people still face barriers throughout their lives: housing is inadequate, as too is childcare, and many disabled people are unable to access the right to form relationships. Life is extremely challenging for disabled people, particularly those in the Global South (WHO, 2011; Grech & Soldatic, 2016).

Violence against disabled people continues to be high. In the United Kingdom, for example, research by the disability organization Mencap indicates that 88% of people with a learning disability had experienced a hate crime in the previous 12 months and that 66% of those were frequent victims, with nearly a third bullied on a daily or weekly basis. The impact this has on people's well-being is now emerging (Wiseman & Watson, 2021). Given these and many other inequalities, it is no wonder that people with learning disabilities have as many health conditions at age 20 and over as the rest of the population aged 50 and over, and live 20 years less than their nondisabled peers (Kinner et al., 2018).

Seeing these statistics it is easy to see why a strong, barriers approach is appealing. However, the social model has come under criticism for its failure to account for the bodily dimensions of both disablement and impairment—impacting pain, incontinence, sexual function, and fatigue. These become marginalized within the rhetoric associated with the social model (Shakespeare & Watson, 2001; Morris, 1991; Crow, 1996). It also homogenizes the disability experience, denying differences in terms of gender, age, ethnicity, culture, class, and geographical location (Shakespeare & Watson, 2001).

Carol Thomas, in an attempt to meet these criticisms, has developed what she describes as a relational social model. Her revisions involve the incorporation of what she terms impairment effects, and psycho-emotional disablement. Impairment effects are "restrictions of bodily activity that are *directly attributable* to bodily variations designated impairments rather than those *imposed upon* people" (Thomas, 2007, p. 136). She employs the term psycho-emotional disablism to distinguish between barriers to doing and barriers to being. These are:

> the impacts and effects of the social behaviours that are enacted between the "impaired" and the "non-impaired," for example in familial relationships, in interactions in communities, and in encounters with health, welfare and educational services.
>
> (Thomas, 2004)

Thomas (2012) has argued that the sociology of disability should present disability—like gender—as a key dimension of global social divisions and inequity that can be approached from a multiplicity of analytical directions, using a rich mix of theoretical perspectives, methodologies, and research techniques. While attractive, there are numerous problems with this formulation, not least that, unlike disability, there are no rational reasons to consider homosexuality, ethnicity, or gender undesirable characteristics whatever the social context, but there are many impairments that can reasonably be seen as undesirable (Shakespeare, 2013, Vehmas & Watson, 2014). Motor neurone disease, depression, or spinal cord injury cause suffering irrespective of the social or cultural environment.

There is also a danger that impairment and disablement become envisaged as dual systems rather than a complex interwoven matrix, and a debate about boundary maintenance can emerge. Is this a disability issue or is this an impairment issue? Shakespeare (2013) argues it is almost impossible to divide complex experiences into "social" and "medical." In fact, anyone who does empirical research with disabled people experiences this difficulty. Lived experience is messy: while social structures undoubtedly impact people with impairments, extricating and labelling different factors at work is hard. For example, above we highlighted evidence that people with intellectual disabilities, on average, live shorter lives than non-disabled people. Some of this is because the impairment itself is associated with a shorter life span. Some of it is associated with poverty, housing, and social exclusion (Wiseman & Watson, 2021). Some of it is associated with failures of health and social care services, for example the inadequate care that has led to the deaths of people with a learning disability living in care homes or hospitals (Ryan, 2017). Some of it is associated with eating poorer food in great quantity, sometimes because care and support staff lack time or skills to cook better. Some of this premature mortality of people with profound and multiple intellectual disabilities results from aspiration pneumonia, partly caused by food going down the wrong way. Some of this may be the result of being fed too quickly by a poorly paid and inadequately managed care worker who is in a hurry, and some of which is very hard to avoid in a person who has profound intellectual disability. It would be a very difficult task to neatly divide social and medical factors.

EXPLORING THE DIVIDE

These and other critiques were used within medical sociology in the United Kingdom to reject, almost outright, the claims of the social model theorists. The early 1990s saw two key, and very bitter, engagements between leading UK medical sociologists and disability scholars, one on research, later published as a special issue in what was then called *Disability, Handicap and Society* (1992), and the other on theory published in a collection edited by Barnes and Mercer, *Exploring the Divide* (1996).

Given the very strong support within British medical sociology for a materialist understanding of the causes of ill health and the links between poverty and health inequality (Whitehead et al., 1990), it is perhaps surprising that the claims of scholars such as Oliver and Barnes and the disabled people's movement were dismissed out of hand. When it came to disability, medical sociology simply failed to follow the same social deterministic account that it applied to poverty and ill health. This was equally true in the post-structuralist or postmodern accounts that were appearing in the then newly emerging sociology of the body, where again the disabled body was naturalized

(Shilling, 1993). Physical inadequacy was taken as the defining element of disabled people's experiences. For other inequality groups, the tendency within sociology was to deconstruct it, whereas if it was disability, it naturalized it.

There has of course been a change in this, but the dominant perspective within medical sociology at that time was to focus on the experience of living with a chronic illness. Symbolic interactionist and phenominological accounts predominated developing concepts such as biographical disruption (Bury, 1982), narrative reconstruction (Williams, 1984), and the impact of chronic illness on the self (Charmaz, 1983). The approaches explored and documented the impact of chronic illness on people's sense of identity and its influence on daily living and social relationships.

Work in this paradigm focuses on the difficulties that chronic conditions raise in interpersonal relationships and how individuals negotiate their way through these difficulties. Management problems are at the forefront of much of the analysis; the emphasis is on the process of "normalization" and the tactics employed by individuals in "symptom control."

Medical sociology has provided some very useful avenues of research. Biographical disruption remains a very useful concept and stigma is a perennial interest. Studies exploring narrative reconstruction or the experiences of living with a chronic condition provide important and vital perspectives on the lives of disabled people (Reeve et al., 2010; Wilson, 2007). But this does not provide any analysis as to what happens after the biography has been disrupted, the identity spoiled, or the narrative reconstructed. Further impairment and social suffering are not a reliable or useful indicator of social justice. The uncritical subjectivism that emerges does not allow an unpacking or exploration of social oppression or provide avenues for tackling that oppression. These researchers failed to examine cultural meanings ascribed to impairments or chronic conditions or address why disabled people felt excluded. They presented disabled people as "vulnerable" and failed to explore fully the cultural context within which the experience of social isolation, segregation, and poor self-image are lived. As Gareth Williams (1996) pointed out, prior to the emergence of disability studies it was rare to see disability discussed in terms of equality, oppression, violence, or discrimination. It took the disability studies approach, and the emergence of disabled scholars (e.g., Oliver, Barnes, Abberley, Morris, Thomas, Roulstone, Shakespeare, Watson), to bring this to the fore. Ironically, many of the "chronic illness" tendency in medical sociology had themselves personal experience of chronic illness but failed to politicize it.

BRINGING THEM TOGETHER

Both approaches described above are incomplete, and neither forms the basis for an adequate theory or methodology through which to explore disability. In this next section we present data from three very diverse studies on disability, selected because they represent different elements of the disability experience, to show the interconnectedness and diversity of the disability experience and of life with an impairment. The first draws on data from a mixed-methods study of people with restricted growth conditions living in the north of England (Thompson et al., 2010). The second draws data from a study based on 28 interviews with older people with CP (Paterson & Watson, 2013.) This is a group traditionally thought of as representing a so-called static, lifelong condition. The third draws on study based on series of longitudinal interviews with 40 people and their families with Motor Neurone Disease (or Amyotrophic Lateral Sclerosis as it is termed in North America) (Ferrie & Watson, 2015).

Restricted Growth: Bio-psycho-social Disablement

The following discussion is based on a mixed-methods study of people with restricted growth conditions living in the north of England (n = 81), more than half of whom had achondroplasia, the most common restricted-growth condition (Thompson et al., 2010). The majority of people with restricted growth live independently, are intellectually unaffected, and do not face communication barriers. Few use wheelchairs. Culturally, therefore, people with restricted growth do not have many of the markers that signal membership within the disability category. Employment rates (57%) in this study were only slightly lower than the non-disabled average (61%). Yet, 60% claimed Disability Living Allowance, and 56% of the sample had a Blue Badge for parking. This suggests that disability identity is strategic: we also found that younger people in the study were more likely to think of themselves as "different," and older people, who had more mobility impairments, were more likely to think of themselves as "disabled."

Key points in the biography where disablement impinges are starting school, teenage years, becoming more impaired in middle age, and retirement. The major disabling factor for all our respondents was the attitude of others, particularly staring and mockery. This impinged when the child went to school, or when the young adult was hoping to date potential partners, or, for all respondents, in public settings.

This was also part of other people's expectations of them. As described by one participant:

> just prior to my leaving [school] I got called into the headmistress's study and she said "we've been thinking about what you're going to do and I think you should stay home and help mother," those were her words. (female, age 78)

Although this may be a dated reaction, people today were advised not to go into professions, such as teaching and medicine, and were steered toward clerical work, nursery nursing, and classroom aide roles. We found that, as a consequence, respondents were more likely to be overqualified for their roles, which were often in clerical or subordinate positions. Having gotten a job, proved themselves, and managed environments, respondents were reluctant to risk what they had achieved by going for promotion. This was not because they were not capable, and it was often not because of direct discrimination. As a result of not being encouraged and supported, and because of their fears, they did not push themselves to have a developing career. Like some people with other impairments like epilepsy or visual impairment, they were in work, but concentrated in lower social positions: these disabled people face a "glass staircase," not a glass ceiling.

A typical example of bodily restrictions—what Thomas (1999) might call impairment effects—was the following:

> and I think my back problem, pains in my legs, it's just deteriorated and deteriorated all the time, in the last 3 years. (female, age 33)

Almost all had pain and mobility limitation; often these physical difficulties resulted in mental-health difficulties as people negotiated limitations and dependencies:

> I get, well, what I consider depression. Because [husband's] deteriorated quite badly and our lives are changing and it's just adapting to the changes, coming to terms with the changes. (female, age 49, husband has same condition)

Many were forced to retire early, in their fifties, due to physical difficulties, with resulting impacts on their economic situation:

> . . . because I'd have liked to work till I was 65. That's annoyed me, that I can't. . . that was hard to accept. (male, age 57, retired due to ill health at 52)

This study shows that disability identity is dynamic and changing. It is the result of medical, social, cultural, and psychological factors. It shifts over the life course. Indeed, the team interviewed two women in the same northern town who had the same impairment and socio-economic situation. One felt that restricted growth had not harmed her life: she was working, married, with children. The other felt that restricted growth had ruined her life: she was single, unemployed, and lonely. The difference could be put down to early childhood experiences, personality, or luck. But both faced many of the same activity limitations and participation restrictions, to use the language of the ICF (WHO, 2001).

Aging and Cerebral Palsy

The experience of impairment and of embodiment was central as people aged with CP. Some of the comments relate to what is called primary aging: these are the "normal; changes associated with growing old" (Haak et al., 2009). People described how carrying out physical tasks and activities becomes more difficult with age:

Everything just gets harder as you get older and I'm getting pains in my legs that I never had. Now I might turn and it's like a cramp just for about 5 or 10 seconds but it kind of stops you in your tracks you know, even just turning and I've obviously pulled a muscle or something and thing like that but it does definitely get harder and my energy levels are not as good.

It is hard to distinguish this sort of aging from aging experienced by non-disabled people. There may be a quantitative difference, but qualitatively there is no separate status for people with impairment. The language is similar to that found in other studies, such as the work of Cunningham-Burley and Backett Milburn (2002).

What distinguishes this experience is the process known as secondary aging, the aging associated with having cerebral palsy. This was a much more dominant topic during the interviews. As one informant neatly put it,

Everything just gets harder as you get older and I'm getting pains in my legs that I never had . . . . We wear out quicker. There's no doubt about it.

Like restricted growth, CP is often described as a static condition, but in reality it is a condition that changes, and these changes can, for some, be dramatic, creating what Bury would describe as a biographical disruption:

In the past, before I was deteriorating with the cerebral palsy I knew my limits and worked within my limits so what happens is when you do deteriorate to the extent that I have, you have to re-educate yourself again and really it's a sense like as though you've not had a disability before compared to the level of disability now. You know if that kind of makes any sense but that's the way I've kind of approached it, because you've had to start again. It has not made me give up but you still have to start again.

One of the key impairment changes that drove this disruption was around mobility— specifically walking and balance. As people aged they got less and less able to walk, and by the time of the interviews all but one of the participants who could in the past walk and had some ability to stand, now no longer could. Some stopped walking because of a fall, but the most typical cause was a prolonged stay in bed or hospital.

Calum: "... I was able to walk until 11 years ago."
Key Worker: And then you just woke up didn't you one morning and he was unable to walk. "I think I got a virus."
Key Worker: Because when you went to your bed and you got up you couldn't walk anymore?
Calum: "Yes."
Key Worker: It was obviously a big shock.
Interviewer: Yes it must have been a big shock
Calum: "Yes it was big shock to my wife as well and my sons."

This is of course interesting in and of itself, as too are participants' comments about how they rebuilt their lives and how, for some, moving into a chair was, in terms of their mobility, actually enabling rather than disabling because they were able to travel further. However, what really stood out was that was nobody was offered support when they started falling, or rehabilitation once they had lost the ability to walk. Which other group would this happen to? It is hard think of any other group where there would be no attempt to help them walk, or at least to boost their mobility. This had real knock-on effects in their ability to live independently, to work and to participate in day-to-day activities. For many, after losing the ability to walk, so too went the ability to transfer in or out of the chair, and with that the ability to toilet independently. We also found a lot of discrimination: people being forced out of the labor market, and when they went to their doctor, all the doctor did was offer to sign them off. Many people wanted to carry on working, but at no point were they offered vocational rehabilitation or were changes in working practice suggested. When people complained that changes in their impairment meant that they were now living in unsuitable housing with inadequate support often the only alternative offered was to move into a care home, a move many did not want to make.

The problems associated with aging with CP are not widely recognized, and support services do not plan for the consequences of CP as a long-term condition. CP is seen as a problem of pediatrics, not life-long complications. We talked to neurologists about this, and they told us it was a care-of-the-elderly problem; when we asked specialists in care of the elderly, they told us it was a neurology problem.

Motor Neurone Disease (MND)

In this next section we look at the intersection between the medical and the biological in people with MND and draw on data from a qualitative study based on interviews with 40 people who had the condition (Ferrie & Watson, 2015). Motor Neuron Disease (MND) encompasses several different conditions whose common feature is the premature degeneration of motor nerves and in the United States is often referred to as Amyotrophic Lateral Sclerosis (ALS). Locock et al. (2009) in their qualitative study exploring the experiences of people with MND argued that for this condition, while some biographical disruption and repair may be present, so great were the effects of MND that rather than what Bury termed "biographical disruption" it became "biographical abruption." There is no denying that MND is a brutal health condition, and in our work on MND we found similar comments to those of Locock et al. People talked about how they could no longer do things that were important to them, such as knitting, woodwork, or another hobby or activity, and that this greatly affected who they were and how they self-identified. With an average life expectancy of 18 months after diagnosis, a poorly defined trajectory, and little or no chance of recovery, biographical abruption may be a distinctive feature of this condition.

However, while it is possible to ascribe this abruption to MND, there is a danger that we might ignore, or at least underplay, some of the surrounding issues. Although biographical abruption may often be present, there is a social element to its production. For example, some local authorities refused to fund adaptations if they felt that there would be no benefit for at least three or in some cases five years:

Martin: *"When Katie was first diagnosed... em... it wasn't good at all. We had a terrible run in with... we had wanted a stair lift fitted and they wouldn't do it. Despite being approached by the MSP and everything, they wouldn't do it... eh..."*
Jo: *"And what reason did they give?"*
Martin: *"They didn't think basically... and again this five year thing came into the equation... to cut a long story short they basically didn't think they would get their money's worth out of it."*

There were also lots of examples of where disablement impacted on people's lives. Respondents talked about not being able to go out, to join friends for meals, or to go to other social events.

Kate: *when was the last time you took your wife out...?*
Phillip: *But it is difficult because I have got splints which mean that I can walk a bit further in them than I can without the splints... however, if there is a step, a kerb, stairs they are dreadful. Or if there is a sloping bit of ground they are dreadful... or if the ground is wet it is terrible... So, I really have to...*
JF: *So, that really limits their use...*
Phillip: *I've got to ask where am I going...? Can I do that? Is there a step there...? Everything has got to be planned like a military operation... Phillip and his wife Kate*

The intersection between the experience of impairment and social barriers was common. Sometimes the reluctance to venture out was the result of impairment-related issues, such as fear of choking, but there was also a lot of discussion around barriers: these could be both physical, as described above, and also cultural, in that respondents did not want people to see them as they now were. There is still a stigma attached to a condition such as MND, much of which the informants described as "felt" rather than "enacted" (Scambler, 2004), This served to constrain and deny people the opportunity to participate.

Rachel: *I feel embarrassed at neighbours seeing me. Embarrassed at friends seeing me. Crazy! Why should I? But I do.*
Jo: *Because of their reaction to you? Rachel 'No! they've been great, it's me. I'm embarrassed*
Jo: *But if it was them...*
Rachel: *I'd be there, with them! But the shoe is on my foot and I'm embarrassed to have this illness. I'd rather die tomorrow that have to deal with this. You have to mentally adjust all the time, its too much.*

The sociology of chronic illness, with its focus on biographical issues to do with meaning and experience and the stigma associated with it would benefit from a more explicit linking to the political agenda, Williams (2010). This is a point often overlooked, and a key point made by Goffman in the conclusion to *Stigma*, when he argued,

> Sociologically, the central issue concerning these groups [the stigmatized] is their place in the social structure; the contingencies these persons encounter in face-to-face interaction is only part of the problem, and something that cannot itself be fully understood without reference to the history, the political development and the current policies of the group.

(Goffman, 1968, p. 151)

Any sociological account of impairment must explore these inequalities, their impact on how people value themselves, and the suffering and restricted flourishing they engender in disabled people. Impairment is not always in and of itself deterministic, but as it gets worse it does have the potential not only to lead to higher levels of disablement, but also to have an even greater impact on the self. On average, the greater the level of impairment, the more the opportunity for both exists. Fatigue, pain, and impairment contribute to exclusion, an exclusion that cannot be extracted from the overall experience of disablism. But the roles of negative attitudes and structures are also central. By ignoring the lived experience of having an impairment, of aging with an impairment, or the very demanding and all-embracing impact of living with a progressive condition, any exploration of disability runs the danger of ignoring an important and central part of disabled people's lives.

The sociology of chronic illness, with its focus on biographical issues to do with meaning and experience, would also benefit from a more explicit linking of these themes to the political agenda, as Williams (2010) and others have argued. Both provide a necessary corrective to each other, but as things currently stand, by not working together they are not achieving the impact they should

DISCUSSION

How can we best theorize disability? The *International Classification of Functioning, Disability and Health* (WHO, 2001) brings together the medical and social models, giving more prominent place to environmental factors, but has failed to analyze personal factors, or to account for the role of culture. Equally, in the search for intellectual resources, we have not found critical disability studies very useful (Vehmas & Watson, 2014). The focus on cultural discourse and the assumption of able-bodiedness is useful, but less helpful when it comes to understanding material social relations (Shakespeare, 2013).

We consider that the idea of critical realism and capability theory could help us better understand disablement. Critical realism distinguishes between the "real" and "observable" world: some things we can see and feel, but other structural relations are not visible. However, we can infer the existence of these real underlying mechanisms from their effects in the observable world. Critical realism also suggests research that uses a laminar approach to explore the various strata of experience in an interactive manner. Bhaskar and Danermark (2006) argue that adopting a critical realist approach allows research on disability on a range of different levels from the cellular to the cultural. For example, the lives of people with restricted growth could be understood according to the schema we present in Table 2.1.

Similar, but subtly different, laminar tables might be relevant to people with cerebral palsy or MND. For example, dwarfism has a particular cultural valence that these other conditions might lack. However, CP may be associated with speech impediments, which members of the public may associate with inferiority or intellectual disability, while MND has an association with dying, which is not relevant to CP or restricted growth. While this gives an approach that can be used to more generally uncover and explore disability across a much broader perspective, it does not provide us with the outcomes-focused agenda we need if we are to develop an adequate model of disability and chronic illness. But it does suggest that interventions at different levels might be needed: the medical, the rehabilitative, the psychological, the legal, and so on.

Table 2.1 A laminar schema for understanding the disability experience of people with restricted growth

Legal	Covered by Equality legislation, may require reasonable accommodation/adaptation.
Cultural	Stigma associated with dwarfism arising from cultural representations.
Social policy	May require support from government benefits or programs to cover additional costs associated with disability. Economic consequences of limited working and early retirement.
Social	Exposure to negative attitudes and limiting expectations when in public settings.
Environmental	Possible requirement for level access for a wheelchair user; provision of accessible parking.
Psychological	Negative attitudes of others; internalized low esteem; depression consequent on medical and functional difficulties and social consequences.
Functional	Limited walking and standing.
Medical	Pain and paralysis.
Anatomical	Dwarfism diagnoses (achondroplasia, SED, etc.).
Genetic	e.g., mutation in FGFR3 gene

In order to understand what could be done to improve lives, it might also be useful to draw on capability theory (CT). It has also been given much attention in disability studies (Mitra & Ruger, 2017; Mitra, 2017; Nussbaum, 2006; Brunner, 2019), and it is one of the few philosophical theories that engages with issues, including disability, in a manner that is not only theoretically illuminating but also politically practical. Arising from the work of Amartya Sen and then Martha Nussbaum and others (Robeyns, 2007), CT aims to improve capabilities, which are the freedoms to act. Functionings refer to states of the person or community, what they are able to do and what they are, and things such as literacy, health, and mobility (Anderson, 2010). Capabilities are real freedoms or opportunities to achieve functionings. They are the set of things that people can do and can be. For example, moving would be a function, and capabilities would describe the opportunity for movement (Robeyns, 2007). Functionings are therefore a subset of the capability set.

CT focuses on what people are actually able to do and be and contrasts with other approaches, which emphasize what people possess or do not possess, have done, or how they feel. In CT, well-being is evaluated in terms of how people are able to live, and it enables an analysis of the "actual opportunities a person has" for example in health, in education or in community engagement (Sen, 2009, p. 253). CT highlights that people will choose different goods and should have the freedom to do so. CT also emphasizes what Sen originally called "Conversion handicap": the barriers and difficulties that mean that disabled people have additional costs when it comes to converting resources into functionings, meaning that the same income goes less far (this is one of the big difficulties for universal basic income schemes). These conversion factors include individual, social, and structural difficulties.

We need an approach that will provide us with the outcomes-focused agenda if we are to develop an adequate model of disability and chronic illness. Andrew Sayer (2011) argues that to have effect, sociology needs careful evaluative descriptions that identify both flourishing and suffering as well as their source. Without these, we cannot develop an adequate account of social life. We need some consistency in the way valuations and values are understood in each of these categories. We need a normative framework through which we can work, it is not enough to talk about biographical disruption or the experience of chronic illness; they have to be linked to processes, structures, or actions that improve outcomes.

In the search for a normative framework, it could be thought that human rights, and in particular the Convention on the Rights of Persons with Disabilities (2006), provides an ample "moral compass." However, rights-based approaches are individualist: a person seeks fulfilment of their personal rights and can take a legal case if these are not respected. They do not, as Rose argues, provide a 'means of formulating reforms or for implementing such reforms' (1985;214). In terms of disability, families and others affected by disability are almost completely excluded from the Convention. Nor is it clear how the Convention can be emancipatory for those who are unable to compete in the economic marketplace. If barriers are removed, then many disabled people, but not all, will be able to earn their living and be independent, thanks to the market. What happens to those with more profound impairments who cannot compete? And indeed, rights-based approaches may empower many disabled people so they access education, employment, and community living, but then may leave them unequal and unable to flourish (Fraser, 2013).

Critical realism has the potential to be emancipatory, because it emphasizes mechanisms underlying experiences—mechanisms that can be changed and improved. Capability theory talks about human development as a process of increasing the freedom that people have to act. We consider that the combination of these approaches has the potential to support the construction, not just of a more adequate model of disability, but also a roadmap for its transformation.

CONCLUSION

We support an engaged, empirically grounded disability research agenda. We consider the two major aspects of this endeavor are to explore the lived experience of disability in different settings and to explore disabling barriers. Obviously, disabling barriers will impact lived experiences, and vice versa.

The experience of disablement is far more complex than the 1976 framing of impairment and disability allowed for, or even Michael Oliver's 1990 sociological exploration, of the social model. Nor does the 2001 *International Classification of Functioning, Disability and Health* resolve the difficulties described in this chapter. Thomas's (2007) recommendation that the sociology of illness should be separate from disability studies is not a solution either. We consider that biological, psychological, and social factors need to be understood in their interrelation. We believe that these interactions will impact people with different impairments differently, and that other dimensions of their biographies—gender, class, ethnicity—will also play a role.

The aim of this paper was to develop theoretical and methodological approaches that are able to fully represent the disability experience, in all its diversity. We have argued that our understanding should be able to not only identify mechanisms, predominantly social, economic, and cultural, that operate to exclude and disadvantage different people who have impairments, but also point to ways they can be reconfigured to enable disabled people to flourish. This requires a multi-layered approach, and a sociology of disability has to engage with the medical and health sciences, and other disciplines. The development and growth of technology, communication, and interaction has the potential to liberate many people if they can access them, just as improvements in healthcare enable more people with illness and impairment to survive and lead flourishing lives. For these to be liberating and to help empower and include disabled people, they have to work with people and meet the needs of disabled people. This is where sociology, and social policy, can come in and help to create a framework through which these potentials can be realized.

REFERENCES

Abberley, P. (1996). Work, utopia and impairment. In L. Barton (Ed.), *Disability and Society: Emerging Issues and Insights*. Longman, 61–79.

Anderson, E., 2010. Justifying the capabilities approach to justice. In H. Brighouse & I. Robyns (Eds.), *Measuring justice: Primary goods and capabilities*, (pp. 81–100). Cambridge, Cambridge University Press.

Barnes, C. (1991). *Disabled people in Britain and discrimination*. Hurst and Co.

Barnes, C., & Mercer, G. (Eds.). (1996). *Exploring the divide: Illness and disability*. Disability Press.

Bhaskar, R., & Danermark, B. (2006). Metatheory, interdisciplinarity and disability research: A critical realist perspective. *Scandinavian Journal of Disability Research, 8*(4), 278–297.

Brunner, R. (2019). Critical realism and the "fourth wave": Deepening and broadening social perspectives on mental distress. In N. Watson & S. Vehmas (Eds.), *Routledge handbook of disability studies* (2nd ed., pp. 189–205). London.

Burke, T. F., & Barnes, J. (2018a). Layering, kludgeocracy and disability rights: The limited influence of the social model in American disability policy. *Social Policy and Society, 17*(1), 101–116.

Burke, T. F., & Barnes, J. (2018b). The civil rights template and the Americans with Disabilities Act. In Lynda G. Dodd (Ed.), *The rights revolution revisited* (pp. 167–196). Cambridge University Press.

Bury, M. (1982). Chronic illness as biographical disruption. *Sociology of Health and Illness, 4*, 167–182.

Campbell, J., & Oliver, M. (1996). *Disability politics: Understanding our past, changing our future*. London.

Charlton, J.. (1998). *Nothing about us without us: Disability, oppression and empowerment*. University of California Press.

Charmez, K. (1983). Loss of self: A fundamental form of suffering in the chronically sick. *Sociology of Health and Illness, 5*, 168–195.

Christie, C. (2011). Commission on the future delivery of public services. Scottish Government.

Crow, L. (1996). Including all of our lives. In C. Barnes & G. Mercer (Eds.), *Exploring the divide: Illness and disability* (pp. 55–72). Leeds, Disability Press.

Cunningham-Burley, S., & Backett-Milburn, K. (2002). The body, health and self in the middle years. In S. Nettleton & J. Watson (Eds.), *The body in everyday life* (pp. 142–59). Routledge.

Driedger, D. (1989). *The last civil rights movement: Disabled people's international*. Hurst and Co.

DWP. (2015). Employment gaps for various characteristics. https://www.gov.uk/government/uploads/system/uploads/attachment_data/file/444508/Chapter_13.csv/preview

Ferrie, J., & N. Watson. (2015). The psycho-social impact of impairments. In T. Shakespeare (Ed.), *Disability Research today: International perspectives* (p. 43). Routledge.

Finkelstein, V. (1988). To deny or not to deny disability. *Physiotherapy, 74*(12), 650–652.

Flynn, M., & Citarella, V. (2013). Winterbourne View Hospital: A glimpse of the legacy. *The Journal of Adult Protection, 15*(4), 173.

Fraser, N. (2013). *Fortunes of feminism: From state-managed capitalism to neoliberal crisis*. Verso Books.

Grech, S., & Soldatic, K. (Eds.). (2016). *Disability in the Global South*. Springer.

Goffman, E. (1968). Stigma-notes on the management of spoiled identity. Penguin.

Haak, P., Lenski, M., Hidecker, M.J.C., Li, M., & Paneth, N. (2009). Cerebral palsy and aging. *Developmental Medicine & Child Neurology*, *51*, 16–23.

Hahn, H. (1996). Antidiscrimination laws and social research on disability: The minority group perspective. *Behavioral Sciences and the Law*, *14*, 41–59.

Hasler, F. (1993). Developments in the disabled people's movement. In J. Swain et al. (Eds.), *Disabling barriers, enabling environments* (pp. 278–283). SAGE Publications.

Kinnear, D., Morrison, J., Allan, L., Henderson, A., Smiley, E., & Cooper, S. A. (2018). Prevalence of physical conditions and multimorbidity in a cohort of adults with intellectual disabilities with and without Down syndrome: cross-sectional study. *BMJ open*, *8*(2), p.e018292.

Levitas, R. (2013). *Utopia as method: The imaginary reconstitution of society*. Springer.

Locock, L., Ziebland, S., & Dumelow, C., 2009. Biographical disruption, abruption and repair in the context of motor neurone disease. *Sociology of health & illness*, *31*(7), 1043–1058.

Miller, E. J., & Gwynne, G. V. (1972). *A life apart: A pilot study of residential institutions for the physically handicapped and the young chronic sick*. Taylor & Francis.

Mitra, S. (2017). *Disability, health and human development*. New York Springer Nature.

Mitra, S., & Ruger, J. P. (Eds.). (2017). *Health, disability and the capability approach*. Routledge.

Morris, J. (1991). *Pride against prejudice*. The Women's Press.

Nussbaum, M. (2006). *Frontiers of justice disability, nationality, species membership*. Harvard University Press

Oliver, M. (1983). *Social work with disabled people*. Basingstoke

Oliver, M. (1990). *The politics of disablement*. Macmillan.

Oliver, M. (1992). Changing the social relations of research production. *Disability, Handicap and Society*, *7*(2), 101–115.

Paterson, K., & Watson, N. (2013). *Ageing with a lifelong condition: The experiences and perception of older people with cerebral palsy*. Edinburgh Capability. https://www.capability-scotl and.org.uk/media/371733/ageing_with_a_lifelong_condition_the_experiences_and_pe rception_of_old.pdf

Reeve, J., Lloyd-Williams, M., Payne, S., & Dowrick, C. (2010). Revisiting biographical disruption: Exploring individual embodied illness experience in people with terminal cancer. *Health*, *14*(2), 178–195.

Robeyns, I. (2007). The capability approach: A theoretical survey. *Journal of Human Development and Capabilities 6* (1), 93–117.

Rose, N. (1985). Unreasonable rights: Mental illness and the limits of the law. *Journal of Law and Society*, *12*(2), 199–218.

Ryan, F. (2019). *Crippled: The austerity crisis and the threat to disability rights*. Verso.

Ryan, S. (2017). *Justice for laughing boy: Connor Sparrowhawk-a death by indifference*. Jessica Kingsley Publishers.

Sayer, A. (2011). *Why things matter to people: Social science, values and ethical life*. Cambridge, Cambridge University Press.

Scambler, G. (2004). Re-framing stigma: Felt and enacted stigma and challenges to the sociology of chronic and disabling conditions. *Social Theory and Health 2*, 29–46.

Sen, A.K. (2009). *The idea of justice*. Harvard University Press.

Shakespeare, T. (2013). *Disability rights and wrongs revisited*. Routledge.

Shakespeare, T., Watson, N. (2001a). The social model of disability: An outdated ideology? *Research in Social Science and Disability*, *2*, 9–28.

Shakespeare, T., & Watson, N. (2001b). Making the difference: Disability, politics, and recognition. In G. L. Albrecht, K. D. Seelman, & M. Bury (Eds.), *Handbook of disability studies* (pp. 546–564). SAGE Publications.

Shakespeare T, Watson N, (2001) The social model of disability: an outdated ideology? in S.Barnartt and B.Altman (eds) *Exploring Theories and Expanding Methodologies: where are we and where do we need to go?*, JAI, Oxford.

Shakespeare, T., & Watson, N. (2010). Beyond models: Understanding the complexity of disabled people's lives. In G. Scambler & S. Scambler (Eds.), *New directions in the sociology of chronic and disabling conditions* (pp. 57–77). Palgrave Macmillan.

Shakespeare, T., Watson, N., Brunner, R., Cullingworth, J., Hameed, S., Scherer, N., Pearson, C., & Reichenberger, V. (2022). Disabled people in Britain and the impact of the COVID-19 pandemic. *Social Policy and Administration 56* (1) 103–117.

Shilling, C. (1993). *The body and social theory*. SAGE Publications.

Social Metrics Commission. (2019). Measuring poverty. https://socialmetricscommission.org .uk/wp-content/uploads/2019/07/SMC_measuring-poverty-201908_full-report.pdf

Thomas, C. (1999). *Female forms: Experiencing and understanding disability*. Open University Press.

Thomas, C. (2004). *Developing the social relational in the social model of disability: a theoretical agenda*. In: C. Barnes & G. Mercer (Eds.), *Implementing the social model of disability*. Disability Press. https://disability-studies.leeds.ac.uk/wp-content/uploads/sites/40/library/ Barnes-implementing-the-social-model-chapter-3.pdf (Accessed January 6 2022).

Thomas, C. (2007). *Sociologies of disability and illness: Contested ideas in disability studies*. Palgrave Macmillan.

Thomas, C. (2012). Theorising disability and chronic illness: Where next for perspectives in medical sociology? *Social Theory & Health, 10*(3), 209–228.

Thompson, S., Shakespeare, T., & Wright, M. (2010). Disability and identity across the life course: The restricted growth experience. *Medische Anthropologie 22* (2), 237–251.

Union of the Physically Impaired Against Segregation. (1976). *Fundamental principles of disablement*. UPIAS.

Vehmas, S., & Watson, N. (2014). Moral wrongs, disadvantages, and disability: A critique of critical disability studies. *Disability & Society, 29*(4), 638–650.

Watson, N. (2012). Theorising the lives of disabled children: How can disability theory help?. *Children & Society, 26*(3), 192–202.

Watson, N. (2019). Agency, structure and emancipatory research: Researching disablement and impairment. In Watson N and Vehmas S (eds) *Routledge handbook of disability studies* Routledge 127–141.

Whitehead, M., Morris, J. N., & Black, S. D. (1990). *Inequalities in health: The health divide. The black report*. Penguin Books.

Williams, G. (1984). The genesis of chronic illness: Narrative reconstruction *Sociology of Health and Illness 6* , 175–200.

Williams, G. (1996). Representing disability: Some questions of phenomenology and politics. In C. Barnes & G. Mercer (Eds.), *Exploring the divide: Illness and disability*. Disability Press.

Williams, S. (2010). The biopolitics of chronic illness: Biology, power and personhood. In G. Scambler & S. Scambler (Eds.), *New directions in the sociology of chronic and disabling conditions: Assaults on the lifeworld* (pp. 205–224). Palgrave Macmillan.

Wilson, S. (2007). "When you have children, you're obliged to live": Motherhood, chronic illness and biographical disruption. *Sociology of Health & Illness, 29*(4), 610–626.

Wiseman, P., & Watson, N. (2021). "Because I've got a learning disability, they don't take me seriously:" Violence, wellbeing, and devaluing people with learning disabilities. *Journal of Interpersonal Violence.* https://doi.org/10.1177/0886260521990828

World Health Organization. (2001). *International classification of functioning, disability and health.* WHO.

World Health Organization. (2011). *World report on disability.* WHO.

CHAPTER 3

....

SOCIOLOGICAL
PERSPECTIVES ON
DISABILITY

....

LAURA MAULDIN

INTRODUCTION

....

RACE, class, and gender are central to sociological analyses. However, scholars of disability in sociology have also long argued for disability to be considered as a social category and analyzed as such by sociologists. The interdisciplinary field of disability studies is based on that exact premise: Disability is a sociopolitical category that fundamentally structures every individual's experiences, regardless of their disability status. Indeed, the foundational concepts that influenced the beginning of the field of disability studies came out of sociological scholarship and continue to inform the subfield of the sociology of disability today.

The roots of this scholarship are often attributed to influential British sociologist Michael Oliver, who coined the term "social model of disability" in 1983 (Shakespeare, 2013). Simply put, the social model argued that disability is socially produced through structural and cultural arrangements that exclude individuals with various types of impairments. In UK disability scholarship, the distinction between impairment and disability became central; disability is a social process and not the inevitable result of an individual body's condition. As Oliver states, the social model goes "beyond the personal limitations that impaired individuals may face, to social restrictions imposed by an unthinking society. Disability is understood as a social and political issue rather than a medical one" (Oliver, 1998, p. 1446).

The social model, however, is only a basic origin and foundation for thinking about disability and has been critiqued by many (e.g., Crow, 1996; French, 1993; Morris, 1999; Shakespeare & Watson, 2001). Since its origins, scholarship on disability has progressed considerably toward more complex conceptualizations of disability. As a result, disability studies scholars are moving toward more relational models of disability that incorporate the realities of impairment, embodiment, *and* social barriers (e.g., Kafer, 2013; Shakespeare, 2006). And scholars theorize how disability is inflected by gender (e.g., Garland-Thomson, 2003) and race (e.g., Schalk & Kim, 2020). Similar to other axes of inequality investigated in sociology, disability is cast as a social phenomenon equivalent to race, class, or gender and as intersecting with these categories. In the discipline of sociology, understanding processes of stratification and inequality are central to the discipline, but disability has not yet been included as a standard axis of analysis.

Perhaps more important here is what the social model is meant to contrast. It is set up in opposition to a medical or individual model that defines disability based on individual condition or pathology, locates the source of the problem on the impaired body, and fails to focus critique and analysis on structural factors that shape, among other things, individual- and community-level experiences of disability (Oliver, 2013; Shakespeare & Watson, 2001). This last problematic aspect of the medical model of disability is one that should resonate across sociology: It is our job as sociologists to examine structural factors and social norms that produce individual and community experiences, not to reproduce norms and values about how individuals, because of particular physical attributes, are "naturally" excluded from some realms of society more than others. Psychologists tend to focus on psychological effects of disability for disabled people and their families or caregivers, anthropologists study human behavior and culture, and others in more health-related fields study the more physical or clinical aspects of disability. Sociology is uniquely positioned to understand how disability as a social category is made through institutional structures, larger patterns of exclusion and inclusion, and emphasis on power and inequality. Indeed, it is anti-sociological to conceive of disability as a physical attribute that naturally excludes or disqualifies individuals from certain social spaces or privileges and/or inevitably impedes social mobility. Nevertheless, much of sociology has either been plagued by a medical model understanding of disability or been outright ignored by sociologists altogether. As Barnartt writes, "Most sociologists ignored the phenomenon of disability until recently" (Barnartt, 2017, p. xv).

This chapter examines how sociology more broadly—that is, outside the subfield of the sociology of disability—has traditionally approached disability. What it reveals is that despite a corpus of scholarship in the subfield of sociology of disability (which is heavily influenced by a social model legacy and disability studies), broader sociology has typically failed to understand the social category of disability and the processes of ableism. In a review of the highest-ranking generalist and medical sociology journals, Stoll and Egner (2021, p. 11) write, "While sociologists view systems of oppression like racism, sexism, and classism as worthy of great theoretical and empirical consideration in our discipline—and we should—when it comes to fatphobia and ableism as we have illustrated, sociologists have been relatively silent by comparison." Meanwhile, theorizing disability has been vital in the interdisciplinary field of disability studies; there are numerous sophisticated theories of disability in the field. However, disability studies is interdisciplinary and often more humanities based. This is a stark contrast from norms in sociology requiring empirical data to make arguments. Even so, theories of disability are a strength that sociology can draw from disability studies, and conversely disability studies can benefit from the empirical capabilities that sociologists bring.

Despite such possibilities, Frederick and Shifrer similarly argue that in the broader discipline of sociology there is "a general neglect of disability as a category of inequality altogether" (2018, p. 200). At the same time, research in the sociology of disability consistently reveals that there are patterns and norms that broadly shape disability experience.[1] It seems odd that a discipline like sociology, which claims to be so attuned to power and stratification, would not apply these ideas to a category such as disability more readily. It may be because society at large is rather used to discussing discrimination when it comes to race, gender, or sexuality, but it has only been in more recent years that disability activism has begun to resonate in larger culture and conversations about discrimination with regard to disability. Perhaps it's the relative lateness, compared to other social movements, of laws like the Americans with Disabilities Act. But that was passed in 1990. It may be that disability has been conflated with impairment and obscured as a matter of "health" in such a way that precludes discussing it as a matter of identity or culture. This has meant studies related to disability often show up in medical sociology, an established subfield. But the American Sociological Association did not establish a Disability in Society Section until 2010 and there are currently no sociology programs that specialize in disability. Disability also remains highly stigmatized in a capitalist society where independence and productivity are prized. Could it be that sociologists too have been socialized such that disability is inconceivable as anything other than a personal tragedy? Why have we not yet been able to see this supposedly "private trouble" as a "public issue," as C. Wright Mills would put it?

Importantly, as disability scholarship has progressed in other disciplines and more nuanced theoretical understandings emerged, there has been a shift from the project of solely understanding disability toward also conceptualizing and understanding ableism as a value system (e.g., Campbell, 2009; Wolbring, 2008). "Ableism, like other "isms" such as racism and sexism, describes discrimination toward a social group, in this case disabled people, but it also describes how certain ideals and attributes are valued or not valued" (Friedman & Owen, 2017). Sociologists are generally inclined toward greater understanding of systems of thought such as "-isms," and their historical origins and effects, yet there has been a surprising absence of considering ableism. In addition to scholarship that aims to better understand sexism and racism, for example, a sociology that acknowledges ableism and incorporates it into research adds a powerful dimension to examinations of inequality and other social phenomenon.

Campbell (2009) and Wolbring (2008) both emphasize that ableism is more than simply a preference for nondisability; it is a set of values that privilege certain bodies and features over others. Wolbring writes that "ableism reflects the sentiment of certain social groups and social structures that value and promote certain abilities, for example, productivity and competitiveness, over others" (2008, p. 253). Wolbring goes so far as to say that ableism is the "umbrella-ism" upon which other isms like racism are based (2008, p. 253). This is echoed by recent disability justice work by Lewis (2019), who defines ableism as "a system that places value on people's bodies and minds based on socially constructed ideas of normalcy, intelligence, and excellence." Lewis goes on to inextricably link this to racism—that these commitments to particular forms of intelligence are rooted in racism, and specifically anti-Blackness (Lewis, 2019). This discussion of ableism and the evolving theoretical work being done in disability studies has not been, for the most part, integrated into sociology, even as such theoretical ideas are clearly compatible with sociological thought and practice.

This brings us to the question: If disability has not largely been seen as an axis of inequality in sociology or considered in the context of ableism, how has it been conceptualized? To answer this question, the sections that follow examine the landscape of the dominant theoretical frames for understanding disability in sociology. First, the primary location of scholarship on disability has been in medical sociology, where it is subsumed under conceptualizations and investigations of illness. Second, the subfield of sociology of the body/embodiment also engages disability, but the dominant approaches here mimic some of the tensions seen in medical sociology. Finally, feminist sociological scholarship, which crosses multiple specializations within sociology, has also included disability in its analyses and, while it is still not commonplace, it has been more likely to treat disability as an axis of inequality. This is particularly seen in scholarship that engages with intersectionality and the concept of disability justice. For this reason, feminist scholarship may be a fertile place for disability to grow in the discipline, as feminist scholarship is increasingly attending to disability in intersectional analyses (Chapple, 2019; Naples et al., 2018; Schalk & Kim, 2020).

In the following sections, I trace various approaches to conceptualizing disability in sociology. What becomes clear are the ways in which these subfields of health and illness, body/embodiment, and feminist scholarship all have areas of overlap and cross pollination but also share similar threads and histories in sociology that limit approaches to or even mentions of disability. Unlike other social sciences like economics, disability is often not even conceptualized as a category or included in measurements or data collection, except in cases such as Acemoglu and Angrist's (2001) work on disability and employment. Throughout the sections, I look at why this exclusion of disability as a category endures in sociology. I also contrast various sociological approaches to disability in mainstream sociology with those in disability studies and the subfield of sociology of a disability to make the departures a bit clearer. Finally, I conclude with some thoughts about where new scholarship in disability might be going in sociology.

Disability's Common Home in Sociology: Medical Sociology

Medical sociology has the longest history of engaging with disability, but it also demonstrates the dominance of a medical model conceptualization in sociology. This is because disability in medical sociology is positioned as a subcategory of illness, specifically chronic illness. In *Sociologies of Illness and Disability* (2007), Carol Thomas provides a deeply researched and comprehensive history of disability in medical sociology and the tensions in approaches to disability in sociology (specifically medical sociology) and disability studies. She characterizes these tensions broadly as two competing frames: medical sociology/sociology of health and illness, informed by symbolic interactionism, frames disability as social deviance, while a sociology of disability, informed by disability studies, frames disability as social oppression.

How did this social deviance frame of disability in medical sociology come to be? As Barnartt (2017) points out, we can look back to Parsons's (1951) concept of the "sick role," a foundational concept in medical sociology, and the long-lasting effect on how disability was seen. Grounded in a time when sociology was developing grand theories to explain overall society, Parsons attempted to map and define social roles for all individuals. The sick role accounted for individuals with an acute illness, providing them a temporary reprieve from their usual social roles and responsibilities. That is, illness was seen as deviating from one's "normal" social role, which assumed being nondisabled, equating this with productivity, efficiency, and contribution to overall society. As a result, illness was seen as disqualifying, incompatible with occupying a social role, with the sick role providing cover for resigning from social roles/obligations through a form of "sanctioned deviance." And while those in the sick role did not choose that fate, they were expected to "work to become well, by cooperating with medical personnel, because it is in the interest of society that illness become minimized" (Barnartt, 2017, p. xviii). That is, being ill is a sanctioned type of deviance, but only if it is a short period of time and resolved through medical intervention. As I elaborate on further later, this expectation to normalize oneself through medical intervention, as part of the processes of medicalization (e.g., Conrad, 2007; Zola, 1972) is also an important subject in both the sociology of disability and medical sociology.

Although Parsons never used the word *disability* and his concept of the sick role did not even account for chronic illness, only acute, these beginnings nonetheless fundamentally linked disability to deviance in medical sociology. As Barnartt writes, "it took little to extend it to chronic illnesses and disabilities" (2017, p. xix), and thus chronic illness and disability came under a deviance lens. Certainly, the sick role has been heavily criticized and for the most part abandoned (e.g., Burnham, 2012; Glenton, 2003; Varul, 2010), but this original framing impacted how chronic illness and disability in medical sociology are seen as forms of deviance. It should be noted that there is a large body of work in the sociology of health/illness devoted to the illness experience (e.g., Charmaz, 1993, and others), but even scholarship on illness experience, as I address further later, still maintains a deficit approach to disability.

I purposefully include chronic illness here in a consideration of disability, broadly defined. This is because various laws in the United States, as well as national and global health and disability organizations, define disability in relation to both physical and mental bodily functions, which would clearly include chronic illness (Thomas, 2007). There is also a large literature in sociology on conceptualizing disability that engages with measurement and type of impairment (see Altman [2016] for a detailed account), and most categorizations adopted by governmental agencies rely on definitions of disability and impairment that would indeed include chronic illness. Furthermore, "As people with impairment, those living with declared or readily apparent characteristics of chronic illnesses share in forms of social exclusion and disadvantage experienced by those whose impairments have other qualities and features" (Thomas, 2007, p. 50). Thus, Thomas argues, people with chronic illness experience ableism, whether or not they identify as disabled, necessitating that we include discussions of chronic illness in disability scholarship informed by a social oppression frame. For all of these reasons, I propose that sociology also adopt a broader universalizing stance on disability for the purposes of research, narrowing to particular type when this is appropriate for the unit of analysis. Indeed, if sociologists were to critically engage with these categorical framings, it would also shape the kinds of data we collect, with implications for survey design and other methods of data collection. Furthermore, embracing ableism as an ideology that assigns value to individuals and groups with regard to their potential for "productivity" would also have the potential to affect how data are analyzed and interpreted.

Even though medical sociology has moved beyond the sick role, an "overarching social deviance paradigm" (Thomas, 2007, p. 15) persists in framing chronic illness and disability in this subfield today. The rise of symbolic interactionism in sociology inspired a turn toward sociology of health/illness and a central line of inquiry became understanding how illnesses are socially constructed and how these meanings shape the experiences of people living with one (e.g., Brown, 1995; Epstein, 1996; Freidson, 1988). Since then, studies have focused on patient experiences with illness and contributed to our understandings of living with a chronic illness in particular (Barker, 2005; Charmaz, 1993; Frank, 1997; Kempner, 2014; Kleinman, 1989). However, many such studies still focus on a personal tragedy model of illness—a medical model derivative—and generally adhere to the deviance paradigm (Scambler & Scambler, 2010).

Charmaz's (1993) classic work on chronic illness centered on the interruption, crisis, and isolation it causes for the individual presents one example. At times, it addresses how chronically ill people interact with others, though it is mainly framed as a personal process of managing stigma. Indeed, in a recent piece, Charmaz (2020) traces the conceptualization of disability as deviance within the symbolic interactionist frame to the influence of Goffman's work on stigma. Charmaz, citing Barnartt's (2016) critique of Goffman on how stigma is seen as "stable" and casts disabled people as embodying a form of deviance, concedes that the symbolic interactionist tradition has ignored structural causes of disability oppression. But she maintains that it is entirely possible for symbolic interactionists to contextualize interactions and experiences within social structure. This reflection might signal an openness for the influence of what Thomas (2007) called a social oppression frame for disability integrated into the subfield of medical sociology/sociology of health and illness. At the very least, taking structural aspects into account and acknowledging that disability is a social process and category that exists because of exclusion, not solely because of a physiological status, bends this work more toward scholarship concerned with inequality. The transformation of disability from a one-dimensional "health status" to an axis of inequality in medical sociology could transform the subfield in generative ways. This is more likely to occur if mainstream sociology would recognize disability as such; the likelihood of such recognition would increase with placement of rigorous empirical and/or theoretical research clearly showing the salience of disability as an axis of inequality in high-impact journals in the field.

Another area of scholarship where disability has appeared in the sociology of health/illness is scholarship interrogating medicalization (Conrad, 2007; Zola, 1972). Irving Zola's work had specific and lasting impacts on this area of scholarship. Indeed, as the person who first conceptualized medicalization (1972) and a central figure in establishing early disability studies, he advocated for and blended a social oppression approach to disability into sociology of health/illness. For example, *Missing Pieces* (Zola, 1982) not only discussed experiences of impairment but also the cultural, structural, and interactional making of disability and devaluation of disability in society. In other words, he integrated both the impairment-related experiences *and* the exclusion of disabled people in society due to disability being a devalued category, linking the individual with social structure. Though he does not use the word *ableism*, he points out the systemic exclusion of disabled or chronically ill people as a social category and the expectation that individuals should "overcome" their impairments or risk being blamed, both of which are results of ableism. He further argues that chronically ill individuals have a minority group experience and that each individual's experience or hardship related to their disability or illness is specific to them, but the "core problem" is not (Zola, 1982, p. 211). That is, the "core problem" he refers to is not the disability or illness itself, but its interaction with social structures and the larger cultural devaluation of disability. Despite his important scholarship, however, as Shakespeare and Watson state, it is still primarily the case that "in medical sociology it is the illness that is the social experience of the impairment, rather than issues of inequality or powerlessness that are placed at the center of research" (2010, p. 65).

There are, however, some examples of scholarship centered on medicalization where the two frames of disability are at times brought together fruitfully and contrasted. This is particularly seen in scholarship focused on pregnancy, mothering, and disability (e.g., Blum, 2015; Green, 2007; Leiter, 2004; Litt, 2004; Mauldin, 2016; Rapp, 2000; Rothman, 1993; Scott, 2010) that bridge sociology of disability, sociology of health and illness, and feminist scholarship in unique ways. In these works, sociologists engage with disability as social oppression insofar as they use it to question the motives, outcomes, and consequences of embracing techniques of normalization. These studies reveal the extent to which normalization is culturally sanctioned, as well as structurally favored/enabled within medical and intervention systems meant to serve families. They show how a dominant ideology of disability as deviance persists and is institutionalized into policy and structure. Scholars in this vein examine the social experiences of mothering children with various types of disabilities, and normalization through medical interventions is held up as questionable, particularly as it links to the unequal care demands that such processes place on women.

In many ways, this scholarship can be seen as bringing disability into sociology of health and illness scholarship through the vector of examining ableism (even if this is not explicitly stated in these works) and its impacts on mothers and their disabled children. Campbell (2009), a scholar of ableism in disability studies, inextricably links projects of normalization as products of ableism: "a chief feature of an ableist viewpoint is a belief that impairment or disability (irrespective of "type") is inherently negative and should the opportunity present itself, be ameliorated, cured or indeed eliminated" (Campbell, 2009, p. 5). In sum, while the social deviance model of disability that dominates medical sociology has been critiqued by some medical sociologists as inadequate due to a shift from acute to chronic illnesses in modernity, an aspect unaccounted for in Parsons's original conceptualization (Conrad & Barker, 2010; Scambler & Scambler, 2010; Varul, 2010), there remains work to be done to better integrate a social oppression framing into this subfield.

DISABILITY IN SOCIOLOGY OF THE BODY AND EMBODIMENT

Another subfield that has considered disability, though to a lesser extent, is sociology of the body and embodiment. While medical sociology and sociology of the body are linked and in conversation with each other, there is a tension between them. Often, sociology of the body is seen as a more critical alternative and to be more committed to the contestation of deviance and normalcy when it comes to bodies. And for this reason, it is a subfield with potential for deeper engagement with disability. This section highlights what sociology of the body does and some of the broad strands of thinking within it and how they apply to disability. However, despite the potential for productive conversation between sociology of the body and sociology of disability, there does not seem to be a substantial body of empirical work on disability in this subfield.

In his piece outlining how disability has been seen in sociology of the body, Bryan Turner (2001) begins with the familiar refrain that disability has been surprisingly neglected and ignored in mainstream sociology, including sociology of health and illness as well as sociology of the body. He begins by broadly characterizing two main strands in sociology of the body: (1) Foucauldian and social constructionist approaches to the body that center on issues of power, normalization, and governmentality, and (2) phenomenological approaches that center experiences of the body in everyday life, many of which connect back to Goffman's works on stigma (Turner, 2001). While these strands have differing approaches to disability and focus on different "levels" of disability, both can challenge the medical model of disability. The poststructuralist or Foucauldian (Foucault, 1980, 1987, 1988) approach understands bodies vis-à-vis the ways they are "produced, categorized, and regulated" (Turner, 2001, p. 255), thus considering the discursive construction of bodies rather than centering some kind of individual pathology as the medical model would. However, this discursive focus denies or erases any material or sensuous experiences of bodies. In contrast, the phenomenological approach privileges those very experiences, revealing how "our perceptions of the world are always grounded in the relationship between our embodiment and the world" (Turner, 2001, p. 255). This counters the medical model because a medical model rejects subjective experiences and only sees the body as a collection of "normal" or "pathological" parts. The emergence of these two strands are consequences of the fact that historically in sociology, it was primarily Goffman and Foucault who examined bodies directly.

Despite the potential of these two strands to consider disability in more nuanced, sociological ways than the medical model, Turner states that a deviance framing of disability persists in this subfield as well. In particular, Goffman (1963) has had an enormous impact in the phenomenological strand of sociology of the body (and clearly his work is an important thread linking the subfields of body/embodiment and health/illness), but once again, deviance is the central frame for understanding disability. Turner explains that the phenomenological approach in sociology of the body "keeps the body in focus as an object of intellectual inquiry . . . [and] recognizes the complex interplay between the objectified body of medical discourse, the phenomenal body of everyday experience, and the body image that, as it were, negotiates the social spaces between identity, experience, and social relationships" (Turner, 2001, p. 254). One study by Seymour (2012) that he highlights does engage with disability and the body through more of a social model–informed lens. But, overall, this symbolic interactionist–informed approach in sociology of the body tends to privilege the concept of stigma. And, as discussed earlier regarding Barnartt's (2016) critique of Goffman, this grounding of disability in stigma has not only been heartily critiqued by disability studies scholars (Brune et al., 2014) but sociologists as well. For example, Oliver (1996) writes that "Goffman's use of the term 'stigma' is based upon perceptions of the oppressor rather than those of the oppressed . . . [and] takes as given the imposed segregation, passivity and inferior status of stigmatized individuals and groups—including disabled people" (Oliver, 1996, p. 22).

Subsuming disability into studies of illness or stigma and doing so in the absence of integrating a social oppression or social model–influenced approach has severely limited what both sociologists of the body and sociologists of health/illness can do. As Freund (2001) points out, "Sociological approaches to the body and disability take the individual body as their point of departure, neglecting (as advocates of the social model might point out), social structure and its enabling as well as disabling features" (2001, p. 691). Turner (2001) suggests that these failures of grappling with disability in sociology of the body are ironic because symbolic interactionism, a major school of thought in sociology, has been influential in problematizing notions of normality and deviance in the first place. Yet serious engagement with work in disability studies that considers the materiality and biological reality of disabled and sick bodies or bodies in pain (Hughes & Paterson, 1997; Kafer, 2013; Siebers, 2010)—that is, work developing critiques of norms regarding the types of bodies and minds that are valued and considered in scholarship— appear to have not been adequately integrated into or informed sociology of the body scholarship since Turner's (2001) critiques. Furthermore, sociology of the body is also especially concerned with the relationship between body-self/identity, as the body has emerged as more central to identity as we have entered high modernity (Giddens, 1991). Once again, disability studies and sociology of disability routinely investigates disability as a social category—and indeed one that results in a cultural group—demonstrating how imperative acknowledging disability as a sociopolitical category is for accurately understanding disability identity (Darling, 2013; Grue, 2016; Shakespeare, 1996). Yet it seems such work remains largely absent in sociology of the body scholarship, despite its potential for better informing sociological analyses of disabled bodies.

In addition to questioning norms about what constitutes valuable bodies/minds and examining the relationship between the body and identity, sociology of the body is also concerned with new capacities for individualization. As biomedical capabilities further develop, technologies that blur the boundaries of bodies and technology or rituals of customization have come under the purview of sociology of the body (Shilling, 2003). This seems again to be a ripe area of possible conversation with disability studies, where the ethics and consequences of medical technologies are debated (Blume, 2010; Galis, 2011; Mauldin, 2014; Moser, 2006; Parens & Asch, 2000) and design and world building with assistive technologies are investigated (Fritsch et al., 2019; Hamraie & Fritsch, 2019). Shilling (2003) does argue for aging, sick, different, or nondefault bodies to be more present and integrated into sociology of the body scholarship and asks how doing so might reflect on and revise social theories about bodies. But without integrating insights from disability studies or sociologists of disability, sociologists of the body are limited in the kind of theoretical and empirical work they can do on disability. This once again shows the need for a broader recognition of disability as a category so that these various subfields can work across one another rather than having smaller areas of foci within them that may address disability in some way, without larger key disciplinary concepts to turn to.

While these two main strands in sociology of the body—discursive/phenomenological or epistemological/ontological—structure the subfield, sociology of the body/embodiment is also fundamentally influenced by feminist scholarship. Indeed, feminists were some of the first to take up the question of the body in sociology and "Feminism as a praxis has taught us to look first for the effects of politics in what is done to bodies" (Frank, 1990, p. 132). And while sociology of the body was dominated by a discursive approach, there has been a biological turn in feminism (Pitts-Taylor, 2016). As this shift occurred, feminists in sociology of the body began to more explicitly consider the materiality of the body and shift toward more ontological questions (e.g., Bendelow et al., 2003; Fausto-Sterling, 2000; Grosz, 1994). And in his work linking this biological turn with scholarship on health, illness, and disability in sociology, Williams (2006) writes there is a need "not simply for an approach to the study of chronic illness which explicitly focuses on the body, but one which incorporates both social and biological facts in doing so" (2006, p. 11). He calls for more engagement with impairment, advocating for integrating Carol Thomas's notion of "impairment effects" into both the subfields of health/illness and body/embodiment. In a similar manner, epistemological/ontological divides in disability studies were also challenged, with scholars pointing to the limitations of a purely constructed body that adhered to a strong social model. For example, this resulted in work like Shakespeare's (2006) proposed "critical realist model," Kafer's (2013) political relational model of disability, and Sieber's work on pain (2010). All of these are examples of disability studies scholarship that laments the removal of disabled bodies and their biological realities.

In sum, even though Arthur Frank (1990) declared that "Bodies are in" (1990, p. 131), sociologists of disability Shakespeare and Watson (1996) responded with, "But what exactly are these bodies that are 'in'? [Sociology of the body] is predominantly theoretically driven with a reliance on avant-garde theory for its own sake." They argue that there is "little or no empirical research" on disabled people in this subfield, and more than twenty years later, this seems to still be the case. It is difficult not to see the influence of Mike Oliver's scholarship in sociology of disability behind this critique of sociology of the body as remaining too theoretical. Oliver advocated for an explicitly "emancipatory" approach to scholarship on disability where the scholarship produced should be "part of the struggle by disabled people to challenge the oppression they currently experience in their daily lives" (Oliver, 1992, p. 102). This overlaps with feminist methodologies and epistemologies, long emphasizing an emancipatory orientation (e.g., Craven & Davis, 2013), which heavily figure into the sociology of the body subfield. And Rosemarie Garland-Thomson's field establishing work in feminist disability studies makes clear that it is about accounting for disabled bodies and identities (Garland-Thomson, 2003). Thus, there is potential for growing the fruitful affinity between sociology of the body and sociology of disability. And I will now more explicitly turn to the contributions of feminist sociological scholarship to investigations of disability.

DISABILITY IN FEMINIST SOCIOLOGICAL SCHOLARSHIP

In this final section, I wish to briefly point out some feminist sociological scholarship on disability, much of which intersects with the main two subfields of health/illness and body/embodiment outlined earlier. It bears mentioning that feminist sociologists have perhaps been some of the few and earliest adopters of social model–influenced conceptualizations of disability in sociology. See, for example, the earlier works of Rothman (1993) and Sandelowski (1994) examining the constructions of disability in prenatal care. Since these earlier engagements, a subset of scholarship on gender, family, and disability emerged, which Blum synthesizes by articulating that "feminists in the social sciences largely engage with disability through the study of families (in all their diversity) and relations of gendered caregiving and interdependence" (Blum, 2020, p. 180). As noted, much of this scholarship, situated at the intersection of health/illness and sociology of disability, examines mothering disabled children. Thus, this is work that engages disability in terms of how it impacts gendered expectations and norms around care. That is, disability is a vector through which norms about care are constructed based on gendered expectations to be a "good" mother and raise a "healthy" child. And it is this aspect of this scholarship that does make it unique; often these studies directly confront systems of care and intervention that insist on normalization of disability and document parents' negotiation of this.

Second, feminist sociological work on disability questions turns toward examining how sociopolitical aspects of disability and ideologies of ableism intersect with gender and gender roles. Importantly, recent work by scholars such as Frederick (2017) examines the experiences of disabled mothers, and Dillaway and Lysack (2014) analyze experiences of disabled women obtaining reproductive healthcare. Both of these turn toward delineating how disability and ableist ideologies work in concert with gender as an axis of inequality shaping disabled women's lives when it comes to mothering. What is important about this is how disability is not relegated to something women care for, but rather that disabled women experience ableism as they have children and parent, all while dealing with oppression at the intersection of their gender and disability. Similarly, Fannon (2016) writes of blind women's negotiation of beauty ideals for women, while Gerschick (2000) argues for developing theories at the intersection of gender and disability and Fine and Asch (2009) address the unique (and magnified) oppression for disabled women across numerous social spheres. And finally, Chapple (2019) argues for the development of a Black Deaf feminism in order to better understand the particular oppression experienced by Black Deaf women. Empirical and theoretical works such as these that develop more sociological evidence demonstrating how disability operates as an axis of inequality; that is, ableism acts in concert with sexism and gender norms, affecting what kinds of assumptions or rights are ascribed to disabled people in relation to their gender.

The desire to integrate disability as an axis of inequality is one commonality between feminist sociological scholarship and sociology of disability, but it is only recently that this has been more robustly developed as a strategy in sociological scholarship. One example of how this has been done is through explicitly positioning disability as an axis of inequality via engagement with the concept of intersectionality. Intersectionality, a concept from Black feminist thought that reveals how systems of domination work across social categories, particularly race/racism as it intersects with sex/sexism (Collins, 1986; Collins & Bilge, 2016; Crenshaw, 1989). To be sure, scholars in critical disability studies have long been doing intersectional work that centers disability an axis of inequality as it interacts with and is co-constructed with other axes of inequality (e.g., Dunhamn et al., 2015; Erevelles, 2014a,b; Erevelles & Minear, 2010; Hirschmann, 2012; Lukin, 2013; Mollow, 2017; Nishida, 2016; Schalk, 2018). Beyond disability studies, disabled people of color working outside academia on a platform of disability justice also produce intersectional scholarship (Berne et al., 2018; Harriet Tubman Collective, 2016; Lewis, 2019; Piepzna-Samarasinha, 2018). However, in the discipline of sociology, as has been reviewed throughout this chapter, there has been far less engagement or taking seriously of disability as a social category much less one to be included in intersectional analyses.

As mentioned, however, more recent scholarship has emerged to critique this omission and begin to address it. For example, Frederick and Shifrer (2018, p. 2) state that "The discipline has not offered much in the way of expansive intersectional analyses of race and disability beyond social determinants of health. This omission is quite stunning, given that racism and ableism are powerful interacting forces in contemporary issues of concern to sociologists, including mass incarceration and the school-to-prison pipeline." Shortly after their publications, a special issue of *Gender & Society* on gender, disability, and intersectionality was published. In the introduction, Naples, Mauldin and Dillaway discuss how "Despite [intersectionality's] analytic power to incorporate analysis of diverse forms of power and inequality into the framework, disability remains consistently missing from most contemporary intersectional studies in sociology" (2018, p. 10). The issue featured work by Bailey and Mobley (2019) developing a Black disability studies framework and Miles (2019) on Black disabled women's experiences with home ownership and the concept of the "Strong Black woman." It also featured articles using various empirical sources to document intersecting inequalities with regard to race, gender, and disability (Maroto et al., 2018); gender, disability, and work (Brown & Moloney, 2018); and the intersection of queerness and disability (Egner, 2019). All of these articles either theoretically or empirically (or both) engage with disability as a social category that is co-constructed with race and gender. They thus contribute to more theoretical sophistication regarding disability in sociology or are examples of how to collect data and conduct quantitative analyses that take disability meaningfully into account in order with regard to gendered patterns of work and economic inequality. Furthermore, these innovative theoretical approaches and research designs have yielded empirical work that demonstrates the importance of including disability as a social category.

In sum, feminist sociologists have been early adopters of a social model/social oppression framework of disability in sociology. More recent work incorporates disability as an axis of inequality that intersects with other social categories like gender and race. But sociological scholarship remains far behind other fields like feminist and critical disability studies in terms of its engagement with these topics both empirically and theoretically. For example, feminist theorist Rosemarie Garland Thomson published her groundbreaking essay on integrating feminist theory into disability studies in 2003.

CONCLUSION

The premise of this chapter has been that understanding patterns and norms of inequality with regard to disability is as central to sociological inquiry as the patterns we examine with regard to other social categories. The preceding sections outline how disability has been approached in sociology in the subfields that it has appeared in most often, medical sociology, sociology of the body/embodiment, and feminist scholarship. In medical sociology or sociology of health/illness, a deviance framing of disability that does not account for structural factors still dominates. Even with the turn toward prioritizing illness experiences, this framing has limited much of sociology of health/illness to a more medical model–influenced approach to disability. In sociology of the body/embodiment, calls for more integration of disabled and sick bodies into scholarship in that subfield have largely not been effective. And the two dominant strands of the subfield have not yet been able to advance theory on disability. Finally, feminist sociological work appeared across both of these subfields as examples of places where a social model–influenced or social oppression approach to disability has been seen.

As reviewed earlier, in contrast to other subfields in sociology, sociologists of disability operate under two assumptions: (1) disability should be seen as an axis of inequality and interrogated as a social problem, and (2) disability is not "marginal" and need not be relegated to a "special case" or specific site of analysis, but rather ableism understood as one of the defining characteristics of bodies as abled/disabled, productive/unproductive, efficient/inefficient, worthy/unworthy in society operate on all of us and such values permeate all of society. This value system is understood as ableism. In other words, sociologists of disability want both disability to be recognized as a social category and for ableism to be understood as a central organizing feature of society. But taking disability seriously as a social category in sociology would mean incorporating an understanding of ableism in society into the work we do, developing theoretical and methodological techniques that consider ableism, and becoming more familiar with research already being done in disability studies.

The three subfields covered in this chapter—medical sociology, body and embodiment, and feminist scholarship—are in dire need of more awareness of ableism and integration of disability as a standard social category. As suggested earlier, medical sociologists can begin to integrate disability by confronting the theoretical histories that have shaped their work and being mindful of not reproducing work that positions disability as a deficit. There is much in disability studies to be learned about the ways that ableism also contributes to health outcomes; ableism is itself disabling! And medical sociologists might begin by engaging sociology of disability and the tools of disability studies in both research design (i.e., critically thinking about categories of analysis or measurement and/or being careful to ask questions of participants in qualitative research about their experiences of ableism). Sociology of body and embodiment might begin by attending more overtly to disability; there was a dearth of examples of body and embodiment scholarship that engaged with disability or used it as its focus outside of the aligned feminist scholarship on gender and disability with regard to beauty norms. Body and embodiment scholars might ask: What generative and creative ways of being in the world, of being in spaces, and of interacting with others does the disabled body bring? Finally, feminist sociological scholarship may be at the forefront of sociological work on disability, particularly with its attention to disability as an aspect of intersectionality. Further work in feminist scholarship, however, could benefit by engaging ableism more deeply, especially ensuring attention to the connection between racism and ableism, and engaging with the work of disability justice scholars and communities that are at the forefront of social change with regard to care systems and care collectives.

Doing this kind of theoretical and methodological work on disability in the discipline of sociology, however, depends on sociologists being reflexive. Zola (1991) warns it is "the danger of sociology's being so analytic that it becomes too distant from those it is trying to study" (1991, p. 2). He states that issues around disability are part and parcel of understanding other social categories like race, class, gender, sexuality, and age. And he argues that sociologists have to consider our own perspectives, including how we have been socialized into thinking about disability, lest our work "reflect the concerns and views of the investigator more than those of the people who have bodies and (in a socially constructed way) illnesses and disabilities" (1991, p. 5). This is echoed by Oliver (1992) when he states that a large part of the problem in sociology is that sociologists are "seeing the problems that disabled people face as being caused by their individual impairments. These rock-bottom explanations not only see disability as an individual problem but in so doing they reject other possible explanations" (Oliver, 1992, p. 108). Thus, if disability is to be taken seriously as a category, sociologists must prioritize better understanding of the social processes of discrimination that individuals are subjected to. The aim of this chapter was to chart where the gaps in sociology are and to suggest some places wherein sociologists might go to try to close them.

NOTE

1. For example, there are currently eleven volumes of the book series *Research in Social Science and Disability*, edited by Sharon Barnartt and Barbara Altman. This series has served as a de facto journal in sociology for the subfield of disability and is one location to find sociological research that is disability specific.

REFERENCES

Acemoglu, D., & Angrist, J. D. (2001). Consequences of employment protection? The case of the Americans with Disabilities Act. *Journal of Political Economy, 109*(5), 915–957. https://doi.org/10.1086/322836

Altman, B. M. (2016). Conceptual issues in disability: Saad Nagi's contribution to the disability knowledge base. In S. Green & S. Barnartt (Eds.), *Sociology looking at disability: What did we know and when did we know it* (Vol. 9, pp. 57–95). Emerald Group. https://doi.org/10.1108/S1479-354720160000009006

Bailey, M., & Mobley, I. A. (2019). Work in the intersections: A Black feminist disability framework. *Gender & Society, 33*(1), 19–40. https://doi.org/10.1177/0891243218801523

Barker, K. (2005). *The fibromyalgia story: Medical authority and women's worlds of pain.* Temple University Press.

Barnartt, S. (2017). Introduction: An historical overview of sociology looking at disability: What did we know and when did we know it? In S. Green & S. Barnartt (Eds.), *Sociology looking at disability: What did we know and when did we know it?* (Vol. 9, pp. xv–xxxiii). Emerald Group.

Barnartt, S. (2016). How Erving Goffman affected perceptions of disability within sociology. In S. Green & S. Barnartt (Eds.), *Sociology looking at disability: What did we know and when did we know it* (Vol. 9, pp. 29–37). Emerald Group. https://doi.org/10.1108/S1479-35472016000 0009004

Bendelow, G., Birke, L., & Williams, S. (2003). Debating biology. In *Debating biology: Sociological reflections on health, medicine and society* (pp. 1–12). Routledge.

Berne, P., Morales, A. L., Langstaff, D., & Invalid, S. (2018). Ten principles of disability justice. *WSQ: Women's Studies Quarterly, 46*(1), 227–230. https://doi.org/10.1353/wsq.2018.0003

Blum, L. M. (2015). *Raising generation Rx: Mothering kids with invisible disabilities in an age of inequality.* NYU Press.

Blum, L. M. (2020). Gender and disability studies. In N. A. Naples (Ed.), *Companion to women's and gender studies* (pp. 175–194). Wiley-Blackwell.

Blume, S. (2010). *The artificial ear: Cochlear implants and the culture of deafness.* Rutgers University Press.

Brown, P. (1995). Naming and framing: The social construction of diagnosis and illness. *Journal of Health and Social Behavior, Spec No,* 34–52.

Brown, R. L., & Moloney, M. E. (2018). Intersectionality, work, and well-being: The effects of gender and disability. *Gender & Society, 33*(1), 94–122. https://doi.org/10.1177/089124321 8800636

Brune, J., Garland-Thomson, R., Schweik, S., Titchkosky, T., & Love, H. (2014). Forum introduction: Reflections on the fiftieth anniversary of Erving Goffman's stigma. *Disability Studies Quarterly, 34*(1). http://dsq-sds.org/article/view/4014

Burnham, J. C. (2012). The death of the sick role. *Social History of Medicine, 25*(4), 761–776. https://doi.org/10.1093/shm/hks018

Campbell, F. K. (2009). *Contours of ableism: The production of disability and abledness.* Palgrave Macmillan.

Chapple, R. L. (2019). Toward a theory of Black Deaf feminism: The quiet invisibility of a population. *Affilia 34* (2) 186–198. doi:10.1177/0886109918818080.

Charmaz, K. (1993). *Good days, bad days: The self and chronic illness in time.* Rutgers University Press.

Charmaz, K. (2020). Experiencing stigma and exclusion: The influence of neoliberal perspectives, practices, and policies on living with chronic illness and disability. *Symbolic Interaction, 43*(1), 21–45. https://doi.org/10.1002/symb.432

Collins, P. H. (1986). Learning from the outsider within: The sociological significance of Black feminist thought. *Social Problems, 33*(6), S14–S32. https://doi.org/10.2307/800672

Collins, P. H., & Bilge, S. (2016). *Intersectionality.* Polity.

Conrad, P. (2007). *The medicalization of society: On the transformation of human conditions into treatable disorders.* Johns Hopkins University Press.

Conrad, P., & Barker, K. K. (2010). The social construction of illness: Key insights and policy implications. *Journal of Health and Social Behavior, 51 Suppl,* S67–S79. https://doi.org/ 10.1177/0022146510383495

Craven, C., & Davis, D.-A. (Eds.). (2013). *Feminist activist ethnography: Counterpoints to neoliberalism in North America.* Lexington Books.

Crenshaw, K. (1989). Demarginalizing the intersection of race and sex: A Black feminist critique of antidiscrimination doctrine, feminist theory and antiracist politics. *The University of Chicago Legal Forum, 140,* 139–167.

Crow, L. (1996). Including all of our lives. In C. Barnes & G. Mercer (Eds.), *Exploring the divide: Illness and disability* (pp. 55–72). Disability Press.

Darling, R. B. (2013). *Disability and identity: Negotiating self in a changing society*. Lynne Rienner.

Dillaway, H., & Lysack, C. (2014). "My doctor told me I can still have children but . . .": Contradictions in women's reproductive health experiences after spinal cord injury. In M. Nash (Ed.), *Reframing reproduction* (pp. 135–149). Palgrave Macmillan.

Dunhamn, J., Harris, J., Jarrett, S., Moore, L., Nishida, A., Price, M., Robinson, B., & Schalk, S. (2015). Developing and reflecting on a Black disability studies pedagogy: Work from the National Black Disability Coalition. *Disability Studies Quarterly*, 35(2). http://dsq-sds.org/article/view/4637

Egner, J. E. (2019). "The disability rights community was never mine": Neuroqueer disidentification. *Gender & Society*, 33(1), 123–147. https://doi.org/10.1177/0891243218803284

Epstein, S. (1996). *Impure science: AIDS, activism, and the politics of knowledge*. University of California Press.

Erevelles, N. (2014a). Crippin' Jim Crow: Disability, dis-location, and the school-to-prison pipeline. In L. Ben-Moshe, C. Chapman, & A. C. Carey (Eds.), *Disability incarcerated: Imprisonment and disability in the United States and Canada* (pp. 81–99). Palgrave Macmillan. https://doi.org/10.1057/9781137388476_5

Erevelles, N. (2014b). Thinking with disability studies. *Disability Studies Quarterly*, 34(2). https://doi.org/10.18061/dsq.v34i2.4248

Erevelles, N., & Minear, A. (2010). Unspeakable offenses: Untangling race and disability in discourses of intersectionality. *Journal of Literary & Cultural Disability Studies*, 4(2), 127–145. https://doi.org/10.3828/jlcds.2010.11

Fausto-Sterling, A. (2000). *Sexing the body: Gender politics and the construction of sexuality*. Basic Books.

Foucault, M. (1980). *The history of sexuality, vol. 1: An introduction*. Vintage.

Foucault, M. (1987). *The history of sexuality: The use of pleasure*. Penguin.

Foucault, M. (1988). *The history of sexuality, vol. 3: The care of the self*. Vintage.

Frank, A. W. (1990). Bringing bodies back in: A decade review. *Theory, Culture & Society*, 7, 131–162. https://doi.org/10.1177/026327690007001007

Frank, A. W. (1997). *The wounded storyteller: Body, illness, and ethics*. University of Chicago Press.

Fannon, T. A. (2016). Out of sight, sill in mind: Visually impaired women's embodied accounts of ideal femininity. *Disability Studies Quarterly*, 36(1). https://doi.org/10.18061/dsq.v36i1.4326

Fine, M., & Asch, A. (2009). *Women with disabilities: Essays in psychology, culture, and politics*. Temple University Press.

Frederick, A. (2017). Risky mothers and the Normalcy Project: Women with disabilities negotiate scientific motherhood. *Gender & Society*, 31(1), 74–95. https://doi.org/10.1177/0891243216683914

Frederick, A., & Shifrer, D. (2018). Race and disability: From analogy to intersectionality. *Sociology of Race and Ethnicity*. https://doi.org/10.1177/2332649218783480

Freidson, E. (1988). *Profession of medicine: A study of the sociology of applied knowledge*. University of Chicago Press.

French, S. (1993). Disability, impairment or something in between? In J. Swain, V. Finklestein, S. French, & M. Oliver (Eds.), *Disabling barriers, enabling environments* (pp. 44–48). SAGE Publications.

Freund, P. (2001). Bodies, disability and spaces: The social model and disabling spatial organisations. *Disability & Society*, *16*(5), 689–706. https://doi.org/10.1080/0968759012 0070079

Friedman, C., & Owen, A. L. (2017). Defining disability: Understandings of and attitudes towards ableism and sisability. *Disability Studies Quarterly*, *37*(1). http://dsq-sds.org/article/view/5061

Fritsch, K., Hamraie, A., Mills, M., & Serlin, D. (2019). Introduction to special section on crip technoscience. *Catalyst: Feminism, Theory, Technoscience*, *5*(1), 1–10. https://doi.org/10.28968/cftt.v5i1.31998

Galis, V. (2011). Enacting disability: How can science and technology studies inform disability studies? *Disability & Society*, *26*(7), 825–838. https://doi.org/10.1080/09687599.2011.618737

Garland-Thomson, R. (2003). Integrating disability, transforming feminist theory. *NWSA Journal*, *14*(3), 1–32.

Gerschick, T. J. (2000). Toward a theory of disability and gender. *Signs*, *25*(4), 1263–1268.

Giddens, A. (1991). *Modernity and self-identity: Self and society in the Late Modern Age*. Stanford University Press.

Glenton, C. (2003). Chronic back pain sufferers—Striving for the sick role. *Social Science & Medicine (1982)*, *57*(11), 2243–2252. https://doi.org/10.1016/s0277-9536(03)00130-8

Goffman, E. (1963). *Stigma: Notes on the management of spoiled identity*. Prentice-Hall.

Green, S. E. (2007). "We're tired, not sad": Benefits and burdens of mothering a child with a disability. *Social Science & Medicine*, *64*(1), 150–163. https://doi.org/10.1016/j.socscimed.2006.08.025

Grosz, E. (1994). *Volatile bodies: Toward a corporeal feminism*. Indiana University Press.

Grue, J. (2016). The social meaning of disability: A reflection on categorization, stigma and identity. *Sociology of Health & Illness*, *38*(6), 957–964. https://doi.org/10.1111/1467-9566.12417

Hamraie, A., & Fritsch, K. (2019). Crip technoscience manifesto. *Catalyst: Feminism, Theory, Technoscience*, *5*(1), 1–33. https://doi.org/10.28968/cftt.v5i1.29607

Harriet Tubman Collective. (2016, September 4). Disability solidarity: Completing the "vision for Black lives." *The Harriet Tubman Collective*. https://harriettubmancollective.tumblr.com/post/150415348273/disability-solidarity-completing-the-vision-for

Hirschmann, N. J. (2012). Disability as a new frontier for feminist intersectionality research. *Politics & Gender*, *8*(3), 396–405. https://doi.org/10.1017/S1743923X12000384

Hughes, B., & Paterson, K. (1997). The social model of disability and the disappearing body: Towards a sociology of impairment. *Disability & Society*, *12*(3), 325–340. https://doi.org/10.1080/09687599727209

Kafer, A. (2013). *Feminist, queer, crip*. Indiana University Press.

Kempner, J. (2014). *Not tonight: Migraine and the politics of gender and health*. University of Chicago Press.

Kleinman, A. (1989). *The illness narratives: Suffering, healing, and the human condition*. Basic Books.

Leiter, V. (2004). Dilemmas in sharing care: Maternal provision of professionally driven therapy for children with disabilities. *Social Science & Medicine (1982)*, *58*(4), 837–849.

Lewis, T. T. (2019). Longmore lecture: Context, clarity and grounding. Talila A. Lewis. http://www.talilalewis.com/1/post/2019/03/longmore-lecture-context-clarity-grounding.html

Litt, J. (2004). Women's carework in low-income households: The special case of children with attention deficit hyperactivity disorder. *Gender & Society*, *18*(5), 625–644. https://doi.org/10.1177/0891243204267399

Lukin, J. (2013). Disability and blackness. In L. J. Davis (Ed.), *The disability studies reader* (4th ed., pp. 308–315). Routledge.

Maroto, M., Pettinicchio, D., & Patterson, A. C. (2019). Hierarchies of categorical disadvantage: Economic insecurity at the intersection of disability, gender, and race. *Gender & Society*, 33(1), 64–93. https://doi.org/10.1177/0891243218794648

Mauldin, L. (2014). Precarious plasticity neuropolitics, cochlear implants, and the redefinition of deafness. *Science, Technology & Human Values*, 39(1), 130–153. https://doi.org/10.1177/0162243913512538

Mauldin, L. (2016). *Made to hear: Cochlear implants and raising deaf children*. University of Minnesota Press.

Miles, A. L. (2019). "Strong Black women": African American women with disabilities, intersecting identities, and inequality. *Gender & Society*, 33(1), 41–63. https://doi.org/10.1177/0891243218814820

Mollow, A. (2017). Unvictimizable: Toward a fat Black disability studies. *African American Review*, 50(2), 105–121. https://doi.org/10.1353/afa.2017.0016

Morris, J. (1999). *Pride against prejudice: A personal politics of disability*. Women's Press.

Moser, I. (2006). Disability and the promises of technology: Technology, subjectivity and embodiment within an order of the normal. *Information, Communication & Society*, 9(3), 373–395. https://doi.org/10.1080/13691180600751348

Naples, N. A., Mauldin, L., & Dillaway, H. (2018). From the guest editors: Gender, disability, and intersectionality. *Gender & Society*. https://doi.org/10.1177/0891243218813309

Nishida, A. (2016). Understanding political development through an intersectionality framework: Life stories of disability activists. *Disability Studies Quarterly*, 36(2), 5–18. https://doi.org/10.18061/dsq.v36i2.4449

Oliver, M. (1992). Changing the social relations of research production? *Disability, Handicap & Society*, 7(2), 101–114. https://doi.org/10.1080/02674649266780141

Oliver, M. (1996). A sociology of disability or a disablist sociology? In L. Barton (Ed.), *Disability and society: Emerging issues and insights* (pp. 18–42). Longman.

Oliver, M. (1998). Theories of disability in health practice and research. *BMJ: British Medical Journal*, 317(7170), 1446–1449.

Oliver, M. (2013). The social model of disability: Thirty years on. *Disability & Society*, 28(7), 1024–1026. https://doi.org/10.1080/09687599.2013.818773

Parens, E., & Asch, A. (Eds.). (2000). *Prenatal testing and disability rights*. Georgetown University Press.

Parsons, T. (1951). *The social system*. Free Press.

Piepzna-Samarasinha, L. L. (2018). *Care work: Dreaming disability justice*. Arsenal Pulp Press.

Pitts-Taylor, V. (Ed.). (2016). *Mattering: Feminism, science, and materialism*. NYU Press.

Rapp, R. (2000). *Testing women, testing the fetus: The social impact of amniocentesis in America*. Routledge.

Rothman, Barbara Katz. (1993). *The Tentative Pregnancy: How Amniocentesis Changes the Experience of Motherhood*. W. W. Norton & Company.

Sandelowski, M. (1994). Separate, but less equal: Fetal ultrasonography and the transformation of expectant mother/fatherhood. *Gender & Society*, 8(2), 230–245. https://doi.org/10.1177/089124394008002006

Scambler, G., & Scambler, S. (2010). Introduction: The sociology of chronic and disabling conditions; Assaults on the lifeworld. In G. Scambler & S. Scambler (Eds.), *New directions in the sociology of chronic and disabling conditions: Assaults on the lifeworld* (pp. 1–7). Palgrave Macmillan.

Schalk, S. (2018). *Bodyminds reimagined: (Dis)ability, race, and gender in Black women's speculative fiction.* Duke University Press.

Schalk, S., & Kim, J. B. (2020). Integrating race, transforming feminist disability studies. *Signs: Journal of Women in Culture and Society, 46*(1), 31–55. https://doi.org/10.1086/709213

Scott, E. K. (2010). "I feel as if I am the one who is disabled": The emotional impact of changed employment trajectories of mothers caring for children with disabilities. *Gender & Society, 24*(5), 672–696. https://doi.org/10.1177/0891243210382531

Seymour, W. (2012). *Remaking the body: Rehabilitation and change.* Routledge.

Shakespeare, T. (1996). Disability, identity, and difference. In C. Barnes & G. Mercer (Eds.), *Exploring the divide: Illness and disability* (pp. 94–113). Disability Press.

Shakespeare, T. (2006). *Disability rights and wrongs.* Routledge.

Shakespeare, T. (2013). The social model of disability. In L. J. Davis (Ed.), *The disability studies reader* (4th ed., pp. 214–221). Routledge.

Shakespeare, T., & Watson, N. (1996). *"The body line controversy": A new direction for Disability Studies?* Hull Disability Studies Seminar, Leeds, UK.

Shakespeare, T., & Watson, N. (2001). The social model of disability: An outdated ideology? In S. Barnartt & B. Altman (Eds.), Research in Social Science and Disability, 2, 9–28.

Shakespeare, T., & Watson, N. (2010). Beyond models: Understanding the complexity of disabled people's lives. In G. Scambler & S. Scambler (Eds.), *New directions in the sociology of chronic and disabling conditions: Assaults on the lifeworld* (pp. 57–76). Palgrave Macmillan.

Shilling, C. (2003). *The body and social theory* (2nd ed.). SAGE Publications.

Siebers, T. (2010). In the name of pain. In J. Metzl & A. Kirkland (Eds.), *Against health: How health became the new morality* (pp. 183–191). NYU Press.

Stoll, L. C., & Egner, J. (2021). "We must do better": Ableism and fatphobia in sociology. *Sociology Compass.* https://doi.org/10.1111/soc4.12869.

Thomas, C. (2007). *Sociologies of disability and illness: Contested ideas in disability studies and medical sociology.* Palgrave Macmillan.

Turner, B. S. (2001). Disability and the sociology of the body. In *Handbook of disability studies* (pp. 252–266). SAGE Publications. https://doi.org/10.4135/9781412976251

Varul, M. Z. (2010). Talcott Parsons, the sick role and chronic illness. *Body & Society, 16*(2), 72–94. https://doi.org/10.1177/1357034X10364766

Williams, S. J. (2006). Medical sociology and the biological body: Where are we now and where do we go from here? *Health, 10*(1), 5–30. https://doi.org/10.1177/1363459306058984

Wolbring, G. (2008). The politics of ableism. *Development, 51*(2), 252–258. https://doi.org/10.1057/dev.2008.17

Zola, I. K. (1972). Medicine as an institution of social control. *The Sociological Review, 20*(4), 487–504.

Zola, I. K. (1982). *Missing pieces: A chronicle of living with a disability.* Temple University Press.

Zola, I. K. (1991). Bringing our bodies and ourselves back in: Reflections on a past, present, and future "medical sociology." *Journal of Health and Social Behavior, 32*(1), 1. https://doi.org/10.2307/2136796

CHAPTER 4

FEMINIST PERSPECTIVES ON DISABILITY, IMPAIRMENT, AND ABLENESS

VERA CHOUINARD

OVER the past several decades, feminist and disability scholars and activists have challenged our thinking about the causes and consequences of disability, impairment, and ableness. In this chapter, I outline how the interdisciplinary field of feminist perspectives on disability has developed and changed. Challenging the "male gaze" or the construction of the normatively "ideal" body as white, able-bodied, heterosexual, and male, and the related objectification and devaluation of women's embodiment (Ponterotto, 2016), has been one aspect of these changes. Feminists have also been critical of the social model of disability developed by disability scholars and activists for neglecting embodiment as a key facet of lived experiences of disability. This, in turn, opened up possibilities for more intersectional accounts of diversity in bodies and minds. More recently, there have been efforts to think more expansively about the production of impairment, disability, and ableness as enmeshed in the dynamics of neoliberal global capitalism. My thesis is that feminist perspectives on disability have shifted from recognition of disability as an important facet of some women's lives to thinking more expansively about the multiple differences shaping disabled women's, men's, and children's lives.

How have feminist perspectives challenged our understanding of disability, impairment, and ableness? One way is by challenging abstract conceptions of able and disabled forms of embodiment as intrinsically male. Recognizing diversity in bodies and minds informed both the women's and disability movements, and this was reflected in the feminist perspectives on disability that emerged in the 1980s and 1990s. Feminist perspectives on disability also force us to consider how multiple social relations of power and oppression are implicated in disabled people's lives. Today it is no longer sufficient to recognize that experiences of disability are gendered—we need to also consider how they are simultaneously racialized, classed, and sexualized. We also need to recognize that experiences of disability and struggles for social change are geographically uneven:

that where in the world we are matters in how these experiences and struggles unfold. Putting experiences of ableness, impairment, and disability in a global geographic context is important in developing a better understanding of the relations of power through which disabled people are oppressed at multiple scales including the transnational. This, in turn, encourages attention to neocolonial relations of power and how these inform disabled people's lives in the Global South and North (see for example Grech & Soldatic, 2016).

These arguments are developed in the following way. In section one, I define impairment, disability, and ableness. Next, I reflect on how the women's and disability movements laid the groundwork for feminist perspectives on disability. Then I consider early contributions to feminist perspectives on disability (i.e., drawing on examples from the 1980s and 1990s). Finally, I turn to feminist perspectives on disability in the new millennium, arguing that at least some of this work is helping to forge new and exciting directions for feminist accounts of disability.

Impairment, Disability, and Ableness

Impairment, disability, and ableness are contested concepts in the feminist and disability studies literatures. In the medical model of disability, which prevailed in the 1960s and 1970s, impairment was generally considered to be a physical or mental limitation in the functioning of the individual body and/or mind. This conception of *impairment* as an individualized state did not disappear with the shift toward a social model of disability in disability studies (Disabled Students Campaign, 2018; Anasiou and Koffman, 2013). Although it emphasized that disability was the outcome of socially constructed physical, social, and attitudinal barriers to inclusion, experiences of impairment were still "bracketed off" from consideration in thinking about disability (Anasiou and Kauffman, 2013). More recently, and at least in part as a result of feminist efforts to bring the "body and mind back in" to critical analyses of disability, there has been renewed recognition that impairment also has social meanings. For example, when losses of mobility are viewed as "tragic" and as making a life less worth living. Impairment is, then, a social and not simply a biological state. In a similar vein, disability is perpetuated by social barriers to inclusion but also includes experiences of what Shakespeare (2006), Thomas (1999), and others refer to as "impairment effects" (e.g., pain, mobility limitations, mental distress).

A key challenge in further developing feminist perspectives on disability, and critical accounts of disability more generally, is conceptualizing what "ableness" entails. By this, I refer to a regime of power and oppression that favors non-disabled bodies and minds and a set of practices disciplining all of us into striving to project an able body and mind. In this regime of power and oppression, able bodily ideals such as being able to walk, talk, and see are more valued than non-able alternative ways of being such as using aids or wheelchairs or walkers to negotiate places. In other words, ableness validates notions that our self- and societal worth depend on how ably we can go about our day to day lives. Feminist perspectives on disability have been important in complicating such conceptions of ableness by recognizing that embodied experiences of ability unfold along multiple, intersecting differences (e.g., ability, class, race, and gender; Erevelles, 2011).

LAYING THE GROUNDWORK: THE WOMEN'S AND DISABILITY MOVEMENTS

The 1960s, 1970s, and 1980s were eras of protest and unrest. Struggles over human rights included the civil-rights movement in countries such as the United States and Canada the anti-war and students' movements, environmental activism, the women's "liberation" movement (as it was then called), and a fledgling disability-rights movement. By calling for greater equality of rights for disadvantaged groups, such as women and disabled people, activists and scholars laid the conceptual and empirical groundwork for the development of feminist perspectives on disability.

The second wave of the feminist or women's movement emerged in the 1960s and 1970s. Women activists and scholars protested women's continued subordination to men and associated restrictions on how women lived their lives. Related themes included the need to free women from traditional social roles such as being suburban housewives (Friedan, 1963) and from male dominance of women's sexuality and desire (Greer, 1971). Oppression and control were thus central issues in feminist scholarship and activism.

Understanding the body as a site of patriarchal oppression and control was important to women's struggles for equality and ultimately in considering multiple embodied differences such as gender, race, and disability. Activists in the women's movement expressed dissatisfaction with their lack of knowledge of and control over their own bodies and with the apparent indifference of medical professionals to these concerns. In 1973 the Boston Women's Collective published a landmark book *Our Bodies/Ourselves* that tackled such issues as women's access to contraception, control over pregnancies, and sexuality and desire. The book was a phenomenal success, selling over 4 million copies and being translated into 29 languages (Wells, 2010). By sharing women's stories of experiences of the body, health, and medical care, the book helped to challenge male ways of gazing upon and objectifying women's bodies and lives.

Encounters between feminist perspectives on disability and disability studies from the 1970s onward were interdisciplinary—involving scholars in the humanities, sociology, political science, women's studies, geography, and philosophy (Thomas, 2007). This work proceeded along two main trajectories. The first of these was concerned with making the voices and lives of disabled women visible in a society in which they were largely ignored. This reflected feminist concerns to demonstrate how personal experiences of disability are political and gendered. It also paralleled concerns among new left scholars to document the lives of disadvantaged groups. E. P. Thompson's (1964) *The Making of the English Working Class*, although not concerned with disability per se, is a classic example of this genre of work. While we know relatively little about whether and how such broader academic developments encouraged feminist life histories, it is clear that feminist disability studies books such as Mairs's (2001) *Waist High in the World* helped to reveal how disabled women are devalued through prevailing misconceptions about their lives—for instance that their lives are not worth living and that these women are unattractive and asexual. Veronica Marris (1996) chronicled the lives of women with chronic illnesses insisting that their social contributions meant that their lives are worth living.

A second trajectory in feminist perspectives on disability was a more critical assessment of the social discourses, policies, and social relations helping to perpetuate disabled women's marginalization in society and space. Martin (1990), for example, criticized malestream scientific discourses that constructed natural bodily processes in women such as menstruation and menopause as dysfunctional. By challenging and unsettling such discourses, it was possible to question gendered and ableist devaluations of women's bodies and lives. In doing so, this created opportunities for critical assessments of the meanings assigned to embodied differences more generally. This included an internal critique of the women's movement and feminist scholarship for being dominated by white middle class women at the expense of others such as women of color—this too was an impetus toward taking women's embodied diversity seriously in understanding women's oppression and the prospects for social change (e.g., Crenshaw, 1991; Soder, 2009).

Disability studies, as an interdisciplinary field of inquiry, first emerged in the 1970s in the United States and United Kingdom and has since become a global phenomenon. It is worth noting that as early as the 1960s, sociologists in the United States had begun to make seminal contributions to disability studies. Particularly important in this regard was the work of Irving Zola and Erving Goffman. Zola was primarily concerned with the power and control over people's lives exercised by medical institutions such as hospitals and the pharmaceutical industry (Zola, 1972). Goffman (1986) focused on stigma and how this was applied to what he characterized as "spoiled identities" that deviated from cultural ideals of embodied life (e.g., by being alcoholic or mobility impaired). While these were not feminist perspectives on disability, they were influential in putting inequalities in social power on the agenda of social scientists concerned with disability and thus helping to make space for the development of various streams of critical disability studies including feminist perspectives (for further discussion of these developments, see Thomas, 2007).

Disability studies and the disability-rights movement continued to gain momentum particularly in the 1980s and 1990s. Disabled university students in California, notably in Berkeley (Neudel, 2011), struggled for rights to attend school and to live independently in their communities (ibid.). Demands for independent living reflected concerns that many disabled people were being "ware-housed" or incarcerated in large institutions and denied their rights to live life on their own terms. Resistance to this found expression in "deinstitutionalization" or efforts to shift disabled people from large-scale institutional settings such as psychiatric institutions to smaller-scale community settings such as group homes. Social scientists were critical of such efforts for failing to provide adequate community supports and services to integrate disabled people into community life and thus creating a geographically uneven patchwork of "asylums without walls" (see for example Dear & Wolch, 1987; Knowles, 2000). And, as the social model of disability became more influential in disability activism and scholarship, there were growing demands that physical and social barriers to disabled people's inclusion be removed, through for example providing accessible public-transit services.

Like the women's movement, disability activists faced challenges in terms of internal political divisions. In the case of the disability movement, this initially took the form of many disability activists organizing according to the type of impairment or illness that they had. This was consistent with the medical model of disability and an associated emphasis on individual rehabilitation for particular conditions. Gradually, however, activists realized they would have greater political influence as cross-disability organizations (an example in the United States context is that of ADAPT; Neudel, 2011).

But there were other insidious, if relatively invisible, divisions in the disability movement and disability studies. One of these was gender. Although there were many women involved in the disability movement, it was men who dominated decision-making and leadership. By the 1980s and 1990s, however, women had begun to challenge male-centric understandings of disability and an exclusionary politics of disability activism. At the same time, disabled women were challenging their marginalization in the women's movement on bases of embodied differences in ability but also other intersecting differences such as sexuality (e.g., Chouinard, 1999). I discuss these developments in the next section of this chapter.

CHALLENGING THE MALE GAZE AND "BRINGING THE BODY AND MIND BACK IN"

As was also the case with regard to the women's movement, the project of feminist perspectives on disability was to challenge the "male gaze" that objectified and devalued women who differed from the ideals of being a white, heterosexual, able, middle-class male (Ponterotto, 2016). Originally developed in film studies, the concept also acknowledged that this gaze constructed able women as objects of male sexual desire. Feminist perspectives on disability had at least three basic aims. The first was to put women's experiences of disability on research and political agendas. The second was to ensure that bodies and minds being bracketed off from consideration in social models of disability remained central to feminist work on impairment and disability. And third was to develop more complex, intersectional approaches to explaining disabled women's lives and identities—as I discuss below.

As Fraser (2000) points out, feminists have engaged with disability through a variety of perspectives. These include liberal and radical feminism, and post-structural and postmodern approaches. From a liberal feminist perspective, disability struggles are about obtaining equal rights within existing social institutions. From a radical feminist vantage point, it is the oppression of people with bodies and minds that differ from able and patriarchal ideals that is key. Recent calls for studies of transgendered people and disabilities reflect this concern with complex embodied subjectivity (Noonan & Gomez, 2011). Post-structural and postmodern approaches emphasize cultural constructions of disability, gender, and other embodied differences and the fluidity of identity formation.

Emerging feminist disability scholars pursued these aims by addressing a variety of topics and issues. Fine and colleagues' groundbreaking edited collection, one of the first to focus on disabled women's experiences, provides a glimpse into what some of these topics and issues were (Fine and Asch, 1988). It includes an account of Diane DeVries' struggles to contend with pressures to "normalize" her body and make it more attractive to others by using protheses to replace limbs missing as a result of being born with quadrilateral limb deficiencies (Frank, 1988). The author, Geyla Frank, makes it clear that this is a story of contested embodiment. She observes that the way most people use the body is culturally prescribed, developmental, and ultimately habitual. For individuals with physical disabilities, however, the challenge is to find new, culturally acceptable ways of integrating identity with having a variant body image and function. Diane, in the course of her struggles over how she would be embodied in an able world, gradually realized that projecting a more able identity was not worth difficulties such as pain endured as a result of using prostheses. In doing so she at least partially reclaimed an identity as a woman with physical impairments. As Frank (1988, p. 41) notes, this is a phenomenological approach that begins with the body as a locus for sensation, perception, and interaction.

Another focus of feminist inquiry in this collection is that of representations of disabled women in novels and plays. The author, Deborah Kent, examined over 30 novels and plays portraying disabled women. What she found was that, despite differences in when and where they were written and in what genre, they were quite similar in the representation of disabled women. She writes:

> Whether she is blind or deaf, facially disfigured or paraplegic, the disabled woman is typically shown to be incomplete not only in body, but in her basic expression of her womanhood. . . . Generally, she is both physically and emotionally dependent upon others, constantly draining their resources and giving little in return.
>
> (Kent, 1988, p. 93)

Kent (1988) goes on to note that disabled women are regarded as being unimportant/unattractive to men. Most of these women are portrayed as bitter, despairing, and engaging in self-loathing. This is usually attributed not to the social stigma with which disabled women deal in real life but to the disability itself.

Disabled women in relationships is another theme in this collection. Simon (1988) shows how older-aged, never-married disabled women use discourses about the realities of an aging body and disability to forge connections with other older women. She argues that disability in old age makes never-married women's lives more like those who have been married so that they find common ground. She concludes that in a sexist and capitalist society, all women lose value as they become less able to satisfy male conceptions of beauty and usefulness—that is, as they age, become infertile, and deal with mobility and other bodily limitations. Work such as this helps to shed light on how important changes in embodiment are to able and disabled women's identities and oppression.

The 1990s proved to be a decade of critical re-appraisal of the social model of disability and of how disability was addressed by social scientists. Jenny Morris's book *Pride Against Prejudice: Transforming Attitudes Toward Disability*, published by the Women's Press in 1991, was an impassioned call to feminist scholars and activists to confront and challenge non-disabled persons' stereotypes about disabled people's lives, for instance that they are not worth living. Morris, herself a physically disabled woman, argued that such views were rooted in intolerance toward diversity in human embodiment and fears about being or becoming physically or mentally impaired. She argued that feminists had failed disabled women by not addressing their experiences and concerns and that, in doing so, both the disability and women's movements had been impoverished—the former by not addressing diversity in experiences of impairment and disability and the latter by failing to connect with disabled women and to address their concerns through scholarly and activist work.

Following an account of the devaluation of disabled people's lives as a result of the eugenics movement, Darwinian evolutionary theory (e.g., "survival of the fittest"), and the brutal murders of disabled women, children, and men by the Nazi regime, Morris goes on to stress how important it is that disabled people reassert their rights to determine how their lives will be portrayed. This includes the ways in which negative as well as positive aspects of being disabled are understood. She writes that scholars and activists require the courage to say that there are awful things about being disabled but also positive things that are a source of pride. This is necessary, she argues, to challenge able-bodied negative judgements about disabled people's lives. Acknowledging that there are awful aspects of being disabled, such as living in poverty, arguably can foster a greater mutual understanding between disabled and non-disabled persons that being disabled is neither bad nor good but both. As such it should be valued and not only feared.

Authors such as Morris (1991) and Begum (1992) offered powerful critiques of the neglect of disabled women's lives and oppression in both the women's and disability movements. Arguing that experiences of disability are gendered, for instance through negative stereotypes of disabled women's bodies as undesirable, these authors were applying a feminist perspective to disabled women's lives by considering how they were constructed as objects of male oppression (e.g., through sexual abuse), and they urged feminist and disability scholars to acknowledge these women's lives and struggles for inclusion.

Inspired by the disability and women's movements, the 1990s were also a time when scholars were critical of the relative invisibility of disabled women in their respective disciplines and of the approaches being used to understand their lives. In *Geography*, Chouinard and Grant (1995) criticized the neglect of disabled and lesbian women's lives. This was occurring even among radical and feminist geographers. Critical reappraisal of the social model of disability in disability studies and activism was also a feature of the 1990s. Feminists arguably led the way by insisting that disability and impairment were embodied experiences although others such as Hughes and Paterson (1997), who called for a sociology of impairment, and Hall (2000), who urged colleagues to take the fleshy body seriously, also contributed. Unlike the social model of disability, with its dichotomous understanding of impairment as a physical state and disability as an outcome of attitudinal and social barriers to inclusion, embodied approaches to disability and impairment took seriously the notion that impairment is social as well as physical (e.g., in terms of how physically impaired and/or ill bodies are assigned meaning) and that social processes disabling those with impairments or illnesses become embodied physically as well as mentally (e.g., in physical exclusion and emotional distress at being marginalized in society and space).

Susan Wendell's (1996) book *The Rejected Body* was an important intervention in philosophical reflections on why mainstream culture rejects bodies that differ from able social norms. She argued that despite shared experiences of the negative or rejected body (such as the body in pain), prevailing cultural conceptions of the normal body allowed people not to confront or try to understand why "abnormal" bodies are rejected. She argues that if the "normal body" is constructed as being young, healthy, energetic, pain free, and fully mobile, then there is no need to come to terms with experiences of disabled bodies as not ordinary and not "us."

Wendell (1996) goes on to describe the "flight from the rejected body," or the complex processes through which people embrace or resist prevailing ideals of bodily life. She argues that although actually existing bodies are diverse, cultural and economic constructions of the desirable body are much narrower and thus cast bodies that deviate from these ideals as rejected and "other." She notes that body ideals include not only ideals of appearance, and that this is especially influential in women's lives, but also strength, energy, movement, function, and proper control and that these assumptions about bodies tend not to be noticed by those who meet these ideals but come to the fore when one is disabled or ill. Moreover, struggles to emulate these ideals are closely linked to the economic dynamics of consumer, and capitalist, societies. Striving to conform to prevailing bodily ideals (with respect to beauty, health, and physical performance) and to embrace new ones translates into tremendous profits and exposes growing numbers of people to the images of real people that meet the latest cultural ideals of embodied life. Wendell notes that one of the repercussions of this is that the images of a few people increasingly depart from the bodily realities of most people we interact with (Wendell, 1996, p. 86).

Auto-ethnographic and auto-biographical accounts of disabled women's lives have played an important role in raising awareness of what it is like to embody impairment and illness and how gender matters in experiences of disability oppression. Mairs (1996), for example, shared her reflections on what it was like to be "waist high" in the world as a wheelchair user who could not move in able ways. Chouinard (1995/96) wrote about how gender, impairment, illness, and radical scholarship marked her out as a woman and a professor who did not belong in the academy. Marris (1996) shared the stories of women with chronic illness, detailing, for example, how difficult it was to continue to fulfill roles such as being a paid worker after becoming chronically ill and how this heightened their financial insecurity. Thomas (1999) shared autobiographical narratives by other disabled women to help illustrate how they struggled to fulfill gendered roles such as motherhood. Much like consciousness raising in the women's movement, these accounts aimed to make personal aspects of disabled women's lives political and thus possible to contest.

By the end of the 1990s, there was a relatively small but influential corpus of feminist work on disability. This had helped to at least partially unsettle social-model understandings of impairment, illness, and disability by bringing the lived body and mind back into embodied accounts of processes of oppression. It is important to note, however, that some disability-studies scholars resisted this change—arguing that the social model remained central to the intellectual and political project of disability studies (see Watson & Vehmas, 2019). A key concern was that its political power, as a call for barrier removal, would be "diluted" if it were modified. Feminist perspectives on disability had also tapped into women's own voices on what it was like for women to live with impairment, disability, and illness. This consciousness raising would help to provide a foundation for feminist perspectives on disability in the new millennium.

Situating Ableness, Impairment, and Disability in Neoliberal Global Capitalism

During the past 20 years, feminists have continued their efforts to make multiple differences in bodies and minds more central to our understanding of disability oppression. This was an impetus to more intersectional analyses of how embodied differences such as ability, gender, class, race, and sexuality helped to construct disabled women and men as negatively other and out of place in their interactions with others. Marta Russell's (1998) work on disability rights and oppression in US capitalism encouraged scholars to forge socialist-feminist accounts of the role of class and economic disadvantage (e.g., poverty and unemployment) in the marginalization of disabled women and men

(Malhotra, 2017). This remains an important theme in feminist thinking about disabling differences (see for example Erevelles, 2014, 2011). Developing more intersectional feminist accounts of impairment, disability, and ableness has also been a challenge (Cho et al., 2013). Valentine (2007), for instance, considered how embodied differences, such as hearing impairment and a lesbian identity, came to the fore in the oppression of a D/deaf woman in spaces such as a deaf club but were less salient in other local contexts. Taking intersectionality seriously, moreover, led to the development of what we might call hybrid approaches to understanding disabled women's and men's lives. By this I mean analyses that blur the boundaries between bodies of knowledge about disability and difference, such as queer and disability studies. Eli Clare's (1999, 2001) work was an explicit call for exploring the potential of queer and gendered accounts of disability.

By the mid-2000s, feminist perspectives on disability had coalesced sufficiently to allow feminist and some disability scholars to claim that a distinctive field of feminist disability studies had been established. Garland-Thomson (2005), for example, argued that feminist disability studies was committed to reimagining disability and that it involved more than scholarship about disabled women—that like feminisms in general it was concerned to critically analyze the "entire gender system." Answering the question of what feminist disability studies is, she stressed that it aims to unsettle "tired stereotypes" about disabled people and prevailing assumptions about life with a disability. Disability experiences are situated in terms of rights and social exclusions.

It also sheds light on identity formation by striving to retrieve dismissed voices and misleading accounts of experiences and by addressing complex relations between bodies and selves (Garland-Thomson, 2005, p. 1557).

Be (2020) notes that feminist disability studies made substantial progress with respect to developing more intersectional approaches to understanding disabled people's identities and lives (see Evans & Lipinard, 2020 on intersectionality in feminist and queer studies). One caveat, however, is that intersectional analyses of disability have been relatively neglected in the sociological literature but are more common in bodies of literature such as disability studies (Naples et al., 2019). Other important contributions to framing disability as an intersectional process, the subject of a recent special journal issue, include Miles (2019) on the complex, multidimensional ways that African American disabled women are marginalized in their struggles to survive and achieve milestones such as being a homeowner. She shows how the trope of the "strong black woman" informs their self-concept and identity and how their marginalization reflects other intersecting differences such as class disadvantage. Egner (2019) enriches intersectionality studies by examining the process of disidentification associated with the "neuroqueer crip project." She argues that this project includes critique of assumptions that minds function in neurotypical ways, a recognition of the fluidity in queer expressions of sexuality, and disidentification with assimilationist strategies such as searching for a medical "cure" for impairment and disability. In a more quantitative vein, Maroto et al. (2019) explore the hierarchies of disadvantage associated with disability, poverty, gender, and race in the United States.

Efforts such as these are contributing to a more nuanced understanding of the kinds of differences that intersect in shaping disabled peoples' lives and identities.

Progress is also being made in drawing on queer conceptions of embodying impairment and disability, as I suggest below. These developments have prompted some noteworthy changes in feminist perspectives on disability. One of these changes has been a broadening of the range of bodies and minds considered to be "disabled." Longhurst (2010), for example, has argued that although large or "fat" women may not identify as disabled that they still experience disabling impacts of being large (such as avoiding beaches where they are sometimes subjected to disapproving gazes that make them feel "out of place") (see also Mollow, 2015). A related change has been growing openness to juxtaposing different areas of inquiry in order to push the boundaries of our ways of conceptualizing and understanding impairment, disability, and ableness. Kafer (2013), for example, considers the interface between disability and reproductive rights and critiques notions that disability justifies abortion in favor of a non-ableist approach that insists on women's fundamental rights to control their reproductive lives.

Recent work in feminist disability studies has built in creative ways on queer scholarship.

In fact, Garland-Thomson (2005) argues that this is one beacon of light in contemporary disability studies. Puar (2017), a feminist and queer scholar, has focused on "bio-power" and how it is exercised in interactions between people with diverse bodies and minds.

Drawing on the Israeli-Palestinian conflict, she argues that an important manifestation of such power is the exercise of the "right to maim." By this she means acts intended to impair and disable other people, such as when Israeli soldiers shoot to "cripple" rather than kill. But the "right to maim" entails more than this. It also includes the destruction of vital infrastructure such as hospitals thus diminishing capacities to treat and assist Palestinian people who have become impaired as a result of this long-standing conflict. Rebuilding such infrastructure is profitable with, ironically enough, Israeli companies being among those who profit from repairing the destruction their government and military have inflicted. This reflects the rise of what Klein (2007) refers to as "disaster capitalism." Rob McRuer (2018), also a feminist and queer scholar, has characterized the current state of our global and capitalist order as "crip times." That is to say, a period in which austerity politics is globalizing and heightening the oppression of disabled and other people with anomalous bodies and minds. One of the examples used to illustrate this is Liz Crow's 2015 ambitious art installation "Figures" in the United Kingdom. For the artist's account of this work as art-activism see Crow (2019). The artist sculpted 650 figures from river clay, many of which represented disabled individuals and how their lives have been impacted by austerity. The figures were publicly displayed and, in a final ceremony, burned while each story was read out loud. Footage of the activities was also posted online. McRuer argues that, in important ways, artistic and political interventions such as this help to "crip" austerity. He explains that *Figures* offers critical disabled perspectives on austerity and identifies a coalition of "left behinds" who do not necessarily identify as disabled but whose lives are connected through a crip analytic that conceptualizes precarity and resistance in expansive ways. *Figures* unsettles or short-circuits austerity—meaning that it works for and against it in its existing forms as scholars and activists strive to observe and comprehend "the totality of austerity's operation."

Alison Kafer (2013) is another feminist, crip, and queer scholar who aims to un-settle or trouble feminist perspectives on disability. She critically assesses, for example, Haraway's feminist theoretical figure of the "cyborg." Noting that Haraway provides examples of cyborgs that equate them with severe physical disability (and hence the use of technologies such as power wheelchairs and ventilators), she argues for a redeploy-ment of the concept of the cyborg in more subversive ways. She insists that it is impor-tant to "push and fill" the concept of the cyborg in order to imagine futures which are crip and queer. She notes that a non-ableist cyborg politics does not separate and isolate persons with a cyborgian identity as a result of disability and illness from those able-bodied people who are subject to the same pervasive technoculture. In this context, cy-borg theory could then allow exploration of the abled/disabled binary. An example that she gives is asking why the same technologies are described as "assistive" when they are used by a disabled person and "time-saving" when used by an able-bodied person (Kafer, 2013, 18). A related challenge is to further interrogate why and how such experiences are simultaneously gendered. The marketing of home appliances in the postwar era as allowing women to be more efficient in their mothering and house-keeping roles is a case in point.

Kafer (2013) sees such explorations as imperative in forging feminist, crip, and queer affinities, political alliances, and futures.

One of the exciting features of the debates outlined above is how they dovetail into more expansive ways of conceptualizing impairment, disability, and ableness as bound up in the dynamics of a neoliberal capitalist order. Puar's (2017) work, for instance, sheds light on how capitalist societies employ bio-power to discipline diverse bodies and minds in more and less oppressive ways. McRuer (2018) insists that compulsory able-bodiedness, austerity, and beliefs that people succeed through a meritocracy are central to neoliberal capitalism and to disciplining able and non-able ways of being in society and space. Kafer (2013) invites us to consider how we can imagine crip futures that move beyond the ability/disability binary so pervasive in capitalist societies. Other scholars have also contributed to this intellectual project. Campbell (2009), for ex-ample, examines the close links that exist between profit-making and the marketing of assistive technologies such as cochlear implants for hearing loss—technologies that are at least sometimes considered to be ill-advised and overly invasive. In a complementary vein, Mitchell (2015) argues that it is bodily and mental imperfections and the selling of remedies for those imperfections that lie at the heart of neoliberal capitalism.

Feminist disability scholars are also recognizing the need for approaches that straddle the boundaries between black studies and disability studies. Bailey and Mobley (2019) critique disability studies for not paying attention to race and black studies for not grap-pling with disability as well as sexism. They argue that doing so would enrich black femi-nism and disability studies and help to identify new theoretical and empirical directions, for instance with respect to why women of color are disproportionately likely to provide care to disabled people and the impact this has on their abilities to care for their own family members. They argue that by taking up disability and gender more comprehensively and confronting ableism, black studies could help scholars and activists move beyond ableist language and find new ways of discursively constructing disability and ability. They also suggest that if disability studies drew upon black studies and critical race theory in ways that challenged the white disabled body as the norm, this could encourage the development of a more flexible and globally relevant framework for critiquing late neoliberal capitalist societies (Bailey & Mobley, 2019, p. 35). This could also include questioning why black women and men are disproportionately likely to be disabled and are further disadvantaged by conditions of life such as poverty. It could also include questioning why and how women are impaired as a result of male violence and constructed as deserving of violence when they are disabled. The geographically uneven production and distribution of impairment and disability is also a concern since the vast majority (80%) of disabled women, men, and children live in countries of the Global South (Chouinard 2012, 2015).

As is the case with queer feminist conceptions of disability, then, such hybrid grounds of work promise to situate impairment, disability, and ableness in the context of neoliberal global capitalism. Everelles (2011, 2014) is among those who take up this challenge. She discusses how race and disability and impairment were intertwined in the slave trade—impairment was often inflicted as a means of controlling those who were enslaved. She also discusses Jim Crow in the southern United States and contemporary modes of segregating and disciplining people of color. She argues that today's school to prison pipeline (particularly for young black and Latino men) works to maintain the segregation and other racialized disadvantages such as lower educational attainment that people of color endure. Erevelles' (2011) work is socialist-feminist—for example in terms of emphasizing the importance of an intersectional perspective on embodied differences in global capitalism.

Feminist perspectives on disability have also continued to include post-modern approaches (Fawcett 2000). Shildrick's work (2002, 2012) is a good example of this. She offers a different, postmodern feminist intersectional approach to understanding how embodied subjects are discursively constructed as negatively "other" than able ideals or norms. She argues that discourses about disability, subjectivity, and sexuality are "dangerous" in that they provide opportunities to disrupt such notions as that disabled subjects are necessarily "monstrous" and asexual. As such, they help to reveal the limits of prevailing ways of governing what we might term "unruly bodies"—that is to say, bodies that in various ways transgress normative assumptions about embodied life. Shildrick (2012) goes a step further and argues that counter-discourses or narratives must remain radically open-ended to ensure that scholars and activists remain receptive to emerging ideas about disability, subjectivity, and sexuality and alert to new possible ways of challenging political organizing around issues of corporeality. She argues that postmodern perspectives are more effective than other approaches in deconstructing destructive normativities about embodied life and finding new and positive ways of feeling and thinking about embodied differences. Engaging with critical disability theory has the potential not just to alter the lives of disabled people but also to challenge the overall relationship between diverse embodied subjects. She suggests, following Deleuze, that a postmodern emphasis shifts attention away from discrete, bounded categories (such as disabled women) to how the disabled body is caught up in the dynamics of assemblages and is just one component of them (Shildrick, 2012, pp. 171–72).

What does it mean to conceptualize disabled bodies as just one component of assemblages of embodied subjects, built environments, and objects (e.g., presence or absence of mobility aids)? While definitions of assemblages differ, in general, the term highlights dynamic configurations of embodied subjects, environments, and inanimate objects. As such it is a concept that points to the ongoing relational nature of disabled people's lives and struggles. It also lends itself to understanding those lives and struggles as processes of "becoming" as opposed to more static notions of being.

Conclusions: What Next?

As the developments discussed in this chapter suggest, feminist perspectives on disability have come of age in recent decades—providing an impressive range of critical accounts of disability and gender and blurring boundaries between bodies of work such as critical disability, black, and queer studies. There is now a burgeoning interdisciplinary field of inquiry and activism that has brought bodies and minds back into our understanding of what it is like to experience impairment, disability, and ableness (an understanding jettisoned in strong versions of the social model of disability) (see Shakespeare, 2006, 2013, 2014). The sheer volume and innovative characteristics of this work make it challenging to convey its many contributions. In some ways the account provided here only scratches the surface of these developments. Readers are therefore encouraged to delve further into this exciting area of endeavor. Incorporating the fleshy body and mind back into feminist perspectives on disability addresses concerns that we need to understand the extent to which people are able to exercise control over their own bodies (e.g., with respect to asserting rights to abortion in the case of women). As outlined in this chapter, recognizing that embodied experiences of disability oppression are complex and intersectional has opened the way toward "hybrid" approaches to disability that, for instance, draw on queer and feminist perspectives on "anomalous bodies and minds" and how these are disciplined in society and space.

As argued in this chapter, thinking more expansively about disability has included efforts to understand impairment, disability, and ableness as part and parcel of a global capitalist order. Related to this has been a growing interest in developing neo-colonial accounts of how these forces are manifest in countries of the Global South (see for example Grech & Soldatic, 2016; Grech, 2012; Meekosha & Soldatic, 2011). These manifestations include imposing ideas from the Global North, such as the social model, in countries of the Global South. By focusing on barrier removal, this model frames disability issues as matters of advancing the individual civil rights of disabled people. But material conditions of daily life in the Global South differ in significant ways from what is encountered in the Global North. It is much harder, for example, to fund initiatives such as income support for disabled women and men (Chouinard, 2014). There are also gender differences, for instance in terms of high rates of endemic violence that produce impairment and disability, especially among women in the Global South. It is vital that such deconstructive neocolonial work continues, especially given that the vast majority of disabled people (80%) live in countries of the Global South. While the literature on disability in the Global South is not always explicitly feminist, there is an urgency to think through how gender and intersecting differences such as disability are at work in shaping the lives of people in the majority world.

Inspired in part by the work of post-modern feminist scholars such as Donna Haraway and Margrit Shildrick, feminist perspectives on impairment and disability have sought to "trouble" conceptualizations of embodied subjects as discrete, independent entities. Instead of a related emphasis on "being," they favor attention to more fluid processes of "becoming" through assemblages of diverse bodies, assistive technologies, and subjectivities. Gibson and colleagues (2012) explain what such an approach entails with respect to understanding forces shaping a young disabled woman's life. They argue that persons, care givers, and assistive technologies should be viewed as assemblages that give rise to specific social practices. These connectivities are transient and in flux but reimagining such aspects of disabled peoples' lives provides theoretical opportunities to rethink goals of independence in treatment, assessment, rehabilitation, and research practices. Rather than use narrow conceptions of function and well-being the challenge is to recognize that assemblages can be harmful or helpful in multiple ways.

These more fluid and expansive conceptualizations of "becoming" promise to destabilize boundaries between the disabled embodied subject, his or her assistive technologies, interactions with others (for instance carers or pets), and the achievement of in/dependence in practices that are also in flux. They also offer a more dynamic and relational way to approach impairment and disability and other intersecting differences such as gender.

Living through extraordinary pandemic times has helped to reveal some of the more pressing challenges associated with further developing feminist perspectives on impairment, disability, and ableness. One such challenge is delving further into the processes through which those without able bodies and/or minds are being devalued and disadvantaged in terms of access to essentials such as health care. Organizations such Age International report, for example, that it has become increasingly common worldwide for older and less able people to be denied access to medical aids such as ventilators and to use these instead for younger and healthier patients deemed more likely to recover from the pandemic viruses. This is a facet of what Butler (2004) refers to as "precarious life." As noted in this chapter, the precarity of embodied life is also being intensified as government supports, including income supports, are being whittled away in the name of austerity (McRuer, 2018).

Finally, it is time for feminist perspectives on disability to focus more intensively on the production of impairment and ableness as matters of global injustice.

The production of impairment is geographically uneven with poorer nations especially vulnerable to events such as factory collapse causing numerous physical and mental impairments (e.g., the 2013 Rana Plaza collapse in Bangladesh). We also see this geographic unevenness within more affluent countries—in the case of Canada's indigenous people lacking basics for health such as clean water in reserve communities. The uneven global production of impairment is a reminder that in contemporary global capitalism many people's lives do not count. At the heart of ableness in neoliberal global capitalism is the desire to "correct" bodily imperfections and a relentless drive to promote the consumption of commodities and services that, for instance, derive profits from restoring sight or hearing or giving the illusion of "youth." Such processes have gendered consequences—historically it has been women's bodies that have been deemed most "imperfect" and in need of "work" such as beauty being associated with consuming commodities such as makeup. We need to know more about why related services such as plastic surgery remain alluring for many women (and increasing numbers of men) and how such phenomena buttress desires for the elusive able embodied ideal.

The feminist perspectives discussed in this chapter promote a more nuanced understanding of how multiple intersecting differences shape disabled people's lives. They also have the potential to advance our understanding of the ways in which impairment, disability, and ableness unfold as matters of global, national, and local injustices. This requires recognition that what counts as viable and valuable embodied life is deeply contested by many of us. We can and must build on such insights as we seek to map out more just and enabling futures.

ACKNOWLEDGMENTS

The author would like to thank the editors, reviewers, and publishers for their helpful suggestions and patience with extensions due to ill health.

REFERENCES

Anasiou, D., & Kauffman, J. M. (2013). The social model of disability: Dichotomy between impairment and disability. *The Journal of Medicine and Philosophy: A forum for bioethics and philosophy of medicine*, 441–459. Oxford University Press.

Bailey, M., & Mobley, I. A. (2019). Work in the intersections: A black feminist disability framework. *Gender & Society*, 33(1), 19–40.

Be, A. (2020). Feminism and disability: A cartography of multiplicity. In N. Watson & S. Vehmas (Eds.), *Routledge international handbook of disability studies* (pp. 421–435). Routledge.

Begum, N. (1992). Disabled women and the feminist agenda. *Feminist Review*, 40(1), 70–84.

Butler, J. (2004). *Precarious life: The powers of mourning and violence*. Verso.

Campbell, F. K. (2009). *Contours of ableism: Territories, objects, disability and desire*. Palgrave Macmillan.

Cho, S., Crenshaw, K. W., & McCall, L. (2013). Toward a field of intersectionality studies: Theory, application and praxis. *Signs: A Journal of Women in Culture and Society*, 38(4), 783–810.

Chouinard, V. (1995/96). Like Alice through the looking glass: Accommodation in academia. *Resources for Feminist Research*, 24(3/4), 3–10.

Chouinard, V. (1999). Body politics: Disabled women's activism in Canada and beyond. In R. Butler & H. Parr (Eds.), *Mind and body spaces: Geographies of illness, impairment and disability* (pp. 279–304). Routledge.

Chouinard, V. (2012). Pushing the boundaries of our understanding of disability and violence: Voices from the Global South (Guyana). *Disability and Society*, 27(6), 777–792.

Chouinard, V. (2014). Precarious lives in the Global South: On being disabled in Guyana. *Antipode*, 46(2), 340–358.

Chouinard, V. (2015). Contesting disabling conditions of life in the Global South: Disability activists' and service providers' experiences in Guyana. *Disability and Society*, 30(1), 1–14.

Chouinard, V., & Grant, A. (1995). On being not even anywhere near the 'project': Ways of putting ourselves in the picture. *Antipode*, 27, 137–166.

Clare, E. (1999). *Exile and pride: Disability, queerness and liberation*. South End Press.

Clare, E. (2001). Stolen bodies, reclaimed bodies: Disability and queerness. *Public Culture*, 13(3), 359–365.

Crenshaw, K. (1991). Mapping the margins: Intersectionality, identity politics, and violence against women of colour. *Stanford Law Review*, 43(6), 1241–1299.

Crow, L. (2019). "Figures: An artist-activist response to austerity." In Borghs,M. Chatacko,T., Labib, Y., and Dube, A.K., (eds.)*The Routledge Handbook of Disability Activism* Routledge, 81–86.

Dear, M. J., & Wolch, J. R. (1987). *Landscapes of despair: From deinstitutionalization to homelessness*. Princeton University Press.

Disabled Students Campaign. (2018). Social model of disability (discussion with Michael Oliver). www.youtube.com.

Egner, J. E. (2019). "The disability rights community was never mine": Neuroqueer disidentification. *Gender and Society*, 33(1), 123–147.

Erevelles, N. (2011). *Disability and difference in global contexts: Enabling a transformative body politic*. Palgrave Macmillan.

Erevelles, N. (2014) Beyond ramps/against work: Marta Russell's legacy and politics of intersectionality. In Mahotra, R., Ben-Moshe, L., Chapman, C., & Carey, A. C. (Eds.). *Disability incarcerated: Imprisonment and disability in the United States and Canada* New York: Palgrave Macmillan, 81–99.

Evans, E., & Lepinard, E. (Eds). (2020). *Intersectionality in feminist and queer movements: Confronting privileges*. Routledge.

Fawcett, G. (2000). *Feminist perspectives on disability*. Routledge.

Fine, M., & Asch, A. (1988). Shared dreams: A left perspective on disability rights and reproductive rights. In M. Fine & A. Asch (Eds.), *Women with disabilities: Essays in psychology, culture and politics* (pp. 297–305). Temple University Press.

Frank. G. (1988). Beyond stigma: Visibility and self-empowerment of persons with congenital limb deficiency. *Journal of Social Issues*, 44(1), 95–115.

Fraser, N. (2000). Rethinking recognition. *New Left Review*, 3, 107.

Friedan, B. (1963). *The feminine mystique*. W.W. Norton and Company.

Garland-Thomas, R. (2005). Feminist disability studies. *Signs, 30*(2), 1557–1587.

Gibson, B. E., Carnavale, F. A., & King, G. (2012). "This is my way": Reimagining disability, in/dependence and interconnectedness of persons and assistive technologies. *Disability and Rehabilitation, 34*(22), 1894–1899.

Goffman, E. (1986). *Stigma: Notes on the management of spoiled identity*. Prentice-Hall.

Grech, S. (2012). Disability and the majority world: A neocolonial approach. In D. Goodley, B. Hughes, & L. Davis (Eds.), *Disability and social theory* (n.p.). Palgrave Macmillan.

Grech, S., & Soldatic, K. (Eds.). (2016). *Disability in the Global South: The essential handbook*. Springer.

Greer, G. (1971). *The female eunuch*. Macgibbon and Kee.

Hall, E. (2000). "Blood, brain and bones": Taking the body seriously in the human geography of health and impairment. *Area, 32*(1), 21–29.

Hughes, B., & Paterson, K. (1997). The social model of disability and the disappearing body: Towards a sociology of impairment. *Disability and Society, 12* (3), 325–340.

Kafer, A. (2013). *Feminist queer crip*. Indiana University Press.

Kent, D. (1988). In search of a heroine: Images of disabled women in fiction and drama. In M. Fine & A. Asch (Eds.), *Women with Disabilities: Essays in Psychology, Culture and Politics*. Temple University Press, 90–110.

Klein, N. (2007). *The shock doctrine: The rise of disaster capitalism*. Metropolitan Books.

Knowles, C. (2000). *Bedlam on the streets*. Routledge.

Longhurst, R. (2010). The disabling affects of fat: The emotional and material geographies of some women who live in Hamilton, New Zealand. In V. Chouinard, E. Hall, & R. Wilton (Eds.), *Towards enabling geographies: "Disabled" bodies and minds in society and space* Famham, U.K.: Ashgate, (pp. 199–216).

Mairs, N. (1996). *Carnal acts: Essays*. Boston: Beacon Press.

Mairs, N. (2001). *Waist high in the world: A life amongst the non-disabled*. Boston:Beacon Press.

Malhotra, R. (Ed.). (2017). *Disability politics in a global economy: Essays in honour of Marta Russell*. London and New York: Routledge.

Maroto, M., Pettinicchio, D., & Patterson, A. C. (2019). Hierarchies of categorical disadvantage: Economic insecurity at the intersection of disability, gender and race. *Gender and Society, 33*(1), 64–93.

Marris, V. (1996). *Lives worth living: Women's experiences of chronic illness*. Pandora/Harper Collins.

Martin, E. (1990). Science and women's bodies: Forms of anthropological knowledge. In M. Jacobus, E. F. Keller, & S. Shuttleworth (Eds.), *Body/politics: Women and the discourses of science* (pp. 69–82). Routledge.

McRuer, R. (2018). *Crip times: Disability, globalization, and resistance*. Volume 1. NYU Press.

Meekosha, H., & Soldatic, K. (2011). Human rights and the Global South: The case of disability. *Third World Quarterly, 32*(8), 1383–1397.

Miles, A. L. (2019). "Strong black women": African American women with disabilities, intersecting differences, and inequality. *Gender and Society, 33*(1), 41–63.

Mitchell, D. T., with Snyder, S. L. (2015). *The biopolitics of disability: Neoliberalism, ablenationalism, and peripheral embodiment*. University of Michigan Press.

Mollow, A. (2015). Disability studies gets fat. *Hypatia, 30*(1), 199–216.

Morris, J. (1991). *Pride against prejudice: Transforming attitudes toward disability*. The Women's Press.

Naples, N. A., Maudlin, L., & Dilliway, H. (2019). Gender, disability and intersectionality. *Gender and Society*, *33*(1), 5–18.

Neudel, E. (2011). Lives worth living: The great fight for disability rights. IMBdPro.

Noonan, A., & Gomez, M. T. (2011). Who is missing? Awareness of lesbian, gay, bisexual and transgender people with disabilities. *Sex and Disability*, *29*, 175–180.

Ponterrotto, D. (2016). Resisting the male gaze: Feminist responses to the "Normatization" of the female body in Western culture. *Journal of International Women's Studies*, *17*(1), 133–151.

Puar, J. K. (2017). *The right to maim: Debility, capacity, disability*. Duke University Press.

Russell, M. (1998). *Beyond ramps: Disability at the end of the social contract: a warning from an uppity crip*. Common Courage Press.

Shakespeare, T. (2006). The social model of disability. In L. J. Davis (Ed), *The disability studies reader*, 2nd ed., Oxfordshire, UK: Taylor & Francis. (pp. 197–204).

Shakespeare, T. (2013). The social model of disability. In L. J. Davis (Ed.), *The disability studies reader*, 4th ed. (pp. 214–221). Routledge.

Shakespeare, T. (2014). *Disability rights and wrongs revisited*. Routledge.

Shildrick, M. (2002). *Embodying the monster: Encounters with the vulnerable self*. SAGE Publications.

Shildrick, M. (2012). *Dangerous discourses of disability, subjectivity and sexuality*. Palgrave Macmillan.

Simon, D. L. (1988). "Never-married old women and disability: A majority experience." In Fine M..and Asch, A.(eds.), *Women with disabilities: Essays in psychology, culture and politics*. Temple University Press, 215–226.

Soder, M. (2009). Tensions, perspective and themes in disability studies. *Scandinavian Journal of Disability Research*, *11*(12), 67–81.

Thomas, C. (1999). *Female forms: Experiencing and understanding disability*. Open University Press.

Thomas, C. (2007). *Sociologies of disability and illness: Contested ideas in disability studies and medical sociology*. Macmillan International and Red Globe Press.

Thompson, E. P. (1964). *The making of the English working class*. Penguin Modern Classics.

Valentine, G. (2007). Theorizing and researching intersectionality: A challenge for feminist geography. *The professional geographer*, *59*(1), 10–21.

Watson, N., & S. Vehmas (Eds.). (2019). *Routledge Handbook of Disability Studies*, 2nd edition, Routledge.

Wells, S. (2010). *Our bodies/ourselves and the work of writing*. Stanford University Press.

Wendell, S. (1996). *The rejected body: Feminist philosophical reflections on disability*. Routledge.

Zola, I. (1972). Medicine as an institution of social control. *The Sociological Review*, *20*(4), 487–504.

CHAPTER 5

THE ABLE BODY AND THE PURSUIT OF POWER

BILL HUGHES

INTRODUCTION

POWER, I argue here, is captured at the dawn of "Western civilization" by the figure of ability. Able, or normate power, was embodied in the organization of the male-dominated, warrior societies to which the contemporary Global North traces its origins. Ability was baked into social and mythical sources of power evident in the militarized, expansionist polities and honor-driven, agrarian-based, slave economies of ancient Greece and Rome (Mann, 1986). It was expressed through the aggressive pursuit of material resources in military conquest and in the deployment of psychosocial attributes associated with competitive "strength" and a sense of superiority with respect to other ethnicities (Sennett, 1980)—what we would call, today, racism. These qualities were putatively possessed by well-born, or eugenic masculine elites. The moral dimension to able power—its self-interested righteousness—was central to its origins and development. In Greek, *eu* means good.

Power was exercised inside the polity through internecine power struggles among elites and geopolitically through imperial dominion over conquered people who were enslaved and depicted as ethnic inferiors. The raison d'être of able, classical "power elites" (Mills, 1956) was to win and retain possession of property at the expense of others and to win and acquire worth and honor—or propriety—at the expense of others. Wealthy elites cultivated glory and esteem to decorate their conquests. The conquered were othered through subjugation and oppression. The others—including disabled people—were materially and axiologically invalidated by the deployment of material and ideological forms of power by able elites. Political power and the able body, being similar in form, had an isomorphic relationship in the "ideology of able-bodiedness" promulgated by the able elites (Siebers, 2008, p. 8).

In Greek culture, *eudemonia* (to flourish) was associated with goodness, nobility, effort, and agency. One had to be able-bodied, that is, have sufficient, power, talent, skill, and resources to make things happen, to transform the world into one's own. Moral strength—signified by the prefix *eu*—was attributed to the aristocratic elite, to "the best of men," to those who were regarded as the natural proprietors of reason and beauty. *Eudemons* possessed the Homeric flame of *ethnos*: the singular racial attribute of Greek men. It was their right, they believed, to conquer, subjugate, and rule over "barbarians" or men of lesser worth (Harrison, 2001). The Romans followed the Greeks in these considerations of the representation and enactment of embodied power.

The power associated with the idealized masculine body represented a bold contrast to the material and moral weakness that Aristotle, for example, associated with feminine deformity. Power and authority in classical Western society were manifest in the deployment of strength and supremacy (Sennett, 1980) embodied in ability, masculinity, property, and the virile ethnicity of Greek (and later) Roman militarism.

I argue, in this chapter, that the modern form of able power, at its most virulent during the fin de siècle period between the end of the 19th and the beginning of the 20th century, draws on a similar ideological arsenal of classical, White, eugenic, self-confident superiority to justify its colonizing and disabling agenda.

In the ancient ideology of able-bodiedness, weakness and inferiority belonged—by virtue of the natural distribution of *capability*—to disability, femininity, poverty, and the barbaric other (Isaac, 2006). The baseline for embodied "strength" was "a sound mind in a sound body" (Hughes, 2019a). Disability was conceived as the antithesis of this benchmark. The hubris and perfectionism of the able ideal that we associate with contemporary social relations have deep roots in the past (Campbell, 2010).

In this chapter, I argue that able power is and has been embodied in what Plato called "those of the best"—men who claim to ennoble the world with their eugenic superiority. Able power, legitimated by this view of congenital superiority, represented the disabled body in a pejorative language of humiliating tropes, the most common of which, in the terminology of antiquity, were deformity, defectiveness, and monstrosity (Hughes, 2019a).

In modernity, able power absorbs scientific and pseudoscientific ideology into its agenda of legitimation by superimposing, on top of the ancient and debilitating, ideological categories, medical terms that pathologize disabled people and ethnic others who are caught in the civilizing web of White European colonialism. The colonizing predilection of Western able power and its racist representations of non-Western ethnicities as inferior and defectively embodied is explored later in a "historical sociology" of disability. Antique and modern imperialisms are examined. In these two moments, able power deploys economic and military might to subdue inferior persons abroad while, simultaneously, oppressing "dysgenic" bodies at home. The focus is on these two sociological moments because they, it is argued, represent the policies and practices of able power and the ideology of able-bodiedness at its most aggressive and violent.

In what follows, I discuss the transformative capacity of able power, its isomorphic relationship to the able body, and the deficits of the disabled body as it is constructed by able power as the weak and crooked antithesis of its embodied nobility. In the two sections that follow, I examine able power in, what I call, the ancient, eugenic Mediterranean and, thereafter, in the modern age of empire in the 19th and the first half of the 20th centuries. This period has been described as the prime time of the "eugenic Atlantic"—an age dominated by White, able imperialism (Mitchel & Snyder, 2010).

ABLE POWER AND THE BODY IN
DISABILITY STUDIES

Disability and nondisability formed the grounding dyad of the discipline of disability studies as it threw off the sovereignty of medical discourse in the last 30 years of the 20th century. In the new millennium, just as critical race studies turned its attention to "Whiteness," so critical disability studies began to interrogate and problematize ability (Goodley, 2013).

"Dis crit," shorthand for the exploration of the intersections between ableism and racism, followed the singular disciplines that preceded it (Connor et al., 2015). These critical disciplines sit well together in contemporary neoliberal society where hegemony is racialized and normate. Critical race studies and critical disability studies also readily call out patriarchal power. Recognizing that male privilege intersects with the interests of White, able bodies make feminism a powerful ally of disabled people and people of color.

Contemporary studies of race, gender, and disability accept the view that the opposing triumvirate of able, male, White power forms a powerful phalanx of interests. "Life," one might argue, in this context of opposing forces, "is subjected to a normative evaluation between higher and privileged forms of *proper* life and lower, degraded and excluded forms of *improper* life" (Agamben, 1998, p. 23, *my italics*).

This view from an advocate of biopower—that "*proper* lives are vitalized by exploiting and appropriating. . . *improper* lives"—has recently entered into disability scholarship in the form of an examination of the maiming regimes of contemporary neoliberalism (Puar, 2017, p. 304). The damage done to identities constructed in the pursuit of power is the key issue in the historical and contemporary intersections of ableism, racism, and sexism (Parekh, 2008; Wolbring, 2008). The burning question of our times is a question of the relations between the ideological constructions of proper and improper persons. The divide arises when we ask, Which lives matter? It is a question about the distribution of power and embodied privilege; or the struggle between ideological or discursive constructions of propriety and impropriety, worthiness and worth-less-ness.

The *history* of the "West," from a proper or, more specifically, able standpoint, unfolds as the triumph of able-centric social relations: strength over weakness, civilization over barbarity, White over Black, men over women. We could add to these binaries of propriety and impropriety other crude polarities like reason and idiocy, order and chaos, truth and error, beauty and ugliness. Power and subordination attach themselves to these categories and, more importantly to the relations between them, for these relations translate into bodies that matter and bodies that do not.

The relationship between power and the body is isomorphic—that is, similar in form, shape, and structure. Think of power in corporeal terms and one thinks of an able-bodied, White male. It is *he* who tells the story of the "West" and it is told from his point of view through a colonized curriculum. In the following, I will return to the discussion of isomorphism, to outline the specific relation between able power and the able body.

The story of the West is a sanitized tale of the successful and progressive pursuit of power by able elites. Impairment appears in the narrative as a shadow, a silence; an improper antithesis to normate candor. The narrator is *eugene* or *well-born*. He is a *eudemon*—a flourishing, dynamic figure; the aristocratic embodiment of Western ideals. *He* adopts the perspective of physical, intellectual, and sensory excellence; a position of superiority. He speaks, authoritatively, from a White, masculine, normate podium of power.

The narrator employs a sharp contrast between himself and his "crooked" antithesis. The charismatic presence of his normate embodiment (Garland-Thomson, 2017) is contrasted to the disgrace and stigma of the disabled other (Elias, 2009). The abject vulnerability of disability is contrasted to the robust purity of ability (Hughes, 2019b). The able, normate figure—in magnified, ideal, proper form (Campbell, 2010)—claims virtue, prowess, and virility. Disabled people with their impaired bodies are represented as emblems of worthlessness and failure; without sufficient, power, skill, or resources to bring about change or make things happen (Linton, 1998).

This "transformative ability" (Giddens, 1990) or the will to make things happen has been regarded, in the sociological canon, as the key to understanding power. Weber (1968, p. 943) argued that "domination" depended on the "ability to realise compliance by virtue of authority." Michael Mann's (1986, p. 8) neo-Weberian view of power proposed four key sources of dominion—economic, political, military, and ideological These are, by virtue of human agency, oriented toward "a generalized means of attaining a goal." To make money, to rule, to make war, and to control ideas are the engines of history, social change, and development. These are the sources of power that have been monopolized by the *eugene*. Beneath the eugenic elite who command and make things happen, there is dependency; followers, foot soldiers, the masses.

Popitz (2017) argues that the first and most fundamental anthropological form of power is the ability to modify or the "disposition" to change the world through the "power of action." Disabled people do not have access to the means to make things happen. They have been in the past and are today excluded from them.

Sociologists warn that one must be careful not to individualize power or reduce it to behavior. It must be examined through the lens of wider social interests, including contexts, institutions, and structures (Lukes, 2005). These include the two main drivers of the pursuit of power which the well-born narrator of "Western" history grasps with both hands. They are (1) unbridled access to the means of violence and hence the tools of economic expropriation and (2) a voice that resonates with seductive—but always self-serving—persuasiveness. These are the two basic forms of power; the two central transformative agents. The first is material, the second ideological.

This double-headed view of power is best expressed in the work of Antonio Gramsci (1971). He uses the term *hegemony* to describe power in terms of wealth and persuasion or force and consent. His theory of power was influenced by Marx and Machiavelli. Gramsci, in turn, influenced the historical materialist view of power proposed by Mike Oliver (1990), the founder of the social model of disability in the United Kingdom. Power is exercised through control over the means of violence and through the ability to construct a consensus that "subjects" are prepared to follow even if doing so is against their interests. Though different in many ways, this dual approach to power finds some common ground beyond Gramsci, in the work of other major theorists of power, including Weber and Foucault.

As Weber (1968, p. 961) recognized, "every sphere of social action is profoundly influenced by structures of dominance." These include (in modernity at least) the "state laying claim to the monopoly of legitimate physical violence" (Weber, 2004, p. 43) as well as the mythologies of "savvy power" (Weber, 1968, p. 213). The latter refers to the standard-bearers of moral authority that smooth the acceptance of "valid norms" (Weber, 1968, p. 948) and sustain the value of normalcy (Davis, 1995). For Gramsci (1971), while the means of violence are concentrated in the state, the most important bulwark in the defense of property is the ideological legitimacy diffused throughout civil society as a "common-sense" world view. To draw an example from the sociology of disability, what Tobin Siebers (2008) called the "ideology of able-bodiedness" serves the interests of normate power and sustains the dominance of the able elite.

Foucault's ideas have been very influential in disability studies as a framework for the analysis of power (Tremain, 2005, 2017) and corporeal resistance to it (O'Brien, 2005). The contrast between the violent coercion of sovereignty and the persuasive power of subjectification that transforms external systems of surveillance into self-discipline animates his early work (e.g., Foucault, 1979). His, more "mature" concept of "bio-power" refers to the vital force for life that can be simultaneously generative and debilitating; the latter, particularly so for disabled people (Kadler, 2019; Kolarova, 2015; Mitchell & Snyder, 2015; Puar, 2017). Foucault's importance as a theorist of power is that he returns our thinking to the question Which lives matter? and, therefore, to the unequal distribution of life chances that privilege White, masculine, able bodies.

The isomorphic relationship between able power and the able body is a useful starting point in explaining the relationship between normate power and the disabled body. The latter, from the perspective of able power, is a crooked, deficient body that needs to be straightened, fixed, or rehabilitated.

In modernity, impairment is a byword for the deficit, represented by morally negative terms such as pathology and abnormality. In the deep history of the West, before disabled bodies were medicalized, impairment was a byword for defectiveness, deformity, and monstrosity (Hughes, 2019a). Disabled people's bodies have been dominated by invalidating representations and associations which contrast them, pejoratively, as the antithesis of able propriety. Ideas of corporeal propriety are "infused with 'able-bodied' notions" (Barnes et al., 1999, p. 65) that disempower corporeal difference.

The wholesome organism projected by able power is a mirror image of what Julia Kristeva (1982, p. 71) has called the "clean and proper body." It is the body of the "normate," the term that Rosemarie Garland Thomson (2017) gives to the body that thinks of itself as invulnerable and entirely properly formed. It is noteworthy that this dominant form of embodiment has no empirical existence per se. It is a normative construct. As Campbell (2008, p. 153) puts it, "ableism" is constructed from "a network of beliefs, processes and practices that produces a particular kind of self and body (the corporeal standard) that is projected as perfect, species-typical and therefore essential and fully human." Able corporeality is an ideal of being that is depicted ideologically in the imaginary of "modernist ontology, epistemology and ethics" as that which is "secure, distinct, closed and autonomous" (Shildrick, 2002, p. 51). The able body embraces "human perfectibility as a normative physical or psychological standard" and involves "a curious disavowal of variation and mortality" (Kaplan, 2000, p. 303).

Able power embraces a physical identity that we are supposed to aspire to but can never become. It promotes the body of our dreams; one that is without grounding in the material or sensible world and is therefore no more than a "body schema, a psychic construction of wholeness that. . . belies its own precariousness and vulnerability" (Shildrick, 2002, p. 79). The able body is "divorced from time and space." It is "a thoroughly artificial affair" (Mitchell & Snyder, 2000, p. 7). It closes itself off from any connection with the animal side of humanity, from imperfection, physical decline, the messiness of existence, and death. Disability is depicted by able power as the opposite of this somatic ideal, the "inverse reflection" (Deutsch & Nussbaum, 2000, p. 13) of the able body. From the grand perspective of ability, the disabled body is portrayed as the epitome of what not to be; flawed identity *par excellence*.

In the next two sections of this chapter, I examine the relationship between able power and the disabled body, in the context of (first) ancient and (second) modern forms of western "imperialism." I argue that eugenic thinking is mobilized by "well-born" elites to subjugate bodily difference at home and undermine the value of bodies abroad, subjugated by territorial expansion and colonization.

ABLE POWER IN THE EUGENIC MEDITERRANEAN

In Western antiquity, intolerant and bellicose regimes of ability governed disabled people's lives. Impaired bodies were used as *pharmakoi* or scapegoats, represented as ominous symbols of catastrophe, selected for infanticide, and singled out for ridicule and maltreatment (Garland, 2010; Hughes, 2019a). Disabled bodies were targeted by able power for elimination and indignity. Historically, the ideology of able-bodiedness constructed disability as "crooked" nature and "constitutional weakness." Disability was conceived in these ancient societies as the embodiment of physical, intellectual, and sensory deficit; and impairments were referred to in pejorative terms as signs of defective, deformed, and monstrous lives.

Able power in classical society expressed itself in projects of social hygiene. For Greece and Rome, "the barbarian" was the foreign monster that the great powers of the eugenic Mediterranean sought to subdue and enslave. The barbarian was represented as a figure of inferiority by the two classical giants. The barbarian body was characterized as "defective *Zoë*" or "deformed biology." Weak bodies and minds were "displaced onto territories that" Greece and Rome sought to conquer. The two greatest military powers of antiquity "evolved a biopolitics of evangelising civilisation" in which "moral legitimacy" was derived from "myths of monsters that must be slain" (Hughes, 2019a, p. 133) by virtuous, "clean and proper bodies."

Military conquest served the desire for land and estates in the colonies and glory at home. The defeated were dishonored by their transformation into the property of the victor. With more than 30% of the working population enslaved, Greece and Rome fulfill the base criterion of "slave societies" (Andreau & Descat, 2011). Land and slaves constituted economic and symbolic capital. They were the two most palpable signs of the able power of classical aristocrats. Civilized, victorious people were sharply delineated from the debilitated and broken bodies of defeated chattels (Bowden, 2005 Hughes, 2019a). The "heroic project" of conquest was founded on a sense of superiority that has been described as "proto-racist" (Isaac, 2006).

Slaves and barbarians were according to Aristotle, defectives, who were, "incapable of reasoning," as if "diseased by the onset of illnesses like epilepsy or madness" (Myrdal quoted in Kendi, 2016, p. 17). Disability was used to depict racial otherness. Meanwhile, eugenic policies at home constituted a project of social hygiene that eliminated or abused disabled Greeks and Romans. Disabled people were treated like "ethnic inferiors," and ethnic inferiors were treated like disabled people.

For the classical doctrine of ethical naturalism that underpinned the possessive, militarized system of social relations and the cult of beauty that accompanied it, the elimination of disabled people was completely intelligible (Stiker, 1999). The *eugenic* project was designed to cut out the cancer of inferior embodiment. Elimination or enslavement of barbaric and defective persons was the political means employed. By contrast, the propertied elite represented itself as a class to which "honor" and honorable employment was attached (Veblen, 1899/1994, p. 2). The landowner/warrior, was *of the best*. He was empowered by his place at the privileged peak of the normate hierarchy to claim that he was the strongest, the wisest, the most noble, and virtuous.

"Those of the worst"—to use Plato's epigram for disabled people—were poor and vulgar, weak and ugly, defective in mind, body, or senses. They were the ostensive negation to *eugene* and *eudemon*; the antithesis of the best of men. The pseudoscience of physiognomy, powerfully ingrained in classical consciousness, "proved" that ugly and deformed bodies were crooked in spirit, devoid of reason, morally compromised, and omens of catastrophe. Eugenics was good sense. It made embodied defectives into candidates for infanticide and for sacrificial rites of expulsion that cast disability out from polity and community (Hughes, 2019a, pp. 117–174).

Plato admired Spartan eugenics and "decreed that 'defective babies' should be left to die" (Carlson, 2010, p. 2). He supported *eu*thanasia for the "useless" and the insane. Weakness, ugliness, deformity, and—most importantly for the philosophers— irrationality were threats to the "stock" of the polity. The insane, should, therefore, "not appear in the city" (quoted in Stiker, 1999, p. 44).

Robust, warrior-citizens were necessary for social reproduction and the maintenance of power. Whatever might dilute their number, muscularity, strength, beauty, or intelligence threatened virtue and the security of the "superior" Greek and (later) Roman way of life. Medical and philosophical expertise agreed on this point: Clinical reason deployed in the decision as to whether "a new born child" was "worth raising" (Stainton, 2008, p. 487) was a political and moral obligation for citizens.

In the able imaginary, defective babies should be eliminated: Raising (only) sound minds in sound bodies was the path to prosperity, virtuous citizenship, and imperial dominance. If "crooked bodies" were not eliminated at birth, they had little value save as objects of ridicule and amusement. Disabled people were, according to Aristotle, "*lusus naturae*," meaning mistakes or "jokes" of nature. The aristocratic elites of Greece and Rome used the power of laughter to humiliate and demean disabled people.

The Greeks were masters of tendentious humor and lovers of schadenfreude. Socrates recommended cruel humor, though he countenanced care in its use. To laugh at the expense of mercurial power was a dangerous business. As jokes of nature, however, disabled people—who had escaped the infanticide medically recommended for "defective bodies"—were fair game for sticks and stones and hurtful names. Aristotle provided a timeless, ecological justification for laughing at disability. Separating disabled people from the usual considerations of proper behavior was commonplace. Deformity, Herodotus, the father of history, argued, was incompatible with virtue and happiness. Compassion for human vulnerability was not in the emotional lexicon of the ancient Greeks. Physical and intellectual differences provided standard targets for normate invective.

Virtue, or, to use the Greek term, *arete*, was entirely dependent on the possession of "a sound mind in a sound body," strength and beauty combined with reason and intelligence. Physical and intellectual impairment in Greece was an abomination. Plato and Aristotle recommended infanticide for disabled infants. Disabled people who survived the murderous disgust of their communities and even wounded war veterans were considered fair game for dehumanizing malice and ridicule.

The symposium—an elite male drinking club—was a vibrant institution in the Greek city states. It thrived on tendentious chatter steeped in eugenic sentiment (Garland, 2010). A night of poetry and serious debate was incomplete for a well-born noble if it did not involve getting drunk and poking fun at defective inferiors. In the moral economy of Greek civilization, disabled people represented the antithesis of the eugene whose claim to virtue and propriety was embodied in beauty, truth, reason, order and justice. . . the ideals that *he* symbolized (Hughes, 2019a).

Disabled people, conceived ideologically, under eugenic hegemony, as the negation of propriety were fit only for humiliation or sacrificial expulsion. The disabled God Hephaestus—source of laughter for fellow Olympians—was cast out from Heaven by his mother who was disgusted by his deformities. During the annual Athenian festival of Thargelia, a *pharmakos* or scapegoat was chosen by the city-state to be ritually humiliated and expelled from the city. Either a criminal or a disabled person—both regarded as *offensive*—was chosen for this role.

The Greek elite could not abide defective, deformed, or monstrous bodies. Disabled people who escaped infanticide or the indignities of ritual exclusion were kept out of sight and mind. Roman ableism, by contrast, indulged the grotesque in carnivals of spectacular embodiment. Pomp and ceremony were grist to the mill of empire. Gladiatorial games, theatrical extravaganzas, staged naval battles, chariot races, and mass executions mapped, in fabulous displays of visual grandeur, the bloody contours of power.

Impairment was woven into the politics of spectacle, providing light relief and counterpoint to the elaborate staging of blood-soaked pageants. Dwarfs were kept as pets by the patrician classes and some were used in the gladiatorial arena, pitted against women slaves in mock, comic intermezzos. The use of wooden swords indicated that dwarfs were far too expensive to be sacrificed for ephemeral pleasure. They fetched huge sums at the *teraton agora* or "monster market." So, too, did fools and "monsters," a term used by Greeks and Romans to describe bodies that were profoundly different to the aesthetic norm.

The more "spectacular" the impairment, the greater the demand and the economic return for sellers who tramped the empire to enslave disabled people and bring extraordinary specimens to market (Barton, 1995, p. 68). Impaired bodies were costly symbols of wealth trotted out at parties by social elites for the amusement of influential guests. Ownership of people with corporeal anomalies was a sign of social standing, a "must have" for an upper-class get-together. In the moral economy of able-centric Rome, disabled people had abuse value as amusements for patricians at play.

Freud argued that tendentious humor arises in the id and expresses itself in bile, lust, and violence. It requires the benign superego of civilized propriety to keep it in check. There was no such check for the Greeks and Romans, who were quick to revulsion, abuse, and mockery in the face of imperfection, weakness, and vulnerability. For the able power brokers, compassion was "womanly"; it was associated with the "loss of moral autonomy and self-control" (Sznaider, 2001, p. 20). Nietzsche suggested that the virile, "master morality" of antique civilization inured it against a sensitive response to human vulnerability. The axiological invalidation of disabled lives in Western antiquity was founded on an ideology of able-bodiedness in which disabled people were reduced to deformity, defectiveness, and monstrosity.

In this section, I have discussed the historical infancy of ability/disability and the noble, propertied *eugenic* or able form of power that constructed impairment as the embodiment of weakness and inferiority. The focus has been on how disability was constructed, like the racially other barbarian, as ontological inferiority and depicted as deformed, defective, and monstrous. Disabled people were regarded as the antithesis of ability, human agency, strength, and excellence and were subjected to demeaning abuse.

THE EUGENIC ATLANTIC AND THE PURSUIT OF POWER IN THE MODERN AGE OF EMPIRE

In the late 19th century and the first half of the 20th century, the powerful "able nations" (Mitchell & Snyder, 2015) of the North Atlantic rim sought to "civilize" at home and abroad by invoking eugenic "missions" (Mitchell & Snyder, 2010). The propaganda employed by the imperial projects of the industrializing, mercantile powers were, charters of White, male superiority that drew heavily, like the classical powers of antiquity, on the ideology of able-bodiedness.

The ancient medical lexicon for disability was re-formed in modernity. Defectiveness, deformity, and monstrosity were still used by the eugenics movement but gave way, in more scientifically inclined discourse, to medical terminology. Teratology substituted for monstrosity while abnormality and pathology offered clinical, supposedly objective, alternatives to the calumnious tropes of the ancients. Those assigned to clinical categories, however, did not escape the trap of the pejorative evaluation and stigma embedded in them (Canguilhem, 1989).

Supremacist philosophies like social Darwinism and racist "civilizing missions" were espoused by Western imperialists as they deployed their mercantile power and industrialized military resources to plunder the "Global South" (Moore, 2002). Western powers drew on intersecting ideologies of race and able-bodiedness to justify an expansionist approach to international relations and to legitimate, on the domestic front, the implementation of eugenic policies of hygienic population control designed to protect "clean and proper bodies" from dysgenic inferiors like Black and disabled people.

Western imperial interests invoked the "standard of civilization" to ideologically justify the disabling agenda of colonialism and to colonize and control non-European people (Bowden, 2005). The hidden agenda was the expansion of markets and the pursuit of profit. A similar agenda was in play in the United States as it sought to justify its expansion toward the Pacific coast. It expropriated indigenous land and exploited the Black labor that produced vast riches for the able beneficiaries of the "white gold" of the American South (Wolfe, 2006, p. 392). It took civil war to undermine the legitimacy of the "peculiar institution," but racism and White supremacism rerooted after the abolition of slavery in the segregationist laws of the Jim Crow era.

"Foreigners," in the White European imperial projects, were depicted as disabled by backwardness, racial inferiority, heathenism, and savagery. Jules Ferry, Prime Minister of France for two periods in the 1880s, justified French colonial expansion on the grounds of Western racial supremacy, which he called "the superior civilising duty":

"The higher races," he argued, "have a right over the lower races. . . superior races. . . have a duty. . . to civilise inferior races" (quoted in Majunder, 2007, p. 23). Albert-Pierre Sarraut—another French statesman of the imperial age—summed up the civilizing mission of his able nation "as the right of the strongest to help the weakest" (Majunder, 2007, p. 24).

Across the English Channel in another of the "able nations" of the Atlantic rim, the British took the view that the mission to civilize the backward native—"half devil and half child"—was, as Rudyard Kipling put it "the white man's burden." His advice to the United States, at the close of the Spanish American War (1898), was to annex (take on the burden of) the Philippines and tie its future to Anglo-Saxon excellence and ability (Kipling, 1970, p. 323–324). The able nations were contestants for the markets opened up by their colonial expropriations, but they agreed that White, normate hegemony would bring benefits to all, most especially the "backward" people of the colonies.

On the American frontier, the New World equivalent of the European civilizing mission was in full swing. The buffalo genocide of the 1880s was the beginning of the end for the traditional, indigenous, tribal life in the United States. The able nation was taking shape as lives and land rights of indigenous people in the Midwest were obliterated by the "logic of elimination" that had been built into White, settler colonialism (Wolfe, 2006). "The frontier" was transformed from—as Theodore Roosevelt put it in his "triumphalist geography" (Shapiro, 1999) *The Winning of the West* (1888/1989, p. 119)—"a game preserve for squalid savages," into a land fit for agrarian profiteering, industrial expansion, and capital accumulation. When greed and ethnocide—the "civilized" bedfellows of "frontier"—finally fused east with west, "an avalanche of assimilationist legislation" killed tribal sovereignty and the independence of the Indian way of life (Wolfe, 2006).

Fredrick Jackson Turner's homage to frontier life, argued that "free land and an abundance of natural resources open to *fit* people" had been the making of American democracy (quoted in Potter, 1954, p. 149; *my italics*). The *fit* people of the able nation were characterized by "coarseness and strength . . . acuteness and acquisitiveness" (Turner, 1893/2007, n.p.). The "savage lands" expropriated by force, over three centuries, finally surrendered completely to the entrepreneurialism, ingenuity, and military might of able, White, self-reliant, rugged, settler-pioneers.

Late 19th-century imperialism, was justified by the "binary typology of advanced and backward. . . races" (Said, 1978, p. 206). It was "interpreted" by the European powers as an invitation to "White civilization" to take the "underdeveloped" world under its wing, and, where necessary, disable its people for their own good. In turning non-European territory from an "alien to a colonial world," the able powers struck-up a "proprietary attitude" toward it that transformed relations to otherness. These relations had been "textual and contemplative." They became "administrative, economic and. . . military" (Said, 1978, pp. 210–211). This is also the argument that Karen Soldatic (2015) makes in her study of the administrative affinities between the subjugation of disabled and indigenous people by the White Anglo-Saxon, Australian state at the beginning of the 20th century. The "decolonising agenda" (Meekosha, 2011) in disability studies is currently central to critiques of able power in settler colonial contexts like Palestine (Jaffee, 2016) and Canada (Hutcheon & Lashewicz, 2020).

Eugenics provided an endogenous "standard of civilization" for the able, occidental elite. Revivified, from its origins in ancient Greece, by Galton in 1883, eugenics was constructed as a weapon to eliminate backwardness and degeneracy on the home front. The pseudoscience legitimated the racial and normate supremacism that animated the ableist imaginary in the late 19th and early 20th centuries.

Acolytes of Galton, like, for example, the biologist Charles Davenport in the United States, invoked a degenerate, menacing underclass of abnormal persons who were afflicted with a range of pathologies. "Feeble-minded," insane, and deformed people were depicted as evidence of widespread "social pathology." The unfit were mired in vagrancy, alcoholism, criminality, pauperism, and prostitution (Jones, 1986, pp. 93–95). The dysgenic classes were "utterly helpless, repulsive in appearance and revolting in manners" (Emerson et al., 2005, p. 13). In the United States, the so-called hereditary inferiority of Black people was associated, in eugenic thinking, with exacerbated individual abnormalities and social pathologies (Kendi, 2016, pp. 301–302).

For the able elites, the dysgenic underclasses were regarded as profoundly dangerous, a threat to social hygiene that, if left unattended, would rip to shreds the social and moral fabric of nation, empire, and future. Segregation, in, for example, the United Kingdom and segregation combined with sterilization in, for example, the United States were deemed to be the best methods to save society from the spreading cancers of pathological defectiveness that were carried by disabled and Black bodies.

Plato's recommendation that disabled people should be put to death was "softened" in modernity (until the Nazis revivified it) to a claim that, for imbeciles and defectives, social death was punishment enough. From the perspective of the able or "clean and proper body"—in circumstances thousands of years apart—what was most important was that the well-born have the opportunity to flourish. The priority was to exclude "those of the worst" and contain their inferiority by population control. The "able nations" exiled pathological defectives from the civilized spaces of propriety in bespoke institutions.

Able anxieties in the modern Age of Empire were filtered through "the conflicting imperatives of laws of kinship that forbade inbreeding on the one hand and phobic responses to foreigners on the other. The fear and shame of defect. . . was powerful enough to smother unions too close to home or too 'hybrid'" (Kaplan, 2000, p. 303). From eugenic perspectives, threats to superiority of nation and race from the pathological underclass of disabled and Black people could be mitigated by appropriate reproductive choices that maintained the purity of the stock. Eugenics offered a flexible ideology anchored in the confidence and anxieties embodied in the kinship of elite, White, Western, able supremacists. Racist and ableist ideas, during the late 19th and early 20th centuries, had significant appeal across the political spectrum, uniting conservatives, liberals, and socialists (Kelves, 1985).

Eugenics in the modern Age of Empire was filtered through ideas of natural selection, the science of evolution, and a pessimistic demography. The fear was that urban improvements in the industrialized conurbations of the imperialist nations of Western Europe and North America created conditions in which too many social degenerates or "freaks of nature" would prosper. This view "like a biological version of entropy, suggested that lower classes, or inferior races would come to predominate over 'superior' beings, who were more likely to reproduce at a slower rate." Furthermore, "it was claimed that deleterious mutations were more common than advantageous mutations, so that the population would inevitably decline" (Shakespeare, 2008, p. 23).

It was imperative, from the perspective of the eugenic ideology of able-bodiedness, that the "unfit" be prevented from breeding and that, conversely, the well-born be encouraged to go forth and multiply. In the United States, city authorities even tried to sweep degenerates from urban spaces while immigration authorities in New York tried to curtail the arrival of "mendicants, cripples, criminals, idiots &C" (Hughes, 2017, pp. 6–9; Schweik, 2009, p. 165). The "ugly laws" were designed to take the maimed, diseased, and mutilated off the streets, to hide their "repulsive countenances" from the gaze of ordinary, "descent," White normates who wished to occupy hygienic spaces of consumption without being bothered by "cripples" and beggars. At the same time post-Reconstruction America was using the stranglehold of "vitality politics" to slowly choke and debilitate any sign of sovereign life among the Black population. In the Age of Empire—(even) in the isolationist United States—"capacity, debility and disability" existed "in a mutually reinforcing constellation" of power (Kadler, 2019, p. 13).

CONCLUSION

For Aristotle, one could not be *eudemon*—could not flourish—without the gift of reason or the strength to prevail over other, weaker competitors. He argued in the *Nicomachean Ethics* (1962, 1099b, pp. 5–6) that, without the proper *eugenic* credentials (excluding those who were, as he put it, "ugly," "not of good birth," or not able to conceive "good children"), a virtuous, happy life was a pipe dream. Disability was conceived, pejoratively, in the shadow of this ennobling roll call of ideas. As I have argued, these ancient ideas of able superiority were alive and well in the ideology and practices of modern Western colonialism and American expansionism. They were welded into the revival of antique eugenics during the Industrial Revolution. Able nations, scrambling to secure parcels of Africa, demonstrated the barbarity their "civilizing missions" and eugenics reached its blood-curdling nadir in the genocide of World War II.

The eugene symbolizes the "good body." The ideological power associated with this figure is derived from his representation as the epitome of ability, including possession of wealth strength, virility, and military might. These "noble" traits represent the narcissistic ideology of able-bodiedness. They represent the legend that the eugenic power elites claimed for themselves in ancient times and reappropriated to legitimate modern colonialism and the oppression of bodily difference. The hegemony of "ability," and the pursuit of power by those who see themselves bold and armored in its mirror, rest on command over the means of force and persuasion (Gramsci, 1971). Able power has depended materially on the wealth of well-born elites whose fortunes were established, in the first place, by conquest and enslavement. Disability, by contrast, represented and continues to represent, spoiled embodiment, crookedness of body and mind, traits of weakness and vulnerability. The bodily perfection promised by able power is alive and well in the contemporary cultural fascination with genetic engineering and its expectations of better bodies and improved nature (Sandal, 2009).

Herodotus, the father of history, argued that the central credential for human happiness, or *eudemonia*, was "freedom from deformity" (quoted in Shapiro, 1999, p. 153). The opportunity to flourish fell to the *eugene* or the well-born. A fulfilled life was not in the nature of disability. However, it was the birthright of the well-born, wealthy elites who served as the symbol of ability, masculinity, and ethnic superiority. Able power and the able body were regarded, at the dawn of "Western civilization," as imperatives for social and cultural success. These views are alive and well today, but challenges to them are well established in progressive intersections where socially disenfranchised people, including women, disabled people, and people of color, claim their rights to express the value of their lives.

References

Agamben, G. (1998). *Homo sacer: Sovereign power and bare life*. Stanford University Press.

Andreau, J., & Descat, R. (2011). *The slave in Greece and Rome* (M. Leopold, Trans.). University of Wisconsin Press.

Aristotle. (1962). *Nicomachean ethics* (H. Rackham, Trans.). Loeb Classical Library, Harvard University Press.

Barnes, C., Mercer, G., & Shakespeare, T. (1999). *Exploring disability: A sociological introduction*. Polity Press.

Barton, C. (1995). *The sorrows of the Ancient Romans: The gladiator and the monster*. Princeton University Press.

Bowden, B. (2005). The colonial origins of international law: European expansion and the classical standard of civilization. *Journal of the History of International Law, 7*(1), 1–24. https://doi.org/10.1163/1571805054545145

Campbell, F. A. K. (2008). Exploring internalised ableism using critical race theory. *Disability & Society, 23*(2), 151–162.

Campbell, F. K. (2010). *Contours of ableism: The production of disability and abledness*. Palgrave Macmillan.

Canguilhem, G. (1989). *The normal and the pathological* (C. Fawcatt, Trans.). Zone Books.

Carlson, L. (2010). *The faces of intellectual disability: Philosophical reflections*. Indiana University Press.

Connor, D., Ferri, B., & Annamma, S. (Eds.) (2015). *DisCrit—disability studies and critical race theory in education*. Teachers College Press.

Davis, L. (1995). *Enforcing normalcy: Disability, deafness and the body*. Verso.

Deutsch, H., & Nussbaum, F. (2000). *Defects: Engendering the modern body*. University of Michigan Press.

Elias, N. (2009). Group charisma and group disgrace. In R. Kilminster & S. Mennell (Eds.), *Essays on sociology and the humanities, volume 16 of the collected works of Norbert Elias* (pp. 73–81). UDC Press.

Emerson, E., Malam, S., Davies, I., & Spencer, K. (2005). *Adults with learning difficulties in England 2003-4*. Health and Social Care Information Centre.

Foucault, M. (1979). *Discipline and punish: The birth of the prison*. Random House.

Garland, R. (2010) *The Eye of the Beholder: Deformity and disability in the Graeco-Roman World*, (2nd Edition) NY and London: Bristol Classical Press

Garland-Thomson, R. (2017). *Extraordinary bodies: Figuring physical disability in American culture and literature* (20th anniversary ed.). Columbia University Press.

Giddens, A. (1990). *Consequences of modernity*. Polity Press.

Goodley, D. (2013). Dis/entangling critical disability studies. *Disability & Society, 28*(5), 631–644.

Gramsci, A. (1971). *The prison notebooks*. Lawrence and Wishart.

Harrison, T. (Ed.) (2001). *Greeks and barbarians*. Routledge.

Hughes, B. (2017). Impairment on the move: The disabled incomer and other invalidating intersections. *Disability & Society, 32*(4), 467–488.

Hughes, B. (2019a). *A historical sociology of disability: Human validity and invalidity from Antiquity to early modernity*. Routledge.

Hughes, B. (2019b). The abject and the vulnerable: The twain shall meet: Reflections on Disability in the moral economy. *The Sociological Review*. https://doi.org/10.1177%2F0038026119854259

Hutcheon, E., & Lashewicz, B. (2020). Tracing and troubling conformities between ableism and colonialism in Canada. *Disability & Society, 35*(5), 695–714.

Isaac, B. (2006). *The invention of racism in classical antiquity*. Princeton University Press.

Jaffee, L. (2016). Disrupting global disability frameworks: Settler colonialism geopolitics of disability in Palestine/Israel. *Disability & Society, 31*(1), 116–130.

Jones, G. (1986). *Social hygiene in twentieth century Britain*. Croom Helm.

Kadler, S. (2019). *Vitality politics: Health, debility and the limits of black emancipation*. University of Michigan Press.

Kaplan, C. (2000). Afterword: Liberalism, feminism and defect. In H. Deutsch & F. Nussbaum (Eds.), *Defects: Engendering the modern body* (pp. 303–318). University of Michigan Press.

Kelves, D. (1985). *In the name of eugenics: Genetics and the uses of human heredity*. Knopf.

Kendi, I. (2016). *Stamped from the beginning: The definitive history of racist ideas in America*. The Bodley Head.

Kipling, R. (1970). *Rudyard Kipling's verse—Definitive edition* (3rd ed.). Doubleday.

Kolarova, K. (2015). Death by choice, life by privilege: Biopolitical circuits of vitality and debility in the times of Empire. In S. Tremain (Ed.), *Foucault and the government of disability* (2nd ed.) (pp. 373–96). University of Michigan Press.

Kristeva, J. (1982). *Powers of horror: An essay on abjection* (L. Roudiez, Trans.). Columbia University Press.

Linton, S. (1998). *Claiming disability*. New York University Press.

Lukes, S. (2005). *Power: A radical view* (2nd ed.). Springer.

Majunder, M. (2007). *Postcoloniality: The French dimension*. Berghahn Books.

Mann, M. (1986). *The sources of social power: Volume 1: A history of power from the beginning to AD 1760*. Cambridge University Press.

Meekosha, H. (2011). Decolonising disability: Thinking and acting globally. *Disability & Society*, 26(6), 667–682.

Mills, C. W. (1956). *The power elite*. Oxford University Press.

Mitchell, D., & Snyder, S. (2000). *Narrative prosthesis: Disability and the dependencies of discourse*. University of Michigan Press.

Mitchell, D., & Snyder, S. (2010). The eugenic Atlantic; race, disability and the making of eugenic science 1800–1945. *Disability & Society*, 18(7), 843–864.

Mitchell, D., & Snyder, S. (2015). *The biopolitics of disability: Neoliberalism, ablenationalism and peripheral embodiment*. University of Michigan Press.

Moore, G. (2002). *Nietzsche, biology, metaphysics*. Cambridge University Press.

O'Brien, R. (2005). *Gender, disability and a workplace ethic of care*. Routledge.

Oliver, M. (1990). *The politics of disablement*. Palgrave Macmillan.

Parekh, P. (2008). *Intersecting gender and disability perspectives in rethinking postcolonial identities* (Wagadu, Volume 4). Xlibris Corporation.

Popitz, H. (2017). *Phenomena of power: Authority, domination and violence* (G. Poggi, Trans.). Columbia University Press.

Potter, D. (1954). *People of plenty: Economic abundance and the American character*. University of Chicago Press.

Puar, J. (2017). *The right to maim: Debility, capacity, disability*. Duke University Press.

Roosevelt, T. (1989). *The winning of the West*. (Original work published 1888). Best Books.

Said, E. (1978). *Orientalism*. Penguin.

Sandal, M. (2009). *The case against perfection: Ethics in the age of genetic engineering*. Harvard University Press.

Schweik, S. (2009). *The ugly laws*. New York University Press.

Sennett, R. (1980). *Authority*. Faber and Faber.

Shakespeare, T. (2008). Disability, genetics and eugenics. In J. Swain & S. French (Eds.), *Disability on equal terms* (pp. 21–30). SAGE Publications.

Shapiro, A. (1999). *Everybody belongs: Changing negative attitudes to classmates with disabilities*. Garland.

Shildrick, M. (2002). *Embodying the monster: Encounters with the vulnerable self*. SAGE Publications.

Soldatic, K. (2015). Post-colonial reproductions: Disability, indigeneity and the formation of the white, masculine, settler state of Australia, *Social Identities*, 21(1), 116–130.

Siebers, T. (2008). *Disability theory*. Michigan University Press.

Stainton, T. (2008). Reason, grace and charity: Augustine and the impact of church doctrine on the construction of intellectual disability. *Disability & Society*, 23(5), 485–496.

Stiker, H. (1999). *A history of disability* (W. Sayers, Trans.). University of Michigan Press.

Sznaider, N. (2001). *The compassionate temperament: Care and cruelty in modern society*. Rowman and Littlefield.

Tremain, S. (2005) *Foucault and the Government of Disability*, Ann Arbor: University of Michigan Press

Tremain, S. (2017). *Foucault and feminist philosophy of disability*. University of Michigan Press.

Turner, F. J. (1893/2007). *The frontier in American history*. Project Gutenberg. http://guttenberg.org.files/22994/22994-h/22994-html

Veblen, T. (1994). *The theory of the leisure class: An economic study in the evolution of institutions* (Original work published 1899). Dover.

Weber, M. (1968). *Economy and society: An outline of interpretative sociology*. University of California Press.

Weber, M. (2004). *The vocation lectures*. Hackett.

Wolbring, G. (2008). The politics of ableism. *Development, 51*, 252–258.

Wolfe, P. (2006). Settler colonialism and the elimination of the native. *Journal of Genocide Research, 8*(4), 307–409.

CHAPTER 6

CONTEXTUALIZING DISABILITY EXPERIENCES

Understanding and Measuring How the Environment Influences Disability

KENZIE LATHAM-MINTUS AND SABRINA CORDON

INTRODUCTION

OVER the past 50 years, multiple definitions and models of disability have been developed by clinicians, researchers, and policymakers (Altman, 2014). Although traditional definitions have typically conceptualized disability as a result of a medical condition such as an injury or disease, increasingly there is recognition that disability is "also a social construct that results from the social and physical environment in which a person lives their life" (Altman, 2014, p. 2). Even today, medical and programmatic definitions of disability often narrowly focus on disease and impairment without adequate consideration to the role of the environment, yet disability scholarship has made large strides in understanding, defining, and measuring disability and the environment. The purpose of this chapter is to examine how the physical and social environment is understood and measured in relation to disability within the current literature.

Guiding our own conceptualization of disability, we draw from multiple models of disability that highlight the role of the environment, including the social model of disability and various hybrid models (e.g., World Health Organization's [WHO] International Classification of Functioning, Disability, and Health) that recognize the health and social dimensions of disability. One of the earliest attempts to move disability past solely medical definitions comes from the social model of disability. The social model of disability makes a clear distinction between disability and impairments, where disability is due to the "disabling barriers" of society such as inaccessible physical environments (e.g., broken and uneven sidewalks, building entrances without ramps, or improper signage) and ableist attitudes, stigmatizing interpersonal interactions, and discriminatory practices (Oliver, 2013). Although this distinction has been criticized for undervaluing the meaning of impairment to people's lives and fully rejecting medical interventions, the social model of disability is lauded for shining a light onto the environmental factors that disable individuals with impairments, and it continues to be featured heavily in Disability Studies (Shakespeare, 2006).

Efforts to integrate the health and social dimensions of disability have taken many forms and create the foundation for hybrid models (Shandra, 2018). Examples of hybrid models include the disablement process model (Verbrugge & Jette, 1994) and the WHO's International Classification of Functioning, Disability, and Health (ICF) (WHO, 2001). The basis of many contemporary hybrid models can be traced to the Nagi (1964) model of disablement, which made important distinctions among pathology, impairment, functioning, and disability (Altman, 2001; Jette, 1994). The Nagi (1964) model predates the social model of disability and represents a biopsychosocial approach to acquired disability; however, the role of the environment is subsumed into the definition of disability (i.e., limitation in social roles within a specific sociocultural context) (Jette, 1994). To varying degrees, hybrid models emphasize the role of the environment for shaping disability experiences, yet each recognizes that disability is contextual and socially situated.

Also included in this body of work are the Institute of Medicine (IOM) models of disability (Pope & Brandt, 1997; Pope & Tarlov, 1991). Similar to other hybrid models, the Nagi model was the foundation of the IOM models of disability (Altman, 2001); however, the definition of disability also drew from the person-environment fit model. According to Pope and Brandt (1997), disability is defined as "the expression of a physical or mental limitation in a social context—the gap between a person's capabilities and the demands of the environment" (Pope & Brandt, 1997, p. 95). In line with the social model of disability, the person-environment fit model views most disability as preventable by removing disabling barriers and lowering environmental demands within the social and physical environment (Pope & Brandt, 1997). From this perspective, disability is the result of the interaction between the person and the environment.

The WHO's ICF (2001) has gained prominence among researchers and scholars from a variety of disciplines. The ICF has been widely adopted internationally; however, its popularity is diluted in the United States. For example, in 2009, a series of guest editorials in the *Journals of Gerontology, Series A: Medical Sciences* discussed the challenges of adopting the ICF within American gerontology (see Freedman, 2009; Guralnik & Ferrucci, 2009; Jette, 2009). Guralnik and Ferrucci (2009) and Freedman (2009) raised concerns about a lack of precision between the activities and participation domains and the loss of pathway from pathology to disability/participation restriction. During the same period, the IOM's Committee on Disability in America noted that the ICF model had important contributions such as nonstigmatizing language and the inclusion of contextual factors, yet the committee also suggested there were key limitations in the ICF model that needed to be addressed (IOM, 2007). Although enthusiasm for the ICF continues to be mixed, it is praised by many stakeholders for its clear articulation of the role of the environment on activity and participation.

Like other hybrid models, the ICF highlights the role of the environment, yet in many ways the environment is more fully centered (Badley, 2008; Schneidert et al., 2003). The ICF includes contextual factors (i.e., personal and environmental factors) as separate components of the larger model and views these factors as influencing all levels of functioning, including activity and participation (WHO, 2001). Environmental factors are further categorized into six subdomains (i.e., chapters): products and technology, natural environment and human-made changes to environment, support and relationships, attitudes, services, and systems and policies (WHO, 2001). The ICF is not without its critics, but its focus on environmental factors has led to increased attention on how to conceptualize and measure environmental barriers and facilitators.

Taken together, the social model and hybrid models of disability have informed the current body of empirical studies examining the relationship between disability and the environment. We provide an overview of the current literature highlighting advancements in measurement and offering recommendations for future research to fill critical gaps. We consider physical and social environments separately and examine how personal factors intersect with the environment to perpetuate inequalities experienced by people with disabilities. Although we examine physical and social environmental factors individually, we recognize that the social environment (e.g., trust among community members) reflects the physical environment (e.g., physical disorder) and vice versa.

We take a place-based approach to the environment and focus on communities and neighborhoods. Although the environment encompasses aspects of physical, social, policy, and attitudinal environments from the macro or societal level to the micro or individual level, we focus on the meso (mezzo) level and on where people with disabilities live, work, learn, and spend their free time. This choice reflects both practical motives (i.e., the majority of research into environmental factors focus on neighborhoods and community-level factors) and theoretical considerations. In particular, we contend that communities hold the most potential for effective interventions that address disabling barriers (Hammel et al., 2015) and, ultimately, it is within one's community that larger macro-level environmental factors such as policy or attitudinal barriers are felt by individuals (e.g., a person with disability experiencing housing or work discrimination in their city).

DEFINING AND MEASURING PHYSICAL ENVIRONMENTS IN RELATION TO DISABILITY

The social model of disability has continuously emphasized the importance of the physical environment as disabling or enabling full participation for people with disabilities

(Hammel et al., 2015). Examining the physical environment on a neighborhood level provides a unique understanding of the relationship between people and their surroundings. The physical and built environments can be defined as the material world in which individuals live, participate, and engage with others. The physical environment encompasses both natural and human-made, or built, elements. Comprehensive models of the physical environment include both natural phenomenon such as weather, light, and naturally occurring terrain (Shumway-Cook et al., 2003) as well as built elements of an area, like transportation systems, land-use patterns, and other aspects of urban design (Rosso et al., 2011). Both natural and human-made components of the environment shape how people with disabilities interact, navigate, and participate in their communities.

Many physical features of the environment can hinder or enhance participation and community engagement for an individual living with a disability. Environmental barriers act as difficulties or obstacles to community engagement that people with disabilities may experience when participating in the community, whereas environmental facilitators permit or foster activity and participation (WHO, 2001). It is often the case that one environmental factor can act as both a barrier and a facilitator, depending on the condition or accessibility of said factor. Take one example: neighborhood sidewalks. Christensen et al. (2010) found that the presence of neighborhood sidewalks was associated with meeting the recommended physical activity levels for adults with physical disabilities. Alternately, one qualitative study found that neighborhood sidewalks of poor quality—that have no or insufficient curb cuts or are in need of repair—are one of the biggest barriers for mobility and transportation within a community for individuals with spinal cord injuries (Newman, 2010). Additional environmental barriers include human-made elements, such as inaccessible buildings, traffic patterns, or insufficient outdoor lighting, or natural elements such as the weather and climate.

Researchers have used many tools to measure the relationship between the physical environment and the lived experiences of people with disabilities. With regard to disability experiences within the community, research is often separated into the two following camps, depending on which reality researchers are trying to understand: the subjective, or experienced reality, or the objective, factual reality. Objective measures aim to understand things that can be measured consistently, while subjective measures account for the perspectives and experiences of the population being studied. Oftentimes research using community-level data about individuals with disabilities aims to analyze both objective and subjective assessments for a more holistic understanding of the relationship between the physical environment and disability.

A variety of methodologies have been used to gather objective and subjective data. In-depth interviews and focus groups are the most common forms of qualitative data collected to study the environment and subjective disability experiences. However, Newman (2010) provides an example of Photovoice, a community-based participatory research approach, being used to gather information about the subjective experiences of interacting with the built environment among people with disabilities. More specifically, participants with spinal cord injuries were given digital cameras to help document their personal experiences within their neighborhoods (Newman, 2010). Disability researchers have also focused on creating objective measures—with high levels of test-retest reliability—to better understand environmental influence on disability. For example, the Craig Hospital Inventory of Environmental Factors (CHIEF) assessment was created to measure both the frequency and magnitude of experiencing environmental barriers in the areas of mobility, self-care, learning, and communication (Whiteneck et al., 2004a), and it has been used in research around the world to study environmental barriers for people with disabilities (Law et al., 2007; Zhang et al., 2015).

Other research has collected a combination of subjective and objective data. For example, Spivock et al. (2008) collected neighborhood-level data about the physical environment via neighborhood observation and completed phone surveys among adults with and without a disability. Participants were asked about their physical activity and their perceptions of their neighborhood quality. Objective, neighborhood-level measures of active living buoys (e.g., walking surface conditions, signage, and adaptations in surrounding areas) were associated with leisure physical activity, while subjective assessments were not (Spivock et al., 2008). Additionally, Shumway-Cook et al. (2003) studied objective physical performance measures, like walking speed and distance of adults with mobility disabilities, and asked participants to self-rate the impact of various environmental factors on their own experiences. The authors found that older adults with mobility disabilities were more likely to avoid environments with barriers such as busy streets, stairs, or unfamiliar places (Shumway-Cook et al., 2003).

Although more limited compared with research into the built environment, features of the natural environment, such as seasonality, weather conditions, and the presence of green space, are all environmental factors that influence physical activity and engagement within the community (Rosenberg et al., 2012; Rosso et al., 2011; Shumway-Cook et al., 2003). In general, features of the built environment were the most commonly cited barriers and facilitators to engagement within the community. Adequate curb ramps, sidewalks, and street crossings are considered facilitators to activity in the community (Rosenberg et al., 2012). Physical environments with a high number of facilitators are positively associated with meeting recommended physical activity levels (Christensen et al., 2010; Spivock et al., 2008). However, there are various problematic aspects of land development and land usage. For example, lack of accessible public transportation, lack of wheelchair ramps, and poor sidewalk quality were related to less physical and social activity within the community (Newman, 2010; Rosso et al., 2011). Access to recreational and leisure activities was positively related to leisure-time physical activity (Christensen et al., 2010; Spivock et al., 2008) as well as more positive self-rated health measures for individuals with intellectual disabilities (Emerson et al., 2014).

Other research provides information that is also tied to the physical environment such as urbanicity and rurality, as well as community deprivation. The physical environment is situated within these larger scene-setting factors. The population density that accompanies urban areas often allows for greater proximity of businesses and other landmarks as well as important facilitators such as sidewalks, street lighting, and curb cuts (Clarke et al., 2008). Botticello et al. (2012) note that life dissatisfaction was higher among urban adults with spinal cord injury, relative to their suburban and rural peers. However, suburban residents with spinal cord injuries reported better employment, compared with their urban peers (Botticello et al., 2012). Rural areas are less densely populated and often have more limited services (e.g., transportation, waste removal, health care), yet research suggests that people with disabilities have better employment opportunities and community participation in rural areas (McPhedran, 2011; Nicholson & Cooper, 2013). A study of adults with disability in South Africa observed key differences in environmental barriers by geography, where urban residents reported more environmental barriers, while rural residents more attitudinal barriers (Maart et al., 2007).

Community or neighborhood deprivation is the source of many environmental barriers. Social inequality leads to unequal environments, and people with disabilities disproportionately reside in communities without critical services and environmental facilitators (Pruchno et al., 2012). Kirby and Kaneda (2005) state that "when individuals who are disadvantaged are concentrated into specific areas, disadvantage becomes an 'emergent characteristic' of those areas" (p. 29). Specifically, Kirby and Kaneda (2005) found that neighborhood disadvantage was associated with more unmet healthcare need, even after controlling for individual factors (or compositional effects) among residents. Neighborhood disadvantage reflects historical and contemporary policies that have resulted in the disinvestment and the loss of tax revenue in certain communities—predominantly poor communities of color who have higher rates of impairment and health conditions (Molina, 2016; Williams et al., 2009).

The lack of investment by policymakers in low-income or socially disadvantaged communities is directly tied to the experiences of residents with disabilities. For example, neighborhood disadvantage is associated with less outdoor mobility (e.g., community participation) in older adults with disability (Beard et al., 2009). Furthermore, Spivock et al. (2007) document fewer active living buoys in low-income areas, which lower environmental demands and enable individuals with functional limitations to navigate their communities more effectively. Schmitz and colleagues (2009) observed a strong association between neighborhood disadvantage and disability among residents with diabetes. These studies highlight the root cause of physical environmental barriers: social inequalities. Community deprivation shapes the physical environment but also the social environment by concentrating people with limited individual resources.

In sum, the current literature underscores the importance of the physical environment for shaping the experiences of people with disabilities. The natural and built environments can be sources of disabling barriers, but environments with ample facilitators enable all residents to engage in their community. The clustering, or social patterning, of environmental barriers and facilitators demonstrates how social inequality, including class- and race-based systems of oppression, generates unequal environments, which disproportionately affect people with disabilities.

DEFINING AND MEASURING SOCIAL ENVIRONMENTS IN RELATION TO DISABILITY

Defining and measuring the social environment has unique challenges compared with the physical environment. While a clear distinction has been made between objective and subjective measures of physical environmental measures, this distinction is harder to make when assessing social environments, which are often conditional on people's perceptions about others and interactions with others. Although different definitions have been applied to the social environment, there are certain features that are regularly cited as belonging to the social environment, including social relationships and support, services, attitudes, and social policies (Whiteneck et al., 2004a; WHO, 2001). Essentially, the social environment is everything that is not the physical environment, including who interacts with one another and how.

Social Relationships and Support

At its core, the social environment is about the people within a community. There are three major approaches to measuring social relationships and support that involve subjective assessments of social cohesion (i.e., perceptions of trust, belonging, and solidarity), social and civic participation, and social networks within the community. Part of the challenge of measuring social relationships and support as a dimension of the social environment is due to the complex individual networks of community members, which transcend social and physical boundaries of neighborhoods and communities. In addition, one's social environment is inherently subjective. To illustrate, two neighbors may have strikingly different experiences in a neighborhood based on their interactions with others through informal and formal networks. This is particularly true for individuals who experience marginalization and social exclusion due to their minority status, such as people with disabilities (Barnes & Mercer, 2005; Bates & Davis, 2004; Milner & Kelly, 2009). Despite these challenges, the extant literature provides important insights into how the social environment shapes the lived experience of people with disabilities.

There is a rich and long-standing literature on the relationship between social support and health, where individuals with high levels of perceived support report better health and quality of life (Umberson & Montez, 2010). Although individual social networks are a part of one's social environment, we focus this overview on the aspects of the social environment rooted in the communities themselves such as community ties and the social integration of residents. We briefly summarize the current research into these social relationships and support, including research into social capital as a multidimensional measure of social networks, social participation, and social integration.

Research into social relationships and support among community members is overwhelmingly quantitative in nature with most data coming from community-based and national surveys. Additionally, most studies rely on self-reports about community members' experiences or perceptions about their local area, but often do not consider multiple levels or nested data (e.g., neighborhood blocks, zip codes, or census tracks). Recognizing the multiple levels at which data are collected enables researchers to consider whether individual characteristics (e.g., individual social capital) or area characteristics (e.g., area social capital) influence a particular outcome (Leyland & Groenewegen, 2020). Most research analyzing multilevel models comes from epidemiological research, and when disability is considered, it typically echoes the medical model perspective (e.g., an emphasis on the prevention of disability). However, this methodological approach allows researchers to disentangle individual (compositional) and community (contextual) effects and provides important information about community-level factors, above and beyond individual experiences (Freedman et al., 2008; Nascimento et al., 2018; Philibert et al., 2013; Pruchno et al., 2012).

Subjective assessments of social cohesion are measured based on self-reports of neighborhood trust (i.e., neighbors are trustworthy), sense of belonging, and solidarity. This area of research is particular active within gerontology, where higher levels of social cohesion are associated with more social participation, higher quality of life, and better health among older adults with disabilities (Friedman et al., 2012; Latham & Clarke, 2018; Mendes de Leon et al., 2009; Nguyen et al., 2016). However, other research examining midlife disability and specific impairments have documented similar findings. A study of British adults with intellectual disabilities documented lower rates of social and civic participation and worse ratings of neighborhood quality among adults with intellectual disabilities (Emerson et al., 2014). Furthermore, among adults with intellectual disabilities, those who had higher levels of participation and favorable perceptions of the neighborhood reported better health—which underscores the importance of the social environment for health promotion among people with disabilities. Cross-cultural research into subjective well-being has shown that the disparities in subjective well-being among people with and without disabilities is mostly due to variation in personal and social resources, including social cohesion (Van Campen & Van Santvoort, 2013).

Within this vein of research, the concept of *social capital* is often employed. The definition of social capital varies depending on tradition and discipline, which is often reflected in a researcher's choice of measures. According to Bates and Davis (2004), social capital suffers from imprecise definitions; however, six key components have been identified, including (1) community participation, (2) reciprocity, (3) feelings of trust and safety, (4) social connections within the community/bridge building, (5) citizen power and civic engagement, and (6) community perception and reputation (Bates & Davis, 2004; Fleming & Boeck, 2005). It is rare for an empirical study to measure all six components, yet more attention is paid in this research area to the multidimensional nature of the social environment and the embedded social networks within the community.

The current body of literature tends to place a greater emphasis on social connections (i.e., social networks) and community participation. Mithen and colleagues (2015) provide an example of this approach. Using data from the 2010 Australian General Social Survey (GSS), Mithen et al. (2015) found that people with disabilities had lower social capital, as measured by informal and formal networks and social support, relative to people without disabilities. Brucker (2015) used data from the 2010 Current Population Survey Civic Engagement Supplement, which emphasizes social connections and civic engagement, to assess social capital disparities among people with disabilities who were employed or unemployed. Current labor force participation was associated with higher social capital among people with disabilities (Brucker, 2015). Among adults with psychological disabilities, perceptions of social capital and neighborhood quality were positively associated with a sense of community and life satisfaction (Yanos et al., 2011).

Services, Attitudes, and Social Policies

Less attention has been paid to the dimensions of the social environment that are not directly tied to individual community members such as the service environment (e.g., transportation availability, including formal and informal options), attitudinal environment within the community, and the (local) policy environment (e.g., accessibility and accommodation by organizations within the community). Because these dimensions of the social environment reflect macro-level factors such as societal and cultural attitudes, systems and policies, and social inequality (Hammel et al., 2015), discerning the local social environment is a difficult task. However, qualitative and mixed-methods research has found these to be important barriers (or facilitators) for full participation in the community among people with disabilities. Much of this research stems from efforts to apply the ICF model and identify environmental barriers and facilitators. For example, Hammel and colleagues (2015) collected information about environmental barriers and facilitators from focus groups and differentiated examples from the micro, meso, and macro levels. Examples of community barriers included a lack of social networking and capital opportunities, a lack of voice and respect in community groups, attitudes from people in a community, and a lack of willingness of people and businesses in the community to make accommodations (Hammel et al., 2015, p. 587).

Similarly, Whiteneck et al. (2004b) examined the separate subdomains of the ICF environmental factors using an inventory checklist approach (i.e., Craig Hospital Inventory of Environmental Factors [CHIEF]). Based on the responses from adults with disabilities and other key informants such as healthcare professionals, five factors and subscales were identified: (1) attitudes and support, (2) services and assistance, (3) physical and structural, (4) policies, and (5) work/school. Within each subscale, items corresponded to community and at-home barriers; results demonstrated that respondents with disabilities experienced more barriers across all subscales, relative to respondents without disabilities (Whiteneck et al., 2004b). Gray et al. (2008) combined elements of the Measure of the Quality of the Environment (MQE), which assesses subjective quality, and the CHIEF to develop the Facilitators and Barriers Survey for people with mobility impairment (FABS/M). Garcia et al. (2015) focused specifically on attitudinal facilitators and barriers and developed an item bank based on focus group interviews. Without the adoption of the ICF model, it seems unlikely that the same types of advancements in measurements of the social environment would be as plentiful. Although more work is needed to operationalize features of the social environment, the increased recognition of the role of services, attitudes, and social policies *within the community* is an important step.

Understanding Intersectionality, Disability, and the Environment

The relationship between the environment and disability is complicated by the intersection of other social identities like age, race, gender, and socioeconomic status. Intersectional approaches to understanding disability emphasize the importance of considering how social identities and structural inequalities act as compounding factors for exposure to health risks or access to health-promoting resources (Warner & Brown, 2011). Environment-based, intersectional disability research often focuses on accessibility to the built environment and how this affects opportunities for work, leisure, socialization, and wellness (Sarma, 2016). Currently, intersectional research on the relationship between disability and the environment focuses on socioeconomic status, race, gender, and age, with less emphasis on other social identities like sexual orientation or immigrant status. Disability represents diversity in the human experience; however, disability experiences are often dependent on an individual's other social identities and social locations (Sarma, 2016), which poses unique conceptual and methodological challenges to researchers. Despite these challenges, disability research using an intersectional approach is a growing field and contributes to our understanding of the human experience.

Race and socioeconomic status are inextricably linked in disability research, particularly when considering the social and physical environments in which people live. In their study of young adults with chronic pain, Green and Hart-Johnson (2012) found an interactional relationship between race and neighborhood socioeconomic status, in which Black residents with lower neighborhood socioeconomic status had worse pain outcomes. Green and Hart-Johnson (2012) also found that living in a neighborhood with lower socioeconomic status is related to increased pain, pain-related disability, and mood disorders. However, neighborhood socioeconomic status was a protective factor for White residents (Green & Hart-Johnson, 2012). Botticello et al. (2016) found that White adults with spinal cord injuries (SCIs) are more likely to report full participation within their communities when compared to Black or Hispanic adults with SCIs. This same study found that racial minorities with SCIs are more likely to live in neighborhoods with lower socioeconomic status, less vehicle access, and less green space (Botticello et al., 2016), factors which we already know lead to decreased social and physical participation within the community.

Age is another key factor in much of the research that examines the relationship between disability and the environment. Neighborhoods can play a unique part in the lived experience of disability as well as the disablement process, particularly for older adults. Older adults with physical disabilities are more likely to avoid more challenging aspects of their immediate environment, such as going out in inclement weather (snow or ice) or the dark when compared to older adults without mobility difficulties (Shumway-Cook et al., 2003). Higher traffic volume was also associated with walking difficulty and avoidance, while housing density was associated with greater levels of walking (Rosso et al., 2011). These physical elements of neighborhoods affect the independence and ability of older adults to manage and maintain their home and health routines as well as engagement in the community (Clarke & George, 2005).

The association between the neighborhood and disability experiences is present for children, too. One American study of Rhode Island children found that one in seven children lived in a distressed neighborhood (defined by higher rates of children living in poverty, high school dropouts, male unemployment, and number of single-mother households), but one in four children with a motor disability and two of seven children with a self-care disability lived in distressed neighborhoods (Msall et al., 2007). Physical and social factors influence recreational, community, and school participation for children and adolescents with physical disabilities (Verschuren et al., 2012). In fact, the same study found that children's and adolescents' perceptions of barriers increase with age, particularly as they start to expand their recreational activities beyond the home and school (Verschuren et al., 2012).

Gender also provides an important context for how environmental factors influence participation within the community among people with disabilities. Disability tends to uniquely disadvantage women, and the environment can act as both a barrier and facilitator. Studies have found that women are more likely to experience disability in voluntary activities (Green & Hart-Johnson, 2012), and older women are more likely to have trouble performing self-care tasks and tasks within the community, like shopping, when compared to their male counterparts (Zeki Al Hazzouri et al., 2011). At the age of 53, women (especially women of color) are more likely to experience functional limitations compared to men of the same age (Warner & Brown, 2011). One New Jersey study of disabled adults found that despite living in similar neighborhoods, men in the sample were more likely to be younger with more education and higher household incomes, while women were more likely to be older and have functional limitations (Wilson-Genderson & Pruchno, 2015).

Different components of the social and physical neighborhood also influence how disabled men and women interact with their environment. One study found that "perceived proximity to neighborhood resources moderates the association between disability and social participation in older men, but not women" (Levasseur et al., 2011). Closer proximity to neighborhood amenities fosters social participation among men with a disability, but the same was not true for women (Levasseur et al., 2011). In terms of the built environment, among women, walking was associated with the presence of local destinations (shops, neighbors, parks, etc.), whereas neighborhood density and design characteristics were significantly associated with walking for men (Gallagher et al., 2014). Although research into intersectionality, disability, and the environment is still emerging, researchers have already documented how the intersection of marginalized social identities intensifies the consequences of disabling environmental barriers and influences opportunities for full participation within the community.

DISCUSSION

This chapter examined the role of the environment in shaping the lives of people with disabilities. We took a place-based approach and focused on the communities where people with disabilities live. We considered the physical and social environment separately; however, this division, in many ways, is artificial. The physical environment and social environments are mirrors of each other—inaccessible physical environments are a choice that reflects societal attitudes and resource allocation based on political influence.

Empirical research into the environmental barriers and facilitators within communities offers important information into how the environment shapes the lives of people with disabilities and what communities can do to foster greater social inclusion. To illustrate, physical environmental barriers and a lack of services in the community are often listed as the most important barriers to participation by people with disabilities (Bodde & Seo, 2009; Centers for Disease Control and Prevention, 2006; Gallagher et al., 2011; Kirchner et al., 2008; Mojtahedi et al., 2008; Newman, 2010; Rimmer et al., 2004; Schopp et al., 2002; Whiteneck et al., 2004b). However, social relationships and support from community members typically serve as facilitators (Hammel et al., 2015). Involvement in community groups and tailored services were frequently listed as facilitators (Henry & Lucca, 2004; Jaarsma et al., 2014). Although certain types of environmental barriers were cited frequently, the effect of environmental barriers and facilitators on people's lives varied by impairment. For people with physical disabilities and/or used mobility devices, physical barriers were the most pressing (Gallagher et al., 2011; Kirchner et al., 2008), whereas people with intellectual and mental disabilities commonly reported a lack of opportunities and attitudinal barriers as most critical (Bodde & Seo, 2009; Emerson et al., 2014; Lippold & Burns, 2009; Yanos et al., 2011).

We also apply an intersectional approach and observe important inequalities across key social statuses related to disability experiences. Disability as an axis of inequality intersects with other axes (Shandra, 2018). Systems of oppression take root in our communities—leading to unequal opportunities for education, work, leisure, and health. We were unable to consider all environments within the scope of this chapter; however, noteworthy work has been done to uncover environmental barriers within people's homes (see Stark, 2001), workplaces (see Martins, 2015), and schools (see Pivik et al., 2002). We also did not fully consider how life course stage changes the relationship between the environment and disability. We focused our review on adults, including older adult experiences, but children with disabilities also experience environmental barriers and facilitators to full participation in their communities. Finally, although we included research from multiple countries and regions, we were unable to discuss in depth how environmental factors vary across sociocultural contexts.

Although it is encouraging to observe the current body of empirical work investigating how the environment shapes disabilities experiences and perpetuates inequalities, there are still critical gaps in the literature and an urgent need for more research. First, we encourage more research into environments across multiple geographic and sociocultural contexts. Broad typologies provide insight into common environmental barriers and facilitators; however, each community is unique, and the specific barriers/facilitators will vary across contexts. Second, we believe there is a need for further refining definitions and measures of the social environment. Imprecise definitions lead to a lack of clarity with regard to findings and measurement. Social capital may be a useful way to think about the social environment, but without consensus on a definition and measurement, we can only learn so much. We would also urge researchers to think about ways to measure aspects of the social environment that transcend social and physical boundaries. Finally, we would like to encourage researchers to foster more interdisciplinary collaborations. So much of the current research reflects disciplinary boundaries with specific theoretical and methodological approaches with little cross-fertilization. By reaching across disciplines and adopting different perspectives, models, and methodological techniques, we believe that many of the current gaps in the literature would be filled.

REFERENCES

Altman, B. M. (2001). Disability definitions, models, classification schemes, and applications. In G. Albrecht, K. D. Seelman, & M. Bury (Eds.), *Handbook of disability studies* (pp. 97–122). SAGE Publications. https://doi.org/10.4135/9781412976251.n4

Altman, B. M. (2014). Definitions, concepts, and measures of disability. *Annals of Epidemiology*, 24(1), 2–7. https://doi.org/10.1016/j.annepidem.2013.05.018

Badley, E. M. (2008). Enhancing the conceptual clarity of the activity and participation components of the International Classification of Functioning, Disability, and Health. *Social Science & Medicine*, 66(11), 2335–2345. https://doi.org/10.1016/j.socscimed.2008.01.026

Barnes, C., & Mercer, G. (2005). Disability, work, and welfare: Challenging the social exclusion of disabled people. *Work, Employment and Society*, 19(3), 527–545. https://doi.org/10.1177/0950017005055669

Bates, P., & Davis, F. A. (2004). Social capital, social inclusion and services for people with learning disabilities. *Disability & Society*, 19(3), 195–207. https://doi.org/10.1080/0968759042000204202

Beard, J. R., Blaney, S., Cerda, M., Frye, V., Lovasi, G. S., Ompad, D., Rundle, A., & Vlahov, D. (2009). Neighborhood characteristics and disability in older adults. *Journals of Gerontology: Series B, 64*(2), 252–257. https://doi.org/10.1093/geronb/gbn018

Bodde, A. E., & Seo, D. C. (2009). A review of social and environmental barriers to physical activity for adults with intellectual disabilities. *Disability and Health Journal, 2*(2), 57–66. https://doi.org/10.1016/j.dhjo.2008.11.004

Botticello, A. L., Boninger, M., Charlifue, S., Chen, Y., Fyffe, D., Heinemann, A., Hoffman, J., Jette, A., Kalpakjian, C., & Rohrbach, T. (2016). To what extent do neighborhood differences mediate racial disparities in participation after spinal cord injury?. *Archives of Physical Medicine and Rehabilitation, 97*(10), 1735–1744. https://doi.org/10.1016/j.apmr.2016.04.007

Botticello, A. L., Chen, Y., & Tulsky, D. S. (2012). Geographic variation in participation for physically disabled adults: The contribution of area economic factors to employment after spinal cord injury. *Social Science & Medicine, 75*(8), 1505–1513. https://doi.org/10.1016/j.socscimed.2012.06.010

Brucker, D. L. (2015). Social capital, employment and labor force participation among persons with disabilities. *Journal of Vocational Rehabilitation, 43*(1), 17–31. https://doi.org/10.3233/JVR-150751

Centers for Disease Control and Prevention (CDC). (2006). Environmental barriers to health care among persons with disabilities—Los Angeles County, California, 2002–2003. *Morbidity and Mortality Weekly Report, 55*(48), 1300.

Christensen, K., Holt, J. M., & Wilson, J. F. (2010). Effects of perceived neighborhood characteristics and use of community facilities on physical activity of adults with and without disabilities. *Preventive Chronic Disease, 7*(5), 1–13.

Clarke, P., Ailshire, J. A., Bader, M., Morenoff, J. D., & House, J. S. (2008). Mobility disability and the urban built environment. *American Journal of Epidemiology, 168*(5), 506–513. https://doi.org/10.1093/aje/kwn185

Clarke, P., & George, L. K. (2005). The role of the built environment in the disablement process. *American Journal of Public Health, 95*(11), 1933–1939. https://doi.org/10.2105/AJPH.2004.054494

Emerson, E., Hatton, C., Robertson, J., & Baines, S. (2014). Perceptions of neighbourhood quality, social and civic participation and the self-rated health of British adults with intellectual disability: Cross sectional study. *BMC Public Health, 14*(1), 1252. https://doi.org/10.1186/1471-2458-14-1252

Fleming, J., & Boeck, T. (2005). Can social capital be a framework for participative evaluation of community health work. In D. Taylor & S. Balloch (Eds.). The politics of evaluation: Participation and policy implementation (pp. 223–237). Bristol: Polity Press.

Freedman, V. A. (2009). Adopting the ICF language for studying late-life disability: A field of dreams? *The Journals of Gerontology Series A: Medical Sciences, 64A*(11), 1172–1174. https://doi.org/10.1093/gerona/glp095

Freedman, V. A., Grafova, I. B., Schoeni, R. F., & Rogowski, J. (2008). Neighborhoods and disability in later life. *Social Science & Medicine, 66*(11), 2253–2267. https://doi.org/10.1016/j.socscimed.2008.01.013

Friedman, D., Parikh, N. S., Giunta, N., Fahs, M. C., & Gallo, W. T. (2012). The influence of neighborhood factors on the quality of life of older adults attending New York City senior centers: Results from the Health Indicators Project. *Quality of Life Research, 21*(1), 123–131. https://doi.org/10.1007/s11136-011-9923-6

Gallagher, N. A., Clarke, P. J., & Gretebeck, K. A. (2014). Gender differences in neighborhood walking in older adults. *Journal of Aging and Health, 26*(8), 1280–1300. https://doi.org/10.1177/0898264314532686

Gallagher, P., O'Donovan, M. A., Doyle, A., & Desmond, D. (2011). Environmental barriers, activity limitations and participation restrictions experienced by people with major limb amputation. *Prosthetics and Orthotics International, 35*(3), 278–284. https://doi.org/10.1177/0309364611407108

Garcia, S. F., Hahn, E. A., Magasi, S., Lai, J. S., Semik, P., Hammel, J., & Heinemann, A. W. (2015). Development of self-report measures of social attitudes that act as environmental barriers and facilitators for people with disabilities. *Archives of Physical Medicine and Rehabilitation, 96*(4), 596–603. https://doi.org/10.1016/j.apmr.2014.06.019

Gray, D. B., Hollingsworth, H. H., Stark, S., & Morgan, K. A. (2008). A subjective measure of environmental facilitators and barriers to participation for people with mobility limitations. *Disability and Rehabilitation, 30*(6), 434–457. https://doi.org/10.1080/09638280701625377

Green, C. R., & Hart-Johnson, T. (2012). The association between race and neighborhood socioeconomic status in younger Black and White adults with chronic pain. *The Journal of Pain, 13*(2), 176–186. https://doi.org/10.1016/j.jpain.2011.10.008

Guralnik, J. M., & Ferrucci, L. (2009). The challenge of understanding the disablement process in older persons: Commentary responding to Jette AM. Toward a common language of disablement. *Journals of Gerontology Series A: Medical Sciences, 64*(11), 1169–1171. https://doi.org/10.1093/gerona/glp094

Hammel, J., Magasi, S., Heinemann, A., Gray, D. B., Stark, S., Kisala, P., . . . Hahn, E. A. (2015). Environmental barriers and supports to everyday participation: A qualitative insider perspective from people with disabilities. *Archives of Physical Medicine and Rehabilitation, 96*(4), 578–588. https://doi.org/10.1016/j.apmr.2014.12.008

Henry, A. D., & Lucca, A. M. (2004). Facilitators and barriers to employment: The perspectives of people with psychiatric disabilities and employment service providers. *Work, 22*(3), 169–182.

Institute of Medicine. (IOM) 2007. *The future of disability in America.* The National Academy Press.

Jaarsma, E. A., Dijkstra, P. U., Geertzen, J. H. B., & Dekker, R. (2014). Barriers to and facilitators of sports participation for people with physical disabilities: A systematic review. *Scandinavian Journal of Medicine & Science in Sports, 24*(6), 871–881. https://doi.org/10.1111/sms.12218

Jette, A. M. (1994). Physical disablement concepts for physical therapy research and practice. *Physical therapy, 74*(5), 380–386. https://doi.org/10.1093/ptj/74.5.380

Jette, A. M. (2009). Toward a common language of disablement. *Journals of Gerontology Series A: Biomedical Sciences and Medical Sciences, 64*(11), 1165-1168. https://doi.org/10.1093/gerona/glp093

Kirby, J. B., & Kaneda, T. (2005). Neighborhood socioeconomic disadvantage and access to health care. *Journal of Health and Social Behavior, 46*(1), 15–31. https://doi.org/10.1177/002214650504600103

Kirchner, C. E., Gerber, E. G., & Smith, B. C. (2008). Designed to deter: Community barriers to physical activity for people with visual or motor impairments. *American Journal of Preventive Medicine, 34*(4), 349–352. https://doi.org/10.1016/j.amepre.2008.01.005

Latham, K., & Clarke, P. J. (2018). Neighborhood disorder, perceived social cohesion, and social participation among older Americans: Findings from the National Health & Aging Trends Study. *Journal of Aging and Health, 30*(1), 3–26. https://doi.org/10.1177/0898264316665933

Law, M., Petrenchik, T., King, G., & Hurley, P. (2007). Perceived environmental barriers to recreational, community, and school participation for children and youth with physical disabilities. *Archive of Physical Medicine and Rehabilitation, 88*, 1636–1642. https://doi.org/10.1016/j.apmr.2007.07.035

Levasseur, M., Gauvin, L., Richard, L., Kestens, Y., Daniel, M., Payette, H., & NuAge Study Group. (2011). Associations between perceived proximity to neighborhood resources, disability, and social participation among community-dwelling older adults: Results from the VoisiNuAge study. *Archives of Physical Medicine and Rehabilitation, 92*(12), 1979–1986. https://doi.org/10.1016/j.apmr.2011.06.035

Leyland, A. H., & Groenewegen, P. P. (2020). Context, composition and how their influences vary. In A. Leyland & P. P. Groenewegen (Eds.). *Multilevel modelling for public health and health services research* (pp. 107–122). Springer. https://doi.org/10.1007/978-3-030-34801-4_7

Lippold, T., & Burns, J. (2009). Social support and intellectual disabilities: A comparison between social networks of adults with intellectual disability and those with physical disability. *Journal of Intellectual Disability Research, 53*(5), 463–473. https://doi.org/10.1111/j.1365-2788.2009.01170.x

Maart, S., Eide, A. H., Jelsma, J., Loeb, M. E., & Ka Toni, M. (2007). Environmental barriers experienced by urban and rural disabled people in South Africa. *Disability & Society, 22*(4), 357–369. https://doi.org/10.1080/09687590701337678

Martins, A. C. (2015). Using the International Classification of Functioning, Disability and Health (ICF) to address facilitators and barriers to participation at work. *Work, 50*(4), 585–593. https://doi.org/10.3233/WOR-141965

McPhedran, S. (2011). Disability and community life: Does regional living enhance social participation? *Journal of Disability Policy Studies, 22*(1), 40–54. https://doi.org/10.1177/1044207310394448

Mendes de Leon, C. F., Cagney, K. A., Bienias, J. L., Barnes, L. L., Skarupski, K. A., Scherr, P. A., & Evans, D. A. (2009). Neighborhood social cohesion and disorder in relation to walking in community-dwelling older adults: A multilevel analysis. *Journal of Aging and Health, 21*(1), 155–171. https://doi.org/10.1177/0898264308328650

Milner, P., & Kelly, B. (2009). Community participation and inclusion: People with disabilities defining their place. *Disability & Society, 24*(1), 47–62. https://doi.org/10.1080/09687590802535410

Mithen, J., Aitken, Z., Ziersch, A., & Kavanagh, A. M. (2015). Inequalities in social capital and health between people with and without disabilities. *Social Science & Medicine, 126*, 26–35. https://doi.org/10.1016/j.socscimed.2014.12.009

Mojtahedi, M. C., Boblick, P., Rimmer, J. H., Rowland, J. L., Jones, R. A., & Braunschweig, C. L. (2008). Environmental barriers to and availability of healthy foods for people with mobility disabilities living in urban and suburban neighborhoods. *Archives of Physical Medicine and Rehabilitation, 89*(11), 2174–2179. https://doi.org/10.1016/j.apmr.2008.05.011

Molina, E. T. (2016). Neighborhood inequalities and the long-term impact of foreclosures: Evidence from the Los Angeles-Inland Empire region. *City & Community, 15*(3), 315–337. https://doi.org/10.1111/cico.12192

Msall, M. E., Msall, E. R., & Hogan, D. P. (2007). Distressed neighborhoods and child disability rates: Analyses of 157,000 school-age children. *Developmental Medicine & Child Neurology*, *49*, 814–817. https://doi.org/10.1111/j.1469-8749.2007.00814.x

Nagi, S. Z. (1964). A study in the evaluation of disability and rehabilitation potential: Concepts, methods, and procedures. *American Journal of Public Health and the Nation's Health*, *54*(9), 1568–1579. https://doi.org/10.2105/AJPH.54.9.1568

Nascimento, C. F. D., Duarte, Y. A. O., Lebrao, M. L., & Chiavegatto Filho, A. D. P. (2018). Individual and neighborhood factors associated with functional mobility and falls in elderly residents of São Paulo, Brazil: A multilevel analysis. *Journal of Aging and Health*, *30*(1), 118–139. https://doi.org/10.1177/0898264316669229

Newman, S. D. (2010). Evidence-based advocacy: Using photovoice to identify barriers and facilitators to community participation after spinal cord injury. *Rehabilitation Nursing*, *35*(2), 47–59. https://doi.org/10.1002/j.2048-7940.2010.tb00031.x

Nicholson, L., & Cooper, S. A. (2013). Social exclusion and people with intellectual disabilities: A rural-urban comparison. *Journal of Intellectual Disability Research*, *57*(4), 333–346. https://doi.org/10.1111/j.1365-2788.2012.01540.x

Nguyen, T. T., Rist, P. M., & Glymour, M. M. (2016). Are self-reported neighbourhood characteristics associated with onset of functional limitations in older adults with or without memory impairment? *Journal of Epidemiology and Community Health*, *70*(10), 1017–1023. https://doi.org/10.1136/jech-2016-207241

Oliver, M. (2013). The social model of disability: Thirty years on. *Disability & Society*, *28*(7), 1024–1026. https://doi.org/10.1080/09687599.2013.818773

Philibert, M. D., Pampalon, R., Hamel, D., & Daniel, M. (2013). Interactions between neighborhood characteristics and individual functional status in relation to disability among Québec urbanites. *Disability and Health Journal*, *6*(4), 361–368. https://doi.org/10.1016/j.dhjo.2013.02.004

Pivik, J., McComas, J., & Laflamme, M. (2002). Barriers and facilitators to inclusive education. *Exceptional Children*, *69*(1), 97–107. https://doi.org/10.1177/001440290206900107

Pope, A. M., & Brandt Jr, E. N. (Eds.). (1997). *Enabling America: Assessing the role of rehabilitation science and engineering*. National Academies Press.

Pope, A. M., & Tarlov, A. R. (1991). *Disability in America: Toward a national agenda for prevention*. National Academy Press.

Pruchno, R. A., Wilson-Genderson, M., & Cartwright, F. P. (2012). The texture of neighborhoods and disability among older adults. *Journals of Gerontology Series B: Psychological Sciences and Social Sciences*, *67*(1), 89–98. https://doi.org/10.1093/geronb/gbr131

Rimmer, J. H., Riley, B., Wang, E., Rauworth, A., & Jurkowski, J. (2004). Physical activity participation among persons with disabilities: Barriers and facilitators. *American Journal of Preventive Medicine*, *26*(5), 419–425. https://doi.org/10.1016/j.amepre.2004.02.002

Rosenberg, D. E., Huang, D. L., Simonovich, S. D., & Belza, B. (2012). Outdoor built environment barriers and facilitators to activity among midlife and older adults with mobility disabilities. *The Gerontologist*, *53*(2), 268–279. https://doi.org/10.1093/geront/gns119

Rosso, A. L., Auchincloss, A. H., & Michael, Y. L. (2011). The urban built environment and mobility in older adults: A comprehensive review. *Journal of Aging Research*. https://doi.org/10.4061/2011/816106

Sarma, J. (2016). Accessibility to the built environment in Delhi, India: Understanding the experience of disablement through the intersectionality paradigm. *Knowledge Management for Development Journal*, *12*(2), 104–121.

Schmitz, N., Nitka, D., Gariepy, G., Malla, A., Wang, J., Boyer, R., Messier, L., Strychar, I., & Lesage, A. (2009). Association between neighborhood-level deprivation and disability in a community sample of people with diabetes. *Diabetes Care, 32*(11), 1998–2004. https://doi .org/10.2337/dc09-0838

Schneidert, M., Hurst, R., Miller, J., & Üstün, B. (2003). The role of environment in the International Classification of Functioning, Disability and Health (ICF). *Disability and Rehabilitation, 25*(11–12), 588–595. https://doi.org/10.1080/0963828031000137090

Schopp, L. H., Sanford, T. C., Hagglund, K. J., Gay, J. W., & Coatney, M. A. (2002). Removing service barriers for women with physical disabilities: Promoting accessibility in the gynecologic care setting. *The Journal of Midwifery & Women's Health, 47*(2), 74–79. https://doi.org/ 10.1016/S1526-9523(02)00216-7

Shakespeare, T. (2006). The social model of disability. *The Disability Studies Reader, 2*, 197–204.

Shandra, C. L. (2018). Disability as inequality: Social disparities, health disparities, and participation in daily activities. *Social Forces, 97*(1), 157–192. https://doi.org/10.1093/sf/soy031

Shumway-Cook, A., Paula, A., Stewart, A., Ferrucci, L., Ciol, M. A., & Guralnik, J. M. (2003). Environmental components of mobility disability in community-living older persons. *Journal of American Geriatric Society, 51*(3), 393–398. https://doi.org/10.1046/ j.1532-5415.2003.51114.x

Spivock, M., Gauvin, L., & Brodeur, J. M. (2007). Neighborhood-level active living buoys for individuals with physical disabilities. *American Journal of Preventive Medicine, 32*(3), 224–230. https://doi.org/10.1016/j.amepre.2006.11.006

Spivock, M., Gauvin, L., Riva, M., & Brodeur, J. M. (2008). Promoting active living among people with physical disabilities: Evidence for neighborhood-level buoys. *American Journal of Preventive Medicine, 34*(4), 291–298. https://doi.org/10.1016/j.amepre.2008.01.012

Stark, S. (2001). Creating disability in the home: The role of environmental barriers in the United States. *Disability & Society, 16*(1), 37–49. https://doi.org/10.1080/713662037

Umberson, D., & Montez, J. K. (2010). Social relationships and health: A flashpoint for health policy. *Journal of Health and Social Behavior, 51*(Suppl. 1), S54–S66. https://doi.org/10.1177/ 0022146510383501

Van Campen, C., & Van Santvoort, M. (2013). Explaining low subjective well-being of persons with disabilities in Europe: The impact of disability, personal resources, participation and socio-economic status. *Social Indicators Research, 111*(3), 839–854. https://doi.org/10.1007/ s11205-012-0036-6

Verbrugge, L. M., & Jette, A. M. (1994). The disablement process. *Social Science & Medicine, 38*(1), 1–14. https://doi.org/10.1016/0277-9536(94)90294-1

Verschuren, O., Wiart, L., Hermans, D., & Ketelaar, M. (2012). Identification of facilitators and barriers to physical activity in children and adolescents with cerebral palsy. *The Journal of Pediatrics, 161*(3), 488–494. https://doi.org/10.1016/j.jpeds.2012.02.042

Warner, D. F., & Brown, T. H. (2011). Understanding how race/ethnicity and gender define age-trajectories of disability: An intersectional approach. *Social Science and Medicine, 72*(8), 1236–1248. https://doi.org/10.1016/j.socscimed.2011.02.034

Whiteneck, G. G., Harrison-Felix, C. L., Mellick, D. C., Brooks, C. A., Charlifue, S. B., & Gerhart, K. A. (2004a). Quantifying environmental factors: A measure of physical, attitudinal, service, productivity, and policy barriers. *Archives of Physical Medicine and Rehabilitation, 85*(8), 1324–1335. https://doi.org/10.1016/j.apmr.2003.09.027

Whiteneck, G., Meade, M. A., Dijkers, M., Tate, D. G., Bushnik, T., & Forchheimer, M. B. (2004b). Environmental factors and their role in participation and life satisfaction after spinal cord injury. *Archives of Physical Medicine and Rehabilitation, 85*(11), 1793–1803. https://doi.org/10.1016/j.apmr.2004.04.024

Williams, D. R., Sternthal, M., & Wright, R. J. (2009). Social determinants: Taking the social context of asthma seriously. *Pediatrics, 123*(Suppl. 3), S174–S184. https://doi.org/10.1542/peds.2008-2233H

Wilson-Genderson, M., & Pruncho, R. (2015). Functional limitations and gender differences: Neighborhood effects. *The International Journal of Aging and Human Development, 81*(1–2), 83–100. https://doi.org/10.1177/0091415015614843

World Health Organization (WHO). 2001. *International classification of functioning, disability, and health*. WHO.

Yanos, P. T., Stefanic, A., & Tsemberis, S. (2011). Psychological community integration among people with psychiatric disabilities and nondisabled community members. *Journal of Community Psychology, 39*(4), 390–401. https://doi.org/10.1002/jcop.20441

Zeki Al Hazzouri, A., Mehio Sibai, A., Chaaya, M., Mahfoud, Z., & Yount, K.M. (2011). Gender differences in physical disability among older adults in underprivileged communities in Lebanon. *Journal of Aging and Health, 23*(2), 367–382. https://doi.org/10.1177/0898264310385454

Zhang, L., Yan, T., You, L., & Li, K. (2015). Barriers to activity and participation for stroke survivors in rural China. *Archives of Physical Medicine and Rehabilitation, 96*, 1222–1228. https://doi.org/10.1016/j.apmr.2015.01.024

CHAPTER 7

HOW TO GET WHAT YOU WANT TO KNOW AND KNOW WHAT YOU'VE GOTTEN IN RESEARCH

Measuring Disability Past, Present, and Future

SHARON N. BARNARTT AND BARBARA M. ALTMAN

RESEARCH methodology needs to accord with the principles of science, which include being based upon observations or data and using methods of investigation that are logical, documented, systematic, replicable, and verifiable (Babbie, 2010). A major component of these principles is that research is based upon variables, so how variables are conceptualized and measured forms a large (although not the only) part of evaluating whether research is scientific.

Measurement is problematic for research in most topic areas, and it can be problematic when focusing on disability-related research because it so often has real world consequences. How disability is defined and measured, especially in surveys that are the basis of "official statistics," has a lasting effect on policies that affect people's lives. What questions are asked (or not asked) or what answer categories are provided influence perceptions about the population, decisions about policy/legislation, and estimates of program costs.

The multiplicity and ambiguity of definitions of disability exacerbate the measurement problem. Altman (2001, pp. 85–88) highlighted this problem when she showed that there are large differences in population estimates (i.e., numbers of people who are categorized as "having a disability") depending upon which measurement is used. Altman (2001) showed that one quarter of respondents said they had role limitations caused by an impairment, while 30% said they had chronic impairments, 4% said they received disability related benefits, but about 2% fit a definition of disability based upon "bed days." Only about 1% of people who were identified as having a disability were so identified on all of these measurements (Altman, 2001).

There have been many articles about issues related to measures of disability as well as critiques of their results. These include Altman et al. (2003), Altman and Barnartt (2006), and, more recently, a special issue of the *Journal of Survey Statistics and Methodology* (2021). Examinations of international measurements of disability have focused on the ICIDH (World Health Organization, 2001) and the Washington Group on Disability Statistics (2020).

This article begins by reviewing principles of measurement as they apply primarily to quantitative[1] studies of disability, especially those conducted through surveys. It asks how measurement must occur, examines historical examples of disability measurement in censuses in the United States conducted in the 19th century and assesses difficulties that may emerge in attempts to measure current concepts of disability.

THE PROCESS OF MEASUREMENT

Measurement is a process of decision-making that permits us to collect data for a specific purpose. Babbie (2010) suggests that the purposes of research in the social sciences are exploration, description, and explanation. We add intervention as a fourth goal and prediction as a fifth. More specifically, measurement is the process by which we become able to categorize people or cases according to our variables of interest. Correct categorization means that we have put our people or cases into the most appropriate categories of our variable, and that different researchers or the same researcher at different times will get the same results. Correct categorization means that a statement, such as "One quarter of all Americans have disabilities," can be dissected so that one knows who has been included in that number, who has not been included, and that both of these designations are correct.

In the measurement of disability, we are asking how many people "have a disability" or "are disabled." In order to produce correct categorizations, we have to know what it is we are trying to measure, and that is where definitions of what we think we are measuring become important. In the case of disability, many meta-models, models, and concepts of disability exist; they include characterizations of disability "as pathology," "as difference," or "as a source of pride" (Barnartt, 2012). Even with the most widely discussed models (the social model and the medical model), we are faced with the question of whether we need to be measuring characteristics of people or of environments. Other types of measurements are used in policy discussions, such as whether people receive Social Security benefits. In order to use any of these as the basis for our research, we need to have clear conceptualizations and operational definitions.

Creating Conceptual and Operational Definitions

Our goal as researchers is to produce correct measurements. This means that researchers must decide what is to be measured and how it is to be measured. Deciding exactly what is to be measured involves choosing definitions that are attached to a theory, or developing our own: the process of conceptualization. Part of that processes involves finding or developing indicators that fit the concept: the processes called "operationalization" or "developing an operational definition."

The process has to start with definitions of what we are measuring. If we want to measure disability, we have to specify what we mean by that word. Do we mean a person or a condition? Is it an attitude, an action, or a characteristic? If we mean a person, what type of person? What characterizes that person? Is it related to the person's perception of themselves or to other people's perceptions? If, as the social model suggests, it is a characteristic of an environment, what is it about the environment which makes it disabling?

Consider a few possibilities. Suppose we were basing our definition on Scotch's (1984) book *From Good Will to Civil Rights*. If we take the title literally, it suggests that a person with a disability is a person worthy either of goodwill or civil rights. If that is our core definition, we need to measure it in a way that addresses a person's acceptability as a recipient of charity. Nothing more, and nothing less. On the other hand, if we equate disability with a specific type of condition, regardless of how a person functions, we need to measure a diagnosis, not a person. If we equate disability with an attribution by other people, we have to measure what it is that other people say, not what a specific person has or does.

According to the deductive method of science, theory must guide the process of deciding on a definition, and it provides us with clues about what to look for. It defines the scope of our phenomenon and provides some characteristics to help us to decide how to define it. A theory is based upon variables and makes predictions about relationships among variables. Variables found in theories are often implicit and have very general definitions, so sometimes they are too abstract to be used easily or directly. In order to define a concept or variable based upon a theory, we have to tease out the characteristics the theory is discussing.

It is possible to measure a concept that is not attached to a theory, although if we are beginning without a theory, we are lacking the help which is provided by the theory. Researchable definitions can begin with an explicit definition of any type, but, if they are not shared among researchers in that field, they may be criticized for lacking credibility, even if the subsequent measurement process is perfect. A conceptualization needs to specify a real definition, a nominal definition, and an operational definition, which also includes categories. Babbie (2010) suggests that the **real** definition picks up the "essential nature" of the phenomenon. However, especially in theories, that essence can be vague, complicated, excessively abstract, or not easily amenable to being used empirically. Additionally, if the phenomenon has received extensive theoretical attention, there may be competing real definitions. These definitions provide a place to start but not a place to end, so the researcher must sort through the competing definitions, choose one, or create an amalgam.

In order to make the real definition more useful, we also need a **nominal** definition. This must specify the one meaning (perhaps out of many) that will be used for the purpose of this specific research. In the same way as there may be more than one real definition, there may be many possible nominal definitions which would fit any one real definition. For example, consider the concept "deafness." We could begin by saying that the real definition is "the inability to hear." But that is extremely broad: Hear what? When? Under what circumstances? We need a more specific definition, so suppose we propose the nominal definition to be "a person's inability to hear what other people are saying in a group when there is noise in the background." This is quite a different nominal definition than one which referred to a person's hearing level as measured by an audiogram and which sets a dB (decibel) loss level above which a person is defined as being deaf.

We have to justify our choice of nominal definition. The key here is that the nominal definition must fit the real definition but must also specify exactly what we are trying to measure. The above example suggests a nominal definition which does not refer to the inability to hear <u>all</u> types of sounds, just spoken words. Is that what we want our definition to be? Perhaps yes. But do we want it also include the inability to hear parts of words as well as full words? Also, what type of noise are we talking about as being "in the background"? If the research is to be conducted within a noisy situation, the nominal definition must indicate that in some way. If, alternatively, the real definition was "an inability to hear a voice in any situation," we would have to make sure that the nominal definition would cover all situations. Thus, the nominal definition clarifies what it is that we want to measure, based upon the real definition with which we started.

Measurement also requires a specific **operational definition** or **operationalization**, which indicates exactly how the concept will be measured in <u>that specific</u> research situation. It may differ from one used in other situations, even if either the real or the nominal definitions are the same. This specifies the situation and methodology to be used in this research. So, for example, if the nominal definition of disability is "lacking the ability to work," the operational definition must measure the ability to work, not the desire to work, the need for assistive technology, amount of training for work, or anything else. On the other hand, if the nominal definition is of disability as a self-perception, the operational definition must measure that. The operational definition has to indicate how the measurement will be conducted, indicating exactly what will be done. This includes what will be asked, what will be looked for in an observation, or what measuring equipment will be used. But no matter how it is constructed, the operational definition must match the nominal definition and the real definition.

In the above example about deafness, the operational definition might be "how much a person could hear of a conversation between 3 people at a table in a restaurant." It must specify the proximity of the other people to the test subject. It must specify the procedure. Here is an example of an operational definition which would fit our nominal definition and would suggest how to measure it: "Listen to 5 sentences with 5 words each against a background of 4 people sitting at the same table and not more than 5 feet away, speaking in normal tones. The subject would type the sentences heard into a computer." An audiogram result would not fit that conceptualization, nor would the "Gallaudet scale" used in survey research (e.g., Schein & Delk, 1974), which asks how much trouble a person has hearing overall. One could argue that this operationalization is not either reliable or valid, but it does fit our conceptualization.

Finally, an operational definition includes the **categories** to be used, which must match the other parts of the measurement. They sometimes can be left unspecified at the beginning of survey research: open-ended survey questions will not specify the categories, while closed-ended questions will. But they must be specified by the time the data are analyzed. In the example above, will the categories be "deaf" and "not deaf," or will they be "not deaf," "hard of hearing," and "deaf"? Alternatively, since the person will be typing what they hear into a computer, the categories could be specific scores. But the categories still need to fit our operational definition. Is "deaf" equal to a score of 0–15 words correct and 'hard of hearing" equal to a score of 16–25 correct? Our theory might help with some of these decisions: If the theory's implicit categorization is "deaf" and "not deaf," it suggests different categories than if three categories are implied.

It is clear that any nominal definition may have many different possible operational definitions and categories. In our example above, an alternative measurement could involve observing the interaction as described but only counting how many times the person asks, "what did you say" or says "I did not understand what you said." But, again, exact definitions of the desired categories must be created.

The process of developing a complete operational definition is neither simple nor obvious, as this discussion of the steps involved in the process has shown. And it is not the only part of the measurement process to which attention must be paid. Other factors are the level of measurement of the categories, the time dimension, the unit of analysis, and measurement quality.

OTHER ASPECTS OF THE MEASUREMENT PROCESS

The **level of measurement** is a characteristic of the categories. If the categories are qualitatively different from each other and cannot be ranked in any way, they are at the **nominal** level of measurement. Categories in variables such as "race," "ethnicity," or "gender" tend to be at this level of measurement, because they are words that cannot be translated into numbers. Categories that can be ranked, with differences between them which are not exact or evenly spaced, are at the **ordinal** level of measurement: Categories such as "strongly," "agree," "disagree," and "strongly disagree" are at this level of measurement Categories which use grouped numbers, such as 1–3, 4–6, and 5–10 are also at this level of measurement. Finally, some categories are integers or actual numbers. If these integers do not have a meaningful zero category, the categories are at the **interval** level of measurement. If the category of "zero" actually means "none," they are at the **ratio** level of measurement.

For example, if disability defined as a "yes-no" characteristic, with categories of disabled and non-disabled, this is at the nominal level of measurement. Alternatively, if disability has levels (for example, of impairment, of pain, or of need for assistance) that can be ranked, such as if the categories range from "severe" to "mild" or from "always impairing" to "only occasionally impairing," the measurement is at the ordinal level. If disability is conceptualized as numbers that are not equally distant, but which can be measured on a scale such as a pain or impairment scale from 1 to 10, the categories are at the interval level of measurement. (It is worth noting that scales such as these assume that the categories are equally spaced, but they are not.). Examples of disability-related ratio variables in which the categories numbers) are equally spaced would be the (actual) number of hours per day a person uses a hearing aid or that the person requires assistance in doing ADLs or IADLs or that the impairment is percentaged, as it is on impairment scales such as those used for military evaluations of disability in the United States.

Why is level of measurement important? Decisions regarding a desired level of measurement for an operationalization may be made based upon several factors, but one important decision criterion is the type of statistical analysis planned. All statistical analyses demand—or permit—certain levels of measurement. If the variables are all at the nominal or ordinal level or analysis, correlations, regressions, and most other types of bivariate or multivariate analysis cannot (correctly) be done. Many types of bivariate and especially multivariate analysis require the ratio level of measurement. Thus, the anticipated type of statistical analysis needs to be considered as the process of conceptualization proceeds.

Measurement quality is evaluated through the validity and reliability of the measurements. **Validity** is concerned with whether the operationalization actually measures what the researcher is attempting to measure. This word is frequently misused in discussions of research, often in relationship to whether samples are "valid." Samples are *representative* or not, but that assessment is based upon sampling criteria, not measurement criteria. Measurement validity asks if the measurement fit the real and nominal definitions of the concept. While philosophers might argue about whether it is ever possible to know for certain if any specific measure is valid, it is often quite clear when a measure is not valid. For example, it is unlikely that a behavioral measurement can be used as a valid measurement for an attitudinal variable or that using a disease diagnosis classification is a valid way to measure the level of impairment produced by that diagnosis. There are a number of ways in which researchers attempt to *estimate* validity, such as face validity, construct validity, and criterion validity (Babbie, 2010, pp. 154–155), but validity cannot be known for sure.

Reliability is concerned with a very different aspect of measurement: its stability or replicability. It is concerned with whether a measurement will get the same results from the same people if it were to be repeated.[2] Again, this cannot be known for certain but it is often estimated. Methods such as split-half or test-retest reliability are often reported, but these provide estimations, not certainties.

Overall, the conceptualization of a variable indicates what it is thought to be as well as how it is to be measured. All of the details mentioned above should be specified in any research report. If parts of that conceptualization are missing. not reported or, more concerningly, not considered, the scientific credibility of the research is decreased. Below we consider how these processes were—or were not—apparently followed in the census measurements of disability conducted during the 19th century in the United States.

INADEQUATE MEASUREMENTS: DISABILITY IN US CENSUSES FROM 1830 TO 1900

Census data collection began in the United States in 1790, as specified in the US Constitution that it must happen every 10 years.[3] However, the collection of data on disability did not begin until 1830 and continued through the 1890 census, until it was discontinued for many decades. In this section, we examine the measurement of disability as it was done in these censuses. This examination helps to illuminate some of the points made above about the parts of measurement and how inadequacies with, or the complete absence of, the required parts of a measurement can result in problematic or meaningless conclusions.

When disability measures were introduced in the 1830 census, the only "conditions" of concern (i.e., categories) were "blindness" and "deafness with accompanying mutism." No instructions were given to the marshals collecting the information regarding identifying appropriate level of deafness or blindness (i.e., operationalizations). Rather, these were left to the interpretation of the person answering the question (or possibly to the person asking the question).

The conditions (categories) of "insanity" and "idiocy" were added in the 1840 census, but, in the resulting statistics, numbers for the two categories were reported jointly. This census also asked whether those people were in "private charge" or "public charge" (The Congressional Globe, 1839). Again, there was no operational definition presented to provide guidance in determining either insanity or idiocy; the decision as to what constituted insanity or idiocy was usually left to the head of household who responded to the questions or to the person conducting the questioning.

There was a minor scandal caused by the collection of this data. In many instances, results of cross-tabulations of race with 'insane/idiotic' within census tracts were impossible. Lakin reported (1979, p. 5), that an Illinois county was listed as having no colored inhabitants, but at the same time was shown to have eight insane or idiotic colored residents. The superintendent of the 1850 census acknowledged the problems with the 1840 data, including the fact that the two classes were captured together and generally not understood. He also acknowledge.d.s that this probably resulted in the large discrepancy in numbers compared to the data reported in 1850 with the categories separated. He concluded that the returns of 1840 must have been deficient or that there was an error in placing the figures on the tables A report of the American Statistical Association to the Congress in 1844 documented the many errors in data collection, particularly attributions of insanity or idiocy to large proportions of the colored population (Lakin, 1979, p. 6).

There were some important changes made to the census in 1850 (and thereafter). Congressional legislators kept the questions related to people who were "deaf, dumb, blind, insane or idiotic" because they were seen as being *customary*. Additionally, Congress proposed a form for use in o collecting the census data, (a change in the method of operationalization), which among other things identified that the unit of analysis be the individual, not the family (The Congressional Globe, 1850).

The 1860 census was the first to include instructions to the enumerators about identification of persons with impairments; these served as operational definitions as well as operational instructions. They stated that a "person is to be noted deaf and dumb who was born deaf, or who lost the faculty of hearing before acquiring the use of speech" (Census Office, 1860, p. 16). Blindness was only to be noted if it was in both eyes. The instructions regarding "insanity" indicated:

> A person may be reputed erratic on some subject, but if competent to manage his or her business affairs without manifesting any symptoms of insanity to an ordinary observer, such persons should not be recorded as insane. Where persons are in institutions for safety or restoration, there can exist no doubt as to how you should classify them. . . . *Idiocy* applies to persons who have never possessed vigorous mental faculties, but from their birth have manifested aberration. The cases wherein it may be difficult to distinguish between insanity and idiocy are not numerous; should such occur, however, you may rely on the opinion of any physician to whom the case is known.

Apportionment information about how Black people (i.e. newly freed slaves) were to be treated occupied most of the attention when the congress planning the 1870 census (Anderson, 1990). Thus, this census kept disability measurement as it had been in 1860; impairments resulting from the Civil War, which ended in 1865, we were not addressed.

The 1880 census introduced a section labeled "health," which included new questions that used the term disabled for the first time. One question included the category of "maimed, crippled, bedridden or otherwise disabled" (Gauthier, 2002, p. 17). Another asked, "Is the person (on the day of the Enumerator's visit) sick or temporarily disabled so as to be unable to attend to ordinary business or duties? If so, what is the sickness or disability?" and was designed to measure illness or temporary disability (Gauthier,

2002). With these questions, "disability" was conceptualized as related to sickness or physical deficiency which caused incapacity, as it tended to be at that time (Liachowitz, 1988). However, no special operationalization instructions were included. Instructions for identifying appropriate level of deafness, blindness, insanity, or idiocy were not provided, and the criteria were left either to the person who responded to the questions or to the person conducting the questioning.

For this census, many changes which had been proposed prior to 1870 census were enacted into law. Although primarily related to procedures, some changes mandated the provision of detailed information and others introduced the term "feeble-minded" to replace "idiocy." Information was to be obtained from officers of the institutions for the care and treatment of these people, instead of having marshals, trained for completely different duties, conducting the enumeration. This changed the operational definition of these terms substantially. Additionally, the 1880 census included a supplemental schedule meant to provide more information about the condition of "idiots." The new schedule included the name of the special school; self-support or partial self-support; age at which idiocy occurred; supposed cause if idiocy was acquired; head size; attendance at a training school for idiots and if yes, what school; length of time spent in any such school or schools; date of discharge; and whether the person also was insane, blind, deaf, epileptic, or paralyzed and if the latter on which side, left or right (Lakin, 1979, p. 115).

Information was published following the 1880 census provided some justification for the implicit concept that underpinned that enumeration:

> It is the case in each of these four classes, their claim to the protecting care of the government is, therefore, based upon a physical or mental defect. . . . there are no other classes of defectives for whose relief the governments of the several states and territories are invoked to make provision for their maintenance, tuition, or medical treatment, in institutions created by law and supported at the expense of the public treasury. It is because of this . . . that they are enumerated in the census, in order that the governments referred to may know the precise extent of the claim which may justly be made in their behalf and the amount of provision to be made for them.
>
> (Wines, 1888, p. 8)

The 1890 census provided the most comprehensive data on persons with disabilities in the 19th century. It included eight supplemental schedules for special information on "defective, dependent and delinquent classes." These included one for persons identified as insane, feeble-minded, deaf and dumb, blind, or diseased and physically defective, whether or not they were at home or in an institution. They included detailed questions about the "defects," including the cause of the problem, when it occurred, whether there were other relatives with the same problem or with one of the other conditions considered defective, and whether the person was wholly or partially supported by public or private charity. The schedule also included questions about the use of assistive devices for walking, whether the person was "crippled or lame, maimed, deformed and paralyzed," and it asked deaf people about defects in speech. For people in institutions, the schedules required data on admission and discharge or transfer over the past nine years (1881–1889) and the expenditures for each year (Wright & Hunt, 1900). The procedures spelled out for the operationalizations were also changed. Data on persons residing in institutions would be collected by institutional enumerators who differed from the district enumerators because they were "official or trustworthy persons connected with the institution," determined partly by the size of the institution.

Legislation for the 1900 census authorized the director to collect statistics relating to "the insane, feeble-minded, deaf and dumb, and blind," but it was *restricted to people in institutions* (Wright & Hunt, 1900, p. 950), thus changing the operational definition again. But this census did collect supplementary information on deaf and blind people. Blindness was defined as "couldn't see well enough to read a book, even with glasses," and "deaf and dumb" was defined as "could not be made to understand what people say, even when they shout, and could not speak as to be understood." There was follow up questioning conducted by Dr. Alexander Graham Bell, who had been appointed as an expert special agent for this census. Questions were asked about total or partial blindness; blindness in one or both eyes; ability to read; and ability to recognize persons or objects, get about the neighborhood without a guide, and the use of glasses. Questions were also asked about age of onset, cause of blindness, if and where the person attended school, if parents were first cousins, if any relatives were blind and if so which ones and what occupation the person had (Bell, 1906, p. 4). This report did not document the questions asked about deaf people, but its tables and charts suggest that the questions were similar to those asked about or to blind people but also included questions about the ability to speak.

As noted above, after the 1990 census, questions relating to disability were not asked again for a number of decades. How did this reduced amount of attention to health and disability after the 1900 census happen? Possibly it was related to the fact that the population with disabilities was perceived to be so small that it did not influence the big picture, so it fell off the methodological and statistical radar (Anderson, 1990). The one exception was that questions related to deafness and deaf people were included in the 1930 census. Otherwise, questions related to health and or disability did not reappear at the national level in any measurement for almost half a century. When they reappeared, it was not as part of the census—because it did not fit into its legislative mandates such as apportionment—but in other national statistical measurements (Altman, 2008).

THE CENSUS CONCEPTUALIZATIONS

What can we learn from these early measurement attempts by the US Census? We can see that there were problems in the conceptualization of "disability"—or the lack thereof, in changing operational definitions, and in definitions of categories.[4] Most conceptualizations did not appear to be based upon any real or nominal definition of "disability." Additionally, in most years operational definitions were lacking or minimal, without instructions to either respondent or to enumerators. The meaning of "disability" apparently was equated with having a specific but not very well-defined condition. This is especially true when in 1840 the categories of "idiocy" and "insanity" were added to those (deafness and blindness) that had been recorded in the 1830 census. With no operational definitions spelled out, what was being measured was simply being labeled—by a family member, a school principal, or a census enumerator—as being one of the conditions. Because the category indicated only a label, it may simply have been a proxy for societal reactions to the person by their family, let alone larger society. It may even have been a proxy for race (see Baynton, 2001). The measurements used in the two earliest censuses did not include either nominal or operational definitions of disability. Instead, they were measuring labeled conditions or conditions that caused a person to live in an institution. The earliest nominal definition included as a conceptualization of "disability" may have been intended to be "having a specific (assumed to be) disabling condition," but the actual nominal definition implicit in the earliest measurements was "institutionalization." The categories were simply "present in the institution" or "not."

By the 1860 census, some clarity was issued for the use of the operational definitions of the categories which formed the basis of the census interest in disability. However, as in the prior censuses, a concept of a non-categorically based disability status, or even of a mixed category disability status, did not appear. In the 1870 census, categories or conditions of injury, which could have emerged after the Civil War, were not specifically included, despite the fact that such discussions had occurred after the Revolutionary War (Liachowitz, 1988, pp. 19–28), or the fact that the "disability concept was essential to the development of a workforce in early capitalism" that was occurring in that period of time (Stone, 1984, p. 179).[5] For the 1880 census, measurements supposedly related to health were added, although the questions did not seem to be about health. Rather, the overarching concept was measure of "less than totally functional" or, in the terminology of the time, "unfortunates" (Kirchner, 2010) Rules for operationalization were not specified, except insofar as indicating that the person collecting the information might be a staff member or administrator of an institution. Specific definitions for categories were also not provided. Thus, although quite a lot of data was collected, as a measurement of disability it was weak.

A larger amount of data about people with disabilities was collected in the 1890 census, but it lacked conceptual coherence. It produced a lot of information, apparently, but as a measurement of disability it was not very good. Finally, in the 1900 census, disability-related questions were *restricted to people in institutions* (Wright & Hunt, 1900, p. 950). Additional information was collected about deaf or blind people, in the former case apparently influenced strongly by Alexander Graham Bell presumably as part of his fights against the use of sign language and to support oral education of deaf children (See Buchanan, 1999, pp. 20–39).

These measurements of disability, were flawed. The censuses collected data about characteristics of people that were assumed to be related to a medical condition, so they appeared guided by a medical model of disability. However, most were only trying to categorize some people, and the rules for the categorizations were not well clarified into an operationalization.

MEASURING DISABILITY: WHAT IS CURRENT, AND WHAT IS NEEDED

What initially replaced the census measurements of disability were not, until quite recently, other national measurements of disability. Rather, surveys were conducted to measure the prevalence of disability on a local or regional level instead of the national level. Early on, these included the Cleveland and Elyria Cripple Surveys (Stern, 1919).

More recently, survey measurements of disability have been either constructed primarily for specific purposes, such as measuring the prevalence of work limitations in the population (the Current Population Survey), or they were imputed from data whose main purpose was not to measure disability but to measure aspects of health and illness (the National Health Interview Survey). Volumes edited by Barnartt and Altman (2001, Altman et. al (2003), and Altman and Barnartt (2006), mentioned above, illustrate how difficult the problem of measuring disability actually is and the degree to which measures are contingent upon theories regarding disability.

There are a multiplicity of models, theories, and concepts that attempt to define the essence of disability. These include the medical and social models, the social constructionist model of disability, the deviance model of disability, and other concepts. The medical model of disability focuses on individuals, while the social model focuses on social factors not at the individual level (Barnartt & Green, 2018). Thus, a measurement based upon the medical model must focus on an *individual*'s medical situation and on aspects of the presence of certain medical (physical or mental) conditions. This model *imputes* perceived limitations but does not measure them. For example, in what was originally called the ICIDH (International Classification of Impairment, Handicap and Disability) scale, diagnostic categories were used to measure disability status (Andersson, 2006). This widely criticized measurement fit the model, but it did not provide much information about actual people in actual environments. Now called the ICF (the International Classification of Functioning), it was revised to add measures of functionality (Hendershot, 2006)—hence the name change.

Two current surveys used in the United States to produce national disability data primarily based upon the medical model are the Survey of Income and Program Participation (SIPP), and the Current Population Survey (CPS). These are based upon six disability types (now called difficulties) of hearing difficulty, vision difficulty, cognitive difficulty, ambulatory difficulty, self-care difficulty, and independent living difficulty. The more recently developed American Community Survey (ACS) is a national survey which is becoming more aware of the need to focus on functioning instead of diagnosis, although that is an effort in progress. (See many publications under www.cen

sus.gov). While these types of measurements do take into account the possibility of individual variations in impairment types, individual reactions and social environments
are not as well measured as we would hope they could be. For example, a deaf person
who lives in a family with all deaf members and who works in an environment in which
communication is maximized signed communication or various recent technical
advancements are common may experience a different level of "inability" than another
person with a similar level of hearing 'difficulty' but a different social/environmental
situation.

In order to measure disability status from the point of view of the social model,
researchers would need to evaluate what it is about the environment that engenders limitations in attitudes, behavior, or potentialities for people who have certain conditions.
As Nagi (1965) argued, the conceptualization of this type requires measuring **both** what
it is about the person which is relevant **and** what it is about the environment which is
disabling. In other words, it is the **interaction** of these two components which has to
be measured. Drawing from Nagi's discussions, a conceptualization of disability which
would focus solely upon the conditions of the environment was suggested by a National
Academy of Sciences panel. This conception envisioned "an environmental mat,"
the strength of which would determine whether a specific condition was likely to be
disabling and which, presumably, could be measured (Brandt & Pope, 1997). However,
this conceptualization does not allow for individual variation in a person's reaction to
one or a set of impairments; such reactions would also need to be measured.

The social model is difficult to operationalize, partly because it conceptualizes a situation which occurs because of the interaction of a person and an environment which is
less likely to be measurable using survey research techniques. However, a survey developed by the Washington Group on Disability Statistics, supported by the United Nations
Statistical Division (Loeb & Eide, 2006), provides an example of using a measurement that attempts to evaluate the effect of the environment on the person in different
situations while not actually evaluating the environment itself. Rather, it uses questions
to evaluate the presence of hearing difficulty, vision difficulty, cognitive difficulty, and
ambulatory difficulty, among others and then it asks how often such a difficulty causes
problems in a number of environmental realms.

A variant of the social model, based upon theories of social construction (Berger &
Luckman, 1966), is the Social Constructionist Model of Disability. That model includes
both the individual and societal levels of analysis, and it examines how any identity (one
assumes, including disability) is produced by and in society.

The Deviance Model of Disability (Freidson, 1965), which also fits Goffman's (1963)
work, was a very commonly used model in the 1950's through 1970's in the United States
(Barnartt & Green, 2018). It combines the social and social constructionist models, but
it suggests different measurement strategies. If the person is defined as being deviant
because of a physical or mental condition (a medical model approach), disability might
be operationalized as an attitude or self-conception as deviant, which can use survey
questions to measure how the person feels. If, however, a more socio-cultural or environmental approach is taken, the measurement would need to focus on aspects of the

social environment such as stigma and discrimination (which would be imputed to cause a type of person to experience the status of deviance even if the person resisted that status).

There are a number of recent conceptions of disability. One is of disability as being a minority group (Stroman, 1982; Deegan, 1981). This concept includes societal inequality in both money and power, experiencing discrimination, being included under the "frame" of civil rights, and possessing a group identity. There have been attempts to measure minority group identity at the individual level as the degree of identification with the idea of disabled people as minority group (e.g., Darling, 2013).

A number of authors have examined the application of the concept of intersectionality, originally suggested to apply to black women, to people with disabilities (Barnartt & Altman, 2013). Mauldin and Brown (2021) broadened the notion by saying that disability is an axis of inequality commensurate with race, class, and gender *and* intersecting with them. It is not clear how these related conceptualizations would be operationalized, since they theorize causation to be at the society level.

A number of concepts are derived from the concept of culture. In the disability community, "disability culture" and "disability pride" are commonly used, and "disability consciousness" is used in discussions related to social movement activity (Barnartt, 1996).

In the deaf community, "deaf culture," and to a lesser extent "deaf pride" are commonly used. "Deaf culture" is not just an indication of deaf pride, but, rather, it is related to usage of sign language and a number of norms, values, and behaviors which are felt to distinguish groups of people with hearing losses. All of these concepts could be used as the basis of a measurement. There are several additional concepts which might be used as the basis for measurement. Barnartt (2016) views disability through the concept of fluidity, or disability as a fluid state, with a focus on social roles and their enactment. Fluidity is based upon the fact that a person may enter and leave a role during an hour, a day, a week, or a month, depending upon the role, and the person may also vary in how well they enact the requirements of the role. A person who has a physical or mental condition may enact a specific role differently than someone without that condition, so the person may (or may not) be impaired or disabled in their enactment of that role according to the cultural conceptions of that role and either in their own eyes or in the eyes of others. This conceptualization of disability would require a measurement that addresses the many and variable social situations, which both occur simultaneously and change over time.

Works by Barnartt (1996; 2017a,b), Barnartt and Scotch (2001), Carey et al. (2020), and others suggest a conceptualization of disability derived from concepts of social movements. Operationalization could be more dependent upon characteristics of social movements than on individuals, it could be behavioral (focusing on movement activities or involvements), or it could focus on a person's degree of identification with the movement.

Among deaf people, in addition to the concepts mentioned above which are variants of concepts used in or by the larger disability community, there are also a number of concepts which have gained popularity but which are not shared with, or applied to, the larger disability community. One is the concept of "deaf gain" (Bauman and Murray, 2009). This concept focuses on possible positive results of a lack of hearing for individuals, such as greater visual capabilities, and for societies, such as attention to visual teaching methods or greater architectural focus on lighting. Again, it may need to be measured on both the individual and societal levels, so operationalization is problematic. Additionally, while a similar concept has not been given much attention relating to general or unspecified disabilities, it could be.

This is by no means an exhaustive list of concepts of disability which are in use or could be, but this multiplicity of models and concepts is part of the reason why measuring disability is so difficult. In order to try to simplify this, we suggest focusing on two major axes on which disability measurements can be located and that, when combined and considered as having yes-no categories, could produce four types of measurements which would require very different measurement characteristics.

One axis is the "unit of analysis," which varies from one individual groups to entire societies. That is, the focus of the measurement can vary from that based upon individuals to that based upon groups of various sizes from pairs to entire societies. For purposes of creating the 4 types of mesasurements, this is categorized as being "single individual" or "more than one individual." The other axis is a "time continuum" that varies from one moment in time (in which the person is answering a question or being evaluated by someone else at one point in time only) to many moments in time—in methodological terms from cross sectional to longitudinal. Thus the unit of analysis and the time format both define and constrain the measurement which is to be used.

Thinking of these as a four-fold table gives us four cells describing different methodological constraints: Individual and cross-sectional, individual and longitudinal, group/society and cross-sectional, and group/society and longitudinal. Thus, for example, a measurement which is individual and cross-sectional must focus within the person's individual characteristics (whether physical or mental) but will also focus on one point in time. (For greatest reliability, this is usually the time at which the measurement is administered.) If the measurement is focused at the individual level but is longitudinal, there are a number of methodological possibilities, including repeated measures and cohort comparisons. (Retrospective measures (asking about the past) which attempt to be longitudinal are unreliable because they are measured at the individual level, so social changes would have to be imputed.)

If the measurement is at larger than the individual level, it must in some way measure groups. This does not mean that it measures groups of people as multiples of individuals; rather, that it measures characteristics of the groups themselves. If it is cross-sectional, again this would mean a singular measurement, at one point in time. However this type of measurement is unlikely to be accomplished as a survey; innovative methodologies, such as measurements of ecological or geographic features, may be required. Finally, a measurement whose focus is a group and which is longitudinal would conduct multiple measurements of those described above.

CONCLUSION

The four different methodological foci we have noted—individual and cross-sectional, individual and longitudinal, group/society and cross-sectional, and group/society and longitudinal—form a template that could guide future measurements of disability. Those measurements, however, must also follow the strictures laid out earlier: There must be a nominal definition, usable in the research situation, that fits the real or abstract definition. There must be an operational definition that actually measures the nominal definition, and the operational definition must have appropriate categories that fit the nominal and operational definitions. The level of measurement must fit the nominal definition (and vice versa), and the categories and the level of measurement of the categories must fit the real and nominal definitions.

This chapter has used the discussion of historical measurements of disability in the US Census to help us understand how problematic such measures can be. Examination of more recent models and concepts expands how we think about the essence of disability, but disability researchers still need to work on creating measurements which better fit the rules of conceptualization and operationalization. Otherwise, statements such as "disabled people are 25% of the population" have no meaning unless they specify *both* the conceptualization *and* the operationalization used to produce it.

There is final caveat here. Measurement is not the only issue for researchers focusing on disability, although it is an extremely important one. Another issue is related to sampling. Research from which generalizations are to be made must pay attention to how representative samples can be chosen from relatively unknown or difficult-to-identify populations, institutionalized populations, and/or populations with different or sometimes less than adequate communications abilities (such as signing deaf people or people with severe cognitive impairments). Sample identification as well as sample selection can present problems which are not as likely to be encountered in populations of people without impairments.

Finally, this chapter has not attempted to address issues relating to qualitative research. While the research processes may differ substantially from quantitative processes, the definitional strictures laid out here are not irrelevant. That is, for example, an observational researcher must still have an implicit conceptualization of disability which must be made explicit in order to understand to whom and under what circumstances the observation apply.

NOTES

1. In qualitative research, the focus is likely to be on processes and relationships whose generality is usually not tested until subsequent research, if at all. Issues raised in the current discussion of measurement are sometimes applicable to qualitative research, but that will not be discussed here.

2. This assumes that there is not a theoretical reason why the results should change, as there would be if a measurement were being used as the dependent variable in an experiment or it were a characteristic which is assumed to change over time. Again, this determination depends partly upon the real and the nominal definitions used.
3. The work of locating and collating this information was done by Barbara Altman.
4. There were also problems related to strategies used to locate respondents, which we will not discuss here. However, there were echoesechoes of similar problems in problems seen in the 2020 census, which also used "informants" to provide information for people who could not easily be located.
5. A number of the papers in Longmore and Umansky's (2001) collection begin to flesh out how definitions of disability were emerging and growing at the end of the century but not so much before that.

REFERENCES

Altman, B., Barnartt, S., Hendershot, G, and S. Larson. (2003). *Using survey data to study disability: results from the national health interview survey.* Research in Social Science and Disability 3. New York, NY: JAI Press.

Altman, B., & Barnartt, S. (2006). *International views on disability measures: Moving towards comparative measurement.* Research in Social Science and Disability 4. New York, NY: JAI Press.

Altman, B. (2008). Disability measurement in a policy context. Presented at the Annual Meeting of the American Sociological Association.

Altman, B. M. (2001). Definitions of disability and their operationalization and measurement in survey data: An update. In S. Barnartt and B. Altman (Eds.), *Exploring Theories and Expanding Methodologies: Where We Are and Where We Need to Go* (pp. 77–100). Research in Social Science and Disability 2. New York, NY: JAI Press.

Andersson, Y. (2006). Reflections on disability language and the ICIDH/ICF. In B. Altman and S. Barnartt (Eds.), *International Views on Disability Measures: Moving Towards Comparative Measurement* (Pp. 55–62). Research in Social Science and Disability 4. New York, NY: JAI Press.

Anderson, M. J. (1990). *The American census: A social history.* New Haven: Yale University Press.

Babbie, E. (2010). *The practice of social research.* 12th edition. Belmont, CA: Wadsworth Publishing Co.

Barnartt, S. (1996). Disability culture or disability consciousness. *Journal of Disability Policy Studies* 7(2), 1–17.

Barnartt, S. (2012). *Deafness and disability discourses: Implications for policies and programs.* Boston, MA: The Society for Applied Anthropology.

Barnartt, S. (2016). Role theory and the fluidity of disability. In P. Devlieger, Beatriz Miranda-Galarza, Steven E. Brown, and Megan Strickfaden Maklu (Eds.), *Rethinking Disability: World Perspectives in Culture and Society* (Pp. 47–58). Antwerp, Belgium: Garant Publishers.

Barnartt, S. (2017a). Introduction: An historical overview of sociology looking at disability: What did we know and when did we know it?" In S. Green and S. Barnartt (Eds.), *Sociology Looking at Disability: What Did We Know and When Did We Know It?*, (Pp. xv–xxxiii). Research in Social Science and Disability 9. Bingley, UK: Emerald Press.

Barnartt, S. (2017b). The sociology of disability. In K. Korgen (Ed.), *The Cambridge Encyclopedia of Sociology* (Pp. 285–294). Cambridge, UK: Cambridge University Press.

Barnartt, S., & Altman, B. (2001). *Exploring theories and expanding methodologies: Where we are and where we need to go*. Research in Social Science and Disability 1. New York, NY: JAI Press.

Barnartt, S., & Altman, B. (2013). *Disability and intersecting statuses*. Research in Social Science and Disability 7. Bingley, UK: Emerald Press.

Barnartt, S., & Green, S. (2018). Disability in [or not in] American social theory. Toronto, Canada: The International Sociological Association Meeting.

Barnartt, S. and Scotch, R. (2001). *Disability Protests: Contentious Politics 1970–1999*. Washington, DC: Gallaudet University Press.

Bauman, D., & Murray, J. J. (2009). Reframing: From hearing loss to Deaf gain. *Deaf Studies Digital Journal* 1.

Bell, A. G. (1906). *The Blind and the Deaf*. Washington, DC: U. S. Printing Office.

Baynton, D. (2001). Disability and the justification of inequality in American history. In Paul K. Longmore and Lauri Umansky (Eds.), *The New Disability History: American Perspectives* (Pp. 33–57). New York: New York University Press.

Berger, P. L., & Luckman, T. (1966). *The social construction of reality*. Garden City, NY: Doubleday Press.

Brandt, E., and & Pope, A. (1997). *Enabling America: Assessing Disability and Rehabilitation in America*. Washington, DC: National Academy Press.

Buchanan, R. (1999). *Illusions of equality: Deaf Americans in school and factory 1850-1950*. Washington, DC: Gallaudet University Press.

Carey, A., Block, P, and Scotch, R. 2020. Disability Aliancesand Allies (Research in social Science and Disability volume 12.) Bingley, UK: Emerald Press.

Darling, Rosalyn Benjamin. 2013. *Disability and identity: Negotiating self in a changing society*. Boulder, CO: Lynne Rienner Press.

Deegan, M. J. (1981). Multiple minority groups: A case study of physically disabled women. *Journal of Sociology and Social Welfare* 8(2), 274–295.

Freidson, E. (1965). Disability as social deviance. In M. B. Sussman (Ed.), *Sociology and Rehabilitation* (Pp. 71–99). Washington, DC: American Sociological Association.

Gauthier, J. G. (2002). *Measuring America: The decennial censuses from 1790 to 2000*. Washington, DC: US Department of Commerce, US Census Bureau.

Goffman, Erving. 1963. *Stigma*. Englewood Cliffs, NJ: Prentice Hall, Inc.

Herndershot, G. (2006). Survey measurement of disability: A review of international activities and recommendations. Pp. 17–40 In B. Altman and S. Barnartt (Eds.), *International Views on Disability Measures: Moving Towards Comparative Measurement* (). Research in Social Science and Disability 4. New York, NY: JAI Press.

Kirchner, Corinne. 2010. From "survival of the fittest" to "fitness for all" to "who defines fitness anyway?" 100 years of (US) sociological theory on disability. In S. Barnartt (Ed.), *Disability as a Fluid State* (Pp. 131–157). Research in Social Science and Disability 5. Bingley, UK: Emerald Press.

Lakin, K. C. (1979). *Demographic studies of residential facilities for the mentally retarded: An historical review of methodologies and findings*. Developmental Disabilities Project of Residential Services and Community Adjustment. Minneapolis: University of Minnesota.

Liachowitz, C. (1988). *Disability as a social construct: Legislative roots*. Philadelphia, PA: University of Pennsylvania Press.

Loeb, M., & A. Eide. (2006). Paradigms lost: The changing face of disability in research. In B. Altman and S. Barnartt (Eds.), *International Views on Disability Measures: Moving Towards Comparative Measurement* (Pp. 111–130). Research in Social Science and Disability 4. New York, NY: JAI Press.

Longmore, P., & Umansky, L. (2001). *The new disability history: American perspectives*. New York, New York: New York University Press.

Mauldin, L., & Brown, R. L. (2021). Missing pieces: Engaging sociology of disability in medical sociology. *Journal of Health and Social Behavior* 62(4), 477–492.

Nagi, S. Z. (1965). Some conceptual issues in disability and rehabilitation. In M. B. Sussman (Ed.) *Sociology and Rehabilitation* (Pp. 100–113). Washington, DC: American Sociological Association.

Schein, J. D., and Delk, M. T. (1974). *The deaf population of the United States*. Silver Spring, MD: National Association of the Deaf.

Scotch, R. (1984). *From good will to civil rights: Transforming federal disability policy*. Philadelphia, PA: Temple University Press.

Stern, Walter G. (1919). A report on the Cleveland and Elyria Cripple Surveys. *Journal of Bone and Joint Surgery* 1(1), 30–39.

Stone, D. (1984). *The disabled state*. Philadelphia, PA: Rutgers University Press.

Stroman, D.F. (1982). *The awakening minorities: The physically handicapped*. Washington, DC: University Press of America

The Congressional Globe. (1850). *Century of lawmaking for a new nation: U.S. congressional documents and debates*. Washington, DC: US Government Printing Office 1778-1875.

The Congressional Globe. (1839, February). *U.S. congressional documents and debates*. Washington, DC: US Governemtn Printing Office.

Washington Group on Disability Statistics. (2020). Disability Measurement and Monitoring using the Washington Group Disability Questions. https://www.washingtongroup-disabil ity.com/fileadmin/uploads/wg/Documents/WG_Resource_Document__4_-_Monitoring _Using_the_WG_Questions.pdf.

World Health Organization. (2001). International classification of functioning, disability and health (ICF). Geneva: World Health Organization. https://apps.who.int/iris/bitstream/ handle/10665/42407/9241545429.pdf;jsessionid=33E82CBBB80558550482733824861786? sequence=1.

Wright, C. D., & Hunt, W. C. (1900). *The history and growth of the United States Census*. Washington, DC.

PART II

Global Perspectives

CHAPTER 8

CRITICAL THINKING ON DISABILITY AND DEVELOPMENT IN THE GLOBAL SOUTH

SHAUN GRECH

INTRODUCTION

THIS chapter is written some 20 years into working in the field that has come to be known as "disability and development" or "global disability" as an academic and a practitioner. In truth, it is not so much a field of study with its own theory, as much as a space of practice and research focused on disability in the so-called Global South, which, following Dados and Connell (2012, p. 12), is employed here to denote an emphasis on geopolitical relations of power that have long historical lineages and manifestations. More specifically, the term "Global South" is used here to delineate power, resource, and epistemological differentials, which though not localized, embrace a substantial portion of the world living in a scenario of profound geopolitical asymmetries, poverty, and isolation confronting deeply entrenched centers of concentrated wealth and power accumulated historically and perpetuated in times of coloniality.

The attention to disability in the Global South is not unwarranted. According to the first World Report on Disability published by the World Health Organization (WHO) and the World Bank in 2011, 15% of the world population is disabled. Among this population, 80% are located in the Global South, the majority living in rural areas in conditions of poverty. However speculative (and likely wrong) these numbers may be, they still create a sense of urgency. Disability has always been there, and it always will be. The numbers also continue to rise, especially in the Global South, on account of extreme poverty and growing inequality amid neoliberal globalization, weakening of social protection measures, hunger and malnutrition, violence and conflict, and forced migration in perilous conditions (Grech, 2019). In practice, no one really knows how many disabled people there are. Several people, especially those in poor rural areas, are unregistered, data are lacking or absent, and national survey and census methods vary considerably across regions. This number, though, we can safely speculate, is far from small.

The need to focus on disability in the Global South as an academic and practice endeavor has found some support in recent years, often backed by frequent references to a disability and poverty relationship, one generally framed as a cycle (see Groce et al., 2011; Pinilla-Roncancio, 2015). Though research (notably critical qualitative research) on this relationship remains scarce (Grech, 2015a), it has helped to direct focus on the inordinate barriers said to be encountered by disabled people, especially in spaces marked by profound deprivation, poverty, and inequality. For example, figures suggest that nine out of ten disabled children in low-income countries do not have access to education (Global Partnership for Education, 2016). Livelihoods are marred by multiple barriers, including access to credit and physical constraints in harsh informal labor contexts (Grech, 2015a; UN, 2018). Transport barriers are rife and limit mobility, and impaired access to health care is dramatic and life threatening (Banks et al., 2017). Disabled people also face higher risks of malnutrition, violence (especially women), access barriers (e.g., to clean water and adapted humanitarian services), and are especially exposed in contexts of conflict (see Pisani & Grech, 2015; UN, 2018).

These are only some of the barriers disabled people face in very complex and often tough and dynamic spaces. It is impossible to capture every barrier here, especially if we consider the various intersectional dimensions, for example those between forced migration, gender, and disability. Still, estimates suggest that 1 in 5 of the world's poorest people are disabled people, experiencing a deep, multidimensional, and frequently chronic poverty (Mitra, 2018; UN, 2018). Elsewhere (see Grech, 2019), I have suggested that this figure may in fact be much higher if one considers the impacts of disability on fragile families, pushing for the need to speak about "disabled families." Overall, disability, has often been linked to broader discussions on vulnerability, or rather disabled people pitched as disproportionately vulnerable, whether to poverty, illness, or violence. As I will be discussing later, such focus on vulnerability comes at the expense of discussions on agency, and it isolates disabled people as somehow "special recipients" for outside intervention in ableist discourses and practices; moreover, critical discussion is still lacking.

These discursive shifts, alongside the strengthening of the international disability movement, have spurred numerous changes, with implications for disability in the Global South. The United Nations Convention on the Rights of Persons with Disabilities (UNCRPD) (UN, 2006) was drafted, signed, and eventually ratified by many countries.[1] The sustainable development goals (SDGs) have replaced the previous millennium development goals (MDGs), providing a development "road map" for the next 15 years, or as some would argue, a set of promises unlikely to be achieved, or only in part, not least because they are not legally binding (see Moyer & Hadden, 2020). The past years have also seen emerging discourse around disability mainstreaming, that is, the need to infuse disability in all areas of development, to ensure disabled people are adequately considered, planned for, and reached in all stages of development (see ADD, 2016). Others supported a twin-track approach to disability, stressing the need to not only mainstream disability in development but also to target disabled people too through disability-specific measures (see UNDP, 2018).

Overall, the focus of international development on the Global South, including through measures such as poverty reduction, has made the discursive link between disability and development inevitable. Many (see Yeo, 2005, for example) have long argued that if disabled people are disproportionately represented among the poorest in the Global South, and if development is indeed set on reducing poverty (amid other priorities), then, it will be impossible to reduce poverty if the needs of disabled people are not flatly addressed.

Over the past two decades, we have seen other changes. In particular, we have witnessed the emergence of the narrative of disability-inclusive development (DID). Taking its lead from earlier calls for "inclusive development" (see van Gent, 2017), DID emphasizes the need for all areas and stages of development to be inclusive of and also accessible to disabled people (see UNDP, 2018). These discursive shifts have helped strengthen the argument that disability in the Global South is a legitimate "object" of development. They also opened a space for research and consultants, including universities to make money.

Despite these twists and turns, many issues haunt the "disability and development" landscape apart from the policies and declarations (e.g., the UNCRPD) with very limited "bite" in practice. The main one is perhaps the most obvious: The emphasis on DID is borne from the fact that disability remains marginalized in international development and programs; otherwise we would not need to echo it at every turn. Disability remains virtually absent in core development studies modules in universities, and scarce in mainstream development journals. It also lingers on the edges of development practice, not quite a legitimate area, ambivalently relegated to the space of medicine or charity, a specialized concern in which development workers feel they have little or no specialization and training, and which is perceived as too costly, and then perpetually (re)framed as someone else's "problem" (see Grech, 2015a; Niewohner et al., 2019). This is unlike gender, which today is a core issue in development theory and practice, backed by decades of a strong feminist movement operating and lobbying from within. On the contrary, the advocacy to include disability in development has always come from outside development, and as such it remains the concern of outsiders.

This marginalization of Global South disability issues, though, occurs not only in development but also within disability studies. Recent critical work has highlighted how this small field remains both Global North–centric and Global North–focused (see Grech, 2011, 2015; Nguyen, 2018; Staples, 2020), imbued with ideological, theoretical, cultural, economic, and historical assumptions and specificities. It is no secret that much of the body of work that constitutes disability studies is largely dominated by concerns pertinent to the Global North, within specific contexts (e.g., presence of some or other social protection system and rights frameworks) and steered by Global

North academics. The United Kingdom and the United States, in particular, continue to lead in what we see as core disability studies literature, research, and orientations. As with most key disability studies textbooks, the Global South is often at best included as a cursory issue (e.g., a stray chapter) or at worst excluded (see, e.g., Davis, 2017; Watson & Vehmas, 2020).

Overall, those working in "disability and development" (e.g., with a background in global health), frequently operate in rather uncritical and/or monodisciplinary ways and on occasion prescriptively.[2] Complexities, heterogeneities, and difficult questions are often forsaken in favor of an approach that seeks to simplify and generalize disability, the Global South, and the methods of research and practice. In this process, multiple and diverse perspectives are often unheard or stifled, especially Southern voices and theory challenging and dislocating hegemonic Global North discourse and practices. This means that accounts on disability and development are not only partial and fragmented, they may also be, as I will argue, neocolonizing (see Durokifa & Ijeoma, 2018, for more on necolonization within the development sector). Neocolonization is used here to mean epistemic, discursive, and also practice domination, where the objective is control, with power concentrated in the Global North.

This chapter reflects critically on some of these concerns. Inspired by critical disability studies (Goodley et al., 2018) and decolonial theory (Castro-Gómez & Grosfoguel, 2007), it addresses emerging issues that arise when Global North disability discourse and "development" confront complex, dynamic, and heterogeneous Southern spaces and disability within. In particular, it engages with how simplifications and generalizations not only have severe epistemological implications but also practical ones, in particular, in creating the conditions for perpetual interventions in and on the Southern disabled subject. The chapter ends with an exploration of some ideas as to what a decolonizing approach to disability in the Global South could look like.

Framing Disability in the Global South

Before discussing the critical issues that emerge, it is perhaps best to first take a step back and explain how disability in the Global South has and continues to be constructed within dominant Global North discourses and practices. Much of what is framed as "global disability" or "disability and development" as an area of study, research, and practice has emerged from and been propagated by Global North universities, research institutes, donors (e.g., the British DFID), and international organizations (INGOs) (see, e.g., ICAI, 2018). These have sought to fashion a defined area of epistemological and practice intervention, and to do this, they have and continue to attempt to contain very complex and heterogenous realities "out there," whether through simplification or generalization. The objective is not only to discursively contain and manage (disability, the Global South, etc.) but also to legitimize the "solutions" and/or research and interventions proposed in and about these spaces and lives from the metropole (see Grech, 2015b; Said, 1993). Such dynamics have strong foundations in colonialism, defined here as the subjugation by discursive, "physical and psychological force of one culture by another—a colonizing power" (McMichael, 2016, p. 4). Framings of the colonial subject, for example, helped not only justify the colonial "mission" built on pillaging, brutality, and murder, but they also rendered the subject docile or savage as required at any time, if anything to legitimize and perpetuate the actions of the colonizer (see Fanon, 1963) as a necessary, even divine mission.

Global North urban academics, consultants, and researchers, as well as INGOs with head offices in the Global North, not only shape discourse and create work for themselves, but they also determine priority areas, methods, and "strategies." These are often molded on Global North values, concepts, and norms, including rights-based approaches to disability, constructions of ethics, and "adequate" rehabilitation practices. This Global North space, as we often see, is where "real expertise" and "learned methods" are seen to reside both by those propagating such discourse and also their privileged associates in the Global South. This knowledge imperialism (Alatas, 2003) has long historical roots and baggage. The Global North university is where authoritative and informed knowledge stems from, and the US- or UK-based INGO is the one with the best tools in the field. This expertise and credible knowledge, as it seems, rarely resides in the Global South. Over the past years, critics calling out White privilege, as well as racism in international development, humanitarian action, and the charity sectors, have solidly stepped up, a dynamic with long historical lineages, imbricated in race and geopolitical asymmetries among others (see ODI, 2020; Wilson, 2012). Decolonial theorists have long called for a "decolonial option" capable of making clear "precisely that master paradigms and abstract universals . . . are still caught in imperial desires" by listening to and prioritizing voices and spaces "that have been silenced, repressed, demonized, devalued" (Mignolo, 2010, pp. 1–2).

How we have come to understand disability in the small space of disability and development, has often been through channels and means that rarely address the necessary contextual, historical, social, cultural, economic, and political complexities. So-called evidence-based studies continue to pile up, informed by a short empirical stint, a brief literature review, or more inferences from quantitative data, articles are published in rapid succession on a range of themes, and onto the next funded project. Researchers within development on occasion also transfer momentarily their own research and methodology focus onto disability, crunch some numbers, publish a paper, and then go back their respective areas (Pinilla-Roncancio & Alkire, 2020). This does not make such work irrelevant or weak. On the contrary, we need more interdisciplinary work, but we also need more informed, contextualized, engaged, and consistent work, where disability is not a momentary add-on, where theoretical understandings are brought in with the depth and time they deserve, and importantly where disabled voices are not stifled.

Within disability and development specifically, criticality is frequently sacrificed, replaced by quick output and often "easy" solutions. These are issues amply discussed in the broader development sector (see Flint & Meyer zu Natrup, 2019). Pressured by their institutions to pull in research money, universities do not so much try and understand disability as much as "sell" easily packaged and communicable synthesized information. Large data sets are processed and presented in tables, and statistics tell us how many people are disadvantaged in different areas, but the methods themselves and the ideological dimensions justifying them are rarely questioned. For example, the assumption that disabled Indigenous people in remote areas are somehow expected to be open to an outsider knocking and asking survey style questions is rarely questioned (see Grech, 2015), for more on power dynamics and differentials in research). Instead, simply using a national researcher seems to solve the problem, even when that researcher is rarely from the same rural community, is not known, and may even be feared. We rarely read about the lack of knowledge of rural areas, and sometimes also fear of these spaces by those doing what I call "hit and run" research. Issues of power and oppression in research are relegated to the back (see Soldatic et al., 2018; Tuhiwai-Smith, 1999). Overall, disabled poor people continue to be spoken for, with dimensions of their lives often simplified and contained in rather meaningless numbers. They are then unable to contest the discourse, methods, and strategies that *we* propose about *them*.

With scarce specific, historical, and contextualized information, these studies, like much of the grey literature published by INGOs and donors on disability in so-called "developing" or "low-income" countries (see, e.g., DFID, 2018; UN, 2018), rarely say much that is new, simply because the critical nuances are not there. These require time and, importantly, grounded approaches open to complexity. We see document after document telling us that disabled people and their families are some or other percentage points poorer (see Pinilla-Roncancio & Alkire, 2020) and how health is a dramatic barrier. Importantly we are regaled with numerous solutions, including how "good" DID should be done, more often than not, in line with what is already being done or what an institution or organization has to offer and how it should be measured (against legitimate benchmarks). This excerpt from the DFID strategy on DID for 2018–2023 (DFID, 2018, p. 11) is representative:

> To achieve the greatest impact we will initially focus on a set of distinct and transformational areas where DFID has the expertise and ability to deliver at scale, whilst continuing to mainstream disability across our portfolio. Over the next five years we will prioritise four strategic pillars for action: (i) inclusive education, (ii) social protection, (iii) economic empowerment, and (iv) humanitarian action. There is a close fit between these areas and the SDGs, and they are areas where DFID has a comparative advantage, and global influence. We will measure success in these four pillars; by doubling the proportion of programmes that are disability inclusive by 2023 – tracked across all areas using the internationally agreed OECD Development Assistance Committee's (OECD-DAC) disability inclusion and empowerment marker.

Within academic circles and research, a few nice snapshots of a White academic on a fleeting trip with a local disabled person rubber-stamp the whole project as "legitimate" and even "participatory," and on we move. This output is then exported/imposed, to use

Stuart Hall's (1996) words "from the West to the rest"—packaged "informed/expert" knowledge for mass consumption. These are what make credible references in papers, books, and reports.

Over the past years, universities and other institutions have backed the supposed "soundness" of their studies by claiming they consulted with and included local DPOs as partners, arguing that the study is then representative of all local voices and locally "owned." The methodology rarely gives much information on who actually determined the research approach and methods to be used, the locations, and the time devoted to developing a relationship with participants, among other critical aspects. But more importantly, we are rarely allowed to question who these local partners are. It is no secret for us who regularly work in the field, that many local partners are, more often than not, privileged urban DPOs and stakeholders. These organizations are close to main thoroughfares, likely to be in touch with foreign institutions, and have structures in place to deal with the demands of research (see Bezzina, 2019; Grech, 2015a). Poor isolated disabled people and their organizations are rarely consulted, and they are hardly considered authoritative enough to even discuss their own lives. Similar arguments have been raised on the limitations of participation in development (see Cooke & Kothari, 2001).

As I have stressed multiple times, "poverty is rarely lived on the skin of those 'doing' policy talk, consultancy or academia" (Grech, 2016a, p. 11). The privileged Southern partners and DPOs may hardly have any contact with or even know poor rural areas in their own countries, simply because they have never been and know little or nothing about disability in these spaces. Their own claim to legitimacy is nationality, not knowledge, and identity politics often come into play when lack of knowledge is in fact contested. Nevertheless, they are assumed to represent all disabled people in their countries, while the foreign institution gets to tick the "participation" box of the university and the donor, and ethically it rings no alarm bells. For all intents and purposes, disabled people were represented by their own organizations and people.

This scenario is not unfamiliar in the international development sector, one framed and perpetuated from the Global North, which some concede is a development sector that ultimately remains unresponsive to Southern voices and priorities, and is possibly neocolonizing (see Escobar, 1995). Langan (2018, p. 1) highlights how many scholars in development "are decidedly squeamish when the term [neocolonialism] is invoked," even when it is undeniable that many of these development practices were far from harmless in continents such as Africa. Similarly, those working in "global disability" are not too quick to even ponder, let alone take on themes such as neocolonialism, or simply power relationships in what they do. These questions not only slow down the process, as it seems, but as I was once told by a consultant, they "stop us from telling them how to do it better for the sake of disabled people."

Despite the emphasis on DID, those working in "disability and development" are not always schooled in international development, its history, or its geopolitical dimensions, including critical discourses questioning and challenging development itself (see Escobar, 1995). Indeed, what we are left with is often a rather atheoretical and unquestioning stance, while interdisciplinarity is lacking dramatically in this work. Those churning out report after report are hardly engaging any theory, and instead stick to familiar terrains, because they may also lack time to read. Ironically, there is little disability studies in there, too.

This does not mean that critical work has not emerged to focus on disability in the Global South. In fact, the last 10 years have seen a surge in critical writings (see Grech, 2011, 2015b; Kamenopoulou, 2020; Meekosha, 2011; Soldatic & Grech, 2014), including dedicated spaces such as the establishment of the international critical journal, *Disability and the Global South* (http://www.dgsjournal.org). The contributions continue to grow to question and dislocate institutionalized Global North discourses and practices. That much of the core of so-called disability and development continues to lazily echo its own discourse is therefore hardly a reflection of lack of critical thinking, research, and literature. Instead, it is the result of an ongoing posture or false sense of epistemic comfort and even superiority.

Overall, disability and the Global South are often simplified in the bid to contain them, to make them intelligible to everyone, especially research funders that include donors and research councils. But what has discourse in disability and development looked like, and how has it been sustained? In the following subsections, I lay out some patterns to illustrate three particularly conspicuous dynamics: (1) the simplification and generalization of disability and the Global South, (2) vulnerability and vanishing agency, and (3) the consequential imperative to intervene.

Simplifying (and Containing) Disability

It would be incorrect to say that research does not exist to highlight the deep contextualized complexity and heterogeneity of disability across space and time. The past few years have seen the emergence of empirical as well as theoretical studies (see, e.g., Devlieger et al., 2013; Friedner, 2017; Grech, 2015a; Ingstad & Whyte, 1995, 2007). These offerings, some of which are ethnographic, carefully frame disability within context, alongside the multiple and complex dimensions that not only surround disability, but through which, as I emphasize elsewhere (see Grech, 2015a), disability is ultimately constructed and understood (even if partially). These contexts include personal circumstances, family situations, poverty, levels of support, access to services, religious beliefs, and attitudes, all of which are complex and diverse. They are also dynamic, meaning that disability can hardly be understood through short research stints, and through static models at one point in time.

Disability in contexts of poverty also impacts family members (Grech, 2015a, 2019), and feeds back into how disability is shaped and understood, including by disabled people themselves. Disability therefore requires longitudinal and even intergenerational research that is dynamic and responsive to change. I will not be the first, surely, to emphasize that disability is not only a profoundly complex human "condition," but importantly, it challenges any fixities, and this has been amply written about in critical disability studies and anthropology among others (see, e.g., Ginsburg & Rapp, 2020; Goodley, 2016; Grech, 2015a). It has also propelled multiple interdisciplinary endeavors, including with feminist theory, postcolonial studies, critical theory, and childhood studies, among others to seek to help understand a disability that defies any attempts at organizing (see Shakespeare, 2013; Shakespeare & Watson, 2010).

When it comes to how disability is often seen and communicated in disability and development, though, it loses this complexity. This research is often backed by now normalized myths, generalizations, and simplifications, and the perpetuation of almost institutionalized guesstimates (Grech, 2009). To be clear, the need to create a case for disability to be considered in policy and practice remains urgent. It is also amply evident that politicians have limited knowledge of these issues, and that numbers do remain reasonably powerful tools in the hands of activists. There is, though, a more nuanced space, where theory meets practice on the ground. Critically, simplifying and trying to contain disability may have its own consequences, including political and practical ones, such as untargeted and decontextualized support and even disabling responses. Communicating simply is one thing. Simplifying (and ignoring) the complex and heterogeneous is another.

But stepping back a minute, it is perhaps better to explain what this simplified discourse has been. When one reads much of the literature that has appeared over the past two decades in disability and development or from outside, one is immediately faced with statements, easily thrown around, asserting that disabled people in so-called developing countries are hidden, killed, neglected, or live in a state of such extraordinary misery and suffering (see, e.g., Rohwerder, 2018). These lives are depicted as ones lived with little to no support whatsoever. In response, some critique has in fact emerged in recent years, including the charge of epistemic neocolonization (see Grech, 2009, 2011; Meekosha, 2011). Indeed, just like INGO images of charity portraying poor undernourished (often Black) children, disabled people have always been great poster material.

Two narratives—the suffering disabled and the grateful disabled—dominate this literature. The first depicts an image of suffering or loss, focused on what is "taken away" by the impairment in these harsh spaces. It creates discomfort, but for that one second there is a sense of utter conviction: that unknown yet assumed place these disabled subjects are staring from is wholly oppressive and inhumane, they need help, and that help must come from outside that dark space. On occasion we get the name below a photo of a sad looking disabled person in hell-like conditions, accompanied by a description of the help that was given. The name will quickly fizzle out of our memory, but the saving action of the organization lingers long enough to ideally donate some money, while framing and legitimizing the benevolence of the organization and the act. There is much critical literature on what is now referred to as "White savior complex" or a variation of this (see, e.g., Walsh, 2020).

Alternatively, the second image or discourse presents smiling disabled people, depicting feelings of happiness and gratitude following an intervention or gift by a Global North INGO. The smiling disabled person confirms that something has been done, they are happy, and that action is good and desired. Academia, too, sometimes has its own moments. It is not unusual to see a photo of some or other Global North academic or NGO person with a poor disabled subject while on a short research or lecturing stint, someone they will likely never see again, or even remember their name. Yet this serves as a timestamp, like the history on a computer. It once again exudes a sense of benevolence, but as Santos (2007) would put it, a kind of benevolent imperialism. The questions are many, as well as the dilemmas: How can we represent and advocate without recolonizing voices and lives? And who said that they need *us* to represent and intervene? When do we take a back seat and when is it OK to take a step forward? How can people represent themselves? On the contrary, when do people call for others to speak with them? (See Elder and Odoyo [2018] and Grech and Soldatic [2016], for more on these issues in the case of disability.)

At this time, I would like to go back to the key point in this section, which is often the homogenization of disability and its assumed "treatment" in an apparently homogenized Southern space. It would be erroneous to state that some of these narratives may not be true, or that they are wholly untrue. Ill treatment does exist, but it exists everywhere. However, while much disability literature, including models of disability, have emerged and evolved to explain the complexity of disability in a diverse Global North space imbued with complex humanity (see Davis, 2017; Oliver, 1990; Shakespeare, 2013), when it comes to the Global South, it is a different story. On the one hand, statements such as "the poverty of disability in developing countries" or "disabled people are oppressed in the Global South" have become standard and all-encapsulating, covering whole regions and countries, without anyone really contesting them. On the other hand, no one would dare say that disabled people in the Global North, or even in a single country such as the United Kingdom, are ill-treated, oppressed, or live in misery. This is despite the fact that in countries such as the United Kingdom, disabled people continue to be killed or abandoned, including by a reckless and inhumane system of austerity and political indifference (see Healy, 2019). The assumption here is that cruelty and inhuman traits are reserved to those historically framed as the "wretched of the earth," to use Fanon's (1963) words.

Such simplifying yet dominant discourses and postures serve not only to homogenize and demonize the Global South and its subjects but to occlude a number of issues—at least not to treat them with the historical and political nuance they deserve. These include structural problems, geopolitical asymmetries, global inequalities, exploitative trade conditions, colonialism, the dumping of waste in the Global South, and the closing of borders in the United States and the European Union in the current politics of containment, where the body of the migrant is criminalized and rejected. These seem to conveniently be less persistent issues to discuss than the assumed pathologies and lack of the Southern subject.

Vulnerability and the Agency That Withers

Framing the aforementioned arguments requires a connection with the notion of vulnerability and how disability is positioned and even constructed through ideas and discourses around who is deemed vulnerable and what this vulnerability implies. Development actors will often rebut the suggestion that disabled people are not considered or included in international development. They will instead most likely suggest that if not specifically mentioned, they (disabled people) are somehow there alongside the long list of populations framed as "vulnerable." Indeed, reports by international organizations and institutions such as the United Nations (UN) and the World Bank will often have such a list of "vulnerable people." This group is assumed to incorporate women, children, older adults, refugees, and perhaps disabled people, too, in truth anyone who hasn't been quite well served enough by thought and strategy, but who it is important, we need to give the impression are somehow in there. The following excerpts taken from the UN (2019) Global Sustainable Development Report serve as clear examples of such discourse:

> A 2030 Agenda city will be compact and accessible to all, including women, youth, persons with disabilities and other vulnerable populations, with sufficient public transit and active mobility options. (p. xxviii)

> Such management should avoid maldistribution and seek to repair the damage already caused by poor technical, financial and political interventions, especially where indigenous communities and other vulnerable groups are concerned, with concerted efforts to leave no one behind. (p. xxx)

The statements are generally big if not unrealistic, and they are meant to promote an all-encapsulating feel. As is evident in the earlier excerpts, the category "vulnerable" and who fits in is expandable, depending on necessity (of the sentence), but, and more sincerely, to create the impression that no one is left behind. Very evident in many of these reports, though, is that such statements are rarely followed by a clear strategy and commitment to resources as to how this situation will be addressed or redressed, whether in leveling technologically inaccessible spaces or simply poverty reduction for all.

Built on the notion that some are weaker than others, the concept of vulnerability has served lobbyists well in development, to address the needs of those who are more susceptible to stresses and shocks, and for whom these would have dramatic, even life-threatening consequences. This includes a focus on children as populations who are vulnerable to violence, trafficking, or kidnapping, and on older adults who may need health care, but live in isolated areas (see, e.g., EC, 2016). Including disability within the list of vulnerable populations has supported the calls for "inclusive development" or "mainstreaming" and the need to "intervene" in this space, whether through policy or through services (see House of Commons International Development Committee, 2019).

The notion of vulnerability is imbued with ideas around weakness and critically focuses this supposed vulnerability as a characteristic of the person tagged as "vulnerable." This is not to suggest that some families and individuals may not be in a weaker position to weather stresses and shocks. Some suffer disproportionately because of where they live (e.g., in remote environmentally dangerous areas), just like some disabled people with certain physical impairments may be heavily impacted if they cannot farm the land and contribute to covering the food basket (see Grech, 2015a). However, there is little attempt to reengage critically with the notion of vulnerability as a shared human condition, something that binds rather than separates, and whereby surviving despite this vulnerability is a sign of resilience and resistance, the virtue of being human. This is where "investments" (including epistemological) need to perhaps be made. And there are few better places than those of rural extreme poverty where this resilience and will to survive is more evident, lives survived with little or no formal safety nets. Unfortunately, though, disabled people are often those pitched as victims, weak and dependent, where their own bodies are the problem, and with the implication that these need to be intervened in with an assistance specific to them and their needs. As a result, the focus is often on preventing or eliminating problems rather than strengthening what it is that works (Sözer, 2019).

Authors, such as Mirza (2011), for example, have illustrated how while toolkits on disability exist in forced migration, they frequently only emphasize screening, prevention, and treatment, internalizing disability as a personal "problem" that needs to be fixed or removed—"aberrations in need of therapeutic intervention" by others to "return them to the natural order of things, either back into the fold of the nation-state or back into the state of normalcy" (p. 217). Siebers (2008) similarly highlights what he calls an "ideology of ability" that frames disability as a burden or an object of fear, simultaneously banishing it and turning it into a "principle of exclusion" (p. 10). Critically, an approach emphasizing vulnerability leaves the broader system, structures, and barriers that produce so-called vulnerability unprobed, while generalizing the needs and demands of disabled people and perhaps the "solutions," too. The voices of disabled people as agentic bodies continue to be stifled, drowned in a narrative of helplessness and hopelessness.

The notion of vulnerability needs to be challenged while seeking to understand barriers, lives, and experiences through an optic of agency and subjectivity to highlight how disabled people navigate, resist, and negotiate these barriers and ultimately survive. It is in these spaces that support lies. We need to do this, at the very least to ensure that people's own strategies of survival are not trampled upon, discursively or practically. The suggestion here is not to diminish or divert attention away from specific problems confronted by these populations, but instead to understand collective experiences and hurdles in a collective state of human vulnerability—"our common vulnerability" (Turner, 2006, p. 9). A challenging of the vulnerable/nonvulnerable binary is required in order to provide a more nuanced and fluid understanding of human experience.

Although disability may intensify vulnerability to suffering, poverty, and other barriers, it does not necessarily mean that disabled people are weaker or more vulnerable. It also does not mean that this suffering is experienced on more vulnerable terms, or is incremental and dependent on the level of vulnerability (Grech, 2015a). There is indeed much to be learned from pulling disability out of the familiar space of lack and victimhood (a space poor people know too well) and recasting it into a space of resource and determined survival. Only then do we have a clearer and contextualized picture, and a narrative premised on survival and will to live. More practically, it opens a fertile space for understanding what it is that actually works on the ground, as opposed to what we believe disabled people need and want. Devlieger et al. (2013, p. 19 cited in Ginsburg & Rapp, 2020) capture this succinctly:

> the radical presentation of disability as a resource . . . that moves disability out of the realm of victimized people, or as an insurmountable barrier . . . the experience of disability provides the opportunity to enter into networks that recognize strengths of different abilities and that include considering resilience, survival, vulnerability, body knowledge, and performativity as resources.

The Need to Intervene: The Healing Power of "Development" and Rights

Theorists and activists from within, on the edges, or outside of postcolonial theory (see Fanon, 1963; Said, 1993) have long written about the discursive formations of a Southern subject and space that are not only lacking and/or demonized. They are also those, who as a consequence, need an intervention that is inevitable, framed as the "human" thing to do, in other words, for their own good. And this intervention must come from the civilized, White, Global North space, subject, and institutions, "legitimised as a moral endeavour for 'progress'" (Langan, 2018, no. 2), and sanctioned by a long history defining who holds illuminated civility and humanity and has the power to spread these to others.

Disabled bodies are therefore repositioned as neocolonized subjects, or better still, what I have called "neocolonized bodies"—those positioned at the anxious intersection of the discursive, the economic, the cultural and (geo)political, the global, and the local (Grech, 2015b). These are the docile bodies ruled over indefinitely by virtue of and through their specific geopolitical, historical, and ontological location within Global North imaginaries. One critical space for such intervention has been and remains that of international development.

Undeveloping Development?

Disabled bodies have long been intervened in. From the colonial missionaries to organized medical expeditions to more contemporary efforts at prevention and "treatment," interventions from outside are not unfamiliar terrain. Many also contend that the roots of development as we know it lie in the colonial encounter itself (see Kothari, 2006).

Over the past two decades, the need to intervene in disability has been cast as an object of development, hence the discursive turns toward DID. However, and while many, including women, have long contested what it means to be included in development and its consequences (see Moser, 2006), this has not quite happened among those lobbying to include disability in development. Not only is development rarely understood or questioned, but it is also based in assumptions, including that development is necessarily good and not harmful to disabled people. Even more basic questions are rarely posed by those pushing for DID, including whether despite the changes in talk, the development sector is really willing and importantly equipped to include disabled people (see, e.g., UNDP, 2018).

It is difficult to address these issues with the nuance they deserve in this chapter (see Grech, 2016a, for an in-depth discussion). However, several key points are worth mentioning. First, it is clear that those arguing for DID have often not worked in international development, may not know much about the subject and area, and are detached (perhaps knowingly) from the problematic aspects of development, despite the long history of such debates (see, e.g., Escobar, 1995; Horner, 2019). Unfortunately, the need for a convenient narrative supersedes the need to understand what development actually is and whether it may be indeed harmless to disabled people and their families, how and when, and what to do to avert this. Langan (2018, p. 2), in his work on the neocolonial dimensions of development, highlights how "many interventions are in fact undertaken on the basis of a donor (and at times, corporate) language of altruism, despite the fact that the tangible consequences of such action more often than not exacerbate conditions of ill-being and poverty." Some (see Orbie & Delputte, 2019) have recently taken to even claiming that we should do away with development altogether, since, rather than serving the needs of the poorest and those who need it most, it simply accommodates an economic agenda. In response, Bogaert et al. (2019) call for "justice" and not "aid" as the way forward.

Second, if we are pushing to include disabled people in development, it is surely apt, responsible, and important to ask the question: Inclusion into what? Contemplating if and how disability fits within the development narrative and sector raises many issues, including the neoliberal ideologies, tool kits, and practices propping up development, and what the impacts on disabled people may be. From the 1950s model of development as economic growth through to contemporary and hegemonic notions of development as neoliberal globalization, disability has either been invisible, marginal, or constructed as problematic or even inimical to development, generally as a cost (see, e.g., Banks & Polack, 2015; UN, 2018). Economic growth (premised on strong individualized bodies) has and continues to be the main driver of development, premised on hard work, and where resources are allocated to realize predetermined development goals in a short time span. More basically, where development means quick results, disabled people may become invisible, or are seen as too "slow," "unproductive," or "burdensome" (see Grech, 2011; Wolbring et al., 2013).

Overall, when numbers dominate the research, subjective noneconomic dimensions are too easily sacrificed. Those who need more time, or where "development" may not be too quickly seen and enumerated, can all too often slip out of sight and out of mind. This means that development projects will more readily undertake the construction of a highly visible school rather than investing in less visible programs that ensure education is inclusive of all children backed by adequate training and resources. Disabled people, as well as those entrapped in chronic poverty who "require extended time and resources, fundamental organizational changes (including ideological ones), flexibility, and who may not produce immediately visible and quantifiable results over the short term . . . are (re)constructed as *the problem*, responsible for their own predicament, and even unreceptive and resistant to development efforts" (Grech, 2016a, p.b, 15, italics in original).

These debates need to be had, and they need to be sparked by those lobbying for inclusive development, to understand what it is they are pushing for and how. But, and importantly, to do this, they need to understand international development, its history, its discourse, and its practices. This requires not only time and theoretical investments but also collaborations with others working inside development, who can help inform DID, and importantly provide informed cross-sectoral support.

A Decolonizing Approach: Some Insights and Tentative Routes

This chapter has addressed a small number of critical issues emerging from attempts at speaking about disability in the Global South. These are only a few of a myriad complex and often interconnected issues that arise. At this juncture, it is important to reflect on what a decolonizing approach might mean. The word is increasingly thrown around (including here) but often with little engagement as to what this might mean in practice.

A decolonizing approach forms the core part of what I have called a critical global disability studies (CGDS), a project that "is transdisciplinary, transboundary, open to debate and, before anything else, willing to decolonise debates" (Grech, 2016b, p. 17). It is also a project that is "(self)reflexive, emphasises uncertainty and contingency, and encourages a great deal of critical questioning, learning and the challenging of epistemological, ontological and practical fixities" (p. 17). Importantly, and cutting across any attempts at doing this, is the critical and urgent need to make "present and credible, suppressed, marginalized and disaccredited knowledges" (Santos, 2007, p. 16 cited in Grech, 2016a, p. 17), especially those of disabled people and their families and those living in poverty—the real experts in their own lives. Our role is that of learning, and supporting the articulation of these voices and their own priorities on their own terms.

Decolonizing disability and development, in line with a decolonial approach, means challenging and dislocating an array of assumptions. These include assumptions made about the Global South, the treatment of disability within, and also about the assumed "healing" powers of international development and rights, not least to ensure that any development practice does not harm or trample upon people's own means of survival, that is, their own strengths. We must challenge and shift the fixities in our discourse and practices to understand their boundedness to history, and the structural, geopolitical, and other factors and processes that persistently prop them up. Within our work, a critical disability studies lens has helped with this, including interdisciplinarity, reflected in a growing body of critical work on disability in the Global South.

A decolonizing approach focuses on agency and shared vulnerability, turning attention away momentarily from the disabled person and on to the context, the structural and other barriers, and to find and understand within these agencies, the power to survive. We need to focus on strengths, rather than personal deficits, and to build upon these. We need genuine participatory and locally owned approaches to produce knowledge *with* people as genuine partners. We need a conceptual approach prioritizing the critical role that disabled people play in interpreting, living, resisting, and reframing discourse, policy, and practice, and hence addressing power dynamics as well as finding solutions for their own lives.

Finally, we require an approach that understands context with the complexity it deserves, alongside the heterogeneity and dynamic nature of disability across space and time. This needs not only investments of time but also interactions between disciplines and fields of studies, to understand aspects such as local informal economies, agricultural cycles in rural areas, water systems, local health care services, and so much more, and to start anew in every single place. These are ultimately the spaces where disability is lived and survived, what I call the "spaces of poverty" (Grech, 2015a)—and, I would add, the "spaces of resources and resilience."

NOTES

1. See https://www.un.org/development/desa/disabilities/convention-on-the-rights-of-pers ons-with-disabilities.html for full list.
2. See, for example, much of the work by the World Health Organization (WHO): (https:// www.who.int/news-room/fact-sheets/detail/disability-and-health

REFERENCES

ADD. (2016). *The value of mainstreaming: Why disability-inclusive programming is good for development.* ADD.

Alatas, S. H. (2003). Academic dependency and the global division of labour in the social sciences. *Current Sociology, 51,* 599–633

Abosede Durokifa, A., & Chikata Ijeoma, E. (2018). Neo-colonialism and Millennium Development Goals (MDGs) in Africa: A blend of an old wine in a new bottle. *African Journal of Science, Technology, Innovation and Development, 10*(3), 355–366.

Banks, L. M., & Polack, S. (2015). *The economic costs of exclusion and gains of inclusion of people with disabilities: Evidence from low and middle income countries.* CBM.

Banks, L. M., Kuper, H., & Polack, S. (2017). Poverty and disability in low- and middle-income countries: A systematic review. *PLoS ONE, 13*(9). https://pubmed.ncbi.nlm.nih.gov/29267388/

Bezzina, L. (2019). *Disability and development in Burkina Faso: Critical perspectives.* Palgrave Macmillan.

Bogaert, K., Carlier, J., De Smet, B., Casier, M., Vanden Boer, D & Mazijn, B. (2019). "Justice" not "aid" for the Global South. http://www.developmentresearch.eu/?p=512

Castro-Gómez, S., & Grosfoguel, R. (2007). *El giro decolonial. Reflexiones para una diversidad epistémica más allá del capitalismo global.* Siglo del Hombre Editores.

Cooke, B., & Kothari, U. (2001). *Participation: The new tyranny?* Zed Books.

Dados, N., & Connell, R. (2012). The Global South. *Contexts, 11*(1), 12–13.

Davis, L. (Ed.) (2017). *The disability studies reader* (5th ed.). Routledge

Devlieger, P., Miranda-Galarza, B., Brown, S. E., & Strickfaden, M. (Eds.). (2013). *Rethinking disability: World perspectives in culture and society.* Garent.

DFID. (2018). DFID's Strategy for Disability Inclusive Development 2018-23. DFID.

EC. (2016). Vulnerability up close: An exploratory study into the vulnerability of children to human trafficking. EC.

Elder, B. C.. & Odoyo, K. O. (2018). Multiple methodologies: Using community-based participatory research and decolonizing methodologies in Kenya. *International Journal of Qualitative Studies in Education, 31*(4), 293–311.

Escobar. A. (1995). *Encountering development: The making and unmaking of the third world.* Princeton University Press.

Fanon, F. (1963). *The wretched of the earth.* Grove Press.

Flint, A., & Meyer zu Natrup, C. (2019). Aid and development by design: Local solutions to local problems. *Development in Practice, 29*(2), 208–219,

Friedner, M. (2017). How the disabled body unites the national body: Disability as "feel good" diversity in urban India. *Contemporary South Asia, 25*(4), 347–363.

Ginsburg, F., & Rapp, R. (2020). Disability/anthropology: Rethinking the parameters of the human: An introduction to Supplement 21. *Current Anthropology, 61*(S21), S4–S15.

Global Partnership for Education. (2016). Children with disabilities face the longest road to education. https://www.globalpartnership.org/blog/children-disabilities-face-longest-road-education

Goodley, D. (2016). *Disability studies: An interdisciplinary introduction.* SAGE Publications.

Goodley, D., Liddiard, K. & Runswick-Cole, K. (2018) Feeling Disability: Theories of Affect and Critical Disability Studies. *Disability & Society, 33*(2), 197–217.

Grech, S. (2009). Disability, poverty and development: Critical reflections on the majority world debate. *Disability & Society, 24*(6), 771–784.

Grech, S. (2011). Recolonising debates or perpetuated coloniality? Decentering the spaces of disability, development and community in the global South. *International Journal of Inclusive Education, 15*(1), 87–100.

Grech, S. (2015a). *Disability and poverty in the Global South: Renegotiating development in Guatemala.* Palgrave Macmillan.

Grech, S. (2015b). Decolonising Eurocentric disability studies: Why colonialism matters in the disability and global South debate. *Social Identities, 21*(1), 6–21.

Grech, S. (2016a). Disability and development: Critical (dis)connections. In J. Gruger & D. Hammett (Eds.), *The Palgrave handbook of international development* (pp. 513–534). Palgrave Macmillan.

Grech, S. (2016b). Disability and development: Critical connections, gaps and contradictions. In S. Grech & K. Soldatic (Eds.), *Disability in the Global South: The critical handbook* (pp. 3–19). Springer.

Grech, S. (2019). Disabled families: The impacts of disability and care on family labour and poverty in rural Guatemala. *Societies, 9*(4), 1–16.

Grech, S., & Soldatic, K. (Eds.) (2016). *Disability in the Global South: The critical handbook.* Springer.

Groce, N., Kett, M., Lang, R., & Trani, J. (2011). Disability and poverty: the need for a more nuanced understanding of implications for developing policy and practice. *Third World Quarterly, 32*(8), 1493–1513. https://doi.org/10.1080/01436597.2011.604520.

Hall, S. (1996). The West and the rest: Discourse and power. In S. Hall D. Held, D. Hubert & K. Thompson et al. (Eds.), *Modernity: An introduction to modern docieties* (pp. 184–224). Blackwell.

Healy, J. C. (2019). "It spreads like a creeping disease": Experiences of victims of disability hate crimes in austerity Britain. *Disability & Society, 35*(2), 176–200.

Horner, R. (2019). Towards a new paradigm of global development? Beyond the limits of international development. *Progress in Human Geography, 44*(3), 415–436.

House of Commons International Development Committee. (2019). DFID's work on disability-inclusive development: Thirteenth Report of Session 2017–19. House of Commons.

ICAI. (2018). DFID's approach to disability in development A rapid review. ICAI.

Ingstad, B., & Whyte, S. R. (1995). *Disability and culture.* University of California Press.

Ingstad, B., & Whyte, S. R. (2007). *Disability in local and global worlds.* University of California Press.

Kamenopoulou, L. (2020). Decolonising inclusive education: An example from a research in Colombia. *Disability and the Global South, 7*(1), 1792–1812.

Kothari, U. (2006). From colonialism to development: Reflections of former colonial officers. *Commonwealth and Comparative Politics, 44*(1), 118–136.

Langan, M. (2018). *Neo-colonialism and the poverty of 'development' in Africa.* Palgrave Macmillan.

McMichael, P. (2016). *Development and social change: A global perspective* (6th ed.). SAGE Publications.

Meekosha, H. (2011). Decolonising disability: Thinking and acting globally. *Disability & Society, 26*(6), 667–682.

Mignolo, W. (2010). Introduction: Coloniality of power and de-colonial thinking. In W. D. Mignolo & A. Escobar (Eds.), *Globalization and the decolonial option* (pp. 1–21). Routledge.

Mirza, M. (2011). Disability and humanitarianism in refugee camps: The case for a travelling supranational disability praxis. *Third World Quarterly, 32*(8), 1527–1536.

Mitra, S. (2018). *Disability, health and human development.* Palgrave Macmillan.

Moser, C. (2006). Has gender mainstreaming failed? A comment on international development agency experiences in the South. *International Feminist Journal of Politics, 7*(4), 576–590.

Moyer, J. D., & Hedden, S. (2020) Are we on the right path to achieve the sustainable development goals? *World Development, 127*, 1–13

Niewohner, J., Pierson, S., & Meyers, S. J. (2019) "Leave no one behind"? The exclusion of persons with disabilities by development NGOs. *Disability & Society, 35*(7), 1171–1176.

Nguyen, T. (2018). Critical disability studies at the edge of global development: Why do we need to engage with Southern theory? *Canadian Journal of Disability Studies*, 7(1), 1–25.

ODI. (2020). How to confront race and racism in international development. ODI. https://www.odi.org/blogs/17407-how-to-confront-race-and-racism-international-development

Oliver, M. (1990). *The politics of disablement*. Palgrave Macmillan.

Orbie, J., & Delputte, S. (2019). Let's abolish the EU Commissioner for Development. EUObserver. https://euobserver.com/opinion/144841

Pinilla-Roncancio, M. (2015). Disability and poverty: Two related conditions. A review of the literature. *Revista de la Facultad de Medicina*, 63(1), 113–123.

Pinilla-Roncancio, M., & Alkire, S. (2020). How poor are people with disabilities? Evidence based on the Global Multidimensional Poverty Index. *Journal of Disability Policy Studies*, 31(4), 206–216.

Pisani, M., & Grech, S. (2015). Disability and forced migration: Critical intersectionalities. *Disability and the Global South*, 2(1), 421–441.

Rohwerder, B. (2018). *Disability stigma in developing countries*. K4D.

Said, E. (1993). *Culture and imperialism*. Knopf.

Santos, B. (2007). Beyond abyssal thinking: From global lines to ecologies of knowledges. *Eurozine*, 1–33.

Shakespeare, T. (2013). *Disability rights and wrongs revisited*. Routledge.

Shakespeare, T., & Watson, N. (2010). Beyond models: Understanding the complexity of disabled people's lives. In G. Scambler & S. Scambler (Eds.), *New directions in the sociology of chronic and disabling conditions* (pp. 57–76). Palgrave Macmillan.

Siebers, T. (2008). *Disability theory*. University of Michigan Press.

Soldatic, K., & Grech, S. (2014). Transnationalising disability studies: Rights, justice and impairment. *Disability Studies Quarterly*, 34(2) https://dsq-sds.org/article/view/4249

Soldatic, K., Melboe, L., Kermit, P., & Somers, K. (2018). Challenges in global Indigenous—Disability comparative research, or, why nation-state political histories matter. *Disability and the Global South*, 5(2), 1450–1471.

Sözer, H. (2019). Humanitarianism with a neo-liberal face: Vulnerability intervention as vulnerability redistribution. *Journal of Ethnic and Migration Studies*, 46(11), 2163–2180.

Staples, J. (2020). Decolonising disability studies? Developing South Asia–specific approaches to understanding disability. In M. Mehrotra (Ed.), *Disability studies in India*. (pp. 1–17). Springer.

Tuhiwai-Smith, L. (1999). *Decolonizing methodologies: Research and indigenous peoples*. Zed Books.

Turner, B. S. (2006). *Vulnerability and human rights*. Pennsylvania State University Press.

UN. (2006). *Convention on the Rights of Persons with Disabilities*. UN.

UN. (2018). Disability and Development Report: Realizing the Sustainable Development Goals by, for and with persons with disabilities. https://www.un.org/development/desa/disabilities/wp-content/uploads/sites/15/2018/12/UN-Flagship-Report-Disability.pdf

UN. (2019). *Global Sustainable Report 2019: The future is now—Science for achieving sustainable development*. UN.

UNDP. (2018). *Disability inclusive development in UNDP guidance and entry points*. UNDP.

van Gent, S. (2017). Beyond buzzwords: What is "inclusive development"? Synthesis report August 2017 ASC. INCLUDE Secretariat.

Walsh, G. M. (2020). Challenging the hero narrative: Moving towards reparational citizenship education. *Societies, 10*, 34.

Watson, N., & Vehmas. S. (Eds.) (2020). *Routledge handbook of disability studies*. Routledge.

WHO and World Bank. (2011). *World report on disability*. WHO.

Wilson, K. (2012). *Race, racism and development: Interrogating history, discourse and practice*. Zed Books.

Wolbring, G., Mackay, R., Rybchinski, T. & Noga, J. (2013). Disabled people and the post-2015 development goal agenda through a disability studies lens. *Sustainability, 5*(10), 4152–4182

Yeo, R. (2005). Disability, poverty and the new development agenda. London: Disability Knowledge and Research (KaR)

CHAPTER 9

DISABILITY, GENDER, AND HEALTH CARE IN THE GLOBAL SOUTH

AIZAN SOFIA AMIN

INTRODUCING DEBATES IN DISABILITY, GENDER, AND HEALTH CARE STUDIES

THIS chapter seeks to explore how disability status intersects with gender in the health care experiences of disabled women in the Global South. To address this question, an intersectional framework of disability feminist and critical realist approaches is employed to examine the complex intersections between disability and gender experiences in health care. The chapter begins with a discussion on debates in disability, gender, and health care studies. Later, the chapter conceptualizes the intersectionality of disability and gender in the Global South from the viewpoint of the disability feminist framework and critical realist approaches. Following this, the chapter maps some fundamental issues underlying gendered experiences in health care. The chapter then discusses findings from disability and gender research in Malaysia, which highlights how disability status intersect with gender in three main themes: access to modern medicine, the role of traditional medicine, and sexual abuse in health care settings.

The World Health Organization (WHO) and the World Bank, in their World Report on Disability, estimate that over one billion or 15% of the world population have some form of disability (WHO, 2011). WHO estimates that the prevalence of disability is more common among the poor and those living in lower-income/developing countries where 80% of disabled people live (WHO, 2011). However, Pettinicchio and Maroto (2021) recently found that the estimation process of people with disabilities across the globe is more complicated to measure. Therefore, disability should be defined within a particular society from an understanding of how local people think and respond to disability and impairment to ensure effective intervention plans can be prepared (Coleridge, 2000).

What is suitable for a given society in the west may not be appropriate for a particular society in the east. For instance, societies in the Global South may have different and pessimistic attitudes toward disability compared to the Global North. Swartz and Bantjes (2016, p. 23) argue that "in many cases, impairments, like ill-health, do not just 'happen'—they are the consequence of social and political arrangements. And the consequences of impairment and ill health are equally socially mediated." Therefore, disability definition is socially constructed and may vary across societies. A complete understanding of disability and gender experiences requires localized investigation that incorporates the economic and socio-historical assumptions and the circumstances of a particular society.

In relation to gender experiences, females of all ages with disability are recognized to be among the most vulnerable and marginalized groups in society (United Nations General Assembly, 2000). Furthermore, disability is found to be more widespread amongst women than men (WHO, 2011). The Global Burden of Diseases study estimated that females have a higher percentage of disability than males (WHO, 2011). Despite this, feminist disability writers argue that the issues of disabled women have been neglected within disability studies and feminist theories (see, e.g., Morris, 1993; Begum, 1992; Thomas, 1999; Garland-Thomson, 2002; Ghai, 2002). As such, it is crucial to incorporate the agenda of disabled women into disability and feminist research and not to be excluded from mainstream society.

In addition, the personal experience of impairment and gender are equally crucial to social oppression and should not be excluded from the disability research (Morris, 1991, 1993). Often, the issues faced by disabled women are different from those faced by disabled men (Be, 2012), and thus women's experiences should be explored from a feminist epistemology (Stanley & Wise, 1990). Disabled women across the globe may experience their lives differently, they are generally subjected to more significant and more numerous disadvantages than disabled men. They encounter not only disabling barriers but also gender discrimination (WHO, 2011).

Besides social oppression and disadvantages experience by disabled men and women, disabled people across the globe have poorer access to health care and lower health outcomes than non-disabled people as indicated by the World Health Organization and the World Bank in their World Report on Disability (WHO, 2011). The health disparities are more common in low-income countries where most people live. Among the health disparities experienced by disabled people are related to greater risks for nonintentional injuries, premature death, access to health care services, barriers to sexual and reproductive health services, and greater risk of HIV infection (WHO, 2011).

In some low- and middle-income countries, health policies are not inclusive to disabled people (MacLachlan et al., 2012). Consequently, many disabled people especially women with disabilities are at a greater disadvantage in getting adequate health care services that can intensify their impairment. Furthermore, with the current global health situation caused by the COVID-19 pandemic outbreak, the needs of disabled people in health care must be highly considered to ensure that they are not excluded from global health. Thus, this chapter focuses on the question of how disability status intersects with gender in the global South from the feminist disability framework and critical realist approach that will be discussed next.

Conceptualizing the Intersectionality of Disability and Gender in the Global South

The complexity of disability and gender experiences require a multifaceted level of analysis in understanding the intersectionality of both in the Global South. While the incidence of disability is higher in developing countries or the Global South, empirical research involving disabled women from this part of the world is scarce (Grech, 2009; WHO, 2011; Shakespeare, 2012). It is crucial to understand the disability and gender experiences from the Global South perspective while incorporating empirical research within the local context of the developing countries. Thus, this section conceptualizes the intersectionality of disability and gender in the Global South from the feminist disability framework and critical realist approach.

Since the 1980s, feminism has played a significant role in shaping disability studies (Thomas, 2007; Be, 2012). Morris and other disabled feminists advocate for the documentation of disabled people's experiences to develop a shared understanding of what it is to be disabled. They refuse to distinguish between "the personal and the political which is strongly utilized in the emancipatory paradigm, which denies the reality of disability" (Watson, 2000; Thomas, 2007). They applied the feminist slogan "the personal is political" in researching disability (Morris, 1992) in opposition to the social model approach, which focuses on the material, social and political, rather than "personal experiences" (Oliver, 1996; Finkelstein, 1996).

Feminists argue that disability studies should embrace the physical and emotional realities involved in living with impaired bodies, including pain, fear of dying, and coping with physical change (Morris, 1996; Wendell, 1996; Garland-Thomson, 1997). Feminists also emphasize "publishing research-based and biographical material detailing personal struggles with both impairment and disablism" (Thomas, 2007). The feminist approach has made essential contributions to disability studies which acknowledge that disabled people do not represent a homogenous social group (Shakespeare, 2006: Thomas, 2007) but rather that the experiences of disablism and living with impairment are intersected "with other cultural markers of social 'difference': gender, 'race,' sexuality, age and class" (Thomas, 2007, p. 70). These aspects of research are vital in understanding disability in the Global South, which is made up of different dimensions of socio-cultural facets of disability experiences and identities.

For example, in ancient cultures, disability was directly observed as something related to sin and evil (Mackelprang & Salsgiver, 1999). As perceived in Indian society, disability may be associated with bad karma (evil deeds) done in a present or a past life (Yamney & Greenwood, 2004; Vidya, 2011). Disabled women in India may also be subjected to more significant social disadvantages for being disabled, being a woman, and coming from a lower-class family. Jewish society also has a different attitude toward disabled people. Many people with impairment and illness are considered symbols of offense, which accounted for them being exiled from the community (Barnes & Mercer, 2010). Researching disability thus requires careful attention to the complex interaction between different facets of a given culture or society.

In addition to the feminist framework, the critical realist approach offers a broader perspective into researching disability in the global South. It draws from the feminist literature and the works of Watson (2012a, b), Shakespeare (2006, 2014), and Shakespeare and Watson (2001, 2010). Critical realism emphasizes a non-reductionist perspective (Danermark & Gellerstedt, 2004; Bhaskar & Danermark, 2006), focusing on both structural barriers to inclusion and the individual agency that gives value to the different dimensions of disability experience (Shakespeare, 2006). This approach emphasizes that phenomena exist whether or not we have conscious knowledge of them, yet the existence of phenomena (ontology) should not be conflated with the knowledge about them (epistemology) (Thomas, 2007; Watson, 2012a; Shakespeare, 2006). For example, impairment has always existed and has its experiential truth even when we have different opinions or attitudes across cultures (Shakespeare, 2006). As such, we cannot deny the existence of impairment and its experiential reality as it is embodied within us.

In addition, agency and structure are considered equally important as they are shaped and reshaped by one another across time (Williams, 1999). A critical realist approach thus allows us to move beyond debates about disability and impairment, how they should be defined, and the relationship between impairment and disablement (Watson, 2012a). This non-reductionist approach enables us to explore the experiential reality of impairment and observe the possible daily problems of living with impairment (Scambler, 2005).

Therefore, the critical realists' approaches seek to explore different levels of analysis in the complex disability experience as Williams (1999) stresses that disability is an emergent condition that involves the biological reality of physiological impairment, structural conditioning, and socio-cultural interaction. Disability is thus being examined from different angles of analysis and not from a single lens of inquiry. Danermark and Gellerstedt (2004) argue that inequalities to disabled people can be understood neither as generated by solely cultural mechanisms nor by solely cultural socio-economical mechanisms or by biological mechanisms.

Disability can also be understood as an interaction between individual (intrinsic) factors and structural (extrinsic) factors (Shakespeare, 2014). The intrinsic factors may include the nature and severity of impairment, personality, individual attitudes, abilities, and qualities. The extrinsic factors can be the attitudes and reactions of others, environment, economy, policy and cultures (Shakespeare, 2006, 2014). Contextual factors (extrinsic) may influence the internal factors (intrinsic): "impairment may be caused by poverty or war, personality may be influenced by upbringing and culture, etc." (Shakespeare, 2014, p. 75). For example, a girl in India may become blind due to trachoma because her family is too poor to get her antibiotics. She may not have a formal education because of her family's poverty and a cultural upbringing that places less value on females' education than males. As a result of her impairment and low education, she may have restricted opportunities for broader economic and social activities. Therefore, disability is always an interaction between different contextual and intrinsic factors that vary across individuals, cultures, and locations.

Likewise, disability can be examined within a stratified or laminated system (Collier, 1998), in which Watson (Watson, 2012a, b) cites the work of Bhaskar and Danermark (2006). Therefore, disability can be explored at different physical, biological, psychological, psycho-social and emotional, socio-economic, cultural, and normative levels. This stratified system of analysis offers a practical understanding of the disability experience. Thus, the feminist and critical realist approaches provide valuable insight into understanding disabled women's lives in Global South countries and this chapter uses Malaysia as a case study. These two paradigms offer a more comprehensive understanding of the health care experiences of disabled women with mobility impairment within the many aspects of Malaysian society: including the exploration of both the agency and structures. Therefore, both approaches are fundamental in providing an alternative framework for disability and gender research in the global South.

POSITIONING DISABILITY AND GENDER IN HEALTH CARE SETTING

As previously noted, many disabled people have poorer access to health care and lower health outcomes than non-disabled people especially for those living in developing countries (WHO, 2011). It is argued that disability has often been associated with poverty, but few empirical studies examine the relationship between these two in developing countries (Groce et al., 2011; Braithwaite & Mont, 2009). Sen (2009) and Elwan (1999, p. i) suggests a two-way relationship between disability and poverty as "disability may increase the risk of poverty and poverty may increase the risk of disability" (Sen, 2009). The World Bank indicates that poverty and disability have a strong mutual relationship in which poverty may lead to disability through poor health care, malnutrition, and difficult living conditions (The World Bank Group, 2013).

The World Bank Poverty Assessment review found that many developing countries acknowledge that there is a strong relationship between poverty and disability but little data regarding this phenomenon is available (Braithwaite & Mont, 2009). The World Bank further estimated in 1999 that in developing countries, about 20% of those who are living on or below poverty line were disabled people (Levinsohn, 2002). For example, in Uganda, "at least 2.4 million disabled people remain poor" (Lwanga-Ntale, 2003, p. 1) this shows that disabled people are liable to live in poverty or that poor people are at greater risk of developing an impairment, especially in the Global South.

Low economic status hinders people from acquiring proper medical treatment, prevents them from having sufficient nutrition (especially for children), and makes them vulnerable to many dangers by living in poor neighborhoods. Likewise, disability may herald the onset of poverty by preventing disabled people from full participation in social and economic activities (WHO, 2011). For instance, disabled children have less opportunity to attend school (Filmer, 2008; Jonsson & Wiman, 2001) and they may become an economic burden on families and society (Jonsson & Wiman, 2001, p. 1). Exclusion from education may reduce employment opportunities among disabled youth and thus increase the risk of poverty. Disabled people are also more likely to experience unemployment and discrimination in employment (WHO, 2011). Furthermore, they may receive low wages, marginal promotion prospects and encounter a lack of access to transportation. As such we can observe that intersectionality between disability and poverty may not only impede the opportunity for adequate health care but also may have profound impact on the opportunities for accessible education, employment, and transportation.

Moreover, the impact of disability on disabled women requires particular attention especially for those living in the Global South countries. For instance, disabled women are not only subjected to the strong traditional gender roles and stereotypes within society, but they also have less access to healthcare and rehabilitation services (Thomas & Thomas, 1998; Nosek & Simmons, 2007). This is most apparent in developing countries like for instance Malaysia, with a diverse geographical population. Although the accessibility of health care to the general population is relatively adequate, rural populations, especially in the largest states like Sarawak, Sabah and Pahang, have limited access to the local health facilities (NGO Shadow Report Group, 2005). Hospitals or local clinics are usually located in highly populated areas. People living far from the heart of medical facilities may have limited access to proper medical treatment and information, especially mobility impairments. The Ministry of Women Family and Community Development reported to CEDAW (First and Second Report) in 2004 that some groups of women (disabled/migrant/aboriginal or indigenous women) are marginalized regarding access to health services and facilities (NGO Shadow Report Group, 2005).

Moreover, the government does not have gender-disaggregated data and analysis on health care issues although women are more likely to develop impairments later due to women having a higher life expectancy than men in Malaysia (Department of Statistics Malaysia, 2011). The NGO Shadow Report Group (2005) argues that there is a critical need to have gender-disaggregated data and analysis for the Malaysian population. The health data collected for the country has not been subjected to gender analysis despite it being utilized in identifying the prevalence of common diseases for males and females for intervention and treatment planning at the national level. For example, the incidence of hypertension, psychiatric morbidity, and cancers (all sites) was more common among females than males in the National Health and Morbidity Survey II (Ministry of Health,

1997). Therefore, Malaysian women may be subjected to a greater risk of acquiring disability at a later age without an appropriate intervention and treatment plan at the national level due to the absence of gender-disaggregated data and analysis.

In addition, disabled women in Malaysia may experience socio-cultural barriers to proper health care treatment and rehabilitation. Some women may be unable to leave the house without their husband's permission, lack alternative childcare arrangements, or lack education (NGO Shadow Report Group, 2005). Likewise, many women in a traditional society such as India, especially those who live in a village, do not go out of their houses to seek health care assistance if the care provider is a male (Thomas & Thomas, 1998). Thus, the cultural attitudes toward gender, coupled with a lack of women practicing in rehabilitation professions, may dissuade disabled women from receiving adequate assistive devices and treatments (Thomas & Thomas, 1998; The World Bank Group, 2013). Moreover, McFarlane (2004) and Young et al. (1997) argue that disabled women with physical impairments are at higher risk of being abused sexually and physically by their healthcare providers. As a result, such conditions may restrict equal access and opportunity for adequate health care services for disabled women especially those from the Global South.

Therefore, this chapter presents the evidence from Malaysian disabled women's health care accounts that observe the complex intersections of disability with gender, poverty, rurality and culture from the feminist disability and critical realist perspectives.

RESEARCH METHODOLOGY

The findings presented in this chapter draw from empirical research into the lived experiences of disabled women when accessing health care in Malaysia. This study was conducted with reflexivity processes to integrate self-awareness and thoughts throughout the research process (Etherington, 2004). "Reflexive analysis in research encompasses continual evaluation of subjective responses, intersubjective dynamics, and the research process itself" (Finlay, 2002, p. 532). The interpretation of the data is based on the author's expertise and experience as a Malaysian woman with a physical disability. The author shares a similar position to the research participants—a Malaysian woman with mobility impairment (an insider)—albeit she has some differences with the participants (an outsider). Some feminist researchers outlined the importance of a reflexive sociology in which sociologists locate their own social identity and values within their work (Roberts, 1990; Stanley & Wise, 1993).

Drawing on a feminist approach "writing the self" (Thomas, 1999) and biographical research "telling my own story" (Roberts, 2002), the author felt committed to locating her role in this research as a disabled Malaysian woman studying and reconstructing the lives of Malaysian disabled women. It is fundamental to provide readers with an insight into the subjective understandings and interpretations across the research from the initial design to the final write up. Also, it is important to make visible the author's identity and reflect on how her personal story (e.g., impairment, gender, social class, ethnicity, and religion) may influence this research at the personal and political level whilst adhering to the feminist methodology on the principle of making the personal political (Morris, 1992). Although the author's role as a researcher may have been perceived as that of an "insider" to those participating in this research, at times she also had an "outsider" position in some aspects of the participant's life story. Both roles are important to the research as Dwyer and Buckel (2009) argue that the personhood of the researcher both as an insider and an outsider is important and an ever-present aspect in the research.

This qualitative study was conducted in Peninsular Malaysia: Kuala Lumpur, Selangor, and Negeri Sembilan. However, most informants formerly lived in other states in Malaysia, all over the country, including states in Borneo. The data of this study were collected from in-depth interviews with 33 Malaysian women with physical (mobility) impairments. The ethics approval was obtained in August 2011 from the ethics committee—College of Social Sciences, University of Glasgow. The interview was conducted from October 2011 to March 2012 (6 months) in Malaysia. The participants were recruited via six non-governmental organizations (NGOs) for disabled people, disabled friends' networking, and snowballing.

The research used a narrative approach (Creswell, 2007) that explores the participants' lived experiences on their access to health care. For 6 months, 17 Malay, 8 Chinese, and 8 Indian women were interviewed twice. The time interval between the first and second interviews were 3 to 6 months. The in-depth interviews were conducted twice to give space to the research participants to share experiences that are more sensitive in the second interview. They were interviewed in a conducive environment, such as at the non-governmental organization (NGO) premises or at the research participants' homes.

The research participants' ages ranged from 21 to 57 years old. The participants were physically impaired due to spinal cord injury, polio, spinal muscular atrophy, muscular dystrophy, Marfan syndrome, systemic lupus erythematosus, traumatic brain injury, gestational diabetes mellitus, osteosarcoma, spina bifida, teratoma, dysmelia, leg amputation or leg injury. In terms of the highest education level, 16 women have skills certificates; 8 attended secondary school, 5 have a diploma, 3 have a master's degree, and 1 a doctorate. Of the 33 women, 23 are working, and 10 are not. Table 9.1 presents an overview of the participants' demographic characteristics.

Most of the women (28 of the 33) were born and raised in rural areas and 15 of the 17 participants who were Malay came from villages, estates or rural areas. Similarly, 7 out of the 8 of the Chinese interviewees formerly lived in rural areas, and 6 out of the 8 Indian participants lived in estates or rural areas. People from the rural communities in Malaysia tend to have limited access to information, facilities and developments compared to those living in big cities. Many of the women later moved to urban areas, which is reflected in the rest of the Malaysian community since 1957 due to the rapid population migration from rural regions to urban centres (Tarmiji et al., 2012). For instance, in 1950, only about 20% of the country's total population lived in urban areas: this had risen dramatically to 71% by 2010 (Department of Statistics Malaysia, 2011). Thus, most women grew up in low socio-economic conditions, which hindered their access to adequate health care.

Table 9.1 Overview of the participants' demographic characteristics

Characteristics	Items	Frequency (N=33)
Age	20–29	6
	30–39	10
	40–49	11
	50–59	6
Ethnicity	Malay	17
	Chinese	8
	Indian	8
Religious denomination	Muslim	19
	Christian	3
	Buddhist	6
	Hindu	5
Highest education level	Secondary school	8
	Skills certificate	16
	Diploma	5
	Masters	3
	Doctorate	1
Employment status	Working	23
	Not working	10
Assistive equipment	Wheelchair	23
	Crutch (s)	4
	Prosthetic (s)	1
	Calliper (s)	1
	None	4

The data gathered from the in-depth interviews were transcribed and then organized in computer software—QSR NVivo 9—and analyzed using thematic analysis (Bazeley, 2007; Creswell, 2007; Gibbs, 2011). After several transcription readings, the researcher constructed a list of codes/categories in the NVivo 9 system. Some codes were combined with other codes, removed, or renamed after re-checking transcripts multiple times. Three major themes were finally identified, analyzed and discussed: i) access to modern medicine, ii) the role of traditional medicine, and iii) sexual abuse in health care settings that are further explained in the next section.

FINDINGS

Since its independence in 1957 from Britain 64 years ago, Malaysia has gradually improved its health care system and now medical care is dominated by Western bio-medicine (Kamil & Khoo, 2006). Traditional medicine is also widely practiced by much of the population (Ministry of Health, 2005; Kuno, 2007). This examination recognizes that the women interviewed pursue treatment within this varied health care context.

Access to Modern Medicine

Access to modern (Western) health care was difficult for many of the participants. There were many reasons for this, including finance, geography, poor transport, and cultural influences. For example, Jiaying[1] (45, Chinese, crutch user, rural) described how her family's poverty prevented her from getting modern medical treatment:

> From what I learned from my mother, I got Polio because of a high fever. I was about one year old at that time. My mother had very little money because she was only a rubber tapper. My father was a carpenter. Our life was so hard at that time because I had many brothers and sisters. I have 14 siblings. So, when they knew that I fell sick, they took me to see a Buddhist monk. They never took me to see doctors, but they always took me to pray.

Poverty was not the only barrier to accessing modern health care among the participants; rurality was another factor, as described by Farah (31, Malay, wheelchair user, rural) who lived in a village and had limited transportation:

> I never went to the hospital. It's quite far. My mother is poor. We were using a bicycle to travel from one place to another. That's why we never thought to go to the hospital; never going for any treatment. I went to see a doctor at the vocational center for disabled people while I was studying there.

In the early years after independence, the Malaysian health care system was predominantly focused on catering to the needs of people in urban areas rather than those in rural communities (Chen 1981 cited in Kamil & Teng, 2002). "Rural health services were largely non-existent and, if available, were based in health centers located in small country towns" (Kamil & Teng, 2002, p. 99). Therefore, people in rural areas had limited access to the health care services provided by the state. This was confirmed by many of the women interviewed who lived far from the city.

The absence of health care services in rural areas, and the high incidence of poverty meant that many women were brought by their families to receive traditional treatments from local traditional healers. As Ika (21, Malay, wheelchair user, rural) described:

> When I was 2 years old, my bone was not bending – it was normal. Then when I was in standard 1 [seven years old], it started to bend. I never went to see doctor. I just went to traditional massage – my mother took me to have a normal massage.

Consequently, many of the rurally located women interviewed received traditional rather than modern medical treatments, due to the difficulties of accessing modern health care. This showed a strong intersection of disability with poverty and rurality. Therefore, the remedies available to them tended to be the ones offered by the local traditional healers, shamans, or religious person. It would however be wrong to claim that participants only turned to traditional medicine because they could not access western medicine, the use of traditional medicine was widespread amongst all the participants and it was clear that most of them, regardless of age, ethnicity, class, or location, had obtained some form of traditional treatment at least once in their lifetime, often by choice. This suggests a pervasive cultural influence in their health care experience, which this section will now turn to.

The Role of Traditional Medicine

In the section above, in explaining their choice of pursuing traditional medical treatments, the participants expressed that it was primarily driven by their economic background (poverty) and their location (rurality). Nevertheless, regardless of geographical background, many of the participants had sought traditional treatments at least once. This suggests a greater cultural influence than that of just economics and geography.

For example, a Malay woman Yasmin (52, wheelchair user, Malay-Muslim), who came from a rural area, mentioned that her family brought her to seek various traditional treatments instead of modern medical medicine because they had little faith in the hospital:

> When I was in my hometown, my family took me to seek traditional treatments from many traditional healers. You know, villagers don't really have faith in the hospital. They thought my condition had resulted from evil spirits.

Many families believed that their daughters' impairment resulted from demonic possession or evil spirits as described by the two women below, on Hindu and the other Muslim:

> I have tried many traditional treatments since I was small. I think the last time was 10 years ago. That Hindu monk said that I was possessed by an evil spirit, so he asked me to stay in his place for two weeks, Prema (40, wheelchair user, Indian-Hindu, rural).

> I went to see a religious person. He said it had something to do with an evil spirit. So he used Quranic verses to treat me. He asked me to recite some verses frequently Nora (34, crutch user, Indian-Muslim, urban).

These common cultural beliefs and a tendency to seek help from traditional healers or religious persons were evident across different races or ethnic groups, religious beliefs and socio-locations. It, therefore, indicated that there were significant cultural and religious influences in meeting the need for a cure amongst the participants. Despite the wide availability of modern health care services accessible to rural and remote populations in Malaysia, the Malaysian communities still use traditional health care services for health and psychosocial problems (Kamil & Teng, 2002).

For example, Cuifen (33, wheelchair user, Chinese-Buddhist), who lived in a city and acquired her impairment at age seven talked about the role of traditional medicine in her life:

> No matter whether it was Indian, Malay or Chinese, we went to them all. Whenever my father heard about any good traditional healer, he took me there. He wanted me to be cured. But, it didn't work.

The actions of Cuifen's family, with their strong reliance on traditional medicine, were driven by the quest for cure. People were not interested in the type of health care or in its origin; all they wanted was a cure. This cultural representation of healing is complex and should be understood from different ontological levels: biomedical and psychological intervention (see Shakespeare, 2006, pp. 112–117). Disability in Malaysian culture, as in most other cultures, is generally seen as a negative attribute that people do not want to be associated with. Many women and their families were culturally informed that having an impairment was defective and actions should be taken to eliminate it.

However, the women included in this study and their families also commonly believed that modern medicine "failed" to cure them and consequently they turned to traditional remedies. This caused significant psycho-emotional damage to these women as they grew up, reminding them that they were seen as "not perfect" and "different." Moreover, they were influenced by their cultural and religious beliefs that created a self-perception that their impairment might be linked to demonic possessions or evil spirits and must be treated. "Among Malaysians, and especially the Malays, the traditional belief that spiritual forces play a great role over physical and mental health is dominant" (Haque & Masuan, 2002, p. 277). Thus, we can appreciate that health care choices are shaped by culture, as well as poverty and rurality.

Sexual Abuse in Health Care Settings

In both traditional and modern health care settings, the women I interviewed commonly experienced abuse.

Ainul (41, wheelchair user, Malay-Muslim, urban) for example described, how she was traumatized when her private parts were touched by her traditional healer without her consent:

> The man (traditional healer) touch my private part (the vagina). When he touched it I felt scared. Then I tried to avoid him whenever he came to my parents' house. When I thought about the incident, I felt scared. I had a spinal injury and I don't feel anything from the waist to the bottom of my body. I was scared of not realising that people were taking advantage on me.

Ainul felt even more under pressure because of her parent's belief in the traditional healer—a respected man in her village and a family friend. Therefore, she was reluctant to inform her parents of the incidents as she felt that they would not believe her, and this could create tension over their relationship with that man. As a result, she kept it to herself, and this caused an intense emotional impact over her bodily experience.

Close relationships between the traditional healers and the families of disabled women also prevented them from exposing such incidents to their family and seeking justice. This was reinforced by the collective nature of Asian society which values religious figures and those in higher authority. Yasmin (52, wheelchair user, Malay-Muslim) for instance, confided that she had nearly been raped by a well-known shaman in her village:

> I was nearly raped by a shaman in my hometown. I was given a medicine and fell asleep. Then the man asked my father to wait outside the room. When we were alone in the room, he switched off the light. Fortunately, my father secretly watched through the holes of the room. When he saw the man try to rape me, he rushed into the room and saved me.

Despite the seriousness of this incident and her father's awareness of it, they did not report the sexual assault to the police. Yasmin noted that she has remained traumatized by the incident and has never received justice for herself. Indeed, of the 33 women interviewed, 5 of them confirmed they had experienced sexual assaults from their traditional healers, and none of them reported it to the local authority. This can be regarded as a cultural constraint where the Malaysian culture was embedded in these women to such a degree that they were unable to challenge the respect given to religious figures and those in higher authority within their local area. As a result, this cultural influence led to significant life-course impact to their physical and psychological wellbeing.

Experiences of sexual abuse in modern healthcare settings also challenged the agency of the women interviewed. For instance, two women described how they were sexually abused by their healthcare professionals. Eryna (36, Malay-Muslim, wheelchair user) for example, told of how she was traumatized by the sexual abuse experienced in her early years:

> Then it happened in the hospital. It was my first time going to the X Hospital. Before I was referred to a specialist, I was checked by a medical doctor. He took off my clothes, everything including my underwear. I don't know what he was trying to check by doing that. But it shouldn't be [like that] as it has nothing to do with my leg. He took advantage as I was only 14 years old at that time. Why did he want to take off my underwear right? It wasn't right. It happened once before when I went to see a specialist. I didn't tell my family, I just kept it to myself.

As mentioned in the previous section, regarding the traditional settings, Eryna was also prevented from expressing her concerns over her physician's misconduct toward her as she felt that he was superior to her. By contrast Wei Yin (47, Chinese-Buddhist, calliper user, rural) strongly objected to what she perceived as inappropriate treatment undertaken by her physician:

> When I was in standard 1 or 2 [seven years old], my father brought me to see a doctor in the X Hospital. During our second or third meeting, the doctor asked me to take off all my clothes. I am a girl right and I felt embarrassed. I refused but my father convinced me to follow the doctor's will. I felt oppressed! At that time I felt humiliated you know. It was just like my dignity as a human being was gone. Although my father protected me, he could not object to his order at that time. Why did my father follow his will? Is that because he was a doctor? Because he was highly educated? I felt it was unfair to me! This is unfair to me I said!

Although Wei Yin had exercised her agency by expressing her objections, she remained helpless because she was overshadowed by a significant male figure in her life—her father. Such an unforgettable incident created tension for her, and it made her feel oppressed and vulnerable, even 40 years later. Since that incident, she refused to continue her medical treatment and never wanted to go to the hospital again. Therefore, the sexual abuse experienced by these women in healthcare settings, both in traditional or modern medical healthcare, significantly impacted upon them over time and violated their dignity as women. It not only "bruised" their physical and psychological personas, but also prevented them from getting appropriate health care services.

It is important to point out that these are not uncommon experiences for disabled women in other countries. As McFarlane (2004) noted, disabled women with physical impairments 'are more likely to experience physical or sexual abuse by attendants and healthcare providers. Young et al. (1997, p. 43) likewise found that "women with physical disabilities also were more likely to be abused by their attendants and by healthcare providers." This lack of power appears to be an almost universal characteristic for disabled women and a unifying feature of the female disabled experience.

The above examples highlight the imbalance of power between the research participants and their physicians, again a situation prevailing in other parts of the world, as Lundgren et al. (2004) have demonstrated, "it is the power-imbalance between professional and patient that allows healthcare professionals to exploit or abuse as well as to heal." Such types of exploitation made the women in this study develop negative attitudes toward medical practice. Consequently, it prevented them from getting adequate medical advice and services, and resulted in an intensification of their impairment and disability experiences.

In brief, getting access to adequate healthcare was not a simple issue for many of the women interviewed. It involved a complex intersection between disability, gender, poverty, rurality, and cultural influence that impeded their opportunities to get equal access to health care services.

CONCLUSION

This chapter demonstrates the need to consider the complexity of gendered disability experiences within a local context to understand experiences of health care in the Global South. The data presented in this chapter observed that due to their poverty and rurality factors, many women had little access to modern health care, which led to the onset of their impairment or intensified their impairment conditions. This study found that disabled women from deprived family backgrounds, and those who lived far from cities, experienced transportation barriers when seeking medical treatment and rehabilitation services from physicians and rehabilitation therapists. Consequently, many of them never had the opportunity to treat their impairment conditions properly, and thus they were left permanently disabled.

Lack of health care services in rural areas often made them dependent on the traditional treatments offered by the local shaman or religious persons. It encouraged a solid cultural belief in the effectiveness of traditional remedies rather than modern medical treatments. Due to a strong dependence on traditional medicines, some women were exposed to sexual abuse by traditional healers. However, these incidents were never revealed to the authorities as the perpetrator was usually known to these women's families. Likewise, unethical practices also occurred in modern medical healthcare as some of the women described how they were subjected to sexual abuse by their physicians. Such unethical practices prevented some of the women from continuing their medical treatment, leaving them permanently disabled. This narrative shows that disabled women experiences in health care are a complex issue, and they require better access and protection in preserving their rights and dignity as an individual and woman.

The women involved in this study had long-term psychological trauma or psycho-emotional disablism (Thomas, 2007) that made them felt oppressed and some of them discontinued their medical treatments. The study is consistent with the previous findings elsewhere that found disabled women with physical impairments are subjected to physical and sexual abuse by their healthcare providers (Young et al., 1997; McFarlane, 2004). This universal characteristic of the female disabled experience that observes an explicit lack of power exhibited by these women toward their healers/physicians profoundly impacted their life course. It not only tainted their psychological well-being but also prevented them from getting adequate healthcare assistance. It can be intensified by cultural attitudes, which is demonstrated by many women in a traditional society such as India, particularly villagers, do not seek healthcare assistance from male practitioners. Thus, it implies that disabled women may be reluctant to seek assistance from male care providers (Thomas & Thomas, 1998). Therefore, it is vital to ensure that health care settings have an adequate number of female practitioners.

Thus, to overcome the sexual abuse in healthcare settings—in both the traditional and the modern healthcare practice, the state should vigorously address this issue by instructing the Ministry of Health to protect disabled women from being sexually exploited by their physicians or attendants. The state should take all appropriate measures to educate disabled children and women and their families about different scenarios that may occur during physical examinations and what may be considered an unethical practice in modern medicine. For instance, sexual education for disabled young people could be introduced. The imbalance of power between healthcare providers and patients should also be reduced. At the same time, disabled children and women should be empowered to report any malpractice done by their healthcare providers. In so doing, disabled children and women could hopefully be protected from such disturbing occurrences that may act to impede their wellbeing.

Equally important is that this issue should also be addressed in the context of traditional medicine whilst traditional medicine is culturally acceptable amongst many Malaysians. Across different ethnic groups and religions, parents of disabled children should be aware of potential dangers to protect their children from being sexually exploited. For example, disabled children and women should not be allowed to attend appointments with traditional healers alone, and they should be always accompanied by at least one family member or friend. They should also be encouraged to report such experiences to the state or local authorities, even if it involves someone known to their family or a respected figure in their hometown.

In conclusion, many women faced constant challenges in exercising their agency in getting access to health care which are significantly related to financial and geographical barriers and the result of the powerful influence of culture and male-dominant figures (traditional healers and physicians). Therefore, all these factors undermined the wellbeing of disabled women and restricted their full access to health care. Consequently, their disability status may expose them to limited opportunities in education and employment. Their full potential to be an active agent in society was constrained, and it denied their rights to be equally included in Malaysian society. Therefore, disabled women's right to get equal access to health care and be protected while getting health care services in the traditional and modern healthcare settings should be vigorously addressed to protect their dignity and rights as individuals and women.

NOTE

1. All the participants' names were referred to using pseudonyms to protect their identity and to ensure anonymity.

REFERENCES

Barnes, C., & Mercer, G. (2010). *Exploring disability: A sociological introduction*. 2nd ed. Polity Press.
Bazeley, P. (2007). *Qualitative data analysis with NVivo*. SAGE Publications.

Be, A. (2012). Feminism and disability. In N. Watson et al. (Eds.), *Routledge Handbook of Disability Studies* (pp. 363–375). Routledge Taylor & Francis Group.

Begum, N. (1992). Disabled women and the feminist agenda. *Feminist Review 40*, 70–84. http://www.jstor.org/stable/1395278.

Bhaskar, R., & Danermark, B. (2006). Metatheory, interdisciplinarity and Disability research: A critical realist perspective. *Scandinavian Journal of Disability Research 8*(4), 278–297. http://dx.doi.org/10.1080/15017410600914329.

Braithwaite, J., & Mont, D. (2009). Disability and poverty: A survey of World Bank Poverty Assessments and implications. *ALTER, European Journal of Disability Research 3*(3), 219–232. http://www.sciencedirect.com/science/article/pii/S1875067209000261.

Collier, A. (1998). Explanation and emancipation. In M. S. Archer et al. (Eds.), *Critical Realism: Essential Readings* (pp. 444–472). Routledge.

Coleridge P. (2000). Disability and culture. In Thomas, M. and Thomas, M. J. eds. Selected Readings in CBR. *Asia Pacific Disability Rehabilitation Journal 1*, 21–39.

Creswell, J. W. (2007). *Qualitative inquiry and research design: Choosing among five approaches.* 2nd ed. SAGE Publications.

Danermark, B., & Gellerstedt, L. C. (2004). Social justice: Redistribution and recognition—a non-reductionist perspective on disability. *Disability & Society 19*(4), 339–353. http://www.tandfonline.com/doi/abs/10.1080/0968759041000168945 8#.U3jqzRsU-ic.

Department of Statistics Malaysia. (2011). *Population distribution and basic demographic characteristic report 2010.* http://www.statistics.gov.my/portal/index.php?option=com_content&id=1215.

Dwyer, S. C., & Buckle, J. L. (2009). The space between: On being an insider-outsider in qualitative research. *International Journal of Qualitative Methods 8*(1), 54–63.

Elwan, A. (1999). *Poverty and disability: A survey of the literature.* Social Protection Discussion Paper No. 9932. The World Bank. http://www.handicap-international.fr/bibliographie-handicap/4PolitiqueHandicap/hand_pauvrete/HandPovSurvey.pdf.

Etherington, K. (2004). *Becoming a reflexive researcher: Using our selves in research.* Jessica Kingsley Publishers.

Filmer D. (2008). Disability, poverty and schooling in developing countries: Results from 14 household surveys. *The World Bank Economic Review 22*(1), 141–163. http://siteresources.worldbank.org/.

Finkelstein, V. (1996). Outside, "inside out." *Coalition* 30–36. https://disability-studies.leeds.ac.uk/wp-content/uploads/sites/40/library/finkelstein-Inside-Out.pdf

Finlay, L. (2002). "Outing" the researcher: The provenance, process, and practice of reflexivity. *Qualitative Health Research 12*(4), 531–545. http://qhr.sagepub.com/content/12/4/531.

Garland-Thomson, R. (1997). Extraordinary bodies: Figuring physical disability in American culture and literature. University Press.

Garland-Thomson, R. (2002). Integrating disability, transforming feminist theory. *Feminist Disability Studies 14*(3), 1–32. http://www.jstor.org/stable/4316922.

Ghai, A. (2002). Disabled women: An excluded agenda of Indian feminism. *Hypatia 17*(3), 49–66. http://muse.jhu.edu.ezproxy.lib.gla.ac.uk/journals/hypatia/v017/17.3ghai.pdf.

Gibbs, G. R. (2011). *Analyzing qualitative data.* SAGE Publications.

Grech, S. (2009). Disability, poverty and development: Critical reflections on the majority world debate. *Disability & Society 24*(6), 771–784. http://www.tandfonline.com/doi/abs/10.1080/09687590903160266#.U3NZvRsU-ic.

Grech, S. (2009). Disability, poverty and development: Critical reflections on the majority world debate. *Disability & Society* 24(6), 771–748.

Groce, N., et al. (2011). *Poverty and disability-a critical review of the literature in low and middle-income countries.* Leonard Cheshire Disability and Inclusive Development Centre working paper series no. 16. London: LCDIDC. http://www.ucl.ac.uk/.

Haque, A., & Khairol A. M. (2002). Perspective: Religious psychology in Malaysia. *International Journal for the Psychology of Religion* 12(4), 277–289. http://dx.doi.org/10.1207/S15327582IJPR1204_05.

Jonsson, T., & Wiman, R. (2001). *Education, poverty and disability in developing countries.* A Technical Note Prepared for the Poverty Reduction Sourcebook. Finnish Consultant Trust Fund. http://www.congreso.gob.pe/comisiones/2006/discapacidad/tematico/educacion/Poverty-Education-Disability.pdf.

Kamil, M. A., & Teng, C. L. (2002). Rural health care in Malaysia. *Aust. J. Rural Health* 10(2), 99–103. http://www.ncbi.nlm.nih.gov/pubmed/12047504.

Kamil, M., A., & Khoo, S. B. (2006). Cultural health beliefs in a rural family practice: A Malaysian perspective. *Aust. J. Rural Health* 14(1), 2–8. http://www.ncbi.nlm.nih.gov/pubmed/16426425.

Kuno, K. (2007). *Does community based rehabilitation really work? Community based rehabilitation (CBR) and participation of disabled people.* ISM Research Monograph Series 5. Kuala Lumpur: Social Institute Malaysia.

Levinsohn, J. (2002). *The World Bank's poverty reduction strategy paper approach: Good marketing or good policy?* World Bank. http://www.g24.org/levintgm.pdf.

Lundgren, K. S., Needleman, W. S., & Wohlberg, J. W. (2004). Above all, do no harm: Abuse of power by health care professionals. *Therapy Exploitation Link Line.* http://www.therapyabuse.org/p2-abuse-of-power.htm.

Lwanga-Ntale, C. (2003). *Chronic poverty and disability in Uganda.* International Conference on Staying Poor: Chronic Poverty and Development Policy, Manchester.

Mackelprang, R. W., & Salsgiver, R. O. (1999). *Disability: A diversity model approach in human service practice.* Brooks/Cole Publishing Company.

MacLachlan, M., Kavanagh, B., & Kay, A. (2012). Maritime health: A review with suggestions for research. *Int. Marit. Health* 63, 1–6.

McFarlane, H. (2004). *Disabled women and socio-spatial "barriers" to motherhood* [Doctoral dissertation]. University of Glasgow.

Ministry of Health Malaysia. (2005). *Oral healthcare in Malaysia.* http://www.whocollab.od.mah.se/wpro/malaysia/data/oral_healthcare_in_malaysia_05.pdf.

Ministry of Health. (1997). *Report of the second national health and morbidity survey conference.* Kuala Lumpur Hospital.

Morris, J. (1991). *Pride against prejudice: A personal politics of disability.* The Women's Press Ltd.

Morris, J. (1992). Personal and political: A feminist perspective on researching physical disability. *Disability, Handicap & Society* 7(2), 157–166. http://dx.doi.org/10.1080/02674649266780181.

Morris, J. (1993). Feminism and disability. *Feminist Review* 43, 55–67. http://www.freelists.org/archives/sig-dsu/10-2013/pdfQdPhEkBApd.pdf.

Morris, J. (1996). *Encounters with strangers: feminism and disability.* The Women's Press Ltd.

NGO Shadow Report Group. (2005). *NGO shadow report on the initial and second periodic report of the government of Malaysia: Reviewing the government's implementation of the Convention on the Elimination of All Forms of Discrimination against Women (CEDAW).* Kuala Lumpur: NCWO and WAO. http://www.iwraw-ap.org/resources/pdf/Malaysia_SR.pdf.

Nosek, M. A., & Simmons, D. K. (2007). People with disabilities as a health disparities population: the case of sexual and reproductive health disparities. *Californian Journal of Health Promotion* 5(special issue), 68–81. http://cjhp.fullerton.edu/Volume5_2007/IssueSp/068 -081-nosek.pdf.

Oliver, M. (1996). *Understanding disability: From theory to practice.* Palgrave Macmillan.

Pettinicchio, D., & Maroto, M. (2021). Who counts? Measuring disability cross-nationally in census data. *Journal of Survey Statistics and Methodology* 9(2), 257–284.

Roberts, B. (2002). *Biographical research.* Open University Press.

Roberts, H. (1990). Women and their doctors: Power and powerlessness in the research process. In H. Roberts (Ed.)., *Doing Feminist Research* (pp. 7–29). Routledge.

Scambler, S. (2005). Exposing the limitations of disability theory: The case of Juvenile Batten Disease. *Social Theory & Health* 3, 144–164. http://www.palgrave-journals.com/sth/journal/ v3/n2/abs/8700045a.html.

Sen, A. (2009). *The idea of justice.* The Belknap Press of Harvard University Press.

Shakespeare, T., & Watson, N. (2010). Beyond models: Understanding the complexity of disabled people's lives. In G. Scrambler & S. Scambler (Eds.), *New Directions in the Sociology of Chronic and Disabling Conditions: Assaults on the Lifeworld* (pp. 57–76). Palgrave Macmillan.

Shakespeare, T. (2006). *Disability rights and wrongs.* Routledge.

Shakespeare, T. (2012). Disability in developing countries. In N. Watson et al. (Eds.), *Routledge Handbook of Disability Studies* (pp. 271–284). Routledge Taylor & Francis Group.

Shakespeare, T. (2014). *Disability rights and wrongs revisited.* 2nd ed. Routledge.

Shakespeare, T., & Watson, N. (2001). The social model of disability: An outdated ideology? In S. Barnart & B. M Altman (Eds.)., *Exploring Theories and Expanding Methodologies: Where we are and where we need to go? Research in Social Science and Disability*, vol. 2, (pp. 9–28). http://www.emeraldinsight.com/books.htm?chapterid=1783286

Stanley, L., & Wise, S. (1990). Method, methodology and epistemology in feminist research processes. In L. Stanley (Ed.), *Feminist Praxis: Research, Theory and Epistemology in Feminist Sociology* (pp. 20–62). Routledge.

Stanley, L., & Wise, S. (1993). Breaking out again: Feminist ontology and epistemology. Routledge.

Swartz, L., & Bantjes, J. (2016). Disability and global health. In S. Grech & K. Soldatic (Eds.), *Disability in the Global South: The Critical Handbook* (pp. 21–33). Springer.

Tarmiji, M., et al. (2012). Population and spatial distribution of urbanisation in Peninsular Malaysia 1957–2000. *Geografia: Malaysian Journal of Society and Space* 8(2), 20–29. http:// pkukmweb.ukm.my/geografia/v1/index.php.

The World Bank Group. (2013). *Malaysia overview.* http://www.worldbank.org/en/country/ malaysia/overview.

Thomas, C. (1999). *Female forms: Experiencing and understanding disability.* Open University Press.

Thomas, C. (2007). *Sociologies of disability and illness: Contested ideas in disability studies and medical sociologies.* Palgrave Macmillan.

Thomas, M., & Thomas, M. J. (1998). Status of women with disabilities in South Asia. *Asia Pacific Disability Rehabilitation Journal* 9(2), 60–64.

United Nations General Assembly resolution. (2000). *Further actions and initiatives to implement the Beijing Declaration and Platform for Action.* A/RES/S-23/3, 23rd special session. http://www.un.org/womenwatch/daw/followup/ress233e.pdf.

Vidya, B.G. (2011). How Hindus cope with disability. *Journal of Religion, Disability & Health* 15(1), 72–78. http://www.tandfonline.com/doi/abs/10.1080/15228967.2011.540897#.U3PZf RsU-ic.

Watson, N. (2000). *Impairment, disablement and identity* [Doctoral dissertation]. University of Edinburgh.

Watson, N. (2012a). Researching disablement. In N. Watson et al. (Eds.), *Routledge Handbook of Disability Studies* (pp. 271–284). Routledge Taylor & Francis Group.

Watson, N. (2012b). Theorising the lives of disabled children: how can disability theory help? *Children & Society* 26, 192–202. http://onlinelibrary.wiley.com/doi/10.1111/j.1099 -0860.2012.00432.x/full.

Wendell, S. (1996). *The rejected body: Feminist philosophical reflections on disability*. Routledge.

WHO. (2011). *World report on disability*. World Health Organization.

Williams, S. J. (1999). Is anybody there? Critical realism, chronic illness and the disability debate. *Sociology of Health & Illness* 21(6), 797–819. http://onlinelibrary.wiley.com/doi/10.1111/ 1467-9566.00184/abstract.

Yamney, G., & Greenwood, R. (2004). Religious views of the "medical" rehabilitation model: A pilot qualitative study. *Disability and Rehabilitation* 26(8),455–462. http://www.ncbi.nlm .nih.gov/pubmed/15204467.

Young, C.R. et al. (1997). The differential diagnosis of multiple sclerosis and bipolar disorder. *Journal of Clinical Psychiatry* 58(3), 123. http://www.ncbi.nlm.nih.gov/pubmed/9108815.

CHAPTER 10

......

DISABILITY AND
HUMAN RIGHTS

......

PAULA CAMPOS PINTO

HUMAN rights are the rights we all have because we are human beings. The concept can be traced back to the 17th and 18th centuries in Europe when philosophers such as Jean-Jacques Rousseau and John Locke asserted the centrality of the individual in political and social systems and called upon states to protect and ensure their natural and inalienable rights. Yet the international system of human rights, as we know it today, mostly emerged following World War II in reaction to the horrors of the Holocaust. Since then, an increasingly complex system has developed to respect, protect, and fulfill the human rights of all human beings, everywhere in the world.

Although persons with disabilities have been part of this system since its foundation, their specific concerns have been largely ignored (Quinn and Degener et al., 2002). Disability emerged as a human rights issue only over the last four decades. Applying a rights-based approach to disability means recognizing the inherent human dignity and worth of all disabled persons, regardless the complexity of their needs, and putting into place all necessary means to ensure that they enjoy their status as citizens with equal rights and freedoms to all others (Stein & Stein, 2007). The rights approach marks a "paradigm shift" in attitudes to and treatment of persons with disabilities, as it moves away from a medicalized paternalistic view, recasting them as "subjects" with rights, able to make decisions on their lives and be active members of society (Quinn and Degener et al., 2002).

Although the rights discourse around disability preceded the adoption of the UN Convention on the Rights of Persons with Disabilities (CRPD) in 2006, the treaty is usually seen as the hallmark of this paradigm shift (e.g. Berghs et al., 2016; Degener, 2016; Kanter, 2015; Harpur, 2012), given its consequences for how societies and states understand and respond to disability. The CRPD creates binding obligations to the states that sign and ratify it, while serving as an internationally agreed-upon roadmap for states that do not. As of today, 182 nations have ratified the convention, which makes it one of the most widely accepted treaties.

Yet, as sociologists are aware, social change does not necessarily follow legal change. Moreover, there may be a myriad of reasons that lead states to sign and ratify treaties, and not all of them are related to a real commitment to change state's practices (Kanter, 2015). Furthermore, the lack of strong enforcement procedures in the UN system limits the transformative power of international human rights law (Hathaway, 2002; Berghs et al., 2016). Hence, over a decade after coming into effect, many tensions and challenges remain around the full implementation of the CRPD and its rights agenda, in countries of both the Global North and South.

This chapter contributes to a better understanding of some of these tensions and challenges by examining the conditions, scope, and political effects of realizing the paradigm shift that the CRPD calls for. Drawing from a sociological perspective, it sheds light on the social and political conditions that enabled the emergence of a human rights model of disability and its rapid worldwide dissemination. Next, it reviews the CRPD, its Optional Protocol, and the seven General Comments that have been issued so far by the CRPD Committee to support State Parties in the implementation of specific norms of the convention. This section highlights the scope and the main features entailed by the human rights model of disability, enshrined in the CRPD. Finally, drawing on the experience gathered from the implementation of Disability Rights Promotion International (DRPI)[1], a global initiative to monitor disability rights worldwide, we discuss opportunities and challenges facing a sociologist from the Global North conducting research on disability rights in the Global South.

DISABILITY IN THE INTERNATIONAL HUMAN RIGHTS SYSTEM

Although the preamble to the *United Nations Charter* (UN, 1945) affirms that "all human beings are born free and equal in dignity and rights" and gives primary importance to the promotion of social justice, the explicit inclusion of disability in the international human rights agenda has been a slow process, eagerly supported by the advocacy efforts of an increasingly organized and stronger international disability movement. Figure 10.1 provides a timeline for the inclusion of disability within the UN system, highlighting this slow process from 1948 through 2021.

The United Nations General Assembly established the foundation for the promotion and protection of human rights in 1948 when it proclaimed the *Universal Declaration of Human Rights*. Article 25 of the *Declaration* states that each person has "the right to security in the event of unemployment, sickness, *disability*, widowhood, old age or other lack of livelihood in circumstances beyond his control" (UN, 1948; my emphasis). Reflecting the lack of awareness of the rights dimension of disability at that time, founding human rights instruments such as the *International Covenant on Civil and Political Rights* (UN, 1966a) and the *International Covenant on Economic, Social and Cultural Rights* (UN,

1966b) do not make explicit reference to disabled people. Still, the standards that they uphold, particularly the over-arching right to non-discrimination, are relevant in the context of disability, as General Comment no. 5 on *Persons with Disabilities*, issued by the Committee on Economic, Social and Cultural Rights in 1995 reminds us (CESCR, 1995).

Throughout the seventies, however, the concept of human rights for disabled persons began to achieve greater visibility internationally (UN Enable, 2008). The adoption by the General Assembly of the *Declaration on the Rights of Disabled Persons*, in 1975 (UN,

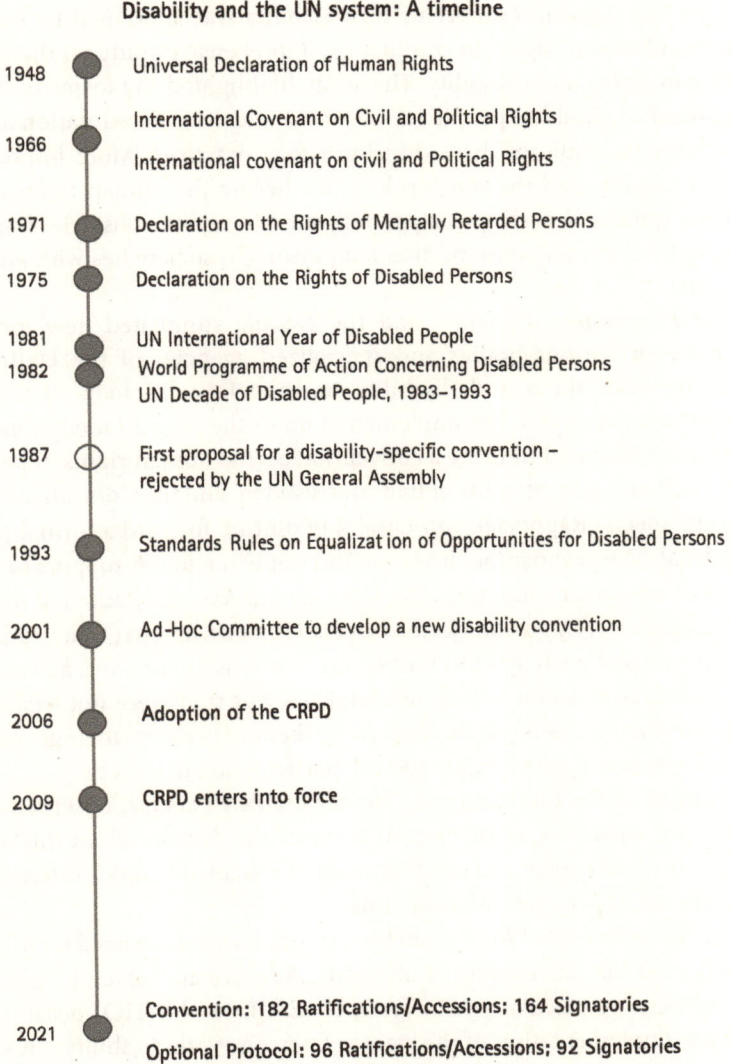

Disability and the UN system: A timeline

1948 — Universal Declaration of Human Rights

1966 — International Covenant on Civil and Political Rights
International covenant on civil and Political Rights

1971 — Declaration on the Rights of Mentally Retarded Persons

1975 — Declaration on the Rights of Disabled Persons

1981 — UN International Year of Disabled People
1982 — World Programme of Action Concerning Disabled Persons
UN Decade of Disabled People, 1983–1993

1987 — First proposal for a disability-specific convention – rejected by the UN General Assembly

1993 — Standards Rules on Equalization of Opportunities for Disabled Persons

2001 — Ad-Hoc Committee to develop a new disability convention

2006 — Adoption of the CRPD

2009 — CRPD enters into force

2021 — Convention: 182 Ratifications/Accessions; 164 Signatories
Optional Protocol: 96 Ratifications/Accessions; 92 Signatories

FIGURE 10.1 Disability and the UN system: A timeline

1975), following the *Declaration on the Rights of Mentally Retarded Persons*, issued in December 1971 (UN, 1971), marked the beginning of this new approach.

The year of 1981 was declared the *UN International Year of Disabled People*, which prompted several important initiatives at national, regional, and international levels aimed at promoting "full participation and equality" for disabled persons. The main result of the activity undertaken before and during that year was the elaboration of the *World Programme of Action concerning Disabled Persons* (UN, 1982), and the proclamation of the *UN Decade of Disabled People, 1983–1992*. The *World Programme of Action* explicitly recognized the right of every human being to equal opportunity, thus actually expanding the concept of human rights.

In 1984, the first Special Rapporteur on Disability was appointed by the UN Sub-Commission on Human Rights to conduct a comprehensive study on the relationship between human rights and disability. The study highlighted the forms of discrimination experienced by disabled people in the world and considered national and international policies to eradicate these discriminatory practices. More importantly, the report explicitly addressed the state's role in furthering the human rights of disabled citizens by recognizing that the principal obligation to remove obstacles hindering the integration and full participation of disabled persons in society lies with governments (Despouy, 1991).

The *World Programme of Action* and the *Decade* stimulated new forms of cooperation between various bodies and specialized agencies of the United Nations system, and between them and disability organizations. In 1987, during the first major international review of the implementation of the *World Programme of Action*, participants recommended drafting a convention on the human rights of persons with disabilities—with the governments of Italy and Sweden, and the Commission for Social Development's Special Rapporteur on Disability putting forward a formal proposal to achieve that goal. The proposition, however, did not win enough support to lead to the negotiation of a new treaty and, thus, the UN General Assembly adopted the *Standard Rules on Equalization of Opportunities for Disabled Persons*, in 1993 (UN, 1993). The *Rules* targeted areas of equal participation for persons with disabilities and advanced implementation measures and monitoring mechanisms, but they were not legally binding. This did not prevent disabled people from using them to pressure their governments to move forward in ensuring their rights and full participation in society.

The celebration of the International Day of Disabled Persons, observed ever since on December 3rd each year, is another outcome of the decade. All of this has further contributed to the emergence and establishment of Disabled People's International, the first global network of persons with disabilities.

During the 1990s, five UN World Conferences emphasized the need for a "society for all" and reaffirmed the universality of all rights. Additionally, several United Nations specialized agencies (particularly ILO, FAO, UNESCO, and WHO) became more involved with the implementation of the rights of persons with disability, thus reflecting the increasing mainstreaming of disability issues in the human rights agenda.

Despite this growing visibility, disabled persons all over the world continued to face discrimination and denial of fundamental human rights (Quinn and Degener et al., 2002). It became clear that, while existing human rights instruments offered considerable potential to further the rights of disabled people, this potential was not being adequately tapped. Hence, a legally binding document, setting out states' obligations to protect and promote the rights of persons with disabilities, was needed. With the mounting pressure of the international disability movement, in December 2001 the UN General Assembly accepted the Mexican government's proposal and established an Ad Hoc Committee, tasked with the development of a comprehensive and integral international convention to fulfill and protect the rights of persons with disabilities.

The Ad Hoc Committee met eight times between 2002 and 2006—a record number for any negotiation of a UN treaty—and on December 13, 2006, the UN General Assembly adopted by consensus the Convention on the Rights of Persons with Disabilities and its Optional Protocol (UN, 2006).[2] The first convention of the new millennium and its Optional Protocol opened for signature at the UN Headquarters in New York on March 30, 2007, collecting an historic number of 82 signatures in the opening day. The instruments entered into force on May 3, 2008, after receiving the 20th ratification of the *Convention* and the 10th ratification of the Optional Protocol.

The Convention on the Rights of Persons with Disabilities

The Disability Convention is an international human rights instrument. It fundamentally asserts that *all* persons with *all* types of disabilities must enjoy *all* human rights and freedoms on an equal basis with others. Although it is often stated that the convention does not create new rights, rather it clarifies and qualifies how all categories of rights apply to persons with disabilities, this is also disputable. While conceding that the CRPD reaffirms some of the basic human rights already contained in other human rights treaties, Mégret (2008) argues that the CRPD is a good example of the current phenomenon of "pluralization of rights." Indeed, it not only modifies the content of existing rights by reformulating or significantly expanding their meaning, but it also "comes very close to creating new rights, rights that inhere in the experience of disability and are arguably, at least in the particular form in which they are presented, specific to persons with disabilities" (p. 498). Examples of these last categories include the right to live in the community, and the principle of respect for autonomy of persons with disabilities, which is one of the General Principles enshrined in the *Convention* (art. 3), and one that is further taken up in other rights, such as the right to personal mobility, the right to accessibility, and the right to live independently.

Importantly, the new treaty does not offer a rigid definition of disability. Moving away from medical and individualized conceptions, in the Preamble it acknowledges that disability is "an evolving concept." Article 1 states that:

Persons with disabilities include those who have long-term physical, mental, intellectual, and sensory impairments which in interaction with various barriers may hinder their full and effective participation in society on an equal basis with others.

Even though the language chosen avoided politicized terms to define the status of disabled people, such as the notion of oppression, the role of society in creating disability is clearly acknowledged in the convention.

Figure 10.2 presents an overview of the CRPD, dividing its 50 articles into four main categories: norms dealing with general principles, norms about rights and freedoms, norms addressing the situation of special groups, and norms about other provisions. The arrows connecting the four categories in Figure 10.2 highlight how these separate categories of norms intersect and interact with each other. For instance, in discussing measures to implement the right to work, women with disabilities are often faced with multiple and intersecting forms of discrimination that may place them in more disadvantaged positions in the labor market. Similarly, in developing job opportunities catered for persons with disabilities, principles of inclusion and non-discrimination must be ensured. In this sense, forced work or work under conditions of segregation due to disability is not permitted under the CRPD.

As shown in the Figure 10.2, the CRPD promotes and protects the human rights and freedoms of people with disabilities in all spheres of life encompassing both civil and political rights, as well as social, economic, and cultural rights. Recognizing that some groups are more exposed than others to multiple and intersecting forms of discrimination based on age, sex, or other grounds, the treaty calls special attention to the situation of women and girls, as well as children with disabilities.

The instrument further enunciates areas where states need to intervene so that persons with disabilities can fully enjoy their rights. These articles, gathered under the category of special provisions (see Figure 10.2) address issues such as raising awareness about disability and disability discrimination; promoting accessibility to the built environment, transportation, and information; ensuring access to justice for people with disabilities; and undertaking the systematic collection of data on disability issues as a basis for the formulation of policy to implement the convention, among others.

Finally, to guide states and other actors in the implementation of these obligations, the convention spells out eight general principles for a human rights approach to disability (Figure 10.2). The first, the principle of human dignity underscores the idea that human beings are intrinsically worthy, just by nature of their humanity and regardless of any consideration of their economic or social value. The principle is linked to the notion of autonomy to remind us that as "subjects" on their own right, persons with disabilities must be entitled to exercise their right to self-determination and enjoy the freedom to choose how and with whom they want to live their lives.

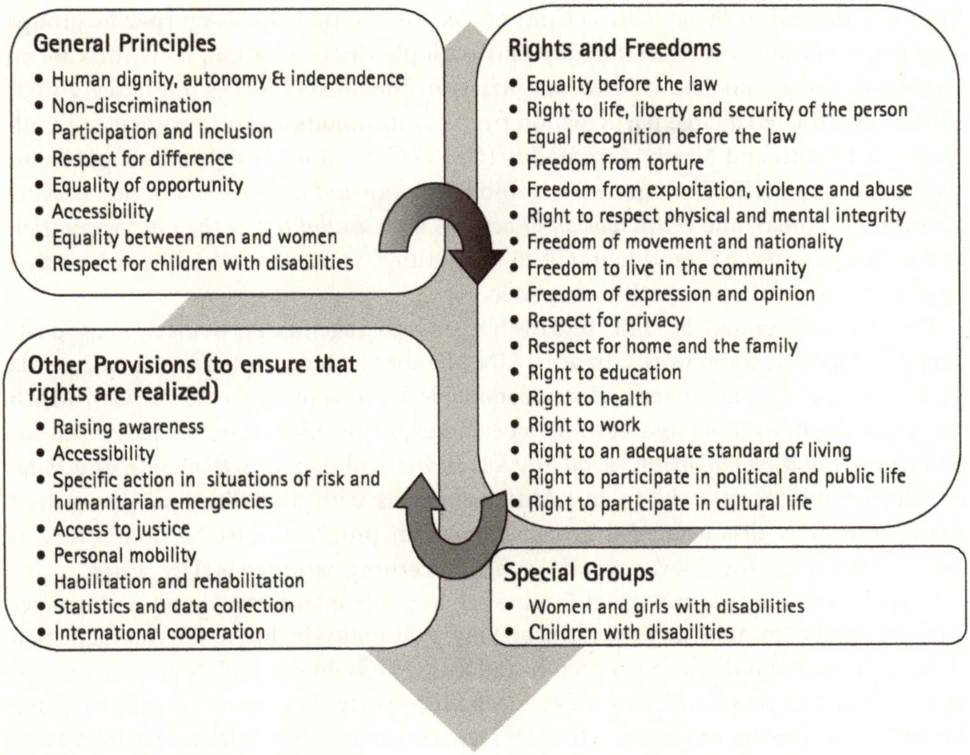

General Principles

- Human dignity, autonomy & independence
- Non-discrimination
- Participation and inclusion
- Respect for difference
- Equality of opportunity
- Accessibility
- Equality between men and women
- Respect for children with disabilities

Rights and Freedoms

- Equality before the law
- Right to life, liberty and security of the person
- Equal recognition before the law
- Freedom from torture
- Freedom from exploitation, violence and abuse
- Right to respect physical and mental integrity
- Freedom of movement and nationality
- Freedom to live in the community
- Freedom of expression and opinion
- Respect for privacy
- Respect for home and the family
- Right to education
- Right to health
- Right to work
- Right to an adequate standard of living
- Right to participate in political and public life
- Right to participate in cultural life

Other Provisions (to ensure that rights are realized)

- Raising awareness
- Accessibility
- Specific action in situations of risk and humanitarian emergencies
- Access to justice
- Personal mobility
- Habilitation and rehabilitation
- Statistics and data collection
- International cooperation

Special Groups

- Women and girls with disabilities
- Children with disabilities

FIGURE 10.2 The CRPD at a glance

With the entry into force of the convention in 2008, a specialized body was established to monitor the implementation of the CRPD worldwide. Currently, the CRPD Committee comprises 18 independent experts who review state party reports and make recommendations to improve compliance with the CRPD norms and principles. Many of these experts are persons with disabilities themselves, appointed and elected by the state parties during the Annual State Parties' Conference while considering "equitable geographical distribution, representation of the different forms of civilization and of the principal legal systems, [and] balanced gender representation" (art. 4.3).

In addition to its monitoring role, the committee issues General Comments to provide interpretation of specific articles of the convention and offer guidance to state parties on measures and steps to take to make human rights a reality. The adoption of a General Comment is always a very participative process in which civil society organizations and governments take part. The process typically starts with a call for submissions, often followed by a day of public discussion, based on which the committee prepares a draft that is open to further public discussion before the final version is adopted.

As of May 2021, seven General Comments have been adopted, covering a range of rights. Some deal with those provisions that have been identified as the most challenging norms of the CRPD: *Equality before the law* (CRPD Committee, 2014a), and the

Right to independent living (CRPD Committee, 2017). Others focus on specific groups drawing attention to intersectionality and multiple discrimination, as is the case of General Comment no. 3 on *Women and girls with disabilities* (CRPD Committee, 2016a) which has attracted a large participation from organizations and governments of both the Global South and North. *Accessibility* (CRPD Committee, 2014b), the *Right to inclusive education* (CRPD Committee, 2016b), *Equality and non-discrimination* (CRPD Committee, 2018a), and *Participation of persons with disabilities in the implementation and monitoring of the Convention* (CRPS Committee, 2018b) are other provisions that have received attention from the committee.

The CRPD integrated disability into the human rights agenda, particularly in the post-2015 development frameworks. In 2015, UN Member States adopted the 2030 Agenda for Sustainable Development and its Sustainable Development Goals (SDGs), which recognize disability as a cross-cutting issue and explicitly address it the areas of *education*; *growth and employment*; *inequality*; *accessibility of human settlements*; and *data, monitoring, and accountability*. In addition, persons with disabilities are recognized among the most disadvantaged groups for whom progress must be monitored, as member states aim to achieve universal goals concerning basic needs (UN, 2015).

Despite providing an important framework to guide international and national actors and local communities towards achieving a disability-inclusive development that "leaves no one behind," the 2030 agenda and its 17 SDGs do not replace the convention and, indeed, can be viewed as a softer mechanism since they are not legally binding. Nevertheless, a recent report from the UN Department of Economic and Social Affairs, assessing disability and the Sustainable Development Goals of the 2030 Agenda for Sustainable Development at the global level, concluded that despite the progress made over the last years, huge gaps remain, and many persons with disabilities, in both the Global North and South, continue to face barriers to exercise their rights and participate as full members of their communities (UN, 2018). In this sense, the call for a disability-inclusive development, advanced by the 2030 agenda and the SDGs, reinforces the mainstreaming of disability in human rights debates and actions at local, national, and global levels.

A Paradigm Shift? What Really Changed with the CRPD?

The adoption of the Disability Convention is often said to mark a "paradigm shift" with profound repercussions in how disability is described, explained, and dealt with by society and the state. These changes are encapsulated in the so-called human rights model of disability (Kanter, 2003, 2015; Harpur, 2012; Stein, 2007; Stein & Stein, 2007).

Emerging from the social model of disability, which described disability as the consequence of "social" rather than "individual pathology" (Rioux & Valentine 2006), with root causes in society's barriers that impose restrictions on what disabled people can do and be, the human rights model of disability has been most clearly outlined by the disability legal scholar Theresia Degener (2016). According to Degener (2016), a distinctive characteristic of the human rights model is its assertion of the inherent dignity of all persons with disabilities, regardless the complexity of their needs and impairments. In this sense, the Convention operates what Nash (2015) calls "the cultural politics of human rights," challenging and expanding traditional representations of "who counts as 'human'" (p. 13), notably those based on the capacity contract. This is clear from the preamble, when it is recognized that the rights of all persons with disabilities, including those with more intensive support needs, must be protected (preamble, para. j) or when legal capacity is asserted as a right for all (art. 12).

Moreover, the human rights model embodied in the CRPD embraces all categories of human rights—social, economic, cultural, civil, and political. Previous rights-based legislation for persons with disabilities tended to merely focus on civil rights (as in anti-discrimination laws, such as the American with Disabilities Act). Although necessary, these have proved insufficient to address the range of inequalities that affect persons with disabilities (Kanter, 2015; Stein & Stein, 2007). In the CRPD, several provisions call upon different sets of rights, recapturing the notions of universality, indivisibility, and interdependence of all human rights that were proclaimed in the Vienna Declaration. Such is the case, for example, of the right to equality before the law, which although being categorized as a civil right may require the provision of social supports to be exercised. Other authors have similarly claimed that the disability human rights paradigm is "holistic" (Stein & Stein, 2007), as it requires states to support the freedom and equality of all individuals, including those with more complex needs (Kanter, 2003).

In addition, the human rights model values impairment as part of human diversity. It addresses issues of identity politics and intersectionality, recognizing multiple discrimination faced by women and girls with disability (art. 6) and providing support for the "specific culture and cultural identity, including sign languages and deaf culture" (art. 30). And even though it rejects an understanding of disability as a medical condition, it does not neglect the experience of pain and impairment in the lives of many persons with disabilities, viewing access to health and rehabilitation as an important human right and a necessary condition to ensure social participation and the quality of life of persons with disabilities (Harpur, 2012). In doing so, the human rights model also challenges the notion of the autonomous individual, which constitutes the mythic standard against which persons with disabilities, especially those who need care and support, are often compared and devalued (Kanter, 2015, p. 301). By asserting that we are all interdependent, the human rights model emphasizes that every individual has specific talents and unique contributions to give to our global society, provided they are granted the opportunity and the resources they need to fully participate (Kanter, 2015; Harpur, 2012).

Finally, the human rights model "offers a roadmap for change" (Degener, 2016), detailing states and society's full range of obligations in the process of societal transformation that will allow persons with disabilities to achieve their potential and participate as full members of their communities (Harpur, 2012; Stein & Stein, 2007). The power of this message is now being tapped by disability activists who increasingly claim their right to participate and have a saying in the distribution of resources and the design and implementation of development strategies. Worldwide, the momentum generated by the adoption of the CRPD has stimulated the creation of many disability organizations, run and led by persons with disabilities themselves, who are using the CRPD as a tool for policy change. By taking a leading role and making their voice heard in the public space, these activists are also contributing to shift social representations of persons with disabilities from dependent subjects to active citizens (Kanter, 2015; Harpur, 2012).

The rapid spread of the human rights model of disability is now visible in the adoption of a rights discourse to frame disability debates and politics at both national and international levels (Lawson & Beckett, 2021). Yet, this often translates more into a rhetorical shift than an actual change of attitudes and practices since these latter frequently remain hostage of medical and charity-based perspectives. Hathaway (2002) has already demonstrated the limited impact that the signature of human rights treaties may have and the significant level of noncompliance with human rights norms that can be found among signatory states. Still, many (e.g. de Beco, 2020; Kanter, 2015; Harpur, 2012; Stein & Stein, 2007) agree in categorizing the CRPD as a ground-breaking treaty. Certainly, relationships of power and inequality at the local level impact on the realization of rights, as when disability rights travel they do not do so in the void. Rather, they meet with domestic institutional logics, local politics, and the evolving meanings that social movements attribute to disability and rights at national level. From these encounters, and the shifting balance among actors at all these levels, new tensions emerge. Often this results in hybrid law and policy models that keep some of the old features while adopting new ones (Pinto, 2018, p. 148).

In assessing the impact of the human rights model, non-enforcement of the CRPD is viewed as a potential weakness (Berghs et al., 2016). Indeed, governments and large segments of society are still failing with their responsibilities to ensure the realization of human rights for persons with disabilities (Isaac et al., 2010; Pinto, 2018). This has led Berghs and colleagues (2016) to conclude that a social model of human rights is needed to address disability-based discrimination and inequalities more effectively. Taking the argument further, Lawson and Beckett (2021) claim that the social and the human rights models are not oppositional, but indeed complementary. The social model offers a heuristic tool to understand disability as a form of social oppression, and the human rights model provides a framework to analyze disability policy. Hence, they must be used in tandem in struggles to overturn a disabling society. Today, such struggles are taking place all over the world, largely led by an increasingly stronger and cohesive disability movement, itself an outcome of the CRPD (Kanter, 2015). And although their success is often lengthy and limited, this, I would argue, is the greatest achievement, and conceivably hope too, for the realization of disability rights.

THE SOCIOLOGY OF HUMAN RIGHTS

In the face of these debates, what is the role for sociology? Sociologists arrived late to the human rights arena (Frezzo, 2015; Nash, 2015; Woodiwiss, 2005), but an increasingly populated body of literature is now becoming available in the new field of the sociology of human rights. Sociology's traditional attention to social problems and the theories and methods of the discipline make it particularly apt to research human rights. In analyzing the social world, sociologists seek to understand the power relations that create and sustain social, economic, and cultural inequalities among individuals and social groups. Given that human rights are moral and legal claims aimed to redress inequalities, it does not come as a surprise to find sociologists interested on the study of human rights (Polanska, 2016).

Drawing from a critical sociology perspective, Armaline and colleagues (2015) coined the term "human rights enterprise" to characterize the struggles over power, resources, and voice that mobilize social movements and the often contradictory role of state actors and other international institutions when engaging with human rights. According to the authors, the main task for the new sociology of human rights is to analyze the complexities of these human rights struggles. Highlighting the crucial role of social movements in challenging states and other powerful interests to advance human rights in contemporary societies, researchers seek to move beyond traditional approaches that tended to portrait states as the main responsible for human rights innovations—an argument that clearly resonates with the disability movement efforts to achieve social justice that culminated in the passage of the CRPD.

Taking a similar approach, Nash (2015) develops a political sociology of human rights to examine "the range of actors involved in making human rights claims, the types of actions in which they are engaged, and the organizations through which claims are addressed" (p. 6). Viewing human rights as "always open to being re-articulated in different ways," she argues in favor of the sociological study of the tensions and paradoxes of the global human rights field, suggesting another promising avenue of research when it comes to analyzing disability rights. One such paradox evolves around the emancipation/governance pole. Although human rights are intrinsically emancipatory, for they involve claims for equality and freedom for all, "the global governance that is needed to realise human rights in practice itself produces inequalities" (Nash, 2015, p. 166). Such a paradox, Nash (2015) continues, cannot be overturned, but it can be better addressed through strong grassroots mobilization. This argument resonates with trends observable in the disability rights field, where a strong international movement of persons with disabilities is organizing around the CRPD to make their voice heard in national and international arenas. Constructing disability as a human rights issue is key to these processes. It carries a "symbolic power" enabling these activists to put pressure on states and make use of international resources to achieve a greater degree of justice for persons with disabilities at local and global levels.

Expanding previous understandings, Frezzo (2015) offers a comprehensive overview regarding how sociology can provide useful perspectives to researching human rights. According to the author, sociological analyses complement the contributions from other disciplines (e.g., law, philosophy, political science, anthropology) as they "elucidate the economic, political, social and cultural forces that impact the construction, interpretation, implementation and enforcement of human rights" (pp. 1–2). Frezzo identifies four core areas of work for a sociology of human rights: analyzing "rights conditions" (i.e., the economic, political, social, cultural, and environmental circumstances that originate grievances), "rights claims" (i.e., the conditions under which such grievances become rights demands), "rights effects" (i.e., the outcomes of rights codification in power dynamics), and "rights bundles" (i.e., groups of rights that go beyond the conventional classifications of rights). All these strands hold enormous potential for the understanding of disability rights struggles and achievements.

The edited volume organized by Brunsma, Smith, and Gran (2015) provides examples of a sociology of human rights in practice by analyzing the human rights experiences of traditionally excluded groups such as women, racial and ethnic minorities, children, elders, LGBTQ people, persons with mental illness, and others. The authors present evidence regarding the enforcement and denial of human rights for different social groups in different parts of the world, the social forces and pressures behind these patterns, and the consequences of selective implementation of rights in the lives of these groups. They also show the epistemological, theoretical, and methodological perspectives involved in a sociological inquiry of human rights, by drawing from sociological frameworks such as that of social construction (the idea that society creates things such as categories of people—e.g., the dependent and vulnerable vs. the autonomous being) while using quantitative and qualitative sociological research methods.

Despite this growing literature, the sociological engagement with human rights research is not exempt from tensions, dilemmas, and difficulties. It is to the examination of these challenges, particularly in the context of disability rights in the Global South, as well as of ways of dealing with them, that we turn now.

Developing a Sociology of Human Rights in the Context of the Global South: Challenges and Ways Forward

As noted elsewhere (Rioux et al., 2016), the usefulness of disability human rights discourses, practices, and research in the context of the Global South has been questioned because of the cultural bias embedded in human rights frameworks (Freeman, 2018), and the continuing global dominance of Northern disability discourses in such discussions and practices (Meekosha & Soldatic, 2011, p. 1392). In this section, we address these debates and suggest how they can be transcended. To do so, as an illustration of a sociology of human rights in practice, we draw from the fieldwork experience gathered through over 20 projects conducted in countries around the globe by Disability Rights Promotion International (DRPI), an international initiative to monitor disability rights worldwide.

One of the criticisms more often raised about human rights approaches concerns the binary universalism/cultural relativism. Universality is a fundamental principle of human rights theory, yet the idea of human rights universalism reflects "Western cultural imperialism" (Freeman, 2018, p. 122). In the field of disability rights, Meekosha and Soldatic (2011) argue that the universalistic perspective is "embedded in a grand tradition emerging from the North," and human rights discourse perpetuates colonialism, "whereby the hegemonic North determines the constitution of human rights, ignoring the inherent global power imbalances" (p. 1388).

Northern conceptions of disability, for example, tend to accentuate the disability/impairment divide, focusing on disability as the outcome of barriers to social participation and sidelining impairment as belonging to the biological/natural realm, which is reflected in the definition of disability embraced by the CRPD. However, the authors claim, "the politics of impairment is particularly significant for understanding 'disability' within the Global South, particularly those impairments deeply associated with processes of colonisation and imperialism" (p. 1390). The devastating impacts on women's fertility and reproduction of the depleted uranium from ammunitions used during the Gulf War, or the introduction of alcohol in white colonial settler communities as means to exert social control over "the native" are just two examples that illustrate their point.

Following Mutua (2008), who maintains that Western hegemony in human rights discussions, translate in the classic narrative of "savages," "victims," and "saviors," Meekosha and Soldatic (2011) contend that human rights approaches often depict persons with disabilities from the Global South as victims of "traditional" cultural norms and beliefs, in need of being rescued by NGOs and development agencies from the North. This reproduces colonialist views and practices and reinforces the subordinate position of Southern peoples and cultures, in the context of North-South power relations.

Another problematic point raised in these debates stresses the clash between individualistic conceptualizations of rights, originated in the Western liberal tradition, and the collectivist approaches to rights as understood in the Global South, including by many disability movements and groups. Individualistic and legalist constructions of human rights are thus viewed as useless to address structural causes of rights violations, as those that result from the dynamics of North-South relationships (Freeman, 2018).

Despite these criticisms, the ongoing universal project of human rights remains of strategic importance for persons with disabilities across the Global South and North (Meekosha & Soldatic, 2011). It is worth noting that the proposal for the Disability Convention emanated from a Southern country (Mexico) and was greatly supported by disability activists in the Global South who continue to be active in the annual Conference of State Parties and the workings of the CRPD Committee. Grassroots movements of persons with disability in countries of the Global South (as in the Global North) also continue to mobilize around human rights to place demands on their states for the ratification and implementation of the CRPD.

Moreover, as evident throughout the DRPI projects, disability rights are "as precarious in the North as in the South" (Rioux et al., 2016, p. 537), and thus, emancipatory struggles of persons with disabilities for respect, resources, and collective voice in all corners of the world are often framed around the discourse of human rights. In a similar vein, Freeman (2018) concedes that human rights may have strong Western roots but "the value of human rights as a defence against oppression is now universal" (p. 123). Expanding the argument, others (e.g., Ife, 2012; Nash, 2015) have underlined that the potential of human rights to confront oppression everywhere lies in its socially constructed nature, and, thus, pure universalism and pure relativism reflect a naive understanding of the nature of human rights. Only a critical perspective will enable us to transcend the binary universalism/relativism and recognize their interdependence, since "all universals are inevitably contextually based" (Ife, 2012, p. 115). For Freeman (2018), though, it is not so much cultural differences but more often "practical circumstances" that drive diversity in the interpretation of human rights. And Frezzo (2015, p. xxi) reminds us that universalism, rather than an established achievement, must be addressed as a *project* that "entails and open-ended dialogue across civilizations." All these arguments resonate with the work developed by DRPI.

DRPI projects are grounded in three key principles. First, monitoring is led by persons with disabilities. Second, the research reflects the human rights approach by documenting the discrimination and rights violations experienced by persons with disabilities around the world. Third, sustainability is sought, and projects promote capacity building and partnerships to create multi-actor networks in local communities, equipped to undertake disability rights monitoring. These three principles have enabled us to move beyond universalism/relativism and individual/collective rights debates in the human rights sociological research conducted.

Placing persons with disabilities at the center of disability rights research has provided an opportunity to adequately consider cultural and regional differences while working to find a common ground on disability rights discussions across the globe. This has been accomplished at various levels, from defining the focus of each research project, to strategies of data collection and analysis. Local disability organizations, not Northern researchers, defined the scope of the research projects to address local priorities. Thus, in some countries DRPI projects covered all areas of rights and all types of disability. In others, by choice of the local DPO(s) leading the research, monitoring activities concentrated on specific topics, such as access to social protection (Marocco, Tunisia, and Algeria), work and employment (Nepal, Bangladesh, and India), or particular groups of the population, such as persons with psychosocial disabilities (Colombia).

In addition, the DRPI research tools, including the interview guide and coding scheme, have taken a rights-based approach to research to offer a common framework with which to assess the context-specific experiences of exercise or denial of human rights of persons with disabilities in a variety of countries. The interview guide starts with an open question—"*Which things have you found more satisfying in your life over the last five years? And which things have presented the greatest obstacles or barriers?*" This approach enabled each person interviewed to identify the issues that are more relevant to them, rather than imposing a fixed script on everyone and forcing them to address specific themes. During the interview, the issues raised by each interviewee are then probed to explore their human rights implications.

The analysis of the reports collected in each country serves to identify country patterns of rights violations. However, the aim of this research is not counting how many services people use or are available in their community (as in traditional human rights gap analyses). We study the extent to which five human rights principles are embedded in the laws, policies, programs, are reflected in the social attitudes, and are experienced in the everyday lives of persons with disabilities in those communities.

The five human rights goals that structure the DRPI coding scheme—*dignity; autonomy; non-discrimination and equality; participation, inclusion, and accessibility;* and *respect for difference*—are directly driven from the CRPD. However, the ways in which persons with disabilities make sense of these rights principles in everyday life vary greatly, even among countries in the Global South, in consequence of their different social, economic, and political realities. For instance, for a blind man in the Philippines, discrimination and erosion of dignity meant being forced to use a t-shirt with the word "blind" written in capital letters on his back to signal his enhanced abilities to perform massages to tourists in the streets of Manila. For a woman in Cameroon, it meant being denied the opportunity to pursue an education because the family could only afford to send one child to school and the parents felt they should rather invest in the more promising future of her younger non-disabled brother. In short, everywhere it has been the "practical circumstances" of people's lives that grant meaning and content to their rights talk (Freeman, 2018).

Finally, while working to build sustainable networks of disability rights activists and researchers, DRPI projects have supported advocacy strategies of grassroots local disability communities by submitting parallel reports to the CRPD Committee. In every country this work has been developed under the leadership of a disabled people's organization. We have been always amazed by the vitality and rights awareness of the DPOs in countries of the Global South we worked with, which typically are extremely active and efficient in advancing a rights-based agenda for persons with disabilities in their countries even if their resources are often very weak. For them, the CRPD has clearly become a powerful tool to pressure their national government and raise national and international attention for the rights violations experienced by persons with disabilities in their communities. The CRPD provides them with a common language that unites their struggles with those of the rest of the world, which also contributes to their empowerment.

At a more individual level, even in face of severe economic and social deprivation and poverty, persons with disabilities interviewed rarely emerged as passive victims. Rather, from their individual experiences of discrimination and exclusion they were able to deploy strategies of resistance that challenged the *status quo*, voicing a new agenda to bring about positive change in their lives and those of their peers. Many asked for awareness raising campaigns to overcome widespread ignorance and misconceptions about disability and increase respect for the contributions that persons with disabilities make to their communities. Others demanded increased state accountability to reduce levels of corruption and bureaucracy in access to services and supports, largely a legacy of colonial administration that continues to serve as gatekeeper to control demand. More importantly, whether by publicly telling their stories and making the personal political, or actively joining forces with other disability activists, they intertwined individual and collective understandings of rights and positioned themselves, not as human rights victims, but as "agents of their own social change" (Meekosha & Soldatic, 2011, p. 1394).

CONCLUDING REMARKS

This chapter examined, from a sociological perspective, the social and political conditions that have enabled the emergence and wide dissemination of the human rights model of disability. Taking the CRPD as the hallmark of this paradigm shift, it provided an overview of the treaty and discussed the meaning and scope of the change that is enshrined in the convention. This discussion highlighted the strengths and limitations of the right-based approach, particularly its recognition of the inherent dignity of all persons, regardless the complexity of their needs; the holistic perspective adopted by the CRPD and its emphasis on the interdependency of all rights; and, above all, the assertion of the central role of persons with disabilities in any efforts to transform society and achieve social justice. The CRPD offers "a roadmap for change" (Degener, 2016), detailing the range of obligations that bind states that ratify the treaty. Although the lack of strong enforcement mechanisms may hinder full implementation of rights-based approaches, the increasingly strong activism of persons with disabilities and their representative organizations, at both national and international levels, is pivotal to overturn traditional representations of disability while placing added pressure on states for accelerating needed change.

By bringing in the epistemological, theoretical, and methodological tools of sociology to the inquiry of human rights, the new sociology of human rights may help understand these processes. In the final section of the chapter, the experience of DRPI provided the ground on which to discuss opportunities and challenges that emerge for a Northern researcher doing research on disability rights in the Global South.

Beyond the difficulties highlighted for sociologists engaging in human rights research—mostly concerning the danger of developing new forms of colonialism due to the Western cultural bias embedded in human rights frameworks—there is still another challenge: that of reconciling our scientific profession with an interest in social justice

(Frezzo, 2015). Our concern with social inequalities and injustice brings us closer to activism (which many of us also are doing) but as much as we want our research to support rights struggles, we need to keep the rigor of our theories, methods, and results, and remain open to scientific scrutiny (Pinto, 2020).

There is a debate to whether the new sociology of human rights should "connect scholarship with advocacy" (Frezzo, 2015). I am on the side of those who believe that this is the right thing to do. "Transformational research" (Rioux et al., 2020) is the way forward to achieve this goal. Grounded on the understanding that "rights, justice and power cannot be separated in the fundamental design and implementation of research and in the transfer of knowledge," transformational research considers the research process as important as the outcome. In doing such, it refuses to be value neutral (Frezzo, 2015, p. 152), rather embracing human rights as normative principles shaping the research questions, processes, and relationships.

As a researcher coming from the Global North to develop sociological research on disability rights in the Global South, this requires refraining from imposing a research agenda of my own interest and convenience. Furthermore, it necessitates adopting a permanent critical stance and being considerate of North-South relations of power and colonial legacy. It requires being committed to address local priorities and interests, to provide a voice to persons with disabilities, and to work to strengthen local ownership of research processes and outcomes. In other words, it demands that I place myself at the service of local disability communities as resource, and engage with them in a dialogue to produce knowledge that is useful for local struggles for dignity, inclusion, and the human rights of persons with disabilities. My sociological journey with DRPI shows this is not just possible but, indeed, more necessary than ever.

Notes

1. DRPI is a collaborative initiative that developed a worldwide system to monitor the human rights of persons with disabilities. The project was launched in 2002, following an international Seminar that discussed measures to strengthen the rights of persons with disabilities, convened by Bengt Lindqvist, then the UN special rapporteur on disability. DRPI focuses on three areas of monitoring: systems monitoring (i.e., laws, policies, and programs), individual monitoring (i.e., reports individual experiences gathered from persons with disabilities) and societal monitoring (i.e., social representations of disability as conveyed by the media), taking the norms of the CRPD as benchmarks. Over 40 DRPI disability-rights-monitoring projects have been conducted in countries all over the world. For more information on DRPI visit http://drpi.research.yorku.ca.

2. The Optional Protocol establishes procedures for strengthening and monitoring the implementation of the convention, notably an individual communications procedures allowing individuals or groups of individuals to make claims as victims of violations of rights and an inquiry procedure giving the Committee on the Rights of Persons with Disabilities (a new body established by the convention) authority to conduct inquiries on disability rights violations.

References

Armaline, W., Glasberg, D. S., & Purkayastha, B. (2015). *The human rights enterprise*. Polity Press.

Berghs, M., Atkin, K., Graham, H., Hatton, C., & Thomas, C. (2016). Implications for public health research of models and theories of disability: a scoping study and evidence synthesis. *Public Health Research*, 4(8). https://doi.org/10.3310/phr04080

Brunsma, D., Smith, K. E. I., Gran, B. K. (Eds.). (2015). *Expanding the human in human rights: Towards a sociology of human rights*. Paradigm Publishers.

Committee on the Rights of Persons with Disabilities (CRPD Committee). (2014a). *General comment No. 1 (2014) Article 12: Equal recognition before the law*. CRPD /C/GC/1. United Nations.

Committee on the Rights of Persons with Disabilities (CRPD Committee). (2014b). *General comment No. 2 (2014) Article 9: Accessibility*. CRPD /C/GC/2. United Nations.

Committee on the Rights of Persons with Disabilities (CRPD Committee). (2016a). *General comment No. 3 (2016) Article 6: Women and girls with disabilities*. CRPD /C/GC/3. United Nations.

Committee on the Rights of Persons with Disabilities (CRPD Committee). (2016b). *General comment No. 4 (2016) Article 24: Right to inclusive education*. CRPD /C/GC/4. United Nations.

Committee on the Rights of Persons with Disabilities (CRPD Committee). (2017). *General comment No. 5 (2017) Article 19: Right to independent living*. CRPD /C/GC/5. United Nations.

Committee on the Rights of Persons with Disabilities (CRPD Committee). (2018a). *General comment No. 6 (2018) Article 5: Equality and non-discrimination*. CRPD /C/GC/6. United Nations.

Committee on the Rights of Persons with Disabilities (CRPD Committee). (2018b). *General comment No. 7 (2018) Articles 4.3 and 33.3: Participation of persons with disabilities in the implementation and monitoring of the Convention*. CRPD /C/GC/7. United Nations.

De Beco, G. (2020). Intersectionality and disability in international human rights law. *The International Journal of Human Rights*, 24(5), 593–614.

Degener, T. (2016). Disability in a human rights context. *Laws*, 5(35). https://doi.org/10.3390/laws5030035

Despouy, L. (1991). Human rights and disability: final report. E/CN.4/Sub.2/1991/31.

Freeman, M. (2018). *Human rights*. Polity Press.

Frezzo, M. (2015). *The sociology of human rights*. Polity Press.

Harpur, P. (2012). Embracing the new disability rights paradigm: The importance of the Convention on the Rights of Persons with Disabilities. *Disability & Society*, 27(1), 1–14.

Hathaway, Oona A. (2002). Do human rights treaties make a difference? *Yale Law Journal*, 111. Boston Univ. School of Law Working Paper No. 02–03. Available at SSRN: https://ssrn.com/abstract=311359

Ife, J. (2012). *Human rights and social work: Towards rights-based practice*. Cambridge University Press.

Isaac, R., , Raja, B. W. D., & Ravanan, M. P. (2010). Integrating people with disabilities: Their right – our responsibility. *Disability & Society*, 25(5), 627–630.

Kanter, A. (2003). The globalization of disability rights. *Syracuse Journal of International Law and Commerce*, 30, 241–263.

Kanter, A. (2015). *The development of disability rights under international law: From charity to human rights.* Routledge.

Lawson, A., & Beckett, A. (2021). The social and human rights models of disability: Towards a complementarity thesis. *Disability & Society, 25*(2), 348–379. https://doi.org/10.1080/13642987.2020.1783533

Meekosha, H., & Soldatic, K. (2011). Human rights and the global South: The case of disability. *Third World Quarterly, 32*(8), 1383–1397. http://dx.doi.org/10.1080/01436597.2011.614800

Mégret, F. (2008). The disabilities convention: Human rights of persons with disability or disability rights? *Human Rights Quarterly, 30*(2), 494–516. https://doi.org/10.1353/hrq.0.0000.

Mutua, M. (2008). *Human rights: A political and cultural critique.* University Press.

Nash, K. (2015). *The political sociology of human rights.* University Press. https://doi.org/10.1353/hrq.0.0000

Pinto, P. C. (2018). From rights to reality: Of crisis, coalitions, and the challenge of implementing disability rights in Portugal. *Social Policy and Society, 17*(1), 133–150. https://doi.org/10.1017/S1474746417000380

Pinto, P. C. (2020). When academia meets activism: The place of research in struggles for disability rights. In K. Soldatic & K. Johnson (Eds.), *Global perspectives on disability activism and advocacy* (pp. 315–327). Routledge.

Polanska, K. (2016). Human rights equals human survival? *International Sociology, 31*(2): 149–157. https://doi.org/10.1177/0268580915627083

Quinn, G., & Degener, T., with A. C. Burke, J. Castellino, P. Kenna, U. Kilkelly, & S. Quinlivan. (2002). *The current use and future potential of United Nations human rights instruments in the context of disability.* Office of the United Nations High Commissioner for Human Rights.

Rioux, M., & Valentine, F. (2006). Does theory matter? Exploring the nexus between disability, human rights and public policy. In D. Pothier & R. Devlin, *Critical disability theory: Essays in philosophy, politics, policy and law* (pp. 47–69). UBC Press.

Rioux, M., Pinto, P. C., Viera, J., & Keravica, R. (2016). Disability research in the Global South: Working from a local approach. In S. Grech & K. Soldatic (Eds.), *Disability in the global South: The critical handbook* (pp. 531–544). Springer.

Rioux, M., Pinto, P. C., Wakene, D., Keravica, R., & Viera, J. (2020). Reinventing activism: Evidence-based participatory monitoring as a tool for social change. In M. Berghs, T. Chataika, Y. El-Lhib, & K. Dube (Eds.), *The Routledge handbook of disability activism* (pp. 369–382). Routledge.

Stein, M. (2007). Disability human rights. *California Law Review, 95*, 75–121.

Stein, M., & Stein, P. (2007). Beyond disability civil rights. *Hastings Law Journal, 58*(6), 1203–1240.

United Nations (UN). (1945). *Charter of the United Nations.* Signed in San Francisco on June 26, 1945.

United Nations (UN). (1948). *Universal declaration of human rights.* Adopted and proclaimed by the United Nations General Assembly Resolution 217A (III), December 10, 1948. United Nations.

United Nations (UN). (1966a). *International covenant on civil and political rights.* Resolution 2200A/21 of December 16, 1966, UN Doc. A/6316. United Nations.

United Nations (UN). (1966b). *International covenant on social, economic and cultural rights.* Resolution 2200A/21 of December 16, 1966, UN Doc.E/6316. United Nations.

United Nations (UN). (1971). *Declaration on the rights of mentally retarded persons.* Resolution 2856 (XXVI) of December 20, 1971. United Nations.

United Nations (UN). (1975). *Declaration on the rights of disabled persons*. Resolution 3447 (XXX) of December 9, 1975. United Nations.

United Nations (UN). (1993). *The standard rules on the equalization of opportunities for persons with disabilities*. Resolution 48/96, annex, of December 20. United Nations.

United Nations (UN). (2006). *Convention on the rights of persons with disabilities*. Resolution A/61/106 of December 6, 2006. United Nations.

United Nations (UN). (2015). *Transforming our world: the 2030 Agenda for Sustainable Development*. Resolution A/RES/70/1 of September 25, 2015. United Nations.

UN Committee on Economic, Social and Cultural Rights (CESCR). (1995). *General Comment no. 5, Persons with disabilities*. U.N. Doc E/1995/22. United Nations.

UN Department of Economic and Social Affairs (UN). (2018). *Disability and Development Report: Realizing the Sustainable Development Goals by, for and with persons with disabilities*. United Nations.

UN World Programme of Action Concerning Disabled Persons (UN) (1982). Resolution A/RES/37/52 of December 3. United Nations.

UN Enable. (2008). Rights and dignity of persons with disabilities. http://www.un.org/disabilities/

Woodiwiss, A. (2005). *Human rights*. Routledge.

PART III

Representations of Disability in Culture and Media

....

CHAPTER 11

INEQUALITY AND DAY-TO-DAY ENCOUNTERS WITH MEDIA

....

KATE PRENDELLA AND MERYL ALPER

INTRODUCTION

....

DISABLED people have a complex and contested relationship with media—be it mass media, social media, or media technologies—as content consumers, activist organizers, and technological innovators. For many people with disabilities around the world, the societal, legal, and philosophical ideals of media access and accessibility have yet to be fully realized (Alper, 2021; Dobransky & Hargittai, 2006; Goggin, 2017). Rates of technological underconnectivity, for instance, are high among people with disabilities globally (Scholz et al., 2017). In the United States, disabled adults are three times less likely than nondisabled adults to say that they go online and are approximately 20 percentage points less likely to report owning a computer or smartphone (Anderson & Perrin, 2017). Beyond material access issues, disabled people also encounter narrow, stereotypical, and limited portrayals of disability throughout media and popular culture (Haller, 2010).

Such underconnectivity and underrepresentation impact the daily lives of disabled individuals in concrete ways, including those with physical, sensory, communicative, intellectual, and psychosocial disabilities. This includes gaps in accessing educational resources, receiving important news, finding health information, getting remote medical treatment through online telehealth platforms, contacting government services, and searching for jobs (Dobransky & Hargittai, 2016; Kim & Hwang, 2019). These needs have become even more pressing for disabled people amid the heightened uncertainties and anxieties of the coronavirus era (Barker, 2020). At the same time, people with disabilities are not merely beneficiaries of media access and representation. They have been central to the growth and culture of online communities since the inception of the Internet (Ellis & Kent, 2017). Computer-mediated communication has also offered significant space for linguistic, sensory, and social adaptability not found by individuals with disabilities in many physical environments (Sinclair, 2005).

Sociological approaches to media and culture have much to contribute to better understanding the everyday mediated lives of disabled people and making sense of the tensions described earlier. Though there is no canonical definition of media sociology, it broadly focuses on how "the media' [is] embedded in sociological thought and questions" (Waisbord, 2016, p. 1). It encompasses the study of social forces that shape and are shaped by media institutions, industries, audiences, representations, and technologies (Gurevitch et al., 1982; Waisbord, 2014). Both media and disability theorists are invested in unpacking social constructions of identity and community, as well as the structural power to make, unmake, and remake these aspects of society (Goggin & Newell, 2003).

In disability studies, a central concept is the idea that people with disabilities are in part made disabled by way of their societal interactions and social environments (Taylor, 2004), or what is known as the "social model of disability" (Shakespeare, 2006). Media and technology play an essential part, for example, in both enabling political participation for disabled people through online activism and creating barriers to voting through inaccessible materials and machinery (Trevisan, 2016). Recent work, however, has challenged a dichotomous model of individual impairment and social disability (Kafer, 2013). The pains and pleasures of disability are negotiated in complex ways through interactions across physical and digital spaces (Hamraie, 2017), such as how media and technology are bound up with contemporary models of care, modes of care work, and networks of mutual aid (Bennett et al., 2020). Media studies scholars and sociologists of media are similarly committed to exploring how public and private digital spaces can be understood in nuanced ways in relation to broader societal institutions such as law, policy, and education (Silverstone, 1999), though less attention has been paid to how these considerations are further informed by disability.

The benefit of locating disability within the scholarly traditions of media studies and media sociology is to situate it—alongside and entwined with race, class, gender, and sexuality—as a constructed phenomenon that reflects and produces social order (Ellcessor & Kirkpatrick, 2017). The goals of this chapter are thus to highlight underexplored theoretical connections between critical disability studies, cultural studies, media and communication studies, and sociology; to consider these overlaps through multiple forms of media and communication technology; and to suggest fruitful areas for future research at the intersections of disability and media sociology. We argue two main points: first, that people with disabilities have multifaceted yet ordinary daily encounters with media that have significant political, social, and cultural implications; and second, that the everyday experiences that nondisabled people have with media are already always influenced by disability.

We begin by briefly outlining cultural theories and concepts relevant to analyzing how dominant values and attitudes become associated with disability through contemporary media and communication technologies, as well as how inequalities and asymmetries are perpetuated by these largely limiting social constructs. Together, these theoretical traditions draw attention to how disabled people's meaning-making as citizens and audience members is shaped by dynamic interactions between structural forces (i.e., economic, social, cultural) and individual agency. The rest of the chapter delves into the daily media encounters of individuals with disabilities in three respects—media technologies, social media, and mass media—and how each might be understood through a sociological lens concerned with social distinction and differentiation. We conclude by discussing how media sociology might better account for disability and the disabled experience and, in turn, how disability can inform and improve the sociological study of media.

THEORETICAL BACKGROUND

A sociological approach to culture, focused on how human activity is embedded in networks of affect and meaning (Swidler, 1986), offers important insights into the everyday lives of disabled people and the ways that media artifacts, rituals, and institutions shape their individual and collective experiences (Lupton, 2012). Three analytical frameworks from the intellectual tradition of cultural studies in particular offer critical perspectives from which intersections between media and disability can be understood: Raymond Williams's notion of "culture as ordinary" (1989); the "circuit of culture" model, introduced by Stuart Hall and his collaborators (du Gay et al., 1997, 2013); and Elizabeth Ellcessor's "access kit" (2016). Though this overview is not exhaustive (e.g., encompassing Bourdieuian [1972, 1984] approaches to culture, power, and distinction), taken together, these theoretical and conceptual tools help us begin to explore how disability is defined, measured, and understood within society, culture, and media.

Culture as Ordinary

Raymond Williams's foundational work in cultural studies ([1958] 1989) questioned the essential relationship between society and culture. In his insistence that "culture is ordinary," Williams converges and diverges from Marxist framings of cultural production by arguing that culture is a way of life, and the arts (including media) are part of social organization, which economic change necessarily affects. Beyond cultural elites, working people have their own institutions outside of and often in opposition to strictly bourgeois culture. Culture is ordinary because it is created and reworked through lived experiences and rituals, and cultural meanings cannot be prescribed. Moreover, paralleling Stuart Hall's encoding/decoding model of communication (1980), which theorized that messages can be understood and adopted in alternate ways depending on one's positionality, individuals process and decipher cultural meanings differently based on their unique embodiment and location.

Though the process of ascribing marginalized identities to social practices was outside of Williams's conceptualization (Lewis, 2007), a focus on the body, culture, and everyday life is useful for recognizing disabled individuals as audiences, users, and producers of media. Dolmage (2014) notes that one cannot understand disability solely through dominant cultural rhetoric that seeks to devalue and isolate it from the central concerns and priorities of a society. Media, as "socially realized structures of communication" (Gitelman, 2006, p. 7), often fail to resonate with the common experiences and concerns of disabled individuals and disability communities, who regularly develop their own media practices, productions, and advocacy groups that directly reflect their interests, desires, and priorities (Ellcessor & Kirkpatrick, 2017; Siebers, 2010). One such example is the coordinated social media efforts of the Disability Visibility Project, founded and led by Asian American disability rights activist Alice Wong (2019). The cultural terms and contexts within which disability is deemed ordinary or extraordinary, normal or deviant—and the power in making those distinctions—are constantly being negotiated by disabled artists, writers, and media creators.

Circuit of Culture

Utilizing the "culture is ordinary" framework, we can interrogate what culture is, how it is made, and its potential to reflect and reconfigure society. However, understanding the cultural factors that shape media in relation to broader historical, social, and economic forces requires a deeper investigation of institutional and organizational processes. One tool for such an analysis is the "circuit of culture" model developed by Hall and fellow British Centre for Contemporary cultural studies theorists (du Gay et al., 1997, 2013). This model was a significant development in the sociology of culture as it called for analysis beyond the production of cultural commodities, but also their consumption, regulation, representation, and relationship to identity. The framing of this model as a "circuit" emphasizes how each element, distinct for analytic purposes, is connected to the others in a reciprocal process.

The circuit of culture model is a valuable framework for a sociological interrogation of the relationship between disability and media (Ellis, 2016) because it allows for analysis of how a cultural artifact is brought about through regulation, legislation, and production, as well as encoded with meaning. Those regulatory, technological, and ideological processes directly and indirectly impact the lived experience of disability. One rich example is the critically acclaimed 2020 documentary film *Crip Camp*, which chronicles the US disability rights movement and passage of the Americans with Disabilities Act (ADA) (1990). The film, an exemplar of media directed and produced by disabled people, was accompanied by "Crip Camp 2020: The Virtual Experience," a remote workshop series that offered a community-building experience for contemporary grassroots disability activists and advocates. The circuit of culture model prompts questions about how disability representation and identity are contested and reconstructed through a given media artifact like *Crip Camp*, and it encourages an understanding of disabled individuals as active producers and consumers of mainstream and independent media.

Access Kit

Though circuit models for the study of media culture allow for analysis at the macro and micro levels of society, they do not offer specific insights into the accessibility of information, media, and communication technologies. Elizabeth Ellcessor's "access kit" (2016) guides ongoing critical examination of media accessibility as a relational and variable phenomenon. Paralleling the circuit of culture, the access kit consists of five elements: regulation, use, form, content, and experience. Ellcessor argues that media access must be recognized beyond basic "availability, affordability and choice" and calls for analysis of "what is being accessed, and for what purposes" (Ellcessor, 2016, p. 8). The ability for those with sensory and communication disabilities to participate in the physical and digital world often relies on "access work," or the situated and affective labor that makes information and technical accessibility possible. The access kit framing enables an evaluation of media as more than just accessible or inaccessible, but to instead consider access itself as a critical object of inquiry and in/accessibility as a work in progress (Hamraie, 2017; Williamson, 2019).

Ellcessor's model is naturally suited for a sociological consideration of the relationship between disability and media, as she is specifically interested in how bodies and technologies co-constitute one another and reestablish norms of culture and identity. Outside the fields of media and communication studies, such discussions of power, culture, and society are of vital importance for sociologists. Ellcessor (2016) details the "preferred user position" created through the access conditions of media technologies, an expansion upon Hall's notion of a dominant-hegemonic position assumed among the media-viewing audience. Such an imagined audience rarely includes, for instance, d/Deaf and hard-of-hearing people who generate affective meaning from descriptive closed captioning on video content. The preferred user position situates digital media content within a neoliberal hierarchy for disabled users, with information being prioritized, communication ranking a distant second, and entertainment constructed as a luxury. In this context, the assertion that disabled people should be prioritized as media audiences for the purposes of leisure and entertainment becomes a political act.

As these theoretical frameworks illustrate, culture, media, and disability are not abstract concepts, but are made highly material through the frictions that they generate in the struggle for societal power, autonomy, and agency. The "culture is ordinary" framing underscores disabled people's resistance against ableist media cultures. The "circuit of culture" model illustrates how media depictions and technical arrangements taken up by individuals with disabilities do not operate solely at the level of the artifact, but broader social processes as well. And lastly, the "access kit" employs a similar dynamic approach as the circuit of culture but centers disability and in/accessibility in all forms of cultural production. In what follows, we apply these models to discuss three broad types of media—access work, social media, and mass media—and specific instances in which they are co-configured through disability, with a limited focus on the US context.

Everyday Interactions with Media and Technology

Critical sociological approaches to culture and meaning-making have much to add to discussions of disability as it is enacted, performed, and lived through media and communication technologies. First, we review media "access work," or the paid and voluntary efforts of individuals who labor to make media technologies accessible, and how this work has historically been devalued and rendered invisible, though this is shifting in the post-coronavirus era. Next, we consider social media and online communities as powerful resources for generating and sharing knowledge among people with disabilities, while contending with major structural limitations to their participation. Lastly, we explore mass media and the tensions inherent in disability media representation both on- and off-screen.

Media Technologies and Access Work

People with disabilities regularly rely on an assemblage of tools to access technology for creating, consuming, and circulating media (e.g., visual description of televisual content for blind and low vision audiences). Many also require a set of media technologies to access face-to-face communication (e.g., CART, or communication access real-time translation, which involves steganography software and computer screens for the captioning of live speakers and events). These tools in and of themselves do not provide access; they require the skilled labor of people doing media access work (making media accessible) and mediated access work (making access through media) (Alper, 2021). While flows of information have always relied on human labor, the often-invisible technical and cultural work that disabled and nondisabled people do to enable political, social, and economic participation via what Downey terms "accessibility labor" (2014, p. 158) is consistently undervalued in society.

Access work has taken on new meaning—and increased societal importance—in the age of COVID-19. The "social distancing" (or more accurately, physical distancing) required to slow the spread of coronavirus brought both the successes and failures of mediated access to the forefront of society. The global health disaster demanded an unprecedented move toward virtual work, learning, and gathering, completely altering the pace of daily life worldwide, concerns which were not new for disabled people and those with chronic illnesses. This population has long been met with denials or encountered major barriers in order to receive accommodations, and many wondered if the flexibility afforded to the nondisabled would extend to individuals with disabilities after the pandemic subsided (Meng, 2020). In the sudden move toward remote telepresence across workplaces and learning environments, many disabled people's media access needs were still left behind (Hamraie, 2020). For instance, US parents of disabled students reported significant difficulty obtaining the same level of support as was outlined in their child's individualized education plan (IEP) while learning from home through online instruction (Nadworny, 2020).

Those who enact the paid, and at times precarious, labor of media and mediated access in person and from a distance include click workers, web designers, software developers, user experience researchers, sign language interpreters, closed captioners, audio describers, and real-time stenographers (Downey, 2008; Gray & Suri, 2019; Zdenek, 2015). The temporality of media access work varies across scales of time, be it through routine uses of media, real-time translations of public speeches replayed at a later date, or the long-term technological care, maintenance, repair, and replacement of hardware and software (Hickman, 2019). People with disabilities are central to such work in formal and informal ways. They may be employed in media accessibility professions or informally design and develop multimodal interventions (Titchkosky, 2011). This can include providing printed text copies of spoken talks and describing visual images that appear projected on presentation slides. Such efforts draw on the collective knowledge-making practices of what feminist disability science and technology studies scholars Hamraie and Fritsch (2019) term "crip technoscience."

Distinguishing between accessibility work and mainstream usability work is complicated, considering multiple media audiences and underlying incentive structures (Ellcessor, 2015). For example, a growing number of online videos on Instagram have stylized open captions (i.e., cannot be turned off by the viewer) accompanying short audio clips. These videos reflect increasing rates of global mobile consumption and the likelihood that smartphone users might not be able to hear audio clearly in a loud place (Butler, 2020). Such captions have the additional benefit of being useful for d/Deaf and hard-of-hearing individuals. The economic incentives of usability work can sometimes dovetail with accessibility work, but more often than not, solutions like closed captioning or screen reading software exist under "legislative determinism," or cultural change that only occurs when legal action demands it, and even then the laws may not be followed unless accompanied by economic or reputational penalties (Ellis, 2019; Petrick, 2015).

Whether media or mediated access work is best done by humans or machines, amateurs or professionals, or some combination is also up for debate. It is hard to imagine, for instance, a robot replacing the mediated access work of passing around the microphone during the question-and-answer period of a lecture, nor the affective and situated labor of encouraging others to do so (Hickman, 2019). The poor quality of auto-generated captions on YouTube (of such low quality that they garnered the Twitter hashtag campaign #NoMoreCRAPtions, developed by deaf YouTuber Rikki Poynter in 2016), along with a lack of regulation, has resulted in a mix of paid and voluntary work and alternative captioning platforms like Amara (Ellcessor, 2016; Hollier et al., 2017). Even "automated" access work involves humans, generally paid minimally for sorting or labeling tasks (Gray & Suri, 2019).

There is a cruel irony to the fact that accessibility labor may finally become more valuable in a post-COVID-19 world after so many nondisabled people by necessity—and profitably—made media accessible remotely. For example, the exclusive South by Southwest (SXSW) film festival announced in Spring 2020 that it would allow films scheduled to premiere in person at the canceled Austin, Texas-based festival to be viewed on Amazon Prime's streaming video platform, free to anyone with an Amazon account. Meanwhile, disabled filmmakers have argued for years that the lack of physical and media access at festivals limits their opportunities for career advancement (Lopez, 2020). Media access work and mediated access work underlie all communication technologies, whether or not nondisabled people know about or appreciate such efforts.

Social and Digital Media

Turning to social media as a site of cultural interaction and interactivity, the use of digital spaces by people with disabilities tends to be understood in relation to its creative and political potential. This includes possibilities for disabled users to gain access to information, build robust networks, and engage in production that challenges the limiting models of disability ever-present in mass media. Through the relative ease of content creation and publication in digital spaces, we have seen a rise in global disability cultures and subcultures (Goggin & Newell, 2003). Such formations have significant implications for disabled social media users and social media writ large, including conceptions of self-representation and community formation.

The Internet is a critical space for marginalized groups to advocate for greater equity, justice, and authentic visibility (Jackson et al., 2020), and people with disabilities are no exception. Interactive sites like YouTube and the livestream gaming platform Twitch allow for disabled creators to share content and directly engage with audiences via comments and chat functionality (Ellis, 2010; Johnson, 2019). Disabled adolescents and adults craft personal narratives, share slices of life, and generate memes through social media platforms such as Facebook, Twitter, TikTok, and Instagram. One of the distinguishing features of digital spaces is that it makes production and distribution more accessible to those outside of traditional media industries. In comparison to mass media, social media platforms provide people with a much wider distribution venue at a lower cost.

Social media generate space for self-representation that can also defy the narrow presentation of disability normalized and perpetuated in culture. Disabled people, especially those who are LGBTQ + and people of color, have utilized social media to address and challenge the lack of media representation and media attention paid to issues most concerning them (Thompson, 2019). #FilmDis, a hashtag and Twitter discussion created by trans disabled filmmaker Dominick Evans (2020), provides a regular site for interrogating the lack of people with disabilities behind and in front of the camera. Acts of self-representation in these spaces are also inherently political, such as the #HospitalGlam Instagram hashtag developed in 2015 by queer disabled artist Karolyn Gehrig to reassert agency and pride over a body made to feel disempowered in doctor's offices and medicalized spaces (Hill, 2017). In these contexts, social media is an important advocacy tool for confronting a patriarchal and ableist society.

Though normative narratives may be challenged through social media, there are also drawbacks. Hill (2017) argues that within "neoliberal inclusionism," disabled content creators must at once position themselves as personally motivated and socially motivating for their audiences. Nondisabled audiences often place demands on disabled media figures that their messages of advocacy and justice be made more palatable and less radical. Further, the work of self-representation in digital spaces involves physical, economic, and affective labor on the part of disabled producers. Beyond the time to produce content, creators devote significant energy to strategically disclosing intimate details of their lives (Ellcessor, 2017). Social media presents real opportunities for challenging prevailing representations of disability, but such work is not undertaken without risk.

Another key component of social media is community building. Long before the Internet, disabled people forged strategic coalitions out of necessity both among themselves and across other populations fighting for civil rights (Shapiro, 1993). Over the 20th century, daily engagements with media became part of a larger community experience, especially for minoritized audiences (Gross, 1991). Social connection is consistently a leading reason why people with disabilities report engaging in social media (Hynan et al., 2014). The promises of digital spaces for community formation are significant for disabled people as they can reduce physical, temporal, economic, and spatial barriers (Goggin & Newell, 2003; Trevisan, 2016). Digital spaces also allow for different forms of activism to flourish, such as the #DisabilityTooWhite movement started in 2016 by Vilissa Thompson (2019). Thompson developed the campaign to speak back to the disability community by addressing racial inequities present within the disability rights movement and challenge the whitewashing of disability activism. Other hashtags such as #CripTheVote and #SuckItAbleism enable disabled activists to form community often denied to them, assert political power, and amplify a diverse range of stories told from their perspectives.

MASS MEDIA

Portrayals of disability through mass media—be it radio, television, film, or literature—also impact the lives of individuals with disabilities and the way that they are viewed in everyday social interactions and cultural encounters (Kent, 1987; Zhang & Haller, 2013). Historically, disability representation has been sensationalist and detrimental; disabled individuals were simultaneously on display and removed from society, both politically and physically (Schweik, 2009). There has been a surge in disability visibility in recent decades, both feeding into and boosted by passage of legislation such as the ADA. With increased attention to disability comes the potential for mass media that will move beyond stereotypes to tell more authentic, intersectional stories.

The history of disability media representation has overwhelmingly been one of presentation through a deficit model, in which disability is marked as an inherently negative identity (Scott-Hill, 2004). There are a number of major stereotypes that have characterized disability representation over the years (Garland-Thomson, 1996; Longmore, 1987). The charity model of disability forms the basis of one such stereotype, in which disabled individuals are seen as objects of pity in need of saving, popularized in the 20th century by fundraising telethons such as the Jerry Lewis-hosted MDA (Muscular Dystrophy Association) Labor Day Telethon (Longmore, 2016). Disability is also often linked with morality, which positions disabled characters as evil, as in the classic film *Peter Pan* and the sinister, one-handed Captain Hook. Overcoming narratives featuring a "supercrip"—a disabled individual who achieves astonishing things—also dominate, like autistic Dr. Shaun Murphy in ABC's drama series *The Good Doctor*. Such representations have the potential to undermine people with disabilities and serve to justify ableism (Jaeger, 2011).

Popular disability discourses unjustly come to stand in for all disabled people. Hollywood portrayals of disability have been essentially standardized as White, male, straight, and cisgender. This results in a monolithic presentation of disability and its intersections with race, gender, and sexuality. Such production choices are often made in an effort to "universalize" the narrative. These inaccuracies are exacerbated by the casting of nondisabled actors to play disabled characters (Ellcessor, 2017), also known as "disability drag" or "cripping up" (Siebers, 2008). Moreover, nondisabled actors are regularly rewarded for these portrayals with Oscar nominations and awards. A study by the Ruderman Family Foundation (2019) found, however, that 55% of film and television audiences are more likely to watch a production that casts a disabled actor, and they want not only more representation of disability but more accurate depictions as well (Nissim, 2019). Key to creating such content is the cultivation and promotion of disabled people in media executive leadership positions, as well as the behind-the-scenes crew. More diverse production teams, as seen in television programs like Netflix's *Special* and ABC's *Speechless*, have led to representations of disability that move away from regressive, unidimensional stereotypes.

Beyond the screen, stereotypical disability representation has an impact on both disabled and nondisabled audiences. Negative media coverage may be directly internalized by disabled individuals (Zhang & Haller, 2013), which then shapes the broader culture of ableism. Media stereotypes do not necessarily have to be perceived as negative to have a harmful societal impact. Activist Stella Young (2012) popularized the phrase "inspiration porn," which describes narratives that objectify disabled individuals for the benefit of nondisabled people. Such messages proliferate in media and are meant to inspire or motivate nondisabled audiences. Young argued that such reductive narratives dehumanize people with disabilities and distract nondisabled audiences from working to remove structural obstacles that individuals with disabilities face. It is not only how disability is represented on-screen and behind the screen that matters but also the off-screen emotional and psychological effects of said representation on audiences.

In addition to direct impacts on viewers, mass media representations of disability operate in tandem with structures and hierarchies that impact the daily lives of disabled individuals. One outcome of deficit-oriented media representation is the erasure of disability culture, whereby disabled individuals are seen as having an identity that must be "eradicated or normalized" (Scott-Hill, 2004, p. 88). This is exemplified through the media trope of individually focused "overcoming" narratives (e.g., viral videos of deaf people with new cochlear implants "hearing" for the first time). If one disabled person cannot "overcome" or "succeed," then it is explained within this discourse as a personal failure rather than the mark of a system of societal hierarchies and oppression (Mauldin, 2016; Puar, 2017). Such perceptions of disability normalize the neglect of disabled bodies and removal from public life (Longmore, 1987). Mass media representations of disability operate in conjunction with ableist policies, systems, and histories.

Conclusion

This chapter has proposed disability as an important but overlooked lens in media sociology through a cultural analysis of disabled individuals' day-to-day interactions with media in a variety of forms, from transcription software to Twitch to television networks. We have reviewed a number of theoretical approaches to the study of culture, media, and society in relation to disability, and employed these frameworks to understand mediated labor practices, social and digital media, and mass media as sites within which disability is at once enacted, erased, and negotiated. Powerful social institutions, including but not limited to media, largely perpetuate neoliberal notions of access, success, and work. Within these constraints, disabled people also find and generate community, solidarity, and knowledge across a range of media and communication technologies.

In our reflection on relevant theories and concepts, we have found new links between multiple areas of study, namely media sociology, cultural studies, disability studies, and sociology of culture. These points of connection highlight how media representations and media technologies comprise a major component of the social model of disability, while recognizing the limits of such a model to contain the complexity of the disabled experience. Williams's "culture is ordinary" framing, du Gay et al.'s "circuit of culture," and Ellcessor's "access kit" each offer novel critical approaches to sociological theorizations of disability, media, and culture, with an emphasis on the power dynamics at play in the meaning-making and knowledge production enabled by digital technologies. Taken together, these conceptualizations are of significant value for media sociologists and communication scholars as they help to articulate how marginalization occurs, nondisabled privilege is generated, and ableist distinctions are perpetuated by media industries.

We conclude by suggesting areas for future research that take seriously the mediated work of disabled individuals, employ explicitly anti-ableist approaches, and recognize "cultural accessibility" (Ellcessor, 2016) as a promising direction for media scholarship. First, be it through producing media, conducting media access work, or sharing best practices for mediated access, disabled activists, artists, and scholars have long been engaging in material and affective labor, often outside of and apart from resources within academia (Oliver, 2009). They have and are performing accessibility labor by forming communities in digital spaces and challenging problematic media productions of disability. Such work is vital and yet often undervalued in scholarship on media industries. Increased recognition necessitates shifting present conceptions of media and information production to include this labor within and outside of the academy (Titchkosky, 2011).

Second, disability is vital to the work of media sociologists as it exposes underlying, but largely overlooked, structures and systems of exclusion (Moser, 2006). Expanding opportunities for media ownership, policymaking, and production among disabled people will occur not through "normalizing" efforts, but anti-ableist ones. Normalizing rhetorics calls for the extension of dominant cultural values to create equality, without disrupting the systems that created said inequality (Gleeson, 1997). These discourses also perpetuate the idea that abnormality resides with individuals, in line more broadly with neoliberal notions of individualization. Attempts at inclusion often fail to attend to the impact of compounding marginalized identities (Crenshaw, 1990). Age, gender, race, ethnicity, class, and disability each play a key role in shaping the type of media interaction individuals experience. The path forward is not in normalizing then, but anti-ableist approaches that challenge oppressive systems and institutions, and acknowledge intersectionality in disabled people's relationships to digital and mass media.

Lastly, to confront the power structures and hegemonic notions of disability discussed throughout this chapter, cultural accessibility is central. Introduced by Ellcessor (2016), cultural accessibility moves "past accommodation, or tolerance, to integration and calls upon society to include and integrate the different bodies, knowledges, perspectives, and possibilities offered within disability cultures" (p. 184). Through the active inclusion of disabled perspectives, social activists are better equipped to push back against neoliberalism and capitalist structures that presently define mediated spaces. In the wake of COVID-19, for instance, disabled and chronically ill media makers already had ample experience writing, collaborating, and producing from a distance (Wong, 2020). Cultural accessibility involves centering and rewarding the expertise of marginalized people, as well as recognizing the role of systems and institutions across culture in perpetuating inequality.

In closing, centering disability within the sociology of media and culture, and its concurrent focus on distinction, differentiation, inequalities, and asymmetries, generates an important space for social theorization and political activation. Disability contains both cultures onto itself and is shaped in myriad ways by the cultural accessibility and inaccessibility of media and communication technologies. As critical social scholars analyze how media artifacts, cultural institutions, and technological infrastructures are raced, classed, and gendered, so, too, should disability be recognized as a vital component of media use among both disabled and nondisabled people.

REFERENCES

Alper, M. (2021). Critical media access studies: Deconstructing power, visibility, and marginality in mediated space. *International Journal of Communication*, 15, 840–861.

Americans With Disabilities Act of 1990, Pub. L. No. 101–336, 104 Stat. 328 (1990).

Anderson, M., & Perrin, A. (2017). Disabled Americans are less likely to use technology. *Pew Research Center*. https://www.pewresearch.org/fact-tank/2017/04/07/disabled-americans-are-less-likely-to-use-technology/

Barker, A. Z. (2020, March 30). Those with disabilities have a right to survive the coronavirus pandemic. *Boston Globe*. https://www.bostonglobe.com/2020/03/30/opinion/those-with-disabilities-have-right-survive-coronavirus-pandemic/

Bennett, C. L., Rosner, D. K., & Taylor, A. S. (2020). The care work of access. In *Proceedings of the 2020 CHI Conference on Human Factors in Computing Systems* (CHI '20) (pp. 1–15). ACM.

Bourdieu, P. (1972). *Outline of a theory of practice*. (R. Nice, Trans.). Cambridge University Press. https://doi.org/10.1525/aa.1979.81.1.02a00940

Bourdieu, P. (1984). *Distinction: A social critique of the judgment of taste* (R. Nice, Trans.). Harvard University Press.

Butler, J. (2020). The visual experience of accessing captioned television and digital videos. *Television & New Media*, 21(7), 679–696. https://doi.org/10.1177/1527476418824805

Crenshaw, K. (1990). Mapping the margins: Intersectionality, identity politics, and violence against women of color. *Stanford Law Review*, 43, 1241. https://doi.org/10.2307/1229039

Dobransky, K., & Hargittai, E. (2006). The disability divide in internet access and use. *Information, Communication & Society*, 9(3), 313–334. doi:10.1080/13691180600751298

Dobransky, K., & Hargittai, E. (2016). Unrealized potential: Exploring the digital disability divide. *Poetics*, 58, 18–28. https://doi.org/10.1016/j.poetic.2016.08.003

Dolmage, J. (2014). *Disability rhetorics*. Syracuse University Press.

Downey, G. J. (2008). *Closed captioning: Subtitling, stenography, and the digital convergence of text with television*. Johns Hopkins Press. https://doi.org/10.2307/j.ctt1j2n73m

Downey, G. J. (2014). Making media work: Time, space, identity, and labor in the analysis of information and communication infrastructures. In T. Gillespie, P. J. Boczkowski, & K. A. Foot (Eds.), *Media technologies: Essays on communication, materiality, and society* (pp. 141–165). MIT Press. https://doi.org/10.7551/mitpress/9780262525374.003.0008

du Gay, P., Hall, S., Janes, L., Mackay, H., & Negus, K. (1997). *Doing cultural studies: The story of the Sony Walkman* (1st ed.). SAGE Publications.

du Gay, P., Hall, S., Janes, L., Madsen, A. K., Mackay, H., & Negus, K. (2013). *Doing cultural studies: The story of the Sony Walkman* (2nd ed.). SAGE Publications.

Ellcessor, E. (2015). Blurred lines: Accessibility, disability, and definitional limitations. *First Monday*, 20(9). https://doi.org/10.5210/fm.v20i9.6169

Ellcessor, E. (2016). *Restricted access: Media, disability, and the politics of participation*. New York University Press. doi:10.18574/nyu/9781479867820.001.0001

Ellcessor, E. (2017). Kickstarting community disability, access, and participation in 'My Gimpy Life'. In E. Ellcessor & B. Kirkpatrick (Eds.), *Disability media studies* (pp. 31–51). NYU Press. https://doi.org/10.18574/nyu/9781479867820.001.0001

Ellcessor, E., & Kirkpatrick, B. (Eds.) (2017). *Disability media studies*. NYU Press. https://doi .org/10.18574/nyu/9781479867820.001.0001

Ellis, K. (2010). A purposeful rebuilding: YouTube, representation, accessibility and the socio-political space of disability. *Telecommunications Journal of Australia*, *60*(2), 21.1–21.12. https://doi.org/10.2104/tja10021

Ellis, K. (2016). *Disability and popular culture*. Routledge. https://doi.org/10.4324/978131 5577326

Ellis, K. (2019). *Disability and digital television cultures: Representation, access, and reception*. Routledge. https://doi.org/10.4324/9781315755663

Ellis, K., & Kent, M. (Eds.) (2017). *Disability and social media: Global perspectives*. Routledge. https://doi.org/:10.4324/9781315577357

Evans, D. (2020, March 1). How #FilmDis is transforming the conversation about disability in film. *Daily Dot*. https://www.dailydot.com/upstream/filmdis-disability-film-twitter/

Garland-Thomson, R. (1996). *Extraordinary bodies: Figuring physical disability in American culture and literature*. Columbia University Press.

Gitelman, L. (2006). Introduction: Media as historical subjects. In *Always already new: Media, history, and the data of culture* (pp. 1–22). MIT Press. https://doi.org/10.7551/mitpress/1208.001.0001

Gleeson, B. J. (1997). Disability studies: A historical materialist view. *Disability & Society*, *12*(2), 179–202. https://doi.org/10.1080/09687599727326

Goggin, G. (2017). Disability and digital inequalities: Rethinking digital divides with disability theory. In M. Ragnedda & G. W. Muschert (Eds.), *Theorizing digital divides* (pp. 69–80). Routledge. https://doi.org/10.4324/9781315455334

Goggin, G., & Newell, C. (2003). *Digital disability: The social construction of disability in new media*. Rowman & Littlefield.

Gray, M., & Suri, S. (2019). *Ghost work: How to stop Silicon Valley from building a new global underclass*. Houghton Mifflin Harcourt.

Gross, L. (1991). Out of the mainstream: Sexual minorities and the mass media. In M. Wolf & A. P. Kielwasser (Eds.), *Gay people, sex, and the media* (pp. 19–46). Haworth Press.

Gurevitch, M., Bennett, T., Curran, J., & Woollacott, J. (Eds.) (1982). *Culture, society, and the media*. Routledge.

Hall, S. (1980). Encoding/decoding. In S. Hall, D. Hobson, A. Love, & P. Willis (Eds.), *Culture, media, language* (pp. 128–138). Hutchinson.

Haller, B. A. (2010). *Representing disability: Essays on mass media*. Advocado Press.

Hamraie, A. (2017). *Building access: Universal design and the politics of disability*. University of Minnesota Press.

Hamraie, A. (2020). Accessible teaching in the time of COVID-19. *Mapping access* [blog]. https://www.mapping-access.com/blog-1/2020/3/10/accessible-teaching-in-the-time-of-covid-19

Hamraie, A., & Fritsch, K. (2019). Crip technoscience manifesto. *Catalyst: Feminist, Theory, Technoscience*, *5*(1), 1–33.

Hickman, L. (2019). Transcription work and the practices of crip technoscience. *Catalyst: Feminism, Theory, Technoscience*, *5*(1), 1–10.

Hill, S. (2017). Exploring disabled girls' self-representational practices online. *Girlhood Studies*, *10*(2), 114–130. https://doi.org/10.3167/ghs.2017.100209

Hollier, S., Ellis, K. M., & Kent, M. (2017). User-generated captions: From hackers, to the disability digerati, to fansubbers. *M/C Journal*, *20*(3).

Hynan, A., Murray, J., & Goldbart, J. (2014). "Happy and excited": Perceptions of using digital technology and social media by young people who use augmentative and alternative communication. *Child Language Teaching and Therapy*, *30*(2), 175–186. https://doi.org/10.1177/0265659013519258

Jackson, S. J., Bailey, M., & Foucault Welles, B. (2020). *# HashtagActivism: Networks of race and gender justice*. MIT Press.

Jaeger, P. T. (2011). *Disability and the internet: Confronting a digital divide*. Lynne Rienner.

Johnson, M. R. (2019). Inclusion and exclusion in the digital economy: Disability and mental health as a live streamer on Twitch.tv. *Information, Communication & Society*, *22*(4), 506–520. https://doi.org/10.1080/1369118X.2018.1476575

Kafer, A. (2013). *Feminist, queer, crip*. Indiana University Press.

Kent, D. (1987). Disabled women: Portraits in fiction and drama. In A. Gartner & T. Joe (Eds.), *Images of the disabled, disabling images* (pp. 47–69). Praeger.

Kim, K. M., & Hwang, J. H, (2019) Exploring gaps in the online economic inclusion of persons with disabilities in Korea. *Information, Communication & Society*, *22*(4), 570–581. https://doi.org/10.1080/1369118X.2018.1545039

Longmore, P. K. (1987). Screening stereotypes: Images of disabled people in television and motion pictures. In *Why I burned my book and other essays on disability* (pp. 131–146). Temple University Press.

Longmore, P. K. (2016). *Telethons: Spectacle, disability, and the business of charity*. Oxford University Press. doi:10.1093/acprof:oso/9780190262075.001.0001

Lopez, K. (2020, April 3). It's hard being cut off from society? Welcome to my world. *IndieWire*. https://www.indiewire.com/2020/04/disability-media-health-crisis-1202220789/

Lewis, G. (2007). Racializing culture is ordinary. *Cultural Studies*, *21*(6), 866–886.

Lupton, D. (2012). *Medicine as culture: Illness, disease and the body* (3rd ed.). SAGE Publications.

Mauldin, L. (2016). *Made to hear: Cochlear implants and raising deaf children*. University of Minnesota Press.

Meng, A. (2020, March 13). The coronavirus response shows how crucial accessibility is. *BuzzFeed News*. https://www.buzzfeednews.com/article/amymeng/coronavirus-working-from-home-disability-accessibility

Moser, I. (2006). Sociotechnical practices and difference: On the interferences between disability, gender, and class. *Science, Technology & Human Values*, *31*(5), 537–564. https://doi.org/10.1177/0162243906289611

Nadworny, E. (2020, March 27). With schools closed, kids with disabilities are more vulnerable than ever. *National Public Radio (NPR)*. https://www.npr.org/2020/03/27/821926032/with-schools-closed-kids-with-disabilities-are-more-vulnerable-than-ever

Nissim, H. S. B. (2019). *Disability inclusion in movies and television: Market research, 2019*. https://rudermanfoundation.org/white_papers/disability-inclusion-in-movies-and-television-market-research-2019/

Oliver, M. (2009). *Understanding disability: From theory to practice* (2nd ed.). Palgrave Macmillan.

Petrick, E. (2015). *Making computers accessible: Disability rights and digital technology*. Johns Hopkins University Press.

Puar, J. K. (2017). *The right to maim: Debility, capacity, disability*. Duke University Press.

Scholz, F., Yalcin, B., & Priestley, M. (2017). Internet access for disabled people: Understanding socio-relational factors in Europe. *Cyberpsychology: Journal of Psychosocial Research on Cyberspace*, *11*(1), Article 4. https://doi.org/10.5817/CP2017-1-4

Schweik, S. M. (2009). *The ugly laws: Disability in public*. NYU Press.

Scott-Hill, M. (2004). Impairment, difference and "identity." In J. Swain, S. French, C. Barnes, & C. Thomas (Eds.), *Disabling barriers—enabling environments* (2nd ed., pp. 87–93). SAGE Publications.

Shakespeare, T. (2006). The social model of disability. In L. J. Davis (Ed.), *The disability studies reader* (2nd ed., pp. 197–204). Routledge.

Shapiro, J. P. (1993). *No pity: People with disabilities forging a new civil rights movement.* Times Books.

Siebers, T. (2008). *Disability theory.* University of Michigan Press. https://doi.org/10.3998/mpub.309723

Siebers, T. (2010). *Disability aesthetics.* University of Michigan Press.

Sinclair, J. (2005). *Autism Network International: The development of a community and its culture.* http://www.autreat.com/History_of_ANI.html

Silverstone, R. (1999). *Why study the media?* SAGE Publications.

Swidler, A. (1986). Culture in action: Symbols and strategies. *American Sociological Review, 51*(2), 273–286.

Taylor, S. (2004). The right not to work: Power and disability. https://monthlyreview.org/2004/03/01/the-right-not-to-work-power-and-disability/

Thompson, V. (2019). How technology is forcing the disability rights movement into the 21st century. *Catalyst: Feminism, Theory, and Technoscience, 5*(1), 1–5. doi:10.28968/cftt.v5i1.30420

Titchkosky, T. (2011). *The question of access: Disability, space, meaning.* University of Toronto Press.

Trevisan, F. (2016). *Disability rights advocacy online: Voice, empowerment and global connectivity.* Taylor & Francis.

Waisbord, S. (2014). *Media sociology: A reappraisal.* Polity.

Waisbord, S. (2016). Media sociology. In K. B. Jensen & R. T. Craig (Eds.), *The international encyclopedia of communication theory and philosophy* (Vol. 3, pp. 1–18). Wiley. https://doi.org/10.1002/9781118766804.wbiect161

Williams, R. (1989). *Resources of hope: Culture, democracy, socialism.* Verso.

Williamson, B. (2019). *Accessible America: A history of disability and design.* NYU Press.

Wong, A. (2019). The rise and fall of the plastic straw: Sucking in crip defiance. *Catalyst: Feminism, Theory, and Technoscience, 5*(1), 1–12. doi:10.28968/cftt.v5i1.30435

Wong, A. (2020). I'm disabled and need a ventilator to live. Am I expendable during this pandemic? *Vox.* https://www.vox.com/first-person/2020/4/4/21204261/coronavirus-covid-19-disabled-people-disabilities-triage

Young, S. (2012). We're not here for your inspiration. *Ramp Up.* https://www.abc.net.au/rampup/articles/2012/07/02/3537035.htm

Zdenek, S. (2015). *Reading sounds: Closed-captioned media and popular culture.* University of Chicago Press.

Zhang, L., & Haller, B. (2013). Consuming image: How mass media impact the identity of people with disabilities. *Communication Quarterly, 61*(3), 319–334. https://doi.org/10.1080/01463373.2013.776988

CHAPTER 12

FRAMING DISABILITY IN FASHION

JORDAN FOSTER

INTRODUCTION

DESPITE a long history of exclusion from the fashion industry, models with disabilities have—quite literally—come into focus. Among them are Kate Grant for *Benefit Cosmetics* and Special Olympics athlete Chelsea Werner for American-based retailer *Aerie*. Notable others include Jillian Mercado for the September cover of *Teen Vogue* and, more recently, Sofía Jirau, who walked the runway during New York City Fashion Week (Delgado, 2020). These models have emerged in the context of greater diversity along a number of axes, with runway designers and major fashion brands featuring a larger number of plus-size models, trans models, and women of color in their ready-to-wear shows and campaign advertisements (Foster & Pettinicchio, 2021; Friedman, 2018; Schneier, 2018).

Teen Vogue's September cover featuring Chelsea Werner stands out as particularly striking in an industry that has historically neglected diversity and difference. In response to the publication's effort and to others in the industry, news media and editorial columnists offer support and praise, suggesting in one instance that they "reflect new-found awareness of inclusive design" (Jackson, 2019), and in another, that change in the industry has produced "the most inclusive" set of designer collections in recent history (Friedman, 2018). Consumers also praise fashion advertisements, shows and magazine images featuring disability, reposting these to their social media pages and commending the cultural producers and brands who back them (Foster & Pettinicchio, 2021).

For many, these efforts on behalf of the fashion industry toward diversity and inclusivity come as a surprise. Among the world's most financially lucrative and widely influential producers of cultural iconography, the fashion industry has long neglected people with disabilities (Burke, 2018), opting instead for a cast of uniformly slender, White, and able-bodied models (Mears, 2010). This is an omission that has not gone unnoticed.

Reflecting on her own experience growing up with a disability, model Jillian Mercado remarked that "even as a very young girl and adolescent, I always knew that there was a hole in the fashion industry, and that it wasn't fair that I did not see myself reflected" (Brown, 2018). Mercado's observation extends beyond fashion, capturing a larger issue at work across cultural industries—the stigmatization and erasure of men and women with a disability.

In the absence of any concrete representation, the fashion industry has drawn from (and often maligned) "the objects and devices associated with the disabled" (Burke, 2018). In 2016, for example, fashion photographer Steven Klein was met with criticism after photographing celebrity Kylie Jenner in a wheelchair for a cover story with *Interview* magazine (Benham, 2018; Burke, 2018). The photograph sparked intense public debate surrounding the appropriateness of casting able-bodied individuals in the seat of people with a disability. This debate, however, did not stop retailer Kimhekim from posturing runway models with IV bags and bandages in their Spring/Summer show just 1 year later (Nesvig, 2019).

Though fashion's relationship with disability is not without flaws, recent efforts toward diversity and inclusion in the industry suggest that change may be underway. In this chapter, I examine these changes with a focus on the representation of disability in online fashion media. Specifically, I look to a collection of editorial articles posted online by *Teen Vogue*. As one of the first mainstream fashion magazines to place a model with a disability on its cover, and with a unique focus on editorial content and broader social and political issues, *Teen Vogue* provides a revealing opportunity for an analysis of the representation of disability in fashion media. Looking to *Teen Vogue*, I ask how editorial articles published online frame disability for consumers, and whether these frames reproduce or challenge widely shared norms surrounding disability and difference. Throughout, I use mainstream representations of disability to speak to sociologically relevant questions surrounding the production and maintenance of inequality.

STUDYING FASHION AND STYLING DIFFERENCE

Fashion media provide an ideal vehicle through which to assess mainstream norms and widely shared cultural ideals (Baumann, 2008; Laan & Kuipers, 2016), including norms and ideals surrounding disability. This media is ideal for at least two reasons. First, fashion media is both widely circulated and highly influential, shaping a range of commercial, cultural, and economic endeavors, including Hollywood film and mainstream politics. Second, and relatedly, fashion media play an important role in establishing sartorial trends and in challenging or reinforcing widely shared notions surrounding beauty and appearance (Milkie, 1999; Press, 2011). Not unlike other media products (Baumann, 2008; Johnston & Baumann, 2007), fashion media legitimate appearances along the lines of existing social privileges (Mears, 2014), defining which of these are noteworthy and, correspondingly, which are not. To borrow from Schudson (1984, p. 215), these media reify lifestyles "worth emulating."

To date, sociological studies of fashion—and fashion media specifically—have taken an important look at the implications of mainstream fashion images for the men and women they feature or exclude, the cultural producers and industry creatives who craft them, and the structural organization of the industry itself (Aspers & Godart, 2013; Crane, 1997; Godart & Mears, 2009). This includes Giselinde Kuipers's (2015) systematic evaluation of fashion magazines in Europe and Shyon Baumann's (2008) critique of print advertisements in the West. In his work, for example, Baumann found that mainstream advertisements reflected widely shared beliefs surrounding femininity and ideals related to complexion. Whereas women with light or fair complexions were depicted as "angelic" and "innocent," women with dark complexions were often sexualized, reinforcing negative beliefs surrounding Black women's sexuality (Baumann 2008, p. 18). Kuipers (2015) provides a similar set of findings, leveraging fashion magazines to show how representations of beauty distinguish between individuals and groups, cementing existing appearance norms and social privileges.

Together, this literature speaks to sociologically relevant questions surrounding the maintenance and reproduction of inequality especially and including the micro-mechanisms through which inequality becomes normalized and legitimated. Building on this literature, I use fashion as an avenue through which to analyze the representation of diversity and difference in online media. I do this with a critical eye toward disability—a theorized but understudied area of research in sociological studies of fashion. The fashion industry and its media products can tell us a great deal about representation, inclusion, and inequality. This is, at least in part, because the structural organization of the fashion industry allows us to trace how market forces, firms, and figures combine to enable and constrain cultural change (Crane, 1997). And it is because the images it promotes and produces necessarily rely on aesthetic judgments related to the body's appearance (Laan & Kuipers, 2016). Importantly, these judgments entail processes of *both* inclusion *and* exclusion. Former model and associate professor at Boston University, Ashley Mears (2010, 2011, 2014) demonstrated as much in her own work, leveraging contacts in the fashion industry to better understand how cultural producers, including photographers and model bookers, enable and constrain opportunities for diversity in fashion.

Bookers play a particularly important role in selecting (and rejecting) models, deciding which of these possess "a look" that will resonate with consumers and sell effectively for clients (Mears, 2011, p. 124). As Mears points out, "beauty is in the eye of the booker" (2011, p. 127), and theirs is an eye that has been well trained. So well, in fact, that bookers exhibit remarkable consensus with one another, typically opting for (and sharing) just a handful of young, able-bodied models (Godart & Mears, 2009; Mears, 2011).

Importantly, bookers' search for and selection of models take place against a backdrop of constraints and industry conventions. Taken together, these constraints and conventions explain why men and women with a disability are so often excluded from fashion media like editorial images and mainstream advertisements. To explain, cultural products—from high-end fashion editorials to commercial fashion advertisements—are costly to produce with no guarantee that they will resonate with consumers (Crane, 1997; Entwistle, 2002; Mears, 2010). For this reason, producers seldom diverge from industry norms and conventions or from existing market successes, trusting instead that "safe bets" will reduce ambiguity and generate "hits" (Bielby & Bielby, 1994; Dowd, 2004; Godart & Mears, 2009; Mears, 2010; Radway, 1991). In this case, safe bets refer to models who are "conventionally attractive," slender, or else "edgy" in their appearance (Entwistle, 2002; Mears, 2011). The suggestion being that models with a disability are somehow or somewhat "riskier" than their "conventional" counterparts.[1]

Industry constraints and conventions thus reinforce and reproduce "social structural patterns of inequality" that limit opportunities for inclusion among those who diverge from widely shared ideals surrounding appearance in the fashion industry (Mears, 2011, p. 171). Models with a disability, along with trans models, models of color, and plus size models are thus routinely dismissed from mainstream fashion advertisements and high-end editorial images presumably because their bodies are not "ideal" enough to be placed within them (Barry, 2015, 2019; Czerniawski, 2016; Hargreaves & Hardin, 2009; Panol & McBride, 2001). If and when cultural producers diverge from one another or from broader industry conventions constraining the representation of diversity, their efforts tend to be narrow in scope and, often, naïve. In fashion, for example, editorial images and mainstream advertisements featuring models with a disability are routinely sanitized for consumers, eclipsing questions surrounding the variety of ways in which disability might shape the lives of everyday people, or how disability may intersect with other elements of consumers' identities (Foster & Pettinicchio, 2021).

Of course, fashion is not the only cultural industry from which people with disabilities have been excluded. In the mainstream news, people with a disability are, by and large, missing. If their stories are included, they tend to be told from the perspective of their able-bodied counterparts, including parents, siblings, or friends, and so erase opportunities for readers to see and understand the disability community in more intimate terms (Billawalla & Wolbring, 2014). The same can be said of television shows and Hollywood films where people with a disability are either absent from set (Appelbaum, 2019), or else, cast to inspire pity (Barnes, 1992; Panol & McBride, 2001). Reporting on representation and diversity in television, GLAAD recently showed that people with a disability represent only a fraction of all primetime characters, rounding off at just 3.1% of actors and actresses appearing on TV between 2018 and 2019.[2] And while exclusion is not "inherently negative" (Baumann & de Laat 2012, p. 515), it raises a number of questions related to the contexts and conditions under which men and women with a disability might be represented in the media.

It is possible, for instance, that online media afford new opportunities for inclusion and diversity (Trevisan, 2014).[3] Absent the constraints that accompany the production of print content, advertisements, or television (Bielby & Bielby, 1994; Radway, 1991), online editorials may allow cultural producers somewhat more flexibility to craft innovative products and flex their creative muscles (so to speak). In order to assess whether these media do in fact present a more inclusive and diverse portrayal of men and women with a disability, I turn to a sample of 50 editorial articles posted online by *Teen Vogue*. I compare these articles to earlier findings related to print magazines (Foster & Pettinicchio, 2021) in fashion in order to assess whether online media is more inclusive than print content.

TEEN VOGUE

Teen Vogue provides a revealing look at fashion media. Sister to a family of fashion media held under the Condé Nast label, *Teen Vogue* targets teen readers with an interest in fashion and style content. The magazine also features editorial columns on politics, culture, and identity, drawing a diverse audience of young people to its online platform. But this was not always the case. In fact, the magazine had, until quite recently, struggled to engage with readers, ultimately closing its print portfolio in December 2017 following significant and consistent declines in the magazine's sales (Fernandez, 2017).

Today, *Teen Vogue* is published exclusively online, where according to industry reports, Web traffic and online advertising revenue have risen substantially (Fernandez, 2017). This is consistent with broader industry trends. Consumers are increasingly enchanted by online appearances, with digital mavericks and marketing mavens forecasting market growth for those brands who can generate the greatest share of online innovation, while simultaneously driving "social media buzz" (Dalton, 2018). And while online media, no doubt, represent a new way to capture consumers and to keep ahead of industry competitors, these media may also afford an opportunity for more diverse and inclusive fashion content. As Chantal Fernandez, a columnist for *Business of Fashion*, pointed out, *Teen Vogue* is not only more profitable today than it has been in the past, but more "progressive" as well (Fernandez, 2017). This suggests, at least anecdotally, that the magazine's movement online may have played a role in the production of more diverse and inclusive editorial content.

To assess the ways in which online media might enable or constrain the representation of diversity in fashion, I look to a set of editorial articles published online by *Teen Vogue*. Specifically, I offer an analysis of 50 online articles surrounding disability. Drawing on my previous work with print magazines (Foster & Pettinicchio, 2021), I look for differences in the posturing and portrayal of disability between mainstream print and online fashion media. In order to locate editorial articles, I employed a keyword search using a number of terms including "disability" and "disabled." My search was guided by a modified version of PRISMA (Preferred Reporting Items for Systematic Reviews and Meta-Analyses) guidelines and followed a four-step process to identify articles for inclusion (Moher et al., 2009). With the help of *Teen Vogue*'s online selection tools, I refined each keyword search to the most relevant editorial articles, screening these to determine their eligibility for analysis. Articles that featured a man or woman with a physical or intellectual disability and/or that reflected on disability or issues related to the disability community more broadly were included for analysis.

Consistent with my research objectives, my search was narrowed to align more closely with the period in which *Teen Vogue* shuttered the doors to its printed press. That is, I drew articles published online between January 2018 and January 2020. This allowed me to make comparisons between online editorials and my previous work with print magazines (Foster & Pettinicchio, 2021). It also provided an opportunity to better understand how online editorials, removed as they are from the costly world of print publishing, might provide opportunities for greater representation, diversity, and inclusion.

Once collected, I applied an inductive and open-coding procedure to identify the ways in which these articles framed disability for readers (Rodney et al., 2017). Specifically, I evaluated each article to capture patterns and narrative dimensions as they appeared across the sample (Baumann, 2008; Billawalla & Wolbring, 2014). For instance, I recorded whether or not the article featured an image with a man or woman with a disability and whether this disability was a visible or nonvisible disability. I also looked to the ways in which *Teen Vogue* had sorted and categorized each article for readers (e.g., Politics, News, Culture, Identity, etc.) and made note of whether or not the article had itself been written by a man or woman with a disability. This allows me to assess the range of ways in which men and women with a disability have been included (or excluded) from the magazine and to comment on the relative import the magazine places on each story.

With these patterns and dimensions in mind, I observed three key frames emerge across the sample. These frames postured disability in terms of (1) representation, (2) disability rights, and (3) individual profiles and personal biographies. Editorials framed around representation were often couched within conversations surrounding movies, television, music, and fashion, emphasizing existing barriers to inclusion and the issues that accompany the appropriation of disability. Somewhat differently, editorials framed around disability rights covered mainstream public policy debates and American legislation affecting men and women with a disability, as well as the politics surrounding protests broadly speaking. These editorials, while removed from the magazine's ostensible focus on beauty and style, reflect fashion's broader reach into public discourse and the field of politics. Finally, editorials framed around individual profiles and personal biographies connected readers to young men and women with a disability, providing an intimate snapshot of their day-to-day lives.

Comparing these frames and the stories they captured to my previous findings related to the representation of disability in mainstream fashion press, *Teen Vogue*'s editorial articles on disability were not only more numerous than editorials postured elsewhere in the fashion landscape (Foster & Pettinicchio, 2021) but also more comprehensive. Specifically, editorial articles published by *Teen Vogue* covered a wider range of issues related to or affecting the disability community. These editorials were more often written by people who were themselves disabled and were more likely to include a photograph featuring a person with a disability or an image related to disability. In fact, 26% of all editorial articles were written by a man or woman with a disability, and a full 50% of editorial articles posted by *Teen Vogue* included a photograph related to disability. To compare, a 5-year longitudinal analysis of three mainstream fashion press produced only 29 editorials related to disability, and fewer than five of these included a photograph featuring a person with a disability (Foster & Pettinicchio, 2021).

Representation and the Inappropriateness of Appropriation

Teen Vogue presented a significant number of editorials stressing the importance of representation for people with a disability. Reporting in this vein included editorials covering the "appropriateness of appropriation" or the issues associated with borrowing the signs and symbols of the disability community. One such editorial, quoting disability activist Annie Segarra, reminded readers that "disability is not something we can just take on and off, attempting to use it as a prop is a mockery of the privilege one has in order to do such a thing" (as quoted by McNamara, 2018a). Another covered criticism issued by actor Nyle DiMarco. These criticisms came quickly after the actor witnessed an on-screen portrayal of a young character pretending to speak sign on-screen. "Pretending to be deaf," he remarked, "is NOT ok" (as quoted by McNamara, 2018b).

Social media outlets, the blogosphere, and other online press have devoted considerable attention to the subject of appropriation, but they have rarely touched on what it means to appropriate the signs and symbols associated with disability and the consequences of this appropriation for the disabled. Namely, the appropriation of disability runs the risk of further stigmatizing disability, and of trivializing the ways in which visible and nonvisible disabilities shape the day-to-day experiences of people who live with them.

Outside of covering issues related to appropriation, editorials stressing the importance of representation detailed the ways in which people with a disability have been excluded (or included) in such cultural industries as film, television, and fashion. For instance, one editorial detailed the rise of young Hollywood actress, Millicent Simmonds. Millicent, who lost her hearing at a young age, the editorial explains, routinely enrolled in local drama programs and auditioned for theatrical roles in mainstream productions. When asked what on-screen characters she related to growing up, Millicent replied to *Teen Vogue*: "Honestly, I don't know if I ever saw one character on screen that I felt I could relate to as a deaf person" (as quoted by Williams, 2020). Elaborating on the current state of film and television, Millicent observed that existing roles for people with a disability are quite narrow: "I'd like to see more roles for people with disabilities that you don't feel sorry for" (Williams, 2020).

Millicent's comments confirm what disability scholars have long shown us; that when it comes to the star-studded screens of Hollywood cinema and commercial television, people with a disability are practically nonexistent (Appelbaum, 2019; Parsons et al., 2017). When they are included, people with a disability are often cast to "pull at our heart strings" (Pettinicchio, 2019; Foster & Pettinicchio, 2021), to emphasize the importance of physical sameness and difference, or to highlight an ability to overcome the body's physical limitations (Parsons et al., 2017; Rainey, 2019). Here, it is worth pointing out that *Teen Vogue*'s reporting often departed from these cast types and tropes, offering readers a more expansive vision of disability. As one such editorial put it, "authentically" cast characters that move beyond *and* challenge negative stereotypes surrounding the disabled are absolutely essential (Bergado, 2020). In another, on the representation of disability in film, *Teen Vogue* reminded readers that all sorts of stories are possible for people with a disability, and that with time, "the hope" is to see more complex, honest, and thoughtful portrayals "you can fall in love with" (Bergado, 2019).

But not all reporting on the importance of representation was so expansive. For instance, *Teen Vogue* rarely discussed the representation of disability in terms explicitly related to style or fashion. In fact, over the 2-year period of time sampled here, *Teen Vogue*'s online columnists released only six articles sorted under "style" accounting for just 12% of all editorials included in the present sample. By the website's own doing, editorials relating to disability were far more likely to be sorted under such categories as "identity," which made up 22% of all articles included here. This is more or less consistent with my previous findings in mainstream fashion print (Foster & Pettinicchio, 2021), revealing that when it comes to the representation of disability and diversity more broadly, the fashion industry, obsessed as it is with appearance, has yet to take a look at itself in the mirror.

What reporting did exist in this vein was not without issue. Consider, for example, *Teen Vogue*'s editorial coverage of clothing retailer *Aerie* and their collaboration with model Brenna Huckaby. Brenna, a Paralympic athlete (and gold medalist), was signed to the brand as one of several models cast to represent "unique stories, real bodies, and influential voices" (Ware, 2019). The editorial spends some time reporting on Brenna's disability and her effortless style, before explaining that Brenna often encounters obstacles when shopping for clothing—an important issue facing the disability community. The solution to these obstacles: "Brenna had to build up the mindset to know that the clothing she wore didn't define her, but her confidence does" (Ware, 2019). Here, we see an important limitation of the editorial's reporting. That is, by insisting that Brenna's confidence made the biggest difference to her shopping experience, the editorial ultimately shifts blame away from retailers who do not manufacture garments for people with a disability or else fail to make their storefronts and online websites accessible to all shoppers. The editorial insists instead that confidence is all that's necessary to address the obstacles people with a disability encounter while shopping for clothing and styling their bodies.

The Politics of Inclusion

Teen Vogue's editorial articles often situated disability within broader conversations related to issues outside of the fashion industry. For instance, *Teen Vogue*'s editorial articles on disability drew from a well-worn vocabulary tying disability to the field of politics. This vocabulary extends to include conversations within the US Congress surrounding client and consumer rights, the provision of services, and the political elites and entrepreneurs responsible for protecting each (Pettinicchio, 2019). The inclusion of editorial articles related to the field of politics within a fashion magazine might strike some readers as surprising. But fashion has long shaped *and* been shaped by broader public discourse, including and especially political discourse (see Ford, 2015).

Consider, for example, *Teen Vogue*'s coverage of the US Democratic primary debate in January 2020. The editorial chastised primary candidates, including Joe Biden and Cory Booker, for their ill-preparedness and poor planning, revealing that these candidates had developed no concrete plans to assist people with a disability. The editorial praised candidates Andrew Yang and Elizabeth Warren, who, in contrast, were ready to address issues facing the disability community such as those related to education and employment. "By empowering and amplifying the voices of people with disabilities," read the article, "Democratic candidates have a huge opportunity to excite a population that has felt ignored in previous elections" (Moss, 2020). To be sure, people with a disability make up a significant share of the electorate; with over 14.3 million voters reporting a disability of some kind in the 2018 election, and another 10.2 million voters estimated to reside with someone who has a disability (Abrams, 2019). And still, people with a disability are often looked over by politicians or else addressed in ways that ultimately reinforce and reproduce narrow and often negative beliefs about the disabled. Explaining perhaps why "even everyday Americans find it hard to see the disability community as they do other historically marginalized and oppressed groups" (Pettinicchio, 2019, p. 136).

Somewhat differently, a number of editorial articles surrounding disability rights emphasized the political conversations from which people with a disability have been excluded. These include ongoing debates related to gun violence and sexual assault. One such editorial on gun-control rallies pointed out that "some disabled people were unable to attend at all, while others dealt with access issues that made it difficult to participate" (Smith, 2018). Reporting of this kind calls to mind activists' concerns that when it comes to the issues affecting people with a disability, conversation too often proceeds in the absence of any meaningful consultation or inclusion (Pettinicchio, 2012, 2019).

Another article focused on the #MeTooMovement similarly reported that women living with a disability had been excluded from public debate centering on women's sexuality and threats of sexual violence. As the editorial writer, a young woman with a disability, rightly pointed out, "excluding sexuality from conversations with and about the disability community not only reinforces stigmas about disabled people being undesirable, but it can perpetuate rape culture toward disabled people as well" (Flores, 2018). She isn't wrong. In fact, her statement echoes scholarly work surrounding disability and sexuality. This work illustrates the narrow and often negative ways in which people with a disability have been represented by the mainstream media (Brodwin & Frederick, 2010; Tilley, 1996).

Women with a disability, for example, are often perceived as violating traditional norms of sexuality and femininity particularly among those who already hold rigid beliefs around men and women's gender roles (Parsons et al., 2017). Owing to these perceptions, the sexual practices of women with a disability are, in turn, viewed less favorably by able-bodied people (Parsons et al., 2017). That *Teen Vogue* addressed women's sexuality vis a vis the #MeTooMovement marks a significant challenge to existing stereotypes and perceptions, pushing readers to consider disability and sexuality in new terms.

Profiles and Personal Biographies

In addition to editorial articles focused on the representation of men and women with a disability and on disability rights, *Teen Vogue* published a number of articles that provided a comprehensive profile or personal biography related to disability. These editorials were often written by people who were themselves disabled and so provided an honest and intimate reflection on their daily lives and on their experience growing up within a culture in which their stories are, so often, neither seen nor heard.

Take, for example, Madison Lawson's (2018) editorial for *Teen Vogue*: "I'm in a Wheelchair, and This Is What It Meant to See Someone Like Me in a Fashion Ad." Here, Madison reflects on her childhood and late adolescence, explaining to readers that fashion has always played a "big part" in her life. As she writes, growing up "people knew me as the girl with really good style rather than the girl in the wheelchair, I felt seen, not just looked at" (Lawson, 2018). But achieving Madison's signature looks came with significant effort. This is because many garments are not designed for people with a disability in mind, meaning that these may fall awkwardly on the body or else produce a silhouette that is less flattering for some than for others.

Innovative designers and creative entrepreneurs can change this. Tommy Hilfiger's recent line of adaptive garments, for example, makes dressing more straightforward. These garments have been cut and tailored with disability in mind. They feature adjustable closures and custom zippers, as well as flexible hemlines and necklines. Commenting on this innovation, Madison explains that Hilfiger's efforts toward inclusive design represent a significant step forward in fashion. Whereas "traditional, ableist clothing can remind you that your body is fallible and flawed every time you get dressed" (Lawson, 2018), Hilfiger's line of adaptive garments serves as an important affirmation of the wearers' independence and allows greater freedom to both look and feel beautiful.[4]

Sarah Kim provides a similarly revealing look at what it means to live with a disability. A young woman with cerebral palsy, Kim's (2019) life is one "full of endless paradoxes and contradictions." Excluded from the movies and books she loved, Sarah felt that her story wasn't one worth telling. This feeling was amplified by daily mistreatment she experienced growing up in New York City. From strangers on the street to security guards at her campus, Sarah (2019) often came up against criticism and "condescension." Determined to set a new course for herself, Sarah (2019) concluded her editorial by writing that "I am worthy of receiving respect from other people and I should hold myself to a higher standard. I don't need to live in a world where I expect mistreatment—I can, and will, demand more."

For Haley Moss (2019), a young woman with autism, confronting friends and strangers wasn't easy. Haley spent most of her childhood hiding the fact that she was autistic for fear that others wouldn't understand. She likened her own diagnosis to a set of "magical powers" that set her aside as "unique" and "full of differences and an inability to fit in" (Moss, 2019). That was until Haley shared her diagnosis and her thoughts on this with a noteworthy publisher, and soon after, her teachers and classmates. In Haley Moss's (2019) own words, "I went from being the girl with secret magic, disclosing on a need-to-know basis, to telling different people in my life." She continued, "with neurodiversity in my arsenal of magic, I am able to publicly change the narrative toward greater autism acceptance in all aspects of life" (Moss, 2019).

Across the profiles and individual biographies shared by *Teen Vogue*, it is worth highlighting that there exists a focus that cuts across a range of disability types and status characteristics. In fact, many of the profiles included here reflected on how disability intersects with race and gender to shape the lives of people with a disability. Sarah, for instance, explained to readers that her disability, and the treatment she received because of it, was sometimes made worse by her status as a Korean-born woman (Kim, 2019). In this way, *Teen Vogue* sheds a light on the various ways in which our identities collide to determine our lived experiences and the complexities that these identities produce.

Taken together, these powerful profiles and individual biographies provide readers with an opportunity to better understand disability in new terms, pushing the boundaries of existing and widely shared beliefs about diversity and difference. This includes a move away from stories emphasizing the pitiable nature of disability (Foster & Pettinicchio, 2021; Parsons et al., 2017; Pettinicchio, 2019) and toward stories that destabilize taken-for-granted stereotypes and empower men and women with a disability. This is in sharp contrast to previous research surrounding the representation of men and women with a disability (Parsons et al., 2017), and in opposition to my own findings across mainstream fashion print (Foster & Pettinicchio, 2021), suggesting that online media are significantly more inclusive than print content. The findings further suggest that a larger shift in the fashion industry is underway.

CONCLUSIONS

In the fashion industry, slender and impossibly tall models "strut down the runway as though they are giving an ode to able-bodied walking" (Brown, 2018). In press pages and fashion advertisements too, able-bodied models look out as though to remind consumers exactly who is (and isn't) worthy of our consideration. Perfectly polished, models' posturing reflects widely shared norms surrounding the body and prescribes directives for its comportment and appearance (Laan & Kuipers, 2016; Mears, 2011). As Mears (2011) explains, these "representations do work" (p. 175), constraining opportunities for the representation of men and women with a disability and limiting our understanding of diversity and difference, broadly speaking (Foster & Pettinicchio, 2021).

Whether for runway shows or mainstream fashion press, these representations are crafted by a team of fashion bookers and creative agents including photographers and stylists located within the fashion industry. Together, they play a key role in selecting (and rejecting) models. Fashion bookers, for example, decide which models are most likely to succeed in the industry and resonate with clients and consumers (Entwistle, 2002; Godart & Mears, 2009). Owing in large part to industry conventions and market constraints (Mears, 2010, 2011), fashion bookers tend to favor models who are uniformly slender, White, and able-bodied in their appearance, trusting that these models will be well received by clients and consumers. In so doing, bookers reinforce and reproduce existing appearance norms and the concomitant inequalities that these norms are so intimately tied to.

More recently, however, a handful of bookers and industry creatives have diverged in their selection process and begun producing sartorial content with disability in mind. In the last 2 years alone, we have seen models with a disability move to the cover of mainstream fashion magazines and to the fore of fashion advertisements (Foster & Pettinicchio, 2021). Some designers have even begun to revise their manufacturing processes, creating adaptive fashion garments for people with a disability (Rivas, 2018). These changes have been met with significant praise and suggest that change in the fashion industry is *finally* underway.

To assess the nature of these changes and their implications for people with a disability, I took a careful look at *Teen Vogue*'s editorial reporting online. Sampling from across a 2-year time period and with an eye toward editorials surrounding the disability community, I compared the representation of disability online in *Teen Vogue* to my previous work surrounding disability in mainstream fashion press (Foster & Pettinicchio, 2021). Specifically, I looked to the ways in which editorial articles framed men and women with a disability. Throughout, I drew comparisons between editorial articles published online and those published in the printed press. This allowed me to speak to industry dynamics that might constrain opportunities for inclusion: namely, the cost of print production and the implications of representation for men and women with a disability.

As this chapter has shown, *Teen Vogue*'s fashion content offers a more expansive vision of disability for consumers of fashion. This vision includes editorial work surrounding the importance of representation and inclusion for people with a disability, work on disability rights, and editorials featuring individual profiles and personal biographies. Many of these editorials were written by a person with a disability and featured images that helped to fashion the author's story, conveying its truth and complexity. While the editorials are themselves noteworthy in an industry that has historically neglected people with a disability, the images they feature are also worth attending to. Images of people with a disability are incredibly infrequent in the media and especially so in mainstream fashion press (Foster & Pettinicchio, 2021). The number of images included in *Teen Vogue*'s editorial articles thus stands out as incredibly unique. What is more, these images cut across disability types and status characteristics, reflecting on the ways in which disability intersects with race, gender, and sexuality—an often neglected feature in reporting of this kind.

Taken together, *Teen Vogue*'s editorials and images—whether related to the importance of representation or the provision of rights and services in the American political landscape—frame disability in a number of ways that challenge widely shared and taken-for-granted beliefs about the disabled. For instance, *Teen Vogue*'s editorials posture people with a disability within stories that reflect on personal biographies, drawing readers' attention to the disability community and its neglect from the glitter and glamour of fashion, as well as from film, television, and even the field of politics. These frames empower people with a disability to share their stories and are significantly more solicitous of the contemporary issues facing the disability community, including social stigmatization and a range of institutional barriers to cultural inclusion. In this way, *Teen Vogue* broadens our understanding of disability, allowing consumers of fashion to see the disability community in a new and more complex light.

Still, more work is needed. Whether we are looking to fashion or Hollywood film, the representation of people with a disability has been, until quite recently, lackluster. Popular among these representations are cast types and tropes of men and women with disabilities who are either "inconceivable to non-disabled people" or else, stereotypically "dependent . . . asexual, and/or pitiful" (Wendell, 2013, p. 485). While the fashion industry has made some significant strides forward, departing in some instances from these more popular (and damaging) portrayals, efforts toward diversity and the inclusion of people with a disability have taken place slowly and, in some cases, have been short-lived. In others, the representation of people with a disability remains neglected.

The underrepresentation and erasure of people with a disability carry significant implications for the reproduction and maintenance of inequality. Specifically, their erasure and underrepresentation further stigmatize people with a disability while blinding everyday consumers to the cultural, political, and economic realities that the disability community continues to face. The question now turns to whether or not representations of disability are here to stay, and if so, what these representations will mean for members of the disability community. Will the fashion industry continue to broaden its castings to include diverse men and women in their advertisements, images, and runway shows? Will these efforts challenge or reinforce existing portrayals of disability, and will the industry invite members of the disability community to assist with decision-making, to collaborate on creative projects, and to comment on product design, or will it proceed without them? Looking forward, let's hope that disability remains in vogue.

NOTES

1. The neglect of diversity and difference in the fashion industry takes place in spite of the fact that greater inclusivity can increase product sales and brand profitability; see Ben Barry's interview with Ava Baccari (2012) for *Elle Canada*.
2. See GLAAD's 2019 report on diversity and representation in television: "Where We Are on TV."
3. Trevisan (2014) reports that online media tools possess a number of strengths for the mobilization and empowerment of disabled users, but these are also accompanied by a set of weaknesses and a host of tensions for the men and women who use them.
4. See Barry (2019, p. 300) for a fuller discussion on how fashion can be worn and used to reimagine the body and empower "wearers."

REFERENCES

Abrams, A. (2019). Why disabled voters could be a key voting bloc in 2020. *Time*. https://time.com/5622652/disability-voter-turnout-2020/.

Appelbaum, L. (2019). Representation of characters with disabilities increases on TV but still lacking. *Respect Ability*. https://www.respectability.org/2018/10/characters-with-disabilities-2018/.

Aspers, P., & Godart, F. (2013). Sociology of fashion: Order and change. *Annual Review of Sociology*, 39(1), 171–192.

Baccari, A. (2012). Q&A with Ben Barry on the fashion industry: Our chat with the model agent and author of "Can diversity in modelling benefit brands?" *Elle Canada*. https://www.ellecanada.com/fashion/q-a-with-ben-barry-on-the-fashion-industry-our-chat-with-the-model-agent-and-author-of-can-diversity-in-modelling-benefit-brands

Barnes, C. (1992). *Disabling imagery and the media: An exploration of the principles for media representations of disabled people*. The British Council of Organisations of Disabled Peopl/Ryburn Publishing.

Barry, B. (2019). Fabulous masculinities: Refashioning the fat and disabled male body. *Fashion Theory*, 23(2), 275–307.

Barry, B. (2015). Op-ed: Diversity in fashion advertising does sell. *The Business of Fashion*. https://www.businessoffashion.com/community/voices/discussions/why-isnt-the-fashion-industry-more-diverse/op-ed-diversity-in-fashion-advertising-does-sell.

Baumann, S. (2008). The moral underpinnings of beauty: A meaning-based explanation for light and dark complexions in advertising. *Poetics*, 36(1), 2–23.

Baumann, S., & de Laat, K. (2012). Socially defunct: A comparative analysis of the underrepresentation of older women in advertising. *Poetics*, 40(6), 514–541.

Bergado, G. (2019). 4 feet: *Blind Date* is a captivating film showing that disabled people have a right to their sexuality. *Teen Vogue*.

Benham, J. (2018). Fabulous Fetishization: Kylie Jenner's Interview Cover and Wheelchair Identity Politics. *Gender Forum* 68, 4–72.

Bergado, G. (2020). "Sex Education" newcomer George Robinson on Isaac's relationship with Maeve and disability representation." *Teen Vogue*.

Bielby, W., & Bielby, D. (1994). "All hits are flukes": Institutionalized decision making and the rhetoric of network prime-time program development. *American Journal of Sociology*, 99(5), 1287–1313.

Billawalla, A., & Wolbring, G. (2014). Analyzing the discourse surrounding Autism in the New York Times using an ableism lens. *Disability Studies Quarterly*, 34(1):1–28.

Brodwin, M., & Frederick, P. (2010). Sexuality and societal beliefs regarding persons living with disabilities. *Journal of Rehabilitation*, 76(4), 37–41.

Brown, K. (2018). What It's Like to Be a Disabled Model in the Fashion Industry. *Teen Vogue*. https://www.teenvogue.com/story/cover-story-representation-fashion-industry-jillian -mercado-mama-cax-chelsea-warner

Burke, S. (2018). The limits of fashion's inclusivity. *The New York Times*. https://www.nytimes .com/2018/09/30/fashion/disabled-beauty.html.

Crane, D. (1997). Globalization, organizational size, and innovation in the French luxury fashion industry: Production of culture theory revisited. *Poetics*, 24(6), 393–414.

Czerniawski, A. (2016). Beauty beyond a size 16. *Contexts*, 15(2), 70–73.

Dalton, M. (2018). At fashion week, Gucci is king of social-media buzz. *The Wall Street Journal*. https://www.wsj.com/articles/fashion-houses-work-to-build-buzz-off-the-runway -1538000399.

Delgado, O. (2020). Latina model with Down syndrome rocks runway at New York Fashion Week. *LatinLife*. https://www.wearelatinlive.com/article/13400/latina-model-with-down -syndrome-rocks-runway-at-new-york-fashion-week.

Dowd, T. (2004). Concentration and diversity revisited: Production logics in the U.S. mainstream recording market, 1940–1990. *Social Forces*, 82(4), 1411–1455.

Entwistle, J. (2002). The aesthetic economy: The production value in the field of fashion modelling. *Journal of Consumer Culture*, 2(3), 317–339.

Fernandez, C. (2017). Transforming Condé Nast's problem child. *The Business of Fashion*. https://www.businessoffashion.com/articles/intelligence/transforming-conde-nasts -problem-child.

Flores, E. (2018). The #MeToo movement hasn't been inclusive of the disability community. *Teen Vogue*.

Ford, T. (2015). *Liberated threads: Black women, style, and the global politics of soul*. University of North Carolina Press.

Foster, J., & Pettinicchio, D. (2021). A model who looks like me: Communicating and consuming representations of fashion. *Journal of Consumer Culture*, 1–19. https://doi.org/ 10.1177/14695405211022074.

Friedman, V. (2018). The most diverse fashion season ever on the runway, but not the front row. *The New York Times*. https://www.nytimes.com/2018/10/11/fashion/the-most-diverse -fashion-season-ever-on-the-runway-but-not-the-front-row.html.

Godart, F., & Mears, A. (2009). How do cultural producers make creative decisions? Lessons from the catwalk. *Social Forces*, 88(2), 671–92.

Hargreaves, J., & Hardin, B. (2009). Women wheelchair athletes: Competing against media stereotypes. *Disability Studies Quarterly*, 29(2):1–18.

Jackson, L. (2019). Why 2019 was a landmark year for disabled fashion *The Guardian*. https://www.theguardian.com/fashion/2019/dec/30/why-2019-was-a-landmark-year-for -disabled-fashion.

Johnston, J., & Baumann, S. (2007). Democracy versus distinction: A study of omnivorousness in gourmet food writing. *American Journal of Sociology*, 113(1), 165–204.

Kim, S. (2019). I spent years accepting mistreatment because of my disability. *Teen Vogue*.

Kuipers, G. (2015). Beauty and distinction? The evaluation of appearance and cultural capital in five European countries. *Poetics*, 53, 38–51.

Laan, E., & Kuipers, G. (2016). How aesthetic logics shape a cultural field: Differentiation and consolidation in the transnational field of fashion images, 1982–2011. *Poetics, 56*, 64–84.

Lawson, M. (2018). I'm in a wheelchair, and this is what it meant to see someone like me in a fashion ad. *Teen Vogue*.

McNamara, B. (2018a). Why it's not OK to dress up as someone with a disability for Halloween. *Teen Vogue*.

McNamara, B. (2018b). Nyle DiMarco called out "Sierra Burgess is a loser" for a storyline that mocked deafness. *Teen Vogue*.

Mears, A. (2010). Size zero high-end ethnic: Cultural production and the reproduction of culture in fashion modeling. *Poetics, 38*(1), 21–46.

Mears, A. (2011). *Pricing beauty: The making of a fashion model*. University of California Press.

Mears, A. (2014). Aesthetic labor for the sociologies of work, gender, and beauty. *Sociology Compass, 8*(12), 1330–1343.

Milkie, M. (1999). Social comparisons, reflected appraisals, and mass media: The impact of pervasive beauty images on black and white girls' self-concepts. *Social Psychology Quarterly, 62*(2), 190–210.

Moher, D., Liberati, A., Tetzlaff, J., & Altman, D. (2009). Preferred reporting items for systematic reviews and meta-analyses: the PRISMA statement. *British Medical Journal* 339(7716), 78–336.

Moss, H. (2019). Telling my high school class that I'm autistic is the best thing I've ever done. *Teen Vogue*.

Moss, H. (2020). Which 2020 Democratic candidates are taking disability rights seriously? *Teen Vogue*.

Nesvig, K. (2019). This fashion brand is being called out on Instagram for using IV bags as an accessory. *Teen Vogue*. https://www.teenvogue.com/story/kimhekim-pfw-2020.

Panol, Z., & McBride, M. (2001). Disability images in print advertising: Exploring attitudinal impact issues. *Disability Studies Quarterly, 21*(2):1–21.

Parsons, A., Reichl, A., & Pedersen, C. (2017). Gendered ableism: Media representations and gender role beliefs' effect on perceptions of disability and sexuality. *Sexuality and Disability, 35*(2), 207–225.

Pettinicchio, D. (2012). Institutional activism: Reconsidering the insider/outsider dichotomy. *Sociology Compass, 6*(6), 499–510.

Pettinicchio, D. (2019). *Politics of empowerment: Disability rights and the cycle of American policy reform*. Stanford University Press.

Press, A. (2011). "Feminism? That's so seventies": Girls and young women discuss femininity and feminism in America's next top model. In R. Gill & C. Scharff (Eds.), *New femininities* (pp. 117–133). Palgrave Macmillan.

Radway, J. (1991). *Reading the Romance: Women, patriarchy, and popular literature* (2nd ed.). University of North Carolina Press.

Rainey, S. (2019). Loving the other: Fantastic films and unlikely couples. *Disability Studies Quarterly, 39*(10). https://doi.org/10.18061/dsq.v39i1.4394

Rivas, M. (2018). Tommy Hilfiger's new campaign features models with disabilities. *Teen Vogue*. https://www.teenvogue.com/story/tommy-hilfiger-spring-2018-adaptive-collection.

Rodney, A., Cappeliez, S., Oleschuk, M., & Johnston, J. (2017). The online domestic goddess: An analysis of food blog femininities. *Food, Culture & Society, 20*(4), 685–707.

Schneier, M. (2018). The stars of September. *The New York Times*. https://www.nytimes.com/2018/08/09/style/diversity-september-issue-magazines.html.

Schudson, M. (1984). *Advertising, The uneasy persuasion: Its dubious impact on American society*. Basic Books.

Smith, S. (2018). The disability community is being excluded from the gun control conversation. *Teen Vogue*.

Tilley, C. (1996). Sexuality in women with physical disabilities: A social justice or health issue? *Sexuality and Disability*, 14(2), 139–151.

Trevisan, F. (2014). Scottish disability organizations and online media: A path to empowerment or "business as usual"? *Disability Studies Quarterly*, 34(3):1–29.

Ware, A. (2019). Aerie real role model Brenna Huckaby on the difficulties of shopping with a disability. *Teen Vogue*.

Wendell, S. (2013). *The Rejected Body: Feminist Philosophical Reflections on Disability*. New York: Routledge.

Williams, W. (2020). Millicent Simmonds is a force to be reckoned with. *Teen Vogue*.

CHAPTER 13

....

INTELLECTUAL DISABILITY AND THE DIMENSIONS OF BELONGING

....

ALLISON C. CAREY

WHAT does it mean to belong? Who experiences the privileges of belonging? In 1966, American disability rights activist Jacobus tenBroek asserted that people with disabilities should have "the right to live in the world" (tenBroek, 1966, p. 841). tenBroek's statement was, and continues to be, a radical idea, entailing a dramatic shift away from the ableist and eugenic practices that have long characterized American society. This shift may be particularly challenging with regard to people with intellectual disabilities, who have been among those most systematically marginalized in America's civic and moral body.

A complex web of social structures enforces exclusion, and, if radically transformed, could instead foster belonging. In this chapter, we focus on four structural dimensions of belonging to show how social structures and policies have enforced exclusion or, alternatively, fostered belonging. The dimensions include legal rights, culture and the accordance of moral value, power, and access. We begin with legal rights because the denial of rights has served as a tool of sweeping exclusionary force, and much of disability activism since the late 1960s has focused on securing basic civil rights. Rights on paper, though, do not always translate into significant change in the lives of people. Paul Longmore (2003) argued that disability culture constituted the "second phase" of disability activism in which people with disabilities use the tools of culture to demand recognition and respect. Thus, after rights we turn to a discussion of role of culture in exclusion and the ways in which policies can instead support cultural workers. Third, we examine the issue of power, including economic, political, and relational power. To belong as equals and as valued members of society, people with disabilities must have the power to make their own choices and to shape the systems that claim to serve them. Finally, we discuss access to consider how to foster meaningful, self-determined access to the range of relationships and roles that enable one to be a vibrant member of one's community. For each dimension, we examine how exclusion is enacted via informal social patterns and formal policy, and we offer examples of potential avenues to creating and embracing a broad sense of belonging that includes people with intellectual disabilities. Only a multifaceted approach to belonging can dissemble the complex structural factors that continue to enforce exclusion.

A Note about Intellectual Disability

Because this chapter focuses on intellectual disability, it is important to explain this concept in sociological terms. Intellectual disability is a socially constructed and contested label (Bogdan & Taylor, 1976; Carey, 2009; Trent, 1994). As a medical diagnosis, intellectual disability is associated with three key components: (1) an IQ significantly lower than average (typically defined as 70 and below), (2) combined with significant limitations in "adaptive behavior" reducing a person's ability to meet the cultural and social expectations given their age, (3) which originates before the age of 18 (Schalock et al., 2010). Rather than being an objective biological fact, though, labels related to intelligence are created by society, and these labels, the assumptions embedded in them, the bases on which they are given, and the response to them vary tremendously through history.

Throughout American history, many labels have been used to refer to deficits in intelligence, including "slow," "backward," "idiot," "imbecile," "feebleminded," "special," "mentally retarded," "mentally challenged," and "intellectually disabled" (Carey, 2009; Trent, 1994). Each label carried its own set of assumptions and provoked particular responses. For example, in early America's agricultural economy, formal education was uncommon and many people were illiterate. Under these conditions, the label of "idiot" (a legal construct, not yet a medical one) marked only serious deficits; most people who today would be labeled with mild intellectual disability went unnoticed (Nielsen, 2012; Wickham, 2001). In contrast, modern competition for scarce, well-paying, white-collar jobs fuels academic hypercompetition. In these conditions, schools sort children by ability, and disability labels serve as a mechanism by which to give or deny children resources (Blum, 2015; Ong-Dean, 2009; Pitts-Taylor, 2010). The educational and administrative uses of the label increased labeling. Thus, labels are connected to and embedded in a wider system of norms, relational power, and resources. Furthermore, because labels carry meanings, evoke values, and provide or deny access to resources, the labels are not only constructed; they are contested as groups fight to shape meaning and the distribution of resources. When people are assigned the label of intellectual disability, it positions them within a web of structures and policies which shape how they are perceived and what opportunities and resources they can access.

The Dimensions of Belonging

Legal Rights

Rights serve as a key indicator of belonging, marking one as a respected and valued member of a community and providing a tool to influence others and pursue one's interests (Hirschmann & Linker, 2015). Because rights can be formally established and contested, they are one of the most apparent indicators of belonging or exclusion. People with intellectual disabilities have been formally and informally denied many rights, and thus experience a form of second-class citizenship (Carey, 2009; Carlson, 2009; Trent, 1994).

The early architects of American government built the exclusion of people with intellectual disabilities, as well as many other groups, directly into the framework of the American government (Minow, 1990; Nielsen, 2012). Drawing on liberal political philosophy, the founding fathers argued that a properly functioning democracy required citizens to be both rational and autonomous. According to this logic, rationality would ensure that citizens understood the meaning and consequences of their decisions, and autonomy would allow citizens to act to pursue their self-interests without undue influence by others. People with intellectual and mental disabilities, though, were portrayed as irrational and dependent, representing the antithesis of the good citizen (Carey, 2009; Carlson, 2009), and America's earliest laws denied "idiots" and "the insane" the rights to vote, contract, and marry. The denial of rights to other groups, such as women, African Americans, and Indigenous peoples, hinged on associations with disability; they, too, were depicted as too irrational and incapable of independence—too disabled—to exercise rights (Baynton, 2001; Nielsen, 2012). America thereby established a dual-track legal system, in which some citizens received rights, while others received exclusions and "protections" (Minow, 1990). Although predicated on the requirements of rationality and autonomy, the denial of rights rarely entailed an assessment of actual skills or functioning. Rather, exclusion relied heavily on ascriptive traits, the perceived unworthiness of whole categories of people, and the conferring of the label of intellectual disability.

Medicalization obscured these exclusionary impulses by depicting the denial of rights via institutionalization and sterilization as benevolent "treatment." Institutional patients lived as prisoners with almost no recognized rights (Ben-Moshe, 2020; Ben-Moshe et al., 2014), and even the worst of institutional conditions went largely unaddressed (Ferguson, 1994). In 1937, Pennsylvania Governor George H. Earle reported institutional conditions "so lacking in humaneness as to be almost unbelievable in the great civilized Commonwealth." Conditions continued to deteriorate. In 1965, after Senator Robert Kennedy toured New York's Willowbrook State School, he described it as a "snake pit." Patients' powerlessness and isolation left them highly vulnerable to abuse, with almost no mechanisms to protest or even to reveal that abuse (Burghardt, 2018; Johnson, 2002; Reaume, 2009). Meanwhile institutional residents performed most of the work of the institution, usually without pay, under the guise of treatment and training. They washed the laundry, raised crops, cooked food, and provided care to other patients who needed assistance with bathing, eating, and toileting.

Activists, using a variety of social movement strategies, including lawsuits, protests, and lobbying, fought to establish basic rights for people with disabilities (Fleischer & Zames, 2011; Pelka, 2012). They demanded the right to an education, secured in the 1975 Individuals with Disabilities Education Act (IDEA). Lawsuits in multiple states led to deinstitutionalization and the establishment of community-based services. The

1990 Americans with Disabilities Act prohibited discrimination on the basis of disability, giving people with disabilities the right to compete in the workplace and to access public services (Davis, 2015). These legal achievements establish people with intellectual disabilities as valued members of society and provide them with the tools to demand their rights.

Even with these successes, though, laws still curtail the rights of people with intellectual and mental disabilities. For example, through guardianship, people can be stripped of their rights. Guardianship can be an important support in making decisions in one's life, but too often guardianship is a superficial bureaucratic process with few safeguards to ensure the welfare of the guardianee. As another example, in many states, parents with disabilities can lose custody of their children on the basis of disability alone, with no proof of abuse or neglect (NCD, 2012). And, despite the IDEA, many children with intellectual disabilities still experience educational segregation based on outdated assumptions and bureaucratic efficiencies.

Therefore, securing and protecting rights remain key priorities among activists. Parents still take uncooperative school districts to court and lobby for funding to pay for disability services in schools. Self-advocates and their allies continue to fight against institutionalization and the delivery of services in large-scale segregated settings (Carey et al., 2020; Friedman & Beckwith, 2014). Activists work state by state to reform guardianship laws to limit the power of guardians, center the interests of people with disabilities, and protect them from possible exploitation and abuse. Indeed, the passage of rights legislation is not the end of a battle but rather just a stepping-stone, as activists continually work to have rights recognized, protected, enforced, and expanded.

In addition to the passage of laws that articulate the rights of people with disabilities, policies can fund an infrastructure of support for self-advocacy which enables people with disabilities to keep fighting for their rights. For example, policies can fund training for people with intellectual disabilities to learn about their rights and pay for self-advocacy facilitators who assist self-advocates in the variety of self-advocacy activities such as reading and understanding complex material, creating meeting agendas and recording meeting minutes, speech-writing and preparation, disseminating information, and getting to events. States may also fund provide protection, advocacy, and legal services for people with disabilities. The fight for rights relies on legal action, which requires expertise and money, but people with intellectual disabilities are disproportionately poor. Thus, legal advocacy provides critical resources. Legal advocacy became central, for example, in the Justice for Jenny campaign. In 2013, Jenny Hatch, a woman with an intellectual disability, was placed under guardianship. Her guardians removed her from her preferred living situation, placed her in a group home against her wishes, and denied her access to her friends. With support from disability organizations and legal advocacy, Hatch won the right to make decisions for herself using supported decision-making so that her preferences could be the cornerstone of decision-making regarding her life (Ross et al. v. Hatch, 2013). Hatch successfully ensured her right to control her life through the use of laws that protected her from discrimination, the development of her self-advocacy, and the provision of legal services.

Culture, Cultural Work, and the Accordance of Moral Value

The presence of formal rights on the books does not ensure their enactment in practice (Engle & Munger, 2003). Claiming rights requires, among other things, the recognition of one's moral value as a person. Via cultural discourse, some persons are set outside the bounds of humanity and defined as "other" or nonpersons (Du Bois 1903/1994; Ilyes, 2020; Opotow, 1990, 2018; Snyder & Mitchell, 2005). Once defined as such, atrocities can be committed against them, including violence, the denial of rights, and disregard for even the most basic of needs. In the case of intellectual disability, several of the most powerful of these discourses are social Darwinism, eugenics, and neoliberalism.

Social Darwinism centers on the maxim of the survival of the fittest. This maxim suggests that humans and society evolve toward perfection under conditions of unhindered competition which allow the strong to rise to the top and the weak to fall to the bottom. As such, social Darwinists discourage government aid to the poor, believing that such programs serve only to undercut the positive influence of "natural selection." Eugenicists build on this ideology but articulate a more proactive approach to "improving" population quality (Snyder & Mitchell, 2006; Trent, 1994). Rather than leaving genetic selection to nature, eugenicists encourage professionals to identify, categorize, and surveil the national population in order to mark the unfit. With this information, the state may deploy tactics, including institutionalization, compulsory sterilization, and immigration restrictions, to ensure that those they deemed "unfit" do not procreate or otherwise destroy the moral fiber of America.

The ideals of social Darwinism provide the framework for modern neoliberalism, an ideology which promotes individual freedom based on a laissez-faire approach to capitalism with little government regulation or public provision of services (Fritsch, 2013, 2017; Giroux, 2008). People are encouraged to rely on their own initiative and merit to attain success and discouraged from expecting public support. Neoliberalism has devastating consequences for people with disabilities (and other Americans as well) who rely on regulations and public supports (Fritsch, 2013, 2017; Mitchell, 2015; Rosenthal, 2019; Russell, 1998). Regulations mandate, for instance, the provision of accommodations for education, accessibility standards for housing units, and nondiscrimination guidelines in places of employment. Public benefits ensure that those excluded from the workplace have shelter, food, and healthcare. Without these types of government interventions, capitalists (and workers caught up in a competitive world with little safety net of their own) have little incentive to ensure accessibility, inclusion, or even subsistence for others.

Through these varied discourses, able bodies and minds are positioned as valued, while others are treated as an unexpected and undesirable deviations—at best "special" circumstances that require accommodations, at worst threatening deviations requiring eradication (Davis, 1997; Garland-Thomson, 1996). Consequently, people with intellectual disabilities face stigma and devaluation throughout their entire lives. The devaluation begins even before birth. Not yet embodied or manifest with and alongside other traits, prenatal intellectual disability is constructed by medical professionals through the rhetoric of birth "defect" into a master status of only negative traits. Due to this narrow portrayal of intellectual disability, and the associated fears of stigma, perceived burdens of a child with a disability, and paucity of services available, more than 90% of women with fetuses identified as having Down syndrome choose to abort (Berger, 2013).

As children grow, they face a world that values achievement, individualism, and intelligence. Their progress is carefully measured, compared, and rank ordered against the progress of other children. In our modern hypercompetitive environment, each success/failure serves to herald future glories or predict later doom (Blum, 2015; Pitts-Taylor, 2010). In this context, children with intellectual disabilities rarely find themselves and their talents appreciated. In the following quote, parent Heather Kirn Lanier's (2015) expresses her frustration at being told by her doctor that her daughter Fiona was "way behind."

> *Way, way behind*, he said. I saw a race. Numbers on the backs and fronts of runners, all children. The able-bodied kids charging ahead, the whites of their brains all fatty and luxurious with myelin, sending and receiving impulses with standard issue speed. I saw them racing toward a finish line. I saw a ribbon fall when their chests touched it, and I saw arms raised in victory. In the metaphor, my daughter is *way, way behind*. In the metaphor, my daughter is a turtle creeping along the asphalt, and no, there is no fabled "Tortoise and Hare" ending. The metaphor makes a competition of human development, one in which my daughter is ultimately dismissed because, let's face it, in this competition, she will never "catch up."

Kinlanier's blog criticizes a culture that values only people who can attain a particular version of "success" and relegates others to the junk pile, discarding them in segregated environments with few opportunities and little respect. Typical achievements—working one's first teenage job, high school graduation, getting a driver's license, building a career, and starting a family—may elude or be delayed for people with intellectual disabilities because of their specific limitations and/or because of the social isolation and discrimination they experience. The attainment of wealth and occupational prestige presents an even greater problem given that people with disabilities are disproportionately unemployed, underemployed, and in poverty. Thus, people with disabilities may struggle to feel respected, given the narrow definition of achievement commonly extolled in America.

Transforming culture and its associated beliefs and values is no small feat. However, some activists use the tools of culture, such as mass media and performance, to present a world in which people with intellectual disabilities are included and valued. For example, in 1975, Emily Kingsley, a writer for the children's show *Sesame Street*, wrote an episode featuring her son Jason, who has Down syndrome. Jason went on to appear in 55 episodes. In so doing, he opened the door for other actors with intellectual disabilities and helped the audience imagine the possibilities of inclusion. British punk rock band Heavy Load, which includes musicians with and without intellectual disabilities, more loudly and adamantly challenges the cultural norms around intellectual disability. In a society in which people with intellectual disabilities are infantilized and their choices limited by service agencies, Heavy Load's aggressive music and late-night performances in bars demand that people with disabilities be allowed to engage as equal adults who can have fun, drink, and stay out late into the evening. The troupe Drag Syndrome wields the power of drag performance to challenge the stereotypes of incompetence and asexuality surrounding Down syndrome and radically assert their power of self-definition. Although varied, these performers reimagine the cultural landscape to include and empower people with intellectual disabilities (Piepzna-Samarasinha, 2018).

Other cultural work more directly intersects with politics and lobbying to challenge the cultural elements of disability oppression. For example, language is one of the most important elements of culture, and the language around disability often carries negative connotations. The label "mental retardation" began as a progressive alternative to eugenic ideas of disability as deviant, drawing instead on a model of slowed childhood development. However, over time, the term "retarded" became associated with low educational expectations, segregation, and even playground insults. At the 2009 Special Olympics, self-advocates and their allies launched the Spread the Word to End the Word campaign to encourage people to stop using the term "mental retardation" and instead rely on language, attitudes, and behaviors that value human diversity.

Policy can support the cultural work of people with intellectual disabilities in numerous ways. Organizations can transform their language, symbols, and cultural practices to reflect contemporary, positive attitudes. They can also support cultural workers with intellectual disabilities (e.g., artists, actors, writers, performers) through the creation of paid art fellowships, the provision of art education, the targeted hiring of people with disabilities in the arts, and the prioritization of disability perspectives and accessibility throughout cultural organizations.

Challenging neoliberalism and its devastating impact on people with disabilities requires profound cultural, economic, and political transformation. In a world where human worth is based on one's production of profit, people with intellectual disabilities will not thrive. In contrast to neoliberalism, discourses of human rights portray all people as worthy of dignity. They directly challenge the sharply unequal distribution of resources produced by transnational capitalism and promote policies that foster greater economic equality and ensure social welfare through universal healthcare, high-quality education, and income benefits (Berne, 2015).

Empowerment

As legal rights and cultural acceptance grow, people with disabilities still often find themselves on the bottom of the social hierarchy with little control over their lives. For example, rights activism has expanded education and broadened access to community-based services, but in both arenas (education and the service system) people with intellectual disabilities tend to exercise little power and instead experience surveillance and social control. Rights and acceptance have opened the opportunity to be in society, but often on someone else's terms. Power enables people to make their own choices, to influence others, and to shape their social context to meet their needs and preferences (Weber, 1922/1978). As such, power is inherently a relational concept. People with disabilities, though, typically exercise very little power. Whether it be in the realms of politics, economics, the service system, or interpersonal interaction, people with intellectual disabilities have few opportunities to influence the people around them to act in accordance with their interests.

People with intellectual disabilities are largely shut out of political power. Indeed, although there have been recent strides made in the election of people with varied disabilities, it may be that no person identified with an intellectual disability has ever been elected in America to a federal, state, or local-level political office (Garcia, 2020). Moreover, people with intellectual disabilities have struggled to have a seat at the political table regarding the policies that shape their lives. Disability policy has traditionally been controlled by medical professionals. Parent activists fought to establish their own authority and political access, but this does not necessarily increase the political power of their disabled offspring (Carey et al., 2020; Rottier & Gernsbacher, 2020).

Political power is not the only type of power. Economic power ensures control over one's labor and access to the resources needed to pursue one's interests. As already discussed, in capitalism people who do not meet the capitalist ideals of efficient and exploitable labor are demeaned, segregated, and controlled (Russell, 1998). With little access to the resources they need to survive, people with disabilities struggle to meet their most basic needs such as healthcare or housing. Furthermore, they are transformed into commodities as care, treatment, and support are placed on the market in the pursuit of profit, prioritizing profit over the actual needs of disabled people (Charlton, 2000; Erevelles, 2011; Oliver, 1990; Rosenthal, 2019).

Given the relentless focus on profit, capitalists resist hiring people with intellectual disabilities; only 44% of people with intellectual disabilities are employed compared to 83% of people without disabilities (Siperstein et al., 2013). Their position on the bottom of the economic stratification system is reinforced by policy, rather than challenged by it. The Americans with Disabilities Act only protects people who are "otherwise qualified" from job discrimination, so employers can turn away people with intellectual disabilities relatively easily. Sheltered workshops in many states still pay disabled workers wages below minimum wage. Income supports for people with disabilities typically are set below the poverty line. These policies, combined with the lack of competitive employment and low wages, ensure the poverty of people with intellectual disabilities and enforce their dependency on the service system (Beckwith, 2016; Maroto & Pettinicchio, 2015).

In addition to political and economic power, people with disabilities lack power over the very services that claim to serve them. Within the social service system, services are organized hierarchically with people with disabilities on the bottom of the hierarchy. Relationships between staff and "consumers" are structured to enforce this hierarchy, including surveilling and recording consumer behavior and transforming it into fodder for team meetings (Chapman et al., 2014; Chapman & Withers, 2019). Many people with intellectual disabilities live completely within the confines of social service bureaucracies—for example, group homes, sheltered workshops, day programs. As such, they experience the routine denial of their rights to privacy, to sexuality, and to make independent decisions about the most basic of things like what or when to eat. People with disabilities rely on these services yet lack the relational power to claim or exercise their rights within them.

The broad devaluation of intellectual disability in American culture, combined with the lack of economic and political power, strips people of interpersonal power. In this context, people with intellectual disabilities too often are subjected to violence. A study by the World Health Organization (Hughes et al., 2012) found that children with disabilities are almost 4 times more likely to be victims of violence than children without disabilities, and adults with disabilities are 1.5 times more likely to be victims of violence. People with intellectual disabilities are 7 times as likely to be victims of sexual assault than those without disabilities. They are more likely to be victimized by someone they know, in a setting designated as a service setting, and during the day (Shapiro, 2018). Indeed, from a perpetrator's perspective, people with intellectual disabilities represent an ideal victim—socially isolated, discredited, uninformed of their rights, and disempowered in their interpersonal contacts.

Self-advocacy is one of the primary paths to empowerment. Through self-advocacy, people with intellectual disabilities learn to articulate and pursue their self-interests. Self-advocates with intellectual disabilities began organizing to pursue their own interests on the local and state level in the 1970s, and in 1990 they established the national organization, Self-Advocates Becoming Empowered (SABE). SABE fights vehemently to close institutional and segregated settings and to ensure access to the community, but they have faced resistance from parent and professional organizations (Friedman & Beckwith, 2014). Policies which support self-advocacy are crucial to empowerment. Currently though, support of self-advocacy by parent and professional organizations often comes in the form of cooptation, in which self-advocates are provided with some opportunity to voice their opinions while organizational control remains in the hands of parents and professionals (Beckwith et al., 2016). To exercise power, self-advocates must have the funding and supports to pursue their own political agenda, even if that places them in conflict with parent and professional organizations.

In addition to self-advocacy organizations, other initiatives address political power. Beyond Tokenism, for example, is a project by Mark Friedman and Ruthie-Marie Beckwith that advocates for the meaningful inclusion of people with intellectual disabilities on the board of directors of the companies and organizations that shape disability policy and services (http://www.beyondtokenism.com/). Get Out the Vote campaigns tailored to people with intellectual disabilities offer training in the logistics of voting, ensure accessible polling places and voting machines, and provide transportation.

Activists also work to transform power within the social service system. The closure of segregated settings is an essential step toward empowerment; however, many community-based services continue to rely on hierarchical models that deny power to people with disabilities. In contrast, recent policy models, such as person-centered planning and Medicaid waivers, strive to increase the power of people with disabilities. Rather than channeling money directly to service agencies, Medicaid waiver programs provide a flexible state-funded budget to people with disabilities who can choose their services in an individualized and flexible way to best meet their self-identified needs. This strategy transforms the "client" into a "consumer" with the purchasing power to decide what services they want, where they want the services delivered, and by whom.

Increasing access to economic power is one of the most intractable problems in disability politics. Recent policy efforts include prohibiting subminimum wages for disabled workers, increasing access to competitive employment, using the Americans with Disabilities Act to ensure accommodations in the workplace, and supporting self-entrepreneurship by people with disabilities. Recognizing the high level of unemployment for this population, disability benefits through Social Security could be increased and modified to foster income and economic security. Another path may be to ensure broader economic security for all people regardless of disability, such as raising the minimum wage for workers and providing a social safety net to decrease poverty and ensure that those on the bottom of the economic ladder have the ability to meet their basic needs such as shelter, food, and healthcare.

Access to Valued Roles, Opportunities, and Social Capital

While moral value, rights, and power are key ingredients, belonging is perhaps most fundamentally centered on the degree to which we enjoy meaningful and fulfilling relationships. Disability policy often focuses on issues related to productivity, including education and employment. However, people with intellectual disabilities express a more holistic view of their lives, including a desire for meaningful and intimate relationships. Many people with intellectual disabilities are lonely and socially isolated. Compared to people without disabilities, people with intellectual disabilities report far fewer friends and social supports, and their social networks are dominated by family members and paid service providers (Friedman & Rizzolo, 2018). While staff may be caring, high turnover and bureaucratic constraints prevent staff from acting as friends in the traditional sense. In this final section, we focus on relationships as a central feature of human fulfillment and belonging.

The barriers to dating, sexuality, and marriage are tremendous. Students with disabilities are less likely to be taught sexual education, and the sexual education they receive lacks attention to disability issues (Frank & Sandman, 2019; Saxe & Flanagan, 2016). Parents often hold conservative views on sexuality; they often portray sexuality as a problem to be managed rather than a healthy part of their maturing offspring's life (Gill, 2015; Santinele Martino, 2019). Service agencies claim to uphold the human rights of their consumers, but people with intellectual disabilities report a lack of support in attaining and maintaining sexual lives (Alexander & Gomez, 2017; Santinele Martino, 2017, 2019). Social service professionals express ambiguity about their responsibilities and liabilities in supporting access to sexuality, and they often assert the right to refuse to support sexual development, especially if a consumer's sexual choices contradict their own moral code (Achey, 2020; Saxe & Flanagan, 2016).

Eighty percent of American adults 25 years of age and older marry, but policies present obstacles to people with intellectual disabilities who want to make this commitment (Wang & Parker, 2014). Laws in some states restrict marriage on the basis of intellectual disability, and guardianship may also block access. Furthermore, in determining eligibility for public benefits, the government uses a married couple's combined income/assets (rather than the disabled individual's income/assets), which results in the loss of public benefits upon marriage and discourages people with disabilities from marrying. Self-advocate B. J. Stasio (2010) states, "People with disabilities want to get married. We fall in love and want to make a commitment to the person that we love and become a family. For many it is a religious choice to get married. Yet, too many people with disabilities must choose between getting married and continuing to receive the benefits they need to live from federal programs such as Supplemental Security Income (SSI) and Medicaid." Furthermore, many agencies will not serve married couples in group homes nor assist with parenting tasks. Overall, policies continue to adhere to eugenic principles, focusing on ensuring productivity and independence while limiting procreation and even intimate relationships among people with disabilities.

In addition to the profound benefits of intimacy with friends and loved ones, relationships also serve as social capital. In other words, relationships serve as a resource that helps one accrue additional resources (Putnam, 2000). For example, social connections may help one find a job, identify appropriate healthcare professionals, gain entry to a desirable social club, or make introductions to potential romantic partners. The constrained social networks of people with intellectual disabilities hinder their personal growth and access to opportunities (Condelucci & Fromknecht, 2014). For example, most people find their first jobs through their social networks; however, people with disabilities lack connections to the employers (Nelson Bryen et al., 2006). Many people are recruited into social activism and political activities through their networks, but these channels are similarly limited for people with intellectual disabilities. A broad set of social ties also serves to protect one from abuse and violence, whereas the social isolation of people with intellectual disability heightens their vulnerability.

Fifty years after the shift to deinstitutionalization and 30 years after the passage of the Americans with Disabilities Act, systemic inclusion for people with intellectual disabilities remains uncommon in many ways. To focus on schools, evidence suggests the benefits of educational inclusion are extensive and that, overall, inclusive education is a more effective educational strategy than segregation by disability/ability. A 2018 report by the National Council on Disability (NCD) documents that educational inclusion led to greater academic success, improved communication skills, more satisfying and diverse friendships, more social skills, fewer absences, fewer behavioral problems, less formal discipline, more engagement with school, *and* better postsecondary education outcomes, including higher rates of employment and attending college. Students with significant disabilities showed the greatest benefits of inclusion.

Regarding educational inclusion and intellectual disability, we see both promising and disappointing news. The rate of inclusion for students with disabilities has improved over time. Ninety-five percent of students with disabilities now attend neighborhood schools that serve children with and without disabilities. Furthermore, the percent of special education students who spend 80% or more of their school day in a general education classroom increased from 47% in 2000 to 64% in 2018 (Hussar et al., 2020). However, children with intellectual disabilities have been largely left behind in this progress. Children with intellectual disabilities are still more likely to be placed in segregated settings and are given less access to high-quality educational programming. In 2015–2016, only 17% of students with intellectual disabilities spent 80% of more of their school day in a general education setting (NCD, 2018). Moreover, African American students are more likely to be labeled with intellectual disability; 9% of Black children in special education carry this label versus 6% of White children (US Department of Education, NCES, 2019), and among children with labels of intellectual disabilities, racial minorities experience disproportionate segregation (Ferri & Connor, 2006; Fish, 2019; Losen & Orfield, 2002).

At the end of K–12 education, the opportunities for inclusion further diminish. As students emerge as young adults, they and their families face the "disability cliff"— the loss of services at age 21 or upon high school graduation, when young adults with disabilities lose access to a host of services provided through public schools and enter adulthood facing a far more precarious, unsupportive, and fragmented service environment (Bérubé, 2016; Bérubé, 2018). Whereas a public education is guaranteed, one is only *eligible* for adult services (Leiter, 2012). Attaining adult services requires extensive research and planning to investigate, apply for, and secure social services. This complicated process privileges families with capital (Grossman, 2019; Leiter, 2012). Moreover, there are extensive waitlists for services; in Illinois, as an example, the average time on the waitlist for developmental disability services is 7 years (Fazio, 2019).

The legal rights to liberty and access to the community have been inscribed in law in the Americans with Disabilities Act and in Supreme Court decisions (Olmstead v. L.C., 1999); however, America still heavily relies on institutional care and large-scale, disability-specific service settings. Again, we see that policy enforces the social isolation and relational disempowerment of people with disabilities. Medicaid funding retains its "institutional bias," a term which refers to the ways in which Medicaid funding policies encourage the channeling of people with disabilities into large-scale, segregated settings rather than community settings. Even for those in the community, Medicaid funding rules greatly constrain life choices. Because Medicaid is administered on the state level, people cannot move to a different state without losing services (Grossman, 2019). Moreover, the service system ignores the fluidity of disability and life trajectories (Carey et al., 2020). The service system assumes and enforces developmental stagnation; people are "placed" in homes and occupational programs, and they are expected to remain there. People are not encouraged to grow through trying new jobs, finding new roommates, or moving to new areas. While imposing stagnation, the service system itself is anything but stagnant; worker turnover is high, budget cuts common, and agencies close. Thus, much of the change in people's lives is imposed by political and bureaucratic demands, not their own goals.

Policy, though, can also transform and improve people's relational experience. Inclusion is not as a physical place or a ratio of nondisabled to disabled participants. Rather, inclusion involves a philosophy and a set of practices in which people with disabilities, in settings and relationships of their own choice, are valued and active participants with the supports needed to succeed (McLeskey et al., 2014). Inclusive environments embrace disability perspectives and needs, instead of sidelining them, and focus on ensuring that people have choices, relationships, and human fulfillment.

In education, policies have slowly shifted toward inclusion through policies like requiring teachers to receive training in disability. The IDEA mandates the least restrictive environment (LRE); however, this language has been used liberally to preserve educational segregation (Taylor, 2004). A legal focus on inclusion instead of LRE, with clear definitions, expectations, and supports, might encourage more rapid educational transformation. Inclusive programs in higher education have also begun emerging. Millersville University's program for inclusive higher education offers an example. At Millersville University, program staff create an individualized educational plan with students with intellectual disabilities. These students have access to the same classes as other Millersville students, and program staff support faculty and students in making appropriate accommodations. Students receive academic mentorship and tutoring, as well as social coaching to enable students to identify and participate in clubs and social activities of interest. Social coaches explicitly facilitate the growth of the student's social networks on campus. Internships and job coaching then extend these inclusive experiences off campus, as students and local employers build connections and skills in creating accessible workplaces.

In social services, some agencies now use tools to increase social relationships, such as person-centered planning, which includes social network mapping and activities expressly designed to increase the networks of people with intellectual disabilities. Medicaid has also begun shifting toward an inclusive framework, tying funding for disability services to their efforts to build inclusion in the community.

Regarding intimacy, the University of Chicago at Illinois, along with other organizations, has created a sexual education curriculum that supports engagement in healthy sexuality and pleasure. Activists are working to change the Social Security disability benefit formula so that marriage does not incur an economic penalty for people with disabilities. Lawsuits and lobbying efforts have taken aim at laws which threaten parental rights based on disability. Individualizing funding for disability services through Medicaid waiver services and separating service provision from residential placement also enables people to create the homes they want, with the people they want, without forfeiting necessary services.

Conclusion

In the 1950s, America's dominant policy response to intellectual disability enforced segregation and exclusion. Times have changed, mostly due to dramatic shifts in the social and political landscape opening opportunities for people with intellectual disabilities. Indeed, changes such as deinstitutionalization showcase the ability for radical transformation (Ben-Moshe, 2020). However, inclusion requires far greater social change. The good news is that through policy and other social reforms, we have the capacity to transform lives. For example, in 1960, the life expectancy of people with Down syndrome was on average 10 years; in 1983, 25 years; in 2007, 47 years; and in 2020, 60 years (NDSS, n.d.). In addition to medical advances, people with intellectual disabilities live longer lives because they now are largely free from mass institutionalization, and they live with their families, receive education, and have supports. The organization of society deeply shapes the opportunities and experiences of people with intellectual disabilities. This chapter has not listed all of the necessary changes or provided a cohesive blueprint for reform. More simply, we have examined several components of belonging and the relationship between policy, exclusion, and inclusion for each component in order to document the need for and capacity for broad-scale social change.

References

Achey, N. (2020). *Direct support professional's perspectives on sexuality issues of adults with intellectual disabilities: A qualitative analysis of interviews with providers in Maine* [Doctoral dissertation, University of Maine].

Alexander, N., & Gomez M. T. (2017). Pleasure, sex, prohibition, intellectual disability, and dangerous ideas. *Reproductive Health Matters, 25*(50), 114–120.

Baynton, D. C. (2001). Disability and the justification of inequality in American history. In P. K. Longmore & L. Umansky (Eds.), *The new disability history: American perspectives* (pp. 33–57). New York University Press.

Beckwith, R.-M. (2016). *Disability servitude: From peonage to poverty.* Palgrave Macmillan.

Beckwith, R.-M., Friedman, M. G., & Conroy, J. W. 2016. Beyond tokenism: People with complex needs in leadership roles: A review of the literature. *Inclusion, 4*(3), 137–155.

Ben-Moshe, L. (2020). *Decarcerating disability: Deinstitutionalization and prison abolition.* University of Minnesota Press.

Ben-Moshe, L., Chapman, C., & Carey, A. (Eds.). (2014). *Disability incarcerated: Disability and imprisonment in the United States and Canada.* Palgrave Macmillan.

Berger, R. (2013). *Introducing disability studies.* Lynn Reinner.

Berne, P. (2015). Disability justice—A working draft. *Sins Invalid.* www.sinsinvalid.org/blog/disability-justice-a-working-draft-by-patty-berne

Bérubé, M. (2018, April 2). Don't let my son plunge off the "disability cliff" when I'm gone. *USA Today.* https://www.usatoday.com/story/opinion/2018/04/02/dont-let-my-son-plunge-off-disability-cliff-column/443138002.

Bérubé, M. (2016). *Life as Jamie knows it: An exceptional child grows up*. Beacon.

Blum, L. M. 2015. *Raising generation Rx: Mothering kids with invisible disabilities in an age of inequality*. New York University Press.

Bogdan, R., & Taylor, S. (1976). The judged, not the judges: An insider's view of mental retardation. *American Psychologist, 31*, 47–52.

Burghardt, M. C. (2018). *Broken: Institutions, families, and the construction of intellectual disability*. McGill-Queen's University Press.

Carey, A. C. (2009). *On the margins of citizenship: Intellectual disability and civil rights in twentieth century America*. Temple University Press.

Carey, A. C., Block, P., & Scotch, R. (2020). *Allies and obstacles: Disability activism and parents of children with disabilities*. Temple University Press.

Carlson, L. (2009). *The faces of intellectual disability: Philosophical reflections*. Indiana University.

Chapman, C., & Withers, A. J. (2019). *A violent history of benevolence: Interlocking oppression in the moral economies of social working*. University of Toronto Press.

Chapman, C., Carey, A. C., & Ben-Moshe, L. (2014). Reconsidering confinement: Interlocking locations and logics of incarceration. In L. Ben-Moshe, C. Chapman, & A. C. Carey (Eds.), *Disability incarcerated: Imprisonment and disability in the United States and Canada* (pp. 3–24). Palgrave Macmillan.

Charlton, J. I. (2000). *Nothing about us without us: Disability oppression and empowerment*. University of California Press.

Condeluci, A., & Fromknecht, J. (2014). *Social capital: The key to macro change*. LASH & Associates.

Davis, L. J. (2015). *Enabling acts: The hidden story of how the Americans with Disabilities Act gave the largest US minority its rights*. Beacon Press.

Davis, L. J. (1997). Constructing normalcy: The bell curve, the novel, and the invention of the disabled body in the nineteenth century. In L. Davis (Ed.), *The disability studies reader* (pp. 9–28). Routledge.

Du Bois, W. E. B. (1994). *The souls of black folk*. (Original work published 1903). Dover.

Earle, George H. (1937). Remarks of Governor George H. Earle, governor of Pennsylvania, at ground-breaking ceremonies, Laurelton State Village, Thursday 23, 1937, at 11 am EST. Papers of the Governor George Howard Earle III, Pennsylvania State Archives, Manuscript Group 342, Official Papers, Speeches 1937–1938, box 15.

Engel, D., & Munger, F. (2003). *Rights of inclusion: Law and identity in the life stories of Americans with disabilities*. University of Chicago Press.

Erevelles, N. (2011). *Disability and difference in global contexts: Enabling a transformative body politic*. Palgrave Macmillan.

Fazio, M. (2019, December 10). Why those with disabilities wait years for programs they need to live on their own. Disability Scoop. *Chicago Tribune*. https://www.disabilityscoop.com/2019/12/10/why-disabilities-wait-years-programs-need-live-own/27553/

Ferguson, P. M. (1994). *Abandoned to their fate: Social policy and practice toward severely disabled people in America, 1820–1920*. Temple University Press.

Ferri, B. A., & Connor, D. J. (2006). *Reading resistance: Discourses of exclusion in desegregation and inclusion debates*. Peter Lang.

Fish, R. E. (2019). Standing out and sorting in: Exploring the role of racial composition in racial disparities in special education. *American Educational Research Journal, 56*(6), 2573–2608.

Fleischer, D. Z., & Zames, F. (2011). *The disability rights movement: From charity to confrontation*. Temple University Press.

Frank, K., & Sandman, L. (2019). Supporting parents as sexuality educators for individuals with intellectual disability: The development of the home B.A.S.E curriculum. *Sexuality and Disability*, *37*, 329–337.

Friedman, C., & Rizzolo, M. C. 2018. Friendship, quality of life, and people with intellectual and developmental disabilities. *Journal of Developmental and Physical Disabilities*, *30*(1), 39–54.

Friedman, M., & Beckwith, R.-M. (2014). Self-advocacy: The emancipation movement led by people with intellectual and developmental disability. In L. Ben-Moshe, C. Chapman, & A. Carey, *Disability incarcerated* (pp. 237–254). Palgrave Macmillan.

Fritsch, K. (2013). The neoliberal circulation of affects: Happiness, accessibility and the capacitation of disability as wheelchair. *Health, Culture and Society*, *5*(1), 135–149.

Fritsch, K. (2017). Contesting the neoliberal affects of disabled parenting: Toward a relational emergence of disability. In Michael Rembis (Ed.), *Disabling domesticity* (pp. 243–267). Palgrave Macmillan.

Garcia, E. (2020). Autistic people are coming into their own as political players. *Spectrum.* https://www.spectrumnews.org/opinion/autistic-people-are-coming-into-their-own-as-political-players/.

Garland-Thomson, R. (1996). *Freakery: Cultural spectacle of the extraordinary body*. New York University Press.

Gill, M. (2015). *Already doing it*. University of Minnesota Press.

Giroux, H. A. (2008). *Against the terror of neoliberalism: Politics beyond the age of greed*. Routledge.

Grossman, B. R. (2019). Disability and corporeal (im)mobility: How interstate variation in Medicaid impacts the cross-state plans and pursuits of personal care attendant service users. *Disability and Rehabilitation*, *41*(25), 3079–3089.

Hirschmann, N. J., & Linker, B. (2015). Disability, citizenship, and belonging: A critical introduction. In N. J. Hirschmann & B. Linker (Eds.), *Civil disabilities: Citizenship, membership, and belonging* (pp. 1–21). University of Pennsylvania Press.

Hughes, K., Bellis, M. A., Jones, L., Wood, S., Bates, G., Eckley, L., McCoy, E., Mikton, C., Shakespeare, T., & Officer, A. (2012). Prevalence and risk of violence against adults with disabilities: A systematic review and meta-analysis of observational studies. *Lancet*, *379*(9826), 1621–1629.

Hussar, B., Zhang, J., Hein, S., Wang, K., Roberts, A., Cui, J., Smith, M., Bullock Mann, F., Barmer, A., & Dilig, R. (2020). The condition of education 2020 (NCES 2020-144). U.S. Department of Education. National Center for Education Statistics. https://nces.ed.gov/pubsearch/pubsinfo.asp?pubid=2020144

Ilyes, E. (2020). *Social production of intellectual disability and the mechanics of moral exclusion: Past, present, and future* [Doctoral dissertation, The City University of New York].

Johnson, R. (told to Karl Williams). (2002). *Lost in a desert world*. Speaking for Ourselves.

Lanier, H. K. (2015). Breaking up with Dr. Normal. *Star in Her Eye* [blog]. https://starinhereye.wordpress.com/2014/01/05/breaking-up-with-doctor-normal/

Leiter, V. (2012). *Their time has come: Youth with disabilities on the cusp of adulthood*. Rutgers University Press.

Longmore, P. K. (2003). *Why I burned my book and other essays*. Temple University Press.

Losen, D. J., & Orfield, G. (2002). *Racial inequality in special education*. Harvard Education Press.

Maroto, M., & Pettinicchio, D. (2015). Twenty-five years after the ADA: Situating disability in America's system of stratification. *Disability Studies Quarterly, 35*(3). https://dsq-sds.org/article/view/4927.

Minow, M. (1990). *Making all the difference*. Cornell University Press.

Mitchell, D. T. (2015). *The biopolitics of disability: Neoliberalism, ablenationalism, and peripheral embodiment*. University of Michigan Press.

McLeskey, J., Waldron, N. L., Spooner, F., & Algozzine, B. (2014). What are effective inclusive schools and why are they important? In J. McLeskey, N. L. Waldron, F. Spooner, & B. Algozzine (Eds.), *Handbook of effective inclusive schools* (pp. 3–16). Routledge.

National Council on Disability (NCD). (2018). *IDEA series: The segregation of students with disabilities*. NCD. https://ncd.gov/sites/default/files/NCD_Segregation-SWD_508.pdf.

National Council on Disability (NCD). (2012, August 10). *Chapter 13: Supporting parents with disabilities and their families*. NCD. https://ncd.gov/publications/2012/Sep272012/Ch13

National Down Syndrome Society (NDSS). (n.d.) Down syndrome facts. https://www.ndss.org/about-down-syndrome/down-syndrome-facts/

Nelson, B., Potts, D., Blyden, B. & Carey, A. C. (2006). Job-related social networks and communication technology. *Augmentative and Augmentative Communication, 22*, 1–9.

Nielsen, K. (2012). *A disability history of the United States*. Beacon Press.

Oliver, M. (1990). *The politics of disablement*. Macmillan Education.

Ong-Dean, C. (2009). *Distinguishing disability: Parents, privilege and special education*. University of Chicago Press.

Opotow, S. (1990). Moral exclusion and injustice: An introduction. *Journal of Social Issues, 46*(1), 1–20.

Opotow, S. (2018). Social justice theory and practice: Fostering inclusion in exclusionary contexts. In *The Oxford Handbook of Social Psychology and Social Justice* (pp. 41–56). Oxford University Press.

Pelka, F. (2012). *What we have done: An oral history of the disability rights movement*. University of Massachusetts Press.

Piepzna-Samarasinha, L. L. (2018). *Care work: Dreaming disability justice*. Arsenal Pulp Press.

Pitts-Taylor, V. (2010). The plastic brain: Neoliberalism and the neuronal self. *Health, 14*(6), 635–652.

Putnam, R. (2000). *Bowling alone: The collapse and revival of American community*. Simon and Schuster.

Reaume, G. (2009). *Remembrance of patients past: Patient life of the Toronto Hospital for the Insane, 1870–1940*. University of Toronto Press.

Rosenthal, K. (Ed.). (2019). *Capitalism and disability: Selected writings by Marta Russell*. Haymarket Books.

Rottier, H., & Gernsbacher, M. A. (2020). Autistic adult and non-autistic parent advocates: Bridging the divide. In A. C. Carey, J. M. Ostrove, & T. Fannon (Eds.), *Disability alliances and allies: Opportunities and challenges* (pp. 155–166). Emerald Press.

Russell, M. (1998). *Beyond ramps: Disability at the end of the social contract*. Common Courage Press.

Santinele Martino, A. (2017). Cripping sexualities: An analytic review of theoretical and empirical writing on the intersection of disabilities and sexualities. *Sociology Compass, 11*(5), 1–15.

Santinele Martino, A. (2019). Power struggles over the sexualities of individuals with intellectual disabilities. In K. Malinen (Ed.), *Dis/Consent: Perspectives on sexual consent and sexual violence*, (pp. 98–107). Fernwood.

Saxe, A. & Flanagan, T. (2016). Unprepared: An appeal for sex education training for support workers of adults with developmental disabilities. *Sexuality and Disability, 35*, 21–38.

Schalock, R. L., Borthwick-Duffy, S. A., Bradley, V. J., Buntinx, W. H. E., Coulter, D. L., Craig, E. M. (Pat), Gomez, S. C., Lachapelle, Y., Luckasson, R., Reeve, A., Shogren, K. A., Snell, M. E., Spreat, S. Tasse, M. J., Thompson, J. R., Verdugo-Alonso, M. A., Wehmeyer, M. L., & Yeager, M. H.. (2010). *Intellectual disability: Definition, classifications and systems of support.* 11th ed. American Association on Intellectual and Developmental Disabilities.

Shapiro, J. (2018). The sexual assault epidemic no one talks about. *National Public Radio.* https://www.npr.org/2018/01/08/570224090/the-sexual-assault-epidemic-no-one-talks-about.

Siperstein, G. N., Parker, R. C., & Drascher, M. (2013). National snapshot of adults with intellectual disabilities in the labor force. *Vocational Rehabilitation, 39*, 157–165.

Snyder, S. L., & Mitchell, D. T. (2005). *Cultural locations of disability.* University of Chicago Press.

Snyder, S. L., & Mitchell, D. T. (2006). Eugenics and the racial genome: Politics at the molecular level. *Patterns of Prejudice, 40*(4–5), 399–412.

Stasio, B. J. (2010). People with disabilities and the federal marriage penalties. *Impact, 32*(2). University of Minnesota, Institute on Community Integration. https://publications.ici.umn.edu/impact/23-2/people-with-disabilities-and-the-federal-marriage-penalties.

Taylor, S. (2004). Caught in the continuum: A critical analysis of the principle of the least restrictive environment. *Research and Practice for Persons with Severe Disabilities, 29*(4), 218–230.

tenBroek, J. (1966). The right to live in the world: The disabled in the law of torts. *California Law Review, 54*(2), 841–919.

Trent, J. W. Jr. (1994). *Inventing the feeble mind: A history of mental retardation in the United States.* University of California Press.

US Department of Education, National Center for Education Statistics. (2019). Status and trends in the education of racial and ethnic groups. https://nces.ed.gov/programs/raceindicators/indicator_RBD.asp#:~:text=In%20school%20year%202015%E2%80%9316,13%20percent)%2C%20Hispanic%20and%20Pacific

Wang, W., & Parker, K. (2014). Record share of Americans have never married. PEW Research Center. https://www.pewsocialtrends.org/2014/09/24/record-share-of-americans-have-never-married/.

Weber, M. (1978). *Economy and society: An outline of interpretive sociology.* (Original work published 1922). University of California Press.

Wickham, P. (2001). Idiocy and the laws in colonial England. *Mental Retardation, 39*(2), 104–113.

SECTION II

EXPERIENCING DISABILITY ACROSS THE LIFE COURSE

PART IV

Disability and the Life Course

CHAPTER 14

DISABILITY AND FAMILY CARE WORK OVER THE LIFE COURSE

J. DALTON STEVENS

INTRODUCTION

THE likelihood of experiencing disability, and the likelihood of needing care, rises with age. Estimates from the Behavioral Risk Factor Surveillance System assessing serious difficulty in hearing, vision, cognition, ambulation, self-care, and independent living suggest disability rates have increased in the United States across all age groups, rising from 24.6% of the population, or 62.6 million people, in 2016 to 26.7%, or 67.2 million people, in 2019 (CDC, 2019). Fifty percent of those ages 75 and older and 25% of those ages 65–74 report a disability requiring care, and estimates suggest the costs of care are likely to double by 2050 due to population aging (Kaye et al., 2010; US Department of Health and Human Services, 2003). Moreover, people with intellectual and developmental disabilities, including many needing care, have seen substantial increases in life expectancy since 1960 due to various social improvements (Landes et al., 2020a). Unpaid family members provide most care for people of all ages with disability; thus, serious policy discussions concerning the provision of such care have intensified (Folbre & Wright, 2012; Harrington Meyer & Abdul-Malak, 2020; Hess et al., 2020). Sociological literatures focusing on disability and family care work have also grown over the last 50 years. However, sociologists tend to theorize and study disability and family care work in isolation (Carey et al., 2020; Cranford, 2020; Kröger, 2009; Morris, 2001), leaving fissures between the two literatures despite disability-related policy needing insights from both. In this chapter, I synthesize life course theory, theories of disability, and care work theories to begin bringing disparate literature on disability and care work together by accounting for the dyad of care worker and care recipient more holistically in an integrated theoretical model. I then identify key areas of scholarship that feature paths forward using a hybrid theoretical model of disability and family care work over the life course.

How can sociologists blend these separate theoretical and empirical literatures to develop a more comprehensive understanding of care work in the context of disability? I develop the Life Course Disability Care Work Integrated Model (LCDCW) to illustrate the potential for analyzing, understanding, and explaining care work in the context of disability over the life course. The life course principles of social structure and linked lives and the focus on aging-related changes lay a foundation for scholarship and policy to account for the experiences of both those who provide and receive care in the context of disability. Structural and interpersonal contexts unite the dyad of care worker and care recipient. I argue that researchers can comprehensively account for care experiences in their research and policy recommendations if they consider both in tandem to identify the contexts that unite and divide them. I consider the social, economic, and policy factors that increase demand for family care in the lives of people with disability and critiques of life course theory from disability studies in the theoretical synthesis. I then turn to the empirical literature on family care work and disability to demonstrate the usefulness of the LCDCW in identifying the unique and shared contexts that shape and problems that arise in care relationships. I highlight that people with disability are both care recipients and providers, a critical linkage between the reviewed literatures. The conclusion summarizes the contributions of the review, highlights existing gaps in the literature, identifies opportunities for future research, and suggests how the literature on disability and family care work can influence disability policy.

THEORETICAL ORIENTATIONS: LIFE COURSE, DISABILITY, AND CARE WORK

Life Course Theory

Life course theory provides a valuable entry point to study people's experiences with disability receiving and providing care because it connects various aspects of life that shape human development and life outcomes (Elder, 1994; Landes & Settersten, 2019; Leiter, 2012; Priestley, 2003). The provision of care is complex and fluctuates over the life course. Scores of family members, friends, and neighbors provide care to and receive care from people in their lives in various forms and for different durations (Kaye et al., 2010). Some provide intensive support, requiring multiple forms of support simultaneously with some medical or nursing skill (Folbre & Wright, 2012; Harrington Meyer & Abdul-Malak, 2020; Reinhard et al., 2019). Others provide infrequent, nonintensive support. Over time, care needs, and therefore care provisions, change. For example, people with cerebral palsy often experience accelerated aging in early adulthood, leading to increased pain and fatigue and modest decreases in functional status (Turk &

Fortuna, 2019). Consequently, care demands shift in tandem with needs, and life course theory can help account for these variations in care. Life course theory converges and diverges with care work and disability theories in several key respects, however.

Life course theory helps theorize the fluctuating objectives, experiences, and need for care work throughout life stages. Life course theory posits that historical, social, and cultural contexts; timing of transitions and critical life events; linked lives; and human agency influence lifelong human development (Elder, 1994; Settersten & Mayer, 1997). Life course theory considers the implications of aging on life experiences and future outcomes. Age is particularly consequential in care provision (Grossman & Magaña, 2016; Settersten & Mayer, 1997). In many regards, childcare is qualitatively different from elder care. The type of care, desired outcomes of care, amount of care required, and experiences of care receipt vary by age. For example, people *aging with disability*, acquired early in life, often see the goal of care as developing independence (Hogan, 2012; Monahan & Wolf, 2014; Stevens, 2019). Conversely, people who *age into disability*, acquired in later life, emphasize retaining as much independence as possible (Monahan & Wolf, 2014). Moreover, for people with intellectual and developmental disabilities, family care work often extends beyond parents and into siblings and grandparents (Harrington Meyer & Abdul-Malak, 2020; Sanchez, 2016; Seltzer et al., 2005). As for the linked lives of siblings, care expectations frequently arise from a young age, and as parents grow older, siblings often expect to assume care responsibilities when parents are no longer able to provide daily care (Seltzer et al., 2005). The focus of the literature on sibling experiences of disability shifted away from a medical-burden model of disability and toward positive and social experiences of siblings in the 1980s, but both strands of research continue (Roper et al., 2014; Sanchez, 2016).

Because interactions between care worker and care recipient are central to the care relationship (Cranford, 2020), scholars must attend to linked lives—the interdependencies that emerge through sustained interaction between individuals (Elder, 1994). Interpersonal relationships, including the care provider and recipient dyad, change over the life course, and how people use connections depends on social contexts—characteristics such as disability and age, and structure (Elder, 1994; Hogan, 2012; Seltzer et al., 2005; Van Asselt-Goverts et al., 2013). Glen Elder (1994) considered *linked lives* the most central principle of life course thinking because relations are formative in human development and correspond with macro-historical change (Elder, 1994, p. 6). For example, the assumption that children with disability would be kept in residential facilities directed how parents responded to disability in the early 20th century (Leiter & Waugh, 2009). Now, the state relies on families comprised of parents, siblings, grandparents, and other informal care workers to provide a bulk of care for children with disability because we have seen a shift to home and community-based services (HCBS); implementation of educational service delivery; neoliberal retrenchment and gatekeeping of social benefit programs; and the rise of single, working, and intensive care work (Harrington Meyer & Abdul-Malak, 2020; Leiter & Waugh, 2009). In the rise of intensive care work, mothers and grandmothers are the gold-standard care providers for children. Women are also more likely to assume care roles over the life course when family members need support (Harrington Meyer & Abdul-Malak, 2020; Roper et al., 2014).

Disability, then, is a life course phenomenon that is best studied when age and linked lives are considered salient to experiences. By accounting for lifelong development and linked lives, researchers can situate disability within a life course framework to critique and extend the literature on disability and the life course. In one such project, Landes and Settersten (2019) use the life history of Pattie Burt to challenge the life course assumption that human agency is an individual property of developmentally normal people. They argue that interpersonal relationships, or the life course concept *linked lives*, always contribute to how one expresses agency. For Burt, foster parents, institutional staff, and care workers engaged in explicit efforts to constrict her agency in many ways—ranging from dictating what foods she ate to what she was able to learn (Landes & Settersten, 2019). After leaving institutional settings, Burt struggled to enact her agency. Still, Burt's pastor and a friend from church taught her how to grocery shop, compare prices of goods, and ultimately continue developing agency as she aged. Burt's life history gives empirical evidence that interpersonal relationships are instrumental to agency, and agency extends beyond those deemed developmentally normal.

Some disability scholars argue that life course theory fails to incorporate lives of people with disability by normalizing specific life course pathways and stigmatizing others, often rendering disability as dependence or disadvantage (Priestley, 2003; Stevens, 2019). In the case of adulthood, researchers explore how people make the transition to adult status, frequently relying on high school graduation, college completion, employment, independent living, marriage, and parenthood (Hogan, 2012; Leiter, 2012; Shandra, 2011). Because the assumption is that achieving these social transitions distinguishes successful adulthood, disability scholars argue that life course theory reproduces marginalization of people with disability by focusing attention on how disability status, not society, limits social transitions (Priestley, 2003, p. 27; Stevens, 2019). For some people with disability, social transitions do not correspond with their actual lived experiences nor conceptualization of adulthood (Leiter, 2012; Stevens, 2019). However, some people with disability do find social transitions salient to adulthood, and they pursue and achieve these goals throughout adulthood to varying degrees (Shandra, 2011; Stevens, 2019). In this context, many young adults with disability find themselves needing support while pursuing independence in adulthood (Stevens, 2019). Despite the variation in dependencies, independencies, and interdependencies of people with disability, life course theory tends to conceptualize care from a supply-side perspective, centering the burden of care on the care worker through the concept of linked lives (Caputo et al., 2016; Grossman & Magaña, 2016). Correspondingly, life course theory primarily relies on a conceptualization of disability as dependence or an outcome of disadvantage (Priestley, 2003). Ultimately, studying variation in life course transitions and pathways is integral to understanding how historical, social, and cultural contexts; timing; linked lives; and human agency shape people's lives (Elder, 1994; Priestley, 2003). However, without a critical understanding of disability, life course theory struggles to conceptualize disability outside of frameworks of dependency or disadvantage. Priestley

(2003) argues that studying normative life patterning reveals why accommodating disability is challenging in the modern era. In doing so, Priestley (2003) calls attention to the importance of blending life course theory and social models of disability.

Theorizing Disability: Individual and Social Models

There are two primary types of models of disability—*individual models* and *social models*, reviewed in Chapter 1 of this handbook and elsewhere (Oliver, 2004; Union of the Physically Impaired Against Segregation and The Disability Alliance, 1975). The models differ in what causes disability, responses to disability, and how to study disability. This section reviews these significant differences between individualistic and social models of disability and identifies how the different models can inform theories of care work and life course theory.

Individual models take a medicalized view of disability as a person's trait. Consequently, the person's atypical body, thinking, or sensory integration causes disability (Oliver, 2004). The response to disability is equally individualistic—medical definition and intervention are necessary to identify and correct one's inability to perform any given task. For example, when a child is diagnosed with attention-deficit/hyperactivity disorder (ADHD), medical professionals often prescribe a stimulant, Ritalin, to increase neurotransmitter levels in the brain in the hopes the child begins to sit still, pay attention, and control their behavior (Conrad, 2010). Individual models define the problem through medical diagnosis and correct via treatment. When treatment fails, rehabilitation is necessary to help people adapt to their disability. For children with ADHD, rehabilitation takes the form of behavioral therapy to modify habits, skills, and responses to the environment—adaptation of the individual is the final solution to fix disability within individualistic models. Care provided from a medicalized notion of disability can encourage treatment seeking that can help people with disabilities, though treatment can also be harmful (Conrad, 2010).

Social models of disability argue that society and its organization, not the individual nor their body, produce disability. The unifying theme of social models of disability, inclusive of the sociopolitical model, is the assumption that disability, or more accurately *impairment*, is not inherently negative nor in need of correction (Oliver, 2004; Union of the Physically Impaired Against Segregation and The Disability Alliance, 1975). Rather, social organization through social structures, institutions, practices, and culture perpetuates the exclusion, isolation, stigma, and overall marginalization of people with impairments. Moreover, social models contend that people with disability are experts in their own lives, counter to individual models that prioritize medical perspectives (Hughes & Paterson, 1997; Sherry, 2016). Social models direct scholars, policymakers, and people with disability to identify social contexts and environments that disadvantage people with impairments, challenging the conflation of disability with illness, pain, suffering, disadvantage, and dependency. The social model of disability has significantly impacted research and policy (Carey et al., 2020).

Sociologists employing social models of disability argue that *impairment*, the concept used in the sociology of disability to refer to biological aspects associated with disability, is conceptually distinct from disability and can limit personal capability and, similar to disability, is socially and culturally defined (Hughes & Paterson, 1997; Oliver, 2004; Sherry, 2016). Sociologists have developed a sociomedical model of disability, the disablement process, over the last 20 years (Verbrugge & Jette, 1994). The disablement process holds that disability is the gap between personal capability and environmental demand. This model is particularly effective in measuring disability rates; theorizing the interaction between human bodies and environments; and drawing conceptual boundaries between disability and associated concepts pathology, impairment, functional limitation, and intervention (Verbrugge & Jette, 1994). Morris (2001, p. 2) argues separating *impairment* and *disability* is the "cornerstone of what is known as the social model of disability." By neglecting this distinction, care needs are challenging to identify. Providing too little or too much care may harm those providing and receiving care (Harrington Meyer, 2014; Pyke & Bengtson, 1996; Stevens, 2019).

The sociopolitical model of disability identifies and addresses the external barriers people with disability experience when attempting social, economic, and political activities (Hahn, 1985). Barriers emerge from social and physical environments, and policy and social change that focus on barriers in transportation, education, employment, architecture, and public accommodations and attitudes can alleviate disability (Hahn, 1985). The sociopolitical model relies on a political-economic view of disability and is therefore suited to theorize the distribution of resources, such as care, and how the state and market guide this process (Hahn, 1985; Harrington Meyer & Abdul-Malak, 2020; Kröger, 2009). In terms of care, the barriers people with disability face are tremendous and emerge at the structural, organizational, and interpersonal levels (Grossman & Magaña, 2016). For example, at the structural level, state variation in Medicaid policy can prevent cross-state moves for beneficiaries with disabilities who rely on services (Grossman, 2019). While neglected in many studies taking this approach, parents and families of children with developmental disability report difficulty finding informal care providers at the interpersonal level, situating the burden of care squarely on families' shoulders (Cranford, 2020; Harrington Meyer & Abdul-Malak, 2020; Hogan, 2012). However, like the medical model, the sociopolitical model assesses disability along one dimension, sectioning off essential facets of the disability experience (Hughes & Paterson 1997; Sherry, 2016). The sociopolitical model of disability constructs disability as disembodied, focusing on politics and citizenship and limiting the conceptualization of impairments (Hughes & Paterson, 1997; Sherry, 2016). The section on care work expands on this limitation.

By integrating life course perspectives with the sociopolitical model of disability, researchers have conceptual tools to better theorize interpersonal barriers and facilitators in the lives of people with disability. Specifically, because life course theory considers interpersonal relationships in conjunction with social and historical contexts (Elder, 1994; Grossman & Magaña, 2016), blending life course theory with the sociopolitical model can better account for disability-related interpersonal and structural barriers. For example, during the COVID-19 pandemic and vaccine distribution, most US states prioritized vaccination for individuals with intellectual and developmental disabilities living in congregate living facilities (National Governors Association, 2021) due to the increased risk of severe symptoms and mortality given comorbid health conditions and group living quarters (Landes et al., 2020b; Turk et al., 2020). Despite elevated case-fatality rates among adults with intellectual and developmental disabilities generally, and those younger especially (Turk et al., 2020), states did not prioritize people with disability receiving family care simultaneously (National Governors Association, 2021). Therefore, people with disabilities receiving only unpaid care remained at heightened risk while those receiving paid care had the opportunity to prevent severe effects of COVID-19. The type of interpersonal relationship between the care recipient and care provider dictated the political response to vaccine distribution. While researchers and policymakers made a crucial step in protecting some people with disabilities, public health response during the pandemic neglected the linked lives of unpaid family care workers and recipients.

Embedding the sociopolitical model of disability within the life course framework theorizes how family care is organized, distributed, and received as a necessary yet scarce resource while emphasizing the civil and human rights of people with disability. By acknowledging that impairments contribute to functional limitations within the framework (Hughes & Paterson, 1997; Sherry, 2016; Stevens, 2019), scholars can account for the labor involved in care work (Folbre & Wright, 2012; Kröger, 2009; Verbrugge & Jette, 1994). In uniting experiences of care providers and recipients in the context of impairment and disability, academics may be able to make policy suggestions that address the care relationship and context more holistically (see Figure 14.1).

Theorizing Care Work

Care work exists between the public and private spheres. The oscillation of domestic and economic responsibilities, desires, and motivations shape family care work for people with disability (Kaye et al., 2010; Reinhard et al., 2019). Care workers often find themselves juggling care responsibilities, careers, and other life demands. Indeed, parents, most often mothers, of children with disability, like many parents, often choose between providing unpaid care and maintaining employment (Hogan, 2012; McCall & Starr, 2018; Scott, 2018), stretching their budgets, lowering lifetime earnings, and straining relationships (Bianchi et al., 2012; Harrington Meyer, 2014; Hogan, 2012). This section defines care work and reviews prominent theories of care work to begin expanding these theories to include life course and disability principles.

Sociologists define care work in a variety of ways. Herd and Harrington Meyer (2002, p. 666) define care work as "the daily physical and emotional labor of feeding and nurturing citizens, [and] is an active form of participatory citizenship with far-reaching civic benefits." Folbre and Wright (2012) define care work differently, outlining three forms of care work—*interactive care*, *support care*, and *supervisory care*. Interactive

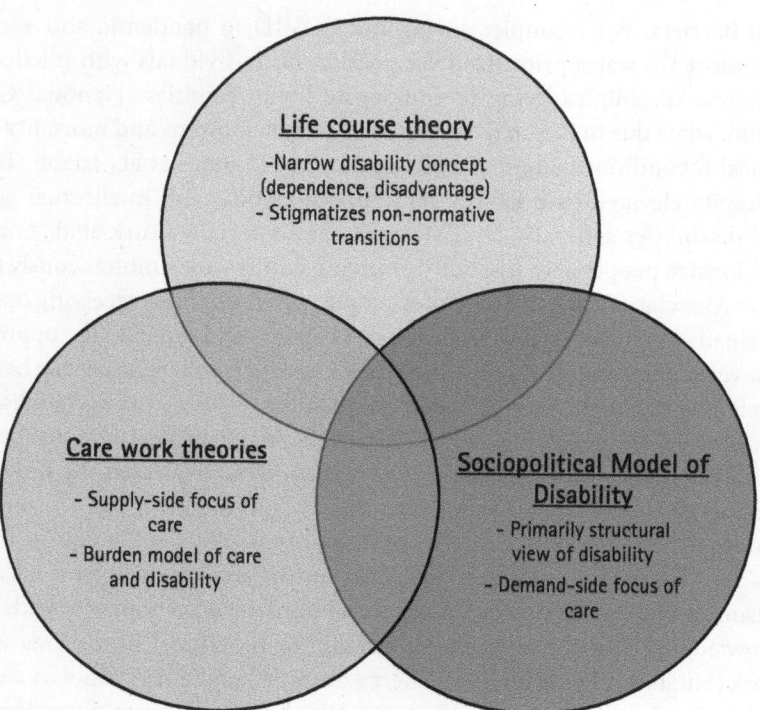

FIGURE 14.1 Shortcomings of life course theory, sociopolitical model of disability, and theories of care work.

care involves the in-person support typically associated with assisting in activities of daily living (ADLs: toileting, bathing, dressing, grooming, feeding, and transferring). Support care provides assistance with instrumental activities of daily living (IADLs: cooking, finances, laundry, shopping, and transportation), often considered household labor (Folbre & Wright, 2012). Supervisory care refers to being on-call to provide care but does not involve physical duties. The definition of care that fits best with life course and disability theory must acknowledge care work as a form of emotional, mental, and physical labor that provides various types of support to individuals, including those with disability, while contributing to broader political and social projects.

A prominent strand of care work theory conceptualizes how various social structures—namely gender, economy, and politics—shape care work and the lives of care workers (Harrington Meyer & Abdul-Malak, 2020). Prevailing structural theories of care argue that because women perform most care work, and because women's status is devalued by society, a significant wage gap between men and women persists (Bianchi et al., 2012; Budig & England, 2001; Hess et al., 2020). Empirical analyses seem to support the devaluation theory by specifying the mechanisms causing the pay gap. Using data from the 1982–1993 National Longitudinal Survey of Youth with fixed-effects models, Budig and England (2001) show that married and unmarried mothers, on average, experience a 7% wage penalty due to reduced employment experience and hour reductions associated with care provision. Time-use studies suggest that women average 5.7 hours per day performing unpaid care work across the life course while men average 3.6 hours, a 37% disparity (Hess et al., 2020). The social expectation of women to provide unpaid care devalues women's contributions to their societies, communities, and families.

Given the disproportional effects of unpaid care work on women's labor force participation and earnings, the market and state play a significant role in structuring care work (Cranford, 2020; Harrington Meyer & Abdul-Malak, 2020). Structural paradigms of care work rely on political economy theories that suggest that demand for care work fluctuates in response to sociodemographic trends, economic shifts, and social assistance program availability as unpaid care workers respond to unmet needs (Harrington Meyer & Abdul-Malak, 2020). The market has failed to provide adequate services for people who need care and family-friendly policies for those who provide care, unsurprising given the difficulty of translating intangible social benefits of care into profit (Harrington Meyer & Abdul-Malak, 2020). Additionally, traditional gender and family assumptions shape US welfare programs, often at the detriment of women's economic and social security (Bianchi et al., 2012; Harrington Meyer & Abdul-Malak 2020; Herd & Harrington Meyer, 2002). Negative consequences of providing unpaid family care are immense and often force women to accept lower-paying jobs or reduce paid work, decreasing lifetime earnings and pension contributions (Bianchi et al., 2012; Harrington Meyer, 2014; Hogan, 2012). Moreover, research demonstrates negative physical and mental consequences of unpaid family care for care providers, such as higher rates of chronic health conditions, depression, inadequate nutrition, and early death (Caputo et al., 2016; Ciciurkaite & Brown, 2017; Vitaliano et al., 2003).

In many ways, the complex web of state and federal social assistance programs that comprise the US welfare state has also undersupplied and underfunded care. The state does so to defray costs, relying on targeted programs with strict means-tests to limit social benefit program uptake instead of adopting universal programs (Harrington Meyer & Abdul-Malak, 2020). For example, the red tape that potential beneficiaries encounter when applying to Medicaid, the largest payer of long-term services and supports for people with disability, increases perceived stigma, application burden, and learning costs and decreases uptake among the eligible (Harrington Meyer & Stevens, 2020; Herd et al., 2013). By delaying approval, the state saves millions of dollars annually, $470 million in 2017, according to the most recent estimates, shifting labor to unpaid families (Harrington Meyer & Abdul-Malak, 2020; Herd et al., 2013; Reinhard et al., 2019).

Care work theorists also study the motivations for providing care, benefits of care, and labor associated with care and its effects (Bianchi et al., 2012; Folbre & Wright, 2012; Herd & Harrington Meyer, 2002). Social psychological theories of care work note that motivations for providing care are intrinsic and extrinsic (England et al., 2012). For unpaid care work, intrinsic motivations may include love, altruistic worldviews, and early socialization for care work. Extrinsic motives such as a lack of affordable and high-quality alternatives, avoidance of penalties, social approval, and reciprocity expectations encourage women to perform care work (England et al., 2012; Harrington Meyer & Abdul-Malak, 2020). The benefits of care accrue individually and socially. Providing care involves an investment in the care recipient; care can provide cognitive skills to increase earnings, develop healthy habits, and build relationships. Resulting individual benefits provide returns to society by improving the next generation's skills and allowing others to earn a paycheck. However, people who provide unpaid care often lack choice due to sparse options (Cranford, 2020; Harrington Meyer & Abdul-Malak, 2020).

Given these dynamics in care provision policy, it becomes clear that the care dyad is interdependent. Therefore, theories of care work would benefit from integrating a life course perspective and the sociopolitical model of disability. Some care work literature already integrates life course theory into theories of care (Harrington Meyer & Abdul-Malak, 2020). For example, scholars of care work have used life course theory to theorize the multiple care relationships a person engages with that change with aging and can include *simultaneous* and *sequential care work*. This theorization of care considers life course aging and the numerous interpersonal relationships involving care among grandparents providing care to grandchildren with disabilities (Harrington Meyer & Abdul-Malak, 2020). However, sociologists studying care work tend to focus on care impacts on care workers (Bianchi et al., 2012; England et al., 2012), emphasizing supply-side contexts and workers' rights while neglecting care receipt (Kröger, 2009). By blending life course theory with theories of care work, scholarship and policy can identify converging and diverging experiences, needs, and rights of care workers and recipients.

The blended life course and care work literature must account for the sociopolitical model of disability to fully attend to the care dyad. Not only should care workers have rights to compensation for their labor and contributions to the state and to refuse and limit how much care work they are providing (Budig & England, 2001; Herd & Harrington Meyer, 2002; Hess et al., 2020), people receiving care have rights to decide what that care looks like, how it is provided, who provides it, and to ensure their need for support does not supersede their rights as citizens or self-direction (Cranford, 2020; Kröger, 2009; Morris, 2001). The linked rights of the care dyad often conflict (Carey et al., 2020). However, using the sociopolitical model of disability informed by life course theory and care work theory that assesses converging and diverging needs of the care dyad across the life course may account for the conflict (Carey et al., 2020; Cranford, 2020). Recent research supporting this notion from Carey and colleagues (2020) calls attention to the allied and unique contributions to disability rights and policy agenda made by parents and people with disability. In their analysis of disability and parent activism, Carey and colleagues (2020) argue that human rights are central to policy change moving forward. However, parents' rights and disability rights often clash because the disability community advocates for more control over services while parents advocate for safety. Assessing this dynamic in social scientific theorizing necessitates integrated disability and care work theories over the life course.

Integrating Disability and Care Work Theories through Life Course Principles

Existing perspectives overlook the extent to which the care relationship is comprised of independencies, dependencies, and interdependencies. The disparate foci of disability and care work theorists have produced fractured literatures, with the former taking a demand-side perspective and the latter taking a supply-side perspective on care work. Some sociologists have started to mend this fissure by considering the care relationship more holistically by accounting for shared experiences and structural contexts of care workers and recipients with disability (Carey et al., 2020; Cranford, 2020; Leiter, 2012; Shandra & Penner, 2017). Historically, scholars of care work have focused on the physical, emotional, financial, and social ramifications of providing care to the care worker (Caputo et al., 2016; Green, 2007; National Academies of Sciences, Engineering, and Medicine, 2016). Alternatively, disability scholars studying care often focus on the control or lack thereof that care recipients experience in their care relationships at the interpersonal, organizational, and structural levels (Cranford, 2020; Grossman, 2019; Morris, 2001).

Life course principles, especially social structure, linked lives, and attention to aging-related change, provide insight into the twin experiences of providing and receiving care in the context of disability. Interpersonal and structural contexts bind the dyad of care worker and care recipient, and I argue that researchers can account for care experiences comprehensively if they consider both care workers and recipients in unison to identify the contexts that unite and divide the care dyad. Moreover, the tripartite orientation of the LCDCW (Figure 14.2) can attend to the converging and diverging needs and rights of care workers and care recipients over the life course. This framework for theorizing disability and care over the life course reveals potential areas of scholarship that are underdeveloped.

Issues in care manifest at the individual and interpersonal level—care burden among care providers and control of care among care recipients. For example, care workers, and unpaid care workers especially, face higher levels of burden when providing more physically and emotionally intensive care—an artifact of the labor involved in providing consistent, strenuous, and indispensable assistance to someone (Green, 2007; Roper et al., 2014). Despite experiencing care burden, research also demonstrates family care providers report benefits of providing care for children and adults with disability, such as increasing the importance of family closeness and appreciation for life (Green, 2007; Harrington Meyer & Abdul Malak, 2020; Myers et al., 2009). However, some people with disability receiving care express lacking control in care relationships, a frequent point of contention for disability scholars studying care (Grossman & Magaña, 2016; Kröger, 2009; Morris, 2001). People with disability often have little control over who is

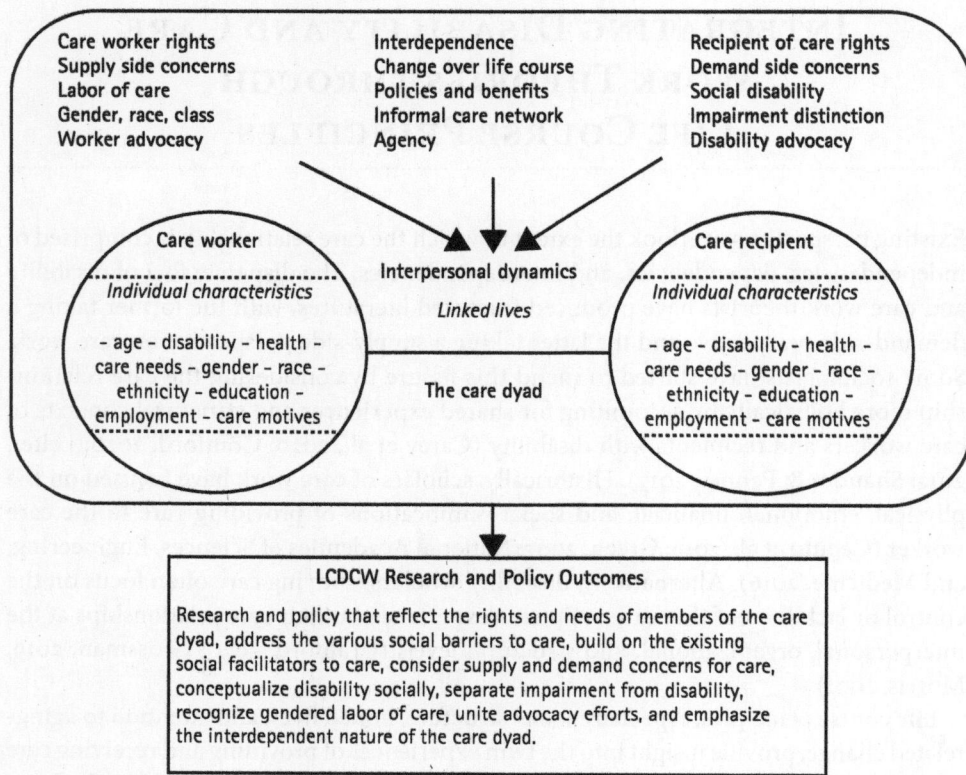

FIGURE 14.2 Visual representation of the Life Course Disability Care Work Integrated Model.

providing care. The limited pool of care workers who can provide quality care that is attentive to recipients' desires and needs has contributed to a heavy reliance on family care (Harrington Meyer & Abdul Malak, 2020; Kröger, 2009; Morris, 2001). Alternatively, people with disability recognize that the support they receive from parents contributes to their ability to live their lives and reach levels of independence regardless of care needs (Leiter, 2012; Stevens, 2019).

Structural contexts further unite the dyad of care worker and care recipient. Ten million Americans report needing assistance with ADLs/IADLs (Kaye et al., 2010), 92% of which receive unpaid, mainly family, support. The lack of policy support for care workers is a major contributing factor to why family members provide so much care in the United States. Kaye et al. (2010) analyzed 2005 data from the Survey of Income Program Participation. They find that of the 10 million noninstitutionalized individuals in need of ADL/IADL support, only 13%, or 1.4 million people, rely on paid care workers, while over 90% receive unpaid support. Medicaid also provides some long-term services and supports through HCBS waivers to 1.8 million individuals (Kaiser Family Foundation, 2018), but these programs' availability varies by state. For example, all 50 states extend HCBS waivers through Medicaid to individuals with intellectual and developmental disabilities. However, only certain states extend waivers to seniors with physical impairments (21 states), nonelderly adults with physical impairments (16 states), traumatic brain or spinal cord injuries (21 states), children with high medical needs (18 states), mental health disabilities (11 states), and those with HIV/AIDS (5 states) (Musumeci & Chidambaram, 2020). Smaller programs, such as the National Family Caregiver Support Program, have provided some support for family care workers. In 2014, the most recent year data were available, the program provided 604,000 care workers with respite services, nearly 6 million labor hours (Administration for Community Living, 2019). The existing programs help some families, but a sizeable population remains unsupported (Kaye et al., 2010; Reinhard et al., 2019).

As researchers continue to study the intersection of care work and disability, they must recognize that care recipients and care workers are rowing the same boat. The same policy gaps that affect care providers affect care recipients. For example, families must choose between providing care for children with disability and paid labor, increasing the burden associated with care. Reciprocally, people with disability receiving care from their family members have limited say over who provides care if no alternatives are available. Lacking robust family care policies exacerbates these issues. To be sure, blending life course theory, sociopolitical models of disability, and theories of care work enables researchers to think through how social structures such as social assistance policy shape care relationships, and the interpersonal dynamics that play out within them (Cranford, 2020; Grossman & Magaña, 2016; Priestley, 2003). Research that focuses solely on care workers or on people with disability who need care has provided significant insight into various social problems. Nevertheless, researchers can account for care experiences more comprehensively if they are attentive to care workers and recipients by identifying shared and unique issues that arise and their effects (Carey et al., 2020; Cranford, 2020; Kröger, 2009; Morris, 2001).

Care Experiences

Care experiences of people with disability demonstrate how the integration of the literatures on disability and care work can help researchers balance the civil and human rights of people with disability with the labor involved in providing care, especially unpaid family care. Importantly, putting care recipients' and care workers' experiences in conversation highlights the effects of care on both. The dual information allows us to understand how to craft policy that responds to and supports the care dyad with disability over the life course. Moreover, research and policy must attend to the fact that people with disability often provide care, challenging the idea that people with disability are simply dependent beneficiaries of care (Carey et al., 2020; Shandra & Penner, 2017; Thorpe et al., 2015). This section reviews work that, when read together, best exemplifies this intersection that aligns with the LCDCW—a hybrid theoretical model blending life course theory, sociopolitical models of disability, and theories of care work.

PEOPLE WITH DISABILITY RECEIVING CARE

Though care benefits are numerous at individual and social levels, care recipients frequently experience adverse outcomes associated with care, such as feelings of dependency, stigmatization, lowered self-esteem, and powerlessness. Relatedly, care workers providing support to family members with disability often experience feelings of captivity, courtesy stigma, and relationship dissatisfaction. Others report positive outcomes of care provision, such as increased autonomy and the ability to forge close relationships. The LCDCW insists that research and policy consider care experiences and outcomes of the care dyad simultaneously. This section demonstrates how the LCDCW integrated framework operates by reviewing the literature on these experiences and concluding with a review of the literature that proposes interpersonal and structural interventions to mitigate harmful effects.

Receiving care from a family member can be exceptionally difficult for people with disability. The limited empirical research on experiences of care receipt demonstrates the impacts of the type of relationship, age, and type of care on receiving care. Parents with disability who receive care from their children report feelings of infantilization (Pyke & Bengston, 1996). In a qualitative study on how elder care is performed by families using 67 interviews with members of 20 three-generation families, Pyke and Bengston (1996) report *overcaring*—providing care an individual does not need—leads to animosity between the care recipient and provider. In one case, Alfred, a 91-year-old father, reported that instances of family overcaring left him feeling less independent, fostering family discord (Pyke & Bengtson, 1996). Adult children receiving care from a parent or sibling have reported similar outcomes. Stevens (2019) relies on life-history interviews with nine young men with mobility impairments to assess how they experience interdependence in early adulthood. Some of the young men used family interdependence as a route to increased autonomy. However, others found interdependence infantilizing and prevented advancement, especially after moving in with their parents (Stevens, 2019). Spouses with disability receiving care from their partners report negative care interactions. In one study of 276 spousal pairs, 40% of spouses with disability reported negative care interactions involving either undercaring or overcaring. Negative care interactions decreased self-esteem and increased fatalistic attitudes and marital conflict among care recipients (Newsom & Schulz, 1998).

According to the LCDCW, research and policy must attend to care workers' experiences of providing care in tandem with care recipients' experiences of receiving care. Family care for a person with disability may also have deleterious effects on the care worker. Providing care to a spouse with disability can increase rates of depression, feelings of captivity, and marital dissatisfaction, and researchers frequently observe increased risk among women, who disproportionally provide family care work (Caputo et al., 2016; Ciciurkaite & Brown, 2017). Mothers of children with disability report higher rates of maternal stress than mothers of children without developmental disability (Hogan, 2012; Myers et al., 2009). Hogan's (2012) mixed-methods study of family consequences of children's disability reported that parents of children with disability have fewer interpersonal relationships, and interview participants explained that friends perceive them as overextended. One of Hogan's (2012, p. 50) participants said, "All the ones [friends] I had before he was born are gone. My best friend, Molly, won't call me anymore. She says I have no time for her. They don't understand . . . why I have to take him with me." After autism diagnosis, parents of children with autism report similarly strained social lives (Myers et al., 2009). Narrowing social lives of parents with children with disability may be, in part, due to perceived burdens of childcare. Other research documents that *courtesy stigma*—experiences of negative public perceptions and reactions to individuals close to stigmatized persons—also contributes to social isolation and exclusion of parents (Green, 2007).

Despite the breadth of literature on negative experiences of family care and disability, many care recipients with disability and family care providers report benefits associated with care, such as increased independence and opportunities for care recipients (Hogan, 2012; Leiter, 2012; Stevens, 2019) and increased adaptability, marital and spiritual enrichment, compassion, and appreciation for life for care providers (Green, 2007; Myers et al., 2009). Indeed, many care recipients and, to a lesser extent, providers believe that family care is better for their situation than hiring nonfamily members (Cranford, 2020; Lehnert et al., 2019). In one study assessing the use of Independent Choices, the Arkansas Medicaid program that provides cash to beneficiaries to pay for and arrange their care, Foster and colleagues (2003) report that almost all survey respondents (N = 1,739) hired family or friends as care providers. Moreover, their results also suggest Independent Choices users report higher quality care and fewer incidences of neglect.

Considering the care dyad in unison within the LCDCW identifies potential interpersonal and structural interventions to enhance care benefits and decrease care harms. Some literature suggests that practices of reciprocity, whether pay or other support, can mitigate negative experiences (Cranford, 2020; England et al., 2012; Foster et al., 2003). Although the benefits of reciprocity are potentially limited (Harrington Meyer & Abdul-Malak, 2020), policies extending cash options may offer more control to care recipients with disability and enable them to pay typically unpaid care workers (Foster et al., 2003). Respite care programs may also ease the stress associated with providing care by allowing primary care providers to take needed breaks (Engwall & Hultman, 2020; Frederick, 2018). Moreover, respite care can also give those receiving care an opportunity to form relationships and lives outside of the purview of their parents, which can be liberating (Engwall & Hultman, 2020).

People with Disability Providing Care

Historically, society and state policies have treated people with disability as dependent and in need of care, neglecting the fact people with disability are often care workers

(Harrington Meyer, 2014; Priestley, 2003; Shandra & Penner, 2017; Thorpe et al., 2015). Thorpe and colleagues (2015) estimate that 38% of informal care providers, most typically family members, have some sort of sensory, cognitive, physical, or multiple functional limitations. Moreover, parents with various types of disability have reported experiences of state scrutiny as their ability to parent has been questioned by medical and state professionals (Frederick, 2017). This section reviews the small literature on care work performed by people with disability to illustrate the importance of considering disability as a part of the care worker experience, an extension of the LCDCW.

Research on care work often overlooks the proportion of care provided by people with disability. Shandra and Penner (2017) use the American Time Use Survey (2008–2015) to assess the extent to which people with disability are benefactors of care. Their analysis reveals some heterogeneity in the types of care people with and without disability provide. For example, mothers with a mental or cognitive disability provide less secondary childcare than mothers without any disability, and men with disability report providing less care to adults and nonhousehold members than men without disability. However, in almost all other comparisons, people with disability report providing similar or even more care than people without disability (Shandra & Penner, 2017).

Research on care providers with disability frequently centers on their ability to provide quality care. For example, Thorpe and colleagues (2015) study the impact of functional limitations of care providers on care recipient use of preventive services. Their analysis of MEPS (2000–2008) shows that care recipients with care providers with cognitive, mobility, or emotional health limitations were less likely than care recipients with care providers without functional limitations to receive preventive services, such as influenza vaccines and routine checkups. In line with a social model of disability, Thorpe and colleagues (2015) identify that distrust of medical professionals, inaccessible and unaccommodating facilities, and inadequate time with providers likely contribute to the disparity in preventive care receipt. Frederick's (2017) research on mothers' experiences with physical or sensory impairments finds that they face extreme scrutiny, especially from medical providers, of their mothering ability. Deemed "risky mothers" by medical professionals, these women face unwarranted competency investigations, recommendations to make adoption or abortion plans, and discrimination from physicians (Frederick, 2017). The LCDCW can help researchers and policymakers address the particular issues that arise when care providers have disabilities.

While impairments can increase the amount of time and difficulty some people have parenting, most experts agree the focus should be on improving services to parents with disability to assist them in their care responsibilities. The United Nations' Convention on the Rights of Persons with Disability (CRPD), signed by the United States in 2009 but rejected for ratification in 2012, outlines the parenting rights of people with disability, calling for nations to eliminate discrimination against parents with disability. Part of this chapter of the CRPD encourages authorities to keep families intact unless professionals prove the child is in danger. Moreover, the CRPD seeks to ensure the right to fertility, making involuntary sterilization procedures and treatment illegal (Tilley et al., 2012). While eugenics thinking is often considered a thing of the past, Washington

State considered adopting broader pathways for parents of people with disability to have their children sterilized as recently as 2017, an apparent clash of rights between care providers and recipients (Ne'eman, 2018). Research informed by the LCDCW is needed to understand fertility choices and decisions of people with disability and identify the constraints and facilitators to parenthood.

CONCLUSION

This chapter brings together theoretical and empirical literatures on disability and care work by employing a life course framework informed by sociopolitical models of disability and care work theories to consider the shared and unique experiences of care providers and care recipients at the interpersonal and structural levels. While the theoretical and empirical literatures on disability and care work have blossomed in isolation as primarily structural paradigms (Cranford, 2020; Hughes & Paterson, 1997), life course theory provides substantial theoretical insight to unite these literatures and begin to address the experiences of people with disability receiving and providing family care work more holistically. Fundamental life course principles, linked lives and social structure, are particularly useful in theorizing the care relationship and how political and economic systems shape care provision and consequences thereof. The LCDCW considers the rights of both care worker and care recipient, accounts for the needs of the care dyad, recognizes that aging impacts the care relationship, assesses social barriers and facilitators to care, and conceptualizes people with disability as both providers and recipients of care. Researchers can use the integrated model to explore how care is received and provided by persons with disability, the barriers and facilitators to high-quality care, and the impact of social policy on the care dyad. Specifically, assessing how policies shape the care relationship from the perspectives of care workers and recipients can highlight what policy changes are necessary to ensure the rights and needs of both parties.

This review also highlights potential areas for growth in disability policy and research. Expanding Medicaid services, especially cash options and respite services, is a meaningful policy change that could address both rights for care recipients and burdens for care workers (Cranford, 2020; Engwall & Hultman, 2020). Specifically, the combined literatures on disability and care work suggest that expanding access to HCBS waivers through Medicaid, strengthening beneficiary control over their care, expanding Medicaid eligibility to include more families that likely rely on unpaid family care, and investing in the training and retention of paid care workers would begin to address the problems faced by both care workers and recipients. However, more research is needed to determine how people with disability experience respite and nonfamily care because most of the literature focuses on care providers' experiences, not recipients (Engwall & Hultman, 2020). Moreover, the LCDCW adds theoretical clarity to the growing number of voices that call for understanding disability as an experience of care workers, challenging the idea disability means dependence (Shandra

& Penner, 2017; Thorpe et al., 2015). Future research should consider the experiences of disabled care providers, parents, and workers generally. Most importantly, sociological researchers must begin attending to the convergences and divergences in the care dyad's experiences, needs, and rights to provide a more holistic accounting for care work and disability over the life course. To date, sociology has neglected disability as an essential dimension of inequality, and sociological literatures must begin attending to how disability influences, is represented in, and intersects with other areas of the discipline. This chapter provides one way to start integrating disability into the discipline more broadly.

References

Administration for Community Living. (2019). National family caregiver support program. https://acl.gov/programs/support-caregivers/national-family-caregiver-support-program

Bianchi, S., Folbre, N., & Wolf, D. A. (2012). Unpaid care work. In N. Folbre (Ed.), *For love and money: Care provision in the United States* 2 (pp. 40–64). Russell Sage Foundation.

Budig, M. J., & England, P. (2001). The wage penalty for motherhood. *American Sociological Review, 66*(2), 204–225.

Caputo, J., Pavalko, E. K., & Hardy, M. A. (2016). The long-term effects of caregiving on women's health and mortality. *Journal of Marriage and Family, 78*(5), 1382–1398. https://doi.org/10.1111/jomf.12332

Carey, A. C., Block, P., & Scotch, R. K. (2020). *Allies and obstacles: Disability activism and parents of children with disabilities.* Temple University Press.

Centers for Disease Control and Prevention, National Center on Birth Defects and Developmental Disabilities, Division of Human Development and Disability. (2019). Disability and health data system. *DHDS Online Data.* https://dhds.cdc.gov

Ciciurkaite, G., & Brown, R. (2017). Food insecurity and mental health: A gendered issue?. In Sara Shastak (Ed), *Advances in Medical Sociology: Food Systems and Health,* (p. 59–76) Emerald Group.

Conrad, P. (2010). The changing social reality of ADHD. *Contemporary Sociology, 39*(5), 525–527. https://doi.org/10.1177%2F0094306110380381

Cranford, C. J. (2020). *Home care fault lines.* Cornell University Press.

Elder, G. H. 1994. Time, human agency, and social change: Perspectives on the life course. *Social Psychology Quarterly, 57*(1), 4. https://doi.org/10.2307/2786971

England, P., Folbre, N., & Leana, C. (2012). Motivating care. In N. Folbre (Ed.), *For love and money: Care provision in the United States* (pp. 21–39). Russell Sage Foundation.

Engwall, K., & Hultman, L. (2020). Constructions of childhood: The assessment of respite care for children with disabilities in Sweden. *European Journal of Social Work,* 1–12. https://doi.org/10.1080/13691457.2020.1763260

Folbre, N., & Olin Wright, E. (2012). Defining care. In N. Folbre (Ed.), *For love and money: Care provision in the United States* (pp. 1–20). Russell Sage Foundation.

Foster, L., Brown, R., Phillips, B., Schore, J., & Carlson, B. P. (2003). Improving the quality of Medicaid personal assistance through consumer direction. *Health Affairs (Project Hope),* Suppl Web (March). https://doi.org/10.1377/hlthaff.w3.162

Frederick, A. (2017). Risky mothers and the normalcy project: Women with disabilities negotiate scientific motherhood. *Gender and Society, 31*(1), 74–95. https://doi.org/10.1177%2Fo891243216683914

Frederick, D. (2018). Mitigating burden associated with informal caregiving. *Journal of Patient Experience*, 5(1), 50–55. https://doi.org/10.1177%2F2374373517742499

Green, S. E. (2007). "We're tired, not sad": Benefits and burdens of mothering a child with a disability. *Social Science and Medicine*. https://doi.org/10.1016/j.socscimed.2006.08.025

Grossman, B. R. (2019). Conflicting narratives of corporeal citizenship: Medicaid personal care attendant (PCA) policy and program users' experiences of cross-state moves. In S. E. Green & D. R. Loseke (Eds.), *New narratives of disability: Constructions, clashes, and controversies* (pp. 185–202). Emerald.

Grossman, B. R., & Magaña, S. (2016). Introduction to the special issue: Family support of persons with disabilities across the life course. *Journal of Family Social Work*, 19(4), 237–251. https://doi.org/10.1080/10522158.2016.1234272

Hahn, H. (1985). Toward a politics of disability: Definitions, disciplines, and policies. *The Social Science Journal*, 22(4), 87–105.

Harrington Meyer, M. (2014). *Grandmothers at work: Juggling families and jobs.* New York University Press.

Harrington Meyer, M., & Abdul-Malak, Y. (2020). *Grandparenting children with disabilities.* Palgrave Macmillan.

Harrington Meyer, M., & Stevens, J. D. (2020). Medicaid for people with disabilities. In D. Lanford (Ed.), *Medicaid: Enrollment, eligibility, and key issues* (pp. 261–300). Nova Science.

Herd, P., Deleire, T., Harvey, H., & Moynihan, D. P. (2013). Shifting administrative burden to the state: The case of Medicaid take-up. *Public Administration Review*, 73(Suppl. 1), 69–81. https://doi.org/10.1111/puar.12114

Herd, P., & Harrington Meyer, M. (2002). Care work invisible civic engagement. *Gender and Society*, 16(5), 665–688. https://doi.org/10.1177%2F089124302236991

Hess, C., Ahmed, T., & Hayes, J. (2020). *Providing unpaid household and care work in the United States: Uncovering inequality: The gender gap in unpaid household and care work: Across all.* Institute for Women's Policy Research.

Hogan, D. P. (2012). *Family consequences of children's disabilities.* Russell Sage Foundation.

Hughes, B., & Paterson, K. (1997). The social model of disability and the disappearing body: Towards a sociology of impairment. *Disability and Society*, 12(3), 325–340. https://doi.org/10.1080/09687599727209

Kaiser Family Foundation. (2018). Home and community-based services waivers participants. https://www.kff.org/medicaid/state-indicator/medicaid-section-1915c-home-and-community-based-services-waivers-participants/?currentTimeframe=0&andsortModel=%7B%22colId%22:%22Location%22,%22sort%22:%22asc%22%7D

Kaye, H. S., Harrington, C., & Laplante, M. P. (2010). Long-term care: Who gets it, who provides it, who pays, and how much? *Health Affairs*, 29(1), 11–21. https://doi.org/10.1377/hlthaff.2009.0535

Kröger, T. (2009). Care research and disability studies: Nothing in common?" *Critical Social Policy*, 29(3), 398–420. https://doi.org/10.1177%2F0261018309105177

Landes, S. D., McDonald, K. E., Wilmoth, J. M., & Grosso. E. C. (2020a). Evidence of continued reduction in the age-at-death disparity between adults with and without intellectual and/or developmental disabilities. *Journal of Applied Research in Intellectual Disabilities* (November), 1–5. https://doi.org/10.1111/jar.12840

Landes, S. D., & Settersten, R. A. (2019). The inseparability of human agency and linked lives. *Advances in Life Course Research*, 42(December), 100306. https://doi.org/10.1016/j.alcr.2019.100306

Landes, S. D., Turk, M. A., Formica, M. K., Mcdonald, K. E., & Stevens, J. D. (2020b). COVID-19 outcomes among people with intellectual and developmental disability living in residential group homes in New York State. *Disability and Health Journal*, 13(4), 1–5.

Lehnert, T., Heuchert, M., Hussain, K., & König, H. H. (2019). Stated preferences for long-term care: A literature review. *Ageing and Society*, *39*(9), 1873–1913. http://dx.doi.org/10.1017/S0144686X18000314

Leiter, V. (2012). *Their time has come: Youth with disabilities on the cusp of adulthood*. Rutgers University Press.

Leiter, V., & Waugh, A. (2009). Moving out: Residential independence among young adults with disabilities and the role of families. *Marriage and Family Review*, *45*(5), 519–537. https://doi.org/10.1080/01494920903050847

McCall, B. P., & Starr, E. M. (2018). Effects of autism spectrum disorder on parental employment in the United States: Evidence from the National Health Interview Survey. *Community, Work and Family*, *21*(4), 367–392. https://doi.org/10.1080/13668803.2016.1241217

Monahan, D. J., & Wolf, D. A. (2014). The continuum of disability over the lifespan: The convergence of aging with disability and aging into disability. *Disability and Health Journal*, *7*(1 Suppl.), S1–S3. https://doi.org/10.1016/j.dhjo.2013.02.002

Morris, J. (2001). Impairment and disability: Constructing an ethics of care that promotes human rights. *Hypatia: A Journal of Feminist Philosophy*, *16*(4), 1–16. https://doi.org/10.1111/j.1527-2001.2001.tb01046.x

Musumeci, M., & Chidambaram, P. (2020). Medicaid home and community-based services enrollment and spending. *Kaiser Family Foundation*. https://www.kff.org/medicaid/issue-brief/medicaid-home-and-community-based-services-enrollment-and-spending/

Myers, B. J., Mackintosh, V. H., & Goin-Kochel, R. P. (2009). "My greatest joy and my greatest heart ache:" Parents' own words on how having a child in the Autism Spectrum has affected their lives and their families' lives. *Research in Autism Spectrum Disorders*, *3*(3), 670–684. https://doi.org/10.1016/j.rasd.2018.10.004

National Academies of Sciences, Engineering, and Medicine. (2016). *Families caring for an aging America*. The National Academies Press.

National Governors Association. (2021). State COVID-19 vaccine resources. *Policy Memos*. https://www.nga.org/memos/state-covid-19-vaccine-resources/

Ne'eman, A. (2018). Washington state may make it easier to sterilize people with disabilities. *ACLU: Speak Freely*. https://www.aclu.org/blog/disability-rights/integration-and-autonomy-people-disabilities/washington-state-may-make-it

Newsom, J. T., & Schulz, R. (1998). Caregiving from the recipient's perspective: Negative reactions to being helped. *Health Psychology*, *17*(2), 172–181. https://psycnet.apa.org/doi/10.1037/0278-6133.17.2.172

Oliver, M. (2004). The social model in action: If I had a hammer. *Implementing the Social Model of Disability: Theory and Research*, *2*, 18–31.

Priestley, M. (2003). *Disability: A life course approach*. Polity Press.

Pyke, K. D., & Bengtson, V. L. (1996). Caring more or less: Individualistic and collectivist systems of family eldercare. *Journal of Marriage and the Family*, *58*(2), 379. http://dx.doi.org/10.2307/353503

Reinhard, S. C., Feinberg, L. F., Houser, A., Choula, R., & Evans, M. (2019). Valuing the invaluable: 2019 update. *AARP Public Policy Institute* (November). (https://www.aarp.org/content/dam/aarp/ppi/2019/11/valuing-the-invaluable-2019-update-charting-a-path-forward.doi.10.26419-2Fppi.00082.001.pdf).

Roper, S. O., Allred, D. W., Mandleco, B., Freeborn, D., & Dyches, T. (2014). Caregiver burden and sibling relationships in families raising children with disabilities and typically developing children. *Families, Systems and Health*, *32*(2), 241–246. https://doi.org/10.1037/fsh0000047

Sanchez, M. (2016). The sibling disability experience: An analysis of studies concerning non-impaired siblings of individuals with disabilities from 1960 to 1990. In S. Green & S. Barnartt (Eds.), *Research in social science and disability* (Vol. 9, pp. 241–259). Emerald Group.

Scott, E. K. (2018). Mother-ready jobs: Employment that works for mothers of children with disabilities. *Journal of Family Issues*, 39(9), 2659–2684. https://doi.org/10.1177/0192513X18756927.

Seltzer, M. M., Greenberg, J. S., Orsmond, G. I., & Lounds, J. (2005). Life course studies of siblings of individuals with developmental disabilities. *Mental Retardation*, 43(5), 354–359. https://doi.org/10.1352/0047-6765(2005)43[354:LCSOSO]2.0.CO;2

Settersten, R. A., & Mayer, K. U. (1997). The measurement of age, age structuring, and the life course. *Annual Review of Sociology*, 23(1), 233–261. https://doi.org/10.1146/annurev.soc.23.1.233

Shandra, C. L. (2011). Life-course transitions among adolescents with and without disabilities. *International Journal of Sociology*, 41(1), 67–86. https://doi.org/10.2753/IJS0020-7659410104

Shandra, C. L., & Penner, A. (2017). Benefactors and beneficiaries? Disability and care to others. *Journal of Marriage and Family*, 79(4), 1160–1185. https://doi.org/10.1111/jomf.12401

Sherry, M. (2016). A sociology of impairment. *Disability and Society*, 31(6), 729–744. https://doi.org/10.1080/09687599.2016.1203290

Stevens, J. D. (2019). Stuck in transition with you: Variable pathways to in(ter)dependence for emerging adult men with mobility impairments. In S. Green & D. Loeseke (Eds.), *New narratives of disability: Constructions, clashes, and controversies* (pp. 169–184). Emerald Group.

Thorpe, J. M., Thorpe, C. T., Schulz, R., Van Houtven, C. H., & Schleiden, L. (2015). Informal caregiver disability and access to preventive care in care recipients. *American Journal of Preventive Medicine*, 49(3), 370–379. https://doi.org/10.1016/j.amepre.2015.02.003

Tilley, E., Walmsley, J., Earle, S., & Atkinson. D. (2012). "The silence is roaring": Sterilization, reproductive rights and women with intellectual disabilities. *Disability and Society*, 27(3), 413–426. https://doi.org/10.1080/09687599.2012.654991

Turk, M. A., & Fortuna, R. J. (2019). Health status of adults with cerebral palsy. In V. P. Prasher & M. P. Janicki (Eds.), *Physical health of adults with intellectual and developmental disabilities* (pp. 87–126)Springer.

Turk, M. A., Landes, S. D., Formica, M. K., & Goss, K. D. (2020). Intellectual and developmental disability and COVID-19 case-fatality trends: TriNetX analysis. *Disability and Health Journal*, 13(3), 1–4. https://doi.org/10.1016/j.dhjo.2020.100942

Union of the Physically Impaired Against Segregation, and The Disability Alliance. (1975). Fundamental principles of disability. In M. Priestley (Ed.), *The Union of the Physically Impaired Against Segregation and The Disability Alliance discuss fundamental principles of disability* (pp. 1–64). UPIAS and The Disability Alliance.

US Department of Health and Human Services. (2003). The future supply of long-term care workers in relation to the aging baby boom generation. *Report to Congress*, 1–64. https://aspe.hhs.gov/system/files/pdf/72961/ltcwork.pdf

Van Asselt-Goverts, A. E., Embregts, P. J. C. M., & Hendriks, A. H. C. (2013). Structural and functional characteristics of the social networks of people with mild intellectual disabilities. *Research in Developmental Disabilities*, 34(4), 1280–1288. https://doi.org/10.1016/j.ridd.2013.01.012

Verbrugge, L. M., & Jette, A. M. (1994). The disablement process. *Social Science and Medicine*, 38(1), 1–14. https://doi.org/10.1016/0277-9536(94)90294-1

Vitaliano, P., Zhang, J., & Scanlan, J. (2003). Is caregiving hazardous to one's physical health? A meta-analysis. Psychological Bulletin 129(6), 946–71. https://doi.org/10.1037/0033-2909.129.6.946

CHAPTER 15

....

WOMEN'S REPRODUCTIVE TRAJECTORIES AFTER SPINAL CORD INJURY

A Life Course Perspective on Acquired Disabilities

....

HEATHER DILLAWAY, ALYMAMAH MASHRAH, BRIANNA MARZOLF, HEATHER FRITZ, WASSIM TARRAF, AND CATHERINE LYSACK

INTRODUCTION

THIS chapter focuses on how the acquisition of physical disabilities can impact individuals and their life trajectories differently depending on timing of onset, individuals' pre-injury experiences, and expectations for future life stages. In this chapter we first review the prevalence of different types of disabilities, with specific attention to the sociological patterns present in the acquisition of physical disabilities. We then present data from a qualitative study of 20 women with spinal cord injuries (SCI) to examine how these injuries may occur at a variety of critical moments during the life course, and how individual women (and their partners/families) navigate different sexual and reproductive decisions and experiences post-injury depending on both the timing of their injury and other social locations. We apply a life-course perspective in this chapter to understand the impact of acquired disabilities on normative life transitions as well as women's expectations for those transitions post-injury. We argue that researchers and practitioners must pay close attention to both the social patterns in disability acquisition and groups' experiences of normative life transitions pre- and post-acquisition, to understand the varied meanings and experiences of disability and the different needs and expectations that individuals with disabilities have post-injury.

Globally, disability rates hover around 15%, which is an increase when compared to decades past (WHO, 2011, p. 7). This means that more than one billion people in the world live with some form of disability (WHO, 2011, p. 5). The US Centers for Disease Control and Prevention (CDC, 2019) estimates that one out of every four adults (26%) has a disability. Types and onsets of disabilities vary considerably, however. The most common disability type is physical mobility limitations, followed by impairments in thinking and/or memory, and then vision and hearing. Furthermore, over 53 million US adults—that is, 13%, or one of every eight—have a physical disability in any given year (CDC, 2015; CDC, 2019). Approximately 11% have a diagnosed cognitive disability, 6% have hearing difficulties or deafness, and 5% have diagnosed vision impairments or blindness (CDC, 2015). One in every four women in the United States has a diagnosed disability (CDC, 2015), and approximately one out of every ten women of reproductive age in the United States has a disability (Signore, 2016, p. 95).

Thinking about *when* individuals encounter disabilities is crucial if we are investigating the impact of disabilities on different social groups in the United States. According to the CDC (2019), disabilities can be the result of conditions that are present at birth that may affect functions later in life, such as muscular dystrophy or Down syndrome. Disabilities can also be associated with other congenital, developmental conditions such as autism spectrum disorder or attention-deficit/hyperactivity disorder (ADHD). Sensory impairments such as blindness or deafness can be present at birth, or can develop later in life due to injury or progressive disease. Conditions of aging, such as Alzheimer's Disease or other forms of dementia, can create progressive, acquired forms of disability in later life. Other chronic conditions that develop across the life course (e.g., post-stroke mobility limitations, post-traumatic stress, type 2 diabetes, fibromyalgia, multiple sclerosis, rheumatoid arthritis, mental illness, cancer-related conditions) are representative of yet another group of acquired disabilities (CDC, 2019). Finally, disabilities can be obtained through an unexpected injury or accident, such as spinal cord injuries, traumatic brain injuries, injuries during paid work, sports-related injuries, or war-related injuries (Tepperman & Meredith, 2016; CDC, 2019).

As a broad category, then, acquired disabilities are *any* disabilities that specifically develop during a person's lifetime and, therefore, could include chronic illnesses, aging-related impairments, as well as unexpected or accidental injuries. There is no definitive list of acquired disabilities, but these types of disabilities can be visible or invisible, and severe, moderate, or mild. Even though limitations in our aggregate data sometimes mask exactly how many physical, cognitive, or sensory impairments are congenital versus acquired, it is estimated that about 85% of working-age adults with a disability have acquired their disability at some point during their life course (National Disability Authority, 2004). Higher rates of disability worldwide are largely attributed to the aging of populations, higher incidence of chronic diseases such as cardiovascular disease and diabetes, and greater risk of accidental injuries such as in motor vehicle accidents or war-related injuries (WHO, 2011, p. 7; see also CDC, 2019). That is, rates of disability are increasing in large part because rates of acquired disability are increasing (WHO 2002).[1]

Thinking Sociologically about Acquired Disabilities

Sociologically, it is important to think about how individuals acquire, interpret, and live with their disabilities across the life course and track the disparate impacts on certain social groups. Furthermore, it is important to question social patterns that might exist in the onset of acquired disabilities. We assume that many injuries and accidents are "unexpected" and truly "accidents," but sociologists Tepperman and Meredith (2016) suggest otherwise. When evaluating who is at most risk for "unexpected" injuries, for instance, researchers find that the elderly and young males are at most risk of motor-vehicle related injuries (Tepperman & Meredith, 2016). Workplace injuries (e.g., injured limbs, carpal tunnel syndrome) may be more likely in certain groups of employees by gender, age, and type of employment. Children are most at risk of disability and death due to traumatic brain injuries, although we also see increased risk among elderly populations due to falls (WHO, 2006). Men are also more likely to be the recipients of gunshot wounds that lead to permanent injury or death, with young Black men most at risk of gunshot wound due to assault, and older, non-Hispanic White men most at risk due to attempted suicide (Cook et al., 2017; WHO, 2006). Even some chronic illnesses, such as fibromyalgia, currently affecting 4 million adults in the United States (CDC, 2017), are more prevalent among women (Fitzcharles et al., 2016). Tepperman and Meredith (2016) propose that our definitions of "accidental" injuries or "unexpected" illnesses are faulty because we can notice clear patterns in onset across social groups. In fact, the word "accident" masks very significant patterns in injury or illness acquisition, incidence, prevalence, life-course outcomes, and, more generally, the structural or system-level causes of acquired disabilities. Ultimately, by defining many acquired disabilities as "accidental" injuries, we hide the very chronic and permanent nature of the physical disabilities created by patterned events and make it more difficult to measure or track the sociological reasons for acquired disabilities.

Consequently, while two people may have the same type of acquired disability, they can attain a disability for distinct, status-based reasons and be impacted by the disability in very different ways (CDC, 2019; Shuey & Wilson, 2008; Tepperman & Meredith, 2016). That is, disabilities can occur at varying stages of life as a result of many different—and often expected—social causes (US Department of Health and Human Services, 2005). Tepperman and Meredith (2016) urge us to focus on the important sociological reasons why we see distinct groups acquire certain types of disabilities at key moments in the life course. Sociologists who study adolescence have documented extensively the societal pressures on teenagers (especially young men, but women too) to engage in rites of passage, such as the transition to driving and drinking, that increase the likelihood of involvement in motor vehicle crashes and the acquisition of permanent physical injuries (Furstenberg, 2000). Furthermore, until recent decades, organized sports has been a predominantly male institution (Messner, 1992; Tepperman & Meredith, 2016); therefore, boys and young men have frequently demonstrated masculinity while playing sports and have incurred more sports-related injuries as a result (although this gendered gap in sports-related injuries is now narrowing with women's greater participation). Additionally, with women's increased involvement in the "second shift" of housework and childcare (Hochschild, 2003) and greater vulnerability to intimate partner violence (Walton-Moss et al., 2005) because of culturally prescribed power imbalances within the home (even though these imbalances may be changing), adult women are more likely than adult men to incur permanent physical injuries in this space (e.g., falls down stairs, kitchen-related injuries, burns) (see also Tepperman & Meredith, 2016). Therefore, individuals' social locations such as gender, age, race, social class, type of employment, marital status, and parental status can affect their propensity for certain types of injuries.

When we acquire a particular disability also matters because outcomes can be shaped by timing of onset. The timing of an injury or illness, for instance, can determine how disruptive it might be for life course expectations and experiences. Outcomes of acquired disabilities are shaped not only by the timing of onset, however, but also the person's social locations, pre-disability experiences, and their expectations for future life stages. Finally, the effects of acquired disabilities on a life course are also determined by whether individuals can receive relevant and life-stage-specific interventions and treatment. For instance, a child may need very different interventions, rehabilitation, and treatment than a middle-aged individual at the onset of an acquired physical disability. Additionally, depending on individuals' social locations, they may be more or less likely to secure quality healthcare after the acquisition of a disability. For example, research has shown that women with fibromyalgia and other invisible chronic illnesses have difficulty securing timely diagnoses and that, even after diagnosis, doctors can have difficulty coming up with a treatment plan (Undeland & Malterud, 2007). Depending on type of employment and health insurance coverage, individuals may also find themselves unable to afford critical medications and rehabilitative treatments post-injury (Andrulis, 1998). Tepperman and Meredith (2016) urge us to examine how the consequences of acquired disabilities might be different by one's social location. Shuey and Wilson (2008, p. 202) further suggest that the relationship between social locations (e.g., race, SES, gender, and age) and health across the life course "has not been adequately examined as a dynamic process that incorporates time and age." Sociologists have much work to do to investigate the cumulative advantage or disadvantage associated with intersections of individuals' social locations and the timing, type, and outcomes of acquired disabilities.

According to the WHO (2002), almost everyone will be temporarily or permanently impaired at some point in life, because of eventual acquired disabilities. Living with acquired disabilities can be a life-long experience for some, depending on timing of onset. That is, not only are rates of disability increasing, but the years that individuals live with disabilities are increasing because of the growing prevalence of chronic illnesses as well as the aging of the population (CDC, 2019; WHO, 2011). Those who survive to old age will experience increasing difficulties in functioning (WHO, 2002). Approximately 46% of adults aged 60 years and older report a moderate or severe disability, for instance (WHO 2008). As individuals age, many experience multiple, acquired disabling conditions that occur simultaneously including chronic medical conditions, sensory disorders, genetic predispositions to late-onset illnesses, or comorbidities relating to other medical conditions (such as amputations secondary to diabetes) (US Department of Health and Human Services, 2005). Globally, the total burden of disability increased from 562 million to 853 million between 1990 and 2017, representing a 52% increase in the total years lived with disabilities (GBD, 2017; Disease and Injury Incidence and Prevalence Collaborators, 2018). Between 2007 and 2017, the leading causes of years lived with disabilities were low-back pain, headache disorders, depressive disorders, diabetes, age-related hearing loss, and COPD (GBD, 2017; Disease and Injury Incidence and Prevalence Collaborators, 2018). Considering the likelihood of disability acquisition across the life span as well as the increasing amount of time that individuals will be living with acquired disabilities, it is important to explore how individuals think about and experience the onset of a disability within one life stage as well as across an entire life course.

Applying a Life Course Perspective

Emerging first in the 1960s, the life course perspective is a theoretical framework developed to examine "continuity and change of human lives in relation to interpersonal, structural, and historical forces" (Elder, Johnson, & Crosnoe, 2003, p. 4). Sociologists, anthropologists, social historians, demographers, social workers, economists, political scientists, and developmental psychologists, among others, have all worked to advance this theoretical lens in different ways. Collectively, scholars working in these disciplines have called attention to the significance of historical events and social change, cohort and generational differences, pathways to adulthood and old age, normative life transitions and turning points, and the timing and sequencing of personal events and decisions (Harrington Meyer, 2014). Relevant for this chapter, a life-course analysis enables researchers not only to observe how individuals navigate a particular disability experience within one single life stage (and examine the well-being of an individual before and after something happens within that stage) but also, in other cases, to watch individuals go through "sequential life stages" (Harrington Meyer, 2014) and navigate a particular disability experience over time. An emphasis on the life course (rather than one particular moment in time) therefore allows us to see the immediate, cumulative, and/or longstanding effects of disability experience.

Life course scholars also recognize that, "depending on one's life stage, different factors or issues take on differing degrees of importance, and that these varying factors and issues may affect attitudes and behaviors" as well as the ability to accomplish certain normative life transitions and trajectories (Roehling, Roehling, & Moen, 2001, p. 146; Elder, Johnson, & Crosnoe, 2003). To date, most life course researchers define life stages by age, parental status, or employment status (Roehling, Roehling, & Moen, 2001). In this study we broaden the application of the life course perspective to explore the interplay of pre-disability experiences and timing of onset on expectations and trajectories post-disability. We find that this focus provides an excellent theoretical lens for exploring how life course trajectories can be affected (or not, as the case may be) by acquired disabilities. As an example, we present an analysis of qualitative data from our own interviews with 20 women with spinal cord injury, to better understand futures envisioned and secured post-injury.

Pairing the concept of "biographical disruption" with a life-course perspective facilitates our analysis of the varied impacts of particular types of disability, depending on timing of onset and pre-disability experiences and expectations. Bury (1982) defines "biographical disruption" as the process by which those with chronic illnesses confront changes in their life situations and, perhaps, their life trajectories as well, due to an acquired impairment. This may include ways in which individuals strategically withdraw from social interactions (or from their own expectations) post-disability under the impact of symptoms (or in thinking about the social-relational impacts of the impairment) (Bury, 1982, p. 169). Biographical disruptions could also include tangible changes in relationships or life-stage moments due to newly acquired disability. While research suggests that the impact of acquired disabilities on quality of life may decrease over time (Schulz & Decker, 1985), a major newly acquired disability not only can have a significant impact on daily life, but can alter expectations for health across one's remaining life span. Adler et al. (2021) discuss how those with chronic illnesses or other types of acquired disabilities may face a period where new life meanings—redefining life with illness—are constructed, and there may be a process by which individuals settle into their altered bodies and their new life. The experience of acquiring a physical disability is not only associated with physical, psychosocial, and economic challenges, it may also introduce a potential gap in (or shock to) one's identity, however temporary (Adler et al., 2021). Bury (1982) makes it clear that meanings, identities, and contexts cannot easily be separated. Thinking about whether and how acquired disabilities might shift and/or disrupt expectations, experiences, and identities at different points across the life course helps us understand why there is such variety in the individual trajectories of disability post-onset.

A Concrete Example of Acquired Disabilities: Women with Spinal Cord Injuries

For the remainder of this chapter we examine research on one group of women with a very specific type of acquired physical disability: spinal cord injury (SCI). Traumatic SCI refers to a sudden injury that causes paralysis and loss of sensation. As discussed in Dillaway et al. (2013) and Fritz et al. (2015), some persons lose the ability, partial or complete, to use their legs and lower body (paraplegia), whereas others lose this ability from the neck down (tetraplegia or quadriplegia). Complete or partial motor paralysis necessitates wheelchair use and lifelong coping with a range of serious medical complications (Jensen et al., 2007). Thus, survivors of SCI must deal with the physical effects of their impairment while also struggling with the social-relational barriers created by an ableist society that defines their bodies as "abnormal" (Hughes & Patterson, 1997).

Based on 2012 world population estimates, 250,000 to 500,000 people suffer a SCI every year (WHO, 2013). Approximately 296,000 people were currently living with SCI in the United States, and almost 18,000 new injuries occur each year (NSCISC, 2021). The average age at injury in the United States has moved from 29 years in the 1970s to 43 years in 2021; this increase can also be seen internationally (NSCISC, 2021; WHO, 2013). Both in the United States and abroad, motor-vehicle crashes are the most common cause of SCI (38–40% of all injuries depending on the reporting country), followed by falls (14–36%), acts of violence (including war-related injuries and intimate partner violence) (11–15%), and sports accidents (8%) (NSCISC, 2021; WHO, 2013). Historically, about 90% of SCIs have been traumatic in nature, but non-traumatic SCIs are also growing in number due to a variety of chronic diseases including osteoporosis and even from the unintended consequences of cancer treatment, which can leave bones of the spinal cord decalcified and weakened and subject to fracture (WHO, 2013). Unfortunately, persons with SCI are more disadvantaged and more dissatisfied than the able-bodied population on many quality-of-life indicators including employment, financial well-being, family life, psychological adjustment, and a range of personal health outcomes (Hammell, 2007). Women with SCI face poorer quality of life outcomes than men overall (Hammelll, 2007; Nosek, 2000).

The focus on women's issues after SCI is a relatively new phenomenon, in part because men are the majority of SCI patients worldwide (approximately 70%) (Rutberg et al., 2008). More women and older adults are suffering from SCI in recent years (WHO, 2013). However, we know little about women's everyday experiences post-injury, and even less about their everyday reproductive and sexual health experiences after SCI, even though there is more research on women with SCI than on women with other disabilities overall. Questions remain about how women with SCI make decisions about reproductive and sexual health within a context of limited medical knowledge and negative attitudes toward women with disabilities.

For most individuals, readjustment after injury is challenging. Quality-of-life indicators ranging from employment and financial well-being, to family life and psychological adjustment, to a range of personal health outcomes, indicate that persons with SCI are disadvantaged (Hammell, 2004; Krause & Broderick, 2004; Whiteneck et al., 2004).[2] Especially concerning is the evidence that women face poorer health-related outcomes than men (Isaksson et al., 2007; Pentland et al., 2002). For example, women report lower satisfaction with health, more poor mental health days, and lower subjective well-being in their home lives than men (Krause & Broderick, 2004). After injury, rates of depression and obesity are also higher in women than men (Tate et al., 2004).

Despite the growing weight of evidence suggesting gender disparities during acute rehabilitation and afterward, the scientific literature about health and quality of life after spinal cord injury continues to be largely focused on men. Some scholars have argued that the longstanding inattention to health-related outcomes of women with disabilities is due to their "double disadvantage" as women *and* disabled persons (Lombardi et al., 2010; Deegan & Brooks, 1985). Much of the research about women's reproductive experiences after spinal cord injury focuses on female fertility and whether women conceive and carry a pregnancy to term. This research argues that women *can* still become pregnant post-injury, furthering knowledge of when or how it is most likely or whether unique obstetric management issues arise (Bughi et al., 2008; Colantino et al., 2010; DeForge et al., 2005). Existing research on women's reproductive health post-injury, then, is often still written in response to myths about the non-reproductive and asexual nature of disabled women, and study conclusions often include the fact that we must acknowledge the reproductive capacities of severely disabled women, in addition to their problems with accessing quality care. Other research is undertaken to inform healthcare providers about special treatment issues that arise (e.g., bladder management, labor management, amenorrhea, osteoporosis, cardiac problems) or the risks of particular birth control methods and hormone therapies (Reame, 1992; Kalpakjian & Lequerica, 2006; Alexander et al., 2007). These literatures provide baseline knowledge on potential reproductive health experiences of women with SCI.

Existing literature does not address that fact that SCI has the potential to alter, delay, or disrupt reproductive trajectories. In other words, we know little about whether or how SCIs present as biographical disruptions (Bury, 1982; Adler et al., 2021) for women. Specifically, the literature lacks basic empirical knowledge on how factors such as pre-injury experiences, or timing of injury, affects women's reproductive expectations or trajectories post-injury. For example, while women may hold expectations for their reproductive experiences pre- and post-injury, previous researchers have not explored how these expectations may be altered, reshaped, or interrupted by injury, depending on women's previous reproductive history and what point in these women's lives the injury occurs. More generally, we know little about how women think about and experience their reproductive lives post-injury.

The literature on women's reproductive experiences post-injury also lacks attention to how factors such as previous intimacy experiences and pre-injury expectations for both intimacy and parenthood might also influence post-injury life course trajectories. Despite the fact that sexual intimacy and reproductive capacity are so closely tied together (and are both part of women's reproductive health broadly defined), the topic of intimacy after injury has often been overlooked (Fritz et al., 2015). Existing research that does directly talk about intimacy inevitably focuses on injury-related conditions that can affect women's sexual activity, such as urinary and bowel incontinence, rather than women's actual involvement in intimate relationships or expectations for intimacy post-injury. We believe it is important to view intimacy potentially as a lifelong pursuit and expectation, and to think about reproductive health holistically so as to include intimacy. To do this, we must understand that previous reproductive experiences include experiences of intimacy pre-injury, and that these pre-injury experiences and the timing of injury may influence women's intimate and reproductive lives post-injury.

LEARNING FROM INTERVIEWS WITH WOMEN WITH SCI

To address the research gaps described above, we highlight examples of how women in our own research have talked about reproductive and family experiences to indicate the complexities of disability, reproductive health, and sexuality across the life span. Specifically, we draw on data from 20 in-depth qualitative interviews with women with SCI in a Midwestern city in the United States to highlight their everyday experiences of menstruation, fertility, pregnancy, childbirth, and sexual relationships (see Dillaway et al., 2013, for a detailed description of our methods). For the purposes of this chapter, we extracted study data that broadly spoke to reproductive experiences and then focused on data that highlighted descriptions of sexual and reproductive experiences pre- and post-injury, and our emergent interpretations of the theoretical connections between women's life stage, timing of injury, and pre-injury experiences.

Researchers who study disabilities tend to focus on experiences post-injury, forgetting how important pre-injury experiences are in framing life-course expectations and post-injury experiences. To apply a life course perspective and emphasize the importance of reproductive histories, however, we organize our analysis based on the sexual and reproductive experiences of the women in our study pre-injury. We then further analyze the reproductive trajectories of these women based on the timing of their SCIs. Specifically, we examine similarities and differences among women who were injured before experiences of sexual intimacy, often during adolescence (age 18 or younger), and after experiences of sexual intimacy and/or motherhood, often in young adulthood (ages 19–34) or late reproductive years (age 35 or older). In organizing our findings based on pre-injury experiences and timing of injury, we attempt to present the most common concerns of each group. While still sharing data from a range of interviewees, we focus only on select participants within each subsection of findings.

FINDINGS

Sample Profile

The average age of the sample was 46 years (range: 27–66), and the average time since injury was 19.5 years on average (range: 3–41 years). Seven participants were injured during adolescence (age 18 or earlier), 9 were injured during the "young adult" years (19–34), and the remaining 4 were injured at age 35 or older. Eleven interviewees were European American/White, while 8 were African American/Black, and 1 self-identified as multiracial. Eleven women were paraplegic and nine were tetraplegic.[3]

Participants had a broad range of sexual and reproductive health experiences. All but 5 women were sexually active prior to injury. Fifteen of the 20 women reported a pregnancy at some point in their lives, and 5 bore children after injury. Eight women reported that they had gone through or were going through menopause at time of interview. Five women had hysterectomies, and 4 of these occurred post-injury; of these 4, 2 hysterectomies occurred to solve menstrual hassles and 2 to eradicate fibroid problems post-injury.

For the remainder of our chapter we show the variation of reproductive events that women experienced pre- and post-injury and how, depending on life stage at time of injury and pre-injury reproductive experiences, an injury may affect expectations and trajectories in different ways. In addition, we illustrate that pre-injury experience and timing of injury shape expectations for reproductive experiences post-injury. We use each subsection of findings to illustrate these themes.

No Intimacy Experience Prior to Injury

For some women in our sample, early onset of injury meant that sexual and reproductive experience would be curtailed—especially if women did not already have expectations for intimacy or reproductive experience pre-injury. Five women in our study were not sexually active prior to their injury, and all 5 of these women were injured in adolescence (age 18 or younger). Janet[4] (age 55, 40 years post-injury, tetraplegic) was injured at age 15. Janet's recovery entailed a 22-month period of institutional rehabilitation. Janet reported no romantic activity prior to injury, and her prolonged institutionalization may have reduced opportunities for courtship, partnering, and sexual exploration among same-aged peers. Perhaps related to her lack of experience, Janet voiced uncertainty about what being sexually intimate entailed, stating, "I really don't know for sure [what being sexually active means], when your body parts are really involved with each other?" Janet did seek out information about reproductive health topics, however, from her care aides.

> I've asked my aides some stuff. They've experienced it all. It's a little embarrassing at times but I feel like a pre-teen . . ., hearing this stuff for the first time, you know?
>
> [Laughs]

At age 55, Janet remained abstinent and had never married, and her remarks suggest unresolved feelings: "I never carried [sexual relationships] that far so . . . I don't know. . . . I did have a couple of boyfriends [post-injury]. . . . We did kiss, nothing real serious, no serious making out."

While Janet noted some curiosity about sexual intimacy, Lana (age 58, 40 years post-injury, tetraplegic) matter-of-factly blamed her lack of sexual and reproductive experiences directly on her injury, stating, "My body doesn't do anything." Like Janet,

Lana had limited exposure to romantic relationships pre-injury (with the exception of some experience kissing boys). Lana reportedly had no expectations for intimacy or reproduction post-injury and said "yes" when we asked if she was as sexually active as she would like to be. She was straightforward about her lack of experience post-injury and said, "I don't even think about it." By the time we interviewed her, she had shifted her identity post-injury to match what she felt her current contexts dictated. Being single and without children felt normal to Lana, and her outlook was at least partially determined by her understanding of her own physical limitations. In contrast Janet still wondered about the possibility of intimate relationships. In both cases, however, lack of experience pre-injury combined with very high-level injuries made it difficult for these women to expect to attain intimate relationships. Both women required daily care due to the severity of their injuries, and their opportunities for socializing were determined mostly by others at the time of their interviews (e.g., their mothers and other state-funded home healthcare workers provided these women with daily care).

Sexual and Reproductive Experience Prior to Injury

An additional 2 women injured as adolescents and nine women injured as young adults (age 19–34) had already experienced a variety of sexual and reproductive events pre-injury, however. As we analyzed our interview conversations with these 11 women, we find that pre-injury experiences formed a potential basis for expectations, decision-making, and perceptions of experiences post-injury. All 11 of these women experienced sexual intercourse prior to injury. Seven of these women experienced a pregnancy, and 6 women experienced childbirth pre-injury. All but 1 desired to have children post-injury, yet many had concerns about what it would be like to reproduce post-injury. Some were worried about whether they should have children post-injury whereas others were concerned about how particular reproductive events would actually occur. Therefore, instead of questioning *whether* they could participate in intimacy or reproductive activity, these 11 women were more likely to be concerned about *how* they would engage in intimacy or reproductive experiences. Here, we can see how women with pre-injury experience had different identities and expectations post-injury than the group without this pre-injury experience.

While her injury was similar in severity to Janet's and Lana's, Candace (age 57, 40 years post-injury, tetraplegic) had been in an intimate relationship pre-injury and was initially fearful that she might have been pregnant at time of injury. When asked how long she experienced amenorrhea (typical after injury), she replied: "Only about 2 months, and I was scared because my boyfriend and I were intimate and I thought I was pregnant."

Unlike Janet and Lana who had no intimacy experience prior to their injury, Candace had high expectations for reproductive experience post-injury, and married and bore 2 children. When asked what advice she would give to other women post-injury, Candace stated:

[J]ust be who you are. . . 'Cause I met my husband at a Halloween party - and this is after I got hurt - and in December he asked me to marry him. We got married in July and we've been married for 32 years.

Perhaps because of her intimate experiences pre-injury and an established expectation for intimacy and reproductive experience post-injury, Candace did not see the injury as limiting her sexual and reproductive options. Expectations for intimacy and mother-hood seemed to dictate Candace's post-injury trajectory, and she did not view her injury as limiting.

Some participants without childbearing experience pre-injury still maintained their expectations for motherhood post-injury. Nonetheless, they still might have felt a temporary uncertainty in identity (Adler et al., 2021) as they confirmed with doctors whether they could still have children. Damita (age 44, 25 years post-injury, paraplegic) did not experience pregnancy pre-injury, and this influenced the strength of her repro-ductive expectations post-injury. She wanted to become a mother and expressed her concerns very directly.

I remember asking the doctor, "Could I still have children?" . . .[T]hat was far more important than being able to get back on my legs. . . . It was good to find out that I could have children.

Not only were some women concerned about whether they could become pregnant, but they were also concerned about the sensory and/or bodily experience of reproduc-tive events post-injury. Anxieties about what pregnancy and labor might be like, and whether there might be more risk to mother and baby post-injury, were voiced during interviews. Women in our sample looked to doctors for reassurance and did not always get it. Many interviewees still went ahead and became biological mothers post-injury, however, despite these initial safety concerns.

On the other hand, for Kelsey (age 31, 9 years post-injury, tetraplegic), injury caused a very real disruption of potential motherhood. Kelsey miscarried an early pregnancy at the time of injury: "I didn't even know I was pregnant. . . . . If I was farther along [in the pregnancy] they would have been able to take the baby and deal with me." At the time of her interview, Kelsey did not expect to have children post-injury. She and her husband were intimate "because the 'apparatus' [body parts, her quotations] that I have are [still] fully functional," but

[W]e have talked about it and we don't want any children. . . . I'm afraid if there are side effects that could complicate my spinal cord injury. . . . I'm afraid of the complications. [A]nother [reason] is we're both in school and we can't afford to have a child. . . . He would get a vasectomy but right now he has no health insurance. . . . [and] I would use birth control but I know there are side effects that could complicate my spinal cord injury.

Kelsey was only just starting to think about motherhood at time of injury. She discusses how she would have become a mother at that point if her pregnancy had come to term, but is forgoing the opportunity now for fear of safety and also because of economic concerns. In this case, then, tentative motherhood was derailed due to injury. It was the experience of this unplanned pregnancy and pregnancy loss that, combined, made her even more tentative about her reproductive future post-injury. At the time of interview, she was trying her best to protect against pregnancy while still being sexually active.

There is variation in how women's reproductive trajectories might be affected if they are injured in young adulthood, depending on pre-injury experiences, exact timing of injury, and consequent expectations for reproductive experience. Although we did not ask women about other life situations that might shape their reproductive expectations, Kelsey's narrative also illustrates that women may have social locations (e.g., low income and no health insurance) that can simultaneously alter or disrupt reproductive trajectories. Nonetheless, if participants had sexual and reproductive experience pre-injury, they at least contemplated motherhood post-injury. That is, with their pre-injury experience providing a roadmap, women injured in young adulthood expected that they would partner and mother regardless of injury. If they did not reach their expectations for motherhood, other life contexts (such as prioritizing school or worrying about finances) sometimes affected trajectories more than the physical impairment itself. And even if they did not pursue biological motherhood, women in the sample were often still sexually active after injury.

Having Children Before Injury

As mentioned earlier, 6 women in our study had children prior to their spinal cord injury. Terry (age 40, 13 years post-injury, paraplegic) had 2 children before injury and thought about having additional children post-injury. Thus, like Candace, Damita, and Kelsey above, Terry's expectations for her life trajectory did not initially change post-injury.

> We hadn't totally decided that we didn't want any other children. I mean, when I first had my accident that was a real concern . . ., having more children. . . . I was only 27. . . . [I]t would have been more devastating to know that not only I lost my legs but that I had also lost the ability to be a woman and to be able to [bear children] . . . I didn't lose that, I still had that.

Eventually Terry and her spouse decided not to have more children because of concerns about safety: "It's scarier [post-injury] than it was before because. . . .We didn't know what risk it was going to put on me and so it was better to go without having another child."

Terry was firm in this decision to forgo having more children, however ambivalent she was about the alterations to her initial expectations for motherhood. Our conversations with Terry were framed by the fact that she was already a mother pre-injury and was happily married both pre- and post-injury. In addition, Terry's two children were aged 6 years and 7 months at time of injury; thus, she was actively mothering immediately post-injury and declared that her kids were important in facilitating her initial recovery. Motherhood was already central to her life and, while her expectations for additional children were curtailed, she could still maintain her identity as a mother both pre- and post-injury.

Terry's and Kelsey's stories do highlight women's apprehensions about safety risks, however, and their desire for more and better information about the impact of acquired disability on reproductive experience at critical life stages. Their stories illustrate how some women's reproductive expectations were not realized post-injury in part because of these concerns. Participants who were injured in young adulthood also uniformly proposed that they desired more information about what it is like to actually experience reproductive events post-injury, as well as information on the safety of birth control, pregnancy, and birth post-injury—affirming once again that they expected to continue being sexually and reproductively active post-injury.

Injured at Midlife

Four interviewees were injured in their late reproductive years (i.e., age 35 or older). All 4 had children prior to injury, and, at time of interview, 2 were married and 2 were divorced. This group had experienced menstruation, sexual intercourse, marriage, pregnancy, childbirth, and motherhood prior to injury, as women without physical disabilities. Narratives from these women draw attention to how the timing of injury could sometimes affect perimenopause, daily activities of motherhood, and the quality of intimate relationships. But pre-injury experiences with intimacy and reproduction were so extensive that these participants' focus was often very different.

Participants varied in their perimenopause experiences, and the management of per-imenopausal symptoms could be burdensome post-injury. Nina (age 55, 7 years post-injury, paraplegic) explains:

> I wish I could have had something [i.e., a hormone therapy prescription], because the night sweats are terrible. I get completely soaked and, when you're stuck in bed, you're stuck in bed. I can't get up and change my nightgown in the middle of the night.

Seemingly simple acts such as having the ability to change clothes in the middle of the night, which could improve comfort, are, at times, major tasks for a woman post-injury. Dealing with perimenopausal symptoms was primary in Nina's mind at the time of interview.

On the other hand, Justine (age 48, 5 years post-injury, tetraplegic) illustrates how SCI can disrupt familial dynamics. At time of injury Justine was married with 2 children.

As a woman without injury, then, she had already followed a culturally normative, age-based, reproductive trajectory, getting married and having children during her late 20s/early 30s. She was injured in a car accident while driving her younger child to visit colleges, long after she had finished childbearing. Managing responsibilities associated with marriage and motherhood post-injury proved difficult for her and her family because of side effects associated with her injury. Justine openly discussed her difficulties in re-engaging in sexual intimacy with her spouse post-injury, explaining, "I can't feel it. . . I have no sensation. [We] tried once but it wasn't productive—he was afraid he was going to hurt me. I think that was the first and last time [i.e., four years ago]." Her mother also came to live with her soon after the accident: "My mom's here but she's got dementia—Alzheimer's—and she stays here even though she has her own home. I have 3 sisters, but none of them can handle her."

Simultaneously caring for elderly parents and children is a strain on any middle-aged woman, but caregiving challenges were compounded by Justine's new physical limitations. The strain on her and her spouse was substantial, resulting in a divorce: "[Her husband left] a year later. . . . he was just fed up." In addition, Justine's college-aged children did not grasp the significance of her injury and, despite receiving counseling, continued to have difficulty coping with the fact that she could not attend to their immediate needs within the home as quickly as they desired or accompany them to public settings very often. Justine explains:

> My kids don't understand it. . . . One is 28 and one is 21, . . . [and] they're like, "Get over it!" They want their mom back like she used to be. . . . [They say they] wish I would just be their mom again. That's hard to hear. The inside is still you. It's really hard.

Mallory (age 56, 2 years post-injury, tetraplegic) had gone through menopause approximately 10 years before injury and was also divorced and done raising 2 kids. When asked about the impact of her injury, she said, "It doesn't bother me. . . . I just try to be as independent as I can." Mallory lived alone, and her only reproductive health concern was going for a mammogram; she talked about scheduling that appointment soon. The comparison of Nina's, Justine's, and Mallory's cases highlights that there can be considerable variation in the impact of injury on reproductive experiences even when women are injured in late adulthood. Of the 4 women injured in this life stage, Nina and Justine experience their injuries most negatively, specifically because they saw their injuries as impacting how they dealt with perimenopausal symptoms and complicated family relationships. Expectations for post-injury sexual and reproductive experience were not met in these two cases.

DISCUSSION

Using findings highlighted above, we propose that, based on the extent of women's pre-injury experiences, the exact timing of injury, and expectations post-injury, women may experience both intimacy and parenthood post-injury in vastly different ways. Likewise, reproductive trajectories can be disrupted, delayed, altered, or seemingly unaffected by SCI, depending on pre-injury experiences, timing of injury, and women's expectations. Thus, we cannot assume women with SCI have uniform experiences and trajectories post-injury, or that life trajectories are permanently interrupted post-injury. For a few women in the study, expectations for intimate relationships and motherhood did remain unfulfilled or permanently disrupted, particularly if they had not been in an intimate relationship before their injury or if they were concerned about the medical risks of giving birth post-injury. For most interviewees, however, reproductive trajectories were only temporarily delayed and reshaped, and in a handful of cases women's reproductive lives continued just as women expected (pre- and post-injury), despite the existence of a physical impairment. This means that Bury (1982) is correct that biographical disruptions may only be temporary, while women adjust to a new physical body and social reality, and that the impact of SCI on women's sexual or reproductive lives may lessen over time depending on women's pre-injury experiences and timing of injury. Only a few women in our sample who incurred a high-level injury in their teenage years, coupled with no sexual or reproductive experience pre-injury, seemed blocked from certain life trajectories long-term. While other women in our sample experienced pregnancy loss or relationship dissolution, and birthed fewer children than they initially desired, their expectations were only altered and not permanently curtailed.

This does not mean, however, that all women did not go through a period during which they developed new identities and redefined what their life trajectories might be post-injury. As stated earlier, all individuals who acquire physical disabilities must engage in a process (however temporary or ongoing) of settling into a post-injury life (Adler et al., 2021). Findings also suggest that women with SCI may compare themselves to their own pre-injury selves and/or adhere to cultural narratives about able-bodied sensory experience at particular moments, and that expectations for sexual activity and reproductive events are sometimes shaped by these comparisons (in the absence of other reference points). Our findings therefore imply that women with SCI may need very different information and examples, reproductive healthcare and provider expertise, and types of familial and community support, depending on pre-injury experiences, timing of injury, and expectations post-injury. Especially since we cannot assume that all individuals with a certain acquired disability may experience the same levels of biographical disruption because of their changing contexts, women with SCI need to be able to access varied types of support and informational resources as they go through distinct periods of adjustment at every life stage.

Using a life-course approach, we contribute to the literature by finding that the effects of acquired disabilities themselves cannot uniformly explain individuals' life-course trajectories. For example, attempts to understand the reproductive expectations and intimacy experiences of women post-injury must incorporate the fact that the onset of injury occurs within a particular moment in the life course and within the context of individual women's sexual and reproductive histories. Therefore, the onset of acquired disabilities may affect post-injury expectations and decision-making in varied ways, and individual life-course trajectories may look very different as a result. Unless we understand life-course contexts both before and after the onset of acquired disabilities, we

cannot truly understand the outcomes of physical impairments or the social and rehabilitative needs of affected individuals. Thus, a life-course analysis allows us not only to
observe how women navigate acquired disabilities in any one life stage but also to understand the effects of previous expectations and experiences on women's current sexual
and reproductive lives. Furthermore, a life-course perspective also allows us to see how
women and men might have very different experiences of SCI because the meanings
attached to normative life transitions and trajectories are gendered. Women may be
more concerned about whether they can still have children post-injury, for example,
because all women face a "motherhood mandate" (McQuillan et al., 2008). Men, on the
other hand, may be more concerned than women about whether they can still perform
sexually post-injury, due to normative expectations of masculinity (Fritz et al., 2015).
An emphasis on the life course (rather than one particular moment in time) therefore
allows us to see the immediate, cumulative, and/or longstanding effects of both acquired disabilities and these gendered sexual and reproductive experiences across the
life course.

Our findings are tempered by our own study's limitations. First, data were gathered
from a small sample of primarily White and African American women living with SCI
in a Midwestern city, and insights generated cannot be generalized beyond the sample.
Second, this research included questions on and participant descriptions of intimacy,
reproduction, gynecological examinations, menstruation, menopause, and other sensitive topics; thus, some personal data might have been withheld, reducing data quality.
Third, we did not ask systematically about the non-reproductive life contexts that
shaped reproductive expectations and trajectories. We know that Kelsey's decision to
forgo having children post-injury was related in part to economic concerns, and this
may have been true for more interviewees. We also do not have enough data on racial
differences to produce any definitive findings about racial-ethnic differences in pre- or
post-injury experience. Fourth, severity of injury may have had more of an impact on
women's experiences than we note here because we did not systematically engage in interview discussions about the impact of level of injury on expectations and trajectories.
We encourage future researchers to investigate thoroughly the impact of women's level
of physical injury on post-injury reproductive health.

ACKNOWLEDGMENTS

Study recruitment was made possible through a previously-funded project: "Community
Living after Spinal Cord Injury: Models and Outcomes"; R01#1HD43378, funded by the
National Institutes of Health (PI: Last Author).

NOTES

1. Before moving on, we find it necessary to note that the definitions of "disability" vary and
   continue to evolve. For purposes of this chapter we are adopting the conceptual distinction
   between "impairment," "disability," and "handicap" made by the World Health Organization

(WHO) (WHO, 2002). According to the WHO framework, impairment exists as an objective medical reality (e.g., a diseased body part), whereas a disability comprises the functional consequences of that impairment on the person. Finally, handicap is the extent to which larger structural forces in the environment prevent an individual from fully inhabiting a culturally normative role (WHO, 2002). In this paper we focus mostly on examining disability, but a discussion of the possible alteration of life trajectories does ultimately lead into a discussion of structural forces that impinge on an individual's ability to carry out their expectations for the life course. In addition, as we explain in the next section, there are sociological reasons why certain groups experience impairment and disability, which keep us attuned to structural contexts. Keeping the focus on macro-level patterns in impairment acquisition and disability experience, as well as the structural barriers individuals face once they have an impairment or disability, becomes extremely important.

2. Schulz and Decker (1985) found, however, that individuals with spinal cord injuries are most disadvantaged right after their injury, and, as time goes by, their quality of life increases. This increase is dependent on social support and their feelings about whether they can control their lives and be independent, however.

3. Exact level of injury was self-reported in the original study, including whether the injury was "complete" (severing of the spinal cord) or "incomplete" (anything less than completely severed) and at which vertebra the injury occurred. The last author and her original research team then categorized participants as paraplegic or tetraplegic using clinical guidelines.

4. Pseudonyms are used to protect confidentiality.

References

Adler, J. M., Lakmazaheri, A., O'Brien, E., Palmer, A., Reid, M., & Tawes, E. (2021). Identity integration in people with acquired disabilities: A qualitative study. *Journal of Personality*, 89(1), 84–112. https://doi.org/10.1111/jopy.12533

Alexander, M. S., Bodner, D., Brackett, N. L., Elliott, S., Jackson, A. B., & Sonksen, J. (2007). Development of international standards to document sexual and reproductive functions after spinal cord injury: Preliminary report. *Journal of Rehabilitation Research & Development*, 44(1), 83–90. https://doi.org/10.1682/JRRD.2005.10.0166

Andrulis, D. (1998). Access to case is the centerpiece in the elimination of socioeconomic disparities in health. *Annals of Internal Medicine*, 129, 412–416.

Bughi, S., Shaw, S., Mahmood, G., Atkins, R., & Szlachcic. (2008). Amenorrhea, pregnancy, and pregnancy outcomes in women following spinal cord injury: A retrospective cross-sectional study. *Endocrine Practice*, 14(4), 437–441. https://doi.org/10.4158/EP.14.4.437

Bury, M. (1982). Chronic illness as biographical disruption. *Sociology of Health and Illness*, 4(2), 167–182. https://doi.org/10.1111/1467-9566.ep11339939

Centers for Disease Control and Prevention. (2019). *Disability and health overview*. https://www.cdc.gov/ncbddd/disabilityandhealth/disability.html

Centers for Disease Control and Prevention. *Fibromyalgia*. (2017, October 11). https://www.cdc.gov/arthritis/basics/fibromyalgia.htm

Centers for Disease Control (CDC). (2015). *Disability impacts all of us: Infographic*. https://www.cdc.gov/media/releases/2015/p0730-us-disability.html

Colantino, A., Mar, W., Escobar, M., Yoshida, K., Velikonja, D., Rizoli, S., Cusimano, M., & Cullen, N. (2010). Women's health outcomes after traumatic brain injury. *Journal of Women's Health*, 19(6), 1109–16. https://doi.org/10.1089/jwh.2009.1740

Cook, Alan, Osler, Turner, Hosmer, David, Glance, Laurent, Rogers, Frederick, Gross, Brian, Garcia-Filion, Pamela, & Malholtra, Ajai. (2017). Gunshot wounds resulting in hospitalization in the United States: 2004–2013. *Injury, 48*(3), 621–627. https://doi.org/10.1016/j.injury.2017.01.044

Deegan, M. J. & Brooks, N. A. (Eds). (1985). *Women and disability: The double handicap.* Transaction Books.

DeForge, D., Blackmer, J., Garrity, C., Yazdi, F., Cronin, V., Barrowman, N., Fang, M., Mamaladze, V., Zhang, L., Sampson, M., & Moher, D. (2005). Fertility following spinal cord injury: A systematic review. *Spinal Cord, 43*, 693–703. https://doi.org/10.1038/sj.sc.3101769

Dillaway, H., Cross, K., Lysack, C. & Schwartz, J. (2013). Normal and natural, or burdensome and terrible? Women with spinal cord injuries discuss ambivalence about menstruation. *Sex Roles, 68*, 107–120. https://doi.org/10.1007/s11199-011-0092-4

Elder, G., Jr., Johnson, M. K., & Crosnoe (2003). The emergence and development of life course theory. In J. T. Mortimer and M. J. Shanahan (Eds.), *Handbook of the life course* (pp. 3–19). Kluwer Academic/Plenum Publishers.

Fitzcharles, M., Ste-Marie, P. A., Rampakakis, E., Sampalis, J. S., & Shir, Y. (2016). Disability in fibromyalgia associates with symptom severity and occupation characteristics. *The Journal of Rheumatology, 43*(5), 931–936. https://doi.org/10.3899/jrheum.151041

Fritz, H., Dillaway, H., & Lysack, C. (2015). "Don't think paralysis takes away your womanhood": Sexual intimacy after SCI. *American Journal of Occupational Therapy, 69* (1), 69022–60030. https://doi.org/10.5014/ajot.2015.015040.

Furstenberg, Frank F. (2000). The sociology of adolescence and youth in the 1990s: A critical commentary. *Journal of Marriage and the Family 62*, 896–910. https://doi.org/10.1111/j.1741-3737.2000.00896.x

GBD 2017 Disease and Injury Incidence and Prevalence Collaborators. (2018). *Global, regional, and national incidence, prevalence, and years lived with disability for 354 diseases and injuries for 195 countries and territories, 1990–2017: A systematic analysis for the Global Burden of Disease Study 2017.* https://doi.org/10.1016/S0140-6736(18)32279-7

Hammell, K. (2004). Quality of life among people with high spinal cord injury living in the community. *Spinal Cord, 42*, 607–620. https://doi.org/10.1038/sj.sc.3101662

Hammell, K. W. (2007). Quality of life after spinal cord injury: A meta-synthesis of qualitative findings. *Spinal Cord, 45*, 124–139. htps://doi.org/10.1038/sj.sc.3101992

Harrington Meyer, M. (2014). *Grandmothers at work: Juggling families and jobs.* New York University Press.

Hochschild, Arlie R. (2003). *The second shift.* Penguin Books.

Hughes, B., & Patterson, K. (1997). The social model of disability and the disappearing body: Towards a sociology of impairment. *Disability & Society, 12*(3), 325–340. https://doi.org/10.1080/09687599727209

Isaksson, G., Josephsson, S., Lexell, J., & Skar, L. (2007). To regain participation in occupations through human encounters – narratives from women with spinal cord injury. *Disability & Rehabilitation, 29*(22), 1679–1688. https://doi.org/10.1080/09638280601056061

Jensen, M., Kuehn, D., Amtmann, D., & Cardenas, D. (2007) Symptom burden in persons with spinal cord injury. *Archives of Physical Medicine and Rehabilitation, 88*(5), 638–645. https://doi.org/10.1016/j.apmr.2007.02.002

Kalpakjian, C. Z., & Lequerica, A. (2006). Quality of life and menopause in women with physical disabilities. *Journal of Women's Health, 15*(9), 1014–1027. https://doi.org/10.1089/jwh.2006.15.1014

Krause, J., & Broderick, L. (2004). Outcomes after spinal cord injury: Comparisons as a function of gender and race and ethnicity. *Archives of Physical Medicine & Rehabilitation*, 85, 355–362. https://doi.org/10.1016/S0003-9993(03)00615-4

Lombardi, G., Del Popolo, G., Marchiarella, A., Mencarini, M., & Celso, M. (2010). Sexual rehabilitation in women with spinal cord injury: A critical review of the literature. *Spinal Cord*, 48(12), 842–849. https://10.1038/sc.2010.36

Messner, Michael. (1992). *Power at play: Sports and the problem of masculinity*. Beacon Press.

McQuillan, J., Greil, A. L., Shreffler, K. M., & Tichenor, V. (2008). The importance of motherhood among women in the contemporary United States. *Gender & Society*, 22(4), 477–496. https://doi.org/10.1177/0891243208319359

National Disability Authority (NDA). (2004). http://nda.ie/Disability-overview/Disability-Statistics/.

National Spinal Cord Injury Statistics Center (NSCISC). (2021). *Fact and figures at a glance*. NSCISC SCI Facts and Figures 2021.pdf (umich.edu)

Nosek, M. (2000) Overcoming the odds: The health of women with physical disabilities in the United States. *Archives of Physical Medicine and Rehabilitation*, 81(2), P135–138. https://doi.org/10.1016/S0003-9993(00)90130-8

Pentland, W., Walker, J., Minnes, P., Tremblay, M., Brouwer, M., Gould. (2002). Women with spinal cord injury and the impact of aging. *Spinal Cord*, 40(8), 374–387. https://doi.org/10.1038/sj.sc.3101295

Reame, N. (1992). A prospective study of the menstrual cycle and spinal cord injury. *American Journal of Physical Medicine & Rehabilitation*, 71(1): 15–21. https://doi.org/10.1097/00002060-199202000-00005

Roehling, P. V., Roehling, M. V., & Moen, P. (2001). The relationship between work-life policies and practices and employee loyalty: A life course perspective. *Journal of Family and Economic Issues*, 22(2), 141–170. https://doi.org/10.1023/A:1016630229628

Rutberg, L., Friden, B., & Karlsson, A-K. (2008). Amenorrhea in newly spinal cord injured women: An effect of hyperprolactinaemia? *Spinal Cord*, 46, 189–191. https://doi.org/10.1038/sj.sc.3102095

Schulz, R., Decker, S. (1985). Long-term adjustment to physical disability: The role of social support, perceived control, and self-blame. *Journal of Personality and Social Psychology*, 48(5), 1162–1172. https://doi.org/10.1037//0022-3514.48.5.1162

Shuey, K. M., & Wilson, A. E. (2008). Cumulative disadvantage and black-white disparities in life-course health trajectories. *Research on Aging*, 30(2), 200–225. https://doi.org/10.1177/0164027507311151

Signore, C. (2016). Reproductive and sexual health for women with disabilities. In S. E. Miles-Cohen & C. Signore (Eds.), *Eliminating inequities for women with disabilities: An agenda for health and wellness* (pp. 93–114). American Psychological Association.

Tate, D. G., Forcheimer, M. B., Krause, J. S., Meade, M. A., & Bombardier, C. H. (2004). Patterns of alcohol and substance use and abuse in persons with spinal cord injury: Risk factors and correlates. *Archives of Physical Medicine and Rehabilitation*, 85(11), 1837–1847. https://doi.org/10.1016/j.apmr.2004.02.022

Tepperman, L., & Meredith, N. (2016). *Waiting to happen: The sociology of unexpected injuries*. Oxford University Press.

Undeland, M., & Malterud, K. (2007). The fibromyalgia diagnosis: Hardly helpful for the patients? A qualitative focus group study. *Scandinavian Journal of Primary Health Care*, 25(4), 250–255. https://doi.org/10.1080/02813430701706568

U.S. Department of Health and Human Services. (2005). *The surgeon general's call to action to improve the health and wellness of persons with disabilities.* US Department of Health and Human Services, Office of the Surgeon General.

Walton-Moss, Benita J., Manganello, Jennifer, Frye, Victoria, & Campbell, Jacquelyn C. (2005). Risk factors for intimate partner violence and associated injury among urban women. *Journal of Community Health, 30*(5), 377–389. https://doi.org/10.1007/s10900-005-5518-x

Whiteneck, G., Meade, M., Dijkers, M., Tate, D., Bushnik, T., & Forchheimer, M. (2004). Environmental factors and their role in participation and life satisfaction after spinal cord injury. *Archives of Physical Medicine and Rehabilitation, 85*(11), 1793–17803. https://doi.org/10.1016/j.apmr.2004.04.024

World Health Organization. (2002). *Towards a common language for functioning, disability and health: ICF the international classification of functioning, disability and health.* https://cdn.who.int/media/docs/default-source/classification/icf/icfbeginnersguide.pdf

World Health Organization. (2006). *Neurological disorders: Public health challenges.* https://www.who.int/publications/i/item/9789241563369

World Health Organization. (2008). *The global burden of disease: 2004 update.* 2004 Update. https://apps.who.int/iris/bitstream/handle/10665/43942/9789241563710_eng.pdf

World Health Organization. (2011). *World report on disability 2011.* Geneva.

World Health Organization. (2013). *International perspectives on spinal cord injury.* https://www.who.int/publications/i/item/international-perspectives-on-spinal-cord-injury

....

CHAPTER 16

DISABILITY AND THE TRANSITION TO ADULTHOOD IN THE UNITED STATES

....

ANTHONY R. BARDO AND ASHLEY VOWELS

INTRODUCTION

THE population of young people with disabilities in the United States is sizeable and has increased in the past 30 years (Houtrow et al., 2014; Kaye et al., 1996). Currently, approximately 4% of all individuals under the age of 18 years have a disability, and disability prevalence increases to 6% when considering only those between the ages of 15 and 17 years (Young, 2021). This sizable population has warranted the attention of federal legislation, which has ensured the right to free and appropriate public education for children with disabilities with the overarching goal to ensure equality of opportunity in the transition to adult roles (e.g., economic self-sufficiency and independent living) (IDEA, 2006). Despite such efforts, little is known about the transition to adulthood among people with disabilities, and this is especially concerning given that the path to adulthood has recently become more arduous and unordered for all (Settersten & Ray, 2010).

Indeed, not all youth experience educational attainment, employment, independent living, marriage, and parenthood in a predictable manner, or at all. This may be especially true for those with disabilities who face relatively greater social barriers (Janus, 2009; Lester, 2014), which highlights a need to understand how the transition to adulthood differs by disability status. Yet sociologists have paid very little attention to postadolescents with disabilities who are in the throes of becoming adults. In fact, even though approximately 6% of transition-age youth have a disability, it is almost as if this group is invisible within the general social science scholarship devoted to the transition to adulthood (Leiter & Waugh, 2009; Wells et al., 2003). Thus, their needs are poorly understood and cannot be adequately considered in pertinent programs and policies, although they are of great concern to parents, educators, and service professionals (Braun et al., 2006).

One major factor that has contributed to a lack of knowledge on transition-age youth with disabilities is that there are few longitudinal studies that use nationally representative samples of adolescent respondents with disabilities, and those that do exist have important limitations (Queirós et al., 2015). For example, existing nationally representative longitudinal studies tend to focus on students, particularly secondary students enrolled in special education programs, and they exclude youth with severe disabilities. Additionally, post–high school follow-up periods tend to be relatively short, and disability onset and severity are typically measured in school but not after school exit (Mann & Honeycutt, 2014). Moreover, these data generally include measures that capture normative assumptions of what constitutes a "good" adulthood, and they overwhelmingly focus on traditional role transitions.

The lion's share of transition to adulthood research on youth with disabilities is located within the fields of special education and rehabilitation, which is steeped in pathologizing understandings of disability (e.g., medical model) (Lester, 2014). This is problematic because the medical model situates disability as a personal problem, while ignoring the social and environmental circumstances that present challenges in the first place. Moreover, much of this research has been conceptual or descriptive. Little attention has been paid to the process by which youth take up and/or resist new roles, which is further concerning because youth with disabilities likely have experiences that differ substantially from their counterparts without disabilities. In sum, there is almost no research based on a critical understanding of disability that problematizes notions of *normal* adulthood. Thus, more often than not disability is entangled with health and results are overgeneralized, with little or no attention paid to disability type or severity as well as intersecting social identities (e.g., gender, race/ethnicity, and sexual orientation) (Shandra, 2018). This chapter reflects a starting point from which sociologists can begin to engage this literature.

The structure of this chapter is as follows: We begin by providing a life course perspective on the transition to adulthood. First, we give a historical overview of the transition to adulthood to show how adulthood is a socially constructed versus natural status, which further situates the circumstances of transition-age youth with a disability within the contexts of a social versus medical model of disability. This historical overview is followed by a short summary of demographic trends in central adult roles (e.g., education, work, and family) to demonstrate the emergent ambiguity surrounding the transition to adulthood. After addressing the complexities of assessing the attainment of adulthood status in general, we summarize the current state of the literature on the transition to adulthood among people with a disability. We conclude with a general summary and a sense of potential ways to develop the field.

The Transition to Adulthood

A Brief History through the Lens of the Life Course

One way of understanding the transition to adulthood in a historical sense comes from the life course paradigm. The life course developed out of a need to understand human experiences in the context of structural and historical forces, as prior scholarship typically separated the individual from such circumstances (Elder et al., 2003). From a life course perspective, human development does not exist in a vacuum; rather, it happens within sociohistorical contexts.

First, this is evident if one acknowledges that the human life span has historically been divided into segments that sequentially reflect a normal and expectable trajectory. The life course in premodern societies centered on biological changes. That is, adulthood was universally determined by the onset of puberty. Coming-of-age rituals fell under the purview of religious institutions, which signified adulthood as an ascribed status that came with clear expectations (Mintz, 2012). However, the autonomy typically affiliated with contemporary adulthood was largely absent: Work was designated, marriages were arranged, and reproduction was far from a choice (Berlin et al., 2010; Waters et al., 2011).

With the progression of modernity, one's position in life was no longer fully determined at birth. Individuals now had some choice in work (i.e., accumulation of property) and family formation (i.e., allocation of property). Governments recognized that these choices required some level of individual accountability (e.g., maturity), and the designation of adulthood status shifted from the sole purview of religious institutions (e.g., from an ascribed to an achieved status) (James, 1960). Hence came the establishment of an age of majority, more commonly recognized by its antecedent (i.e., minors). Consequently, adulthood was then understood to include both physical and psychological changes within the context of the social environment (Hogan & Astone, 1986).

Around the turn of the 20th century, expected psychological development was standardized by age. That is, commonly understood developmental milestones were normalized (e.g., formal operational reasoning and an individual's identity necessary for intimacy, e.g., Freud, Piaget, Erickson) (Hock, 1995). Simultaneously, childhood became a protected life stage intended to foster development (deMause, 1995). Both the physical and psychological capacities necessary to be considered an adult were thus *normalized* at a time when the social environment became increasingly complex (Mintz, 2012). For example, by the 1920s extreme changes in courtship practices were underway (i.e., dating), and options for lifelong mate selection (i.e., marriage) burgeoned (Bailey, 1989).

A new preadult life stage earmarked for self-exploration and identity development emerged in the 1940s (i.e., the teenager) (Nichols & Good, 2004). Post–World War II reconstruction brought about a vast array of never-before-seen options for education, work, and marriage (even divorce and remarriage). By the 1960s parents became poignantly aware that their expectations for adulthood did not match those of their teenagers (Silva, 2012). This period was marked by the breakdown of a gender-based division of labor, as women's participation in the labor market increased (Furstenberg, 2010). Changes in family life soon followed with couples postponing marriage and childbearing or foregoing parenthood all together. Significantly, the development of effective methods of contraception resulted in women postponing childbearing. This meant that the ultimate marker of adulthood (i.e., parenthood) became a "choice" (Umberson et al., 2010). Ultimately, an adult is now understood to be someone that is accountable for their choices and fully responsible for their life outcomes.

While earlier conceptions of human development and the transition to adulthood heavily relied on biological and psychological changes, the life course perspective has made it apparent that this transition is culturally dependent and fluid over time. In this sense, cultural age deadlines provide a timeline for when and under what circumstances certain transitions should occur, and they establish the order in which events should occur within the life course (Settersen & Hagestad, 1996a). These timelines are supported by the collective view of society and enforced through both formal and informal mechanisms of social control.

Cultural age deadlines have been found to provide flexible guidelines for transitions such as education, employment, and marriage, which reflect expectations for life course trajectories (Settersten & Hagestad, 1996b). For instance, historical shifts in women's labor force participation have shaped the cultural age deadlines related to both employment and family (Hagestad & Uhlenberg, 2007). Additionally, they provide context for why nonnormative transitions (i.e., those perceived to be off time or out of order) often negatively impact outcomes across the life course. For instance, "early" transitions into parenthood may negatively impact mothers' well-being (Pearlin & Skaff, 1996; Umberson et al., 2010).

The life course perspective underscores that adulthood is *not* a natural state one can simply reach through a process of human development. Conversely, it is a socially constructed status bound by the social institutions (i.e., education, work, marriage, family) that govern the multifaceted roles that constitute adulthood. The historical overview provided earlier should not be taken to suggest that coming of age was previously easy and predictable (Mintz, 2015). Rather, it provides a backdrop to demonstrate how a relatively recent hyperfocus on individuality and independence has turned adulthood into an ambiguous (possibly unobtainable) status. In fact, the events which historically marked the transition to adulthood have become less of a predictable sequence (Berlin et al., 2010; Furstenberg, 2010; Waters et al., 2011).

Next we provide an overview of trends in the institutions that historically constituted adulthood to show how contemporary cohorts are left without a shared social script that can be used to determine when adulthood status is reached. This preface to our focus on transition-age youth with disabilities highlights the complexities surrounding the conceptualization of adulthood as a series of normative role transitions (e.g., cultural age deadlines). Yet, and as later discussed, this normative transition model closely aligns with the dominant strategies designed to prepare youth with disabilities for the transition to adulthood (i.e., IDEA, 2006).

Demographic Trends in Education, Work, and Family

Adulthood was a relatively salient status prior to the second half of the 20th century, denoted by one's transition from their family of origin to family of procreation, which was traditionally established through marriage and solidified by parenthood (Hogan & Astone, 1986; Modell, 1991). For example, in 1970, approximately 70% of the population age 18 years or older was married, and the vast majority of the remaining 30% would eventually marry or had been married and were widowed. Currently, only 50% are married, and only a slight majority of the remaining one half want to get married someday (Parker & Stepler, 2017). Over this same time the median age at first marriage increased 7 years, from approximately 21 to 28 years for females and 23 to 34 years for males (US Census, 2020). These trends in marriage underlie a prolongation of the transition to adulthood, and they point to a possible deinstitutionalization of the life course (i.e., an emergent ambiguity in what it means to be an adult).

Before getting married one was expected to pass through and/or enter other social institutions. Prior to 1970 this seemingly entailed a hop, skip, and a jump from high school to the workforce, and ideally a career trajectory—at least for males. Postsecondary educational attainment, while on the rise, was still relatively rare: 8% of females and 14% of males age 25 years or older had at least a bachelor's degree in 1970 (NCES, 2019). The female labor force participation rate had steadily increased following World War II by 10 points to 43%, compared to 80% for males (US Department of Labor, 2016). In general, men were at work and women were running the house or bearing a double burden by also bringing home a wage.

Over the next 50 years, postsecondary educational attainment became increasingly important to meet the demands of a rapidly evolving labor market, and sex disparities in both education and the economy began to diminish. Currently 36% of those age 25 years or older have at least a bachelor's degree (with a slightly greater proportion among females) (NCES, 2019), and the labor force's sex ratio is near parity (US Department of Labor, 2016). An increasing number of years spent in education has led to a prolongation of entrance into the labor force. For example, in 1980, nearly 70% of those in their early twenties had secured a full-time paid job, whereas that percentage is currently closer to 50%. Moreover, the age at which the average full-time worker could expect to obtain a salary equivalent to the median US salary has increased over this same period from age 24 to 34 years old (Carnevale et al., 2013). These trends potentially explain a prolonged transition to adulthood, as more time spent in education has led to delays in work, marriage, and parenthood.

Like the trend in age at first marriage, the average maternal age at first birth has increased 6 years since 1970, from age 21 to 27 years (Guzzo & Payne, 2018). Over this same time the total fertility rate dropped from 2.48 to 1.73 (Livingston, 2019).

However, recent cohorts are not only delaying parenthood and having fewer children, but a growing proportion is also forgoing parenthood all together. For example, in 1970 only 24% of 25- to 34-year-olds were childless, and that share has soared to 62% (Schondelmyer, 2017). Of course, some folks beyond the age of 34 still become parents, but reports indicate that intentions to remain childless are especially prevalent among more recent cohorts (Rybińska, 2020).

While debates surrounding trends in marriage and fertility are somewhat contentious, they are often explained by increasing rates of educational attainment and a related prolonged entrance into full-time paid employment (Carnevale et al., 2013). Nonetheless, what is clear is that although an overwhelming amount of attention has been paid to the delays by which traditional adulthood markers are being met, there is an increasing amount of heterogeneity in both the sequencing of these transitions and the rate at which they are being obtained or even sought after all together (Berlin et al., 2010; Waters et al., 2011). Subsequently, this foreshadows an increasingly precarious road to adulthood for those who may face additional barriers, such as postadolescents with disabilities.

THE TRANSITION TO ADULTHOOD AND DISABILITY

Twenty-first-century life course scholarship has uncovered the rapidly growing mismatch between existing institutions and young people making the transition to adulthood, which has elongated, postponed, reordered, and even sometimes eliminated, traditional adult role transitions (Eliason et al., 2015). The life course can be understood as the "universal escalator on which everyone rides" (Glaser & Strauss, 1971, p. 171). Historically this escalator ride was assumed to be somewhat normal and expectable (Hagestad & Neugarten, 1985), but more recent research has shown that some rides occur at different speeds that lead some to arrive at adulthood at different times and with different outcomes (Furstenberg et al., 2004; Settersten & Ray, 2010; Shanahan, 2000; see also Leiter & Waugh, 2009).

In this section we summarize the current state of the literature on the transition to adulthood among people with a disability. As noted in the Introduction, sociological literature on this topic is scant, and most of the information comes from the fields of special education and rehabilitation. Thus, we have organized our review to mimic the normative or expectable life course, and we give careful attention to the social and structural barriers that transition-age youth face. We begin by reviewing the literature on education, which is relatively rich compared to other life domains. However, as evidenced in the following sections, relatively little is known in terms of postgraduation outcomes. Thus, we provide an overview of federal mandates for public education, and then follow this up with details surrounding the circumstances of current secondary educational programs. Next, we begin to address post–high school outcomes by reviewing the postsecondary literature on the transition to work, independent living, and family among youth with disabilities.

Education

Secondary Education

High school graduation signifies a time of many challenges and transitions, such as postsecondary education and/or employment. However, prior to the mid-1970s youth with disabilities were largely excluded from public education and this initial rite of passage into adulthood. The Rehabilitation Act of 1973 required accommodations for students with disabilities. This act was shortly followed by the Education for All Handicapped Children Act of 1975 that enforced the right of youth with disabilities to receive an education. Over the next several decades, disability legislation underwent numerous changes, including the landmark Americans with Disabilities Act of 1990. This landmark legislation coincided with the Individuals with Disabilities Education Act (IDEA), which is updated about every 5 years.

IDEA brought about several important changes in education for youth with disabilities centered on a shifted focus from the disability to the individual. Namely, public schools are required to create an individualized education program (IEP) for each eligible student, which is designed to ensure that students receive appropriate placement in both special education and regular classrooms as well as a chance to participate in school culture and academics as much as possible. There are more than 2 million transition-age students with disabilities, and most of these students spend at least 40% or more of their school day in regular classes (Trainor et al., 2020).

IEPs for students ages 16 or older must also include transition goals. Transition services are defined as "a coordinated set of activities for a child with a disability designed to be within a results-oriented process, focused on improving the academic and functional achievement of the child's movement from school to post-school activities" (IDEA, 2006: p. 855). This *results-oriented* mandate ignited research aimed at identifying best practices, which has accelerated the systematic study of evidence-based practices to teach transition-related skills. These skills include both academic (e.g., math and reading) and functional (e.g., socioemotional and employment) skills recognized as necessary to move from school to adult life (Rowe et al., 2021).

Upwards of 30 evidence-based practices to teach both academic and functional transition-related skills have been identified. Academic practices broadly encompass literacy and numeracy skills, whereas functional practices overwhelmingly focus on teaching self-determination and vocational skills. There is an absence of evidence-based practices to teach needed skills across domains such as financial literacy and benefits planning, as well as sex education. Overall, experts emphasize the need for IEPs and their related programs to match students' goals, and for ensuring programs offer students opportunities in general education, paid employment/work experience, self-care/independent living skills, and student support (Test et al., 2009).

In sum, 68% of secondary students with a disability graduate on time compared to 86% of their counterparts without a disability (NCES, 2019). Despite the notion of established "evidence-based" practices, very little is known about the postgraduation status of people with disabilities. This is a critical oversight given that current practices overwhelmingly emphasize the importance of preparing for a self-sufficient and independent future. Instead of considering school systems, much greater emphasis is placed on individuals with disabilities and their families, and qualities that may or may not be conducive to future success.

Goal Setting, Self-Determination, and Family Involvement

In line with the *results-oriented* IDEA mandate, goal setting is an important aspect of an IEP. In general, goal-setting strategies span both school and home settings, and they often include academic, behavioral, and self-care goals for the student with a disability. To facilitate the transition from high school to postschool life, school-based transition components of a student's IEP should be based on their goals and be designed around their strengths, needs, and interests. Ideally, postschool goals (e.g., postsecondary education, employment, and independent living) should be entertained by at least the middle school years, but they are not typically included in a student's IEP until their transition phase (i.e., when their inclusion is mandated) (Francis et al., 2020).

Self-determined individuals are recognized to have the ability to evaluate options, set goals, and take initiative to reach goals (Rowe et al., 2015). Hence, an emphasis is placed on teaching self-determination skills among evidenced-based transition practices, which has been guided by a stream of research that has found a strong correlation between postschool outcomes for students with disabilities and self-determination skills (see Test et al., 2009). While goal setting is a self-directed skill, it occurs within the IEP process that includes school staff and sometimes family. A student's special education teacher is often the only person responsible for teaching critical self-determination skills (Lingo et al., 2018). Nonetheless, families are generally the only remaining safety net after high school graduation for postadolescents with disabilities.

Schools are encouraged to engage families to plan and prepare for their child's transition from high school to adult roles. All parents face challenges during their children's transition to adulthood, but this is especially true for parents raising children with disabilities. Specifically, parents may have to modify their goals for their children's future roles as an adult (Hogan & Shandra, 2012). Family support includes collaborating, decision-making, instructing, and advocating for their children. Yet families often feel that they have little or no meaningful engagement in school-based transition efforts, and this is particularly felt among families from historically marginalized populations (Wilt et al., 2020).

A major barrier to family involvement in school-based transition efforts is a lack of resources (e.g., time, travel, and money) required to actively participate in the planning process. Another barrier is that families often become "burned out" due to their children's ongoing medical needs and increased problem behavior, which can compound existing stressors. These barriers have been recognized to occur within broader social contexts (e.g., neighborhood, social welfare, and health care services), which suggest that structural issues are the root cause (e.g., lack of options and resources) (Hirano et al., 2018).

Family involvement is viewed as extremely important for the postschool outcomes of students with disabilities. Yet collaborative school-home partnerships are rare, particularly for racial/ethnic minority and low-income families. This double-edge sword contributes to furthering a process of cumulative disadvantage, which is exacerbated by a near absence of transition-related supports and services available to postadolescents with disabilities after high school graduation. Some scholars have noted that policy makers should consider options available in other economically advanced nations, such as dedicated vocational supports in Denmark and the Netherlands, and a dedicated agency to support transition-age folks in Australia (Mann & Honeycutt, 2014). In the meantime, postadolescents with disabilities and their families must continue to face less than full inclusion into "normal" adulthood after high school graduation (Certo et al., 2003).

While secondary education has come a long way toward meeting the needs of students with disabilities, it is clearly in need of major improvements. However, as Trainor et al. (2020) point out in their proposed framework for research in transition, reformation is not an easy task, given a wide array of complexities: (1) extensive heterogeneity among students, schools, and communities; (2) vast variation in policy priorities, and resources across school districts and states; (3) the breadth of life domains that require assessment, planning, and instruction; (4) the range of postschool goals held by students; (5) the number of involved service systems, community partners, and disciplines; (6) special education's overarching commitment to inclusion, individualization, and intensity; (7) the varying degree of preparation professionals receive to carry out this work; and (8) the broader contexts within which transition to adulthood takes place. Sociologists have the skill set to address many of these issues, specifically point (1) and (8), and opportunities for such research appear boundless, given a near absence of sociological transition research on youth with disabilities.

Postsecondary Education

Although people with disabilities are federally protected from discrimination in education, they have relatively lower levels of educational attainment. Completion of high school is a challenge for individuals with disabilities and continuing to postsecondary education presents a new set of challenges. For example, while access to a secondary education is guaranteed, access to a postsecondary education is not. Youth with disabilities are often not less likely to enroll in postsecondary education due to their disability-related limitations, but because their experience has limited their aspirations (Hogan & Shandra, 2012). Expectations for youth with disabilities are relatively low among both teachers and parents, and this has a negative impact on college enrollment for people with disabilities (Shandra & Hogan, 2009). Additionally, families that have youth with disabilities are more likely to experience financial hardship, which limits both their expectations for, and access to, postsecondary education (Shandra, 2011).

Despite these barriers to postsecondary education, students with disabilities are enrolling in postsecondary schools at an increasing rate—though they lag far behind their counterparts without disabilities (Targett et al., 2013). The exact proportion is unknown because disability disclosure is voluntary, but the proportion of undergraduate students with a disability appears to have quadrupled since the 1970s (Carroll et al., 2020). Currently, approximately 11% of undergraduates report having a disability. Despite this nonnegligible number of students with disabilities, research on student success and outcomes is scant and findings are inconclusive (Scott, 2019).

Postsecondary enrollment, and its related outcomes, differ substantially by disability severity and type (Braun et al., 2006). For example, rates for postsecondary attendance range from 31% for students with multiple disabilities to 70% for students with a visual disability. Rates of attendance also differ substantially by institution type (e.g., 2-year vs. 4-year). For example, the respective rates for attendance at a 4-year institution are 8% and 43% (Sanford et al., 2011). Yet disability type and severity, as well as institution type, are rarely disaggregated. Sometimes research will focus on a specific disability type, or category. Categories are sometimes separated into "apparent" versus "nonapparent," "visible" versus "invisible," and "cognitive" versus "noncognitive."

Apparent and visible categories largely include physical disabilities, which are associated with barriers to facilities (e.g., classrooms), learning materials, and instructional strategies. Also, students with physical disabilities may experience social stigma in different ways than those with nonapparent or invisible disabilities and have difficulty cultivating a sense of belonging (Brown, Silny, & Brown, 2021). Nonapparent or invisible categories often include psychological and/or cognitive impairments, which are broadly associated with barriers to instructional processes. For example, such students may require alternative assessments or extra time to complete assignments (Carroll et al., 2020).

All students face challenges as they begin their postsecondary education, but for students with disabilities this transition requires them to become familiar with a new system for accessing support systems. Students with disabilities often report that they are confused about what types of disability are eligible for accommodations, that they are unaware of services, that they have difficulty navigating bureaucratic procedures, and that available accommodations are inadequate. Students with a disability must also learn a new system for disability disclosure, and they often find that faculty are uninformed about campus procedures. Moreover, college students with disabilities often face physical barriers on campuses and in classrooms, as well as stigma related to disability (Scott, 2019).

In general, course performance is one of the strongest predictors of degree completion. Yet adjustment to a new academic and social environment may be more difficult for students with disabilities compared to those without. Reported rates of college completion vary, but it is generally understood that students with disabilities are less likely to complete their secondary education than students without disabilities. Also, there is some evidence to suggest that students with psychological disabilities are less likely to complete a bachelor's degree compared to students with a physical disability—who do not differ substantially in degree completion from students without disabilities (Carroll et al., 2020).

Employment and Financial Independence

Due to being the most direct normative route toward economic self-sufficiency and independent living, employment is commonly recognized as the central adult role (Braun et al., 2006). Specifically, full-time employment is viewed as a key step toward adulthood because of its strong ties to financial and residential independence (Lester, 2014). Most school-age youth with disabilities desire and intend to work after high school graduation. In fact, over 95% of high school students age 15 years and older with a disability expect to be employed by at least age 30 (Carter et al., 2020). However, transitions from school to work present new challenges for all youth, but especially for those with disabilities.

Even though almost all youth with disabilities have goals to work, and despite federal legislation that prohibits employers from disability-based discrimination, a disproportionate percentage of students with disabilities who graduate from high school secure gainful employment (Shandra & Hogan, 2008). In fact, issues surrounding both securing and maintaining employment directly contribute to the greatest negative discrepancy between those with and those without disabilities (Certo et al., 2003). To paraphrase Test and colleagues (2009), being unemployed or underemployed most clearly exemplifies what it means to be disabled.

Over 70% of working-age people without disabilities, versus only 30% of their counterparts with disabilities, are employed. There are also stark inequalities in full- versus part-time employment by disability status. For example, only 17% of employees without disabilities, versus 29% of those with disabilities, work part-time (Shandra, 2018). Employment outcomes also differ substantially by disability type. For example, employees with a cognitive disability are less likely to hold professional or managerial positions, and they are more likely to occupy lower-paying jobs and hold positions in blue-collar occupations. Though somewhat less likely to be employed, there is some evidence to suggest that among those who work with a physical disability that their employment outcomes are relatively comparable to those without disabilities (Queirós et al., 2015).

Test and colleagues' (2009) statement is further exemplified by findings that show the greatest differences in time use by disability status are in the domain of paid work (Anand & Ben-Shalom, 2014). Indeed, full-time employment typically demands a large proportion of one's waking hours. There is only so much time in a day, and everyone is constrained to the same 24 hours. However, those with disabilities face a disproportionate burden regarding the number of hours they must commit to other essential life domains, such as transportation, personal care, and medical care. Time use constraints likely differ substantially by disability type and severity. However, relevant studies rarely disaggregate disabilities, and they typically conflate disabilities with health impairments. The implications of time use for full-time employment remain largely unknown, and this reflects a ripe area of study for sociologists (Shandra, 2018).

A large proportion of evidence-based transition practices are focused on teaching vocational and employment-related skills (Rowe et al., 2021). Yet postadolescents with disabilities are substantially less likely to work for pay after high school graduation compared to their counterparts without disabilities. Given that many postsecondary educators report that they do not feel that students with disabilities are well-prepared to enter the workforce, or that these students would be successful in achieving their employment goals, such disparities should not be surprising (Carter et al., 2020). This brings to question the success of both school- and work-based transition programs (Certo et al., 2003), which remains unknown due to a lack of available data. There is a great need for more thorough data on the efficacy of existing practices and their long-term outcomes by disability type and severity (Shandra & Hogan, 2008).

Youth with disabilities are at a relatively greater risk of financial hardship and poverty after high school due to a lack of employment. Yet, after leaving high school, very few safety nets are in place to assist with either securing or maintaining employment. Some services and supports exist, but they are typically designed to broadly serve those with disabilities rather than cater to the unique needs of those who are presently transitioning into the workforce (Targett et al., 2013). One exception is the Workforce Innovation and Opportunity Act of 2014, which mandates that vocational rehabilitation agencies allocate 15% of their federal funds toward transition services for youth with disabilities (Carter et al., 2020). Given the unique challenges faced by postadolescents with disabilities, especially considering the current economic climate for all youth transitioning to the workforce, more targeted services and supports efforts are needed to help ensure integration into this essential adult role.

Most of the employment research by disability status during the transition to adulthood focuses on the transition from high school to the workforce. Very little is known about the employment outcomes of postadolescents with disabilities after completing postsecondary education. However, there appears to be an ambiguity within postsecondary institutions of who is responsible for addressing the employment needs of students with disabilities. This highlights a need for stronger partnerships between postsecondary career services and disability resource offices (Kutscher et al., 2019). Additionally, much of the relevant employment research is descriptive, and a greater understanding of the experience of postadolescents transitioning to work is sorely needed. Some transition-age youth who are unable to work may be eligible for financial assistance through the Supplemental Security Income (SSI) program, which is a means-tested program intended to help keep beneficiaries only slightly above the federal poverty line. However, the extent to which young people with disabilities adopt SSI benefits instead of employment is unknown (Davies et al., 2009). These gaps in research are particularly important to address, given the key role that employment plays in establishing independent living.

Independent Living

While recent statistics show that transition-age youth are living with their parents much longer than in previous decades, relatively little is known about the residential circumstances of those with disabilities. Independent living is a major goal among youth with disabilities and their families, but this differs substantially by disability type and severity. Historically, youth with disabilities, particularly those with severe disabilities (and those who were deaf, blind, or had severe cognitive disabilities), often left home early in childhood to enter state-run residential facilities. Starting in the 1960s, the parents' movement began to push for a shift from institutionalized living to community-based living for children with disabilities. Special education legislation in the 1970s helped make this possible. As such, the bulk of responsibility shifted to families (Leiter & Waugh, 2009).

While the exact statistics are ambiguous, there is some evidence to suggest that 73% of postadolescents with disabilities continue to live at home after high school, and that less than 1% move to an institutional setting (Test et al., 2009). As noted earlier, there are large disparities in employment outcomes by disability status, and financial independence is a major barrier to those with disabilities who desire to establish their own residence during the transition to adulthood. A lack of financial resources substantially constrains housing choices and largely prevents youth with disabilities from moving out of their parents' home.

Some postadolescents with disabilities face additional barriers to setting up an independent residence. Specifically, some folks with disabilities may require assistance with daily living that is not readily available outside of the family. People with severe or multiple disabilities may require ongoing daily assistance with basic activities of living, whereas others may only need minimal or intermittent assistance. There is tremendous heterogeneity in the daily care needs among youth with disabilities. Nonetheless, while youth with disabilities and their families often advocate for an independent living situation, aside from family support, there are few available options that do not require substantial financial resources (Leiter & Waugh, 2009). Yet there is a paucity of data on the independent living outcomes and experiences of youth with disabilities transitioning to adulthood, and a greater understanding of this matter is needed.

Sex, Marriage, and Parenthood

The emergence of sexual expression during adolescence is nearly universal. While addressing sex-related issues is difficult for all parents, this is particularly true for parents of adolescents with disabilities. Many such parents expect that their children will marry and become parents, but discussions regarding sexual development, prevention of sexually transmitted diseases, and partner choice are rarely had (Hogan & Shandra, 2012). There is a great amount of stigma surrounding sexual activity involving people with disabilities in society at large, but this even carries over to health professionals who often stigmatize people with disabilities as asexual (Becker et al., 1997).

In general, health care professionals appear uninformed about, or unwilling to address, the reproductive health care needs of their patients with disabilities. They often deem their sexual behavior as unsafe or sometimes even inappropriate or not acceptable (Shandra & Chowdhury, 2012). In fact, practitioners often do not even share sexual health information with their patients with disabilities, which is largely due to reported concerns surrounding their abilities to consent to sex (Linton et al., 2015). Attempts to legitimize these concerns are often made by pointing to research findings that suggest people with disabilities are relatively more likely to experience sexual victimization (Martin et al., 2006). Conversely, such issues should encourage health care providers to address the sexual and reproductive needs of their patients with disabilities.

Extant knowledge of sexual activity among transition-age youth with disabilities is limited. However, there is some evidence to suggest that initial sexual experiences are more likely to happen at younger ages for girls versus boys, and that these experiences are more likely to involve an older partner (Hogan & Shandra, 2012). There is a dearth of research on sexual activity by disability type and severity, though there are likely vast differences in sexual activity between those with physical versus psychological disabilities (Kahn & Halpern, 2018). Exacerbating the need to develop a general understanding of sexual behavior among youth with disabilities is an underlying need to improve school-based sex education in general and as a standard part of transition-related curriculum for students with disabilities (Schalet et al., 2014).

Emerging adults are also often found to have difficulty establishing and maintaining romantic relationships. For example, adolescents with cognitive disabilities (e.g., autism spectrum disorder [ASD]) may have trouble differentiating between friendships and romantic relationships (Heifetz et al., 2020). Persons with disabilities generally begin dating later and have fewer romantic and sexual partners in their lifetime. Among young persons with disabilities, parents may serve as the primary source of information about romantic relationships and may therefore influence the age at which such individuals begin dating (Rintala et al., 1997). Moreover, this may differ by sex, as gender norms have been shown to influence stereotypes regarding romantic relationships in the context of disability. Specifically, women are especially likely to face difficulties in forming romantic relationships (Howland & Rintala, 2001).

Individuals with disabilities are likely to partner with other individuals with disabilities, and individuals without disabilities are often unwilling to engage in romantic partnerships or to marry persons with disabilities—this is especially true for persons with cognitive disabilities (Gill, 1996; Miller et al., 2009). Rates of marriage are generally lower among young adults with disabilities when compared to their peers without a disability (MacInnes, 2011; Newman et al., 2011). However, the probability of marriage among adults with disabilities is not uniform, as individuals with learning disabilities and multiple disabilities are especially disadvantaged (MacInnes, 2011). Despite such difficulties, romantic relationships as well as sexuality remain important to the lives of persons with disabilities (Bates et al., 2017; Siebelink et al., 2006).

Persons with disabilities have been shown to especially value the companionship and support provided by their partners (Bates et al., 2017). Recent research has shown that while online dating may pose challenges for individuals with disabilities, it may also have potential for improving the dating experience for individuals with disabilities helping them to form romantic relationships (Mazur, 2017). It should also be noted that persons with disabilities are at increased risk of abuse and interpersonal violence such as name calling and physical violence within the contexts of relationships (Ward et al., 2010). However, there is some evidence to suggest that those who had encountered abuse in previous relationships were able to subsequently form satisfying romantic relationships (Bates et al., 2017).

Such trends in romantic relationships among persons with disabilities coupled with the fact that sexual activity is rarely addressed within such contexts means that fertility and parenthood among this population remains an underresearched topic. An emerging body of research has pointed out that childless women with disabilities are equally likely to want, and equally likely to intend to have, children as those without disabilities (Bloom et al., 2017). Yet women with disabilities may face barriers to fertility and motherhood, despite the abolishment of compulsory sterilization. The overwhelming focus of related policies and medicine is on controlling the reproductive capacity of women with disabilities through contraceptives and hysterectomies. Even when this is not the case, women with disabilities face other barriers such as social stigma and legal issues regarding child custody (Shandra et al., 2014).

Most of the research on fertility among transition-age youth with disabilities focuses on desires and intentions, and almost no attention is paid to parenthood or other postfertility outcomes. Limited evidence has suggested that nearly 30% of young adults with disabilities have had a child, which is comparable to the percentage of their peers without disabilities. Of these parents with disabilities, 83% reported that their children lived with them (Newman et al., 2011). Despite large numbers of children whose parents have disabilities, parenthood among this population is also relatively underresearched. Previous research about parenthood within the context of disability has been largely driven by the assumption that such families are problematic in some way and that disability among parents will lead to negative outcomes among children (Kirshbaum & Olkin, 2002). Research has found that parents with disabilities may face unique challenges related to the stigma of disability such as negative attitudes and prejudice regarding their parenting abilities (Conley-Jung & Olkin, 2001; Kirshbaum & Olkin, 2002). They may also face legal barriers and challenges regarding custody of their children (Shandra et al., 2014).

Nonetheless, parenthood has become an important part of the transition to adulthood for persons with disabilities. Changes in policies regarding fertility and legal rights over the last several decades mean that persons with disabilities will continue to become parents in the future. As such, parenting among this population should be a priority in future research. Given that extant literature almost exclusively focuses on women with disabilities, future research should consider taking a male or nonfemale perspective. An expanded focus beyond women would provide a better understanding of the institutional hurdles that people with disabilities face.

CONCLUSION

What does it mean to become an adult, and how does one know when they are one? It means that one has choices surrounding important life domains (e.g., postsecondary education, employment, independent living, marriage, and parenthood). Sociologists have long pointed out that these choices are constrained by one's sex, race/ethnicity, and class, and when challenges to these choices are unevenly distributed, sociologists have aptly identified the central underlying reasons—structural barriers. Yet, with few exceptions, sociologists have ignored people with disabilities, especially transition-age youth. This is particularly problematic, given the relatively large number of "choices" that occur during this phase of life. Based on our review of the related special education and rehabilitation literature, it is clear that the choices afforded transition-age youth are extremely limited. Furthermore, these choices are fervently expedited, given a lack of post–high school services and supports to navigate a social structure that was not designed for the inclusion of people with disabilities.

In turn, one knows that they are an adult when they have the capacity to fulfill their desired outcomes for the choices they are presented. The childhood and adolescent educational and social experiences of those with disabilities undoubtedly set transition-age youth on a path of cumulative disadvantage. The desires of these folks are fairly well documented. They want to obtain higher education and/or full-time employment, establish an independent residence, be involved in romantic relationships, and they are just as likely to want to have children as those without disabilities. Yet the degree to which these desires remain unfulfilled remains largely unknown. What is known is that transition-age youth face substantial social and structural barriers to achieve their desires, which are actually rights and privileges afforded to all other "adults." In conclusion, we provide a suggested direction for further study.

Emerging Adulthood: A Potential Path Forward

Sociologists have recognized, but have yet to seriously engage, a growing body of literature that asserts that individualistic criteria (e.g., the development of an adult identity and belief system) are more important for transitioning to adulthood than role transitions (Arnett, 2000; see also Shandra, 2011). In other words, educational attainment, employment, independent living, marriage, and parenthood are recognized as important goals, but their attainment is not understood to define adulthood. This new theory, coined "emerging adulthood," suggests that the value of such accomplishments has changed among emerging adults compared to previous generations (Arnett, 2006).

Emerging adulthood refers to the period of life between the late teens through the twenties, and it is defined as a developmental period characterized by five distinct principles: (1) self-exploration (e.g., identity development); (2) uncertainty; (3) self-focus; (4) transition; and (5) optimism. As a developmental period, emerging adulthood is universally applicable, and thus includes those with disabilities. However, youth with disabilities have yet to be thoroughly examined through an emerging adulthood perspective, although there are some studies that focus on 18- through 29-year-old people with disabilities that do invoke some emerging adulthood principles (Meyer et al., 2015).

Emerging adulthood scholarship highlights the idea that recent generations of youth are presented with relatively greater opportunities, and extended time to devote to the exploration of life goals and the self (Tanner & Arnett, 2011). Changes in relationships, living arrangements, and occupations that characterize 21st-century America (and most other economically developed nations) that once would have been considered detrimental are viewed by emerging adulthood proponents as beneficial and as part of the natural developmental process that occurs during this stage of life.

While emerging adulthood research on people with disabilities is currently limited, scholars have noted that those with disabilities may require additional time to complete this developmental process (Meyer et al., 2015). Although seemingly reasonable, concerns like these elucidate key issues that sociologists typically have with developmental stage theories in general. In sum, sociologists are quick to point out that structural changes are responsible for the phenomena characterized by emerging adulthood, and that nothing developmentally has changed nor been newly identified (Cote, 2014; see also Eliason et al., 2015). One benefit of adopting an emerging adulthood approach is that it may encourage scholars to move away from an emphasis on comparing people with and without disabilities. This approach may also and more generally address the important research gaps noted in this review.

References

Anand, P., & Ben-Shalom, Y. (2014). How do working-age people with disabilities spend their time? New evidence from the American Time Use Survey. *Demography, 51,* 1977–1998. https://doi.org/10.1007/s13524-014-0336-3

Arnett, J. J. (2000). Emerging adulthood: A theory of development from the late teens through the twenties. *American Psychologist, 55,* 469–480. https://doi.org/10.1037//0003-066X.55.5.469

Arnett, J. J. (2006). The psychology of emerging adulthood: What is known, and what remains to be known? In J. J. Arnett and J. L. Tanner (Eds.), *Emerging adults in America: Coming of age in the 21st century* (pp. 303–330). APA. https://doi.org/10.1037/11381-013

Bailey, B. L. (1989). *From front porch to back seat: Courtship in twentieth-century America.* John Hopkins University Press.

Bates, C., Terry, L., & Popple, K. (2017). The importance of romantic love to people with learning disabilities. *British Journal of Learning Disabilities, 45*(1), 64–72. https://doi.org/10.1111/bld.12177

Becker, H., Stuifbergen, A., & Tinkle, M. (1997). Reproductive health care experiences of women with physical disabilities: A qualitative study. *Archives of Physical Medicine and Rehabilitation, 78*(12), S26–S33. https://doi.org/10.1016/S0003-9993(97)90218-5

Berlin, G., Furstenberg Jr, F. F., & Waters, M. C. (2010). Introducing the issue. *The Future of Children, 20*(1) 3–18. https://www.jstor.org/stable/27795057

Bloom, T. L., Mosher, W., Alhusen, J., Lantos, H., & Hughes, R. B. (2017). Fertility desires and intentions among U.S. women by disability status: Findings from the 2011–2013 National Survey of Family Growth. *Maternal and Child Health Journal, 21*(8), 1606–1615. https://doi.org/10.1007/s10995-016-2250-3

Braun, K. V. N., Yeargin-Allsopp, M., & Lollar D. (2006). A multi-dimensional approach to the transition of children with developmental disabilities into young adulthood: The acquisition of adult social roles. *Disability and Rehabilitation, 28*(15), 915–928. https://doi.org/10.1080/09638280500304919

Brown, R., Silny, M., & Brown, J. T. (2021). Ableism in the academy? A systematic review and meta-analysis of experiences of students with disabilities in U.S. higher education. In W. Pearson Jr., and V. Reddy (Ed.), *Social justice and education in the 21st century: Research from South Africa and the United States* (pp. 293–335). Springer.

Carnevale, A. P., Hanson, A. R., & Gulish, A. (2013). *Failure to launch: Structural shift and the new lost generation.* Georgetown University Center on Education and the Workforce.

Carroll, J. M., Pattison, E., Muller, C., & Sutton, A. (2020). Barriers to bachelor's degree completion among college students with a disability. *Sociological Perspectives, 63*(5), 809–832. https://doi.org/10.1177/0731121420908896

Carter, E. W., Awsumb, J. M., Schutz, M. A., & McMillan, E. D. (2020). Preparing youth for the world of work: Educator perspectives on pre-employment transition services. In *Career development and transition for exceptional individuals, 44*(3), 161–173. https://doi.org/10.1177/2165143420938663

Certo, N. J., Mautz, D., Pumpian, I., Sax, C., Smalley, K., Wade, H. A., Noyes, D., Luecking, R., Wechsler, J., & Batterman, N. (2003). Review and discussion of a model for seamless transition to adulthood. *Education and Training in Developmental Disability, 38*(1), 3–17. https://www.jstor.org/stable/i23874986

Conley-Jung, C., & Olkin, R. (2001). Mothers with visual impairments who are raising young children. *Journal of Visual Impairment & Blindness, 95*(1), 14–29. https://doi.org/10.1177/0145482X0109500103

Cote, J. E. (2014). The dangerous myth of emerging adulthood: An evidence-based critique of a flawed developmental theory. *Applied Developmental Science, 18*(4), 177–188. https://doi.org/10.1080/10888691.2014.954451

Davies, P. S., Rupp, K., & Wittenburg, D. (2009). A life-cycle perspective on the transition to adulthood among children receiving supplemental security income payments. *Journal of Vocational Rehabilitation, 30*, 133–151. https://doi.org/10.3233/JVR-2009-0459

deMause, L. (Ed.) (1995). *The history of childhood.* Rowan & Littlefield.

Elder, G. H., Johnson, M. K., & Crosnoe, R. (2003). The emergence and development of life course theory. In J. T. Mortimer and M. J. Shanahan (Ed.), *Handbook of the life course* (pp. 3–19). Springer.

Eliason, S. R., Mortimer, J. T., & Vuolo, M. (2015). The transition to adulthood: Life course structures and subjective perceptions. *Social Psychology Quarterly, 78*(3), 205–227. https://doi.org/10.1177/0190272515582002

Francis, G. L., Duke, J. M., & Raines, A. (2020). Goal setting to support mental wellness among adolescents with disabilities and co-occurring mental health needs. *Teaching Exceptional Children, 53*(5), 350–358. https://doi.org/10.1177/0040059920974706

Furstenberg Jr, F. F. (2010). On a new schedule: Transitions to adulthood and family change. In *The future of children, 20*(1), 67–87. https://www.jstor.org/stable/27795060

Furstenberg, F. F., Kennedy, S., McLoyd, V. C., Rumbaut R. G., & Settersten Jr., R. A. (2004). Growing up is harder to do. *Contexts, 3*, 33–41. https://doi.org/10.1525/ctx.2004.3.3.33

Gill, C. J. (1996). Dating and relationship issues. *Sexuality and Disability, 14*(3), 183–190. https://doi.org/10.1007/BF02590076

Glaser, B., & Strauss, A. (1971). *Status passage*. Aldine.

Guzzo, K. B., & Payne, K. K. (2018). https://www.bgsu.edu/content/dam/BGSU/college-of-arts-and-sciences/NCFMR/documents/FP/guzzo-payne-age-birth-fp-18-25.pdf

Hagestad, G. O., & Neugarten, B. L. (1985). Age and the life course. In V. L. Bengston (Ed.), *Adulthood and aging: Research on continuities and discontinuities, a tribute to Bernice Neugarten* (pp. 35–61). Springer.

Hagestad, G. O., & Uhlenberg, P. (2007). The impact of demographic changes on relations between age groups and generations: A comparative perspective. In K. W. Schaie & P. Uhlenberg (Ed.), *Social structures: Demographic changes and the well-being of older persons* (pp. 239–261). Springer.

Heifetz, M., Lake, J., Weiss, J., Isaacs, B., & Connolly, J. (2020). Dating and romantic relationships of adolescents with intellectual and developmental disabilities. *Journal of Adolescence, 79*, 39–48.

Hirano, K. A., Rowe, D., Lindstrom, L., & Chan, P. (2018). Systemic barriers to family involvement in transition planning for youth with disabilities: A qualitative metasynthesis. *Journal of Child and Family Studies, 27*, 3440–3456. https://doi.org/10.1007/s10826-018-1189-y

Hock, R. R. (1995). *Forty studies that changed psychology: Explorations into the history of psychological research* (2nd ed.). Prentice-Hall.

Hogan, D. P., & Astone, N. M. (1986). The transition to adulthood. *Annual Review of Sociology, 12*, 109–130. https://doi.org/10.1146/annurev.so.12.080186.000545

Hogan, D. P., & Shandra, C. L. (2012). Parents, adolescent children with disabilities, and the transition to adulthood. In *Family consequences of children's disabilities*, by Dennis P. Hogan (pp. 58–74). Russell Sage.

Houtrow, A. J., Larson, K., Olson, L. M., Newacheck, P. W., & Halfon, N. (2014). Changing trends of childhood disability, 2001–2011. *Pediatrics, 134*(3), 530–538. https://doi.org/10.1542/peds.2014-0594

Howland, C. A., & Rintala, D. H. (2001). Dating behaviors of women with physical disabilities. *Sexuality and Disability, 19*(1), 41–70. https://doi.org/10.1023/A:1010768804747

IDEA. (2006). Individuals With Disabilities Act, 20 U.S.C § 1400 et seq.

James, T. E. (1960). The age of majority. *The American Legal History, 4*(1), 22–33. https://doi.org/10.2307/844549

Janus, A. L. (2009). Disability and the transition to adulthood. *Social Forces, 88*(1), 99–120. https://doi.org/10.1353/sof.0.0248

Kahn, N. F., & Halpern, C. T. (2018). Experiences of vaginal, oral, and anal sex from adolescence to early adulthood in populations with physical disabilities. *Journal of Adolescent Health, 62*, 294–302. https://doi.org/10.1016/j.jadohealth.2017.08.003

Kaye, H. S., LaPlante, M. P., Carlson, D., & Wenger B. L. (1996). Trends in disability rates in the United States, 1970–1994. *Disability Statistics Abstract*, No. 17. U.S. Departments of Education, National Institute on Disability and Rehabilitation Research.

Kirshbaum, M., & Olkin, R. (2002). Parents with physical, systemic, or visual disabilities. *Sexuality and Disability*, 20(1), 65–80. https://doi.org/10.1023/A:1015286421368

Kutscher, E., Naples, L., & Freund, M. (2019). Students with disabilities and post-college employment: How much do we know? National Center for College Students with Disabilities, Association on Higher Education and Disability (AHEAD). http://www.NCCSDonline.org

Leiter, V., & Waugh, A. (2009). Moving out: Residential independence among young adults with disabilities and the role of families. *Marriage & Family Review*, 45(5), 519–537. https://doi.org/10.1080/01494920903050847

Lester, J. N. (2014). Young adulthood, transitions, and dis/ability. In C. Amelia Davis and Joann S. Olson (Eds.), *New directions for adult and continuing education* (p. 39–49). Jossey Bass. https://doi.org/10.1002/ace

Lingo, M. E., Williams-Diehm, K. L., Martin, J. E., & McConnell, A. E. (2018). Teaching transition self-determination knowledge and skills using the ME! Bell ringers. *Career Development and Transition for Exceptional Individuals*, 41(3), 185–189. https://doi.org/10.1177/216514341 7753582

Linton, K. F., Rueda, H. A., Williams, L. R., Sandoval, A., & Bolin, S. (2015). Reproductive and sexual healthcare needs among adults with disabilities as perceived by social workers. *Sexuality and Disability*, 34(2), 145–156. https://doi.org/10.1007/s11195-015-9416-6

Livingston, G. (2019). Is U.S. fertility at an all-time low? Two of three measures point to yes. https://www.pewresearch.org/fact-tank/2019/05/22/u-s-fertility-rate-explained/

MacInnes, M. D. (2011). Altar-bound? The effect of disability on the hazard of entry into a first marriage. *International Journal of Sociology*, 41(1), 87–103. https://doi.org/10.2753/IJS002 07659410105

Mann, D. R., & Honeycutt, T. C. (2014). Is timing everything? Disability onset of youth and their outcomes as young adults. *Journal of Disability Policy Studies*, 25(2), 117–129. https://doi.org/10.1177/1044207313484176

Martin, S. L., Ray, N. Sotres-Alvarez, D., Kupper, L. L., Moracco, K. E., Dickens, P. A., Scandlin, D., & Gizlice, Z. (2006). Physical and sexual assault of women with disabilities. *Violence Against Women*, 12(9), 823–837. https://doi.org/10.1177/1077801206292672

Mazur, E. (2017). Diverse disabilities and dating online. In M. F. Wright (Eds.), *Identity, sexuality, and relationships among emerging adults in the digital age* (pp. 150–167). IGI Global. https://doi.org/10.4018/978-1-5225-1856-3.ch010

Meyer, J. M., Hinton, V. M., & Derzis, N. (2015). Emerging adults with disabilities: Theory, trends, and implications. *Journal of Applied Rehabilitation Counseling*, 46(4), 3–10. https://doi.org/10.1891/0047-2220.46.4.3

Miller, E., Chen, R., Glover-Graf, N. M., & Kranz, P. (2009). Willingness to engage in personal relationships with persons with disabilities: Examining category and severity of disability. *Rehabilitation Counseling Bulletin*, 52(4), 211–224. https://doi.org/10.1177/0034355209332719

Mintz, S. (2012). Why the history of childhood matters. *The Journal of the History of Childhood and Youth*, 5(1), 15–28. https://doi.org/10.1353/hcy.2012.0012.

Mintz, S. (2015). *The prime of life: A history of modern adulthood*. Harvard University Press.

Modell, J. (1991). *Into one's own: From youth to adulthood in the United States, 1920–1975*. University of California Press.

NCES. (2019). https://nces.ed.gov/programs/digest/d19/tables/dt19_104.10.asp

Newman, L., Wagner, M., Knokey, A. M., Marder, C., Nagle, K., Shaver, D., & Wei, X. (2011). The post–high school outcomes of young adults with disabilities up to 8 years after high school: A report from the National Longitudinal Transition Study-2 (NLTS2). NCSER 2011-3005. National Center for Special Education Research.

Nichols, S. L., & Good, T. L. (2004). *America's teenagers—Myths and realities: Media images, schooling, and the social costs of careless indifference.* Lawrence Erlbaum.

Parker, K., & Stepler, R. (2017). As U.S. marriage rate hovers at 50% education gap in marital status widens. https://www.pewresearch.org/fact-tank/2017/09/14/as-u-s-marriage-rate-hovers-at-50-education-gap-in-marital-status-widens/

Pearlin, L. I., & Skaff, M. M. (1996). Stress and the life course: A paradigmatic alliance. *The Gerontologist, 36*(2), 239–247. https://doi.org/10.1093/geront/36.2.239

Queirós, F., Wehby, G. L., & Halpern, C. T. (2015). Developmental disabilities and socioeconomic outcomes in young adulthood. *Public Health Reports, 130,* 213–221. https://doi.org/10.1177/003335491513000308

Rintala, D. H., Howland, C. A., Nosek, M. A., Bennett, J. L., Young, M. E., Foley, C. C., Rossi, C. D., & Chanpong, G. (1997). Dating issues for women with physical disabilities. *Sexuality and Disability, 15*(4), 219–242. https://doi.org/10.1023/A:1024717313923

Rowe, D. A., Mazzotti, V. L., Fowler, C. H., Test, D. W., Mitchell, V. J., Clark, K. A., Holzberg, D., Owens, T. L., Rusher, D., Seaman-Tullis, R. L., Gushana, C. M., Castle, H., Chang, W-H., Voggt, A., Kwiatek, S., & Dean, C. (2021). Updating the secondary transition research base: Evidence- and research-based practices in functional skills. *Career Development and Transition for Exceptional Individuals, 44*(1), 28–46. https://doi.org/10.1177/2165143420958674

Rowe, D. A., Mazzotti, V. L., Hirano, K., & Alverson, C. Y. (2015). Assessing transition skills in the 21st century. *Teaching Exceptional Children, 47*(6), 301–309. https://doi.org/10.1177/0040059915587670

Rybińska, A. (2020). Trends in intentions to remain childless in the United States. *Population Research and Policy Review,40,* 661–672 https://doi.org/10.1007/s11113-020-09604-9

Sanford, C., Newman, L., Wagner, M., Cameto, R., Knokey, A-M., Shaver, D. (2011). *The post high school outcomes of young adults with disabilities up to 6 years after high school: Key findings from the National Longitudinal Transition Study-2 (NLTS2).* SRI International. https://eric.ed.gov/?id=ED523539

Schalet, A. T., Santelli, J. J., Russell, S. T., Halpern, C. T., Miller, S. A., Pickering, S. S., Goldberg, S. K., & Hoenig, J. M. (2014). Invited commentary: Broadening the evidence for adolescent sexual and reproduction health and education in the United States. *Journal of Youth and Adolescence, 43*(10), 1595–1610. https://doi.org/10.1007/s10964-014-0178-8

Schondelmyer, E. (2017). Fewer married households and more living alone. https://www.census.gov/library/stories/2017/08/more-adults-living-without-children.html

Scott, S. (2019). Access and participation in higher education: Perspectives of college students with disabilities. NCCSD Research Brief, 2(2). National Center for College Students with Disabilities, Association on Higher Education and Disability. http://www.NCCSDclearinghouse.org

Settersten Jr, R. A., & Hägestad, G. O. (1996a). What's the latest? Cultural age deadlines for family transitions. *The Gerontologist, 36*(2), 178–188. https://doi.org/10.1093/geront/36.2.178

Settersten Jr, R. A., & Hagestad, G. O. (1996b). What's the latest? II. Cultural age deadlines for educational and work transitions. *The Gerontologist, 36*(5), 602–613. https://doi.org/10.1093/geront/36.5.602

Settersten, R. A., Jr., & Ray, B. (2010). What's going on with young people today? The long and twisting path to adulthood. *Future of Children*, 20(1), 19–41. https://muse.jhu.edu/article/381974

Shanahan, M. J. (2000). Pathways to adulthood in changing societies: Variability and mechanisms in life course perspective. *Annual Review of Sociology*, 26, 667–692. https://doi.org/10.1146/annurev.soc.26.1.667

Shandra, C. L. (2011). Life-course transitions among adolescents with and without disabilities: A longitudinal examination of expectations and outcomes. *International Journal of Sociology*, 41(1), 67–86. https://doi.org/10.2753/IJS0020-7659410104

Shandra, C. L. (2018). Disability as inequality: Social disparities, health disparities, and participation in daily activities. *Social Forces*, 97(1), 157–192. https://doi.org/10.1093/sf/soy031

Shandra, C. L., & Chowdhury, A. R. (2012). The first sexual experience among adolescent girls with and without disabilities. *Journal of Youth and Adolescence*, 41(4), 515–532. https://doi.org/10.1007/s10964-011-9668-0

Shandra, C. L., & Hogan, D. P. (2008). School-to-work program participation and the post-high school employment of young adults with disabilities. *Journal of Vocational Rehabilitation*, 29(2), 117–130.

Shandra, C. L., & Hogan, D. P. (2009). The educational attainment process among adolescents with disabilities and children of parents with disabilities. *International Journal of Disability, Development and Education*, 56(4), 363–379. https://doi.org/10.1080/10349120903306616

Shandra, C. L., Hogan, D. P., & Short, S. E. (2014). Planning for motherhood: Fertility attitudes, desires and intentions among women with disabilities. *Perspectives on Sexual and Reproductive Health*, 45(4), 203–210. https://doi.org/10.1363/46e2514

Siebelink, E. M., de Jong, M. D., Taal, E., & Roelvink, L. (2006). Sexuality and people with intellectual disabilities: assessment of knowledge, attitudes, experiences, and needs. *Mental Retardation*, 44(4), 283–294. https://doi.org/10.1352/0047-6765(2006)44[283:SAPWID]2.0.CO;2

Silva, J. M. (2012). Constructing adulthood in an age of uncertainty. *American Sociological Review*, 77(4), 505–522. https://doi.org/10.1177/0003122412449014

Tanner, J. L., & Arnett, J. J. (2011). Presenting emerging adulthood: What makes it developmentally distinctive? In J. J. Arnett, M. Kloep, L. B. Hendrty, & J. L. Tanner (eds.), *Debating emerging adulthood: Stage or process?* (pp. 13–31). Oxford University Press. https://doi.org/10.1093/acprof:oso/9780199757176.003.0002

Targett, P., Wehman, P., West, M., Dillard, C., & Cifu, G. (2013). Promoting transition to adulthood for youth with physical disabilities and health impairments. *Journal of Vocational Rehabilitation*, 39, 229–239. https://doi.org/10.3233/JVR-130653

Test, D. W., Mazzotti, V. L., Mustian, A. L., Fowler, C. H., Kortering, L., & Kohler, P. (2009). Evidence-based secondary transition predictors for improving postschool outcomes for students with disabilities. *Career Development for Exceptional Individuals*, 32(3), 160–181. https://doi.org/10.1177/0885728809346960

Trainor, A. A., Carter, E. W., Karpur, A., Martin, J. E., Mazzotti, V. L., Morningstar, M. E., Newman, L., & Rojewski, J. W. (2020). A framework for research in transition: Identifying important areas and intersections for future study. *Career Development and Transition for Exceptional Individuals*, 43(1), 5–17. https://doi.org/10.1177/2165143419864551

Umberson, D., Pudrovska, T., & Reczek, C. (2010). Parenthood, childlessness, and well-being: A life course perspective. *Journal of Marriage and Family*, 72(3), 612–629. https://doi.org/10.1111/j.1741-3737.2010.00721.x

US Census. (2020). Historical marital status tables. https://www.census.gov/data/tables/time-series/demo/families/marital.html

US Department of Labor. (2016). Women in the labor force. https://www.dol.gov/agencies/wb/data/facts-over-time/women-in-the-labor-force#civilian-labor-force-by-sex

Ward, K. M., Bosek, R. L., & Trimble, E. L. (2010). Romantic relationships and interpersonal violence among adults with developmental disabilities. *Intellectual and Developmental Disabilities, 48*(2), 89–98. https://doi.org/10.1352/1934-9556-48.2.89

Waters, M. C., Carr, P. J., & Kefalas, M. J. (2011) Introduction. In M. C. Waters, P. J. Carr, M. J. Kefalas, & J. Holdaway (Eds.), *Coming of age in America: The transition to adulthood in the twenty-first century* (pp. 1–27). University of California Press.

Wells, T., Sandefur, G. D., & Hogan, D. P. (2003). What happens after the high school years among young persons with disabilities? *Social Forces, 82*(2), 803–832. https://doi.org/10.1353/sof.2004.0029

Wilt, C., Hirano, K., & Morningstar, M. E. (2020). Diverse perspectives on transition to adulthood among families: A qualitative exploration. *Journal of Disability Policy Studies, 32*(1), 34–35. https://doi.org/10.1177/1044207320934098

Young, N. A. E. (2021). Childhood disability in the United States: 2019. ACSBR-006, *American Community Survey Briefs*. US Census Bureau.

PART V

Education

CHAPTER 17

DISABILITY IN THE TRANSITION FROM K–12 TO HIGHER EDUCATION

DARA SHIFRER

INTRODUCTION

AN increasing share of US youth with disabilities[1] enroll in higher education (Hong et al., 2007; Katsiyannis et al., 2009; Stodden & Whelley, 2004). This is true even among youth with disabilities linked to more substantial effects on learning, such as intellectual disabilities (formerly called "mental retardation") and autism (Hart et al., 2010; Plotner & Marshall, 2014). Nonetheless, undergraduates with disabilities remain less likely to obtain a higher-education degree than undergraduates without disability (Haber et al., 2016; National Center for Education Statistics, 2000). People with disabilities are much less likely to be employed than people without disabilities (18% versus 65% in 2016) (Bureau of Labor Statistics, 2017), and employed disabled people experience significant earnings disparities (Maroto & Pettinicchio, 2015). This chapter problematizes the notion that the poorer educational and occupational outcomes of persons with disabilities are natural or inevitable. Increasing access to higher-education degrees for young adults with disabilities is one important means of improving their occupational and health outcomes and general social attainment. And then, society benefits from the increased participation of diverse persons, through the unique insights, creativity, and empathy of people with disabilities.

Research on the disabilities most common across youth is limited by a lack of data and by the persistence of medicalized views of disability, even among sociologists (Altman & Barnartt, 2000; Gordon & Rosenblum, 2001; Naples et al., 2019). This chapter draws connections along the educational trajectory from kindergarten through grade twelve (K–12), and then into higher education. This chapter also delineates distinctions in conceptions of and responses to disability in higher education in contrast to earlier levels of schooling. Understandings of educational inequality are incomplete without the regular and intersectional consideration of disability. Moreover, ideas from disability studies have important implications and insights for core theories from sociology of education. This chapter integrates theories and empirical findings from disability studies, stratification theory, medical sociology, critical special-education research, and sociology of education. With a novel demonstration of the tensions between disability ideology and dominant US educational ideals of *merit*, *individual accountability*, and *standardization*, this chapter illuminates the structural barriers youth with disability face in entering and succeeding in higher education, and it provides a framework to help sociologists of education develop and extend their literature by integrating disability topically and ideologically.

THE DISABLED POPULATION IN HIGHER EDUCATION AND K–12 SETTINGS

The disabilities of older Americans are most often related to injury, accident, or aging (Centers for Disease Control and Prevention, 2009). Younger Americans, in contrast, are most likely to be considered disabled on the basis of cognitive differences (e.g., learning disabilities, attention deficit hyperactivity disorder [ADHD], autism), with physical disabilities (e.g., deafness, blindness) composing a small minority of the youth classified with disabilities (McFarland et al., 2019). Although adults are increasingly classified with some of these disabilities (e.g., ADHD), in this chapter, I refer to them as "educational disabilities" to distinguish them from the broader group of disabilities experienced by people of all ages. Definitions are variable, but learning disabilities, encompassing diagnoses like dyslexia and dyscalculia, typically describe youth who struggle despite an average or high IQ (Fletcher et al., 2005). Broadly speaking, ADHD describes issues with attention and focus, and autism describes issues with social skills (American Psychiatric Association, 2000). Only intellectual disabilities ostensibly relate to a low IQ (US Government Printing Office, 2010), but intellectual disabilities and autism tend to be perceived as the most severe disabilities (Hart et al., 2010).

Per a federal report, 19% of young adults in the United States who were undergraduates in the 2015–16 school year reported a disability (Snyder et al., 2019). In this report, disability included "deafness or serious difficulty hearing; blindness or serious difficulty seeing; serious difficulty concentrating, remembering, or making decisions because of a physical, mental, or emotional condition; or serious difficulty walking or climbing stairs" (Snyder et al., 2019, p. 268). Most diagnoses of educational disabilities occur during elementary school (Ong-Dean, 2009). Yet, the distribution of disability types in the higher-education population differs from the distribution in the K–12 population, largely because youth with disability experience limited access to higher education. A relatively high proportion of youth with physical disabilities (75%) proceed into higher education (Hinz et al., 2017). And so, while youth with physical disabilities compose 2% of the pre-K to grade 12 (preK–12) special-education population[2] (McFarland et al., 2019), they make up 14% of the population of undergraduates with disabilities (Raue & Lewis, 2011). Similarly, whereas 5% of the preK–12 special education population qualifies through the emotional disturbance category (McFarland et al., 2019), 15% of the college population receive resources for a psychological disorder (e.g., anxiety, depression) (Raue & Lewis, 2011).

About two-thirds of youth with learning disabilities, autism, or ADHD proceed into some sort of postsecondary education, in contrast to only half of youth with intellectual disabilities (Hinz et al., 2017). Learning disabilities make up the largest share of students with disability in both the preK–12 (35%) and higher-education (31%) settings (McFarland et al., 2019; Raue & Lewis, 2011). Estimates are rough,[3] but a slightly higher share of undergraduates may report ADHD (18%) relative to the preK–12 special education population (15%). The rates of autism (2% versus 10%) and more substantial disabilities like intellectual disabilities (5% versus 6%) are lower among undergraduates than among the preK–12 special-education population (McFarland et al., 2019; Raue & Lewis, 2011). These differences in the populations of youth with disability mirror distinctions in the missions of K–12 and higher-education settings.

Understandings of Educational Disabilities

This section describes how understandings of educational disabilities vary along the continuum from the medical model to social constructionism. These theories, dominant in the sociology-of-health and disability-studies literatures, have been routinely applied to educational disabilities only in the last decade or so. In the *medical model*, conditions are discrete individualized biological differences. For instance, the highest-incidence educational disabilities (e.g., learning disabilities, ADHD, autism, emotional disturbance) are either defined or associated with conditions in the *Diagnostic and Statistical Manual of Mental Disorders* (*DSM*), a volume with substantial control over psychiatric diagnoses in the United States (Kokanovic et al., 2013). Because the *DSM* largely takes a biomedical view (McGann, 2011), their inclusion implies that these educational disabilities represent an objective neurological distinction. Yet, like other conditions in the *DSM* (e.g., depression, schizophrenia) (Kokanovic et al., 2013; Vallee, 2011; Vanheule, 2012), the neurological basis for educational disabilities is only inferred through subjective and socially rooted diagnostic criterion. That is, with no biomarkers (excepting the low-incident Down syndrome, deafness, blindness), the vast majority of educational disabilities are diagnosed based on educational performance, behaviors, and emotions, characteristics known to vary on the basis of early childhood environment, culture, and school influences (Shonkoff & Phillips, 2000; Vellutino et al., 2004).

Nonetheless, Jay Dolmage (2014), taking a disability-studies lens, argues that the medical model remains a "prominent disability rhetoric."

Understandings of disability that recognize *environmental causes* are a first step from a medical to a social model, with Altman (2016) crediting medical sociologist Saad Nagi as instrumental in advancing understandings of disability as a social rather than individual phenomena in the 1960s. For instance, the higher incidence of cognitive disabilities among lower SES children may be due to environmental factors (e.g., toxins, lead poisoning, household resources) that shape learning (Konkel, 2012; Margai & Henry, 2003; Shonkoff & Phillips, 2000). Racial disparities in the prevalence of cognitive disabilities are similarly in part a product of the centering of achievement levels as a diagnostic criterion, and racial differences in SES and subsequently in achievement (Hibel et al., 2010; Shifrer, 2018; Shifrer et al., 2011). James Carrier (1983, p. 970), a British sociologist who took an early interest in educational disabilities, argued that the medical model of learning disabilities effectively masked "the social nature of learning and academic performance in the United States." From the lens of medical model, Black children are disproportionately biologically deficient. The social model, in contrast, demonstrates the central contributions of racial and economic inequality (Shifrer, 2018).

Yet, Dolmage (2014, p. 36) criticizes the emphasis on environmental factors, describing disability as "Sign of Social Ill" or as "Symptom of Human Abuse of Nature" as two dominant disability myths. Researchers employing the social model locate social causes not only in the environment but also in other *people and contexts*. Subjective diagnostic criteria and variable guidelines provide fertile ground for inconsistent and potentially inaccurate classifications, particularly for cognitive educational disabilities (Donovan & Cross, 2002; Proctor et al., 2006; Shifrer & Fish, 2020). Biased classifications are a dominant focus among critical special-education researchers, with racial disproportionality attributed to a range of factors from cultural misunderstanding to the use of special education as a means of re-segregating racial minority students within schools (Anyon, 2009; Blanchett, 2006; Eitle, 2002; Ferri & Connor, 2005; Klingner & Harry, 2006; McDermott et al., 2006; Reid & Knight, 2006; Sullivan et al., 2014). Recent empirical evidence supports hypotheses that teachers' racialized perspectives and schools' racialized contexts are partially the source of racial differences in cognitive-disability classifications (Elder et al., 2019; Fish, 2017; Fish, 2019; Shifrer, 2018; Shifrer & Fish, 2020; Thompson et al., 2020). Like other neurological and cognitive outcomes, cognitive-disability classifications seem to reflect a complicated array of biological, environmental, and social factors. So why do we choose the word "disabled" for these differences? Who created this label?

These are the questions emphasized by *social constructionists*, the most extreme variant of the social model. Disability studies specifically examines the "social, political, cultural, and economic factors that define disability and help determine personal and collective responses to difference" (Society for Disability Studies, 2016). In his research on stigma, Goffman (1963) documented how we decide which differences represent deviance or deficiency. Erevelles (2000, p. 40) similarly states: "it is not really their 'differences' . . . rather, what is at issue is how the social world has 'read' these differences." Erevelles (1996, 2000) uses a Marxist perspective to argue that disabilities were constructed to undergird capitalism, providing a means of justifying the unequal distribution of work and resources.

The socially constructed nature of educational disabilities is evidenced in variable definitions across time and place (Jenkins, 1998), with the relative emphasis on these disabilities in the United States and other Westernized countries attributed to cultural priorities for individualism, productivity, and efficiency (Dudley-Marling, 2004; Nuttall, 1998). Social constructionists show how learning disabilities emerged to be more prevalent among middle-class White students in the 1970s, as parents sought explanations for their children's low achievement, and then transitioned to being more prevalent among low SES and racial minority youth in the 1990s, as schools sought explanations for their failure to exact equal educational outcomes (Blanchett, 2006; Ong-Dean, 2006; Sleeter, 2010). Additionally, sociologists document multiple ways the increasing prevalence of autism reflects social forces rather than actual shifts in the prevalence of a condition (Eyal, 2013; King & Bearman, 2011; Liu et al., 2010). Peter Conrad (1992) was potentially the first medical sociologist to use ADHD as an example of medicalization, that is, when human differences perceived as natural or unimportant come to be perceived as medical conditions requiring treatment. These various perspectives of disability not only shape scholars' understandings of educational disabilities, but also inform institutional policy and the experiences and attitudes of practitioners, parents, the public, and young people themselves.

SOCIAL CONSEQUENCES OF DISABILITY LABELS

This section focuses on how the social model influences our perceptions of the causes of the outcomes of youth with disability. According to the medical model, the poorer outcomes of youth with educational disabilities are a result of their individual deficiencies. Labeling theory, in contrast, builds on social constructionism to present a more sociological understanding of why youth with educational disabilities might have poorer outcomes. Intersectionality facilitates an even more nuanced understanding of the social effects of disability labels.

Labeling theory was first applied to educational disabilities by sociologist of education Hugh "Bud" Mehan et al. (1986), in *Handicapping the Handicapped*. Mehan et al. (1986, p. 160) argued that student identities are constructed by the school and become labels, with the "main difference between normal and deviants" being "that deviants have been apprehended by the formal institution... while so-called normals have not been caught." Labeling theory predicts that labeled persons' poorer outcomes are the result of the label itself, with labels altering others' perceptions and behaviors and eventually those of the labeled person. Educational outcomes of adolescents labeled with a learning disability are poorer than their similarly achieving and behaving peers without a disability label, in part as a function of their teachers' lower expectations for them and their own lowered expectations for themselves (Shifrer, 2013b, 2016). Youth with disability have long experienced educational separation, first through institutionalization and then through separate classrooms within mainstream schools (Erevelles, 2000; Goode et al., 2013). Although most K–12 students now receive special-education accommodations in the regular education classroom because of the shift toward inclusion (Idol, 2006; Spellings et al., 2007), they still experience separation through ability grouping or lower-level course placements (Shifrer, 2013b; Shifrer et al., 2013; Shifrer, 2016). For reasons like this, Ho (2004) argues that labels should be eradicated from schools.

The assumption that disability labels and special education are wholly disadvantageous undergirds much of the critical literature. For instance, the disproportionate placement of Black youth in special education would not be problematic if special education were perceived of as beneficial. Selection bias complicates any attempts at assessing the effects of special education. In other words, it is difficult to determine whether disability labels produce poor outcomes through stigma and stratification, or if the outcomes of youth with disability would have been just as poor, or even worse, without the disability label because of the individual differences that led to the disability label. Because of these substantial data and methodological limitations, findings remain mixed, with some studies finding null or negative effects of special education (Morgan et al., 2010; Shifrer, 2016; Shifrer et al., 2013), and some finding benefits (Hanushek et al., 2002; Hurwitz et al., 2020; Schwartz et al., 2019). Answering these questions is important for the teachers who want to facilitate learning for their students and for the children whose needs are not currently met by schools. Similar needs motivate broader criticisms of social constructionism for failing to provide practical solutions, and for failing to acknowledge tangible pain (e.g., physical, psychological) related to disability (Erevelles, 1996; Shakespeare, 2006; Sommo & Chaskes, 2013). Ho (2004) tempers her anti-label stance with acknowledgment that labels also establish eligibility for legal protections and potentially beneficial resources. Similarly, medical sociologist Bruce Link and colleagues (1989) developed a *modified labeling theory* that acknowledges the individual realities of impairment by attributing people's outcomes to both their individual outcomes and to social consequences of labels.

As much as it is difficult to assess the benefits and costs of disability labels in a straightforward way, assuming that effects are the same for diverse children promotes dichotomous understandings of disability. Dichotomous understandings legitimate and perpetuate disability as a category of inequality by disregarding the heterogeneity of the group of children labeled with disability. Moving beyond a simple dichotomy, Shifrer and Frederick (2019), who focused on disability specifically, call for sociologists to begin rather than end at intersectionality when investigating inequality.

Intersectionality, a product of 1970s Black feminism (McCall, 2005), outlines the interlocking nature of systems of power and oppression (Collins, 1999; Crenshaw, 1989, 1991). Considering whether one category operates differently depending on a person's status along other categories is an important aspect of intersectionality (Hancock, 2007). Although disability is rarely considered in intersectional research (Maroto et al., 2019), some studies find that socially disadvantaged youth (racial minorities, low SES) with educational disabilities experience more negative effects from disability labels than socially advantaged youth (Blanchett, 2010; Ong-Dean, 2009; Saatcioglu

& Skrtic, 2019). Disability-studies theorists particularly point to long-term harm for racial minority youth, linking the disproportionate classification of racial minority youth with disabilities to the disproportionate discipline and the school-to-prison-pipeline literatures (Annamma et al., 2017; Moore, Jr., et al., 2018). In addition to structural inequities and direct bias, these patterns may reflect Latinx, and especially Black, children's increased risk of being categorized with more stigmatizing disabilities (Fish, 2017; Fish, 2019; Saatcioglu & Skrtic, 2019; Tenenbaum & Ruck, 2007), or perceptions that reflect the stigmatized qualities of the students most likely to carry the disability category.

Because labels initiate services that are potentially desired and beneficial (Ho, 2004), some seek disability classifications while others receive disability classifications, that is, they are "labeled." Those who seek recognition as disabled sometimes must establish their *legitimacy*. They must overcome skepticism reflecting disability myths on faking or embellishing disabilities (Dolmage, 2014), more broad suspicion of the ability of socially advantaged families to game the system (Harrison et al., 2007), and then widely publicized cases of actual disability fraud (Lovett, 2020). Ironically, the qualities that produce stigma and stratification are often the same that legitimize deservingness. Biological attributions reinforce perceptions that differences are immutable and resistant to intervention (Pescosolido & Martin, 2007). Yet, by transferring culpability away from behaviors (Martin et al., 2007), biological attributions can legitimize claims of disability. Transgender persons face a similar conundrum of experiencing pathologization through inclusion in the *DSM*, in exchange for biological legitimation and initiation of services (Johnson, 2019; Serano, 2007). Although homosexuality was removed from the *DSM* in the 1970s, gay civil rights still revolve around homosexuality not being a choice, that is, being a function of biological difference (Drescher, 2015). And then, while people with invisible disabilities (e.g., learning disabilities) may face less daily stigma (Dolmage, 2014), they may find it more difficult to legitimate their disability claims than people with visible differences (e.g., Down syndrome) (Blum, 2015). These conundrums produce social psychological challenges for youth with disabilities in higher education.

Finally, a person's *access to disability legitimacy*, and to particular disability categories, may depend on their other status markers. Consistent with the emphasis in the social model on the subjectivity and inconsistency of classification processes, the distinction across disability categories is unclear (Mayes et al., 2000; Stanford & Hynd, 1994). ADHD, autism, and intellectual disabilities can each be characterized by inattention, hyperactivity, and impulsivity, just as psychological disorders, learning disabilities, ADHD, autism, and intellectual disabilities can be characterized by social-skill deficits (Bender & Wall, 1994; Bradley & Isaacs, 2006; Donfrancesco et al., 2005; Gresham, 1992; LoVullo & Matson, 2009; Matson et al., 2010; Stanford & Hynd, 1994). These fluid delineations across disability categories allow for educator bias and parental intervention to shape which category a child's differences are recognized by, with Black children disproportionately categorized with more stigmatizing categories (intellectual disabilities, learning disabilities), and White children with less stigmatizing categories (autism, ADHD) (Eyal, 2013; Ong-Dean, 2009; Saatcioglu & Skrtic, 2019). And then, researchers document actual cases of socially advantaged parents securing extra resources for their children (e.g., extra time on test, stimulants) through fraudulent, or at least less pressing, disability claims (Harrison et al., 2007; King et al., 2014; Lovett, 2020). Ralph Turner (1960, p. 858) described how the United States conceptualizes schools and status attainment as a "sporting event," such that "anything that gives special advantage to those who are ahead at any point in the race" inspires great distrust. The socially differentiated access to and experience of disability labels increases disability skepticism, potentially impairing legitimacy and resources for those who truly need them.

EDUCATIONAL DISABILITIES AND EDUCATIONAL IDEALS

Interweaving ideas from disability studies with classic theory from sociology of education, this section documents tensions between disability ideology and the educational ideals of *merit, individual accountability,* and *standardization* to illuminate the structural barriers youth with disability face in entering and succeeding in higher education. This new theoretical framing is a useful contribution for sociologists of education hoping to more frequently engage with disability ideology and disability as a category of inequality.

A meritocracy is a system in which people attain status and upward social mobility based on their own *merit* (e.g., talent, effort, achievement) rather than their social advantages (e.g., wealth, power) (Shifrer, 2013a). In Turner's (1960) sporting event metaphor, the United States supports the illusion of meritocracy by assuming that everyone starts on "equal footing," with the educational rewards distributed to those who demonstrate merit. Disability marks a tangible departure from this ideology, an explicit acknowledgement that all do not start on equal footing, that all children do not have equal access to what society deems as "merit." We attempt to reconcile this tension, and maintain that the sporting event of education is still fair, by describing special-education accommodations as a way of "leveling the playing field" (Fuchs et al., 2000). Nonetheless, just as conflict theorists frame sorting and selecting in schools as a means of reproducing social disadvantage, problematizing whether selection actually coincides with merit and problematizing the way merit is defined (Collins, 1971), Dolmage (2014) describes how disability myths construct disability as "improper, lesser."

The ideas of merit and meritocracy parallel neoliberal emphasis on *individual accountability* over structural factors (Hill Collins & Bilge, 2016). Although sociologists have established that everybody actually does not start on equal footing (Coleman, 1990; Gamoran & Long, 2006; Hill, 2016), the power of this ideology is evident in how it remains taboo for educators to acknowledge the impact, for instance, of low SES on student learning (Skiba et al., 2006). Disability, tied to an ask for more structural support within schools, explicitly challenges the notion that individuals are entirely accountable for their outcomes. Similarly, Erevelles (2000) describes how capitalistic ideology privileging individualism over dependence underlies portrayals of people with disabilities as "parasitic," just as Shallish (2015) documents how receiving disability accommodations in higher-education settings can be perceived as "an unfair advantage."

Finally, building on the fallacy that we all start on equal footing, neoliberalist educational policy emphasizes *standardization* as a central means of achieving equality of educational opportunity (Ambrosio, 2013; Ball, 2016; Morgan & Shackelford, 2018). Standardized testing was first mandated in 2011 through No Child Left Behind (NCLB), and then continued, in 2015, through the Every Student Succeeds Act (Ambrosio, 2013; Morgan & Shackelford, 2018). NCLB also marked the advent of standardized curriculum, particularly in schools serving larger shares of socially disadvantaged students (Ravitch, 2011; Sleeter & Carmona, 2017). The emphasis on standardization implies that equal inputs are sufficient for equal outcomes. What happens when this paradigm is disrupted, when equal inputs do not result in equal outcomes? Children's risk of being labeled as disabled and deficient increases. In the latest model for classifying educational disabilities, Response to Intervention (RTI), the focus is explicitly on students who appear to not learn despite receiving "high-quality instruction" (RTI Action Network, 2020). Erevelles and Minear (2010, p. 142) similarly argue that special education is "used to segregate students who disrupt the 'normal' functioning of schools." Likewise, ableism involves the assumption that people who are not "standard" are by default "defective" (Campbell, 2009; Wolbring, 2008). Representing another tension with education ideals, disability classifications are a specific means of seeking differentiated[4] rather than standardized instruction.

The neoliberal value for standardization equates *equality of educational outcomes* with equal inputs. James Coleman (1990), a foundational sociologist of education, not only challenged educational thinkers to clarify whether the goal is equal inputs or equal outcomes, but also encouraged a shift toward acknowledging that equality of educational opportunity may require unequal inputs. Although Coleman discussed this in terms of lower SES and racial minority youth, this vision of equality also applies to youth with disability. Nonetheless, this vision of equality can be perceived to run counter to ideals of *merit, individual accountability*, and *standardization*. Is it fair that some students receive more from schools? Who decides who is deserving of receiving more? Has the sporting game of social mobility been rigged? Do grades and degrees still reflect actual merit? The next section explores how these tensions between educational disabilities and educational ideals shape access to higher education and differentiation in postsecondary classrooms for youth with disabilities.

DISTINCTIONS BETWEEN HIGHER EDUCATION AND K-12 SETTINGS

The tensions between disability ideology and US educational ideals are more evident in institutes of higher education than in K-12 schools, partially because of the more enduring history of exclusion in higher education (Higbee & Katz, 2010). In the early 1960s, Ed Roberts faced great resistance after being accepted at the University of California, Berkeley, perceived as "too crippled" with polio to succeed (White et al., 2010). He arranged his own accommodations (living at the university hospital because of a lack of other options) and ultimately banded together with other students with disabilities to form the "Rolling Quads" (White et al., 2010). Roberts and the Rolling Quads established the Physically Disabled Students Program in Berkeley in 1970 (Dolmage, 2017; White et al., 2010), setting a precedent for the disability programs that are now evident at virtually every college and university, and that now serve cognitive as well as physical disabilities (Brown, 2000). In the early 1970s, Roberts was also involved in growing the first Center for Independent Living (CIL) in Berkeley, which emphasized independence, and consumer sovereignty/choice (Dolmage, 2017; White et al., 2010). There are now hundreds of CILs across the nation (Brown, 2000; White et al., 2010). With the Ed Roberts Campus, a building of unprecedented inclusivity, a testament to Roberts (Kullman, 2019), Roberts is considered the father of the Independent Living Movement.

The *Independent Living Movement*, emerging in the late 1960s and early 1970s, advocated for community-based services to facilitate the independence and life quality of people with disabilities (Frieden, 2015; Frieden & Cole, 1985; Nosek et al., 2015). The Independent Living Movement is based on the philosophy that each individual should have "control over one's life based on the choice of acceptable options" (Nosek et al., 2015, p. 1), or as Judy Heumann stated, "To us, independence does not mean doing things physically alone. It means being able to make independent decisions. It is a mind process not contingent upon a 'normal' body . . . " (Nosek et al., 2015, p. 3). The Independent Living Movement was a reaction against the medical model and emphasized disability as an environmental limitation rather than an individual deficit (Frieden & Cole, 1985). With the 1978 Rehabilitation Act Amendments, Congress appropriated funds to establish independent-living programs across the country (Nosek & Smith, 1982; White et al., 2010). Independent-living programs, typically managed by people with disabilities, provide information, referrals, advocacy, counseling, independent-living skills training, and social/community outreach (Nguyen et al., 2019; Nosek & Smith, 1982). They are explicitly meant to help "individuals meet basic needs without the paternalistic involvement of well-meaning social agencies" (White et al., 2010, p. 238). The Disability Rights Education and Defense Fund, national civil rights law, and policy centers established in 1979 in Berkeley and Washington DC were outgrowths of the Independent Living Movement (Dolmage, 2017).

Yet, *legislation* coincident to these movements altered the learning environments of K–12 schools more than colleges and universities. The Rehabilitation Act of 1973 and the Education for All Handicapped Children Act (EHA) of 1975 established the foundations of K–12 special education by requiring states to provide children with disabilities (primarily deaf, blind, and "mentally retarded" children) a "free, appropriate education" in public schools rather than in separate institutions (Brown, 2000). EHA was reauthorized in 1997 as the Individuals with Disabilities Education Act (IDEA), initiating Individual Education Plans (IEPs), that is, individualized differentiation, for students with disability (Gil, 2007; Stodden & Whelley, 2004). Services for adolescents have expanded more recently (Leiter, 2012), with legislation on preparing adolescents for the transition into adulthood in the 1983 and 1990 Amendments to EHA and the IDEA Amendments of 1997 (Office of Special Education Programs, 2003). Providing aid in transitioning from secondary to higher education is also now a central focus of independent-living programs (Luftig & Muthert, 2005; Nguyen et al., 2019). The 1990 Americans with Disabilities Act (ADA) established civil rights for students with disabilities by prohibiting actions that deny them an "equal opportunity" to participate in educational programs or activities (Frieden, 2015; Simon, 2011). Although the ADA applies to higher education, it is interpreted in terms of physical accessibility.

In other words, institutes of higher education are still permitted to enact exclusion based on academic performance. Whereas access to the "student role" in K–12 schools is legally mandated for youth with disabilities, many institutions of higher education can legally prohibit access to the student role through standardized measures of "*merit*" (e.g., SAT/ACT scores, course attainment, course grades). For K–12 settings, Section 504 of the Rehabilitation Act of 1973 describes all youth of an educable age as eligible "qualified handicapped persons"; whereas in higher-education settings, that pool only includes young adults who meet "the academic and technical standards requisite to admission or participation in the recipients' education program or activity" ($104.3 (k)(3)) (Madaus & Shaw, 2004, p. 82).

Turner's (1960) depiction of the US education system as a sporting event is perhaps particularly evident in higher education. Public K–12 schools in the United States are at least ostensibly founded in a mission for the common good, "the American answer to the European welfare state, to massive waves of immigration, and to demands for the abolition of subordination based on race, class, or gender" (Hochschild & Scovronick, 2003, p. 9). In another example, whereas providing meals to lower SES students is institutionalized in K–12 schooling, undergraduates' lack of access to food and housing is increasingly documented (Broton & Goldrick-Rab, 2018). Turner (1960, p. 858) notes how Americans expend "special admiration for the slow starter who makes a dramatic finish." Dolmage (2014) similarly describes an "Overcoming or Compensation" disability myth, the "super crip." In this spirit, we extend extra resources to the slow starters so they can "compete for the final stakes" (Turner, 1960, p. 863). Higher education appears to be the "final stakes," when we become less generous with extra resources and begin sorting and selecting in earnest. Distinctions in the missions of higher education institutions relative to K–12 schools shape perceptions of who has merit and who is deserving of access to education.

The distinct missions of K–12 schools and colleges not only shape the qualities of the respective disabled populations, but also affect access to disability legitimacy and differentiation. We generally culturally perceive the transition from adolescence to adulthood as a transfer of *individual accountability* from adults around youths, to the youths themselves (Furstenberg, 2000). In the K–12 setting, teachers are the individuals primarily held accountable for the progress of students. For instance, teachers are increasingly ranked (sometimes publicly) on the basis of their students' test-score gains, despite widespread criticism that these approaches do not sufficiently account for structural influences on student learning (Morgan & Shackelford, 2018; Schneider et al., 2011; Shifrer, 2020). Teachers' specific accountability for students with disabilities was legislated through NCLB, which made the standardized test scores of students with disabilities part of schools' accountability ratings (Browder & Cooper-Duffy, 2003). With the shift in governance of disability services from IDEA in K–12 settings to the ADA in higher-education settings, accountability for legitimating disability shifts from schools to students (Gil, 2007; Madaus & Shaw, 2004; Stodden & Whelley, 2004). Approximately 60% of students with a disability diagnosis do not report it to their college (Burrelli, 2011; Higher Education Research Institute at UCLA, 2010; Newman & Madaus, 2015; Wagner et al., 2007). Undergraduates describe the legitimation process as costly, time consuming, and confusing (Leiter, 2012; Madaus et al., 2010; Weis et al., 2012). Moreover, earlier experiences with stigma and stratification may reduce undergraduates' willingness to disclose (Lehmann et al., 2000). Critical researchers describe the postsecondary emphasis on disability compliance, on meeting legal obligations, as indicative of a lack of real institutional commitment to supporting undergraduates with disabilities (Shallish, 2015; Simon, 2011; Voulgarides, 2018). The general demand for legitimation increases perceptions of disability services as an "unfair advantage" (Simon, 2011) and restricts the pool of undergraduates perceived as deserving of differentiation.

Nature of Differentiation in Higher Education

Tensions between disability and dominant educational ideals are also evident in the nature of differentiation in institutes of higher education, particularly relative to K–12 schools. Like disability legitimation, the *accountability* for securing and managing accommodations shifts from the school to individual students in the higher-education setting (Gil, 2007; Madaus & Shaw, 2004; Stodden & Whelley, 2004). Self-advocacy skills are frequently cited as essential for the success of undergraduates with disabilities (Lehmann et al., 2000; Morningstar et al., 2010; Mull et al., 2001; Roberts, 2010; Shaw et al., 2009; Trainor, 2008), and high schools are more often taxed with building these skills than colleges (Banks, 2014; Hitchings et al., 2005; Newman et al., 2016; Newman & Madaus, 2015; Trainor, 2008). Similarly, IDEA grants parents the right and responsibility to intervene on the behalf of their K–12 child with disability, but college records are only released to parents with student permission (Stodden & Whelley, 2004). Newman & Madaus (2015) find that only 23% of undergraduates who were in special education in high school receive accommodations once in higher education. Whereas schools and teachers are responsible for modifying the learning environment for K–12 students, individual students are accountable for securing differentiation and accommodations for their disabilities in higher education.

And then, undergraduates experience a more *standardized* level of accommodations, which typically involves less differentiation than what K–12 students with disability experience (Weis et al., 2016). The law specifically dictates that, unlike K–12 settings, accommodations in higher-education settings should not alter basic program or course requirements; expectations surrounding individualized services and devices are also lower in higher-education settings (Gil, 2007). Colleges, for instance, do not use IEPs, the documents that detail the individualized differentiation for each special-education student, and that shifts accountability to a community of adults instead of the student (Gil, 2007). Shallish (2015) describes a 2009 study that found that half of the nation's colleges reported limited staff resources for training in accessibility, as well as an institutional focus on priorities other than disability support. Turner (1960, p. 863) depicts universities in the United States as "run like the true contest: standards are set competitively, students are forced to pass a series of trials each semester, and only a minority of the entrants achieve the prize of graduation." Shallish (2015) argues that the "standardized focus on merit" in higher education more broadly fails to account for the diversifying population of learners.

Ironically, universal design, a dominant emphasis for inclusivity in higher education, can also be perceived as *standardized* differentiation. Universal design is based in the idea that the success of students with disabilities can be supported in ways that increase success for all students (Baglieri & Knopf, 2004; Basham et al., 2010; Basham & Marino, 2013; Izzo, 2012; Scott et al., 2003). Universally designed courses are clear and transparent, rely on multiple methods to deliver information and assess learning, accept diversity as the norm, and incorporate flexibility (Hong et al., 2007; Orr & Hammig, 2009; Scott et al., 2003). Universal design was a policy response to the IDEA Amendments of 1997 "stating that students with disabilities must be given the opportunity to be involved in and progress in the same general curriculum taught to all other students" (Orkwis & McLane, 1998, p. 3). And so proponents frame universal design as a social-justice effort aimed at facilitating mainstreaming rather than separation (Liasidou, 2014). Proponents also depict universal design as a shift from the medical to the social model of disability, with disability framed as individual deficit in the accommodations approach but as just one more aspect of student diversity in the universal design approach (Thornton & Downs, 2010).

In contrast to higher-education settings, pedagogical approaches like this have been prevalent in K–12 settings for decades, with "universal design" now nearly synonymous with special education. Problematically, faculty are often encouraged to embrace universal design while university disability centers simultaneously persist in the traditional medical-model approach (Thornton & Downs, 2010). And then, some use a disability-studies lens to argue that universal design does not sufficiently attend to the intersectional nature of diversity (Hamraie, 2013), nor to destabilizing broader power inequities (Liasidou, 2014). In many higher-education settings, there is no real focus on universal design, with faculty instead required to direct students to the disability center through a statement on their syllabus.

Finally, the higher-education emphasis on *merit* and *individual accountability* negatively impacts the social experiences of undergraduates with disabilities. Jack (2019) describes how youth with less privileged socioeconomic backgrounds not only have less access to higher education itself but also are barred access to the higher-education culture. The legislative and bureaucratic treatment of disability as a point of compliance rather than as an aspect of diversity relieves higher-education institutions of collective responsibility for ensuring the success of undergraduates with disability, or of fostering a climate that supports them as a diverse community (Shallish, 2015). Youth with disability are precluded from the sort of community-building efforts targeting other diverse youth (e.g., racial minorities, sexual minorities) (Shallish, 2015). From an intersectional perspective, the social barriers that undergraduates with disabilities face in higher-education settings are likely exacerbated for undergraduates with multiple marginalizing categories (Banks, 2014; Dowrick et al., 2005; Madaus et al., 2014).

College faculty are often unprepared to support students with disabilities. They already receive far less pedagogical training than K–12 teachers (Andersen & McCombs, 2017; Burgstahler et al., 2000), and likely no training in pedagogy for youth with disabilities (Bell, 2014; Burgstahler & Doe, 2006). With few mechanisms in place to assess the quality and continued growth of postsecondary instructors (Austin & Barnes, 2005) and with disability misunderstood or negatively stereotyped (Shallish, 2015), college faculty, especially more senior faculty, may even feel resentful at these relatively new expectations of accommodation and differentiation (Lehmann et al., 2000; Rickerson et al., 2004; Shallish, 2015).

Faculty relieve themselves of *individual accountability* for the success of undergraduates with disability and other diverse undergraduates by attributing undergraduate failure to their prior educational experiences (Shallish, 2015) or even to a lack of will and motivation, that is, a lack of merit. From a disability-studies lens, the higher-education emphasis on *merit* is an explicit masking of the transmission of privilege (Shallish, 2015), with ableism especially pernicious in academia and higher-education settings (Dolmage, 2014; Miles et al., 2017; Price, 2011). Just as disabled characters in movies are either "killed or cured" (Dolmage, 2014), our education system is structured so that youth with disability either conform to standardized measures of *merit* by higher education or exit the system.

CONCLUSION

This chapter outlines the structural underpinnings of the educational experiences of young adults with disability in the United States, drawing connections and distinctions along the trajectory from kindergarten through grade 12 and then into higher education. I integrate perspectives from disability studies, stratification theory, medical sociology, and critical special-education research with classic theory and empirical findings from sociology of education. After summarizing the main points of this chapter, this conclusion documents how sociologists of education can enrich their work through more frequent engagement with disability. This chapter contributes a theoretical framing for understanding disability in higher-education settings by integrating ideas from disability studies and classic sociology-of-education literature, particularly documenting tensions between disability ideology and dominant US educational ideals of *merit*, *individual accountability*, and *standardization*.

Social models of disability contest the individualized biological focus of medical models by demonstrating social causes of disability and even how the very idea of disability is a social construction. While the idea that people with disabilities are treated unfairly is straightforward, the notion of disability as socially constructed facilitates a more nuanced understanding of the social consequences of declaring some differences as disabilities, squarely centering the culpability for these consequences on social structure. Labeling theory, for instance, argues that the poorer outcomes of labeled persons are a function of the negative social correlates of the label itself rather than of individual differences. Disability, more specifically, represents a tension with US educational ideals of *merit*, *individual accountability*, and *standardization*. These tensions are particularly marked in higher-education settings, with a mission distinct from the mission of K–12 schools, and with a longer history of exclusion. These tensions are evident in how undergraduates are required to legitimize their disability and then in the nature of the differentiation they experience. In higher-education settings, individual accountability shifts from teachers and parents to the students themselves, the extent of differentiation is limited, and the emphasis on merit and ableism compounds the barriers that undergraduates with disability face.

This chapter advocates for nuance and moderation by highlighting the strengths and limitations of varying perspectives. Modified labeling theory, for instance, acknowledges the inherent rather than social struggle of some individual differences (e.g., physical pain, psychological pain) while still emphasizing the important contributions of social responses to difference. Intersectional theory points to how understanding stratification more broadly, and understanding the effects of specific categories more specifically, requires consideration of the entire matrix of oppression. Confirming multiple marginalization, empirical evidence shows that youth with disability disadvantaged along other status markers experience greater stratification and stigma than youth with disability advantaged along other status markers.

The theoretical richness and empirical rigor of sociology of education requires the more regular consideration of disability as a category of inequality. Stratification, tracking, and processes of sorting and labeling are of central interest to sociologists of education but are incompletely understood without a focus on how disability is interwoven in each of these processes. Students with disability represent a large and increasingly expanding minority group. More pressing, disability ideology is central in the social construction of the categories of class, race, gender, and sexuality, and in their legitimation and perpetuation (Shifrer & Frederick, 2019). By disregarding disability, our understanding of how class, race, gender, and sexuality continue to shape experiences within schools is undeveloped. From another perspective, the social institution of education is fundamental in the construction of disability ideology. Recognizing these mutually constitutive relationships is essential for more holistic understandings of both education and disability. Finally, studies of educational inequality should begin with intersectionality rather than including it as an afterthought or a less central nuance. For instance, investigations into the educational experiences of Black boys that do not include disability are simply inadequate, with disability ideology instrumental in the construction of the Black category and used in contemporary times to regulate perceptions of Black boys, as well as their social mobility.

In addition to contributing to research and theory, this chapter seeks to outline the practical and policy-relevant implications of intertwining ideas from disability studies with ideas from the sociologies of education and health. Disability is legitimated and perpetuated as a category of inequality through moral and biological attributions, dichotomization, and separation (Shifrer & Frederick, 2019). Practitioners and parents can disrupt the reproduction of disability as a category of inequality by recognizing that learning differences can simultaneously reflect neither immutable neurological differences nor moral failings. They can refute portrayals of disability classifications as markers of objective difference, or as indicators of low potential. Categories imply an objective, clear, and consistent delineation of human difference, which is almost never the truth. Moral and biological attributions are used to hierarchically organize categories, linking one side to ability, goodness, and worth, and the other side to inability, amorality, and unworthiness. In a seeming total rebuttal of these perspectives, categories are currently proliferating along other lines, like sexuality, gender, ethnicity. The difference may be in ownership. Some categories are applied and some are chosen. Youth labeled with disability must take ownership of their category. Question the validity of the category. Recognize that they are more complex and multidimensional than any one category. Take the information from the category that is useful and leave the rest. Never let the category determine their destiny.

ACKNOWLEDGMENTS

This chapter was supported by the National Science Foundation (DRL-1652279) and the National Institutes of Health funded Build EXITO program at Portland State University (UL1GM118964). This chapter benefits from previous collaborations with and targeted suggestions from Drs. Laura Mauldin, Angela Frederick, Rachel Fish, and Jennifer Pearson.

NOTES

1. Respecting varying language preferences in disability communities, I alternate between person-first language (people with disabilities) and identity-first language (disabled people) throughout this article.
2. Federal statistics are not disaggregated more specifically than ages 3 to 21. With this federal report's focus on students covered by IDEA, Part B, which does not apply in higher-education settings, the youth aged 18 to 21 included in this count are not in college.
3. K–12 students with ADHD qualify for special-education services through the federal disability category Other Health Impairment, but this category is also used for other disabilities or illnesses like epilepsy. Although youth with ADHD are also more likely than youth with

other disabilities to receive less intensive services through Section 504 (Harrison et al., 2007), rates of participation in Section 504 are even less well documented than rates of participation in special education.
4. Differentiation has a specific meaning to special education practitioners (Iris Center, 2020). While "differentiated instruction" describes the more general practice of varying and adapting instruction based on students' individual needs (e.g., flexible grouping, immediate feedback), "accommodations" describe the specific supports special-education students receive in order to access the general education curriculum. "Modifications," in contrast involve actual changes to the general education content or expectations. This chapter uses "differentiation" more theoretically and broadly to reference any attempts made to meet the individual needs of students with disabilities.

REFERENCES

Altman, B. M. (2016). Conceptual issues in disability: Saad Nagi's contribution to the disability knowledge base. In S. Green & S. Barnartt (Eds.), *Research in social science and disability (Volume 9: Sociology looking at disability: What did we know and when did we know it)* (pp. 57–95). Emerald Group Publishing.

Altman, B. M., & Barnartt, S. N. (2000). Introducing research in social science and disability: An invitation to social science to "get it." In B. M. Altman & S. N. Barnartt (Eds.), *Research in social science and disability (Volume 1: Expanding the scope of social science research on disability)* (pp. 1–30). Emerald Group Publishing.

Ambrosio, J. (2013). Changing the subject: Neoliberalism and accountability in public education. *Educational Studies, 49*(4), 316–333.

American Psychiatric Association. (2000). *Diagnostic and statistical manual of mental disorders, fourth edition.* American Psychiatric Association.

Andersen, C., & McCombs, M. (2017). *When data are not enough: Barriers to broadening participation of STEM students with disabilities.* Accelerating systemic change in STEM higher education. https://ascnhighered.org/ASCN/SMTI_ASCN_2017/when_data.html

Annamma, S. A., Jackson, D. D., & Morrison, D. (2017). Conceptualizing color-evasiveness: Using dis/ability critical race theory to expand a color-blind racial ideology in education and society. *Race Ethnicity and Education, 20*(2), 147–162.

Anyon, Y. (2009). Sociological theories of learning disabilities: Understanding racial disproportionality in special education. *Journal of Human Behavior in the Social Environment, 19*(1), 44–57.

Austin, A. E., & Barnes, B. J. (2005). Preparing doctoral students for faculty careers that contribute to the public good. In A. Kezar, A. C. Chambers, & J, C. Burkhardt (Eds.), *Higher Education for the Public Good: Emerging Voices from a National Movement* pp. 272–292). Wiley.

Baglieri, S., & Knopf, J. H. (2004). Normalizing difference in inclusive teaching. *Journal of Learning Disabilities, 37*(6), 525–529.

Ball, S. J. (2016). Neoliberal education? Confronting the slouching beast. *Policy Futures in Education, 14*(8), 1046–1059.

Banks, J. (2014). Barriers and supports to postsecondary transition: Case studies of African American students with disabilities. *Remedial and Special Education, 35*(1), 28–39.

Basham, J. D., Israel, M., & Maynard, K. (2010). An ecological model of STEM education: Operationalizing STEM for all. *Journal of Special Education Technology, 25*(3), 9–19.

Basham, J. D., & Marino, M. T. (2013). Understanding STEM education and supporting students through universal design for learning. *Teaching Exceptional Children, 45*(4), 8–15.

Bell, A. V. (2014). Diagnostic diversity: The role of social class in diagnostic experiences of infertility. *Sociology of Health & Illness, 36*(4), 516–530.

Bender, W. N., & Wall, M. E. (1994). Social-emotional development of students with learning disabilities. *Learning Disability Quarterly, 17*(4), 323–341.

Blanchett, W. J. (2006). Disproportionate representation of African American students in special education: Acknowledging the role of white privilege and racism. *Educational Researcher, 35*(6), 24–28.

Blanchett, W. J. (2010). Telling it like it is: The role of race, class, and culture in the perpetuation of learning disability as a privileged category for the White middle class. *Disability Studies Quarterly, 30*(2), 1–13. http://dsq-sds.org/article/view/1233/1280

Blum, L. M. (2015). *Raising generation RX: Mothering kids with invisible disabilities in an age of inequality.* New York University Press.

Bradley, E. A., & Isaacs, B. J. (2006). Inattention, hyperactivity, and impulsivity in teenagers with intellectual disabilities, with and without autism. *Canadian Journal of Psychiatry, 51,* 598–606.

Broton, K. M., & Goldrick-Rab, S. (2018). Going without: An exploration of food and housing insecurity among undergraduates. *Educational Researcher, 47*(2), 121–133.

Browder, D. M., & Cooper-Duffy, K. (2003). Evidence-based practices for students with severe disabilities and the requirement for accountability in "No Child Left Behind." *Journal of Special Education, 37*(3), 157–163.

Brown, S. E. (2000). Zona and Ed Roberts: Twentieth century pioneers. *Disability Studies Quarterly, 20*(1), 26–42.

Bureau of Labor Statistics. (2017). *Persons with a disability: Labor force characteristics summary.* https://www.bls.gov/news.release/disabl.nr0.htm

Burgstahler, S., & Doe, T. (2006). Improving postsecondary outcomes for students with disabilities: Designing professional development for faculty. *Journal of Postsecondary Education and Disability, 18*(2), 135–47.

Burgstahler, S., Duclos, R., & Turcotte, M. (2000). *Preliminary findings: Faculty, teaching assistant, and student perceptions regarding accommodating students with disabilities in postsecondary environment.* ERIC Clearinghouse on Disabilities and Gifted Education.

Burrelli, J. (2011). *What the data show about students with disabilities in STEM.* Division of Science Resources Statistics, National Science Foundation.

Campbell, F. K. (2009). *Contours of ableism: The production of disability and abledness.* Palgrave Macmillan.

Carrier, J. G. (1983). Masking the social in educational knowledge: The case of learning disability theory. *The American Journal of Sociology, 88*(5), 948–974.

Centers for Disease Control and Prevention. (2009). Prevalence and most common causes of disability among adults—United States, 2005. *Morbidity and Mortality Weekly Report, 58*(16), 421–426.

Coleman, J. S. (1990). *Equality and achievement in education.* Westview Press.

Collins, P. H. (1999). Learning from the outsider within: The sociological significance of Black feminist thought. In S. Hesse-Biber, C. Gilmartin, & R. Lydenberg (Eds.), *Feminist approaches to theory and methodology: An interdisciplinary reader* (pp. 155–178). Oxford University Press.

Collins, R. (1971). Functional and conflict theories of educational stratification. *American Sociological Review, 36*(6), 1002–1019.

Conrad, P. (1992). Medicalization and social control. *Annual Review of Sociology, 18,* 209–232.

Crenshaw, K. W. (1989). Demarginalizing the intersection of race and sex: A Black feminist critique of antidiscrimination doctrine, feminist theory, and antiracist politics. *University of Chicago Legal Forum, 1989*, 139–167.

Crenshaw, K. W. (1991). Mapping the margins: Intersectionality, identity politics, and violence against women of color. *Stanford Law Review, 43*(6), 1241–1299.

Dolmage, J. T. (2014). *Disability rhetoric.* Syracuse University Press.

Dolmage, J. T. (2017). *Academic ableism: Disability and higher education.* University of Michigan Press.

Donfrancesco, R., Mugnaini, D., & Dell'Uomo, A. (2005). Cognitive impulsivity in specific learning disabilities. *European Child & Adolescent Psychiatry, 14*(5), 270–275.

Donovan, M. S., & Cross, C. T. (2002). *Minority students in special and gifted education.* National Research Council, National Academies Press.

Dowrick, P. W., Anderson, J., Heyer, K., & Acosta, J. (2005). Postsecondary education across the USA: Experiences of adults with disabilities. *Journal of Vocational Rehabilitation, 22*(1), 41–47.

Drescher, J. (2015). Out of DSM: Depathologizing homosexuality. *Behavioral Sciences, 5,* 565–575.

Dudley-Marling, C. (2004). The social construction of learning disabilities. *Journal of Learning Disabilities, 37*(6), 482–489.

Eitle, T. M. (2002). Special education or racial segregation: Understanding variation in the representation of Black students in educable mentally handicapped programs. *The Sociological Quarterly, 43*(4), 575–605.

Elder, T. E., Figlio, D. N., Imberman, S. A., & Persico, C. L. (2019). *School segregation and racial gaps in special education identification (working paper 25829).* National Bureau of Economic Research.

Erevelles, N. (1996). Disability and the dialectics of difference. *Disability & Society, 11*(4), 519–537.

Erevelles, N. (2000). Educating unruly bodies: Critical pedagogy, disability studies, and the politics of schooling. *Educational Theory, 50*(1), 25–47.

Erevelles, N., & Minear, A. (2010). Unspeakable offenses: Untangling race and disability in discourses of intersectionality. *Journal of Literary & Cultural Disability Studies, 4*(2), 127–145.

Eyal, G. (2013). For a sociology of expertise: The social origins of the autism epidemic. *American Journal of Sociology, 118*(4), 863–907.

Ferri, B. A., & Connor, D. J. (2005). In the shadow of Brown: Special education and overrepresentation of students of color. *Remedial and Special Education, 26*(2), 93–100.

Fish, R. (2017). The racialized construction of exceptionality: Experimental evidence of race/ethnicity effects on teachers' interventions. *Social Science Research, 62,* 317–334.

Fish, R. E. (2019). Standing out and sorting in: Exploring the role of racial composition in racial disparities in special education. *American Educational Research Journal, 56*(6):2573–2608.

Fletcher, J. M., Denton, C., & Francis, D. J. (2005). Validity of alternative approaches for the identification of learning disabilities: Operationalizing unexpected underachievement. *Journal of Learning Disabilities, 38*(6), 545–552.

Frieden, L. (2015). *The impact of the ADA in American communities.* The University of Texas Health Science Center at Houston.

Frieden, L., & Cole, J. A. (1985). Independence: The ultimate goal of rehabilitation for spinal cord-injured persons. *The American Journal of Occupational Therapy, 39*(1), 734–739.

Fuchs, L. S., Fuchs, D., Eaton, S. B., Hamlett, C., Binkley, E., & Crouch, R. (2000). Using objective data sources to enhance teacher judgments about test accommodations. *Exceptional Children, 67*(1), 67–81.

Furstenberg, F. F., Jr. (2000). The sociology of adolescence and youth in the 1990s: A critical commentary. *Journal of Marriage and Family, 62*(4), 896–910.

Gamoran, A., & Long, D. A. (2006). *Equality of educational opportunity: A 40-year retrospective (WCER working paper no. 2006-9)*. University of Wisconsin-Madison.

Gil, L. A. (2007). Bridging the transition gap from high school to college. *Teaching Exceptional Children, 40*(2), 12–15.

Goffman, E. (1963). *Stigma: Notes on the management of spoiled identity*. Prentice-Hall.

Goode, D., Hill, D. B., Reiss, J., & Bronston, W. (2013). *History and sociology of the Willowbrook State School*. American Association of Intellectual and Developmental Disabilities.

Gordon, B. O., & Rosenblum, K. E. (2001). Bringing disability into the sociological frame: A comparison of disability with race, sex, and sexual orientation statuses. *Disability & Society, 16*(1), 5–19.

Gresham, F. M. (1992). Social skills and learning disabilities: Causal, concomitant, or correlational? *School Psychology Review, 21*(3), 348–360.

Haber, M. G., Mazzotti, V. L., Mustian, A. L., Rowe, D. A., Bartholomew, A. L., Test, D. W., & Fowler, C. H. (2016). What works, when, for whom, and with whom: A meta-analytic review of predictors of postsecondary success for students with disabilities. *Review of Educational Research, 86*(1), 123–162.

Hamraie, A. (2013). Designing collective access: A feminist disability theory of universal design. *Disability Studies Quarterly, 33*(4).

Hancock, A.-M. (2007). When multiplication doesn't equal quick addition: Examining intersectionality as a research paradigm. *Perspectives on Politics, 5*(1), 63–79.

Hanushek, E. A., Kain, J. F., & Rivkin, S. G. (2002). Inferring program effects for specialized populations: Does special education raise achievement for students with disabilities. *Review of Economics and Statistics, 84*(4), 584–599.

Harrison, A. G., Edwards, M. J., & Parker, K. C. H. (2007). Identifying students faking ADHD: Preliminary findings and strategies for detection. *Archives of Clinical Neuropsychology, 22*(5), 577–588.

Hart, D., Grigal, M., & Weir, C. (2010). Expanding the paradigm: Postsecondary education options for individuals with autism spectrum disorder and intellectual disabilities. *Focus on Autism and Other Developmental Disabilities, 25*(3), 134–150.

Hibel, J., Farkas, G., & Morgan, P. L. (2010). Who is placed into special education? *Sociology of Education, 83*(4), 312–332.

Higbee, J. L., & Katz, R. E. (2010). Disability in higher education: Redefining mainstreaming. *Journal of Diversity Management, 5*(2), 7–16.

Higher Education Research Institute at UCLA. (2010). *Degrees of success: Bachelor's degree completion rates among initial STEM majors*. Higher Education Research Institute at UCLA.

Hill Collins, P., & Bilge, S. (2016). *Intersectionality*. Polity.

Hill, H. C. (2016). 50 years ago, one report introduced Americans to the Black-White achievement gap. Here's what we've learned since. Chalkbeat.

Hinz, S., Arbeit, C. A., & Bentz, A. (2017). *Characteristics and outcomes of undergraduates with disabilities (NCES 2018-432)*. National Center for Education Statistics, Institute of Education Sciences.

Hitchings, W. E., Retish, P., & Horvath, M. (2005). Academic preparation of adolescents with disabilities for postsecondary education. *Career Development For Exceptional Individuals, 28*(1), 26–35.

Ho, A. (2004). To be labeled, or not to be labeled: That is the question. *British Journal of Learning Disabilities*, 32(2), 86–92.

Hochschild, J., & Scovronick, N. (2003). *The American Dream and the Public Schools* (pp. 9–27). Oxford Press.

Hong, B. S. S., Ivy, W. F., Gonzalez, H. R., & Ehrensberger, W. (2007). Preparing students for postsecondary education. *Teaching Exceptional Children*, 40, 32–38.

Hurwitz, S., Perry, B., Cohen, E. D., & Skiba, R. (2020). Special education and individualized academic growth: A longitudinal assessment of outcomes for students with disabilities. *American Educational Research Journal*, 57(2), 576–611.

Idol, L. (2006). Toward inclusion of special education students in general education: A program evaluation of eight schools. *Remedial and Special Education*, 27(2), 77–94.

Iris Center. (2020). *To meet the needs of the widest range of students, what should teachers consider when planning their instruction?* Nashville, TN: Vanderbilt University.

Izzo, M. V. (2012). Universal design for learning: Enhancing achievement of students with disabilities. *Procedia Computer Science*, 14, 343–350.

Jack, A. A. (2019). *The privileged poor: How elite colleges are failing disadvantaged students.* Harvard University Press.

Jenkins, R. (1998). Towards a social model of (in)competence. In R. Jenkins (Ed.), *Questions of competence: Culture, classification and intellectual disability* (pp. 222–230). Cambridge University Press.

Johnson, A. H. (2019). Rejecting, reframing, and reintroducing: Trans people's strategic engagement with the medicalisation of gender dysphoria. *Sociology of Health & Illness*, 41(3), 517–532.

Katsiyannis, A., Zhang, D., Landmark, L., & Reber, A. (2009). Postsecondary education for individuals with disabilities: Legal and practice considerations. *Journal of Disability Policy Studies*, 20(1), 35–45.

King, M. D., & Bearman, P. S. (2011). Socioeconomic status and the increased prevalence of autism in California. *American Sociological Review*, 76(2), 320–346.

King, M. D., Jennings, J., & Fletcher, J. (2014). Medical adaptation to academic pressure: Schooling, stimulant use, and socioeconomic status. *American Sociological Review*, 79(6), 1039–1066.

Klingner, J. K., & Harry, B. (2006). The special education referral and decision-making process for English language learners: Child study team meetings and placement conferences. *Teachers College Record*, 108(11), 2247–2281.

Kokanovic, R., Bendelow, G., & Philip, B. (2013). Depression: The ambivalence of diagnosis. *Sociology of Health & Illness*, 35(3), 377–390.

Konkel, L. (2012, June 6). Pollution, poverty and people of color: Children at risk. *Scientific American*. https://www.scientificamerican.com/article/pollution-poverty-people-color-living-industry/

Kullman, K. (2019). Politics of dissensus in geographics of architecture: Testing equality at Ed Roberts Campus, Berkeley. *Transactions of the Institute of British Geographers*, 44, 284–298.

Lehmann, J. P., Davies, T. G., & Laurin, K. M. (2000). Listening to student voices about postsecondary education. *Teaching Exceptional Children*, 32(5), 60–65.

Leiter, V. (2012). *Their time has come: Youth with disabilities on the cusp of adulthood.* Rutgers University Press.

Liasidou, A. (2014). Critical disability studies and socially just change in higher education. *British Journal of Special Education*, 41(2), 120–135.

Link, B. G., Cullen, F. T., Struening, E., Shrout, P. E., & Dohrenwend, B. P. (1989). A Modified Labeling theory approach to mental disorders: An empirical assessment. *American Sociological Review*, 54(3), 400–423.

Liu, K.-Y., King, M., & Bearman, P. S. (2010). Social influence and the autism epidemic. *American Journal of Sociology*, 115(5), 1387–1434.

Lovett, B. J. (2020). Disability identification and educational accommodations: Lessons from the 2019 admissions scandal. *Educational Researcher*, 49(2), 125–129.

LoVullo, S. V., & Matson, J. L. (2009). Comorbid psychopathology in adults with autism spectrum disorders and intellectual disabilities. *Research in Developmental Disabilities*, 30(6), 1288–1296.

Luftig, R. L., & Muthert, D. (2005). Patterns of employment and independent living of adult graduates with learning disabilities and mental retardation of an inclusionary high school vocational program. *Research in Developmental Disabilities*, 26, 317–325.

Madaus, J. W., Banerjee, M., & Hamblet, E. C. (2010). Learning disability documentation decision making at the postsecondary level. *Career Development For Exceptional Individuals*, 33(2), 68–79.

Madaus, J. W., Grigal, M., & Hughes, C. (2014). Promoting access to postsecondary education for low-income students with disabilities. *Career Development and Transition for Exceptional Individuals*, 37(1), 50–59.

Madaus, J. W., & Shaw, S. F. (2004). Section 504: Differences in the regulations for secondary and postsecondary educators. *Intervention in School and Clinic*, 40(2), 81–87.

Margai, F., & Henry, N. (2003). A community-based assessment of learning disabilities using environmental and contextual risk factors. *Social Science & Medicine*, 56(5), 1073–1085.

Maroto, M., & Pettinicchio, D. (2015). Twenty-five years after the ADA: Situating disability in America's system of stratification. *Disability Studies Quarterly*, 35(3), 1–34.

Maroto, M., Pettinicchio, D., & Patterson, A. C. (2019). Hierarchies of categorical disadvantage: Economic insecurity at the intersection of disability, gender, and race. *Gender & Society*, 33(1), 64–93.

Martin, J. K., Pescosolido, B. A., Olafsdottir, S., & McLeod, J. D. (2007). The construction of fear: Americans' preferences for social distance from children and adolescents with mental health problems. *Journal of Health and Social Behavior*, 48(1), 50–67.

Matson, J. L., Mahan, S., Hess, J. A., & Fodstad, J. C. (2010). Effect of developmental quotient on symptoms of inattention and impulsivity among toddlers with autism spectrum disorders. *Research in Developmental Disabilities*, 31(2), 464–469.

Mayes, S. D., Calhoun, S. L., & Crowell, E. W. (2000). Learning disabilities and ADHD: Overlapping spectrum disorders. *Journal of Learning Disabilities*, 33(5), 417–424.

McCall, L. (2005). The complexity of intersectionality. *Signs: Journal of Women in Culture and Society*, 30(3), 1771–1800.

McDermott, R., Goldman, S., & Varenne, H. (2006). The cultural work of learning disabilities. *Educational Researcher*, 35(6), 12–17.

McFarland, J., Hussar, B., Zhang, J., Wang, K., Hein, S., Diliberti, M., Cataldi, E. F., Mann, F. B., & Barmer, A. (2019). *The condition of education 2019 (NCES 2019-144)*. National Center for Education Statistics, US Department of Education.

McGann, P. (2011). Troubling Diagnoses. In P. McGann & D. J. Hutson (Eds.), *Advances in medical sociology: Sociology of diagnosis* (Vol. 12, pp. 331–362). Emerald.

Mehan, H., Hertweck, A., & Meihls, J. L. (1986). *Handicapping the handicapped: Decision making in students' educational careers*. Stanford University Press.

Miles, A. L., Nishida, A., & Forber-Pratt, A. J. (2017). An open letter to White disability studies and ableist institutions of higher education. *Disability Studies Quarterly, 37*(3).

Moore, Jr., L. F., Lewis, T. A., & Brown, L. X. Z. (2018). *Accountable reporting on disability, race, and police violence: Community response to the "Ruderman white paper on the media coverage of use of force and disability"*. Harriet Tubman Collective, Inc.

Morgan, P. L., Frisco, M., Farkas, G., & Hibel, J. (2010). A propensity score matching analysis of the effects of special education services. *The Journal of Special Education, 43*(4), 236–254.

Morgan, S. L., & Shackelford, D. T. (2018). School and teacher effects. In B. Schneider (Ed.), *Handbook of the sociology of education in the 21st century* (pp. 513–534). Springer International Publishing.

Morningstar, M. E., Frey, B. B., Noonan, P. M., Ng, J., Clavenna-Deane, B., Graves, P., Kellems, R., McCall, Z., Pearson, M., Wade, D. B., & Williams-Diehm, K. (2010). A preliminary investigation of the relationship of transition preparation and self-determination for students with disabilities in postsecondary educational settings. *Career Development for Exceptional Individuals, 33*(2), 80–94.

Mull, C., Sitlington, P. L., & Alper, S. (2001). Postsecondary education for students with learning disabilities: A synthesis of the literature. *Exceptional Children, 68*(1), 97–118.

Naples, N. A., Mauldin, L., & Dillaway, H. (2019). From the guest editors: Gender, disability, and intersectionality. *Gender & Society, 33*(1), 5–18.

National Center for Education Statistics. (2000). *Postsecondary students with disabilities: Enrollment, services, and persistence*. Institute for Educational Sciences.

Newman, L. A., & Madaus, J. W. (2015). An analysis of factors related to receipt of accommodations and services by postsecondary students with disabilities. *Remedial and Special Education, 36*(4), 208–219.

Newman, L. A., Madaus, J. W., & Javitz, H. S. (2016). Effect of transition planning on postsecondary support receipt by students with disabilities. *Exceptional Children, 82*(4), 497–514.

Nguyen, V., Limlek, I., & Frieden, L. (2019). *Knowledge and capacity of Centers for Independent Living on providing training and technical assistance on the Americans with Disabilities Act*. Southwest ADA Center, TIRR Memorial Hermann-ILRU.

Nosek, P., Narita, Y., Dart, Y., & Dart, J. (2015). *A philosophical foundation for the Independent Living & Disability Rights movements*. The Independent Living Research Utilization Project.

Nosek, P., & Smith, Q. (1982). *On the right track: Foundations for operating an independent living program*. The Independent Living Research Utilization Project.

Nuttall, M. (1998). States and categories: Indigenous models of personhood in northwest Greenland. In R. Jenkins (Ed.), *Questions of competence: Culture, classification and intellectual disability* (pp. 176–193). Cambridge University Press.

Office of Special Education Programs. (2003). *History: 25 years of progress in educating children with disabilities through IDEA*. Office of Special Education and Rehabilitative Services, U.S. Department of Education.

Ong-Dean, C. (2006). High roads and low roads: Learning disabilities in California, 1976–1998. *Sociological Perspectives, 49*(1), 91–113.

Ong-Dean, C. (2009). *Distinguishing disability: Parents, privilege, and special education*. University of Chicago Press.

Orkwis, R., & McLane, K. (1998). *A curriculum every student can use: Design principles for student access (ERIC/OSEP Topical Brief No. ED423654)*. The ERIC Clearinghouse on Disabilities and Gifted Education, The Council for Exceptional Children.

Orr, A. C., & Hammig, S. B. (2009). Inclusive postsecondary strategies for teaching students with learning disabilities: A review of the literature. *Learning Disability Quarterly*, 32(1), 181–196.

Pescosolido, B. A., & Martin, J. K. (2007). Stigma and the sociological enterprise. In W. R. Avison, J. D. McLeod, & B. A. Pescosolido (Eds.), *Mental health, social mirror* (pp. 307–328). Springer Science+Business Media, LLC.

Plotner, A. J., & Marshall, K. J. (2014). Navigating university policies to support postsecondary education programs for students with intellectual disabilities. *Journal of Disability Policy Studies*, 25(1), 48–58.

Price, M. (2011). *Mad at school: Rhetorics of mental disability and academic life*. University of Michigan Press.

Proctor, B. E., Prevatt, F. F., Adams, K. S., Reaser, A., & Petscher, Y. (2006). Study skills profiles of normal-achieving and academically-struggling college students. *Journal of College Student Development*, 47(1), 37–51.

Raue, K., & Lewis, L. (2011). *Students with disabilities at degree-granting postsecondary institutions (NCES 2011-018)*. U.S. Department of Education, National Center for Education Statistics. Washington DC: US Government Printing Office.

Ravitch, D. (2011). *The death and life of the great American school system: How testing and choice are undermining education*. Basic Books.

Reid, D. K., & Knight, M. G. (2006). Disability justifies exclusion of minority students: A critical history grounded in disability studies. *Educational Researcher*, 35(6), 18–23.

Rickerson, N., Burgstahler, S., & Souma, A. (2004). *Psychiatric disabilities in postsecondary education: Universal design, accommodations and supported education*. National Center on Secondary Education and Transition, University of Hawaii at Manoa.

Roberts, K. D. (2010). Topic areas to consider when planning transition from high school to postsecondary education for students with autism spectrum disorders. *Focus on Autism and Other Developmental Disabilities*, 25(3), 158–162.

RTI Action Network. (2020). *What is RTI?* National Center for Learning Disabilities. http://www.rtinetwork.org/learn/what/whatisrti

Saatcioglu, A., & Skrtic, T. M. (2019). Categorization by organizations: Manipulation of disability categories in a racially desegregated school district. *American Journal of Sociology*, Published online first.

Schneider, B., Grogan, E., & Maier, A. (2011). Improving teacher quality: A sociological presage. In M. T. Hallinan (Ed.), *Frontiers in sociology of education, frontiers in sociology and social research* (Vol. 1, pp. 163–180). Springer.

Schwartz, A. E., Hopkins, B. G., & Stiefel, L. (2019). *The effects of special education on the academic performance of students with learning disabilities (Ed WorkingPaper No. 19-86)*. Annenberg Institute for School Reform, Brown University.

Scott, S. S., Mcguire, J. M., & Shaw, S. F. (2003). Universal design for instruction: A new paradigm for adult instruction in postsecondary education. *Remedial and Special Education*, 24(6), 369–379.

Serano, J. (2007). *Whipping girl: A transsexual woman on sexism and the scapegoating of femininity*. Seal Press.

Shakespeare, T. (2006). *Disability rights and wrongs*. Routledge.

Shallish, L. (2015). Just how much diversity will the law permit?': The Americans with disabilities act, diversity, and disability in higher education. *Disability Studies Quarterly*, 35(3), 8.

Shaw, S. F., Madaus, J. W., & Banerjee, M. (2009). 20 ways to enhance access to postsecondary education for students with disabilities. *Intervention in School and Clinic*, *44*(3), 185–190.

Shifrer, D. (2013a). Meritocracy. In J. Ainsworth (Ed.), *Sociology of education: an A-to-Z guide*. SAGE Publications. https://sk.sagepub.com/reference/sociology-of-education

Shifrer, D. (2013b). Stigma of a label: Educational expectations for high school students labeled with a learning disability. *Journal of Health and Social Behavior*, *54*(4), 462–480.

Shifrer, D. (2016). Stigma and stratification limiting the math course progression of adolescents labeled with a learning disability. *Learning and Instruction*, *42*(1), 47–57.

Shifrer, D. (2018). Clarification of the social roots of the disproportionate labeling of racial minorities and males with learning disabilities. *The Sociological Quarterly*, *59*(3), 384–406.

Shifrer, D. (2020). Contextualizing educational disparities and the evaluation of teacher quality. *Social Problems*. https://academic.oup.com/socpro/advance-article-abstract/doi/10.1093/socpro/spaa044/5957219?redirectedFrom=fulltext.

Shifrer, D., Callahan, R., & Muller, C. (2013). Equity or marginalization? The high school course-taking of students labeled with a learning disability. *American Educational Research Journal*, *50*(4), 656–682.

Shifrer, D., & Fish, R. E. (2020). Contextual reliability in the designation of cognitive health conditions among U.S. children. *Society and Mental Health*, *10*(2), 180–197.

Shifrer, D., & Frederick, A. (2019). Disability at the intersections. *Sociology Compass*, *13*(e12733), 1–16.

Shifrer, D., Muller, C., & Callahan, R. (2011). Disproportionality and learning disabilities: Parsing apart race, socioeconomic status, and language. *Journal of Learning Disabilities*, *44*(3), 246–257.

Shonkoff, J. P., & Phillips, D. A. (2000). *From neurons to neighborhoods: The science of early childhood development*. National Research Council and Institute of Medicine, National Academies.

Simon, J. A. (2011). Legal issues in serving students with disabilities in postsecondary education. *New Directions for Student Services*, *134*, 95–107.

Skiba, R., Simmons, A., Ritter, S., Kohler, K., Henderson, M., & Wu, T. (2006). The context of minority disproportionality: Practitioner perspectives on special education referral. *Teachers College Record*, *108*(7), 1424–1459.

Sleeter, C. E. (2010). Why is there learning disabilities? A critical analysis of the birth of the field in its social context. *Disability Studies Quarterly*, *30*(2), 210–237.

Sleeter, C. E., & Carmona, J. F. (2017). *Un-standardizing curriculum: Multicultural teaching in the standards-based classroom*. Teachers College Press.

Snyder, T. D., De Brey, C., & Dillow, S. A. (2019). *Digest of education statistics 2018 (NCES 2020-009)*. National Center for Education Statistics, Institute of Education Sciences, U.S. Department of Education.

Society for Disability Studies. (2016). *What is disability studies?* https://disstudies.org/index.php/about-sds/what-is-disability-studies/

Sommo, A., & Chaskes, J. (2013). Intersectionality and the disability: Some conceptual and methodological challenges. In *Research in social science and disability (Volume 7: Disability and intersecting statuses)* (pp. 47–59). Emerald Group Publishing Limited.

Spellings, M., Knudsen, W. W., & Guard, P. J. (2007). *27th annual (2005) report to Congress on the implementation of the Individuals with Disabilities Education Act* (Vol. 1). Office of Special Education Programs, Office of Special Education and Rehabilitative Services, US Department of Education.

Stanford, L. D., & Hynd, G. W. (1994). Congruence of behavioral symptomatology in children with ADD/H, ADD/WO, and learning disabilities. *Journal of Learning Disabilities*, *27*(4), 243–253.

Stodden, R. A., & Whelley, T. (2004). Postsecondary education and persons with intellectual disabilities: An introduction. *Education and Training in Developmental Disabilities*, 39(1), 6–15.

Sullivan, A. L., Artiles, A. J., & Hernandez-Saca, D. I. (2014). Addressing special education inequity through systemic change: Contributions of ecologically based organizational consultation. *Journal of Educational and Psychological Consultation*, 25, 1–19.

Tenenbaum, H. R., & Ruck, M. D. (2007). Are teachers' expectations different for racial minority than for European American students? A meta-analysis. *Journal of Educational Psychology*, 99(2), 253–273.

Thompson, M., Wilkinson, L., & Woo, H. (2020). Social characteristics as predictors of ADHD labeling across the life course. *Society and Mental Health*, 11(2), 91–112.

Thornton, M., & Downs, S. (2010). Practice brief—Walking the walk: Modeling social model and universal design in the disabilities office. *Journal of Postsecondary Education and Disability*, 23(1), 72–78.

Trainor, A. A. (2008). Using cultural and social capital to improve postsecondary outcomes and expand transition models for youth with disabilities. *The Journal of Special Education*, 42(3), 148–162.

Turner, R. H. (1960). Sponsored and contest mobility and the school system. *American Sociological Review*, 25(6), 855–867.

U.S. Government Printing Office. (2010). *S. 2781 (111th): Rosa's Law*. https://www.govtrack.us/congress/bills/111/s2781/text

Vallee, M. (2011). Resisting American psychiatry: French opposition to *DSM-III*, biological reductionism, and the pharmaceutical ethos. In P. McGann & D. J. Hutson (Eds.), *Advances in medical sociology: Sociology of diagnosis* (Vol. 12, pp. 85–110). Emerald.

Vanheule, S. (2012). Diagnosis in the field of psychotherapy: A plea for an alternative to the DSM-5.x. *The British Psychological Society*, 85, 128–142.

Vellutino, F. R., Fletcher, J. M., Snowling, M. J., & Scanlon, D. M. (2004). Specific reading disability (dyslexia): What have we learned in the past four decades? *Journal of Child Psychology and Psychiatry*, 45(1), 2–40.

Voulgarides, C. K. (2018). Does compliance matter in special education? IDEA and the hidden inequities of practice. In A. J. Artiles & E. B. Kozleski (Eds.), *Disability, Culture, and Equity Series*. Teachers College Press.

Wagner, M., Newman, L., Cameto, R., Levine, P., & Marder, C. (2007). *Perceptions and expectations of youth with disabilities: A special topic report of findings from the National Longitudinal Transition Study-2 (NLTS2) (NCSER 2007-3006)*. SRI International.

Weis, R., Dean, E. L., & Osborne, K. J. (2016). Accommodation decision making for postsecondary students with learning disabilities: Individually tailored or one size fits all? *Journal of Learning Disabilities*, 49(5), 484–498.

Weis, R., Sykes, L., & Unadkat, D. (2012). Qualitative differences in learning disabilities across postsecondary institutions. *Journal of Learning Disabilities*, 45(6), 491–502.

White, G. W., Simpson, J. L., Gonda, C., Ravesloot, C., & Coble, Z. (2010). Moving from independence to interdependence: A conceptual model for better understanding community participation of centers for independent living consumers. *Journal of Disability Policy Studies*, 20(4), 233–240.

Wolbring, G. (2008). The politics of ableism. *Development*, 51, 252–258.

....

CHAPTER 18

VOCATIONAL REHABILITATION AND EMPLOYMENT OUTCOMES

....

FABRICIO E. BALCAZAR AND NORMA RAMIREZ

INTRODUCTION

....

HISTORICALLY, individuals with disabilities have experienced lower rates of employment than individuals without disabilities, a disparity which is seen across all sociodemographic groups. According to the US Bureau of Labor Statistics (BLS), in 2019 only 30.9% of individuals with disabilities ages 18 to 64 were employed and 66.4% were no longer in the labor force, while 74.6% of people without a disability were employed and 22.7% were not in the labor force (US Department of Labor Bureau of Labor Statistics, 2020). This disparity extends to other aspects of employment, including monthly earnings (i.e., $1,961 for people 21 to 64 with a disability, compared with $2,724 for those with no disability). This translates into an earnings gap where individuals with disabilities earn about 72% of what workers without disabilities earn (US Department of Labor Bureau of Labor Statistics, 2020). In addition, poor employment outcomes for people with disabilities are often related to the severity of the disability, limited education, and limited previous work experience (Krause & Terza, 2006; Ozawa & Yeo, 2006; Phillips & Stuifbergen, 2006; Walker et al., 2006).

Relative to the general population of youth with disabilities, those from disadvantaged backgrounds and minority race and ethnic groups are at even greater risk of poor employment outcomes (Cameto et al., 2003; National Council on Disability, 2008; Wagner et al., 2005, 2006). Nationally, almost half of all Black, Hispanic, and Native American youth drop out of public schools each year in the United States (Bridgeland et al., 2006). Reviewing trends in high school dropout and completion rates, McFarland et al. (2016) found that in 2013, young adults with disabilities had a lower high school status completion rate (81.3%) than their peers without disabilities (92.4%). In addition, during the 2012–2013 school year, the national adjusted graduation rate for White students (87%) was 16 percentage points higher than the national rate for Black students (71%) and 12 percentage points higher than the national rate for Hispanic students (75%). In the 2017–2018 school year, however, the national adjusted graduation rate for public high school students rose to 85%, the highest it has been since the rate was first measure in 2010–2011. The rate for White students was 89%, Hispanic 81%, and for Black students was 79% (National Center for Educational Statistics, 2020). These rates represent significant improvements for Hispanic and Black students. However, although the data is still not available, a new decline is expected because of the pandemic.

The economic costs of unemployment and underemployment of youth and other individuals with disabilities are numerous (Hernandez et al., 2007). First, the poverty rate for the disability community far exceeds the rate for the general population. Second, living in poverty limits the full participation of people with disabilities in economic and social aspects of society. Third, the unemployment of people with disabilities is often linked to reliance on Social Security Administration (SSA) benefits (Rusch et al., 1993). According to the US BLS (2013), 58.4% of people 15 to 64 with severe disabilities receive public assistance, 33% receive social security benefits, 28% receive food stamps, and 11% receive public housing assistance. Hernandez et al. (2007) suggest that socially, the diversity of the American workforce suffers when the disability community is not represented. Workplaces lose out on the perspectives and talents of workers with disabilities, and unemployed people with disabilities also miss out on opportunities to build professional and social relationships. As Vernon (1999) argues, racism, classism, and disablism oppress marginalized populations simultaneously or independently depending upon context:

> Multiple oppressions refer to the fact that the effects of being attributed several stigmatized identities are often multiplied (exacerbated) and they can be experienced simultaneously and singularly depending on the context. It also takes account of the fact that the experience of disability or any other form of oppression may be modified by the presence of some privileged identities (for example, being of higher social class status or male). Impairment, which is a precondition of disability, settles upon anyone but the effect on any individual is very largely modified, minimized or exacerbated by who that person is in terms of their ethnicity, gender, sexual orientation, age and class.
>
> (Vernon, 1999, p. 395)

Our own research suggests that the transition outcomes for ethnic minority youth with disabilities who live in poverty in urban communities are very limited (Awsumb et al., 2016; Hasnain & Balcazar, 2009). The social needs of these youth challenge educators and include limited English proficiency, high rates of mobility and dropout, and teenage parenthood (Taylor-Ritzler, 2007). In Chicago, many minority students who complete high school do not have high levels of success in enrolling in postsecondary educational settings, obtaining support from the vocational rehabilitation agency, and securing jobs that pay above minimum wage or include benefits (Awsumb et al., 2016). Graduating students with disabilities who do not have the appropriate training and preparation have a very low likelihood of finding a job with career advancement opportunities, which translate into fewer opportunities for social mobility (National Secondary Transition Technical Assistance Center, 2009). In addition, students with disabilities have a much lower rate of completing postsecondary education compared to students without disabilities (Lindsay et al., 2019).

This chapter begins with a review of the 1973 Rehabilitation Act, which aimed to improve employment outcomes for people with disabilities and established the Vocational Rehabilitation Program (VR), followed by related policies like the Workforce Innovation and Opportunity Act (WIOA) and the Ticket to Work Program (TTW). We then introduce a conceptual framework to help understand the individual, organizational, and contextual factors affecting employment outcomes for youth with disabilities and how those factors interact. We also share our experiences with an innovative program to promote entrepreneurship experiences among high school youth with disabilities.

US POLICIES THAT PROMOTE EMPLOYMENT FOR PEOPLE WITH DISABILITIES

The Rehabilitation Act of 1973 as amended prohibits discrimination on the basis of disability in programs conducted by federal agencies, programs receiving federal financial assistance, federal employment, and in the employment practices of federal contractors. The Rehabilitation Act established the Rehabilitation Services Administration, which oversees Vocational Rehabilitation Agencies (VR) in every state and the US territories. VR agencies are required to assist individuals with disabilities to prepare for, obtain, maintain, or regain employment. The Act calls upon the federal government to play a leadership role in promoting the employment of individuals with disabilities, especially individuals with severe disabilities, in part by assisting states and service providers in fulfilling the aspirations of individuals with disabilities for meaningful and gainful employment and independent living (29 U.S.C. 701(b)(2)). In the regulations for the VR program, an employment outcome is defined as entering or retaining full-time or, if appropriate, part-time competitive employment, as defined in 34 CFR 361.5(b)(11), in the integrated labor market, supported employment, or any other type of employment in an integrated setting, including self-employment, telecommuting, or business ownership, that is consistent with an individual's strengths, resources, priorities, concerns, abilities, capabilities, interests, and informed choice (see 34 CFR 361.5(b)(16)).

According to fiscal year (FY) 2015–2016 data from the Rehabilitation Services Administration (RSA) Report (US Department of Education, Rehabilitation Services Administration, 2019), there were approximately 540,877 new applicants in federal fiscal year 2016. Of this number, 469,962 (87%) were determined eligible to participate and

186,713 individuals (39.73%) achieved employment outcomes. The RSA monitoring report also indicated that there are 80 VR agencies in the country that are evaluated on the basis of the employment outcomes achieved by individuals with disabilities after receiving VR services, with particular emphasis on individuals who achieved competitive employment (US Department of Education, RSA, 2019). In FY 2016, the average cost per employment outcome for all state VR agencies was $16,698. However, there are large disparities in the expenditures by state, which have a direct impact on the types of services provided to consumers and the resulting employment and educational outcomes.

Even though VR system services have undergone many transformations, the services have not changed much, and the eligibility requirements remain unchanged. Services are still primarily for individuals with a major physical or mental impairment that limits their ability to work. Priority is given to individuals who have the most severe disabilities. This includes working-age high school students (16 + years) and adults (18–65 years). Once a person is considered eligible, a VR counselor helps the person create an individualized plan for employment (IPE). This plan is used to identify the client's vocational goal and the services needed to best meet that goal. Students with disabilities can begin arranging services as early as high school (generally the last 2 years of high school) in preparation for postsecondary plans.

In Illinois, the coordination of postsecondary services is done through the Secondary Transitional Experience Program—Transition/STEP—DHS 4663 (see Illinois Department of Human Services, 2020) outlined in Table 18.1. Eligibility for high school students to the STEP in Illinois includes individuals with a physical/mental disability who receive 504 services (Section 504 of the Rehabilitation Act), special education services, or other assistance due to a disability. This program offers youth with disabilities the opportunity to gain work experience while in school to prepare them in making the transition from high school to employment and community participation.

Table 18.1 The Secondary Transitional Experience Program (STEP) Program in Illinois*

The STEP program helps students identify goals that include:
- Assisting students in developing desirable work habits and realistic career goals
- Providing opportunities for students to explore careers
- Offering meaningful work experience through on-the-job placement
- Encouraging students to develop the social and personal skills needed to maintain successful employment

STEP services also include:
- Job exploration counseling
- Work-based learning experiences and internships
- Counseling postsecondary education
- Workplace readiness training
- Introduction to self-advocacy

* Illinois Department of Human Services, 2020

The Workforce Innovation and Opportunity Act (WIOA, 2014), which was signed into law by President Obama in 2014, expanded the requirements for, and opportunities available to serve low-income young adults. Specifically, WIOA requires VR agencies to allocate 15% of their funding allotment towards pre-employment transition services (PreETS) to students with disabilities aged 16–21. PreETS are intended to provide job exploration and related services early in the transition process to prepare students with disabilities for employment. The five primary PreETS include job exploration counseling, work-based learning experiences, counseling in postsecondary education opportunities, workplace readiness training, and instruction in self-advocacy.

While increased transition services are meant to close the education, employment, and independent living gaps between youth with and without disabilities, the WIOA mandates come with implementation concerns. For VR, the 15% transition allotment is difficult to meet because community infrastructure to deliver transition services is undeveloped and evidence-based practices are lacking in some of the PreETS content areas (WIOA, 2014). The case story illustrates some of these issues that Latino parents of high school students with disabilities experience in the Chicago area, which was collected as part of the Taylor-Ritzler et al. (2010) study. These families are often unaware of the services and supports available to their youth after high school graduation. For that reason, they can miss opportunities to receive services related to employment, education, and/or independent living (see Case Story in Box 18.1).

The Ticket to Work (TTW) is a program developed by the Social Security Administration to support career development for social security disability beneficiaries age 18 to 64 who want to work. The program is a good fit for people who want to improve their earning potential and are committed to preparing for long-term success in the workplace (Social Security Administration, 2020). The program is available to individuals receiving Supplemental Security Income (SSI) and/or Social Security

Box 18.1 Case Story

A case manager at a local high school believes there is a lack of knowledge about VR services because the parents in his school who are mostly Latino immigrants are not aware that these programs exist. He thinks that because of the demographic characteristics of his students, the parents are busy working, struggling financially, and have many obligations and very little time to research services after graduation for their youth. He stresses to the parents that they may not be there forever for their children, asking questions like "Who is going to take care of your daughter or son when the time comes?" He says that he worries about his students because he doesn't want them to finish high school and end up sitting at home doing nothing. He believes that the parents don't want that either because once they turn 18, and even though most of them can sign up for benefits (e.g., Social Security), they have to navigate these agencies on their own and they often do not know how. He tries to give them options and tells them what they need to do to help their children as much as he can.

Disability Insurance (SSDI), which are the main welfare programs that support people with disabilities.

Despite such programs, people with disabilities continue to experience significant barriers related to employment. For instance, Hernandez et al. (2007) conducted a qualitative study to explore the employment, VR, and TTW experiences of people with disabilities. Across 12 focus groups with 74 working-age adults from ethnically diverse backgrounds and with various disabilities, respondents reported major barriers to employment that included negative employer attitudes toward hiring workers with disabilities, lack of or unreliable transportation to and from job sites, and insufficient levels of formal education to compete successfully within the labor market. Regarding VR services, participants expressed concerns about their counselors, whom they perceived as unresponsive and noncollaborative. Although clients were generally aware of the TTW program, accurate knowledge and utilization of the program were quite limited. Of those clients reporting TTW awareness, over one third feared that participating in the program would result in their loss of existing medical and cash benefits.

Programs like the Social Security Disability Insurance (SSDI) have been associated with poor employment outcomes because many people are concerned about losing their health benefits (Ipsen, 2006; Marini et al., 2008). As mentioned in the previous section, people with disabilities experience high incidence of secondary health conditions and those also affect their VR experience (Field et al., 2006; Kinne et al., 2004), and many of these conditions (such as pain, fatigue, sleep problems, and depression) have a negative effect on a person's ability to become or remain employed (Ipsen et al., 2010; Jiang & Hesser, 2006). However, poverty itself often pushes families to pursue Supplemental Security Income (SSI) to meet their basic financial needs.

For minorities with disabilities, employment may be harder to secure because they experience discrimination and multiple disadvantages from service providers. Many are also unsure of what accommodations would help, unaware of their rights, or lack self-advocacy and conflict resolution skills needed to request and successfully negotiate for reasonable accommodations (e.g., Johnson et al., 2004). It is especially difficult for persons with disabilities who are part of underrepresented groups to not only locate jobs but to gain entrance into the VR systems when compared to their White counterparts. For example, Wilson (2000) investigated differences in acceptance rates for VR services among African Americans, Whites, Native American or Alaskan Natives, and Asian or Pacific Islanders with disabilities in the United States using the Rehabilitation Services Administration Database (RSA-911). Controlling for education, type of major disability, and socioeconomic status, African Americans were more likely to be found ineligible for VR services. People with disabilities who are part of underrepresented groups are less likely to find jobs after being accepted for VR services when compared to White clients (Wilson et al., 2001). Although a preponderance of VR research indicates that White Americans are more likely to be accepted for VR services than African Americans, after accounting for differences in education, type of major disability, and socioeconomic status, differences between underrepresented groups and the majority group declined (Wilson, 2002). This trend is continuing, as Wilson and Senices (2005) reported that

Hispanics were more likely to be accepted for VR services than non-Hispanics in the US at the time.

Although the Rehabilitation Act, Workforce Innovation and Opportunity Act, and the Ticket to Work program all aim to increase employment opportunities for people with disabilities, it is clear that employment barriers that are exacerbated by racism and racial disparities remain. Importantly, improving employment outcomes through VR also requires that people take advantage of the services offered. Many, however, continue to leave programs early or completely miss out on the program.

Entering and Exiting VR Programs

Little is known about why VR clients choose to exit the program before completing services. However, researchers have noted various conditions associated with poorer employment outcomes. These include weak counselor–client relationships (Donnell et al., 2004; Lustig et al., 2004); racial or cultural differences between counselor and clients related to perceptions, beliefs, or expectations for services (Day-Vines et al., 2007; Hanson & Kerkhoff, 2007); work disincentives, such as receipt of SSI or SSDI (Ipsen, 2006; Marini et al., 2008); and incidence of secondary health conditions (Ipsen et al., 2010, 2011).

Data from the Longitudinal Study of the Vocational Rehabilitation Services Program indicate that, on average, each VR counselor has a caseload of 123 clients. With this high caseload, each counselor spends less than 15 minutes per month per client on eligibility determination, less than 20 minutes a month counseling each client, and about 20 minutes per month per client on file management (Hayward & Schmidt-Davis, 2003). Thus, building strong counselor–client relationships may be difficult due to limited client–counselor contact, and this may be a factor that contributes to premature exit from the program (Arnold & Seekins, 1998).

In addition, not all individuals who qualify for VR services accept them. According to a longitudinal study of the VR program (Hayward & Schmidt-Davis, 2003), 12% of persons accepted for VR services chose not to enter services. Several factors appear to affect the likelihood that an individual with a disability who is accepted for services will complete an individual plan for employment (IPE) and obtain VR services. Two factors that decreased the likelihood of a person receiving services were receiving SSI or SSDI and lacking a work history (i.e., never having worked at a job two consecutive weeks).

Premature exit is also problematic for both VR clients and agencies. For clients, exiting prematurely has been correlated with poorer economic outcomes when compared to those who stay and become employed (Hayward & Schmidt-Davis, 2003). For instance, longitudinal data show that 82.9% of VR clients whose cases were closed due to competitive employment (status 26) were still employed after 1 year. In contrast, only 33.4% of individuals choosing to forego VR services reported being employed at the 1-year follow-up (Hayward & Schmidt-Davis, 2003, pp. 4–6).

For VR agencies, the cost of premature exit is also high. For example, in 2006, RSA data indicated that of the total number of cases closed that year (617,154), 17.05% were closed as "refused services," and another 13.67% of the cases were closed as "failure to cooperate." VR spends an average of $1,077 per client who refuses services (totaling $113,353,173 in costs), and an average of $1,115 per client who fails to cooperate (totaling $94,099, 310 in costs). These figures underestimate the true costs because they exclude program administration costs, including staff salaries, and services provided by rehabilitation programs that are not directly billed on an individual basis (US Department of Education Rehabilitation Services Administration, 2008).

VR programs have the ability to improve employment outcomes for people with disabilities, but premature exit of such programs can be costly, and participants' outcomes also depend on more than just the program. The next section introduces the conceptual framework that we are using to better understand how individual, organizational, and contextual factors impact employment outcomes for youth with disabilities. The framework highlights the critical role that teachers, case managers, VR counselors, and the youth themselves play in attaining those outcomes.

CONCEPTUAL FRAMEWORK

Our activities are grounded in the sociopolitical understanding of disability, defined as "a product of the interaction between the individual and the environment" (Hahn, 1993, p. 741). According to this framework, disability-related challenges are seen as a product of limiting environments and negative societal attitudes. The capacity of the individual to succeed reflects the environment's accessibility and the supports available for them to function and perform effectively.

Figure 18.1 presents a conceptual framework that emphasizes the interaction of individual, organizational, and environmental factors on employment outcomes, based on reviews of the literature and our own research. Access to VR programs becomes one of many factors that influences employment outcomes. In this interactive framework, the ongoing participation and voice of individuals with disabilities, schoolteachers, and VR counselors/administrators is essential and required when designing feasible, utilized, and replicable interventions. Several individual and contextual factors contribute to the pervasive high rate of unemployment of people with disabilities. Such factors are further explained later.

Individual Factors

Individuals with disabilities are a heterogeneous group. Employment-related outcomes for people with disabilities appear to be associated with individual-level characteristics, such as severity of disability and sociodemographic characteristics (Crisp, 2005).

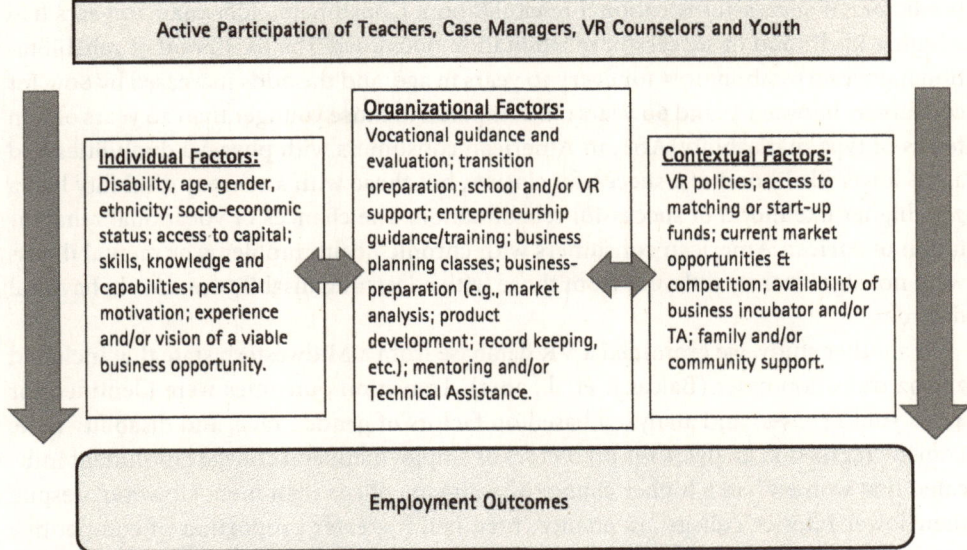

FIGURE 18.1 Individual, organizational, and contextual factors affecting employment outcomes.

Many studies of individual-level characteristics and employment-related outcomes of individuals with disabilities have been based on samples of individuals with a specific disabling condition, such as spinal cord injury (SCI). For example, Schopp et al. (2007) found that many persons with SCI experience low rates of participation in social activities (Tasiemski et al., 2000), limited employment opportunities (Tasiemski et al., 2000), low life satisfaction (Nosek et al., 1995), and high rates of depression (Krause et al., 2000). Similar findings were reported for individuals with traumatic brain injury (Wehman et al., 2005) and mental illness (Stuart, 2006), among other disability types.

Our research emphasizes the role of individual factors, particularly race, gender, age, and type of disability, as predictors of employment-related outcomes in VR. For example, we examined the VR records from a Midwestern state that included 2,122 African American and 4,284 White individuals who reported mental illness as their primary disability (Lukyanova et al., 2014). We found that African Americans had significantly more closures at referral and overall were closed as nonrehabilitated more often than Whites. Controlling for key variables, African American VR consumers were less likely to be employed compared to Whites. Gender differences were also present where women were more likely to find jobs than men. This finding was surprising, since previous literature consistently attributes better employment outcomes to men than women (e.g., Arango-Lasprilla et al., 2008). We also found differences in age, as middle-aged consumers with disabilities between 36 and 50 were more likely to find jobs than younger consumers (18 to 35 years old).

In a similar study, we examined a VR database that included 37,404 African Americans who were referred or self-referred over a period of 5 years (Balcazar et al., 2012). Logistic regression analyses indicated that age and disability type were significant predictors of successful vocational rehabilitation. Consumers older than 20 years had a higher likelihood of successful rehabilitation outcomes. The likelihood of rehabilitation increased by about 10% for every 10 years in age, and the odds increased by 80% for consumers between 51 and 60 years old compared to those younger than 20 years old. In terms of type of disability, African American consumers with physical disabilities had a 15% lower likelihood of a successful closure, but those with a sensory disability had a 72% higher likelihood of successful rehabilitation. The chances of vocational rehabilitation of African American consumers with chronic health problems or mental illness were not significantly different from those with a learning disability and/or behavioral disorder.

In another study, we examined a VR database from a Midwestern state that included 26,292 transition cases (Balcazar et al., 2013). Transition outcomes were identified for 4,010 youth (15.3%) and analyzed based on factors of gender, race, and disability type. Logistic regression analyses for predictors of employment and college enrollment indicated that women had a higher chance of going to college than men. However, despite their lower rates of college attendance, men had a greater proportion of competitive employment outcomes compared to women. Regarding race, White and Asian youth had a significantly higher percentage of identifiable transition outcomes than African Americans. Finally, disability type was also predictive of transition outcomes; and individuals with sensory and physical disabilities attended college in a larger proportion compared to individuals with other disabilities.

Finally, we studied the risk factors for failure of individuals with disabilities to enter the VR program, including the cases where they had been formally accepted but were yet to receive any service (Langi & Balcazar, 2017). We used a prospective cohort data from a Midwestern US state and analyzed 126,251 and 94,517 individuals, respectively, for acceptance and admission into VR services. The results indicated that individuals with a visual disability, those who had a prior history of employment, and those who received public support tended to have lower risks of nonacceptance and nonadmission. However, being non-White, with a higher level of education, ever or currently married, and with a physical/orthopedic disability appeared to increase the risks of both nonacceptance and nonadmission into VR.

To conclude, several characteristics of persons who received VR services affected their odds of obtaining an employment outcome. In terms of disability type, persons with vision, hearing, orthopedic impairments, or mental retardation were more likely than those with other types of disabilities to obtain employment. Receipt of SSI, SSDI, or other types of financial assistance reduced the likelihood of achieving an employment outcome following VR services. Higher gross motor function, higher self-esteem, having been working at a job application, need for assistive technology services or services as a motive for applying for VR, and having more dependents all increased the odds of an employment outcome. Being non-White or seeking help for postsecondary education decreased those odds. These disparities suggest the need to revise VR programs and improve the supports and services available to make employment outcomes more likely to all types of consumers.

Contextual Factors

Environmental or contextual factors can also drastically limit community and employment participation for individuals with disabilities. These factors include the physical, social, and attitudinal environments in which people live (Schopp et al., 2007). Products and technology for personal use in daily living, attitudes of community members, and availability of health and social support services are examples of such environmental factors (World Health Organization, 2001).

Our research also shows that contextual factors, particularly VR policies related to eligibility and expenditures, impact rehabilitation outcomes and often explain a larger proportion of the variance in the individual factors. For example, Lukyanova et al. (2014) found that VR case expenditures between $1,000 and $4,999 were significantly lower for African Americans than for Whites, which explains, in part, the differences in employment outcomes between the two groups of consumers. Balcazar et al. (2012) also found that when analyzed alone, none of the 22 types of VR services available was a significant predictor of rehabilitation for African Americans with disabilities. However, the number of services a consumer received was a significant predictor; each additional service received by a consumer increased their chances of rehabilitation by 47%. Further, as the amount of money spent on a case increased, the chances of successful rehabilitation increased such that each additional thousand dollars spent on a case doubled the consumers' likelihood of successful rehabilitation. Most importantly, according to the analysis, spending between $5,000 and $8,000 per consumer is associated with the maximum rate of rehabilitation (a 1,360% higher likelihood of getting rehabilitated) compared with consumers receiving less than $500 or no funding at all. Balcazar et al. (2013) reported that the chances of a youth gaining competitive employment increased as the amount of money spent by VR on the case increased. The study also found that youth who received vocational guidance and on-the-job supports had higher chances of obtaining competitive employment than of going to college.

Beyond spending, the sociopolitical understanding of disability leads us to emphasize the importance of improving counselors' effectiveness in recognizing and removing contextual barriers to consumer success, including organizational practices and policies (Hayward & Schmidt-Davis, 2003). Combined with strategies that can help consumers become more engaged in setting and pursuing their rehabilitation goals (Kundu et al., 2018), there are many potential benefits of promoting environmental changes for improving employment outcomes.

According to Hirano and colleagues (2018), family involvement is particularly important to the postschool success of young adults with disabilities who typically experience fewer education and employment opportunities after leaving high school than their same-age peers without disabilities. They concluded that despite mandates for family involvement, school–home partnerships remain elusive, particularly for low-income and culturally and linguistically diverse families. They also found that families cited multiple sources of stress and a lack of resources as factors that inhibit their active and ongoing participation in planning and preparing for their student's transition from high school to adulthood. In addition to a family's own personal health and well-being, families experience needs specific to the developmental periods of late adolescence and emerging adulthood, as well as needs related to their youth's disabilities. Increases in youth problem behavior (e.g., violence, truancy, criminal behavior) or ongoing medical needs (e.g., medications, doctors' visits) can compound existing stress, leading families to become burned out and less engaged in a young adult's education or provision of community service supports. Edelman and colleagues (2006) suggested that "policies to raise the numbers of young men connected to the labor market should focus not only on their academic achievement and postsecondary educational attainment, but also on improving their occupational skills, early work experience and on-the-job training, especially before they leave high school or just afterwards" (p. 7). At the same time, the authors concluded that we must improve the incentives for the youth to remain connected to school or work, and we have to address the special needs of youth offenders and young noncustodial fathers.

Organizational Factors

The third set of factors within the conceptual framework outlined in Figure 18.1 occur at the organizational level. These serve to link individual and contextual factors and highlight the important role of VR programs. One concrete way to benefit individuals with disabilities at risk of poor employment outcomes is to improve their experience with the vocational rehabilitation system. With the right tools and services, youth with disabilities can better participate in society. Services from VR programs, especially when received early on, have shown positive outcomes, including access to higher education, employment, independence, inclusion, self-advocacy, and work hours and salary (Lindsay et al., 2019). Jun et al. (2015) examined the effects of school transition programs in combination with VR services and found that individuals receiving VR services at an early age (14–18 years) achieved better employment outcomes than those who start later in life (19–21 years). Similar outcomes can also be achieved for individuals who stay in a VR program longer (1+ years).

Regarding attainment of rehabilitation outcomes, Hayward and Schmidt-Davis (2003) found that about two thirds of persons who received VR services achieved an employment outcome as a result of those services. In effect, the type of services that VR customers receive appears to predict employment outcomes. Hayward and Schmidt-Davis (2003) found that controlling for consumer characteristics, environmental factors, and VR office characteristics, the services received account for nearly 30% of the variance. Services reported to have increased the odds of an employment outcome include quality of the consumer–counselor relationship individual plan for employment (IPE) amendments (as a result of changes in goals, circumstances, or interests); job placement; supported employment; on-the-job training; college or university training;

work adjustment training; driver training and licensing; business or vocational training; and the provision of tools, uniforms, equipment, or stock.

VR programs can be a good resource for youth with disabilities seeking training and employment; however, this program is not flawless. One of the common issues is the lack of adequate coordination between schools and VR services (US Government Accountability Office [GAO], 2012). The US GAO (2012) recommended better co-ordination of services among government agencies and concluded that students with disabilities face several challenges accessing federally funded programs that can provide transition services as they leave high school for postsecondary education or the work-force. These include difficulty navigating multiple programs that are not always coor-dinated; possible delays in service as they wait to be served by adult programs; limited access to transition services; a lack of adequate information or awareness on the part of parents, students, and service providers of available programs that may provide transi-tion services after high school; and a lack of preparedness for postsecondary education or employment.

It is important to notice that Hayward and Schmidt-Davis (2003) emphasized the role of organizational and contextual variables, which is consistent with our efforts to move away from the individual with a disability as the main source of success and often the scapegoat for failure that have characterized the traditional medical model of disability. However, we also recognize that each individual is responsible for taking the necessary steps to achieve rehabilitation and independent living goals. In conclusion, these three factors can impact the employment outcomes of people with disabilities in significant ways, and it is very important to understand how each one can be adjusted to better serve the needs of each individual. Each is also important to consider when studying dif-ferent avenues for transitioning out of VR programs.

TRANSITION BEST PRACTICES

With regards to transition services, Lee and Carter (2012) suggested that there are at least seven important elements of high-quality transition services that should be considered as best practices for schools, including (1) individualized, strengths-based transition services and supports; (2) positive career development and early work experiences; (3) meaningful collaboration and interagency involvement; (4) family supports and expectations; (5) fostering self-determination and independence; (6) social and employment-related skill instruction; and (7) establishing job-related supports. This in-formation is very useful because counselors often do not have a clear sense of the rela-tive benefit of one type of service over another. In addition, the list supports the three components of our conceptual framework, as each one contributes to the success or failure of the transition preparation process at schools. In fact, Johnston et al. (2009) advocated for the need to use evidence-based practices in the delivery of VR services as a way to involve the best available evidence—integrated with clinical expertise and the values and experiences of people with disabilities and other stakeholders—to guide decisions about clinical and community practices.

Wagner and colleagues (2017) reported that taking a concentration of career and technical education courses in a specific occupational area in high school can help students achieve their employment goal in the first few post–high school years. In turn, this helps establish an employment history that may contribute to further employment success in later years. Plotner and Dymond (2017) reported efforts to involve a team of VR transition specialists in the development and implementation of transition-related curricula for students with severe disabilities in several school districts in a midwestern state. Participating VR transition specialists reported that they were able to influence curricula through a collaborative approach and focused on resources and knowledge sharing. These professionals also reported delivering several direct-service activities to students inside and outside of the school sites. A core finding from this study is that participants believed the nature of their position (jointly funded by VR and the school districts, and physically located within the school buildings) served as a catalyst for encouraging high levels of collaboration, which had a positive impact on the transition outcomes of the students. We now introduce the concept of entrepreneurship that can also help youth with disabilities prepare for transitioning out of high school.

INNOVATION THROUGH ENTREPRENEURSHIP

Another strategy that is often overlooked as a viable alternative for youth with disabilities preparing to transition out of high school is entrepreneurship. Kaufmann and Stuart (2007) defined entrepreneurship as the process of finding and evaluating opportunities and developing and executing plans for translating those opportunities into financial self-sufficiency. Entrepreneurship allows people to customize their work experiences specifically to their needs and strengths and to design a work environment that optimizes flexibility and personal accommodation (US Department of Labor, Office of Disability Employment Policy [ODEP], 2013). The ODEP report adds that entrepreneurial education and training programs can help in the development of a young person in the transition to adulthood. Youth entrepreneurship programs may include group projects with youth working together to develop a new product or service or working with existing products or services. The possibility of earning money can also be a motivator and incentive for most youth.

In addition, Bronte-Tinkew and Redd (2001) reported that youth who are involved in vocational and entrepreneurial activities through programs or in education settings may experience a variety of positive outcomes. Some of these include improvements in academic performance; improved school attendance; development of practical skills such as teamwork, money management, decision-making, personal responsibility, and public speaking; and job readiness. The authors also mentioned that the experience can facilitate improvements in student's knowledge of entrepreneurship and entrepreneurial attitudes, short-term economic advantages, and consistent gains in factual knowledge related to the entrepreneurial experience. From a psychological perspective, the authors identified social skills development; enhanced development in self-esteem, ego development, and self-efficacy; and increased problem-solving ability and leadership skills (Bronte-Tinkew & Redd, 2001). Although youth with disabilities as participants in these efforts were not mentioned, it is likely that such programs would also benefit this population.

Beginning in 2006 and continuing through 2009, ODEP sponsored three national demonstration projects to research effective policies and practices that improve entrepreneurship outcomes for people with disabilities. These projects represented a diversity of locations, economic environments, and stakeholder groups, and they resulted in new knowledge, as well as local policy and program improvements, that could help more individuals with disabilities achieve their entrepreneurship career goals. Of the 194 persons with disabilities enrolled in the program, 137 achieved at least one major milestone. The most frequently achieved milestone was initiation of a business plan. During the follow-up period of data collection, 56 entrepreneurs (28.8% of participants) reported an operating business (US Department of Labor, ODEP, 2013). Also, state grantees noted that they considered a successful outcome to be an informed decision not to start a business or pursue self-employment. Going through the discovery process led some people to conclude that entrepreneurship was not the right avenue for them, thereby enabling them to focus on wage employment opportunities.

VR state agency involvement in facilitating self-employment outcomes varies substantially from state to state, particularly for persons with intellectual disabilities. In states, such as Florida and Ohio, VR agencies are involved in initiatives to implement policies and practices that expand participation in self-employment. These agencies are implementing a step-by-step vocational rehabilitation process that provides a variety of resources to the individual with a disability potentially interested in self-employment. This process focuses on individual support needs and emphasizes the development of a business design team to assist and support the self-employment initiative. It also focuses on the ongoing supports needed for the development of a viable business plan and the successful implementation and maintenance of the self-employment venture.

In 2007, the National Foundation for Teaching Entrepreneurship (NFTE)[1] commissioned research to evaluate the effectiveness and impact of its programs (Kaufmann & Stuart, 2007). Evaluation studies conducted by Brandeis University (1993–1997), the Koch Foundation (1998–1999), and the Harvard Graduate School of Education (2002–2006) showed that when youth participated in entrepreneurship programs, interest in attending college increased 32%, occupational aspirations increased 44%, and leadership behavior increased 8.5% as starters/founders of activities and 13.2% as leaders. Importantly, 99% of former participants recommended NFTE programs to others.

Although entrepreneurship allows people to customize their work experiences specifically to their needs, it remains a marginal practice in Departments of Vocational Rehabilitation Services across the country, and the implementation and promotion of entrepreneurship skills among VR customers is very limited. This is one of the reasons why we included entrepreneurship as part of the contextual component of our conceptual framework. The first author is currently developing a comprehensive approach for promoting entrepreneurship skills in high schools with support from a grant from the National Institute on Disability Independent Living and Rehabilitation Research (Balcazar, 2019). This grant presents two main goals. First, it aims to understand the barriers and facilitators to entrepreneurship among low-income minority individuals with disabilities. Second, it will conduct formative and summative evaluations of a school-based model intended to promote self-employment outcomes among transition-aged youth with disabilities. We plan to develop a classroom-based curriculum and intervention model to promote and support youth's efforts to start their own small businesses. The entrepreneurship intervention will include skill development and training on areas like how to prepare a business plan, mentoring from existing business owners, access to small capital to start the businesses (up to $500 in supplies or equipment), and technical assistance and support. We will collect both quantitative and qualitative data using participatory research methods and examine individual, organizational, and contextual factors that contribute to the success or failure of the entrepreneurial efforts.

Conclusions

Racial and ethnic minority individuals with disabilities are underserved when it comes to rehabilitation services, including both independent living and VR. As a result, they are more likely to experience more social, economic, educational, and vocational disadvantages than their White counterparts. These differences have persisted, even though the US Congress passed amendments to the Rehabilitation Act in 1992 and 1998 and WIOA in 2014 to ensure equal treatment to all regardless of race and other characteristics.

Although several national programs and policies have been implemented to address unemployment among people with disabilities, employment continues to be a significant issue for the disability community with severe economic, social, and psychological implications. WIOA expanded the requirements and opportunities available for serving youth with disabilities and calls for an increased focus on serving the most vulnerable populations and expanding the education, training, and work experience opportunities provided to them. It has also played a critical role in the development of more internships and field work experiences, as well as intervention components related to self-employment among youth with disabilities in high school. Employment training and work experiences in high school are critical for success in post–high school competitive employment (Wehman et al., 2015), and it can complement parental expectations for the youth's future.

Unfortunately, the broader impact of programs like WIOA is not very clear, as program implementation varies across schools and states. Low-income communities need more help. They not only struggle with the limited resources available to support their schools based on local tax revenues and property taxes but also with issues of violence and limited public transportation and social services. These environments make it a challenge for youth with disabilities and their families to overcome or even survive. VR services can help, but those services must be adapted to address the complex needs of those youth and their families. This is a good example of how our conceptual model helps us understand the way in which personal, organizational, and contextual factors interact to—in many cases—make the desired outcomes more difficult to attain. Counselors, teachers, and school administrators need to do a better job of informing families and students about the resources available to support post–high school education or vocational training (as mentioned in the Case Story), as not every student is interested or prepared to pursue regular college education. But the problem is that in many communities, particularly among Latinx, the awareness and understanding of VR resources and supports is often minimal or nonexistent.

There are many barriers to successful employment for minority youth with disabilities and self-employment is an underutilized strategy—particularly in urban areas—which has the potential to increase the earning capacity of individuals who otherwise struggle to find and/or keep a regular job. Unfortunately, many youths have no idea of the potential opportunities and benefits of self-employment, or as the Start-UP USA researchers found, benefit from being able to make an informed decision *not* to start a business or pursue self-employment.

To conclude, Plotner and Dymond (2017) suggested that more collaboration between VR and school personnel can have very positive effects on the transition preparation of students with severe disabilities. The VR transition specialists were able to build rapport with school personnel and influence the curriculum in ways that might not otherwise have been possible. Given the positive results from that study, more states should consider implementing a model that supports increased collaboration around curriculum by school personnel and VR transition specialists. The findings from our own studies also support the critical role of VR professionals in transition service delivery for students with disabilities. We also hope that our entrepreneurship intervention will open new opportunities, particularly among low-income minority youth with disabilities, to start and operate their own small business.

NOTE

1. See https://www.nfte.com/impact-stories/

REFERENCES

Arango-Lasprilla, J. C., Ketchum, J. M., Williams, K., Kreutzer, J. S., Marquez de la Plata, C. D., O'Neil-Pirozzi, T. M., & Wehman, P. (2008). Racial differences in employment outcomes after traumatic brain injury. *Archives of Physical Medicine and Rehabilitation*, 89(5), 988–995.

Arnold, N., & Seekins, T. (1998). Rural and urban vocational rehabilitation: Counselors perceived strengths and problems. *Journal of Rehabilitation*, 64(1), 5–13.

Awsumb, J. M., Balcazar, F. E., & Alvarado, F. (2016). Vocational rehabilitation transition outcomes of youth with disabilities from a Midwestern state. *Rehabilitation Research, Policy, and Education*, 30, 48–64.

Balcazar, F. E. (2019). *Promoting entrepreneurship among low-income youth with disabilities*. Grant funded by the National Institute on Disability Independent Living and Rehabilitation Research, US Department of Education.

Balcazar, F. E., Oberoi, A., & Keel, J. M (2013). Predictors of employment and college attendance outcomes for youth in transition: Implications for policy and practice. *Journal of Applied Rehabilitation Counseling*, 44(1), 38–45.

Balcazar, F. E., Oberoi, A. K., Suarez-Balcazar, Y., & Alvarado, F., (2012). Predictors of rehabilitation outcomes for African Americans in a vocational rehabilitation state agency: Implications for policy and practice. *Rehabilitation Research, Policy and Education*, 26(1), 43–54.

Bridgeland, J. M., Dilulio, J. J., & Morrison, K. B. (2006). *The silent epidemic: Perspectives of high school dropouts*. Civic Enterprises. https://docs.gatesfoundation.org/documents/thesilentep idemic3-06final.pdf

Bronte-Tinkew, J., & Redd, Z. (2001). *Logic models and outcomes for youth entrepreneurship programs, DC children and youth investment trust corporation*. http://www.cyitc.org/cyitc/outcomes/LogicModels_YouthEnt.pdf

Cameto, R., Marder, C., Wagner, M., & Cardoso, D. (2003). *Youth employment. NLTS2 Data Brief: A report from the National Longitudinal Transition Study-2*, pp. 1–5. http://www.ncset.org/publications/nlts2/NCSETNLTS2Brief_2.2.pdf

Crisp, R. (2005). Key factors related to vocational outcome: Trends for six disability groups. *Journal of Rehabilitation*, 71(4), 30–37.

Day-Vines, N., Wood, S., Grothaus, T., Craigen, L., Holman, A., Dotson-Blake, K., & Douglass, M. (2007). Broaching the subjects of race, ethnicity, and culture during the counseling process. *Journal of counseling & Development*, 85(4), 401–409.

Donnell, C., Strauser, D., & Lustig, D. (2004). The working alliance: Rehabilitation outcomes for persons with severe mental illness. *Journal of Rehabilitation*, 70(2), 12–18.

Edelman, P., Holzer, H. J., & Offner, P. (2006). *Reconnecting disadvantaged young men*. Urban Institute Press.

Field, M., Jette, A., & Martin, L. (Eds.). (2006). *Workshop on disability in America: A new look*. The National Academic Press.

Hahn, H. (1993). The potential impact of disability studies on political science (as well as vice versa). *Policy Studies Journal*, 21, 740–751.

Hanson, S., & Kerkhoff, T. (2007) Ethical decision-making in rehabilitation: Consideration of cultural factors. *Rehabilitation Psychology*, 52(4), 409–420.

Hasnain, R., & Balcazar, F. (2009). Predicting community- versus facility-based employment for transition-aged, young adults with disabilities: The role of race, ethnicity, and support systems. *Journal of Vocational Rehabilitation*, 31, 175–188.

Hayward, B. J., & Schmidt-Davis, H. (2003). *Longitudinal Study of the Vocational Rehabilitation Services Program. Final Report 1: How consumer characteristics affect access to, receipt of, and outcomes of VR services.* http://www2.ed.gov/rschstat/eval/rehab/vr-final-report-1.pdf

Hernandez, B., Cometa, M. J., Velcoff, J., Rose, J., Schober, D., & Luna, R. D. (2007). Perspectives of people with disabilities on employment, vocational rehabilitation, and the Ticket to Work program. *Journal of Vocational Rehabilitation, 27*(3), 191–201.

Hirano, K. A., Rowe, D., Lindstrom, L., & Chan, P. (2018). Systemic barriers to family involvement in transition planning for youth with disabilities: A qualitative meta- synthesis. *Journal of Child and Family Studies, 27*, 3440–3456.

Illinois Department of Human Services (2020). Transition/STEP—DHS 4663. Illinois Department of Human Services. http://www.dhs.state.il.us/page.aspx?item=35174

Ipsen, C. (2006). Health, secondary conditions, and employment outcomes for adults with disabilities. *Journal of Disability Policy Studies, 17*(2), 77–87.

Ipsen, C., Seekins, T., & Arnold, N. (2011). A prospective study to examine the influence of secondary health conditions on vocational rehabilitation client employment outcomes. *Journal of Disability Health, 4*(1), 28–38.

Ipsen, C., Seekins, T., & Ravesloot, C. (2010). Building the case for delivering health promotion services within the vocational rehabilitation. *Rehabilitation Counseling Bulletin, 53*(2), 67–77.

Jiang, Y., & Hesser, J. (2006). Associations between health-related quality of life and demographics and health risks. Results from Rhode Island's 2002 behavioral risk factor survey. *Health and Quality of Life Outcomes, 4*, 14–24.

Johnson, K. L., Amtmann, D., Yorkston, K. M., Klasner, E. R., & Kuehn, C. M. (2004). Medical, psychological, social, and programmatic barriers to employment for people with multiple sclerosis. *Journal of Rehabilitation, 70*, 38–49.

Johnston, M. V., Vanderheiden, G. C., Farkas, M. D., Rogers, E. S., Summers, J. A., & Westbrook, J. D. (2009). *The challenge of evidence in disability and rehabilitation research and practice: A position paper.* SEDL for the NCDDR Task Force on Standards of Evidence and Methods. https://ktdrr.org/ktlibrary/articles_pubs/ncddrwork/tfse_challenge/tfse_challenge.pdf

Jun, S., Kortering, L., Osmanir, K., & Zhang, D. (2015). Vocational rehabilitation transition outcomes: A look at one state's evidence. *Journal of Rehabilitation, 81*(2), 47–53.

Kaufmann, B., & Stuart, C. (2007). *Road to self-sufficiency: A guide to entrepreneurship for youth with disabilities.* National Collaborative on Workforce and Disability for Youth, Institute for Educational Leadership. http://www.ncwd-youth.info/wp-content/uploads/2016/11/entrepreneurship_guide.pdf

Kinne, S., Patrick, D., & Doyle, D. (2004). Prevalence of secondary conditions among people with disabilities. *American Journal of Public Health, 94*(3), 442–445.

Krause, J. S., Kemp, B., & Coker, J. (2000) Depression after spinal cord injury: Relation to gender, ethnicity, aging, and socioeconomic indicators. *Archives of Physical Medicine and Rehabilitation, 81*(8), 1099–109.

Krause, J., & Terza, J. (2006). Injury and demographic factors predictive of disparities in earnings after spinal cord injury. *Archives of Physical Medicine and Rehabilitation, 87*, 1318–1326.

Kundu, M., Dutta, A., & Chang, F. (2018). Developing international standards for return-to-work professionals: An overview. In Gudrun Wansing, Felix Welti, Markus Schäfers (Eds.), *The right to work for persons with disabilities: International perspectives.* Nomos Verlag, Germany (p. 169–182).

Langi, F. L. F. G., & Balcazar, F. E. (2017). Risk factors for failure to enter vocational rehabilitation services among individuals with disabilities. *Disability and Rehabilitation*, *39*(26), 2640–2647.

Lindsay, S., Lamptey, D.L., Cagliostro, E., Srikanthan, D., Mortaji, N., & Karon, L. (2019). A systematic review of post-secondary transition interventions for youth with disabilities. *Disability and Rehabilitation*, *41*(21), 2492–2505.

Lee, G. K., & Carter, E. W. (2012). Preparing transition-age students with high-functioning Autism Spectrum Disorders for meaningful work. *Psychology in the Schools*, *49*, 988–1000.

Lukyanova, V., Balcazar, F.E., Oberoi, A., & Suarez-Balcazar, Y. (2014). Employment outcomes among African Americans and Whites with mental illness. *Work*, *48*(3), 3219–3328.

Lustig, D., Strauser, D., & Weems, G. (2004). Rehabilitation service patterns: A rural/urban comparison of success factors. *Journal of Rehabilitation*, *70*(23), 13–19.

Marini, I., Lee, G., Chan, F., Chapin, M., & Romero, M. (2008). Vocational rehabilitation service patterns related to successful competitive employment outcomes of persons with spinal cord injury. *Journal of Vocational Rehabilitation*, *28*, 1–13.

McFarland, J., Stark, P., & Coi, J. (2016). Trends in high school dropout and completion rates in the United States: 2013. Compendium Report. *National Center for Education Statistics*. 2016–2017.

National Center for Educational Statistics. (2020). *Public high school graduation rates*. https://nces.ed.gov/programs/coe/indicator_coi.asp

National Council on Disability. (2008). *The Rehabilitation Act: Outcomes for transition-age youth*. http://www.ncd.gov/newsroom/publications/2008/publications.htm

National Secondary Transition Technical Assistance Center. (2009). *Evidence-based secondary transition practices*. http://www.nsttac.org/ebp/evidence_based_practices.aspx

Nosek, M. A., Fuhrer, M. J., & Potter, C. (1995). Life satisfaction of people with physical disabilities: Relationships to personal assistance, disability status, and handicap. *Rehabilitation Psychology*, *40*(3), 191–202.

Ozawa, M. N., & Yeo, Y. H. (2006). Work status and work performance of people with disabilities. *Journal of Disability Policy Studies*, *17*, 180–190.

Phillips, L., & Stuifbergen, A. (2006). Predicting continued employment in persons with multiple sclerosis. *Journal of Rehabilitation*, *72*, 35–43.

Plotner, A. J., & Dymond, S. K. (2017). How Vocational Rehabilitation Transition Specialists influence curricula for students with severe disabilities. *Rehabilitation Counseling Bulletin*, *60*(2), 88–97.

Rehabilitation Act of 1973, as amended. 29 U.S.C. 701 et seq. https://www.gpo.gov/fdsys/pkg/USCODE-2011-title29/pdf/USCODE-2011-title29-chap16.pdf

Rusch, F. R., Conley, R. W., & McCaughrin, W. B. (1993). Benefit–cost analysis of supported employment in Illinois. *Journal of Rehabilitation*, *59*(2), 31–36.

Schopp, L. H., Good G. E., Mazurek, M. O., Barker, K. B., & Stucky, R. C. (2007). Masculine role variables and outcomes among men with spinal cord injury. *Disability and Rehabilitation*, *29*, 625–633.

Social Security Administration. (2020). *The Ticket to Work Program: Access to employment support services for social security disability beneficiaries who want to work*. https://choosework.ssa.gov/index.html

Stuart, H. (2006). Mental illness and employment discrimination. *Current Opinion in Psychiatry*, *19*, 522–526

Tasiemski, T., Bergstrom, E., Savic, G., & Gardner B. P. (2000). Sports, recreation, and employment following spinal cord injury—A pilot study. *Spinal Cord, 38*(3), 173–184.

Taylor-Ritzler, T., Balcazar, F. E., Suarez-Balcazar, Y., Kilbury, R., Alvarado, F., & James, M. (2010). Engaging ethnically diverse individuals with disabilities in the vocational rehabilitation system: Themes of empowerment and oppression. *Journal of Vocational Rehabilitation, 33,* 3–14.

Taylor-Ritzler, T. (2007). A grounded theory of first high school dropout for urban, ethnic minority teenage mothers with learning disabilities. *The Community Psychologist, 40*(2), 18–20.

US Department of Education, Rehabilitation Services Administration. (2008). *Vocational rehabilitation services program: Draft strategic performance plan goals, objectives, and measures.* https://www2.ed.gov/policy/speced/guid/rsa/strategic_performance_plan_2008.pdf

US Department of Education, Rehabilitation Services Administration. (2019). *Report for fiscal year 2016: Report on federal activities under the Rehabilitation Act of 1973, as amended.* https://www2.ed.gov/about/reports/annual/rsa/2016/rsa-2016-annual-report.pdf

US Department of Labor Bureau of Labor Statistics. (2020, February). *Persons with a disability 2019.* Current Population Survey, Division of Labor Force Statistics. https://www.bls.gov/news.release/pdf/disabl.pdf

US Department of Labor, Office of Disability Employment Policy. (2013, December). *Self-employment for people with disabilities.* GS-10F-0042M. https://www.dol.gov/odep/pdf/2014startup.pdf

US Government Accountability Office (2012, July). *Students with Disabilities: Better Federal Coordination Could Lessen Challenges in the Transition from High School.* GAO-12-594 https://www.gao.gov/assets/gao-12-594.pdf

Vernon, A. (1999). The dialectics of multiple identities and the disabled people's movement. *Disability & Society, 14*(3), 385–398.

Wagner, M., Newman, L., Cameto, R., Garza, N., & Levine, P. (2005). *After high school: A first look at the postschool experiences of youth with disabilities: A report from the National Longitudinal Transition Study-2* (NLTS2). SRI International. https://files.eric.ed.gov/fulltext/ED494935.pdf

Wagner, M., Newman, L., Cameto, R., Garza, N., & Levine, P (2006). *An overview of findings from Wave 2 of the National Longitudinal Transition Study-2 (NLTS2).* SRI International. https://ies.ed.gov/ncser/pdf/20063004.pdf

Wagner, M. M., Newman, L. A., & Javitz, H. S. (2017). Vocational education course taking and post-high school employment of youth with emotional disturbances. *Career Development and Transition for Exceptional Individuals, 40*(3), 132–143.

Walker, W., Marwitz, J., Kreutzer, J., Hart, T., & Novack, T. (2006). Occupational categories and return to work after traumatic brain injury: A multicenter study. *Archives of Physical Medicine and Rehabilitation, 87,* 1576–1582.

Wehman, P., Targett, P., West, M., & Kregel, J. (2005). Productive work and employment for persons with traumatic brain injury: What have we learned after 20 years? *Journal of Head Trauma Rehabilitation, 20*(2), 115–127.

Wehman, P., Sima, A. P., Ketchum, J., West, M. D., Chan, F., & Luecking, R. (2015). Predictors of successful transition from school to employment for youth with disabilities. *Journal of Occupational Rehabilitation, 25*(2), 323–334.

Wilson, K. B. (2000). Predicting vocational rehabilitation acceptance based on race, education, work status, and source of support at application. *Rehabilitation Counseling Bulletin, 43*(2), 97–105.

Wilson, K. B. (2002). Exploration of VR acceptance and ethnicity: A national investigation. *Rehabilitation Counseling Bulletin, 45*(3), 168–176.

Wilson, K. B., Harley, D. A., & Alston, R. (2001). Race as a correlate of vocational rehabilitation acceptance: Revisited. *Journal of Rehabilitation, 67*(3), 35–41.

Wilson, K.B & Senices, J. (2005). Exploring the Vocational Rehabilitation Acceptance Rates for Hispanics Versus Non-Hispanics in the United States. *Journal of Counseling and Development, 83*(1), 86–96.

Workforce Innovation and Opportunity Act. (2014). *Public Law 113 – 128. 128 STAT. 1425.* https://www.govinfo.gov/content/pkg/PLAW-113publ128/pdf/PLAW-113publ128.pdf

World Health Organization. (2001). *International classification of functioning, disability and health, ICF short version.* WHO. http://www.who.int/whr/2001/en/

CHAPTER 19

DISABILITY, EDUCATION, AND WORK IN A GLOBAL KNOWLEDGE ECONOMY

SALLY TOMLINSON AND STACY HEWITT

All must be set to work that are in any ways able, and scrutiny should be made even among the infirm.

Bernard Mandeville (1714)

INTRODUCTION

GOVERNMENTS in modern nation states, whatever their political ideologies, increasingly believe their countries cannot prosper unless their economies are growing. They press for higher levels of education and skills for whole populations as necessary for successful competition in a global economy. They believe, despite recessions and job losses, that people who invest in their education and training, described as "human capital," will prosper individually and help grow the economy (Brown et al., 2011). This view persists even though globalization—the removal of barriers to the movement of capital, goods, and labor around the world—is now questioned, which has implications for both education and work.

Additionally, the effects of a global COVID-19 pandemic on employment are only beginning to be understood, although it was clear that into the 21st century the youth labor market had collapsed in developed countries, and a majority were eventually required to stay in some form of education and training to age 18. Questions about what kind of education and work will be available for young people must be asked, especially as it is now recognized that people are largely disabled by current social and work organization rather than impairments or learning disabilities. The rise of competitive market ideologies has placed educational changes and reforms firmly within economic imperatives, with public institutions encouraged to deregulate, privatize, and contract out services. Much of education and skills training in England[1] and other countries has been reconstructed into semiprivate businesses. Political claims are still made that economic development and global competition requires more and higher levels of education with flexible enterprising workers prepared for a knowledge-based digitalized economy (Ainley, 2016). Where does that leave the large numbers of students who have been labeled in schools, colleges, universities, and employment centers as having special needs and disabilities?

In England in 2019, disabled adults made up 20% of potential workers, but only half were employed (Schuelka et al., 2019). Changes in labor markets globally made it even more likely that those who have learning difficulties and disabilities would still be relegated to lower levels of education and skill training and less likely to obtain work. This relationship is also intersectional. Disability, social class, and gender all combine to impact how both young and old are treated in the labor market (Frederick & Shifrer, 2018; Maroto, Pettinicchio, and Patterson, 2018; Piketty, 2014).

This chapter begins by discussing the nature of changing economies and labor markets and the place of young people labeled as having special needs or disabilities in education and training and their likely futures in England. It notes the shift to a social model of disability in which a social and work environment often fails to adapt to people with disabilities, especially through cuts in funding for education and training. Education and training are usually associated with lower level vocational training (Richardson et al., 2017), and the chapter notes the history and current realities of the assumptions that this will continue. But, as the UK Office for Students has pointed out, disabled students are now a significant part of university life and are not only destined for lower level vocational training. The chapter examines how attempts in universities in England to include disabled students mitigate the disadvantages faced by some disabled students. It contrasts the situation in England with Germany, where the dual system of vocational education and training still operates, and Finland, where there is a commitment to equality and more support for young disabled people in well-resourced colleges. Finally, the chapter discusses how accepted or developing ideas about preparing young people for greater inclusion in education and skill training were thrown into confusion with the global COVID-19 pandemic that in 2021 was damaging economies around the world.

A GLOBAL KNOWLEDGE ECONOMY

The international acceptance of the notion of a global economy called into question what counts as "knowledge" in a world rapidly changing with global trade and communication, and new kinds of knowledge emerging. Definitions of "work" were also changing. As Farrell and Fenwick (2007) asked, "What counts as 'work' in different work sectors and what kinds of knowledge are needed in each sector now?" (p. 3). All political parties in the United Kingdom in the late 20th and early 21st centuries endorsed the notion that high levels of knowledge were required for economies to compete (DTI, 1998).

The World Bank announced in 2003 that a knowledge-based economy that relied primarily on ideas rather than physical labor and the application of technology rather than the use of cheap labor would become the norm (World Bank, 2003). That may have been news to the millions worldwide still laboring physically and cheaply, but the analysis was endorsed in Britain by Prime Ministers Blair and Brown and later Cameron, May, and Johnson. They believed that the economy should be structured around financial services, website developers, games production, and ITC consultants rather than the manufacturing of goods, leaving out much of the service industry (Brown, 2017). These governments gave less attention to the expansion of both public and private service industries from professional, health, care. and education services to the employment by the wealthier of butlers and nannies. This economy employed over 80% of the workforce by 2018 (ONS, 2019). Disabled people were both recipients of service industries, especially care, and also employed by the services.

Early in the 21st century the Department for Education in England took the view that it was the duty of individuals to achieve well at school, train and retrain, skill and upskill, and engage in lifelong learning. It claimed that "the global economy has made extinct the notion of a job for life, the imperative now is employability for life" (DfES/DTI, 2003, p. 15). This put the responsibility to train, retrain, and seek employment on young people even if governments had failed to restructure their economies to provide jobs. Much discussion centered on the speed with which information can be shared and the increased digitalization of information, but whether this is dramatically different from the historical accumulation of knowledge was questionable. The work required to build material goods, such as computers, aircraft, and pharmaceuticals, is a development of 19th-century brain work that built bridges, railways, and sewage systems, and physical labor is still required despite automation. On the one hand, a knowledge economy appears to refer to the newer technical knowledge associated with aerospace engineering, and, on the other, it refers to ensuring that motor vehicle maintenance students know how to use computers (Tomlinson, 2013).

Problems with a global economy were quickly apparent. Joseph Stiglitz, former chief economic adviser to the World Bank, has consistently pointed out that that economies dominated by transnational companies with little national regulation have increased national and global inequalities, mass unemployment, social injustice, and economic inefficiency. Those who benefit from unequal global markets benefit financially in ways unbelievable to ordinary tax-paying workers (Stiglitz, 2007). This may change in the near future as inequalities in developed countries become more obvious and unsustainable (Dorling, 2019, 2021). Richard Sennett drew attention to the "spectre of uselessness," which hung over professional and manual workers alike, leading to whole populations feeling insecure and turning their anxieties onto immigrant and foreign workers (Sennett, 2006), a consequence clearly apparent in England after the vote to leave the European Union in 2016. Brown et al. (2011) produced a devastating critique, pointing out that the "opportunity bargain" supported by governments, especially in the United Kingdom and United States, was now broken. The bargain that more education, even if fueled by student debt, would lead to well-paid jobs and a comfortable lifestyle no longer holds. The global market now includes many well-educated low-cost workers from non-Western countries, and Western faith that the knowledge economy would secure upward mobility for Western workers has gone. The encouragement of individual self-interest by governments had, even before Western economies were affected by the virus pandemic, contributed to a fear among the middle classes that their children and grandchildren might not benefit in this globalized economy.

By the second decade of the 21st century, this realization appeared to be spreading. Political philosopher Michael Sandal wrote in 2013 that the era of market triumphalism was dead, although people still did not accept that the financial crash of 2008 was due to the immorality of unregulated markets (Sandal, 2012). The realization that the benefits of globalization had largely benefited the rich owners of capital and created inequality was more apparent. Governments were seemingly less able to control their economies in a globalized world, and faith in free markets and free trade was beginning to be questioned. Larry Elliott noted early in 2020, "The world is changing: we're in the era of deglobalisation" (Elliott, 2020a). In particular, a greater understanding of climate change was forcing governments to question the movement of goods and services, and the notion that nations can "take back control" of their economies unilaterally was questionable. Economists and political groups around the world were attempting to produce scenarios for the future of work and the nature of the education and skill training that might be needed in the future. In England, the chief executive of the Royal Society of Arts (RSA) wrote that by early 2020, "Economic insecurity is the new normal for millions of people in this country" (Taylor, 2020, 20). He noted an Royal Society of Arts (RSA) survey, which found that only 43% of people were confident they will be able to maintain a decent quality of life, and economic insecurity was widespread among all ages. There was also a dismal forecast that automation, robotics, and e-commerce would continue to create winners and losers, with women, the low paid, and the disabled bearing the brunt of job losses (ILO, 2020).

Where then does even a partial retreat from a global economy leave young people with disabilities in terms of education, training, work, or a workless future?

BEING DISABLED IN A GLOBAL ECONOMY

Hannah Arendt pointed out that before industrialization and mass elementary education, divisions between the skilled and unskilled were of little importance (Arendt, 1998). It was accepted that all activity, whether manual or mental, required some form of skill. Economies demanded that all, even the "infirm," do some kind of work. With industrial notions of the division of labor and hierarchies of schooling, contrast between intellectual and manual labor developed. The construction of separate schooling for those regarded as disabled, originally the physically impaired, deaf-dumb, blind, and feeble-minded, led inexorably to links between those coming from "special" education to vocational training for lower level work (Richardson et al., 2017; Tomlinson, 2017). This persisted into the 21st century, with vocational ed-ucation and training being associated with second-class provision, and from elite perspectives, something "for other people's children." Vocational courses were presented as lower prestige alternatives to academic schooling and associated with manual work. Lower level courses were advertised as suitable for those with disabilities (Tomlinson, 2013).

The notion that children and adults living with the various labels of disability should be able to join mainstream society is, in historical terms, relatively recent. Into the 1970s individualistic models of disability as medical problems, "individual tragedies," or learning difficulties that should lead to separation and segregation were still dom-inant. Challenges to the segregation of children in special schools, units, and classes became more prominent in the 1980s when integration—later "inclusion"—into main-stream schooling became the accepted understanding. For postschool young adults the challenges came largely from disabled people themselves and their organizations, espe-cially in the United Kingdom, the United States, and Sweden. In Britain the social model of disability—the view that people with impairments are disabled by society's failure to accommodate to their needs—slowly became acceptable (see Barnes et al., 2002). The first Disability Studies course in Britain was an Open University Course, which aimed to help students improve their social and professional skills for employment (Finklestein, 1997). This was followed by a range of undergraduate and postgraduate courses in main-stream further and higher education institutions across the United Kingdom. Ayesha Vernon, herself a blind university lecturer, was one of the first to study the simultaneous discrimination against disabled Black women in education and employment (Vernon, 1998). In one of their first reports, the Office for Students noted that students and staff with several disabilities needed special help, suggesting that all buildings put in ramps and elevators (OfS, 2020).

Disability in industrial societies has long been linked to poverty, unskilled work, exclusion from the labor market, and stigmatization of social benefit claimants. Globalization of the world economy was unlikely to change this without delib-erate policies. It will still be the case that "the removal of disabling physical and social structures [was] unlikely to be prioritized within the imperatives of the globalized economy" (Holden & Beresford, 2002, p. 194). Although worldwide calls for education and skill training have created an expansion of institutions, courses, and guidance for groups previously excluded (especially working classes and lower castes, women and disabled people), state intervention in providing funding and resources is still prob-lematic. Moves toward inclusive education have meant that a range of schools, colleges, and universities now incorporate students regarded as having learning difficulties, and physical and mental health disabilities. All young people are expected to participate in some kind of education and training for a potential working future, or failing that, be prepared for independent living. But despite a concern for expanding the labor supply by the "inclusion" of disabled people, governments are reluctant to provide the neces-sary funding and resources, and have pushed much of the assessment, provision, and care into the private sector.

People with disabilities in developed economies are still more likely to be in poverty. The austerity measures brought in as a response to the 2008 financial crash by David Cameron's government in England led to a raft of damaging social consequences, including to the 8 million people living with some kind of a disability. Disabled people are more likely to be less qualified and unemployed, paid less than nondisabled people, and incur more costs as they live with impairments in lower income families (UNISON, 2019). The policy in England of a Universal Credit system of social security payments led to a court judgment that disabled people were treated unlawfully over claims for disabilities. Universal credit merged six previous benefits people were entitled to claim, including disability, housing, and child benefits. Claims have to be made online, which further disadvantages many people. Those with learning disabilities, even when not severe, found that the abuse and stigmatization leveled over the centuries, was still directed at them if they failed to complete complex requirements to perform required bureaucratic tasks (Rogers, 2016). One of us recently observed a claimant for Universal Credit with learning difficulties and without access to a computer being told that payments would be calculated on months of 4 weeks and thus for 1 month she would receive no money and must "budget accordingly."

VOCATIONAL EXPECTATIONS

Despite the predominantly negative views of disabled young people, parents and students in developed and developing countries have demanded more recognition and resources for those who have extra difficulties in learning in competitive education environments. Richardson and colleagues (2017), examining the effects of mass schooling globally, pointed out that one effect is a closer convergence of special and vocational educational. They noted that an expanding knowledge economy plus neoliberal market ideologies has raised the level of skills deemed necessary for social and economic functioning (Richardson et al., 2017). Globally, links between those with descriptive special educational labels are still closely linked to vocational education. While SEND (Special Educational Needs and Disabilities) is the catch-all label recognizable in England, as is NEET (Not in Education, Employment, or Training), in Japan "Freeters" describes low education levels, possible disability, and unemployment (Richardson et al., 2017, p. 13).

In England, government was expected to take a lead in providing opportunities for those with lower school attainments and SEND labels by providing skill training in colleges of further education or with employer-led apprenticeships. On the positive side, the effects of more inclusion and recognition of difficulties in school education over the past 20 years were to some extent successful. In 2002, just less than 20% of 16-year-olds labeled as having special educational needs and disabilities but without what was then a Statement of Special Needs (now an Education, Health, and Care Plan [EHCP]) gained five good GCSEs.[2] In 2012, this had risen to 59%. For those disabled students with a Statement/Plan, only 8.7% gained the five GCSEs in 2002, but in 2012 this rose to nearly 25%. Thus, there were more students who are qualified go on to vocational and further education and enter university courses.

Historically, having large numbers of people, especially young people, not in work has been a focus for government anxiety on both economic and political levels. Nineteenth-century links between assumed low ability, disabilities, poverty, and unemployment have resonated into the 21st century. In 2010, the International Labour Organization forecast that failure to find work would have dramatic results. "An inability to find employment creates a sense of uselessness and idleness among young people that can lead to increased crime, mental problems, violence, conflicts and drug-taking" (ILO, 2010, p. 1). All young people in England were required after 2008 to stay in some form of education or training until 18, and those with an Education Health and Care Plan were the responsibility of their local council until aged 25. A plethora of training courses at a range of skill levels were offered in colleges of further education and by employers (Tomlinson, 2013). While it was the responsibility of students over 16 to declare if they had a learning difficulty or disability, colleges were often reluctant to take students who were badly behaved or were disengaged from education. In 2011, 2.5 million young people aged 14–19 were taking some form of vocational course, but a third had little or no value in the labor market (Wolf, 2011). Wolf (2011) recommended that young people should not be tracked irreversibly into vocational courses, and only good qualifications recognized by employers should be acceptable.

Central government took no responsibility for the effects of funding cuts to the Further Education sector from 2010 and claimed they had increased the number of apprenticeships. The Department for Education insisted that all students should attain the GCSE qualification in math and English and announced that schools should be held accountable for these attainments and preparing students for postschool success. In 2017, after pressure from disability charities, apprentices with learning difficulties were exempted from these required standards for math and English, and by 2018 some 12.3% of all apprenticeship starters had declared a learning difficulty (Jolin, 2021). Under David Cameron's government, apprenticeships were to be paid for by a levy (tax) on businesses and there appeared to be an increase in those taking up apprenticeships. Much of this was due to employers renaming existing workers as apprentices with fewer school leavers being taken on. Some apprenticeships were at high academic or technical levels and not available for those with lower attainments. A new T-level course (technical) introduced as an equivalent to the A-level (advanced-level GCSE) by 2023, was also unlikely to be taken up by many students with a disability. Although disability inclusion consultancies sprang up, employers continued to be reluctant to take on those with disabilities, especially the "neurodiverse"—those with dyslexia, dyspraxia, and attention-deficit/hyperactivity disorder, for example (Fuller, 2020). As Keep (2019) pointed out, "some issues have been hanging over the vocational sector for forty years. If we truly want to transform education and society, we can't keep passing the buck" (Keep, 2019, p. 4). Policies have created a set of quasi-markets, funded by government through employers, with little advice for students over their "choice," and not generally serving, as intended, to raise the skill levels of potential workers in the country.

There had been some expectations that after Britain left the European Union there would be more control over immigration of low-skilled workers and more chances for disabled young people to be trained for jobs, but this has remained highly problematic, especially in the economic situation created by the COVID-19 pandemic. The government hastily put together a Plan for Jobs portfolio, which included the Section-based Work Academy Programme (SWAP), a sector-based work program pairing businesses with skilled people, and Kickstart, a program for young people 16–24 on benefits, who were at risk of long-term unemployment (gov.uk/jobhelp 2021). Charities set up more training programmes for disabled adults, and a report on Further Education set out a series of reforms and programs intended to include all young people (DfE, 2021). But a study published in the same month suggested that 10 years of progress on employment for all, especially in old industrial areas, had been wiped out (Beatty & Fothergill, 2021). In addition, by 2021 the coronavirus pandemic was limiting numbers and kinds of apprenticeships, with six out of ten employers reporting they had ceased recruiting apprentices (Little, 2021).

HIGHER EDUCATION

Although vocational education and training was still the destination of a majority of young disabled people, by 2010 more were now qualifying for entry to higher levels of education. As noted, governments had come to believe that a higher education at the university level was necessary in a knowledge-driven economy. From the 1990s institutions and participation rates in higher education rapidly grew around the world. In Canada, Japan, and South Korea, over 50% of young people were enrolled in higher education by 1991, closely followed by China and the United States (Roser & Ortiz-Ospina, 2010). Prime Minister Blair announced in 1999 that he, too, wanted England to reach this target, and by 2017, 49% were in higher education in some form. In 2017/18, 2.34 million students (1.77 million undergraduates and 0.57 million postgraduates) were studying in the 164 institutions offering higher education, which included some colleges of further education (Higher Education Statistics Authority, 2017).

The expansion of higher education institutions, more being granted university status, and the increased number of young people gaining required entry qualifications had the positive effect of bringing in more students with disabilities. Into the 1980s, students with disabilities in higher education were not recorded in separate tables, being notionally included under the "disadvantaged." Under the 2004 Higher Education Act (part 3), higher education institutions could set their own fees, but had to submit plans to promote equality of opportunity and encourage access of underrepresented groups. Up to 2009, higher education institutions could set fees of up to £3000 pounds sterling. This went up to £9000 by 2012 and £9250 by 2019. This encouraged higher education institutions to count the numbers of students who were now required to declare if they had a disability, encourage applications from disabled young people, and make provisions for them. Students who, for a variety of reasons, chose not to declare a disability would of course not be counted.

By 2017, 13.2% of students in English universities reported having at least one disability. The Office for Students estimated that this translated to almost 300,000 students and declared that "Disabled students make up a significant part of the student population" and "disabled students contribute to a more diverse student body and bring a wider variety of views into the seminar room" (OfS 2019, p. 1). The Office for Students was established in 2017 out of a merger of the previous Higher and Further Education Council for England and an Office for Fair Access. It does not fund students directly but gives advice and guidance under the remit of ensuring access and success in higher education, especially for disadvantaged and disabled students. The Office defined disabled students as those with specific learning differences such as dyslexia or attention-deficit disorder, mental health conditions, physical disabilities, sensory impairments, and social or communication impairments, such as autistic spectrum disorders, and long-term health conditions. The disadvantaged and disabled still needed to take loans for their £9,250 tuition fee and any maintenance loans, although bursaries and allowances were available. For students with disabilities, a Disabled Student Allowance (DSA) has been available for nearly 20 years. Figure 19.1 indicates the percentages of UK-based students receiving

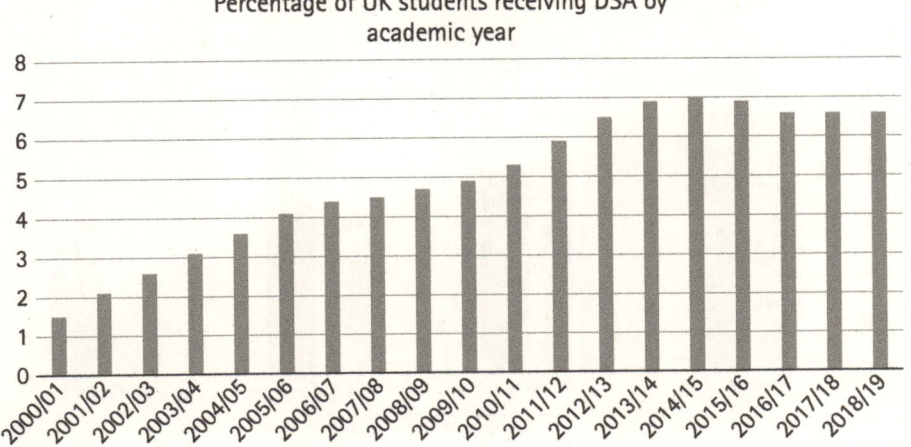

FIGURE 19.1 Percentage of UK domiciled full-time first-degree students in receipt of Disabled Students' Allowance by academic year.

Source: Data taken from Table C in *Inclusive Teaching and Learning in Higher Education—A Route to Excellence*. Higher Education Student Access.

a Disabled Students Allowance up to 2019. This shows that from 1.5% in 2001, 6.9% were in receipt of the allowance by 2016, leveling off at 6.6% for the following 3 years.

Some 40 years after the social model of understanding disability had been formulated and elaborated (Oliver 1990), the OfS now incorporated it. They state: "The social model of disability is widely accepted as the most effective way that universities and colleges can respond to the needs of disabled students" (Office for Students, 2019, p. 1). Although the social model stressed that disability was not something medical to be treated but a failing on the part of society and the environment, the Office was concerned that it was not always applied in universities and many institutions saw disabled students as a "problem to be solved" rather than a structural issue requiring institutional changes. In keeping with the English obsession with performance tables and competitive comparisons, the Office was concerned that there was a gap of 2.8% between disabled and nondisabled students graduating with good first- and upper-second-class degrees and set up another Centre for Transforming Access and Student Outcomes in Higher Education. In addition, information is now collected on the employment rates of students graduating from higher education, especially as compared to those who do not gain good school examination results.

Figure 19.2 compares employment rates for people with and without disabilities in March 2019, broken down by degree attainment. While it is a very positive advance that 73% of disabled students with degrees went on into employment in 2019, there was little information on the kind of work or its permanence. A downside to employment information is that only 21% of disabled young people without any school qualifications are actually in employment. Disabled people in England, especially those with low attainments, get very little help from their colleges or government agencies.

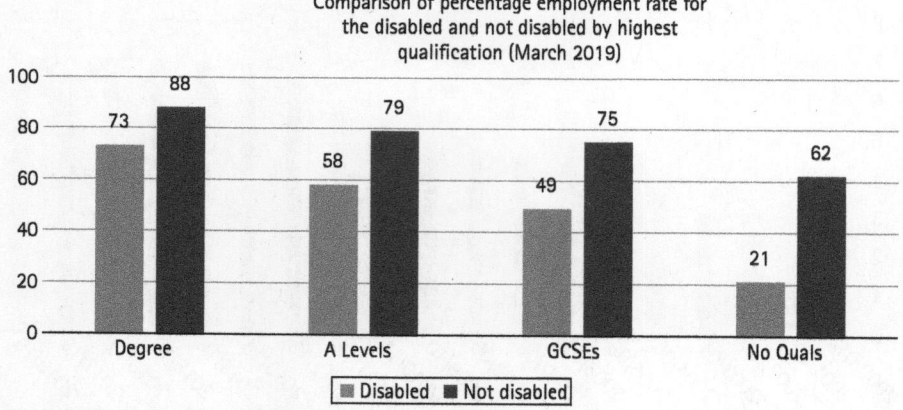

FIGURE 19.2 Employment rates of disabled and not disabled people by highest qualification achieved.

Source: HM Government. DfE Statistics Higher Education. Data from https://assets.publishing.service.gov.uk/governm ent/uploads/system/uploads/attachment_data/file/875199/employment-of-disabled-people-2019.pdf

TRANSITION TO WORK IN GERMANY

After the global economic crash of 2008, Germany played a leading role in helping stabilize other economies, and its own economy continued to function well. Much of the credit went to a strong manufacturing sector and a highly skilled workforce, trained in a dual system of apprenticeships in all industrial and commercial areas and where, until recently, vocational training was offered to all young people who were not going on to higher education or immediate employment. There was less rhetoric about a "knowledge economy" as in other countries, but it was assumed that the economy needed a highly educated and qualified workforce at all levels. The English had long admired German education and training, especially for those with lower attainments. In 1916, the Master of University College, Oxford, wrote, with class and academic snobbery, that "German education makes good use of all its second-grade ability, which in England is far too much of a waste product" (Sadler, 1916). Sadler (1916) misunderstood the notion of *Beruf*—the trade or occupation which defined German vocational training and included the notion of the full development of all young people. By 2016 there were around 350 state-regulated occupations made up of every aspect of economic life, with 45% of young people over 16 being in the dual system of apprenticeship training (Gomolla, 2020).

After World War II, the dual system where apprentices spent time in colleges and with employers, with cooperation and funding from central and local Lander (states), employers and trade unions worked well, but a selective school system persisted. Children with special educational needs and disabilities were usually placed in the *Hauptschule*—the lower level secondary school—or in special schools. The label "Kruppelschulen" (Cripples school), only translated as for the physically impaired in 1964, and special school teachers and their unions were reluctant to accept inclusion in mainstream education. By the 1990s, the dual system and training for one job became less acceptable as globalization increased the need for new kinds of skill. There was, for example, no dual system for jobs in information technology. The transition to work for those with no school leaving certificates—mainly the lower attainers and disabled students—and no place in the dual system became an issue of concern. Additionally, in the first international educational attainment tests for 15-year-olds in 2001, German students overall did not perform well in the tests, despite students from special schools not being entered. Political and public debates around these new developments in the education and training system did not lead to structural and democratizing reforms; the lobbies for selection rather than a fully comprehensive system were too strong (Zapp & Powell, 2018).

Recognition of the existence of disability increased from 2001, when the federal government passed a Rehabilitation and Participation of Disabled Persons Act. This promised to promote equal participation and counter disadvantage and discrimination. More students with a recognized disability were able to enter higher education, and they accounted for around 2% of the student body in 2001. In 2009, Germany signed the UN Convention of the Rights of Persons with Disabilities, and by law German universities became responsible for recognizing and assisting students with disabilities. As in England, the organizations to assist students with disabilities were in the administration, rather than the academic area. One unforeseen issue was that, as employment possibilities globally became more problematic, middle-class and nondisabled young people, armed with higher level school leaving certificates, began to apply for the good apprenticeships, further disadvantaging those coming from special schools or with disabilities. As in other countries, the coronavirus pandemic affected numbers of apprenticeships offered by employers, and students with disabilities were likely to have fewer chances of starting good apprenticeships. Even before the pandemic, a study found that almost a quarter of all students in German higher education institutions reported some kind of a disability and especially a mental health issue (Poskowsky et al., 2017). All Western European countries are finding that many students felt their mental health was affected by a shortage of good jobs, and then by the pandemic.

FINLAND: A MODEL FOR THE WORLD?

Comparing education systems and their results, especially for lower attaining students, is now of permanent interest to governments. It was in 1958 that a group of scholars, led by Martii Takala from Finland, developed an International Assessment for the Evaluation of Educational Achievement. Since then many large-scale international tests have been developed, the best known being the Programme for International Student Assessment (PISA) tests for 15-year-olds. The results of tests provide much anxiety for governments globally.

Finland, a country which usually outperforms other countries, became a magnet for educationalists and policymakers, anxious to examine how good results were achieved. One lasting feature of the Finnish test results was that the lowest quartile of student achievers—mainly those with special needs and disabilities—obtained higher scores than similar groups in other countries. After completing their lower secondary comprehensive schooling, around 55% of students go on to upper secondary school and university, including some students with disabilities. Apart from a small number of students with more severe impairments who go on after 16 to special vocational colleges and training centers, over 40% of students go on to well-resourced vocational colleges, leading to recognized qualifications and employment. For other countries, the question becomes: If Finland can prepare all young people, including those with special needs and disabilities for higher educational and good vocational training levels, should Finland become a model for other education systems around the world?

One explanation for Finland's success was provided by eminent Professor Pasi Sahlberg at Helsinki University, who has studied education and training systems around the world and advised the World Bank and education leaders globally. In 2015, he wrote that "The key factor in Finland's development of a successful knowledge economy with good governance, and a respected education system, has been its ability to reach a broad consensus on most major issues concerning Finland's future direction as a nation" (Sahlberg, 2015, p. 49). It is difficult to find any other country that boasts a respected education system and consensus about the future.

After a contested development toward a comprehensive education system (*peruskoulu*) for all children and young people, education in Finland was accepted as a public good and a strong force in economic and social nation-building. The education and skill training system was based on the belief that all young people should have free and equal access to education to the highest possible levels. A system of excellent teacher education and a culture of trust between political leaders, education authorities, teachers, and parents developed, and all children, whatever their disability, had a right to enrol in their local school. A Basic Education Act in 1998 required an individual education plan for all young people requiring extra support, and at any time around 30% of students are receiving support. A common claim is for help with dyslexia, but it is noteworthy that in any kind of further education all students are required to learn another language. There is no national testing or inspection, although children are subject to regular formative tests to check on their progress and help with any learning problems. All schools must have special education teachers and classroom assistants, and prevention of learning difficulties is the aim. Students who go on at 15/16 to upper secondary education study an academic curriculum leading to university, and as in Germany and other Nordic countries, those going on to vocational colleges study well-organized, well-resourced courses leading to recognized employment qualifications. In addition, Finland is consistently reported as being the happiest country in the world (Dorling & Koljonen, 2020).

The success of the education system, however, does not always translate into success in the economy. Finland suffered economic problems in the 2008 global financial crash, and although it claimed by the early 21st century to have the fourth most successful "knowledge economy," especially in telecommunications and electronics, there were problems in 2012 with the collapse of the mobile phone business Nokia. Although the labor market at this time still provided a range of opportunities, there was a 16% youth unemployment rate and only 20% disabled young people were in permanent employment, with 50% in part-time or temporary work (Lamsa, 2012). In addition, 10% of children were still living in low-income households, and immigrant children and young people faced more challenges in learning and working. Vocational education suffered funding reductions, but even after the global financial crash, the labor market continued to provide a wide range of opportunities for those with skills learned in vocational colleges (Silliman & Virtanen, 2019).

Finland could still provide a model for other countries to follow. It is one of the most equal countries by income in the world and has a high rate of social and educational mobility (Dorling & Koljonen, 2020). Mobility is defined as the freedom to make life choices, irrespective of birth origins, rather than "becoming better" than others in a social hierarchy. As Dorling and Koljonen noted, "Finland offers an example of what policies can produce. Policies put the equality of individuals at the heart, with the aim of building a fairer, happier, and more prosperous society" (p. xviii).

CONCLUSIONS

In 2020, the notion of a global economy had become problematic, as the global spread of COVID-19, a new virus, affected all countries. The pneumonia-type coronavirus was detected in China in early January. By the end of March 2020, countries around the world from European countries, including Germany, France, and Spain, to Asian countries, including Singapore and Malaysia, were in "lockdown" with citizens required to stay indoors, work from home, and isolate themselves to prevent passing on the virus. By early 2021, there was a fear of a global recession worse than that of 2008 and many countries, including the United Kingdom, were in "lockdown" measures again, although more key workers were carrying on their employment. Globally, stock markets suffered losses, and despite interventions by the International Monetary Fund, the US Federal Reserve, and the Bank of England, "there has been a growing fear that the world faces a perfect storm" (Partington & Kollowe, 2020). Economists claimed that central banks could do little to prevent a global recession. Larry Elliot forecast a prolonged recession—with "travel bans, sporting events cancelled, mass gatherings prohibited, stock markets in free-fall, deserted shopping centres" (Elliott, 2020b)—which did indeed come to be the norm by 2021.

In England, schools, including special schools and colleges of further education, faced closures, and more disabled people relying on carers for daily help needed assistance. The years of austerity and cuts to local authority funding from 2010 became all too apparent, as local councils struggled to provide necessary services. Universities and colleges in England and other European countries closed most face to face tuition, and expectations were that students would study online. Students from deprived backgrounds or with disabilities, who had struggled to arrive in higher education, struggled with online learning, especially if they lacked access to a smartphone or a laptop (Fazackerly, 2020).

For some people there may be some short-term positives resulting from the pandemic. An Oxford primary school special needs teacher noted that students with learning difficulties did not seem as far behind as expected in the autumn of 2020. For some students this may have been due to more attention being available at home than at school. However, as almost all students had been out of school due to national lockdown, it was also the case that teachers were not assuming prior knowledge and so were going back over material, benefitting those with learning disabilities. Another positive, observed at the higher education level, was that lectures were now routinely recorded. Students with disabilities who struggled to attend lectures and tutorials in person were no longer missing out. Students with learning disabilities had more opportunity to listen to lectures at their own pace. Some autistic students have said that they prefer working remotely.

Despite these potential positives, the consequences of the pandemic on the disabled may be long term. At the start of COVID-19 restrictions, local authorities in England were asked to carry out risk assessments for students with an EHCP to consider whether they were able to attend their usual education setting. Schools, including special schools, largely remained open for vulnerable students. However, government data (see Figure 19.3) showed that in January 2021, only 34% of students with an EHCP were attending school compared to 75% when not in lockdown. Among the third who were in school, it was not possible to meet their EHCP objectives. One teaching assistant said: "We are meant to be helping them (their students with disabilities) to interact and socialize, but we are in a room on our own with hardly anyone else in school" (personal communication).

The UK Chancellor of the Exchequer, Rishi Sunak, in post for only a month in the Johnson Conservative government, announced in mid-March 2020 that "The coronavirus is a public health emergency; it is also an economic emergency" and claimed that a £350 billion package of loans and grants, mainly for large businesses and airlines, would be made available (Elliot & Stewart, 2020). Immediate assistance in the form of social security money for those losing their jobs, the already unemployed, those on poverty wages, and the sick and disabled was notionally to be dealt with by a Corona Virus Retention Scheme and the furloughing[3] of workers. But as always the future of those with any sort of disability in a global knowledge economy which demanded higher levels of skill and education remained problematic.

In the new deglobalizing economy, ravaged by a pandemic, the future for those with disabilities does not look promising. The UK Office for National Statistics had noted in 2019 that disabled people were 28% less likely to be in work than the nondisabled,

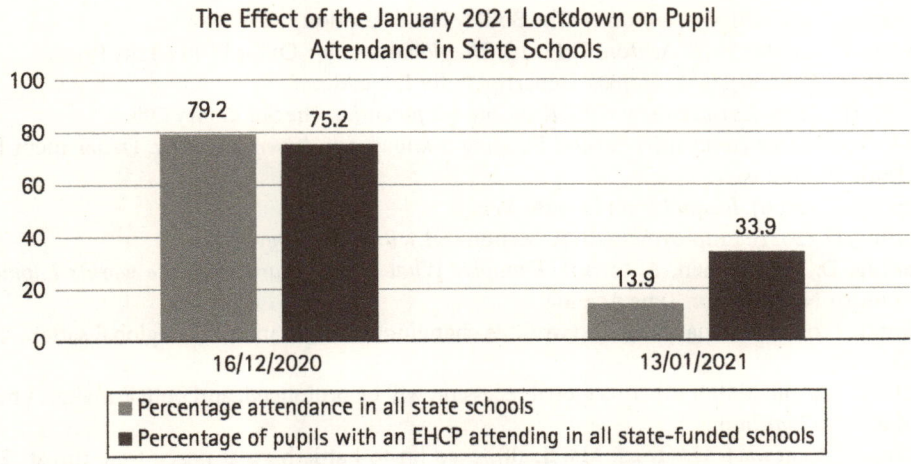

FIGURE 19.3 The effect of the January 2021 lockdown on pupil attendance in state schools.

Source: Data from https://explore-education-statistics.service.gov.uk/find-statistics/attendance-in-education-and-early-years-settings-during-the-coronavirus-covid-19-outbreak/2021-week-6

and by early 2021 the effects of Brexit leaving the European Union were beginning to affect all employment. How much bureaucratic benevolence will there be when the profits of large companies and stock markets are at risk? Despite any upskilling of the workforce and technical developments that allow for more flexible working practices, will employers choose to hire disabled employees when there is a surfeit of potential workers available for the promised global knowledge economy?

NOTES

1. Legislation in this chapter refers to England and Wales until 1999. Under devolution, responsibility for their systems of education and training was transferred to Wales and Northern Ireland in 1999. Scotland had been responsible for its education and training system from 1945.
2. The General Certificate of Secondary Education (GCSE) is the public examination taken by young people aged 15/16 from 1988. The advanced-level GCSE (A level) is taken at 18 and was the main qualification for university entrance.
3. The furlough scheme was part of the UK governments plan to protect jobs. Initially 9 million workers had 80% of their wages paid with government help to employers. The scheme was due to end in April 2021.

REFERENCES

Ainley, P. (2016). *Betraying a generation: How education is failing young people*. Policy Press.

Arendt, H. (1998). *The human condition* (2nd ed.). Penguin Books.

Barnes, C., Oliver, M., & Barton, L. (2002). *Disability studies today*. Cambridge Polity Press.

Beatty, C., & Fothergill, S. (2021). *The impact of the corona virus on older industrial Britain*. Centre for Regional and Social Research, Sheffield Hallam University.

Brown, G. (2017). *My life, our times*. The Bodley Head: London.

Brown, H., Lauder, H., & Ashton, D. (2011). *The global auction*. Oxford University Press.

DfE. (2021, January). *Skills for jobs*. Department for Education.

DfES/DTI. (2003). *21st century skills: Realising our potential*. The Stationary Office.

DTI. (1998). *Our competitive future: Building a knowledge driven economy*. Department for Trade and Industry.

Dorling, D. (2019). *Inequality and the 1%*. Verso.

Dorling, D. (2021). Employment. In A. Menon (Ed.), *Brexit and beyond*.

Dorling, D., & Koljonen, A. (2020). *Fintopia: What we can learn from the world's happiest country*. Newcastle on Tyne Agenda.

Elliot, L. (2020a, February 14). The world is changing: We're in an era of deglobalisation. *The Guardian*.

Elliot, L. (2020b, March 16). This global recession will be prolonged, and policy-makers know that. *The Guardian*.

Elliot, L., & Stewart, H. (2020, March 18). £350 bn to battle biggest peace time threat. *The Guardian*.

Farrell, L., & Fenwick, T. (Eds.) (2007). *Educating the global workforce*. Routledge.

Fazakerley, A. (2020, March 17). Corona virus: Universities having to adapt fast in face of crisis. *The Guardian*.

Finkelstein, V. (1997). Emancipating disability studies. In T. Shakespeare (Ed.), *The disability studies reader*. Cassell.

Frederick, A., & Shifrer, D. (2018). Race and disability: From analogy to intersectionality. *Sociology of Race and Ethnicity*.

Fuller, G. (2020, February 4). Autism to ADHD: Thinking differently about recruitment. *The Guardian*.

Gomolla, M. (2020). School reform, educational governance, and discourses on social justice and democratic education in Germany. Oxford Research Encyclopedia of Education.

Higher Education Statistic Authority. (2017). Higher education student statistics: UK, 2017/18—Student numbers and characteristics. https://www.hesa.ac.uk/news/17-01-2019/sb252-higher-education-student-statistics/numbers.

Holden, C., & Beresford, P. (2002). Globalization and disability. In C. Barnes, M. Oliver, & L. Barton (Eds.), *Disability studies today*. Cambridge Polity Press.

ILO. (2010). *World joblessness soars*. Geneva International Labour Organization.

ILO. (2020). *Uncertain and uneven recovery expected to follow labour market crisis*.Geneva International Labour Organization.

Jolin, L. (2021, February 9). Disability: What can be done to make training more inclusive? *Apprentices* (supplement). *The Guardian*.

Keep, E. (2019). Some ideas have been hanging over the vocational sector for forty years. *FE Weekly, 298*.

Lamsa, A.-L. (2012). *Active inclusion of young people with disabilities and health problems in Finland*. Europa Foundation.

Little, J. (2021, February 9). The Covid effect: Apprenticeships hit hard, but well placed to recover. *Apprentices* (supplement). *The Guardian*.

Mandeville, B. (1714). *The fable of the bees*. Liberty Classics (republished 1988).

Maroto, M., Pettinicchio, D., & Patterson, A. C. (2018). Hierarchies of categorical disadvantage: Economic insecurity at the intersection of disability, gender, and race. *Gender & Society, 33*(1), 64–93.

OfS. (2019). *Beyond the bare minimum: Are universities and schools doing enough for disabled students?* Office for Students.

OfS. (2020). *Annual report*. Office for Students.

Oliver, M. (1990). *The politics of disablement*. Macmillan.

ONS. (2019). *Employment in the UK*. Office for National Statistics.

Partington, R., & Kollowe, J. (2020, March 17). Global recession fear as markets plunge despite joint central banks. The Guardian.

Piketty, T. (2014). *Capital in the 21st century*. The Belknap Press for Harvard University Press.

Poskowski, J., Heissenberg, S., Zassinger, S., & Brenner, J. (2017). *Studying with impairments in Germany*. National Association for Student Affairs.

Richardson, J. G., Jinting, W., & Judge, D. M. (2017). *The global convergence of vocational and special education*. Routledge.

Rogers, C. (2016). *Intellectual disability and being human*. Routledge.

Roser, M., & Ortiz-Ospina, S. (2010). Tertiary education of the world population. Our World in Data. Oxford Martin School.

Sadler, Sir M. (1916, January 14). Need we imitate the German system. *The Times*.

Sahlberg, P. (2015). *Finnish lessons*. Teachers College Press.

Sandel, M. S. (2012). *What money can't buy*. Penguin Books.

Sennett, R. (2006). *The culture of the new capitalism*. Yale University Press.

Shuelka, M. J., Johnstone, C. J., Thomas, G., Artiles, A. J. (2019). *The Sage handbook of inclusion and diversity*. SAGE Publications.

Silliman, M., & Virtanen, H. (2019) Labour market returns to vocational secondary education. ETLA Working paper no 65. Research Institute of the Finnish Economy.

Stiglitz, J. (2007). *Making globalisation work*. Penguin Books.

Taylor, M. (2020). The feeling of insecurity is widely shared: It can help us empathise with others. *Royal Societiey of Arts Journal*, 4, 3.

Tomlinson, S. (2013). *Ignorant yobs: Low attainers in a global knowledge economy*. Routledge.

Tomlinson, S. (2017). *A sociology of special and inclusive education*. Routledge.

UNISON. (2019). *Disabled people and cuts*. UNISON.

Vernon, A. (1998). Multiple oppression and the disabled people's movement. In T. Shakespeare (Ed.), *The disability reader*. Cassell.

Wolf, A. (2011). *Review of vocational education (The Wolf Report)*. Department for Education.

World Bank. (2003). *Life-long learning in a global knowledge economy: Challenges for developing countries*. World Bank.

Zapp, M., & Powell, J. W. (2018). Shaping the educational research field in Germany and the impact of international large-scale assessment. In M. Zapp, M. Marques, & J. W. Powell (Eds.), *European educational research (re) constructed*. Didcot Symposium Books.

PART VI

Work and Economic Wellbeing

....

CHAPTER 20

RELATIONAL INEQUALITY AND THE STRUCTURES THAT DISADVANTAGE

....

MICHELLE MAROTO AND DAVID PETTINICCHIO

QUANTITATIVE research is essential for documenting the different dimensions of disadvantage that marginalized groups face. Poverty rates, graduation rates, and employment rates tell us how different groups are doing relative to one another and how their situations have changed over time. Citing such statistics without considering the *structures that disadvantage*, however, can lead to a focus on deficits where individuals from different historically disadvantaged groups get blamed for their circumstances (Valencia, 2012; Walter & Andersen, 2013). When connected to racism, capitalism, colonialism, and, as we argue, ableism, disparities then implicate dimensions of the larger social structure. Only when structural dimensions of disadvantage are considered do we avoid the pitfalls associated with deficit models. It is not that micro-level accounts do not provide important insights on the (re)production of inequality, but explanations focused on individual traits, behaviors, and preferences, often assign responsibility to marginalized groups for their situations. These drawbacks can easily be seen in educational contexts when people believe that a student with disabilities does poorly because they "just don't get it" or when working disabled people living on the edge of poverty are considered "irresponsible" and "bad with money" because they have no savings. Much needed is a theoretical framework that accounts for the interrelated processes and spaces that structure disadvantage and inequality.

The present de-emphasis of structure in accounts of disability-based inequality is in part why disability is often left out of studies of stratification. Still anchored in medical and client-service models of disability (Pettinicchio, 2013, 2019; Watson & Shakespeare, Handbook), people wrongly assume that disability leads to unemployment, poverty, and homelessness *only* due to the disability itself—that disability is a personal shortcoming (albeit out of a person's control)—but that nonetheless demands special treatment, charity, and dependence. These models overlook the structures that turn disability into disadvantage. Viewing disability-based inequality through a structural lens illustrates the importance of policy that supports people with disabilities, organizational willingness to provide necessary accommodations, and enabling environments that empower rather than marginalize disabled people. In other words, a structural lens spotlights anti-ableist cultural and institutional contexts.

This chapter reviews three key dimensions of disadvantage in education, employment, and wealth associated with disability while emphasizing the social structures that create and maintain such disadvantages. Drawing on *relational inequality theory*, we discuss how disability has come to be a key categorical distinction around which status, resources, and opportunities are distributed. We focus on how inequality within and between organizations emerges through social relationships informed by the organizations individuals inhabit, which are themselves embedded in broader cultural and institutional fields. We further emphasize how disadvantage is the product of ableist inequality regimes that value certain bodies and minds, assigning worth to some individuals and rendering others worthless.

Status and Disadvantage

Approximately 15% of the adult population globally has at least one disability (World Bank, 2021; WHO, 2011; Mitra & Sambamoorthi, 2014). Rates vary cross-nationally with higher-income countries reporting greater prevalence (Kostanjsek et al., 2013; Pettinicchio & Maroto, 2021). Variation in prevalence, however, is often the result of the way disability is defined, asked about, and reported on, which has important implications for quantitative analyses (Altman, 2001; Barnartt & Altman, this Volume). The United Nations Washington Group on Disability Statistics (WG) and the International Classification of Functioning, Disability and Health (ICF) have been working for over 20 years now to promote a definition of disability based on the occurrence and severity of a broad set of functional limitations. Still, definitions across surveys and studies vary considerably (Me & Mbogoni, 2006). As our systematic analysis of cross-national IPUMS micro-census data across 65 countries showed, definitions, terminology, measurement, and instructions to respondents and enumerators matter for understanding disability prevalence (Pettinicchio & Maroto, 2021). This, in addition to problems of ex-post survey harmonization, makes prevalence difficult to compare cross-nationally.

Disability is also a broad category that encompasses a host of lived experiences tied directly to social, economic, and political barriers within ableist structures and cultures. Functional limitations associated with disabilities are but one dimension, and sociological insight tells us that we cannot fully understand disability without knowing about the *context that is disabling* (Altman, 2001; Shakespeare, 1996). For instance, the common use by quantitative social scientists of work-limiting measures of disability (see Maroto & Pettinicchio, 2015; Pettinicchio & Maroto, 2017) raises questions about why disability may or may not be present yet not disabling at work if, indeed, a person does not believe their disability limits work (Burkhauser, Daly, Houtenville, & Nargis, 2001; Burkhauser, Houtenville, & Tennant, 2014). Conversely, the lack of employer-provided workplace accommodations may be the primary disabling factor for an individual, which means that individuals with similar functional limitations in different jobs could have totally different experiences with what a work-limiting disability looks like. Some firms may be more inclined to provide accommodations than others—a function of organizational norms and cultures (Weil, 2001; Jolls & Prescott, 2004; Maroto & Pettinicchio, 2020). And so, disabling environments are the result of disadvantage, inequality, and marginalization perpetuated by structures that limit access to resources and opportunities for social citizenship and integration.

Similarly, in the United States and other countries, disability has often been understood in terms of its so-called mitigated state (Lee, 2003; Maroto & Pettinicchio, 2014a). That is, if individuals can mitigate their disability with medicines or aides, they are *not really disabled* because they can perform everyday activities—including work tasks—adequately (see for example, the Sutton v. United Airlines US Supreme Court Case). This way of thinking, ironically, acknowledges that experiencing disability is not just an individual "condition" but one resulting from accessing external measures like mitigating aides, which are themselves unequally distributed in the population. Although experiences with disability are inherently shaped by broader forces, inequality in access to such medicines, aides, and technologies is typically unrecognized.

Access is further determined by other statuses and categorical distinctions, including class, race, and gender. Groce's (2006) example of accessing toilets highlights the intersection of disability and socioeconomic status. If a toilet is in the home, often the case with wealthier households, a person with a mobility-related limitation can access it relatively easily. But, if the toilet is outside the home, often the case with poorer households, that person might experience much greater difficulty in accessing it. Thus, considering how individuals experience barriers because they cannot access their environments captures broader forms of gender, race, and class-based inequality (Kostanjsek et al., 2013; Maroto, Pettinicchio, & Patterson, 2019). Two individuals with the same disability may have widely different experiences with environmental barriers and obstacles depending on status and location.

Consequently, and despite being largely ignored by sociologists of stratification, inequality, and discrimination, disability is, like gender, race, and class, a diffuse status characteristic influencing experiences, social interaction, and well-being (Markus, 2008), making it one of the most important global dimensions of inequality. Diffuse status characteristics are socially relevant characteristics where different states (e.g., disabled and not disabled) hold differential status evaluations with some states being valued more than others (Ridgeway, 1991; Berger & Fisek, 2006). Status characteristics confer advantage and disadvantage, affect interpersonal interactions, and influence access to resources (Ridgeway, 1991; Webster & Hysom, 1998). And so, these categorical distinctions reward some groups and marginalize others. Disability is no exception.

Disability is a stigmatizing status characteristic (Brown & Ciciurkaite, 2021; Brown & Batty, this Volume) that continues to disadvantage and oppress an historically marginalized community. In studies incorporating implicit measures of disability attitudes, respondents indicated implicit preferences for people without disabilities, treating disabled people as hazardous, weak, and even childlike (Greenwald & Krieger, 2006; Tajfel, 1982; Robey et al., 2006; Vaughn et al., 2011). Not surprisingly, important calls are periodically made to further uncover how responses to status create inequality (Reskin, 2003; Ridgeway, 2014).

According to Ridgeway (2014, p. 3) "status is based on widely shared beliefs about the social categories or 'types' of people that are ranked by society as more esteemed and respected by others." By tying status and resources together, status beliefs legitimate and transform inequality beyond the control of resources to also include status differences. Consequently, disguised as meritocracy, it becomes widely assumed that groups with more resources are simply more competent than the groups without them. As these beliefs—divisions that now rest on status differences between groups—grow increasingly more prevalent, they constitute an independent factor perpetuating and justifying inequality.

These kinds of persistent disadvantages based on disability and other intersecting statuses can be found across a host of interrelated areas like education, employment, and wealth, all of which affect rates of poverty, insecurity, and overall economic well-being.

Education, particularly obtaining a university-level education, is critical in limiting disadvantage among people with disabilities. People with disabilities with a post-secondary degree earn more than those without one, and they are less likely to experience poverty (Barnard-Brak et al., 2010; She & Livermore, 2007; Dong et al., 2016; Maroto & Pettinicchio, 2020). With higher education as a pathway to overcome institutional and cultural barriers in the labor market, the number of students with disabilities entering colleges and universities has increased. Yet, students with disabilities are less likely to finish their degrees and more likely to get poor grades (DuPaul et al., 2017).

Although *employment levels* among people with disabilities vary globally, they tend to fall well below those of the general population. In the United States, disability employment rates hover around 30% (BLS 2020), in Canada they remain at about 50% (Morris et al., 2018; Maroto & Pettinicchio, 2014a), and they are closer to 60% in the United Kingdom (UK Annual Population Survey, Office for National Statistics, 2020). In the Global South, however, these often fall below 20% (Hanass-Hancock & Mitra, 2016). People with disabilities who find work earn less than other workers, which partly stems from occupational segregation, the rise of precarious work, and discriminatory practices within workplaces (Kaye, 2009; Maroto & Pettinicchio, 2014b; Schur & Kruse, this Volume).

Labor market barriers—whether delayed entry into the labor market, occupational clustering in low-paying jobs, or lack of upward mobility—contribute to lower earnings and, in turn, limit the ability to buy homes, save, and build wealth. As a result, households where at least one member reports a disability are less likely to own their homes, have lower overall net worth, and accumulate less in financial assets (Maroto, 2016; Maroto & Pettinicchio, 2020; Parish et al., 2010). These disparities are exacerbated by intersecting statuses (Miles, 2019). For instance, we describe a "hierarchy of categorical disadvantage" where women of color with disabilities are most likely to experience unemployment, low earnings, and poverty (Maroto et al., 2019; see also Pettinicchio & Maroto, 2017).

The dimensions of disadvantage experienced by people with disabilities are many. In addition to the intersectional nature of inequality, dimensions of disadvantage also build on one another (Brooks, this Volume; Egner, this Volume). Family and household situations affected by one or more household members having a disability may limit economic resources and create barriers in accessing health, social services, and education and, in turn, securing a well-paying job. In line with cumulative disadvantage and life course perspectives, disability at different points in adulthood, especially in one's active years, can also lead to negative economic outcomes further down the road (Clarke & Latham, 2014; this Volume). Stressor exposure across multiple life domains is also additive, which further affects the wellbeing of people with disabilities (Brown 2017; Ciciurkaite, Marquez-Velarde, and Brown 2021). This means that understanding structural disadvantage requires having a relatively fuller picture of both intersecting statuses, as well as overlapping organizational spaces.

DISABILITY AND THE STRUCTURES THAT DISADVANTAGE

Considering the interplay between categorical inequality and structural, organizational, institutional, and cultural milieus provides many clues about the large and lasting disparities in education, employment, and wealth. When rewards are assumed to be deserved, earned, and distributed via merit, it becomes easy to assume that those with less have less because of their own personal failings. They did not work hard enough, they were not smart enough, they did not have the needed skills, or, in the case of disability, they have a physical or cognitive limitation that kept them from getting ahead. Yet, more often than not, talent, skill, and hard work are not the factors that define winners and losers. A person's place in the structure of opportunities, their access to education and training, and their ability to move through life without experiencing discrimination often have a much greater influence on outcomes than individual-level factors. These structural factors are then linked to status characteristics like race, class, gender, and disability.

Relational Inequality Theory

Relational inequality theory (RIT) provides a framework describing how structures shape inequality through social interaction. Recently outlined by Tomaskovic-Devey and Avent-Holt (2019, p. 3), RIT focuses on "how categorical distinctions, when wed to organizational divisions of labor, become the interactional bases for moral evaluation, inclusion and exclusion from opportunities, and the exploitation of effort and value." The theory incorporates two central building blocks—categorization and organizations. Humans divide their world into categories to make it easier to navigate social life, and organizations, which are structured by categorical distinctions, become the primary place for generating and reproducing inequalities around these social categories.

There is a human tendency to place individuals into distinct socially constructed categories—like disability, for example—that are assigned different value and worth. Some categories are given high status *relative* to others. This is important because resource allocation and (re)distribution are informed by these categories and statuses. Drawing from the Marxist understanding on the exploitative relationship between capitalists and workers, connecting status to resource hoarding and exploitation is the relative power that groups and actors receive based on status to make claims. Relational claims-making serves as a mechanism explaining how social interaction based on categories and meanings produces inequality. It is "the discursive articulation of why one actor is more deserving of organizational resources than others" (Tomaskovic-Devey & Avent-Holt 2019, p. 163). Simply put, an actor makes claims on different organizational resources, and if these claims are recognized as legitimate, resources then flow to the actor. Resources usually flow through the exploitation of those seen as having low status. Through *social closure*, more powerful groups exclude others from important resources, and through opportunity hoarding, well-connected in-groups monopolize resources for themselves. These main tenets of RIT echo both Tilly (1999) and Weber's (1922, 1978) accounts of power, exclusion, and inequality.

The source of legitimacy underlying claims-making is influenced by local organizational cultures and broader institutions. And so, the second dimension to RIT involves organizations that shape interactions and meanings associated with categories and status. Organizations refer to "social inventions which coordinate the efforts of human beings, through interactions with each other, to accomplish some set of tasks" (Tomaskovic-Devey & Avent-Holt, 2019, p. 48). This aspect of RIT largely builds on Charles Tilly's (1999) *durable inequality* and Joan Acker's (2006) *inequality regimes*. For Tilly (1999), durable inequalities are "those that last from one social interaction to the next, with special attention to those that persist over whole careers, lifetimes, and organizational histories" (p. 6). Such inequalities are made durable when broader status characteristics like race, class, gender, and disability are matched to different organizational hierarchies again and again across organizations, partly through mechanisms of social closure, exploitation, adaptation, and emulation. This perspective is inherently relational as the causal mechanisms behind durable inequality "operate in the domains of collective experience and social interaction" (Tilly, 1999, p. 25).

Through inequality regimes, Acker (2006) focuses on "specific organizations and the local, ongoing practical activities of organizing work that, at the same time, reproduce complex inequalities" (p. 442). She notes that "All organizations have inequality regimes, defined as loosely interrelated practices, processes, actions, and meanings that result in and maintain class, gender, and racial inequalities within particular organizations" (Acker, 2006, p. 443). This perspective shows how inequality differs across organizations in relation to each organization's varying resources, social relations, practices, and cultures.

Drawing from these concepts, RIT identifies proximate social networks, developed within and between organizations, as powerful social locations that generate, maintain, and can even challenge inequality, while making sure to place these proximate relationships within broader institutions cross-cutting social fields. Akin to Bourdieu's (1984) field theory that specifically invokes positionality, class, status, and power relations, as well as other iterations emphasizing the normative aspect of fields (Fligstein & McAdam, 2012; Pettinicchio, 2013), RIT explicitly acknowledges that organizations are not isolated entities. Each exists at the intersection of multiple social fields, or the structured social relations among actors and positions.

Larger criss-crossing fields include markets, communities, and political contexts. Organizations are also affected by the pull of many different institutions that span social fields. Following Nee (1998), we understand institutions as "webs of interrelated rules and norms that govern social relationships, comprise the formal and informal social constraints that shape the choice-set of actors" (Nee, 1998, p. 8). Institutions create expectations regarding how organizations should function and how individuals should interact, pushing and pulling organizations and actors in certain directions. These cross-cutting fields imply isomorphic processes involving the production of inequality (DiMaggio & Powell, 1983). As Tomaskovic-Devey and Avent-Holt point out, the principles of RIT—categorization, exploitation, hoarding, and claims-making—transcend organizational boundaries. What is context specific are the meanings and legitimacy attached to these processes that are shaped by different organizations.

RIT is useful for understanding where inequality comes from and how it endures. It centers organizations as locations producing inequality, with the understanding that individual organizations—while informing specific meanings attached to status—are also constrained by their broader institutional environments. Our contribution to this perspective incorporates ableism into relational inequality theory and demonstrates how ableism, as an institution, supports inequality regimes that structure disadvantage for people with disabilities.

Ableism Is an Institution

Like racism and sexism, much of the discussion around ableism has focused on how individual perceptions, beliefs, attitudes, and prejudice support the discrimination and oppression of people with disabilities (Bogart & Dunn, 2019). Common stereotypes regarding disability, especially the assumption that people with disabilities are less productive, are continually used to justify their exploitation and exclusion from various organizations (Robey et al., 2006; Vaughn et al., 2011). Even when explicit bias is suppressed, implicit biases that associate disability with dependence and slowing action remain (Friedman & Owen, 2017).

Attitudes and assumptions about disability are only one dimension of ableism, however. Notably, Campbell (2009) and Wolbring (2008) refer to this definition as *disablism*, not ableism. Disablism concerns the negative attitudes and assumptions that support the unequal treatment of people with disabilities. Ableism, however, is also linked to the compulsory preference for non-disability (Campbell, 2009). It "reflects the sentiment of certain social groups and *social structures* that value and promote certain abilities" (Wolbring, 2008, p. 253). In Campbell's (2001, p. 44) words, ableism is a "network of beliefs, processes and practices that produces a particular kind of self and body (the corporeal standard) that is projected as the perfect, species-typical and therefore essential and fully human. Disability then is cast as a diminished state of being human."

Despite civil and human rights frameworks for disability—even when accepted as legitimate and important—this perspective does more to draw from medical and client-service models of disability by emphasizing deficits among a group sharing a broad status or category. Ableism is inherently relational; it explicitly or implicitly situates disability as an abnormal state compared to able-bodiedness. Based on so-called abilities that are given value and worth, it shapes relationships between actors, groups, and their environments (Wolbring, 2007a, b, 2008). This has important implications for the production of inequality, for as Chouinard (1997, p. 380) explains, "This presumption, whether intentional or not, means that one's ability to approximate the able-bodied norm, influences multiple facets of life: such as the character and quality of interpersonal relations, economic prospects, and degrees of physical and social access to various life spaces."

These definitions bring many core ideas together, highlighting the beliefs, processes, and practices that set a certain type of body and mind as standard. It serves to lift some— the preferred who are not disabled (Friedman & Owen, 2017)—*while* marginalizing others. Individuals in groups whose status is disassociated with inhabiting or embodying "compulsory" able-bodied roles (even slightly since, according to McRuer, 2002, they are impossible to embody anyway), are assigned lower status.

Ableism *is* discrimination against a social group based on values assigned to attributes of disability. Ableism clearly points to the structural bases of inequality and marginalization. A central organizing institution, it remains, like racism and sexism, both omnipresent yet masked, often performed under the guise of ability (loosely defined), meritocracy, deservedness, responsibility, and independence, patterning social behavior with important consequences across fields and organizations. It informs practices and policies that render disability and disabled people invisible, if not deviant, or aberrant (Foster & Pettinicchio, 2021).

Ableism *is* an institution that influences the practices of different organizations and structures social relations in ways that exploit people with disabilities and limit disabled people's full participation in society. It sets the norms that limit people with disabilities from making claims on resources. It rests on a discriminatory belief system that defines what is valued and worthy based on ascribed characteristics. Disability falls outside those.

When we conceive of ableism as an institution, not just an ideology, we can better begin to understand how and why disability-based disadvantage is so prevalent in our society. Categories of "disabled" and "non-disabled" are assigned status, value, and privilege. Through claims-making, those deemed "disabled" are assigned lower status, legitimizing their exploitation by those with higher status—those able-bodied who are deemed as living up to a certain ideal. People with disabilities are cut off from resources by ableist structures that favor the privileged able-bodied. Manifesting through organizational spaces—from education to work to wealth—inequality regimes maintain and make durable disability-based inequality.

Applying RIT: Exploitation, Social Closure, and Claims-Making in Higher Education, Employment, and Wealth

The central components of RIT—categorization and organizations—are clearly present and particularly helpful in making sense of how ableism reproduces disadvantage. Ableism's ubiquity across different social fields means that people with disabilities experience both exploitation and social closure across many spheres of life. Assigned a lower status, they have little influence in making legitimate claims over resource flows within and across organizations. Ableist systems at work in higher-education, employment, and housing and credit markets render people with disabilities a group deemed less deserving and closed off from organizational resources where exploitive practices further entrench and reproduce inequality.

Higher Education

Higher education is a pathway for disrupting poverty, mitigating disadvantage, and decreasing economic inequality. Education teaches skills, satisfies job requirements and demands, and provides opportunities for developing network ties and social capital. Higher education offers resources to groups often excluded via social closure and exploitive resource flows (Hout, 2012). Educational degrees increase status among an already low-status group—and while albeit unfairly used to contradict erroneous low expectations about disability—education has been a resource in helping to empower this community. Perhaps not surprisingly, sociologists have often used education as a proxy for class (Hout 2008) and as a sieve for sorting and stratifying groups (Stevens, Armstrong, & Arum, 2008).

Importantly, education is also organized around and governed by inequality regimes and defined by ableist attitudes and practices (Collins, 1971; Hanselman, Domina, & Hwang, 2021; Shifrer, this Volume). These extend not only to the more manifest academic or knowledge transfer and acquisition side of education, but also to more latent aspects including the broader participation of different groups in the social life of the organization (Dolmage, 2017; Dong et al., 2016).

In line with the principles of the social and human rights models of disability, activists and scholars alike have emphasized the "disabling" nature of higher educational environments through supports (or lack thereof), teaching practices, and social interactions that undermine student success (Dolmage, 2017; Leyser & Greenberger, 2008). The way universities are organized around the provision of on-campus disability-related supports matters for how students receive and make use of accommodations (DuPaul et al., 2017). This is critical because not receiving appropriate accommodations is associated with increased attrition rates (Collins et al., 2015; Lombardi et al., 2013; Marshak et al., 2010).

Accommodations within universities are both resources themselves and the means to access additional educational resources. As a specific status within education, "disability" is ultimately defined not only by the lived experiences of a disabled student, but by medical, social-welfare, and educational professionals through formal institutional processes that have important impacts on whether individuals can make claims over resources like accommodations. The requirements that disabled students must seek out accommodations on their own and prove their disabilities through documentation (Barnard-Brak et al., 2010; Getzel, 2008) demonstrate the many disadvantages that students with disabilities experience in attempting to engage in claims-making over key educational resources. A system that relies on "special accommodations" to make its resources accessible only to students with documented disabilities clearly limits access. For students who are unable to navigate university structures, it also often leads to "silenced" claims (Tomaskovic-Devey & Avent-Holt, 2019), where many ultimately avoid engaging in claims-making altogether (Lyman et al., 2016).

A successful claim in this context first requires that students seek out accommodations, which is often contingent on students' backgrounds and their past experiences informed by intersecting statuses like race, class, and gender. Whether students seek out accommodations depends on their prior experiences managing their learning needs with university professors and instructors (Hartman-Hall & Haaga, 2002; Junco & Salter, 2004). Once a claim is initiated, student success also depends on the presence of disability resource centers and the amount of contact students have with them (Troiano et al., 2010), as well as the willingness of faculty to support accommodations.

Although faculty are overwhelmingly positive about supporting accommodations (Norton, 1997), seeing it as "doing the right thing" (Jensen et al., 2004), increases in the number of students requesting accommodations may lead faculty to interpret these as personal burdens (Bourke et al., 2000). Additionally, support varies by the nature of the accommodation. Faculty perceptions of fairness, influenced by ableism and ideas of meritocracy, matter a great deal in their attitudes about accommodations. Accommodations seen as distributively unfair (giving unfair advantage where disabled students might outperform others) and procedurally unfair (where accommodations make things harder for others who are not benefiting from these) are viewed unfavorably (Paetzold et al., 2008).

Faculty seek consultation with disability resource centers and may see these campus-wide centers as taking on more of the work making accommodations more favorable for faculty. Murray et al. (2008) found that faculty who think there are not enough campus resources are less likely to provide accommodations. As Newman et al. (2015) explain, there is an important distinction between requesting accommodations directly through faculty and through disability resource centers where the former typically result in weaker, inappropriate, or no accommodations. These aspects of social relations between groups with varying access to power and resources within organizations showcases broader ableist systems that structure disadvantage.

This inherently points to how organizational practices, including the provision of accommodations, are, in effect, ableist. They do not inherently challenge ableist systems when the claims-making capacity of low status groups is weakened and tied directly to rules established by organizational spaces that are themselves governed by inequality regimes. This further contributes to exploitive relations and unequal distribution of resources. It also points to the unequal power relations between those seeking support and those making decisions about the worthiness of those claims. As such, and in line with RIT, one cannot ignore power relations in negotiating resource flows.

Attitudes and practices reflect how higher-education settings are organizational spaces where social closure and claims-making keeps some groups in subordinate positions. However, such places can also empower individuals and groups when organizational practices and procedures for claims making are altered (Acker, 2006). The push for universal design (UD) in learning within higher education provides one example for challenging inequality regimes (Bowe, 2000; Dolmage, 2017).

Universal design, which originated as an architectural movement and has now become much broader, refers to "the design of products and environments to be usable by all people, to the greatest extent possible, without the need for adaptation or specialized design" (Mace, 1985, p. 147). UD specifically acknowledges that many of our current models for sharing information, designing buildings, and supporting education are, in fact, ableist. As Dolmage (2017) notes, "The push toward the universal is a push toward seeing space as open to multiple possibilities, as being in process. More simply, the universal is an acknowledgment that our design practices have long been biased" (p. 117).

With this understanding, UD emphasizes equitable use across people with diverse abilities, flexibility in use to accommodate people with different abilities, simple and intuitive use that is easy to understand, perceptible information regardless of sensory abilities, a tolerance for error, low physical effort in access, and a constant consideration of the appropriate size and space for all use (Dolmage, 2017). Although it has been most successful for changing physical environments, UD offers many opportunities within higher education as it seeks to change the current system of individual-based accommodations to one that is more open and accessible. (Dolmage, 2005).

The potential benefits of UD extend beyond higher education. Considering similar dimensions within the labor market, for example, where accommodations are primarily distributed to only those who go through the burdensome process of requesting them, would make employment more accessible to people with disabilities. Yet, the barriers to implementing UD in workplace organizations are often much greater.

Employment, Labor Markets, and Workplaces

Education and work organizations are part of broader ableist institutional fields. They share many of the same values, assumptions, and practices that (re)produce inequality. When it comes to work, Wolbring's (2008) definition of ableism is especially haunting. He writes, "Ableism reflects the sentiment of certain social groups and social structures that value and promote certain abilities, for example, productivity and competitiveness, over others, such as empathy, compassion and kindness. This preference for certain abilities over others leads to a labelling of real or perceived deviations from or lack of 'essential' abilities as a diminished state of being, leading or contributing to justifying various other isms."

Common theories seeking to explain labor market outcomes among people with disabilities can generally be understood in terms of supply and demand; explanations have either emphasized characteristics of workers, such as education and human capital (supply), or characteristics and preferences of employers, firms, sectors, and broader economic contexts (demand). Disability informs both demand- and supply-side factors in related ways because disability status is understood as limiting productivity regardless of whether it does or does not. Structural and attitudinal barriers tied to disability in health, social supports, and education limit inputs that then limit access to the labor market. Then, employers and others in power with access to resources including hiring, promotion, and firing decisions hold negative attitudes about disability, especially when it comes to productivity and work. These are reflected in their norms and practices, legitimized and structured by the organizations in which they operate.

From the supply side, as an individual-level worker characteristic, the nature of disability can shape performance in specific work duties and tasks. It may indeed be limiting in some areas of a job but have little bearing on other areas. More broadly, as a social status and category, disability can contribute (often negatively) to other supply factors like educational attainment, up-to-date job skills and training, and network ties.

At the same time, disability is not independent of demand-side factors. These go far in accounting for how social closure limits access to entire sectors or access to certain jobs within a sector. These preferences restrict access to higher-paying occupations, contributing to social closure and exploitation of workers relegated to so-called bad jobs (Kalleberg, 2011). Employer preferences for certain kinds of workers include implicit biases about disability, and ableist work norms and cultures limit horizontal and vertical mobility within occupations. Low expectations among gatekeepers, such as hiring managers, about performance and competence based on group generalizations (see Ridgeway, 1991, 1997), bar disabled people from the labor market. This, coupled with weakly enforced legislation, has no doubt contributed to low employment rates among Americans with disabilities (Maroto & Pettinicchio, 2014a).

For years, employment rates following the landmark Americans with Disabilities Act (ADA) continued to decline, apparently baffling lawmakers. As Harken noted at a

Senate Committee on Health, Education, Labor, and Pensions hearing, "That's the one thing that has bedeviled me since the passage of the ADA, we made wonderful strides in accommodations and transportation, a lot of the things, and that coupled with IDEA, mainstreaming it, getting kids into school. But we really haven't cracked that nut on employment . . . " (Pettinicchio, 2019, p. 147). Efforts over the years to delegitimize the ADA by describing it as creating unintended harms, increasing the costs of hiring disabled people, or forcing employers to hire unqualified workers, illustrate how ableist institutional arrangements undermine the goals of civil-rights legislation. These claims made by those with power and money are couched in a neo-liberal framework reifying the notion that and, to echo Marta Russell's (2002) point, the ADA is but a free market bill of rights, meaning that in the end, the free market is still the best mechanism dictating labor market outcomes and that the law it is not there to challenge inherent inequalities. It also provides a structural context for understanding micro-level outcomes. Much has been said about experiences of discrimination in the labor market, but less in terms of how discriminatory practices transcend organizational and institutional boundaries— that is, how ableism is structurally embedded in virtually all spheres of life, including the labor market.

Linking individual-level factors to labor market factors demonstrates the *relational aspects* behind where disabled workers are located in the labor market and why that is. Within the labor market, processes of social closure contribute to disability-based occupational segregation, or the unequal distribution of groups, including people with disabilities, across occupations and industries, which has significant impacts on earnings. As we have demonstrated, people with disabilities tend to be clustered in low paying service, retail, and manufacturing jobs for which they are over-skilled, and they still earn less than their non-disabled counterparts within those jobs and occupations (Maroto & Pettinicchio, 2014b). The over-skilling of disabled individuals (Jones & Sloane, 2010) suggests that employers use educational credentials to assuage their fears that disabled people are less productive, are dependent and need "hand-holding," and "can't get ahead." Isolation and tokenism in the labor market then support further discrimination (Robert & Harlan, 2006), compounding disadvantage.

This demonstrates how ableist workplace inequality regimes, resting on stereotypes and assumptions that people with disabilities are less productive, limit people with disabilities from making claims for income and other resources. Like within educational spaces, accommodations are often negotiated and contested—they are a means to even the playing field. The "reasonableness" of accommodations has historically had little input from the disability community and accommodations are not always viewed positively as a mechanism for achieving equality by higher-status groups who make hiring and promotion decisions. So-called reasonable accommodations are seen as a form of redistribution (Pettinicchio, 2019; Basas, 2008)—as taking resources from one group and applying them to a "special" circumstance. Furthermore, individuals from lower status groups in the labor market are concerned about disclosing their status especially if that intersects with another status. Fear of disclosure precludes receiving appropriate accommodations (Pilling, 2012).

American social policy has historically emphasized making disabled people "taxpayers rather than tax burdens" through work—no matter how precarious and low paying those jobs might be. Vocational rehabilitation programs touted the number of previously "untrainable" and "uneducable" people with disabilities now working, ignoring low expectations about the kinds of work people with disabilities are can do (Balcazar & Ramirez, this Volume; Pettinicchio, 2019). And so, an institutional legacy of keeping disabled people out of good jobs and placing some into jobs paying subminimum wages, a practice that is still allowed under the FLSA through special waivers (see Bradley, 2017; Friedman, 2019; Tomaskovic-Devey & Avent-Holt, 2019), further entrenched processes of social closure and exploitation. Through social closure, people with disabilities are kept out of higher-paying and higher-prestige jobs, including upper-management and supervisory roles. They are segregated into low-pay and low-prestige jobs and, among its most extreme form through sheltered workshops and wage theft, are paid subminimum wages.

If work training programs, anti-discrimination legislation, and provisions for reasonable accommodations have not changed organizational practices enough to truly improve employment and earnings outcomes for people with disabilities, what can? Here, it is helpful to broaden our perspective to consider different policies and practices that support and legitimize workers' claims to resources. Through collective bargaining, unions give workers leverage, increase worker wages, and improve employment conditions (Cornfield, 1991; Finnigan & Hale, 2018; Mishel, 2012). By standardizing agreements and creating venues for claims-making among workers, they also help to reduce inequality across groups (Kerrissey & Meyers, 2021; VanHeuvelen, 2018).

This is also the case for disability (Maroto & Pettinicchio, 2020). Using nine years of US data, we show that union membership reduces earnings inequality between workers with and without disabilities, particularly those with more severe disabilities. However, people with disabilities first need access to union jobs, which have been on the decline (Western & Rosenfeld, 2011; Rosenfeld & Kleykamp, 2012). And, as organizations that are not immune to inequality, unions must also recognize their own ableist practices and proactively support efforts to challenge workplace inequality regimes (Lurie, 2017). Otherwise, people with disabilities will continue to have fewer paths to workplace equality, especially as protections against discrimination continue to be weakly enforced (Pettinicchio, 2019). The barriers to employment and income then reverberate into other areas, limiting wealth building and housing options.

Housing and Credit Markets

The same ableist notions about productivity and competence that limit people with disabilities' access to higher education and employment continue to limit their access to housing, lending, and, ultimately, wealth accumulation. Scholars have pointed to the barriers and discrimination faced by racial minority groups when it comes to accessing credit markets, financial institutions, and products that help to build assets (Campbell & Kaufman, 2006; Pager & Shepherd, 2008; Zhang, 2003), but much less is known how this applies to people with disabilities.

We do know from the few studies on disability and credit markets that households with disabilities have less wealth and are less likely to own their own homes (Maroto, 2016; McKnight, 2014; Parish et al., 2010). We show that Canadian households with disabilities had 25% fewer non-housing assets than households without disabilities, partly because of their limited earnings (Maroto & Pettinicchio, 2020). Our findings not only point to the distinction and relationship between employment income and wealth and assets, but how the latter greatly contributes to inequality and economic precarity. Individuals with fewer assets and household wealth are left with different choices when it comes to health and personal care, overall lifestyle, and education. And, in light of the recession of the late-2000s and the recent global COVID-19 pandemic, those with savings are better equipped to weather these exogenous shocks, further highlighting increasing individual risk as states divest from their roles, and the inherently ableist policies of capitalist and liberal welfare regimes.

From this perspective, the chief factor shaping asset-building is access to credit markets and financial literacy, including knowledge of savings institutions and financial products (see Sherraden, Schreiner, & Beverly, 2003 on the institutional theory of saving). This ignores how access and information is largely determined by race, class, and gender (Lusardi & Mitchell, 2007; Van Rooij, Lusardi, & Alessie, 2011). These structural dimensions are clear within the numerous programs and schemes to entice people to save. Many of the policies in place to help households build wealth—tax-free savings and retirement accounts, mortgage deductions, and first-time home-buyer benefits—assume that individuals have extra money to put aside. These do not address broader structural inequalities when it comes to building savings, providing affordable housing, and securing financial futures.

Labor and credit markets are linked, in part because much of the wealth that individuals accumulate is influenced by the money earned from working (Maroto & Pettinicchio, 2020). Employment earnings are not the only source of income, as is the case of disabled people. Income may also come from other sources including government supports (Maroto et al., 2019), but most of these supports come with means- and asset-testing, available only to those with very limited incomes and assets. This also means that disability benefits can limit saving and wealth building, as recipients are penalized for saving by being excluded from much-needed income supports.

Wealth inequality is also directly linked to housing inequality. For most families, their homes are their most important assets. Like other minority groups, people with disabilities are less likely to own their own homes (Maroto, 2016). When it comes to accessing housing more generally, evidence shows that people with disabilities are discriminated against—from the application process to inaccessible physical structures (Aranda, 2015). The problem in the US context is so significant that, according to the National Fair Housing Alliance (2016), more than half of all complaints about discrimination in the rental housing market were disability based.

As policies continue to emphasize the right of individuals with disabilities to live in their own homes and communities rather than in institutionalized or congregate care settings where freedoms are restricted and large power imbalances exist between staff and residents (Olive et al., 2020), access to affordable and suitable housing is ever more critical. Inaccessible housing supports ableist and disablist understandings of community, housing, and "the home" (Marcum, 2017), feeding into a continued reliance on segregated housing in restrictive environments.

Like labor and credit markets, people with disabilities are excluded from the housing market through ableist practices creating obstacles to accessing basic rights to fair housing. Housing is so fundamental that it affects other areas as well. As the title of a study by Devine, Vaughan, and Kavanagh (2020) so poignantly illustrates, "*If I had stable housing, I would be a bit more receptive to having a job.*" Housing insecurity reveals how structural disadvantage plays out both concretely, as in the built environment, and more abstractly, through interrelated institutions, norms, and practices. Ableist policies governing housing limit, exclude, segregate, and, in some cases, render people homeless because of membership in a group defined as having low status.

CONCLUSION

We write this chapter during a time of upheaval and change in the world. The COVID-19 pandemic has led many to question how we structure education, work, and social relationships. It has also led to devastating losses and immense suffering. And yet, the pandemic is not the only imminent threat to humans' ways of existing. As the consequences of climate change expand, we will continually see significant disruptions to daily living around the world. And, if the results of COVID-19 tell us anything, it is likely that already disadvantaged groups, with few means to make claims on limited resources, will bear the brunt of such changes.

This has been the case with people with disabilities and chronic health conditions who experience more fear, stress, and anxiety about getting the virus (as they are a more at-risk group), while facing numerous challenges in taking the necessary precautions to stay safe (Pettinicchio, Maroto, & Lukk, 2021). Illustrating how ableist neo-liberal welfare regimes come into play during moments of crisis, disabled people have been largely ignored by policymakers on a host of issues disproportionately affecting them, including income supports, access to care, and mental health (Pettinicchio, Maroto, Chai, & Lukk, 2021; Maroto, Pettinicchio, & Lukk, 2021).

Exogenous shocks brought on by health pandemics and economic crises highlight the importance of taking a structural approach toward understanding inequality and disadvantage. On the one hand, they demonstrate how broader forces shape outcomes for individuals and groups. They have brought suffering and inequality to the surface across many interrelated discussions, especially regarding racism and sexism. On the other hand, they also show how easy it is to overlook the needs of groups who have little voice in policymaking, as has been the case with disability.

In our recent work on the effects of COVID-19 on people with disabilities and chronic health conditions, we sought to include the voices of those most affected by this crisis.

We did this by supplementing analyses of quantitative survey data with open-ended survey questions and subsequent in-depth interviews with survey participants. This qualitative data contributed greatly in showcasing how different factors—from family and government supports to savings and employment—are in fact interrelated in explaining precarity. It also uncovered subjective perceptions of economic well-being and how they are shaped by interactions with different organizations and institutions, including numerous policies. Perhaps most importantly, qualitative data shed light on these in respondents' own words.

Supporting Research that Emphasizes Structures that Disadvantage

We understand that the agenda we have laid out above complicates our research. How can we actually support research that emphasizes structure? This is a tough question, especially for researchers like us who often rely on individual-level survey data. Part of the answer involves framing and situating our research questions about disadvantage and inequality within theories that speak to how individuals experience marginalization based on social categories within and across the organizational and institutional spaces they inhabit. RIT, for example, emphasizes "relationships between people, positions, and organizations" (Tomaskovic-Devey & Avent-Holt, 2019, p. 14). Individual-level interview and survey data often do not provide this type of important relational information. But, there are opportunities for expanding on these.

First, organizational data, especially when matched with employee data, provide an important avenue for understanding the organizational processes that facilitate exploitation and social closure. Such data might include organizational administrative data or data collected from employees within specific firms. Robert and Harlan's (2006) study on disability discrimination within organizations provides one example.

Based on 63 interviews with people with different disabilities in government jobs, Robert and Harlan (2006) underscore how proximate social relationships as seen in day-to-day interactions support disability-based discrimination through the marginalization, fictionalization, and harassment of people with disabilities. They then clearly tie these mechanisms to organizational aspects, demonstrating, for instance, how marginalization resulted in the physical segregation of people with disabilities, and how fictionalization, particularly the construction of disabled workers as "liability workers," limited disabled workers' abilities to make claims for promotions and reasonable accommodations. Thus, by incorporating workplace contexts, Robert and Harlan (2006) were able to uncover aspects of how ableism determined inequality regimes within specific organizations.

Second, and following from this, research that emphasizes institutions and inequality regimes more broadly offers another important avenue for understanding disability from a relational inequality perspective. Incorporating this perspective helps to demonstrate the many nuances present within the creation and implementation of organizational policies. For instance, we show that although unions work to decrease within-group inequality for disabled workers, they also increase between-group inequality, expanding the distance between unionized and non-unionized workers with disabilities (Maroto & Pettinicchio, 2020).

Qualitative studies have contributed a lot in this area. Mauldin's (2014) research further illustrates the importance of relational work when it comes to understanding the implantation of cochlear implants. Interactions around the use of cochlear implants across settings highlights not only how deafness is constructed, but the social construction of ableism as well. Mauldin's work inherently situates disability within organizations and via the imbalanced power relations across actors including the Deaf community, parents, and medical professionals.

Third, and on a much larger level, this body of research would benefit from more studies that bring together political sociology with stratification, as some comparative work has done. As intersectional research (Acker, 2006) shows, the institutions of ableism, sexism, racism, classism, heterosexism, and ageism are linked. For instance, Mauldin's (this Volume) chapter situates disability alongside race and gender as axes of inequality, and Chouinard's (this Volume) chapter explores the gendered aspects of disability drawing important parallels between racism, sexism, and ableism.

Scholars have also increasingly linked colonialism to ableism. Meekosha (2011) and Hutcheon and Lashewicz (2020) emphasize how ableism serves colonial interests and how colonial policies, including environmental destruction, produce disability, and Soldatic (2019) extends this framework using a gendered and indigenous lens. In line with the decolonization of disability studies, Velarde (this Volume) examines various forms of oppression based on the intersection of disability and indigeneity. In their (this Volume) chapter, Hughes links white colonialism to "able power" and the "able body," rendering all others as inferior and abhorrent. These intersecting dynamics shed much-needed light on how disability-based inequality is organized, institutionalized, and reproduced. It provides a framework for understanding how access to resources is constrained by the politics and policies surrounding disability inclusion (Bruyère and Saleh this Volume) and the role of human rights frameworks to empower disabled people as they challenge ableist regimes (Gran, Bryden, & Shick, this Volume).

In addition to suggesting pathways for new research on disability and inequality, our goal in this chapter, like many before us (Jenkins, 1991; Omansky & Rosenblum, 2001), has been to better link disability to studies of stratification through a discussion of relational inequality theory and ableism as an institution. By providing such a framework for explicitly linking disability with structural disadvantage, we also aim to bring sociology, stratification, and disability studies into deeper conversation with each other.

Social relationships between and within organizations are influenced by the push and pull of different institutions. As an institution, ableism goes beyond disablist attitudes. It shows how organizations define certain bodies as the normative standard, excluding others and making it close to impossible for those outside to access resources. Addressing the structures that disadvantage, therefore, means tackling the ableist notions of disability and disabled people, as well as the ableist organizational practices and policies that continue to exploit people with disabilities and limit their access to key corners of society—a task that goes far beyond research.

REFERENCES

Acker, J. (2006). Inequality regimes: Gender, class, and race in organizations. *Gender & Society*, *20*(4), 441–464.

Altman, B. M. (2001). Disability definitions, models, classification schemes and applications. In G. L. Albrecht, K. D. Seelman, & M. Bury (Eds.), *Handbook of Disability Studies* (pp. 123–144). SAGE Publications.

Aranda, C. L. (2015). Targeting disability discrimination: Findings and reflections from the national study on housing discrimination against people who are deaf and people who use wheelchairs. *Cityscape*, *17*(3), 103–122.

Barnard-Brak, L., Lechtenberger, D., & Lan, W. Y. (2010). Accommodation strategies of college students with disabilities. *Qualitative Report*, *15*(2), 411–429.

Basas, C. G. (2008). Back rooms, board rooms—Reasonable accommodation and resistance under the ADA. *Berkeley Journal of Employment and Labor Law*, *29*(1), 59–116.

Berger, J., & Fişek, M. H. (2006). Diffuse status characteristics and the spread of status value: A formal theory. *American Journal of Sociology*, *111*(4), 1038–1079.

Bogart, K. R., & Dunn, D. S. (2019). Ableism special issue introduction. *Journal of Social Issues*, *75*(3), 650–664.

Bourdieu, P. (1984). *Distinction: A social critique of judgement and taste*. Harvard University Press.

Bourke, A. B., Strehorn, K. C., & Silver, P. (2000). Faculty members' provision of instructional accommodations to students with LD. *Journal of Learning Disabilities*, *33*(1), 26–33.

Bowe, F. G. (2000). *Universal Design in education: Teaching non-traditional students*. Bergin and Garvey, 2000.

Bradley, D. H. (2017). The federal minimum wage: In brief. *Congressional Research Service*.

Brown, R. L. (2017). Perceived stigma, discrimination and mental health among people with disabilities: The conditional effects of coping resources. *Stigma and Health*, *2*(2), 98–109.

Brown, R. L., & Ciciurkaite, G. (2021). The "own" and the "wise" revisited: Physical disability, stigma, and mental health among couples. *Journal of Health and Social Behavior*, *62*(2), 170–182.

Burkhauser, R. V., Houtenville, A. J., & Tennant, J. R. (2014). Capturing the elusive working-age population with disabilities: Reconciling conflicting social success estimates from the Current Population Survey and American Community Survey. *Journal of Disability Policy Studies*, *24*(4), 195–205.

Burkhauser, R. V., Daly, M. C., Houtenville, A. J., & Nargis, N. (2001). The employment of working-age people with disabilities in the 1980s and 1990s: What current data can and cannot tell us. *FRB of San Francisco Working Paper* (2001-20).

Campbell, F. K. (2009). *Contours of ableism: The production of disability and abledness*. Palgrave Macmillan.

Campbell, F. K. (2001). Inciting legal fictions: "Disability's" date with ontology and the ableist body of the law. *Griffith Law Review*, *10*(1), 42–62.

Campbell, L. A., & R. L. Kaufman. (2006). Racial differences in household wealth: Beyond Black and White. *Research in Social Stratification and Mobility*, *24*, 131–152.

Chouinard, V. (1997). Making space for disabling difference: Challenges ableist geographies. *Environment and Planning D: Society and Space*, 15, 379–387.

Clarke, P., & Latham, K. (2014). Life course health and socioeconomic profiles of Americans aging with disability. *Disability and Health Journal*, 7(1), S15–S23.

Ciciurkaite, G., Marquez-Velarde, G., & Brown, R. L. (2021). Stressors associated with the COVID-19 pandemic, disability, and mental health: Considerations from the intermountain West. *Stress and Health*. https://doi.org/10.1002/smi.3091

Collins, M. A., & Carol T. Mowbray. 2015. Higher education and disabilities: National survey of campus disability services *American Journal of Orthopsychiatry*, 75, 304–315.

Collins, R. (1971). Functional and conflict theories of educational stratification. *American Sociological Review*, 36(6), 1002–1019.

Cornfield, D. (1991). The U.S. labor movement: Its development and impact on social inequality and politics. *Annual Review of Sociology*, 17(1), 27–49.

Devine, A., Vaughan, C., & Kavanagh, A. (2020). If I had stable housing I would be a bit more receptive to having a job: Factors influencing the effectiveness of Disability Employment Services reform. *Work*, 65, 775–787.

DiMaggio, P. J., & Powell, W. W. (1983). The iron cage revisited: Institutional isomorphism and collective rationality in organizational fields. *American Sociological Review*, 48(2), 147–160.

Dolmage, J. T. (2017). *Academic ableism: Disability and higher education*. University of Michigan Press.

Dolmage, J. T (2005). Disability studies pedagogy, usability and Universal Design. *Disability Studies Quarterly*, 25(4).

Dong, S., & Lucas, M. S. (2016). An analysis of disability, academic performance, and seeking support in one university setting. *Career Development and Transition for Exceptional Individuals*, 39(1), 47–56.

DuPaul, G. J., Pinho, T. D., Pollack, B. L., Gormley, M. J., & Laracy, S. D. (2017). First-year college students with ADHD and/or LD: Differences in engagement, positive core self-evaluation, school preparation, and college expectations. *Journal of Learning Disabilities*, 50(3), 238–251.

Finnigan, R., & Hale, J. M. (2018). Working 9 to 5? Union membership and work hours and schedules. *Social Forces*, 96(4), 1541–1568.

Fligstein, N., & McAdam, D. (2012). *A theory of fields*. Oxford University Press.

Foster, J., & Pettinicchio, D. (2021). A model who looks like me: Communicating and consuming representations of disability. *Journal of Consumer Culture*, June. doi:10.1177/14695405211022074

Friedman, C. (2019). Ableism, racism, and subminimum wage in the United States. *Disability Studies Quarterly*, 39(4).

Friedman, C., & Owen, A. L. (2017). Defining disability: Understandings of and attitudes towards ableism and disability. *Disability Studies Quarterly*, 37(1).

Getzel, E. E. (2008). Addressing the persistence and retention of students with disabilities in higher education: Incorporating key strategies and supports on campus. *Exceptionality*, 16(4), 207–219.

Greenwald, A. G., & Krieger, L. H. (2006). Implicit bias: Scientific foundations. *California Law Review*, 94(4), 945–967.

Groce, N. (2006). Cultural beliefs and practices that influence the type and nature of data collected on individuals with disability through national census. In B. M. Altman & S. N. Barnartt (Eds.), *International views on disability measures: moving toward comparative measurement* (Research in Social Science and Disability) (pp. 41–54). Emerald Group Publishing Limited.

Hanass-Hancock, J., & Mitra, S. (2016). Livelihoods and disability: The complexities of work in the global south. In S. Grech & K. Soldatic (Eds.), *Disability in the Global South* (pp. 133–149). Springer, Cham.

Hanselman, P., Domina, T., & Hwang, N. (2021). Educational inequality regimes amid algebra-for-all: The provision and allocation of expanding educational opportunities. *Social Forces*. https://doi.org/10.1093/sf/soab052

Hartman-Hall, H. M., & Haaga, D. A. (2002). College students' willingness to seek help for their learning disabilities. *Learning Disability Quarterly*, 25(4), 263–274.

Hout, M. (2012). Social and economic returns to college education in the United States. *Annual Review of Sociology*, 38, 379–400.

Hout, M. (2008). How class works: Objective and subjective aspects of class since the 1970s. In A. Lareau & D. Conley (Eds.), *Social Class: How Does it Work?* (pp. 25–64). Russell Sage Foundation.

Hutcheon, E. J., & Lashewicz, B. (2020). Tracing and troubling continuities between ableism and colonialism in Canada. *Disability & Society*, 35(5), 695–714.

Jenkins, R. (1991). Disability and social stratification. *British Journal of Sociology*, 42(4), 557–580.

Jensen, J. M., McCrary, N., Krampe, K., & Cooper, J. (2004). Trying to do the right thing: Faculty attitudes toward accommodating students with learning disabilities. *Journal of Postsecondary Education and Disability*, 17(2), 81–89.

Jolls, C., & Prescott, J. J. (2004). Disaggregating employment protection: The case of disability discrimination. https://www.nber.org/papers/w10740

Jones, M. K., & Sloane, P. J. (2010). Disability and skill mismatch. *Economic Record*, 86, 101–114.

Junco, R., & Salter, D. W. (2004). Improving the campus climate for students with disabilities through the use of online training. *NASPA Journal*, 41(2), 263–276.

Kalleberg, A. L. (2011). *Good jobs, bad jobs: The rise of polarized and precarious employment systems in the United States, 1970s–2000s*. Russell Sage Foundation, American Sociological Association Rose Series in Sociology.

Kaye, S. H. 2009. Stuck at the bottom rung: Occupational characteristics of workers with disabilities. *Journal of Occupational Rehabilitation*, 19(2), 115–128.

Kerrissey, J., & Meyers, N. (2021). Public-sector unions as equalizing institutions: Race, gender, and earnings. *ILR Review*. doi: 10.1177/00197939211056914.

Kostanjsek, N., Good, A., Madden, R. H., Üstün, T. B., Chatterji, S., Mathers, C. D., & Officer, A. (2013). Counting disability: Global and national estimation. *Disability and Rehabilitation*, 35(13), 1065–1069.

Lee, B. A. (2003). A decade of the Americans with Disabilities Act: Judicial outcomes and unresolved problems. *Industrial Relations: A Journal of Economy and Society*, 42(1), 11–30.

Leyser, Y., & Greenberger, L. (2008). College students with disabilities in teacher education: Faculty attitudes and practices. *European Journal of Special Needs Education*, 23(3), 237–251.

Lombardi, A., Murray, C., & Dallas, B. (2013). University faculty attitudes toward disability and inclusive instruction: Comparing two institutions. *Journal of Postsecondary Education and Disability*, 26(3), 221–232.

Lurie, L. (2017). Do unions promote rights for people with disabilities? *Indiana Journal of Law and Social Equality*, 5(2), 477–497.

Lusardi, A., & Mitchell, O. S. (2007). Baby Boomer retirement security: The roles of planning, financial literacy, and housing wealth. *Journal of Monetary Economics*, 54(1), 205–224.

Lyman, M., Beecher, M. E., Griner, D., Brooks, M., Call, J., & Jackson, A. (2016). What keeps students with disabilities from using accommodations in postsecondary education? A qualitative review. *Journal of Postsecondary Education and Disability*, 29(2), 123–140.

Mace, R. L (1985). Universal Design, barrier free environments for everyone. *Designers West*, 33(1), 147–52.

Marcum, A. (2017). Rethinking the American dream home: The disability rights movement and the cultural politics of accessible housing in the United States. In M. Rembis (Eds.), *Disabling domesticity* (pp. 103–135). Palgrave Macmillan.

Markus, H. R. (2008). Pride, prejudice, and a of race and ethnicity. *American Psychologist*, 63(8), 651–670.

Maroto, M. L. (2016). Fifteen years of wealth disparities in Canada: New trends or simply the status quo? *Canadian Public Policy*, 42(2), 152–167.

Maroto, M. L., & Pettinicchio, D. (2014a). The limitations of disability antidiscrimination legislation: Policymaking and the economic well-being of people with disabilities. *Law and Policy*, 36(4), 370–407.

Maroto, M., & Pettinicchio, D. (2014b). Disability, structural inequality, and work: The influence of occupational segregation on earnings for people with different disabilities. *Research in Social Stratification and Mobility*, 38, 76–92.

Maroto, M. L., & Pettinicchio, D. (2015). Twenty-five years after the ADA: Situating disability in America's system of stratification. *Disability Studies Quarterly*, 35(3), 1–34.

Maroto, M., & Pettinicchio, D. (2020). Barriers to economic security: Disability, employment, and asset disparities in Canada. *Canadian Review of Sociology*, 57(1), 53–79.

Maroto, M., Pettinicchio, D., & Lukk, M. (2021). Working differently or not at all: COVID-19's effects on employment among people with disabilities and chronic health. *Sociological Perspectives*, 64(5), 876–897.

Maroto, M., Pettinicchio, D., & Patterson, A. (2019). Hierarchies of categorical disadvantage: Incorporating disability into intersectional analyses of economic insecurity. *Gender & Society*, 33(1), 64–93.

Mauldin, L. (2014). Precarious plasticity: Neuropolitics, cochlear implants, and the redefinition of deafness. *Science, Technology, & Human Values*, 39(1), 130–153.

Marshak, Laura, Van Wieren, Todd, et al. (2010). Exploring barriers to college student use of disability services and accommodations. *Journal of Postsecondary Education and Disability*, 22, 151–165.

McKnight, A. (2014). Disabled People's Financial Histories: Uncovering the disability wealth-penalty. *Centre for Analysis of Social Exclusion* (CASE).

McRuer, R. (2002). Critical investments: AIDS, Christopher Reeve, and queer/disability studies. *Journal of Medical Humanities*, 23(3), 221–237.

Me, A., & Mbogoni, M. (2006). Review of practices in less developed countries on the collection of disability data. In B. Altman & S. Barnartt (Eds.), *Research in Social Science and Disability*, vol. 4 (pp. 111–129). Elsevier Ltd.

Meekosha, H. 2011. "Decolonising disability: Thinking and acting globally." *Disability & Society*, 26(6), 667–682.

Miles, A. L. (2019). "Strong black women": African American women with disabilities, intersecting identities, and inequality. *Gender & Society*, 33(1), 41–63.

Mishel, Larry. 2012. *Unions, inequality, and faltering middle-class wages.* Issue Brief 342, Economic Policy Institute.

Mitra, S., & Sambamoorthi, U. (2014). Disability prevalence among adults: estimates for 54 countries and progress toward a global estimate. *Disability and rehabilitation, 36*(11), 940–947.

Morris, S. P., Fawcett, G., Brisebois, L., & Hughes, J. (2018). A demographic, employment and income profile of Canadians with disabilities aged 15 years and over, 2017. *Statistics Canada.*

Murray, C., Wren, C. T., & Keys, C. (2008). University faculty perceptions of students with learning disabilities: Correlates and group differences. *Learning Disability Quarterly, 31*(3), 95–113.

National Fair Housing Alliance. (2016). A landmark year: 2016 fair housing trends report. https://nationalfairhousing.org/wp-content/uploads/2017/04/2016_NFHA_Fair_Housing_Trends_Report.pdf

Nee, V. (1998). Sources of new institutionalism. In M. C. Brinton & V. Nee (Eds.), *The New Institutionalism in Sociology* (pp. 1–16). Russell Sage Foundation.

Newman, L. A., & Madaus, J. W. (2015). An analysis of factors related to receipt of accommodations and services by postsecondary students with disabilities. *Remedial and Special Education, 36*(4), 208–219.

Norton, S. M. (1997). Examination accommodations for community college students with learning disabilities: How are they viewed by faculty and students? *Community College Journal of Research & Practice, 21*(1), 57–69.

Oliver, S., Gosden-Kaye, E. Z., Winkler, D., & Douglas, J. M. (2020). The outcomes of individualized housing for people with disability and complex needs: A scoping review. *Disability and Rehabilitation, 9*, 1–15.

Omansky Gordon, B., & Rosenblum, K. E. (2001). Bringing disability into the sociological frame: A comparison of disability with race, sex, and sexual orientation statuses. *Disability & Society, 16*(1), 5–19.

Paetzold, R. L., García, M. F., Colella, A., Ren, L. R., Triana, M. D. C., & Ziebro, M. (2008). Perceptions of people with disabilities: When is accommodation fair? *Basic and Applied Social Psychology, 30*(1), 27–35.

Pager, D., & Shepherd, H. (2008). The sociology of discrimination: Racial discrimination in employment, housing, credit, and consumer markets. *Annual Review of Sociology, 34*, 181–209.

Parish, S. L., Grinstein-Weiss, M., Yeo, Y. H., Rose, R. A., & Rimmerman, A. (2010). Assets and income: Disability-based disparities in the United States. *Social Work Research, 34*(2), 71–82.

Pettinicchio, D. (2013). Strategic action fields and the context of political entrepreneurship: How disability rights became part of the policy agenda. In P. G. Coy (Ed.), *Research in social movements, conflicts and change* (pp. 79–106). Emerald Group Publishing Limited.

Pettinicchio, D. (2019). *Politics of empowerment: Disability rights and the cycle of American policy reform.* Stanford University Press.

Pettinicchio, D., & Maroto, M. (2017). Employment outcomes among men and women with disabilities: How the intersection of gender and disability status shapes labor market inequality. In Barbara Altman & Sharon Barnartt (Eds.), *Factors in Studying Employment for Persons with Disabilities*, vol. 10 (pp. 3–33). Emerald.

Pettinicchio, D., & Maroto, M. (2021). Who counts? Measuring disability cross-nationally in census data. *Journal of Survey Statistics and Methodology, 9*(2), 257–284.

Pettinicchio, D., Maroto, M., & Lukk, M. (2021). Perceptions of Canadian Federal Policy responses to COVID-19 among people with disabilities and chronic health conditions. *Canadian Public Policy, 47*(2), 231–251.

Pettinicchio, D., Maroto, M., Chai, L., & Lukk, M. (2021). Findings from an online survey on the mental health effects of COVID-19 on Canadians with disabilities and chronic health conditions. *Disability and Health Journal, 14*(3), 101085. doi:10.1016/j.dhjo.2021.101085

Pilling, M. D. (2012). Invisible identity in the workplace: Intersectional madness and processes of disclosure at work. *Disability Studies Quarterly, 33*(1).

Reskin, B. (2003). Including mechanisms in our models of ascriptive inequality: 2002 presidential address. *American Sociological Review, 68*(1), 1–21.

Ridgeway, C. L. (1991). The social construction of status value: Gender and other nominal characteristics. *Social Forces, 70,* 367–386.

Ridgeway, C. L. (1997). Interaction and the conservation of gender inequality: Considering employment. *American Sociological Review, 62,* 218–235.

Ridgeway, C. L. (2014). Why status matters for inequality. *American Sociological Review, 79*(1), 1–16.

Robert, P. M., & Harlan, S. L. (2006). Mechanisms of disability discrimination in large bureaucratic organizations: Ascriptive inequalities in the workplace. *The Sociological Quarterly, 47*(4), 599–630.

Robey, K. L., Beckley, L., & Kirschner, M. (2006). Implicit infantilizing attitudes about disability. *Journal of Developmental and Physical Disabilities, 18*(4), 441–453.

Rosenfeld, J., & Kleykamp, M. (2012). Organized labor and racial wage inequality in the United States. *American Journal of Sociology, 117*(5), 1460–1502.

Russell, M. (2002). What disability civil rights cannot do: Employment and political economy. *Disability & Society, 17*(2), 117–135.

Shakespeare, T. (1996), Disability, identity, difference. In C. Barnes & G. Mercer (Eds.), *Exploring the Divide: Illness and Disability* (pp. 94–113). The Disability Press.

She, P., & Livermore, G. A. (2007). Material hardship, poverty, and disability among working-age adults. *Social Science Quarterly, 88*(4), 970–989.

Sherraden, M., Schreiner, M., & Beverly, S. (2003). Income, institutions, and saving performance in individual development accounts. *Economic Development Quarterly, 17,* 95–112.

Soldatic, K. (2019). Disability and postsocialism. *Disability & Society, 34*(3), 504–505.

Stevens, M. L., Armstrong, E. A., & Arum, R. (2008). Sieve, incubator, temple, hub: Empirical and theoretical advances in the sociology of higher education. *Annual Review of Sociology, 34,* 127–151.

Tajfel, H. (1982). Social psychology of intergroup relations. *Annual review of psychology, 33*(1), 1–39.

Tilly, C. (1999). *Durable inequality.* University of California Press.

Tomaskovic-Devey, D., & Avent-Holt, D. (2019). *Relational inequalities: An organizational approach.* Oxford University Press.

Troiano, P. F., Liefeld, J. A., & Trachtenberg, J. V. (2010). Academic support and college success for postsecondary students with learning disabilities. *Journal of College Reading and Learning, 40*(2), 35–44.

UK Annual Population Survey, Office for National Statistics, 2020.

U.S. Bureau of Labor Statistics (BLS). (2020). Persons with a disability: Labor force characteristics—2019. USDL-20-0339. https://www.bls.gov/news.release/pdf/disabl.pdf

Valencia, R. R. (Ed.). (2012). *The evolution of deficit thinking: Educational thought and practice.* Routledge.

VanHeuvelen, T. (2018). Moral economies or hidden talents? A longitudinal analysis of union decline and wage inequality, 1973–2015. *Social Forces, 97*(2), 495–530.

Van Rooij, M., A. Lusardi, and R. Alessie. (2011). Financial literacy and stock market participation. *Journal of Financial Economics, 101,* 449–472.

Vaughn, E. D., Thomas, A., & Doyle, A. L. (2011). The multiple disability implicit association test: Psychometric analysis of a multiple administration IAT measure. *Rehabilitation Counseling Bulletin, 54*(4), 223–235.

Walter, M. & Andersen, C. (2013). *Indigenous statistics: A quantitative research methodology.* Taylor & Francis Group.

Weber, M. 1978. *Economy and society*, vol. 2, edited by G. Roth and C. Wittich. University of California Press.

Weber, M. [1922] 1946. Class status and party. In H. H. Gerth & C. W. Mills (Eds.), *From Max Weber: Essays in Sociology* (pp. 180–195). Oxford University Press.

Webster Jr, M., & Hysom, S. J. (1998). Creating status characteristics. *American Sociological Review, 63*(3), 351–378.

Weil, D. (2001). Valuing the economic consequences of work injury and illness: A comparison of methods and findings. *American Journal of Industrial Medicine, 40,* 418–437.

Western, B., & Rosenfeld, J. (2011). Unions, norms, and the rise in US wage inequality. *American Sociological Review, 76*(4), 513–537.

World Health Organization. 2011. *World report on disability.*

Wolbring, G. (2008). The politics of ableism. *Development, 51*(2), 252–258.

Wolbring, G. (2007a). NBICS, other convergences, ableism and the culture of peace. http://www.innovationwatch.com/choiceisyours/choiceisyours-2007-04-15.htm

Wolbring, G. (2007b). New and emerging sciences and technologies, ableism, transhumanism and religion, faith, theology and churches. *Madang: International Journal of Contextual Theology in East Asia, 7,* 79–112.

World Bank. (2021). *Disability inclusion.* https://www.worldbank.org/en/topic/disability#1

Zhang, X. (2003). *The wealth position of immigrant families in Canada.* Statistics Canada.

CHAPTER 21

··

DISABILITY AND
PRECARIOUS WORK

··

LISA SCHUR AND DOUGLAS L. KRUSE

DOES precarious employment increase economic well-being for people with disabilities, or does it simply add to the precariousness of life with a disability? Recognizing the barriers that people with disabilities often face in getting and keeping standard jobs, the 2006 United Nations Convention on the Rights of Persons with Disabilities ("UN Convention") adopted language promoting some forms of precarious work for people with disabilities (Harpur, 2017). While precarious employment can increase employment opportunities for some people with disabilities, these jobs generally have fewer employment protections, including coverage by anti-discrimination law, dismissal protections, sick leave, annual leave, and workers compensation (Harpur, 2017, p. 52). The UN Convention focused on self-employment, which would include most independent contractors, on-call workers, day laborers, and gig workers. In addition to these jobs, people in temporary employment relationships are also generally considered to be precarious workers due to the instability of their employment and their reduced employment protections.

We explore the potential positive and negative aspects of precarious employment for people with disabilities by looking at evidence on its prevalence, causes, and consequences. In line with prior research, we define precarious employment broadly to include work arrangements that do not have an explicit or implicit guarantee of continuity, and are typically accompanied by low pay, few employment protections, unpredictable schedules, limited training, lack of union representation or other employee voice mechanisms, and power imbalances that leave workers vulnerable to intimidation, discrimination, harassment, and being unable to exercise their rights (Julia et al., 2017). Despite these negative characteristics, some precarious arrangements can provide valued flexibility and control to workers, such as high-skill workers who can provide specialized well-paid services in a series of temporary jobs with little fear of extended joblessness.

Although some people argue that any work is beneficial for people with disabilities, determining how precarious employment affects the well-being of people with disabilities is complicated both by the great variety in types of precarious jobs and by the wide variation in types and severity of disability. On the one hand, a precarious job may be very beneficial to people who have disabilities that require substantial time and energy in activities of daily living, and who may prefer to have access to gig work that can be scheduled flexibly. On the other hand, a precarious job may be an undesirable alternative for workers with disabilities who are victims of job discrimination that prevents them from obtaining standard full-time jobs with good pay, benefits, and job protections.

The variation across individuals with disabilities and precarious jobs means there is no simple answer as to whether such employment is generally good or bad for people with disabilities. In this chapter we provide a broad overview of the evidence regarding disability and precarious employment. We first set the stage by reviewing the overall economic and employment situation of people with disabilities and the types of barriers they face, followed by the potential advantages and disadvantages of precarious work as they relate to these barriers. We then organize the evidence using three questions:

1. How common is precarious employment among workers with disabilities?
2. What accounts for higher levels of precarious employment among workers with disabilities?
3. What are the consequences of precarious employment for people with disabilities?

For each question we review the available research literature. We also add new evidence from a large 2017 survey conducted by the US Bureau of Labor Statistics containing data from 47,851 employed people, of whom 2,051 have disabilities. This survey has data on major types of precarious employment: temporary jobs (including but not limited to temporary agency employment), on-call and day labor, contract employment, independent contracting where the worker is highly reliant on one client, and gig work where the worker performs tasks for a client with coordination by a company, such as Uber or Lyft for ride sharing or MTurk for computer tasks.

Disability may interact with other identities, such as race and gender, requiring an intersectional analysis of how disability combines with other disadvantaged identities to affect the likelihood and effects of precarious work. A growing amount of research has explored connections of precarious work to gender and race (e.g., Branch & Hanley, 2017; Kalleberg & Vallas, 2018). In the context of disability, Maroto et al. (2019) find strong support for "hierarchies of disadvantage, where women and members of racial minority groups with disabilities and less education experience the highest poverty levels, report the lowest total income, and have a greater reliance on sources outside the labor market for economic security" (2019, p. 64; also see Pettinicchio & Maroto, 2017). Our survey data allow us to address intersectionality by looking at how disability and precarious work may vary by gender, race, ethnicity, age, and education.

We do not analyze telework or other home-based work in this chapter. Such work can be precarious or non-precarious; it can offer some of the flexibility advantages of precarious work, but has its own set of advantages and disadvantages for workers. The research shows that people with disabilities in the US were more likely than those without disabilities to be working at home before the pandemic, but had a smaller increase in working at home during the pandemic, largely due to their greater likelihood of being in blue-collar and service jobs that are not amenable to telework (Schur et al., 2020; Kruse et al., forthcoming).

EMPLOYMENT BARRIERS FACED BY PEOPLE WITH DISABILITIES

The employment barriers faced by people with disabilities provide context for considering their relationship to precarious work. Employment rates among working-age people with disabilities are low around the world (Jones, 2021; World Bank, 2011). The negative effect of disability on employment is apparent not just in cross-sectional comparisons but also in longitudinal comparisons before and after the onset of a disability (e.g., Butler et al., 2006; Campolieti & Krashinski, 2006; Jones, 2008; Jones & McVicar, 2020; Jones, 2021).

Why do people with disabilities have lower employment levels? It is not generally due to an inability or less desire to work; a large majority of nonemployed people with disabilities say they would prefer to be working and are able to do so (Ali et al., 2011), and unemployment rates (reflecting those actively searching for jobs) are generally higher among people with disabilities (Grammenos, 2010). In the United States, the unemployment rate is consistently over twice as high among working-age people with disabilities as among their nondisabled counterparts (US BLS, 2020). People with disabilities are not only less likely to be hired but also more likely to be laid off than workers without disabilities (Mitra & Kruse, 2016). Being "last hired, first fired" is consistent with the discriminatory pattern faced by Blacks in the United States (Cherry & Rodgers, 2000).

Potential personal factors contributing to lower employment of people with disabilities include the following:

- Extra costs of working—extra time, energy, or financial costs of getting ready for work, transportation, and medical care
- Extra need for flexibility—extra time and flexibility for self-care, therapy, and medical appointments, due to medical conditions that create pain, uncertainty, or other difficulties in daily schedules.
- Lower levels of education and training that limit potential productivity, earnings, and career growth.

Employment outcomes can be shaped by government policies that affect these factors and that establish access to disability income and health care. Disability income systems may decrease employment both by providing non–work income and by creating disincentives to employment due to potential reduction or loss of disability benefits.

Employer attitudes and practices can also limit job opportunities for people with disabilities, reflecting either outright discrimination or uncertainty about how they will fit into an organization. Field experiments find that employers are less likely to respond to job applications from qualified workers with disabilities, even when the specific disability would not decrease productivity (e.g., a person with a spinal cord injury applying for an accounting position) (Ameri et al., 2018; Baert, 2018). Studies have shown that workers with disabilities often encounter stigma and negative stereotypes on the job, resulting in poor wages, mistreatment from coworkers and supervisors, and fewer employment opportunities (Baldwin & Johnson, 2006; Beatty et al., 2019; Colella et al., 1998; Colella, 2001; Kruse et al., 2018; Louvet, 2007; Louvet et al., 2009; Ren et al., 2008; Stone & Colella, 1996). For example, Snyder et al., (2010) found that people with disabilities were more likely than others to cite explicit bias or microaggressions at work. Such experiences reflect unwelcoming corporate cultures (Schur et al., 2005, 2009), and they can discourage workers with disabilities from searching for or maintaining employment. Occupational segregation of people with disabilities contributes to their lower wages (Maroto & Pettinicchio, 2014).

In addition, some employers are reluctant to make needed accommodations even when required by law, due to the perceived cost or potential disruption in the workplace (reviewed in Schur et al., 2013, pp. 75–79). This partly reflects "ADA-recalcitrant employers" who are "known or reputed to be reluctant to comply with disability non-discrimination laws," of whom 81% cited the cost of accommodations as a major reason for not hiring people with disabilities (Kaye et al., 2011). While workers with disabilities are more likely than those without disabilities to request accommodations, the reported costs are generally low and similar for workers with and without disabilities. Also, supervisors and coworkers often report positive coworker reactions; in fact, accommodations tend to have positive spillover effects on the attitudes of coworkers toward the organization (Schur et al., 2014).

The reluctance of employers to hire people with disabilities persists despite many research studies showing that hiring people with disabilities often leads to improved business performance and competitive advantage (Lindsay et al., 2018).

As advocates for workers, unions may help alleviate some of the employment inequities associated with disability. Over the 2009–2017 period, US unions appear to have raised wages more for workers with disabilities (30%) than for workers without disabilities (24%), which decreased but did not eliminate the disability pay gap (Ameri et al., 2019). Exploratory data show that both union coverage and disability status increased the likelihood of requesting accommodations, supporting the idea that unions can serve as a voice for workers. While workers with disabilities had greater job retention in unionized jobs, they were also less likely to be hired into unionized jobs, indicating that employers appear reluctant to give union protections to workers with disabilities. In the union context, workers with disabilities appear more likely to be "last hired," but less likely to be "first fired." The net result is that the percent unionized decreased faster among workers with disabilities than workers without disabilities in the 2009–2017 period (Ameri et al., 2019). The higher retention rate among unionized workers with disabilities—compared both to unionized workers without disabilities and non–union workers with disabilities—may help decrease the likelihood that workers with disabilities will be laid off and have to turn to precarious work.

ADVANTAGES AND DISADVANTAGES OF PRECARIOUS WORK

Factors that affect the overall likelihood of employment are related to the potential advantages and disadvantages of precarious work. People with disabilities may particularly benefit when precarious jobs:

- Provide economic resources and useful work experiences without substantial training or commitments tied to a specific job or employer.
- Provide flexibility for people with disabilities in when and where to work. This can be particularly valuable to people with unpredictable conditions (e.g., lupus) and those that place demands on time and energy (e.g., weekly therapy schedules) or otherwise create uncertainties (e.g., transportation or medical difficulties) that make it difficult to commit to a standard fixed workweek.
- Support a transition to more permanent full-time work as people test their abilities through "job shopping" after an illness or injury or after finishing their education. Employers may use temporary jobs as a way to "audition" workers for new permanent jobs, which may especially benefit workers with disabilities by providing information to employers that helps correct biases and uncertainty that employers often have about hiring people with disabilities.

On the other hand, precarious jobs can have negative consequences for people with disabilities:

- Most obviously, job insecurity creates income insecurity, making financial planning difficult or impossible.
- People in precarious jobs tend to be paid less in general, and they are less likely to receive employer-sponsored training and benefits such as pension coverage and health insurance.

- Many workers in precarious jobs are considered independent contractors rather than employees, removing them from many employment protections.
- As with employment in general, the receipt of income through precarious employment may jeopardize disability benefits.
- Rather than providing a pathway to secure employment, people with disabilities may be stuck in these insecure jobs if employer discrimination keeps them out of more secure and high-paying jobs.

We examine the evidence related to these potential advantages and disadvantages next.

How Common Is Precarious Employment among Workers with Disabilities?

People with disabilities are more likely to work in precarious jobs. Evidence from 1995–2001 surveys in the United States shows that among people reporting work disabilities, between 18.0% and 20.8% of those who were employed could be classified as precarious or contingent workers (Schur, 2003). This was almost twice as high as the rates for workers without work disabilities that ranged from 11.1% to 11.9%. Workers with disabilities were more prevalent in each type of precarious work in 2001: those expecting the job to last for a "limited time" (7.2% for workers with disabilities compared to 3.3% for workers without disabilities), temporary help agency workers (2.0% compared to 0.8%), workers provided by contract firms (0.7% compared to 0.5%), on-call or day laborers (3.4% compared to 1.6%), and independent contractors who are highly reliant on one client (10.3% compared to 6.0%) (Schur, 2002, pp. 598–599).

A separate 2000 US survey used a broader definition of disability but narrower definition of precarious employment, finding that workers with disabilities in California were only slightly more likely than those without disabilities to be in jobs they expected to last less than 12 months (12.1% and 10.8%, respectively) (Yelin & Trupin, 2003). A Canadian study found that labor force participants with disabilities were slightly more likely than those without disabilities to be in nonstandard work arrangements over the 1989–2001 period (Tompa et al., 2006). Another Canadian study found that 10.1% of workers with disabilities in 2006 were in temporary, contract, or on-call jobs, but the data did not allow comparisons to precarious work among workers without disabilities (Shuey & Jovic, 2013).

Buttressing the idea that they are more likely to work in precarious job arrangements, people with disabilities generally express higher levels of job insecurity (Schur et al., 2009, 2017). Such feelings are clearly justified. Workers with disabilities in the United

States face higher rates of layoff than do otherwise similar workers without disabilities (Baldwin & Schumacher, 2002; Kaye, 2010; Mitra & Kruse, 2016; Schur et al., 2017; Yelin & Trupin, 2003). Combined with the evidence on employer reluctance to hire people with disabilities, these results support the idea that people with disabilities are "last hired, first fired."

We present new evidence from the 2017 US Current Population Survey Contingent Work Supplement (CPS CWS). The survey is very similar in methods and questions to earlier surveys done between 1995 and 2005 (analyzed through 2001 in Schur 2002, 2003). The major difference is that the earlier surveys could only be linked to a work disability measure (whether the person reports being limited in the kind or amount of work they can do), whereas the 2017 survey uses a more extensive set of six disability identifiers covering vision, hearing, cognitive, and mobility impairments, and difficulty with self-care (dressing or bathing) or going outside alone. Another difference from the earlier surveys is that the 2017 survey has a measure of gig work—whether the person took short tasks or jobs through companies that connect them directly with customers. We include gig work as an additional form of precarious work. All estimates use survey weights.

The 2017 survey has a total sample size of 47,851 workers—including both employees and self-employed—of whom 2,051 are identified as having a disability. Instead of limiting to working age, we include all workers age 18 or older since the experiences of precarious workers age 65 or older are also of interest. The rate of precarious work is higher in general among workers age 65 or older, but the disability gap in this rate is very similar to the gap among those of working age.[1]

This survey shows that workers with disabilities in the United States were more likely than those without disabilities to be precarious workers in 2017. Figure 21.1

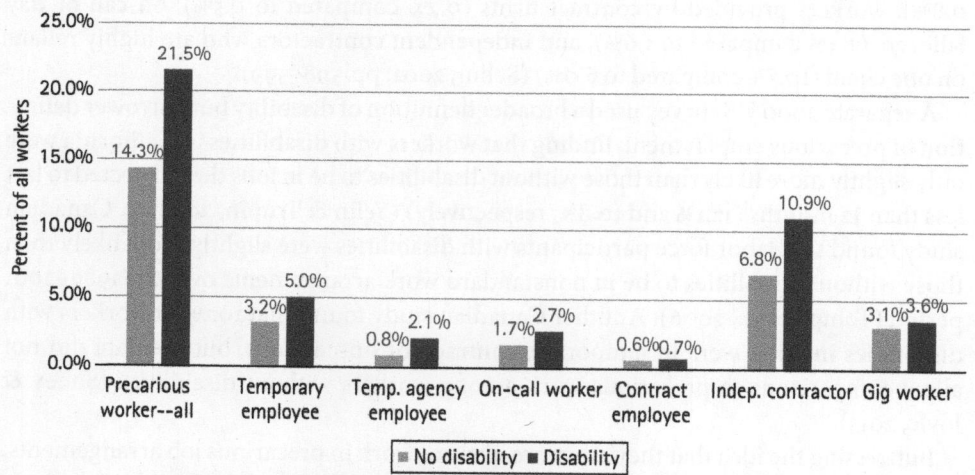

Based on 2017 Current Population Survey Contingent Work Supplement, with sample sizes of 2,051 workers with disabilities and 45,600 workers without disabilities. See Table 21.1.

FIGURE 21.1 Precarious work by disability status.

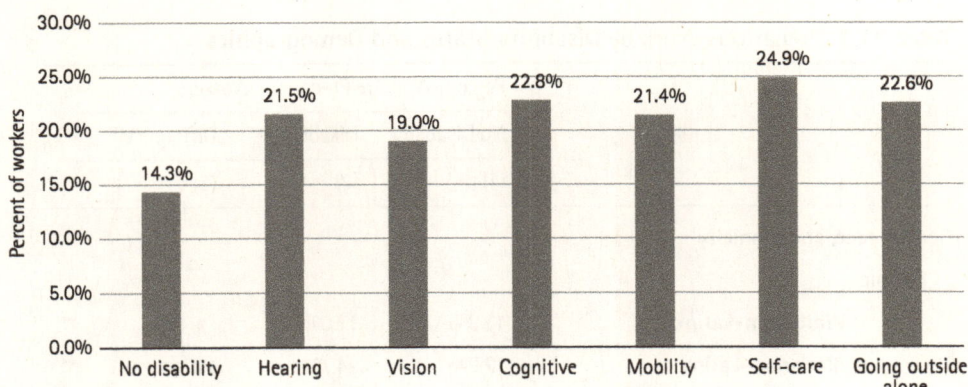

Based on 2017 Current Population Survey Contingent Work Supplement, with sample sizes of 2,051 workers with disabilities and 45,600 workers without disabilities. See Table 21.1.

FIGURE 21.2 Precarious work by type of disability.

shows that one-fifth (21.5%) of workers with disabilities were in precarious jobs, compared to one-seventh (14.3%) of workers without disabilities. This difference is significant, as are the higher rates among workers with disabilities for each type of precarious work except contract employee and gig worker. The most common type of precarious job for workers both with and without disabilities was independent contracting with reliance on a single client, followed by temporary employees in jobs that will "last only for a limited time or until the completion of a project." Workers with disabilities were more likely than those without disabilities to hold these jobs and to be temporary agency employees or on-call workers. There was no significant difference, however, in the likelihood that workers with disabilities were contract employees or gig workers.

The higher rate of precarious work held true for each of the six types of disability as shown in Figure 21.2, except that the higher rate for people with vision impairments is not strong enough to be statistically significant.

Intersectional analysis is very important in studying precarious employment, as White men have typically held the most high-status and secure jobs while women and people of color are more likely to work in lower-paying, less stable jobs. Table 21.1 looks at precarious work in the United States as it relates to disability intersected with gender, race, ethnicity, marital status, and presence of children in the household. As can be seen in column 3, in almost all of these groups, people with disabilities are more likely than those without disabilities to be precarious workers. Precarious work is especially common among workers with disabilities who are Black women, Black men, Latinx men, and unmarried men with children under 18 living in the household. The economic status of Blacks in the United States is generally lower than that of Whites (Cherry & Rodgers, 2000), and these results indicate that precarious employment may contribute to lower well-being for Blacks with disabilities. In results not shown, we also find that

Table 21.1 Precarious Work by Disability Status and Demographics

	Percent Who Are Precarious Workers		
	No Disability	Disability	Difference
	(1)	(2)	(3)
Gender, race, and ethnicity			
Female			
White non-Latinx	12.9%	17.0%	4.1% **
Black non-Latinx	12.2%	24.7%	12.5% **
Latinx	13.2%	21.9%	8.7% *
Other race/ethnicity	13.9%	10.2%	-3.7%
Male			
White non-Latinx	15.8%	24.3%	8.5% **
Black non-Latinx	14.0%	25.5%	11.6% *
Latinx	16.1%	27.3%	11.2% **
Other race/ethnicity	14.9%	21.7%	6.8%
Gender, marital status, and children			
Female			
Not married, no kids under 18	12.8%	20.4%	7.6% **
Not married, kids under 18	12.1%	17.3%	5.3%
Married, no kids under 18	13.6%	16.6%	3.0%
Married, kids under 18	12.8%	14.1%	1.4%
Male			
Not married, no kids under 18	15.8%	24.4%	8.6% **
Not married, kids under 18	14.8%	30.7%	16.0% **
Married, no kids under 18	16.5%	25.9%	9.3% **
Married, kids under 18	14.7%	19.1%	4.4%

* Significant difference between disability and no disability at $p < .05$.
** $p < .01$.
Source: Based on analysis of US Current Population Survey Contingent Work Supplement, May 2017.

the disability gap in precarious employment is fairly similar across age and education groups.

These results clearly point to disability as an important factor in the prevalence of precarious work, over and above other personal characteristics. However, there are many potential reasons for this higher prevalence.

WHAT ACCOUNTS FOR HIGHER LEVELS OF PRECARIOUS EMPLOYMENT AMONG WORKERS WITH DISABILITIES?

The reasons for the higher rate of precarious employment among workers with disabilities are not obvious. There may be no direct causal link but simply a correlation with a third variable such as poverty that puts people at greater risk for developing disabilities (Lustig & Strauser, 2007; WHO/World Bank 2011, pp. 36–37). People in poverty are both more likely to take precarious jobs and to develop disabilities, and the precarious jobs provide incomes that are too low to pull them out of poverty. In this case, precarious work is a symptom of economic difficulties rather than a direct contributor.

There may, however, be a causal link. Precarious work itself may play a role in increasing disability, either directly through injuries or indirectly through worsened health that can lead to disability (Krahn et al., 2015). In the opposite direction, having a disability may lead many workers to take precarious jobs, as a result of worker preferences or employer decisions. Next we discuss these causal links going in both directions.

Why Precarious Work May Lead to Disability

Some studies show a direct link from precarious work to disability. For instance, MacEachen et al. (2014) find that temporary agency employees are at greater risk for work injuries than regular employees. This may be due to increased exposure to hazards, less safety training, lack of safety equipment, worker unfamiliarity with equipment and tasks, inferior knowledge on standards and regulations, inadequate supervision or staff, lack of adequate accommodations, or a lower likelihood of reporting hazards due to job insecurity (Ekberg et al., 2016; McNamara, 2006).

In addition to direct effects on disability, numerous studies have found that workers are at greater risk of developing ill health in more precarious jobs, which can lead to disability (Lustig & Strauser, 2007; Lewchuk, 2017; Ronnblad et al. 2019; Farina et al., 2020). Precarious employment may lead to bad health outcomes through reduced control, increased job strain and stress, and high workload. As noted by Lewchuk et al., "simply by showing up to work, workers in standard employment relationships have a degree of control over whether they will be employed the next day and the terms and conditions of their future employment" (2006, p. 144), while a lack of control and predictability for precarious workers creates adverse health consequences. In a review of 93 studies, 76 showed a connection between precarious employment and poor health (Quinlan et al., 2015). Another review of 16 studies of young people concluded that they were especially vulnerable to health problems when working in precarious conditions (Vancea and Utzet 2017). Across several longitudinal studies, precarious work was linked to worsening health in Italy (Pirani & Salvini, 2015); poorer mental health in

Sweden (Canivet et al., 2016); poorer self-rated health and serious psychological distress in Japan (Tsurugano et al., 2012); increased mortality and longer depression-related disability episodes in Finland (Natti et al., 2009; Ervasti et al., 2014), and worse health in Canada (Scott-Marshall & Tompa, 2011).

Why Disability May Lead to Precarious Work

There are several ways in which workers with disabilities may be channeled into precarious jobs: their own choices and preferences, the income constraints created by various public policies, and the discrimination they face from employers.

Worker Preferences

A key characteristic of most precarious work arrangements is greater flexibility, which may be at the discretion of the employer or employee. Some people with disabilities prefer precarious work arrangements due to the flexibility provided in coping with the demands of a disability, such as medical or therapy appointments, unpredictable medical issues, or greater required time, effort, or need for assistance in activities of daily living. People with mobility issues can face transportation problems both with personal vehicles and public transportation, creating uncertainty in reliably meeting fixed work schedules. All of these potential demands and problems can make it difficult to maintain a commitment to a standard long-term job with a fixed schedule.

Apart from the desire for flexibility, one attraction of temporary jobs is that they can allow workers to test their abilities and interests in different work environments. The testing of abilities may be especially important for workers who are attempting to return to work after an injury or disability onset, and may find temporary work a good bridge to more permanent work. More generally, this may be true for workers who want to explore how their disability affects pay and performance in alternative jobs, or who want to use a temporary job to dispel employer uncertainty about their disability as they "audition" for a more secure job.

Indirect data point to worker preferences as a factor in the higher rate of precarious work. As unemployment rates go down and labor markets tighten, workers have more choice among jobs and their preferences should play a stronger role. A US study found that while the rate of permanent full-time employment increases for workers both with and without disability when labor markets tighten, the rate of contingent or part-time work declines for people without disabilities but increases for people with disabilities (Schur, 2003). The higher rate of contingent and part-time work as labor markets tighten indicates that many workers with disabilities prefer these types of work arrangements as work becomes available. This conclusion is echoed in findings from the United Kingdom showing that greater work limitations from a disability are linked to a higher rate of self-employment. This suggests that "self-employment may provide an important means by which those with work-limiting disabilities can accommodate their impairment" (Jones & Latreille, 2011, p. 4161).

More direct data on preferences, however, do not support the idea that people with disabilities generally place a higher priority on flexibility. In one US survey, nonemployed people with disabilities did not significantly differ from people without disabilities in their preferences regarding desirable job characteristics (Ali et al., 2011, p. 206).

The 2017 CPS CWS sheds further light on this issue with data on the primary reasons given by precarious workers for being in these jobs. As shown in Table 21.2, there is no significant difference between precarious workers with and without disabilities in citing "personal/family reasons" (columns 1 and 2). Within the personal/family reasons, workers with disabilities are less likely to cite "flexibility of schedule" as a reason, but more likely to simply cite "health limitations," which may reflect some of the time, energy, and scheduling factors that lead people with disabilities to favor precarious work.

Although the overall reports of personal/family reasons are similar, precarious workers with disabilities are more likely than those without disabilities to report economic or labor market constraints (26.4% compared to 20.5%). In particular, temporary employees with disabilities were significantly more likely to report that temporary work was the "only type of job [they] could find" (columns 3 and 4).

Precarious workers with disabilities were also significantly less likely to report being in such work due to being in school or training (1.4% compared to 6.4%). Workers with disabilities tend to be older and less likely to be in school or training, but even among workers age 18–34, those without disabilities are almost three times more likely than those with disabilities to cite being in school or training as a primary reason for their precarious job (19.7% compared to 7.6%). Precarious jobs may help to finance schooling and training while maintaining flexibility to accommodate school and training schedules. Precarious work is therefore more likely to be seen as a temporary stepping stone to career success for workers without disabilities than for those with disabilities.

These new data indicate that preferences are not necessarily the main driver of precarious work for people with disabilities. People with and without disabilities are just as likely to cite personal/family reasons, and temporary employees with disabilities are more likely than those without disabilities to say that this is the only work they could find. Further evidence from the survey also points away from worker preferences and toward labor market constraints as a driving factor.

Figure 21.3 illustrates comparisons of job search and preferences for other jobs from the 2017 US survey. The results show that precarious workers with disabilities are significantly more likely than those without disabilities to say they would like a different type of job (32.8% compared to 26.9%). In addition, precarious workers with disabilities are more likely to have searched for another type of job within the past 4 months (13.3% compared to 7.3%). In results not shown, the differences by disability status exist across all of the types of precarious work, although small sample sizes contribute to a lack of statistical significance for most differences within precarious work types.

These results do not permit a clean conclusion on the importance of worker preferences as a driver of precarious employment among people with disabilities. The importance of worker preferences is suggested by the finding that precarious work goes

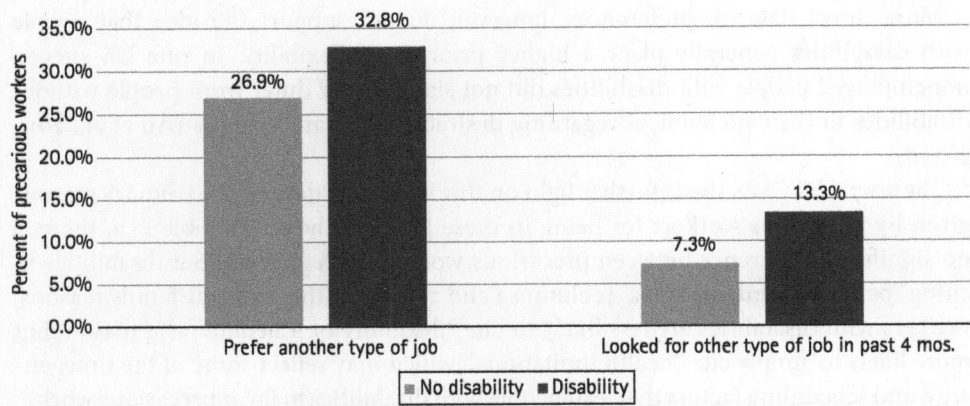

Based on 2017 Current Population Survey Contingent Work Supplement. Respective sample sizes are 5,297, 375, 6,606, and 433.

FIGURE 21.3 Job search and preferences for another job among precarious workers.

up among people with disabilities as labor markets tighten when workers have more choice among jobs. The directly reported data on preferences, however, cast doubt on the role of preferences. They show that workers with disabilities are no more likely to report personal or family reasons for precarious work; temporary employees with disabilities are more likely than those without disabilities to report that they could only find precarious work; and precarious workers with disabilities are more likely than those without disabilities both to say they would like another type of job and to be searching for another job.

Disability Income Constraints

Apart from worker preferences, the constraints imposed by disability income systems may affect the type and amount of work chosen by workers. While disability income systems vary substantially across countries, they are generally based on an assessed limitation or incapacity for work (Mitra, 2009; OECD, 2010; WHO/World Bank, 2011). Those who qualify for disability income may be limited in the jobs they can take in order to remain eligible for disability income.

In the United States, Social Security Disability Income (SSDI) is available to those with an earnings record who are judged to no longer be able to engage in "substantial gainful activity." SSDI recipients can, however, earn small amounts of income that fall under the threshold for substantial gainful activity, so they may take part-time or precarious jobs that provide supplemental income. Following recipients over time, Schur (2003) found that an increase in the earnings threshold was linked to a change in the earnings distribution of people with disabilities, but only about 5% of recipients increased their earnings to move closer to the new threshold, leading to the conclusion that SSDI earnings limits "account for only a small portion of the higher rates of contingent and part-time work among people with disabilities" (Schur, 2003, p. 611). This conclusion is reinforced by the 2017 survey data in Table 21.2 where only 3.1% of precarious

Table 21.2 Reported Reasons for Precarious Work and Self-Employment

	Any Precarious Worker		Temporary Employee		On-Call Worker		Independent Contractor Relying on Single Client	
	No Disability	Disability	No Disability	Disability	No Disability	Disability	No Disability	Disability
	(1)	(2)	(3)	(4)	(5)	(6)	(7)	(8)
All	100.0%	100.0%	100.0%	100.0%	100.0%	100.0%	100.0%	100.0%
Personal/family reasons	56.1%	59.5%	26.2%	29.8%	41.7%	31.0%	73.0%	80.2% *
Flexibility of schedule	23.5%	17.5% *	11.1%	6.6%	24.7%	10.7% **	29.5%	23.8%
Health limitations	0.6%	9.7% **	0.6%	11.6% **	0.8%	12.6% *	0.5%	9.6% **
Child care problems	3.0%	2.9%	1.0%	0.0% **	3.6%	0.6% **	3.6%	4.2%
Only wanted to work for a short period of time	0.4%	0.2%	1.5%	0.8%	NA	NA	NA	NA
Enjoys being own boss/independence	18.5%	16.4%	NA	NA	NA	NA	30.8%	27.6%
Other personal	8.1%	10.5%	7.9%	6.0%	10.8%	3.4% **	7.3%	14.3% *
Other family/personal obligations	2.0%	2.2%	4.1%	4.7%	1.8%	3.7%	1.2%	0.8%
Economic/labor market constraints	20.5%	26.4% *	37.5%	60.4% **	32.5%	34.3%	9.5%	8.3%
Only type of work could find	13.4%	17.0%	24.1%	43.4% **	23.9%	20.9%	6.1%	4.6%
Employer laid off and hired back as temporary worker	1.1%	0.6%	1.9%	0.9%	0.0%	0.0%	1.0%	0.7%
Hope job leads to permanent employment	4.0%	5.6%	8.5%	11.4%	5.0%	6.6%	1.1%	1.3%
Retired/Social Security earnings limit	1.9%	3.1%	3.0%	4.7%	3.6%	6.8%	1.3%	1.7%
Skill investment	7.8%	1.4% **	25.8%	5.5% **	5.4%	0.0% **	0.7%	0.0% **
In school/training	6.4%	1.4% **	21.9%	5.5% **	4.5%	0.0% **	0.3%	0.0% *
To obtain experience/training	1.4%	0.0% **	3.8%	0.0% **	0.9%	0.0% *	0.4%	0.0% **

(continued)

Table 21.2 Continued

	Any Precarious Worker		Temporary Employee		On-Call Worker		Independent Contractor Relying on Single Client	
	No Disability	Disability	No Disability	Disability	No Disability	Disability	No Disability	Disability
	(1)	(2)	(3)	(4)	(5)	(6)	(7)	(8)
Other reasons								
Money is better	7.1%	4.2% *	1.8%	2.0%	5.6%	4.4%	9.9%	5.4% **
Nature of work/seasonal	3.6%	4.8%	4.7%	0.0% **	9.1%	20.1%	2.3%	3.4%
Other economic	4.9%	3.7%	4.1%	2.4%	5.8%*	10.2%	4.6%	2.7%
n	5,233	374	1,328	99	773	62	3127	214

Figures represent the primary reason reported for the given work arrangement (column percentages).

* Significant difference between disability and no disability at $p < .05$;

** $p < .01$.

Source: Based on analysis of US Current Population Survey Contingent Work Supplement, May 2017.

workers with disabilities cited "retired/Social Security earnings limit" as their primary reason for precarious employment.

Employer Discrimination

The high rate of precarious work may also reflect employer discrimination that limits access to standard permanent jobs for people with disabilities. As reviewed earlier, there is good evidence that prejudice and discrimination contribute to the overall low employment levels of people with disabilities, and it is very possible that people with disabilities are forced to take precarious jobs as a result of not being able to obtain standard permanent jobs.

The potential role of discrimination is revealed in part by examining precarious work across the business cycle, as employers can more easily engage in discrimination when unemployment is high and they have substantial choice among job applicants. This fits the employment pattern of Black workers, who face well-documented discrimination and whose employment especially goes up in tight labor markets as employers are more eager to attract workers (Cherry & Rodgers, 2000). This overall pattern is also generally true for people with disabilities (Tompa et al., 2006), but there is an interesting and informative divergence between precarious and nonprecarious employment. While overall employment increased but contingent and part-time employment decreased for Black workers as labor markets tightened, among people with disabilities contingent and part-time jobs increased along with permanent full-time jobs, pointing to the role of worker preferences rather than discrimination as a key driver of precarious and part-time employment (Schur, 2003).

Looking at direct reports of discrimination, temporary workers in a Canadian study were more likely to report perceived job discrimination in the past 5 years than were permanent employees who felt their skills were fully utilized (Konrad et al., 2012, 2013). While this suggests temporary employees experience greater discrimination (which may have led to the temporary employment in the first place), this conclusion is muddied by the finding that there were even higher reports of job discrimination among the unemployed and the permanent employees who felt their skills were underutilized.

There is some support for the idea that discrimination plays a role in Table 21.2's finding that temporary employees with disabilities were almost twice as likely as those without disabilities to say this is the only type of work they could find (43.4% compared to 24.1%) (columns 3 and 4). One other piece of evidence is that while discrimination may lead employers to disproportionately try out workers with disabilities as temporary workers, Table 21.2 shows that precarious workers with disabilities were no more likely than those without disabilities to say they were hoping the job would lead to permanent employment.

In short, there is mixed evidence on whether worker preferences or employer discrimination are primarily responsible for driving workers into precarious employment.

WHAT ARE THE CONSEQUENCES OF PRECARIOUS EMPLOYMENT FOR PEOPLE WITH DISABILITIES?

The most important aspect of precarious employment is by definition a lack of employment security. This is consistent with higher reported job insecurity and greater rates of layoff among workers with disabilities (Mitra & Kruse, 2016; Schur et al., 2009, 2017). While employment insecurity is a problem for any worker, it is especially difficult for those who are poor, and people with disabilities are more likely than those without disabilities to live in poverty (Brucker et al., 2015; Tompa et al., 2006).

Other important outcomes that may be affected by precarious employment include health, pay and benefits, accommodations, eligibility for disability income, and general well-being. The effects of precarious employment on health were reviewed earlier, while the effects on these other outcomes follow.

Pay and Benefits

Precarious jobs pay less and are less likely to provide employment-related benefits than other jobs. In the 2017 US study, workers in three alternative work arrangements (on-call workers, temporary agency employees, and independent contractors) had lower median weekly pay than workers in traditional arrangements, although contract employees had higher median weekly pay (US BLS, 2018). On-call workers, temporary agency employees, and contract employees were all less likely to have employer-provided health insurance or to be included in an employer-provided pension plan.

On top of the generally lower pay in these jobs, precarious workers with disabilities earn even lower pay than those without disabilities. The pay gaps combine such that temporary employees with disabilities in the United States earned 4.5% less per hour than temporary employees without disabilities, and 14.1% less than permanent employees without disabilities in 1995–2001 (Schur, 2002). The equivalent pay gaps facing independent contractors with disabilities were 17.2% and 21.9%, respectively. Schur (2002) also found the precarious employees with disabilities were especially unlikely to participate in employer-provided health insurance or pension plans, relative both to permanent employees with disabilities and to precarious employees without disabilities. This pattern is also evident in Canadian data where Tompa et al., found that over 1989–2001 the annual earnings of people with disabilities in nonstandard work were "consistently lower than those for people without disabilities in the same type of arrangements" (2006, p. 112).

Data from the 2017 US survey are consistent with this pattern. As shown in Table 21.3, precarious workers with disabilities have 25.0% lower median weekly pay, and 23.5%

Table 21.3 Pay and Benefits by Work Arrangement and Disability Status

	Median Weekly Pay			Median Hourly Pay			Health Insurance from Employer		Participate in Employer Pension Plan		Union Coverage	
	No Disability	Disability	% Gap	No Disability	Disability	% Gap	No Disability	Disability	No Disability	Disability	No Disability	Disability
	(1)	(2)	(3)	(4)	(5)	(6)	(7)	(8)	(9)	(10)	(11)	(12)
All												
Permanent employee	$769	$673	−12.5% *	$13.00	$12.00	−7.7% **	61.1%	51.3% **	57.6%	49.1% **	12.7%	10.5%
Precarious worker	$600	$450	−25.0% **	$14.37	$11.00	−23.5% **	20.5%	12.6% **	32.8%	23.1% **	6.5%	3.0% **
Type of precarious worker												
Temporary employee	$438	$365	−16.7% *	$12.00	$10.00	−16.7% **	22.8%	8.4% **	18.2%	8.2% **	10.2%	3.5% **
Temporary agency employee	$480	$450	−6.3%	$12.00	$10.00	−16.7% **	14.6%	2.6% **	8.3%	2.5%	6.3%	0.0% **
On-call worker	$500	$384	−23.2%	$15.00	$10.50	−30.0% **	30.8%	19.3%	34.1%	33.9%	12.8%	9.2%
Contract employee	$962	$438	−54.5% *	$20.00	$16.00	−20.0%	43.1%	28.8%	42.4%	47.5%	11.0%	2.1% **
Independent contractor relying on single client	$692	$488	−29.5% **	$25.00	$25.00	0.0%	2.8%	1.7%	18.1%	8.3%	3.4%	1.3% *
Gig worker	$720	$525	−27.1% **	$15.00	$10.00	−33.3% **	44.6%	43.2%	53.6%	48.7%	8.2%	6.5%
Overall n	15,549	776		12,991	775		42,463	1,919	36,856	1,562	15,549	776

* Difference from no disability at p < .05;

** p < .01.

Source: Based on analysis of US Current Population Survey Contingent Work Supplement, May 2017.

lower median hourly pay, than precarious workers without disabilities (columns 3 and 6). These gaps are larger than the disability gaps among permanent employees (–12.5% and –7.7%, respectively). In addition, precarious workers with disabilities are less likely to be covered by employer-provided health insurance or pension plans (columns 7 to 10), and they are less likely to have union coverage (columns 11 and 12). The disability gaps in pay, benefits, and union coverage exist across most of the comparisons within different types of precarious workers, although some of the differences are not large enough to be statistically significant.

Disability Accommodations

The principle of accommodation is key to improving employment opportunities and outcomes for people with disabilities (Blanck, 2020). In many precarious jobs, there is no traditional employer who is covered by an anti-discrimination law (such as the ADA) and required to make reasonable accommodations. The legal status of many precarious workers is murky, and there is a need for regulatory reforms to clarify and extend employment protections and accommodations (Blanck, 2020).

Employers are more likely to provide accommodations to workers who they expect to keep employed for a long time, so that the cost of accommodations is amortized over a longer period. This would lead to lower rates of accommodation for precarious workers with disabilities who are not expected to stay with the organization. Consistent with this, among workers with disabilities who had accommodation needs, 45.6% of precarious workers in Canada reported their needs were not fully met, compared to 33.5% of permanent employees with disabilities, and a significant difference remained after controlling for other worker and job characteristics (Shuey & Jovic, 2013). It is, of course, possible that this pattern of greater unmet needs is also true for precarious workers without disabilities.

Our analysis of the US Current Population Survey Disability Supplement in July 2019 finds that among workers with disabilities who requested a "change in your workplace to help you do your job better," those in temporary jobs were twice as likely as other workers to say their request was not fully met (38% compared to 18%). This difference was smaller when comparing workers without disabilities who requested changes in temporary and nontemporary jobs (25% compared to 19%). Although these differences were not statistically significant, the pattern is consistent with the idea that temporary employees with disabilities are more likely to have unmet accommodation needs compared both to temporary employees without disabilities and to nontemporary employees with disabilities.

While employers may be less willing to accommodate precarious workers, the increased flexibility of precarious work may give workers more opportunity to create accommodations for themselves. As noted by Harpur and Blanck in discussing gig workers with disabilities, "often it is easier for people with disabilities to create and manage inclusive and flexible work arrangements when they own and operate the businesses in question" (2020, p. 511). In addition, people with disabilities are more likely than those without disabilities to work from home (Schur et al., 2020), which can help accommodate the needs of many people with disabilities through, for example, easier access to "individualized medical or assistive devices and supports that they have arranged in their residences" (Harpur & Blanck, 2020, p. 513). The greater use of home-based work during the COVID pandemic may increase the long-term acceptability of home-based work as a disability accommodation, and possibly also increase on-site work accommodations as employers rethink how essential tasks can be performed (Schur et al., 2020).

Eligibility for Disability Income

The lower earnings and more intermittent nature of precarious employment can make it harder to apply for disability income, as the award of disability income is often based on one's earnings record. Precarious employment may lower a person's eligibility for disability income as well as their potential benefits, if eligible. A US study of workers in their fifties and sixties found that the Social Security Disability Income application rate among those with a history of precarious work arrangements was one-quarter lower than among other workers (Rutledge et al., 2019). In addition, the award rate was about one-third lower for those with a history of precarious employment.

These results may, of course, differ by the rules of disability income systems. Following Finnish workers over the period of 1984–2003, Ojala and Pyöriä (2019) found that those with a history of precarious employment were more likely to receive a disability pension. The precarious job feature that most strongly predicted receiving a disability pension was poor employability (low likelihood of finding a new job). In this case precarious employment appears to be a symptom rather than a cause of the poor employability that predicted eligibility for a disability pension.

Worker Well-Being

How do precarious workers with disabilities feel about their jobs? Job quality appears to be lower for precarious workers in general. A Finnish study found they had decreased levels of skill and discretion, and worked in a less supportive environment (Pyöriä & Ojala, 2016). We know from Figure 21.3 that they are more likely than precarious workers without disabilities to prefer another type of job and to have looked for another type of job in the past 4 months. A Canadian study of people with disabilities found that temporary workers reported lower life satisfaction than permanent employees who felt their skills were fully utilized, although similar satisfaction as underemployed permanent employees who felt their skills were moderately underutilized, and higher satisfaction than underemployed permanent employees who felt their skills were highly underutilized (Konrad et al., 2012). Compared to those not working, their life satisfaction was higher than among people with disabilities who were unemployed and looking for work, but equivalent to that of nonparticipants in the labor force. No comparison was available to see if this pattern was the same among workers without disabilities.

Overall, for a person with a disability, having a temporary job appears to be better for life satisfaction than being unemployed, and better than being highly underutilized in a permanent job, but worse than having one's skills fully utilized in a permanent job. This pattern matches the earlier-noted reports of job discrimination. Temporary workers with disabilities report fewer experiences of discrimination within the past 5 years than do the unemployed and permanent employees with disabilities who feel underutilized, but report more discrimination than permanent employees with disabilities who feel their skills are fully utilized.

SUMMARY AND CONCLUSION

Based on a review of the relevant literature and our own original analyses of 2017 US CPS Contingent Worker data, we find the following:

- Workers with disabilities are more likely than those without disabilities to work in precarious jobs.
- The difference in precarious employment between workers with and without disabilities exists within most demographic groups, indicating that disability is an independent contributor to the higher prevalence.
- The higher prevalence of precarious work may reflect both a greater likelihood that precarious work leads to disability and a greater likelihood that workers with disabilities choose or are constrained to take precarious jobs.
- The evidence on worker preferences as a driver of the higher rate of precarious work among people with disabilities is mixed. Labor market transitions indicate that many people with disabilities choose precarious jobs as labor markets tighten and their options expand, but survey data indicate that workers with disabilities are more likely than those without disabilities to feel constrained to a temporary job, and to want and search for a nonprecarious job. The latter results are more consistent with the idea that employer discrimination is limiting many workers with disabilities to precarious jobs.
- Workers without disabilities are more likely to say they are in these jobs due to being in school or training, indicating that precarious work is more likely to be seen as a stepping stone for workers without disabilities.
- A number of studies find that precarious employment can lead to ill health and disability.
- Workers with disabilities tend to earn less than those without disabilities in every type of precarious employment arrangement, have less access to employer-provided

health insurance and pensions, and have lower union coverage. The disability pay gap is higher in precarious jobs than in full-time permanent jobs.

• Whether precarious work leads to higher overall well-being among workers with disabilities depends on the comparison group. Precarious workers with disabilities report higher satisfaction compared to unemployed people with disabilities and to permanent employees with disabilities who feel their skills are greatly underutilized, but they report lower life satisfaction than permanent employees with disabilities who feel their skills are fully utilized.

Overall, it is difficult to reach general conclusions about the value of precarious work for people with disabilities given the tremendous variety in types of disability and types of precarious jobs. The accumulated data do not allow us to tease out how many workers adopt precarious jobs as a result of their voluntary choices as opposed to decisions constrained by employers, labor markets, and other institutions.

The mixed evidence indicates that, depending on the circumstances, precarious jobs create good outcomes for some workers with disabilities but bad outcomes for others. Precarious work is clearly appropriate for people whose disabilities make it difficult or impossible to commit to a standard full-time job with a fixed schedule. For these people, precarious jobs may provide an important opportunity both to earn some income and to be at least somewhat more integrated into the mainstream of economic and social life. Given the greater isolation faced by people with disabilities, any employment opportunity can be valuable not only economically but also socially and psychologically (Schur, 2003).

Precarious work clearly presents problems, however, for many workers with disabilities who want and need more secure and rewarding employment. There is evidence that disability prejudice and discrimination continue to limit people with disabilities in obtaining standard jobs with good pay, and many of the people who are turned down for standard jobs end up in precarious jobs with less security, lower pay and benefits, and other undesirable characteristics.

A question that should be investigated further is the potential role of unions. Future research can explore whether and how unions help provide employment protections to precarious workers while preserving some of the advantages of flexibility (although not many precarious jobs are unionized). Another important set of questions concerns accommodations for precarious workers. What obligations do employers have when their workers are not traditional employees? To what extent can precarious workers with disabilities make their own accommodations? How can public policy ensure that precarious workers with disabilities have access to needed accommodations?

Clearly people with disabilities need greater access to standard jobs. Whether workers with disabilities freely choose or are constrained to take precarious jobs, however, a common concern is that they receive lower pay and benefits than do workers without disabilities. Also, these jobs typically provide few employment protections, unpredictable schedules, limited training, no upward mobility, lack of union representation or other employee voice mechanisms, and power imbalances that increase worker vulnerability (Julia et al., 2017). These negative job characteristics may especially disadvantage workers with disabilities within these jobs. As noted by Harpur, "precarious work structures have not been developed to promote equality" (2018, p. 70). In line with principles laid out in the UN Convention, efforts to expand social and legal norms to bring higher pay and greater protections to precarious workers would especially benefit workers with disabilities.

ACKNOWLEDGMENTS

This line of study was supported in part by grants from the National Institute on Disability, Independent Living, and Rehabilitation Research (NIDILRR) for the Rehabilitation Research & Training on Employment Policy: Center for Disability-Inclusive Employment Policy Research Grant #90RTEM0006-01-00, and the Disability Employer Practices RRTC Grant #90RTEM0008-01-00 The views provided herein do not necessarily reflect the official policies of NIDILRR nor do they imply endorsement by the federal government.

NOTE

1. The rate of precarious work among workers with disabilities age 65 or older is 30.9% among those with disabilities and 24.7% among those without disabilities (gap of 6.2%), while the rate among those age 18-64 is 19.6% and 13.7% respectively (gap of 5.9%).

REFERENCES

Ali, M., Schur, L., & Blanck, P. (2011). What types of jobs do people with disabilities want? *Journal of occupational rehabilitation*, 21(2), 199-210.

Ameri, M., Ali, M., Schur, L., & Kruse, D. (2019). Disability in the unionized workplace. In S. Bruyere (Ed.), *Employment and disability: Issues, innovations, and opportunities* (pp. 65–97). Cornell University Press.

Ameri, M., Schur, L., Adya, M., Bentley, F. S., McKay, P., & Kruse, D. (2018). The disability employment puzzle: A field experiment on employer hiring behavior. *ILR Review*, 71(2), 329–364.

Baert, S. (2018). Hiring discrimination: An overview of (almost) all correspondence experiments since 2005. In S. Gaddis (Ed.), *Audit studies: Behind the scenes with theory, method, and nuance* (vol. 14, 63–77). Springer.

Baldwin, M. L., & Johnson, W. G. (2006). A critical review of studies of discrimination against workers with disabilities. In W. M. Rodgers (Ed.), *Handbook on the economics of discrimination* (pp. 119–160). Edward Elgar Publishing.

Baldwin, M., & Schumacher, E. (2002). A note on job mobility among workers with disabilities. *Industrial Relations*, 41(3), 430–441.

Beatty, J. E., Baldridge, D. C., Boehm, S. A., Kulkarni, M., & Colella, A. J. (2019). On the treatment of persons with disabilities in organizations: A review and research agenda. *Human Resource Management*, 58(2), 119–137.

Blanck, P. (2020). Disability inclusive employment and the accommodation principle: emerging issues in research, policy, and law. *The Journal of Occupational Rehabilitation*, 30, 505–510.

Branch, E. H., & Hanley, C. (2017). A racial-gender lens on precarious nonstandard employment. In Kalleberg, A. L., & Vallas, S.P. (Eds.) *Precarious Work* (*Research in the Sociology of Work* Vol. 31, pp. 183–213). Emerald.

Brucker, D. L., Mitra, S., Chaitoo, N., & Mauro, J. (2015). More likely to be poor whatever the measure: Working-age persons with disabilities in the United States. *Social Science Quarterly*, 96(1), 273–296.

Butler, R. J., Baldwin, M. L., & Johnson, W. G. (2006). The effects of occupational injuries after returns to work: Work absences and losses of on-the-job productivity. *Journal of Risk and Insurance*, 73(2), 309–334.

Campolieti, M., & Krashinsky, H. (2006). Disabled workers and wage losses: Some evidence from workers with occupational injuries. *ILR Review*, 60(1), 120–138.

Canivet, C., Bodin, T., Emmelin, M., Toivanen, S., Moghaddassi, M., & Östergren, P. O. (2016). Precarious employment is a risk factor for poor mental health in young individuals in Sweden: A cohort study with multiple follow-ups. *BMC Public Health*, 16(1), 687.

Cherry, R., & William III, M. (Eds.). (2000). *Prosperity for all?: The economic boom and African Americans*. Russell Sage Foundation.

Colella A. (2001). Coworker Distributive Fairness Judgments of the Workplace Accommodation of Employees with Disabilities. *Academy of Management Review* 26: 100–116.

Colella, A., DeNisi, A. S., & Varma, A. (1998). The impact of ratee's disability on performance judgments and choice as partner: The role of disability-job fit stereotypes and interdependence of rewards. *Journal of Applied Psychology*, 83, 102–111.

Ekberg, K., Pransky, G. S., Besen, E., Fassier, J. B., Feuerstein, M., Munir, F., & Blanck, P. (2016). New business structures creating organizational opportunities and challenges for work disability prevention. *Journal of Occupational Rehabilitation*, 26(4), 480–489.

Ervasti, J., Vahtera, J., Virtanen, P., Pentti, J., Oksanen, T., Ahola, K., Kivimaki, M., & Virtanen, M. (2014). Is temporary employment a risk factor for work disability due to depressive disorders and delayed return to work? The Finnish Public Sector Study. *Scandinavian Journal of Work, Environment & Health*, 40(4), 343–352.

Farina, E., Green, C. P., & McVicar, D. (2020). Is precarious employment bad for worker health? The case of zero hours contracts in the UK. IZA Discussion Paper 13116.

Grammenos, S. (2010). *Indicators of disability equality in europe, ANED 2010 task 4*. Leeds, UK: Academic Network of European Disability experts, Centre for Disability Studies, University of Leeds.

Harpur, P. (2017). Collective versus individual rights: The able worker and the promotion of precarious work for persons with disabilities under conflicting international law regimes. *Loyola of Los Angeles International and Comparative Law Review*, 41, 51.

Harpur, P., & Blanck, P. (2020). Gig workers with disabilities: Opportunities, challenges, and regulatory response. *Journal of Occupational Rehabilitation*, 30(4), 511–520.

Jones, M. (2021). Disability and labor market outcomes. *IZA World of Labor*, 253v2, doi: 10.15185/izawol.253.v2.

Jones, M. K. (2008). Disability and the labour market: A review of the empirical evidence. *Journal of Economic Studies*, 35(5), 405–424.

Jones, M. K., & Latreille, P. L. (2011). Disability and self-employment: Evidence for the UK. *Applied Economics*, 43(27), 4161–4178.

Jones, M. K., & McVicar, D. (2020). Estimating the impact of disability onset on employment. *Social Science & Medicine*, 255, 1–6.

Julià, M., Vanroelen, C., Bosmans, K., Van Aerden, K., & Benach, J. (2017). Precarious employment and quality of employment in relation to health and well-being in Europe. *International Journal of Health Services*, 47(3), 389–409.

Kalleberg, A. L., & Vallas, S. P. (2018). Probing precarious work: Theory, research, and politics. *Research in the Sociology of Work*, 31(1), 1–30.

Kaye, H. S., Jans, L. H., & Jones, E. C. (2011). Why don't employers hire and retain workers with disabilities?. *Journal of Occupational Rehabilitation*, 21(4), 526–536.

Kaye, H. S. (2010). The impact of the 2007–2009 recession on workers with disabilities. *Monthly Labor Review*, October, 19–30.

Konrad, A. M., Moore, M. E., Doherty, A. J., Ng, E. S., & Breward, K. (2012). Vocational status and perceived well-being of workers with disabilities. *Equality, Diversity and Inclusion: An International Journal*, 31(2), 100–123.

Konrad, A. M., Moore, M. E., Ng, E. S., Doherty, A. J., & Breward, K. (2013). Temporary work, underemployment and workplace accommodations: Relationship to well-being for workers with disabilities. *British Journal of Management*, 24(3), 367–382.

Krahn, G. L., Walker, D. K., & Correa-De-Araujo, R. (2015). Persons with disabilities as an unrecognized health disparity population. *American Journal of Public Health*, 105(S2), S198–S206.

Kruse, D., Schur, L., Rogers, S., & Ameri, M. (2018). Why do workers with disabilities earn less? Occupational job requirements and disability discrimination. *British Journal of Industrial Relations*, 56(4), 798–834.

Kruse, D., Park, S., Rodgers, Y., & Schur, L. (forthcoming). Disability and Remote Work During the Pandemic with Implications for Cancer Survivors. *Journal of Cancer Survivorship*.

Lewchuk, W. (2017). Precarious jobs: Where are they, and how do they affect well-being?. *The Economic and Labour Relations Review*, 28(3), 402–419.

Lewchuk, W., de Wolff, A., King, A., & Polanyi, M. (2006). The hidden costs of precarious employment: Health and the employment relationship. In Vosko L. (Ed.), *Precarious employment: Understanding labour market insecurity in Canada* (pp. 141–162). McGill-Queen's Press.

Lindsay, S., Cagliostro, E., Albarico, M., Mortaji, N., & Karon, L. (2018). A systematic review of the benefits of hiring people with disabilities. *Journal of Occupational Rehabilitation*, 28(4), 634–655.

Louvet, E. (2007). Social judgment toward job applications with disabilities: Perception of personal qualities and competencies. *Rehabilitation Psychology*, 52, 297–303.

Louvet E., Rohmer O., & Dubois N. (2009). Social judgment of people with a disability in the workplace: How to make a good impression on employers. *Swiss Journal of Psychology*, 68, 153–159.

Lustig, D. C., & Strauser, D. R. (2007). Causal relationships between poverty and disability. *Rehabilitation Counseling Bulletin*, 50(4), 194–202.

MacEachen, E., Saunders, R., Lippel, K., Kosny, A., Mansfield, L., & Carrasco, C. (2014). *Understanding the management of injury prevention and return to work in temporary work agencies*. Institute of Work & Health.

Maroto, M., & Pettinicchio, D. (2014). Disability, structural inequality, and work: The influence of occupational segregation on earnings for people with different disabilities. *Research in Social Stratification and Mobility*, 38, 76–92.

Maroto, M., Pettinicchio, D., & Patterson, A. (2019). Hierarchies of categorical disadvantage: Economic insecurity at the intersection of disability, gender, and race. *Gender & Society*, 33(1), 64–93.

McNamara, M. (2006). The hidden health and safety costs of casual employment. Industrial Relations Research Centre. Research supported by Bartier Perry. http://wwwdocs.fce.unsw .edu.au/orgmanagement/IRRC/CasualEmploy.pdf.

Mitra, S. (2009). Temporary and partial disability programs in nine countries: What can the United States learn from other countries? *Journal of Disability Policy Studies*, 20(1), 14–27.

Mitra, S., & Kruse, D. (2016). Are workers with disabilities more likely to be displaced? *International Journal of Human Resource Management*, 27(14), 1550–1579.

Nätti, J., Kinnunen, U., Mäkikangas, A., & Mauno, S. (2009). Type of employment relationship and mortality: Prospective study among Finnish employees in 1984–2000. *European Journal of Public Health*, 19, 150–156.

OECD, (2010). *Sickness, disability, and work: Breaking the barriers*. Organisation for Economic Co-operation and Development.

Ojala, S., & Pyöriä, P. (2019). Precarious work and the risk of receiving a disability pension. *Scandinavian Journal of Public Health*, 47(3), 293–300.

Pettinicchio, D., & Maroto, M. (2017). Employment outcomes among men and women with disabilities: How the intersection of gender and disability status shapes labor market inequality. In B. Altman (Ed.), *Factors in studying employment for persons with disability* (pp. 3–33). Emerald.

Pirani, E., & Salvini, S. (2015). Is temporary employment damaging to health? A longitudinal study on Italian workers. *Social Science & Medicine*, 124, 121–131.

Pyöriä, P., & Ojala, S. (2016). Precarious work and intrinsic job quality: Evidence from Finland, 1984–2013. *The Economic and Labour Relations Review*, 27(3), 349–367.

Quinlan, M., Bohle, P., & Rawlings-Way, O. (2015). Health and safety of homecare workers engaged by temporary employment agencies. *Journal of Industrial Relations*, 57(1), 94–114.

Ren, L., Paetzold, R., & Colella, A. (2008). A meta-analysis of experimental studies on the effects of disability on human resource judgments. *Human Resource Management Review*, 18, 191–203.

Rönnblad, T., Grönholm, E., Jonsson, J., Koranyi, I., Orellana, C., Kreshpaj, B., . . . & Bodin, T. (2019). Precarious employment and mental health: A systematic review and meta-analysis of longitudinal studies. *Scandinavian Journal of Work, Environment & Health*, 45(5), 429–443.

Rutledge, M. S., Zulkarnain, A., & King, S. E. (2019). How does contingent work affect SSDI benefits? (Working paper no. wp2019-4). Center for Retirement Research.

Schur, L., Kruse, D., & Blanck, P. (2005). Corporate culture and the employment of persons with disabilities. *Behavioral Sciences & the Law*, 23(1), 3–20.

Schur, L., Kruse, D., & Blanck, P. (2013). *People with disabilities: Sidelined or mainstreamed?* Cambridge University Press.

Schur, L., Kruse, D., Blasi, J., & Blanck, P. (2009). Is disability disabling in all workplaces? Workplace disparities and corporate culture. *Industrial Relations: A Journal of Economy and Society*, 48(3), 381–410.

Schur, L., Nishii, L., Adya, M., Kruse, D., Bruyère, S. M., & Blanck, P. (2014). Accommodating employees with and without disabilities. *Human Resource Management*, 53(4), 593–621.

Schur, L., Han, K., Kim, A., Ameri, M., Blanck, P., & Kruse, D. (2017). Disability at work: A look back and forward. *Journal of Occupational Rehabilitation*, 27(4), 482–497.

Schur, L. A. (2002). Dead end jobs or a path to economic well being? The consequences of non-standard work among people with disabilities. *Behavioral Sciences & the Law*, 20(6), 601–620.

Schur, L. A. (2003). Barriers or opportunities? The causes of contingent and part-time work among people with disabilities. *Industrial Relations: A Journal of Economy and Society*, 42(4), 589–622.

Schur, L. A., Ameri, M., & Kruse, D. (2020). Telework after COVID: A "silver lining" for workers with disabilities? *Journal of Occupational Rehabilitation*, 30(4), 521–536.

Scott-Marshall, H., & Tompa, E. (2011). The health consequences of precarious employment experiences. *Work*, 38(4), 369–382.

Shuey, K. M., & Jovic, E. (2013). Disability accommodation in nonstandard and precarious employment arrangements. *Work and Occupations*, 40(2), 174–205.

Snyder, L. A., Carmichael, J. S., Blackwell, L. V., Cleveland, J. N., & Thornton, G. C., III. (2010). Perceptions of discrimination and justice among employees with disabilities. *Employee Responsibilities and Rights Journal*, 22, 5–19.

Stone, D. L. & Colella, A. (1996). A model of factors affecting the treatment of disabled individuals in organizations. *Academy of Management Review*, 21, 352–401.

Tompa, E., Scott, H., Trevithick, S. & Bhattacharyya, S. (2006). Precarious employment and people with disabilities. In L. Vosko (Ed.), *Precarious employment: Understanding labour market insecurity in Canada* (pp. 90–114). McGill-Queen's Press.

Tsurugano, S., Inoue, M., & Yano, E. (2012). Precarious employment and health: Analysis of the Comprehensive National Survey in Japan. *Industrial Health*, 50(3), 223–235.

US Bureau of Labor Statistics. (2018, June 7). Contingent and alternative employment arrangements—May 2017. USDL-18-0942, Bureau of Labor Statistics.

US Bureau of Labor Statistics. (2020, February 26). Persons with a disability: Labor force characteristics summary. USDL-20-0339, Bureau of Labor Statistics.

Vancea, M., & Utzet, M. (2017). How unemployment and precarious employment affect the health of young people: A scoping study on social determinants. *Scandinavian Journal of Public Health*, 45(1), 73–84.

WHO/World Bank (2011). *World report on disability*. World Health Organization and World Bank.

Yelin, E. H., & Trupin, L. (2003). Disability and the characteristics of employment. *Monthly Labor Review*, 126, 20.

CHAPTER 22

SERVICE-CONNECTED DISABILITY AND POVERTY AMONG US VETERANS

ANDREW S. LONDON, SCOTT D. LANDES,
AND JANET M. WILMOTH

SOCIAL, economic, and health inequalities are rooted in social structures that variably influence childhood and adolescent development, shape experiences within institutions, and compound (dis)advantage as individuals transition into adulthood, move through mid-life, and segue to later life (Dannefer, 2003; Ferraro & Shippee, 2009). The influences of cumulative (dis)advantage and inequality processes emerge along and are variably moderated by socially constructed, intersecting axes of differentiation, such as gender, race/ethnicity, ability, and sexual orientation (Maroto, Pettinicchio, & Patterson, 2019), and contribute through multiple mechanisms to the risk of impairment, access to resources, and disability outcomes across the life course (Elder, Johnson, & Crosnoe, 2003; Elder & Shanahan, 2006). Variation in the effects of these processes within and between cohorts and subpopulations is in part produced by the unique historical experiences their members encounter at critical life stages, including economic cycles, demographic changes, periods of war and peace, policy environments, and technological changes. As the modern welfare state evolved over the course of the twentieth century, the US federal government increasingly developed public policies and ground-level programs to promote population health and well-being by mitigating the negative and enhancing the positive influences of macro-level social forces that directly and indirectly shape life-course inequality (Wilmoth & London, 2021).

Building on the foundational early work of Glen H. Elder Jr. and his colleagues (Elder, 1986, 1987; Elder & Clipp, 1988a, 1988b, 1989; Elder, Shanahan, & Clipp, 1994, 1997), sociologists of aging and the life course have been at the forefront of efforts to understand the influence of military service on lives and how it shapes inequality in mid- and later-life outcomes related to educational and socioeconomic attainment, marriage and family, and health, disability, and mortality (Landes, London, & Wilmoth, 2021; London & Wilmoth, 2016; Modell & Haggerty, 1991; Sampson & Laub, 1996; Settersten & Patterson, 2006; Spiro, Settersten, & Aldwin 2018; Wilmoth & London, 2013). Processes of cumulative (dis)advantage and inequality affect the lives of veterans in ways that are similar to their influences on those who never serve in the military. However, those who serve in the military also face a historically variable set of risk factors (Wilmoth & London, 2011), including but not limited to combat exposure, that can contribute in distinct ways to impairment, disability, and inequality across the life course (MacLean, 2010; Wilmoth, Landes, & London, 2019).

To date, sociologists who study disability have paid limited attention to the influence of military service on disability and life-course inequality even though there are potential insights that could emerge from the incorporation of a focus on the military into sociological studies of disability. Military service is limited to those aged eighteen and over, and few adults enter military service with existing, observable impairment or disability because the Department of Defense (DoD) uses extensive pre-induction physical- and mental-health screenings to help them determine who can join the military (Wolf, Wing, & Lopoo, 2013). As a result, SCD is best conceptualized as a distinct category of adult-onset, occupationally acquired, medically defined disability that may affect life-course inequality differently than disability conceptualized and measured in other terms (Maroto & Pettinicchio, 2014a, 2014b; Pettinicchio & Maroto, 2017).

This chapter examines Department of Veterans Affairs (VA) service-connected disability (SCD) status and poverty among veterans in the United States. We focus on the military and SCD because the military is a policy-relevant, highly selective, potentially transformative social institution that can have life-long consequences in multiple domains even though it tends to engage individuals in early adulthood for relatively short durations of time (Settersten, 2006; Spiro, Settersten, & Aldwin, 2018; Wilmoth & London, 2013). We also focus on SCD because it is notably different from other forms of adult-onset and occupationally acquired disability. Additionally, SCD connects veterans who have an SCD to a specific part of the US welfare state and an array of federally funded benefits that are unavailable to non-veterans and veterans without an SCD (Landes, London, & Wilmoth, 2021; US Department of Veterans Affairs, 2020a; Wilmoth, London, & Heflin, 2015a).

The VA is a Department of the US government that is independent of the DoD and, though not typically recognized as such, in many ways functions as an arm of the US welfare state that provides targeted benefits to veterans with SCD as a prioritized part of its mission (Wilmoth & London, 2021). Relying on a medical model of disability, the VA's initial focus is on the diagnosis of disability, disease, or injury, and on making a determination about the extent to which it is service connected (Jette, 2006; Holder, 2016). Unlike sociopolitical, biopsychosocial, and minority models of disability, the medical model used by the VA does not recognize the ways in which societal norms and/or environments work to define and stigmatize disability (McNally & Frueh, 2013; Scotch, 2000; Thomas, 2007). While other federal agencies, such as the Social Security Administration (Jette, 2006), also rely on a medical model of disability, SCD is distinct as it is limited to occupationally acquired disability, disease, or injury among an adult population with specialized institutional and occupational as well as citizenship-based ties to the state. The assignment of an SCD rating determines compensation and priority access to a range of benefits, including tax-free income maintenance. Some of these benefits are available to all veterans, while others are limited to those with SCD. As stated by the VA: "We assign you a disability rating based on the severity of your service-connected condition. We use your disability rating to determine how much disability compensation you'll receive each month, as well as your eligibility for other VA benefits" (U.S. Department of Veterans Affairs, 2020b). Because access to these resources is based on the enduring linkage of veterans with SCD to the VA and does not preclude employment, SCD may not have the same association with poverty as early-onset disability and other kinds of adult-onset, occupationally acquired disability.

In this chapter, we include an examination of SCD and its relation to poverty among veterans, paying particular attention to the role of VA benefits and employment. We begin with a discussion of military service and SCD. We then consider the benefits provided to veterans with SCD and how those relate to socioeconomic status and poverty. We descriptively examine VA SCD in relation to poverty and employment using data from the 2019 American Community Survey (ACS) downloaded from the IPUMS USA website (Ruggles, Flood, Foster, Goeken, Pacas, Schouweiler, & Sobek, 2021). We use the ACS because it is a high-quality, large, nationally representative data source that includes veterans, as well as a participant-reported measure of SCD. Importantly, among those with an SCD, the public-use file of the ACS also includes participant-reported information on the SCD rating, which indicates the VA's assessment of the severity of the impairment and its functional impact on earnings capacity. Unless otherwise indicated, the descriptive analyses that are presented in this chapter are based on the same analytic sample, which is limited to veterans and non-veterans who are eighteen years old or older and have complete data on all of the analytic variables (N=2,552,527). To focus our discussion and simplify the exposition of the descriptive results, we exclude ACS respondents who were active-duty personnel or were training in the Reserves or National Guard at the time of the survey even though some of them have SCD ratings. All analyses include non-veterans and veterans with no SCD, which allows us to compare the outcomes of veterans with different SCD ratings with each other and those of other subgroups of the population. We conclude with a discussion of the lessons that may be learned for poverty reduction among all people living with disability from a consideration of the military's response to SCD.

THE SELECTIVITY OF US MILITARY SERVICE

The modern US military is a gate-keeping organization that shapes the distribution of disability in the civilian, active-duty, and veteran populations by excluding some and selectively enrolling others. As a result of their service, some military service members enter the veteran period of the life course with an SCD, or with illnesses or injuries acquired during military service that will eventually result in SCD. Through exclusion, individuals with early-onset disability, and social characteristics that may contribute to cumulative (dis)advantage and inequality across the life course, are concentrated in the non-veteran population. Those who become active-duty service members undergo systematic, pre-induction screening for health and the absence of impairment, but attain military statuses and roles that expose them to a set of institutionally embedded risks for injury and disability. Thus, through inclusion, the military generates a unique subpopulation of adults with disability and, by definition, concentrates them in the veteran population once they exit active-duty status.

During the era of conscription and since the advent of the All-Volunteer Force in 1973, the US military has used pre-induction mental- and physical-health screenings, vocational aptitude tests, and other assessments to selectively recruit young men, and increasingly women (see Wilmoth & London, 2021), with characteristics deemed compatible with military readiness and national security (Wolf, Wing, & Lopoo, 2013). As a consequence of not meeting one standard or another, substantial numbers of potential active-duty personnel have been denied entry into the military (Theokas, 2010). According to the National Research Council (2006), the characteristics that disqualify an individual from service have varied historically, especially during periods of war, but have included: physical- and mental-health problems, obesity, disability, low IQ, lack of a high school diploma or equivalent, heavy drug use, and having a felony conviction. From 1950 to 1971, rates of rejection based solely on the pre-induction physical exam were always over 30%, but mostly at or over 40%, and varied substantially from year to year (Wolf, Wing, & Lopoo, 2013). Thus, given the stringent, systematic health screening that takes place prior to accession, at the outset of their time on active duty, service members have few detectable physical or mental impairments.

US MILITARY SERVICE AND IMPAIRMENT

Once individuals enter one of the branches of the US Armed Forces, they face a variety of risks that have the potential to cause injury and illness. The military functions like a total institution and variably exposes members to risks that can be, as a whole, unlike those of any other occupation. This organizationally embedded potentiality, which Wilmoth, Landes, and London (2019) have termed the "military hazard effect," is rooted in many aspects of the active-duty experience. Service members may incur substantial, long-term physical- and mental-health impairments from accidents, over-training injuries, combat experiences, environmental exposures (e.g., chemical agents, smoke, radiation), and military sexual trauma (MST) (MacLean, 2010; Wilmoth, London, & Oliver, 2018; US Department of Veterans Affairs, 2018a, 2018b; Wolff & Mills, 2016). Military service members can acquire impairments leading to disability while they are on active duty or after it has ended. In either instance, a medical model of disability

(Drum, 2009; Thomas, 2007), with a focus on disability as a physical or mental impairment, is the framework within which the disability is defined.

If acquired while a service member is still on active duty in one of the US Armed Services, the DoD determines whether the impairment reduces the service members' ability to perform their required duties (Buddin & Kapur, 2005; Buddin & Han, 2012). Typically, service members who acquire a disability that prevents performance of duties are medically discharged from duty. After separation from the US Armed Services, these veterans have the choice of receiving disability-related benefits through the DoD, or applying for an SCD. While DoD-designated disability statuses are at times referred to as service-connected disabilities, they should not be confused with SCD, which is distinct and the specific focus of this chapter. The majority of service members who acquire a disability while in the armed services choose to transition to an SCD designation after separating from the military because any assigned DoD disability compensation offsets VA disability compensation, DoD disability compensation is taxed, and VA disability compensation is not taxed (Buddin & Han, 2012; Kregel & Miller, 2016).

Although they have varied across time and in relation to specific populations, the VA has developed detailed protocols for making official determinations about SCD. The VA defines service members as having an SCD if they have "disabilities that are the result of a disease or injury incurred or aggravated during active military service" or "disabilities that are considered related or secondary to disabilities occurring in service and for disabilities presumed to be related to circumstances of military service, even though they may arise after service" (US Department Veterans Affairs, 2019a, p. 14). Importantly, SCD designations are rated in relation to severity of impairment and future earnings capacity. Specifically, when evaluated for SCD, veterans are assigned a "percentage rating," which represents "as far as can practicably be determined the average impairment in earning capacity resulting from such diseases and injuries and their residual conditions in civil occupations" ("Schedule for Rating Disabilities," 1994, p. 4.1–2). As such, while an SCD rating is a medically defined disability, it is important to understand that it also incorporates a socioeconomic status designation.

SCD ratings range from 0% to 100% and are assigned in 10% increments (US Department of Veterans Affairs, 2020b). The VA utilizes different rating schedules for different parts of the body that may have incurred injury, illness, or impairment during military service. These schedules have been developed for the musculoskeletal system, visual impairment, hearing impairment, infectious diseases, immune disorders, nutritional deficiencies, the respiratory system, the cardiovascular system, the digestive system, the genitourinary system, gynecological conditions, disorders of the breast, the hemic and lymphatic systems, the skin, the endocrine system, neurological conditions, convulsive disorders, mental disorders, and dental and oral conditions ("Schedule for Rating Disabilities," 2021). Multiple ratings of different injuries, illnesses, and impairments can be assigned, which yields a combined rating that may be different than the sum of the individual ratings. However, in circumstances when more than one SCD rating is assigned, the military uses "a method called the 'whole person theory'" to determine the combined rating to ensure that the "total VA disability rating doesn't add up to more than 100% . . . because a person can't be more than 100% able-bodied" (US Department of Veterans Affairs, 2020b). As discussed in greater detail in Landes, Wilmoth, and London (2019), SCD ratings are determined in relation to such factors as degree of functional limitation, chronicity of symptoms, medication requirements, and degree of interference with occupational and social functioning. A 100% SCD rating represents severe impairment (e.g., "near-constant disabling symptoms") that is deemed at the time of adjudication to substantially reduce if not preclude future labor-force participation and earnings.

Generally, SCD ratings and compensation decisions are finalized after the service member transitions from active-duty to veteran status. While most determinations are made close to the time of separation, adjustments to SCD ratings and new determinations about compensation can be made across the life course, long after separation from the military has taken place. Some evidence suggests that such adjustments vary by gender (Murdoch et al., 2019; Murdoch et al., 2021). There is also evidence that there have been post-separation increases in the number of Vietnam veterans who have received VA disability compensation for type-2 diabetes associated with exposure to Agent Orange during their wartime military service and in the number of Gulf War veterans diagnosed with chronic fatigue, fibromyalgia, and environmentally induced illnesses (Duggan, Rosenheck, & Singleton, 2010; Duggan, 2014).

The relative contributions of the different military-service-connected exposures and experiences to SCD across the military and veteran life course is not known. During wartime, combat exposure is undoubtedly a primary contributor to both physical- and mental-health-related SCD (Eggleston et al., 2019; Dismuke-Greer et al., 2018). Experiencing the stress of chronic threat, killing or wounding others, witnessing the wounded or dead, being wounded by gunfire, or acquiring a traumatic brain injury (TBI) from a landmine or an improvised explosive device are combat-service-connected experiences that can have immediate and long-term consequences (McNally & Frueh, 2013). Post-traumatic stress disorder (PTSD) and other "invisible wounds of war" are common among combat veterans (Tanielian & Jaycox, 2008), are associated with such health behaviors as inadequate sleep and everyday drinking (London, Burgard, & Wilmoth, 2014; London, Wilmoth, Oliver, & Hausauer, 2020), and may (re)-emerge in later life (Davison, Kaiser, Spiro, Moye, King, & King, 2016). Improvements in battle-field medicine have resulted in more service members surviving what would have been mortal wounds in previous eras. As a result, more service members are returning to civilian life as veterans with life-long, trauma-related impairments (Butler, 2017; Lenhart, Savitsky, & Eastridge, 2012).

Non-combat, service-connected factors can also contribute to both physical- and mental-health-related SCD. One study that focused on active-duty personnel used data from the US Army Physical Disability Agency, the Naval Disability Evaluation Board, and the Air Force Physical Disability Division from the early 1980s to 1994 to examine the role of injuries in physical disability (Songer & LaPorte, 2000). Across the different services, 30% to 50% of physical disability cases that had been awarded DoD compensation were due to injury, especially lower-back and knee conditions. Upon separation from the military, these injuries incurred during service may contribute to SCD ratings that carry forward into the veteran period of the life course. Female military personnel have a higher risk of service-connected injury than male military personnel (Kaufman, Brodine, & Shaffer, 2000). They also have a higher risk of MST: a meta-analysis conducted by Wilson (2018) found that among military personnel and veterans, the percentages reporting MST involving harassment only, harassment and assault, or assault only were 52.5%, 38.4%, and 23.6%, respectively, among women, and 8.9%, 3.9%, and 1.9%, respectively, among men. MST is associated with range of physical- and mental-health issues, including physical symptoms, chronic conditions, depression, and PTSD and often leads to a designation of SCD (Suris and Lind 2008).

SCD AMONG VETERANS

The National Center for Veterans Analysis and Statistics (2021) estimates that there were nineteen million living US veterans as of September 30, 2021. It is well documented that SCD among veterans is increasing in the United States (Holder, 2016; US Department of Veterans Affairs, 2019a). From 1986 to 2016, the number of veterans with SCD increased by 96%, from 2,225,289 to 4,356,443, while over the same period, the number with SCD ratings of 0% to 20% increased by 5% (from 1,255,399 to 1,318,939), the number with SCD ratings of 30% to 40% increased by 59% (from 495,655 to 785,687), the number with SCD ratings of 50%-60% increased by 201% (from 224,588 to 675,865), and the number with SCD ratings of 70% or more increased by 531% (from 249,647 to 1,575,952) (US Department of Veterans Affairs, 2020c). Using data from the ACS, the US Census Bureau (2016) reports that the percentage of veterans with an SCD increased from 15.1% in 2008 to 21.7% in 2016.

As seen in Table 22.1, we use data from the 2019 ACS to estimate self-reported SCD among veterans and find that 25.5% self-report an SCD. The modal category in the distribution is 70% or more (9.6% of veterans); 7.7% have SCD ratings in the 0% to 20% range, 7.1% have SCD ratings in the 30%–60% range, and 1.2% report an SCD but do not specify the level. These self-reported rates are likely to be under-estimates. Some veterans may be hesitant to acknowledge an SCD because they may believe that it connotes weakness and conflicts with the military mindset and military values, and because, at times, it is juxtaposed in popular culture and community life to images of the "wounded warrior" that veterans experience as inaccurate and stigmatizing (Griffin & Stein, 2015; Montgomery, 2018).

There is an extensive literature on approaches to the measurement of disability and how survey-based estimates of disability are affected by question wording and other methodological issues (Pettinicchio & Maroto, 2021). It is important to note that self-reported SCD captures a broad array of conditions that are not well represented by the six measures of disability status used by the ACS, which are based on suggestions from the Washington Group on Disability Statistics—cognitive difficulty, ambulatory

Table 22.1 Sample Description and Percent of Veterans
with Service-Connected Disability (SCD), 2019
American Community Survey

	N[1]	Percent[2] of Veterans (N=204,190)[1]
No SCD	153,132	74.5
0% SCD	2,206	1.0
10%–20% SCD	14,243	6.7
30%–40% SCD	7,625	3.8
50%–60% SCD	6,493	3.3
70% or More SCD	18,645	9.6
SCD % Unknown	1,846	1.2

Source: Author calculation.
Notes:
1. Unweighted.
2. Weighted.

difficulty, independent living difficulty, self-care difficulty, vision difficulty, and hearing difficulty (Holder, 2016; Madans, Loeb, and Altman, 2011). To illustrate this, Figure 22.1 presents the percent reporting none of the six ACS-defined disability statuses by veteran status and SCD rating. Overall, among non-veterans and veterans combined, 84.3% report no ACS disability. Notably, all veteran groups, regardless of SCD, have a lower percentage reporting no ACS disability. While this likely reflects demographic differences in the composition of the non-veteran and veteran populations (e.g., veterans are older, on average, than non-veterans) and under-reporting, the percentage with no ACS disability declines substantially among veterans as SCD rating increases. Among non-veterans, the percentage with no ACS disability is 85.5%, while it is 73.4% among veterans with no SCD, between 62.4% and 67.4% among veterans with SCD ratings in the 0% to 60% range, and 46.6% among veterans with SCD ratings of 70% or more. These results affirm that self-reported SCD rating is associated with ACS-measured disability, but also underscores the notion that self-reported SCD encompasses considerably more than is measured by these six measures of disability status. It is probable that some of the unmeasured functional limitation and disability is related to service-connected mental-health and substance-use disorders (Holder, 2016). However, it is also possible that not all impairments that result in an SCD designation and VA disability compensation are readily identified by ACS respondents as disability, and that some veterans with service-connected injuries or illnesses do not seek or obtain SCD designation from the VA for various reasons, including service-member choice, lost records, and gender- and race-related biases (Fried et al., 2015; Murdoch et al., 2003a, 2003b; Sayer et al., 2004; Wherry, 2017).

Table 22.2 provides a bit more detail on the correspondence, or lack thereof, between SCD and ACS-defined disability statuses by providing estimates of the prevalence of each of the six ACS disability statuses by veteran status and SCD rating. Participants can report more than one ACS disability status and are included in the prevalence rate for each of the six types of ACS disability that they report. Although these results do not adjust for age or other compositional differences across the veteran status and SCD rating groups, several patterns are evident. First, overall, 15.7% report any ACS disability status, but there is variation in the prevalence of the six disability statuses, ranging from 2.9% for vision difficulty to 8.6% for ambulatory difficulty. Second, for each of the six ACS disability statuses, non-veterans have a lower prevalence than all categories of veterans, regardless of SCD rating. This includes veterans with no SCD. Third, generally, the prevalence of each ACS disability status increases as SCD rating increases, with the highest prevalence for those with SCD ratings of 70% or more for all but hearing difficulty. Consistent with other reports of severe hearing impairment among US veterans (Groenewold, Tak, & Masterson, 2011), for hearing difficulty, the prevalence is above 20% for veterans with SCD ratings of 10% or higher. The prevalence of hearing difficulty among non-veterans is 3.7%. Finally, the prevalence of each ACS disability among veterans with an SCD rating of 70% or more is many times higher than it is among non-veterans, ranging from 2.7 times higher for vision difficulty to 6.3 times higher for hearing difficulty. Taken together, these patterns suggest, in a very limited way, that there is an association between increasing SCD rating and increasing prevalence of ACS-measured disability. However, they also draw attention to the fact that

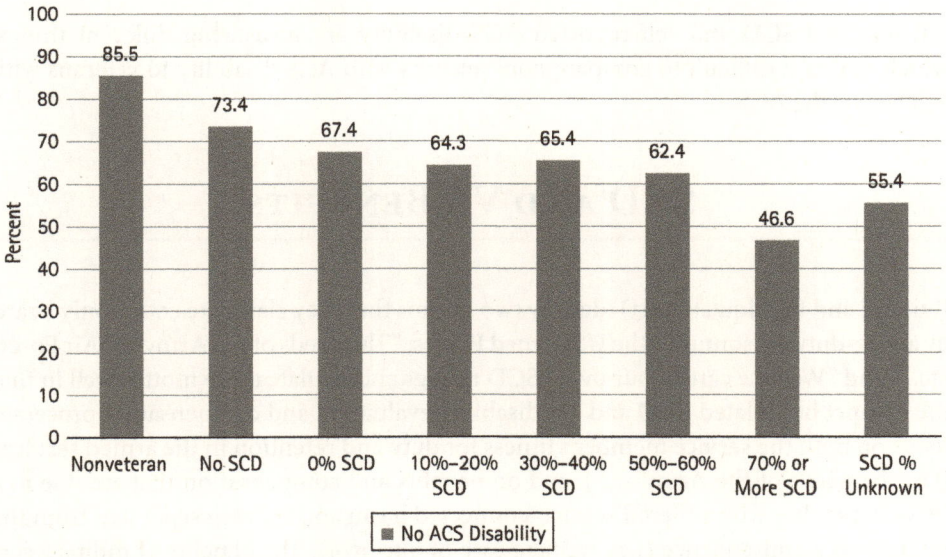

FIGURE 22.1 Percent with No ACS Disability, by Veteran Status and Service-Connected Disability Rating, 2019 American Community Survey.

Source: Author calculation.

Table 22.2 Type of ACS Disability by Veteran Status and Service-Connected Disability Rating, 2019 American Community Survey

	Any ACS Disability (%)	Cognitive Difficulty (%)	Ambulatory Difficulty (%)	Independent Living Difficulty (%)	Self-Care Difficulty (%)	Vision Difficulty (%)	Hearing Difficulty (%)
Total	15.7	5.8	8.6	6.4	3.4	2.9	4.5
Nonveteran	14.6	5.6	8.0	6.1	3.2	2.7	3.7
No SCD	26.6	6.9	14.7	9.0	5.5	4.3	12.9
0% SCD	32.7	8.6	15.3	9.1	5.9	5.1	18.4
10%–20% SCD	35.7	6.7	14.4	6.7	3.9	4.8	24.8
30%–40% SCD	34.6	8.2	15.3	6.7	3.7	4.8	21.4
50%–60% SCD	37.7	11.2	18.1	7.7	4.6	5.2	21.1
70% or More SCD	53.4	23.3	29.7	18.1	11.2	7.3	23.3
SCD % Unknown	44.6	15.6	25.5	16.3	10.4	9.2	23.6

Source: Author calculation.

self-reported SCD and self-reported ACS disability are measuring different things, which makes it difficult to compare non-veterans with ACS disability to veterans with SCD using the ACS.

SCD AND VA BENEFITS

Burland and Lundquist (2013) identify two mottos that they claim are commonly heard by active-duty personnel in the US Armed Forces: "The needs of the Army [or Air Force, etc.]" and "We take care of our own." SCD ratings encapsulate these mottos well in that the distinct but related DoD and VA disability evaluation and compensation processes focus on both the service member's fitness for duty and retention in the armed services (i.e., the needs of the Army . . .), and on benefits and compensation that are due to a service member who suffered service-connected harm and is being separated from the military as a consequence (i.e., we take care of our own). The benefits of military service, including but not limited to the compensation and services that are made available to veterans with SCD, have been conceptualized as a military capital effect (Wilmoth,

Landes, & London, 2019). Through a variety of mechanisms, military service provides a range of exposures and experiences that have the potential to be beneficial for a range of life-course outcomes (Wilmoth & London, 2013).

The military capital effect operates through various mechanisms that are broadly available to, albeit not realized by, all service members, and some that are specifically targeted to those who were harmed by their military service. Broadly, participation in the military may be beneficial because it includes: participation in a range of potentially health-promoting activities (e.g., physical training and exercise), the establishment of social networks that broaden ties to the community and labor-market opportunities, the development of social and occupational skills that can translate into better post-military outcomes, and access to a broad range of DoD and VA benefits (e.g., education, health care, and home-loan guaranty benefits) (US Department of Veterans Affairs, 2020a; Wilmoth & London, 2013). Since the mid-1980s, military policies have also been effective at discouraging certain types of substance use during both the active-duty and veteran periods of the life course (Miech, London, Wilmoth, & Koester, 2013). Additionally, entry into the armed forces can produce positive turning points in the life course of persons from socioeconomically disadvantaged backgrounds by "knifing off" the influence of early-life disadvantages and providing a "bridging environment" to opportunities. Military job training, educational opportunities through the GI Bill, and socialization to adult roles may give veterans from disadvantaged backgrounds an advantage in the labor market that they otherwise would not have (Bennett & McDonald, 2013; Kleykamp 2007, 2013; Sampson & Laub, 1996).

The SCD-specific benefits component of the military capital effect reflects a specific social contract that is anchored in the service member's occupational tie to the military and serves as a counter-weight to the military hazard effect. A financial benefit is provided to compensate veterans for possible losses to civilian earnings due to the SCD (Duggan, 2014). Compensatory benefits and services are given specifically to those who are seen as deserving of such support because they have sacrificed in defense of the nation (Gerber, 2000). Consider, for example, this quote from the State of Vermont's Office of Veterans Affairs (2021) website that aims to encourage veterans to undergo medical assessment to document conditions early in the life course in case SCD emerges later in the life course: "Disability Compensation is for veterans who have conditions that were caused or aggravated by their service in the military. These conditions cover the full range of human physical and emotional experience. Has your ankle bothered you ever since you twisted it at boot camp? Have your ears rung ever since you spent a year driving a tank in a combat zone? Have you felt anxious ever since going on patrol in hostile territory? The bottom line: If you have a current physical or mental condition, and it is related to your military service, then apply for Disability Compensation. Even if the condition seems minor now, don't wait to apply. When you're 25, that "bum" left knee may just be a minor inconvenience; when you're 55, the early onset arthritis you developed in that knee because of your service may mean you can barely walk. You should apply regardless of your income and regardless of your ability to find work. In short: if the military broke it, the VA owns it."

For veterans who qualify, the VA disability compensation rate is based on the veteran's SCD rating and, for those with SCD ratings of 30% or higher, dependent status (US Department of Veterans Affairs, 2020d). Current-year rates are available at https://www.va.gov/disability/compensation-rates/veteran-rates/. In 2020, the monthly compensation rate was $142.29 for veterans with a 10% SCD rating and $281.27 for veterans with a 20% SCD rating. Veterans with a rating of 30% or higher are entitled to additional payments for dependent parents, a spouse, and children. Compensation rates increase substantially at higher SCD rating levels. For example, in 2020, a veteran with a spouse and one dependent child receives $1636.17 per month if they have a 70% SCD rating and $3,406.04 per month if they have a 100% SCD rating. Notably, over the period 1990 to 2018, the VA has documented that the growth in the number of veterans with SCD has been concentrated among those with SCD above 50%, and that the rate of increase in cash payments (8.0%) has outpaced the rate of increase in the number of veterans with SCD (2.9%) (US Department of Veterans Affairs, 2019b).

Veterans can receive VA disability compensation even if they and/or their family members work. In that sense, VA disability compensation is administered as an entitlement that is not conditional on the absence of labor-force participation. Additionally, regardless of SCD rating or level of VA disability compensation, veterans may also apply for compensation under the civilian Social Security Disability Insurance (DI) program (Social Security Administration, 2021a). However, having an SCD rating does not guarantee that a veteran will qualify for DI benefits given different eligibility criteria between the programs. In order to qualify for DI benefits, veterans must meet the standard program requirements, which include two earnings tests related to "recent work" and "duration of work." Work activity includes employment in both the civilian and military sectors. Like non-veteran applicants, veterans must also provide evidence of a work-limiting "medical condition that is expected to last at least one year or result in death" (Social Security Administration, 2019). Medical conditions can be due to either physical or mental disorders. The requirement that DI recipients have a long-term, work-limiting disability limits program receipt to that portion of the general population (non-veteran and veteran) with a severe disability that precludes work.

While it is possible for veterans to be "dually eligible" for VA disability and DI programs, some research indicates that more veterans participate in VA disability than DI, and joint participation in both VA and DI programs is very low (Wilmoth, London, & Heflin, 2015a). One recent study indicates that older veterans are more likely than their non-veteran peers to report work-limiting disability and to receive DI benefits, which suggests that older veterans are facing increasing challenges in the labor market, which may be due to their health, a growing skills gap, or poorly aligned incentives (Ben-Shalom, Tennant, & Stapleton, 2016). Most likely, joint participation is low due to differences between the programs in eligibility rules, particularly related to definitions of SCD that are used to determine eligibility for VA disability programs versus definitions of long-term work-related disability that are used to determine eligibility for DI disability compensation.

SCD and Poverty

Recent studies that have used the ACS to study disability and socioeconomic outcomes have reported critically important findings related to disability, economic security, and the social production of inequality (Maroto & Pettinicchio, 2014b; Pettinicchio & Maroto, 2017). For example, Maroto, Pettinicchio, and Patterson (2019) build on their earlier work related to "hierarchies of disadvantage" to document that women and racial minority groups with disabilities and lower educational attainments experience the highest poverty levels, report the lowest total income, and rely most on sources of income external to the labor market. Relatedly, Maroto and Pettinicchio (2014a) document the heterogenous influence of occupational segregation on earnings conditional on type of disability and report that people with disabilities are overrepresented in low-skilled, low-paid occupations for which they are over-skilled. While an extension of these studies to include SCD is beyond the scope of this handbook chapter, we hope that the descriptive analysis that follows suggests the value of undertaking such research in the future.

Individuals have variable connections to institutions and the state, which provide them differential access to resources. The disability compensation, access to health care, and other resources available to veterans with SCD, as well as the broad set of benefits available to all veterans, create a social welfare safety net that is fundamentally different than that available to non-veterans living with disability. Military capital has the potential to reduce poverty among veterans with SCD and others in their households to whom their lives are linked. An examination of poverty among veterans with different SCD ratings, as well as among veterans without an SCD rating and non-veterans, can provide insight into how public policies for non-veterans living with disability could be changed to improve their economic well-being.

It is not clear the extent to which existing disability programs sufficiently compensate veterans with SCD for income losses. Buddin and Han (2012) prospectively followed cohorts of veterans who left active military service between fiscal years 1993 to 2004 and compared the civilian earnings and labor-force participation of veterans with and without SCD over a twelve-year period. They found that the losses in civilian earnings among veterans with SCDs are more than offset by the tax-free disability payments they received; however, veterans with disability-related separations from active duty had much lower earnings than comparable veterans with the same SCD ratings. Similarly, Heaton, Loughran, and Miller (2012) report estimated replacement rates among injured veterans of the Iraq and Afghanistan Wars that are above 100%, which similarly indicates that disability benefits are offsetting injury-related earnings loss. However, previous research indicates that disabled veterans—as measured by the six disability status questions in the 2007 ACS—have substantially lower income relative to persons without disabilities and non-veterans who report the same number of disabilities (Fulton, Belote, Brooks, & Coppola, 2009). However, as noted above, there are reasons to believe that SCD is not adequately captured by the six ACS disability status measures. Additionally, as discussed below, many veterans with SCD combine VA disability compensation receipt with employment, and it is the combined influence of these two sources of income, as well as the income of others in the household, that shapes poverty status.

A small body of evidence underscores the notion that SCD may not be associated with poverty in the same way as other forms of disability among adults (London, Heflin, & Wilmoth, 2011; Wilmoth, London, & Heflin, 2015b). Figure 22.2 presents the percent poor, defined using the US federal poverty threshold, for five types of households defined in relation to the work-limiting disability and veteran statuses of all household members. Based on their composition and for ease of presentation, households are identified as: No Disabled Person or Veteran, Disabled Non-Veteran, Disabled Veteran, Non-Disabled Veteran, and Non-Disabled Veteran and Disabled Non-Veteran. The category Disabled Veteran includes the very small number of households that include a Disabled Veteran and a Disabled Non-Veteran, which is the sixth logical category obtained from the cross-classification of statuses. In Figure 22.2, results are presented for households that do not include any household member who is sixty-five years old or older and for households in which at least one member is sixty-five years or older. The patterns are similar across both subpopulations, although, possibly due to the influence of Social Security, the level of poverty is somewhat lower in households that include an older adult than among households that do not. Overall, these results indicate that households that include a disabled non-veteran and no veteran are the most likely to be in poverty, while households that include a non-disabled veteran, regardless of whether the household includes a disabled non-veteran, have substantially lower

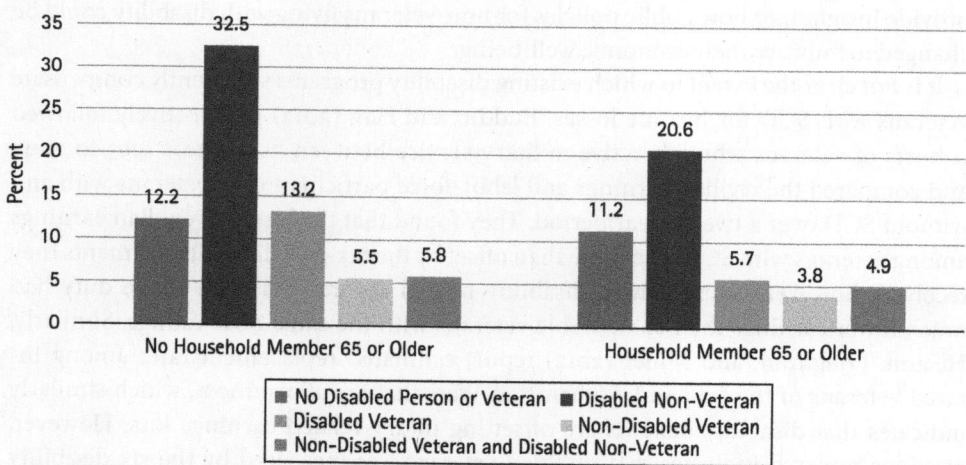

FIGURE 22.2 Percent Poor in Households by Members' Work-Limiting Disability, Veteran Status, and Age.

Source: Data for this figure were drawn from London, Heflin, and Wilmoth (2011) and Wilmoth, London, and Heflin (2015 b).

levels of poverty. The disability status of the veteran in the household influences the poverty status of the household substantially. Households that include a disabled veteran fare better than households that include a disabled non-veteran but no veteran, but they fare worse than households that include a non-disabled veteran. This suggests that some—but not all—of the veteran advantage with respect to poverty is reduced by work-limiting disability, which may to some extent be service connected.

In order to examine the association between SCD and poverty more directly, we analyzed data from the 2019 ACS. Overall, we estimate that 13.4% of the population is living below the federal poverty level (FPL), 14.9% are in the 100%–199% of the FPL category, 15.0% are in the 200%–299% of the FPL category, 13.6% are in the 300%–399% of the FPL category, 10.7% are in the 400%–499% of the FPL category, and 32.4% are 500+ % of the FPL. Figure 22.3 presents the percent of federal poverty level (FPL) distribution by veteran status and SCD rating. Notably, all of the veteran groups, regardless of SCD, have rates of poverty that are below the 13.8% poverty rate among non-veterans. Moreover, as SCD rating increases, the percent in and near poverty decreases. Overall, non-veterans, veterans with no SCD, and veterans with a 0% SCD rating, all of whom do not qualify for VA disability compensation, have the highest rates of poverty (<100% of the FPL) and are also more likely to be in the 100%–199% of the FPL category. Among the groups eligible for some level of disability compensation (i.e., categories 10%–20% and higher disability ratings), the distributions look very similar, with about 53%–56% of each group having income 400+% above the FPL.

In considering the association between SCD and poverty, it is important to keep in mind veterans who applied for but were denied SCD compensation. One study

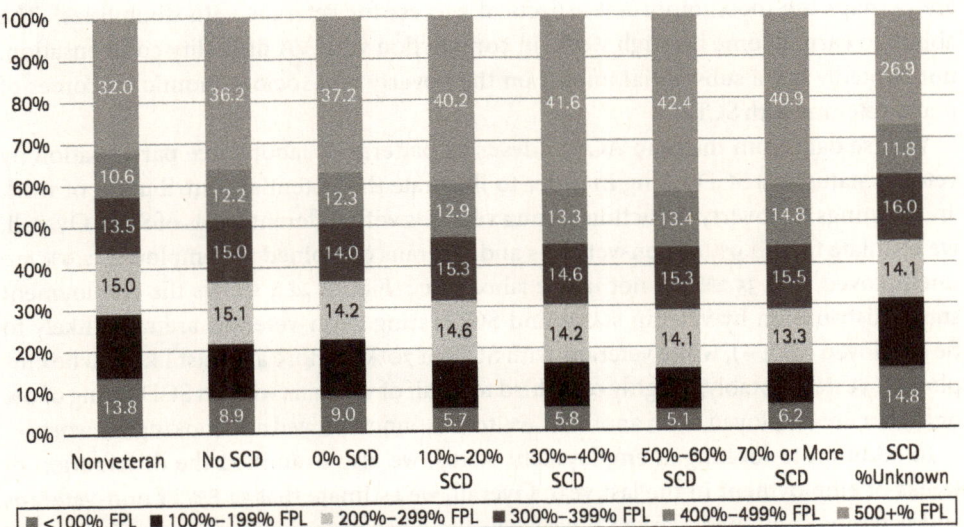

FIGURE 22.3 Percent of Federal Poverty Level (FPL) Distribution by Veteran Status and Service-Connected Disability Rating, 2019 American Community Survey.

Source: Author calculation.

compared veterans who applied for but were denied VA disability compensation to veterans who received VA disability compensation and found that applicants who were denied benefits: were more likely to have poor health and functional limitations; had physical- and mental-functioning composite scores that were not clinically different than those who received benefits; experienced higher levels of social isolation; and were more likely receive means-tested public assistance, which is associated with poverty (Fried, Passannante, Helmer, Holland, & Halperin, 2017). Another study compared the long-term outcomes of veterans with PTSD who were denied benefits to those who received VA disability compensation and found similar rates of employment, but much higher rates of poverty among those denied benefits than among those who received them (44.8% versus 15.2%) (Murdoch et al., 2011). These results underscore the potential role of VA disability compensation in helping to reduce poverty.

SCD AND EMPLOYMENT

Veterans with SCD are able to work and continue to receive VA disability compensation. Although not all are able to do so or choose to do so if they are able, it is well documented that many veterans with SCD are employed to some extent (Buddin & Han, 2012; Olsen et al., 2018; Stern, 2017). In fact, promoting return-to-work among veterans with SCD is an area of substantial policy focus and clinical intervention (Moore et al., 2016; Merritt et al., 2020; National Conference on State Legislatures, 2019). As Moore et al. (2016, p. 159) note: "The reintegration to occupational functioning and prevention of job loss are perhaps the most important aspects of success for veterans with disabilities." The ability to earn income through work, in conjunction with VA disability compensation, undoubtedly has a substantial impact on the poverty and socioeconomic outcomes of many veterans with SCD.

We use data from the 2019 ACS to describe patterns of labor-force participation by veteran status and SCD rating in order to illustrate the potential contribution of work and earnings to poverty reduction among veterans with different levels of SCD. Overall, we estimate that 61.9% of non-veterans and veterans combined are employed, 2.9% are unemployed, and 35.2% are not in the labor force. Figure 22.4 shows the employment status distribution by veteran status and SCD rating. Non-veterans are most likely to be employed (63.2%), while veterans with SCD of 70% or more are least likely to be employed (33.1%). Notably, roughly one-third to a half of veterans with an SCD rating of 0% or higher are employed, with another 1.6% to 2.6% unemployed and looking for work.

In addition to looking at employment status, we also examined the distribution of weeks of employment in the last year. Overall, we estimate that 32.8% of non-veterans and veterans combined worked 0 weeks in the prior year, while 13.8% worked one to forty-nine weeks, and 53.4% worked fifty to fifty-two weeks. Figure 22.5 shows the annual weeks worked distribution by veteran status and SCD rating. Non-veterans are the only groups with more than half working fifty to fifty-two weeks in the prior year (54.4%), and they are also the group with the highest percentage working one to forty-nine weeks

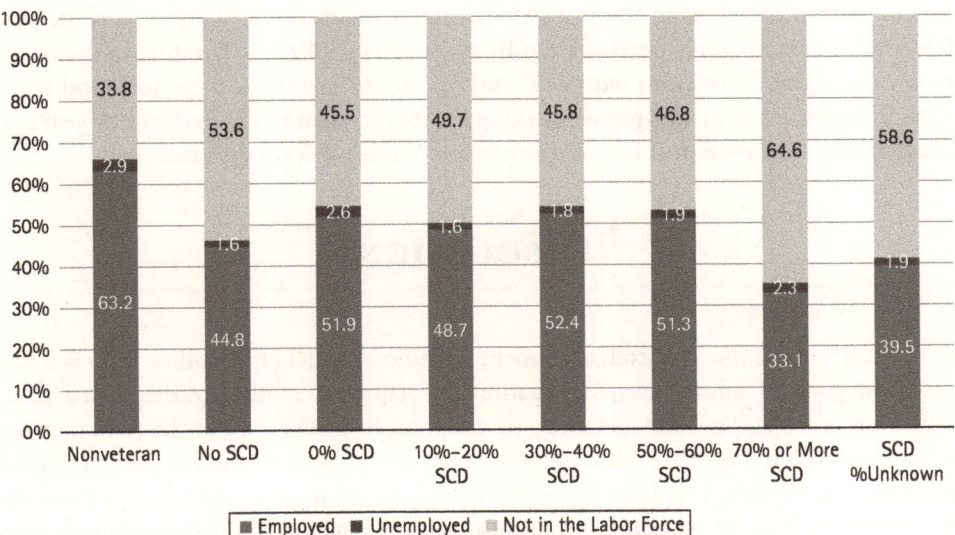

FIGURE 22.4 Employment Status Distribution by Veteran Status and Service-Connected Disability Rating, 2019 American Community Survey.

Source: Author calculation.

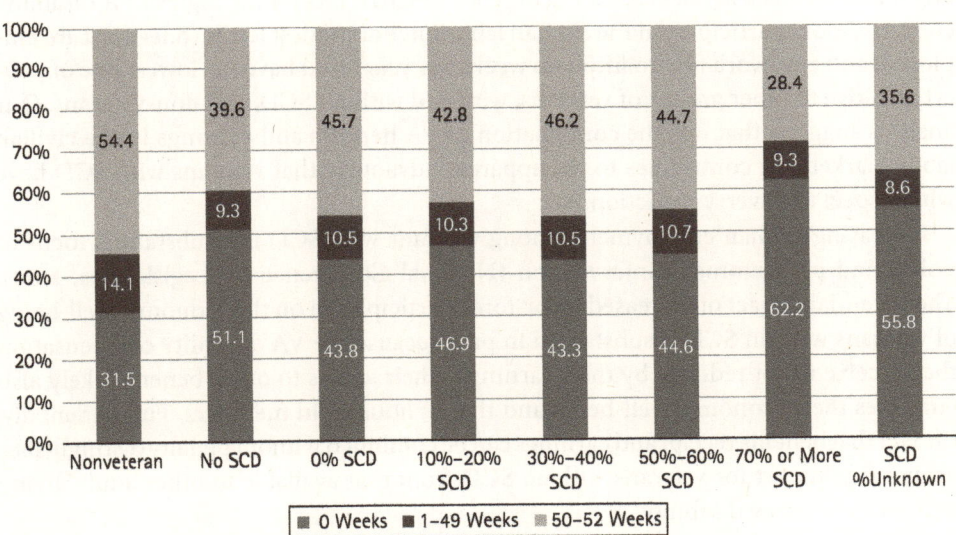

FIGURE 22.5 Usual Weeks of Work in the Past Year Distribution by Veteran Status and Service-Connected Disability Rating, 2019 American Community Survey.

Source: Author calculation.

in the prior year (14.1%). This high rate of labor-force participation may in part reflect the fact that non-veterans are, on average, younger than veterans. Veterans with an SCD rating of 70% or more are the least likely to report working fifty to fifty-two weeks in the prior year, but still, 28.4% report working that much and another 9.3% report working one to forty-nine weeks in the prior year. Veterans with no SCD report a somewhat lower level of labor-force participation than veterans with an SCD rating in the 0% to 60% range. Among veterans with SCD ratings of 0%, 10%–20%, 30%–40%, and 50%–60%, between 43% and 46% report working fifty to fifty-two weeks in the prior year and another 10.3%–10.7% report working one to forty-nine weeks in the prior year.

DISCUSSION

Based solely upon the VA's exclusive use of a medical model of disability, SCD is a distinct category of adult-onset, occupationally acquired, medically diagnosed disability, disease, or injury. Veterans may be assigned an SCD rating at the time they are separated from the military, although they may also acquire or modify an SCD rating subsequently. Veterans with an SCD rating have access to all of the benefits available to veterans in general, as well as a subset of specific benefits targeted to veterans with SCD. Targeted benefits include priority access to VA health care, receipt of supportive services, and tax-free disability compensation. Importantly, veterans with an SCD are allowed to work if they desire and are able to do so, and a large percentage do work. Notably, veterans with an SCD rating of 70% or higher: receive the highest VA disability compensation; participate in the civilian labor force at modest levels (one-third are employed, and 28% work fifty to fifty-two weeks per year); and have the lowest rate of poverty relative to other groups of veterans, with and without SCD, and non-veterans. Our analysis suggests that it is the combination of VA benefits and earnings in the civilian labor market that contributes to the apparent advantage that veterans with SCD have with respect to poverty reduction.

Increasing civilian employment among veterans with SCD is a substantial focus of policy and programmatic intervention (National Conference on Legislatures, 2019). The potential impact of increased labor-force participation on the economic well-being of veterans with an SCD is substantial in part because the VA disability compensation they receive is not reduced by their earnings. Their access to other benefits likely also enhances their economic well-being and that of household members. Fundamentally, the fact that benefits receipt and earnings can be combined without penalty distinguishes economic support for veterans with an SCD from that available to other adults living with work-limiting disability.

Increasing employment among non-veteran adults living with work-limiting disability is also a priority of policy makers (Social Security Administration, 2021b). Receipt of DI benefits is limited to individuals with long-term, work-limiting disability. While benefit receipt has generally been contingent on recipients refraining from labor-force participation, the Social Security Administration has been expanding opportunities for DI recipients to earn income without losing benefits. Most recently, beginning in 2021, recipients DI are able to participate in a work-incentive program through which they can work for up to nine months over a rolling sixty-month period and not have their

DI benefit cut (Social Security Administration, 2021c). The Trial Work Period (TWP), which was instituted as part of the Ticket to Work Program, allows DI recipients who report work to earn more than $940 per month for nine months over a five-year period and retain their benefit. Months in which they earn $940 or less do not count toward the TWP. While not allowing the same level of work as the VA disability compensation program, which is structured as an entitlement for those who were harmed while serving their country, this policy change is consistent with the notion that both disability income and earnings can benefit many adults living with disability, regardless of their veteran and SCD status.

The VA's response to SCD has the potential to provide generalizable lessons for poverty reduction and the enhancement of economic well-being. Yet, there is a need for additional research at the nexus of service-connected harm, access to and acceptance of an SCD designation, and the consequences of VA disability compensation on labor-force participation. Such research might address a number of different issues. For example, based on a systematic review of the literature on employment among persons with SCD, Stern (2017) suggested that future research should examine what facilitates work for veterans with disabilities, veteran-civilian career identity conflict, and the lived experiences of veterans with service-connected disabilities and their employers. Research might also take a life-course perspective and ask questions about how SCD affects work at different ages. This is important given that there is some evidence that disability compensation receipt may disincentivize the labor-force participation of younger-adult veterans with an SCD at a critical period of the life course when careers are established and employment experiences begin to cumulate (Ben-Shalom, Tennant, & Stapleton, 2016). A life-course perspective might also focus on how the lives of those who are linked to veterans with an SCD are affected by their access or lack thereof to VA resources. Additional research might also recognize the inherent limitations in attempting to study SCD with data that use competing models of disability, none of which may be accepted by the population in question. Such research would require that greater attention be paid to social versus medical definitions of disability, identification of who does and does seek and/or act upon an SCD rating, and the ways in which military culture and veteran culture may shape the ways in which veteran self-define disability status and benefits. Finally, future research should address whether and how the relationship between SCD and poverty varies by gender, race/ethnicity, and cohort/time period served. Pursuing these avenues of research will elucidate the most effective policy approaches to strengthen the social safety net in ways that reduce poverty among persons with disability.

In recent years, sociologists of disability have made substantial contributions to the literature on disability, employment, and socio-economic and life-course inequality (Maroto & Pettinicchio, 2014a, 2014b; Maroto, Pettinicchio, & Patterson, 2019; Pettinicchio & Maroto, 2017). These studies have taken up important questions related to occupational segregation, income and poverty, and the intersecting influences of race, gender, and disability on economic inequality. However, in these studies and in the field of disability studies more generally, the influence of military connectedness remains a hidden, but potentially consequential, variable. This point is similar to the point made by Settersten and Patterson (2006) a decade and a half ago that "wartime experiences may be important but largely invisible factors underneath contemporary knowledge about aging" (p. 5). They made this claim because very few studies of older adults included veteran status despite the fact that very high proportions of men in the cohorts under investigation had served in the military earlier in their lives (Wilmoth & London, 2011). Relatedly, Wilmoth and London (2016) focused on publications in the seven top aging journals for the thirty-four-year period from January 1980 through December 2013 and documented an average of three articles per year were published that included any mention of veterans or military service. This represents less than 1% of the nearly 12,000 articles published in these mainstream aging-focused journals over this period.

The ACS measures of disability do not fully capture SCD, thus it is hard to know how the apparent SCD advantage affects overall levels of disability-related inequality. If SCD was included, the size of the disabled population would be larger than is generally estimated, but estimated employment, wage, earnings, and poverty gaps might be smaller than estimated in other ACS-based studies that focus on disability-related employment, occupational segregation, and economic outcomes (e.g., Maroto & Pettinicchio, 2014a, 2014b; Maroto, Pettinicchio, & Patterson, 2019; Pettinicchio & Maroto, 2017). There is a need for research on a range of life-course processes and outcomes that includes veteran status and takes veterans with disability that is not service connected, as well as veterans with SCD, into account. By not taking veteran status and SCD into account, studies that focus on disability may be missing an important variable that contributes to variation in disability-related outcomes. More importantly, they may be missing a substantial component of the disability population since, as documented above, the general measures of disability included in data sets like the ACS do not fully capture the population of persons with SCD. Collaboration between sociologists of disability and sociologists of aging and the life course who study the consequences of military service would benefit both subfields and substantially enhance our sociological understanding of a range of life-course inequalities among nonveterans, veterans, and those whose lives are linked to them.

REFERENCES

Ben-Shalom, Yonatan, Jennifer R. Tennant, and David C. Stapleton. 2016. "Trends in Disability and Program Participation among U.S. Veterans." *Disability and Health Journal* 9, 449–56.

Bennett, Pamela R., and Katrina Bell McDonald. 2013. "Military Service as a Pathway to Early Socioeconomic Achievement for Disadvantaged Groups." Pp. 119–43 in *Life-Course Perspectives on Military Service*, edited by Janet M. Wilmoth and Andrew S. London. New York: Routledge.

Buddin, Richard, and Kanika Kapur. 2005. "An Analysis of Military Disability Compensation." Santa Monica, CA: RAND.

Buddin, Richard, and Bing Han. 2012. "Is Military Disability Compensation Adequate to Offset Civilian Earnings Losses from Service-Connected Disabilities?" Santa Monica, CA: RAND.

Burland, Daniel, and Jennifer Hickes Lundquist. 2013. "The Best Years of Our Lives: Military Service and Family Relationships—A Life-Course Perspective." Pp. 165–84 in *Life-Course Perspectives on Military Service*, edited by Janet M. Wilmoth and Andrew S. London. New York: Routledge.

Butler. Frank K. 2017. "Two Decades of Saving Lives on the Battlefield: Tactical Combat Casualty Care Turns 20." *Military Medicine 182* (3-4), e1563–e1568. doi: 10.7205/MILMED-D-16-00214.

Dannefer, Dale. 2003. "Cumulative Advantage/Disadvantage and the Life Course: Cross-Fertilizing Age and Social Science Theory." *The Journals of Gerontology, Series B: Psychological Sciences and Social Sciences 58* (6): S327–S337.

Davison Eve H., Anica Pless Kaiser, Avron Spiro III, Jennifer Moye, Lynda A. King, and Daniel W. King. 2016. "From Late-Onset Stress Symptomatology to Later-Adulthood Trauma Reengagement in Aging Combat Veterans: Taking a Broader View." *The Gerontologist 56* (1), 14–21.

Dismuke-Greer, Clara Elizabeth, Tracy L. Nolen, Kayla Nowak, Shawn Hirsch, Terri K. Pogoda, Amma A. Agyemang, Kathleen F. Carlson, Heather G. Belanger, Kimbra Kenney, Maya Troyanskaya, and William C. Walker. 2018. "Understanding the Impact of Mild Traumatic Brain Injury on Veteran Service-Connected Disability: Results from Chronic Effects of Neurotrauma Consortium." *Brain Injury 32* (10), 1178–87.

Drum, Charles E. 2009. "Models and Approaches to Disability." Pp. 27–44 in *Disability and Public Health*, edited by C. E. Drum, Gloria L. Krahn, and Hank Bersani Jr.. Washington, DC: American Public Health Association.

Duggan, Mark. 2014. The Labor Market Effects of the VA's Disability Compensation Program. Stanford, CA: Stanford University. https://drive.google.com/file/d/1Q2jRA10t5t8wCYG6SVayyFAQUUWhwhm3/view

Duggan, Mark, Robert Rosenheck, and Perry Singleton. 2010. "Federal Policy and the Rise in Disability Enrollment: Evidence for the Veterans Affairs' Disability Compensation Program." *Journal of Law and Economics 53* (2): 379–98.

Eggleston, B., Clara Elizabeth Dismuke-Greer, Terri K. Pogoda, J. H. Denning, B. C. Eapen, Kathleen F. Carlson, S Bhatnagar, R Nakase-Richardson, Maya Troyanskaya, Tracy Nolen, and William C. Walker. 2019. "A Prediction Model of Military Combat and Training Exposures on VA Service-Connected Disability: A CENC Study." *Brain Injury 33* (13–14), 1602–14.

Elder, Glen H Jr. 1986. "Military Times and Turning Points in Men's Lives." *Developmental Psychology 22* , 233–45.

Elder, Glen H. Jr. 1987. "War Mobilization and the Life Course: A Cohort of World War II Veterans." *Sociological Forum 2* , 449–72.

Elder, Glen H. Jr., and Elizabeth C. Clipp. 1988a. "Wartime Losses and Social Bonding: Influences Across 40 Years in Men's Lives." *Psychiatry 51*, 177–98.

Elder, Glen H. Jr., and Elizabeth C. Clipp. 1988b. "Combat Experience, Comradeship, and Psychological Health. Pp. 131–56 in *Human Adaptation to Extreme Stress: From the Holocaust to Vietnam*, John P. Wilson, Zev Harel, and Boaz Kahana. New York: Plenum.

Elder, Glen H. Jr., and Elizabeth C. Clipp. 1989. "Combat Experience and Emotional Health: Impairment and Resilience." *Journal of Personality 57* (2): 311–41.

Elder, Glen H. Jr., Michael J. Shanahan, and Elizabeth C. Clipp. 1994. "When War Comes to Men's Lives: Life-Course Patterns in Family, Work, and Health." *Psychology and Aging 9* (1), 5–16.

Elder, Glen H. Jr., Michael J. Shanahan, and Elizabeth C. Clipp. 1997. "Linking Combat and Physical Health: The Legacy of World War II in Men's Lives." *American Journal of Psychiatry* 154 (3), 330–36.

Elder, Jr., Glen H., Johnson, Monica K., and Crosnoe, Robert. 2003. "The Emergence and Development of Life Course Theory." Pp. 3–19 in *Handbook of the Life Course*, edited by Jeylan T. Mortimer and Michael J. Shanahan. New York: Kluwer Academic/Plenum.

Elder, Jr., Glen H., and Shanahan, Michael J. 2006. "The Life Course and Human Development." pp. 665–715 in *Theoretical Models of Human Development* (Volume 1: *The Handbook of Child Psychology*, 6th Edition), edited by Richard E. Lerner, series editor William Damon. New York: Wiley.

Ferraro Kenneth F., and Tetyana Pylypiv Shippee. 2009. "Aging and Cumulative Inequality: How Does Inequality Get Under the Skin?" *The Gerontologist* 49 (3): 333–343.

Fried, Dennis A., Drew Helmer, William E. Halperin, Marian Passannante, and Bart K. Holland. 2015. "Health and Health Care Service Utilization among U.S. Veterans Denied VA Service-Connected Disability Compensation: A Review of the Literature." *Military Medicine* 180 (10): 1034–40.

Fried, Dennis Adrian, Marian Passannante, Drew Helmer, Bart K. Holland, and William E. Halperin. 2017. "The Health and Social Isolation of American Veterans Denied Veterans Affairs Disability Compensation." *Health & Social Work* 42 (1) 7–14.

Fulton, Lawrence V., Janna M. Belote, Matthew S. Brooks, and M. Nicholas Coppola. 2009. "A Comparison of Disabled Veteran and Nonveteran Income: Time to Revise the Law?" *Journal of Disability Policy Studies* 20 (3), 184–91.

Gerber, David A. 2000. *Disabled Veterans in History*. Ann Arbor: University of Michigan.

Griffin, Christopher L., and Michael Ashley Stein. 2015. "Self-perception of Disability and Prospects for Employment among U.S. Veterans." *Work* 50 (1), 49–58.

Groenewold, Matthew R., Sangwoo Tak, and Elizabeth Masterson. 2011. "Severe Hearing Impairment Among Military Veterans—United States, 2010." *MMWR* 60 (28), 955–58.

Heaton, Paul, David S. Loughran, and Amalia Miller. 2012. *Compensating Wounded Warriors: An Analysis of Injury, Labor Market Earnings, and Disability Compensation among Veterans of the Iraq and Afghanistan Wars*. Santa Monica, CA: RAND.

Holder, Kelly Ann. 2016. *The Disability of Veterans*. Washington, DC: US Census. Bureau. https://www.census.gov/content/dam/Census/library/working-papers/2016/demo/Holder-2016-01.pdf

Janet M. Wilmoth, Scott D. Landes, and Andrew S. London. 2019. "The Health of Male Veterans in Later Life." *Annual Review of Gerontology and Geriatrics*, 39(1): 23–48. doi:10.1891/0198-8794.39.1.

Jette, Alan M. 2006. "Toward a Common Language for Function, Disability, and Health." *Physical Therapy* 86 (5): 726–34.

Kaufman, Kenton R., Stephanie Brodine, and Richard Scaffer. 2000. "Military Training-Related Injuries: Surveillance, Research, and Prevention." *American Journal of Preventive Medicine* 18 (3 Suppl), 54–63.

Kregel, John, and Lucy Miller. 2016. "Disability Benefits for Veterans: Interactions among Department of Defense, Department of Veterans Affairs, and Social Security Administration Programs." Mathematica Policy Research. file://hd.ad.syr.edu/02/11c150/Documents/Downloads/DRC%20Brief%20Veterans.pdf

Kleykamp, Meredith. 2007. "A Great Place to Start: The Effects of Prior Military Service on Hiring." *Armed Forces & Society* 35 (2), 266–85.

Kleykamp, Meredith. 2013. "Labor Market Outcomes among Veterans and Military Spouses." Pp. 144–64 in *Life-Course Perspectives on Military Service*, edited by Janet M. Wilmoth and Andrew S. London. New York: Routledge.

Landes, Scott D., Andrew S. London, and Janet M. Wilmoth. 2021. "Service-Connected Disability and the Veteran Mortality Disadvantage." *Armed Forces & Society* 47 (3), 457–79.

Lenhart, Martha K., Eric Savitsky, and Brian Eastridge. 2012. *Combat Casualty Care: Lessons Learned from OEF and OIF*. Falls Church, VA: Office of the Surgeon General, United States Army.

London, Andrew S., Colleen M. Heflin, and Janet M. Wilmoth. 2011. "Work-Related Disability, Veteran Status, and Poverty: Implications for Family Well-Being." *Journal of Poverty* 15, 330–49.

London, Andrew S., Sarah A. Burgard, and Janet M. Wilmoth. 2014. "The Influence of Veteran Status, Psychiatric Diagnosis, and Traumatic Brain Injury on Inadequate Sleep." *Journal of Sociology & Social Welfare XLI* (4), 49–67.

London, Andrew S., and Janet M. Wilmoth. 2016. "Military Service in Lives: Where Do We Go From Here?" Pp. 277–300 in *Handbook of the Life Course*, vol. 2, edited by Michael J. Shanahan, Jeylan T. Mortimer, and Monica Kirkpatrick Johnson. Switzerland: Springer International Publishing.

London, Andrew S., Janet M. Wilmoth, William J. Oliver, and Jessica A. Hausauer. 2020. "The Influence of Military Service Experiences on Current and Everyday Drinking." *Substance Use & Misuse* 55 (8), 1288–99.

MacLean, Alair. 2010. "The Things They Carry: Combat, Disability, and Unemployment among Men." *American Sociological Review* 75 (4), 563–85.

Madans, Jennifer H., Mitchell E. Loeb, and Barbara M. Altman. 2011. "Measuring Disability and Monitoring the UN Convention on the Rights of Persons with Disabilities: The Work of the Washington Group on Disability Statistics." *BMC Public Health* 11 (Suppl 4): S4. http://www.biomedcentral.com/1471-2458/11/S4/S4

Maroto, Michelle, and David Pettinicchio. 2014a. "Disability, Structural Inequality, and Work: The Influence of Occupational Segregation on Earnings for People with Different Disabilities." *Research in Social Stratification and Mobility* 38, 76–92.

Maroto, Michelle, and David Pettinicchio. 2014b. "The Limitations of Disability Antidiscrimination Legislation: Policymaking and the Economic Well-being of People with Disabilities." *Law and Policy* 36 (4), 370–407.

Maroto, Michelle, David Pettinicchio, and Andrew C. Patterson. 2019. "Hierarchies of Categorical Disadvantage: Economic Insecurity at the Intersection of Disability, Gender, and Race." *Gender & Society* 33 (1), 64–93.

McNally, Richard J., and B. Christopher Frueh. 2013. "Why Are Iraq and Afghanistan War Veterans Seeking PTSD Disability Compensation at Unprecedented Rates?" *Journal of Anxiety Disorders* 27 (5), 520–26.

Merritt, Victoria C., Sarah M. Jurick, Laura D. Crocker, Amber V. Keller, Samantha N. Hoffman, and Amy J. Jak. 2020. "Factors Associated with Employment and Work Perception in Combat-Exposed Veterans." *Rehabilitation Psychology* 65 (3), 279–90.

Miech, Richard A., Andrew S. London, Janet M. Wilmoth, and Stephen Koester. 2013. "The Effects of the Military's Anti-Drug Policies Over the Life Course: The Case of Past-Year Hallucinogen Use." *Substance Use & Misuse* 48 (10), 837–53.

Modell, John, and Timothy Haggerty. 1991. "The Social Impact of War." *Annual Review of Sociology* 17, 205–224.

Montgomery, Sidra. 2018. "Coming Home as 'Wounded Warriors': Identity, Stigma, and Status among Post-9/11 Wounded Veterans." Department of Sociology, University of Maryland, College Park, MD.

Moore, Corey L., Ningning Wang, Jean Johnson, Edward O. Manyibe, Andre L. Washington, and Atashia Muhammad. 2016. "Return-to-Work Outcome Rates of African American Versus White Veterans Served by State Vocational Rehabilitation Agencies: A Randomized Split-Half Cross-Model Validation Research Design." *Rehabilitation and Counseling Bulletin 59* (3), 158–71.

Murdoch Maureen, James Hodges, Carolyn Hunt, Diane Cowper, Nancy Kressin, and Nancy O'Brien. 2003a. "Gender Differences in Service Connection for PTSD." *Medical Care 41* (8), 950–61.

Murdoch, Maureen, James Hodges, Diane Cowper, Larry Fortier, and Michelle van Ryn. 2003b. "Racial Disparities in VA Service Connection for Posttraumatic Stress Disorder Disability." *Medical Care 41* (4), 536–49.

Murdoch Maureen, Shannon Kehle-Forbes, Michele Spoont, Nina A. Sayer, Siamak Noorbaloochi, and Paul Arbisi. 2019. "Changes in Post-traumatic Stress Disorder Service Connection Among Veterans Under Age 55: An 18-Year Ecological Cohort Study." *Military Medicine 184* (11–12), 715–22.

Murdoch Maureen, Michele R. Spoont, Nina A. Sayer, Shannon M. Kehle-Forbes, and Siamak Noorbaloochi. 2021. "Reversals in Initially Denied Department of Veterans Affairs' PTSD Disability Claims After 17 Years: A Cohort Study of Gender differences." *BMC Women's Health 21* (1), 70. Published online February 16, 2021. http://doi:10.1186/s12905-021-01214-7

Murdoch, Maureen, Nina A. Sayer, Michele R. Spoont, Robert Rosenheck, Siamak Noorbaloochi, Joan M. Griffin, Paul A. Arbisi, and Emily Hagel. 2011. "Long-term Outcomes of Disability Benefits in US Veterans with Posttraumatic Stress Disorder." *Archives of General Psychiatry 68* (10), 1072–80.

National Conference of State Legislatures. 2019. *A Path to Employment for Veterans With Disabilities*. Denver, CO and Washington, D.C. https://www.ncsl.org/research/military-and-veterans-affairs/a-path-to-employment-for-veterans-with-disabilities.aspx#:~:text=According%20to%20the%20U.S.%20Bureau%20of%20Labor%20Statistics%2C%20veterans%20with,also%20vary%20across%20the%20country.

National Center for Veterans Analysis and Statistics. 2021. Number of Projected Veterans by Urban and Rural in 50 States, DC and PR, from 9/30/2019 to 9/30/2021. https://www.va.gov/vetdata/Veteran_Population.asp.

National Research Council. 2006. *Assessing Fitness for Military Enlistment: Physical, Medical, and Mental Health Standards*. Washington, DC: National Academies Press.

Olsen, Donald C., Chelsea C. Hays, Henry J. Orff, Amy J. Jak, and Elizabeth W. Twamley. 2018. "Correlates of Employment and Postsecondary Education Enrolment in Afghanistan and Iraq Veterans with Traumatic Brain Injuries." *Brain Injury 32* (5), 544–49.

Pettinicchio, David, and Michelle Maroto. 2017. "Employment Outcomes Among Men and Women with Disabilities: How the Intersection of Gender and Disability Status Shapes Labor Market Inequality." *Research in Social Science and Disability 10* , 3–33.

Pettinicchio, David, and Michelle Maroto. 2021. "Who Counts? Measuring Disability Cross-Nationally in Census Data." *Journal of Survey Statistics and Methodology 9* (2), 257–84.

Ruggles, Steven, Sarah Flood, Sophia Foster, Ronald Goeken, Jose Pacas, Megan Schouweiler, and Matthew Sobek (2021). IPUMS USA: Version 11.0 [dataset]. Minneapolis, MN: IPUMS. https://doi.org/10.18128/D010.V11.0

Sampson, Robert J., and John H. Laub. 1996. "Socioeconomic Achievement in the Life Course of Disadvantaged Men: Military Service as a Turning Point, Circa 1940–1965." *American Sociological Review 61* (3), 347–67.

Sayer, Nina A., Michele Spoont, and Dave Nelson. 2004. "Veterans Seeking Disability Benefits for Post-Traumatic Stress Disorder: Who Applies and the Self-Reported Meaning of Disability Compensation." *Social Science & Medicine 58* (11): 2133–43. https://doi.org/10.1016/j.socscimed.2003.08.009

Schedule for Rating Disabilities, 38 U.S.C. § 1155 C.F.R. 1994.

Schedule for Rating Disabilities, 38 C.F.R. Book C. 2021. https://www.benefits.va.gov/WARMS/bookc.asp

Scotch, Richard K. 2000. "Models of Disability and the Americans with Disabilities Act." *Berkeley Journal of Employment & Labor Law 21*, 213–22.

Settersten Jr., Richard A. 2006. "When Nations Call: How Wartime Military Service Matters for the Life Course and Aging." *Research on Aging 28* (1), 12–36.

Settersten, Richard A., Jr., and Patterson, Robin S. 2006. "Military Service, the Life Course, and Aging: An introduction." *Research on Aging 28* (1), 5–11.

Songer, Thomas J., and Ronald E. LaPorte. 2000. "Disabilities Due to Injuries in the Military." *American Journal of Preventive Medicine 18* (3 Suppl), 33–40.

Spiro III, Avron, Richard A. Settersten, Jr., and Carolyn M. Aldwin (Eds.). 2018. *Long-Term Outcomes of Military Service: The Health and Well-Being of Aging Veterans*. Washington, DC: American Psychological Association.

State of Vermont's Office of Veterans Affairs. 2021. *VA Disability*.https://veterans.vermont.gov/benefits-and-services/veteran-benefits/va-disability.

Stern, Lisa. 2017. "Post 9/11 Veterans With Service-Connected Disabilities and their Transition to the Civilian Workforce: A Review of the Literature." *Advances in Developing Human Resources 19* (1), 66–77.

Social Security Administration. 2019. *Disability Benefits*. Social Security Administration in Washington, D.C. https://www.ssa.gov/pubs/EN-05-10029.pdf.

Social Security Administration. 2021a. *Disability Benefits For Wounded Warriors*. Social Security Administration in Washington, D.C. https://www.ssa.gov/pubs/EN-05-10030.pdf.

Social Security Administration. 2021b. *Working While Disabled: How We Can Help*. Social Security Administration in Washington, D.C. https://www.ssa.gov/pubs/EN-05-10095.pdf.

Social Security Administration. 2021c. "What's New in 2021?" https://choosework.ssa.gov/blog/2021-01-21-whats-new-in-2021

Suris, Alina, and Lind, Lisa. 2008. "Military Sexual Trauma: A Review of Prevalence and Associated Health Consequences in Veterans." *Trauma, Violence, & Abuse 9* (4), 250–69.

Tanielian, Terri., and Lisa H. Jaycox (Eds.). 2008. *Invisible Wounds of War: Psychological and Cognitive Injuries, Their Consequences, and Services to Assist Their Recovery*. Santa Monica, CA: RAND.

Theokas, Christina. 2010. "Shut Out of the Military: Today's High School Education Doesn't Mean You're Ready for Today's Army." Available at https://edtrust.org/wp-content/uploads/2013/10/ASVAB_4.pdf

Thomas, Carol. 2007. *Sociologies of Disability and Illness: Contested Ideas in Disability Studies and Medical Sociology*. London: Red Globe Press.

U.S. Census Bureau. 2016. American Community Survey, 2008–2016.https://factfinder.census.gov/bkmk/table/1.0/en/ACS/16_1YR/B21100

U.S. Department of Veterans Affairs. 2018a. Public Health. Veterans' Diseases Associated with Agent Orange.https://www.publichealth.va.gov/exposures/agentorange/conditions

U.S. Department of Veterans Affairs. 2018b. Public Health. Veterans' Diseases Associated with Ionizing Radiation Exposure. https://www.publichealth.va.gov/exposures/radiation/disea ses.asp

U.S. Department of Veterans Affairs. (2019a). *Statistical Trends: Veterans with a Service-Connected Disability, 1990 to 2018*. Washington, DC: National Center for Veterans Analysis and Statistics. https://www.va.gov/vetdata/docs/Quickfacts/SCD_trends_FINAL_2018.pdf

U.S. Department of Veterans Affairs. 2019b. *Federal Benefits for Veterans, Dependents, and Survivors* (2019 Edition). U.S. Department of Veterans Affairs in Washington D.C. https:// www.va.gov/opa/publications/benefits_book.asp.

U.S. Department of Veterans Affairs. 2020a. *VA Utilization Profile FY 2017*. Washington, DC: National Center for Veterans Analysis and Statistics. U.S. Department of Veterans Affairs in Washington D.C. https://www.va.gov/vetdata/docs/Quickfacts/VA_Utilization_Profile _2017.pdf

U.S. Department of Veterans Affairs. 2020b. *About Disability Ratings*. U.S. Department of Veterans Affairs in Washington D.C. https://www.va.gov/disability/about-disability -ratings/.

U.S. Department of Veterans Affairs. 2020c. *Service Connected Disability (SCD) Veterans by Disability Rating Group: FY1986 to FY2016*. U.S. Department of Veterans Affairs in Washington D.C. https://www.data.va.gov/dataset/Service-Connected-Disability-SCD -Veterans-by-Disab/vne6-2zez.

U.S. Department of Veterans Affairs. 2020d. *Veterans Disability Compensation Rates*.https:// www.va.gov/disability/compensation-rates/veteran-rates/

Wherry, Jessica Lynn. 2017. "Interminable Parade Rest: The Impossibility of Establishing Service Connection in Veterans Disability Compensation Claims When Records Are Lost or Destroyed." *Brooklyn Law Review 83* (2), 477–515.

Wilmoth, Janet M., and Andrew S. London. 2011. "Aging Veterans: Needs and Provisions." Pp. 445–61 in *Handbook of Sociology of Aging*, edited by Richard A. Settersten Jr. and Jacqueline L. Angel. New York: Springer.

Wilmoth, Janet M., and Andrew S. London (Eds.). 2013. *Life-Course Perspectives on Military Service*. New York: Routledge.

Wilmoth, Janet M., Andrew S. London, and Colleen M. Heflin. 2015a. "The Use of VA Disability Compensation and Social Security Disability Insurance among Working-Aged Veterans." *Disability and Health Journal 8* (3), 388–96.

Wilmoth, Janet M., Andrew S. London, and Colleen M. Heflin. 2015b. "Economic Well-Being Among Older-Adult Households: Variation by Veteran and Disability Status." *Journal of Gerontological Social Work 58* (4), 399–419.

Wilmoth, Janet M., and Andrew S. London. 2016. "The Influence of Military Service on Aging." Pp. 227–50 in *Handbook of Aging and the Social Sciences*, 8th edition, edited by Linda K. George and Kenneth F. Ferraro. Boston: Elsevier

Wilmoth, Janet M., Andrew S. London, and William J. Oliver. 2018. "Military Service Experiences and Older Men's Trajectories of Self-Rated Health." Pp. 125–45 in *Long-Term Outcomes of Military Service: The Health and Well-Being of Aging Veterans*, edited by Avron Spiro III, Richard A. Settersten, Jr., and Carolyn M. Aldwin. Washington, DC: American Psychological Association.

Wilmoth, Janet M., and Andrew S. London. 2021. "The Role of the Military in Women's Lives." Pp. 181–200 in *Handbook of Aging and the Social Sciences*, 9th edition, edited by Kenneth F. Ferraro and Deborah Carr. Boston, MA: Elsevier.

Wilson, Laura C. 2018. "The Prevalence of Military Sexual Trauma: A Meta-Analysis." *Trauma, Violence, & Abuse* 19 (5), 584–97.

Wolf, Douglas A., Coady Wing, and Leonard M. Lopoo. 2013. "Methodological Problems in Determining the Consequences of Military Service." Pp. 254–74 in *Life-Course Perspectives on Military Service*, edited by Janet M. Wilmoth and Andrew S. London. New York: Routledge.

Wolff, Kristina B., and Peter D. Mills. 2016. "Reporting Military Sexual Trauma: A Mixed-Methods Study of Women Veterans' Experiences Who Served From World War II to the War in Afghanistan." *Military Medicine* 181 (8), 840–48.

CHAPTER 23

CUMULATIVE DISADVANTAGE IN EMPLOYMENT

Disability over the Life Course and Wealth Inequality in Later Life

KIM SHUEY AND ANDREA WILLSON

INTRODUCTION

SOCIAL models of disability recognize disability as a process whereby impairments become disabling within the context of social institutions, such as labor markets that lack adequate workplace supports (see, e.g., Oliver, 1996; Oliver & Barnes, 2012; Priestley, 2005). The interaction between impairment and social institutions varies over the life course and according to the individual's social structural location, making it part of a larger system of stratification and inequality (Nagi, 1991; Priestley, 2005; Verbrugge & Jette, 1994). The life course perspective within sociology (for discussion see Elder et al., 2003) that emerged in the 1970s provides a lens with which to study disability, focusing attention on time and process and how the intersection of individual lives and social structures at various life stages affects later life outcomes. Of particular relevance for understanding social inequality associated with disability are life course principles highlighting the importance of timing and duration of disability and their relationship with the accumulation of risks and opportunities across the life course.

The timing of a life course transition such as the onset of disability affects both its meaning and potential consequences, as the same event can affect individuals differently depending on when it occurs (Elder et al., 2003; George, 1993). Depending on the timing of disability onset, barriers to educational attainment, discrimination in hiring, a lack of workplace accommodation, and employers' discriminatory attitudes present obstacles to career advancement, job retention, and other labor-market experiences (Schur, 2003; Schur et al., 2009). Disability-related labor-market disadvantages encountered over the work life course contribute to future disadvantage, affecting the process of wealth accumulation and access to benefits such as employer pensions that set the stage for either economic security or precarity into old age.

Within sociology, this accumulative process is elaborated by theories of cumulative dis/advantage, which provide key frameworks for understanding socioeconomic status across the life course at the individual level and growing inequality with age within cohorts at the population level (Dannefer, 2003; Ferraro & Shippee, 2009; O'Rand, 1996). These theories describe an accumulative process whereby early-life advantage provides opportunities to access additional resources as well as to avoid many sources of adversity, while early disadvantage generates exposure to risk and further losses (O'Rand, 2006).

In this chapter we discuss the contribution of these theories of accumulation to our understanding of the implications of disability for economic insecurity. In addition, we utilize 40 years of longitudinal data from the US Panel Study of Income Dynamics (PSID 2019) to illustrate the association between the timing and duration of work disability and accumulated wealth at the end of the work life course.

DISABILITY AND THE LIFE COURSE

The Accumulation of Disadvantage

Theories of cumulative dis/advantage outline a dynamic, accumulative process whereby early-life advantages provide greater opportunities to access additional resources and to avoid sources of adversity (Crystal & Shea, 1990; Dannefer, 2003; Ferraro & Shippee, 2009; O'Rand, 1996). This can be contrasted to the experience of early-life disadvantage, which generates exposure to a chain of risks resulting in further losses (O'Rand, 2006). These concepts advance traditional theories of stratification through an emphasis on the dynamics of change over the life course, suggesting a process through which initial relative advantage generates greater divergence in resources across individuals or groups over time (Crystal & Shea, 1990; Dannefer, 1987, 2003).

The accumulation of financial resources is one of the most straightforward applications. Operating through the process of compound interest, money invested early accumulates interest that, if reinvested, generates a return that grows exponentially over time and increases the advantage of those who invest greater initial sums (for discussion see DiPrete & Eirich, 2006). A central idea of a process of cumulative advantage is the growing advantage of one group relative to another, with smaller initial differences in important resources such as income, wealth, or health becoming magnified over time, making it increasingly difficult for the group that falls behind to catch up (DiPrete & Eirich, 2006).

Theoretical formulations of the accumulation of dis/advantage consider the potentially harmful interaction between initial status and societal institutions across the life course (e.g., Crystal & Shea, 1990). In the case of disability, the systematic barriers associated with the treatment of disability within various societal institutions vary across the life course (for further discussion see Putnam, 2002; Schur, 2003; Shuey et al., 2016). For those experiencing early disability onset, inequality in the treatment of disability within educational institutions affects access to higher education and impacts labor-market entry and future wages. Whereas persons experiencing disability from birth or childhood experience the potential to accumulate disadvantage beginning very early in the life course through encounters with systemic barriers across various social institutions including the educational system, those experiencing disability in midlife and beyond start the accumulation clock much later in life. Once in the labor market, the experience of disability, including marginalization and exclusion, can affect wages, wage growth, and the ability to stay in the labor market. The barriers and experiences of individuals facing early disability onset are quite different from those encountering aging-associated disability near the end of their work lives. Thus, the *timing* of disability onset within the life course provides an indicator of the life stage at which individuals may encounter the structural barriers embedded within social institutions and is key to understanding the accumulation of disability-associated disadvantages (also see Shuey et al., 2016).

In addition, understanding this process of accumulation is complicated by the fact that disability is not a static state. Individuals may enter and exit disability multiple times over the life course, as disability is often a fluid rather than a fixed status. This means that not only is the concept of timing relevant, but *duration* of disability is also an important consideration. Within the cumulative dis/advantage tradition, the idea of cumulative exposure highlights the deleterious effects of long-term exposure to a particular state on the process of accumulation. The duration of exposure to "disadvantageous opportunity structures" has the potential to exert "a kind of social gravity" on future resources and reduce the ability to reverse the harmful effects of earlier disadvantage (DiPrete & Eirich, 2006; O'Rand, 2009, p. 135). Whereas theoretical models often assume a linear accumulation of advantage or disadvantage over time relative to initial level of resources, relatively little empirical attention has been given to examining changing statuses and the effect of persistent (or transient) disadvantage on later outcomes (but see McDonough & Berglund's 2003 examination of poverty history, Ferraro & Kelley-Moore's 2003 examination of obesity, Willson & Shuey's 2016 examination of pathways of economic hardship and health, and Shuey & Willson's 2019 examination of work disability and economic outcomes). Overall, the fluid nature of disability across the life course makes things complex, with additional questions arising. These include whether moving in and out of disability across the life course is as detrimental for the accumulation of subsequent resources as experiencing a persistent disability.

Disability and the Accumulation of Labor Market Disadvantage

Individuals living with a disability have lower rates of labor force participation, higher rates of unemployment and involuntary part-time work, lower wages, and fewer benefits (Baldwin & Schumacher, 2002; Maroto & Pettinicchio, 2014, 2015;

Schur et al., 2009). Although varying in magnitude, a sizable employment gap holds across countries, worldwide (Heymann et al., 2014). In the United States, for example, over half of people report a work disability at least once between the ages of 25 and 60, and only approximately one-third of individuals reporting a disability are employed compared to three-quarters of their nondisabled counterparts (Lauer & Houtenville, 2017; Rank & Hirschl, 2014). These labor-market disadvantages have contributed to greater economic insecurity for disabled individuals and households with a disabled member. Reports suggest a poverty rate that is two times higher for working-age people with disabilities than for those without, as well as significant asset and home ownership gaps (Erickson et al., 2015; Maroto, 2016; Maroto & Pettinicchio, 2020).

One challenge to understanding the relationship between disability and economic resources, however, relates to the strong, reciprocal relationship between socioeconomic status and health more generally. Having fewer resources is associated with worse health outcomes across nearly every health measure, with lower-income individuals more likely to experience earlier health declines and disability onset. The accumulation of both health and economic advantages are interrelated processes that begin early in life. Early disadvantage of either type initiates a pathway involving lower educational attainment and employment in jobs with lower wages and fewer benefits that are also more likely to generate additional health penalties (Shuey & Willson, 2019; also see Pais, 2014). Health disadvantages negatively affect labor-force participation, compensation, and resource acquisition, and the resulting economic penalties in turn have the potential to negatively affect future health in a reciprocal manner across the life course (also see Haas, 2006; Haas et al., 2011; Warren, 2009). In previous research we have argued that work disability operates across the life course as both an outcome and a mechanism of stratification connecting early-life disadvantage to later-life economic insecurity through a temporal chain of risks involving exposure to structural barriers, discrimination, and unequal labor-market outcomes (Shuey & Willson, 2019).

In recognition of these complexities, disability is often theorized as a dynamic process and a sizeable body of research conceptualizes disability in the form of a trajectory across the life course rather than as a static, point-in-time state (see Verbrugge & Jette, 1994). Studies of disability trajectories have incorporated various conceptualizations of disability, including functional limitations, activities of daily living (ADLs), and chronic conditions, and addressed a variety of questions such as cohort differences in trajectories of disability, disability onset and progression, and mediating mechanisms such as education (see, e.g., Deeg, 2005; Liang et al., 2009; Nusselder et al., 2006; Taylor, 2011; Taylor & Lynch, 2011; Verbrugge et al., 2017; Wolf et al., 2015). A lack of longitudinal data that captures a large portion of the life course has limited research explorations of individual variations in long-term disability pathways associated with concepts such as timing and duration. In addition, limited attention has been given to understanding the extent to which disability is associated with the accumulation of disadvantage across the life course and the economic and labor-market outcomes of various trajectories of disability (but see Clarke & Latham's 2014 analysis of the economic consequences of disability in early mid-life and Shuey & Willson's 2019 examination of economic insecurity approaching retirement).

In the next section we use long-term panel data to further illustrate these dynamic relationships by empirically investigating the relationship between patterns of work disability across the life course and wealth inequality. Individuals accumulate wealth as they age and may draw upon it both to create opportunities and bequests for their children, as well as to buffer the effects of exits from the labor force, both during the working years and in retirement (Oliver & Shapiro, 2006). Wealth is strongly associated with individual health, independent of education and income (e.g., Boen, 2016). Wealth accumulation is an important life course status-attainment process, and inequalities in wealth reflect cumulative disadvantage across various domains, such as race-ethnicity and family background. Wealth inequality emerges early in the life course and widens over time within cohorts to levels much higher than those based on income (Brown, 2016; Willson, Shuey, & Elder, 2007). The accumulation of economic dis/advantage associated with disability can be seen in findings discussed below from models examining the relationship between the timing and duration of work disability and accumulated wealth approaching retirement.

DATA AND METHODS

Data

From a life course perspective, work disability can be conceptualized as a long-term process that takes the form of a trajectory operating across biographical and historical time. Examining trajectories of work disability therefore requires long-term panel data that observes individuals throughout their entire work life course. Data for this analysis are drawn from the US Panel Study of Income Dynamics (PSID), an ongoing survey that began in 1968 with a nationally representative sample of approximately 5,000 households and individuals residing in those households (PSID 2019). The PSID interviewed families annually until 1997, when interviewing became biennial. The latest wave of data available for this analysis was collected in 2017, making the PSID the longest-running longitudinal survey in the world.

Our goal was to observe work disability over the entire work life course and examine its relationship with wealth acquisition approaching retirement. In this analysis we followed men who were between the ages of 20 to 25 years old between 1968 and 1975 until they turned 62 to 65 between the years 2007 and 2017. We limited our analytic sample to men for several reasons. Women who were 20 to 25 years old between 1968 and 1975 (born between 1943 and 1955) experienced employment histories with shorter job tenure, more frequent job changes, and a greater likelihood of part-time work than men, and they took more time out of the labor force to raise children than current cohorts of employed women. Research also suggests that women have higher disability prevalence rates than men, are more likely to suffer from chronic health problems, and have multiple comorbidities (Laditka & Laditka, 2002; Warner & Brown, 2011). Given the gender differences in both disability profiles and employment histories, the dynamic relationship between work disability and wealth acquisition likely differs for men and women. Additionally, information on work disability was not consistently collected for women in the PSID, unless they were the household head, until 1981, which does not allow for observation of the entire adult work life course.

Thus, our analytic sample includes men who were 20 to 25 years of age between 1968 and 1975 ($N = 1,615$), observed until they turned 62 to 65 between the years 2007 to 2017 (the youngest cohort in the sample turns 62 in 2017). After attrition and minimal missing data on variables, our final analytic sample consists of 1,054 men observed at 25 time points for 26,350 total observations.

Although the sample size of the PSID has declined over time through attrition, extensive studies of attrition have demonstrated that the weighted sample maintains its representativeness (Fitzgerald, 2011). Our previous investigations suggest that the effect of attrition likely results in conservative estimates of the strength of the association of disability pathways and measures of economic security (Shuey & Willson, 2019).

Measures

Wealth Quartile

The dependent variable in this analysis is the wealth quartile of the respondent in the survey year during which they were 62 to 65 years old. We use the PSID-constructed measure of imputed household net worth, excluding housing equity, to calculate wealth quartiles. Before calculating the quartiles, wealth in each year observed was adjusted for inflation to 2017 dollars using the Consumer Price Index because respondents turned 62–65 in different years. The resulting variable was weighted because the PSID includes an oversample of families from low-income neighborhoods. Quartile 1 includes respondents with the highest wealth and quartile 4 the lowest. Quartile cut-points are as follows: quartile 1 = > $694,000; quartile 2 = $157,301–$694,000; quartile 3 = $24,961–$157,300; quartile 4 = Negative wealth –$24,960.

Work Disability

In each cycle, respondents were asked, "Do you have any physical or nervous condition that limits the type of work or the amount of work you can do?" If respondents answered yes to this question, they were coded as having a work disability. This measure focuses on the intersection of impairment and social context, rather than on the impairment or health condition itself, therefore linking health with the socioeconomic consequences of an individual's ability to participate in social institutions, such as work (Kelley-Moore, 2010; Nagi, 1991; Priestley, 2005; Verbrugge & Jette, 1994). Work-limiting impairments may include chronic conditions, short-term physical injuries, long-term disabilities, mental-health issues, and any other health-related issue that prevents someone from working to the extent they would have without the condition. Patterns of responses over the approximately 34-year period were evaluated using latent class analysis, described below.

Control Variables

In the United States, large racial disparities exist in both wealth and health (Boen et al., 2020). For example, the average wealth of white families is eight times the wealth of African American families and five times the wealth of Hispanic families (Bhutta et al., 2020). Large and persistent racial disparities in health mean that racial minorities in the United States experience illness and death at younger ages than whites, and have higher rates of disability that affect labor-force attachment (Bound et al., 1996; Courtney-Long et al., 2017; for review, see Williams, 2012). As well, there are differences in educational attainment between persons with and without disabilities, with lower rates of university completion among those with disabilities, especially among older cohorts (e.g., Arim, 2015). Education is also strongly related to wealth accumulation. To allow us to focus on the long-term economic implications of disability, our models control for race-ethnicity with a variable that compares non-white and white respondents, and for the highest degree completed by respondents, measured as less than a high school degree, high school degree but less than college, and college degree or post-graduate degree.

There are other factors that may affect the relationship between work disability and wealth and that vary over time, including family structure, occupation, and wages (e.g., Brown 2016; Maroto & Pettinicchio, 2020). Because the purpose of the present analysis is illustrative and descriptive rather than explanatory, we include only education and race as two key dimensions of inequality associated with both wealth and health that may be expected to occur causally prior to family structure and employment characteristics.

Analytic Strategy

The life course perspective conceptualizes trajectories as long-term patterns of stability and change that often include multiple transitions (George, 1993, p. 358; Elder et al., 2003). Trajectories can be described, studied, and compared by considering their different qualitative dimensions (see Pavalko, 1997; Clipp et al., 1992). Such qualities include broader patterns defined by characteristics indicating stability or change. For example, trajectories of disability could remain stable following onset or could be intermittent or reversible, with someone moving in and out of work disability over time. Trajectories can also be characterized by their timing, with age of work disability onset representing the life course stage at which someone encounters disadvantage through processes such as social exclusion and disabling social institutions (as discussed above and in Shuey et al., 2016).

Latent class analysis (LCA) is a statistical technique that allows for the modeling of trajectories that capture various dimensions of life course change (Collins & Lanza,

2010; Shuey & Willson, 2014; Taylor & Lynch, 2011). It has been used to examine life course processes such as trajectories of socioeconomic status and health risk (e.g., O'Rand & Hamil-Luker, 2005; Willson & Shuey, 2016), cohort variations in the long-term experiences of disablement (Taylor & Lynch, 2011), and race differences in trajectories of work-limiting health impairments (Pais, 2014). When latent classes are estimated with repeated measures of a single item, such as work disability status, the results are the common trajectories of work disability observed over time, enabling us to identify groups (classes) of individuals who differ in their timing and pattern of work disability during their work life course (Collins & Lanza, 2010; Lanza et al., 2015; Lynch & Taylor, 2016). To empirically examine the relationship between patterns of work disability across the life course and the accumulation of economic disadvantage, we model trajectories of work disability using latent class analysis with PROC LCA in SAS 9.4 (Lanza et al., 2015). In the second stage of the analysis, we include the classes of work disability as independent variables in multinomial logistic regression models predicting wealth quartile at retirement age.

Results

Estimating Work Disability Trajectories

The first step in the analysis is to identify trajectories of work disability and specify the appropriate number of latent classes. Model selection in RMLCA is theoretically motivated and determined by sequentially fitting models, starting with a one class model and continuing until there is a lack of improvement in model fit, based on a combination of statistical criteria, parsimony, and interpretability (Collins & Lanza, 2010). Relative model fit, or the optimal balance of fit and parsimony, is assessed by comparing information criteria associated with each model. The Akaike information criterion (AIC; Akaike, 1987) and the Bayesian information criterion (BIC; Schwarz, 1978) are the two most commonly used tools for model comparison, and for both, a smaller value indicates a better model fit. However, theory and interpretability remain important guides for model fit as AIC and BIC do not always identify the same model as optimal, and they are best used as guides for ruling out models. Models with one through six classes were fit to the data, and our interpretation of the above tests indicated that a four-class model provided the best fit to the data.

RMLCA estimates the proportion of the sample in each latent class, as well as item-response probabilities, which show the association between the indicators of work disability at each time point and the latent classes of work disability. Figure 23.1 plots the item-response probabilities over time by age to visually depict the four latent classes of work disability trajectories—No Work Disability, Early Onset Disability, Midlife Onset Disability, and Episodic Work Disability.

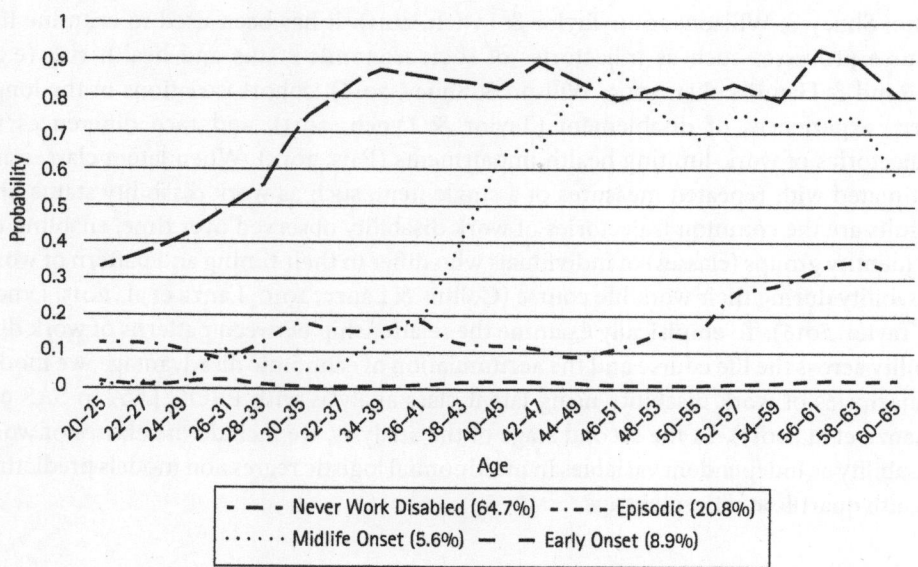

FIGURE 23.1 Item-response probabilities for a four-class longitudinal latent class model of work disability trajectories, panel study of income dynamics (*N* = 1,054).

Most of the sample (64.7%) had a low probability of experiencing a work disability from their 20s to mid-60s. Early onset of work disability was experienced by approximately 9% of the sample; these respondents had an elevated probability of work disability in their early 20s, which rapidly increased into their 30s and was maintained at a high level into their 60s. Approximately 6% of respondents had a low probability of experiencing work disability until their 40s, when the likelihood of reporting a work disability increased sharply and was maintained until respondents entered their 60s (Midlife Onset). For Early Onset and Midlife Onset respondents, the drop in probability of a work disability evident at the end of the observation period could indicate a shift to respondents defining themselves as retired. Finally, approximately 21% of the sample experienced episodic health conditions that limited their ability to work (Episodic Work Disability).

To interpret the item-response probabilities of this latent class, we plotted a random subset of cases and their trajectories of work disability indicated frequent movement in and out of work disability over the analysis period (not shown), resulting in an average probability of work disability that is elevated over the observation period. These findings are similar to trajectories identified by Pais (2014) using the NLSY79.

Table 23.1 presents means and proportions by work disability class (weighted). The Never Work Disabled latent class is more highly educated than the other classes—over half have a college degree compared to less than 20% in the Early Onset latent class and just over 30% in the Episodic and Midlife Onset latent classes. Almost 25% of those in the Early Onset and 20% of those in the Midlife Onset latent classes did not graduate

Table 23.1 Proportions by Disability Trajectory and Wealth Quartile, Weighted. Panel Study of Income Dynamics, (N = 1,054)

	Work Disability Trajectories			
	Never Work Disabled	Episodic	Midlife Onset	Early Onset
Education				
Less than high school	4.60	9.66	21.22	24.07
High school degree	44.80	59.35	42.47	57.01
College degree	50.61	30.99	36.31	18.92
Race-ethnicity				
White	65.19	21.04	6.06	7.71
Non-white	61.17	19.29	2.59	16.95

	Wealth Quartile 1 (highest)	Wealth Quartile 2	Wealth Quartile 3	Wealth Quartile 4 (lowest)	
Work Disability Trajectories					
Never Work Disabled	30.19	26.27	23.51	20.03	100%
Transient	19.10	26.05	26.51	28.34	
Midlife Onset	16.59	21.34	34.00	28.07	
Early Onset	3.91	17.29	26.96	51.84	
Education					
Less than high school	0.00	7.17	37.32	55.51	100%
High school degree	16.27	23.61	26.62	33.50	
College degree	39.27	30.38	20.85	9.49	
Race-ethnicity					
White	27.21	26.72	24.50	21.57	100%
Non-white	7.69	14.08	28.20	49.42	

from high school compared to approximately 5% of those in the Never Work Disabled latent class and 10% of those in the Episodic Work Disability latent class. Non-whites are approximately twice as likely as whites to experience early onset (17% vs. 8%) and midlife onset (6% vs. 2.6%) of work disability in their working years. Similar proportions of whites and non-whites comprise the Episodic Work Disability and Never Work Disabled latent classes.

Bivariate analyses also indicate that long-term patterns of work disability, as well as race-ethnicity and education, influence wealth accumulation at traditional retirement ages (bottom panel of Table 23.1). Among those with early onset work disability, 52% are in the bottom wealth quartile compared to one-fifth of those who never experience a work disability. In contrast, one-third of those who never experience a work disability are in the top wealth quartile. Those with midlife onset or episodic patterns of work disability are more evenly distributed across wealth quartiles, but less likely than the never disabled to be in the top wealth quartile. Results based on education and race-ethnicity are consistent with previous research demonstrating the important role of education in wealth accumulation as well as the large disparities in wealth between whites and non-whites in the United States.

Table 23.2 presents odds ratios from a multinomial logistic regression predicting wealth quartiles including latent classes of work disability trajectories, education, and race-ethnicity. The top wealth quartile is the reference category. Results indicate that, compared to the never disabled, episodic work disability increases the likelihood that one's wealth will fall in the bottom half of the wealth distribution, and compared to the never work disabled, respondents with episodic work disability are almost three times as likely to have wealth in the bottom wealth quartile (quartile 4) than the top (quartile 1). Compared to the never disabled, those with early onset work disability are significantly more likely to be in all other wealth quartiles than the top, and they are almost seven times as likely as the never disabled to fall into the bottom quartile compared to the top quartile. Results suggest that those with midlife onset of work disability are not significantly different from the never disabled in wealth accumulation, although odds ratios suggest that they are less likely to be found in the top wealth quartile.

Table 23.2 Multinomial Logistic Regression Predicting Wealth Quartile, Panel Study of Income Dynamics, (N = 1,054)

	Wealth Quartile 2	Wealth Quartile 3	Wealth Quartile 4
	Odds Ratio	Odds Ratio	Odds Ratio
Work Disability Trajectories (ref=Never Work Disabled)			
Episodic	1.40	1.87*	2.78***
Midlife Onset	1.23	2.48	3.02
Early Onset	2.89***	3.93***	6.74***
Education (ref=Less than college degree)			
College degree	0.46***	0.24***	0.11***
Race-ethnicity (ref=White)			
Nonwhite	1.91*	5.05***	10.62***

Note: Wealth quartile 1 (highest wealth) is the reference category.
* $p<.05$;
** $p<.01$;
*** $p<.001$.

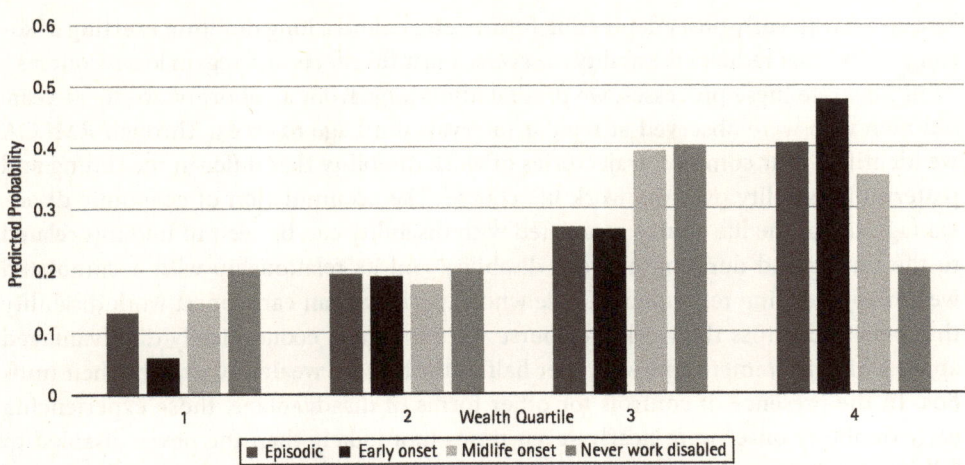

FIGURE 23.2 Predicted probabilities of wealth quartile by work disability latent class, panel study of income dynamics ($N = 1{,}054$).

To further illustrate these findings, predicted probabilities of location in each of the wealth quartiles are presented in Figure 23.2 (calculated from Table 23.2, model 1). Probabilities across the wealth quartiles vary considerably. Respondents who were never work disabled are approximately 70% more likely to have wealth accumulation that falls into the top quartile (quartile 1) than those with early onset work disability (20% vs. 6%), and in turn, those with early onset work disability are almost 60% more likely than the never work disabled to be in the bottom quartile (quartile 4; 48% vs. 20%). Those with midlife onset work disability are 42% more likely to be located in quartile 4 than the never work disabled (35% vs. 20%) and those with episodic work disability are twice as likely.

DISCUSSION

Theories on the accumulative nature of disadvantage across the life course suggest that, as with other forms of disadvantage, experiencing disability during the working years shapes wealth accumulation and sets the stage for economic precarity that continues into old age. Understanding this process of accumulation is complicated by the often fluid nature of disability with some individuals entering and exiting disability multiple times over the life course, as well as its intersection with other structures of social stratification and inequality that also impact both wealth and health. Temporal aspects of disability, including timing and duration, affect the potential economic consequences of disability. The cumulative dis/advantage tradition suggests that both early and long-term exposure to disability have deleterious effects on the accumulation of economic resources, with early onset depressing future returns and a long duration exerting a "social gravity" that reduces the ability to reverse harmful effects and regain lost resources.

To illustrate these processes, we presented findings from a cohort of 20- to 25-year-old men who were observed at regular intervals until age 62 to 65. Through RMLCA we identified four common trajectories of work disability that differ in the timing and pattern of disability over the work life course. The accumulation of economic disadvantage across the life course associated with disability can be seen in findings related to the timing and duration of work disability and its relationship with accumulated wealth approaching retirement. Those who experienced an early onset work disability that persisted across the work life course were the most economically disadvantaged approaching retirement age, with over half in the bottom wealth quartile by their mid-60s. In the presence of controls for other forms of disadvantage, those experiencing early disability onset were nearly seven times more likely than the never disabled to fall into the bottom wealth quartile. In comparison, midlife onset was not as harmful to asset accumulation as disability experienced early on and in fact, the midlife onset group was not significantly different from those who were never disabled in terms of the measure of wealth accumulation used here. Experiencing episodic work disability (off and on multiple times over the work life course), however, does have harmful effects on wealth accumulation, with individuals following this trajectory almost three times more likely than the never work disabled to have wealth in the bottom wealth quartile. Overall, both early onset and episodic groups were less likely than the never disabled to be in the top wealth quartile.

In the present descriptive analysis, the mechanisms through which disadvantage associated with disability initiates and accumulates are not identifiable. Is wealth disadvantage primarily driven by the loss of income associated with labor market exit, job switching, or part-time employment? There is some evidence to suggest this is the case (see, e.g., Clarke & Latham, 2014; Maroto & Pettinicchio, 2020). In addition, different mechanisms of inequality and exclusion are salient across the various stages of the work life course, with disability trajectories characterized by early onset potentially involving additional discrimination in hiring, training, promotion, and wage growth—all likely contributing to a more enduring impact on wealth accumulation associated with early rather than midlife onset disability.

As there is much research on the importance of interlocking forms of disadvantage, it is likely that the opportunities for wealth accumulation associated with various trajectories of disability will vary along other dimensions of disadvantage, such as social class, gender, and race/immigrant status—inequalities that also affect the opportunity for wealth accumulation more generally. For example, midlife disability onset may have less of an impact on wealth accumulation for more advantaged workers who have already had the opportunity to amass savings over a large portion of their work lives, or for married women, who have historically had a looser attachment to the labor market. Also, of particular interest is the episodic work disability latent class, which made up approximately 21% of our sample. The inclusion of other dimensions, such as disability severity and occupational location, could help us to understand the disadvantage experienced by this group. In sum, the findings here suggest the importance of the timing and duration of work disability for the accumulation of wealth. Work disability, particularly when early or episodic, contributes to wealth inequality in later life, and more work is needed to add the additional nuance that is important to this complex story. The life course perspective and theories of cumulative dis/advantage provide a valuable framework for this research.

References

Akaike, H. (1987). Factor analysis and AIC. *Psychometrika, 52*, 317–332.

Arim, R. (2015). A profile of persons with disabilities among Canadians aged 15 years or older, 2012. Statistics Canada Publication 89-654-X. http://www.statcan.gc.ca/pub/89-654-x/89-654-x2015001-eng.htm

Baldwin, M. L., & Schumacher, E. J. (2002). A note on job mobility among workers with disabilities. *Industrial Relations, 41*, 430–441. https://doi.org/10.1111/1468-232X.00255

Bhutta, N., Chang, A. C., Dettling, L. J., & Hsu, J. W. (2020). Disparities in wealth by race and ethnicity in the 2019 Survey of Consumer Finances. Fed Notes. https://www.federalreserve.gov/econres/notes/feds-notes/disparities-in-wealth-by-race-and-ethnicity-in-the-2019-survey-of-consumer-finances-20200928.htm

Boen, C. (2016). The role of socioeconomic factors in Black-White health inequalities across the life course: Point-in-time measures, long-term exposures, and differential health return. *Social Science & Medicine, 170*, 63–76.

Boen, C., Keister, L., & Aronson, B. (2020). Beyond net worth: Racial differences in wealth portfolios and black-white health inequality across the life course. *Journal of Health and Social Behavior*, online first May 23, 2020.

Bound, J., Schoenbaum, M., & Waidmann, T. (1996). Race differences in labor force attachment and disability status. *The Gerontologist, 36*(3), 311–321.

Brown, T. H. (2016). Diverging fortunes: Racial/ethnic inequality in wealth trajectories in middle and late life. *Race and Social Problems, 8*(1), 29–41.

Clarke, P., & Latham, K. (2014). Life course health and socioeconomic profiles of Americans aging with disability. *Disability and Health Journal, 7*, S15–S23. https://doi.org/10.1016/j.dhjo.2013.08.008

Clipp, E. C., Pavalko, E. K., & Elder, G. H., Jr. (1992). Trajectories of health: In concept and empirical pattern. *Behavior, Health, and Aging, 2*(3), 159–179.

Collins, L. M., & Lanza, S. T. (2010). *Latent class and latent transition analysis.* Wiley.

Courtney-Long, E. A., Romano, S. D., Carroll, D. D., & Fox, M. H. (2017). Socioeconomic factors at the intersection of race and ethnicity influencing health risks for people with disabilities. *Journal of Racial and Ethnic Health Disparities, 4*, 213. https://doi.org/10.1007/s40615-016-0220-5

Crystal, S., & Shea, D. (1990). Cumulative advantage, cumulative disadvantage, and inequality among elderly people. *The Gerontologist, 30*, 437–443. https://doi.org/10.1093/geront/30.4.437

Dannefer, D. (1987). Aging as intercohort differentiation: Accentuation, the Matthew effect, and the life course. *Sociological Forum, 2*, 211–236. https://doi.org/10.1007/BF01124164

Dannefer, D. (2003). Cumulative advantage/disadvantage and the life course: cross-fertilizing age and social science theory. *The Journals of Gerontology, Series B: Psychological Sciences and Social Sciences, 58*, S327–S337. https://doi.org/10.1093/geronb/58.6.s327

Deeg, D. J. H. (2005). Longitudinal characterization of course types of functional limitations. *Disability and Rehabilitation, 27,* 253–261. https://doi.org/10.1080/09638280400006507

Diprete, T. A., & Eirich, G. M. (2006). Cumulative advantage as a mechanism for inequality: A review of theoretical and empirical developments. *Annual Review of Sociology, 32,* 271–297.

Elder, G. H., Jr., Johnson, M. K., & Crosnoe, R. (2003). The emergence and development of life course theory. In J. Mortimer & M. Shanahan (Eds.), *Handbook of the life course* (pp. 3–19). Kluwer Academic/Plenum Publishers. https://doi.org/10.1007/978-0-306-48247-2_1

Erickson, W., Lee, C., & von Schrader, S. (2015). Disability statistics from the 2013 American Community Survey (ACS). Cornell University Yang Tan Institute (YTI).

Ferraro, K. F., & Kelley-Moore, J. A. (2003). Cumulative disadvantage and health: Long-term consequences of obesity? *American Sociological Review, 68,* 707–729.

Ferraro, K. F., & Shippee, T. P. (2009). Aging and cumulative inequality: How does inequality get under the skin? *The Gerontologist, 49,* 333–343. https://doi.org/10.1093/geront/gnp034

Fitzgerald, J. (2011). Attrition in models of intergenerational links in health and economic status in the PSID. *The B.E. Journal of Economic Analysis & Policy, 11,* 1–61. http://doi.org/10.2202/1935-1682.2868

George, L. K. (1993). Sociological perspective on life transitions. *Annual Review of Sociology, 19,* 353–373. https://doi.org/10.1146/annurev.so.19.080193.002033

Haas, S. A. (2006). Health selection and the process of social stratification: The effect of childhood health on socioeconomic attainment. *Journal of Health and Social Behavior, 47,* 339–354. https://doi.org/10.1177%2F002214650604700403

Haas, S. A., Glymour, M. M., & Berkman, L. F. (2011). Childhood health and labor market inequality over the life course. *Journal of Health and Social Behavior, 52,* 298–313. https://doi.org/10.1177%2F0022146511410431

Heymann, J., Stein, M. A., & de Elvira Moreno, M. R. (2014). Disability, employment, and inclusion worldwide. In J. Heymann, M. A. Stein, & M. R. de Elvira Moreno (Eds.), *Disability and Equity at Work* (pp. 1–9). Oxford University Press.

Kelley-Moore, J. (2010). Disability and ageing: The social construction of causality. In D. Dannefer & C. Phillipson (Eds.), *The Sage Handbook of Social Gerontology* (pp. 96–110). SAGE Publications. http://dx.doi.org/10.4135/9781446200933.n7

Laditka, S. B., & Laditka, J. N. (2002). Recent perspectives on active life expectancy for older women. *Journal of Women & Aging, 14*(1/2), 163–184.

Lanza, S. T., Dziak, J. J., Huang, L., Xu, S., & Collins, L. M. (2015). *Proc LCA and Proc LTA users' guide (Version 1.3.2).* The Methodology Center, Penn State. http://methodology.psu.edu

Lauer, E. A., & Houtenville, A. J. (2017). *Annual disability statistics compendium: 2016.* University of New Hampshire, Institute on Disability.

Liang, J., Xu, X., Bennett, J. M., Ye, W., & Quiñones, A. R. (2009). Ethnicity and changing functional health in middle and late life: A person-centered approach. *The Journals of Gerontology, Series B: Psychological Sciences and Social Sciences, 65,* S470–S481. https://doi.org/10.1093/geronb/gbp114

Lynch, S. M., & Taylor, M. G. (2016). Trajectory models in aging research. In L. K. George & K. F. Ferraro (Eds.), *Handbook of Aging and the Social Sciences* (8th ed., pp. 23–51). Academic Press.

Maroto, M. L., & Pettinicchio, D. (2014). Disability, structural inequality, and work: The influence of occupational segregation on earnings for people with different disabilities. *Research in Social Stratification and Mobility, 38,* 76–92.

Maroto, M. L. (2016). Fifteen years of wealth disparities in Canada: New trends or simply the status quo? *Canadian Public Policy*, 42(2), 152–167.

Maroto, M. L., & Pettinicchio, D. (2015). Twenty-five years after the ADA: Situating disability in America's system of stratification. *Disability Studies Quarterly*, 35, 1–34.

Maroto, M. L., & Pettinicchio, D. (2020). Barriers to economic security: Disability, employment, and asset disparities in Canada. *SSRN Electronic Journal* http://dx.doi.org/10.2139/ssrn.3532036

McDonough, P., & Berglund, P. (2003). Histories of poverty and self-rated health trajectories. *Journal of Health and Social Behavior*, 44(2), 198–214.

Nagi, S. (1991). Disability concepts revisited: Implications to prevention. In A. M. Pope & A. R. Tarlove (Eds.), *Disability in America: Toward a national agenda for prevention* (pp. 307–327). National Academy Press.

Nusselder, W. J., Looman, C. W. N., & Mackenback, J. P. (2006). The level and time course of disability: Trajectories of disability in adults and young elderly. *Disability and Rehabilitation*, 28(16), 1015–1026. https://doi.org/10.1080/09638280500493803

Oliver, M. (1996). *Understanding disability: From theory to practice*. Macmillan.

Oliver, M., & Barnes, C. (2012). *The New Politics of Disablement*. Palgrave Macmillan.

Oliver, M. L., & T. M. Shapiro. 2006. *Black wealth/White wealth*. Routledge.

O'Rand, A. M. (1996). The precious and the precocious: understanding cumulative disadvantage and cumulative advantage over the life course. *The Gerontologist*, 36(2), 230–238. https://doi.org/10.1093/geront/36.2.230

O'Rand, A. M. (2006). Stratification and the life course: Life course capital, life course risks, and social inequality. In R. H. Binstock & L. K. George (Eds.), *Handbook of Aging and the Social Sciences* (6th ed., pp. 145–162). Academic Press. https://doi.org/10.1016/B978-012088388-2/50012-2

O'Rand, A. (2009). Cumulative processes in the life course. In G. H. Elder, Jr., & J. Giele (Eds.), *The Craft of Life Course Research* (pp. 121–140). SAGE Publications.

O'Rand, A. M., & Hamil-Luker, J. (2005). Processes of cumulative adversity: Childhood disadvantage and increased risk of heart attack across the life course. *The Journals of Gerontology, Series B, Psychological Sciences and Social Sciences*, 60(Ii), 117–124.

Pais, J. (2014). Cumulative structural disadvantage and racial health disparities: The pathways of childhood socioeconomic influence. *Demography*, 51, 1729–1753. https://doi.org/10.1007/s13524-014-0330-9

Panel Study of Income Dynamics. (2019). Public use dataset produced and distributed by the Institute for Social Research, University of Michigan, Ann Arbor, MI.

Pavalko, E. K. (1997). Beyond trajectories: Multiple concepts for analyzing long-term process. In M. Hardy (Ed.), *Studying Aging and Social Change* (pp. 129–147). Sage Publications.

Priestley, M. (2005). Disability and social inequalities. In M. Romero & E. Margolis (Eds.), *The Blackwell Companion to Social Inequalities* (pp. 372–395). Blackwell. https://doi.org/10.1002/9780470996973.ch17

Putnam, M. (2002). Linking aging theory and disability models: Increasing the potential to explore aging with physical impairment. *The Gerontologist*, 42, 799–806. https://doi.org/10.1093/geront/42.6.799

Rank, M. R., & Hirschl, T. A. (2014). The risk of developing a work disability across the adulthood years. *Disability and Health Journal*, 7, 189–195. https://doi.org/10.1016/j.dhjo.2013.12.001

Schur, L. (2003). Barriers or opportunities? The causes of contingent and part-time work among people with disabilities. *Industrial Relations, 42*, 589–622. https://doi.org/10.1111/1468-232X.00308

Schur, L., Kruse, D., Blasi, J., & Blanck, P. (2009). Is disability disabling in all workplaces? Workplace disparities and corporate culture. *Industrial Relations, 48*, 381–410. https://doi.org/10.1111/j.1468-232X.2009.00565.x

Schwarz, G. (1978). Estimating the dimension of a model. *Annals of Statistics, 6*(2), 461–464.

Shuey, K. M., Willson, A. E., & Bouchard, K. (2016). Disability and social inequality in Canada. In E. Grabb & N. Guppy (Eds.), *Social inequality in Canada: Dimensions of Disadvantage* (6th ed., pp. 258–273). Oxford University Press.

Shuey, K., & Willson, A. (2014). Economic hardship in childhood and adult health trajectories: An alternative approach to investigating life-course processes. *Advances in Life Course Research, 22*, 49–61. https://doi.org/10.1016/j.alcr.2014.05.001

Shuey, K. M., & Willson, A. E. (2019). Trajectories of work disability and economic insecurity approaching retirement. *The Journals of Gerontology, Series B: Psychological Sciences and Social Sciences, 74*(7), 1200–1210.

Taylor, M. (2011). The causal pathway from socioeconomic status to disability trajectories in later life: The importance of mediating mechanisms for onset and accumulation. *Research on Aging, 33*(1), 84–108. http://dx.doi.org/10.1177/0164027510385011

Taylor, M. G., & Lynch, S. M. (2011). Cohort differences and chronic disease profiles of differential disability trajectories. *The Journals of Gerontology, Series B: Psychological Sciences and Social Sciences, 66*, 6, S729–S738. https://doi.org/10.1093/geronb/gbr104

Verbrugge, L. M., & Jette, A. M. (1994). The disablement process. *Social Science & Medicine, 38*, 1–14. https://doi.org/10.1016/0277-9536(94)90294-1

Verbrugge, L. M., Latham, K., & Clarke, P. J. (2017). Aging with disability for midlife and older adults. *Research on Aging, 39*(6), 741–777 https://doi.org/10.1177%2F0164027516681051

Warner, D. F., & Brown, T. H. (2011). Understanding how race/ethnicity and gender define age-trajectories of disability: An intersectionality approach. *Social Science & Medicine, 72*, 1236–1248.

Warren, J. R. (2009). Socioeconomic status and health across the life course: A test of the social causation and health selection hypotheses. *Social Forces, 87*, 2125–2153. https://doi.org/10.1353/sof.0.0219

Williams, D. R. (2012). Miles to go before we sleep: Racial Inequalities in health. *Journal of Health and Social Behavior, 53*(3), 279–295.

Willson, A. E., & Shuey, K. M. (2016). Life course pathways of economic hardship and mobility and midlife trajectories of health. *Journal of Health and Social Behavior, 57*(3), 407–422. https://doi.org/10.1177%2F0022146516660345

Willson, A. E., Shuey, K. M., & Elder, G. H., Jr. (2007). Cumulative advantage processes as mechanisms of inequality in life Course health. *American Journal of Sociology, 112*(6), 1886–1924.

Wolf, D. A., Freedman, V. A., Ondrich, J. I., Seplaki, C. L., & Spillman, B. C. (2015). Disability trajectories at the end of life: A "countdown" model. *The Journals of Gerontology, Series B: Psychological Sciences and Social Sciences, 70*, 5, S745–S752. https://doi.org/10.1093/geronb/gbu182

PART VII

Stigma, Discrimination, and Systems of Inequality

CHAPTER 24

EVOLVING PERSPECTIVES ON DISABILITY, STIGMA, AND DISCRIMINATION

ROBYN LEWIS BROWN AND EVAN BATTY

INTRODUCTION

PEOPLE with disabilities experience a dichotomy of persisting bias and social progress. On the one hand, they continue to face considerable challenges. In the United States, for example, people with disabilities earn less, are more likely to be unemployed, experience higher levels of stress and greater material hardship, and are involved in fewer social activities than their non-disabled peers, on average (Iezzoni et al., 2001; National Council on Disability, 2008; Shandra, 2018; Weil et al., 2002). Public-opinion research also indicates that common views toward persons with disabilities are devaluing. For example, a US national opinion poll conducted in 2000 found that 60% of those surveyed felt that persons with disabilities have little influence in society, and 65% said there is some or a lot of prejudice and discrimination against persons with disabilities (Kaiser Public Opinion Spotlights, 2004). More recently, about half (48%) of those responding to a national opinion poll about the Americans with Disabilities Act indicated that they oppose workplace accommodations for people with disabilities (Lake, 2016).

While these examples highlight disability as a potent form of social disadvantage, there is also clear indication that conditions for people with disabilities have improved and are continuing to improve. Over the past several decades, people with disabilities and their advocates have challenged political ideologies, advanced civil rights, and questioned the medical field's practical limits, shifting both public and scholarly attention to the prevention of illness rather than the restoration of health, and holistic approaches to health that promote personal efficacy and stress management (Albrecht & Verbrugge, 2000). Because of these important advances, individuals with disabilities have gained social acceptance and achieved considerable autonomy in personal and public spheres. This is supported, for example, by a 1999 US national opinion poll, which found that 82% of those surveyed felt that the quality of life of persons with disabilities has improved in the past 50 years (Pew Research Center 1999). Similarly, most US adults think people should not face discrimination in public places on the basis of disability (90%) and that employers should not discriminate against qualified candidates on the basis of a disability (88%) (Harris Poll, 2015).

The dual indications that people with disabilities are achieving social progress and that some degree of social devaluation toward persons with disabilities continue to highlight some of the lasting effects of ableism. Friedman and Owen (2017) define ableism as thus: "Ableism, like other 'isms' such as racism and sexism, describes discrimination towards a social group, in this case disabled people, but it also describes how certain ideals and attributes are valued or not valued." They, and others, have linked social norms concerning people's bodies and minds with discriminatory experiences at the micro, meso, and macro levels (Campbell, 2009; Friedman & Owen, 2017).

Extending this literature, the central theme of this chapter is that efforts to meaningfully address ableism, and the constraints it poses for the life experiences and opportunities of people with disabilities, must confront enduring forms of discrimination *and* the feelings of personal devaluation (i.e., stigmatization) it engenders. To better contextualize this critical point, this chapter first provides an abridged social and sociological history of stigma and discrimination toward people with disabilities. This discussion draws from the two-tiered construct introduced by disabled activists in the 1970s that, as noted elsewhere in this handbook, differentiates "impairment," or the presence of a biological condition, from "disability," which refers to the inability of a society to meet or address the needs of people with impairments (UPIAS, 1975). This definition of impairment, which initially signified only physical conditions, has been expanded to include intellectual, behavioral, and psychological conditions to match the World Health Organization's definition of disability and legal definitions used in federal and state policies (Barnes, 2000).

There appears to be less clear endorsement for an expanded definition of disability in general populations, however. For example, the 2015 Harris Poll indicates that the majority of US adults agree that blindness, cerebral palsy, deafness or hearing loss, and multiple sclerosis should be legally considered a disability, whereas less than half think schizophrenia (46%), depression (29%), or drug or alcohol dependence (10%) should be legally considered a disability (Harris Poll, 2015). Psychological and behavioral disabilities have also received comparatively little theoretical and empirical attention in research on disability relative to physical and developmental impairments (Beresford, 2000; Lewis, 2006; Price, 2011). To this point, in the latter part of this chapter we argue that academic efforts to address ableism will be incomplete if they do not engage with disabilities in their various forms, including the coexistence of multiple disabilities. We draw on work concerning psychiatric disability to illustrate several consequences of underinclusion, and discuss challenges in incorporating physical, psychological and intellectual conditions into a more universal conception of impairment. We conclude by outlining an intersectional approach to the study of stigma and discrimination that acknowledges comorbidity of impairment conditions within a sociology of disabilities framework.

A Semi-brief Social and Sociological History

A Long History of Hardship

General distinctions have been drawn between individuals with physical, intellectual, and psychological impairments and those without since antiquity. Historical accounts provide poignant examples of the pervasive devaluation of persons identified as disabled, illustrating that societies have long expressed ambiguity, at best, as well as derision toward persons with a variety of impairments (for reviews, see Braddock & Parish, 2003; Longmore, 2000, 2003). For example, Braddock and Parish (2003) suggest that the texts of the Old Testament/Hebrew Bible reflect mixed feelings toward individuals with disabilities since ancient times. On the one hand, disability was feared and viewed as a manifestation of the wrath of God, as is evident in the edict from Deuteronomy, "If you do not carefully follow His commands and decrees . . . all these curses will come upon you and overtake you; the Lord will afflict you with madness, blindness and confusion of mind" (Deuteronomy 28:15, 28–29). On the other hand, individuals with disabilities were also viewed with sympathy and as persons worthy of charity, as is reflected in the Leviticus command, "Thou shalt not curse the deaf nor put a stumbling block before the blind, nor maketh the blind to wander out of the path" (Leviticus 19:14).

Such a sense of ambiguity apparently persisted into the early modern period (Braddock & Parish, 2003; Longmore, 2000). The Renaissance and period of Enlightenment brought advancing scientific methods to bear on the experience of disability (Braddock & Parish, 2003; Longmore, 2000, 2003). The proliferation of scientific inquiry during this time can be characterized by the development of increasingly complex classifications of physical impairments and treatment regiments, as well as the waning belief that disability resulted from supernatural forces (Braddock & Parish, 2003; Longmore, 2000, 2003). As Longmore (2000) has argued, the emerging medicalization of physical disability was intended to rehabilitate individuals with disabilities so that they could fulfill social and occupational roles. However, in practice, the crude rehabilitation services then available had limited success, thus often reifying notions of persons with disabilities as incompetent in core roles. Braddock and Parish (2003) further remark that, in the United States, persons with disabilities were often viewed as threats to the economic viability of communities in the extent to which they were unable to perform occupational roles. As a consequence, families commonly auctioned off the care of persons with disabilities (Braddock & Parish, 2003). Banishing persons with disabilities from their homes and communities was also common in this period of history (Braddock & Parish, 2003).

Gallagher (1985) suggests that considerable social devaluation toward persons with physical disabilities persisted well into the early twentieth century because of stigmatizing beliefs upheld by the field of medicine. As an illustration, Gallagher (1985) cites an influential orthopedic text from 1911, which suggested that "a failure in the moral training of the cripple means the evolution of an individual detestable in character, a menace and burden to the community, who is only too apt to graduate into the mendicant and criminal classes" (Gallagher, 1985, p. 30). Consistent with medical views, individuals with disabilities, broadly defined, were viewed as morally inferior and separated from mainstream society (Gallagher, 1985; Tyor & Bell, 1984), "kept at home, out of sight, in back bedrooms, by families who felt a mixture of embarrassment and shame about their presence" (Gallagher, 1985, p. 29).

Entering the Modern Era

The United States's entry into World War I is cited as influential in changing medical perceptions of physical disabilities, as the permanent impairments sustained by veterans in the name of national service could not readily be attributed to personal deficiencies or a lack of moral character (Braddock & Parish, 2003; Longmore, 2000). Rehabilitation services for persons with physical impairments were vastly improved throughout the first half of the twentieth century (Braddock & Parish, 2003); yet, it is suggested that the improved services were accompanied by increased expectations that medicine could "cure" poor health (Freund & McGuire, 1995; Longmore, 2000). This meant that, for individuals who experienced chronic impairments, clear socially sanctioned exemptions from normal social obligations were typically not made (Braddock & Parish, 2003; Freund & McGuire, 1995).

Indeed, while medical practitioners adopted increasingly scientific rather than moralistic understandings of disability, general social views were slower to change. As an illustration, into the 1960s, "ugly laws" in American cities prohibited the "diseased, maimed, mutilated or in any way deformed" from public places (Kleinfeld, 1977, p. 35). Sociological viewpoints occupied a somewhat intermediary position. Parsons' (1951) description of the "sick role," for example, is consistent with a rehabilitation-based understanding of physical impairment, but also addresses disability as a potential form of social deviance. This theory reflects a somewhat idealized understanding of poor health as a temporary exemption from normal social obligations contingent upon an individual's willingness to seek treatment and become well (Parsons, 1951). Parsons elaborated:

> The sick role is a mechanism which channels deviance so that the two most dangerous potentialities, namely group formation and successful establishment of the claim of legitimacy, are avoided. The sick are tied up, not with other deviants to form

a "subculture" of the sick, but each with a group of nonsick, his personal circle, and, above all, physicians. The sick thus become a statistical status and are deprived of the possibility of forming a solidary collectivity.

(Parsons, 1951, p. 477)

While Parsons saw disability as temporary and clearly not a social category, Goffman (1963) conceptualized disability as a more enduring category of identity. Although Goffman provides a general assessment of stigma in the book *Stigma*, two of the three categories of stigmatization he proposes derive from physical or mental impairments, and he devotes considerable attention to stigma resulting from disability or, more broadly, "abominations of the body" (Cahill & Eggleston, 1995; Goffman, 1963; Susman, 1994). Goffman (1963) observed disability to be a deeply discrediting social identity characterized by often insurmountable interpersonal difficulties that challenge individuals' fundamental sense of value and worth (Goffman, 1963). Goffman (1963) also suggested that it is not the experience of an impairment that poses the greatest challenge to persons with disabilities but, rather, being distinguished as a "disabled person" because of the social devaluation that accompanies this social status.

What is perhaps most striking in considering the enduring influence of *Stigma* is that subsequent early work on disability did not question the application of negative labels to individuals with disabilities, and assumed that negative consequences would result (Cahill & Eggleston, 1995; Joachim & Acorn, 2000; Miller & Major, 2000; Susman, 1994). Fine and Asch (1988), for example, remark that much research assumed that disability is central to a disabled person's self-concept and social comparisons and took for granted that disability is synonymous with lacking social support. This is despite the social milieu of the civil rights movements of the 1960s, which encouraged political organizing among people with various physical impairments for the cause of disability rights (Braddock & Parish, 2003; Longmore, 2003).

Making Progress

Advocacy groups for disability rights emerged in the late 19th century, most notably among deaf rights activists, but collective action for the rights of individuals with disabilities did not gain widespread momentum until the 1970s (Braddock & Parish, 2003; Cahill & Eggleston, 1995; Longmore, 2000, 2003; Silverstein, 2000). The extent to which this shift toward activism was historically significant cannot be understated—as Charlton (1998, p. 24) notes, "People with disabilities, at least as a group, may have been the first to join the ranks of the underclass. Since feudalism and even earlier, they have lived outside the economy and political process."

Although it is beyond the scope of this chapter to describe disability social movements in depth, several key developments in the United States forecast our understanding of stigma and discrimination today. Advocacy groups championed Congress's passing of Section 504 of the Rehabilitation Act in 1973, which prohibited discrimination against persons with disabilities by any entity that received federal funds, and, later, the Americans with Disabilities Act (ADA) of 1990, which banned discrimination against persons with disabilities in employment and public accommodations (Braddock & Parish, 2003; Cahill & Eggleston, 1995; Kudlick, 2003; National Council on Disability, 1997). The disability rights movement has also been instrumental in challenging cultural belief systems that reify notions of impairment as abnormal or deficient (Davis, 1999; Kudlick, 2003; Shakespeare, 1997). This is reflected, in part, in the discrepancy between viewing physical impairment as an abnormality as opposed to a normal aspect of life for many and a typical part of the aging process for most (Davis, 1999). The movement has been further instrumental in addressing alienation or feelings of demoralization among people with disabilities across various spheres of life (Charlton, 1998; Davis, 1999; Pfeiffer, 2002). This is evident, for example, in the now relatively standard use of "people first" language to describe or communicate about people with various impairments or disabilities (i.e., a person with epilepsy as opposed to an epileptic, or person who uses a wheelchair as opposed to a handicapped or crippled). Reclaiming one's sense of agency and autonomy in clinical encounters has, moreover, been a catalyst for activism in its own right (Charlton, 1998).

It is perhaps not surprising, thus, that since the late 1980s, as scholarly considerations increasingly adapted an "insider's perspective" on the experience of disability, research on disability has also increasingly departed from the conceptualization of disability as inherently stigmatizing (Brown, 2015; Cahill & Eggleston, 1995; Charmaz, 2000; Miller & Major, 2000; Susman, 1994). This has been a slow shift rather than a radical one. For example, a meta-analysis of 20 qualitative studies conducted during the 1980s indicates that research on disability during this time overwhelmingly focused on negative adaptational outcomes among persons with disabilities, such as interpersonal difficulties, a diminished sense of self-worth, and psychological suffering (Thorne & Paterson, 1998).

Research since the 1990s has provided a more detailed acknowledgment of the potential for variation in experiences of disability and its consequences. This orientation derives, in part, from the rejection of the medical model of disability and other deficit models by disability scholars (Davis, 1999; Pfeiffer, 2002; Swain & French, 2000). Also noteworthy is more recent study directly challenging earlier scholarship, such as Goffman's work on stigma. One current thread of scholarship, for example, emphasizes that it is inappropriate to assume that persons with disabilities necessarily experience social stigma and suffer emotional distress as a consequence. This research provides compelling evidence that, contrary to prior views, there is considerable variation in experiences of stigmatization or social devaluation among people with disabilities (Brown, 2015; Crocker, Major, & Steele, 1998; Diener & Diener, 1995; Friedman & Brownell, 1995; Miller & Major, 2000). Specifically, this research shows that, while some people with disabilities do recognize stigma and discrimination as enduring strains in their lives, others report very low levels of social devaluation, and still others raise the possibility of experiencing disability without stigma altogether (Brown, 2015; Lock

& Scheper-Hughes, 1996; Hughes & Paterson 1997; Major, 1994; Paterson et al., 1999; Scheer & Groce, 1988; Susman, 1994).

Further research has considered the potential for positive adaptation to disability, which is reflected in research documenting a positive restructuring of social relationships and personal identity following the onset of an impairment (Major, 1994; Thorne & Paterson, 1998; see also Charmaz, 1983, 2000; Kadner, 1989), as well as work indicting that people with disabilities draw on various resources and metaphors to cope with experiences of discrimination and maintain a positive sense of self-worth (Charmaz, 2002; Cooper & Burnside, 1996; Miller & Major, 2000; Woloshin, Schwartz, & Tosteson, 1997). There is also some indication that people with disabilities can experience both social acceptance and social rejection simultaneously, and that these experiences will have varying effects on one's sense of self and quality of life (Bodgan & Taylor, 1987; Brown, 2015; Cahill & Eggleston, 1995).

Indeed, some recent scholarship challenges the notion that a disability must be associated with diminished quality of life altogether. This is exemplified in research demonstrating that persons with disabilities, in fact, often report very positive levels of life satisfaction despite discriminatory experiences (Crocker, Major, & Steele, 1998; Diener & Diener, 1995; Friedman & Brownell, 1995; Miller & Major 2000). This work demonstrates that it is inappropriate to assume that persons with disabilities necessarily experience social stigma and devaluation and suffer emotional distress as a consequence (Bogdan & Taylor, 1987; Brown, 2015; Crocker et al., 1998; Thorne & Paterson, 1998). To the contrary, research suggests that there is considerable variation in disability-related stigma and discrimination and their personal relevance (Charmaz, 2000; Kadner, 1989; Major, 1994).

Current Reckonings

It must also be acknowledged, however, that this body of work has primarily focused on experiences of physical disability as opposed to intellectual, psychological, and behavioral forms of impairment. It has long been recognized that there is a hierarchy of preference toward disability groups (Thomas, 2000; Tringo, 1970) that is said to privilege people with physical disabilities over those with intellectual or psychiatric disabilities. Tringo's (1970) influential work on this topic, for example, assessed perceived social distance from various disability groups based on one's willingness to marry, accept as a close kin by marriage, have as a next door neighbor or casual friend, or alternately keep away from, keep in an institution, send out of the country, or put to death. This work found that people report the least social distance from individuals with various chronic health conditions such as arthritis, asthma, diabetes, and heart disease, greater distance from people with intellectual disabilities and the greatest social distancing from people with psychiatric disabilities (Tringo, 1970). This set of findings has been replicated numerous times over several decades (e.g., Thomas, 2000). Some have suggested that this hierarchy extends to the field of disability studies itself (Thomas, 2007). This is a key area in which sociologists of disability can address ableism.

With respect to scholarship on psychological disability, for example, psychiatric viewpoints have tended to play a more tenuous role within disability research than perspectives from other social and behavioral sciences, and tensions have persisted over the tendency of psychiatrists and psychologists to view physical and developmental disabilities as abnormal, deficient, or deviant (Asch, 1984; Gleeson, 1997; Olkin & Pledger, 2003; Thorne & Paterson, 1998). Nevertheless, when psychological disability or "poor mental health" more generally is discussed in the context of disabilities, it tends to be cited as a worst-case outcome of physical disability or disabling social environments (Jones & Brown, 2012). This approach fails to distinguish psychological distress from psychological diversity and may, in fact, serve to strengthen the framing of psychological disabilities as entirely negative outcomes of (physical) disability-related oppression and disadvantage, rather than equivalent instances of human variation and diversity. To be sure, a challenge to the discipline is not only the framing of physical, psychological, intellectual, and behavioral conditions by researchers and practitioners in the field, but also the absence of a more universal conception of impairment. The more basic point for the field put forth here is that the exclusion or underinclusion of certain disabilities within the discipline is ableist, and has negative consequences for scholarship and, ultimately, those who are underrepresented.

TOWARD A FRAMEWORK OF INCLUSION?

As an illustration of the negative consequences of underrepresentation, one striking difference between the literature on disability, generally defined, and that which is specific to psychological disability is that social models of psychological disability do not have the prominent role within discourses on psychiatric issues that social models of physical disability occupy. Emphasis is placed instead on biomedical understandings of psychological disorder, particularly in the case of serious psychological disabilities such as schizophrenia, schizoaffective disorder, bipolar disorder, or major depressive disorder.

A Largely Unchallenged Biomedical Perspective

A number of scholars have suggested that the lack of attention to social or psychological models of mental illness has influenced the more widespread acceptance of medically derived understandings of psychological disability (Horwitz, 2003; Luhrmann, 2000; Schwartz & Corcoran, 2010). Somewhat paradoxically, medical models of psychiatric disability were slower to find acceptance because early psychodynamic theories of mental illness rooted in psychotherapeutic approaches were highly varied (Horwitz, 2003; Luhrmann, 2000). However, the psychiatric disease models that emerged in the 1950s (e.g., Lewis, 1953) led to the development of more uniform diagnostic criteria such as that provided by the Diagnostic and Statistical Manual of Mental Disorders (DSM). Additionally, the emergence in the 1970s of new technologies that made it possible to study the brain for the first time (e.g., CAT, MRI, and PET technologies) and accompanying psychopharmacological developments swiftly shifted the focus among researchers and practitioners from psychological understandings for mental illness to biologically derived explanations (Horwitz, 2003; Luhrmann, 2000).

This shift is not entirely without its critics, and social histories of mental-health care often characterize the ascendancy of the biomedical model as therapeutically inefficient (Lewis, 2006; Morrison, 2009). Nonetheless, since the biomedical perspective has become the dominant paradigm for understanding psychological disability, the low degree of scientific confirmation of many psychological disorders (particularly compared to physical disorders) has not been well recognized publicly (Eberstadt, 1999; Gernsbacher, Dawson, & Goldsmith, 2005). Additionally, there is little appreciation for the social constructionist nature of diagnostic criteria within scientific discourse, which is evidenced by the lack of specificity of diagnostic criteria. White and Bloch (1970), for example, long ago demonstrated that between one-quarter and one-half of patients receiving ambulatory psychiatric care were not able to be diagnosed based upon existing criteria.

Stalled Progress and Social Disadvantage

Perhaps more critical is the lack of evidence that biomedical understandings of psychological impairment have improved the life experiences of people with psychological disabilities. This stands in contrast to the significant positive changes witnessed over time among people with other forms of disability. In fact, there is some indication that biological and genetic attributions of psychological disability, and particularly psychotic disorders such as schizophrenia, have exacerbated public stigma toward people with psychiatric disabilities, including concerns about the seriousness, permanence, and dangerousness of various psychiatric disabilities (Pescosolido et al., 2010; Schnittker, 2008; Sheehan & Corrigan, Handbook). For example, according to public opinion research, the general population is now less interested, compared to 50 years ago, in marrying someone with a serious mental illness because of possible genetic causes (Pescosolido et al., 2010). There is also some indication that the current focus on genetics may be damaging to relationships among family members who share a disorder, at least partly because of shared social stigma based on genetic explanations (Corrigan & Miller, 2004). As an illustration of this point, Corrigan and Miller (2004) cite a personal communication in *Schizophrenia Bulletin* by Ben-Dor (2001, p. 330): "My then 13-year-old daughter summed it up this way: 'If David's body were hurting, people would send gifts, but because it is his mind that is hurting, they throw bricks.' And so we were thrust into the stigma/blame loop. [People would say] 'She's the one with the crazy son. Maybe he's crazy because she is?'"

Stigma and discrimination also undermine economic advancement among people with psychological disabilities (Cook, 2006; Elliott & Reuter, Handbook). Characterizing employment trends related to psychiatric disability, Cook's (2006) synthesis of four nationally representative surveys conducted between 1989 and 1998 found that people who reported any mental illness had lower employment rates (48 to 73%) than those who did not (76 to 87%). This assessment found even lower rates of employment among people with diagnoses associated with higher levels of disability such as schizophrenia and other psychotic disorders—just 22 to 40% (Cook 2006). People with psychological disabilities identify discrimination in the workplace as one of their most frequent stigma experiences. They are twice as likely as people with physical disabilities to report that they expect to experience employment-related stigma (Roeloffs et al., 2003). And, an estimated one in three people with psychological disabilities in the United States have reported being denied employment or having employment rescinded once their disability became known, despite the protections provided by the ADA (Wahl, 1999).

Moreover, in the decades since widespread deinstitutionalization of state psychiatric institutions occurred, people with psychological disabilities have encountered new challenges as the community mental-health services that were intended to provide care in the post-institutionalization era have not materialized (Dowdall, 1999). People with severe psychological disabilities, for example, now experience considerably higher rates of homelessness and incarceration than the general population (Baum & Burnes, 1993; Lamberti, 2007). Between one-third and one-half of all adults in the United States who are homeless have a serious psychological disability, and as much as 75% of the adult homeless population is estimated to have either a psychological disability or substance-related disorder or both (Baum & Burnes, 1993). There is also indication that there is a correlation between the patient populations who were displaced through deinstitutionalization and the large numbers of people with psychological disabilities who are now incarcerated (Lamb & Baumrach, 2001; Lamb & Weinberger, 1998; Teplin, 1983; Torrey, 1997). These unfortunate trends are tied to stereotypes about mental illness and dangerousness, which a number of scholars have linked with discriminatory social policies that further undermine people with psychological disabilities in vulnerable situations (Dowdall, 1999; Lamb and Baumrach, 2001).

Unmet Challenges

These examples of enduring difficulties associated with psychological disabilities, coupled with evidence for the primacy of biomedical understandings of psychological disability, reinforce the need for further study of the discriminatory conditions that influence the onset, course, and treatment of psychological disability within a sociology of disability perspective (Jones & Brown, 2012; Lewis, 2006). Admittedly, these are issues being taken up in the burgeoning field of mad studies (Ingram, 2016), and this field may ostensibly seem better suited to the study of psychological disabilities as they are largely addressed in autonomous systems, infrastructures, and policies. This is, indeed, partly why the trajectories of many social movements associated with psychological disability issues have diverged substantially from the more mainstream disability rights movements. However, this split seems shortsighted for the simple reason that many people do not experience discrete disabilities.

To better put this in context, and in keeping with the physical disability/non-physical disability distinction we've made thus far, consider that one recent meta-analysis indicates that an estimated 36% of people with physical disabilities also experience a psychological disability (Dare et al., 2019). Analyses of the National Survey on Drug Use and Health further estimate the prevalence of substance abuse among people with physical disabilities at 40% (Glazier & King, 2013). There is considerably greater comorbidity even still between mental-health- and substance-use-related disorders, with the National Comorbidity Study and Replication indicating that the majority of substance use disorders are a consequence of primary psychological disabilities (Kessler et al., 1997; Merikangas et al., 2007), but the point is that comorbidity is a fundamental issue rarely addressed in the sociology of disability literature. This challenges us to grapple with the social problems and forms of oppression that are unique to those who experience not only non-physical disabilities but also multiple disabilities.

New Directions in the Study of Stigma

One promising avenue for further study of multiple disability categories—not to mention the experience of disabilities among individuals who experience other disadvantaged social statuses—derives from interpretations of the intersectionality perspective in the stigma literature. In considering how to move the field forward, we describe the potential of an intersectional stigma perspective, and provide more general suggestions based upon the discussion of psychological disability in the previous section.

Incorporating intersectionality in one's research recognizes the unique forms of marginalization that are experienced by individuals who occupy multiple disadvantaged social statuses (Crenshaw, 1991; Egner, Handbook). The experience of stigmatization is one form or dimension of marginalization, and an intersectional stigma perspective seeks to articulate how the convergence of stigmatized statuses defines life experiences. A stigma analytic more generally emphasizes that the life experiences of those who are stigmatized are a product of the social and institutional contexts within which they occur (Brown, 2015; Brown & Ciciurkaite, 2021). One of the earliest examples of research in this area was Crandall's (1991) comparison of AIDS-related stigmatization based on HIV transmission (e.g., same-sex intercourse and intravenous drug use compared to blood-transfusion or health-care contact) and having a particular disease (e.g., AIDS and hepatitis compared to paraplegia and flu). This study demonstrated the significance of understanding AIDS-related stigma through both transmission and disease type and, importantly, identified the additive effect of behavioral stigma statuses related to drug use and same-sex intercourse on disease-related stigma for individuals with HIV/AIDS (Crandall, 1991).

Research on intersectional stigma has gained significant traction relatively recently, but it has rarely considered disabilities (Turan et al., 2019; Medina-Perucha et al., 2019; Quinn et al., 2002; Rice et al., 2018; Logie et al., 2011; Crockett et al., 2018; Goodin et al., 2018; Sangaramoorthy et al., 2017; Logie et al., 2019; English et al., 2018; Pachankis, J. E. (2017; Remedios & Snyder, 2015; Remedios & Snyder, 2018; Oexle et al., 2018; Jackson-Best & Edwards, 2018). In this literature, different terminology has been used to reflect the number of conditions assessed and provide consistency in the theoretical implications of findings. One strand of this literature is primarily quantitative and began with research on the possession of two stigmatized statuses addressing "double" or "dual" stigma (Knesebeck et al., 2017; Bejenk et al., 2019; Daftary, 2012; Staiger et al., 2018; Vanderlinden, 2009). Investigations of dual or double stigma are predominantly focused on documenting the additive effects of possessing two stigmatized statuses. In the limited literature in this area concerning disability, for example, Merikangas and colleagues (2007) report greater role disability for people with physical and psychological disabilities compared to those who experience only one form of disability.

An extension of this literature is found in work on multiple stigma, which is methodologically and conceptually similar to dual stigma research, but considers more than two dimensions of stigmatization analytically. The multiple stigma literature typically includes findings related to the distinct effect of each stigmatized status on an outcome, compares effects, and considers interactive effects between stigma statuses (e.g., Daftary, 2012; Gausel & Thorrisen, 2014; Makowski et al., 2019). While some work on multiple stigma does aim to understand the complexity of navigating the social world with multiple stigmatized statuses (Kidd, S. A., Veltman, A., Gately, C., Chan, K. J., & Cohen, J. N. (2011); Gausel & Thorrisen, 2014; Treloar et al., 2016), the convergence of multiple stigmatized positions typically appears as a consequence of a moderation analysis rather than the focus of investigation. McCall (2005) describes most dual/double and multiple stigma studies as deconstructive given their focus on identifying and differentiating different groupings of stigmatized statuses.

In contrast, layered and multilayered stigma research, which increasingly is referred to instead as intersectional stigma research, evolved from the theoretical position that the effects of occupying multiple disadvantaged statuses are not simply additive. Rather, conceptualizing multiple stigmas as layered assumes a convergence of statuses to produce a *new* stigmatized status that cannot be adequately explained through looking at any one status individually (Crockett et al., 2018; Quinn et al., 2002; Medina-Perucha et al., 2019; Staiger et al., 2018; English et al., 2018). Understanding this unique status requires thick description of its complexities through qualitative (intracategorical) methods (McCall, 2005). For example, Whittle and colleagues' (2017) investigation of people with chronic and work-limiting physical impairments who receive disability benefits documents a unique stigma associated with "shirking and malingering" (p. 187), and describes the challenges of navigating a complex bureaucratic structure while in poor health.

Each of the approaches described may be useful in extending a sociology of disability-informed understanding of ableism, and form the basis for four recommendations we have to move the field forward. These are: (1) to utilize mixed methods, (2) to incorporate an insider's perspective into the study of non-physical disabilities, (3) to investigate structural drivers of stigma and discrimination, and (4) to explore pathways to positive adaptation.

First, the complementary potential of the intersectional approaches should not be dismissed. As an illustration, more remains to be learned about what constellations of conditions are most stigmatized and discriminated against—this is an important step in establishing a priori relationships. The checklist measures of discriminatory experiences frequently used in survey research might also be effective in documenting the potentially intersectional nature of ableism. They could provide straightforward information, for example, on the cumulative burden of discrimination experienced because of a physical disability and discrimination exposure due to a psychological disability. But, these investigations must also not overlook *why* discrimination is occurring and *why* some people are subjected to greater stigmatization than others. They also cannot address whether the layering of stigma categories creates unique stigma experiences. Quantitative analysis can provide some information on key drivers and mechanisms but, to deepen these analyses, future work utilizing a qualitative or mixed-methods approach is needed to more clearly document the lived, intersectional experiences of people with multiple disabilities.

Second, pursuing these considerations would further benefit from an insider's perspective and, indeed, firsthand experiences of oppression are a cornerstone of intersectional research. As Mauldin and Brown (2021) note, integrating such a perspective into disability research requires that cultural knowledge from the disability community one is studying is fully incorporated into your research agenda. It also involves the inclusion of people with disability as experts on your research design team (Mauldin & Brown, 2021). This is relatively typical in the study of physical disabilities, but is not common practice in the study of non-physical disabilities. With respect to the study of psychological disability, for example, lived experience is still described as a deterrent to quality research because it may introduce bias, subjectivity, personal overinvolvement, weak boundaries, or a general lack of rigor (Rose, 2015; Saks, 2009). This is unfortunate for a number of reasons, but perhaps especially because it contributes to a lack of alternatives to a biomedical understanding of psychological disability. Further research based upon first-hand accounts of psychological disability and other disabilities is, thus, a critical area for extending our understanding of individual and intersecting disabilities alike.

Third, in applying various strands of intersectional stigma research to the study of disabilities, it is imperative that conceptualizations of ableism move beyond explanations rooted in personal prejudice (Maroto & Pettinicchio, Handbook). The utility of a stigma analytic is that it directs our attention to the structural constraints that further undermine problematic social relationships (Brown & Ciciurkaite, 2021). An illustration is provided in the qualitative research on clinical encounters among those with comorbid physical and psychological disabilities. This research indicates that clinicians tend to attribute physical symptoms to mental illness, and that they tend not to treat or advise follow-up medical evaluation for physical symptoms among patients with a diagnosed psychological disorder (Corrigan et al., 2014; Mittal et al., 2013). The implication is that prejudicial viewpoints held by clinicians are an impediment to quality healthcare among people with comorbid physical and psychological disabilities. We do not doubt or dispute this, but note that clinical decisions are further constrained by insurance coverage for physical versus psychological conditions, limitations in medical education, coordination of care among multiple specialties, the aggressive marketing of psychotropic drugs, and so on.

Finally, there remains a need for intersectional stigma research on disabilities to acknowledge the potential for positive adaptation. Research on physical disability shows that positive adaptation is the norm rather than the exception and in most spheres of life. In contrast, research on positive adaptation associated with psychological conditions is almost entirely focused on the absence of symptoms and, similarly, research on positive adaptation among people with comorbid physical and psychological disabilities tends to conceptualize positive adaptation as the reduction of psychological symptoms. However, and without minimalizing psychological distress, we wish to point out that psychological symptoms are not universally understood as negative. For example, research on depressive symptoms shows that rumination is not always viewed as a maladaptive cognition; people with depression often believe that a tendency to ruminate makes them more analytical and better problem solvers (Horwitz 2003). Such framing of symptoms is one way that positive adaptation can occur. It is also hardly a stretch to imagine having comorbid physical and psychological disabilities and *not* experiencing social devaluation or negative self-views. We must be mindful of both variation in experiences of ableism among people with psychological disabilities and multiple disabilities, and variation in its consequences.

Concluding Thoughts

In addition to articulating four recommendations for intersectional research on disability, stigma, and discrimination, we have illustrated in this chapter the constraints that ableism imposes on the individual life experiences and opportunities of people with disabilities, and especially those with non-physical disabilities. This review acknowledges that it is challenging to conceptualize disability in a way that is not partial to the experience of physical disability. This intellectual challenge, however, is overshadowed by the far greater challenge of living in an ableist society. Thus, our imperative as researchers should be to study the experiences of people with different and multiple types of disability more intentionally and with the goal of addressing needs and improving lives.

REFERENCES

Albrecht, Gary L., & Lois M. Verbrugge. (2000). The global emergence of disability. In G. L. Albrecht, R. Fitzpatrick, and S. C. Scrimshaw (Eds.), *The Handbook of Social Studies in Health and Medicine* (pp. 293–307). SAGE Publications.

Asch, Adrienne. (1984). The experience of disability: A challenge for psychology. *American Psychologist, 39*, 529–536.

Barnes, Colin. (2000). A working social model? Disability, work and disability politics in the 21st century. *Critical Social Policy, 20*, 441–457.

Baum, Alice S., & Donald W. Burnes. (1993). *A nation in denial: The truth about homelessness.* Westview Press.

Ben-Dor, Sarah. (2001). Personal account. *Schizophrenia Bulletin, 27*, 329–332.

Benjenk, I., Buchongo, P., Amaize, A., Martinez, G. S., & Chen, J. (2019). "Overcoming the Dual Stigma of Mental Illness and Aging: Preparing New Nurses to Care for the Mental Health Needs of Older Adults." *American Journal of Geriatric Psychiatry, 27*, 664–674.

Beresford, Peter. (2000). What have madness and psychiatric system survivors got to do with disability and disability studies? *Disability & Society, 15*, 167–172.

Bogdan, Robert, & Taylor, Steven. (1987). Toward a sociology of acceptance: The other side of the study of deviance. *Social Policy, 18*, 34–39.

Braddock, David L., & Parish, Susan L. (2003). An institutional history of disability. In Gary L. Albrecht, Katherine D. Seelman, and Michael Bury (Eds.), *Handbook of Disability Studies* (pp. 11–68). SAGE Publications.

Brown, Robyn Lewis. (2015). Perceived stigma among people with chronic health conditions: The influence of age, stressor exposure, and psychosocial resources. *Research on Aging, 37*, 335–360.

Brown, Robyn Lewis, & Ciciurkaite, Gabriele. (2021). The "own" and the "wise" revisited: Physical disability, stigma, and mental health among couples." *Journal of Health and Social Behavior, 62*(2), 170–182.

Cahill, Spencer E., & Eggleston, Robin. (1995). Reconsidering the stigma of physical disability: Wheelchair users and public kindness. *The Sociological Quarterly, 36*, 681–698.

Campbell, Fiona K. (2009). *Contours of ableism: The production of disability and abledness.* Springer.

Charlton, James I. (1998). *Nothing about us without us: Disability, oppression and empowerment.* University of California Press.

Charmaz, Kathy. (1983). Loss of self: A fundamental form of suffering in the chronically ill. *Sociology of Health and Illness, 5*, 168–195.

Charmaz, Kathy. (2000). Experiencing chronic illness. In Gary L. Albrecht, Ray Fitzpatrick, and Susan C. Scrimshaw (Eds.), *Handbook of Social Studies in Health and Medicine* (pp. 277–292). SAGE Publications.

Charmaz, Kathy. (2002). The self as habit: The reconstruction of self in chronic illness. *The Occupational Therapy Journal of Research, 22*(supplement), 31S–41S.

Cook, Judith A. (2006). Employment barriers for persons with psychiatric disabilities: Update of a report for the president's commission. *Psychiatric Services, 57*, 1391–1405.

Cooper, R., & Burnside, I. (1996). Three years of an adult burns support group: An analysis. *Burns, 22*, 65–68.

Corrigan, Patrick W., & Miller, Frederick E. (2004). Shame, blame, and contamination: A review of the impact of mental illness stigma on family members. *Journal of Mental Health*, 13, 537–548.

Corrigan, Patrick W., Mittal, Dinesh, Reaves, Christina M., Haynes, Tiffany F., Han, Xiaotong, Morris, Scott, & Sullivan, Greer. (2014). Mental health stigma and primary health care decisions. *Psychiatry Research*, 218, 35–38.

Crandall, C.S. (1991). "Multiple stigma and AIDS: Illness stigma and attitudes toward homosexuals and IV drug users in AIDS-related stigmatization." *Journal of Community and Applied Social Psychiatry*, 1, 165–172.

Crenshaw, Kimberle. (1991). Mapping the margins: Intersectionality, identity politics, and violence against women of color. *Stanford Law Review*, 43(6), 1241–1299.

Crocker, Jennifer, Major, Brenda, & Steele, Claude. (1998). Social stigma. In D. T. Gilbert & S. T. Fiske (Eds.), *The Handbook of Social Psychology* (pp. 504–553). McGraw-Hill.

Crockett, C., Cooper, B., & Brandl, B. (2018). "Intersectional Stigma and Late-Life Intimate-Partner and Sexual Violence: How Social Workers Can Bolster Safety and Healing for Older Survivors." *The British Journal of Social Work*, 48(4), 1000–1013. https://doi.org/10.1093/bjsw/bcy049

Daftary, A. (2012). "HIV and tuberculosis: The construction and management of double stigma." *Social Science and Medicine*, 74, 1512–1519.

Davis, Lennard J. (1999). Crips strike back: The rise of disability studies. *American Literary History*, 11, 500–512.

Dare, Labante O., Bruand, Pierre-Emile, Gerard, D., Marin, Benoit, Lameyre, V., Boumediene, F. Preux, Pierre-Marie. (2019). "Co-morbidities of mental disorders and chronic physical diseases in developing and emerging countries: A meta-analysis." *BMC Public Health*, 19(304), 1–12.

Diener, Ed, & Diener, Marissa. (1995). Cross-cultural correlates of life satisfaction and self-esteem. *Journal of Personality and Social Psychology*, 68, 653–663.

Dowdall, George W. (1999). Mental hospitals and deinstitutionalization. In Carol S. Aneshensel & Jo C. Phelan (Eds.), Handbook of the Sociology of Mental Health (pp. 519–537). Springer.

Eberstadt, Mary. (1999). Why Ritalin rules. *Policy Review*, 94, 24–44.

English, D., Rendina, H. J., & Parsons, J. T. (2018). "The effects of intersecting stigma: A longitudinal examination of minority stress, mental health, and substance use among Black, Latino, and multiracial gay and bisexual men." *Psychology of Violence*, 8, 669–679. https://doi.org/10.1037/vi00000218

Fine, Michelle, & Asch, Adrienne. (1988). Disability beyond stigma: Social interaction, discrimination, and activism. *Journal of Social Issues*, 44, 3–21.

Friedman, Carli, & Owen, Aleksa L. (2017). Defining disability: Understandings of and attitudes towards ableism and disability. *Disability Studies Quarterly*, 37(1). http://dsqsds.org/article/view/5061/4545

Friedman, Michael A., & Brownell, Kelly D. (1995). Psychological correlates of obesity: Moving to the next research generation. *Psychological Bulletin*, 117, 3–20.

Freund, Peter E. S., & McGuire, Meredith B. (1995). *Health, illness and the social body: A critical sociology*. 2nd ed. Prentice Hall.

Gallagher, Hugh Gregory. (1985). *FDR's Splendid Deception*. Dodd, Mead and Company.

Gausel, N., & Thørrisen, M. M. (2014). "A theoretical model of multiple stigma: ostracized for being an inmate with intellectual disabilities." *Journal of Scandinavian Studies in Criminology and Crime Prevention*, 15, 89–95.

Gernsbacher, Morton Ann, Dawson, Michelle, & Goldsmith, H. Hill. (2005). Three reasons not to believe in an autism epidemic. *Current Directions in Psychological Science, 14,* 55–58.

Glazier, R. E. (2013). "Recent trends in substance abuse among persons with disabilities compared to that of persons without disabilities." *Disability and Health Journal, 6,* 107–115.

Gleeson, Brendan. (1997). Community care and disability: The limits to justice. *Progress in Human Geography, 21,* 199–224.

Goffman, Erving. (1963). *Stigma: Notes on the management of spoiled identity.* Simon & Schuster.

Goodin, B. R., Owens, M. A., White, D. M., Strath, L. J., Gonzalez, C., Rainey, R. L., . . . & Merlin, J. S. (2018). "Intersectional health-related stigma in persons living with HIV and chronic pain: implications for depressive symptoms." *AIDS care, 30,* 66–73.

Harris Poll. (2015). *Overwhelming public support for the Americans with disabilities act, but disagreements exist on what should qualify as a disability.* Data Summary from Harris Poll #43. Retrieved June 24, 2015, from https://theharrispoll.com

Horwitz, Allan V. (2003). *Creating mental illness.* University of Chicago Press.

Hughes, Bill, & Paterson, Kevin. (1997). The social model of disability and the disappearing body: Towards a sociology of impairment. *Disability & Society, 12,* 325–240.

Iezzoni, Lisa I., McCarthy, Ellen P., Davis, Roger B., & Siebens, Hilary. (2001). Mobility difficulties are not only a problem of old age. *Journal of General Internal Medicine, 16,* 235–243.

Ingram, Richard A. (2016). "Doing Mad Studies: Making (Non)sense Together." *Intersectionalities: A Global Journal of Social Work Analysis, Research, Polity, and Practice, 5*(3), 11–17. ISSN 1925-1270.

Jackson-Best, Fatimah, & Edwards, Nancy. (2018). "Stigma and intersectionality: A systematic review of systematic reviews across HIV/AIDS, mental illness, and physical disability." *BMC Public Health, 18,* 1–19.

Joachim, Gloria, & Acorn, Sonia. (2000). Living with chronic illness: The interface of stigma and normalization. *Canadian Journal of Nursing Research, 32,* 37–48.

Jones, Nev, & Brown, Robyn Lewis. (2012). The absence of psychiatric C/S/X perspectives in academic discourse: Consequences and implications. *Disability Studies Quarterly, 33,* 1–10.

Kadner, K. D. (1989). Resilience: Responding to adversity. *Journal of Psychosocial Nursing, 27,* 20–25.

Kaiser Public Opinion Spotlight. (2004). *Americans' views of disability.* Kaiser Family Foundation.

Kessler, R.C., Crum, R.M., Warner, L.A., Nelson, C.B., Schulenberg, J., Anthony, J.C. (1997). "Lifeime co-occurrence of DSM-III-R alcohol abuse and dependence with other psychiatric disorders in the National Comorbidity Survey." *Arch Gen Psychiatry, 54,* 313–321.

Kidd, S. A., Veltman, A., Gately, C., Chan, K. J., & Cohen, J. N. (2011). "Lesbian, gay, and transgender persons with severe mental illness: Negotiating wellness in the context of multiple sources of stigma." *American Journal of Psychiatric Rehabilitation, 14,* 13–39.

Kleinfeld, Sonny. (1977). *The hidden minority: America's handicapped.* Little, Brown.

Knesebeck, O. von dem, Kofahl, C., & Makowski, A. C. (2017). "Differences in depression stigma towards ethnic and socio-economic groups in Germany – Exploring the hypothesis of double stigma." *Journal of Affective Disorders, 208,* 82–86. https://doi.org/10.1016/j.jad.2016.08.071

Kudlick, Catherine J. (2003). Disability history: Why we need another "other." *The American Historical Review, 108,* 763–93.

Lake, Celinda. (2016). Public *opinion on disability issues*. Lake Research Partners.

Lamb, H. Richard, & Bachrach, Leona L. (2001). Some perspectives on deinstitutionalization. *Psychiatric Services, 52*, 1039–1045.

Lamb, H. Richard, & Weinberger, Linda E. (1998). Persons with severe mental illness in jails and prisons: A review. *Psychiatric Services, 49*, 483–492.

Lamberti, J. Steven. (2007). Understanding and preventing criminal recidivism among adults with psychotic disorders. *Psychiatric Services, 58*, 773–781.

Lewis, Aubrey. (1953). Health as a social concept. *The British Journal of Sociology, 4*, 109–124.

Lewis, Bradley. (2006). A mad fight: Psychiatry and disability activism. In Lennard J. Davis (Ed.), *The Disability Studies Reader* (pp. 339–54). Routledge.

Lock, Margaret, & Scheper-Hughes, Nancy. (1996). A critical-interpretive approach in medical anthropology: Rituals and routines of discipline and dissent. In C. F. Sargent and T. M. Johnson (Eds.), *Medical Anthropology Contemporary Theory and Method* (pp. 41–70). Greenwood Publishing Group.

Logie, C. H., James, Ll., Tharao, W., & Loutfy, M. R. (2011). "HIV, gender, race, sexual orientation, and sex work: A qualitative study of intersectional stigma experienced by HIV-positive women in Ontario, Canada." *PLoS Medicine, 8*, e1001124. https://doi.org/10.1371/journal.pmed.1001124

Logie, C. H., Williams, C. C., Wang, Y., Marcus, N., Kazemi, M., Cioppa, L., Kaida, A., Webster, K., Beaver, K., de Pokomandy, A., & Loutfy, M. (2019). "Adapting stigma mechanism frameworks to explore complex pathways between intersectional stigma and HIV-related health outcomes among women living with HIV in Canada." *Social Science & Medicine, 232*, 129–138. https://doi.org/10.1016/j.socscimed.2019.04.044

Longmore, Paul K. (2000). Disability policy and politics: Considering consumer influences. *Journal of Disability Policy Studies, 11*, 36–44.

Longmore, Paul K. (2003). *Why I burned my books and other essays on disability*. Temple University Press.

Luhrmann, Tanya M. (2000). *Of two minds: The growing disorder in American psychiatry*. Alfred A. Knopf.

Major, Brenda. (1994). From social inequality to personal entitlement: The role of social comparisons, legitimacy appraisals and group membership. In M. P. Zanna (Ed.), *Advances in Experimental Social Psychology* (pp. 293–348). Academic Press.

Makowski, A. C., Kim, T. J., Luck-Sikorski, C., & von dem Knesebeck, O. (2019). "Social deprivation, gender and obesity: multiple stigma? Results of a population survey from Germany." *BMJ open, 9*, e023389.

Mauldin, Laura, & Brown, Robyn L. (2021). Missing pieces: Engaging sociology of disability in medical sociology. Journal of Health and Social Behavior, 62(4), 477–492.

McCall, L. (2005). "The complexity of intersectionality." *Signs: Journal of Women in Culture and Society, 30*, 1771–1800.

Medina-Perucha, L., Scott, J., Chapman, S., Barnett, J., Dack, C., & Family, H. (2019). "A qualitative study on intersectional stigma and sexual health among women on opioid substitution treatment in England: Implications for research, policy and practice." *Social Science & Medicine, 222*, 315–322. https://doi.org/10.1016/j.socscimed.2019.01.022

Merikangas, K. R., Akiskal, H. S., Angst, J., Greenberg, P. E., Hirschfeld, R. M. A., Petukhova, M., & Kessler, R. C. (2007). "Lifetime and 12-Month Prevalence of Bipolar Spectrum Disorder in the National Comorbidity Survey Replication." *ARCH GEN PSYCHIATRY, 64*, 11.

Miller, Carol T., & Major, Brenda. (2000). Coping with stigma and prejudice. In T. F. Heatherton, R. E. Kleck, Michelle R. Hebl, and J. G. Hull (Eds.), *The Social Psychology of Stigma* (pp. 243–272). The Guilford Press.

Mittal, Dinesh, Drummond, Karen L., Blevins, Dean, Curran, Geoffrey, Corrigan, Patrick, & Sullivan, Greer. (2013). Stigma associated with PTSD: Perceptions of treatment seeking combat veterans. *Psychiatric Rehabilitation Journal, 36*(2), 86–92.

Morrison, Linda J. (2009). *Talking back to psychiatry: The psychiatric consumer/survivor/ex-patient movement.* Routledge.

National Council on Disability. (1997). *Equality of opportunity: The making of the Americans with Disabilities Act.* Author.

National Council on Disability. (2008). *Keeping track: National disability status and program performance indicators.* http://www.ncd.gov/newsroom/publications/2008/Indicators_Report.html

Oexle, N. & Corrigan, P.W. (2018). "Understanding mental illness stigma toward persons with multiple stigmatized conditions: Implications of intersectionality theory." *Psychiatric Services, 69,* 587–589.

Olkin, Rhoda, & Pledger, Constance. (2003). Can disability studies and psychology join hands? *American Psychologist, 58,* 296–304.

Pachankis, J. E. (2017). "The Geography of Sexual Orientation: Structural Stigma and Sexual Attraction, Behavior, and Identity Among Men Who Have Sex with Men Across 38 European Countries." *Arch Sex Behav, 46,* 1491–1502.

Parsons, Talcott. (1951). *The social system.* The Free Press.

Paterson, B., Thorne, S., Crawford, J., & Tarko, M. (1999). Living with diabetes as a transformational experience. *Qualitative Health Research, 9,* 786–802.

Pescosolido, Bernice A., Martin, Jack K., Long, J. Scott, Medina, Tait R., Phelan, Jo C., & Link, Bruce G. (2010). "A disease like any other"? A decade of change in public reactions to schizophrenia, depression, and alcohol Dependence. *American Journal of Psychiatry, 167,* 1321–1330.

Pew Research Center. (1999). *People and the press 1999 millennium survey.* http://www.people-press.org/reports

Pfeiffer, David. (2002). The philosophical foundations of disability studies. *Disability Studies Quarterly, 22.*

Price, Margaret. (2011). *Mad at school: Rhetorics of mental disability and academic life.* University of Michigan Press.

Quinn, Gerard, Degener, Theresia, Bruce, Anna, Burke, Christine, Castellino, Joshua, Kenna, Padraic, Kilkelly, Ursula, & Quinlivan, Shivaun. (2002). *Human rights and disability.* United Nations.

Remedios, J. D., & Snyder, S. H. (2015). "Where Do We Go From Here? Toward an Inclusive and Intersectional Literature of Multiple Stigmatization." *Sex Roles, 73*(9–10), 408–413. https://doi.org/10.1007/s11199-015-0543-4

Remedios, J. D., & Snyder, S. H. (2018). "Intersectional Oppression: Multiple Stigmatized Identities and Perceptions of Invisibility, Discrimination, and Stereotyping: Intersectional Oppression." *Journal of Social Issues, 74*(2), 265–281. https://doi.org/10.1111/josi.12268

Rice, W. S., Logie, C. H., Napoles, T. M., Walcott, M., Batchelder, A. W., Kempf, M.-C., Wingood, G. M., Konkle-Parker, D. J., Turan, B., Wilson, T. E., Johnson, M. O., Weiser, S. D., & Turan, J. M. (2018). "Perceptions of intersectional stigma among diverse women living with HIV in the United States." *Social Science & Medicine, 208*, 9–17. https://doi.org/10.1016/j.socscimed.2018.05.001

Roeloffs, Carol, Sherbourne, Cathy, Unützer, Jürgen, Fink, Arlene, Tang, Lingqi, & Well, Kenneth B. (2003). Stigma and depression among primary care patients. General Hospital Psychiatry, 25(5), 311–315.

Rose, Diana. (2015). The contemporary state of service-user-led research. The Lancet Psychiatry, 2(11), 959–960.

Saks, Elyn R. (2009). Some thoughts on denial of mental illness. American Journal of Psychiatry, 166(9), 972–973.

Sangaramoorthy, T., Jamison, A., & Dyer, T. (2017). "Intersectional stigma among midlife and older Black women living with HIV." *Culture, Health, & Sexuality, 19*, 1329–1343.

Scheer, Jessica, & Groce, Nora. (1988). Impairment as a human constant: Cross-cultural and historical perspectives on variation. *Journal of Social Issues, 44*, 23–37.

Schnittker, Jason. (2008). An uncertain revolution: Why the rise of a genetic model of mental illness has not increased tolerance. *Social Science & Medicine, 67*, 1370–1381.

Schwartz, Sharon, & Corcoran, Cheryl. (2010). Biological theories of psychiatric disorders: A sociological approach. In Teresa L. Scheid and Tony N. Brown (Eds.), *A Handbook for the Study of Mental Health: Social Contexts, Theories, and Systems*, 2nd ed. (pp. 64–88). Cambridge University Press.

Shakespeare, Tom. (1997). The social model of disability. In Lennard J. Davis (Ed.), *The Disability Studies Reader*, 3rd ed. (pp. 266–273). Routledge.

Shandra, Carrie L. (2018). Disability as inequality: Social disparities, health disparities, and participation in daily activities. *Social Forces, 97*(1), 157–192.

Silverstein, R. (2000). *Disability policy framework: A guidepost for analyzing public policy*. Center for the Study and Advancement of Disability Policy and the Arc of the United States.

Staiger, T., Waldmann, T., Oexle, N., Wigand, M., & Rüsch, N. (2018). Intersections of discrimination due to unemployment and mental health problems: the role of double stigma for job- and help-seeking behaviors. *Social Psychiatry and Psychiatric Epidemiology, 53*, 1091–1098.

Susman, Joan. (1994). Disability, stigma and deviance. *Social Science and Medicine, 38*, 15–22.

Swain, John, & French, Sally. (2000). Towards an affirmation model of disability. *Disability & Society, 15*, 569–582.

Teplin, Linda A. (1983). The criminalization of the mentally ill: Speculation in search of data. *Psychological Bulletin, 94*, 54.

Thomas, Adrian. (2000). Stability of Tringo's hierarchy of preference toward disability groups: 30 years later. *Psychological Reports, 86*, 1155–1156.

Thomas, Carol. (2007). *Sociologies of disability and illness: Contested ideas in disability studies and medical sociology*. Palgrave Macmillan.

Thorne, Sally, & Paterson, Barbara. (1998). Shifting images of chronic illness. *Image: Journal of Nursing Scholarship, 30*, 173–178.

Torrey, Edwin Fuller. (1997). *Out of the shadows: Confronting America's mental illness crisis*. John Wiley.

Treloar, C., Jackson, L. C., Gray, R., Newland, J., Wilson, H., Saunders, V., Johnson, P., & Brener, L. (2016). "Multiple stigmas, shame and historical trauma compound the experience of Aboriginal Australians living with hepatitis C." *Health Sociology Review, 25*, 18–32. https://doi.org/10.1080/14461242.2015.1126187

Tringo, John L. (1970). The hierarchy of preference toward disability groups. *The Journal of Special Education, 4*, 295–306.

Turan, J. M., Elafros, M. A., Logie, C. H., Banik, S., Turan, B., Crockett, K. B., Pescosolido, B., & Murray, S. M. (2019). "Challenges and opportunities in examining and addressing intersectional stigma and health." *BMC Medicine*, *17*, 1–15.

Tyor, Peter L., & Bell, Leland V. (1984). *Caring for the retarded in America: A history. Contributions in medical history, number 15*. Greenwood Press.

UPIAS. (1975). *Fundamental principles of disability*. The Union of the Physically Impaired Against Segregation & The Disability Alliance.

Vanderlinden, L. K. (2009). "German genes and Turkish traits: Ethnicity, infertility, and reproductive politics in Germany." *Social Science & Medicine*, *69*, 266–273.

Wahl, Otto F. (1999). Mental health consumers' experience of stigma. Schizophrenia Bulletin, 25(3), 467–478.

Weil, Evette, Wachterman, Melissa, McCarthy, Ellen P., Davis, Roger B., O'Day, Bonnie, Iezzoni, Lisa I., & Wee, Christina C. (2002). Obesity among adults with disabling conditions. *Journal of the American Medical Association*, *288*, 1265–1268.

White, Warren, & Bloch, Sidney. (1970). Psychiatric referrals in a general hospital. *Medical Journal of Australia*, *1*(19), 950–954.

Whittle, H. J., Palar, K., Ranadive, N. A., Turan, J. M., Kushel, M., & Weiser, S. D. (2017). "The land of the sick and the land of the healthy": disability, bureaucracy, and stigma among people living with poverty and chronic illness in the United States. *Social Science & Medicine*, *190*, 181–189.

Woloshin, Steven, Schwartz, Lisa M., Tosteson, Anna N. A., Chang, Chiang Hua, Wright, Brock, Plohman, Joy, & Fisher, Elliott S. (1997). Perceived adequacy of tangible social support and health outcomes in patients with coronary artery disease. *Journal of General Internal Medicine*, *12*, 613–618.

CHAPTER 25

DISCLOSURE, DISCRIMINATION, AND IDENTITY AMONG WORKING PROFESSIONALS WITH BIPOLAR DISORDER OR MAJOR DEPRESSION

MARTA ELLIOTT AND JORDAN C. REUTER

INTRODUCTION

PREVAILING stereotypes of bipolar disorder and major depression suggest that people who are diagnosed with these conditions are unlikely to be successful working professionals, but the evidence suggests otherwise. While symptoms of bipolar disorder and depression may impact one's ability to function in the workplace, most people with these diagnoses report no work impairment whatsoever the majority of the time when followed over a 15-year period (Judd et al., 2008). Moreover, being employed may improve mental health for these individuals. According to a randomized experimental study of social security disability recipients diagnosed with schizophrenia, bipolar disorder, or depression, the experimental group who received employment support had significantly better mental health over 2 years than the control group (Drake et al., 2013). Other research demonstrates that work provides a sense of purpose and identity among people being treated for bipolar disorder, although it can provoke symptoms if sufficient supports are not in place (Borg et al., 2013).

Nonetheless, having a mental illness such as bipolar disorder or major depression can present barriers to success on the job short of being completely disabling, including the exacerbating effects of working conditions on psychiatric symptoms and discrimination on the part of employers against people with mental illness (Sevak & Khan, 2017).

These barriers reflect the distinction between impairment and disability that is fundamental to the social model of disability, wherein impairment may be intrinsic to mental
illness, whereas disability involves social forces that exclude or marginalize the people
with mental illness (Shakespeare, 2013).

Most people with mood or anxiety disorders who express a need for workplace
accommodations do not receive them, even though receiving accommodations is associated with a reduced odds of meeting disorder symptom criteria 1 year later (Bolo
et al., 2013). Working professionals with mental illness are often disinclined to seek
accommodations on the job owing to fear of negative consequences if their condition
is exposed (Boyd et al., 2016; Price et al., 2017). This is unfortunate, given evidence that
accommodations are cost effective for employers and helpful for people with mental
illnesses (Zafar et al., 2019), including for people with bipolar disorder and depression. Reportedly beneficial accommodations for people with bipolar disorder include
frequent breaks, the opportunity to work from home, and schedule control (Tremblay,
2011). For people with a range of mood or anxiety disorders (including bipolar disorder and depression), weekly meetings with one's supervisor, exchanging tasks with
coworkers, individualized training, and a relatively quiet workspace are useful (Wang et
al., 2011).

To receive workplace accommodations for mental illness, an individual must disclose
their condition indirectly via vocational program staff members (if eligible) or directly
to their employer (Jones, 2011), but stigma deters people from doing so (Rotenberg et al.,
2016). The effect of disclosure is unpredictable, sometimes leading to support from one's
supervisor and sometimes leading to interpersonal strain (Jones, 2011), suggesting that
the decision to disclose on the job must be made cautiously. Despite protections ostensibly afforded to employees by the Americans with Disabilities Act (ADA), employment
discrimination still occurs against people whose mental illness is disclosed during the
hiring process and on the job (Stefan, 2002). During hiring, employers are significantly
less likely to call back job applicants who disclose a history of mental illness (Hipes et
al., 2016). Among the employed, people with serious mental illness who experience exposure to stigma on the job earn significantly less than those who do not have a mental
illness (Baldwin & Marcus, 2006). The guidelines for when people with mental illness
qualify for disability accommodations under the ADA are ambiguous, and the ADA
cannot protect people with mental illness from the indirect effects of stigma on their
willingness to apply or the reaction they receive if they do apply (Cummings et al., 2013).
Little is known about how people with mental illness consider the issue of applying for
disability accommodations, let alone what happens when they do so (Zafar et al., 2019).

MENTAL ILLNESS AND IDENTITY

Being diagnosed with a mental illness poses an identity threat owing to the public
stigma that characterizes people with mental illness as less than fully human (Goffman,
1963; Steele et al., 2002). The causes and the constitution of most major mental illnesses

are poorly understood (Paris, 2015), putting people diagnosed as such in the position of piecing together limited information as to the nature of their condition. This process may be particularly relevant to identity processes when mental illnesses are characterized as biologically based lifelong conditions, such as bipolar disorder. Confronted with such a diagnosis, individuals may be compelled to revise their identity to incorporate an apparently unalterable and fundamental aspect of self that may have wreaked significant havoc on their lives. In contrast, people diagnosed with conditions from which they presumably may fully recover, such as major depression, may not experience the same level of identity threat or need to revise their self-understanding.

Bipolar disorder is characterized by psychiatry as a chronic condition requiring lifelong adherence to treatment primarily in the form of psychotropic prescription medications (Grande et al., 2016). In addition, bipolar disorder is highly stigmatized in US society (Hawke et al., 2013) and stereotyped as being associated with violence, dangerousness, and instability (Wong et al., 2017). As such, receiving a diagnosis of bipolar disorder is likely to provoke questions about one's self and identity, including the implications of having a purportedly defective brain for one's capacity to function professionally, and the connotations of the label for one's self-esteem. Several aspects of having bipolar disorder challenge identity, including the stigmatized diagnosis itself, symptoms that seem out of character, and medications that symbolize dependence and can dull one's emotions (Chapman, 2002).

Qualitative studies about people diagnosed with bipolar disorder indicate that accepting the biomedical model corresponds to adopting a "patient" identity in which the self becomes indistinguishable from the illness, and the "sick" individual must cede control to prescribed treatments (Fernandez et al., 2014). The identity or sense of self of people with bipolar disorder varies with mood state leading to identity confusion and loss of self (i.e., is it me or is it my illness?), contradictory selves (i.e., depressed vs. manic self), self-doubt, and low self-esteem (Inder et al., 2008; Michalak et al., 2006; Lim et al., 2004; Proudfoot et al., 2009). Loss of self is associated, in part, with perceiving that the brain disorder has taken control of one's feelings and behaviors (Goldberg, 2007).

Major depressive disorder, unlike bipolar disorder, is presented as a condition from which one may recover, although recurrence is common (Colman et al., 2011). While psychotropic medications are the treatment of choice by psychiatry (Gelenberg et al., 2010), they are not necessarily prescribed for life, as is typically the case for bipolar disorder. Depression is not as stigmatized as bipolar disorder (Ellison et al., 2013). Nonetheless, being diagnosed with depression is likely to have important ramifications for identity. People who adopt an illness identity by attributing their depression to a chemical imbalance are relieved of culpability yet may feel a loss of control and victimization (Karp, 2017). People who experience discrimination on the basis of having a depression diagnosis may socially identify with other people with the same diagnosis. However, unlike social identities that are protective, the identity of being a depressed person tends to exacerbate the negative impact of discrimination on well-being because of the unhealthy social norms associated with depression (e.g., thinking negative thoughts or engaging in self-harm) (Cruwys & Gunaseelen, 2016).

Although meeting criteria for bipolar disorder or major depression is negatively associated with socioeconomic status (Smith et al., 2013), it clearly does not preclude occupational success. Occupying a role as a working professional (unlike having a mental illness) is a marker of achievement, and people with higher occupational status tend to have higher self-esteem (Twenge & Campbell, 2002). Nonetheless, the stressors associated with high-status occupations are a risk factor for mental illness, as suggested by high rates of depression among lawyers (Krill et al., 2016) and physicians (Mata et al., 2016). People who simultaneously succeed professionally and live with serious mental illness exhibit status inconsistency; that is, they hold two positions in society that do not normatively coincide (Stryker & Burke, 2000). Professional success may help individuals cope with the identity threat associated with their mental illness by demonstrating their competence in the workplace.

This chapter challenges stereotypes associated with serious mental illnesses by giving voice to working professionals who are successful on the job while coping with the symptoms of bipolar disorder or depression, often in secret. It asks how people with serious mental illness handle revealing versus concealing their diagnoses on the job, seeking accommodations when indicated (which necessitates disclosure), dealing with forced ends to employment, and identifying with their inconsistent statuses.

Lastly, it compares how they identify with their illness versus their profession in an effort to maintain their sense of self-worth. These questions are addressed via an analysis of data from 45 individuals who were interviewed in depth, each of whom identified as having either bipolar disorder ($n = 24$) or major depression ($n = 21$) and who described themselves as working professionals. The results reveal how judiciously people handle disclosure, how difficult it is to seek accommodations, how devastating it is to be severed from employment, and how important it is to have a professional identity in the face of one's illness. We discuss these findings in terms of how workplaces could accommodate the needs of working professionals with mental illnesses whose contributions are many and whose needs may go unrecognized or ignored.

DATA AND METHODS

The results presented in this chapter are based on semistructured in-depth interviews conducted by the first author with 45 adults living throughout the United States who volunteered to discuss their experiences as working professionals diagnosed with mental illnesses. While this chapter describes issues related to managing mental illness in the workplace, the broader goals of the project included understanding participants' explanatory models of mental illness vis-à-vis their personal and social histories and their experiences with mental health treatment. The study was reviewed by the Institutional Review Board (IRB) at The University of Nevada, Reno (UNR), and deemed of minimal risk to human subjects. The interviews took place in person, by video, or by phone between 2015 and 2018, and they were audiotaped (with the participants' permission) and transcribed for analysis.

About two thirds (64%) of the sample was female (58% with bipolar disorder and 71% with depression) and age ranged from 31 to 68 years. Most participants were White, with the exception of four Asian Americans and two African Americans. All but three participants had college degrees, and 28 (62%) had postgraduate degrees. There were doctors, lawyers, professors, psychologists, computer scientists, bankers, authors, and assorted other types of professionals in the sample. The majority of those with bipolar disorder (22 or 92%) were currently in a romantic relationship (many of them married), in contrast with 12 (57%) of those with depression.

The stated purpose of the study printed on the recruitment flyer was to "give voice to the many individuals in the US who play a vital role in society while simultaneously dealing with the symptoms and stigma of mental illness." The flyers were posted on campus and instructed potential participants to email the first author to learn more about the study. At the completion of each interview, participants were asked to refer people they knew to the study if they thought it was a valuable experience. The word spread and a snowball sample accumulated such that when the interviewing ended, there were 56 completed interviews, 45 of which are the subject of this study because they identified as either having bipolar disorder or depression.

In the case of in-depth interviewing, it is important to consider the position of the researcher/interviewer in relation to the participant and how similarities and differences in their social statuses might affect the interview process. There are advantages and disadvantages of sharing an "insider" status with the participant versus being an outsider (Gair, 2012; Gruys & Hutson, 2020). In this study, the first author presented as a working professional. However, she did not share her identity as someone with a history of mental illness unless asked, which was rare, and she made clear she was not a mental health professional. Thus, she was positioned as an insider with respect to social class and an outsider with regard to illness experience. While her status as a researcher lent credibility to the study, her presentation as naïve to serious mental illness granted participants the role of expert on the subject, potentially putting them at ease to speak more freely.

The interview questions were guided by a priori expectations based on our prior research (e.g., Elliott & Doane, 2015), and the research objectives of the study, yet the interviews were sufficiently open-ended to allow unexpected findings to emerge. Each interview had three parts. In part one, participants described their history of mental illness, including treatment they had received and their beliefs about the causes of their condition. During this part, they also described their educational and career trajectories and how they intersected with their mental illness. In part two, participants were asked about with whom they share they mental health information and from whom they keep it a secret and why, both in and outside of the work setting. During this portion, they were prompted to discuss how others reacted upon learning of their mental illness with a focus on feeling rejected and maligned versus accepted and supported. In the third part, participants were asked to share their perceptions of public stigma toward people with mental illness and how it affects their sense of self or identity. They were also asked about how being a working professional affects their identity. This chapter focuses on decision-making and experiences surrounding revealing versus concealing one's mental illness in the workplace (as opposed to with family, friends, and partners), attitudes toward and experience seeking accommodations at work on the basis of having a mental illness, losing a job owing to mental illness, and personal identity in relation to being a working professional with a mental illness.

The interview data were analyzed according to the flexible coding method (Deterding & Waters, 2021), which consists of four stages. During the first stage, "attributes" of participants were coded into mutually exclusive, exhaustive categorical variables such as gender, age, occupation, and psychiatric diagnosis. In stage two, index codes were applied to the transcripts to organize them for further analysis. An index code indicates that a given portion of a transcript contains material related to a topic of interest, such as disclosure of one's mental illness on the job. Multiple index codes were applied to the same text when more than one topic was discussed simultaneously, such as when the topic of stigma came up in the context of whether or not to reveal one's mental illness in the workplace. These two stages of the analysis were carried out by a team of student research assistants, including the second author.

The third stage of flexible coding is known as analytic coding, which occurs when one index code is thoroughly analyzed for evidence of similarities, differences, and common themes across participants. This stage of coding was carried out by the second author and resulted in preliminary analytic codes for each topic of interest. Three index codes were analyzed for this study: (1) disclosure of one's mental illness in the workplace, (2) prejudice and discrimination on the basis of mental illness in the workplace, and (3) identity as a person with a mental illness and as a working professional.

The final stage of flexible coding, cross-case theoretical validity testing, served to check the reliability and validity of the analytic codes, and to search for patterns of association between analytic codes (or between analytic codes and participant attributes) across participants. During this stage, the first author cross-checked each analytic code against the original index code from which it was derived, as well as examined the surrounding text of the transcript to ensure nothing was taken out of context.

Results

Disclosure on the Job: Reputation Protection and Judicious Disclosure

The analysis of the disclosure index code indicated that almost half of all participants, regardless of their type of profession, felt compelled to conceal their mental illness on the job, although the majority revealed it selectively. We describe these results in terms of two themes: reputation protection and judicious disclosure.

Twenty of the 45 (44%) participants (46% of those with bipolar disorder and 43% of those with depression) described feeling like they needed to conceal their condition on the job to preclude risking their reputation and being perceived as incompetent, especially from their supervisor or the people they supervised. Emma, a college instructor with depression and social anxiety, explained why: "You just don't want people to look at you like you're incompetent in some way, even though you're doing fine at work." For Jessica, a supervisor in an IT department with bipolar disorder, it was about maintaining her authority: "I need to be passing for normal to preserve my respectability and my authority at work." If everyone knew about her diagnosis, then whenever she had to "take a hard line with them, or when I have to do like discipline or talk about poor performance or something like that, then they'll be like dismissive." Elizabeth, a development officer for a hospital, kept her bipolar disorder a secret because she thought it would prevent her from rising into a supervisory position: "the fear is that people would either be scared of me, scared I might act out, or just wouldn't think of me as somebody with leadership potential."

Some described concealing their condition until they established themselves, whereas others said they concealed it at all costs. Peggy, a social worker who directed a health care company and had bipolar disorder, explained that "I want them to see me as competent and effective before I let them know something like this, because I'm very concerned that it will impact the way that they see me." Annie, a research project manager, thought the better of disclosing after overhearing someone at work say, "Oh, so and so has bipolar. We're just waiting for them to have their next episode this week so we can fire them." Lastly, Megan, an insurance adjuster with a history of depression and self-harm, knew she could never disclose: "It's just not possible to ever have my employer or a judge or whomever have me walk in and sit down and say, 'Let's negotiate for a million dollars of your money,' and expose all my scars to the world literally and figuratively."

Most people (79% of those with bipolar disorder and 67% of those with depression), regardless of their profession, had disclosed to someone on the job at some point, yet they tended to be selective about to whom they disclosed and which aspects of their illness they described. Sam, a university professor with a history of depression and suicidal ideation, only shared with certain people for two reasons: "I don't trust some people to understand that this is something serious, and there's other people I don't trust to take it too seriously." Richard, also a university professor with bipolar and avoidant personality disorders, had no qualms about sharing his bipolar diagnosis because it was "an illness just like any other illness." However, when it came to the personality disorder, he "would be a lot more leery about talking about it" because he thought people would react by saying, "Your life is great. Why do you feel this way?"

No one reported an outright negative experience when they chose to reveal to a trusted colleague or supervisor. Rather, the participants tended to describe fairly positive experiences, such as Owen, a computer engineer with bipolar disorder. Disclosing to his boss "makes me feel more welcome, too. If he can treat me like that, then I certainly want to give him my best as an employee." Similarly, Linda, a director of human resources (HR) with a history of depression and an eating disorder, had a positive experience, explaining that "once I started to talk about it with my management, with other colleagues, it really became more freeing, and it was healing to me." Nonetheless, coworkers who found out indirectly about a participant's mental illness were not always so supportive. Eloise felt degraded when a colleague reacted to the revelation that she had bipolar disorder by exclaiming, "Oh really? You seem so smart!" For May, it was much worse. She eventually left a job after taking time off for depression because her coworkers "didn't appreciate that I took time off" and were "unsupportive, which was pretty disappointing."

Disclosure sometimes transformed into advocacy when participants felt a moral imperative to reduce the stigma of mental illness so that other people would not have to endure ongoing hardship. Linda, for example, went beyond disclosing on the job to forming an informal group for other employees struggling with mental illness and posting a video testimonial of her own experiences. Others made a point of outing themselves when they overheard anyone speaking ill of people with mental illness, like Sandra, a therapist with bipolar disorder and a history of borderline personality disorder (BPD). After hearing another mental health professional disparage people with BPD, she confronted him, saying, "You didn't make me feel bad, but we don't walk around with Bs on our chest you know." Karen, a business consultant with depression, kept her story secret for "probably 5 years" based on the counsel of her business strategist, who said "you cannot go public with this. You're gonna wreck your business." Eventually she bucked that advice, describing the publication of her memoir and self-help books as "empowering and healing."

The experience of disclosing to HR in the interest of qualifying for FMLA leave or on-the-job accommodations was generally not as positive for participants as judiciously disclosing to trusted supervisors or colleagues. In the next section we describe why some people decided not to seek accommodations, whereas others felt shamed when they did.

Disability Accommodations: Fear and Shame

The vast majority of participants did not report a need for special accommodations in order to be successful at work, but each of the eight (18%) who did describe some degree of fear, shame, or perceived rejection in relation to it. Whether they were completely deterred from asking or felt treated unfairly when they did ask, they all encountered obstacles. For Harriet, a director of diversity with a history of depression, the obstacle was a workplace culture in which asking for accommodations was simply impermissible, and she knew this from day one in a previous job as a business consultant. During orientation, the facilitator emphasized how easily replaceable she was, declaring "for every one of you sitting here we had a thousand applicants." To her the message was discouraging in that it "breeds a lot of fear and it makes it much less likely that people will ask for what they need or ask for accommodations because they're afraid that it's going to be interpreted as a weakness."

In David's case, the obstacle was not his lack of knowledge of the legal system or his rights, but the fact that his pride prevented him from asking. As a lawyer with bipolar disorder, he used to interact with high-profile clients regularly until the day he lost his temper on the job after forgetting to take his medications. From then on, his boss stopped scheduling him to meet in-person with clients, which left him feeling stuck: "The sad part about this is that they don't really let me talk to people anymore," he said, explaining that "I know the legal way out of it . . . to provide ADA notice that I request reasonable accommodations . . . but there's still that very powerful aspect of shame."

Jessica (the IT supervisor with bipolar disorder) could have used accommodations at work, but she did not want to ask for them because she kept her condition "top-secret at work." Instead, she kept a close eye on herself and made informal adjustments, having learned to "watch very carefully and plan time off and plan breaks and you know, manage things very proactively." One work-around she discovered was to apply for intermittent FMLA leave on the basis of bipolar disorder, but never let on to her direct supervisor the reason why she qualified for it: "If I'm really having a mental health day today, like, I'm gonna call in sick, I'm not going to tell them what I'm sick with, but I'm gonna do that, rather than go to work and be a wreck." However, there were plenty of days where she had to go to work regardless of how she felt where she hoped "my boss doesn't notice that I'm depressed out of my mind and I don't really want to be here."

Melody, a software consultant, also qualified for FMLA owing to her bipolar disorder, but for her the process of applying for it was humiliating: "The human resources department was very judgmental of me" and one of the staff was "extremely unhelpful with the forms I needed to fill out" and "just cold."

Sally, an executive assistant with bipolar disorder, also had a terrible experience with HR, although ultimately it worked out well. Initially she took a temporary leave from work without disclosing the reason why, and the HR director was "very unsupportive. Like very sort of suspicious and she wasn't helpful." Once she received a "really brutal" performance evaluation, she realized she had to exercise her rights or she would lose her job, so she "did ask for accommodations and . . . reveal my diagnosis." The result was that "they were super supportive" and arranged for her to work an earlier shift so she could "take care of myself more effectively."

Lastly, Emma sought and received an accommodation to prerecord her lectures so as to avoid the intense anxiety she experienced while teaching in a live classroom. It took a long time and a lot of pestering to finally get the request approved, and even then, she still faced obstacles when her new boss made light of it. Explaining that he too had "significant anxiety," he suggested that she could overcome it the same way that he did by "basically just talking."

Given the reported obstacles to receiving accommodations in the workplace, it is not surprising that some jobs did not work out at all for some participants. The next section describes various ways in which participants were severed from professional employment in relation to their mental illness.

Perceived Discrimination: Shown the Door

Nine of the 45 participants (20%) described ways in which their mental illness led them to separate from their job under various forms of duress. These included getting fired, being forced to resign, and having one's job eliminated.

Of the five who got fired, none of them could pin it directly on their mental illness, but they had their suspicions. Dirk, for example, had a job in the same hospital where he had been a patient on the psychiatric unit, and he was asked to leave on the basis of a minor infraction soon after he confided in his manager about his recent hospitalization. Annie was told not to come back after just one day on the job because she "got manic over the weekend" and was emailing the boss concerned that "my identity is being compromised, someone is stealing my information, please lock down my account." Rather than ask her what was going on, she "showed up on Monday and they're like, you're gone."

Tammy also lost her job in the midst of a manic phase. Having just been hired as a director of a social service center, her voices became belligerent for the first time and she started warning people about impending lawsuits. Having disclosed her mental illness during the hiring process, she wished she had been offered an accommodation, given she had a long-standing good reputation in the community: "for that to happen and not be offered any options was kind of a slap in the face," she explained. Instead of working with her, they "just thought, you know what, let's just cut it now, let's just cut ties now, don't even open this can of worms." Richard also felt like he should have been given an opportunity to address his work issues before getting fired. Instead, "I was shown the door." When asked if he thought it was because of his mental illness, he felt "singled out" for more than his less than stellar work performance, yet he couldn't be sure, given "you don't know what you don't know, right?"

Alfred lost his investment banking job on the basis of being severely depressed owing to bipolar disorder, but he didn't blame his employer: "it was poor work performance," he said, adding that "I missed work a lot." Amber also attributed the behavior that forced her to resign to her bipolar disorder, yet she did not let the people she worked for off the hook, noting that "racism reared its ugly head" and they made a lot of "horrible remarks" to her. Rather than repress her reaction, "I cussed them all out on Facebook. I mean, I just went at it," after which she realized she was "so sick. I have to go to the hospital."

Ellie found herself demoted when her university administrative position was eliminated during her lengthy medical leave for severe depression: "They decided to restructure the position" while she was away which she attributed to her understanding that "if you change the job significantly enough, you don't have to give it back to the person who was on medical leave." Convinced this was a case of outright discrimination, she consulted an attorney, but "I was just exhausted" and didn't "have the energy to fight this right now," deciding instead to go on the market and find a new job, which she did.

When describing the various ways they lost their jobs, participants often spoke about the importance of professional success for their sense of self or identity. We turn next to a presentation of how participants thought of themselves vis-à-vis their mental illness and their profession.

Identity: I Am Not My Mental Illness

Participants were asked how having a mental illness affects their identity, and of the 45, 22 (49%) responded in terms of whether or not they directly identify as a person with a mental illness. Some described how they distanced themselves from their illness, possibly as a means of protecting themselves from the implications of public stigma. For example, Monica, a therapist with treatment-resistant depression, explained: "I am not my mental illness. These things that happen in my brain are not me." Annette, an advocate for people with mental illness with depression, said it's "on my medical chart, but it's not who I am." Alfred saw it "as an aspect of my personality, but I don't see it as my core." Similarly, Linda did not "think the mental illness defines who I am as a person."

Others described how it was an important, albeit problematic, aspect of their identity. Marianne, a writer with depression, was "working on coming to grips with the fact that it's chronic and there is no cure, that I'm stuck with this . . . I've got to own it." Don, a researcher, also spoke of living with a chronic condition (depression and anxiety), saying that while some recover and "they put it on the shelf and go on with life" for people like him, "it becomes a big part of whom we are . . . of our identity." For Jessica, it was less prominent, yet "it's definitely a part of who I am, but I like to say that I'm living with bipolar and not constantly suffering from bipolar." Rather than let her illness define her, she clarified that "it's not all consuming . . . I'm also a wife and a mom. I'm a daughter and a sister and an employee and a manager . . . bipolar is a big piece, like I have to manage it, I have to deal with it every single day, but it's not the total and sum of my personality and identity."

For working professionals, having a meaningful career was an alternative identity that seemed preferable to identifying closely with their mental illness. Edward, a lawyer with bipolar disorder, took refuge in his professional role, explaining that he "took a lot of my identity in the sense that I was doing okay from my career." Danielle, a social worker with depression and anorexia, also identified more strongly in her professional identity because in comparison to the symptoms of her mental illness "at least one thing is semi steady." For Carrie, work provided not just a refuge or stability, but a positive source of identity with her team: "Even before I knew that I had this mental illness I've always felt different, but when I'm with my group of workers I do feel like I belong." Moreover, being at work made her feel special because "I have a certain knowledge" that "makes me feel like a professional."

The importance of having a professional identity was especially clear when mental illness forced time off from work or (as described earlier) resulted in the end of employment. Annie "really identified a lot with my work and what kind of work I'm interested in, accomplishing things" such that being unemployed was a real hardship. Alfred also took it hard when he lost his job: "It really was, kind of, a slap in the face because I'd been very successful and a star in my career, so I went from kind of being a star to being unemployed." While both of them eventually worked their way back into professional success, the period between jobs compounded their symptoms and feelings of worthlessness. In sum, participants' identity strategies mirrored the disparate statuses of having a mental illness versus being a working professional. While most distanced themselves from their illness identity, identifying as a successful professional was a source of pride, especially in the face of the challenges posed by their illness.

DISCUSSION

The sociology of disability centers on physical conditions while neglecting mental illness as a source of impairment and a cause for exclusion from the workplace (Mulvaney, 2000). Moreover, sociology as a discipline marginalizes disability studies, especially in relation to mental distress (Inckle, 2018). When it comes to making the workplace more accommodating to people with mental illness, little is known about the types of accommodations that are most beneficial and cost-effective (Zafar et al., 2019). Moreover, few studies have focused on the subjective experience of identifying as having a mental illness and considering applying for disability on that basis. This study addresses that imbalance by focusing on people who self-identify as having bipolar disorder or major depression, and describing their experiences balancing illness with professional careers. In so doing, it challenges the stereotype that people with serious mental illness cannot be successful working professionals while lending insight into the unique struggles they face on the job. From keeping one's illness a secret to being too ashamed to seek accommodations to getting fired, the individuals who contributed to this chapter each shared stories of struggles in the workplace. Nonetheless, they exemplified the fact that productivity in professional positions is possible for people with bipolar disorder or major depression.

Before turning to the implications of these findings, we compare and contrast individuals' experiences based on whether their primary diagnosis was bipolar disorder or depression. Similar percentages of people with bipolar disorder versus depression concealed their condition on the job to protect their reputation and only disclosed it judiciously to trusted individuals or when absolutely necessary. In contrast, three of the four individuals who sought some kind of accommodation such as FMLA leave or flexible work hours had bipolar disorder, although these absolute numbers are too small to draw any conclusions.

The contrast is more striking when it comes to the end of employment. Of the nine who reported the most extreme consequence of losing their job, seven (78%) had bipolar disorder, which is consistent with research indicating the bipolar disorder is more stigmatized in US society than major depression (Ellison et al., 2013). Moreover, it may suggest that employers are less willing to work with people showing symptoms of bipolar disorder than symptoms of depression. Annie, for example, got fired after sending "paranoid" emails to her boss, which admittedly did not make much sense. Although she was in too poor a state at the time to challenge the situation, she felt later that it would have been nice if her boss had explored what was behind her behavior and given her a second chance. Similarly, Amber got fired after publicly shaming her employer for ignoring sexual abuse of minors on the job. Had they known that she was a victim of incest herself, was very upset about what she was aware of, and was in the throes of her bipolar disorder, perhaps they might have acted to investigate her claim and ensure her well-being so she could return to work. Ellie, in contrast, was not outright fired after taking a long leave of absence for depression, but she was pushed out of her supervisory position at a time when she was too exhausted by her illness to protest. Perhaps her employer thought it was for her own good, but they did not consult her about the situation, leaving her feeling demoralized and even more depressed.

None of the participants, regardless of diagnosis, identified strongly with their mental illness, but people with bipolar disorder more often described their professional identity as a great source of pride for them, especially in light of their illness. This difference may reflect the fact that bipolar disorder is characterized by psychiatry as a permanent brain disorder requiring lifelong psychiatric treatment (Grande et al., 2016). Such a portrayal may intensify the identity threat faced by people with bipolar disorder versus depression to the extent that it suggests professional success is unlikely.

Although the results of this study are noteworthy, the data have limitations. The sample of 45 is not necessarily representative of working professionals with these conditions, given it is small and was not selected randomly. Instead, respondents opted into the study when they learned about it based on their self-identification as a working professional diagnosed with mental illness and their interest in and willingness to talk about it. As such, the data do not represent those who did not have an opportunity to participate, or who chose not to for various reasons. In addition, the results cannot be extended to people diagnosed with mental illness who identify as other than a working professional, such as those who identify as working class, or as fully disabled, or who are diagnosed with other conditions such as schizophrenia. Lastly, the study is limited by the lack of racial diversity and overrepresentation of women in the sample, rendering analysis of how illness identity intersects with race or gender in shaping people's experiences beyond the scope of the data.

Another limitation of the study, which is simultaneously a strength, is its reliance on people's subjective perceptions of workplace experiences. While the data cannot confirm or deny prejudice or discrimination toward people with mental illness in the workplace, they do reveal in graphic detail how it feels to believe one is being stigmatized. Documenting actual discrimination is challenging for researchers, but listening to people who believe they have been discriminated against is one way to better understand the phenomenon, even in the absence of concrete evidence.

This study is also limited by what participants were willing to share in their 1- to 2-hour interviews, and to how the researchers interpret their accounts, which do not necessarily align perfectly with the participants' understanding. While we endeavored to stay close to the data and avoid speculation, it remains possible that what people said in the interview came across differently to the researchers than was intended.

Despite these limitations, the results of this analysis have important implications for the sociology of disability with respect to people who identify as having serious mental illness and are nonetheless functioning well on the job in professional positions. The limited research conceptualizing mental illness as a disability typically focuses on people so disabled that they qualify for vocational rehabilitation and are placed in low-skilled jobs (e.g., Dean et al., 2017), whereas this study highlights people who have serious mental illness *and* have meaningful and successful professional careers. While most of the participants in this study did not identify as impaired or disabled (perhaps because the label is so stigmatizing), those who did reported a variety of troubling experiences when it came to seeking disability accommodations. Moreover, almost half the participants, whether they needed accommodations or not, were deeply concerned about widely disclosing their mental illness. Taken together, these patterns suggest that public stigma toward mental illness is a powerful force in the workplace that deters even the most successful professionals from being willing to identify as having a mental illness, let alone ask for help.

The participants in this study appreciated caring supervisors, schedule flexibility, the opportunity to take "mental health days," and support for their advocacy work on behalf of all people with mental illness. As such, we concur with the recommendations of the Centers for Disease Control (CDC, 2018) that employers are in a position to create a culture of health by providing health insurance coverage of mental health care, on-the-job programs that promote mental health such as exercise or meditation, and working conditions that minimize stress. We also recommend that employers implement evidence-based workplace anti-stigma campaigns that promote awareness and inclusion of people with mental illness on the job, which could reduce the occurrence of rejection and hostility reported by some of our participants on the part of their coworkers and increase the success of implementation of the ADA for people with mental illness (McDowell & Fossey, 2015). Such campaigns have demonstrated success in increasing knowledge and understanding of mental illness and willingness to help as well as reduced social distance from and stigma toward people with mental illness (Hanisch et al., 2016; Szeto & Dobson, 2010).

In conclusion, being diagnosed with a serious mental illness such as bipolar disorder or major depression does not preclude the possibility of thriving as a working professional, but much remains to be done to improve the working conditions of people in this situation. As society evolves to prioritize mental health in the workplace, more people may be willing to reveal their diagnosis publicly, sending the message to everyone that having a serious mental illness does not equate with total and permanent disability.

REFERENCES

Baldwin, M. L., & Marcus, S. C. (2006). Perceived and measured stigma among workers with serious mental illness. *Psychiatric Services, 57*(3), 388–392.

Bolo, C., Sareen, J., Patten, S., Schmitz, N., Currie, S., & Wang, J. (2013). Receiving workplace mental health accommodations and the outcome of mental disorders in employees with a depressive and/or anxiety disorder. *Journal of Occupational and Environmental Medicine*, 55(11), 1293–1299.

Borg, M., Veseth, M., Binder, P., & Topor, A. (2013). The role of work in recovery from bipolar disorders. *Qualitative Social Work*, 12(3), 323–339.

Boyd, J. E., Zeiss, A., Reddy, S., & Skinner, S. (2016). Accomplishments of 77 VA mental health professionals with a lived experience of mental illness. *American Journal of Orthopsychiatry*, 86(6), 610–619.

Centers for Disease Control (CDC). (2018). *Mental health in the workplace.* https://www.cdc.gov/workplacehealthpromotion/tools-resources/pdfs/WHRC-Mental-Health-and-Stress-in-the-Workplac-Issue-Brief-H.pdf

Chapman, J. R. (2002). Bipolar disorder: Responding to challenges to identity (Publication No. 3099430) [Doctoral dissertation, The University of Texas at Austin]. ProQuest Dissertations and Theses Global.

Colman, I., Naicker, K., Zeng, Y., Ataullahjan, A., Senthilselvan, A., & Patten, S. B. (2011). Predictors of long-term prognosis of depression. *Canadian Medical Association Journal*, 183(17), 1969–1976.

Cruwys, T., & Gunaseelan, S. (2016). "Depression is who I am": Mental illness identity, stigma and wellbeing. *Journal of Affective Disorders*, 189, 36–42.

Cummings, J. R., Lucas, S. M., & Druss, B. G. (2013). Addressing public stigma and disparities among persons with mental illness: The role of federal policy. *American Journal of Public Health*, 103(5), 781–785.

Dean, D., Pepper, J. V., Schmidt, R., & Stern, S. (2017). The effects of vocational rehabilitation services for people with mental illness. *Journal of Human Resources*, 52(3), 826–858.

Deterding, N. M., & Waters, M. C. (2021). Flexible coding of in-depth interviews: A twenty-first-century approach. *Sociological Methods & Research*, 50(2), 708–739.

Drake, R. E., Frey, W., Bond, G. R., Goldman, H. H., Salkever, D., Miller, A., Moore, T. A., Riley, J., Karakus, M., & Milfort, R. (2013). Assisting social security disability insurance beneficiaries with schizophrenia, bipolar disorder, or major depression in returning to work. *American Journal of Psychiatry*, 170(12), 1433–1441.

Elliott, M., & Doane, M. J. (2015). Stigma management of mental illness: Effects of concealment, discrimination, and identification on well-being. *Self and Identity*, 14(6), 654–674.

Ellison, N., Mason, O., & Scior, K. (2013). Bipolar disorder and stigma: A systematic review of the literature. *Journal of Affective Disorders*, 151(3), 805–820.

Fernandez, M. E., Breen, L. J., & Simpson, T. A. (2014). Renegotiating identities: Experiences of loss and recovery for women with bipolar disorder. *Qualitative Health Research*, 24(7), 890–900.

Gair, S. (2012). Feeling their stories: Contemplating empathy, insider/outsider positionings, and enriching qualitative research. *Qualitative Health Research*, 22(1), 134–143.

Gelenberg, A. J., Freeman, M. P., Markowitz, J. C., Rosenbaum, J. F., Thase, M. E., Trivedi, M. H., & Van Rhoads, R. S. (2010). American Psychiatric Association practice guidelines for the treatment of patients with major depressive disorder. *The American Journal of Psychiatry*, 167(Suppl. 10), 9–118.

Goffman, E. (1963). *Stigma: Notes on the management of spoiled identity.* Simon and Schuster.

Goldberg, S. G. (2007). The social construction of bipolar disorder: The interrelationship between societal and individual meanings [Unpublished Doctoral dissertation, Fielding Graduate University].

Grande, I., Berk, M., Birmaher, B., & Vieta, E. (2016). Bipolar disorder. *The Lancet*, *387*(10027), 1561–1572.

Gruys, K., & Hutson, D. J. (2020). The aesthetic labor of ethnographers. In N. Boero & K. Mason (Eds.), *The oxford handbook of the sociology of the body and embodiment*, (pp. 327–344). Oxford University Press.

Hanisch, S. E., Twomey, C. D., Szeto, A. C. H., Birner, U. W., Nowak, D., & Sabariego, C. (2016). The effectiveness of interventions targeting the stigma of mental illness at the workplace: A systematic review. *BMC Psychiatry*, *16*(1), 1–11.

Hawke, L. D., Parikh, S. V., & Michalak, E. E. (2013). Stigma and bipolar disorder: A review of the literature. *Journal of Affective Disorders*, *150*(2), 181–191.

Hipes, C., Lucas, J., Phelan, J. C., & White, R. C. (2016). The stigma of mental illness in the labor market. *Social Science Research*, *56*, 16–25.

Inckle, K. (2018). Irrational perspectives and untenable positions: Sociology, madness and disability. In S. Holland & L. Spracklen (Eds.), *Subcultures, bodies and spaces: Essays on alternatively and marginalization* (pp. 169–188). Emerald.

Inder, M. L., Crowe, M. T., Moor, S., Luty, S. E., Carter, J. D., & Joyce, P. R. (2008). "I actually don't know who I am": The impact of bipolar disorder on the development of self. *Psychiatry: Interpersonal and Biological Processes*, *71*(2), 123–133.

Jones, A. M. (2011). Disclosure of mental illness in the workplace: A literature review. *American Journal of Psychiatric Rehabilitation*, *14*(3), 212–229.

Judd, L. L., Schettler, P. J., Solomon, D. A., Maser, J. D., Coryell, W., Endicott, J., & Akiskal, J. S. (2008). Psychosocial disability and work role function compared across the long-term course of bipolar I, bipolar II and unipolar major depressive disorders. *Journal of Affective Disorders*, *108*(1–2), 49–58.

Karp, D. A. (2017). *Speaking of sadness: Depression, disconnection, and the meanings of illness.* Oxford University Press.

Krill, P. R., Johnson, R., & Albert, L. (2016). The prevalence of substance use and other mental health concerns among American attorneys. *Journal of Addiction Medicine*, *10*(1), 46–52.

Lim, L., Nathan, P., O'Brien-Malone, A., & Williams, S. (2004). A qualitative approach to identifying psychosocial issues faced by bipolar patients. *The Journal of Nervous and Mental Disease*, *192*(12), 810–817.

Mata, D. A., Ramos, M. A., Bansal, N., Khan, R., Guille, C., Di Angelantonio, E., & Sen, S. (2016). Prevalence of depression and depressive symptoms among resident physicians: A systematic review and meta-analysis. *Survey of Anesthesiology*, *60*(4), 2373–2383.

McDowell, C., & Fossey, E. (2015). Workplace accommodations for people with mental illness: A scoping review. *Journal of Occupational Rehabilitation*, *25*(1), 197–206.

Michalak, E. E., Yatham, L. N., Kolesar, S., & Lam, R. W. (2006). Bipolar disorder and quality of life: A patient-centered perspective. *Quality of Life Research*, *15*(1), 25–37.

Mulvany, J. (2000). Disability, impairment or illness? The relevance of the social model of disability to the study of mental disorder. *Sociology of Health & Illness*, *22*(5), 582–601.

Paris, J. (2015). *Overdiagnosis in psychiatry: How modern psychiatry lost its way while creating a diagnosis for almost all of life's misfortunes.* Oxford University Press.

Price, M., Salzer, M. S., O'Shea, A., & Kerschbaum, S. L. (2017). Disclosure of mental disability by college and university faculty: The negotiation of accommodations, supports, and barriers. *Disability Studies Quarterly*, *37*(2).

Proudfoot, J. G., Parker, G. B., Benoit, M., Manicavasagar, V., Smith, M., & Gayed, A. (2009). What happens after diagnosis? Understanding the experiences of patients with newly-diagnosed bipolar disorder. *Health Expectations, 12*(2), 120–129.

Rotenberg, M., Zafar, N., Akhtar, N., & Rudnick, A. (2016). Addressing workplace accommodations for people with mental illness. *Journal of Psychosocial Rehabilitation and Mental Health, 3*(2), 117–118.

Sevak, P. H., & Khan, S. (2017). Psychiatric versus physical disabilities: A comparison of barriers and facilitators to employment. *Psychiatric Rehabilitation Journal, 40*(2), 163–171.

Shakespeare, T. (2013). The social model of disability studies. In L. J. Davis (Ed.), *The Disability studies reader* (pp. 214–221). Routledge.

Smith, D. J., Nicholl, B. I., Cullen, B., Martin, D., Ul-Haq, Z., Evans, J., Gill, J. M. R., Roberts, B., Gallacher, J., Mackay, D., Hotopf, M., Deary, I., Craddock, N., & Pell, J. P. (2013). Prevalence and characteristics of probable major depression and bipolar disorder within UK biobank: Cross-sectional study of 172,751 participants. *PloS One, 8*(11), 1–7.

Steele, C. M., Spencer, S. J., & Aronson, J. (2002). Contending with group image: The psychology of stereotype and social identity threat. *Advances in Experimental Social Psychology, 34*, 379–440.

Stefan, S. (2002). *Hollow promises: Employment discrimination against people with mental disabilities.* American Psychological Association.

Stryker, S., & Burke, P. J. (2000). The past, present, and future of an identity theory. *Social Psychology Quarterly, 63*(4), 284–297.

Szeto, A. C. H., & Dobson, K. S. (2010). Reducing the stigma of mental disorders at work: A review of current workplace anti-stigma intervention programs. *Applied and Preventive Psychology, 14*(1–4), 41–56.

Tremblay, C. H. (2011). Workplace accommodations and job success for persons with bipolar disorder. *Work, 40*(4), 479–487.

Twenge, J. M., & Campbell, W. K. (2002). Self-esteem and socioeconomic status: A meta-analytic review. *Personality and Social Psychology Review, 6*(1), 59–71.

Wang, J., Patten, S., Currie, S., Sareen, J., & Schmitz, N. (2011). Perceived needs for and use of workplace accommodations by individuals with a depressive and/or anxiety disorder. *Journal of Occupational and Environmental Medicine, 53*(11), 1268–1272.

Wong, N. C., Lookadoo, K. L., & Nisbett, G. S. (2017). "I'm Demi and I have bipolar disorder": Effect of parasocial contact on reducing stigma toward people with bipolar disorder. *Communication Studies, 68*(3), 314–333.

Zafar, N., Rotenberg, M., & Rudnick, A. (2019). A systematic review of work accommodations for people with mental disorders. *Work, 64*(3), 461–475.

....

CHAPTER 26

A CRITICAL REVIEW OF APPROACHES TO ERASING THE STIGMA OF MENTAL ILLNESS

....

LINDSAY SHEEHAN AND PATRICK W. CORRIGAN

SOCIOLOGIST Irving Goffman (1963) first described stigma as occurring when physical or mental characteristics signal that a person is different from others. Subsequent scholars have posited that several conditions lead to the perpetuation of stigma once that difference has been perceived (Link & Phelan, 2001). First, members of the society develop negative conceptions about the group (e.g., people with disabilities are weak) and mentally categorize members of that stigmatized group as being substantially different from themselves. Then, when people are labeled as belonging to the stigmatized group, they experience discrimination, along with loss of status and social power in relation to the majority culture (Link & Phelan, 2001). Building on this, the social-cognitive model of public stigma consists of stereotypes, prejudice, and discrimination that hinder people with disabilities from engaging fully in their communities and from fulfilling social, occupational, educational, and health goals (Sheehan et al., 2017). Stereotypes (overgeneralized beliefs) about people with disabilities form the basis for subsequent unfair emotional (prejudicial) and behavioral (discriminatory) reactions. People with disabilities can internalize the public's stigma toward their health condition (i.e., self-stigmatize) and experience negative consequences as a result (Corrigan et al., 2011). Although stigma applies broadly to individuals with all types of disabilities, much theoretical and empirical work on disability stigma has focused on that experienced by individuals with psychiatric disabilities. Thus, this chapter focuses on strategies to reduce public stigma and self-stigma related to mental illness. The goal of the chapter is not to advocate for one strategy versus another, but to provide an overview of anti-stigma efforts and present research on the efficacy of various approaches.

Table 26.1 Social–Cognitive Model of Public Stigma and Progressive Model of Self-Stigma

	Public Stigma	Self-Stigma
Stereotype (cognitive)	People with mental illness are unpredictable.	As a person with bipolar disorder, I am <u>aware</u> of the stereotype that people with mental illness are a burden to others.
Prejudice (affective)	An employer mistrusts employees with mental illness because he/she views them as unpredictable.	I <u>agree</u> with the stereotype and I feel worthless—who would want to date me?
Discrimination (behavioral)	Employee with mental illness is turned down for a promotion.	I <u>apply</u> the self-prejudice to my own life, and stop looking for a relationship, resulting in <u>harm</u> to my social support network.

In regards to *public stigma*, Table 26.1 illustrates how stereotypes ("people with mental illness are dangerous") and prejudice ("I'm afraid of them") can result in discriminatory behavior ("I don't want a mental hospital in my neighborhood"). Similarly, with *self-stigma* individuals with mental illness who internalize the public assumptions about them ("I guess I *am* crazy") can experience shame and self-limit their own behaviors ("I'm never going to measure up, so why even try"). In the progressive model of self-stigma development, an individual must first be "aware" of stereotypes about their disability group, "agree" that these stereotypes are true, "apply" these stereotypes to themselves, and experience "harm" as a result (Corrigan et al., 2011). Self-stigma is associated with reduced self-worth and failure to pursue opportunities, goals, and relationships, often through a strong expectation of rejection (Corrigan et al., 2011; Picco et al., 2016). Additionally, self-stigma is connected with worse mental and physical health outcomes, such that reductions in self-stigma are associated with decreased symptoms, increased functioning, and enhanced quality of life (Pearl et al., 2017).

Stigma Agendas

Efforts to ameliorate stigma are motivated by the three following agendas: 1) a services agenda, 2) a rights agenda, and 3) a self-worth agenda (Corrigan & Al-Khouja, 2018). The *services agenda* assumes that people with mental illness who would otherwise benefit from mental health services avoid counseling, psychiatry, medication, or social work services to prevent being labeled as "mentally ill." Stigma may also interfere with services by impacting quality and availability of services (Corrigan et al., 2014a). Thus, the services agenda to stigma-change seeks to decrease stigma so people better engage in evidence-based care and manage their illness. In contrast, a *rights agenda* recognizes people with disabilities as deserving of fair and equitable treatment in employment, education, housing, relationships, and healthcare. As with the civil-rights movement, the rights agenda seeks to reduce stigma so people are able to meet their life goals and aspirations. In the *self-worth* agenda, individuals internalize prejudice and are harmed by shame and self-stigma. The self-worth agenda includes ways to replace this sense of shame with self-esteem and self-efficacy. This agenda emphasizes hope, confidence, self-esteem, and personal goals (Corrigan & Al-Khouja, 2018).

However, these three agendas might compete with one another. For example, anti-stigma programming that emphasizes a services agenda may focus on identifying and labeling people with a diagnosis, thereby emphasizing the differences between "us" (members of the public) and "them" (people with mental illness), and undermining recovery beliefs (Corrigan & Al-Khouja, 2018). In this way, a services agenda might actually worsen the self-worth of people with mental illness. Hence, scholars and advocates must be aware of unintended consequences in stigma change, while incorporating the perspectives and agendas of other stigma stakeholders into their work. Next, we summarize anti-stigma efforts for public stigma.

ADDRESSING PUBLIC STIGMA

Efforts to reduce the public stigma of mental illness have consisted primarily of three strategies: protest, education, and contact (Corrigan et al., 2001). These strategies are summarized in Table 26.2. Protest strategies involve actively advocating for reductions

Table 26.2 Approaches to Reducing Public Stigma

Type of Intervention	Description	Examples
Protest	Actions to decrease perpetuation of mental illness stigma in media, organizational practices, policy, or legislation	Active Minds' Transform Your Campus https://www.activeminds.org/programs/transform-your-campus/
Contact	Involves persons with a mental illness talking about their own mental health experiences, recovery, and/or experiences with prejudice and discrimination (either face-to-face or virtually)	NAMI's In Our Own Voice https://www.nami.org/Support-Education/Mental-Health-Education/NAMI-In-Our-Own-Voice
Education	Involves dissemination of information about mental illness risk factors and symptoms and/or myths about mental illness; May provide skills-training in how to help a person with mental health challenges	Mental Health First Aid https://www.mentalhealthfirstaid.org/

in stigma for people with psychiatric disabilities. They include pursuits such as marches and petitions against objectionable policies and systems (Arboleda-Flórez & Stuart, 2012). For example, legislative reform and advocacy led to the passage of the Americans with Disabilities Act and mental health parity laws. Another strategy, education, entails communicating information about disabilities, with the primary aim of challenging negative beliefs and assumptions. Social media has facilitated an expansion of education-based anti-stigma messages that can reach individuals via a variety of platforms and formats (e.g., Twitter, Facebook; Betton et al., 2015). Finally, in contact-based strategies, individuals with disabilities speak about their personal experiences with disability, either in person or through another medium such as video. Social media has also fueled opportunities for people to share their experiences with mental illness more widely. While anti-stigma programs have typically targeted healthcare providers and the public in general, fewer have targeted employers, coworkers, family, friends, policymakers, landlords, or religious leaders (Sheehan, 2015).

Outcome Measures

Most evaluations of public anti-stigma interventions measure either: 1) knowledge, 2) attitudes, or 3) behaviors/behavioral proxies (Hanisch et al., 2016). Tests of knowledge include pre-post surveys on mental health awareness or knowledge of research data that challenges common mental illness myths. Attitude tests may ask participants to read a vignette about a person with mental illness and respond to items about the target person in terms of stereotypes ("how dangerous is Harry?") or social distance ("how likely are you to rent your apartment to Harry?"; Corrigan et al., 2002). Attitude tests can also include more subtle questions that reduce social desirability in responses (e.g., "how different are you from Harry?") or reaction times to computer-generated pairing tasks (e.g., Teachman et al., 2006). Behavioral proxy measures, such as self-efficacy in identifying or providing support to a person with mental illness, are often used as well (Hanisch et al., 2016). Less frequently, researchers have measured actual behavior changes such as how often police used force following the anti-stigma intervention (Thornicroft et al., 2016). However, scholars have argued that eliminating negative attitudes and behaviors toward people with mental illness is insufficient to make a difference; anti-stigma programs are successful when people replace prejudice with attitudes of recovery and self-determination (Corrigan et al., 2014c).

Approaches to Reducing Public Stigma

In this section, we examine the research evidence for the three primary anti-stigma approaches.

Protest

Protest strategies are meant to repress stigma that is enacted through media, advertising, policies, practices, or legislation (Corrigan et al., 2001). Examples of protest activities include email campaigns to remove stigmatizing advertisements or letters to company management about sick leave policies for people with disabilities. Interventions utilizing protest strategies are challenging to evaluate empirically. Changes to policies and practices resulting from protest may be enacted over longer time periods, making it difficult to isolate the effects on the public's attitudes and behaviors. In meta-analyses on anti-stigma interventions for mental illness, researchers did not locate a sufficient number of protest-based interventions needed to empirically assess this approach (Corrigan et al., 2012; Griffiths et al., 2014).

Although protest has rarely been studied in randomized trials, legislation resulting from protest and advocacy (most notably the Americans with Disabilities Act) have certainly reduced overt acts of discrimination and removed barriers to community participation for people with disabilities. However, the immediate reaction to acts of protest themselves or toward enactment of protective policies might be one of psychological reactance ("why do they need all these special treatments?") that could actually strengthen negative public attitudes (Corrigan et al., 2001).

Education

Based on the notion that enhanced knowledge of mental health will reduce stigma, mental health literacy interventions deliver information about identification, prevention, and treatment, and then teach skills to respond to mental health crises (Jorm, 2012). For example, Mental Health First Aid is a well-known program that teaches participants to recognize symptoms of various mental illness, identify associated risk factors, and respond to individuals who are experiencing mental health challenges.

Critics argue that trainings on mental health literacy may inadvertently emphasize stereotypes and differences, or the "otherness" of people with mental illness, failing to change more meaningful stigma indices such as behaviors toward people with mental illness or even potentially enhancing discrimination (Corrigan et al., 2015c). For example, a German population survey found that while mental health knowledge increased, comfort in social contacts with people with mental illness did not (Angermeyer et al., 2009). However, in general, education-based interventions lead to reductions in public stigma (Griffiths et al., 2014) that also endure over time (Corrigan et al., 2015b).

As the most frequently evaluated approach, the positive effects of educational anti-stigma interventions have been found for people with mental illness in general and also for those with particular diagnoses (Griffiths et al., 2014; Quinn et al., 2013). Online approaches have been shown equally effective when compared to face-to-face interventions (Griffiths et al., 2014) and adolescents in particular seem to benefit from educational approaches (Borschmann et al., 2014).

Contact

Contact-based interventions involve persons with a mental illness sharing their own experiences with mental illness, recovery, and/or prejudice and discrimination. For example, the National Alliance on Mental Illness (NAMI) conducts the In Our Own Voice (IOOV) program in which trained speakers talk about their own recovery (Brennan & McGrew, 2013). Contact-based interventions have a significant effect on public stigma, in many cases outperforming education-based interventions (Borschmann et al., 2014;

Corrigan et al., 2012). A meta-analysis that included 79 studies and 38,000 participants concluded that effects of contact-based interventions on attitudes and behavioral intentions were roughly twice that of education-based interventions (Corrigan et al., 2012). However, youth may not see the same benefits of contact interventions and may glean more from educational interventions (Borschmann et al., 2014).

Another caveat of contact-based findings is that meta-analytic findings do not support the long-term effects of contact (Corrigan et al., 2015b), perhaps due to limited number of studies that included long-term post-intervention follow-up. Furthermore, not enough studies examine actual behavior change over time (Maunder & White, 2019). In a meta-analysis of contact-based interventions (101 studies in 24 countries), contact led to stigma change both immediately after the intervention, and in the short and medium term (Maunder & White, 2019). Overall, contact interventions were most effective for non-Western individuals, healthcare workers, and college students.

In reality, education and contact interventions are often merged, such that an individual with mental illness educates the audience about mental health and related myths while sharing the story of their own recovery. Another meta-analysis compared combined contact-education interventions with education-only interventions (due to lack of sufficient contact-only studies), finding that contact-education interventions were just as impactful as education-only (Griffiths et al., 2014). Other findings indicate that contact-only interventions are as effective as contact-education (Maunder & White, 2019; Morgan et al., 2018).

Simulation Interventions

Some interventions use simulation of mental illness to reduce stigma, such as having participants use headphones to imitate the voice-hearing experiences of people with psychosis. However, research on anti-stigma simulation activities is mixed (Morgan et al., 2018). Wan and Lam (2019) found six peer-reviewed studies on virtual reality interventions targeting stigma in healthcare providers. Studies focused primarily on simulations of auditory hallucinations or dementia, with some showing increases in knowledge, positive attitudes, and empathy.

Media Campaigns

Media interventions target large audiences via television, mail, internet, apps, or other media. A review of mass media anti-stigma interventions found small to medium reductions in prejudice, but no changes in discrimination (Clement et al., 2013). Video interventions of all types show promise for changing attitudes in adolescents and young adults (Janoušková et al., 2017). A systematic review of serious mental illness and the impact of news and social media on stigma found 12 studies, concluding that positive news stories are connected to reductions in stigma and negative stories are associated with increased stigma (Ross et al., 2019). However, only a few of these studies (n = 3) evaluated anti-stigma programs targeted at reporters or journalism students; of these, the study designs were weak, and there was no evidence for a change in stigmatizing news content occurring post-intervention.

National Anti-stigma Initiatives

Several nations have implemented large-scale strategies to reduce stigma of mental illness over the past several decades (e.g., Australia's beyondblue campaign). National campaigns generally use educational strategies to target mental health literacy, but also include elements of contact (Quinn et al., 2013). While national initiatives to reduce stigma are challenging to appraise due to confounding variables, lack of rigorous research designs, and failure to account for baseline stigma levels (Evans-Lacko et al., 2014), these initiatives are associated with increased help-seeking behaviors, reductions in suicide rates, and decreases in negative attitudes about people with mental illness (Quinn et al., 2013). Large anti-stigma campaigns may increase recognition and sensitivity to stigma as an injustice for people with mental illness (Jorm et al., 2006; Corker et al., 2013).

Unfortunately, relatively few interventions in the research literature have demonstrated the ability to change real-world behaviors; however, both education- and contact-based approaches have an impact on knowledge, attitudes, and behavioral intentions. While education-based strategies are most commonly employed, contact-based strategies appear to have an advantage over educational programming, with effects that persist over time and have an equivalent impact when conducted in video formats. Protest strategies of public stigma reduction may have power to "force" behavior changes through structural transformation (e.g., new laws or policies), but these movements are difficult to evaluate in controlled settings, and it remains unclear whether positive attitude changes accompany protest-initiated structural changes. Conversely, mass-media campaigns appear effective in changing attitudes, but have not demonstrated accompanying behavioral changes. Despite the difficulty in accurately evaluating national anti-stigma initiatives, several countries have measured positive changes in attitudes and behaviors with sustained implementation of comprehensive anti-stigma programming. Interventions have been largely education-based, suggesting an untapped potential for implementation of contact-based strategies overall.

Key Components of Contact-Based Anti-Stigma Interventions

Given the plethora of interventions and anti-stigma campaigns globally, researchers have sought to identify key components of successful contact-based programs. We review the evidence on program format, targets, presenters, message, and follow-up below.

Format

Contact interventions with lived-experience persons can take a variety of forms, including in-person contact, video contact, written stories, or online contact through text or social media (Stuart et al., 2013). Meta-analytic research indicates that in-person contact is about twice as impactful as video contact (Corrigan et al., 2012). Yamaguchi and colleagues (2013) conducted a systematic review of stigma programs in college students, which included 23 RCTs. The authors determined that both video contact and in-person contact had advantages for changing attitudes and social distance over educational programs. People with lived experience who facilitate programs tend to endorse in-person and discussion-based programs (Corrigan et al., 2014b). A study of 22 anti-stigma interventions targeted at healthcare providers found that programs where participants were exposed to more than one type of contact and/or lived experience story were more effective (Knaak et al., 2014). Multiple contacts in these interventions included multiple lived-experience speakers or a combination of speakers and videos.

Targets

Stigma interventions appear most effective when they are targeted at specific groups and adapted to meet the needs of local communities (Borschmann et al., 2014; Corrigan et al., 2014b; Parcesepe & Cabassa, 2013). This may include targeting by age, gender, ethnicity, or occupation (Stuart et al., 2019; Thornicroft et al., 2016). Given that the impact of stigma is most detrimental when perpetrated by those with social influence and power over the stigmatized group (Corrigan & Fong, 2014), anti-stigma interventions for mental health have traditionally targeted health professionals, student trainees, employers, and law enforcement (Dalky, 2012; Livingston et al., 2012). Here we more fully describe effects on healthcare workers and employers.

Addressing stigma related to healthcare has a large potential impact. Despite findings that contact reduces stigma, mental health providers may still perpetrate stigma and may develop more negative attitudes toward people with mental illness because they see patients at the height of their struggles, rather than having a view of their entire recovery trajectory (Ungar et al., 2016). For example, many mental health clinicians have lowered beliefs in the ability of people with mental illness to recover (Magliano et al., 2004; Wahl & Aroesty-Cohen, 2010), often blame people with mental illness for their problems (Ross & Goldner, 2009), believe that people with mental illness are dangerous and unpredictable (Kingdon et al., 2004; Magliano et al., 2004), and desire social distance (Reavley et al., 2014). In a review of contact-based anti-stigma interventions with healthcare professionals, those that were recovery-focused and included multiple methods of contact (e.g., multiple lived-experience speakers) were associated with the best outcomes (Knaak et al., 2014).

Workplace stigma may prevent people with mental illness from retaining their jobs, getting promotions, receiving workplace accommodations, or obtaining future employment (Oexle et al., 2018). Most interventions with employers have been education-based, and the research on these interventions have methodological limitations such as a lack of experimental and longitudinal designs, and inadequacies in scale validity (Malachowski & Kirsh, 2013; Szeto & Dobson, 2010). A systematic review of workplace interventions found 16 studies, including evidence that some interventions increased knowledge, positive attitudes, and supportive actions (Hanisch et al., 2016). Most of the studies that met criteria for the review evaluated educational rather than contact-based approaches to stigma reduction, and the authors did not draw conclusions about key ingredients of these programs. The longest follow-up period for a workplace intervention in this review was two years, with overall follow-up data showing retentions in knowledge and confidence to provide help, but not in attitude change (Hanisch et al., 2016).

Presenter Characteristics

The practice of having intervention facilitators talk about their personal experience with mental illness is a key component of contact-based interventions (Corrigan et al., 2014b; Knaak et al., 2014). The presence of a lived-experience person in a leadership role (e.g., facilitating the training) can implicitly challenge stereotypes about incompetence and impossibility of recovery, in addition to being a source of social contact during the intervention. Lived-experience facilitators can give examples of their own experiences with prejudice, discrimination, and self-stigma, allowing the presentation to take on a real-life flavor. Evidence also suggests that both facilitator passion and use of a person-focused (rather than illness-focused) approach result in better outcomes (Knaak et al., 2014).

Message

The content or messages conveyed through stigma interventions have varied. These include recovery-oriented messages, biogenetic explanations, myth-challenging, and skill-building. First, substantial research (e.g., Corrigan et al., 2014b; Knaak et al., 2014) indicates that recovery-oriented approaches to anti-stigma interventions are most likely to be impactful. To emphasize recovery, facilitators express hopefulness about recovery from mental illness and relate recovery (or "on-the-way up") stories (Corrigan et al. 2014b; see Figure 26.1). Speakers focus on both their current accomplishments and the (often) difficult journey to those accomplishments.

Second, anti-stigma interventions that emphasize biogenetic causes of mental illness ("depression is a brain disease") may seem on the surface to combat stigmatizing attitudes such as blaming the person with mental illness for their condition ("you're not trying hard enough to recover"). However, biogenetic attributions can strengthen negative attitudes and behaviors when they accentuate the idea that people with mental

---

Sample Recovery Story

Hi everyone, my name is Mandy and I'm a nurse practitioner. I'm so excited to be here with you today and share my story. If you met me on the street or at my job, you probably would not be able to tell it, but I have bipolar disorder. I've actually been struggling with mental health since I was a teenager, including a suicide attempt when I was 22. It took me about 8 years to finally get the treatment that would help me and for the past about 4 years, I've really been doing well—in both my personal life—I've just started a family—and my professional life. Along the way, I've had some people who judged me for having a mental illness, but I've also met people who are great supports in my life. As we get to know each other better today, feel free to ask me questions about my experiences with mental health and stigma.

FIGURE 26.1 Sample Recovery Story

illness are different and question recovery potential ("if depression is a brain disease, they'll need medication for the rest of their life"). In fact, when biogenetic causes of mental illness are emphasized, blame is decreased, but endorsement of recovery potential is also reduced (Kvaale et al., 2013). Biogenetic explanations might also result in the "why try" effect, in which individuals endorse the notion that they are biologically inferior, lose hope, and cease efforts in pursuing recovery goals (Kvaale et al., 2013).

Third, anti-stigma interventions have frequently included activities that directly combat stereotypes about people with mental illness ("they're unpredictable, dangerous, and weak"). These activities can take on additional salience when presented by a person with lived experience who can describe how it felt when others mistreated them based on these stereotypes. Myth-challenging has been identified as a key ingredient for programs targeting healthcare professionals (Knaak et al., 2014).

Fourth, some interventions help participants develop specific skills for changing behaviors and reducing the impact of stigma on individuals with mental illness (Knaak et al., 2014). For example, skill-building activities could provide guidance on using person-first forms of address (use "person with schizophrenia" vs. "schizophrenic"), improving body language (making changes in patronizing tone when addressing a person with mental illness), or empathically responding to a person who is in distress.

Follow-Up

Although most interventions are short-term (1–2 hours), some interventions also include follow-ups such as booster sessions, process groups, or evaluations (Stuart et al., 2019). Interventions can also establish future goals such as having attendees write down action steps that they can implement following the training (Corrigan et al., 2014b). Research indicates that follow-up activities may increase the usefulness of the intervention (Knaak et al., 2014; Stuart et al., 2019).

ANTI-STIGMA EFFORTS FOR SELF-STIGMA

Stigma resistance refers to the ability of individuals in a stigmatized group to reject public misperceptions about them and resist the internalization of stereotypes (Firmin et al., 2017). Various interventions have been proposed to address internalized stigma (i.e., self-stigma). Although interventions vary in length, most are designed as small-group interventions (Yanos et al., 2015). We explore approaches to addressing self-stigma below.

Approaches to Addressing Self-Stigma

Although some interventions use multiple strategies, there are five basic approaches to addressing self-stigma: psychoeducation, cognitive-behavioral, strategic disclosure, peer support, and self-help. These are summarized in Table 26.3.

Table 26.3 Approaches to Reducing Self-Stigma

Type of Intervention	Description
Psychoeducational	Provides information on mental illness and mental health–related myths
Cognitive-Behavioral	Helps participants to recognize and challenge self-stigmatizing cognition
Strategic Disclosure	Provides support and guidance to people with mental illness in whether and how to talk to others about their mental health
Peer Support	Organized support group of people with lived experience of mental illness providing mutual support (often manualized and conducted in a group setting)
Self-Help	Self-guided activities such as pamphlets or books to combat self-stigma

Psychoeducation

Like education-based public stigma programs, psychoeducational interventions provide information and counter myths about mental illness (e.g., mental illness is not a sign of weakness). For example, Uchino and colleagues (2012) implemented a manualized intervention for individuals with schizophrenia. This included a video of a person with schizophrenia being interviewed on television, along with a discussion and activity challenging misconceptions about people with schizophrenia perpetrating violence. Participants who completed this program exhibited increased knowledge of mental health, along with reduced endorsement of social distance from people with schizophrenia, as compared to those in the usual care group.

Cognitive-Behavioral

Cognitive-behavioral strategies guide participants in challenging the false stereotypes that might cause personal shame. The Ending Self-Stigma (ESS) program guides participants in identifying stereotypes and challenging automatic thoughts that might result from these stereotypes (Lucksted et al., 2011). For example, a stereotype such as "people with mental illness are weak" might result in an automatic thought ("I'm weak and worthless"). The cognitive-behavioral approach encourages people with mental illness to challenge and replace negative thoughts with more affirming cognitions ("I've been struggling, but the struggle is just showing me how strong I am") and adaptive behaviors (e.g., trying a new wellness goal or making a new social connection). The ESS program also addresses issues related to self-concept and guides participants in responding to discrimination. Similarly, narrative enhancement and cognitive therapy (NECT) is an anti-stigma intervention that uses cognitive restructuring techniques, along with psychoeducation and storytelling, to challenge self-stigma (Yanos et al., 2011).

Strategic Disclosure

The strategic disclosure approach reflects insights about the harm of being in the "stigma closet." People with a mental illness may stay silent about their experiences out of shame, resulting in decrements to self-esteem and self-efficacy. People who decide to talk about their mental health experiences report less self-stigma and greater empowerment (Livingston & Boyd, 2010). Disclosure may also benefit mental health by making additional social and health supports available, releasing the burden of secrecy, and challenging public stigma. A program using strategic disclosure, Honest, Open, Proud (HOP) includes three peer-facilitated group sessions to help participants weigh the pros and cons of disclosure, consider disclosure in different contexts (e.g., at work), develop disclosure scripts, and prepare for the responses of those they disclose to (Corrigan et al., 2013).

Peer Support

Peer support programs to serve people with mental illness have proliferated in recent years. Advocates and researchers suggest that peer support may impact self-stigma and its converse, empowerment, through peers serving as roles models, better engagement in programming, and a reorientation to services that focuses more on the service-user as a human with goals rather than a patient to be treated (Burke et al., 2019). Although peer services can be provided one-to-one, many are designed as curriculum-based groups that are peer-led and include components such as illness self-management strategies, crisis planning, psychoeducation, or group discussion (Burke et al., 2019). Some self-stigma interventions are facilitated by peers (e.g., HOP; Corrigan et al., 2013), but few research studies have explicitly examined the impact of peer support on self-stigma (Burke et al., 2019).

Self-Help

Some individuals are alienated by the healthcare system, feel the impact of self-stigma more acutely, or have significant symptoms (e.g., social anxiety) that prevent them from being able to avail face-to-face services. Self-help strategies have been posited as an option for people with mental illness to utilize written information (e.g., pamphlets, books, blogs) or media (videos, apps) to address self-stigma. A systematic review (2007–2019) located eight studies on self-help interventions that measured self-stigma as an outcome (Mills et al., 2020). However, only one published study had developed a self-help intervention specifically addressing self-stigma. Given the lack of evidence, this may be an area for future study.

Research Evidence on Self-Stigma Interventions

Overall, most self-stigma interventions evaluated in the research literature are group interventions that combine multiple approaches (Alonso et al., 2019; Büchter & Messer, 2017). However, the evidence on self-stigma interventions is mixed. A review of self-stigma interventions found that 8 of 14 of the interventions demonstrated improvements in self-stigma (Mittal et al., 2012). A more recent meta-analysis found 9 of 14 studies reduced self-stigma (Tsang et al., 2016), concluding that the psychoeducational interventions were the most promising approaches, with small to moderate effect sizes. In the most recent systematic review, Alonso and colleagues (2019) also found that 9 of 14 interventions were associated with reductions in self-stigma. In terms of long-term impact, a review of five randomized controlled trials (RCTs) on self-stigma interventions found that there were no effects at a three-month follow-up on recovery, help-seeking, or self-stigma (Büchter & Messer, 2017).

In an RCT of narrative enhancement and cognitive therapy (NECT; n = 87), the intervention group had reductions in self-stigma and increases in self-esteem in comparison to the treatment-as-usual group, in addition to a dosage effect (Hansson et al., 2017). Another trial of NECT (n = 170) for people with schizophrenia found a positive impact on self-stigma (Yanos et al., 2019). Several studies have also examined the impact of the Honest, Open, Proud (HOP) program, a peer-led strategic disclosure program. The HOP program (n = 98) showed significant improvement in stigma stress, self-stigma, help-seeking, disclosure intentions, and depression in adolescents (Mulfinger et al., 2018). A second study, completed with college students, showed similar benefits (Conley et al., 2019). Two additional RCTs have been conducted with adults, finding reduced shame/self-stigma (Corrigan et al., 2015a), and stigma-related stress (Rüsch et al., 2014).

Addressing Self-Stigma at Work

While most self-stigma interventions are facilitated through traditional mental health programming, workplaces may also want to consider how they support employees with mental illness. Self-stigma for employees with mental illness threatens to increase stress levels, cause problems with attendance, and reduce productivity (Fox et al., 2016). Workplace stigma interventions in the research literature have mostly focused on addressing public stigma of employees, highlighting the need for research to develop and evaluate the efficacy of workplace anti-stigma interventions (Oexle et al., 2018). Ensuring the confidentiality of employees who utilize these interventions will be an important consideration in these endeavors (Oexle et al., 2018).

In summary, most self-stigma programs are group interventions that are conducted in mental health settings. Psychoeducational approaches have been identified in meta-analyses as promising, and more recent studies on cognitive-behavioral and disclosure approaches have shown some effectiveness. More research is needed to examine peer support and self-help groups and their role in addressing self-stigma. Overall, however, meta-analyses have shown mixed to little evidence on the efficacy of self-stigma interventions. More efforts might be focused on identification of key components of interventions (e.g., peer vs. professional facilitator, group vs. individual). Research and theory development around individuals who successfully resist self-stigma, such as work by Firmin and colleagues (2017), might identify methods to combat self-stigma that are not included in current interventions. However, efforts to reduce self-stigma might prove difficult until public and structural stigma are substantially reduced. Fear of prejudice and discrimination, combined with the shame of internalized stigma, discourages people from talking about their mental illness, strengthening the misconception that mental illness should be a shameful secret, and reinforcing society's stigmatizing beliefs.

CONCLUSION

In this chapter, we described three agendas that drive stigma research: the services agenda, rights agenda, and self-worth agenda. We also provided a review of strategies to address public stigma including an analysis of key contact-based intervention components and discussions of media influence and national anti-stigma initiatives. Strategies to address public stigma generally fall into three categories: protest, education, and contact. Reviews and meta-analyses on efforts to change public stigma find that, overall, contact-based interventions are most effective but education-based interventions are most commonly implemented. Protest strategies are difficult to evaluate but might lead to changes in behaviors and structural stigma. Overall, there is a need for enhanced program fidelity and more rigorously designed research studies (Corrigan & Fong, 2014). Few studies have examined public stigma change in children (Livingston et al., 2012; Mellor, 2014), long-term outcomes (Thornicroft et al., 2016), cost-effectiveness (Clement et al., 2013), or actual behavior changes resulting from the intervention (Dalky, 2012). Programs may also benefit from focusing on promotion of positive attitudes and actions in conjunction with decreasing stigma (Corrigan et al., 2012; Evans-Lacko et al., 2014).

Finally, we reviewed strategies for reducing self-stigma. Most self-stigma interventions are group-based and conducted through mental health agencies. The most common strategies for addressing self-stigma include psychoeducation, cognitive-behavioral, and disclosure interventions. Peer support and self-help groups might also have an impact on self-stigma. Unlike with public stigma, research is not completely clear about the success of self-stigma interventions, and more evidence is needed to evaluate approaches and components of anti-stigma interventions.

REFERENCES

Alonso, M., Guillén, A. I., & Muñoz, M. (2019). Interventions to reduce internalized stigma in individuals with mental illness: a systematic review. *The Spanish Journal of Psychology*, 22(e27), 1–14. https://doi.org/10.1017/sjp.2019.9

Angermeyer, M. C., Holzinger, A., & Matschinger, H. (2009). Mental health literacy and attitude towards people with mental illness: a trend analysis based on population surveys in the eastern part of Germany. *European Psychiatry*, 24(4), 225–232. https://doi.org/10.1016/j.eurpsy.2008.06.010

Arboleda-Flórez, J., & Stuart, H. (2012). From sin to science: Fighting the stigmatization of mental illnesses. *The Canadian Journal of Psychiatry / La Revue canadienne de psychiatrie*, 57(8), 457–463. https://doi.org/10.1177%2F070674371205700803

Betton, V., Borschmann, R., Docherty, M., Coleman, S., Brown, M., & Henderson, C. (2015). The role of social media in reducing stigma and discrimination. *The British Journal of Psychiatry*, 206(6), 443–444. https://doi.org/10.1192/bjp.bp.114.152835

Borschmann, R., Greenberg, N., Jones, N., Henderson, R. C. (2014). Campaigns to reduce mental illness stigma in Europe: A scoping review. *Die Psychiatrie: Grundlagen &*
Perspektiven, 11(1), 43–50. https://doi.org/10.1055/s-0038-1670735

Brennan, M., & McGrew, J. H. (2013). Evaluating the effects of NAMI's consumer presentation program, In Our Own Voice. *Psychiatric Rehabilitation Journal*, 36(2), 72–79. https://
doi.org/10.1037/h0094974

Büchter, R. B., & Messer, M. (2017). Interventions for reducing self-stigma in people with
mental illnesses: a systematic review of randomized controlled trials. *GMS German Medical*
Science, 15, 1–12. https://doi.org/10.3205/000248

Burke, E., Pyle, M., Machin, K., Varese, F., & Morrison, A. P. (2019). The effects of peer support
on empowerment, self-efficacy, and internalized stigma: A narrative synthesis and meta-
analysis. *Stigma and Health*, 4(3), 337–356. https://doi.apa.org/doi/10.1037/sah0000148

Clement, S., Lassman, F., Barley, E., Evans-Lacko, S., Williams, P., Yamaguchi, S., Slade, M.,
Rüsch, N., & Thornicroft, G. (2013). Mass media interventions for reducing mental health-
related stigma. *The Cochrane Library*, 7(7), 1–15. https://doi.org/10.1002/14651858.cd009
453.pub2

Conley, C. S., Hundert, C. G., Charles, J. L., Huguenel, B. M., Al-khouja, M., Qin, S., . . . &
Corrigan, P. W. (2019). Honest, open, proud–college: Effectiveness of a peer-led small-group
intervention for reducing the stigma of mental illness. *Stigma and Health*, 5(2), 168–178.
https://doi.apa.org/doi/10.1037/sah0000185

Corker, E., Hamilton, S., Henderson, C., Weeks, C., Pinfold, V., Rose, D., . . . & Thornicroft,
G. (2013). Experiences of discrimination among people using mental health services in
England 2008–2011. *The British Journal of Psychiatry*, 202(s55), s58–s63. https://doi.org/
10.1192/bjp.bp.112.112912

Corrigan, P. W., & Al-Khouja, M. A. (2018). Three agendas for changing the public stigma
of mental illness. *Psychiatric Rehabilitation Journal*, 41(1), 1–7. https://doi.org/10.1037/prj
0000277

Corrigan, P. W., Druss, B. G., & Perlick, D. A. (2014a). The impact of mental illness stigma on
seeking and participating in mental health care. *Psychological Science in the Public Interest*,
15(2), 37–70. https://doi.org/10.1177%2F1529100614531398

Corrigan, P. W., & Fong, M. W. M. (2014). Competing perspectives on erasing the stigma of
illness: What says the dodo bird? *Social Science & Medicine*, 103, 110–117. https://doi.org/
10.1016/j.socscimed.2013.05.027

Corrigan, P. W., Kosyluk, K. A., & Rüsch, N. (2013). Reducing self-stigma by coming out
proud. *American Journal of Public Health*, 103(5), 794–800. https://doi.org/10.2105/
AJPH.2012.301037

Corrigan, P. W., Larson, J. E., Michaels, P. J., Buchholz, B. A., Del Rossi, R., Fontecchio, M. J.,
Castro, D., Gause, M., Krzyzanowski, R., & Rüsch, N. (2015a). Diminishing the self-stigma
of mental illness by coming out proud. *Psychiatry Research*, 229(1-2), 148–154. https://doi
.org/10.1016/j.psychres.2015.07.053

Corrigan P. W., Michaels P. J., & Morris S. (2015b). Do the effects of anti-stigma programs persist over time? Findings from a meta-analysis. *Psychiatric Services*, 66(5), 543–546. https://
doi.org/10.1176/appi.ps.201400291

Corrigan, P. W., Michaels, P. J., Vega, E., Gause, M., Larson, J., Krzyzanowski, R., & Botcheva,
L. (2014b). Key ingredients to contact-based stigma change: A cross-validation. *Psychiatric*
Rehabilitation Journal, 37(1), 62. https://doi.org/10.1037/prj0000038

Corrigan, P. W., Morris, S. B., Michaels, P. J, Rafacz, J. D., & Rüsch, N. (2012). Challenging the public stigma of mental illness: A meta-analysis of outcome studies. *Psychiatric Services*, *63*(10), 963–973. https://doi.org/10.1176/appi.ps.201100529

Corrigan, P. W., Powell, K. J., & Al-Khouja, M. A. (2015c). Examining the impact of public service announcements on help seeking and stigma: Results of a randomized controlled trial. *The Journal of Nervous and Mental Disease*, *203*(11), 836–842. https://doi.org/10.1097/nmd.0000000000000376

Corrigan, P. W., Powell, K. J., & Michaels, P. J. (2014c). Brief battery for measurement of stigmatizing versus affirming attitudes about mental illness. *Psychiatry Research*, *215*(2), 466–470. https://doi.org/10.1016/j.psychres.2013.12.006

Corrigan, P. W., Rafacz, J., & Rüsch, N. (2011). Examining a progressive model of self-stigma and its impact on people with serious mental illness. *Psychiatry Research*, *189*(3), 339–343. https://doi.org/10.1016/j.psychres.2011.05.024

Corrigan P. W., River L. P., Lundin R. K., Penn D. L., Uphoff-Wasowski K., Campion, J., . . . & Kubiak, M. A. (2001). Three strategies for changing attributions about severe mental illness. *Schizophrenia Bulletin*, *27*, 187–195.

Corrigan, P. W., Rowan, D., Green, A., Lundin, R., River, P., Uphoff-Wasowski, K., . . . & Kubiak, M. A. (2002). Challenging two mental illness stigmas: Personal responsibility and dangerousness. *Schizophrenia Bulletin*, *28*(2), 293–309. https://doi.org/10.1093/oxfordjournals.schbul.a006939

Dalky, H. F. (2012). Mental illness stigma reduction interventions: Review of intervention trials. *Western Journal of Nursing Research*, *34*(4), 520–547. https://doi.org/10.1177%2F0193945911400638

Evans-Lacko, S., Corker, E., Williams, P., Henderson, C., & Thornicroft, G. (2014). Effect of the Time to Change anti-stigma campaign on trends in mental-illness-related public stigma among the English population in 2003–13: An analysis of survey data. *The Lancet Psychiatry*, *1*(2), 121–128. https://doi.org/10.1016/s2215-0366(14)70243-3

Firmin, R. L., Luther, L., Lysaker, P. H., Minor, K. S., McGrew, J. H., Cornwell, M. N., & Salyers, M. P. (2017). Stigma resistance at the personal, peer, and public levels: A new conceptual model. *Stigma and Health*, *2*(3), 182. https://doi.org/10.1037/sah0000054

Fox, A. B., Smith, B. N., & Vogt, D. (2016). The relationship between anticipated stigma and work functioning for individuals with depression. *Journal of Social and Clinical Psychology*, *35*(10), 883–897. http://dx.doi.org/10.1521/jscp.2016.35.10.883

Goffman, E. (1963). Stigma: Notes on the management of spoiled identity. Prentice-Hall.

Griffiths, K. M., Carron-Arthur, B., Parsons, A., & Reid, R. (2014). Effectiveness of programs for reducing the stigma associated with mental disorders: A meta-analysis of randomized controlled trials. *World Psychiatry*, *13*(2), 161–175. https://doi.org/10.1002/wps.20129

Hanisch, S. E., Twomey, C. D., Szeto, A. C., Birner, U. W., Nowak, D., & Sabariego, C. (2016). The effectiveness of interventions targeting the stigma of mental illness at the workplace: a systematic review. *BMC Psychiatry*, *16*(1), 1. https://doi.org/10.1186/s12888-015-0706-4

Hansson, L., Lexén, A., & Holmén, J. (2017). The effectiveness of narrative enhancement and cognitive therapy: A randomized controlled study of a self-stigma intervention. *Social Psychiatry and Psychiatric Epidemiology*, *52*(11), 1415–1423. https://doi.org/10.1007/s00127-017-1385-x

Janoušková, M., Tušková, E., Weissová, A., Trančík, P., Pasz, J., Evans-Lacko, S., & Winkler, P. (2017). Can video interventions be used to effectively destigmatize mental illness among young people? A systematic review. *European Psychiatry*, *41*, 1–9. https://doi.org/10.1016/j.eurpsy.2016.09.008

Jorm, A. F. (2012). Mental health literacy: Empowering the community to take action for better mental health. *American Psychologist*, *67*(3), 231–243. https://content.apa.org/doi/10.1037/a0025957

Jorm, Christensen, & Griffiths. (2006). Changes in depression awareness and attitudes in Australia: the impact of beyondblue: The national depression initiative. *Australian and New Zealand Journal of Psychiatry*, *40*(1), 42–46. https://doi.org/10.1080/j.1440-1614.2006.01739.x

Kingdon, D., Sharma, T., & Hart, D. (2004). What attitudes do psychiatrists hold towards people with mental illness? *Psychiatric Bulletin*, *28*(11), 401–406. https://doi.org/10.1192/pb.28.11.401

Knaak, S., Modgill, G., & Patten, S. B. (2014). Key ingredients of anti-stigma programs for health care providers: A data synthesis of evaluative studies. *Canadian Journal of Psychiatry*, *59*(10 Suppl 1), S19–S26. https://doi.org/10.1177%2F070674371405901S06

Kvaale, E. P., Haslam, N., & Gottdiener, W. H. (2013). The "side effects" of medicalization: A meta-analytic review of how biogenetic explanations affect stigma. *Clinical Psychology Review*, *33*(6), 782–794. https://doi.org/10.1016/j.cpr.2013.06.002

Link, B. G., & Phelan, J. C. (2001). Conceptualizing stigma. *Annual Review of Sociology*, *27*(1), 363–385. https://doi.org/10.1146/annurev.soc.27.1.363

Livingston, J. D., & Boyd, J. E. (2010). Correlates and consequences of internalized stigma for people living with mental illness: A systematic review and meta-analysis. *Social Science & Medicine*, *71*(12), 2150–2161. https://doi.org/10.1016/j.socscimed.2010.09.030

Livingston, J. D., Milne, T., Fang, M. L., & Amari, E. (2012). The effectiveness of interventions for reducing stigma related to substance use disorders: A systematic review. *Addiction*, *107*(1), 39–50. https://doi.org/10.1111/j.1360-0443.2011.03601.x

Lucksted, A., Drapalski, A., Calmes, C., Forbes, C., DeForge, B., & Boyd, J. (2011). Ending self-stigma: Pilot evaluation of a new intervention to reduce internalized stigma among people with mental illnesses. *Psychiatric Rehabilitation Journal*, *35*(1), 51. https://doi.org/10.2975/35.1.2011.51.54

Magliano, L., Fiorillo, A., De Rosa, C., Malangone, C., & Maj, M. (2004). Beliefs about schizophrenia in Italy: A comparative nationwide survey of the general public, mental health professionals, and patients' relatives. *The Canadian Journal of Psychiatry*, *49*(5), 323–331. https://doi.org/10.1177%2F070674370404900508

Malachowski, C., & Kirsh, B. (2013). Workplace anti-stigma initiatives: A scoping study. *Psychiatric Services*, *64*(7), 694–702. https://doi.org/10.1176/appi.ps.201200409

Maunder, R. D., & White, F. A. (2019). Intergroup contact and mental health stigma: A comparative effectiveness meta-analysis. *Clinical Psychology Review*, *72*, 101749. https://doi.org/10.1016/j.cpr.2019.101749

Mellor, C. (2014). School-based interventions targeting stigma of mental illness: Systematic review. *Psychiatric Bulletin*, *38*(4), 164–171. https://doi.org/10.1192/pb.bp.112.041723

Mills, H., Mulfinger, N., Raeder, S., Rüsch, N., Clements, H., & Scior, K. (2020). Self-help interventions to reduce self-stigma in people with mental health problems: A systematic literature review. *Psychiatry Research*, *284*, 112702. https://doi.org/10.1016/j.psychres.2019.112702

Mittal, D., Sullivan, G., Chekuri, L., Allee, E., & Corrigan, P. W. (2012). Empirical studies of self-stigma reduction strategies: a critical review of the literature. *Psychiatric Services*, *63*(10), 974–981. https://doi.org/10.1176/appi.ps.201100459

Morgan, A. J., Reavley, N. J., Ross, A., San Too, L., & Jorm, A. F. (2018). Interventions to reduce stigma towards people with severe mental illness: Systematic review and meta-analysis. *Journal of Psychiatric Research*, 103, 120–133. https://doi.org/10.1016/j.jpsychires.2018.05.017

Mulfinger, N., Müller, S., Böge, I., Sakar, V., Corrigan, P. W., Evans-Lacko, S., . . . & Ruckes, C. (2018). Honest, Open, Proud for adolescents with mental illness: Pilot randomized controlled trial. *Journal of Child Psychology and Psychiatry*, 59(6), 684–691. https://doi.org/10.1111/jcpp.12853

Oexle, N., Sheehan, L., & Rüsch, N. (2018). Empowering people with mental illness in workplace settings. *Psychiatric Services*, 69(4), 494–495. https://doi.org/10.1176/appi.ps.201700501

Parcesepe, A. M., & Cabassa, L. J. (2013). Public stigma of mental illness in the United States: A systematic literature review. *Administration and Policy in Mental Health and Mental Health Services Research*, 40(5), 384–399. https://doi.org/10.1007/s10488-012-0430-z

Pearl, R. L., Forgeard, M. J., Rifkin, L., Beard, C., & Björgvinsson, T. (2017). Internalized stigma of mental illness: Changes and associations with treatment outcomes. *Stigma and Health*, 2(1), 2–15. https://psycnet.apa.org/doi/10.1037/sah0000036

Picco, L., Pang, S., Lau, Y. W., Jeyagurunathan, A., Satghare, P., Abdin, E., . . . & Subramaniam, M. (2016). Internalized stigma among psychiatric outpatients: Associations with quality of life, functioning, hope and self-esteem. *Psychiatry Research*, 246, 500–506. https://doi.org/10.1016/j.psychres.2016.10.041

Quinn, N., Knifton, L., Goldie, I., Van Bortel, T., Dowds, J., Lasalvia, A., . . . & Thornicroft, G. (2013). Nature and impact of European anti-stigma depression programmes. *Health Promotion International*, 29(3), 403–413. https://doi.org/10.1093/heapro/das076

Reavley, N. J., Mackinnon, A. J., Morgan, A. J., & Jorm, A. F. (2014). Stigmatising attitudes towards people with mental disorders: A comparison of Australian health professionals with the general community. *Australian & New Zealand Journal of Psychiatry*, 48(5), 433–441. https://doi.org/10.1177%2F0004867413500351

Ross, A. M., Morgan, A. J., Jorm, A. F., & Reavley, N. J. (2019). A systematic review of the impact of media reports of severe mental illness on stigma and discrimination, and interventions that aim to mitigate any adverse impact. *Social Psychiatry and Psychiatric Epidemiology*, 54(1), 11–31. https://doi.org/10.1007/s00127-018-1608-9

Ross, C. A., & Goldner, E. M. (2009). Stigma, negative attitudes and discrimination towards mental illness within the nursing profession: A review of the literature. *Journal of Psychiatric and Mental Health Nursing*, 16(6), 558–567. https://doi.org/10.1111/j.1365-2850.2009.01399.x

Rüsch, N., Abbruzzese, E., Hagedorn, E., Hartenhauer, D., Kaufmann, I., Curschellas, J., . . . & Kawohl, W. (2014). Efficacy of Coming Out Proud to reduce stigma's impact among people with mental illness: Pilot randomised controlled trial. *The British Journal of Psychiatry*, 204(5), 391–397. https://doi.org/10.1192/bjp.bp.113.135772

Sheehan, L. (2015). Strategies for changing the stigma of behavioral healthcare. Commissioned paper for the National Academy of Sciences: Committee on the Science of Changing Behavioral Health Norms. http://sites.nationalacademies.org/DBASSE/BBCSS/DBASSE_170049

Sheehan, L., Nieweglowski, K., & Corrigan, P. W. (2017). Structures and types of stigma. In W. Gaebel, W. Rössler, W., & N. Sartorius (Eds.), *The stigma of mental illness: End of the story?* (pp. 43–66). Springer.

Stuart, H., Koller, M., & West Armstrong, A. (2013). Opening Minds in a post-secondary environment: results of an online contact-based anti-stigma intervention for college staff:

Starting the conversation. *Mental Health Commission of Canada*. https://campusmentalhea lth.ca/wp-content/uploads/2018/03/AC-Research-Results-MHCC1.pdf

Stuart, H., Sartorius, N., & Thornicroft, G. (2019). Fighting mental illness-related stigma: What we have learned. In A. Javed & K. Fountoulakis (Eds.), *Advances in Psychiatry* (pp. 621–635). Springer. https://doi.org/10.1007/978-3-319-70554-5_36

Szeto, A. C., & Dobson, K. S. (2010). Reducing the stigma of mental disorders at work: A review of current workplace anti-stigma intervention programs. *Applied and Preventive Psychology*, 14(1–4), 41–56. http://dx.doi.org/10.1016/j.appsy.2011.11.002

Teachman, B. A., Wilson, J. G., & Komarovskaya, I. (2006). Implicit and explicit stigma of mental illness in diagnosed and healthy samples. *Journal of Social and Clinical Psychology*, 25(1), 75–95. http://dx.doi.org/10.1521/jscp.2006.25.1.75

Thornicroft, G., Mehta, N., Clement, S., Evans-Lacko, S., Doherty, M., Rose, D., . . . & Henderson, C. (2016). Evidence for effective interventions to reduce mental-health-related stigma and discrimination. *The Lancet*, 387(10023), 1123–1132. https://doi.org/10.1016/s0140-6736(15)00298-6

Tsang, H. W., Ching, S. C., Tang, K. H., Lam, H. T., Law, P. Y., & Wan, C. N. (2016). Therapeutic intervention for internalized stigma of severe mental illness: A systematic review and meta-analysis. *Schizophrenia Research*, 173(1–2), 45–53. https://doi.org/10.1016/j.schres.2016.02.013

Uchino, T., Maeda, M., & Uchimura, N. (2012). Psychoeducation may reduce self-stigma of people with schizophrenia and schizoaffective disorder. *The Kurume Medical Journal*, 59(1.2), 25–31. https://doi.org/10.2739/kurumemedj.59.25

Ungar, T., Knaak, S., & Szeto, A. C. (2016). Theoretical and practical considerations for combating mental illness stigma in health care. *Community Mental Health Journal*, 52(3), 262–271. https://doi.org/10.1007/s10597-015-9910-4

Wahl, O., & Aroesty-Cohen, E. (2010). Attitudes of mental health professionals about mental illness: A review of the recent literature. *Journal of Community Psychology*, 38(1), 49–62. https://doi.org/10.1002/jcop.20351

Wan, W. H., & Lam, A. H. Y. (2019). The effectiveness of virtual reality-based simulation in health professions education relating to mental illness: A literature review. *Health*, 11(6), 646–660. https://doi.org/10.4236/health.2019.116054

Yamaguchi, S., Wu, S. I., Biswas, M., Yate, M., Aoki, Y., Barley, E. A., & Thornicroft, G. (2013). Effects of short-term interventions to reduce mental health–related stigma in university or college students: A systematic review. *The Journal of Nervous and Mental Disease*, 201(6), 490–503. https://doi.org/10.1097/nmd.0b013e31829480df

Yanos, P. T., Lucksted, A., Drapalski, A. L., Roe, D., & Lysaker, P. (2015). Interventions targeting mental health self-stigma: A review and comparison. *Psychiatric Rehabilitation Journal*, 38(2), 171. https://doi.org/10.1037/prj0000100

Yanos, P. T., Lysaker, P. H., Silverstein, S. M., Vayshenker, B., Gonzales, L., West, M. L., & Roe, D. (2019). A randomized-controlled trial of treatment for self-stigma among persons diagnosed with schizophrenia-spectrum disorders. *Social Psychiatry and Psychiatric Epidemiology*, 54(11), 1363–1378. https://doi.org/10.1007/s00127-019-01702-0

Yanos, P. T., Roe, D., & Lysaker, P. H. (2011). Narrative enhancement and cognitive therapy: A new group-based treatment for internalized stigma among persons with severe mental illness. *International Journal of Group Psychotherapy*, 61(4), 576–595. https://doi.org/10.1521/ijgp.2011.61.4.576

PART VIII

Intersectionality and Inequalities

....

CHAPTER 27

AN INTERSECTIONAL ANALYSIS OF LABOR MARKET OUTCOMES

....

JENNIFER D. BROOKS

INTRODUCTION

....

PEOPLE with disabilities constitute one of the largest minority groups in the United States, with 10.2% of Americans aged 18 to 64 reporting some type of physical or mental limitation (Lauer & Houtenville, 2018). Disability prevalence rates are especially high among women, racial minorities, and those with multiple marginalized statuses (Warner & Brown, 2011). According to 2010 age-adjusted disability rates, 19.8% of women and 23.2% of non-Hispanic (NH) Black people report a disability (Brault, 2012).

Despite the diversity within this population, some literature frames disability as a "master status," dominating over all other statuses (Barnartt, 2013). While recent work has called the "disability as an all-encompassing experience" paradigm into question (Caldwell, 2010; Conejo, 2013; Frederick & Shifrer, 2019), the majority of the work on disability still constructs a raceless, genderless, heteronormative disabled subject, the "normate" with a disability to borrow from Garland-Thomson (2005). Thus, the question still remains as to whether, and how, other status-based characteristics matter in the lives of those with disabilities.

Answering this question requires a deep and complex understanding of how disability, as a status-based characteristic, interacts with an individual's other statuses to shape their experiences. That is, people with disabilities inhabit multiple other statuses, such as race/ethnicity and gender. These intersecting statuses come together, shaping everything from their educational trajectories to their labor market outcomes (Erevelles & Miner, 2010; Pettinicchio & Maroto, 2017). For instance, recent work reveals how race, education, and gender interact with disability status to create hierarchies of economic and labor market inequalities (Brown & Moloney, 2019; Maroto et al., 2019). These hierarchies reveal that, even among people with disabilities, those with multiple marginalized statuses face more disadvantages in society.

This chapter builds on previous work pointing to the intersectional effects of race/ethnicity and gender on poverty and government assistance receipt among persons with disabilities by examining whether similar intersectional effects are present among disabled people's employment outcomes. Moving beyond an empirical test of this intersectional paradigm, this chapter also expands on previous literature by examining whether the intersectional effects experienced in one aspect of an individual's life (i.e., government assistance) intertwine with the labor market to shape racial and gendered employment disparities. In other words, can the disadvantages and/or advantages produced by intersectional effects in one life domain shape experiences and outcomes in others? In doing so, this chapter addresses the following questions: How do race/ethnicity, gender, and disability status simultaneously shape employment outcomes? And how can potential disparities among the race/ethnicity-gender-disability groups be explained by the receipt of government assistance?

To capture the nature of intersectionality, this chapter examines the intersection between race/ethnicity, gender, and disability status to create 16 race/ethnicity-gender-disability groups. I then use a series of logistic regression models to examine how these three statuses intersect to shape employment. Doing so helps shed additional light on how an intersectional framework furthers our understanding of labor market outcomes among people with disabilities. First claimed by Black feminist scholars, intersectionality points to how multiple statuses come together to shape individuals' experiences (Crenshaw, 1989). From this perspective, researchers must consider individuals' multiple statuses to fully capture their multiple layers of oppression and privilege. Building off of this foundational work, the current chapter will apply the key principles of intersectionality to the study of the labor market inequalities of those with disabilities. In doing so, this chapter highlights the complex ways in which race/ethnicity, gender, and disability status simultaneously affect employment and how the multiplicative effects of these statuses can create disadvantages in certain areas of an individual's life that may spill over to impact their employment probabilities.

RACIAL AND GENDERED EMPLOYMENT DISPARITIES AMONG PERSONS WITH DISABILITIES

Research on the employment inequalities of persons with disabilities expands on the broader sociological stratification literature by asserting that disability is an axis of inequality, like race/ethnicity, gender, and other status-based characteristics (Brown & Moloney, 2019; Maroto et al., 2019; Mauldin et al., 2020; Shandra, 2018). According to data from the US Bureau of Labor Statistics (BLS), 33.6% of adults with disabilities ages 16 to 64 were employed in 2019, compared with 77.3% of adults without disabilities (BLS, 2021). This substantial gap in labor force participation alludes to disability-specific barriers that substantially limit the employment potential of people with disabilities.

Policy factors, such as disability-related social safety net programs (specifically Social Security Insurance [SSI] and Social Security Disability Insurance [SSDI]), force some with disabilities to forgo gainful employment in lieu of needed disability-related government benefits and services. While these programs provide access to vital disability-related supports (which many private insurers do not offer), such as wheelchairs, hospital visits, medications, and attendant care, they also provide small amounts of cash transfers which can drive some with disabilities into a "poverty trap" in order to receive life-sustaining supports and services (Stapleton et al., 2006).

Those who bypass the work disincentives created by these programs face other barriers related to employer demand for disabled employees. Specifically, research by Ameri and colleagues (2018) found that when application materials (resumes and cover letters) indicated that the applicant had a disability, employers were 23% less likely to express interest. This discrimination is the product of false attitudes and assumptions held by employers that workers with disabilities are incapable of performing the work required for the job, are less productive than those without disabilities, take longer to learn and complete tasks, require expensive accommodations, will not get along with customers, clients, and coworkers, and will have to take numerous sick days (Chan et al., 2010).

Studies indicate that race/ethnicity shapes how these barriers affect labor market outcomes. Recent statistics show that only 23% of NH Black people with disabilities ages 21–65 were employed in 2017, compared with 36% of similar White people (Brooks, 2019). Underlying this 13-percentage-point gap are racial and ableist structures working in tandem to create compounding labor market disadvantages for NH Black people with disabilities. The multiplicative effects of these two systems of oppression have direct consequences for employment outcomes. For instance, while Vocational Rehabilitation (VR) programs offer individuals with disabilities assistance with finding employment, NH White consumers have higher rates of earnings than NH Black consumers after program exit. In fact, research indicates that the Black-White disability earnings gap increases after receiving VR services (Mwachofi et al., 2009). This increase may be because, on average, VR counselors devote more time and resources to NH White consumers than their NH Black counterparts, indicating the effects of systemic racism even in an agency designed to reduce the barriers created by ableism.

Gender and disability have a more complicated relationship within labor market contexts. Statistics from 2017 show a 4-percentage-point employment gap between men and women with disabilities ages 18–64 (39.3% vs. 34.6%) (Lauer & Houtenville, 2018). The employment gap between women with and without disabilities, however, is slightly smaller (37.6%) than between men with and without disabilities (43.2%). Thus, disability appears to weaken the strong labor market attachment for men while further restricting women's access to employment and earnings (Pettinicchio & Maroto, 2017).

The complex relationship between gender, disability, and employment may be explained in part by the different ways that disability-specific employment barriers affect women and men with disabilities. For instance, while recipients of SSI are more likely to be women with disabilities, men with disabilities represent the majority of SSDI recipients (Caplan, 2014). Disabled men's higher levels of SSDI receipt (a program based on previous earnings) may signal their stronger attachment to the labor market until a point at which they can no longer work. However, women with disabilities' higher rates of receipt of SSI—a means-tested program—may indicate their weaker attachment to the labor market, increasing their vulnerability to falling into the benefits poverty trap. Women with disabilities' weaker attachment to the labor market may also be due to their greater likelihood of having parental and other caregiving responsibilities (Pettinicchio & Maroto, 2017; Shandra & Penner, 2017).

Studies that account for how race/ethnicity and gender affect the labor market experiences of those with disabilities advance our understanding of how membership in other social categories may shape disabled people's employment outcomes (Brooks, 2019; Caplan, 2014; Lauer & Houtenville, 2018; Mwachofi et al., 2009; Pettinicchio & Maroto, 2017). This line of research, however, tends to cite explanations such as "double jeopardy" or "triple disadvantage" (Conejo, 2013) for the lower employment rates and earnings of multiple marginalized people with disabilities. Yet the literature on the gendered employment inequalities among people with disabilities suggests a more complicated relationship among disability, employment, and other status-based characteristics. To fully capture the nuances behind how multiple statuses operate within an individual to shape their labor market outcomes, researchers must account for the various ways these statuses intersect.

AN INTERSECTIONAL APPROACH
TO DISABILITY

Intersectionality points to how various status-based characteristics work in tandem to shape an individual's experiences of power, prejudice, and privilege. First coined by Black feminist scholar Kimberlé Crenshaw (1989) to identify the invisibility of Black women in the workplace, intersectionality calls upon scholars to consider various statuses (i.e., race/ethnicity, gender, disability status, and sexuality) as pieces of a puzzle. While the individual pieces contain some information about the puzzle, scholars must put the pieces together and understand how one piece affects the meaning of another to fully grasp the whole picture. In this same vein, intersectionality suggests that it is not enough to study one aspect of an individual's identity, but rather, an individual's membership in multiple categories must be considered to fully address how these categories shape their experiences within social institutions, their relationships, and their social identity.

Scholars who study disability as an axis of inequality have adopted an intersectional approach to highlight how membership in certain other marginalized categories complicates the experience of living with a disability (Frederick & Shifrer, 2019; Maroto et al., 2019; Mauldin et al., 2020). These studies point to how an individual's other status-based characteristics merge with their disabilities, creating various multiplicative effects.

For instance, women with disabilities experience a specific type of gendered ableism, which denies some disabled women access to traditional female roles, leaving them in a state of "rolelessness" in society (Schur, 2003). These narratives have implications for a disabled woman's educational, economic, and labor market outcomes (Arms et al., 2008; Parish et al., 2009; Pettinicchio & Maroto, 2017).

Less attention, however, has been paid to how this gendered ableism affects men with disabilities. The handful of studies that address the intersection of disability and masculinity point to how male scripts portraying the ideal man as strong, independent, and autonomous come into direct conflict with social constructions of disability as weak, child-like, and dependent (Shuttleworth et al., 2012). These two conflicting roles that men with disabilities must simultaneously inhabit may explain why they experience more labor market and economic disadvantages than their female counterparts (Pettinicchio & Maroto, 2017). That is, studies suggest that dominant notions of masculinity may result in a stronger (more negative) effect on men's employment outcomes when compared to women (Maroto et al., 2019).

Although the compounding effects of gender and disability have been well-documented, much of this research has been conducted on predominantly White samples, paying little attention to how race/ethnicity might also impact these relationships. This reduction of the experience of gender and disability to a White, Western perspective is problematic, given that other research indicates that race/ethnicity has its own effect on disability (Frederick & Shifrer, 2019). In fact, studies document that, due to the intersection of racism and ableism, NH Black people experience disability very differently than their White counterparts (Erevelles & Miner, 2010; Frederick & Shifrer, 2019).

Despite overwhelming evidence that intersectionality is imperative to the study of disability, most research that addresses disability's intersection with other marginalized statuses considers at most one other status-based characteristic. These studies examine how labor market outcomes vary depending on an individual's disability status and an individual's race/ethnicity, gender, or immigration status (Sevak et al., 2017; Xiang et al., 2010). As a result, most of these studies arrive at the same conclusion: Those with disabilities who possess other marginalized statuses experience greater labor market disadvantage.

Other studies contradict this theoretical paradigm, indicating that those with the most marginalized statuses do not always experience the greatest disadvantages (see, e.g., Pettinicchio & Maroto, 2017). An intersectional perspective may help explain these contradictory findings. For instance, labor market studies that examine the intersection of gender and disability consistently find that women with disabilities have the lowest employment rates, compared to both men with disabilities and people without disabilities (Randolph & Andresen, 2004). However, evidence indicates a larger gap in employment probabilities between men with and without disabilities than between women with and without disabilities (Sevak et al., 2017). Addressing two seemingly contradictory findings, Pettinicchio and Maroto (2017) use an intersectional framework to explain how the interaction between masculinity and disability may play a role in shaping the labor market outcomes of men with disabilities. Specifically, they point to the fact that because traditionally men have a stronger attachment to the labor market than women, having a disability, which is associated with the inability to work, may have a stronger effect on men's employment rates.

While research has captured the nuances within the relationship between gender, disability, and the labor market, less attention has been paid to how race/ethnicity may also affect employment outcomes among those with disabilities. The handful of studies that address the multiplicative effects of race/ethnicity and disability from an intersectional perspective tend to focus on compounding systems of oppression, such as ableism, racism, and xenophobia. For instance, studies find that Hispanics with disabilities who are more assimilated into US society have better labor market outcomes than those who are not (Velcoff et al., 2010). Thus, while there is evidence to suggest that intersectionality does matter, more attention must be paid to how race/ethnicity, gender, and disability status work in tandem to create employment disparities among individuals with disabilities. As a result, the first aim of this study will be to address the following: *How do race/ethnicity, gender, and disability status work together to shape employment probabilities?*

OVERLAPPING INSTITUTIONS OF OPPRESSION

The potential joint effects that race/ethnicity and gender may have on the employment inequalities of those with disabilities do not occur within a vacuum. Rather, in theory, the multiplicative effects of race/ethnicity, gender, and disability status on multiple institutions, such as employment, education, and government assistance, may intertwine with one another, creating what I call *overlapping institutions of oppression*. In other words, the intersectional effects that individuals experience in one area of their lives can "spill over" into others, reinforcing existing systems of social stratification.

For instance, a spillover effect may occur with government assistance receipt. Specifically, studies have shown that persons with disabilities who have other marginalized statuses are more vulnerable to government assistance dependency than their more privileged disabled counterparts (Caplan, 2014; Maroto et al., 2019). Yet little attention has been given to how this greater reliance on government assistance affects other aspects of a disabled individual's life. This lack of knowledge is especially concerning given the link between government assistance and employment among individuals with disabilities (Stapleton et al., 2006). The potential link between government assistance dependency, employment, and intersectionality, however, may be bidirectional. That is, studies indicate that the low levels of employment among individuals with disabilities can be both a cause and consequence of their high rates of government assistance receipt. For instance, while the income and asset limits of certain government assistance programs, specifically SSI, may prevent some who experience disability onset in childhood from entering employment, restrictions imposed by other programs, such as SSDI, may create substantial barriers to employment re-entry for those who develop disabilities while working (Livermore, 2011). However, literature has yet to examine whether the connections between government assistance and employment are stronger among multiply marginalized disabled people. This leads to the following: *How can receipt of government assistance explain potential disparities in employment among the race/ethnicity-gender-disability groups?*

AIMS

Expanding on prior research, this chapter examines how the multiplicative effects of race/ethnicity, gender, and disability status on government assistance and employment simultaneously shape one another, reinforcing existing systems of social stratification. In doing so, this chapter has two primary objectives. First, it examines how race/ethnicity, gender, and disability status work in tandem to shape employment probabilities and how an intersectional approach can provide insight into certain nuances of disabled persons' employment inequalities. Second, it investigates whether accounting for government assistance receipt explains the disparities among race/ethnicity-gender-disability groups.

METHODS

Data

To examine how the likelihood of being employed varies by race/ethnicity, gender, and disability status, this chapter analyzes data from the 2017 single-year public use file of the American Community Survey (ACS). The ACS is an ideal dataset for this analysis because of its large size, questions regarding disability, and coverage of employment outcomes.

The analytic sample for this study includes noninstitutionalized respondents aged 25–61 to capture those who have already completed their education and account for early retirement (Maroto & Pettinicchio, 2014). Due to varying levels of access to government assistance programs, the employment trajectories of native-born and non-native-born respondents with disabilities may differ substantially (Xiang et al., 2010). As a result, the sample is further limited to native-born respondents. Once these restrictions are taken into account, the final sample for this analysis contained 1,895,629 individuals.

Measures

The primary outcome variable is employment. Employment status is measured dichotomously, where one represents those who reported active employment and zero represents those who are either unemployed or not in the labor force.

The primary predictor variables capture disability, sex, and race/ethnicity. In 2008, the ACS implemented a six-item disability question sequence to more fully capture the population of individuals with physical/mental limitations (Brault, 2009). Specifically, this sequence includes items for (1) serious difficulty hearing; (2) blindness or serious difficulty seeing even when wearing glasses; (3) serious difficulty concentrating, remembering, or making decisions; (4) serious difficulty walking or climbing stairs; (5) difficulty dressing or bathing; and (6) difficulty doing errands alone, such as visiting a doctor's office or shopping. These questions were combined into one overall binary indicator of disability, with those answering at least one of the six questions in the affirmative coded as having a disability.

Gender is a dichotomous variable with one indicating female and zero indicating male. Race/ethnicity is coded into a four-category variable, representing those who identify as either NH White, NH Black, Hispanic, or NH other.

Interacting gender, and race/ethnicity resulted in 16 race/ethnicity-gender-disability groups (Maroto et al., 2019). I use this to help demonstrate the multiplicative effects of various status-based characteristics. All models also control for age, which is measured continuously on a scale from 25 to 61, marital status, and education. Marital status is a single dichotomous indicator with one as currently married and zero representing those who reported being widowed, divorced, separated, or never married. Educational attainment is measured continuously as the number of years of completed education (1–24 years).

In addition to the compounding effects of race/ethnicity, gender, and disability, this chapter also examines how policy characteristics mediate the potential racial and gendered employment disparities among individuals with disabilities. Receipt of government assistance has been shown to create work disincentives for people with disabilities (Stapleton et al., 2006). Thus, the following analysis includes four dichotomous measures of government benefit receipt during the survey year: (1) Supplemental Security Income (SSI), (2) Social Security Income, (3) public assistance income, and (4) survivor benefits or disability pensions. Accounting for these factors should reduce the possible employment disparities among the race/ethnicity-gender-disability groups.

Analysis

The analysis begins by examining the characteristics of the sample by disability status. Next, to determine how race/ethnicity, gender, and disability status combine with the work disincentives of government assistance programs to shape employment outcomes, this chapter estimated two logistic regression models. Model 1 predicts employment from disability status, race/ethnicity, gender; a series of two-way and three-way interaction terms for race/ethnicity, gender, and disability; and the individual characteristics of age, educational attainment, and marital status. Model 2 accounts for the four government assistance variables mentioned earlier. All models were estimated with Stata 16.1 and were adjusted using appropriate sample weights.

RESULTS

Descriptive Statistics

Table 27.1 provides key demographic information by disability status. As shown in this table, approximately 12% of working-age adults reported at least one of the six disabilities. As expected, disability prevalence varies by race/ethnicity and gender. For instance, people with disabilities are more likely than their nondisabled counterparts to identify as NH Black (15.6% vs. 10.1%) or as NH other (5.3% vs. 4.8%), but they are less likely to identify as Hispanic (9% vs. 9.3%) than those without disabilities. People with disabilities are slightly less likely to identify as female (48.4% vs. 50.7%). This smaller proportion of women is inconsistent with other research that indicates that women are more likely to report disabilities than men (Brault, 2012).

People with and without disabilities also vary on measures of social participation and other individual characteristics. For example, Table 27.1 shows that those with disabilities are substantially less likely to be employed than individuals without disabilities (35.1% vs. 81.0%). Those with disabilities also have lower levels of educational attainment and lower marriage rates. They are also more likely to receive government assistance of any type. People with disabilities are also older than those without disabilities. These percentages are consistent with previous research (Maroto et al., 2019; Pettinicchio & Maroto, 2017; Shandra, 2018).

Employment by Disability, Race/ethnicity, and Gender

Table 27.2 presents results from logistic regression models predicting employment from disability status, race/ethnicity, gender, individual characteristics, government assistance, and a set of two-way and three-way interactions. These models point to how disability interacts with gender and race/ethnicity to create substantial employment disparities. Model 1, which only accounts for the individual characteristics, indicates that NH White men with disabilities have 90% lower odds of employment than their counterparts without disabilities. Disability is associated with 57% lower odds of employment for NH White women than NH White men. Compared to NH White men, disability is associated with 17% lower odds of employment for NH Black men and 23% lower odds for NH other men.

Table 27.1 Descriptive Statistics by Disability Status

	Disability; n = 235,536 (12%)		No Disability; n = 1,660,093 (88%)	
	Estimate (%)	SE	Estimate (%)	SE
Female	48.4	0.001	50.7	0.0004
Race/ethnicity				
NH White	70.2	0.001	75.8	0.0003
NH Black	15.6	0.001	10.1	0.0002
Hispanic	9.0	0.001	9.3	0.0002
Other	5.3	0.000	4.8	0.0002
Employment	35.1	0.001	81.0	0.0003
Individual-level characteristics				
Age (average in years)	47.67	0.022	43.31	0.0085
Education (average in years)	15.9	0.008	17.9	0.0022
Married	39.3%	0.001	59.7%	0.0004
Policy variables				
SSI	19.1	0.001	1.2	0.0001
SSDI	22.5	0.001	1.7	0.0001
Public assistance income	4.9	0.000	1.2	0.0001
Survivor benefits or disability pensions	9.3	0.001	3.4	0.0001

Descriptive statistics presented as percentages and standard errors unless otherwise specified.
Source: 2017 American Community Survey (ACS), adults age 25–61, N = 1,895,629.

How Are Employment Probabilities Simultaneously Raced and Gendered?

According to results reported in Model 1 of Table 27.3 and Figure 27.1, employment probabilities among those with disabilities vary jointly by race/ethnicity and gender. Specifically, while NH White women, Hispanic women, NH other women, and NH other men with disabilities have similar employment probabilities, ranging from 41% to 43%, employment probabilities among those with disabilities from other race/ethnicity-gender groups vary more substantially. For instance, NH White and Hispanic men with disabilities have the highest employment probabilities among those with disabilities (49% and 45%, respectively), while NH Black women and men with disabilities have the lowest (38% and 33%, respectively).

Examining employment probabilities among those with disabilities from an intersectional perspective also reveals that the gender employment probabilities gap indicated by prior work varies by race/ethnicity (Pettinicchio & Maroto, 2017;

Table 27.2 Results from Logistic Models Predicting Employment

	Model 1		Model 2	
	b	SE	b	SE
Disability	–2.059***	0.016	–1.467***	0.018
Female	–.809***	0.008	–.843***	0.009
Race				
Non-Hispanic Black	–.788***	0.013	–.783***	0.014
Hispanic	–.110***	0.021	–.154***	0.021
Non-Hispanic Other	–.470***	0.025	–.501***	0.024
Interaction terms				
Disability*Female	.470***	0.019	.467***	0.021
Disability*Non-Hispanic Black	.088**	0.029	0.04	0.030
Disability*Hispanic	–0.068	0.043	–0.077	0.048
Disability*Non-Hispanic Other	.196***	0.051	.111*	0.056
Non-Hispanic Black*Female	.944***	0.020	1.050***	0.021
Hispanic*Female	.122***	0.024	.182***	0.025
Non-Hispanic Other*Female	.391***	0.032	.434***	0.033
Disability*Non-Hispanic Black*Female	–.392***	0.043	–.294***	0.050
Disability*Hispanic*Female	0.104	0.065	0.105	0.073
Disability*Non-Hispanic Other*Female	–0.032	0.071	0.026	0.072
Individual characteristics				
Age	–.013***	0.000	–.001***	0.000
Education	.155***	0.001	.143***	0.001
Marital status	.251***	0.006	.094***	0.006
Government assistance				
Supplementary Security Income (SSI)			–2.461***	0.023
Social Security income			–2.472***	0.021
Public assistance income			–1.251***	0.033
Survivor benefits or disability			–1.506***	0.017
Intercept	–.287***	0.027	–.304***	0.028

Results from logistic models predicting the probability of employment from disability status. Model 1 includes the two- and three-way interaction terms for race/ethnicity, gender, and disability and accounts for education, age, and marital status. Model 2 adds receipt of government assistance.

* $p < .05$;

** $p < .01$;

*** $p < .001$.

Source: 2017 American Community Survey (ACS), adults age 25–61, N = 1,895,629.

Table 27.3 Average Predicted Probabilities of Employment

Interaction Effects	Model 1	Model 2
Disability		
Non-Hispanic White Women	0.412	0.544
Non-Hispanic Black Women	0.379	0.547
Hispanic Women	0.423	0.556
Non-Hispanic Other Women	0.432	0.559
Non-Hispanic White Men	0.492	0.623
Non-Hispanic Black Men	0.332	0.463
Hispanic Men	0.450	0.575
Non-Hispanic Other Men	0.427	0.541
No Disability		
Non-Hispanic White Women	0.759	0.737
Non-Hispanic Black Women	0.785	0.777
Hispanic Women	0.761	0.741
Non-Hispanic Other Women	0.745	0.726
Non-Hispanic White Men	0.872	0.846
Non-Hispanic Black Men	0.763	0.746
Hispanic Men	0.859	0.830
Non-Hispanic Other Men	0.813	0.787

This table contains average predicted probabilities of employment for race/ethnicity-gender-disability group.

Model 1 controls for individual characteristics, and Model 2 adds receipt of government assistance.

Source: 2017 American Community Survey (ACS), adults age 25–61, N = 1,895,629.

Sevak et al., 2015). For instance, while NH White women with disabilities have employment probabilities that are 8 percentage points lower than disabled NH White men, this gender gap flips for NH Black people with disabilities. NH Black women with disabilities have employment probabilities that are 5 percentage points higher than their male counterparts. Hispanic women with disabilities have employment probabilities that are 3 percentage points higher than their male counterparts, while the gap is nearly nonexistent between NH other women and men with disabilities. Racial disparities among individuals with disabilities also vary by gender. For instance, among women with disabilities, there is only a 4-percentage-point gap between NH Black and NH other women (38% vs. 42%, respectively). This racial gap in employment probabilities increases to 16 percentage points among men with disabilities (NH White men = 49% vs. NH Black men = 33%).

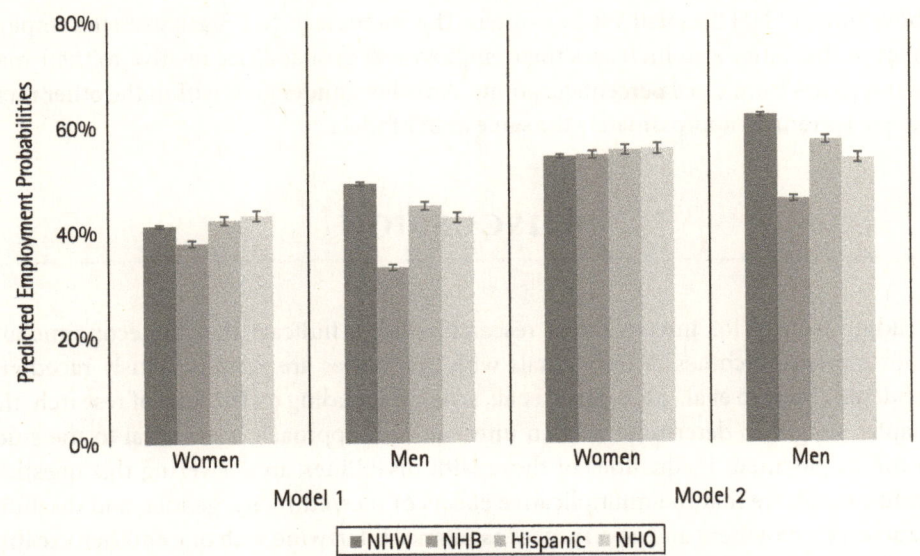

FIGURE 27.1 Predicted employment probabilities for people with disabilities by race/ethnicity-gender group. Figure presents predicted probabilities of employment by gender and race/ethnicity and 95% confidence intervals based on results from Models 1–2 in Table 3. Model 1 controls for individual characteristics and Model 2 for receipt government assistance.

Source: 2017 American Community Survey [ACS], adults age 25–61, N = 1,895,629

How Are Employment Probabilities Shaped by Receipt of Government Assistance?

Controlling for government assistance in Model 2 further increases employment probabilities among those with disabilities. While increases in employment probabilities range from 11 percentage points among Hispanic men with disabilities to 17 percentage points for NH Black women with disabilities, employment probabilities increase by approximately 13 percentage points for most race/ethnicity-gender groups (see Figure 27.1). Taking these increases into account, women with disabilities from all racial categories and NH other men with disabilities have similar employment probabilities, ranging between 54% and 56%. NH White men (62%) and Hispanic men (58%) with disabilities have the highest employment probabilities among those with disabilities, while NH Black men with disabilities have the lowest (46%).

Despite these increases, racial and gendered disparities in employment probabilities among those with disabilities remain. For instance, while there is a substantially smaller racial gap in employment probabilities among women with disabilities (3 percentage points), there is still a 16-percentage-point gap between NH Black and NH White men with disabilities. Notably, however, the smaller racial gap among women with disabilities is primarily due to the large 17-percentage-point increase in employment probabilities among NH Black women with disabilities, placing their employment probabilities above those of NH disabled White women. This increase in NH Black women's employment probabilities also increases their employment probabilities relative to their male counterparts from 5 to 8 percentage points. All other gender gaps within the other racial categories remain approximately the same as in Model 1.

DISCUSSION

Building from prior intersectional research, studies indicate that the economic and labor market outcomes of individuals with disabilities are simultaneously raced and gendered (Maroto et al., 2019; Shaw et al., 2012). Expanding on this line of research, this chapter sought to determine why an intersectional approach is essential to the study of the employment inequalities of those with disabilities. In answering this question, findings indicate that the multiplicative effects of race/ethnicity, gender, and disability status on employment and government assistance intertwine with one another, creating *overlapping institutions of oppression.*

More specifically, results from this research support several key conclusions. First, this chapter found evidence that the gender gap in employment among those with disabilities (Pettinicchio & Maroto, 2017; Sevak et al., 2017) varies by race and ethnicity. In fact, while NH White men have employment probabilities that are 8 percentage points higher than their female counterparts, this gender gap flips for NH Black people with disabilities, where NH Black women have employment probabilities that are 5 percentage points higher than NH Black men. This flip may be explained through an intersectional perspective. Specifically, because men have a stronger attachment to the labor market, disability has a greater (more negative) effect on men's employment rates (Pettinicchio & Maroto, 2017), making them the more disadvantaged group in this particular context. In other words, the multiplicative effects of being male, Black, and disabled have a greater impact on employment than any other combination of statuses examined in this chapter.

Second, as expected, employment probabilities among those with disabilities are simultaneously raced and gendered, which aligns with prior research (Maroto et al., 2019; Pettinicchio & Maroto, 2017). Specifically, examining disabled persons' employment inequalities from an intersectional perspective reveals that several race/ethnicity-gender groups examined in this chapter have similar employment probabilities, even before accounting for government assistance. These probabilities, however, vary more substantially for the most and least marginalized people with disabilities. That is, while the most marginalized individuals with disabilities, specifically NH Black women and men, have the lowest employment probabilities among those with disabilities, those with the most privilege—NH White men—have the highest. These findings point to a kind of "spillover effect," where the disadvantages or advantages an individual acquires from the combination of their status-based characteristics spill over to affect their employment probabilities.

This spillover effect is likely the result of two competing mechanisms. First, research indicates that those with disabilities who have other marginalized statuses, specifically women with disabilities and disabled people of color, are more likely to experience certain barriers that are directly related to employment, such as lower levels of education (Blackorby & Wagner, 1996; Sanford et al., 2011), greater dependency on government assistance (Maroto et al., 2019), and discrimination (Shaw et al., 2012) than their more privileged counterparts. These disadvantages may affect how they interact with the labor market, reducing their chances of employment. Simultaneously, those with disabilities who hold more privilege in society (i.e., White men with disabilities) can use their money, knowledge, resources, and power to minimize the effects of disability-specific employment barriers, increasing their chances of finding and maintaining gainful employment.

Third, this chapter finds evidence that this spillover effect may be the result of *overlapping institutions of oppression*. While prior intersectional research indicates how certain systems of oppression, such as racism, sexism, and ableism, overlap to shape an individual's experience of social institutions (Crenshaw, 1989), this chapter suggests that the multiplicative effects of race/ethnicity, gender, and disability status on such institutions, including employment and government assistance, intertwine with one another to both create and maintain hierarchies of disadvantage (Maroto et al., 2019). This process plays out most prominently when examining the employment probabilities among NH Black women with disabilities. Specifically, after accounting for government assistance receipt, employment probabilities among disabled NH Black women increase by 17 percentage points (38% to 55%), placing their employment probabilities above those of their NH White female counterparts. This substantial increase suggests that disabled NH Black women's higher likelihood of government assistance receipt (Maroto et al., 2019) directly connects to their lower employment probabilities. The connection between higher levels of government assistance receipt and lower employment probabilities may be bidirectional to the extent that the low employment probabilities among NH Black women with disabilities can be both a cause and a consequence of their high levels of government assistance receipt.

Thus, the multiplicative effects of race/ethnicity, gender, and disability on employment and government assistance simultaneously spill over onto one another, creating multiple pathways through which the effects of intersectionality can flow. That is, the interplay between intersecting status-based characteristics, employment, and government assistance highlighted in this chapter demonstrates how the intersectional effects experienced in one life domain can leak into others. Thus, if we think of intersectionality as an elevator, race/ethnicity, gender, and disability do not step on, only intending to visit one floor. Instead, they will press all the buttons on the elevator, ensuring that their experiences on one floor shape their experiences on others.

Policy Implications

Findings from this chapter speak to the ways in which new disability legislation must consider the effects of racism, sexism, and other systems of oppression to create more inclusive disability policies. Although legislation, such as the Americans with Disabilities Act (ADA), may have bolstered the employment potential for some with disabilities, these policies did little to advance the equity of those with more marginalized identities. This lack of protection of those with multiple marginalized statuses under anti-discrimination laws is a common issue in the US legal system (Crenshaw, 1989) and is one of many examples of how those who are the most marginalized are rendered invisible in society (Caldwell, 2010). This invisibility is compounded by the fact that, to date, disability-specific legislation does not address the barriers related to the systemic racism and sexism experienced by disabled people of color and women with disabilities, which are tied to their labor market outcomes. Thus, these policies provide downstream solutions to upstream problems. Until policymakers center the experiences of the most marginalized individuals with disabilities, we will continue to see racial and gendered disparities in employment.

One example of how disability policy can create a more inclusive and equal society is through reforming the network of disability-specific government assistance programs. Currently, these programs, specifically SSI and SSDI, are designed to provide assistance to those with an "inability to engage in any substantial gainful activity by reason of any medically determinable physical or mental impairment" (Autor & Duggan, 2006). As a result, many people with disabilities choose to forgo gainful employment to access these programs and the disability-specific supports and services they provide. Without access to these programs, many people with disabilities, especially those with multiple marginalized statuses, would likely not be able to live independently in the community and be segregated into congregate care facilities where they are more vulnerable to abuse, neglect, and illness (Mauldin et al., 2020).

Thus, disability-specific government assistance programs must be reformed to ensure the health, economic, and social well-being of persons with disabilities, especially those from multiple marginalized communities. Specifically, SSI/SSDI should be redesigned from programs meant to support those with disabilities who "cannot work" to federal subsidies intended to offset the extra costs associated with living with disabilities (Goodman & Morris, 2020). In doing so, financial and material supports from these programs should be allocated based on an individual's physical and/or mental disabilities as well as any social and cultural barriers they may experience. Within this reconfigured government assistance system, NH Black women with disabilities may receive more supports and services than their NH White counterparts with similar disabilities to counteract the multiplicative effects of racism, sexism, and ableism.

LIMITATIONS

Despite this study's important contributions to research on intersectionality and disability, it has a few shortcomings. For instance, because of data limitations, this analysis does not contain measures for sexuality, gender identity, and smaller racial groups, which are fundamental to the study of intersectionality and disability (Caldwell, 2010;

Maroto et al., 2019; Mereish, 2012). Further, because of its cross-sectional design, the ACS does not contain detailed information about respondents' background characteristics, such as work histories, family background, and health records (Montez et al., 2017). The ACS also does not contain information about timing of disability onset, severity, and detailed information about impairment type. The individual section of the ACS also does not have information on parental status. Lastly, because both educational attainment and receipt of government assistance can be both a cause and consequence of joblessness among individuals with disabilities, researchers must be careful not to draw any causal conclusions from the mediation analysis.

Conclusion

The current political and cultural moment calls upon informed citizens to both educate and examine the micro and macro effects of various systems of oppression, such as racism, sexism, and ableism. Intersectionality asserts that to truly understand how these systems of oppression operate, it is imperative to examine how they work alongside each other to create both disadvantage and advantage. Similar to other studies, this chapter found that employment probabilities are both raced and gendered. The analysis, however, moves beyond traditional additive approaches to reveal that the multiplicative effects of race/ethnicity, gender, and disability status on employment, education, and government assistance intertwine with one another, creating overlapping institutions of oppression. That is, the intersectional effects that individuals experience in one area of their lives can "spill over" into others, reinforcing existing systems of social stratification. Thus, employment disparities among those with disabilities are the by-product of barriers operating on multiple levels. This chapter provides further evidence of the fact that in order to create a more fair and just society we must center those with the most marginalized identities, for true equality only will be achievable when all individuals, regardless of race/ethnicity, gender, disability, or any other status-based characteristics, have equal access to society and its social institutions.

References

Ameri, M., Schur, L., Adya, M., Bentley, S., McKay, P., & Kruse, D. (2018). The disability employment puzzle: A field experiment on employer hiring behavior. ILR Review 71(2), 329–364.

Arms, E., Bickett, J., & Graf, V. (2008). Gender bias and imbalance: Girls in US special education programmes. *Gender and Education*, 20(4), 349–359.

Autor, David H. and Mark G. Duggan. 2006. "The Growth in the Social Security Disability Rolls: A Fiscal Crisis Unfolding." The Journal of Economic Perspectives 20(3):71–96

Barnartt, S. N. (2013). Introduction: Disability and intersecting statuses. In *Research in social science and disability*, Vol. 7. Emerald Group. 1–20

Blackorby, J., & Wagner, M. (1996). Longitudinal postschool outcomes of youth with disabilities: Findings from the National Longitudinal Transition Study. *Exceptional Children*, 62(5), 399–413.

Brault, M. (2009). Review of changes to the measurement of disability in the 2008 American Community Survey. *Program*, 1–17.

Brault, M. W. (2012). Americans with disabilities. *U.S. Census Bureau, 1990* (July), 1–18. https://doi.org/10.1300/J138v05n04_03

Brooks, J. D. (2019). Having a disability reduces chances of employment for all racial/ethnic groups. The Lerner Center for Public Health Promotion at The Maxwell School at Syracuse University Research Brief Series.

Brown, R. L., & Moloney, M. E. (2019). Intersectionality, work, and well-being: The effects of gender and disability. *Gender & Society*, 33(1), 94–122.

Caldwell, K. (2010). We exist: Intersectional in/visibility in bisexuality and disability. *Disability Studies Quarterly*, 30(3/4). http://dx.doi.org/10.18061/dsq.v30i3/4.1273

Caplan, M. A. (2014). Financial coping strategies of mental health consumers: Managing social benefits. *Community Mental Health Journal*, 50(4), 409–414.

Chan, F., Strauser, D., Gervey, R., & Lee, E. J. (2010). Introduction to demand-side factors related to employment of people with disabilities. *Journal of Occupational Rehabilitation*, 20(4), 407–411.

Conejo, M. A. (2013). At the intersection of feminist and disability rights movements. From equality in difference to human diversity claims. In *Disability and intersecting statuses*, Barnartt S. N. & Altman, B. M. Eds. (pp. 23–45). Emerald.

Crenshaw, K. (1989). Demarginalizing the intersection of race and sex: A black feminist critique of antidiscrimination doctrine, feminist theory and antiracist politics. *University of Chicago Legal Facts*, 1989(1). 139–167.

Erevelles, N., & Minear, A. (2010). Unspeakable offenses: Untangling race and disability in discourses of intersectionality. *Journal of Literary & Cultural Disability Studies*, 4(2), 127–145.

Frederick, A., & Shifrer, D. (2019). Race and disability: From analogy to intersectionality. *Sociology of Race and Ethnicity*, 5(2), 200–214.

Garland-Thomson, R. (2005). Feminist disability studies. *Signs: Journal of Women in Culture and Society*, 30(2), 1557–1587.

Goodman, N., & Morris, M. (2020). The extra costs of living with a disability in the U.S.—Resetting the policy table. Washington, D.C.

Lauer, E. A., & Houtenville, A. J. (2018). *2017 Annual Disability Statistics Compendium*. Institute on Disability, University of New Hampshire, 1–156.

Livermore, Gina A. 2011. "Social Security Disability Beneficiaries with Work-Related Goals on Expectations."Soc.Sec.Bull. 71(3):61.

Maroto, M., & Pettinicchio, D. (2014). The limitations of disability antidiscrimination legislation: Policymaking and the economic well-being of people with disabilities. *Law and Policy*, 36(4), 370–407. https://doi.org/10.1111/lapo.12024

Maroto, M., Pettinicchio, D., & Patterson, A. C. (2019). Hierarchies of categorical disadvantage: Economic insecurity at the intersection of disability, gender, and race. *Gender & Society*, 33(1), 64–93.

Mauldin, L., Grossman, B., Wong, A., Barnartt, S., Brooks, J., Frederick, A., & Volton, A. (2020). Disability as an axis of inequality: A pandemic illustration. *ASA Footnotes*, 48(3). https://www.asanet.org/sites/default/files/attach/footnotes/may-june_2020_0.pdf

Mereish, E. H. (2012). The intersectional invisibility of race and disability status: An exploratory study of health and discrimination facing Asian Americans with disabilities. *Ethnicity and Inequalities in Health and Social Care* 5 (2), 52–60.

Montez, J. K., Hayward, M. D., & Wolf, D. A. (2017). Do US states' socioeconomic and policy contexts shape adult disability? *Social Science & Medicine, 178*, 115–126.

Mwachofi, A. K., Broyles, R., & Khaliq, A. (2009). Factors affecting vocational rehabilitation intervention outcomes: The case for minorities with disabilities. *Journal of Disability Policy Studies, 20*(3), 170–177.

Parish, S. L., Rose, R. A., & Andrews, M. E. (2009). Income poverty and material hardship among US women with disabilities. *Social Service Review, 83*(1), 33–52.

Pettinicchio, D., & Maroto, M. (2017). Employment outcomes among men and women with disabilities: How the intersection of gender and disability status shapes labor market inequality. In Research in Social Science and Disability (Vol. 10, pp. 3–33). https://doi.org/10.1108/S1479-354720170000010003

Randolph, D. S., & Andresen, E. M. (2004). Disability, gender, and unemployment relationships in the United States from the behavioral risk factor surveillance system. *Disability and Society, 19*(4), 403–414.

Sanford, C., Newman, L., Wagner, M., Cameto, R., Knokey, A.-M., & Shaver, D. (2011). The post-high school outcomes of young adults with disabilities up to 6 years after high school: Key findings from the National Longitudinal Transition Study-2 (NLTS2). NCSER 2011-3004. National Center for Special Education Research.

Schur, L. (2003). Contending with the "double handicap" political activism among women with disabilities. *Women & Politics, 25*(1–2), 31–62.

Sevak, Purvi, David C. Stapleton, and John O'Neill. 2015. "How Individual and Environmental Factors Affect Employment Outcomes." *Journal of Vocational Rehabilitation* 46(2):117–20.

Sevak, P., Stapleton, D. C., & O'Neill, J. (2017). How individual and environmental factors affect employment outcomes. *Journal of Vocational Rehabilitation.* IOS Press. https://doi.org/10.3233/JVR-160848

Shandra, C. L. (2018). Disability as inequality: Social disparities, health disparities, and participation in daily activities. *Social Forces, 97*(1), 157–192.

Shandra, C. L., & Penner, A. (2017). Benefactors and beneficiaries? Disability and care to others. *Journal of Marriage and Family, 79*(4), 1160–1185.

Shaw, L. R., Chan, F., & McMahon, B. T. (2012). Intersectionality and disability harassment: The interactive effects of disability, race, age, and gender. *Rehabilitation Counseling Bulletin, 55*(2), 82–91.

Shuttleworth, R., Wedgwood, N., & Wilson, N. J. (2012). The dilemma of disabled masculinity. *Men and Masculinities, 15*(2), 174–194.

Stapleton, D. C., O'day, B. L., Livermore, G. A., & Imparato, A. J. (2006). Dismantling the poverty trap: Disability policy for the twenty-first century. *Milbank Quarterly, 84*(4), 701–732.

Velcoff, J., Hernandez. B., & Keys C. (2010). Employment and vocational rehabilitation experiences of latinos with disabilities with differing patterns of acculturation. *Journal of Vocational Rehabilitation, 33*(1), 51–64.

US Department of Labor (Bureau of Labor Statistics, US Department of Labor). (2021). Persons with a disability: Labor force characteristics summary.

Warner, D. F., & Brown, T. H. (2011). Understanding how race/ethnicity and gender define age-trajectories of disability: An intersectionality approach. Social science & medicine, 72(8), 1236-1248.

Xiang, H., Shi, J., Wheeler, K., & Wilkins III, J. R. (2010). Disability and employment among US working-age immigrants. *American Journal of Industrial Medicine, 53*(4), 425–434

CHAPTER 28

INDIGENOUS PERSPECTIVES ON DISABILITY

MINERVA RIVAS VELARDE

INTRODUCTION

THE limited global statistics on Indigenous persons with disabilities show that Indigenous peoples are overrepresented among disabled peoples in comparison to the general population. Of the approximately 1 billion people who have some form of disability, 80% live in low- and middle-income countries. The Permanent Forum on Indigenous Issues (2013) estimates the number of Indigenous persons with disabilities in the world today at approximately 54 million. This a conservative estimate, considering that many countries either do not recognize Indigenous peoples, or when they do, the criteria or proxy measures used for their identification differ significantly from country to country. Together with variation on how disability is measured, the intersectionality between indigeneity and disability poses additional challenges (Inter-Agency Support Group On Indigenous Peoples' Issues (2014). There are several inconsistencies in the use of disability indicators (Pettinicchio & Maroto, 2021). Available data and academic literature tend to be concentrated in high-income countries (Smylie & Firestone, 2016). Caution is necessary when addressing this bias, and in efforts to amplify the voices of people from low- and middle-income countries, which, given concentration of Indigenous persons of disabilities in those regions, is both pertinent and necessary.

Indigenous people around the globe experience higher rates of preventable disabilities, mortality, and poor health than their non-Indigenous counterparts (Anderson et al, 2016, Durojaye, 2018, Verstraete et al, 2017). These indicators are the result of a long history of social and political oppression. Colonial practices were marked by exploitation, inequality, and violence, leading to the systematic neglect and oppression of Indigenous peoples in the Global South (Anderson et al., 2006; Bhopal, 2007;

Barker & Murray, 2010; Hicken et al., 2018). Determining the extent to which colonial practices have affected Indigenous peoples has been a challenge for social scientists. Those who undertake this task tend to fall into one of two camps: those who see colonization as an historical process that ended and those who see it as a contemporary, ongoing process. Indigenous scholars tend to align with the second approach.

Indigenous scholars through decolonial thinking (Quijano, 2007) are shedding light on the hegemonic philosophical frameworks that have rationalized the social neglect and high rates of ill health and preventable disabilities experienced by Indigenous peoples, claiming that Indigenous persons have not adapted to capitalism, contemporary work markets, and "social progress." These hegemonic rationales have normalized and justified the past and present dispossession and devastation of native lives (Soldatic & Fiske, 2009). Violence and dispossession initiated during colonial times contributed to social neglect and high rates of preventable disabilites in the same Indigenous populations while also silencing those very voices.

Identifying the social determinants of health is vital to the well-being of Indigenous peoples with disabilities, but it is only one dimension of this broad issue. It is just as important to respect Indigenous knowledge, cultures, and history, including theoretical accounts of impairment, human functioning, and agency. Failing to do so will reinforce historical oppression and allow non-Indigenous people to theorize illegitimately about disability of Indigenous peoples while ignoring their viewpoints and lived experiences. Non-Indigenous knowledge systems and representations of impairment and disability have been and continue to be imposed on Indigenous comunities around the globe. This chapter contributes to understanding the richness and diversity across Indigenous cultures with regard to their views on the intersectionality between indigeneity and disability. It fosters a better understanding of the role of social inclusion and agency on the lived experience of disability.

I begin this chapter by examining dominant disability models with attention to their methodological and theoretical shortcomings when it comes to Indigenous viewpoints on disability. Then, I explore current Indigenous disability scholarship, highlighting its salience from traditional Western notions of impairment and disability. Lastly, I discuss international initiatives aimed at increasing the agency and representation of members of Indigenous communities by expanding on the conceptualization of social and political participation on the basis of specific Indigenous issues.

This chapter is based on an extensive review of the literature published in English, Spanish, and French, focusing on Indigenous and disability social science research, including but not limited to work in mainstream disability journals like *Disability and Society* and *Disability Studies Quarterly*. As this chapter seeks to identify any pertinent and relevant information, a search was extended beyond peer-reviewed journals to dissertation repositories and online United Nations (UN) documents (Refworld). Available literature addressing indigeneity and disability is rare and scant, and it is important to note that available scholarship tends to be in English and concentrated in high-income countries.

DISABILITY MODELS' RAPPORT WITH INDIGENEITY

This section explores how disability has been defined and explained by dominant Western theoretical models. It begins by describing the impact of the medical model and of theoretical models that have been developed in response, including the social model and the relational model or Nordic approach to disability studies (e.g., the Scandinavian model of disability).

The Medical Model of Disability

From the late 19th century, the medical model of disability has been the prevailing approach to disability studies. It defines disability as a personal characteristic, caused by disease, trauma, or other health conditions (World Health Organization, 2001). Disability was viewed as a deficit within the individual that needed to be adjusted or changed. The medical model takes a biological essentialist approach that stipulates a number of biological attributes that define disability (Hughes & Paterson, 1997). For the medical model, the "problems" arose from the bodily deficits that needed to be fixed. Medical experts were assumed be the experts and clinical interventions were seen as ways to "cure" and "fix" those deficits in the body.

This model is linked to Christian beliefs from the West imposed by colonizers. Christian conquerors disparaged non-Christian beliefs, to impose their own religious beliefs and rituals, as well as new ways of understanding the body and the disabled body (Grech, 2015). Issues of disability and views enshrined in the medical models, such as the assumption of biological norms and abnormalities that resulted from "divine punishment" that were to be "fixed" or "cure," grew out of Judeo-Christian ethics and philosophy (Miles, 1995).

In addition to these religious roots, the medical model is based on the domination of the medical profession. Domination is not new to Indigenous communities, as they have experienced it through colonial domination (Miles, 1995). Neither is the idea of the need to "fix" assimilation policies aimed to adapt Indigenous peoples to Western paradigms as compared with the medical approach that aimed to "fix" disabled people to fit into society (Armitage, 1995; Meekosha & Dowse, 1997).

THE SOCIAL MODEL OF DISABILITY

The social model of disability was initiated in the United Kingdom as a direct challenge to the medical model of disability. The social model of disability arose from the strong political engagement of disabled activists and academics in the United Kingdom. These activists were influenced by the American scholarship on civil rights. It identified disability as a form of financial, social, physical, and environmental oppression, not as a pathology. The social model emphasized the removal of these kinds of oppression. This model claims that disability was not an individual deficit, but an externally imposed restriction in the form of nonaccessible settings, discriminatory laws, and policies.

The main shortcoming of this model is its assumption that the experience of disability in the West, more specifically in the United Kingdom, and the struggle to remove barriers to disability were universal. This rationale failed to recognize the cultural and historical phenomena that shaped the experience of disability (Barker & Murray, 2010). Although the disabling, namely the oppression, experience of Indigenous population has been and continues to be specifically related to colonial power, this explanation has been excluded from the mainstream scholarship, which never cites nonmetropolitan authors and rarely builds on social theory formulated outside the metropole (Meekosha, 2008).

The social model does not address the disenfranchisement of Indigenous peoples nor does it consider the social, cultural, and political oppression experienced by them. It ignores how Indigenous peoples perceive bodily integrity, barriers, and disability, let alone the impact of colonization and its consequences on what it means to be disabled. The model also ignores the bodily aspects of disablement, diseases, trauma, or other health conditions that lead to impairment and disablement caused by colonization and historical neglect (Anderson, 2006; Meekosha, 2008). This relationship is key in understanding the experience of oppression for Indigenous peoples with disability. Furthermore, biomedical or neurological diversity has been acknowledged, embraced, and at times celebrated by some Indigenous cultures (Ariotti, 1999; Múnera Orozco et al., 2011; Pérez Serrano & Sarue Díaz, 2008).

THE NORTH AMERICAN CIVIL RIGHTS APPROACH

In comparison, the North American approach views disability as a part of the overall civil rights movement, with disability perceived as another example of a disadvantaged or minority group alongside African Americans, women, and LGBTQ persons. This approach posits that disabled people should be party to decision-making on policy and law based on their claims of an oppressed group. Proponents of this strategy argue that it gives "disabled people a basis upon which to claim for certain adjustments to the environment (e.g., access to public buildings), instead of having adjustments imposed" (Liggett, 1988, p. 271). Disability as a minority issue has a similar trajectory to that of the civil rights campaign for equality associated with race and ethnicity (Barnes et al., 2002).

Disability studies in the United States is based on a sociopolitical analysis of disability (Blanck, 2004; Liggett, 1988). Even in this context, accountability for the past wrongs of colonization has not entered the debate on disability, social justice, and equity, nor have Native American models of the wholeness of existence, nor their ontologies and conceptualization of personhood, health, and impairment (Lovern & Locust, 2013). This neglect occurs because Western disability rights are interested in bodily impairment and social dynamics, while Indigenous scholars focus on the impact of social dynamics on their bodies (Soldatic & Meekosha, 2012. Indigenous people with disabilities have been sorely mindful that Western human rights discourses are not sympathetic to them. They were excluded from the Convention on the Rights of Person with Disabilities, whose framework underpins the theoretical accounts of the civil rights approach and the social model (Hickey and Wilson, 2017; Rivas Velarde, 2018b). The struggles between the state and the rights of Indigenous self-determination are explained in the section "International Advocacy: Indigenous Agency and Representation."

THE RELATIONAL OR SCANDINAVIAN MODEL

The relational model (Gustavsson et al., 2005) borrows from the barrier-free principle of the UK approach. However, in Scandinavia the social relational model of disability has been more closely linked to the welfare state than to radical disability social movements (Söder, 2009). The relational model or Scandinavian approach centers on the principle of citizenship equality, which encompasses the "basic principles and values of the Scandinavian welfare states" (Kristiansen & Traustadóttir, 2004, p. 6). Its main arguments include that disability is a mismatch between the person and the environment; this is similar to the social model. Thus, it adds other elements that the social model does not, asserting that disability is situational, contextual, and relative (Tøssebro, 2004, 2013). This model advocates that the state has a responsibility to guarantee equal rights and opportunities for all citizens.

However, the relational model does not recognize colonization or the state's disenfranchisement of Indigenous peoples. This model centers on the principle of citizenship; thus, Indigenous peoples had no right to their own land and continue to struggle for self-determination (Moyn, 2010). Nor were they protected by domestic legislation. The relational model does not consider that Indigenous persons with disabilities would not be free of oppression from a colonial state. Consequently, the welfare state has failed to accommodate the needs of Indigenous peoples (Häikiö & Hvinden, 2012), such as the Sami from far northern Norway, Sweden, and Finland. The welfare model reinforces standardized policies and practices and overlooks special measures and ultimately the idea of equity (Gilroy et al., 2018). It sets the ground for assimilation, and it denies self-determination.

THE BIOPSYCHOSOCIAL MODEL OF DISABILITY AND THE INTERNATIONAL CLASSIFICATION OF IMPAIRMENT, DISABILITY, AND HANDICAP

Under the International Classification of Impairment, Disability, and Handicap (ICIDH) and the International Classification of Functioning, Disability, and Health (ICF), disability is the result of the combination of body functions, activity limitations, and environmental factors. The ICF goes beyond the dichotomy of disability and impairment, as well as the simplicity—and primary flaw—of the social model to offer a more comprehensive view of disability that also applies to decrements in functioning comprehensibly in the short or long term.

The ICIDH has undergone several modifications over the years. In 2001, the World Health Assembly endorsed the ICF. Global acceptance of the ICF relied on a comprehensive process of consensus to describe and measure health and disability; it "provides a description of the situation with regards to human functioning and serves as a framework to organise this information" (World Health Assembly, 2001, p. 5). In the ICF, *disability* is:

> An umbrella term for impairments, limitations of activity and restrictions in participation. Disability is the interaction between individuals with a health condition (e.g., cerebral palsy, Down's syndrome or depression) and personal and environmental factors (e.g., negative attitudes, inaccessible transportation and public buildings, and limited social support).
>
> (World Health Organization, 2011)

This approach moved beyond the consequences of diseases and treated functioning as a component of health (Üstün et al., 2003). The ICF and the biopsychosocial model of disability at its core have contributed to a better understanding of disability (Shakespeare, Watson & Alghaib 2017). The ICF conceptualization of disability borrows from previous models but provides a more nuanced portrayal of disability as a complex phenomenon that results from a range of medical and sociopolitical factors. Its virtues lie in its universality, seeking to standardize terminology, data collection, and welfare assessment (Bickenbach, 2019), but this promise has not been fully and clearly attained (Pettinicchio & Maroto, 2021). Thus, the ICF provides essential concepts and language, as well as structure, for clinical and social research (Bickenbach, 2012).

Importantly, the ICF addresses some of the shortcomings of the social model, which, in its challenge to medical models, overlooked the role of health and the body on the lived experience of disability (Shakespeare, 2006). These limitations and improvements were apparent in an Australian study of disability among Aboriginal and Torres Strait

Islander communities (Senior, 2003). The study examined the applicability of concepts of disability to Indigenous people in two communities in Northern Australia, using the ICIDH-2, renamed the ICF. The results showed that disability was a difficult concept to discuss with Aboriginal and Torres Strait Islander people; they did not understand the concept and had differing views on what it meant to be disabled (Senior, 2003). Furthermore, research pointed out that culture should be included under ICF's personal factors component, stating that more awareness was needed about how Indigenous culture influences other elements of the ICF (Beaudin, 2011).

Gilroy & Donelly (2016) argue that the biopsychosocial model enshrined in the ICF may be an appropriate theoretical framework to understand the experience of disability of Indigenous peoples if it integrated colonization as a social determinant of disability, use of Indigenous language, and emancipatory stance. Perhaps Gilroy's & Donelly (2016) suggestions address inefficiencies. The ICF was found inefficient in capturing the context of emotions, spiritual significance of traditional practices, and negative emotions such as isolation, shame, and loneliness of Indigenous peoples (Alford et al., 2013).

HOW CAN THESE KNOWLEDGE GAPS BE ADDRESSED?

This section examines the epistemology of Western approaches to disability research that concentrated on positivism rather than the participatory research (Meekosha, 2011; Rivas Velarde, 2018a,b; Smith, 2013). It elaborates on how research questions or rejects the core concepts of traditional disability scholarship. Indigenous and non-Indigenous scholars writing about indigeneity and disability have insisted that disability scholars will be wrong if they fail to recognize that Indigenous peoples have their own knowledge systems that can augment, extend, and contribute to contemporary disability enquiry (Grech & Soldatic, 2015; Hickey & Wilson, 2017; Lavallée & Poole, 2010).

INDIGENOUS PERSPECTIVES OF DISABILITY

Indigenous scholars have challenged the methodologies, languages, and concepts used by dominant approaches to disability, conceptualizing personhood and human capabilities that incorporate culture and lived experiences with an historical and communal perspective (Barker & Murray, 2010; Gilroy & Donelly, 2016; Hickey & Wilson, 2017; Rivas Velarde, 2018 b,c).

Over the last few years, a small but growing body of work has started to analyze the intersectionality of indigeneity and disability. The literature examines the intersectionality of indigeneity and disability. It highlights community interconectiviness, the importance of family ties and community networks, and spirituality as key concepts tied to the lived experience of disability for Indigenous persons. It simultaneously rejects and challenges the concept of disability as described by the major theoretical models discussed earlier, such as universal expirience of opression, overemphasis of bodily defict, or assimilation. This view tends to put more emphasis on self-detemination and agency. They also share some common grounds regarding the experience of colonization.

More than two decades ago, Ariotti (1999) documented how the Anagu people in Western Australia, South Australia, and the Northern Territory overemphasize impairment. In the Pitjantjatjara language, there is no word for "disability," nor do they have an abstract concept to differentiate people with impairments from people without (Ariotti, 1999). Impairment is viewed as an organic part of life, and community living and persons with impairment were generally accepted (Ariotti, 1999). This moves away from the Western attempt to label and divide people into categories of disabled and nondisabled, a division embedded in médical and social models. The focus of Anagu people regarding impairment and disability is on personhood and agency beyond what the ICF or the relation model offered.

Hollinsworth (2013) pointed out that international frameworks were ignoring Indigenous people's cultural processes, as with the civil rights approach and the relation model critic. Soldatic (2015) elaborates that postcolonial scholarship is falling short in addressing the intersectionality of gender, disability, and indigeneity on legislative frameworks and their theoretical underpinnings. Her research calls for a deconstruction of complex disabled identities that are constructed and negotiated under an unequal framework of power and privilege, marginalization, and stigmatization. Meekosha and Soldatic (2016) highlighted the need to portray the voices of Indigenous peoples and develop the relevant policies and legislation. Gilroy and Donelly (2016) claimed that in Australia since colonization, concepts of "defectiveness," "impairment," and "normality" have been imposed upon Indigenous communities, while proposing that colonization should be accepted as a social determinant of disability.

These claims draw attention to the impact that social dynamics have on the bodies of Indigenous peoples. The scholars noted that neglect imposed during the colonial era continues to harm Indigenous people today. The lack of knowledge production on how disability is perceived within Indigenous communities is another aspect of *othering* Indigenous people and perpetuating Indigenous discrimination (Grech & Soldatic, 2015; Hickey & Wilson, 2017). The absence of the voices in academia and in policymaking perpetuates segregation and social disadvantages.

The Māori community in New Zealand calls for disability to be constructed in a more positive and integrated manner than currently portrayed in Western scholarship (Fitzgerald, 1997), given that Western theoretical accounts tend to build upon the bodily deficit and experience of oppression, rather than self-determination and agency. Hickey and Wilson (2017) describe how Māori run services for persons with disability and have worked with communities and their traditions to coin a term that more accurately describes the experience of disability. With the Māori community, the term *whänau hauä* is referred to as an umbrella term suitable for disabled Māori. Indigenous worldviews encompass "spiritual, holistic, relational and environmental dimensions— all important aspects of an Indigenous Mäori worldview" (Hickey & Wilson, 2017, p. 86). The authors explain that *hauä* means "wind, gale, or breeze," *ä* refers to the drive or urge that propels this wind, and *whanau*, meaning "to be born or to give birth," refers to the extended family network. They explain that *whänau hauä* often face difficulties in achieving balance in their lives as they move through unstable and unfavorable environments. Obtaining a sense of balance therefore depends on the efforts of the collective *whanau* (family) members, not just the individual (Hickey, 2015; Hickey et al., 2014).

Locust (1986) claims that many Native American languages do not have words or phrases that could directly translate into *handicapped*, *crippled*, or *disabled*, stressing that impairments or differences indicated by such words were not used to label people across communities; it was more important than the person's belonging to a biological norm within the community. Lovern (2008) shed light on the ontological frameworks and cultural structures that follow from those frameworks among the more than 500 federal and state-recognized Nations and Tribes in the United States. A trend in this model was a sense of the wholeness of existence, considering communities, nature, family, past and present, and contrasting with traditional Western views on "ability" or "disability" (Lovern & Locust, 2013).

The Kallfulikan community that belongs to Mapuches people in Chile adopted the term *kutranche*. This term has been translated as the Spanish *incompleto* (incomplete), *entre dos mundos* (in-between worlds), or *enfermo en el espiritu* (sick in spirit). Pérez Serrano and Sarue Díaz (2008) explore the views of the Kallfulikan community with regard to disability. Based on an anthropological study, they documented these three terms and then explained their use. *Incompleto* refers to somebody who has learned to live as such incomplete. *Entre dos mundos* is a metaphor used in the community, meaning to live like a toad, an animal that could live in the swamps or marshlands, but it is not well adapted to land nor water and exists between the two in an intermediate zone where its ideal environment is found. *Enfermo en el espiritu* refers to disability as a curse caused by past wrongdoing, perhaps because of a family member who disrespected somebody with a disability.

In Colombia, the Nuquiwanna community adopted the term *Chunco* to identify somebody living with any kind of disability (Múnera Orozco et al., 2011). The term *chunco* resembles the word *chueco*, a colloquial Spanish word which translates to English as "crooked." The authors of these community differences were embraced by their members. A good quality of life was defined in terms of celebrating their Indigenous identity and being part of a family. The Nuquiwanna community is a highly isolated community on the coast of Colombia. In this community, independence, autonomy, and literacy were not as important for the community as were interdependence, living in balance with nature life, accepting life as a continuous change, and celebrating their Indigenous identity. When describing the experience of Indigenous persons with intellectual disabilities, Gotto (2009) found that in the Mixe communities in Mexico, people with intellectual disabilities were valued and respected members of society who were recognized for their contributions and not stigmatized because of their impairments.

While discussing Indigenous knowledge on disability research, Owusu-Ansah and Mji (2013) claimed that key concepts in disability research, such as self-determination and empowerment, need to be deconstructed and expanded in light of the meaning of such concepts for Indigenous persons with disabilities in Africa. Researchers must also consider the spiritual, social, political, and economic elements of African cultures. On the same line, Eide Khupe et al. (2014) mentioned the vacuum of knowledge, and past failings in alleviating neglect and poverty among Indigenous peoples and persons with disabilities in Africa. It is critical to learn about the various understandings of disability on Africa to improve living conditions among people with disabilities and other vulnerable groups.

Some cultures, such as Maori in New Zealand, the Native Americans, the Mixe in Mexico and the Anagu in Australia, tend to portray disability in a less stigmatizing way than the Kallfulikan in Chile or the Nuquiwanna in Colombia. This raises question of whether those more accepting cultures have enviroments that are more conducive to the well-being of people with imperments in comparasion with those more stigmatiszing. Rivas Velarde (2018a) and Hickey, (2017), speaking about the Purepecha people in Mexico and Maori in New Zeland, respectively, claim that in cultures that have a more positive outlook on disability, individuals with disabilities tend to hold more respected jobs and social positions. Alternatively, accounts of a more stigmatizing view of disability documented by Pérez Serrano and Sarue Díaz (2008) in Chile paid little attention to the contribution of the members to their comunities. Each of these cultures shared a history of colonization, with different types of colonial settlement and variation on the recognition of their rights and self-determination. This trajectory had a different effect on each community. The adoption of the term *chunco* from the Spanish language by the Nuquiwanna in Colombia is an example of the imposition of concepts of disability upon Indigenous communities by Spanish colonizers. In contrast, those cultures that do not show this type of conceptual assimilation (Mixe, Native Americans, and Maori) tend to be more positive. This reminds us of the variety of approaches across Indigenous communities, as well as the need to learn about the conceptualization of disability, their history, and their resilience.

This scholarship shows the diversity and complexity enshrined in the intersection of indigenety and disability. It also shows that if the social justice concept enshrined in the civil rights approach is to speak to Indigenous peoples with disabilities, it must take into account the social accountability of colonial states. In this line of reflection, the ICF needs to incorporate colonization as a social determinant of disability. This analysis shows that the cultural, historic, and environmental context are key in conceptualizing disability from an Indigenous perspective, as well as Indigenous identity and agency. Across all these communities, social inclusion and agency are at the heart of the lived experience of disability. This is very important because Indigenous persons' perceptions of disability have profound social, economic, and political implications. Yet the most influential models of disability have failed to engage with common experiences of social oppression, ongoing colonization, and ontologies of disability from the perspective of Indigenous persons with disabilities. Paradoxically, these concepts have received little or no attention from theoretical models of disability.

INTERNATIONAL ADVOCACY: INDIGENOUS AGENCY AND REPRESENTATION

The emerging voices of Indigenous scholars across disability scholarship accompanied a growing force of global advocacy on behalf of Indigenous persons with disabilities that are noting the shortcomings of current disability frameworks, which shed light on the limits of their theoretical underpinning. The Global Network of Indigenous Peoples with Disabilities was created at the 12th session of the United Nations Permanent Forum on Indigenous Issues. Just a year later the establishment of this global network, with support of the United Nations Inter-Agency Support Group (IASG), published the first Thematic Paper on the Rights of Indigenous Peoples/Persons with Disabilities. This paper pointed out the lack of relevant, available, and reliable data. It also drew attention to failures of current measurement tools based on the ICF. Furthermore, it also raised issues about the double layers of discrimination and exclusion, the lack of appropriate services that are leading to higher rates of institutionalization of Indigenous persons with disabilities, and their removal from their families, cultures, traditions, communities, and societies. It stressed the devastating effect that institutionalization has on families with children with disabilities. Indigenous children with disabilities continue to be at a high risk of being separated from their families, evoking intergenerational trauma caused by forced assimilation and the removal of children from their families. These issues draw attention to the noted shortcoming of the relation model and assumed benevolence of the state that shall provide protection to its citizens. This report reminds us that the state is the perpetrator of such atrocities, in a continuation of colonial oppression. This report was followed by the PFII session. The network continues to operate, and its presence and advocacy roles are very significant for Indigenous people with disabilities.

The International Labor Organization commissioned a discussion paper on Indigenous persons with disabilities (Rivas Velarde, 2015). This paper cited the difficulties pertaining to country-level data due to the lack of recognition of Indigenous peoples. It highlighted that available data regarding access to education, livelihoods, and employment showed that most Indigenous persons with disabilities are in precarious situations, as they face high levels of poverty and social neglect. Its calls on the Committee on the Rights of Person with Disabilities, the Permanent Forum on Indigenous Issues (PFII), and the Expert Mechanism on the Rights of Indigenous Peoples (EMRIP) to include Indigenous persons with disabilities in decision-making, and for an increase in emphasis on rights accountability.

Indigenous advocates and scholars have complained that Indigenous peoples are only mentioned in the preamble of the Convention of the Rights of Persons with Disabilities (CRPD) and not on the binding text. All states are obliged to submit regular reports on how the rights are being implemented by the CRPD Committee, which is the body of independent experts that monitors the implementation of the Convention. This reporting mechanism provides an opportunity to engage with Indigenous issues, but to this day CRPD recommendations regarding Indigenous persons with disabilities remain inconsistent and irregular. Harpur and Stein (2018) pointed out while analyzing the recommendations issued by the CRPD committee that: "This irregularity manifests clearly where the CRPD Committee addresses issues that are relevant to Indigenous persons with disabilities in some reports by calling for law and policy reforms, while remaining silent on similar issues in other reports, thereby implicitly condoning the state under review." Again, the social model embedded in the CRPD continues to better serve those in the West and to overlook colonial oppression of Indigenous peoples. It is imperative that such systematic shortcomings are rectified, ensuring that the procedures do not continue to alienate Indigenous people with disabilities by failing to protect their rights.

The nondiscriminatory principles of the CRPD (respect for differences, equity, and self-determination) cannot be achieved if the CRPD fails to address current colonization practices. It is necessary to reinterpret the CRPD for Indigenous issues, posing new questions and raising new issues, while creating a new vocabulary that could successfully engage with every aspect of the lives of Indigenous peoples with disabilities. If human rights are to live up to the expectations to be an emancipatory tool for Indigenous peoples, it is necessary to challenge the language of the CRPD and ask what the CRPD means to Indigenous peoples. This can only occur if international frameworks address the impact of colonization on the bodies of Indigenous people acting as a social determinant of disability. The domestic and international law and policy and theoretical models within which they are grounded shall focus on Indigenous self-determination and agency. Indigenous persons with disabilities who participate within the United National Mechanism have claimed that disability frameworks and their monitoring mechanisms seem to recognize their concerns pertaining to disability rights, but they observe reluctance to recognize their political identity as Indigenous persons first and diversity of their approach to disability and their political agency (Inguanzo, 2020). The civil rights approach or relation model promotes assimilation and denies self-determination of Indigenous peoples.

Pratima Gurung, an activist and an Indigenous scholar with a disability, claimed that the global discourse on disability focuses on the Global North, and it has been difficult to advance the recognition of diversity and political identities with the international diplomacy space that is constructed in silos (Gurung, 2019). Participation in the international governance system is key to the progressive implementation of domestic and international legislation and human rights frameworks that are relevant to Indigenous persons with disabilities, and international structures at the international and domestic levels, as they tend to debilitate representation and render their specific demands invisible.

Historically, it is through international frameworks that progress has been reached in the recognition of Indigenous rights while domestic governments denied them (Moyn, 2010). More needs to be done in international governance, but it is also important to challenge the theoretical models upon which measurement tools, laws, and policies are based to advocate for the rights of Indigenous persons with disabilities and end their social and political invisibility.

CONCLUSION

There is a richness and diversity of Indigenous cultures' views on disability that have been ignored within research and theory, except for the few studies that have addressed the intersectionality of indigeneity and disability. Social theories of disability and political activism are related. The social model that continues to be used as political idelogy behind international disability movements continues to claim universalism, as do the civil rights approach, the relation model, and the ICF. But such models are not as demonstrated by the literature portraying Indigenous scholars all around the globe.

This rejection of Western models raises an important question that is not unique to Indigenous persons with disabilities. The question has appeared in other collectives that assert that being identified or self-identifying as disabled is a categorical classification (Rivas Velarde & Shakespeare, 2019; Shakespeare & Watson 2001; Watson, 2002). The evidence suggests that the empowering discourse that served activists in the United Kingdom (and around the West), promoting barrier removal of the social model or the social justice of the civil rights approach, falls short in engaging with diverse realities. Today, the representatives and allies of Indigenous people with disabilities are saying that intersectionality and double layers of discrimination are unresolved issues in domestic and international policymaking. It is critical that Indigenous epistemologies are at the core of understanding the cultural and social context in which peoples with disabilities have lived and continue to live in. It's also essential that both the impact of colonization and how states have treated their Indigenous peoples are acknowledged and revised.

REFERENCES

Alford, V. M., Remedios, L. J., Webb, G. R., & Ewen, S. (2013). The use of the international classification of functioning, disability and health (ICF) in indigenous healthcare: A systematic literature review. *International Journal for Equity in Health*, 12(1), 32.

Anderson, I., et al. (2006). Indigenous health in Australia, New Zealand, and the Pacific. *The Lancet*, 367(9524), 1775–1785.

Anderson, I., Robson, B., Connolly, M., Al-Yaman, F., Bjertness, E., King, A., . . . & Yap, L. (2016). Indigenous and tribal peoples' health (The Lancet–Lowitja Institute Global Collaboration): a population study. *The Lancet*, 388(10040), 131–157.

Ariotti, L. (1999). Social construction of an Angu disability. *Australian Journal of Rural Health*, 7(4), 216–222.

Armitage, A. (1995). *Comparing the policy of aboriginal assimilation: Australia, Canada, and New Zealand.* UBC Press.

Barker, C., & Murray, S. (2010). Disabling postcolonialism: Global disability cultures and democratic criticism. *Journal of Literary & Cultural Disability Studies*, 4(3), 219–236.

Barnes, C., et al. (2002). Disability, the academy and the inclusive society. *Disability Studies Today*, 250–260.

Beaudin, P. G. (2011). A contemporary socio-cultural exploration of health and healing: Perspectives from members of the Oneida Nation of the Thames (Onyota'a: ka). University of Western Ontario, Canada.

Bhopal, R. S. (2007). *Ethnicity, race, and health in multicultural societies: Foundations for better epidemiology, public health, and health care.* Oxford University Press.

Bickenbach, J. (2012). Ethics, disability and the international classification of functioning, disability and health. American Journal of Physical Medicine & Rehabilitation, 91(13), S163–S167.

Bickenbach, J. E. (2019). The ICF and its relationship to disability studies in Watson, N., & Vehmas, S. (Eds.). (2019). Routledge handbook of disability studies. Routledge. Routledge, 2019P.51–67.

Blanck, P. (2004). First Thornburgh family lecture on disability law and policy-Americans with disabilities and their civil rights: Past, present, and future. *University of Pittsburgh Law Review*, 66, 687.

Durojaye, E. (2018). Human rights and access to healthcare services for indigenous peoples in Africa. *Global Public Health*, 13(10), 1399–1408.

Eide, A. H., et al. (2014). Development process in Africa: Poverty, politics and indigenous knowledge. *African Journal of Disability*, 3(2).

Gilroy, J., & Donelly, M. (2016). Australian indigenous people with disability: Ethics and standpoint theory. In Grech, S and Soldatic, K *Disability in the Global South* (pp. 545–566). Springer.

Gilroy, J., et al. (2018). Yuin, Kamilaroi, Sámi, and Maori people's reflections on experiences as "Indigenous scholars" in "disability studies" and "decolonization." *Disability and the Global South*, 5(2), 1344–1364.

Gotto, G. (2009). Persons and nonpersons: Intellectual disability, personhood, and social capital among the Mixe of Southern Mexico. *Disabilities: Insights from across Fields and around the World*, 1, 193–209.^

Grech, S. (2015). Decolonising eurocentric disability studies: Why colonialism matters in the disability and global South debate. Social identities, 21(1), 6–21

Grech, S., & Soldatic, K. (2015). Disability and colonialism: (Dis)encounters and anxious intersectionalities. *Social Identities*, 21(1), 1–5.

Gurung, P. (2019). Claiming voices and spaces: Indigenous women with disabilities in Nepal. *Peace Prints: South Asian Journal of Peacebuilding*, 5(Special Issue: Summer 2019). 5(1) 1–14.

Gustavsson, A., Sandvin, J., Traustadottir, R., & Tossebro, J. (2005). *Resistance, reflection and change: Nordic disability research.* Studentlitteratur.

Häikiö, L., & Hvinden, B. (2012). Finding the way between universalism and diversity: A challenge to the Nordic model. *Welfare State, Universalism and Diversity*, 69–90.

Harpur, P., & Stein, M. A. (2018). Indigenous persons with disabilities and the Convention on the Rights of Persons with Disabilities: An identity without a home? *International Human Rights Law Review*, 7(2), 165–200.

Hicken, M. T., et al. (2018). Racial inequalities in health: Framing future research. *Social Science & Medicine, 199*, 11.

Hickey, H. (2015). Marginalizing the subaltern within: How to effectively engage with and monitor diverse cultural identities with disabilities when individual identity dominates the collective identity framework. *Disability, Rights Monitoring, and Social Change,* 221–237.

Hickey, H., et al. (2014). Indigenous people with disabilities: The missing link. In M. Sabatello & M. Schulze (Eds.), *Human rights and disability advocacy* (pp. 157–169). University of Pennsylvania Press.

Hickey, H., & Wilson, D. (2017). Whānau hauā: Reframing disability from an Indigenous perspective. *Mai Journal, 6*(1), 82–94.

Hollinsworth, D. (2013). Decolonizing indigenous disability in Australia. *Disability & Society, 28*(5), 601–615.

Hughes, B., & Paterson, K. (1997). The social model of disability and the disappearing body: Towards a sociology of impairment. Disability & society, 12(3), 325–340.

Inguanzo, I. (2020). Construcción de marcos-puente en el movimiento de personas indígenas con discapacidad. *Andamios, Revista de Investigación Social, 17*(42), 355–383.

Inter-Agency Support Group On Indigenous Peoples' Issues (2014) Rights Of Indigenous Peoples/Persons With Disabilities, Thematic Paper Towards The Preparation Of The 2014 World Conference On Indigenous Peoples, Retrieved from https://www.un.org/en/ga/69/meetings/indigenous/pdf/IASG%20Thematic%20Paper_Disabilities.pdf 10 July 2021

Kristiansen, K., & Traustadóttir, R. (2004). *Gender and disability research in the Nordic countries.* Studentlitteratur.

Lavallée, L. F., & Poole, J. M. (2010). Beyond recovery: Colonization, health and healing for Indigenous people in Canada. *International Journal of Mental Health and Addiction, 8*(2), 271–281.

Liggett, H. (1988). Stars are not born: An interpretive approach to the politics of disability. *Disability, Handicap & Society, 3*(3), 263–275.

Locust, C. S. (1986). *Apache beliefs about unwellness and handicaps.* Native American Research and Training Center, University of Arizona.

Lovern, L. (2008). Native American worldview and the discourse on disability. *Essays in Philosophy, 9*(1), 113–120.

Lovern, L. L., & Locust, C. (2013). Traditional beliefs about disabilities. In J. Ziarkowska *Native American communities on health and disability* (pp. 95–111). Springer.

Meekosha, H. (2008). *Contextualizing disability: Developing southern/global theory.* 4th Biennial Disability Studies Conference.

Meekosha, H. (2011). Decolonising disability: Thinking and acting globally. *Disability & Society, 26*(6), 667–682.

Meekosha, H., & Dowse, L. (1997). Distorting images, invisible images: Gender, disability and the media. *Media International Australia, 84*(1), 91–101.

Meekosha, H., & Soldatic, K. (2016). *The global politics of impairment and disability: Processes and embodiments.* Routledge.

Miles, M. (1995). Disability in an Eastern religious context: Historical perspectives. *Disability & Society, 10*(1), 49–70.

Moyn, S. (2010). *Last utopia: Human rights in history.* Harvard University Press.

Múnera Orozco, S., et al. (2011). *Representaciones sociales sobre discapacidad en la comunidad indígena Nuquiwanna, en el Departamento del Chocó.*Universidad CES, Bogota, Colombia.

Owusu-Ansah, F. E., & Mji, G. (2013). African indigenous knowledge and research. *African Journal of Disability*, 2(1-8).

Pérez Serrano, G., & Sarue Díaz, E. (2008). Una aproximación a la identidad en los discapacitados mapuche de la comunidad Kallfulikan, en la Comuna de La Florida. Universidad Academia de Humanismo Cristiano.

Pettinicchio, D., & Maroto, M. (2021). Who Counts? Measuring Disability Cross-Nationally in Census Data. Journal of Survey Statistics and Methodology, 9(2), 257–284.

Quijano, A. (2007). Coloniality and modernity/rationality. *Cultural Studies*, 21(2–3), 168–178.

Rivas Velarde, M. (2015). Indigenous Persons with Disabilities: Access to Training and Employment, Gender, Equity and Discrimination Branch, International Labour Organization (ILO) Geneva Switzerland. P.1–47

Rivas Velarde, M. (2018a). The Convention on the Rights of Persons with Disabilities and its implications for the health and wellbeing of indigenous peoples with disabilities: A comparison across Australia, Mexico and New Zealand. *Disability and the Global South*, 5(2), 1430–1449.

Rivas Velarde, M. (2018b). Indigenous perspectives of disability. *Disability Studies Quarterly*, 38(4-18).

Rivas Velarde, M. (2018c). Addressing double layers of discrimination as barriers to health care: Indigenous peoples with disabilities. *ab-Original: Journal of Indigenous Studies and First Nations and First Peoples' Cultures*, 1(2), 269–278.

Rivas Velarde, M., & Shakespeare, T. (2019). Social participation and inclusion of ex-combatants with disabilities in Colombia. *Disability and the Global South*, 6(2), 1736–1755.

Senior, K. (2003). *Testing the ICIDH-2 with Indigenous Australians: Results of field work in two Aboriginal communities in the Northern Territory: A final report prepared for the Australian Institute of Health and Welfare, ICIDH Collaborating Centre and the Department of Health and Family Services*. Australian Collaborating Centre.

Shakespeare, T. (2006). The social model of disability. *The Disability Studies Reader*, 2, 197–204.

Shakespeare, T., & Watson, N. (2001). The social model of disability: An outdated ideology. *Research in Social Science and Disability*, 2(1), 9–28.

Shakespeare, T., Watson, N., & Alghaib, O. A. (2017). Blaming the victim, all over again: Waddell and Aylward's biopsychosocial (BPS) model of disability. *Critical Social Policy*, 37(1), 22–41.

Smith, L. T. (2013). *Decolonizing methodologies: Research and indigenous peoples*. Zed Books.

Smylie, J., & Firestone, M. (2016). The health of Indigenous peoples. In D. Raphael *Social Determinants of Health: Canadian Perspectives*,Canadian Scholars Press Inc Toronto 434–469.

Söder, M. (2009). Tensions, perspectives and themes in disability studies. *Scandinavian Journal of Disability Research*, 11(2), 67–81.

Soldatic, K. (2015). Postcolonial reproductions: Disability, indigeneity and the formation of the white masculine settler state of Australia. *Social Identities*, 21(1), 53–68.

Soldatic, K., & Fiske, L. (2009). Bodies "locked up": Intersections of disability and race in Australian immigration. *Disability & Society*, 24(3), 289–301.

Soldatic, K., & Meekosha, H. (2012). The place of disgust: disability, class and gender in spaces of workfare. *Societies*, 2(3), 139–156.

Tøssebro, J. (2004). Introduction to the special issue: Understanding disability. Scandinavian Journal of Disability Research, 19, 3–7.

Tøssebro, J. (2013). Two decades of disability research in Norway—1990–2010. *Scandinavian Journal of Disability Research*, 15(Suppl. 1), 71–89.

Üstün, T. B., et al. (2003). The International Classification of Functioning, Disability and Health: A new tool for understanding disability and health. *Disability and Rehabilitation*, 25(11–12), 565–571.

Verstraete, P., Verhaegen, E., Depaepe, M., Hanes, R., Brown, I., & Hansen, N. E. (2017). One difference is enough: Towards a history of disability in the Belgian-Congo, 1908–1960. In Hanes, R., Brown, I., & Hansen, N.E. (Eds.)*The Routledge History of Disability*, (1st ed.). 231–241.

Watson, N. (2002). "Well, I know this is going to sound very strange to you, but I don't see myself as a disabled person": Identity and disability. *Disability & Society*, 17(5), 509–527.

World Health Organization. (2001). *International classification of functioning, disability and health: ICF*. World Health Organization.

World Health Organization. (2011). *World report on disability 2011*. World Health Organization.

....

CHAPTER 29

BEING LGBTQ+ AND DISABLED, A SOCIALLY CONTRADICTING EXPERIENCE

....

JUSTINE E. EGNER

INTRODUCTION

....

THERE is a lack of culturally recognizable narratives about the experiences of identifying as both LGBTQ+ and disabled. This can lead to a lack of acknowledgment of LGBTQ+ disability experiences, which thus can result in the invalidation of their identities and the withholding and denial of important LGBTQ+ and disability sex, gender, and health resources, such as sex education. Moreover, the invisibility of LGBTQ+ disabled people is part of a larger cultural trend of overlooking, ignoring, and contesting the sexualities and genders of disabled people generally. Most culturally recognizable and pervasive narratives of disability rely on oppressive and stereotypical notions that proliferate stigma (Berger, 2013; Hevey, 1993). Further, there are few culturally recognizable narratives of disabled people as gendered and sexual (McRuer, 2006; Kafer, 2013). Disability, gender, and sexuality are deemed so antithetical that media portrayals mitigate the sexuality and gender of disabled characters.

Today, there is certainly disability representation in popular media. One need look no further than their own Netflix queue to see examples of hundreds of stories depicting disabled characters, but they are frequently one-dimensional side characters or fall victim to dehumanizing stereotypes and tropes (Berger, 2013; Meeuf, 2009). For instance, consistent with supercrip stereotypes, disabled characters are often deemed unlovable and unattractive until they have been rehabilitated, overcoming their impairments, and are only then worthy of romance. Or disabled characters are consistently portrayed as burdens to potential partners, relying on the "better off dead" stereotype. This is evident in recent blockbusters like "Me Before You," in which a young man who has been paralyzed refuses to burden his love interest and chooses euthanasia. Or disabled characters are the punchline in romantic comedies as evident by *Atypical*, a Netflix original TV show in which the main character who "has Asperger's" tries to enter the dating world and hilarity ensues. Or they are simply written as asexual and/or agender.

The dearth of representative narratives largely render disabled people's experiences of gender and sexuality invisible. Indeed, gender norms are based on nondisabled bodyminds, and disabled people are frequently "denied recognition" as gendered people (Gerschick, 2000, p. 1264). Moreover, if disabled people are constantly understood as agender and asexual, any marker that highlights sexuality or gender can be contested and removed (Cheng, 2009; Hirschmann, 2012). Consequently, the rejection of disabled people's genders and sexualities has contributed to real-world practices of policing disabled peoples' behaviors and bodies (Hirschmann, 2012). This becomes increasingly apparent when we reflect on queer identities (McRuer, 2006). If there are limited circulating narratives of disabled people as gendered and sexual, certainly there are fewer pertaining to disability and queer positionalities. Narratives of LGBTQ+ disabled people are thus essential to a sociological understanding of disability as the hypervisibility of LGBTQ+ disabled people's sexualities and gender experiences (as marked identities versus the unmarked "norm") highlight the invisibility and processes of marginalization for *all* disabled people. Moreover, LGBTQ+ disabled peoples' personal and community narratives can work to contest invisibility and invalidation.

How do queer disabled people construct and negotiate theses often socially contradicting identities for themselves and their communities in virtual spaces? This chapter begins with an explanation of the importance of narratives specifically for marginalized communities and social-movement organizations. After which, I attend to how the lack of current cultural narratives of LGBTQ+ disabled people lead to experiences of intersectional invisibility. I utilize the analytic concept of intersectional invisibility to explore how LGBTQ+ disabled people construct and communicate their identities through storytelling within virtual spaces. I focus my analysis on virtual spaces as virtual communities and social-media sites give marginalized people a unique opportunity to present and depict their experiences, which are ignored and silenced in other forms of popular media. The findings from this project indicate that cultural narratives construct LGBTQ+ and disability identities as incongruent. As such, those who identify as both LGBTQ+ and disabled are not prototypical members of their identity groups and therefore experience intersectional invisibility. LGBTQ+ disabled people have turned to virtual spaces to contest this invisibility through resistance narratives.

NARRATIVES AND INTERSECTIONAL INVISIBILITY

Narratives are culturally situated and recognizable stories that contribute to the construction of identities and meaning (Loseke, 2019; Melucci, 1995). Because stories feature characters, or "types" of people, they can be utilized as powerful tools for identity communities that lack positive representation and social support (Bradford & Clark, 2011; Polletta, 1998). Through the deployment of narratives, marginalized groups can construct identity, make claims about their oppression, and advocate for social change (Bradford & Clark, 2011; Melucci, 1995; Polletta, 1998). When an activist employs a narrative utilizing the collective "we," they help to "bring that identity into being" (Polletta, 1998, p. 423). Narratives can challenge the status quo and the power of dominant groups, as well as encourage self and community creativity, resilience, pride, and survival (Bradford & Clark, 2011; Egner, 2020). Marginalized identities groups often construct new identity resistance narratives in order to combat stereotypical and negative portrayals (Atkinson, 2006). Therefore, both collective community narratives and individual personal narratives can construct and employ new stories, which "can challenge negative evaluations of existing stories and construct alternative, positive possibilities for 'self-stories' and can contribute to the construction of community culture" (Egner, 2020, p. 264).

Intersectionality and Invisibility

As new stories can contest oppression, the analysis of narratives is especially important when examining intersectionally marginalized identities and groups. I employ an intersectional approach in examining the convergence of disability and LGBTQ+ identities. Feminist disability and DisCrit scholars have implored disability researchers to incorporate intersectionality (Crenshaw, 1991) in their analyses (Asch, 2001; Erevelles & Minear, 2010; Garland-Thomson, 2005; Hirschmann, 2012; Kafer, 2013). As is well documented in research, individuals who hold multiple minority identities experience complex forms of marginalization (Crenshaw, 1989, 1991) and are often further marginalized within their own identity-specific communities (Crenshaw, 1989, 1991; Collins & Bilge, 2016; Giwa & Greensmith, 2012; Vernon, 1999). For instance, scholars and activists have documented the exclusion and marginalization of Black women from and within both anti-racist/civil rights and feminist communities (Crenshaw, 1989, 1991; Collins & Bilge, 2016). Moreover, similar analytical techniques have been applied to the study of other experiences of multiple marginalization, such as the estrangement of lesbian, bisexual, and trans women from feminist, lesbian, and gay movements/communities (Crenshaw, 1989, 1991; Collins, 1986, 1999; Elliot, 2016; Walters, 1996). Because there tends to be a focus on the most privileged group members within a community, those who are "multiply burdened" frequently experience exclusion and marginalization within an often already marginalized community (Crenshaw, 1989, p. 140). The overemphasis on more privileged group members distorts our understandings of how systemic and individual forms of oppressions, such as sexism, racism, heterosexism, ableism, operate because our conceptions of specific identify experiences "become grounded in experiences that actually represent a subset of a much more complex phenomena" (Crenshaw, 1989, p. 140).

Inspired by Crenshaw, Purdie-Vaughns and Eibach (2008) employ the concept of *intersectional invisibility* to describe the specific experience of exclusion based upon intersectional marginalization from an identity group of which one is a marginal member. Intersectional invisibility is the "general failure to fully recognize people with intersecting identities as members of their constituent groups" (p. 381). Marginal members are often relegated to a "position of acute social invisibility" (p. 381). Intersectional invisibility is the direct result of androcentrism (the assumption that the standard person is male), heterocentrism (the assumption that the standard person is heterosexual), ethnocentricism (the assumption that the standard person is a member of the dominant ethnic group [i.e., White Americans in the United States]), and ablecentrism (the assumption that the standard person is able-bodyminded, also referred to as compulsory able-bodieness [see McRuer, 2013]). As an analytical tool, intersectional invisibility is useful in exploring how "distinct forms of oppression" can garner a rich "analysis of the complex field of oppressive forces in which people with intersectional identities are situated" (Purdie-Vaughns & Eibach, 2008, p. 380).

LGBTQ+ Disability Intersectional Invisibility

Disabled and LGBTQ+ people experience institutional and personal discrimination and marginalization (Berger, 2013; Kafer, 2013; McRuer & Mollow, 2012; Oliver & Barnes, 2012; Pilling, 2012; Sherry, 2004; Shakespeare, 1994; Shakespeare, 2013). When they are visible in cultural narratives, they are frequently presented through stereotyping, tokenizing, and oversimplifying (Doty, 1993; Raley & Lucas, 2006). Although accurate portrayals of disabled people and LGBTQ+ people are limited, narratives of identifying as both are fully absent from dominant culture. Disability and sexuality are often understood, depicted, and described as incompatible and contradictory; disabled people are habitually desexualized and de-gendered (McRuer & Mollow, 2012). These beliefs invalidate disabled people's gender and sexuality identities and experiences, and they specifically lead to the invisibility and unique marginalization of LGBTQ+ disabled people (Egner, 2017; Pilling, 2012).

Through processes of medicalization and pathologization, queer and disability identities and experiences have been reduced to medical and social moral problems. The pathologization of sexuality and disability have paralleled histories (Egner, 2017). There is an extensive history of medicalizing and pathologizing queer identities, desires, and behaviors as illness, disability, and disease (Tiefer, 1996). Similarly, the sexualities and genders of disabled people and those with bodymind differences have been pathologized or denied altogether (Dinwoodie, Greenhill, & Cookson, 2016; Hirshmann, 2012; Shakespeare, 2013; Kafer, 2013) through policing of bodies, institutionalization infantilization, forced sterilization, and little to no access to sex education and reproductive technologies.

In the late 19th century, sexologists began defining sexuality as a fact of nature and biology (see: Hirschfeld, 1948; Kinsey, Pomeroy, Martin, & Sloan, 1948; Masters & Johnson, 1970). (Hetero)Sexuality came to be understood culturally as a basic human function and driving force in human behavior (similar to sleeping/eating)

(Tiefer, 1996). Under this model, people who desired or engaged in un-heterosexual behavior were deemed non-normative and diagnosed with sexual disorders (Tiefer, 1996). Sexual deviance was thus directly linked to disability, and medical and cultural narratives conceptualized LGBTQ+ identities as an individual problem in need of medical intervention and personal correction (Egner, 2017). Similarly, through processes of pathologization, disability has also been conceived of as an individual problem in need of cure.

Disability, like queer sexuality and gender, was conceptualized as a moral social problem and was therefore understood as failure, incomplete, and inherently less valuable. Disability fell into the jurisdiction of the medical community, and thus disabled bodyminds were in need of medical intervention through etiology, diagnoses, prevention, and treatment (Berger, 2013; Oliver & Barnes, 2012). These histories make LGBTQ+ and disability identities incompatible outside disease models. Cultural narratives of queer and disability identities rely on medical notions that both are in need of cure and are symptomatic of the other.

Even within these identities communities, there is the reliance on narratives that conceptualize disability and queer positionalities as discordant. Take, for example, one of the most prominent and popular current LGBTQ+ narratives—the "Born This Way" narrative. In this narrative, the protagonist is a "healthy" (i.e., not mentally ill, often wealthy, and usually White) gay or lesbian adult whose sexuality, just like that of heterosexual people, was determined from birth. The Born This Way narrative is a rejection and contestation of the notion that being gay or queer is a perverse "lifestyle choice" and is a successful pushback to the historical pathologization of queer positionalities as mental illness. Yet, in constructing the narrative that LGBTQ+ people are not sick, not mentally ill, not disabled, it excludes and invalidates those who are. This narrative turns on the notions that illness and disability are inherently bad and disabled bodyminds lack value. It constructs these identities at odds, sending the message that if you are queer you cannot be disabled as disability muddies the message. This narrative has been extremely effective at garnering audience support and effecting social change because it is relatable and emotionally resonant. However, it has effectively drawn boundaries around who can be queer and who cannot and contributes to the intersectional invisibility experienced by LGBTQ+ disabled people. Concordantly, disability-rights narratives (especially when not led by disabled people) have relied on child-centric approaches to disability, encouraging silence around issues of sexuality and shunning queer positionalities out of fear of further stigmatization.

METHODOLOGY

The data from this chapter are a culmination of a three-part research project that examines online narratives pertaining to LGBTQ+ disability experiences. To garner a more holistic and complete picture of how both individual and group LGBTQ+ disability narratives are constructed, shared, taken up, and evaluated as salient, I collected data through virtual ethnography, constructing three related but distinct data sets.

Data Set One focused on organizational websites that advocated for LGBTQ+ disabled people, Data Set Two focused on blogs written by LGBTQ+ disabled people (specifically around the notion of neuroqueer), and Data Set Three focused on LGBTQ+ disabled peoples' interactions on a social-media site. In Data Set One, I use content analysis and observation to examine social-movement organization websites (including comment sections), and in Data Set Two and Three, I employ virtual ethnography to observe the interactions and communications of social-media and blog users overtime by utilizing archival functions of these social-media spaces.

Virtual ethnography is a methodological approach of employing traditional ethnographic methodologies in virtual spaces (Hine, 2000; Maloney, 2013), allowing researchers to examine the internet as both culture and cultural artifact and explore the ways in which the internet is socially meaningful (Hine 2000). Virtual ethnographic methods are concerned with not only the content of websites but also the interactions between website and social-media site users via comments, posts, construction and deployment of hashtags, liking/hearting/up-voting of comments and posts, and retweeting/reblogging/reposting. In other words, virtual ethnographers examine both the content and structure of the website as well as the interactions of the website users/ visitors with the site itself and with one another. Similar to traditional ethnography, virtual ethnography can include a variety of methods such as interviewing, participant observation, and analysis of content and documents. Over the last decade, with the rise of social-media sites, scholars have begun applying virtual ethnography to the study of social media (Postill & Pink, 2012). Scholars have used virtual ethnography to examine a variety of virtual communities and spaces, such as nonbinary individuals experiences of gender on the social medium Reddit (Darwin, 2017), how trans disabled Tumblr users engage in micro-resistance (Cavar & Baril, 2021), Black Lives Matter and cultural trauma on Twitter and blogs (Stephens, 2018), and the ways in which youth are impacted by cancer diagnosis as described in videos on social media (Gibson, Hibbins, Grew, Morgan, Pearce, Stark, & Fern, 2016).

A note on names and handles: In this chapter I use scholars' and activists' names as written on their blog spaces (if provided) because it is important to cite their work and ideas. I do change names for social-media users on Tumblr in Data Set One and Three for anonymity as their posts were not as easily accessible, and, in some cases, it was unclear if their posting was intended to do social-justice/scholarly work.

Data Set One

This data set focused on five social movement organizations' (SMOs) websites (Blind LGBT Pride International, Ontario Rainbow Alliance of the Deaf [ORAD], Rainbow Support Group, Queers on Wheels, and Queerability). Utilizing virtual ethnography, I examined over a dozen websites associated with SMOs and selected five for analysis based on a variety of predetermined criteria (see Egner, 2019a, for full list). The criteria relevant to this project are: (1) the SMOs explained their objective as the advocacy and/or support for individuals who identified as both disabled and LGBTQ+, and (2) the SMO's website(s) and online presence were public and accessible without the use of passwords, membership, or login information. In one case, an SMO used the social-media platform Tumblr, in which members are able to sign in and create their own handles and profiles. However, people do not need to be members of Tumblr to engage.

The data from each of the five SMOs' websites were collected from December 2014 to January 2016. Data include but are not limited to: bylaws, mission statements, "frequently asked questions," meeting and convention minutes, announcements for social activities and classes, blog posts, comments from members, posted news articles, pictures, logos, flyers for events, and videos. The data amounted to over 300 pages of type and over 50 images, flyers, and videos. Below, I provide a brief description of each group.

Blind LGBT Pride International is a special-interest group affiliated with the American Council of the Blind (founded in 1996). The purpose of this group is to "offer advocacy, education, programs, alliances, and support for persons who are either blind or vision impaired and who are gay, lesbian, bisexual, or trans- gender." **ORAD**, founded in 2001, is a not-for-profit organization that serves "Deaf, deaf, deafened, hard of hearing, and hearing people who are lesbian, gay, bisexual, trans- sexual, transgendered, intersexual, queer, questioning, two-spirited (LGBTTIQQ2S*) communities in the province of Ontario." **Rainbow Support Group** is an affiliate of New Haven Pride (founded in 1996) and is "for people with intellectual disabilities that identify as GLBT." They define themselves as "a group of friends and caregivers who are, or who are here for, LGBT people with disabilities including people with intellectual disabilities, learning, traumatic brain injury, Asperger's, and other challenges, as well as their families and friends." **Queers on Wheels** is an organization that promotes the sexual well-being of physically disabled communities. They welcome individuals "from all sexual identity groups including those who identify as GLBTQ (gay, lesbian, bisexual, transgender, or queer)." **Queerability** is an LGBTQ and disability rights advocacy organization run by a group of LGBTQ people with disabilities. Queerability works to "ensure that the voices of LGBTQ people with disabilities are heard in the conversation around LGBTQ and disability." This group's website is in the form of a Tumblr blog that is active multiple times a week.

Data Set Two

The data collection for this set was concentrated on blogs written by disabled, autistic, and neurodivergent LGBTQ+ activists and scholars. I collected data from November 2015 to December 2016. The intention of this project was to investigate the deployment of the notion of neuroqueer. Sites were chosen based on predetermined criteria relevant to this study. They had to (1) contain posts or comments from people discussing neuroqueer(ing) and (2) be completely open access. Two blogs fit the above criteria:

neurocosmopolitanism.com and neuroqueer.blogspot.com. The founding authors of the two blogs, IB Grace, Melanie Yergeau, Michael Scott Monje Jr., Zachary Richter, and Nick Walker, collaborate in the construction and exploration of neuroqueer.

Data include posts and comments dated between 2013 and 2016. Many blog commentators remained anonymous, and little demographic information was provided. Those who did self-identify identified with a variety of genders, sexualities, disabilities, and neurodivergent identities. Almost all of the posters who self-identified described themselves as LGBTQ+ and neurodivergent (many autistic), and about half identified with other types of disabilities (such as cerebral palsy, D/deaf, "mobility impaired," chronic illness/pain, mental illness). Most posters did not self-identify their race, and of those who did, most identified as White. I compiled data into more than 700 pages of text and images.

Data Set Three

I conducted a six-month virtual ethnography of a community of LGBTQ+ disabled people on the social-media site Tumblr. I entered Tumblr through Queerability's Tumblr page (the main communication site for Queerability, one of the social-movement organizations examined in Data Set One) and found an active community of people who identify as queer and disabled. I collected data from January to June of 2017. Using the archival and search functions, I collected data over a three-year period beginning in February 2014 and ending on June 30, 2017. Tumblr allows for easy access to users' archives, making for incredibly rich data in that members can engage in conversations over extended periods of time. This allowed me to see how and when stories were taken up, how they change over time, and how narratives are constructed through extended periods of online interaction. Posts needed to fit the following criteria: (1) the post must be publicly available, and (2) the content of the post must pertain to both disability and LGBT/queer identities. This dataset is about 270 single-spaced pages of textual data and images.

Most of the posters represented here self-identified as LGBTQ+ and disabled, and many self-identified as LGBTQ+ disabled people of color. Specifically, posters self-identified with a variety of different disabilities (such as disabled, chronically ill, mentally ill, having PTSD, depressed, wheelchair users, autistic, learning disabled, Deaf/deaf, hard of hearing, having Cerebral Palsy, being blind, experiencing mobility impairment, having an invisible disability, and others), sexualities and romantic orientations (lesbian, asexual, aromantic, omnisexual, monosexual, gay, queer, heterosexual, poly, and bisexual), races and ethnicities (such as White, Black, African American, native, indigenous, Latinx, Indian American, Desi, Asian American, and others), and genders and gender expressions (cisgender, nonbinary, boi, femme, butch, trans, trans masculine, genderqueer).

Methods of Analysis

I conducted a narrative analysis of each data set independently and together. I examined prevalent narratives common across websites, blog posts, and Tumblr posts that were repeatedly shared. The data were inserted into an electronic document and uploaded into qualitative-analysis software Atlas.ti. Drawing on Loseke's (2012) guidelines for narrative analysis, I first began by asking questions to situate the context of these stories: Who are the authors? Who is their audience? What type of story are they attempting to tell? Next, I closely read the data to examine the narratives present and to gain an understanding of the central themes of the stories most prevalently told. I coded each post, comment, or passage based on discursive themes of the passages. In subsequent passes, I then re-coded, using lumping and splitting techniques (Zerubavel, 1996) to begin generating common thematic categories. Through narrative analysis, I examined the construction of narratives in each data site independently, and then I examined what each data set narratively had in common.

Online platforms allow people to express themselves and communicate with wide audiences, which is often done through storytelling. Thus, they are ripe for narrative analysis. Recently, scholars have combined narrative examinations and analysis with virtual methodology in their explorations of digital and social-media sites (Busby & Laviolette, 2006; Egner, 2019a, 2019b, 2020; Geiss, 2019; Geiss & Egner, 2021; Underberg & Zorn, 2013; Webb, 2001). In this chapter I employ narrative analysis to examine each data set. Data Set One attended to organizations' narratives and interactions between groups and members, Data Set Two examined narratives constructed in virtual spaces devoted to LGBTQ+ disability discourses and dialogues, and Data Set Three explored the construction of narratives in an extensive and varied virtual space not designated specifically for LGBTQ+ disabled people.

FINDINGS

Throughout this section I demonstrate how LGBTQ+ disabled people and groups understand their identities as socially contradicting and recognize that prominent cultural narratives construct LGBTQ+ and disability identities as incompatible. I then expound upon how these narrative processes result in intersectional invisibility experienced by LGBTQ+ disabled people. Finally, I detail how LGBTQ+ disabled people and advocacy groups are contesting these experiences of invisibility by taking to virtual spaces to write resistance narratives.

Socially Contradicting Identities

It is important to have access to narratives that are representative of one's experiences in that they contribute to the construction of identity and the building of self-worth, and can serve as a device in combatting stigma. However, the prominent circulating narratives about disability are often oppressive and rely on harmful stereotypes. Although narratives about LGBTQ+ identities have drastically shifted over the last three decades, they remain extremely White and able-bodied centered. Furthermore, narratives of disability still carry extreme stigma. LGBTQ+ and disability identities are rarely depicted as experienced together. This is articulated below by one Tumblr user named Skeptical who self-identifies as a queer, autistic, disabled, Canadian woman and sociology major who writes about comics on her blog, when she posts about the importance of disability representation.

> I'm just frustrated by disability being so big of an afterthought for representation. . . even [in] discussions ABOUT representation...I want, like many people do, for my story to be told. I see people championing for queer stories . . . & as a queer women, I get hope & joy from that. But I'm disabled too. I'm autistic. It's not something you can separate out from me. It's not something I want to get a magic fix for...or an extra super-power so my disability can be treated not-really- a-disability-just-something-kinda-cool-because-REAL-disability-means-you-are-gross- and-useless, like a lot of comic book depictions of disabilities tend to deal in . . . It is as much a part of my voice & experiences as being female...Ignoring disability as a important axis of representation? It silences me . . . Disabled people have stories that are worth telling.

Congruent with current disability literature, bloggers, social-media users, and organizations across every platform stressed that disability and LGBTQ+ identities were understood as incompatible. Current socially circulating narratives depict disabled people as neither gendered nor sexual. Queers on Wheels' website explains that these beliefs about disabled people are accepted as common knowledge:

> There's a common social attitude that disabled people are not sexual that something about disability strips people of their sex drive, and that, moreover, disability makes people inherently sexually unappealing, so it's not like they could find partners even if they wanted them. This is accepted as common knowledge, despite the fact that it creates some extremely harmful social attitudes and social structures.

Not only is this common accepted knowledge, but also, as Michael Scott Monje Jr. on the neuroqueer blogs expressed, this narrative is sometimes encouraged within disability communities and spaces (often by able-bodyminded allies/supporters). Monje writes of the "autism community" that "there was a curious kind of quiet around issues that were not child-centric—issues such as sexuality, negotiating consent and power in adult situations, end-of-life issues, and basic civil rights." The notion that disabled people have neither gender nor sexuality leads to the invalidation of disabled people's gender and sexuality identities and experiences, and it specifically leads to the invisibility and further marginalization of LGBTQ+ disabled people. Below, Rainbow Support Group illustrates that intellectually disabled people are rarely thought of having sexuality, much less LGBQ+ sexualities.

> Although the process is complicated, it is doubtful that even those who are most understanding can imagine the obstacles of trying to navigate the intricacies of a sexual orientation discovery by a person with a developmental disability. Acknowledging that people with [intellectual disability] are sexual is a new development in the

human service field, but one that is still in pre-Stonewall days regarding those who are gay. Although people with [intellectual disability] are given unprecedented freedom to make personal vocational decisions, there is an unfounded expectation that they do not have a sexuality, let alone a homosexuality.

Although these various virtual spaces sometimes focused on different experiences of disability, such as intellectual disabilities, neurodivergency, and mobility impairments, they were consistent in their critique of cultural beliefs embedded with stereotypical understandings that disabled people are not, could not, and should not be sexual.

Queerability created many posts on Tumblr to address the difficulty of identifying as LGBTQ+ and disabled as these identities are perceived to be socially contradicting. On one post titled "When it gets tricky to be LGBT and disabled at once," commenters wrote about their experiences navigating these contested identities. It was common to see Tumblr posters write about the lack of complex and multidimensional disability and LGBTQ+ narratives in media. As poster Broadway-Hamilton wrote, "representation is not having a storyline on a character becoming about their identity or their struggles, [it] is about having tridimensional characters with complex storylines that happen to be poc/queer/trans/disabled/etc." Posters recognize that in searching for representation, the only narratives that exist are often one dimensional and rarely address the experiences of identifying as both queer and disabled. Having only a few positive representations means that there is not a recognizable cultural narrative for that particular experience.

This lack of positive circulating narratives that depict disabled people as sexual and gendered and the lack of narratives that address LGBTQ+ positionalities explicitly lead to harmful consequences, the outcomes of which can be damaging. For instance, in another excerpt from Queerability, it is explained that because disabled individuals are not perceived as sexual, the bodies of disabled individuals who are sexual (specifically ones who identified as gay or engaged in same-sex sexual behavior) are consistently policed by denying them access to their sexuality and genders. The write:

> People with developmental disabilities get degendered and desexualized. And denied basic words to talk about gender, sexuality, and their own bodies. This is an abuse. It is not a liberating rejection of the sex and gender binary. There is such a huge difference between rejecting words like penis/clitoris/vagina/breasts as ways of describing your body and *not having those words in your vocabulary to begin with* because people deny you access to them.

Queers on Wheels states that this denial of sexuality of disabled individuals can lead to social problems such as sexual abuse

> The insistence that disabled people are not sexual. . . plays directly into the denial of sexual abuse and violence committed against disabled people. After all, people claim, these behaviors are rooted in sexuality (why this belief persists despite all evidence to the contrary is beyond me), and since disabled people have no sexuality, this means

they can't be assaulted or abused—it's almost as though people genuinely believe that disabled people are like children's dolls, with a great big void where their genitals would be.

Additionally, there are consequences of the lack of narratives that are explicit to LGBTQ+ disabled people. Rainbow Support Group explains that their members can face severe repercussions for identifying as LGBTQ+

> Members are concerned with being forced into heterosexual social situations, since that is the only available option to socialize. Some members have a fear of being "outed" to peers and staff, which is not without merit, since many people with disabilities are not their own legal guardians. They are acutely sensitive to retaliation from staff and family, such as being ostracized from family functions or ridiculed by unsupportive staff.

Furthermore, every platform examined in this project addressed that the lack of representation and the lack of positive socially circulating narratives about identifying as LGBTQ+ and disabled resulted in the proliferation of negative stereotypes and invisibility. Many posters on Tumblr explained that having no representation and having negative representations both contributed to their invisibility and oppression and that they were equally problematic. Below, an anonymous poster discusses this issue:

> A lack of representation and problematic representation stems from the same place and the same perspective, and there isn't much point in establishing a "better or worse" scenario. Both have a negative impact on how communities perceive themselves, and how others perceive them as well.

Certainly, there was a shared understanding of the importance of representation and being able to identify a positive representative cultural narrative. As one poster simply stated, "We all know representation matters." Posters want stories to be told that are representative of their experiences.

Intersectional Invisibility: Invisibility Within Identity Communities

People with intersecting marginalized identities are often perceived as "non-prototypical of their constituent identity groups" (Purdie-Vaughns & Eibach, 2008, p. 376) and are therefore rendered socially invisible. Social-media users, bloggers, and organizational websites elucidate the experience of intersectional invisibility for themselves and their members as LGBTQ+ disabled people. A poster who refers to herself as Tumblr Mom writes to her LGBTQ+ followers (that she often calls her LGBT+ children) about how a lack of representation of intersectionally marginalized identities can lead to experiencing harassment and invisibility and can contribute to people (especially LGBTQ+ people) questioning the validity of their own identities.

> My dear lgbt+ children, This letter goes out to all of you who are lgbt+ *and*... Lgbt+ and a person of color, Lgbt+ and poor, Lgbt+ and disabled, Lgbt+ and chronically ill, Lgbt+ and a abuse survivor, Lgbt+ and on the autism spectrum... These are just some examples what your "*and*" could be. These things might make it harder for you to feel safe enough to come out. ...maybe, you feel like it did cause it and that leaves you feeling like your identity is less valid. Perhaps people even say people like you can't be lgbt+.... it's even a possibility that you get bullied or harassed for it. Maybe people accuse you of "trying so hard to be special" or they act as if you're a walking contradiction. Or maybe other people are accepting but you struggle to accept yourself....
> You are not alone. With all my love, Your Tumblr Mom.

People who identify with marginalized identities frequently seek out others who identify similarly in order to build community. However, people identifying with more than one marginalized identity often experience a double bind, outsider within, and intersectional invisibility within those communities. Posters detailed feeling excluded and invisible due to their complex identities within disability community spaces, LGBTQ+ communities, and Pride Parades and events, as well as other marches, protests, activities, and events associated with identity-based communities. As on commenter on Queerability writes, "I knew the LGBT community, or the L community, or the T community, could never fully be my community, at least as currently constituted." Bloggers, social-media users, and organizations in each data set described that LGBTQ+ and disability communities and community leaders were often unable and unwilling to accommodate the needs of people who identify as both. Indeed, every organization examined in Data Set One described their founding as in response to the exclusion queer disabled people experience in both LGBTQ+ communities and disability communities. Araneae, who self-identifies as a "disabled, queer, fat, Jewish non-binary femme" describes the racism, transphobia, and ableism within hegemonic gay communities. They explain that LGBT communities have a long history of erasing people with intersectionally marginalized identities. This erasure, therefore, leads to members experiencing intersectional invisibility and continued marginalization.

> The LGBT community has history of erasing QPOC, disabled queers, bisexuals, pansexuals, trans folks especially those who do not pass/do not want "the surgery"/ are not "the right kind of trans," non-binary or genderqueer folks, mentally ill queers, fat queers, ace/aro folks, etc. The usual Image of the queer community is a White, Affluent, Thin, Cis, Lesbian or Gay individual or couple . . . We have an image issue, which then permeates the community, and pushes marginalized queer folks further to the edges, or out of the community altogether...racism, cissexism, ableism, biphobia, acephobia. . . has a tendency to cause us to fight each other over scraps rather than lift each other up.

They then describe the life-threatening material issues (such as youth homelessness, prevalence of STDs, murder of trans women), often faced by [a] "less privileged segment of the community are often downplayed or dismissed in order to focus on marriage equality." Posters and groups recognize that such exclusions can have severe real-life implications.

Intersectional Invisibility and Pride

LGBTQ+ disabled people described Pride events as particularly challenging, expressing intersectional invisibility through both physical and ideological exclusion. All of the organizations examined in Data Set One discussed exclusion of many Pride events or made suggestions on how to make LGBTQ+ spaces disability inclusive. In Data Set Two, neuroqueer bloggers pointed out the long histories of erasing marginalized experiences within gay and lesbian communities. Data Set Three posters focused on Pride events as particularly stigmatizing experiences. Bobbie, a queer disabled Tumblr user, exclaimed, "Sometimes pride feels like the time of year when enabled queer community gathers & reminds disabled people that we do not belong & we do not matter." Bek, a queer poster who identifies as mentally ill, in a plea to Pride goers, stated, "can we take a sec to remember that pride months isn't a whole month for cis white gays? it's for neurodivergent, religious, poc, and disabled queer people too." Another poster describes experiences of intersectional invisibility when they write,

> I have been "left behind" by a Pride march overtaken by the folk carrying the "we are the end of the march" banner and told to get on the pavement out of the road. I have also fallen out of my wheelchair on other marches because they cross a road, or go via a flight of steps which when you're marching as part of a crowd, at bum height, you can't see until you're falling down them!

Yet another Tumblr user, Anne, who uses a wheelchair and identifies herself as bi/polysexual and a "proud mad cripple," expounds on their experiences with being excluded when attempting to participate in a LGBTQ+ Pride march.

> It truly sucks, as a physically/otherwise impaired person, to arrange transport to a gathering (maybe a full hundred miles from your isolated town) at which you hope you'll feel welcomed. . . Except, to realize that you can't march with everyone else because of the shitty city streets and that the organizers, well informed on one axis of oppression, ignored a ton of other kinds. Let the cripples set the pace and do not allow hills segregate us from "normal folk". . . Down with ableism and willful ignorance!

This lack of visibility led to the exclusion of posters from identity-specific groups, and disabled LGBTQ+ social-media users and organizations express that Pride and gay and lesbian spaces and communities were often inaccessible and unsafe. It is clear by the quotations above that the posters felt that identity communities did not and could not accommodate LGBTQ+ disabled members because they did not recognize their intersectional experiences.

Intersectional Invisibility through Pathologization

Data from each stage of collection suggests that experiences of intersectional invisibility, in which one or more of their identities were rendered invisible within their specific identity groups, often rely on the pathologization of disability. A Tumblr poster explains that their illnesses/disabilities are often used to deny their LGBTQ+ identities

> shout out to all the lgbt mentally ill & disabled people who have to put up with their symptoms / coping mechanisms being used to judge & deny the rest of their identity ("are you sure you're trans? what if it's your illness talking" "it's hard to be an ally when you're this hard to deal with" etc) as well as being treated like an absurd and unbelievable checklist of tokens by the mainstream ("what's next, an autistic lesbian woc??").

Processes of medicalization have historically defined LGBTQ+ identities as illness while pathologized conceptions of disability frequently reduce disabled individuals' queerness to a symptom of their disability diagnosis. Narrative pathologization was frequently referenced in each data set. The above quotation speaks to experiences of intersectional invisibility as these posters find themselves excluded from their identity groups through narrative tactics that pathologize and describe LGBTQ+ identities as symptoms of disability. At times, intersectional invisibility functions in ways that make those who are multiply marginalized hypervisible. They stand out as "freaks" against the "silent assumption" that people like them do not exist. Tumblr Mom addresses this in a post about the lack of representation for LGBTQ+ people who also hold another marginalized positionality. They write:

> *The silent assumption there are no lgbt+ people of color The silent assumption there are no lgbt+ people with a disability* ...And if you feel like there's no representation of people like you, i feel your pain and i hope we can change that together—but in the meantime, please know even without any representation, you're valid and real and fantastic!

This is further elucidated on the Neuroqueer blogs when IB Grace writes about how LGBTQ+ disabled people were told they made able-bodyminded LGBTQ+ activists "look bad." They write:

> We all marched together and we said were queer, were here, get used to it. That was desperately shocking, back then. The others told us to stop really, stop, your making us all look bad...your making us all look like freaks, nobody will ever accept us when you act like that...they'll never imagine that we are just like them.

Communities are not necessarily exclusionary; it is how specific narratives are taken up and utilized that leads to the erasure of LGBTQ+ disabled people. Specifically, when narratives rely on stereotypes or pathologized notions of identity, they lead to intersectional invisibility, which gives rise to exclusionary practices. This process of destructive narratives and ideas leading to harm is elucidated when Michael Scott Monje Jr. writes that neuroqueer "is an idea that was born out of my own sense of discomfort, out of my feeling that, in order to find support in an autism community, I needed to 'suck it up' and find solidarity with people who were really holding on to some attitude that I found destructive...dangerous...their effects could reach beyond the person who held these destructive beliefs and weak harm in society."

Resistance Narratives and Contesting Invisibility

Social-media users, bloggers, and organizational websites are actively responding to the lack of cultural narratives by writing resistance stories and narrating themselves into existence. The quotations referenced above function in ways that point out exclusive cultural narratives and practices within specific identity communities and contest intersectional invisibility. The social movement organizations in Data Set One are creating physical and virtual spaces used for sharing information and resources, organizing to advocate on behalf of members, and sharing stories about the experiences of identifying as LBGTQ+ and disabled. As Queers on Wheels writes,

> Since people with disabilities are often overlooked as sexual beings, the mission of Queers On Wheels is to liberate and empower them with information and support. This narrow way of thinking does not value a person as a whole, but rather focuses on an aspect of their identity. Queers On Wheels recognizes that people have multiple identities and that those identities need to be valued and appreciated. We recognize the need for a community that incorporates all identities.

In Data Set Two, neuroqueer bloggers use virtual spaces to share their stories as mostly LGBTQ+ autistic/neurodivergent people and contest invisibility and exclusionary practices within disability communities, autism communities, and LGBTQ+ communities. Neuroqueering as a politic rejects exclusionary practices, pathologization of identity, and assimilationist narratives, especially in describing that assimilation was not worth the price of excluding others (Egner, 2019a). In a conversation on the neuroqueer blog, posters discussed that lesbian- and gay-focused SMOs would exclude more marginal members through assimilation.

> The flagship way of being queer...is to be gay or lesbian, and I am this, which gives me privilege of a relative sort. It gives me the kind of privilege to where I could have choses (if I were that kind of unfortunate person to be one of these unctuous HRC slime balls who though it necessary to throw everyone else under the bus to assimilate).

This poster recognizes that more marginal narratives are made invisible by privileging prototypical and assimilation narratives. A commenter responds to the above post by explaining that this type of exclusion and intersectional invisibility contributes to the construction of hierarchies within identity-based communities.

> As for those being "thrown under the bus for assimilation" I think a hierarchy is followed with some more valued at other's expenses with autistic advocacy. I've heard it suggested that the ones represented. . . are the best and brightest advocates . . . That description honors a value system...most, of what motivates the unfair discrimination, elitism, and bigotry in the society being challenged is echoed in the very advocacy movements presenting the challenge... not much can be gained from one that supports the societies' exclusive ideals which need challenging

The neuroqueer bloggers stressed the importance of making this exclusion visible and strategizing against it through the proliferation of resistance narratives. For example, posters frequently expressed frustration with academia (many consider themselves academics) for its lack of accessibility. They recognize that, for many disabled scholars, taking a position against academia's inaccessibility can mean being shut out of the very gates they are attempting to open and can result in further stigmatization. As a commentator explains, "academia beats the possibility of this response out of us...But we can occupy academia; we can stand against oppression and when we find it in ourselves, respond with the truth even if it is very risky." In explaining that they respond with truth, this poster highlights the use of resistance narrative to contest exclusion and invisibility.

In Data Set Three, social-media posters employ resistance narratives through sharing photos of themselves as forms of representation; sharing personal identity and resistance stories; writing stories and creating art with complex queer disabled protagonists; writing analyses and critiques of social organizations, ideologies, and media representations; connecting with others who identify similarly employing Tumblr as a virtual meeting space; and creating and sharing book, movie, and TV show lists with quality representations—effectively building an online queer, disabled, people-of-color–focused library. In doing so, they are constructing resistance narratives to represent their communities. It was extremely common for posters to ask for and share knowledge of positive diverse representations of characters from popular media. For example, in one post a librarian requests help from other Tumblr users in developing a list of "books written by and featuring POC characters, Characters with physical and/or mental disabilities, LGBTQA+ characters." Posters from this online community responded by re-blogging, and creating and adding to a list of books. As a librarian, she intended to add the recommended books to the shelves of her library; therefore, this community contributed to the availability of accessible representation for people who may not be Tumblr users.

Many posters were writing and creating film and art to fill the gap in representation of intersectionally marginalized people. Some Tumblr users post about writing books and screenplays, while others, like Kym, are creating podcasts with diverse representation. "Help me make a podcast?... It'd be fantasy and maybe sci-fi, containing magic and stuff. I want it to be diverse, as diverse as possible. Meaning:—People of color- All kind of MOGAI[1]/LGBT representation- Disabled people- Neurodiverse people... or you just want to add ideas or your voice, message me, and please spread the word!" In the quotation below, Emerson, a novelist who identifies as agender and autistic, shares a film they made in response to a lack of LGBTQ+ disabled characters in movies and TV. They explain that it is important to have a positive representation of such an identity out in the world and ask people to re-blog and share. "So here is a short film I made in response to #LGBTFansDeserveBetter it's about an LGBT+ disabled couple and superheroes. Please reblog this, seriously! It means a lot to me to **get this positive representation out there**. Please check it out, or at least spread the word! [Film Link]"

Ashe, a self-identified demi-pan, autistic, "white boy," writes about how there will only be enough representation when they no longer have to "beg" for it and encourages posters to continue to create their own narratives as representation.

> Begging for more representation of disabled / queer / feminist / poc / intersectional characters like it's genuinely great that an example does exist, and we should praise and acknowledge that but that doesn't mean it's *good enough*, and oftentimes these comments come across like "here's your one example have fun with it now you're done" . . . the point of *good enough* comes when representation is available in such high abundance we don't have to ask for it anymore.

Posters are using Tumblr as the medium for which they disseminate this representation. Many of the posts collected from this community used hashtags to connect with others and to disseminate resistance narratives. It was common to see tags like: #queeranddisabled, #pride, #Accessibility, #disabilityawareness #weneeddiversebooks, # #Actuallyautistic #queershit, #intersectional, #lgbtawareness, #representation, #asexualdisabled #helloIexist. Alongside these hashtags, posters would include pictures and stories about their experiences, often even citing it as representation of their communities. This is the case with many of Jax's[1] posts. Jax frequently posted about using images and stories about their life to represent and support their community. They engaged in narrative building on Tumblr to, as they explained, combat ableism and queerphobia. Jax writes,

> I'm out here trying to represent other disabled queer/trans Chicanxs/Latinxs since we hardly get any representation. Being Mexican and queer has been hard. There's not many places where I'm from to completely live in my truth without judgement. There's so many layers to my intersecting identities. Most days it's hard as hell. Living in a world where no one wants you to live. Ableism kills, so does queer/transphobia.

It is evident by these excerpts from Tumblr users' posts that they are intending to contest intersectional invisibility through the construction of resistance narratives. Below, Kameron, a self-identified queer, disabled sexual-assault survivor explains the importance of being open about her relatively invisible identities to contribute to the building of a cultural narrative for intersectionally marginalized people.

I don't exist to make other people comfortable. I exist to better my life, and the lives of those I love. This includes the disability community. The identities which matter most to me are largely invisible, which affords me a great deal of privilege. As a queer, disabled survivor of sexual assault + partner violence, I have the option of keeping these key parts of me hidden beneath a white blonde femme exterior. This option is not available to most people. It is important that I openly represent my invisible identities, for as long as I am safely able to do so . . . It is about representation and pushing forward for a better quality of life for my communities.

They are resisting current cultural narratives that construct LBGTQ+ and disability identities as incongruent by constructing complex dynamic self-stories. The organizations, bloggers, and social-media users in each data set are attempting to shift the current cultural narratives that rely on oppressive stereotypes and pathologization, and render non-prototypical members invisible.

CONCLUSION

Although the cultural narratives about disability and LGBTQ+ identities render LGBTQ+ disabled people invisible through processes of pathologization and stigmatization, people who identify with this intersection take to virtual spaces to disseminate positive resistance narratives and story their identities. These new narratives do important resistance work by attempting to shift cultural beliefs about disability, sexuality, and gender. The findings elucidated in this chapter provide practical, empirical, and theoretical implications for social-movement and social-justice work, for sociology of disability, and for general sociology. Additionally, because this project expands such an extensive amount of data, this chapter is limited in detail as themes from the analysis could not be included in depth in this chapter. Specific themes that warrant further investigation include the proliferation of these narratives outside of virtual spaces; specific examinations of how race, age, and class further complexify these narratives; and deeper analysis on the impact of virtual spaces in the personal lives of social-media users. Moreover, this chapter focuses on the narratives that are common across these platforms but not the differences among them (for a comparative examination of the social movement organizations referenced here, please see Egner, 2018).

This study highlights two primary practical implications for social movement actors and disabled peoples' lives. First, the findings indicate that there is clearly a lack of sex and gender resources for disabled people generally and disabled queer people specifically. Resources such as sex education and access to contraceptives and safe sex technologies for both hetero cisgender disabled people and LGBTQ+ disabled people are near nonexistent. Access to in-person LGBTQ+ communities and support networks are particularly absent for disabled people. While LGBTQ+ people experience many challenges in building, joining, and maintaining identity communities, this is especially challenging for disabled LGBTQ+ people who can be beholden upon queerphobic caretakers, inaccessible transportation and community spaces, and a lack of financial resources.

Second, these findings indicate that despite the lack of in-person communities and resources for disabled LGBTQ+ people, virtual communities are prevalent and thriving. Virtual spaces are uniquely efficacious for connecting diverse populations of people who are not bound together by geographical location. Ideas, belief systems, and identity narratives can be constructed and disseminated rapidly through virtual communities, quickly amassing member and audience support. Some social-movement scholars have questioned the efficacy of social-media and virtual activism (Anduiza, Cantijoch, & Gallego, 2009). This study, however, indicates that virtual spaces are conducive to broadening group membership and garnering support for movements and desires of marginalized identity communities, particularly when off-line communities are limited.

The findings of this study are of empirical relevance as they demonstrate the importance of both virtual and narrative data. Our world is increasingly more virtual (this is particularly evident in light of the effects of the COVID-19 pandemic), and, as such, it is imperative that social researchers engage fully with virtual data. Moreover, as our in-person world continues to be embedded with virtual forms of communication and interaction, it is important that researchers do not treat the virtual world and "the real world" as entirely separate entities. This is particularly pertinent in examining experiences of disabled people, who frequently rely on various types of virtual technology in their everyday lives. These findings elucidate that, for disabled people, virtual communities and informational resources are just as imperative (if not more so) than those in person or offline.

Additionally, narrative as both cultural artifact and methodological approach can provide rich sociological data. Of explicit relevance to sociological examinations of disability is the consistency of these resistance narratives from a vast array of virtual spaces and diverse virtual voices that are represented in this study. The data from this project span four years of online interaction of hundreds of social-media and blog users and includes five social movement organizations websites. Consistent within all of this data is one prominent story: despite a lack of cultural narratives and experiences of extreme stigmatization and invisibility, LGBTQ+ disabled people exist and resist. Narratives are thus powerful tools in uniting communities and shifting and contesting cultural belief systems

Of particular relevance to sociological theoretical implications, the findings of this project demonstrate the importance of intersectionality in examination of marginalized experiences. Cultural support for LGBTQ+ people has drastically increased over the last three decades. While LGBTQ+ people have been positively impacted by the changes in public opinion, cultural narratives, and policy, these are often not extended to disabled LGBTQ+ people. For example, many of the hard-won civil rights for LGBTQ+ people all but disappear when disability is introduced. While many LGBTQ+ people have been afforded marriage equality, disabled LGBTQ+ people are still constrained by consent and guardianship policies and court decisions that can deny people with (most prevalently intellectual) disabilities the right to marry or policies that limit marriage by denying supplemental security income, medical coverage, and other disability financial and social-service resources to married disabled people or those with combined incomes, monetary savings, and/or assets.

The histories of pathologization of LGBTQ+ people and disabled people still linger for both communities. However, when examined together we can see the extent of the impact pathologization continues to make today. For instance, LGBTQ+ disabled people often have their non-normative gender and sexualities reduced to symptoms of their disabilities. This is made evident when examining arguments that autism is a manifestation of the extreme male brain (e.g., Baron-Cohen, 2003) and that autistic people experience "cross-gender identity problems"; such research essentializes culturally constructed gendered behaviors and often presents deviations from "typical" gender behaviors as *symptoms* of autism (van Schalkwyk, Klingensmith, & Volkmar, 2015). These understandings lead psychologists and medical practitioners to suspect the authenticity of their clients' gender and "to invest special attention in transgender autistic individuals" (Shapira & Granek, 2019, p. 13). This results in the invalidation of LGBTQ+ disabled experiences; specifically, autistic transgender people report difficulties in receiving social recognition of their gender and permissions for gender-affirmation procedures, treatments, and hormone therapies (Bumiller, 2008; Egner, 2019a). Medical, academic, and cultural pathologization of LGBTQ+ disabled people disempower disabled individuals by constructing their sexuality and genders as problems in need of management by third parties (parents, teachers, therapists . . . etc.) (Barnett, 2014; Egner, 2017).

Moreover, intersectionality allows us to see how multidimensional this pathologization and subsequent stigmatization are for LGBTQ+ people generally and LGBTQ+ disabled people specifically. LGBTQ+ people consistently have to prove that they were "born this way" and are "not sick/mentally ill," constantly separating themselves from their disabled community members. We can see how pathologization still deeply impacts the lives of LGBTQ+ people *and* simultaneously examine how the sexuality and genders of disabled people are pathologized by examining disabled LGBTQ+ experiences. It is imperative to bring disability into intersectional theoretical frameworks and intersectionality into disability research (Erevelles & Minear, 2010). Within sociological research, intersectionality has been applied in ways that point out and delineate differences. However, the findings from this project suggest that intersectionality can be particularly useful by employing Hirschmann's (2012) argument that we should recognize similarities in the experience of difference. In employing an intersectional approach to disability and LGBTQ+ identities, we are able to examine the more subtle or invisible ways oppressive forces (such as pathologization) impact the lives of marginalized people with nuance, thus garnering more complex understandings of marginalized experiences and power structures.

REFERENCES

Atkinson, J. (2006). Analyzing resistance narratives at the North American anarchist gathering: A method for analyzing social justice alternative media. *Journal of Communication Inquiry*, *30*(3), 251–272.

Anduiza, E., Cantijoch, M., & Gallego, A. (2009). Political participation and the Internet: A field essay. *Information, Communication & Society*, *12*(6), 860–878.

Asch, A. (2001). Critical race theory, feminism, and disability: Reflections on social justice and personal identity. *Ohio State Law Journal*, *62*, 391.

Barnett, J. P. (2014). Sexual citizenship on the autism spectrum. [Doctoral dissertation. University of Windsor].

Baron-Cohen, S. (2003). *The essential difference: the truth about the male and female brain*. New York: Basic Books.

Berger, Ronald. 2013. *Introducing disability studies*. Lynne Rienner Publishers.

Bradford, S., & Clark, M. (2011). Stigma narratives: LGBT transitions and identities in Malta. *International Journal of Adolescence and Youth*, *16*(2), 179–200.

Bumiller, K. (2008). Quirky citizens: Autism, gender, and reimagining disability. *signs: Journal of Women in Culture and society*, *33*(4): 967–991.

Busby, Graham, & Laviolette, Patrick. (2006). Narratives in the net: Fiction and cornish tourism. *Cornish Studies 14* (1),142–163.

Cavar, S., & Baril, A. (2021). Blogging to counter epistemic injustice: Trans disabled digital micro-resistance. *Disability Studies Quarterly*, *41*(2), 1–36.

Cheng, R. (2009). Sociological theories of disability, gender, and sexuality: A review of the literature. *Journal of Human Behavior in the Social Environment*, *19*(1), 112–122.

Collins, P. H. (1986). Learning from the outsider within: The sociological significance of Black feminist thought. *Social Problems*, *33*(6), s14–s32.

Collins, P. H. (1999). Reflections on the outsider within. *Journal of Career Development*, *26*(1), 85–88

Collins, P. H., & Bilge, S. (2016). *Intersectionality*. John Wiley & Sons.

Crenshaw, K. (1989). Demarginalizing the intersection of race and sex: A black feminist critique of antidiscrimination doctrine, feminist theory and antiracist politics. The *University of Chicago Legal Forum*, *140*,139–167.

Crenshaw, K. (1991). Mapping the margins: Intersectionality, identity politics, and violence against women of color. *Stanford Law Review 43* (6), 1241–1299.

Darwin, H. (2017). Doing gender beyond the binary: A virtual ethnography. *Symbolic Interaction*, *40*(3), 317–334.

Dinwoodie, R., Greenhill, B. & Cookson, A. (2016). "Them two things are what collide together": Understanding the sexual identity experiences of lesbian, gay, bisexual and trans people labelled with intellectual disability. *Journal of Applied Research in Intellectual Disabilities*, *33*(1), 3–16.

Doty, A. (1993). Making things perfectly queer: Interpreting mass culture. University of Minnesota Press.

Egner, J. (2017). A messy trajectory: From medical sociology to crip theory. In Sara Green and Sharon Barnartt (Eds.), *Sociology Looking at Disability: What Did We Know and When Did We Know It* (pp. 159–192). Emerald Group Publishing.

Egner, J. (2018). Hegemonic or queer? A comparative analysis of five LGBTQIA/disability intersectional social movement organizations. *Humanity & Society*, *43*(2) 140–178. https://doi.org/10.1177%2F0160597618782582

Egner, J. E. (2019a). "The disability rights community was never mine": Neuroqueer disidentification. *Gender & Society*, *33*(1), 123–147.

Egner, J. E. (2019b). Hegemonic or queer? A comparative analysis of five LGBTQIA/disability intersectional social movement organizations. *Humanity & Society*, *43*(2):140–178.

Egner, J. E. (2020). "We love each other into meaning": Queer disabled Tumblr users constructing identity narratives through love and anger. In S. Green and D. Loseke (Eds.), *New Narratives of Disability* (pp. 261–276). Emerald Publishing Limited.

Geiss, C. (2019). Connecting practical doings to cultural meanings: Exploring the work of moral mediators in human service organizations. *Symbolic Interaction*, *42*(4), 539–563.

Geiss, C., & Egner, J. E. (2021). Examining organizational narratives: Public appeals of morality, emotions, and medical logic in the case of sex work for disabled clients. *Sociological Inquiry*, https://onlinelibrary.wiley.com/doi/abs/10.1111/soin.12445

Gibson, F., Hibbins, S., Grew, T., Morgan, S., Pearce, S., Stark, D., & Fern, L. A. (2016). How young people describe the impact of living with and beyond a cancer diagnosis: feasibility of using social media as a research method. *Psycho-oncology*, *25*(11), 1317–1323.

Elliot, P. (2016). *Debates in transgender, queer, and feminist theory: Contested sites*. Routledge.

Erevelles, N., & Minear, A. (2010). Unspeakable offenses: Untangling race and disability in discourses of intersectionality. *Journal of Literary & Cultural Disability Studies*, *4*(2), 127–145.

Garland-Thomson, R. (2005). Feminist disability studies. *Signs*, *30*(2), 1557–1587.

Gerschick, T. (2000). Toward a theory of disability and gender. *Signs 25* (4), 1263–1268.

Giwa, S., & Greensmith, C. (2012). Race relations and racism in the LGBTQ community of Toronto: Perceptions of gay and queer social service providers of color. *Journal of Homosexuality*, *59*(2), 149–185.

Hevey, D. (1993). From self-love to the picket line: strategies for change in disability representation. *Disability, Handicap & Society*, *8*(4), 423–429.

Hine, C. (2000). *Virtual ethnography*. SAGE Publications.

Hirschfeld, M. (1948). Sexual anomalies: The origins, nature and treatment of sexual disorders: A summary of the works of Magnus Hirschfeld MD. Emerson Books.

Hirschmann, N. (2012). Disability as a new frontier for feminist intersectionality research. *Politics & Gender*, *8*(3), 396–405.

Kafer, A. (2013). *Feminist, queer, crip*. Indiana University Press.

Kinsey, A. C., Pomeroy, W. B., Martin, C. E., & Sloan, S. (1948). Sexual behavior in the human male. W.B. Saunders Co.

Loseke, D. R. (2012). *Methodological thinking: Basic principles of social research design*. SAGE Publications.

Loseke, D. R. (2019). *Narrative productions of meanings: Exploring the work of stories in social life*. Rowman & Littlefield.

Maloney, Patricia. (2013). Online networks and emotional energy: How pro-anorexic websites use interaction ritual chains to (re) form identity. *Information, Communication & Society*, *16*(1): 105–124.

Masters, W., & Johnson, V. (1970). Human sexual inadequacy. Little, Brown, and Company.

McRuer, R. (2006). *Crip theory: Cultural signs of queerness and disability*. New York University Press.

McRuer, R. (2013). Compulsory able-bodiesness and queer/disabled existence. In Davis, Lennard J (Ed.), *The Disability Studies Reader*, 4th ed. (pp. 301–308). Routledge.

McRuer, R., & Mollow, A. (2012). *Sex and disability*. Duke University Press.

Meeuf, R. (2009). John Wayne as "supercrip": Disabled bodies and the construction of "hard" masculinity in *The Wings of Eagles*. *Cinema Journal 48* (2), 88–113.

Melucci, A. (1995). The process of collective identity. *Social Movements and Culture*, 4, 41–63.

Oliver, M., & Barnes, C. (2012). *The new politics of disablement*. Palgrave Macmillan.

Pilling, M. D. (2012). Invisible identity in the workplace: Intersectional madness and processes of disclosure at work. *Disability Studies Quarterly*, 33(1).

Polletta, F. (1998). Contending stories: Narrative in social movements. *Qualitative Sociology*, 21(4), 419–446.

Postill, J., & Pink, S. (2012). Social media ethnography: The digital researcher in a messy web. *Media International Australia*, 145(1), 123–134.

Purdie-Vaughns, V., & Eibach, R. P. (2008). Intersectional invisibility: The distinctive advantages and disadvantages of multiple subordinate-group identities. *Sex Roles*, 59(5–6), 377–391.

Raley, A. B., and Lucas. J.L. (2006). Stereotype or success?: Prime-time television's portrayals of gay male, lesbians, and bisexual characters. *Journal of Homosexuality*, 15(2), 19–38.

van Schalkwyk, Gerrit I., Klingensmith, Katherine, and Volkmar, Fred R. (2015). Gender identity and autism spectrum disorders. *The Yale Journal of Biology and Medicine*, 88(1), 81.

Shakespeare, Tom. (1994). Cultural representation of disabled people: Dustbins for disavowal? *Disability and Society*, 9(3), 283–299.

Shakespeare, T. (2013). *Disability rights and wrongs revisited*. Routledge.

Shapira, S., & Granek, L. (2019). Negotiating psychiatric cisgenderism-ableism in the transgender-autism nexus. *Feminism & Psychology*, 29(4), 494–513.

Sherry, M. (2004). Overlaps and contradictions between queer theory and disability studies. *Disability & Society*, 19(7), 769–783.

Stephens, E. M. (2018). *Making #BlackLivesMatter: A social media ethnography of cultural trauma* [Doctoral dissertation, George Mason University].

Tiefer, L. (1996). The medicalization of sexuality: Conceptual, normative, and professional issues. *Annual Review of Sex Research*, 7(1), 252–282.

Underberg, Natalie M., & Elayne Zorn. (2013). *Digital ethnography: Anthropology, narrative, and new media*. University of Texas Press.

Vernon, A. (1999). The dialectics of multiple identities and the disabled people's movement. *Disability & Society*, 14(3), 385–398.

Walters, S. D. (1996). From here to queer: Radical feminism, postmodernism, and the lesbian menace (or, why can't a woman be more like a fag?). *Signs: Journal of Women in Culture and Society*, 21(4), 830–869.

Webb, Stephen. (2001). Avatarculture: Narrative, power and identity in virtual world environments. *Information, Communication & Society*, 4(4):560–594.

Zerubavel, E. (1996). Lumping and splitting: Notes on social classification. In *Sociological Forum* (vol. 11, no. 3, pp. 421–433). Kluwer Academic Publishers-Plenum Publishers.

DISABILITY, POLITICS, AND THE LAW

PART IX

Social Policies and Legal Rights

CHAPTER 30

AN INTERNATIONAL PERSPECTIVE ON DISABILITY SOCIAL POLICY

SUSANNE M. BRUYÈRE AND MATTHEW SALEH

INTRODUCTION

THE presence of disability has been a constant throughout human history. However, culturally shared responses to disability vary greatly across time and social context (Scheer & Groce, 1988). Modern international momentum to standardize certain baseline policies under human-rights principles are underway, but nation-level differences in disability policy and implementation are still the rule, rather than the exception. One important recent development has been the United Nations Convention on the Rights of Persons with Disabilities (UNCRPD) —an international treaty adopted in 2006 and entered into force in 2008—that has served as a catalyst for countries to update, or finally develop, disability policies that adhere to modern human-rights frameworks. Still, many ratifying parties have been slow to implement the UNCRPD framework (Nardodkar et al., 2016), and the recent global COVID-19 pandemic has created unique challenges to implementing disability policy around the globe, particularly in navigating the health crisis, economic shocks, and resulting impacts on employment, in a disability-inclusive way (Armitage & Nellums, 2020).

Different national and local contexts give rise to different frameworks and eligibility criteria for disability coverage, different scope and meaning of nondiscrimination requirements, and different service delivery, benefits, and supports offerings and eligibility criteria. Moreover, disability is just one identity that an individual might experience, among many, so considerations of disability policy implementation are often compounded by complex national and local gender, ethnic, geographic, and other socio-demographic identities (Annable et al., 2003). Certain cross-cultural commonalities and "themes" in the development of disability policies and social supports exist, and these are worth highlighting as some nations aim to modernize their disability programs, and others aim to develop disability policies that comply with current human-rights imperatives. Examples of government-level social policy for people with disabilities can include social insurance and welfare programs, healthcare, independent living services and supports, education and training opportunities, vocational rehabilitation and employment support services, and civil-rights protections across multiple societal domains.

This chapter provides a global overview of the development, structure, and function of disability policy across societies, focusing on some of the commonalities in the development of targeted disability policies, as well as challenges and future directions. We emphasize the development and interrelationship of some of the core concepts in disability policy that have emerged in varying national contexts around the globe. These include disability benefits programs, disability employment efforts and services, nondiscrimination frameworks, and access to independent living and healthcare security. Many of these systems differ in practice and implementation, but also have important similarities that are worth highlighting. We describe how these policies have been shaped across different national contexts, and the ways in which social and cultural context influences philosophy and design. We highlight differences in policy development and implementation for nations based on important factors, such as cultural attitudes, income level, level of industrialization, and other factors. Identifying core concepts from international examples of disability policy around the world can be helpful in developing unifying policy frameworks that also account for regional and cultural differences, and that is the aim of this chapter.

THEMES IN THE DEVELOPMENT OF DISABILITY POLICY ACROSS SOCIETIES

Social Insurance and Benefits Programs

Many nations have long histories of providing public protection, insurance, and welfare for individuals with disabilities. In many middle- and high-income nations, these policies developed out of what has been termed a "politics of vulnerability," where acknowledgment of health-related economic and labor market hardship led to the creation of policies offering social "safety nets" for vulnerable and normatively valued social groups (Flynn, 2017). This has traditionally included the provision of means-tested entitlements for groups that include older populations, dependent children, and occupationally injured workers, veterans, and civil servants. Many programs aiming to reduce the financial burden resulting from disability have sought to do so through cash assistance and other benefits. At the same time, other countries have relatively nascent, or in some cases barely existent, commitments to the provision of disability benefits, supports, services, and civil-rights protections (MacLachlan & Swartz, 2009).

In most industrialized countries, initial efforts to provide economic subsistence are continuing to evolve into more targeted policy solutions. These are aimed at promoting not only the economic welfare and societal inclusion of people with disabilities as a subset of the population, but also equal outcomes across a variety of societal domains in which people with disabilities have historically experienced discrimination and exclusion (Sainsbury & Coleman-Fountain, 2014). One of the most critical areas needing continued attention has been labor market participation, which often contributes not only to increased economic self-sufficiency, but also to meaningful participation in society more broadly. We elaborate further in the sections that follow.

Labor Market Participation

National-level disability policy frameworks continue to vary in terms of the breadth and effectiveness of anti-discrimination requirements, as well as the degree of rehabilitation and social services available to enhance employment, economic, and independent living outcomes (Saleh, 2019). Because of the importance of labor market participation in achieving equitable access to economic security, adequate healthcare, and other fundamental attributes of life, the shift towards civil-rights models that facilitate outcomes in the competitive labor market—while ensuring economic security and access to independent living and healthcare—are of particular interest. At different times in different parts of the world, this emphasis on allowing people with disabilities to participate in the labor market was supplemented by advocacy efforts around civil-rights and independent living outcomes for people with disabilities, including groups with more severe disabilities that were often marginalized even from disability policy considerations (Evans, 2003). Over time, policy efforts have shifted to provide basic subsistence, independent living, and healthcare, and to encourage equal participation and outcomes, including in the competitive labor market.

The disability employment gap is in every way a global problem. Exclusion of people with disabilities from the workplace leads to lost labor, trillions in annual loss in GDP (Metts, 2000; Ozawa & Yeo, 2006), and structural and social costs such as high benefit levels and health and social inequalities (Sainsbury & Coleman-Fountain, 2014). Many nations have far to go in realizing nondiscrimination in education, work, and other sectors, and to realizing equal opportunity across these domains. Nation-level policy frameworks vary in terms of the breadth of anti-discrimination provisions, as well as the availability of rehabilitation and social services offerings to enhance social participation, employment, education, and other outcomes. Nardodkar et al. (2016), for instance, found that of all United Nations member states, 30% had no explicit or implied legal provisions for providing reasonable accommodation to persons with disabilities, and 51% had no explicit legal protections from adverse employment actions on health grounds. The circumstances of the current global pandemic and economic downturn have laid bare the importance of providing such protections; as employers around the world have adapted operations to respond to the crisis, people with disabilities experience a much higher rate of employment termination or exit, as the result of a range of factors related to a lack of workplace accommodations for health-related needs, as well as few protections against adverse actions by employers on health grounds (Jesus, Landry, & Jacobs, 2020; Flynn, 2017). Higher labor market inactivity rates for working-age people with disabilities are a problem worldwide (globally almost 2.5 times higher than for people without disabilities, according to most recent measurements) (World Health Organization [WHO], 2011), and unemployment rates have been found to be higher still for more "severe" disability categories like mental health conditions (e.g., schizophrenia, bipolar disorder) and intellectual disabilities (Turcotte, 2012). At the same time, these groups tend to receive weaker legal protections than other disability categories (Hoffman, Sritharan, & Tejpar, 2016).

Even industrialized nations with well-developed rehabilitation and social service offerings experience these employment gaps (see, e.g., Erickson, Lee, & von Schrader, 2017 [United States]; Organization for Economic Cooperation and Development, 2009 [OECD countries]); UN Economic and Social Commission for Asia and the Pacific, 2015 [Australia, New Zealand, Republic of Korea, Thailand, Cambodia, Turkey]). A range of additional studies also evidence employment gaps in many low- and middle-income contexts worldwide (Hoogeveen, 2005 [Uganda]; Lamichhane & Okubo, 2014 [Nepal]; Mitra & Sambamoorthi, 2008 [India]; Mizunoya, Yamasaki, & Mitra, 2016 [Vietnam]; Trani & Loeb, 2010 [Afghanistan, Zambia]; Mizunoya & Mitra, 2013 [Bangladesh, Brazil, Burkina Faso, Dominican Republic, Mauritius, Mexico, Pakistan, Paraguay, Philippines]; Mitra, 2018 [Tanzania, Uganda, Ethiopia, Malawi]).

In the employment area, the main approach of industrialized welfare states has focused on investment in employment readiness and training programs, anti-discrimination legislation, and hiring quota schemes (Grover & Piggott, 2007). Beyond vocational rehabilitation and training efforts, 59% of United Nations member states have some type of affirmative action policy toward hiring people with disabilities. Policies include tax exemptions, incentives, public and/or private sector quotas, and sanctions for failure to meet hiring guidelines, usually in the form of mandatory contributions to disability welfare funds (Nardodkar et al., 2016).

Even in high-income nations with comparatively robust rehabilitation and social service offerings, 20–40% of people with disabilities report not having their everyday service needs met (WHO, 2011). But here it is important to highlight the different timelines globally in the development of rehabilitation and services frameworks. Analysis of four southern African nations, for instance, found high levels of difficulty accessing rehabilitation services (between 26% and 55% obtaining needed services) and vocational training (between 5% and 23%) (WHO, 2011). Around the world, access to in-person, work-related services has also been substantially affected by the recent pandemic (Golden, 2020). Additionally, in many countries, the historical emphasis on low-skill work within vocational rehabilitation and training of people with disabilities has resulted in particular disparities in the experience of work during the pandemic, as people with disabilities are more likely to experience precarious employment and less likely to experience safe working conditions (Saleh & Bruyére, 2018)—factors like these are potentially (if not certainly) exacerbated by a public health crisis (Brooks, 2020). Successful labor market initiatives must be undergirded by thoughtfully constructed social supports that assist in bridging the transition gap from poverty to employment, without creating untenable choices between insecure work attachment and benefits eligibility. The voice of people with disabilities must be included in this process. For example, inclusion of people with disabilities in global economic development initiatives designed to move people out of poverty, and the provision of adequate preparation for the workforce, which is imbedded in national workforce development initiatives.

Access to Education and Services

One of the most intractable barriers to social and economic participation—and attendant rises in overall quality of life—is the difficulty accessing key social institutions that people with disabilities experience around the world, and especially in low-income contexts. Youth with disabilities, for instance, constitute a "significant proportion of the youth population in every society," and estimates indicate that approximately 80% of youth with disabilities (ages 15 to 24), or between 180 and 220 million people, live in developing countries (UN Division of Social Policy and Development [DSPD], 2010, p. 2). Many countries exclude people with disabilities from mainstream schooling and have inadequate or fragmentary school-to-work transition frameworks (Stewart, 2009). The overall lack of services and coordination often leads to a "difficult period of upheaval and uncertainty" as youth with disabilities "transition from childhood into adulthood, primarily in the area of achieving successful employment and independent living" (DSPD, 2010, p. 4). Policy efforts around nondiscrimination frameworks in accessing education, training, and services are of key importance and extend to considerations of accommodations, supplemental services and instruction, and inclusive program design.

Complex Interaction of Benefits/Entitlements and Employment Issues

In countries where poverty is endemic, the introduction of disability benefits, grants, and pensions has been shown to markedly improve standards of living (Loeb, Eide, Jelsma, Ka'Toni, & Maart, 2007). However, the simple introduction of disability or other means-tested benefits has also had some unexpected outcomes. In certain high-income countries, pure cash assistance programs may serve as potential "poverty traps" that "contribute to exclusion from the labor market and result in a comparably low life income" by making maintenance of benefits levels contingent on low work and minimal outside income (Eide & Ingstad, 2011, p. 5). The components of disability programs changed over time due to factors including "rapid growth in program costs; greater awareness that people with impairments are able and willing to work; and increased recognition that protecting the economic security of people with disabilities might best be done by keeping them in the labor market" (Burkhauser, Daly, & Ziebarth, 2016, p. 367). Because of this, one emerging aspect of policy development in industrialized nations has entailed a shift to pro-work and non-discrimination frameworks aimed at improving labor market outcomes in addition to basic economic subsistence.

In discussing the shift to pro-work policies, however, it is crucial to demonstrate caution against advocating for wholesale restrictions on public assistance in favor of pro-work programs, and such policy efforts must prioritize *transition* to competitive wage work, not merely limitations upon public aid in favor of precarious or low-wage employment. Criticism of "work first" measures—such those recently outlined by the Council of Europe—notes that abrupt institution of such measures can pressure individuals to leave or phase out of benefits programs, sometimes resulting in the deterioration of financial position and security for individuals who struggle to find adequate employment (Waddington et al., 2016). Concerns of this sort have resulted in the development of more nuanced bridging arrangements in many national contexts, where policies allow individuals with disabilities to combine wages with disability benefits until they reach a threshold limit of wages.

In this section, we focused on the policy frameworks that have evolved across various country contexts to provide supports to people with disabilities in social benefits and poverty alleviation, and preparation for and access to employment. In the next section, we elaborate more fully on the role that social context plays in how these policies evolve and play out over time.

CONTEXTUAL FACTORS IN THE DEVELOPMENT AND STRUCTURE OF DISABILITY POLICY EFFORTS

Social context, and the relationship of people with disabilities to the state, has played an important role in *who* received access to services or protections. Many early policy efforts, across a variety of national contexts, reinforced a policy objective of supporting individuals with disabilities derived from normatively valued societal contributions within medical or charitable models of service provision and support. Even as vocational and community support frameworks began to develop, it was often at the exclusion of the broader population of people with developmental, intellectual, and mental-health disabilities, many of whom experienced continued societal exclusion (Dumont & Dumont, 2008).

Culture and economics hold important roles in shaping disability identity. While disability, as now conceived, has been a constant throughout human history, "culturally shared responses to [disability] vary greatly across time and social context" (Scheer & Groce, 1988, p. 23), and are often compounded by complex local gender, ethnic, geographic, and other socio-demographic identities (Annable et al., 2003). This is reflected in how legal and administrative definitions of disability often do not map well to functional and subjective definitions, with other demographic characteristics tending to supersede in given contexts (e.g., age, gender, living arrangement, workplace participation) (Gronvik, 2009).

In this section, we further explore some specific social frameworks that influence cultural and societal perceptions of disability, which play an important role in the position that people with disabilities have in given societies, how society responds to disability, and the resulting influence on policy formulation. These include micro- and macro-level conceptualizations of disability and the productivity of people with disabilities, the effects of medicalization of disability identity, and the impact of multiple (intersectional) identities layered on one another, where multiple cultural stigmas found in gender, ethnic, racial, or sexual-orientation biases may contribute additive cultural devaluation.

Individual and Group-Level Conception of Disability and Productivity

In a range of international contexts, the cause of an impairment matters greatly in individual- and group-level perception, as evidenced by the well-documented identity group-formation of veterans with disabilities in Western societies (Gerber, 2003), and with the differing policy treatment of worker's compensation versus disability unemployment insurance in multiple national examples. Another important consideration involves how productivity is defined societally. Trends toward global capitalism, industrialization, and an attendant materialism led to new understandings of "the ways work, social relations, social attitudes, and family relationships were understood and experienced" (Abbas, 2016, p. 136; Oliver, 1990). Since the 18th century, the meaning of work in industrialized nations has evolved to prioritize profit maximization and individual competitiveness in the labor market. In many cases, this reformulation resulted in further marginalization of individuals with disabilities, imposing "disablement upon those non-conforming bodies deemed less or not exploitable by the owners of the means of production" (Russell, 2001, p. 87). The changes brought about by capitalist development, some argue, "resulted in an ideology of individualism, which, coupled with medicalization and the development of rehabilitation, brought about profound changes in the way that people with disabilities are seen and treated" (Riddell & Watson, 2014).

Effects of the Medicalization of Disability Identity

The effects of the development of a medicalized disability identity, and its interactions with the capitalistic narrative of individualism, manifest themselves in unique ways that meld with community-level dynamics. Important community-level factors include familial structure, gender roles, religious views, and reliance on physical labor (Smart & Smart, 1991). Studies of perceptions of autism and developmental disability in China, for instance, show unique contextual factors. These include efforts within families to hide disability, grounded in the belief that "[d]isclosure of disability within a family (i.e., a child) can result in 'loss of face' and may negatively affect the perceived prestige of the entire family," and contextually relevant coping strategies like positive reinterpretation and suppression of competing activities (Wang, Michaels, & Day, 2011, p. 792). Overcoming bias is one of the fundamental challenges of improving employment outcomes for people with disabilities. For instance, a recent analysis of employment prospects for Jordanians with physical, visual, and hearing impairments cited widespread employer bias and prejudice, compounded by an overreliance among governmental and community providers on institutional schemes (residential settings, sheltered workshops), and vocational training opportunities that provide a limited choice of trade (Turmusani, 2018).

Disability Policy and Intersectionality

Intersectionality is an important area for consideration and discussion when talking about the sociology of disability. On one level, intersectionality is used to describe the interactions of many identities that a person does or will experience in their lifetime. More precisely, it refers to an examination of how factors experienced at individual and group levels are shaped by processes and structures of power (e.g., capitalism, globalization, patriarchy, racism, ableism, nationalism, and xenophobia). Applying an intersectional framework involves analyzing the institutional and systemic factors that reject a hierarchy of vulnerability or universal conception of experience (Hankivsky, 2012).

The purpose of intersectionality as a theory is to identify how overlapping categories of identity impact individuals and institutions, and take these relationships into account when working to promote social and political equity. The term intersectionality, coined by legal scholar Kimberlé Crenshaw, underscores the "multidimensionality" of marginalized subjects' lived experiences (Crenshaw, 1989). Crenshaw asserts that intersectionality has the ability to highlight the variations, for example racial variations within gender and vice versa, that exist within a given identity group. Other researchers have extended this inquiry beyond gender and racial-ethnic identities to gender identities and the LBGT community (Parent, DeBlaere, & Morado, 2013), and class, religion, nationality, and age (Ortbals & Rincker, 2009). By exposing intragroup differences, intersectionality has the power to "mediate tensions between assertions of multiple identity" (Crenshaw, 1989; Crenshaw, 1991).

Intersectionality plays out across country boundaries in different ways among all of the groups named above, as well as with those with disabilities, which adds yet another identity to intersectionality considerations (Erevelles & Minear, 2010). Intersectionality issues vary depending on one's perspective in the global and local levels and presence within the larger system. One's environment determines the extent to which their identities influence their full societal inclusion. The issues of discrimination that occur with intersecting statuses, such as gender, race/ethnicity, or sexual/gender identity, are often made even more complex with disability. In many country contexts, disability is more prevalent in rural and lower socio-economic communities, where healthcare inequities are elevated, and often racial/ethnic minorities are in higher proportion. This is where cultural context adds layers of additional discrimination for people with disabilities, who may also be a racial/ethnic minority, and living in poverty. The impact of intersecting layers of discrimination result in inequality in access to healthcare, education, and employment, as well as equitable participation in the governance of civil society.

The COVID-19 pandemic has provided instructive examples of these interactions. In the United States, for instance, job loss rates were higher for people of color with disabilities during the onset of the pandemic, and personal and health-risk factors, as well as employment-related considerations, are not evenly distributed across groups; for instance, the "care burden" from in-home sheltering has been shown to have a larger impact on women with disabilities, and long-standing racial health and healthcare inequalities can affect work outcomes (National Disability Institute, 2020; Lokot & Avakyan, 2020). The micro/macro level recognizes intersectionality from various lenses in order to recognize the "far-reaching roots and sources of oppression and discriminations" that persist (Steinfield et al., 2019, p. 373).

Relationship between Disability and Poverty

It is also important to address the complex interrelation between disability and poverty. Research from low-, middle-, and high-income nations alike connect the conditions of poverty to exposure to disability conditions (Eide & Ingstad, 2011; Fujiura & Yamaki, 2000). Lower income levels also affect people with disabilities differently and can have the effect of broadening economic and services gaps. For example, additional costs for personal support, medical care, and/or assistive devices can lead to a higher likelihood of experiencing financial hardship, such as catastrophic health expenditure (Loyalka, Liu, Chen, & Zheng, 2014). To bridge these gaps, some countries utilize personal assistance schemes, but these vary in terms of the disability categories covered and other eligibility criteria, levels of funding provided, types of activities, assistance, and tasks funded. However, in many countries, people with disabilities are still not able to obtain funded personal assistance from their government at all (Jolly, 2010).

In contexts where poverty is widespread, disability is often an additional dimension to poverty, rather than the fundamental cause, and the complex interactions that link disability and poverty have been described as a "vicious circle" (Yeo & Moore, 2003; Eide & Ingstad, 2011). The dimensions that link disability and poverty often differ substantially between low- and high-income contexts, and causality can run in either direction: that is, poverty can also lead to disability (Saleh & Bruyère, 2018). Examples of this include the lack of workplace safety regulations, inadequate healthcare interventions, poor nutrition and hygienic conditions, pollution, and higher prevalence of inaccessible and disabling environments (Saleh & Bruyère, 2018).

A CIVIL-RIGHTS MODEL OF DISABILITY

Awareness of the historical inequities for people with disabilities, and how perceptions and frameworks have contributed to these inequities, is fortunately increasing. The UN Convention on the Rights of People with Disabilities presents one example of progress in this regard. Another lies within reframing the concept of disability itself, especially in how it is categorized for purposes of creating regulatory frameworks to address disability inequities. In this section, we provide examples of how this is occurring through the reframing of disability as merely a function of impairment, to a contextually contrived perception. This is occurring through the World Health Organization's International Classification of Functioning, Disability and Health (World Health Organization [WHO], 2001), the evolution of international human rights norms, and a re-exploration of the legal definitions of disability.

Developing Unifying Policy Frameworks and Models of Disability

Bérubé (1998, pp. vii–viii) notes that, across cultural contexts, "disability names thousands of human conditions and varieties of impairment, from slight to severe . . . it is a category whose constituency is contingency itself." Efforts to create uniform theoretical constructs of disability, such as the World Health Organization's International Classification of Functioning, Disability and Health (WHO, 2001), acknowledge that "the functioning and disability of an individual occurs in context," alongside environmental and social factors. The ICF revised the previous health-based classification systems, which overlooked the "relativistic and multifactorial" nature of disability in favor of linear, progressive scales (Dahl, 2002, p. 202). While the ICF holds "considerable promise both as a nosological tool and as a heuristic" for guiding practitioner fields (e.g., rehabilitation) (Bruyère, VanLooy, & Peterson, 2005, p. 114), and despite continued efforts to increase the conceptual clarity, the fact remains that there exists no universal international legal definition of disability with respect to income maintenance, employ-ment measures, and social assistance with daily life activities (Degener, 2006).

Civil and human-rights models were largely influenced by a "social model" of disa-bility, across a number of national contexts, which accounts for the role of society and environmental barriers as disabling factors. Despite many different iterations of "social models" of disability over the past thirty years, modern rights-based understandings of disability tend to share the unifying theme that experiences of disability discrimination and societal marginalization were, in modern times, driven by socially constructed, but nevertheless "medicalized," notions of disability that highlighted normative notions of difference (Samaha, 2007). Although many countries have not yet or have only partly, embraced social model frameworks, policies and laws that adopt a "social model" of dis-ability acknowledge that disability is not inherent in the individual, but rather exists in the interaction of impairment and environment (Oliver, 1990). Samaha (2007, p. 1256) describes this as a reframing of the "causation account" of disability, defining disability "as disadvantage caused by the confluence of . . . personal impairment and . . . a social setting comprising architecture, economics, politics, culture, social norms, aesthetic values, and assumptions about ability." Part of this reframing involved taking a critical historical lens to the "sick role" in Western society (Parsons, 1975, p. 257), which "critics of the medical model associate . . . with belittling norms that relieve impaired persons from social obligations yet demand they abide by professional medical judgment" (Samaha, 2007, pp. 1256–1257). The utility of the social model of disability in advancing substantive equality within law and policy frameworks is still being debated by scholars (e.g., Samaha, 2007; Levitt, 2017), but the model has nevertheless been instrumental in advancing policy objectives such as reasonable accommodations/modifications requirements in private employment and public accommodations, which operate under the understanding (in numerous national contexts) that even private entities have an af-firmative legal duty to mitigate disabling environmental barriers.

International Human-Rights Norms

The UNCRPD was the first binding international human-rights treaty to codify the rights of people with disabilities globally. Adopted by the General Assembly in December of 2006, the UNCRPD currently has 164 signatories and 182 ratifying parties (UN Enable, 2021). The UNCRPD is a modern human-rights instrument, outlining a "substantive" notion of equality that distinguishes identical treatment from equal treat-ment, and extends policies beyond negative rights, toward eliminating the conditions that perpetuate discrimination (Committee on Economic, Social and Cultural Rights, 1994).

Prior to the UNCRPD, binding instruments of international human-rights law ne-glected to recognize the equal rights of people with disabilities, or fell into the common trope of defining such issues through the lenses of welfare, health, charity, and guard-ianship issues (Kayess & French, 2008). The equality clauses of the International Bill of Rights (which includes the Universal Declaration of Human Rights, International Covenant on Civil and Political Rights, and International Covenant on Economic, Social and Cultural Rights) did not explicitly mention disability.

In the 1970s, several non-binding instruments sought to address relevant policy themes, but did so through clear appeal to the medical or deficit models. These included the Declaration on the Rights of Mentally Retarded Persons 1971, Declaration on the Rights of Disabled Persons 1975, and the Principles for the Protection of Persons with Mental Illness and the Improvement of Mental Health Care 1991. Of the major thematic conventions, only the Convention on the Rights of the Child 1989 referred to disability, creating obligations to provide "special care" in children with disabilities' social integration and development (Article 23), while the ILO Convention Concerning Vocational Rehabilitation and Employment (Disabled Persons) 1983 served as an important predecessor to the UNCRPD, acknowledging the importance of national vocational rehabilitation policies promoting employment opportunities for people with disabilities in the open labor market.

Prior to the UNCRPD, many international treaties tended to define the rights of people with disabilities in paternalistic terms, prioritizing "segregation through specialized services and institutions" (Kayess & French, 2008, p. 14). However, there were important exceptions, such as the ILO Convention Concerning Vocational Rehabilitation and Employment (1983), the Inter-American Convention on the Elimination of All Forms of Discrimination Against Persons with Disabilities (1999), and the European Union Directive on Discrimination 2000.

The UNCRPD covers a broad array of human-rights topics, including the right to work, economic security and quality of life, non-discrimination, awareness raising, healthcare, education and training, rehabilitation, and accessibility issues. Work and training topics play a prominent role in the UNCRPD. Article 26(1) requires that parties organize, strengthen, and/or extend comprehensive habilitation and rehabilitation programs and services in the areas of health, employment, education, and social services, including effective measures "to enable persons with disabilities to attain and maintain maximum independence, full physical, mental, social and vocational ability, and full inclusion and participation in all aspects of life." Article 27 outlines the right to work and employment "on an equal basis with others." This includes the "opportunity to gain a living by work freely chosen or accepted in a labor market and work environment that is open, inclusive and accessible." It also prohibits employer discrimination in hiring, retention, and advancement, and it provides rights to equal remuneration, reasonable accommodation, favorable and safe working conditions, systems for redress of grievances, union participation, and access to technical and vocational guidance and training. Article 27 also calls for parties to promote advancement and return-to-work efforts, as well as alternative pathways to employment such as self-employment, entrepreneurship, cooperatives, public-sector employment, and affirmative-action programs/incentives. Article 27(1)(h) holds that state parties shall "promote the employment of persons with disabilities in the private sector through appropriate policies and measures, which may include affirmative action programmes, incentives and other measures." This article,

27(1)(j), also requires that participants "promote the acquisition . . . of work experience in the open labour market." Article 24 further contains language not only implicating a nexus between education and the right to work, but also identifying the importance of vocational training, tertiary education, and lifelong learning as human rights.

The UNCRPD is a powerful international legal instrument, but its effectiveness as a corrective influence on country practices is nevertheless subject to variation at regional, national, and local levels. With any international treaty, ratification makes the terms of the agreement legally binding, although enforcement typically falls within the purview of state parties through processes of domestic incorporation (Lord & Stein, 2008). As such, "substantive rights will often get their complexion from the local cultural environment within which they have to be given concrete, practical meaning" (Ncube, 1998, pp. 14–15). Moreover, depending on the level of centralization in legal, regulatory, and enforcement mechanisms, "regional variations may also shape the prospects of people with disabilities seeking to exercise their rights" (Saleh & Bruyère, 2018, p. 21).

Importance of the Legal Definition of Disability

The UNCRPD does not explicitly define disability, and many nations retain their pre-existing definitions of disability in practice. Defining disability within a social model is a threshold step to embedding a legal framework that facilitates and protects labor market access. Despite the importance of defining disability in congruence with the UNCRPD—as this is the threshold legal step to availing such individuals—analysis by Nardodkar et al. (2016) found that laws in 27% of countries (52 member states) did not explicitly define the term "disability."

Initial analysis of commentaries by the Committee on the Rights of Persons with Disabilities highlights a range of UNCRPD implementation concerns at the most basic levels. These included multiple concepts of disability across policies (Austria), continued use of a medical model of disability (Austria, Azerbaijan, China, Costa Rica, Ecuador, South Korea), lack of coverage for certain disability types (Austria, Spain), unrepealed laws that contradict the convention (Belgium), and insufficient participation of people with disabilities in legislative design (Hungary, Paraguay) (Hoffman, Sritharan, & Tejpar, 2016). Considering the challenges of formulating a legal definition of disability, the Court of Justice of the European Union, for instance, has noted that "it cannot be excluded that . . . certain physical and mental shortcomings are in the nature of 'disability' in one social context, but not in another" (*Chacón Navas v. Eurest Colectividades SA*, 2005, para. 58).

A 2014 analysis of the Middle East and North African regions found that most countries still utilize "narrower, medical definitions in their laws as these have not yet been adapted to the CRPD . . . [t]hese narrow definitions often refer to specific bodily limitations" (Sida, 2014). Some nations still have yet to implement an official legal definition of disability. Among Southeast Asian nations, for instance, Laos and Myanmar have no official definition, while Brunei lacks a common definition across agencies. Many other nations, like Vietnam and Thailand, have updated their legal definition of disability in the past decade to reflect different variations of a social model (Cogburn & Reuter, 2017). Dinerstein (2017) noted that many Southeast Asian countries implicitly perpetuated medical views of disability by choosing social welfare or health agencies as their UNCRPD implementation focal point, rather than justice-based agencies. An analysis of anti-discrimination legislation in 28 European Union (EU) countries, 4 candidate countries, and 3 additional European Economic Area (EEA) countries found that, while "[t]he majority of national legislation contains many examples of definitions of disability . . . these often stem from the context of social security legislation rather than anti-discrimination law" (European Commission, 2017, p. 21).

The definitions of disability in many countries still do not reference the interaction of impairment with environmental and cultural barriers, therefore continuing to adopt more of a deficit model of disability inconsistent with modern human-rights norms (these countries included Austria, Bulgaria, Cyprus, the Czech Republic, Estonia, Ireland, Latvia, Liechtenstein, Norway, Romania, Sweden, and the United Kingdom) (European Commission, 2017). Even countries that do define disability in a legal sense, or within a social paradigm, often do so in different or inconsistent ways. Some, like the United States, have multiple legal and regulatory definitions, tailored to specific policy ends (e.g., anti-discrimination versus social security) and independent criteria for coverage that utilize disparate or inconsistent criteria across both medical and social models of disability (Quinn, 2005; Saleh, Golden, & Switzer, 2019). Mashaw and Reno (1996) documented over 20 definitions of disability used by American programs, government agencies, or researchers and argued that the appropriateness of any definition can be judged only in the context in which it is used. This has only become more complicated with passing time.

CONCLUSION

This chapter provides a big-picture sketch of how social policy and disability have evolved over time, the conceptual and definitional drivers that have contributed to how regulations have been promulgated, and the resulting predominant frameworks now in place. We also discussed the drawbacks of some of their policies, and how they have in many cases contributed to a stigmatizing and patronizing picture of people with disabilities and their ability to determine their own destinies and meaningfully contribute to society. The UN Convention on the Rights of People with Disabilities, as well as the World Health Organization's International Classification of Functioning, Disability and Health (ICF), are more contemporary attempts to change the historical frameworks that have kept people with disabilities captive in social policies that contributed to their being viewed as objects of pity rather than empowerment (WHO, 2015).

The growing global disability rights movement, as well as increasing recognition by the corporate sector of their role in improving positive workforce participation outcomes, is offering new paths forward with an increasingly broader base of public support toward the full inclusion of people with disabilities in society. Rehabilitation International[1] is an almost century-old example of this evolution. Rehabilitation International (RI Global) was originally founded by Americans—a social worker and orthopedic surgeon—who wanted to spearhead legislation to afford people around the world full and productive lives. Over the hundred years of its existence, there have been four major name changes, which reflect the evolving social awareness toward disability: the International Society for Crippled Children, 1922; the International Society for the Welfare of Cripples, 1939; the International Society for the Rehabilitation of the Disabled, 1960; and Rehabilitation International, 1972 (now RI Global) (RI, 2020). RI Global is now a worldwide organization comprising people with disabilities, service providers, government agencies, academics, researchers, and advocates working to improve the quality of life of people with disabilities. With member organizations in more than 100 countries and in all regions of the world, this broadened base of interest reflects the social actors needed across disability advocacy, government, and science to contribute to a more contemporary and useful perspective to frame disability policy for the future.

Cultural and country context has been a significant part of our discussion in this chapter, and socio-economic factors are a critical part of this equation. Private-sector business has an important role to play in assisting people with disabilities to realize their place in society. For far too long, business has been the passive recipient and often reluctant applicant of employment nondiscrimination legislation, such as that which is now a part of the UNCRPD as well as many individual countries' laws globally. Increasingly, we are seeing companies coalescing to proactively promote employment of people with disabilities, as well as putting individual company-sponsored innovative programs in place to do so. The International Labor Organization's Global Business and Disability Network[2] (ILO-GBDN), for example, brings together global companies, national business and disability networks, and not-for-profit organizations "to make sure that employment policies and practices in companies of all types are inclusive of people with disabilities around the world. The ILO-GBDN also works to increase awareness about the positive relationship between disability inclusion and business success" (ILO-GBDN, 2020). These kinds of enterprise alliances at community and global levels are needed to bring disability social policy into the contemporary view to empower people with disabilities to determine their own destinies, and to affirm the value that people with disabilities bring to society as a whole. The future of social and disability policy necessitates this kind of broad-based support to realize needed changes going forward.

NOTES

1. For further information see http://www.riglobal.org/.
2. For further information see http://www.businessanddisability.org/mission/.

REFERENCES

Abbas, J. (2016). Economy, exploitation, and intellectual disability. In R. Malhotra (Ed.), *Disability Politics in a Global Economy: Essays in Honour of Marta Russell* (pp.134–147). Routledge.

Annable, G., Watters, C., Stienstra, D., Symanzik, S., Tully, B. L., & Stuewer, N. (2003). *Students with disabilities: Transition from post-secondary education to work: Phase I report*. Canadian Centre of Disability Studies.

Armitage, R., & Nellums, L. B. (2020). The COVID-19 response must be disability inclusive. *The Lancet Public Health*, 5(5), E257. https://doi.org/10.1016/S2468-2667(20)30076-1

Bérubé, M. (1998). *Claiming disability: Knowledge and identity*. New York University Press.

Brooks, J. D. (2020, June, 15). Workers with disabilities may remain unemployed long after the COVID-19 pandemic. Issue Brief # 30. Syracuse University Lerner Center. https://lernercenter.syr.edu/wp-content/uploads/2020/06/Brooks.pdf

Bruyère, S., VanLooy, S., & Peterson, D. (2005). The international classification of functioning, disability and health (ICF): Contemporary literature overview. *Rehabilitation Psychology*, 50(2), 113–121. https://doi.org/10.1037/0090-5550.50.2.113

Burkhauser, R. V., Daly, M. C., & Ziebarth, N. R. (2016). Protecting working-age people with disabilities: Experiences of four industrialized nations. *Journal of Labour Market Research*, 49(4), 367–386. https://doi.org/10.24148/wp2015-08

Chacón Navas v. Eurest Colectividades SA. (2005). Case C-13/05 [2005] ECR I-6476. http://curia.europa.eu/juris/showPdf.jsf?text=&docid=57698&pageIndex=0&doclang=en&mode=lst&dir=&occ=first&part=1&cid=687930

Cogburn, D. L., & Reuter, T. K. (2017). Making disability rights real in Southeast Asia: Implementing the UN Convention on the Rights of Persons with Disabilities in ASEAN. Lexington Books.

Committee on Economic, Social and Cultural Rights. (1994). General comment no. 5, HRI/GEN/1/Rev 8, Add.1.

Crenshaw, K. (1989). Demarginalizing the intersection of race and sex: A Black feminist critique of antidiscrimination doctrine. *University of Chicago Legal Forum, 1989*, 139–168.

Crenshaw, K. (1991). Mapping the Margins: Intersectionality, identity, and violence against women of color. *Stanford Law Review*, 43(6), 1241–1300.

Dahl, T. H. (2002). International classification of functioning, disability and health: An introduction and discussion of its potential impact on rehabilitation services and research. *Journal of Rehabilitation Medicine*, 34(1), 201–204. https://doi.org/10.1080/165019702760279170

Degener, T. (2006). The definition of disability in German and foreign discrimination law. *Disability Studies Quarterly*, 26(2), 5–5.

Dinerstein, R. (2017). Norm diffusion and CRPD implementation and ASEAN. In D. L. Cogburn & T. Kempin Reuter (Eds.), *Making Disability Rights Real in Southeast Asia: Implementing the UN Convention on the Rights of Persons with Disabilities in ASEAN* (pp. 259–270). Lexington Books.

Dumont, M. P., & Dumont, D. M. (2008). Deinstitutionalization in the United States and Italy: A historical survey. *International Journal of Mental Health*, 37(4), 61–70. https://doi.org/10.2753/IMH0020-7411370405

Eide, A. H., & Ingstad, B. (2011). Disability and poverty: A global challenge. Policy Press.

Erickson, W. A., Lee, C., & von Schrader, S. (2017). 2015 Disability status report: United States. http://www.disabilitystatistics.org

Erevelles, N., & Minear, A. (2010). Unspeakable offenses: Untangling race and disability in discourses of intersectionality. *Journal of Literary & Cultural Disability Studies, 4*(2), 127–145. https://doi.org/10.3828/jlcds.2010.11

European Commission. (2017). A comparative analysis of non-discrimination law in Europe: 2017. ec.europa.eu/newsroom/just/document.cfm?action=display&doc_id=49316

Evans, J. (2003). The independent living movement in the UK. In the English version of: A. J. V. Garcia (Ed.), *The Independent Living Movement: International Experiences* (pp.191–213). www.independentliving.org/docs6/alonso2003.pdf

Flynn, S. (2017). Engaging with materialism and material reality: Critical disability studies and economic recession. *Disability & Society, 32*(2), 143–159. https://doi.org/10.1080/09687 599.2017.1284650

Fujiura, G. T., & Yamaki, K. (2000). Trends in demography of childhood poverty and disability. *Exceptional Children, 66*(2), 187–199.

Gerber, D. A. (2003). Disabled veterans, the state, and the experience of disability in Western societies, 1914–1950. *Journal of Social History, 36*(4), 899–916.

Golden, T. P. (2020, May 18). Impact on the workforce and people with disabilities. Cornell University, ILR School. https://www.ilr.cornell.edu/work-and-coronavirus/public-policy/impact-workforce-and-people-disabilities

Gronvik, L. (2009). Defining disability: Effects of disability concepts on research outcomes. *International Journal of Social Research Methodology, 12*(1), 1–18.

Grover, C., & Piggott, L. (2007). Social security, employment and incapacity benefit: Critical reflections on a new deal for welfare. *Disability & Society, 22*(7), 733–746.

Hankivsky, O. (2012). An intersectionality-based policy analysis framework. Institute for Intersectionality Research and Policy.

Hoffman, S. J., Sritharan, L., & Tejpar, A. (2016). Is the UN Convention on the Rights of Persons with Disabilities impacting mental health laws and policies in high-income countries? A case study of implementation in Canada. *BMC International Health Human Rights, 16*(1), 28. doi: 10.1186/s12914-016-0103-1.

Hoogeveen, J. (2005). Measuring welfare for small but vulnerable groups: Poverty and disability in Uganda. *Journal of African Economies, 14*(4), 603–631.

International Labor Organization Global Business and Disability Network. (2020). ILO-GBDN: Who we are. http://www.businessanddisability.org/mission/.

Jesus, T. S., Landry, M. D., & Jacobs, K. (2020). A "new normal" following COVID-19 and the economic crisis: Using systems thinking to identify challenges and opportunities in disability, telework, and rehabilitation. *Work*, Preprint, 1–10. https://doi.org/10.3233/WOR -203250

Jolly, D. (2010). Personal assistance and independent living: Article 19 of the UN Convention on the Rights of Persons with Disabilities. University of Leeds, Disability Studies. Retrieved from https://disability-studies.leeds.ac.uk/wp-content/uploads/sites/40/library/jolly-Perso nal-Assistance-and-Independent-Living1.pdf

Kayess, R., & French, P. (2008). Out of darkness into light? Introducing the Convention on the Rights of Persons with Disabilities. *Human Rights Law Review, 8*(1), 1–34.

Lamichhane, K., & Okubo, T. (2014). The nexus between disability, education, and employment: Evidence from Nepal. *Oxford Development Studies, 42*(3), 439–453.

Levitt, J. M. (2017). Exploring how the social model of disability can be re-invigorated: In response to Mike Oliver. *Disability & Society, 32*(4), 589–594.

Loeb, M., Eide, A. H., Jelsma, J., Ka'Toni, M., & Maart, S. (2007). Poverty and disability in Eastern and Western Cape Provinces, SA. *Disability and Society, 23*(4), 311–321.

Lokot, M., & Avakyan, Y. (2020). Intersectionality as a lens to the COVID-19 pandemic: Implications for sexual and reproductive health in development and humanitarian contexts. *Sexual and Reproductive Health Matters, 28*(1), 40–43. https://doi.org/10.1080/26410 397.2020.1764748

Lord, J. E., & Stein, M. A. (2008). The domestic incorporation of human rights law and the United Nations Convention on the Rights of Persons with Disabilities. *Washington University Law Review, 83*(4), 449–479.

Loyalka, P., Liu, L., Chen, G., & Zheng, X. (2014). The cost of disability in China. *Demography, 51*(1), 97–118. https://link.springer.com/article/10.1007/s13524-013-0272-7

MacLachlan, M., & Swartz, L. (2009). Disability and international development: Towards inclusive global health. Springer.

Mashaw, J. L., & Reno, V. P. (Eds.). (1996). Balancing security and opportunity: The challenge of disability income policy. National Academy of Social Insurance.

Metts, R. L. (2000). Disability issues, trends and recommendations for the World Bank. The World Bank.

Mitra, S. (2018). Disability, health and human development. Palgrave Macmillan.

Mitra, S., & Sambamoorthi, U. (2008). Disability and the rural labor market in India: Evidence for males in Tamil Nadu. *World Development, 36*(5), 934–952.

Mizunoya, S., & Mitra, S. (2013). Is there a disability gap in employment rates in developing countries? *World Development, 42*(1), 28–43.

Mizunoya, S., Yamasaki, I., & Mitra, S. (2016). The disability gap in employment rates in a developing country context: New evidence from Vietnam. *Economics Bulletin, 36*(2), 771–777.

Nardodkar, R., Pathare, S., Ventriglio, A., Castaldelli-Maia, J., Javate, K. R., Torales, J., & Bhugra, D. (2016). Legal protection of the right to work and employment for persons with mental health problems: a review of legislation across the world. *International Review of Psychiatry, 28*(4), 375–384.

National Disability Institute. (2020, August). Race, ethnicity and disability: The financial impact of systemic inequality and intersectionality. National Disability Institute.

Ncube, W. (1998). The African cultural footprint? The changing conception of childhood. In W. Ncube (Ed.), *Law, Culture, Tradition and Children's Rights in Eastern and Southern Africa* (pp. 1–20). Ashgate Publishing.

OECD. (2009). Sickness, disability and work: Keeping on track in the economic downturn. Paper presented at the High-Level Forum, May 14–15, 2009. https://www.oecd.org/els/emp/ 42699911.pdf

Oliver, M. (1990). The politics of disablement: A sociological approach. Palgrave Macmillan.

Ortbals, C., & Rincker, M. (2009). Fieldwork, identities, and intersectionality: Negotiating gender, race, class, religion, nationality, and age in the research field abroad: Editors' introduction. *PS: Political Science & Politics, 42*(2), 287–290. https://doi.org/10.1017/S104909650909057X

Ozawa, M. N., & Yeo, Y. H. (2006). Work status and work performance of people with disabilities: An empirical study. *Journal of Disability Policy Studies, 17*(3), 180–190.

Parent, M.C., DeBlaere, C. & Moradi, B. (2013). Approaches to research on intersectionality: Perspectives on gender, LGBT, and racial/ethnic identities. *Sex Roles, 68*, 639–645. https:// doi.org/10.1007/s11199-013-0283-2

Parsons, T. (1975). The sick role and the role of the physician reconsidered. *The Milbank Memorial Fund Quarterly. Health & Society*, 53(3), 257–278. https://doi.org/10.2307/3349493

Quinn, P. (2005). Disability policy (United States). In J. M. Herrick & P. H. Stuart (Eds.), *Encyclopedia of Social Welfare History in North America* (pp. 84–86). SAGE Publications. http://dx.doi.org/10.4135/9781412952521.n37

Riddell, S., & Watson, N. (2014). Disability, culture and identity: Introduction. In S. Riddell and N. Watson (Eds.), *Disability, Culture and Identity* (pp. 1–18). Routledge.

RI Global (2020). The story of RI Global. http://www.riglobal.org/about/history/

Russell, M. (2001). Disablement, oppression, and the political economy. *Journal of Disability Policy Studies*, 12(2), 87–95.

Sainsbury, R., & Coleman-Fountain, E. (2014). Diversity and change of the employment prospects of persons with disabilities: The impact of redistributive and regulatory provisions in a multilevel framework. DISCIT Deliverable 5.1. https://www.researchgate.net/profile/Edmund_Coleman-Fountain/publication/310766875_Diversity_and_Change_of_the_Employment_Prospects_of_Persons_with_Disabilities_The_Impact_of_Redistributive_and_Regulatory_Provisions_in_a_Multilevel_Framework/links/5836071408aed45931c649c0/Diversity-and-Change-of-the-Employment-Prospects-of-Persons-with-Disabilities-The-Impact-of-Redistributive-and-Regulatory-Provisions-in-a-Multilevel-Framework.pdf

Steinfield, L., Sanghvi, M., Zayer, L. T., Coleman, C. A., Ourahmoune, N., Harrison, R. L., & Brace-Govan, J. (2019). Transformative intersectionality: Moving business towards a critical praxis. *Journal of Business Research*, 100, 366–375, https://doi.org/10.1016/j.jbusres.2018.12.031

Saleh, M. (2019). Global perspectives on employment for people with disabilities. In S. M. Bruyère (Ed.), *Employment and Disability: Issues, Innovations, and Opportunities* (LERA Research Volumes) (pp 279–305). Labor and Employment Relations Association.

Saleh, M. & Bruyère, S. (2018). Leveraging employer practices in global regulatory frameworks to improve employment outcomes for people with disabilities. *Journal of Social Inclusion*, 6(1), https://doi.org/10.17645/si.v6i1.12

Saleh, M., Golden, T. P., & Switzer, E. (2019). U.S. employment and disability policy framework: Competing legislative priorities, challenges and promising practices. In S. M. Bruyère (Ed.), *Employment and Disability: Issues, Innovations, and Opportunities* (LERA Research Volumes) (pp. 13–32). Labor and Employment Relations Association.

Samaha, A. M. (2007). What good is the social model of disability? *University of Chicago Law Review*, 74(4), 1251–1308.

Scheer, J., & Groce, N. (1988). Impairment as a human constant: Cross-cultural and historical perspectives on variation. *Journal of Social Issues*, 44(1), 23–37.

Sida. (2014). Disability rights in the Middle East and North Africa. https://cdn.sida.se/app/uploads/2021/05/10142325/rights-of-persons-with-disabilities-mena.pdf

Smart, J. F., & Smart, D. W. (1991). Acceptance of disability and the Mexican American culture. *Rehabilitation Counseling Bulletin*, 34(4), 357–367.

Stewart, D. (2009). Transition to adult services for young people with disabilities: Current evidence to guide future research. *Developmental Medicine and Child Neurology*, 51(4), 169–173.

Trani, J., & Loeb, M. (2010). Poverty and disability: A vicious circle? Evidence from Afghanistan and Zambia. *Journal of International Development*, 24(51), S19–S52.

Turcotte, M. (2012). Persons with disabilities and employment. Statistics Canada. https://www.statcan.gc.ca/pub/75-006-x/2014001/article/14115-eng.htm

Turmusani, M. (2018). Disabled people and economic needs in the developing world: A political perspective from Jordan. Routledge.

U.N. (2021). Department of economics and social affairs: Disability. https://www.un.org/development/desa/disabilities/

UN Division of Social Policy and Development. (2010). Fact sheet: Youth with disabilities. https://social.un.org/youthyear/docs/Fact%20sheet%20youth%20with%20disabilities.pdf

UN Economic and Social Commission for Asia and the Pacific. (2015). Disability at a glance 2015: Strengthening employment prospects for people with disabilities in Asia and the Pacific. http://www.unescap.org/sites/default/files/SDD%20Disability%20Glance%202015_Final.pdf

Waddington, L., Pedersen, M., & Ventegodt Liisberg, M. (2016). Get a job! Active labour market policies and persons with disabilities in Danish and European Union policy. *Dublin University Law Journal*, 39(1), 1–24.

Wang, P., Michaels, C. A., & Day, M. S. (2011). Stresses and coping strategies of Chinese families with children with Autism and other developmental disabilities. *Journal of Autism and Developmental Disorders*, 41(6), 783–795.

World Health Organization. (2001). International classification of functioning, disability and health.

World Health Organization. (2015). *Global disability action plan 2014–2021: Better health for all people with disability*.

World Health Organization-World Bank. (2011). World report on disability: Summary, 2011, WHO/NMH/VIP/11.01. http://www.refworld.org/docid/50854a322.html

Yeo, R., & Moore, K. (2003). Including disabled people in poverty reduction work: "Nothing about us, without us." *World Development*, 31(3), 571–590.

CHAPTER 31

DISABILITY PREVALENCE, MEASUREMENT, AND HEALTH IN A GLOBAL CONTEXT

BRYAN L. SYKES AND JUSTIN D. STRONG

INTRODUCTION

ONE billion people in the world live with some form of disability (Groce, 2018). Global age-standardized years lived with disability (YLDs) have decreased slightly over the last three decades, but there is large variation across demographic groups and countries (Spenser et al., 2018). Approximately 80% of all people with disabilities live in low- and middle-income countries (Saran et al., 2020), and disability negatively affects employment, education, and household wealth. Moreover, global initiatives such as developmental and poverty reduction projects have often been critiqued for separating disability from issues related to economic opportunity, resources, and welfare programs, or for hastily assuming that poverty reduction inherently means support for people with disabilities (Grech, 2015, 2016; Riddell, 2010). Healthcare is a significant resource for people with disabilities and one that is restricted by barriers, such as financial costs, architectural design, lack of caregivers, and programmatic resources (Eide et al., 2015; Kabia et al., 2018; Munthali et al., 2019; Tomlinson et al., 2009). The global phenomenon of disability has demanded new approaches and paradigms to policy and public health that center health optimization, rehabilitation, and functioning, as opposed to a strict focus on prevention and amelioration (Mitra & Sambamoorthi, 2013; Spenser et al., 2018; Stucki, 2016; World Health Organization, 2015). In this study, we focus on the relationship between disability policy and egalitarian democracy and their impact on disability health metrics.

Although healthcare and disability policy are linked, they are not synonymous. Disability has historically been reduced to a medical pathology, and global initiatives have either avoided or denied the health needs and experiences of people with disabilities (Swartz & Bantjes, 2016). Not only do people with disabilities experience unequal access to healthcare, but, compared to the general population, they also experience greater unmet healthcare needs and poorer standards of care (Rotarou & Sakellariou, 2017a; World Health Organization, 2015). The World Health Organization's (WHO) 2015 global disability action plan aims to improve the life and health outcomes of people with disabilities through such initiatives as extending rehabilitation and habitation assistive services, expanding community-based programs, and improving access to healthcare services. Indeed, a large proportion of gains in global life expectancy are spent in poor health with large inequalities in healthy life expectancy (HALE) (Kyu et al., 2018). Likewise, healthcare systems in low-income countries are likely to be far less expansive, and people with disabilities face higher rates of catastrophic healthcare expenditure (Shakespeare, 2020; World Health Organization, 2011). Examining global health trends might therefore offer unique vantage on the impacts and material implications of disability policy.

Disability intersects with a range of demographic groups who already experience various forms of marginalization and discrimination, which only increases health inequities and impediments to care. Women, children, ethnic minorities, the elderly, and poor people are more likely to report having a disability and are subjected to additional forms of stigmatization, abuse, and violence (Mitra & Sambamoorthi, 2013; World Health Organization, 2015). Disability also requires serious considerations in planning for states of emergency, natural disasters, wars, pandemics, migration, national emergencies, and climate change, all of which have not been appropriately addressed or prioritized at a global scale (Grech, 2016; Groce, 2018). As is the case in Haiti, the catastrophic earthquake of 2010 has been the second leading cause of disability in the country behind communicable/noncommunicable diseases, and more than half of people with disabilities surveyed have been unable to access necessary health services (Danquah et al., 2015).

While reflective of the shortcomings and failures of policy, social inequities and vulnerabilities are also indicative of the extent to which people with disabilities are able to shape and influence policy agenda and priorities. Despite global and national crises that increase mortality and morbidity risks among members of society who are resource, health, and mobility impaired, people nonetheless retain the capacity to lead rich, meaningful, and active lives (Albrecht & Devlieger, 1999; Levitt, 2017; Swain & French, 2000). Their access to and participation in political institutions are crucial to disability rights initiatives. Thus, understanding the causes, correlates, and consequences of disability policy is not only important for local and national public health but also for global human rights and the incorporation of disabled persons into civil society and humanitarian planning during states of emergency (Stucki, 2016; United Nations, 2007b).

In this chapter, we document global and national disability policies in the context of cross-country disability health estimates. We leverage data from a variety of sources to describe how disability matters across three central axes of inequality—health metrics, social policies, and democratic inclusion. We conclude with future directions for research on social policy and disability rates.

Conceptualizing and Measuring Disability

Disability encompasses a broad range of physical and mental health impairments that can be genetic, developmental, emotional, cognitive, injury-based, or caused by illness and disease. Key factors in understanding disability are the environmental and social barriers that inhibit people's everyday functioning. The World Health Organization conceptualizes disability using the International Classification of Functioning Disability and Health (ICF). The ICF, as well as the Washington Group, uses a biopsychosocial model and definition that focuses on functional limitations and the ways in which disability manifests within environmental contexts of interaction, activity, and participation (Berghs et al., 2017; World Health Organization, 2011). Similarly, the United Nations (UN) Convention on the Rights of Persons with Disabilities (CRPD) describes disability as an evolving concept that "[R]esults from the interaction between persons with impairments and attitudinal and environmental barriers that hinders their full and effective participation in society on an equal basis with others" (United Nations, 2007a, p. 33). While the ICF and UN CRPD provide practical conceptualizations of disability— based in the social model of disability—they are open to fluid circumstances and shifting relational contexts across a globalized world (Bury, 1996; Federici et al., 2017; Stucki, 2016). Focusing on interaction, activity, and participation lends to the optimization of social health and rehabilitation, and addressing health inequities as goals of system-wide strategies of inclusion (Stucki, 2016; World Health Organization, 2015). In this sense, health metrics may be able to provide exploratory insight on the impacts of disability policy, as well as the status and social inclusion of people with disabilities.

The conceptualization of disability offered by the ICF and CRPD extends from the disability rights movement, which has refused a medico-pathological model in support of a broader sociocultural, intersectional, and embodiment framework (Bickenbach, 2019; Haegele & Hodge, 2016; Hughes & Patterson, 1997; Knight, 2015; Oliver, 2013; Shakespeare & Watson, 2001). Still, disability continues to be framed in terms of individual tragedy as opposed to a socially produced phenomenon. Intellectual tensions persist as to whether the emphasis should be placed on the social construction and embodiment of impairment or if the focus should remain on the social and environmental barriers that disable one's participation in society (Oliver, 2013; Shildrick, 2020). How one conceptualizes disability is no doubt an ongoing and contentious endeavor. One of the more critical interventions that has emerged is debate and discussion about what constitutes a "normal," "healthy," and "able body"; the dynamics and nuances that produce a variance in physical health and mental well-being are not monolithic and vary across social contexts (Corker & Shakespeare, 2002; Hall & Wilton, 2017; Shildrick, 2020; Williams, 1999). Certainly oppressive and harmful in its consequences, the normative boundary between ability and disability is a precarious imposition of power. Such critical questions should not be taken as a distraction from the real prejudices and inequities people with disabilities experience, but rather scaffold the work by which one understands, assesses, and responds to lived and embodied vulnerabilities.

These inquiries are particularly important when considering questions of governance, law, and policy, which have often put forward normative and dualistic notions of autonomy and self-stability defined in contradistinction to disabled bodies (Davy, 2015; Foucault, 2013; Shildrick, 2020). Moreover, mobilizing conceptualizations of disability proves challenging when attempting to access lived experiences across global contexts. Harmonizing measures of disability, for instance, is complicated by language, cultural reference, stigma, and data collection practices, which work to either promote or discourage disability disclosure in various ways (Pettinicchio & Maroto, 2021). How disability is conceptualized, measured, and addressed by social policy risks reproducing exclusionary practices and stigmatizing attitudes that perpetuate harm. What Hughes (2019, p. 831) describes as the "ableist moral economy" reflects the social and cultural symbols used to evaluate disability as both pollutant and pitiful. The same sentiment that seeks to address the vulnerabilities of disability—such as health inequities—can all too often reinforce adverse notions of disgust and repudiation (Hughes, 2019). This system of symbolic exchange—the cycling back and forth between dignity and degradation—encapsulates the very logic of our modern, humanitarian institutions and should be kept in constant tension with every effort to affect progressive change (Dayan, 2013; Hughes, 2019; Shildrick, 2020).

DISABILITY RIGHTS AND SOCIAL STRUCTURE

How people with disabilities are included and recognized within democratic institutions shapes how their needs and experiences are understood and potentially addressed by social policy (Clifford, 2012; Raisio et al., 2014). Questions about democratic citizenship and inclusion are at the core of the disability rights movement and assessing their material implications is crucial (Berube, 2009; Knight, 2015). Indeed, democratic institutions often place value on political activity and participation in ways that exclude and paternalize people with disabilities (Raisio et al., 2014).

Beyond arguments about human dignity, including people with disabilities in democratic institutions enriches society because people share their perspectives, experiences, and capacities in meaningful ways (Knight, 2015; Nussbaum, 2009). Democracy is enhanced when differences are recognized, thereby opening up critical dialogue about how democratic institutions function for disabled groups (Fraser, 1990; Nussbaum, 2009; Rawls, 2005; Young, 2002). At a basic level, increasing societal participation and recognition of people with disabilities works to address other forms of exclusion and marginalization in areas like education, employment, and civic engagement (Hastbacka et al., 2016; Kabia et al., 2018). Thus, there is reason to assume that the quality and strength of a democracy are important in considering questions about disability policy. This framework for understanding the quality and inclusiveness of a democracy is important for both disability policy formation and observed health disparities because structural health disadvantages are likely to hinder and discourage political engagement in various ways.

While the rights of people with disabilities have ascended in global importance and institutional recognition, nation-states remain instrumental in setting and achieving material outcomes that address health inequalities (Federici et al., 2017; Mégret, 2008; Roca et al., 2020; United Nations, 2007a; World Health Organization, 2015). Despite the attention given to the rights of people with disabilities, policies have been unable to guarantee structural change (Barnes, 2020). Although 163 member nations and regional integration organizations are signatories of the UN CRPD, this declaration does not provide enough context in understanding how global disabilities, health inequalities, and governmental policies interact. In particular, it is necessary to investigate the interrelationship between disability rates, disability policies, and levels of democracy to assess whether national efforts are successful in mitigating the consequences of disease and disability. As states seek to expand the representation and participation of political constituents and provide material support to human rights, people with disabilities are an important group to consider; their political accessibility, as well as the health inequalities they experience and corresponding rehabilitation deficits further complicate political institutions and national initiatives. In this way, stronger democratic regimes might be more active in addressing health inequities for people with disabilities as they have been able to increase participation and processes of recognition for these specific concerns.

Disability intersects with other forms of marginalization, such as racism and sexism, to create hierarchies of disadvantage in economic security, employment, and wealth, which are all likely to negatively impact democratic participation (Maroto & Pettinicchio, 2020; Maroto et al., 2019; Pilling, 2013). Health inequities are particularly salient to understanding disability, which greatly contribute to hierarchies of disadvantage (Gudlavalleti et al., 2014; Shandra, 2019). For instance, disability is often associated with comorbidity of chronic illnesses, such as diabetes, cardiovascular disease, and depression (Gudlavalleti et al., 2014; Reichard et al., 2011). Access to quality and affordable healthcare is a right for people with disabilities; however, disabled persons often experience unmet health and rehabilitation needs. How to integrate the health needs of people living with disabilities into the broader delivery of healthcare systems remains a subject of considerable research (Tomlinson et al., 2009).

Not only do adults with disabilities devote more time to healthcare needs as compared to adults without disabilities, but such differences are explained further by other sociodemographic disparities, such as education, employment, and marriage (Shandra, 2018, 2019). Research has shown how women with mobility disabilities face significant barriers in cancer screening, which is illustrative of broader institutional disparities (Angus et al., 2012). Issues ranged from scheduling and attending appointments, to confronting assumptions about women's bodies, to receiving reliable healthcare. In low-income and developing countries, healthcare access is significantly inhibited by socioeconomic status, transportation challenges, attitudes about healthcare providers, healthcare coverage, and facility accessibility (Eide et al., 2015; Van Rooy et al., 2012). As Rotarou and Sakellariou (2017a) found in their study on healthcare in Chile, people with disabilities face an array of barriers to basic healthcare access, such as getting to a health facility, obtaining an appointment with a doctor, and receiving necessary treatments. These issues in healthcare access were exasperated further by differences between public and private healthcare coverage, socioeconomic status, and gender. Kabia et al.'s (2018) study of healthcare in Kenya also captured how health inequities lie at the intersection of disability, gender, and poverty. Many women with disabilities opt out of healthcare services due to their roles as primary caregivers, transportation costs, and what is described as "disability-unfriendly" health facilities (p. 6). Socioeconomic disparities exacerbate health disparities by cleaving off healthcare needs for vulnerable populations, including individuals living with cognitive and mobility disabilities. Therefore, the structure, strength, and inclusivity of societies are important factors known to shape both healthcare access and disability policy, thereby potentially observing disparities in disability and health.

HEALTH INEQUALITIES AND CIVIC INCORPORATION

A growing body of research has examined the relationship between health, democracy, and political participation. Studies show that health inequality is negatively associated with democratic participation and representation (Mattila et al., 2013; Ojeda & Pacheco, 2019; Pacheco & Ojeda, 2019; Wass et al., 2017). People in poor health have decreased trust in political institutions, which in turn leads to decreased engagement with institutional forms of participation, such as voting (Mattila, 2020). Similarly, other scholarship finds that people with disabilities tend to have lower voter turnout in the United States but favor a stronger government role in healthcare (Schur & Adya, 2013). Member states in the European Union (EU), for example, have varying degrees of structural exclusion for people with disabilities seeking to engage in political participation. Some EU countries have not ratified the CRPD and deny the right to vote for those living in institutional settings, while other countries have deficient telecommunication capabilities, mobility accessibility, and proper monitoring of voter participation (Priestly et al., 2016).

Similarly, healthcare systems are a direct reflection of the global distribution of power, which can undercut local democratic institutions. Countries in the Global South, for instance, are often reliant upon the flow of healthcare commodities and knowledge from the Global North, which creates systems of dependency that shape the very discourse and provision of disability services in ways that are inattentive to social and political contexts at the local level (Swartz & Bantjes, 2016).

Likewise, entrenched global inequality has intensified population health problems by increasing pressure on governments to respond to complex issues that further subject people with disabilities to structural vulnerabilities (McMichael, 2013). Crucial to this global context is the diminishing capacity of democratic governments in responding to the health disparities of people with disabilities. The adoption of neoliberal logics, and their corresponding social policies, have entrenched health inequalities by winnowing down welfare and safety net programs. For instance, in response to the global financial crises associated with the Great Recession, many governments adopted austerity measures—and other forms of political and economic realignment—that meant people with disabilities lost state-subsidized healthcare services (Labonté & Stuckler, 2016; Rotarou & Sakellariou, 2017b). Consequently, worldwide, disability policies have undergone restructuring, such that state benefits and services have become distributed according to hierarchies of impairment and deservingness (Oliver, 2013; Soldatic, 2020).

DATA, MEASURES, AND METHODS

We seek to understand how disability rates are associated with observed democratic principles, including the enshrinement and protection of disability rights into national laws and constitutional doctrines. To do this, we combine data from four sources to examine disability rates within the context of global and national policies, as well as democratic principles. First, we obtain disability data from the Global Burden of Disease (GBD) collaboration (GBD, 2017), available at the Institute for Health Metrics and Evaluation (IHME). IHME cleans, codes, standardizes, and analyzes each country's input data (surveys, registries, hospital admissions/discharges, satellite, and other data) to construct consistent national, regional, and global population estimates for comparative analyses across the life course (GBD Collaborative Network, 2018). These data allow for an examination of cross-country differences in disability rates.

We extract data on the total number and rate of disability-adjusted life years (DALYs) for each country from the GBD data exchange portal. DALYs are a combination of years of life lost (YLLs) and YLDs, and a DALY represents a year of "healthy" life lost due to ill health, disability, or premature death. This measure is consistent with the ICF and Washington Group's definition of functional limitations, but it expresses, quantitatively, how health loss is locally experienced and spatially concentrated. In the aggregate, the sum or rate of DALYs represents the gap between current and ideal health, constituting the overall burden of disease. Research shows that, "In the past decade, it has become evident that measuring non-fatal health loss is important for tracking progress, as the disease burden, in terms of disability-adjusted life years (DALYs), evolves toward being dominated by years lived with disability (YLDs)" (Spenser et al., 2018, p. 1790). Therefore, we construct a categorical measure of where countries fall on the continuum of disease burden if they are one or more standard deviations below (Low) or above

(High) the mean (Middle) value of the DALYs rate. DALYs are for both sexes and all age groups in the population.

Second, we obtained data from the UN on countries that signed or formally confirmed, accessioned, or ratified the CRPD. The CRPD's purpose was to "promote, protect and ensure the full and equal enjoyment of all human rights and fundamental freedoms by all persons with disabilities, and to promote respect for their inherent dignity" (United Nations, 2007a, p. 36). The convention produced 50 articles that specify the rights and dignity of people with disabilities to, among other things, receive equal access to public spaces, employment, education, health, rehabilitation, an adequate standard of living, social protections, and privacy. The CRPD also specifies that participants agree to collect and maintain data on disability rates and social conditions in order to formulate and implement policies that mitigate hardships and stigma for people living with disabilities. To date, there have been 163 signatories and 181 ratifications of the CRPD by countries and regional integration organizations (United Nations, 2007a). These data are useful for our analysis because they represent a country's sociopolitical commitment to protecting the rights of people with disabilities.

We also include data on whether countries signed or formally confirmed, accessioned, or ratified the Optional Protocol to the Convention on the Rights of Persons with Disabilities (OP-CRPD). The Optional Protocol contains 18 articles that specify the process for filing and adjudicating a complaint with the UN for disabled people who allege that their rights have been violated or denied under the CRPD. To date, there have been 94 signatories and 96 ratifications of the OP-CRPD by countries and regional integration organizations (UN, 2007b). Our use of the UN data is restricted to countries that have signed or ratified either the CRPD or OP-CRPD.

The third source of data is the Disability Rights Education & Defense Fund (DREDF). DREDF provides a reference to national policies and constitutional amendments on disability rights for 249 countries and territories (DREDF, 2020). We count and code the number of constitutional amendments/articles and national laws that govern the treatment of disabled persons for each country. Our use of these data will allow for an examination of how domestic policies and constitutional rights map onto observed disability rates.

Lastly, we leverage data on Varieties of Democracy (VDEM) from the V-Dem Institute, an independent research institute headquartered in the Department of Political Science at the University of Gothenburg, Sweden (Coppedge et al., 2020). Over 50 social scientists across six continents collect and construct measures on different dimensions of democracy for each country over time, drawing on the expertise of more than 3,000 country experts and their global International Advisory Board. We utilize VDEM's egalitarian democracy variable, which measures the extent to which the ideal of egalitarian democracy achieved. VDEM states that, for this measure, "The egalitarian principle of democracy holds that material and immaterial inequalities inhibit the exercise of formal rights and liberties, and diminish the ability of citizens from all social groups to participate. Egalitarian democracy is achieved when 1) rights and freedoms of individuals are protected equally across all social groups; 2) resources are distributed equally across all social groups; and 3) groups and individuals enjoy equal access to power" (Coppedge et al., 2020, p. 44). Egalitarian democracy is an index that includes measures of electoral democracy (freedom of association, fair elections, freedom of expression, election of officials, and suffrage) and the level of societal fairness/integration. This measure ranges from 0 (low) to 1 (high), with Yemen having the lowest (0.037) and Denmark having the highest (0.856) egalitarian democracies in 2016. We constructed a categorical measure of where countries fall on this continuum if they are one or more standard deviations below (Low) or above (High) the mean (Middle) value of egalitarian democracy. These data also allow for an examination of the relationship between democracy and disability.

Because many of these datasets do not contain two or three-digit International Organization for Standardization (ISO) country codes, we constructed a crosswalk file to merge these four datasets into one unique database. First, we constructed a crosswalk file that contains the name of each country and its two- and three-digit ISO code. Second, each of the four data sources was matched to this crosswalk file based on the countries listed in their respective data. Because of country naming differences (e.g., Ivory Coast versus Côte d'Ivoire), the crosswalk file accounted for variation in country names by assigning the correct two- and-three digit ISO code to that country. Once all four data sources were linked to the crosswalk file, either by country name or two-/three-digit ISO code, each dataset was merged into a composite dataset based on the three-digit ISO code carried over from the crosswalk file. The merged result produced a unique dataset that contains measures of disability, disability policies, and variations in democracy for 174 countries. Table 31.1 lists the countries in our study.

DISABILITY METRICS AND DISABILITY POLICIES IN A GLOBAL CONTEXT

Table 31.2 presents the summary measures for our analysis. Of the 174 countries in our study, 170 (or 97.7%) are UN member states, representing almost 9 in 10 of all member states. Globally, there were approximately 7.4 billion people in 2016 (PRB, 2016). Among the global population, there were roughly 2.5 billion disability-adjusted life years (DALYs) lost, with an average of 34,751 DALYs across all countries. Approximately 8.6%, 77.0%, and 14.4% of countries have DALY rates in the low, middle, and high range, respectively.

The average country has an egalitarian democracy score of 40.6%. Roughly 18.4%, 60.3%, and 21.3% of countries have egalitarian democracies in the low, middle, and high ranges, respectively.

Regarding disability policies, nearly two-thirds (66.1%) of counties signed or ratified the UN's CRPD or OP-CRPD, and less than half (47.5%) of all countries have an amendment in their nation's constitution that specifically addresses the rights and dignity of

Table 31.1 Countries with Data on Disability-Adjusted Life Years, Measures of Democracy, the United Nation's Convention on the Rights of Persons with Disabilities, and National Constitutional Amendments and Laws on Disability Rights

Afghanistan	Cameroon	Ethiopia	Jamaica	Mongolia	Republic of the Congo	Taiwan*
Albania	Canada	Fiji	Japan	Montenegro	Romania	Tajikistan
Algeria	Cape Verde*	Finland	Jordan	Morocco	Russia	Tanzania
Angola	Central African Republic	France	Kazakhstan	Mozambique	Rwanda	Thailand
Argentina	Chad	Gabon	Kenya	Namibia	Sao Tome and Principe	The Gambia
Armenia	Chile	Georgia	Kuwait	Nepal	Saudi Arabia	Timor-Leste
Australia	China	Germany	Kyrgyzstan	Netherlands	Senegal	Togo
Austria	Colombia	Ghana	Laos	New Zealand	Serbia	Trinidad and Tobago
Azerbaijan	Comoros	Greece	Latvia	Nicaragua	Seychelles	Tunisia
Bahrain	Costa Rica	Guatemala	Lebanon	Niger	Sierra Leone	Turkey
Bangladesh	Croatia	Guinea	Lesotho	Nigeria	Singapore	Turkmenistan
Barbados	Cuba	Guinea-Bissau	Liberia	North Korea	Slovakia	Uganda
Belarus	Cyprus	Guyana	Libya	North Macedonia	Slovenia	Ukraine
Belgium	Czech Republic	Haiti	Lithuania	Norway	Solomon Islands	United Arab Emirates
Benin	Democratic Republic of the Congo	Honduras	Luxembourg	Oman	Somalia	United Kingdom
Bhutan	Denmark	Hungary	Madagascar	Pakistan	South Africa	United States of America
Bolivia	Djibouti	Iceland	Malawi	Palestine/West Bank*	South Korea	Uruguay
Bosnia and Herzegovina	Dominican Republic	India	Malaysia	Panama	South Sudan	Uzbekistan
Botswana	Ecuador	Indonesia	Maldives	Papua New Guinea	Spain	Vanuatu
Brazil	Egypt	Iran	Mali	Paraguay	Sri Lanka	Venezuela
Bulgaria	El Salvador	Iraq	Malta	Peru	Sudan	Vietnam
Burkina Faso	Equatorial Guinea	Ireland	Mauritania	Philippines	Suriname	Yemen
Burma/Myanmar	Eritrea	Israel	Mauritius	Poland	Sweden	Zambia
Burundi	Estonia	Italy	Mexico	Portugal	Switzerland	Zimbabwe
Cambodia	Eswatini (Swaziland)*	Côte d'Ivoire	Moldova	Qatar	Syria	

Note:

* indicates the country is not a United Nations member state.

Table 31.2 Summary Statistics for Descriptive Analysis of a Unique Dataset for 2016

Countries	174
UN member states	170 (97.7%)
UN member states represented	170 of 193 (88.1%)
DALYs (total)	2,495,077,380
DALYs rate (mean)	34,751
Egalitarian democracy (mean)	40.6%
DALYs rate	% of Countries
Low [0–21,909)	8.6%
Middle [21,909–47,594)	77.0%
High [47,594–90,880]	14.4%
Egalitarian democracy	
Low [0–0.168)	18.4%
Middle [0.168–0.645)	60.3%
High [0.645–0.856]	21.3%
Signed/ratified UN CRPD/OP-CRPD	66.1%
Constitutional amendments/articles	47.5%
National disability laws/policies	66.7%

Note: Authors' calculations. DALYs, disability-adjusted life years.

Source: Author's compilation of data from the Global Burden of Disease (GBD), the United Nations' (UN) Convention on the Rights of Persons with Disabilities (CRPD), the Disability Rights Education & Defense Fund (DREDF), and Varieties of Democracy (VDEM).

people with disabilities. However, two-thirds (66.7%) have at least one law or policy that addresses or protects the rights of people with disabilities.

Spatial estimates of disability counts can conceal significant population differences. First, China and India are the two most populous nations on the planet, with over 1.3–1.4 billion people residing in each country, suggesting that the number of DALYs in their countries may be an inadequate metric with which to measure the prevalence of disabilities globally. Second, there are reasons to believe that population aging and differences in the stages of the demographic and epidemiologic transitions matter for both exposure to changing mortality levels and a shift from acute to chronic, degenerative conditions, thereby altering trends in morbidity and disability across the life course. These trends over time and across countries can complicate analyses that rely on raw

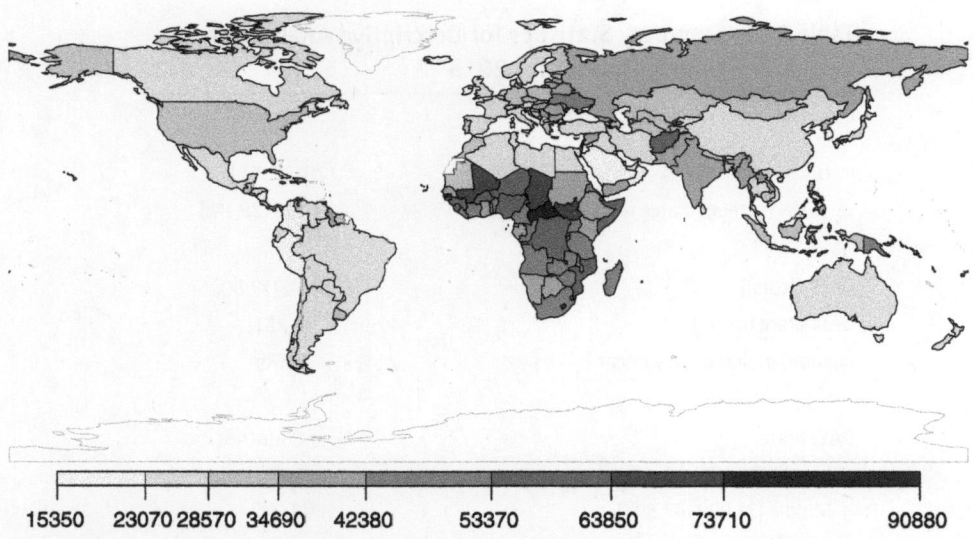

| 15350 | 23070 | 28570 | 34690 | 42380 | 53370 | 63850 | 73710 | 90880 |

FIGURE 31.1 The rate of disability-adjusted life years (DALYs) for both sexes across all age groups by country, 2016.

(*Source*: Author's compilation of data from the Global Burden of Disease [GBD], the United Nations' [UN] Convention on the Rights of Persons with Disabilities [CRPD], the Disability Rights Education & Defense Fund [DREDF], and Varieties of Democracy [VDEM]).

counts or total numbers of DALYs. For these reasons, we present rates of DALYs for each country in Figure 31.1.

Figure 31.1 demonstrates the importance of age and population standardization. While the total number of DALYs is largely concentrated in China, South East Asia, and parts of Eastern Europe (not displayed here), Figure 31.1 shows that the largest concentration of DALY rates is located in Central and Southern Africa. In contrast, countries in Central and Latin America have low rates of DALYs, as do nations in Western Europe, North America, North Africa, and the Middle East.

Figure 31.2 displays the DALYs rate rank order of countries associated with Figure 31.1. The Maldives has the lowest rate of DALYs (15,345 per 100,000), whereas the Central African Republic has the highest rate of DALYs (90,879 per 100,000). Djibouti, ranked 108th on the list, has a DALY rate (34,690 per 100,000) that is closest to the global mean DALY rate (34,751 per 100,000), highlighting the skewed nature of population and epidemiologic dynamics within and across countries.

EGALITARIAN DEMOCRACIES, DALY RATES, AND DISABILITY POLICIES

The number and percentage of countries falling into low, middle, and high ranges for rates of DALYs by level of egalitarian democracy are presented in Table 31.3. Very few

28000

1	Maldives
2	Qatar
3	Kuwait
4	Singapore
5	Bahrain
6	Israel
7	Jordan
8	Oman
9	Saudi Arabia
10	Nicaragua
11	Palestine
12	Lebanon
13	Costa Rica
14	Peru
15	Colombia
16	Iceland
17	Korea, Republic of
18	United Arab Emirates
19	Panama
20	Ireland
21	Cyprus
22	Malaysia
23	Algeria
24	Paraguay
25	Turkey
26	Tunisia
27	Sri Lanka
28	Switzerland
29	Australia
30	Honduras
31	Chile
32	Mexico
33	Ecuador
34	Bhutan
35	Norway
36	Spain
37	Iran
38	Luxembourg
39	France
40	Vietnam
41	New Zealand
42	Canada
43	Taiwan
44	Cape Verde

32000

45	Sweden
46	Venezuela
47	China
48	Netherlands
49	Argentina
50	Kyrgyzstan
51	Iraq
52	Japan
53	Italy
54	Austria
55	Thailand
56	Albania
57	United Kingdom
58	Cuba
59	Malta
60	Denmark
61	Jamaica
62	Belgium
63	El Salvador
64	Egypt
65	Brazil
66	Libya
67	Bolivia
68	Guatemala
69	Finland
70	Seychelles
71	Indonesia
72	Portugal
73	Barbados
74	Morocco
75	Uzbekistan
76	Bangladesh
77	Uruguay
78	Sao Tome and Principe
79	Slovenia
80	Dominican Republic
81	Greece
82	Armenia
83	Timor–Leste
84	Nepal
85	United States
86	Germany
87	North Macedonia
88	Mauritius

FIGURE 31.2 Rank order of countries by disability-adjusted life years (DALYs) rate, 2016.

(*Source*: Author's compilation of data from the Global Burden of Disease [GBD], the United Nations' [UN] Convention on the Rights of Persons with Disabilities [CRPD], the Disability Rights Education & Defense Fund [DREDF], and Varieties of Democracy [VDEM]).

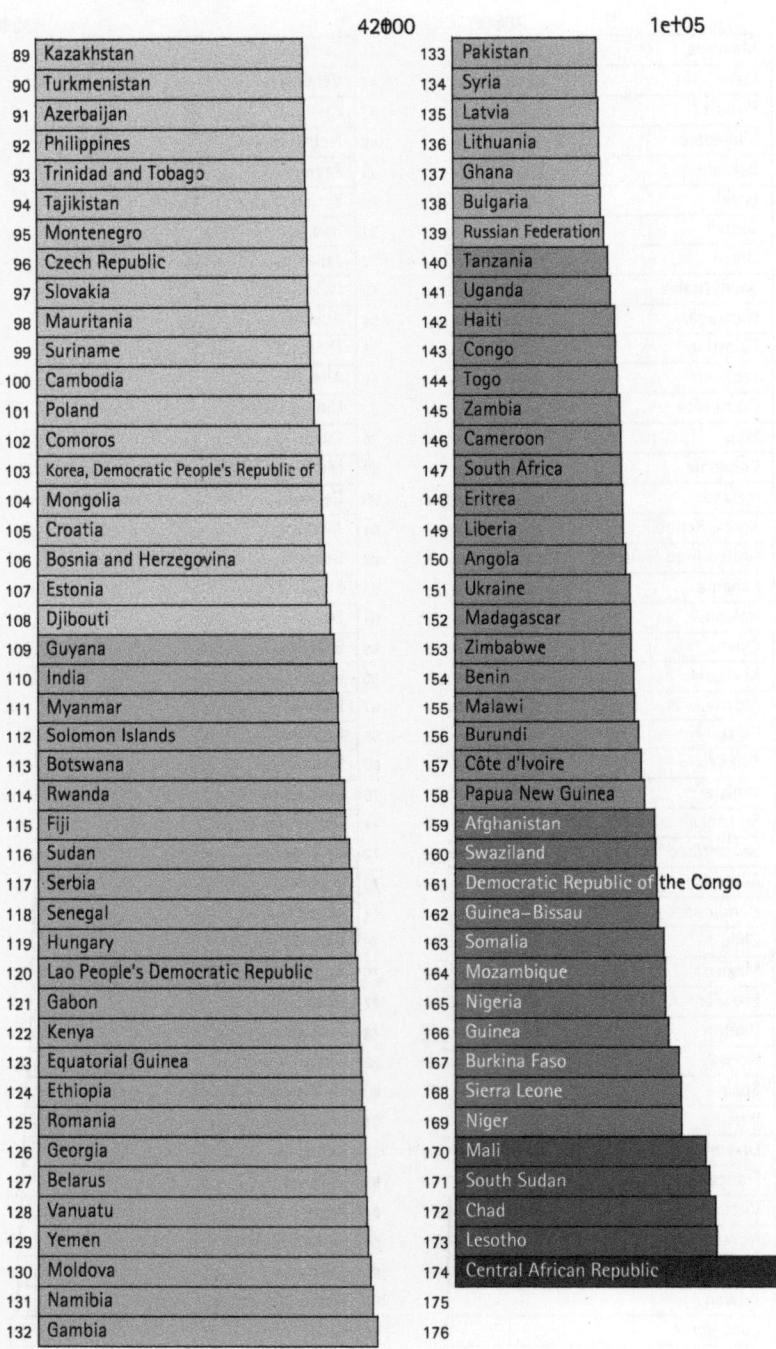

42000   1e+05

89	Kazakhstan
90	Turkmenistan
91	Azerbaijan
92	Philippines
93	Trinidad and Tobago
94	Tajikistan
95	Montenegro
96	Czech Republic
97	Slovakia
98	Mauritania
99	Suriname
100	Cambodia
101	Poland
102	Comoros
103	Korea, Democratic People's Republic of
104	Mongolia
105	Croatia
106	Bosnia and Herzegovina
107	Estonia
108	Djibouti
109	Guyana
110	India
111	Myanmar
112	Solomon Islands
113	Botswana
114	Rwanda
115	Fiji
116	Sudan
117	Serbia
118	Senegal
119	Hungary
120	Lao People's Democratic Republic
121	Gabon
122	Kenya
123	Equatorial Guinea
124	Ethiopia
125	Romania
126	Georgia
127	Belarus
128	Vanuatu
129	Yemen
130	Moldova
131	Namibia
132	Gambia

133	Pakistan
134	Syria
135	Latvia
136	Lithuania
137	Ghana
138	Bulgaria
139	Russian Federation
140	Tanzania
141	Uganda
142	Haiti
143	Congo
144	Togo
145	Zambia
146	Cameroon
147	South Africa
148	Eritrea
149	Liberia
150	Angola
151	Ukraine
152	Madagascar
153	Zimbabwe
154	Benin
155	Malawi
156	Burundi
157	Côte d'Ivoire
158	Papua New Guinea
159	Afghanistan
160	Swaziland
161	Democratic Republic of the Congo
162	Guinea–Bissau
163	Somalia
164	Mozambique
165	Nigeria
166	Guinea
167	Burkina Faso
168	Sierra Leone
169	Niger
170	Mali
171	South Sudan
172	Chad
173	Lesotho
174	Central African Republic
175	
176	

FIGURE 31.2 Continued

Table 31.3 The Number and Percentage of Countries Falling into Low, Middle, and High Ranges for Rates of Disability–Adjusted Life Years (DALYs), by Level of Egalitarian Democracy, 2016

Egalitarian Democracy	DALYs Rate			
	Low	Middle	High	Total
Low	3	22	7	32
	1.7%	12.6%	4.0%	18.4%
Middle	11	76	18	105
	6.3%	43.7%	10.3%	60.3%
High	1	36	0	37
	0.6%	20.7%	0.0%	21.3%
Total	15	134	25	174
	8.6%	77.0%	14.4%	100.0%

Note: Authors' calculations.

Source: Author's compilation of data from the Global Burden of Disease (GBD), the United Nations' Convention on the Rights of Persons with Disabilities (CRPD), the Disability Rights Education & Defense Fund (DREDF), and Varieties of Democracy (VDEM).

countries that score high on egalitarian democracy have low rates of DALYs; in fact, only one country (Costa Rica) meets these standards. The other 36 nations with high egalitarian values tend to have DALY rates that are around the global mean.

At the same time, there are seven countries—Angola, Burundi, Somalia, South Sudan, Eswatini (Swaziland), Chad, and Zimbabwe—that score low on egalitarian democracy and have relatively high DALY rates. Most countries, however, fall somewhere in the middle ranges of both egalitarian democracy and DALY rates. Curiously, three nations (Bahrain, Qatar, and Saudi Arabia) are low on both measures of democracy and disability.

Table 31.4 presents the number and percentage of countries that signed/ratified the UN's CRPD/OP-CRPD, implemented constitutional amendments, and enacted national disability policies/laws, by level of egalitarian democracy. Countries with low levels of egalitarian democracy have lower percentages of policies aimed at recognizing the dignity and protecting the rights of disabled persons. Interestingly, the most egalitarian nations are unlikely to codify and enshrine the rights of disabled persons into their constitutions. Taken together, these findings suggest that instrumental policy adoption and symbolic constitutional recognition of rights are often at odds, with only 47.5% of countries having constitutional articles that recognize disabled persons even though two-thirds of countries afford some national legal protections for people with disabilities (see Table 31.2). The vast majority of countries that do symbolically recognize the rights of disabled persons are largely concentrated among countries with moderate

Table 31.4 The Number and Percentage of Countries That Signed/Ratified the United Nations' CRPD/OP–CRPD, Have Constitutional Amendments/ Articles, and Passed National Disability Policies/Laws, by Level of Egalitarian Democracy, 2016

Egalitarian Democracy	Disability Policy		
	UN CRPD/ OP-CRPD	Constitutional Amendment	National Policies/Laws
Low	18	12	15
	15.7%	15.6%	13.9%
Middle	69	48	60
	60.0%	62.3%	55.5%
High	28	17	33
	24.3%	22.1%	30.6%

Disability Policy	Egalitarian Democracy		
	Low	Middle	High
UN CRPD/OP-CRPD	18	69	28
	15.7%	60.6%	24.3%
Constitutional Amendment	12	48	17
	15.6%	62.3%	22.1%
National Policies/Laws	15	60	33
	13.9%	55.5%	30.6%

Note: Authors' calculations. The top table includes percentages that are measured within-policy across levels of democracy (i.e., column percentages).

Source: Author's compilation of data from the Global Burden of Disease (GBD), the United Nations' Convention on the Rights of Persons with Disabilities (CRPD), the Disability Rights Education & Defense Fund (DREDF), and Varieties of Democracy (VDEM).

(or middle range) egalitarian democracies. Our results point to particular types of countries (i.e., those with less egalitarian democracies) as fruitful areas where international agencies and organizations should concentrate their efforts to affect disability policy development and change.

To draw out the aforementioned point more, Figure 31.3 plots the relationship between egalitarian democracy and DALYs. This figure highlights two key findings. First, there is an inverse relationship between democratic ideals and disability rates: As countries increase in their levels of egalitarian democracy, the rate of DALYs appears to decline. Second, this slightly negative relationship is not linear; the nonlinear fit of these

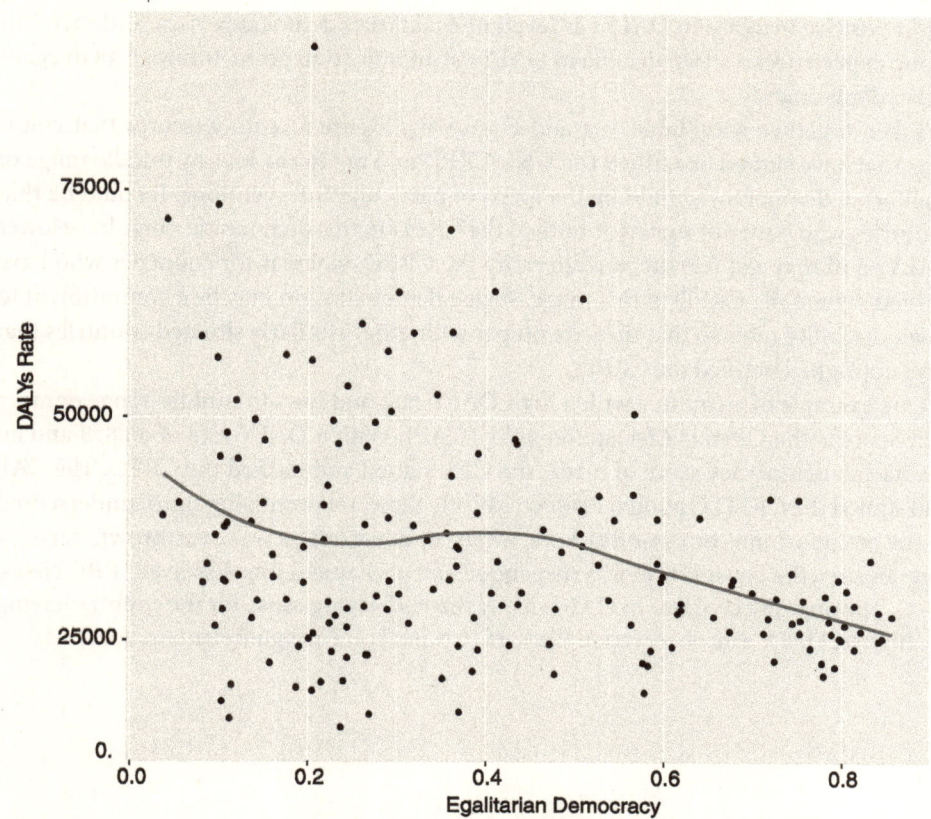

FIGURE 31.3 The relationship between egalitarian democracy and disability-adjusted life years (DALYs), 2016.

(*Source*: Author's compilation of data from the Global Burden of Disease [GBD],
the United Nations' [UN] Convention on the Rights of Persons with Disabilities [CRPD],
the Disability Rights Education & Defense Fund [DREDF], and Varieties of Democracy [VDEM]).

data reflects "health-stalling" in disability rates among countries in the low-to-middle range of egalitarian democracy.

Lastly, we explore whether the "health-stalling" of observed disability rates in the low- to middle-range democracies (in Figure 31.3) depends on whether specific countries have ratified the UN's CRPD. It is theoretically possible that a country's commitment to the UN's CRPD and its observed DALYs rate are independent of the level of egalitarian democracy. Figure 31.4 disaggregates the trend presented in Figure 31.3 into countries that have and have not signed or ratified the UN's CRPD. This figure shows that there are, indeed, two distinct trends for countries that have and have not signed or ratified the UN's CRPD, although most of these differences are not statistically significant. As levels of egalitarian democracy increase, countries that have not signed the CRPD have lower levels of DALYs, and then the trend plateaus, slowly rises, and then begins to fall; by comparison, countries that have signed or ratified the CRPD see a slight positive increase in DALYs as levels of egalitarian democracy rises, and then this group experiences a sharp decline in DALYs at an inflection point around 0.38 in egalitarian democracy.

Taken together with Table 31.4 and Figure 31.3 Figure 31.4 underscores that countries that have signed or ratified the UN's CRPD and are in the low-to-middle range of egalitarian democracy should be the focus of particular interventions. It could be that countries who have not signed or ratified the CRPD in this democratic range have lower DALYs and may not feel the need to ratify the CRPD, whereas for countries who have ratified/signed the CRPD in this range, such a demonstration may be a commitment to lower disability rates so that they are on par with other similarly situated countries that have not signed/ratified the CRPD.

One example of a country with a high DALY rate and low- to middle-range democracy score is the Central African Republic (CAF). With a DALY rate of 90,878 and an egalitarian democracy score of 0.204, the CAF signed and ratified the CRPD. The CAF also signed the CRPD Optional Protocol. While these are promising signs, underscored by the nation's domestic disability laws, when the government was overthrown during a coup in 2013, the constitution was suspended and parliament was dissolved (BBC News, 2013). The ongoing civil war in CAF is likely the underlying cause for the country having the highest DALY rate observed in the data (Council on Foreign Relations, 2021).

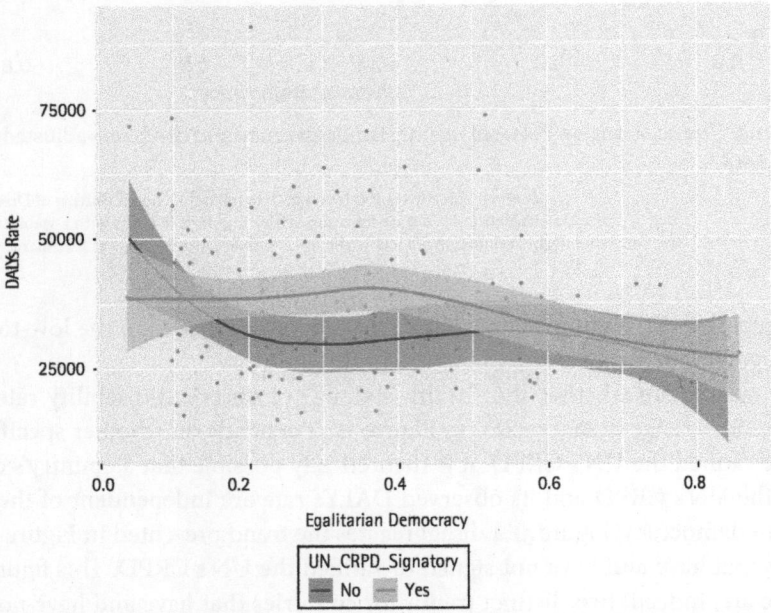

FIGURE 31.4 The relationship between egalitarian democracy and disability-adjusted life years (DALYs), by UN CRPD status, 2016.

(*Source*: Author's compilation of data from the Global Burden of Disease [GBD], the United Nations' [UN] Convention on the Rights of Persons with Disabilities [CRPD], the Disability Rights Education & Defense Fund [DREDF], and Varieties of Democracy [VDEM]).

Nigeria is another example of a country with a low- to middle-range egalitarian democracy score (0.362) and a high DALY rate (59,325). Having ratified both the CRPD and the CRPD Optional Protocol, Nigeria has four national policies aimed at protecting the rights of people with disabilities: National Commission for Rehabilitation Act (1969), the National Provident Fund Act (1961), the Nigerians with Disability Decree (1993), and the Discrimination Against Persons with Disabilities (Prohibition) Act (2018). The 2018 Act provides for the full integration of persons with disabilities into society and creates the National Commission for Persons with Disabilities, vesting in the commission responsibility for national education, healthcare, social, economic, and civil rights on matters related to disability.

Conclusion

If we take seriously the humanist position of our global institutions, all people, including those who are disabled, are entitled to full recognition and enjoyment of human rights and dignity (UN General Assembly, 2002), freedom to make decisions over their lives, equal access to social spaces and opportunities, and free and nondiscriminatory environments. The UN CRPD provides guidance and a set of ideals for how nations can achieve these basic human rights, particularly for the most disadvantaged in society. While a nontrivial number of nations (115 countries) have signed or ratified these principles, the enforcement mechanism (i.e., the Optional Protocol to the Convention) witnessed significantly fewer signatories (89 countries). Holding nations accountable for how they treat their most vulnerable demographic groups is essential for placing disability rates, policies, and protocols in both national and global perspectives. Such structural conditions might be best illustrative of the globalization of the ableist moral economy "in which disability is simultaneous *good to mistreat* and *good to be good to*" (Hughes, 2019, p. 832). While many countries have endorsed the symbolic declaration of rights and dignity for people with disabilities under the UN's CRPD, the lack of accountability and follow-through is perhaps indicative of the degradation and disregard of non-normative bodies.

In this chapter, we have shown that considerable variation exists across three primary axes of inequality: disability-related health metrics (DALY rates), disability policies (the UN's CRPD/OP-CRPD, national constitutional amendments, and domestic laws/ policies), and democratic inclusion (egalitarian democracy). These dimensions of difference matter for tracking the successes and failures of nations to enact social policies aimed at protecting the rights of disabled persons, lessening the burden of disease and disability, and for respecting the inherent dignity of life, regardless of its functional ability or mobility. Future research should assess whether the adoption of social and global disability policies is instrumental in achieving better national and global health outcomes for disabled persons or whether such policy gestures are merely symbolic in nature. These axes of inequality, and others, are important for adjudicating between the instrumental or symbolic policy prescriptions likely to affect global and national population health and disability rates for years to come.

Our findings are also relevant to discussion on the conceptualization and measurement of disability. We have mobilized DALYs, which may be atypical in disability research outside of public and population health (Grosse et al., 2009). While DALYs are standardized across countries, provide acute measures of health issues, and have helped advanced understanding of disability overall, it does reflect part of the normative, medico-pathological model of disability that activists and scholars have struggled to reject (Knight, 2015; Oliver, 2013), and for ascribing specific weights to particular functional limitations experienced at particular ages, with discounting across the life course (Arnesen & Nord, 1999). The tradeoff of using this measure, compared to standard disability measures, is that it captures and combines "information about morbidity and mortality in numbers of healthy years lost" (Arnesen & Nord, 1999, p. 1423), and disability weights are derived from a panel of medical experts and used to adjust the YLDs in the additive component of the DALYs (Grosse et al., 2009). In contrast, the ICF represents the most concerted effort to provide a social model of disability and has been the standard in the design of global disability surveys, such as the Model Disability Survey and Washington City Group on Disability Statistics. At the same time, conceptual and operational issues remain with the ICF, as well as general disparities in global disability estimates.

The conceptual framework between DALYs and the ICF is far from congruent. However, we have tried to leverage the metrical accuracy of DALYs in order to explore the overlap of health inequities, democratic inclusion, and disability policy, which is consistent with "public health professionals need to understand how it relates to contemporary understandings of disability" (Grosse et al., 2009, p. 197). By combining DALYs with such data, and by paying attention to the complexity of disability across different countries, our findings illuminate structural disadvantages that hinder people with disabilities' full participation in society. While there is no getting around the normative ideal of health that motivates the measurement of DALYs, we believe that it can be utilized in creative ways so to explore the global phenomena of health inequities for people living with disabilities in countries of varying democratic ideals.

REFERENCES

Albrecht, G. L., & Devlieger, P. J. (1999). The disability paradox: High quality of life against all odds. *Social Science & Medicine, 48*(8), 977–988. https://doi.org/10.1016/S0277-9536(98)00411-0

Angus, J., Seto, L., Barry, N., Cechetto, N., Chandani, S., Devaney, J., Fernando, S., Muraca, L., & Odette, F. (2012). Access to cancer screening for women with mobility disabilities. *Journal of Cancer Education, 27*(1), 75–82. https://doi.org/10.1007/s13187-011-0273-4

Arnesen, T., & and Nord, E.. (1999). The value of DALY life: Problems with ethics and validity of disability adjusted life years. *British Medical Journal, 319*(7222), 1423–1425. https://www.ncbi.nlm.nih.gov/pmc/articles/PMC1117148/

Barnes, C. (2020). Understanding the social model of disability: Past, present, and future. In N. Watson & S. Vehmas (Eds.), *Routledge handbook of disability studies, Volume 2* (pp. 14–31). Routledge.

BBC News. (2013, March 25). CAR rebel head Michel Djotodia "suspends constitution." BBC News https://www.bbc.com/news/world-africa-21934433

Berghs, M., Atkin, K., Graham, H., Hatton, C., & Thomas, C. (2017). Public health, research and rights: The perspectives of deliberation panels with politically and socially active disabled people. *Disability & Society*, 32(7), 945–965. https://doi.org/10.1080/09687599.2017.1339588

Berube, M. (2009). Citizenship and disability. In R. M. Baird, S. E. Rosenbaum, & S. K. Toombs (Eds.), *Disability: The social, political, and ethical debate* (pp. 205–216). Prometheus Books.

Bickenback, J. E. (2019). The IMF and its relationship to disability studies. In. N. Watson & S. Vehmas (Eds.), *Routledge handbook of disability studies* (pp. 55–71). Routledge.

Bury, M. (1996). Defining and researching disability: Challenges and responses. In C. Barnes & G. Mercer (Eds.), *Exploring the divide: Illness and disability* (pp. 18–38). The Disability Press.

Clifford, S. (2012). Making disability public in deliberative democracy. *Contemporary Political Theory*, 11(2), 211–228. https://doi.org/10.1057/cpt.2011.11

Coppedge, M., Gerring, J., Knutsen, C. H., Lindberg, S. I., Teorell, J., Altman, D., Bernhard, M., Fish, M. S., Glynn, A., Hicken, A., Lührmann, A., Marquardt, K. L., McMann, K., Paxton, P., Pemstein, D., Seim, B., Sigman, R., Skaaning, S.-E., Staton, J., Cornell, A., Gastaldi, L., Gjerløw, H., Mechkova, V. von Römer, J., Sundtröm, S., Tzelgov, E., Uberti, L., Wang, Y.-t., Wig, T., & Ziblatt. D. (2020). "V-Dem Codebook v10" Varieties of Democracy (V-Dem) Project. https://www.v-dem.net/en/

Corker, M., & Shakespeare, T. (2002). Mapping the terrain. In M. Corker and T. Shakespeare (Eds.), *Disability/postmodernity: Embodying disability theory* (pp. 1–17). Cassell.

Council on Foreign Relations. (2021). Violence in the Central African Republic. Council on Foreign Relations. https://www.cfr.org/global-conflict-tracker/conflict/violence-central-african-republic

Danquah, L., Polack, S., Brus, A., Mactaggart, I., Houdon, C. P., Senia, P., Gallien, P., & Kuper, H. (2015). Disability in post-earthquake Haiti: Prevalence and inequality in access to services. *Disability and Rehabilitation*, 37(12), 1082–1089. https://doi.org/10.3109/09638288.2014.956186

Davy, L. (2015). Philosophical inclusive design: Intellectual disability and the limits of individual autonomy in moral and political theory. *Hypatia*, 30(1), 132–148. https://doi.org/10.1111/hypa.12119

Dayan, C. (2013). *The law is a white dog: How legal rituals make and unmake persons.* Princeton University Press.

Disability Rights Education & Defense Fund (DREDF). (2020). International laws. https://dredf.org/legal-advocacy/international-disability-rights/international-laws/

Eide, A. H., Mannan, H., Khogali, M., van Rooy, G., Swartz, L., Munthali, A., Munthall, A., Hem, K., MacLachlan, M., & Dyrstad, K. (2015). Perceived barriers for accessing health services among individuals with disability in four African countries. *PLOS ONE*, 10(5), e0125915. https://doi.org/10.1371/journal.pone.0125915

Federici, S., Bracalenti, M., Meloni, F., & Luciano, J. V. (2017). World Health Organization disability assessment schedule 2.0: An international systematic review. *Disability and Rehabilitation*, 39(23), 2347–2380. Taylor and Francis. https://doi.org/10.1080/09638288.2016.1223177

Foucault, M. (2013). *History of madness.* Routledge.

GBD. (2017). Results. Institute for Health Metrics and Evaluation (IHME), 2018. http://ghdx
    .healthdata.org/gbd-results-tool

Global Burden of Disease Collaborative Network. (2018). Global Burden of Disease Study 2017.

Grech, S. (2015). *Disability and poverty in the global South: Renegotiating development in Guatemala*. Palgrave Macmillan.

Grech, S. (2016). Disability and development: Critical connections, gaps and contradictions. In S. Grech & K. Soldatic (Eds.), *Disability in the global south: The critical handbook* (pp. 1–23). Springer. https://doi.org/10.1007/978-3-319-42488-0

Groce, N. E. (2018). Global disability: An emerging issue. *The Lancet Global Health*, 6(7), E724–E725. https://doi.org/10.1016/S2214-109X(18)30265-1

Grosse, S. D., Lollar, D. J., Campbell, V. A., & Chamie, M. (2009). Disability and disability-adjusted life years: Not the same. *Public Health Reports*, 124(2), 197–202

Gudlavalleti, M. V. S., John, N., Allagh, K., Sagar, J., Kamalakannan, S., Ramachandra, S. S., & South India Disability Evidence Study Group. (2014). Access to health care and employment status of people with disabilities in South India, the SIDE (South India Disability Evidence) study. *BMC Public Health*, 14(1), 1125. https://doi.org/10.1186/1471-2458-14-1125

Fraser, N. (1990). Rethinking the public sphere: A contribution to the critique of actually existing democracy. *Social Text*, 25/26, 56–80. https://doi.org/10.2307/466240

Haegele, J. A., & Hodge, S. (2016). Disability discourse: Overview and critiques of the medical and social models. *Quest*, 68(2), 193–206. https://doi.org/10.1080/00336297.2016.1143849

Hall, E., & Wilton, R. (2017). Towards a relational geography of disability. *Progress in Human Geography*, 41(6), 727–744. https://doi.org/10.1177/0309132516659705

Hästbacka, E., Nygård, M., & Nyqvist, F. (2016). Barriers and facilitators to societal participation of people with disabilities: A scoping review of studies concerning European countries. *Alter*, 10(3), 201–220. https://doi.org/10.1016/j.alter.2016.02.002

Hughes, B. (2019). The abject and the vulnerable: The twain shall meet: Reflections on disability in the moral economy. *The Sociological Review*, 67(4), 829–846. https://doi.org/10.1177/0038026119854259

Hughes, B., & Paterson, K. (1997). The social model of disability and the disappearing body: Towards a sociology of impairment. *Disability and Society*, 12(3), 325–340. https://doi.org/10.1080/09687599727209

Kabia, E., Mbau, R., Muraya, K. W., Morgan, R., Molyneux, S., & Barasa, E. (2018). How do gender and disability influence the ability of the poor to benefit from pro-poor health financing policies in Kenya? An intersectional analysis. *International Journal for Equity in Health*, 17(1), 1–12. https://doi.org/10.1186/s12939-018-0853-6

Knight, A. (2015). Democratizing disability: Achieving inclusion (without assimilation) through "participatory parity." *Hypatia*, 30(1), 97–114. https://doi.org/10.1111/hypa.12120

Kyu, H., & the Global Burden of Disease 2017 DALYs and HALE Collaborators. (2018). Global, regional, and national disability-adjusted life-years (DALYs) for 359 diseases and injuries and healthy life-expectancy (HALE) for 195 countries and territories, 1990–2017: A systematic analysis for the Global Burden of Disease Study 2017. *The Lancet*, 392, 1859–1922.

Labonté, R., & Stuckler, D. (2016). The rise of neoliberalism: How bad economics imperils health and what to do about it. *Journal of Epidemiology and Community Health*, 70(3), 312–318. http://dx.doi.org/10.1136/jech-2015-206295.

Levitt, J. M. (2017). Developing a model of disability that focuses on the actions of disabled people. *Disability and Society*, 32(5), 735–747. https://doi.org/10.1080/09687599.2017.1324764

Maroto, M., & Pettinicchio, D. (2020). Barriers to economic decurity: disability, employment, and asset disparities in canada. *Canadian Review of Sociology/Revue canadienne de sociologie*, 57(1), 53–79. https://doi.org/10.1111/cars.12268

Maroto, M., Pettinicchio, D., & Patterson, A. C. (2019). Hierarchies of categorical disadvantage: Economic insecurity at the intersection of disability, gender, and race. *Gender & Society*, 33(1), 64–93.

Mattila, M. (2020). Does poor health mobilize people into action? Health, political trust, and participation. *European Political Science Review*, 12(1), 49–65. https://doi.org/10.1017/S17557 7391900033X

Mattila, M., Söderlund, P., Wass, H., & Rapeli, L. (2013). Healthy voting: The effect of self-reported health on turnout in 30 countries. *Electoral Studies*, 32(4), 886–891.

McMichael, A. J. (2013). Globalization, climate change, and human health. *New England Journal of Medicine*, 368(14), 1335–1343.

Mégret, F. (2008). The disabilities convention: Human rights of persons with disabilities or disability rights? *Human Rights Quarterly*, 30, 494–516.

Mitra, S., & Sambamoorthi, U. (2013). Disability prevalence among adults: Estimates for 54 countries and progress toward a global estimate. *Disability and Rehabilitation*, 36(11), 940–947. https://doi.org/10.3109/09638288.2013.825333

Munthali, A. C., Swartz, L., Mannan, H., MacLachlan, M., Chilimampunga, C., & Makupe, C. (2019). "This one will delay us": Barriers to accessing health care services among persons with disabilities in Malawi. *Disability and Rehabilitation*, 41(6), 683–690. https://doi.org/10.1080/09638288.2017.1404148

Nussbaum, M. C. (2009). *Frontiers of justice: Disability, nationality, species membership.* Harvard University Press

Ojeda, C., & Pacheco, J. (2019). Health and voting in young adulthood. *British Journal of Political Science*, 49(3), 1163–1186. https://doi.org/10.1017/S0007123417000151

Oliver, M. (2013). The social model of disability: Thirty years on. *Disability & Society*, 28(7), 1024–1026. https://doi.org/10.1080/09687599.2013.818773.

Pacheco, J., & Ojeda, C. (2019). A healthy democracy? Evidence of unequal representation across health status. *Political Behavior*, 42, 1245–1267. https://doi.org/10.1007/s11 109-019-09541-0

Pettinicchio, D., & Maroto, M. (2021). Who counts? measuring disability cross-nationally in census data. *Journal of Survey Statistics and Methodology*, 9(2), 257–284. https://doi.org/10.1093/jssam/smaa046

Pilling, M. D. (2013). Invisible identity in the workplace: Intersectional mad- ness and processes of disclosure at work. *Disability Studies Quarterly*, 33(1), 1–18. http://dx.doi.org/10.18061/dsq.v33i1.3424

Population Reference Bureau (PRB). (2016). 2016 World Population Data Sheet. Population Reference Bureau. https://www.prb.org/wp-content/uploads/2016/08/prb-wpds2016-web-2016.pdf

Priestley, M., Stickings, M., Loja, E., Grammenos, S., Lawson, A., Waddington, L., & Fridriksdottir, B. (2016). The political participation of disabled people in Europe: Rights, accessibility and activism. *Electoral Studies*, 42, 1–9. https://doi.org/10.1016/j.elects tud.2016.01.009

Raisio, H., Valkama, K., & Peltola, E. (2014). Disability and deliberative democracy: Towards involving the whole human spectrum in public deliberation. *Scandinavian Journal of Disability Research*, 16(1), 77–97. https://doi.org/10.1080/15017419.2013.781957

Rawls, J. (2005). *Political liberalism.* Columbia University Press.

Reichard, A., Stolzle, H., & Fox, M. H. (2011). Health disparities among adults with physical disabilities or cognitive limitations compared to individuals with no disabilities in the United States. *Disability and Health Journal, 4*(2), 59–67. https://doi.org/10.1016/j.dhjo.2010.05.003

Riddell, R. C. (2010). Poverty, disability and aid: International development cooperation. In T. Barron & J. Ncube (Eds.), *Poverty and disability.* Leonard Cheshire Disability, 26–80.

Roca, A., Haslam, D., Jolley, E., Ruddock, A., & Schmidt, E. (2020). Moving the global disability agenda forward with scarce data. *The Lancet Global Health, 8*(3), E339. https://doi.org/10.1016/S2214-109X(19)30557-1

Rotarou, E. S., & Sakellariou, D. (2017a). Inequalities in access to health care for people with disabilities in Chile: The limits of universal health coverage. *Critical Public Health, 27*(5), 604–616. https://doi.org/10.1080/09581596.2016.1275524

Rotarou, E. S., & Sakellariou, D. (2017b). Access to health care in the age of austerity: disabled people's unmet needs in Greece. *Critical Public Health, 29*(1), 48–60.

Saran, A, White, H., & Kuper, H. (2020). Evidence and gap map of studies assessing the effectiveness of interventions for people with disabilities in low-and middle-income countries. *Campbell Systematic Reviews, 16*(1), e1070. https://doi.org/10.1002/cl2.1070

Schur, L., & Adya, M. (2013). Sidelined or mainstreamed? Political participation and attitudes of people with disabilities in the United States. *Social Science Quarterly, 94*(3), 811–839. https://doi.org/10.1111/j.1540-6237.2012.00885.x

Shakespeare, T. (2020). Disability in developing countries. In N. Watson & S. Vehmas (Eds.), *Routledge handbook of disability studies* (Vol. 2, pp. 321–335). Routledge.

Shakespeare, T., & Watson, N. (2001). The social model of disability: An outdated ideology? In S. Barnartt & B. Altman (Eds.), *Exploring theories and expanding methodologies: Where we are and where we need to go* (pp. 9–28). Emerald.

Shandra, C. L. (2018). Disability as inequality: Social disparities, health disparities, and participation in daily activities. *Social Forces, 97*(1), 157–192. https://doi.org/10.1093/sf/soy031

Shandra, C. L. (2019). Disability, self-rated health, and time seeking medical care. *Disability and Health Journal, 12*(3), 394–402.

Shildrick, M. (2020). Critical disability studies: Rethinking the conventions for the age of post-modernity. In N. Watson & S. Vehmas (Eds.), *Routledge handbook of disability studies* (Vol. 2, pp. 32–45). Routledge.

Spenser, J., & the Global Burden of Disease 2017 Disease and Injury Incidence and Prevalence Collaborators. (2018). Global, regional, and national incidence, prevalence, and years lived with disability for 354 diseases and injuries for 195 countries and territories, 1990–2017: A systematic analysis for the Global Burden of Disease Study 2017. *The Lancet, 392,* 1789–1858.

Soldatic, K. (2020). Social suffering in the neoliberal age: Surplusisty and the partially disabled subject. In N. Watson & S. Vehmas (Eds.), *Routledge handbook of disability studies* (Vol. 2, pp. 237–250). Routledge.

Stucki, G. (2016). Olle Höök lectureship 2015: The World Health Organization's paradigm shift and implementation of the international classification of functioning, disability and health in rehabilitation. *Journal of Rehabilitation Medicine, 48*(6), 486–493. https://doi.org/10.2340/16501977-2109

Swain, J., & French, S. (2000). Towards an affirmation model of disability. *Disability & Society, 15*(4), 569–582. https://doi.org/10.1080/09687590050058189

Swartz, L., & Bantjes, J. (2016). Disability and global health. In S. Grech & K. Soldatic (Eds.), *Disability in the global south: The critical handbook* (pp. 21–35). Springer. https://doi.org/10.1007/978-3-319-42488-0_2

Tomlinson, M., Swartz, L., Officer, A., Chan, K. Y., Rudan, I., & Saxena, S. (2009, November 28). Research priorities for health of people with disabilities: An expert opinion exercise. *The Lancet.* https://doi.org/10.1016/S0140-6736(09)61910-3

United Nations. (2007a). Convention on the Rights of Persons with Disabilities (CRPD). https://treaties.un.org/doc/Publication/CTC/Ch_IV_15.pdf

United Nations. (2007b). Optional Protocol to the Convention on the Rights of Persons with Disabilities (OP-CRPD). https://treaties.un.org/doc/Publication/CTC/Ch_IV_15.pdf

UN General Assembly. (2002). Progress of efforts to ensure the full recognition and enjoyment of the human rights of persons with disabilities—Report of the Secretary-General [A/58/181]. https://www.un.org/development/desa/disabilities/resources/general-assembly/progress-of-efforts-to-ensure-the-full-recognition-and-enjoyment-of-the-human-rights-of-persons-with-disabilities-report-of-the-secretary-general-a58181.html

Van Rooy, G., Amadhila, E. M., Mufune, P., Swartz, L., Mannan, H., & MacLachlan, M. (2012). Perceived barriers to accessing health services among people with disabilities in rural northern Namibia. *Disability & Society, 27*(6), 761–775. https://doi.org/10.1080/09687599.2012.686877

Wass, H., Mattila, M., Rapeli, L., & Söderlund, P. (2017). Voting while ailing? The effect of voter facilitation instruments on health-related differences in turnout. *Journal of Elections, Public Opinion and Parties, 27*(4), 503–522. https://doi.org/10.1080/17457289.2017.1280500

World Health Organization. (2011). *World report on disability.* WHO Press. https://www.who.int/teams/noncommunicable-diseases/sensory-functions-disability-and-rehabilitation/world-report-on-disability

World Health Organization. (2015). *WHO global disability action plan 2014–2021: Better health for all people with disability.* WHO Press. https://apps.who.int/iris/bitstream/handle/10665/199544/9789241509619_eng.pdf;jsessionid=C90D8096C5613F3FA6F38F4C46D80224?sequence=1

Williams, S. J. (1999). Is anybody there? Critical realism, chronic illness and the disability debate. *Sociology of Health and Illness, 21*(6), 797–819. https://doi.org/10.1111/1467-9566.00184

Young, I. M. (2002). *Inclusion and democracy.* Oxford University Press.

CHAPTER 32

....

DISABILITY RIGHTS
AND CITIZENSHIP

....

BRIAN GRAN AND ANNE BRYDEN

INTRODUCTION

....

AROUND the world, people with disabilities strive to participate in and contribute to the societies in which they live. They hold leadership positions in governments, companies, and non-profit organizations. They are leading scientists and educators. People with disabilities are spouses, parents, and members of civic, religious, and social organizations. Their creativity and hard work make our world a better place. Yet people with disabilities continue to encounter barriers and obstacles to societal membership. People who have disabilities experience limitations on their rights to due process, voting, and education. They encounter barriers to exercising freedoms of speech, movement, and assembly. These persistent barriers prevent many people with disabilities from enjoying the benefits of full societal participation and deprive societies of benefiting from their contributions. These experiences can affect lives of family members, extending negative impacts across generations.

Are citizenship and human rights effective tools to overcoming these barriers and obstacles to societal membership? Here we investigate persistent barriers to social and political participation experienced by people with disabilities in spite of citizenship and human rights they possess according to national laws and international treaties. Through an appraisal of historical literature on citizenship and its conceptualization as a bundle of civil, political, and social rights that are interrelated and interdependent, this chapter examines citizenship as a foundation to the UN's notion of human rights and its contemporary application to disability-rights issues. It examines whether and how rights have become important tools to producing social change for people with disabilities. Furthermore, this chapter investigates the decoupling of disability rights, when a national government ratifies a human-rights treaty but fails to implement it at home. We ask whether rights and their use by disability-rights movements foster citizenship within the context of a human-rights model of disability, which expands the traditional focus from civil, political, and social rights to economic, participation, and cultural rights.

This chapter additionally investigates how disability rights, as forms of citizenship and human rights that belong to individuals who have disabilities, foster societal membership. Disability rights are rights that belong to individuals who have disabilities to assure their societal membership—rights that are necessary to ensure effective use of other interdependent and interrelated rights. Thus, this chapter offers a complex and nuanced approach to studying utility of rights to advancing interests of people who have disabilities. It evaluates evidence to assess whether and how people with disabilities face discrimination when it comes to social and political participation. We conclude with a discussion of new approaches to overcoming barriers that people with disabilities experience in participating in society.

DISABILITY

Disability is a complex phenomenon. According to the World Health Organization (WHO), disability is multi-faceted; it encompasses physical or cognitive impairments, activity limitations, and restrictions on participation in community life (World Health Organization, 2001). Experiences of disability vary widely due to the heterogeneity of impairments and sociodemographic factors. People living with disabilities are disadvantaged from poorer health outcomes, lower educational achievements, fewer opportunities for economic participation, higher rates of poverty, and overall increased dependency and restricted societal participation (Iezzoni, 2011; National Health Interview Survey (US) and National Center for Health Statistics (US), 2008; World Health Organization and World Bank, 2011). While disability does not discriminate, members of some social groups are more likely to experience disabilities, and those with disabilities do not experience disadvantage equally. Greater severity of disability often equals greater disadvantage. Social groups that are already vulnerable to discrimination due to race or sex are at higher risk for disability and experience additional disadvantage as a result of disability (World Health Organization and World Bank, 2011).

MODELS OF DISABILITY: TRANSFORMATION OVER TIME

Two models are commonly employed to understand experiences of disability: the medical and social models. More recently, scholars (Bryden, 2020; Degener, 2017) have employed a new model, the human-rights model, to study and comprehend disability experiences. A human-rights model of disability builds on the medical and social models of disability through inclusion of two important human-rights principles: the inherent dignity and individual autonomy of all human beings, regardless of health or body status (Degener, 2016). The human-rights model of disability acknowledges all aspects of the lived experience with disability and takes issue with the lack of responsiveness of government, business, and civil society to address socially created barriers to ensure respect for dignity and equal rights of all persons (Quinn & Degener, 2002). The human-rights model acknowledges both social and health impacts on experiences of disability and is instrumental to examining interrelationships between human rights and citizenship rights when it comes to disability experiences, including exclusion.

SOCIETAL EXCLUSION AND DISABILITY

Across all societies, people with disabilities face obstacles and barriers to full societal membership. Obstacles and barriers are exhibited in absence of social features that can enable a person with a disability to participate in and contribute to society. They range from physical structures, including the absence of ramps and elevators necessary to enter a building and its space, to lack of social resources and supports for societal engagement, to absence of laws that would enable a person with a disability to be hired to a job or admitted to an educational program.

At the heart of exclusion for people with disabilities is the social construction of disability, which is influenced by ableism and characteristics of the physical majority—those without disabilities. Specifically, people with disabilities face barriers to equal opportunities to participate in the mainstream society, excluding a significant percentage of the population. In some societies, these obstacles and barriers are based in formal laws. People with disabilities are prohibited from participating in parts of society that are components of societal membership. In many societies, children with disabilities cannot exercise their rights to public education. People with disabilities sometimes cannot pursue rights to employment and military service.

Why is societal exclusion "bad?" Predominantly, societal exclusion is bad for the *individual* who is experiencing exclusion, leading to inability to exercise talents, skills, and education. This inability can contribute to withdrawal from society in other ways, such as participation in civil society and political engagement. If such exclusion is experienced across members of a group, this group in toto may become estranged from society.

Societal exclusion also harms *societies*, from economies to science to arts to professions. Societies lose out on economic contributions of people who are excluded. Exclusion undermines scientific progress. Exclusion prevents artists from introducing new perspectives. Exclusion undermines efforts of the professions to care, protect, and advocate. Widespread disengagement of any collective group from civil society in the long term may reduce societal stability and progress (Kätz, 1987; Habermas, 1996;

Putnam, 2000; Skocpol, 2003). Of particular concern is widespread disengagement from politics that may weaken democracy in the long term.

Societal exclusion may increase the risk of weakening civil, political, social, economic, and cultural rights of persons with disability. The more people with disabilities are collectively excluded, the less able they are to participate in their societies. Exclusion can lead to less visibility, thereby producing a vicious circle of exclusion and barriers to participation.

Such exclusion is irrational from any perspective and violates the dignity and autonomy of all human beings (Quinn & Degener, 2002). By and large, however, societies have not enacted plans to reduce exclusion by improving access to structural amenities such as transportation or other public social services. All of us gain when everyone enjoys opportunities to run firms and companies, lead organizations, create and invent, teach students, perform military service, provide care and protection, and all other activities necessary to a strong society. Not to mention taxes. Societal exclusion can undermine and harm politics and civil society.

Given consequences of societal exclusion, it is critical to address the barriers to societal participation experienced by the world's largest minority, people with disabilities. Meaningful change to the experience of disability is not possible without improving access to the social and economic processes of civil society by people with disabilities (Quinn & Degener, 2002). Until then, people with disabilities will be restricted from rights to fully participate in society.

ARE RIGHTS USEFUL TO OVERCOMING SOCIETAL EXCLUSION?

According to the *Stanford Encyclopedia of Philosophy*, "[r]ights are entitlements (not) to perform certain actions, or (not) to be in certain states; or entitlements that others (not) perform certain actions or (not) be in certain states." In most contemporary societies, written laws and policies articulate rights. Constitutions often identify rights important to the country's histories and cultures. Laws, whether established constitutions or legislation or by judges, can identify liberties and freedoms as well as rights to procedures and programs, such as due process and public education. In some societies, we find rights stated in religious texts and cultural traditions, sometimes orally communicated. These traditions may articulate what rights a child has when it comes to property inheritance. Informal norms, including "unwritten rules," can incorporate rights and identify to what the rights holder is entitled. In a workplace, an employee may possess rights to first choice of working hours and other employment conditions due to seniority.

But, rights are more than entitlements and freedoms. Rights can act as glue that keeps society together. Rights can also act as instruments a person or group can deploy to isolate others, socially and from resources. Rights structure how we live together,

660 BRIAN GRAN AND ANNE BRYDEN

both formally and morally. Many societies articulate rights into their government's constitutions and legislation, incorporating rights into policies and procedures. Rights are features that allow individuals and groups to employ rules to shape an organization's behavior, including toward the rights holder. Rights can ensure access to as well as indicate societal membership.

In *The Alchemy of Race and Rights* (1995), as well as her other groundbreaking work, emerita law professor Patricia Williams has argued that rights not only are important to employ the legal system to obtain entitlements arising from rights; rights are also indicators of membership. Even if a person chooses not to exercise a specific right, such as obtaining a court hearing as part of due process rights, possessing a right to a court hearing and due process means that the individual can access the court the same as any other individual. For a person who is a member of a group historically excluded from the legal system, or from voting, or from equal public education, possessing a right and being able to use that right says that the individual "belongs." Like everyone else, as a societal member, this individual can exercise civil, political, social, and other types of rights. Rights are foundations to frameworks around which societies, including relations among societies, are organized. An invaluable framework of rights around which societies are organized is citizenship.

What Is Citizenship?

A classic conception of rights is T. H. Marshall's (1950) notion of citizenship. To Marshall, if an individual possesses citizenship, this person is a member of their society. A claim to citizenship is a claim to full societal membership (1950, p. 8). According to Marshall (1950, p. 28), "Citizenship is a status bestowed on those who are full members of a community." Marshall (1950, pp. 28–29) goes on to say, "All who possess the status [of citizenship] are equal with respect to the rights and duties with which the status is endowed." Marshall's point means that if one does not possess all three types of rights that make up citizenship, one will not be a full member of that society.

In *Citizenship and Social Class*, Marshall (1950) describes citizenship rights as a *bundle* of three types of rights: civil, political, and social. A civil right, such as a right to due process, is based in the legal system and enables an individual to employ the legal system. A political right, including the right to vote, is based in the political system and empowers an individual to use the political system. A social right is based in the welfare state and allows an individual to receive services and benefits through the welfare state.

Why would Marshall conceive of citizenship rights as a bundle? One reason is that he conceived of citizenship rights as interrelated, interdependent, and mutually supportive. Civil, political, and social rights reinforce and support one another. Without possessing all three rights, an individual cannot fully exercise all three rights. For instance, a person who has exercised her right to education can effectively exercise her right to vote. According to Marshall's thinking, if a person's social rights are strong, her civil and political rights will be based on a stronger foundation. If an individual does not possess this bundle of rights, they will not enjoy their status as a citizen and member of society.

Since Marshall published his conception of citizenship as consisting of civil, political, and social rights, experts have called for addition of other rights, including economic, participation, and cultural rights. Perhaps more fundamental is that to truly matter, citizenship rights must be instituted into national law to have meaning and consequence.

Citizenship is tied to the individual's national government. The national government is the organization that is responsible for enabling the individual to exercise her rights. This bundle of citizenship rights enables the individual to hold their national government accountable to implement rights and freedoms that are part of citizenship. Citizenship enables an individual to hold her government accountable to implementing her bundle of rights. The government is expected to set up programs and services to enable an individual to exercise her rights, such as courts, voting operations, and education. The government is expected to set up laws and policies to enable an individual to exercise her freedoms, such as speech and assembly.

We know, however, that many national governments will not and do not recognize and honor citizenship rights, particularly for members of some social groups. Marshall's conception of citizenship seems not to consider barriers to societal membership affecting some social groups. His notion minimizes inequalities that are part and parcel of many societies, inequalities that can lead to vulnerabilities of members of those social groups. Some governments persistently sidestep freedoms of speech and due process, as well as rights to vote and education. Across many countries, communities fail to assure that people with disabilities have access to voting booths and can obtain free and appropriate public education. Societies shortchange their members by failing to prevent discrimination against people with disabilities when it comes to employment, military service, and political leadership. Many governments do not allow members of some social groups to exercise their bundle of rights; in effect, these governments deny citizenship to these social groups. If implementing citizenship depends on a national government, but that national government fails to implement rights, what can be done?

Given questions surrounding citizenship generally, defining citizenship for people with disabilities is even more complex. How is citizenship articulated for people with disabilities? Presuming the dyadic relationship between rights and duties, are persons with disabilities supported in their respective societies to contribute or fulfill their duties to obtain citizenship rights? While Marshall's model provides structure through its concept of bundling of rights, the relationships between different duties and rights are less clear for people with disabilities, and have received little attention in scholarship on citizenship and disability (Sépulchre, 2017). Marshall's notion of a bundle of rights offers insights useful to studying rights of individuals with disabilities. What Marshall had in mind for the bundle is that citizenship requires all three rights (Allars, 2000; Westholm, Montero, & van Deth, 2007).

Nevertheless, some social groups, including minority groups who have experienced discrimination, isolation, and alienation, have used notions of citizenship rights to pursue social change. For an individual to exercise her citizenship rights, however, her national government must recognize and implement these rights. The reality is that many national governments fail to implement citizenship. What does an individual do when she cannot exercise her citizenship rights?

HUMAN RIGHTS

In his groundbreaking article "An Outline of a Theory of Human Rights," Bryan Turner (1993) argued that human rights are useful when a national government fails to honor citizenship rights. Everyone, all of us, is entitled to human rights because we share aspects of humanity, including frailty, according to Turner (1993). What are human rights? How do they work? Do they replace or supplement citizenship rights?

Broadly defined, human rights are "a set of protections and entitlements possessed by all members of the human community regardless of race, class, gender, sexual orientation, cultural background, national origin, or other forms of identity of social standing" (Frezzo, 2015, p. 26). They are universal principles that share a common ontology grounded in the vulnerability of the human state (Turner, 2006). That is, every person possesses these rights because they are members of humanity. Regardless of their societal membership, and whether or not their government recognizes citizenship rights, their identity, and their parents' identities, everyone possesses human rights.

Human rights are interrelated, interdependent, and indivisible. An individual's ability to exercise one right often is dependent upon exercising other rights. Like citizenship, exercising the social right to education can empower an individual to exercise her right to form a contract and her right to vote. All human rights are necessary to human dignity. A hierarchy of human rights does not exist; one human right is not more important than another human right.

We find human rights articulated in multi-lateral treaties. A trio of treaties are considered foundational to human rights and are known as the International Bill of Human Rights, consisting of the Universal Declaration of Human Rights (UDHR), adopted in 1948; the International Covenant on Civil and Political Rights (ICCPR), adopted in 1966; and the International Covenant on Economic, Social, and Cultural Rights (ICESCR), adopted in 1966 (UN General Assembly, 1948, 1966a, 1966b). The UDHR is a declaration, meaning that national governments indicate their agreement with the UDHR's principles. When a national government ratifies a covenant or convention, they are promising to incorporate the respective treaty into their national legal system. The ICCPR articulates civil and political rights, such as a right to self-determination, equality, and voting, as well as freedoms from torture, servitude, and freedoms to travel and liberty. The ICESCR states economic, social, and cultural rights, including rights to education, health, work, and social security.

Even though human rights articulated in the International Bill of Human Rights belong to everyone, treaties beyond the UDHR, ICCPR, and ICESCR have been adopted, including the Convention on the Rights of Persons with Disabilities. Why are these treaties needed? Doesn't the International Bill of Human Rights forbid discrimination? Doesn't the International Bill of Human Rights apply to everyone, including people who have disabilities? If human rights are universal, why are those treaties needed?

DISABILITY RIGHTS

If, by definition, everyone is entitled to human rights without discrimination (United Nations, 2020), why are specific disability rights necessary? There are in existence numerous human-rights instruments targeted toward realizing specific rights for specific groups. Pluralization, or recognition of specialized needs of certain groups requiring more specific protections, is seen in distinct treaties that address discrimination against racial minorities, women, children, migrant workers, indigenous people, and most recently people with disabilities (Mégret, 2008). Despite core human-rights instruments, people with disabilities have not had their full rights realized, necessitating development and adoption of the Covenant on the Rights of Persons with Disability (Harpur, 2012; Kayess & French, 2008; Mégret, 2008). Persistent marginalization of people with disabilities calls for greater attention to the needs of this social group that has only recently been included in the mainstream human-rights discourse (Lynch, 2013) and may be salient in advancing citizenship rights.

The need for specific, disability-focused, human-rights doctrine also arises from recognition that rights are interrelated and interdependent. In order for persons with disabilities to access rights associated with citizenship, they must possess and be able to exercise rights associated with their disability. Disability rights, then, are rights that belong to individuals who have disabilities, ensuring effective use of rights associated with societal membership. Collectively, this interrelation of rights is reflective of the irreducibility of the experience of disability, and is necessary for achieving the best of times for persons with disabilities.

Regarding claims to citizenship and human rights, people with disabilities seek the same or equal opportunities for societal participation, yet also seek differentiation based on their disabled status in order to have necessary supports for successful integration. However, there is irony in the assertion for societal inclusion of people with disabilities who must simultaneously rely on recognition of their "differentness" but also promote group dedifferentiation. This dilemma, as identified by Fraser (1995), stems from tension between redistribution claims and recognition claims. Recognition claims focus on cultural injustice, promote group differentiation, and affirm its value (Fraser, 1995). When social groups experience both cultural and social injustice, "they need to both claim and deny their specificity" (Fraser, 1995, p. 74).

Recognizing these tensions demonstrates that citizenship has different meanings for different social groups and across different societies (Sépulchre, 2018). Sépulchre argues that recognition claims and redistribution claims are simultaneously crucial in establishing disabled people as equal citizens (2018). This aligns, conceptually, with the human-rights model of disability. It acknowledges multifaceted experiences of disability that result from individual, physical impairments (recognition—there are differences across disability) and experiences that are socially constructed (redistribution—the environment is disabling preventing group de-differentiation for people with disabilities). These factors, together with variations in citizenship ideation, suggest an incomplete picture of citizenship rights for persons with disabilities. Fortunately, scholarship on citizenship rights and disability has increased significantly in recent years; however, the conceptual use of citizenship requires further investigation in the context of different state/regional practices and complexity of influencing social and personal situations (Sépulchre, 2017). Such investigation can include the utility of specific human rights, as articulated in the UN Convention on the Rights of Persons with Disabilities, in guiding actions that state parties should take to advance rights of its disabled citizens.

CONVENTION ON THE RIGHTS OF PERSONS WITH DISABILITIES

Adopted on December 13, 2006, the UN Convention on the Rights of Persons with Disabilities (CRPD) is the most recent UN treaty on human rights. Despite its young age, the CRPD is among the most widely ratified of the UN treaties. As of April 2021, over 180 national governments have ratified. The UN member parties that have not ratified include Bhutan, Cameroon, Lebanon, Solomon Islands, St. Lucia, Tajikistan, Tonga, the United States, and Uzbekistan. Widespread ratification of the CRPD should mean that human rights are widely accepted and available to people with disabilities across the world.

Examining the map in Figure 32.1, a zero indicates that the country's national government has ratified neither the CRPD nor its Optional Protocol. A score of one indicates that the country's national government has ratified the CRPD. A score of two means that the country's national government has ratified both the CRPD and its Optional Protocol.

The CRPD is unique in that it engaged civil society, including individuals with disabilities and Disabled Persons Organizations, previously sidelined from discussions of human rights, in treaty formation and monitoring of its implementation (Schulze, 2014). Such partnerships acknowledge the importance of rights and reflect a shared understanding of the importance of including the collective voice of people with disabilities.

The CRPD is organized similarly to other UN treaties. The Convention's preamble reminds us that all people possess inherent dignity and are members of the human family. The preamble reiterates UN principles of human rights, that they are universal, interrelated, interdependent, and indivisible (UN General Assembly, 2006).

FIGURE 32.1 Ratification of the CRPD and its Optional Protocol
0: national government has not ratified CRPD and its Optional Protocol
1: national government has ratified either CRPD or its Optional Protocol
2: national government has ratified CRPD and its Optional Protocol

Source: UN Treaty Dashboard (2021).

Article 3 states powerful and succinct principles that guide the Convention.[1] People with disabilities possess dignity and individual autonomy that empower their independence, equality, and equal opportunity, and that sustain choices they want to make. The Convention states that people with disabilities should live lives free of discrimination and enjoy opportunities to participate in society fully and effectively, with complete accessibility. These principles are neither shocking nor new. The UDHR, for instance, articulates for everyone the principles of inherent dignity, non-discrimination, and equality.

The interrelation of different rights for persons with disabilities is espoused within the CRPD. At its nexus is accessibility, articulated in Article 9, which includes not only built environments, but also access to information and services by persons with disabilities and all stakeholders. Related to accessibility is the right to independent living and being included in the community, articulated in Article 19. Living independently in the community includes one's choice of where and with whom to live, as well as having access to community-based services that foster the right to independence. Associated with accessibility and living independently is the right to personal mobility, which is defined in Article 20 to include personal choice of and access to affordable options for mobility, presumably including a wide range of mobility devices from ambulatory aids to complex rehabilitative technology such as power wheelchairs. Moreover, these rights are all interdependent on rights to education, health, habilitation, and rehabilitation. Better education leads to better health, and better health arises from access to habilitation and rehabilitation, all of which contribute positively to realizing rights that ensure dignity, personal security, choice, and autonomy.

The need for a specific convention to promote rights arises not only from persistent, historic discrimination against persons with disabilities, but also from violations of their humanity and dignity. However, if certain human rights, generally represented in other treaties and conventions, are included and conceptualized to the needs of people with disabilities, are new rights being created, or are existing rights being reformulated? Despite protections under general human-rights treaties and conventions, citizenship and human rights have been systematically denied to people with disabilities. Scholars largely have maintained that while the CRPD does not create new rights in international law, it serves as a shift in the discourse of disability rights, empowering civil society to improve realization of rights for persons with disabilities (Harpur, 2012; Mégret, 2008; Melish, 2014). The CRPD "recognizes the distinct ways that those rights are lived and experienced by persons with disabilities on a daily basis – experiences that often differ quite substantially from those of persons without disabilities" (Melish, 2014, p. 76). Consequently, the CRPD and its focus on dignity and equal human rights are guidance for expansion of citizenship rights.

Of significant importance to realizing rights and ensuring full citizenship of persons with disabilities is Article 8: awareness raising. According to the CRPD, increasing disability awareness at micro, meso, and macro levels of society will foster respect for disabled persons' rights and dignity, reduce stigma and stereotypes, and promote awareness of contributions and capabilities of people with disabilities (UN General Assembly, 2006). Greater recognition of contributions from people with disabilities in conjunction with access to supports or services that facilitate participation is an important aspect of citizenship, emphasizing a balance of rights and duties. Awareness raising is particularly salient for encouraging governments and civil society to take necessary actions to promote the rights of persons with disabilities to ensure full citizenship.

Ensuring Citizenship Rights under the CRPD

A fair question is, to what extent do human-rights treaties shape national policy? When a national government ratifies the CRPD, it is obligated to ensure realization of principles and rights contained within the treaty. *Decoupling* is when a national government ratifies a human-rights treaty, but fails to implement the treaty at home. The fact that national governments ratify the CRPD, but do not take seriously the CRPD, is a policy frustration. This frustration can undermine people's confidence in human rights and the human-rights framework. Even though national governments have ratified the CRPD, many fail to file their reports to the Committee according to the expected timeline. In turn, many national governments fail to implement the Committee's Concluding Observations as a matter of national law.

An expectation of ratification is that the national government will implement the CRPD domestically. One key step to domestic implementation is establishing a constitutional provision that establishes rights of people with disabilities in the particular country. A constitutional provision is considered significant because repealing a constitutional provision is more difficult than repealing national legislation. While a national law that establishes rights of people with disabilities in the particular country is significant, constitutional provisions are considered more powerful.

The map in Figure 32.2 reveals differences across the world in terms of implementing the CRPD domestically. The map indicates widespread adoption across the world of rights of people with disabilities as matters of law. Despite widespread implementation through constitutional provisions and national laws and legislation, national governments of several countries have not taken steps to implement the CRPD at home, including Angola, the Bahamas, Brunei, Burundi, the Central African Republic, Chad, Comoros, Cook Islands, Dominica, The Gambia, Guinea, Haiti, Iraq, Kiribati, Lebanon, Macedonia, Maldives, Mali, Mauritania, Micronesia, Moldova, Monaco, Morocco, Myanmar, Nauru, Oman, Palau, Papua New Guinea, Romania, Rwanda, Saint Lucia, Saint Vincent and the Grenadines, San Marino, Senegal, Solomon Islands, Suriname, Togo, Tonga, Trinidad and Tobago, Tunisia, United Arab Emirates, Vanuatu, and Yemen. All of these countries have ratified the CRPD, except Lebanon, Solomon Islands, and Tonga, which have taken the step of signing the CRPD. While ratifying the CRPD should be applauded, without national implementation of the Convention, ratification merely is a gesture.

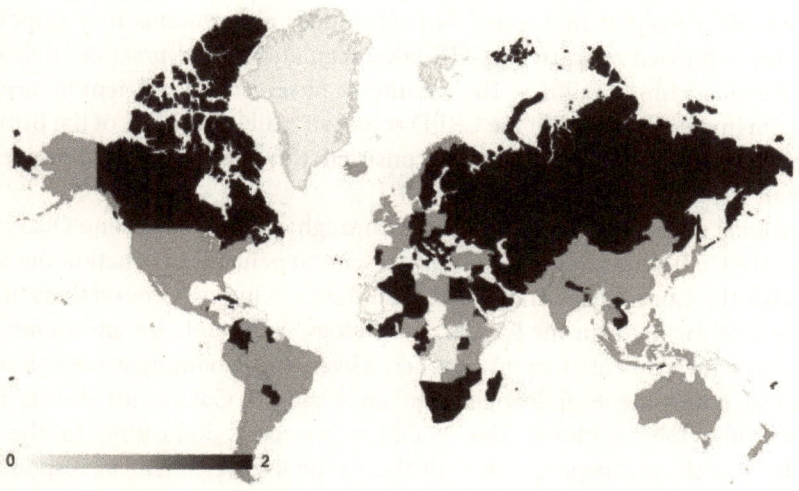

FIGURE 32.2 Incorporation of CRPD into National Constitutions and Laws
0: domestic steps not taken to implement CRPD domestically.
1: national laws or legislation domestically implementing CRPD.
2: constitutional provisions domestically implementing CRPD.

Source: UN Treaty Dashboard (2021) and Disability Rights Education and Defense Fund (2021).

While some experts consider treaty ratification to be an aspiration, national governments can pursue rights of people with disabilities without CRPD ratification. Just because a national government has failed to ratify a human-rights treaty does not mean that those rights are unavailable domestically. Countries whose national governments have not ratified the CRPD but have nevertheless have incorporated rights of people with disabilities into their constitutions are Bhutan, Botswana, Cameroon, Eritrea, Tajikistan, and Timor-Leste.

After a national government ratifies the Convention, it participates in a UN process of providing information to the treaty's Committee, then appearing before the Committee to receive feedback. Like other UN treaties, eighteen experts make up the Committee on the Rights of Persons with Disabilities. After ratifying the Convention, each national government is expected to file with the UN Committee a report on its efforts to implement the CRPD. Initially, the national government is supposed to file this report two years after ratification, then every four years with the Committee. Evidence of timely filing of reports is mixed. Albania's first report was due in 2015, which the Albanian government successfully met. China filed its first report in 2010, but rather than filing its periodic report four years later, China filed its second report in 2018. The United Kingdom filed its initial report in 2011, but has not filed a second report. Finland filed its initial report in 2019, having ratified the CRPD in 2016.

Representatives of the national government appear before the UN Committee. At the conclusion of the process, the Committee files its Concluding Observations. The Concluding Observations typically offer positive feedback to representatives of the national government, then set out changes and improvements the Committee expects of the national government. The Concluding Observations of the United Kingdom's initial report offer insights into how UN Committee's observations may respond. The Committee expressed concern that UK laws, regulations, and practices discriminate against persons with disabilities. The committee observed "insufficient incorporation and uneven implementation" of the CRPD across virtually all aspects of the British government. The Committee noted a lack of consistency in appreciation and responding to the human-rights model of disability.

If a national government does not follow through on the Concluding Observations, what can the Committee do? The Committee cannot penalize or sanction the member party. What the Committee can do is publish the Concluding Observations in the expectation that mainstream media and "watchdogs" will publicize and monitor what the national government does in practice. Given the Committee cannot penalize, do national governments follow through on what the Committee directs through its Concluding Observations? The evidence is mixed. Returning to the United Kingdom, British newspapers called on the national government to respond to the Concluding Observations. The Guardian newspaper challenged the UK government to follow through on the Concluding Observations. The Equality and Human Rights Commission, a British national human-rights institution, filed a report highlighting specific changes the UK government should make in response to the UN Concluding Observations. Since 2019, the British government has undertaken different efforts to respond to the Concluding Observations, including a cross-government approach to disability.

What can an individual do in the wake of rights decoupling? One answer is that an individual can complain about rights violations through the UN procedure called Individual Communications Procedure (sometimes called the Individual Complaints Procedure). This procedure allows an individual to file a complaint directly with the relevant UN Committee. For instance, if an individual believes one of their rights articulated in the CRPD has been violated, they can send an email to the Committee indicating what right has been violated and by what national government. Significant obstacles stand in the way of employing this process, however.

First, for each UN Committee, an optional protocol must be adopted, then ratified by the relevant country, before a person can use the procedure. The optional protocol is a distinct treaty from the relevant convention. Ratification of the CRPD is insufficient; the national government must ratify the optional protocol that establishes the Individual Communications Procedure. Second, if the UN Committee agrees that a right has been violated, it calls upon the national government to acknowledge then respond to the violation. The weak link of the Individual Communications Procedure is its reliance on the national government, which must ratify the optional protocol to the CRPD, then respond to the UN Committee when a complaint is filed. If in the first place the national government does not take seriously a person's citizenship and human rights, should we assume that the Individual Complaints Procedure will make a difference? Limited evidence indicates that the Individual Complaints Procedure can counter decoupling. For the period up to May 2014, the UN Committee found violations against Argentina, Germany, Hungary, and Sweden through the Individual Complaints Procedure. Given recent adoptions of the optional protocol, future research should assess impacts of the Individual Complaints Procedure on advancing rights and interests of people who have disabilities.

The Disability Rights Movement has taken a different approach to rights of people who have disabilities. Rather than concentrate on individual cases, the movement has organized to employ rights collectively to fight against national governments and others to advance rights of people who have disabilities.

THE DISABILITY RIGHTS MOVEMENT

One of the most famous examples of a social movement using rights to produce change is the Disability Rights Movement (DRM). The DRM offers a model of how to pursue social change that leads to international attention and efforts on rights of people who have disabilities, as well as endeavors to achieve national implementation of rights of people with disabilities. Like many social movements, we cannot pinpoint a day or location of the founding of the DRM. Indeed, the DRM is not a single movement. Through the DRM, people have come together with shared goals of improving every aspect of life for people with disabilities, from education and healthcare to employment, housing, and relationships. Emergence of DRM internationally has served as a catalyst for targeted attention to the human rights of persons with disability by the UN.

Degener and Begg (2019) describe four distinct phases of disability issues being recognized as human-rights concerns by the UN. The time period before 1970 was a time of relative invisibility of disabled persons. For the decade of 1970 to 1980, people who have disabilities were seen as objects of care and rehabilitation. For the subsequent two decades, 1980 to 2000, persons who have disabilities were perceived as objects who possess human rights. Since 2000, people who have disabilities are considered active agents of human rights (Degener & Begg, 2019). A significant part of this recent change is the emergence of DRMs as catalysts to new approaches of the United Nations. Indeed, the United Nations formed a panel of experts from disabled-persons organizations who serve as key leaders in UN policy making, rather than turning to experts who have not lived with disabilities (Degener & Begg, 2019). This forward thinking, influenced heavily by international DRMs, led to the creation of the CRPD.

The DRM (Fleischer, Zames, & Zames, 2012) consists of multiple movements across different countries. Because a single source of this information is not available, we selected two countries in each of the World Bank's regions, that is, East Asia and Pacific, Europe and Central Asia, Latin America and Caribbean, Middle East and North Africa, North America, South Asia, and Sub-Saharan Africa. We made this selection employing John Stuart Mill's methods of agreement and difference to identify two countries in each region where in one country the DRM preceded the CRPD, and in the other country the CRPD preceded the DRM (Roig-Tierno, Gonzalez-Cruz, & Llopis-Martinez, 2017, p. 16). (Table 32.1)

The DRM is found in Azerbaijan and Sweden. The Union of Disabled People Organizations (UDPO) of the Republic of Azerbaijan was founded in 2003 and registered in 2005, prior to CRPD adoption (Azerbaijan Republic, 2021). The UDPO is active in multiple ways, including filing reports with the Committee on the Rights of People with Disabilities when Azerbaijan's report is due to the Committee. In Sweden, the Swedish Disability Rights Federation is a powerful representative of the DRM. Composed of over 40 organizations, Funktionsrätt Sveriges was founded in 1942.

In East Asia and the Pacific, we compare China and South Korea. Huang (2019) discusses the work of rights activists in China. After pointing out that rights advocacy commenced in China following CRPD adoption, Huang finds that restrictions on China's civil society have led to weakening of rights advocacy for people with disabilities in China. In their stead, service-oriented disability associations have sprung up and grown. Huang (2019) argues that these organizations have promoted identity work of people with disabilities, sustaining a disability-rights consciousness. In contrast, You and Hwang (2018) find that the DRM in South Korea arose before CRPD adoption. In the last ten years, however, DRM activists have not received support from the government, let alone its sustained attention. Activists struggle to change Korea's system of welfare and services provided to people with disabilities, including residential facilities and schools set up for people with disabilities.

The union Antigua and Barbuda has ratified the CRPD but not its Optional Protocol. The national government has established a component of the national convention

Table 32.1 DRM and CRPD

Country	Region	Which came first?
China	East Asia and Pacific	CRPD
South Korea	East Asia and Pacific	DRM
Azerbaijan	Europe and Central Asia	DRM
Sweden	Europe and Central Asia	DRM
Brazil	Latin America and Caribbean	DRM
Trinidad and Tobago	Latin America and Caribbean	DRM
Egypt	Middle East and North Africa	CRPD
Tunisia	Middle East and North Africa	CRPD
Mexico	North America	DRM
Canada	North America	DRM
Bhutan	South Asia	CRPD
India	South Asia	DRM
Burkina Faso	Sub-Saharan Africa	DRM
Malawi	Sub-Saharan Africa	DRM

articulating rights of people with disabilities. Kirakosyan (2016) documents efforts of Brazil's disability-rights activist organizations to advocate for rights and resources prior to CRPD adoption. Still, Kirakosyan (2016) asserts that after ratification is when Brazil's national government made stronger commitments to rights of people with disabilities. In Trinidad and Tobago, a chapter of Disabled People's International (TT/DPI) has been established. This organization has been an active advocate and provider of services to people with disabilities for decades (D'Aubin 2003). While its history precedes the CRPD, TT/DPI remains active.

According to some reports, a young DRM is gaining traction in Egypt (El-Galil, 2016). This movement appears to have started following CRPD adoption and Egyptian ratification in 2008. One group has called on the Egyptian government to overcome decoupling of human rights of people with disabilities. "There is a vast difference between what the constitution states and what is happening on the ground," said Ghada Mohammed, chairman of Ebtessama Foundation, a non-profit association for people with disabilities. The Ebtessama Foundation was formed in 2007 and is a powerful advocate of people with disabilities, employing research and other means. In Tunisia, the DRM was unable to gain traction until a government changed. Up to 2011, the Tunisian national government was not interested in advancing rights of any social group or rights in general. Since 2011 elections, the new government has paid attention to rights. In this environment, the DRM has moved forward in Tunisia. Starting in 2012, the Tunisian Organization for the Advancement of the Rights of People with Disabilities advocated for inclusion of rights of people with disabilities in the country's constitution.

A key organization in Mexico is the Mexican Confederation of Organizations for the Person with Intellectual Disability. Formed in 1978, this organization is an umbrella of over 100 Mexican organizations that advocate for rights of and provide services to people with disabilities. Similar to Mexico, disability rights was on the minds of Canadians before the CRPD. In 1970, various groups tied to disability rights were formed. The Coalition of Provincial Organizations of the Handicapped was followed by other groups, some of which employed civil-rights strategies (Pierre, 2014).

While Bhutan has not ratified the CRPD or its Optional Protocol, it has established a constitutional provision articulating rights of people with disabilities. The Disabled Persons' Association of Bhutan (DPAB) is founded by a group of individuals with disabilities living in Bhutan. Registered in 2010, and receiving support from Bhutan's Prince Namgyel Wangchuck, the DPAB advocates for interests and rights of individuals with disabilities, including rights to participation, livelihood, and socio-political decision making. In contrast, the DRM has been active in India since the 1970s. A key actor in the DRM is the National Centre for Promotion of Employment for Disabled People (NCPEDP). The NCPEDP was registered in 1996. It seeks to promote awareness of rights of people with disabilities. It seems to move beyond charity to deploy evidence and serving as a watchdog of rights of people with disabilities.

The Fédération Burkinabè des Associations pour la Promotion des Personnes Handicapées (FEBAH) was established in Burkina Faso in 1992. On the face of it, FEBAH is very active. As a federation of organizations, FEBAH concentrates its work on community life, advocacy, training and education, research, and creation of professional unions for people with disabilities. Although FEBAH does not explicitly employ notions of rights in these efforts, among their efforts is seeking Burkina Faso's ratification of the CRPD and other human-rights treaties. A similar federation was established in 1999 in Malawi, the Federation of Disability Organizations in Malawi. As an umbrella of 12 organizations, among its objectives is "to promote and advocate for the rights of persons with disabilities" (https://www.fedoma.org/about/). In addition, the federation is a watchdog that monitors opportunities of people with disabilities according to UN standards.

Of the 14 countries, various forms and aspects of the DRM preceded ratification of the CRPD. In these countries, DRMs engaged individuals and communities as they pursued advancement of rights of people with disabilities. The CRPD preceded activities of DRMs in four of the analyzed countries. For these countries, external activities, including prominent efforts of the United Nations, seem to stimulate efforts to promote rights of people with disabilities.

The DRM has worked to ensure that national governments recognize people who have disabilities as a powerful, socio-political group whose members employ rights "to replace oppression with empowerment, and marginalization with full inclusion" (Winter, 2003, pp. 33–34). The DRM is a social movement led by people with disabilities who are self-advocating for their rights (Sabatello & Schulze, 2014). Rather than rely on political, government, and civil-society leaders, the DRM are groups of people who have come together with shared goals of improving every aspect of life for people who have disabilities.

A Big Picture

The frameworks of citizenship/human rights/disability rights, unfortunately, do include weaknesses. Citizenship rights can be useful to advancing equity and equality, reducing discrimination, and bringing about social, economic, political, and cultural changes. For citizenship to "work," however, a national government must take seriously the bundle of rights that make up citizenship. If a national government does not take citizenship seriously, an individual can turn to human rights. Yet an examination of the human-rights framework reveals reliance on national governments to implement human rights. Even an innovation in the human-rights framework, the Individual Complaints Procedure, depends on a national government's recognition and implementation of an individual's human rights. As a social movement, the DRM is a means by which people who have disabilities can organize to demand social change. The DRM has employed disability rights to change laws, policies, and socio-cultural practices to foster rights and interests of all people who have disabilities. As a social movement, the DRM is a collective group that exercises rights to argue for and achieve broad social change.

A singular focus on rights and legal reforms, however, may be less effective. Instead of strictly relying on rights, other tools and strategies may complement legal reforms to assure that people with disabilities enjoy societal membership and equality in their communities. The US Civil Rights Movement is often considered an exemplary social movement that produced significant social changes. The NAACP Legal Defense Fund used laws and rights to bring about legal change. Case by case, right by right, attorneys and others representing the NAACP Legal Defense Fund dismantled legal segregation. Decades went by, however, while cases were argued in courts. W. E. B. DuBois, a NAACP founder, argued that using the courts took too long. Courts and legislatures can be fickle, legal problems resulting in rights setbacks routinely occur, and strategies to pursue and obtain legal reforms require significant resources, including time. Strategies and efforts outside courts led to changing people's minds about inequalities and barriers to societal membership. Beliefs and opinions about race and segregation were shaped by actions and words of all participants of the Civil Rights Movement.

Perhaps rights should be used at the same time as other strategies. A clear need persists for continuing efforts to ensure human rights and citizenship rights for people with disabilities. What should contemporary DRMs look like, and how can a human-rights model of disability advance economic, social, and cultural rights along with civil and political rights? In its first 15 years, domestic incorporation of CRPD's principles has varied across nations-states. While its long-term influence remains to be seen, the CRPD's framework serves as a vehicle for disability-policy implementation (Lord & Stein, 2008). The use of human rights to guide a government's implementation of citizenship rights for people with disabilities is a strategy for achieving a broader vision that gives discourse to bundling of rights by transcending civil and political inclusion and encompassing economic, social, and cultural rights. The CRPD at this early stage has not been fully tested in its capacity to guide and influence contemporary disability-rights movements in transforming rights for persons with disabilities (Lord & Stein, 2008). As a framework, the CRPD is fluid. Hope bolsters leadership who can not only interpret, but also imagine, how stakeholders will achieve realization of citizenship rights for persons with disabilities.

WHERE DO WE GO FROM HERE?

Citizenship rights, guided by the principles of equality and dignity, are critical for overcoming societal exclusion and marginalization (Kayess & French, 2008; Sépulchre, 2018). A vital step forward in realizing citizenship for people with disabilities is *defining the meaning* of citizenship for this marginalized and excluded group, something that scholars have not fully achieved (Sépulchre, 2017). Scholars have generally defined citizenship as "passive and active membership of individuals in a nation-state with universalistic rights and obligations at a specified level of equality" (Bottomore, 1993; Janoski, 1998). Janoski and Gran (2002, p. 13) offer four main points in the definition of citizenship: determining membership and establishing personhood, active capacities to influence politics, citizenship rights are universal for all citizens, and equality—balancing rights and obligations. Each of these aspects of citizenship has relevant meaning to the experience of disability.

First, determining membership and establishing personhood is a primary objective of the CRPD and human-rights model of disability. A human-rights approach to disability, as articulated in general human-rights treaties as well as the CRPD, recognizes "the inherent dignity and worth and the equal and inalienable rights of all members of the human family"; that "everyone is entitled to all the rights and freedoms set forth therein, without distinction of any kind"; and that "the need for persons with disabilities to be guaranteed their full enjoyment without discrimination" (UN General Assembly, 2006). These principles guide expectations of states parties to extend citizenship rights to persons with disabilities. Second, active capacities to influence politics have been demonstrated through international DRMs, where persons with disabilities have advocated for their rights through legal and political processes. Continued evolution of these movements, particularly to address economic, social, and cultural rights, can further citizenship rights for persons with disabilities.

Unfortunately, citizenship rights are not yet universal for all citizens, as persons with disabilities continue to be marginalized. The third aspect of citizenship, universality of rights for people with disabilities, requires recognition of equal opportunities for participation, yet not necessarily equal experiences as compared to non-disabled citizens. Differentiation based on citizens' disabled status is necessary for successful integration. Simultaneous consideration of both recognition of disability with equality of opportunities aligns with principles of the CRPD that acknowledges the heterogeneity of all humans and recognizes inherent dignity, worth, autonomy, and equal and inalienable rights of all (UN General Assembly, 2006). Fourth, and related to universality, is the concept of equality and balancing rights and obligations. This can only happen when governments recognize capacities and contributions of people with disabilities, requiring a departure from internalized perceptions of persons with disabilities as helpless and as objects of charity. The CRPD as well as the human-rights model of disability promote awareness of capacities and contributions of persons at all levels of ability. The literature on disability and citizenship stops short of examining the mutuality of citizenship rights and obligations for people with disabilities, highlighting a need for additional research on this interrelationship, and examination of the meaning of productive citizenship beyond a narrow, neoliberal view (Sépulchre, 2017).

NOTE

1. General guiding principles: (1) respect for inherent dignity, individual autonomy including the freedom to make one's own choices, and independence of persons; (2) non-discrimination; (3) full and effective participation and inclusion in society; (4) respect for difference and acceptance of persons with disabilities as part of human diversity and humanity; (5) equality of opportunity; (6) accessibility; (7) equality between men and women; (8) respect for the evolving capacities of children with disabilities and respect for the right of children with disabilities to preserve their identities.

REFERENCES

Allars, Margaret. (2000). Citizenship rights, review rights and contractualism. *Law in Context: A Socio-Legal Journal*, 18(2), 79–111.

Azerbaijan Republic. (2021). Union of Disabled People Organizations (UDPO). *Azerbaijan Republic Union of Disabled People Organizations (UDPO)*. (http://www.udpo.az/category .php?lang=2&main=40&content=292).

Bottomore, T. (1993). Citizenship. In W. Outhwaite and T. B. Bottomore (Eds.), *The Blackwell Dictionary of Twentieth-Century Social Thought, Blackwell Reference*. Blackwell.

Bryden, Anne M. (2020). *Navigating resources after spinal cord injury: The utility of human rights*. [Doctoral diss] Case Western Reserve University.

D'Aubin, April. (2003). "'Nothing about us without us:' CCD's struggle for the recognition of a human rights approach to disability issues. In Aldred H. Neufeldt and Henry Enns (Eds.), *In pursuit of equal participation: Canada and disability at home and abroad* (pp. 111–136). Caput Press.

Degener, Theresia. (2016). Disability in a human rights context. *Laws*, 5(4), p. 35. https://doi .org/10.3390/laws5030035

Degener, Theresia. (2017). A new human rights model of Disability. In V. Della Fina, R. Cera, and G. Palmisano (Eds.), *The United Nations convention on the rights of persons with disabilities* (pp. 41–59). Springer International Publishing.

Degener, Theresia, & Begg, Andrew. (2019). Disability policy in the United Nations: The road to the Convention on the Rights of Persons with Disabilities. In T. Degener and M. von Miquel (Eds.), *Aufbrüche und Barrieren* (pp. 43–78). transcript Verlag.

Disability Rights Education and Defense Fund. (2021). International disability rights. https:// dredf.org/legal-advocacy/international-disability-rights/

El-Galil, Tarek Abd. (2016). The nascent disabled-rights movement steps out in Egypt. *Al-Fanar Media Covering Education, Research and Culture.* https://www.al-fanarmedia.org/2016/04/the-nascent-disabled-rights-movement-steps-out-in-egypt/

Fleischer, Doris Zames, & Zames, Frieda. (2012). *The disability rights movement: From charity to confrontation.* Temple University Press.

Fraser, N. (1995). From redistribution to recognition? Dilemmas of justice in a 'post-socialist' age. *New Left Review,* (212), 68–93.

Frezzo, Mark. (2015). *The sociology of human rights: An introduction.* Polity Press, Cambridge.

Habermas, Jürgen. (1996). *Between Facts and Norms: Contributions to a Discourse Theory of Law and Democracy.* Translated by William Rehg. MIT University Press.

Harpur, Paul. (2012). Embracing the new disability rights paradigm: The importance of the convention on the rights of persons with disabilities. *Disability & Society, 27*(1), pp. 1–14. https://doi.org/10.1080/09687599.2012.631794

Huang, S. (2019). Ten years of the CRPD's adoption in China: challenges and opportunities. *Disability & Society, 34*(6), 1004–1009.

Iezzoni, Lisa I. (2011). Eliminating health and health care disparities among the growing population of people with disabilities. *Health Affairs, 30*(10), 1947–1954. https://doi.org/10.1377/hlthaff.2011.0613

Janoski, Thomas. (1998). *Citizenship and civil society.* Cambridge University Press.

Janoski, Thomas, & Gran, Brian. (2002). The foundations of legal and political citizenship. In E. F. Isin and B. S. Turner (Eds.), *Handbook of citizenship studies* (pp. 13–52). SAGE Publications.

Kātz, B. M. (1987). The criticism of arms: The Frankfurt School goes to war. *The Journal of Modern History, 59*(3), 439–478.

Kayess, R., & French, P. (2008). Out of darkness into light? Introducing the convention on the rights of persons with disabilities. *Human Rights Law Review, 8*(1), 1–34. https://doi.org/10.1093/hrlr/ngm044

Kirakosyan, L. (2016). Promoting disability rights for a stronger democracy in Brazil: The role of NGOs. *Nonprofit and Voluntary Sector Quarterly, 45*(1_suppl), 114S–130S. https://doi.org/10.1177/0899764015602129.

Lord, Janet E., & Stein, Michael Ashely. (2008). The domestic incorporation of human rights law and the United Nations Convention on the Rights of Persons with Disabilities Symposium: Framing legal and human rights strategies for change: A case Study of disability rights in Asia. *Washington Law Review, 83*(4), 449–480.

Lynch, Jean. (2013). Disability and society. In D. L. Brunsma, K. E. Iyall Smith, and B. Gran (Eds.), *Handbook of sociology and human rights* (pp. 107–116). Paradigm Publishers.

Marshall, TH. (1950). *Citizenship and social class.* Cambridge at the University Press.

Mégret, Frédéric. (2008). The disabilities convention: Human rights of persons with disabilities or disability rights? *Human Rights Quarterly, 30*(2), 494–516. http://dx.doi.org/10.1353/hrq.0.0000

Melish, Tara. (2014). An eye toward effective enforcement: A technical-comparative report to the drafting negotiations. In M. Sabatello and M. Schulze (Eds.), *Human rights and disability advocacy, Pennsylvania studies in human rights* (pp. 70–96). University of Pennsylvania Press.

National Health Interview Survey (US), & National Center for Health Statistics (US) (Eds.). (2008). *Disability and health in the United States, 2001–2005.* Department of Health and Human Services, Centers for Disease Control and Prevention, National Center for Health Statistics.

Pierre, J. (2014). Disability rights. Retrieved January 2, 2022, from https://eugenicsarchive.ca/discover/encyclopedia/535eeb377095aa000000021b

Putnam, Robert. (2000). *Bowling alone: The collapse and revival of American community*. Simon & Schuster.

Quinn, Gerard, & Degener, Theresia. (2002). *Human rights and disability: The current use and future potential of United Nations human rights instruments in the context of disability*. United Nations.

Roig-Tierno, Norat, Gonzalez-Cruz, Tomas F., & Llopis-Martinez, Jordi. (2017). An overview of qualitative comparative analysis: A bibliometric analysis. *Journal of Innovation & Knowledge*, 2(1), pp. 15–23. https://dx.doi.org/10.1016/j.jik.2016.12.002

Sabatello, Maya, & Schulze, Marianne (Eds.). (2014). *Human rights and disability advocacy*. 1st ed. University of Pennsylvania Press.

Schulze, Marianne. (2014). Monitoring the convention's implementation. In M. Sabatello and M. Schulze (Eds.), *Human rights and disability advocacy, Pennsylvania studies in human rights* (pp. 209–221). University of Pennsylvania Press.

Sépulchre, Marie. (2017). Research about citizenship and disability: A scoping review. *Disability and Rehabilitation*, 39(10), 949–956. https://doi.org/10.3109/09638288.2016.1172674

Sépulchre, Marie. (2018). Tensions and unity in the struggle for citizenship: Swedish disability rights activists claim 'full participation! now!' *Disability & Society*, 33(4), 539–561. https://doi.org/10.1080/09687599.2018.1440194

Skocpol, Theda. (2003). Social provision and civic community: Beyond fragmentation. In J. Rieder (Ed.), *The fractious nation? Unity and division in contemporary American life* (pp. 187–205). University of California Press.

Turner, Bryan S. (1993). Outline of a theory of human rights. *Sociology*, 27(3), 489–512. https://doi.org/10.1177%2F0038038593027003009

Turner, Bryan S. (2006). Crimes against humanity. In *Vulnerability and human rights: essays on human rights* (pp. 1–23). Pennsylvania State University Press.

Turner, B. S. (2006). *Vulnerability and human rights*. Pennsylvania State University Press.

UN General Assembly. (1948). *The universal declaration of human rights*.

UN General Assembly. (1966a). *International covenant on civil and political rights*.

UN General Assembly. (1966b). *International covenant on economic, social and cultural rights*.

UN General Assembly. (2006). *The convention on the rights of persons with disabilities and optional protocol*.

United Nations. (2020). *Human rights*. https://www.un.org/en/sections/issues-depth/human-rights/.

Westholm, Anders, Montero, José Ramón, & van Deth, Jan W. (2007). Introduction: Citizenship, involvement, and democracy in Europe. In A. Westholm, J.R. Montero, & J.W. van Deth, (Eds.), *Citizenship and involvement in European democracies: A comparative analysis* (pp. 1–32). Routledge.

Williams, Patricia J. (1995). *The alchemy of race and rights*. Harvard University Press.

Winter, J. A. (2003). The development of the disability rights movement as a social problem solver. *Disability Studies Quarterly*, 23(1).

World Health Organization. (2001). *International classification of functioning disability and health*. World Health Organization.

World Health Organization, and World Bank (Eds.). (2011). *World report on disability*. World Health Organization.

You, D. C., & Hwang, S. K. (2018). Achievements of and challenges facing the Korean Disabled People's Movement. *Disability & Society*, 33(8), 1259–1279.

United Nations Documents

United Nations Treaty Dashboard. Accessed April 21, 2021. https://indicators.ohchr.org/

PART X

Crime and the Criminal Justice System

CHAPTER 33

....

SOCIAL CONTROL, PUNISHMENT, AND DISABILITY IN THE UNITED STATES

....

APRIL D. FERNANDES AND VICTORIA KURDYLA

WITH the rise of mass incarceration, there has been a wealth of scholarship exploring how social control intersects in the lives of those who traverse the criminal legal system, with mostly detrimental and long-lasting consequences. Of utmost interest is how the system compounds and expands existing inequalities, especially for historically marginalized and disadvantaged groups who are overrepresented within systems of control. From targeted policing and disparities in sentencing to the pains of imprisonment and the enduring scars of criminal legal contact, the system, in its varied forms and throughout time and space, has been the prevailing solution to a host of historical and contemporary social issues, borne out of economic, political, and social inequalities. Chattel slavery, Black codes, the Eugenics movement, asylums, Native American boarding schools, Jim Crow, mass criminalization, and incarceration—these institutions were designed to surveil, incapacitate, warehouse, eradicate, and punish as a means of containing populations that were perceived as progenitors and sustainers of social ills as well as challenges to social control (Davis 2005).

Exploring social control through the lens of disability provides a critical perspective on the use of criminalization and institutionalization as a means of control. The historical and contemporary marginalization of individuals with disabilities in employment, housing, health care, and social and political integration is part and parcel of their current and ongoing representation in the criminal legal system and carceral institutions (Ben-Moshe et al. 2014; Davis 2016). Therefore, the past, present, and future of social control begins with understanding the ways in which individuals with disabilities exist within and are indelibly linked to the patterns, processes, and dysfunctions of systems of control. Examining disability within the context of social-control institutions offers a unique landscape to understand the barriers, challenges, and injustices that pervade the criminal legal and carceral systems in the United States. By outlining how persons with disabilities traverse the system, we highlight the ableist ideologies that are at the heart of these systems.

This chapter details how ableism pervades the ideology, processes, outcomes, and ultimate consequences of contact with the system, contributing to a higher number of arrests, convictions, and incarceration stays for those with disabilities. These ideologies persist in every facet of contact, from the beginning of the encounter with the system during a police stop or arrest through to the process of charge and conviction and then to the point of incarceration. The reading of Miranda rights,[1] for instance, emphasizes the essentializing of ableist ideas of how information should be communicated and how comprehension occurs across populations. The court process itself is riddled with examples of how language, procedure and process, distraction, and insider knowledge, as well as the speed of proceedings, prioritize a certain type of defendant over others. The routinized carceral systems, their structured processing, and their reliance on control clash with the interactional and behavioral variances of individuals with disabilities, upsetting the semblance of control and of total containment. Ableist assumptions of proscribed reactions make the process of going through the system—and the possibility of positive outcome—riddled with difficulties, frustrations, and injustices. The overall institutional response across all contact points has been neither adaptation nor systemic reform, but rather increasingly punitive responses that further isolate, marginalize, and disadvantage individuals with disabilities.

We begin this chapter with what is often the entry point to criminal legal contact—law enforcement contact—and continue through the other systems of criminalization, control, and incapacitation, highlighting the intricacies and variation of the experience of individuals with disabilities in the context of the criminal legal system. The following sections trace the trajectory of criminal legal contact, from police interactions and court hearings to incarceration and reentry, to better understand how disability intersects with the institutions, agents, policies, and procedures of the system. We pay special attention to the ways in which disability intersects with other essential identity markers, such as age, race, gender, sexual orientation, and gender identity, within these social-control institutions to provide a more nuanced understanding of the dynamics, barriers, and inequalities that confront the growing numbers of incarcerated people with disabilities. The issues therein represent only a small fraction of the totality of the complex and varied lived experiences of incarcerated individuals with disabilities.

Disability and Police

Scholars and advocacy groups have argued for an increased focus on interactions between police and persons with disabilities due to heightened contact with law enforcement. Approximately 7–10% of police interactions involve someone with a mental illness or cognitive disability, and people with disabilities have a high cumulative probability of arrest (Vallas, 2016; McCauley, 2017). Additionally, news media analyses report that one-quarter to one-half of officer-involved shootings involved a person with a disability (Appelbaum, 2015; Fuller et al., 2015; Vallas, 2016). Media accounts detail aggressive treatment, including increased use of force, against people with disabilities, as well as their caregivers (Maqbool, 2018; Hollow, 2020). The cases of Adam Trammell and Magdiel Sanchez, among scores of others, suggest patterns of behavior and bias that endanger the health and safety of people with disabilities in their interactions with law enforcement. The police shooting of Charles Kinsey, a Black caregiver for Arnaldo Rios Soto, a man with autism, also highlights the intersection between race and disability in the use of deadly force (Hollow, 2020; Aho et al., 2017). However, scholarly research regarding disability and law enforcement remains limited, and government statistics are nonexistent (Appelbaum, 2015), leaving the topic of policing people with disabilities relatively unexplored. Existing research focuses primarily on cognitive disabilities, sensory disabilities, and mental illness (Appelbaum, 2015; Browning & Caulfield, 2011; Erevelles & Minear, 2010; Myers, 2017; Parsons & Sherwood, 2016; Pecorini, 2016; Vallas, 2016). Researchers argue that people with cognitive and sensory disabilities, and mental illness, are most likely to interact with law enforcement and most likely to face excessive use of force or unnecessary arrest.

FACTORS INCREASING POLICE CONTACT

Two factors related to heightened contact are associated with the increased police contact faced by people with disabilities: the criminalization of homelessness and the shifting role of police as first responders. Following deinstitutionalization, people with disabilities faced increasing risk of homelessness and substance use, with nearly a quarter of individuals with disabilities experiencing chronic homelessness (United States Interagency Council on Homelessness, 2018). Scholars attribute this increase to a lack of affordable, outpatient healthcare and resources for people with disabilities, combined with difficulty obtaining stable employment (Aykanian & Lee, 2016; Vallas, 2016). Homelessness increases the likelihood of police contact for people with disabilities as law enforcement is often used to control homeless populations (Amster, 2008; Aykanian & Lee, 2016; Fitzpatrick & Myrstrol, 2011).

Law enforcement is often used to control certain populations deemed "undesirable" in society, including homeless populations (Fitzpatrick & Myrstrol, 2011). Homeless individuals can symbolize disorder and poverty, threatening the notions of economic stability and aesthetic appeal and societal perceptions of public safety (Aykanian & Lee, 2016; Fitzpatrick & Myrstrol, 2011). As such, numerous laws and policies have been introduced to criminalize behaviors attributed to homeless populations, including laws banning panhandling, loitering, sleeping on the street, and public drunkenness (Aykanian & Lee, 2016). Homelessness combined with experiencing a disability makes individuals hypervisible to police, who may perceive them as a greater threat to public order and safety (Aykanian & Lee, 2016; Stuart, 2015).

In addition to the criminalization of homelessness, police serve as first responders, which heightens their contact with people with disabilities (Appelbaum, 2015; Myers, 2017; Pecorini, 2016; Vallas, 2016). Police are often first to arrive at the scene for crisis situations, such as when a person with a disability or mental illness is being perceived as a threat to themselves or others. Police may be contacted to de-escalate a situation, with the hopes of getting the person with a disability access to resources (Myers, 2017; Pecorini, 2016). Others may contact the police for fear of their own safety, hoping for protection from the person with a disability or mental illness. In each of these scenarios, police are asked to react and respond to these situations, oftentimes with little to no formal training or understanding of disability and mental health (Appelbaum, 2015; Vallas, 2016). Therefore, officers have difficulty identifying a person as having a disability, accommodating their needs, and responding appropriately, and instead increasing the tension of a situation, leading to decisions that may have detrimental impacts on people with disabilities, including the use of force.

IMPACT OF POLICE CONTACT

Police are not properly trained to identify when someone has a disability or mental illness. When they respond to a situation, they may interpret the person as being intentionally disruptive or refusing to follow orders, rather than recognizing that their approach may need to be adjusted to accommodate a person with a disability (Myers, 2017; Pecorini, 2016; Vallas, 2016). Furthermore, even when police are aware of someone's disability or mental illness, they are likely not trained to understand or provide reasonable accommodations for the disability. Instead, they rely on procedure and tactics, such as shouting orders, that could escalate behavior (Dowse, 2017). People with cognitive disabilities or mental illnesses are often viewed as exhibiting "challenging behavior" that is deemed disruptive or dangerous, and police may attempt to control this behavior through aggressive tactics (Dowse, 2017). Police are more likely to use excessive lethal and nonlethal force to restrain someone exhibiting symptoms of a cognitive disability or mental illness (Fuller et al., 2015; Myers, 2017; Pecorini, 2016; Vallas, 2016).

While exploring police interactions with people with disabilities, scholars also highlight the importance of an intersectional analysis (Erevelles & Minear, 2010; Vallas, 2016). Labels of disability have often been disproportionately attached to people of color and LGBT individuals to justify structural inequality, as well as colonization, slavery, and Eugenics (Erevelles & Minear, 2010). Perceptions of dangerousness associated with race and gender may affect police responses, with Black people with disabilities having the highest cumulative probability of arrest (McCauley, 2017). These findings confirm the importance of an intersectional approach, which highlights the multiple structural advantages that individuals of color face that increase their visibility and the likelihood of police contact (Vallas, 2016).

POLICE RESPONSE AND THE ADA

People with disabilities who have been victim to wrongful arrest and excessive use of violence have challenged this behavior in court, arguing that such police contact violates Title II of the Americans with Disabilities Act (ADA), which requires that reasonable accommodations be provided to those with disabilities (Appelbaum, 2015; Myers, 2017; Pecorini, 2016). Although the Supreme Court ruled that the ADA is applicable after arrest (Appelbaum, 2015), courts are indecisive as to whether law enforcement must make accommodations beforehand (Myers, 2017; Pecorini, 2016). This is due to an exception within the ADA for situations that pose a threat to health or safety. Law enforcement has argued that police must make split-second decisions in dangerous situations where being required to make accommodations may lead to higher rates of officer fatalities or harm (Myers, 2017; Pecorini, 2016). Although failing to provide accommodations places people with disabilities at higher risk of harm (Myers, 2017), this exception within the ADA removes accountability and responsibility for law enforcement. After arrest, the court has ruled that ADA is applicable (Myers, 2017), which can be especially important for the issuing of Miranda rights. An individual with a cognitive disability may have difficulty comprehending these rights and may waive them without fully understanding the implications (Parsons & Sherwood, 2016). Additionally, someone with hearing impairments may require the presence of an interpreter to understand these rights (Vernon & Millers, 2005).

Disability and the Courts

Similar to research on policing those with disabilities, scholars exploring disability in the courtroom often focus on mental illness and cognitive disabilities (Kois & Chauhan, 2018; Johnston, 2013; Lowder et al., 2019; Morse, 2011). Due to the frequency of law enforcement encounters for people with disabilities and the resulting higher arrest rates, people with mental illnesses or cognitive disabilities also have more contact with the court system. In response, scholars debate the merits and pitfalls of accommodations made pre-trial, during trial, and post-trial, with the research focusing on physical and sensory disabilities and the barriers to courtroom access (Morse, 2011; Olley, 2013; Tartaro et al., 2018; Pant et al., 2015; Wertlieb, 1991).

PHYSICAL AND SENSORY DISABILITY
IN THE COURTROOM

In an evaluation of New York City courtrooms, Pant et al. (2015) highlight the architectural barriers that make it difficult for individuals with physical impairments to attend trial. Although the courthouses had wheelchair-accessible entrances, as required by the ADA, many of these entrances were hard to find or had some physical barrier that blocked the pathway. Similar obstacles existed inside the courtroom, which often had doors too heavy to open, physical barriers in the walkways, and rows that could not accommodate a wheelchair. For those awaiting trial in a holding cell, there was often no accessible room to talk with a lawyer, and the route from the holding pen to the courtroom sometimes entailed a staircase and no elevator.

Scholars reporting on individuals with hearing impairments in the court system find that they face difficulties communicating with their defense attorney and understanding what was happening during their trial (Miller, 2001; Vernon & Miller, 2005; Vallas, 2016; Wertlieb, 1991). Not all states provide interpreters for trials, and some states have barriers that limit access to an interpreter. For example, some states will not provide an interpreter if not requested far enough in advance (Miller, 2001; Wertlieb, 1991). Additionally, some states may provide an interpreter for the trial, but they will not provide one during meetings with the defendant's lawyer, while other states have allowed court systems to charge the defendant for use of an interpreter (Vallas, 2016). Although an interpreter can be a useful provision, not all hearing-impaired individuals communicate through sign language (Wertlieb, 1991). For these individuals, an interpreter will not help the individual communicate with their lawyer or understand the courtroom proceedings. In these circumstances, individuals have few options, except a competency hearing.

COMPETENCY TO STAND TRIAL

For a defendant to stand trial, they must be able to understand the charges against them and the courtroom proceedings, and be able to assist counsel (Morse, 2011). When this is not possible, the defense attorney, prosecutor, judge, or jailer can request a competency hearing (Morse, 2011; Tartaro et al., 2018). Competency hearing requests are uncommon and typically do not result in a finding of incompetency. Of all cases set for trial, roughly 5% of cases involve a competency hearing, and of these, only 28% result in the defendant being found incompetent to stand trial (Tartaro et al., 2018). Competency hearings often involve a forensic evaluation by a state-appointed mental-health evaluator (Morse, 2011; Tartaro et al., 2018). Within these evaluations, holding a lower IQ increases the likelihood of an incompetency finding (Tartaro et al., 2018). When the defendant is found incompetent to stand trial, they are often committed to a forensic hospital until competence can be restored. Scholars highlight a number of problems with this process, namely that keeping someone hospitalized until competence is restored means an indefinite detention period. Some individuals may never be competent to stand trial, while others may be indefinitely held in detention without having ever been convicted of a crime (Morse, 2011). This could incentivize prosecutors to request a competency hearing, as it keeps a defendant who may be likely to make bail in custody (Tartaro et al., 2018).

The Insanity Defense

Once found competent to stand trial, one proceeds to enter a plea. Individuals with a mental illness or cognitive disability can plead not guilty by reason of insanity (NGI), suggesting that the defendant cannot be held criminally responsible for the crime of which they are accused (Kois & Chauhan, 2018). Of all felony cases, an estimated 0.3–8% of defendants raise questions of criminal responsibility (Kois & Chauhan, 2018, p. 2). When a defendant pleads NGI, they must go through a rigorous evaluation—either the M'Naugten or American Law Institute test[2]—to determine if the court should acquit (Johansen, 2015; Morse, 2011). On average, 25% who plead NGI are acquitted (Kois & Chauhan, 2018). In a study assessing factors associated with a successful NGI plea, Kois and Chauhan (2018) find that having a current diagnosis, previous mental-health treatment, and no criminal history increase the odds of an acquittal.

While an NGI plea should help prevent individuals with severe mental illnesses and cognitive disabilities from being unfairly found guilty and sentenced, scholars critique this option for similar reasons as competency hearings (Morse, 2011). Many individuals who are found NGI can be indefinitely committed to a forensic mental hospital. In addition to an NGI plea, some states allow defendants to plead Guilty but Mentally Ill (GBMI) (Johansen, 2015). Scholars criticize a GBMI option as leading to harsher sentences without any positive benefits (Morse, 2011). A GBMI verdict leads to the same punishment, but it also requires indefinite mental-health treatment during one's sentence, which makes the defendant ineligible for parole, thereby increasing the time incarcerated (Johansen, 2015).

Sentencing

After the defendant is convicted of a crime, they must face sentencing. Studies find that people with a mental illness or cognitive disability often receive longer sentences (Perlin, 2016). Additionally, though the death penalty is prohibited for persons with "mental retardation" according to *Atkins v. Virginia 2002*, people with mental illnesses and cognitive disabilities are disproportionately sentenced to death (Olley, 2013; Perlin, 2013, 2015, 2016). Perlin (2016) suggests that this disproportionality is due to prosecutors playing on fears of mental illness, but Olley (2013) argues that it could result from a lack of clear definition and measurement of cognitive disabilities making it difficult to identify those who do not have a formal diagnosis. Regardless, these findings suggest that despite court procedures meant to protect those with disabilities, people with cognitive disabilities and mental illnesses frequently face injustice in the court system. Even when people with mental illnesses do not face longer sentences than those deemed sane,

Johnston (2013) argued that a similar sentence is unfair as incarceration is experienced differently for both populations.

Disability and Incarceration

In the era of mass incarceration, with prison and jail populations rising to unprecedented levels, scholars have often focused on the impact of incapacitation on those traversing these systems of social control (Kirk & Wakefield, 2018; Travis et al., 2014)[3]. A growing body of literature highlights how disabilities, both visible and invisible, affect the landscape of imprisonment and the experiences of those within the institution. In a recent Bureau of Justice Statistics report, over 30% of state and federal prisoners and 40% of jail inmates reported at least one disability, with cognitive disabilities being most common (Bronson et al., 2015). Although the role that deinstitutionalization has had on these numbers is debated, with some finding a substantial contribution (Raphael & Stoll, 2013), while others call for a more complex recognition of these forces (Kim, 2016; Ben-Moshe, 2017), both sides agree that the historical context becomes imperative when discussing the contemporary state of mass incarceration and disability. From the almshouses and the Eugenics movement, to the push for the closure of asylums and mental-health facilities, and the criminalization and medicalization of mental illness, these historical time points offer a nuanced understanding of the ways those with disabilities have been punished, marginalized, and warehoused, and how our modern systems of formal social control mirrors these historical dynamics (Szasz, 1961; Stanley & Smith, 2011; Rafter, 1997; Ben-Moshe et al., 2014; Ben-Moshe, 2013; Metzl, 2019; Kim, 2016). The state of disability within jail and prison facilities is part and parcel of societal shapes and shifts that undergird the maintenance and persistence of social exclusion and inequalities.

Incarcerated individuals with disabilities are entitled to accommodations and equal access to programming, opportunities, and services under the Americans with Disabilities Act (ADA) (Schlanger, 2017; Maroto & Pettinicchio, 2014; Vallas, 2016). Despite these ADA provisions, the nature and timeliness of accommodations are often lacking, with widespread violations that inhibit accessibility and participation (Schlanger, 2017; Seevers, 2016). Advocates propose that individualized assessments should be done for incarcerated individuals with disabilities to truly capture the complexity of experiences and needs that exist. However, such suggestions have been met with substantial resistance from institutions that are built, operated, and maintained under the ableist assumption of a uniform collective. Investigating the complexity of how disability operates for incarcerated populations offers a unique context for discussions of disability protections and accommodations within the confines of total institutions.

The overrepresentation of people of color in carceral facilities necessitates viewing disability in jails and prisons through an intersectional lens. Both men and women of color—specifically Black men and women—are more likely to be imprisoned in jail or prison and report higher rates of disability while incarcerated (Bronson et al., 2015). Whether these impairments were created or worsened within the institution, they reflect existing social inequalities for people of color. These inequities make the everyday existence of incarceration for people of color with disabilities fundamentally distinct from their White counterparts. In addition, the role of sexual orientation and gender identity offers nuance to the involvement of marginalized individuals within the prison space. These dynamics are then further complicated when discussing the growing elderly population in jail and prison facilities, and their lived experiences in an institution ill-suited to the needs and demands of advanced age (Human Rights Watch [HRW], 2012). Both historical and contemporary inequalities pattern the reality of incarceration, the perceptions of the individual and their disabilities, and the resources that they will have to access during their incarceration.

The following section discusses how institutional confinement in both jail and prison[4] contributes to the creation of impairment and exacerbation of existing disabilities. Throughout the sections, the intersecting dynamics of race, age, gender, sexual orientation, and gender identity will highlight the spectrum of experiences of jail and prison institutions for the various populations who are enmeshed in carceral systems.

Physical Space and Disability

Individuals with disabilities face myriad difficulties in navigating the physical space and daily operational demands of carceral institutions. The design and functionality of jail and prison facilities are focused on punishment, containment, and austerity, constructed with young men in mind. Therefore, the space becomes difficult to use and traverse with all forms of disability. The narrow corridors, the lack of ramps, the organization of cells, and the extended distances between housing units and other essential services become barriers to existing within the institutions for those with mobility concerns (Wertlieb, 1991; ACLU, 2017). For individuals with physical and mobility impairments, the need for proper and functioning mobility aids becomes essential to existing within the institution, but such requests are often delayed or denied due to institutional safety concerns or equipment that is often out of date, broken, or inappropriate for the nature of the impairment (Blanck, 2016; Ware et al., 2014). These accommodation shortfalls can result in missed meals, lack of participation in programs and essential services, and the inability to circulate throughout the institution.

In addition, the building materials and design of carceral institutions maximize noise transmission, resulting in cacophonous surroundings that can trigger or exacerbate existing mental-health or behavioral impairments (Schlanger, 2017). Individuals with autism, for instance, report a worsening of symptoms due to the clashing metal on metal sounds and reverberating noise that radiate throughout prison and jail corridors. The noise levels in correctional institutions can often hinder communication efforts for those with hearing or cognitive impairments, and contribute to increased stress and anxiety (Schlanger, 2017; ACLU, 2017). Such design features were implemented to maximize the harshness of the physical space, making it as uncomfortable and unwelcoming as possible to deter individuals from returning. Consequently, and especially for those with disabilities, the institution is built and maintained to create and sustain unequal access and to heighten the difficulty of daily routines, such as sleeping, eating, bathing, and recreation.

As a result of mandatory minimums that ballooned sentence lengths to decades, the aging population in prisons has increased steadily, with the number of people aged fifty-five or older growing by 282% between 1995 and 2010 (Carson, 2014; HRW, 2012). The steady stream of parole and probation violations that pass through courts means that jail facilities are also facing an increasingly older population in their facilities, with resources and accommodations at a minimum. The growth of the elderly population has resulted in more individuals with disabilities, including mobility impairments, chronic and terminal diseases, and age-related cognitive decline (Maschi et al., 2012a, b). In addition, the physical environment of prisons is not conducive to the dexterity and mobility needs of aging individuals, raising the likelihood of injuries and falls. For individuals with dementia or Alzheimer's, carceral institutions can be a disorienting and chaotic atmosphere that can further impair their cognitive functioning, leading to further isolation and hastening of their mental decline (Maschi et al., 2012a; ACLU, 2012; HRW, 2012). In addition, older individuals can often be targets for victimization by fellow inmates, with research showing that LGBT elderly prisoners report higher rates of sexual and physical assault while incarcerated (Maschi et al., 2012a; ACLU, 2012). The acute physical and psychological needs of the elderly require accommodations beyond the resources of correctional facilities, resulting in seclusion, increased vulnerability, and mounting psychological and physical health concerns.

COGNITIVE IMPAIRMENTS AND BARRIERS TO COMMUNICATION

For individuals with cognitive impairments, the ways that jails and prisons function can pose substantial everyday challenges, but can also result in increased sanctioning due to not understanding commands from correctional officers or not responding in an institutionally acceptable fashion. Correctional officers and administration personnel do not often consider individuals with intellectual disabilities and cognitive impairments when transmitting information or giving orders or directions. The communication of information, demands, changes, and alerts in correctional institutions is often in verbal or written form, which disadvantages those with cognitive or intellectual disabilities when trying to access needed services (Schlanger, 2017).

For instance, acquiring medical, dental, or mental-health services within the institution requires a written request, which inhibits the attainment of such services for illiterate individuals or those who cannot accurately convey their needs in written form. The lack of compliance with verbal commands can result in sanctions, penalties, or extra punishments, such as denial of visitation or participation in programming or isolation in segregated housing (Seevers, 2016; HRW, 2003). Furthermore, institutional grievance procedures often require literacy and the ability to write, making it difficult for individuals with cognitive or intellectual impairments to register complaints or to document violations by correctional staff.

The predominant utilization of verbal commands makes it difficult for those who are deaf or hearing impaired to hear commands, with non-compliance subject to sanctions, isolative segregation, or even violence from correctional officers (Vallas, 2016; Nović, 2017). The barriers to communication often leave those with hearing impairments feeling withdrawn, confused, and excluded from participation in educational or vocational programs and employment opportunities. Insufficient training of correctional staff leads them to misunderstand the complexity of disability, and they thus rely on inappropriate ways of communicating with incarcerated individuals or excluding them from the conversation completely (Blanck, 2016).

Mental Health and Access to Care

Much of the existing research on disability within carceral institutions focus on mental illness and the challenges it presents and its effects on those incarcerated (Yi et al., 2017; Potter et al., 2011). In both jail and prison facilities, the number of people labeled mentally ill has grown substantially, with empirical and advocacy work focusing on both the exacerbation of existing mental illness as a result of incapacitation and the generation of mental-health concerns due to the conditions faced in jails and prisons (Binswanger et al., 2009; Schnittker et al., 2011; Travis et al., 2014). The expansion of correctional institutions has resulted in massive overcrowding and budget shortfalls, resulting in insufficient personnel and resources to provide proper rehabilitative and therapeutic services (Wilper et al., 2009). Other scholars suggest that institutions use the label of mental illness as a method of controlling and containing the incarcerated population, especially those who are perceived as "difficult" or "unruly" (Ben-Moshe et al., 2014; Hatch, 2019). For incarcerated individuals of color, the likelihood of being perceived as a "troublemaker" is increased due to the implicit bias of correctional officers and staff (Ware et al., 2014). For instance, Black women in jails and prisons report that they are considered problematic when they voice concerns about facility conditions or pushback on unsafe or unequal treatment (Chapman et al., 2014; hooks, 1989).

Within the institution, the label of mental illness results in a web of consequences, altering access to opportunities and outside contact, affecting treatment by correctional officers and other incarcerated individuals, and determining the methods to control or neutralize behavior (Metzl, 2009). In addition, the conditions within the facility, and primary and secondary stressors from incapacitation, can trigger mental health concerns and worsen existing levels of anxiety, depression, or other mental illnesses (Ware et al., 2014; World Health Organization, 2007). The "maddening" effect of carceral institutions can be especially salient for elderly individuals who are more prone to depression and isolation and age-related cognitive decline (Barry et al., 2017; Maschi et al., 2012b; HRW, 2012). Furthermore, mental-health concerns can make it more difficult for individuals to voice their concerns and needs, resulting in either isolation or punitive reactions to behavior that is deemed disobedient, and thereby a security risk.

Access to mental-health diagnosis and treatment is paramount to ensuring the well-being, safety, and security of individuals with existing and exacerbated psychological concerns. However, the nature of prison and jail facilities makes effective and sustained treatment difficult, if it is even available. While more than half of individuals in prison receive therapy, less than a quarter of jail inmates have access to such services (Wilper et al., 2009; Freudenberg, 2001). The barriers to diagnosis and treatment are varied. However, most point to the dearth of quality mental-health professionals in both jail and prison facilities and institutional restrictions that hinder therapeutic treatment (Rhodes, 2004; Ware et al., 2014). For individuals with disabilities, the intersection of mental-health concerns and other disabilities can result in the denial of treatment due to the inability to communicate the need for medical or psychological intervention (Reiter & Blair, 2015).

SOCIAL CONTROL: SOLITARY CONFINEMENT

Ample studies show that individuals with disabilities within prisons and jails are often subject to administrative segregation, or solitary confinement, at various points throughout their confinement. Individuals with disabilities are more likely to be sent to administrative segregation for violations of institutional rules and regulations or for failing to comply with the orders of correctional staff (Vallas, 2016; ACLU, 2017). Although the use of solitary confinement, especially for inmates with disabilities, is detrimental to physical and psychological health and well-being, the practice continues as a form of punishment and as an adaptation to the lack of services and spaces available (Smith, 2006; Resnik et al., 2016; Reiter & Blair, 2015; Lobel, 2015).

Generally, administrative segregation exists on a continuum between protective, adaptive, and punitive confinement. Prison officials often cite issues of individual or institutional safety when employing isolation methods for individuals with cognitive, behavioral, or psychological impairments and chronic health conditions such as HIV/AIDS (Velasquez-Potts, 2015; Gaskin, 2009). In addition, protective confinement can be used for individuals identifying as LGBT, those suspected of gang affiliation, or a host of other populations deemed to be "at risk," resulting in intersectional concerns when members of these groups have existing disability concerns (Cammett, 2009; Stanley & Smith, 2011). For transgender or gender non-conforming individuals within the institution, solitary confinement is often the only solution to biological sex-specific housing policies (Sumner & Sexton, 2016; Stanley & Smith, 2011; Cammett, 2009; McCauley & Brinkley-Rubinstein, 2017). Solitary confinement is commonly used as a containment method for individuals deemed as disruptive, combative, or disobedient, often due to cognitive, behavioral, or mental-health impairments that can induce delusions, hallucinations, or outbursts (ACLU, 2017). The lack of alternative communication methods places individuals with cognitive, hearing, and vision impairments at a disadvantage, leading to more punitive sanctions and the loss of access to needed programs and services and social stimulation.

Solitary confinement as punishment has been a hallmark of the incarceration experience; however, for those with disabilities, who are often punished as a result of their impairments, there are differential impacts that result in long-lasting and detrimental repercussions. Those subject to administrative segregation often lose access to in-prison jobs and programs and, in some states, eligibility for work-release programs (Velasquez-Potts, 2015; Bass, 2000; ACLU, 2017). Furthermore, individuals with chronic medical needs or in treatment for mental-health conditions often experience a delay or complete cessation of treatment while in solitary confinement, resulting in further deterioration of existing conditions and increased penalties for non-compliance or other behavioral infractions (ACLU, 2017; Champion, 2007). For individuals with physical impairments, solitary confinement results in the denial of accommodations, such as prosthetic limbs, hearing aids, or wheelchairs, which facilitate communication and everyday functioning (ACLU, 2017). The isolation and sensory and mobility deprivation of solitary confinement can be detrimental for individuals across the disability spectrum, culminating in physical and psychological damage (ACLU, 2017).

Existing empirical research finds stark differences in the use of solitary confinement by race, with people of color constituting nearly half of the solitary population (Resnik, 2016). The overrepresentation of people of color in solitary confinement highlights both the racial disparities inherent in incarceration and the differential responses to Blacks and Latinos in jail and prison facilities (Lantigua-Williams, 2016). Within carceral environments, Black men and women are more likely to be cited for rule violations and disciplined, with more frequent and lengthier stays in solitary (Dolovich, 2011b; Schwirtz et al., 2016). Scholars show how biases pattern interactions with people of color within correctional institutions, with staff relying on prevailing perceptions and stereotypes that cast Black people as threats (Armstrong, 2015). The intersections of race and disability compound these perceptions, resulting in more frequent and extended durations of isolative segregation. For people of color with disabilities, the consequences can be dire, ranging from physical, cognitive, and psychological consequences, and legal ramifications, such as the denial of parole or probation (Wertlieb, 1991; Resnik, 2016).

SOCIAL CONTROL: USE OF FORCE AND CHEMICAL RESTRAINT

Carceral institutions are organized around routine, with the whole day meticulously scheduled to facilitate the semblance of order and control. Individuals with disabilities, especially cognitive and behavioral impairments, often disrupt the predictable functioning of the institution, resulting in clashes with correctional officers, an increase in punitive sanctions, and the use of force (Rhodes, 2004). The social control methods utilized by corrections officers can range from mechanical restraints or straitjackets to the deployment of chemical agents or physical force (HRW, 2015). Force is authorized to protect the safety and security of the institution, mandating that any force be implemented as a last resort and not as part of punishment. However, in practice, the use of force, especially against individuals with disabilities, is common (HRW, 2015; Poole & Regoli, 1980; Dolovich, 2011a). Incarcerated individuals with disabilities are subject to greater use of force due to perceived non-compliance with requests or commands (HRW, 2003).

Implicit bias[5] contributes to how correctional officers view potential threats to the safety and security of the institution (Armstrong, 2015; Bersot & Arrigo, 2011). These biases are often triggered when interacting with an individual with a disability, influencing the decision to use force. For instance, research suggests that individuals with mental-health concerns are more likely to experience cell extractions, physical restraint, or use of force because they are viewed as violent and a threat to correctional-officer safety (Rembis, 2014). Additionally, the potential for the application of physical force is informed by the confluence of correctional-officer biases on the basis of race and disability status. Black men often encounter dual biases, with correctional officers perceiving them as "dangerous" and "violent" due to their race, gender, and disability status, which increases both the likelihood of the use and the severity of force (Castle & Martin, 2006; Mushlin & Galtz, 2009; Spivakovsky, 2014; Dunhamn et al., 2015).

On the opposite end of the spectrum is the increased authorization of psychotropic pharmaceuticals for contained populations, including those in jails and prisons, also known as "chemical restraint" (Fabris, 2011). While the use of force can often be captured through the physical evidence of injury or harm or grievances or lawsuits against correctional personnel, administering psychotropics is a silent form of social control that operates under the radar and without the same oversight as physical force (Hatch, 2019; Fabris & Aubrecht, 2014).

Psychotropic interventions are increasingly used for individuals who have not been diagnosed with a mental illness, but who pose administrative or behavioral difficulties for prison and jail staff, heightening the potential differential use for people of color, especially Black men, women, and those who are gender non-conforming. The non-therapeutic use of psychotropics and sedatives highlight the widespread use of such drugs within correctional institutions without the means to adequately and appropriately treat and accommodate those with existing mental-health conditions. The use of mechanical restraints, sedatives, or psychotropic medications and the deployment of force and chemical agents, such as pepper spray, for those with mental illnesses not only can aggravate existing symptoms, but are also counterproductive for current and future mental-health treatment (HRW, 2015).

Disability and Reentry

There is a wealth of scholarship on the collateral consequences of jail and prison stays, with scholars finding that consequences affect every facet of life from employment (Pettit & Western, 2004; Pager, 2003; Fernandes, 2020; Kirk & Wakefield, 2018; Travis et al., 2014) and housing (Geller & Curtis, 2011; Metraux & Culhane, 2006) to health (Sugie & Turney, 2017; Massoglia, 2008; Schnittker et al., 2011; Schnittker & John, 2007; Patterson, 2010) and family well-being (Comfort, 2016) and economic stability (Harris et al., 2010), decreasing the odds of a successful and sustained reentry. Disability has not been a major focus of the reentry literature, beyond discussions of mental illness as a complicating factor in obtaining employment and housing (for notable exceptions, see Petersilia, 2003; Ben-Moshe et al., 2014). Similarly, work that has investigated the intersections of demographic factors—such as race, gender, gender identity, age, and sexual orientation—with disability and criminal legal contact is at nascent stages (Ben-Moshe & Magaña, 2014; Stanley & Smith, 2011; Maschi & Dasarathy, 2019).

Viewing the process of reentry through a disability lens offers a critical perspective on the challenges and potential pitfalls faced by those who are released from jail and prison. The substantial barriers to reentry are compounded for those with existing disabilities, with these consequences having profound implications for not only reentry, but also levels of inequality and stratification. The exacerbation of existing inequalities raises the specter of continuing or renewed marginalization, either through isolation and disregard post-reentry or recirculation into the criminal justice system.

EMPLOYMENT

Substantial barriers to employment exist for those with any form of a criminal record (Pager, 2003; Apel & Sweeten, 2010; Fernandes, 2020) and those who have existing mental, physical, and developmental disabilities (Maroto & Pettinicchio, 2014; Richardson & Flower, 2014; Darakai et al., 2017; Feist-Price, Lavergne, & Davis, 2014). When these two factors are intertwined, the path to gainful employment becomes fraught with pitfalls related to the stigma that results from these two status categories. For individuals of color, especially Black men and women, with disabilities and criminal records, the path to a sustainable income source is further obscured due to the existing racial discrimination faced in the labor market (Pager, Bonikowski, & Western, 2009). In a similar vein, the existing employment barriers women face thereby complicate the reentry process, with the demand of childcare responsibilities as well as higher rates of being labeled as mentally ill inhibiting stable and flexible employment (Richardson & Flower, 2014). For men, the ability to obtain employment can be predicated on the type of offense and the nature of their disability. Some employers are less likely to offer a job to those with violent or sexual criminal convictions, while others, such as those in the construction industry, may be more willing to overlook the record but the disability becomes a disqualifying factor (Richardson & Flower, 2014). For the aging population with existing disabilities, the barriers to employment are substantial and can result in greater economic and social disadvantage (Williams & Abraldes, 2007; Maschi et al., 2016). The stigma of disability looms over the employment process, with or without a criminal record, with historical inequalities in terms of educational attainment, work history, and perceived assessments of performance linked to lower rates of labor-force participation.

With decreasing prospects for a stable income, individuals with disabilities are not able to manage the costs of staying out of jail or prison. In many jurisdictions, the alternatives to incarceration come with a substantial cost; probation, drug treatment, and electronic home monitoring are all subject to monthly costs that must be borne by the individual (Ruhland, 2019). In addition, these systems are organized for individuals without disabilities, and the training and programming does not offer viable solutions to address the difficulties that individuals with disabilities encounter when applying for, obtaining, and maintaining employment. Furthermore, the monetary sanctions that result from contact with the criminal legal system often create a barrier to successful reentry, forcing the returning individual to choose between medication, food, and other essentials or risk being reincarcerated (Harris, 2016). These sanctions, specifically the fines, fees, costs, and surcharges result from any level of criminal legal contact, from an infraction and misdemeanor to a felony (Harris et al., 2010). For individuals with a disability, the complexity of navigating the court system, matched with the generally chaotic nature of proceedings, can result in difficulty understanding the nature of these charges and the implications for non-payment, which range from debt collection and wage garnishment to reincarceration for failure to pay (Harris, 2016). Without stable income due to the barriers to employment for reentering individuals with a disability, making payments becomes a difficulty, leaving them subject to further indebtedness and economic disadvantage.

HOUSING

The existing work on the consequences of incarceration suggest that a criminal record, whether a misdemeanor or felony conviction, can result in widening residential instability and higher rates of homelessness after release (Geller & Curtis, 2011; Metraux & Culhane, 2006; Petersilia, 2003). The extant criminal record worsens the already established difficulties that individuals with disabilities face in finding secure and affordable housing (Vallas, 2016). With the expanded use of criminal-background checks by potential landlords, the barriers increase exponentially. Therefore, post-release, a substantial portion of individuals with disabilities rely on homeless shelters as their primary source of housing (Vallas, 2016; Ellem, 2012). Due to the "One Strike Policy," a criminal conviction can bar individuals with disabilities from accessing public-housing assistance

(Vallas & Dietrich, 2014). Without access to public housing, individuals with disabilities can often find the process of securing suitable housing with the proper accommodations increasingly difficult (Fontaine, 2013). Existing difficulties in obtaining housing for individuals of color (Pager & Shepherd, 2008), the elderly (Maschi et al., 2016), and members of the LGBT community (Cammett, 2009) can complicate the process of securing housing after release from jail and prison for those with disabilities. In addition, there is an interplay between employment and housing, with decreased labor-force participation making it difficult, if not impossible, to afford rent, utilities, and other housing expenses, and lack of an address depressing the likelihood of obtaining employment.

Health Care

Increasingly, existing scholarship has shown that a prison stay creates physical- and mental-health concerns and exacerbates existing illnesses and impairments (Binswanger et al., 2009; Potter et al., 2011; Wilper et al., 2009; Massoglia, 2008; Schnittker et al., 2011), with recent work finding that even short-term detention in jail can be detrimental to health outcomes (Sugie & Turney, 2017). Incarceration often compounds existing health disparities that exist, especially in socially and economically marginalized communities (Dumont et al., 2013; Housel & Harvey, 2014). For individuals with disabilities, it is not only the access to care once released from the facility, but also the consistency of care to appropriately manage their medical and mental needs.

The reentry process underscores myriad barriers that exist to accessing culturally appropriate care for people of color, the elderly, and members of the LGBT community. For LGBT and gender non-conforming individuals with a disability, it is often difficult to access appropriate care and treatment that do not further marginalize their identity or minimize their medical and mental-health concerns (Housel & Harvey, 2014; Williams & Jackson, 2005; Matthew, 2015). Often, those who have been released from custody report a delay in having their public-health or disability benefits reinstated, which then results in a break in treatment and medication, and the potential worsening of existing illnesses and impairments (Seevers, 2016; Rembis, 2014). The complexity of barriers to a successful reentry, especially for individuals with disabilities, underscores the weight of consequences that arise from criminal legal contact and the dearth of programs, services, and accommodations in place to ameliorate these detrimental effects.

Conclusion

This chapter maps out myriad ways social-control institutions—from law enforcement and the courts to jail and prison systems—exacerbate existing disabilities, while also creating new injuries, illnesses, and diagnoses as a result of traversing the system. We provide a broad understanding of the ways in which disability shapes and complicates reentry processes for those released, often resulting in increased levels of inequality and social stratification. We present the broad strokes of dynamics that have their roots in historical legacies of oppression, alienation, and confinement for individuals with disabilities. In addition, we highlight the intersections between race, age, gender, sexual orientation, and gender identity to capture the interlocking forms of exclusion and marginalization that result from contact with the criminal legal system.

Within the framework of social-control institutions, disability represents disruption of and resistance to the status quo. The reaction from agents of control is often tighter strictures that seek to regain the semblance of dominance that is essential to the power and authority of the institution. The goal then becomes containment rather than treatment, leading to the use of force and profligate administering of powerful medications to keep order and maintain control. If incapacitation is both the overriding goal of these institutions and the penultimate marker of their success, the impetus to change institutional form, function, and practice to accommodate and adapt to the interlocking and complex web of needs of individuals with disabilities is thereby diminished, resulting in institutions locked into patterns of operation that further exclude, marginalize, and stratify. As a result, the reentry process for individuals with disabilities, who face many challenges both inside and outside carceral institutions, is hindered, increasing the potential for continued criminal legal contact.

Notes

1. Miranda rights refer to the Miranda warning, which is a constitutional requirement (*Miranda v. Arizona*) that mandates that a person cannot be questioned by police in the context of a custodial interrogation until they are made aware of the right to remain silent, the right to consult with an attorney and have the attorney present during questioning, and the right to being appointed an attorney if they cannot afford representation.
2. For the M'Naughten test, the defendant must be found to have lack of capacity to distinguish right from wrong at the time of the crime. The American Law Institute test requires the defendant prove they lack cognitive capacity to conform to the law.
3. Scholars, advocates, and activists rightly note that institutionalization and incarceration should include mental-health institutions in addition to prisons and jails, and that the focus solely on carceral institutions limits our understanding of the broader forces that contribute to the growth of these systems and the consequences for individuals with disabilities. Chapman, Carey, and Ben-Moshe (2014) and Ben-Moshe (2017) point out that when taking institutionalization into account, the rise in incarceration in all forms would have begun in the mid-1950s, thereby extending the arc of targeted mass incarceration. We fully agree on this point and the need to include mental-health institutions in future scholarship on incarceration. This section will focus narrowly on carceral institutions due to the availability of scholarship on broader systems of incarceration and control (for notable exceptions, see Ben-Moshe, Chapman, & Carey, 2014; Stanley & Smith, 2011).

4. In the United States, jails generally refer to county or city-level institutions that detain those awaiting trial or adjudication as well as those serving misdemeanor conviction sentences of less than one year. Prison refers to carceral institutions that detain those convicted of felony offenses, ranging from over one year to a life or capital sentence.

5. Implicit bias refers to discriminatory biases based on implicit or unconscious attitudes or implicit stereotypes (Greenwald & Krieger, 2006). This term has been used extensively in scholarship that attempts to analyze the use of force incidents between police and communities of color. However, emerging work has begun to explore how the implicit bias of officers could lead to the escalation of interactions with people with disabilities.

REFERENCES

Aho, T., L. Ben-Moshe, and L. J. Hilton. 2017. "Mad Futures: Affect/Theory/Violence." *American Quarterly 69* (2), 291–302. DOI: 10.1353/aq.2017.0023

American Civil Liberties Union (ACLU). 2012. "At America's Expense: The Mass Incarceration of the Elderly." New York: American Civil Liberties Union report. Retrieved from https://www.aclu.org/sites/default/files/field_document/elderlyprisonreport_20120613_1

American Civil Liberties Union (ACLU). 2017. "Caged In: Solitary Confinement's Devastating Harm on Prisoners with Physical Disabilities." New York: American Civil Liberties Union report. Retrieved from https://www.aclu.org/report/caged-devastating-harms-solitary-confinement-prisoners-physical-disabilities

Amster R. 2008. *Lost in Space: The Criminalization, Globalization, and Urban Ecology of Homelessness*. El Paso, TX: LFB Scholarly Publishing.

Apel, R., and G. Sweeten. 2010. "The Impact of Incarceration on Employment during the Transition to Adulthood." *Social Problems 57* (3), 448–79. https://doi.org/10.1525/sp.2010.57.3.448

Armstrong, A. C. 2015. "Race, Prison Discipline, and the Law." *UC Irvine L. Rev. 5*, 759. https://scholarship.law.uci.edu/ucilr/vol5/iss4/5

Aykanian, A., and W. Lee. 2016. "Social Work's Role in Ending the Criminalization of Homelessness: Opportunities for Action." *Social Work 61* (2), 183–85. https://doi.org/10.1093/sw/sww011

Appelbaum, P. S. 2015. "Can the Americans With Disabilities Act Reduce the Death Toll from Police Encounters with Persons with Mental Illness?" *Psychiatric Services 66* (10), 1012–14. https://doi.org/10.1176/appi.ps.661005

Barry, L. C., D. B. Wakefield, R. L. Trestman, and Y. Conwell. 2017. "Disability in Prison Activities of Daily Living and Likelihood of Depression and Suicidal Ideation in Older Prisoners." *International Journal of Geriatric Psychiatry 32* (10), 1141–49. https://doi.org/10.1002/gps.4578

Bass, E. 2000. "Separate But Equal? Weighting the Pros and Cons of Quarantine." Pp. 156–76 in *HIV Plus*, vol. 6, published December 1999–January 2000. Los Angeles: Here Publishing.

Ben-Moshe, L. 2013. "Disabling Incarceration: Connecting Disability to Divergent Confinements in the USA." *Critical Sociology 39* (3), 385–403. https://doi.org/10.1177%2Fo896920511430864

Ben-Moshe, L. 2017. "Why Prisons Are Not 'The New Asylums.'" *Punishment & Society 19* (3), 272–89. https://doi.org/10.1177%2F1462474517704852

Ben-Moshe, L., C. Chapman., and A.C. Carey. (Eds.). (2014). P. 83 in *Disability Incarcerated: Imprisonment and Disability in the United States and Canada*. New York: Palgrave Macmillan.

Ben-Moshe, L., and S. Magaña. 2014. "An Introduction to Race, Gender, and Disability: Intersectionality, Disability Studies, and Families of Color." *Women, Gender, and Families of Color 2* (2), 105–14. https://doi.org/10.5406/womgenfamcol.2.2.0105

Bersot, H. Y., and B. A. Arrigo. 2011. "The Ethics of Mechanical Restraints in Prisons and Jails: A Preliminary Inquiry from Psychological Jurisprudence." *Journal of Forensic Psychology Practice 11* (2–3), 232–64. https://doi.org/10.1080/15228932.2011.537585

Binswanger, I. A., P. M. Krueger, and J. F. Steiner. 2009. "Prevalence of Chronic Medical Conditions among Jail and Prison Inmates in the USA Compared with the General Population." *Journal of Epidemiology and Community Health 63* (11), 912–19.https://doi.org/10.1136/jech.2009.090662

Blanck, P. 2016. "Disability in Prison." *Southern California Interdisciplinary Law Journal 26* , 309. https://bbi.syr.edu/wp-content/uploads/application/pdf/bio/2017-blanck-disbaility-prison.pdf

Bronson, J., L. M. Maruschak, and M. Berzofsky. 2015. "Disabilities among Prison and Jail Inmates, 2011–12." *US Department of Justice Bureau of Justice Statistics*. Washington, D.C.

Browning, A., and L. Caulfield. 2011. "The Prevalence of Treating People with Asperger's Syndrome in the Criminal Justice System." *Criminology & Criminal Justice 11* (2), 165–80. https://doi.org/10.1177%2F1748895811398455

Cammett, A. 2009. "Queer Lockdown: Coming to Terms with the Ongoing Criminalization of LGBTQ Communities." *The Scholar and Feminist Online, Barnard Center for Research on Women 7* (3), 1–30. http://scholars.law.unlv.edu/facpub/613

Carson, A. 2014. "Aging of the State Prison Population, 1993–2013." Washington, DC: Bureau of Justice Statistics. Retrieved from https://www.bjs.gov/content/pub/pdf/aspp9313.pdf

Castle, T. L., and J. S. Martin. 2006. "Occupational Hazard: Predictors of Stress among Jail Correctional Officers." *American Journal of Criminal Justice 31* (1), 65–80. https://doi.org/10.1007/BF02885685

Champion, M. K. 2007. "Commentary: Seclusion and Restraint in Corrections—A Time for Change." *Journal of the American Academy of Psychiatry and the Law Online 35* (4), 426–30. https://pdfs.semanticscholar.org/21f4/e7218980ee967e89d8c95fdacf03391deb69.pdf

Chapman, C., A. C. Carey, and L. Ben-Moshe. 2014. "Reconsidering Confinement: Interlocking Locations and Logics of Incarceration." Pp. 3–24 in *Disability Incarcerated*. New York: Palgrave Macmillan.

Comfort, M. 2016. "'A Twenty-Hour-a-Day Job' The Impact of Frequent Low-Level Criminal Justice Involvement on Family Life." *The ANNALS of the American Academy of Political and Social Science 665* (1), 63–79. https://doi.org/10.1177%2F0002716215625038

Darakai, A., A. Day, and J. Graffam. 2017. "Public Attitudes towards the Employment of Ex-offenders with a Disability." *Journal of Intellectual Disabilities and Offending Behaviour 8* (1), 3–12. https://doi.org/10.1108/JIDOB-11-2016-0021

Davis, A. 2005. *Abolition Democracy: Beyond Empire, Prisons, and Torture*. New York: Seven Stories Press.

Davis, L. J. 2016. *The Disability Studies Reader*. New York: Routledge.

Dolovich, S. 2011a. "Exclusion and Control in the Carceral State." *Berkeley J. Crim. L. 16*, 259. https://escholarship.org/uc/item/3sg29439

Dolovich, S. 2011b. "Strategic Segregation in the Modern Prison." *Am. Crim. L. Rev. 48*, 1. https://escholarship.org/uc/item/5tt422r2

Dowse, L. 2017. "Disruptive, Dangerous and Disturbing: The 'Challenge' of Behaviour in the Construction of Normalcy and Vulnerability." *Continuum: Journal of Media and Cultural Studies 31* (3), 447–57. http://dx.doi.org/10.1080/10304312.2016.1275148

Dumont, D. M., S. A. Allen, B. W. Brockmann, N. E. Alexander, and J. D. Rich. 2013. "Incarceration, Community Health, and Racial Disparities." *Journal of Health Care for the Poor and Underserved 24* (1), 78–88. https://doi.org/10.1353/hpu.2013.0000

Dunhamn, J., J. Harris, S. Jarrett, L. Moore, A. Nishida, M. Price, and S. Schalk. 2015. "Developing and Reflecting on a Black Disability Studies Pedagogy: Work from the National Black Disability Coalition." *Disability Studies Quarterly 35* (2), 1–18. http://dx.doi.org/10.18061/dsq.v35i2.4637

Ellem, K. 2012. "Experiences of Leaving Prison for People with Intellectual Disability." *Journal of Intellectual Disabilities and Offending Behaviour 3* (3), 127–38.https://doi.org/10.1108/20420921211305873

Erevelles, N., and A. Minear. 2010. "Unspeakable Offenses: Untangling Race and Disability Discourses of Intersectionality." *Journal of Literary & Cultural Disability Studies 3* (2), 127–46.https://doi.org/10.3828/jlcds.2010.11

Fabris, E. 2011. *Tranquil Prisons: Chemical Incarceration under Community Treatment Orders.* Toronto: University of Toronto Press.

Fabris, E., and K. Aubrecht. 2014. "Chemical Constraint: Experiences of Psychiatric Coercion, Restraint, and Detention as Carceratory Techniques." Pp. 185–99 in *Disability Incarcerated*, edited by Ben-Moshe, Chapman and Carey. New York: Palgrave Macmillan.

Feist-Price, S., L. Lavergne, and M. Davis. 2014. "Disability, Race and Ex-offender Status: The Tri-vector Challenge to Employment." *Journal of Applied Rehabilitation Counseling 45* (4), 25–34. doi: 10.1891/0047-2220.45.4.25

Fernandes, A. D. 2020. "On the Job or in the Joint: Criminal Justice Contact and Employment Outcomes." *Crime & Delinquency 12* , 1678–702. https://doi.org/10.1177%2F0011128719901112

Fitzpatrick K. M., and B. Myrstol. 2011. "The Jailing of America's Homeless: Evaluating the Rabble Management Thesis." *Crime & Delinquency 572* , 271–97. https://doi.org/10.1177%2F0011128708322941

Fontaine, J. 2013. "The Role of Supportive Housing in Successful Reentry Outcomes for Disabled Prisoners." *Cityscape 15* (3), 53–76. https://www.jstor.org/stable/10.2307/26326831

Freudenberg, N. 2001. "Jails, Prisons, and the Health of Urban Populations: A Review of the Impact of the Correctional System on Community Health." *Journal of Urban Health 78* (2), 214–35. https://doi.org/10.1093/jurban/78.2.214

Fuller, D. A., H. R. Lamb, M. Biasotti, and J. Snook. 2015. "Overlooked in the Undercounted: The Role of Mental Illness in Fatal Law Enforcement Encounters." Arlington, VA: The Treatment Advocacy Center.

Gaskin, E. H. 2009. *A Prison within a Prison: Segregation of HIV Positive Inmates and Double Stigma* [unpublished master's thesis, Georgia State University]. Retrieved from http://www.antoniocasella.eu/archila/Gaskin_2009.pdf

Geller, A., and M. A. Curtis. 2011. "A Sort of Homecoming: Incarceration and the Housing Security of Urban Men." *Social Science Research 40* (4), 1196–1213. https://doi.org/10.1016/j.ssresearch.2011.03.008

Greenwald, A. G., and L. H. Krieger. 2006. "Implicit Bias: Scientific Foundations." *California Law Review 94* (4), 945–67.

Harris, A. 2016. *A Pound of Flesh: Monetary Sanctions as Punishment for the Poor*. Manhattan, NY: Russell Sage Foundation.

Harris, A., H. Evans, and K. Beckett. 2010. "Drawing Blood from Stones: Legal Debt and Social Inequality in the Contemporary United States." *American Journal of Sociology 115* (6), 1753–99. https://www.jstor.org/stable/10.1086/651940

Housel, T. H., and V. L. Harvey. 2014. "An Introduction to the Loosely Knit Patchwork of LGBT Health Care." Pp. 3–8 in *Health Care Disparities and the LGBT Population*. Lanham, MD: Lexington Books.

Hatch, A. R. 2019. *Silent Cells: The Secret Drugging of Captive America*. Minneapolis: University of Minnesota Press.

Hollow, M. 2020. "When the Police Stop a Teenager with Special Needs." *The New York Times*. https://www.nytimes.com/2020/02/27/well/family/autism-special-needs-police.html

hooks, b. 1989. *Talking Back: Thinking Feminist, Thinking Black*. Boston, MA: South End Press.

Human Rights Watch (HRW). 2003. *Ill-Equipped: U.S. Prisoners and Offenders with Mental Illness*. New York: Human Rights Watch Report. Retrieved from https://www.hrw.org/repo rts/2003/usa1003/

Human Rights Watch (HRW). 2012. *Old Behind Bars: The Aging Prison Population in the United States*. New York: Human Rights Watch report. Retrieved from https://www.hrw.org/report/2012/01/27/old-behind-bars/aging-prison-population-united-states

Human Rights Watch (HRW). 2015. *Callous and Cruel: Use of Force against Inmates with Mental Disabilities in US Jails and Prisons*. New York: Human Rights Watch Report. Retrieved from https://www.hrw.org/report/2015/05/12/callous-and-cruel/use-force-against-inmates-men tal-disabilities-us-jails-and

Kim, D. Y. 2016. "Psychiatric Deinstitutionalization and Prison Population Growth: A Critical Literature Review and Its Implications. *Criminal Justice Policy Review 27* (1), 3–21. https://doi.org/10.1177%2F0887403414547043

Kirk, D. S., and S. Wakefield. 2018. "Collateral Consequences of Punishment: A Critical Review and Path Forward." *Annual Review of Criminology 1* (1), 171–94. https://doi.org/10.1146/annu rev-criminol-032317-092045

Kois, L. E., and P. Chauhan. 2018. "Criminal Responsibility: Meta-analysis and Study Space." *Behavioral Science Law 36* , 276–302. https://doi.org/10.1002/bsl.2343

Johansen, L. G. 2015. "Guilty but Mentally Ill: The Ethical Dilemma of Mental Illness as a Tool of the Prosecution." *Alaska Law Review 32* (1), 1–29. https://scholarship.law.duke.edu/cgi/viewcontent.cgi?article=1489&context=alr

Johnston, E. L. (2013). "Vulnerability and Just Desert: A Theory of Sentencing and Mental Illness." *The Journal of Criminal Law and Criminology 103* (1), 147–229. doi: 0091-4169/13/10301-0147

Lantigua-Williams, J. 2016. "The Link Between Race and Solitary Confinement." *The Atlantic* (December 5). Retrieved from https://www.theatlantic.com/politics/archive/2016/12/race -solitary-confinement/509456/

Lobel, J. 2015. "The Liman Report and Alternatives to Prolonged Solitary Confinement." *Yale LJF 125* , 238. https://www.yalelawjournal.org/pdf/Lobel_PDF_ojfp32mm.pdf

Lowder, E. M., B. R. Ray, and J. A. Gruenewald. 2019. "Criminal Justice Professionals' Attitudes towards Mental Illness and Substance Use." *Community Mental Health Journal 55*, 428–39.https://doi.org/10.1007/s10597-019-00370-3

Maqbool, A. 2018. "Don't Shoot, I'm Disabled." *BBC News*. https://www.bbc.com/news/stories
-45739335

Maroto, M., and D. Pettinicchio. 2014. "The Limitations of Disability Antidiscrimination
Legislation: Policymaking and the Economic Well-being of People with Disabilities." *Law
and Policy 36* (4), 370–407. https://doi.org/10.1111/lapo.12024

Maschi, T., J. Kwak, E. Ko, and M. B. Morrissey. 2012a. "Forget Me Not: Dementia in Prison."
The Gerontologist 52 (4), 441–51. https://doi.org/10.1093/geront/gnr131

Maschi, T., S. L. Sutfin, and B. O'Connell. 2012b. "Aging, Mental Health, and the Criminal
Justice System: A Content Analysis of the Literature." *Journal of Forensic Social Work 2* (2–3),
162–85.http://dx.doi.org/10.1080/1936928X.2012.750254

Maschi, T., J. Rees, and E. Klein. 2016. "'Coming Out' of Prison: An Exploratory Study of LGBT
Elders in the Criminal Justice System." *Journal of Homosexuality 63* (9), 1277–95. https://doi
.org/10.1080/00918369.2016.1194093

Maschi, T., and D. Dasarathy. 2019. "Aging with Mental Disorders in the Criminal Justice System:
A Content Analysis of the Empirical Literature. *International Journal of Offender Therapy and
Comparative Criminology 63* (12), 2103–37. https://doi.org/10.1177%2F0306624X19843885

Massoglia, M. 2008. "Incarceration, Health, and Racial Disparities in Health." *Law and Society
Review 42* (2), 275–306.https://doi.org/10.1111/j.1540-5893.2008.00342.x

Matthew, D. 2015. *Just Medicine: A Cure for Racial Inequality in American Health Care*. New
York: New York University Press. www.jstor.org/stable/j.ctt15zc6c8

McCauley, E. J. 2017. "The Cumulative Probability of Arrest by Age 28 Years in the United States
by Disability Status, Race/Ethnicity, and Gender. *American Journal of Public Health 107* (12),
1977–2014. https://doi.org/10.2105/AJPH.2017.304095

McCauley, E., and L. Brinkley-Rubinstein. 2017. "Institutionalization and Incarceration
of LGBT Individuals." Pp. 149–61 in *Trauma, Resilience, and Health Promotion in LGBT
Patients*. New York, NY: Springer, Cham.

Metraux, Stephen, and Dennis P. Culhane. 2006. "Recent Incarceration History among a
Sheltered Homeless Population." *Crime & Delinquency 52* (3), 504–17. https://doi.org/
10.1177%2F0011128705283565

Metzl, J. 2009. *The Protest Psychosis: How Schizophrenia Became a Black Disease*. Boston:
Beacon Press.

Miller, K. R. 2001. "Access to Sign Language Interpreters in the Criminal Justice System."
American Annals of the Deaf 146 (4), 328–30. https://doi.org/10.1353/aad.2012.0188

Miranda v. Arizona, 384 US 436. 1966. 86 S. Ct. 1602, 16 L. Ed. 2d 694.

Morse, S. J. 2011. "Mental Disorder and Criminal Law." *The Journal of Criminal Law and
Criminology 101* (3), 885–968. doi: 0091-4169/11/10103-0885

Mushlin, M. B., and N. R. Galtz. 2009. "Getting Real about Race and Prisoner Rights." *Fordham
Urb. LJ 36* , 27. http://digitalcommons.pace.edu/lawfaculty/549/

Myers, C. A. 2017. "Police Violence against People with Mental Disabilities: The Immutable
Duty under the ADA to Reasonably Accommodate during Arrest." *Vanderbilt Law Review
70* (4), 1393–1426. https://scholarship.law.vanderbilt.edu/vlr/vol70/iss4/6

Nović, S. (2017). "The Right to Remain Silent." *The New Inquiry*, published March 13, 2017.
https://thenewinquiry.com/the-right-to-remain-silent/

Olley, J. G. 2013. "Definition of Intellectual Disability in Criminal Court Cases." *Intellectual and
Developmental Disabilities 51* (2), 117–21. https://doi.org/10.1352/1934-9556-51.2.117

Pager, D. 2003. "The Mark of a Criminal Record." *American Journal of Sociology 108* (5), 937–75.
http://dx.doi.org/10.1086/374403

Pager, D., B. Bonikowski, and B. Western. 2009. "Discrimination in a Low-Wage Labor Market: A Field Experiment." *American Sociological Review 74* (5), 777–99. https://doi.org/10.1177/000312240907400505

Pager, D., and H. Shepherd. 2008. "The Sociology of Discrimination: Racial Discrimination in Employment, Housing, Credit, and Consumer Markets." *Annual Review of Sociology 34*, 181–209. https://doi.org/10.1146/annurev.soc.33.040406.131740

Pant, N., K. McAnnany, and M. Belluscio. 2015. *Accessible Justice: Ensuring Equal Access to Courthouses for People with Disabilities*. New York: New York Lawyers for the Public Interest.

Parsons, S., and G. Sherwood. 2016. "Vulnerability in Custody: Perceptions and Practices of Police Officers and Criminal Justice Professionals in Meeting the Communication Needs of Offenders with Learning Disabilities and Learning Difficulties." *Disability & Society 31* (4), 553–72.https://doi.org/10.1080/09687599.2016.1181538

Patterson, E. 2010. "Incarcerating Death: Mortality in U.S. State Correctional Facilities, 1985–1998." *Demography 47* (3), 587–607. https://doi.org/10.1353/dem.0.0123

Pecorini, M. 2016. "Trying to Fit a Square Peg in a Round Hole: Why Title II of the American with Disabilities Act Must Apply to All Law Enforcement Services." *Journal of Law and Policy 24* (2), 551–94. https://brooklynworks.brooklaw.edu/jlp/vol24/iss2/5

Perlin, M. L. 2013. *Mental Disability and the Death Penalty: The Shame of the States*. Lanham, MD: Rowan & Littlefield Publishers.

Perlin, M. L. 2015. "Power and Greed and the Corruptible Seed: Mental Disability, Prosecutorial Misconduct, and the Death Penalty." *The Journal of the American Academy of Psychiatry and the Law 43* (3), 266–272.https://dx.doi.org/10.2139/ssrn.2522444

Perlin, M. L. 2016. "Merchants and Thieves, Hungry for Power: Prosecutorial Misconduct and Passive Judicial Complicity in Death Penalty Trials of Defendants with Mental Disabilities." *Washington & Lee Law Review 73* , 1501–45. https://digitalcommons.nyls.edu/cgi/viewcont ent.cgi?article=1469&context=fac_articles_chapters

Petersilia, J. 2003. *When Prisoners Come Home: Parole and Prisoner Reentry*. Oxford: Oxford University Press.

Pettit, B., and B. Western. 2004. "Mass Imprisonment and the Life Course: Race and Class Inequality in U.S. Incarceration." *American Sociological Review 69* (2), 151–69. https://doi .org/10.1177%2F000312240406900201

Poole, E. D., and R. M. Regoli. 1980. "Role Stress, Custody Orientation, and Disciplinary Actions: A Study of Prison Guards.: *Criminology 18* (2), 215–26. https://doi.org/10.1111/j.1745 -9125.1980.tb01360.x

Potter, R. H., H. Lin, A. Maze, and D. Bjoring. 2011. "The Health of Jail Inmates: The Role of Jail Population 'Flow' in Community Health." *Criminal Justice Review 36* (4), 470–86. https:// doi.org/10.1177%2F0734016811415100

Rafter, N. 1997. *Creating Born Criminals*. Chicago: University of Illinois Press.

Raphael, S., and M. A. Stoll. 2013. "Assessing the Contribution of the Deinstitutionalization of the Mentally Ill to Growth in the US Incarceration Rate." *The Journal of Legal Studies 42* (1), 187–222. https://www.jstor.org/stable/10.1086/667773

Reiter, K., and T. Blair. 2015. "Punishing Mental Illness: Trans-institutionalization and Solitary Confinement in the United States." Pp. 177–96 inn *Extreme Punishment*, edited by Keramet Reiter and Alexa Koenig. London: Palgrave Macmillan.

Rembis, M. 2014. "The New Asylums: Madness and Mass Incarceration in the Neoliberal Era." Pp. 139–59 in *Disability Incarcerated*. New York: Palgrave Macmillan.

Resnik, J. 2016. "Aiming to Reduce Time-In-Cell: Reports from Correctional Systems on the Numbers of Prisoners in Restricted Housing and on the Potential of Policy Changes to Bring About Reforms." *Report from Association of State Correctional Administrations, The Arthur Liman Public Interest Program and Yale Law School*. New Haven, CT. https://www.law.yale .edu/centers-workshops/arthur-liman-public-interest-program/limanpublications

Resnik, J., S. Baumgartel, and J. Kalb. 2016. "Time-In-Cell: Isolation and Incarceration." *Yale LJF 125* , 212. https://digitalcommons.law.yale.edu/cgi/viewcontent.cgi?article=6292&cont ext=fss_papers

Rhodes, L. A. 2004. *Total Confinement: Madness and Reason in the Maximum Security Prison*, vol. 7. Oakland, CA: University of California Press.

Richardson, R. L., and S. M. Flower. 2014. "How Gender of Ex-offenders Influences Access to Employment Opportunities." *Journal of Applied Rehabilitation Counseling 45* (4), 35–43. doi: 10.1891/0047-2220.45.4.35

Ruhland, E. 2019. "It's All about the Money: An Exploration of Probation Fees." *Corrections 6* (1), 65–84. https://doi.org/10.1080/23774657.2018.1564635

Schlanger, M. 2017. "Prisoners with Disabilities." Pp. 295–323 in *Reforming Criminal Justice: Punishment, Incarceration, and Release*, vol. 4, edited by E. Luna. Phoenix, AZ: Academy for Justice.

Schnittker, J., and A. John. 2007. "Enduring Stigma: The Long-Term Effects of Incarceration on Health." *Journal of Health and Social Behavior 48* (2), 115–30. https://doi.org/10.1177%2F002 214650704800202

Schnittker, J., M. Massoglia, and C. Uggen. 2011. "Incarceration and the Health of the African American Community." *Du Bois Review 8* (1), 1–9. http://dx.doi.org/10.1017/S1742058X1 1000026

Schwirtz, M., M. Winerip, and R. Gebeloff. 2016. "The Scourge of Racial Bias in New York State's Prisons." *The New York Times* (December 3).

Seevers, R. 2016. "Amplifying Voices of Inmates with Disabilities, Making Hard Time Harder: Programmatic Accommodations for Inmates with Disabilities Under the Americans with Disabilities Act." *AVID Prison Project Report*, pp. 1–40 http://avidprisonproject.org/Mak ing-Hard-Time-Harder/assets/making-hard-time-harder---pdf-version.pdf.

Smith, P. S. 2006. "The Effects of Solitary Confinement on Prison Inmates: A Brief History and Review of the Literature." *Crime and Justice 34* , 441–528. doi: 10.1086/500626

Spivakovsky, C. 2014. "From Punishment to Protection: Containing and Controlling the Lives of People with Disabilities in Human Rights." *Punishment & Society 16* (5), 560–77. https:// www.doi.org/10.1177/1462474514548805

Stanley, E. A., and N. Smith. 2011. *Captive Genders: Trans Embodiment and the Prison Industrial Complex*. Oakland, CA: AK Press.

Stuart, F. 2015. "On the Streets, Under Arrest: Policing Homelessness in the 21st Century." *Sociology Compass 9* (11), 940–50. https://doi.org/10.1111/soc4.12324

Sugie, N. F., and K. Turney. 2017. "Beyond Incarceration: Criminal Justice Contact and Mental Health." *American Sociological Review 82* (4), 719–43. https://doi.org/10.1177%2F000312241 7713188

Sumner, J., and L. Sexton. 2016. "Same Difference: The 'Dilemma of Difference' and the Incarceration of Transgender Prisoners." *Law & Social Inquiry 41* (3), 616–42. https://doi .org/10.1111/lsi.12193

Szasz, T. 1961. *The Myth of Mental Illness: Foundations of a Theory of Person Conduct*. New York: Hoeber-Harper.

Tartaro, C., J. Duntley, S. Medvetz, and N. Hafner. 2018. "Factors That Predict Murder Defendants' Competence to Stand Trial." *International Journal of Law and Psychiatry* 59, 31–37. https://doi.org/10.1016/j.ijlp.2018.05.009

Travis, J., B. Western, and F. S. Redburn. 2014. "The Growth of Incarceration in the United States: Exploring Causes and Consequences. Committee on Causes and Consequences of High Rates of Incarceration." Pp. 1–444 in *National Research Council: Committee on Law and Justice, Division of Behavioral and Social Sciences and Education*, edited by J. Travis, B. Western, and S. Redburn. Washington, DC: The National Academies Press.

United States Interagency Council on Homelessness. 2018. *Homelessness in America: Focus on Chronic Homelessness among People with Disabilities*. Washington, D.C.

Vallas, R. 2016. "Disabled Behind Bars: The Mass Incarceration of People with Disabilities in America's Jails and Prisons." Washington, DC: Center for American Progress. Retrieved from https://cdn.americanprogress.org/wp-content/uploads/2016/07/18000151/2CriminalJustic eDisability-report.pdf

Vallas, R., and S. Dietrich. 2014. *One Strike and You're Out: How We Can Eliminate Barriers to Economic Security and Mobility for People with Criminal Records*. Washington, DC: Center for American Progress. Retrieved from https://cdn.americanprogress.org/wp-content/uplo ads/2014/12/VallasCriminalRecordsReport.pdf

Velasquez-Potts, M. C. 2015. "Regulatory Sites: Management, Confinement, and HIV/AIDS." Pp. 119–32 in *Captive Genders: Trans Embodiment and the Prison Industrial Complex*, 2nd ed., edited by E. A. Stanley & N. Smith. Oakland, CA: AK Press.

Vernon, M., and K. R. Miller. 2005. "Obstacles Faced by Deaf People in the Criminal Justice System." *American Annals of the Deaf* 150 (3), 283–291. https://www.jstor.org/stable/ 26234732

Ware, S., J. Ruzsa, and G. Dias. 2014. "It Can't Be Fixed because It's Not Broken: Racism and Disability in the Prison Industrial Complex. Pp. 163–84 in *Disability Incarcerated*. New York: Palgrave Macmillan.

Wertlieb, E. C. 1991. "Individuals with Disabilities in the Criminal Justice System: A Review of the Literature." *Criminal Justice and Behavior* 18 (3), 332–50. https://doi.org/10.1177%2F0093 854891018003006

Williams, B., and R. Abraldes. 2007. "Growing Older: Challenges of Prison and Reentry for the Aging Population. Pp. 56–72 in *Public Health Behind Bars*, edited by Robert B. Greifinger. New York: Springer.

Williams, D. R., and P. B. Jackson. 2005. "Social Sources of Racial Disparities in Health." *Health Affairs* 24 (2), 325–34. https://doi.org/10.1377/hlthaff.24.2.325

Wilper, A. P., S. Woolhandler, J. W. Boyd, K. E. Lasser, D. McCormick, D. H. Bor, and D. U. Himmelstein. 2009. "The Health and Health Care of US Prisoners: Results of a Nationwide Survey." *American Journal of Public Health* 99 (4), 666–72. https://doi.org/10.2105/ ajph.2008.144279

World Health Organization (WHO). 2007. *Trencin Statement on Prisons and Mental Health*. Copenhagen: World Health Organization, Regional Office for Europe. http://www.euro .who.int/__data/assets/pdf_file/0006/99006/E91402.pdf

Yi, Y., K. Turney, and C. Wildeman. 2017. "Mental Health among Jail and Prison Inmates." *American Journal of Men's Health* 11 (4), 900–09. https://doi.org/10.1177%2F155798831 6681339

CHAPTER 34

DISABILITY, VIOLENCE, AND PRISON

NOMI OSTRANDER

INTRODUCTION

VIOLENCE often surrounds images of prisons, whether it is a violent act that leads to imprisonment or violence within the prison walls. There is the stereotype of the volatile and dangerous prisoner who is locked up for doing untold crimes before going to jail, only to become a hardened criminal behind bars (Edgar et al., 2003). The imagined prisoner is likely a masculine presenting figure and perhaps someone from a minoritized racial or ethnic identity. What is often missing is a broader intersectional image that includes the presence of disability or impairment, along with other identities. Indeed, many carceral analyses ignore intersectionality, particularly around race, gender, and disability (Froman, 2012). As an example, Ritchie (2017) highlighted the official police officer rationale for killing Michael Brown in Ferguson, Missouri, that invoked language that Brown looked demonic, thus stripping Brown of all humanity.

As race, gender, and disability intersect in the media and official police reports, prisons further that process. The violence in prison is often experienced through interpersonal violence from other inmates that may be motivated by group affiliations or bias-related hate crimes against people with disabilities, as well as structural violence within the prison environment. These disabling structural conditions range from the trauma of being housed in closed, tight spaces to public health crises of sexual assaults and drug abuse to a lack of medical supplies and medication—or being overmedicated to induce compliance—to the mental distress solitary confinement induces.

It is useful to define "disability" and "structural disability" at the outset, given how central these concepts will be throughout this chapter. Ben-Moshe and her colleagues (2013) wrote:

> Disability is fluid and contextual rather than biological. This does not mean that bi-ology does not play out in our minds and bodies, but that the definition of disability is imposed upon certain kinds of minds and bodies. . . .But more than that, disa-bility, if understood as constructed through historical and cultural processes, should be seen not as a binary but as a continuum. One is always dis/abled in relation to the context in which one is put. (pp. 210–211)

So, while there are certain physical, psychological, and emotional "conditions" that may be defined medically as a disability, context also plays an integral role. For example, someone who uses a wheelchair is more disabled with stairs and curbs than they are with ramps and curb cuts. In this scenario, the context is the disabling structure.

With this frame in mind, this chapter navigates through the intersection of violence and disability within the prison context.[1] To set the stage for this exploration, I first dis-cuss how the US War on Drugs not only led to the carceral population's rapid expansion but also led to more people with disabilities in prison. Along those lines, this chapter references people with violently acquired disabilities, such as spinal cord injuries and traumatic brain injuries, as important disabled "Ghetto Vets" (Ice Cube, 1998). These kinds of injuries are the urban battle wounds sustained during the War on Drugs. The chapter then shifts to looking at violence toward and exploitation of people with disabilities serving time in prison. Finally, consideration will be given to examining a way forward.

GROWTH OF THE US PRISON POPULATION

Since 1980, the US prison population has grown by 500% (Ghandnoosh, 2020). With more than 2 million individuals in prisons and jails, the United States is the world leader in incarceration. Although it is difficult to estimate how many people in federal and state prisons have physical, cognitive, psychological, sensory, or learning disabilities, it is clear that disabilities and impairments are overrepresented in carceral environments. Although some states, such as Illinois, do not track inmates with disabilities and many individuals do not identify as having a disability, self-report data from the 2011–2012 National Inmate Survey indicate that approximately 30% of state and federal inmates have at least one disability (Bronson, Maruschak, and Berzofsky, 2015). Vallas (2016) estimated that about 40% of the people in local jails have a disability and approximately 32% of the people in prison have a disability.

Compared to the general population, state and federal prisoners are three times more likely to have a disability, and local jail inmates are four times more likely to have a dis-ability. These data support the notion that people with disabilities are overrepresented within prisons and jails, given that approximately 25% of people in the United States have at least one disability (Okoro et al., 2018). Furthermore, as the US prison popu-lation continues to age, a rise in people with some form of physical impairment will likely grow as well. As an example, the carceral population over age 65 grew by 63% just in the years between 2007 and 2010. These are the individuals who received "tough on crime" sentences and have grown old within the prison environment (Fellner and Vinck, 2012).

While this increase in the overall prison population has been managed in part through the construction of new prisons, many prisons have also experienced overcrowding (Franklin et al., 2006). The literature is mixed regarding if overcrowding has led to more violence among inmates, though some research noted that the overcrowding has created more stress on all inmates (National Research Council, 2014). For example, Wooldredge et al. (2001) found that overcrowding was a significant predictor of "inmate misconduct." To the converse, research that found no impact or a reduction of inmate misconduct noted that the carceral staff had a lower tolerance for misconduct and more severe responses to misconduct. What seems counterintuitive is that the overcrowding is more often associated with less interpersonal violence (Franklin et al., 2006). The suggested reasons for this inverse association revolved around stricter penalties from prison guards. However, none of these studies explored specific subpopulations, such as people with disabilities, which then makes it more unclear the ways overcrowding might impact this population.

To understand this rise in prison populations, it is important to look at the primary drivers in the rise of mass incarceration and violence toward people who represent the complex intersectionality of race, gender, and disability. Sentencing laws and policies have led to this prison census growth more directly than an overall population increase in the United States or increase in crime rates. The most impactful policy change during the time in question is the US War on Drugs.

The War on Drugs and Rising Incarceration

Although President Nixon first declared a "war on drugs" in 1971, President Reagan essentially launched the modern War on Drugs in 1982. The "war" included a global focus to address the drug supply from other countries through US military aid and intervention, often destabilizing countries around the world. At home, the policy included a sharp increase in policing and sentencing in the United States, often destabilizing communities across the country. In just over 30 years, this move resulted in the US penal population increasing from 300,000 to more than 2.3 million, lead mostly by drug convictions and hitting African American communities the hardest (Mauer, 2006).

There is a popular misconception that the widespread use of crack cocaine led to Reagan's drug war (Alexander, 2010). The public awareness of crack cocaine, however, came after Reagan's declaration. The Reagan administration hired staff to actively push the narrative of crack cocaine and gather support for his legislation and rapidly increased spending on drug law enforcement (Alexander, 2010). For example, the Drug Enforcement Agency's (DEA) budget increased from $86 million in 1981 to over a billion dollars in under a decade (Alexander, 2010). Despite a lack of empirical research, crack cocaine was seen as a highly addictive drug that caused violent behavior, including gang-related violence in urban areas (Hart et al., 2018; Walker & Mezuk, 2018). Largely driven by media coverage and the emergence of the dehumanizing "crack whore" and "crack baby" stereotypes, public concern reached incredibly high levels. These stereotypes dovetailed with the "welfare mother" narrative that developed simultaneously with the collapse of inner-city communities as manufacturing jobs dried up. Taken in concert, entire communities were demonized and heavily policed to support Reagan's anti-drug policies.

In addition to media reporting about increased violence and addiction stemming from the new form of cocaine, the publicized death of Len Bias, a Boston Celtics draft pick who died in 1986 following an overdose in his college dormitory, solidified the public outcry for action from public officials (Walker & Mezuk, 2018). *Newsweek* went so far as to declare crack cocaine the biggest story since Watergate (Alexander, 2010). This event, among others, ignited a political response to the growing epidemic, which resulted in the enactment of new laws setting mandatory minimum sentences for illicit drug offenses.

The Anti-Drug Abuse Act (ADAA) of 1986 presents one example of these sentencing laws. The ADAA established the federal court sentencing for a typical low level, first-time offense at 5–10 years in prison, while other developed countries around the globe often had that same offense set at no more than 6 months (Alexander, 2010). The ADAA covered most illicit drugs and set differing minimum sentences based on type and quantity of these substances. The structure of the law was based in deterrence, which suggested that the greater the punishment, the less likely people would engage in the behavior. Because it was widely believed in the 1980s that crack cocaine had more abuse potential and was associated social harms than powder cocaine (Beaver, 2010), the ADAA sentencing guidelines established harsher penalties for crack cocaine than powder cocaine. Specifically, the quantity of substance that triggered the mandatory sentencing was a 100:1 ratio of powder cocaine to crack cocaine. Someone caught with 5 grams of crack cocaine would be sentenced as though they were caught with 500 grams of powder cocaine. Although this law was initially directed toward drug trafficking, it was amended in 1988 to include possession offenses (Walker & Mezuk, 2018). The 1988 revision to the ADAA also included additional consequences like disqualifying people with a felony drug offense from public housing or from receiving federal student loans (Alexander, 2010). As a result, the ADAA largely cut off a significant portion of society from the kinds of social programs that might allow for social mobility.

By the early 2000s, evidence mounted that implementation of the ADAA led to significant racial disparities in incarceration (Mustard, 2001). This disparity appeared to be in part because crack cocaine was racialized as a drug favored by low-income African

Americans, while wealthier White businessmen and club-goers preferred powdered cocaine. Black men were also more likely to be prosecuted to the fullest extent of the law than were White men (Mustard, 2001). The ADAA is but one example of the ways the US Congress tied the hands of judges with mandatory sentencing guidelines.

Along with the rise of crack cocaine came increased street gang activity to distribute the drug and protect the gang's market share. Certainly, gangs were not a new phenomenon (Spergel, 1995); however, early gang studies had not tied violence to drug trafficking, and there was very little gang involvement in drugs. In many cases, gang members were pushed out of the gang if they used drugs themselves (Spergel, 1995). A new business model emerged with the rise of crack cocaine. Gang involvement with drug trafficking increased during this time due to cocaine market expansion coupled with price reductions and socioeconomic changes in the United States, specifically large amounts of unemployment after factories closed down and new jobs moved to the suburbs (Fagan, 1993). From a pure business sense, street gangs, with high demand for their product, became the best job option around inner cities that had few other employment options.

Along with the increased drug trade came the more widespread use of firearms among gang members. The routine use of guns in gangs was a recent development starting in the early to mid-1980s (Miller, 1992). This trend continued, and by the mid-1990s, young men in gangs were more likely to carry a gun than their non-gang-affiliated peers (Decker et al., 1997). Data on how many gang members carry guns are difficult to come by; however, one 3-year field study indicated that approximately 81% of gang members at least owned a gun (Decker & Van Winkle, 1996). With more firearms among gang members, the likelihood of getting shot in a disagreement increased. Baumer and colleagues (1998) found in a cross-city longitudinal analysis that crack cocaine was a significant predictor for increased homicide and robbery rates in cities. This connection provides some explanation for the rise in homicide rates in the United States from 1985 to 1995, which also led to increasing numbers of violently acquired disabilities.

VIOLENTLY ACQUIRED DISABILITIES

Although rising homicide rates became an issue of great discussion in the 1980s and 1990s, few politicians, journalists, and researchers talked about situations when people survive gunshots. Between 2000 and 2018, approximately 1.5 million people were shot in the United States. Of those, just over 620,000 people died of gunshots (CDC, 2020). Little is known about the roughly 900,000 people who survived being shot, many of whom ended up with various impairments or disabilities. For those who were shot in the commission of a crime or who were found to have warrants for their arrest while in the hospital, they likely worked their way through the courts and were sentenced to time in prison.

Violently acquired disabilities make up a subset of the disability population within carceral settings. The two most common forms of violently acquired disabilities are spinal cord injuries and traumatic brain injuries (TBIs). To be specific, "violently acquired" refers to penetrating injury (e.g., from a gunshot or stabbing) or an intentional hit with a blunt object (e.g., baseball bat, club, or fists). Gunshot wounds are the third leading cause of these injuries behind falls and motor vehicle accidents, and the number-one cause among males age 16–24 (Jain et al., 2015). This statistic has remained constant over the past 30 years, even though falls account for a greater number of injuries as the US population ages (Jain et al., 2015).

Zeroing in on the 16- to 24-year-old age bracket among men for whom gunshot wounds are a more common etiology, there are insufficient data to indicate the circumstances around those wounds. Thus, they could be accidental shootings, bystander shootings, or assaults. There is, however, a correlation between the number of spinal cord injuries and the number of shooting deaths in this age group during the 1990s when gang violence occurred more frequently and crack cocaine was more prominent in urban environments. Although some of those violently acquired spinal cord injuries were people in the wrong place at the wrong time, there is also the reality that the people who were victims of injuries also caused other injuries (Ostrander, 2008). Specifically, some people with a violently acquired spinal cord injury noted in interviews about their injuries that in previous battles, they shot at rival gang members, and this may have led to injury, disability, or death.

Traumatic brain injuries, defined as a hit to the head or penetrating injury that disturbs the normal functioning of the brain, are not evenly distributed across the population. In the US population, approximately 8%–12% has a TBI (Lasry et al., 2017). The World Health Organization predicted in 2007 that traumatic brain injuries, part of a neurotrauma category that includes spinal cord injuries, would become the leading cause of death and disability in the world by 2020 (Hyder et al., 2007). While that prediction has yet to come true, the impact of TBIs across the globe is significant. They often lead to longer hospitalizations to treat the injury, greater impairment, and more costs than other injuries.

People who are or have been incarcerated have a much higher incidence of TBI than nonprison populations (Fahmy et al., 2020; Schwarts, 2019). Perhaps the most comprehensive meta-analysis of TBI in carceral settings comes from the work of Durand and colleagues (2017). They analyzed 33 publications related to the prevalence of a prior history of TBI among inmates (Durand et al., 2017). The vast majority (66%) involve inmates with TBI housed in the United States, with the remaining articles from Australia, Canada, New Zealand, Spain, and the United Kingdom. Because the studies reviewed had a wide range of reported TBI (9.7%–100%), the authors cited the mean percentage of inmates with a prior history of TBI at 46%. This took into account the total number of inmates across all the studies ($n = 9,342$). Along with TBI, most of the studies noted comorbidities that included psychiatric disorders, substance use disorders, and a great utilization of hospital services while in prison.

VIOLENCE AGAINST PEOPLE WITH DISABILITIES WITHIN PRISONS

The studies referenced in the previous section speak to the large number of individuals who enter prison with violently acquired disabilities. Relatedly, there may be no way to know how many people enter carceral settings with trauma-related psychiatric and emotional disorders based on interpersonal and structural violence within their communities. To then be housed in spaces ill equipped to meet their needs and spaces that may exacerbate mental and emotional distress, the risk for negative outcomes increases. Within carceral settings, approximately 10%–12% of inmates will engage in violence toward another inmate, be charged with a physical assault, or be injured from a violent assault (James & Glaze, 2006). These estimates are aggregates across all segments of the prison population and ignore those intersecting identities that may make people more vulnerable. For example, the Office of Victims of Crime reported that people with disabilities are at least twice as likely to experience a violent crime than people without disabilities (2018). The likelihood of victimization increases if an individual has multiple disabilities. In 2018, which is the most recent year with available data, the Federal Bureau of Investigation (FBI) noted that hate crimes against people with disabilities were on the rise (2019). The FBI defines hate crimes as those motivated in part or entirely by an offender's bias against race, religion, gender, gender expression, sexual orientation, disability, or ethnicity.

There is scant research on hate crimes within prisons globally, let alone in the United States. For the studies that do exist, the focus has been on race ignoring the intersectional nature of identities. For example, Penrice et al. (2019) explored hate crimes among Scottish inmates, interviewing nine inmates who either had committed hate crimes while in prison or who were vulnerable for a racial hate crime. From there, "perceived inequality" emerged as a key motivator for hate crimes across all participants. This "perceived inequality" term means that because of some racial marker, an inmate may receive more sympathy or better treatment than a White inmate. The application of this work to people with disabilities who are behind bars might be that nondisabled inmates may perceive people with a disability as getting special treatment if they spend more time in a medical unit or if they are not in a general population cell. Thus, there may be a perceived inequality that people with disabilities have it easier or get more sympathy while in prison. This perceived inequality may be even greater when someone has a less visible impairment.

Other literature helps explain why people with disabilities are more vulnerable. McMahon and colleagues (2004), for example, suggested three factors that contribute to crimes against people with disabilities: situational contexts, personal features, and societal contributions. First, situational contexts refer to people with disabilities who may experience more isolation and dependence. Because they are cut off from a broader support network, they are more vulnerable to abuse. Second, personal features like the type of impairment may contribute to an individual's vulnerability. Hate crime data indicate that people with cognitive impairments and people with multiple disabilities are more likely to experience victimization (Relia et al., 2019). Finally, societal contributions in terms of negative attitudes and inaccessible environments impact victimization. Inaccessible environments need not be limited to the built environment but also refer to environments that may inhibit reporting a crime or seeking help. All three of these are at play in prisons.

As an example of these three factors, inmates with disabilities may unintentionally become targets for hate crimes due to the inaccessibility of a prison and receiving a perceived benefit because of limitations to the built environment. Many inmates with disabilities may be placed in solitary confinement because there are no accessible cells to accommodate their impairment (Vallas, 2016). Overcrowding likely exacerbates this issue. It may seem easier for prison officials to place someone with a disability in solitary confinement where they are the only person in the cell rather than address issues of accessibility in cells that are shared by multiple inmates, above the cell's intended capacity.

As a practice, solitary confinement is almost total isolation for inmates in prison. Individuals may be placed in solitary confinement because they pose a general threat to the safety of the facility, they are at a heightened risk of serious physical harm or death from the other prisoners, they violated a prison rule, they have a communicable disease, or they have a disability and prison officials determined that solitary confinement is more convenient until permanent and accessible housing can be found (ACLU, 2017). This isolation strips someone of the potential benefits from meaningful social interactions with other inmates and their ability to engage in other social activities within the carceral setting. Solitary confinement negatively affects mental health, with several organizations and researchers calling it torture (United Nations, 2020). These impacts can range an array of negative mental health symptoms that include increased anxiety, hypersensitivity, aggression, suicidal ideation and behaviors, and a slew of other symptoms (ACLU, 2017; Smith, 2006).

More specifically to people with disabilities, however, are the physical harms that come with solitary confinement. These harms can emerge in three key ways. First, there are predictable physical limitations of being isolated in a cell the size of a parking space for 22 hours a day. For many individuals who may have mobility impairments, the inability to continue working on daily functioning can cause a loss of progress and physical deterioration. Considering individuals who may be imprisoned with a more recently acquired disability like a spinal cord injury or an amputation, the drop-off in rehabilitation progress could lead to lifelong limitations or life-threatening complications such as a pressure sore.

Second, prison practices that ban assistive devices in solitary confinement can lead to further impairments. Robert Dinkins, who is paralyzed and uses a wheelchair, noted in a 2017 ACLU report that prison officials confiscated his wheelchair when he entered solitary confinement. Functionally, this meant that he needed to crawl on the ground and eat all of his meals on the ground (ACLU, 2017). This does not appear to be an experience unique to Robert Dinkins. Mark Gizewski filed a lawsuit in 2014 against the New York state prison system for denying him access to his prosthetic devices, cleaning supplies, and a right to a shower for 6 days (*Gizweski v. New York State Department of Corrections*, 2014).

Finally, access to medical care is limited while in prison, and especially so while in isolation—for example, if an individual comes to prison needing to take a prescription at a certain time. While prison medical staff will distribute medications, individual facilities may have limited staff and limited windows of time when prescriptions are distributed. Those windows of time may not be optimal for inmates who need medications at specific times to control symptoms of their impairment. Additionally, prisons are not set up to be rehabilitation centers for people who need regular sessions to work on activities of daily living or other functional exercise.

The COVID-19 pandemic represents another scenario where people with disabilities may experience increased vulnerability and violence. Early on in the pandemic it was clear that the virus spread easily in places where people lived in close contact. Initially this was seen in nursing homes and long-term care facilities, and then in jails and prisons as they became infection hotspots. Compounding the problem was that many carceral facilities doubled-up inmates in cells due to overcrowding (National Academy of Sciences, 2020). Cells as small as 55 square feet that were designed for one person now had two people living in them, making social distancing impossible. As a result, people incarcerated were five times more likely to contract coronavirus and almost three times more likely to die from the disease (Chappell, 2020).

Although disaggregated prison data are not available because prisons do not uniformly count inmates with disabilities, noncarceral based studies have demonstrated greater infection and death rates among some individuals with disabilities due to existing health concerns (Public Health England, 2020; Turk et al., 2020). It is a reasonable extrapolation that people with disabilities within prisons would also be more likely to become infected and have worse outcomes from COVID-19. For example, people with spinal cord injuries often have weaker lung functioning based on injury level, placing them at high risk for respiratory issues. Furthermore, if any personal protective equipment (PPE) was available in prisons or jails, the research cited earlier would suggest that people with disabilities would be targets for theft or manipulation around PPE. Prison officials would likely prioritize medically vulnerable inmates for what little PPE might exist and certainly other inmates would realize that as well. COVID-19 is only one example of the ways people with disabilities are at greater risk when infectious diseases spread through a carceral environment.

A Way Forward

The intersecting issues of violence, disability, and prison are clearly complex, and the way forward is similarly complex. People with disabilities are placed in greater risk of interpersonal and structural violence and inaccessible prison structures exacerbate disabilities. In this light, prisons perpetuate and increase violence and disability. Ultimately, Ruth Wilson Gilmore's (2007) call for community investments and other options for when people "mess up" is the prison abolitionist's dream to mitigate the damages prisons cause. In the meantime, there are at least three immediate and midterm steps that could have a significant impact on the well-being of people with disabilities housed in carceral settings.

First, the most fundamental need is an ongoing, up-to-date census on the number of individuals in carceral settings with disabilities. As the population continues to age, these data will be all the more important. Prisons have long been considered the "new asylum" for people with mental illnesses, and they may soon become the nation's largest long-term care facilities for elder inmates. The experiences of people with disabilities need to be tracked so there is better data on their experiences and vulnerabilities within carceral settings. This allows for better advocacy, program, and policies. Programs like Amplifying Voices of Inmates with Disabilities (AVID) in Washington State offer a glimpse of what advocacy could look like with better understanding of carceral experiences among people with disabilities. Through this program, advocates can help to improve living conditions, medical treatment and services, and community reentry. Unfortunately, this organization is not more widespread, and without a national effort, the outcomes will be hodgepodge and uneven.

Second, if prisons remain the only penological option, then carceral settings must accommodate impairments and disabilities. While this chapter briefly looked at two specific disabilities, this is a pan-disability issue. For example, Abreham Zemedagegehu, a deaf Ethiopian immigrant who spent 6 weeks in a Virginia jail, often missed meals and medications because he was unable to communicate with the carceral staff. Drew Harrison is another individual who suffered unnecessarily in prison. Due to his autism, the carceral setting's abundant stimuli overwhelmed his senses and when he sought relief through wrapping his uniform around his head or trying to stay longer in the prison yard to be free of the fluorescent lights, he was written up as insubordinate and placed in solitary confinement. The author of this chapter has also advocated for individuals with implanted baclofen pumps within carceral settings. Specifically, some individuals with spinal cord injuries have problems with physical spasticity that can only be controlled with baclofen. Prison settings that do not have the ability to monitor the functioning of these pumps have requested that people have them removed, which only worsens the well-being of individuals with spasticity. These stories are not isolated examples. Lawsuits alleging carceral staff's mistreatment of people with disabilities regularly come before the US courts (ACLU, 2017; Morgan, 2017).

Third, COVID-19's tragic trajectory within carceral settings may offer the momentum and direction for significant change. Prisons and jails have already been designated as public health hazards. The rapid spread of COVID-19 in prisons and jails reinforced the reminder that infectious diseases not only spread quickly within the walls, but that corrections officers and other staff are then potent spreaders back in their communities. The National Academy of Sciences (2020) developed guidelines for decarceration in the wake of COVID-19. Their guidelines include the following: (1) increase diversion programs to keep people away from detention; (2) assess current level of overcrowding and release medically vulnerable individuals and individuals at low risk for recidivism; (3) revise compassionate release policies to account for disability, impairment, and medical vulnerability; and (4) improve partnerships between carceral settings and communities to smooth the reentry process. These measures, combined with the other intrainstitutional recommendations around access to testing and treatment, would significantly improve the conditions for people with disabilities.

NOTE

1. Liat Ben-Moshe's *Decarcerating Disability: Deinstitutionalization and Prison Abolition* provides a broader exploration of individuals with cognitive, sensory, and developmental disabilities.

REFERENCES

Alexander, M. (2010). *The new Jim Crow*. The New Press.

American Civil Liberties Union. (2017). *Caged in: The devastating harms of solitary confinement on prisoners with physical disabilities.* https://www.aclu.org/report/caged-devastating-harms-solitary-confinement-prisoners-physical-disabilities?redirect=CagedIn

Baumer, E., Lauritsen, J. L., Rosenfeld, R., & Wright, R. (1998). The influence of crack cocaine on robbery, burglary, and homicide rates: A cross-city, longitudinal analysis. *Journal of Research in Crime and Delinquency, 35*(3), 316–340.

Beaver, A. L. (2010). Getting a fix on cocaine sentencing policy: Reforming the sentencing scheme of the Anti-Drug Abuse Act of 1986. *Fordham Law Review, 78,* 2531.\

Ben-Moshe, L., Nocella, A. J., & Withers, A. J. (2013). Queer-cripping anarchism: Intersections and reflections on anarchism, queer-ness, and dis-ability. In C. B. Darling, J. Rogue, D. Shannon, & A. Volcano (Eds.), *Queering anarchism* (pp. 207–220). AK Press.

Bronson, J., Maruschak, L., and Berzofsky, M. (2015). Disabilities among prison and jail inmates, 2011-2012. Bureau of Justice Statistics. https://www.bjs.gov/index.cfm?ty=pbdetail&iid=5500

Centers for Disease Control. (2020). Traumatic brain injury in prisons and jails. https://www.cdc.gov/traumaticbraininjury/pdf/Prisoner_TBI_Prof-a.pdf

Chappell, B. (2020). Crowded U.S. jails drove millions of COVID-19 cases, a new study says. National Public Radio. https://www.npr.org/2021/09/02/1033326204/crowded-jails-drove-millions-of-covid-19-cases-a-new-study-says

Decker, S. H., Pennell, S., & Caldwell, A. (1997, January). *Illegal firearms; Access and use by arrestees.* Research in Brief. US Department of Justice, Office of Justice Programs, National Institute of Justice.

Decker, S. H., & Van Winkle, B. (1996). *Life in the gang: Family, friends, and violence.* Cambridge University Press.

Durand, E., Chevignard, M., Ruet, A., Dereix, A., Jourdan, C., & Pradat-Diehl, P. (2017). History of traumatic brain injury in prison populations: A systematic review. *Annals of Physical and Rehabilitation Medicine, 60,* 95–101.

Edgar K., O'Donnell, I., and Martin, C. (2003). *Prison Violence: The dynamics of conflict.* Routledge Press.

Fagan, J. E. (1993). The political economy of drug dealing among urban gangs. In R. Davis, A. Lurgicio, & D. P. Rosenbaum (Eds.), *Drugs and community* (pp. 19–54). Charles C. Thomas.

Fahmy, C., Jackson, D. B., Pyrooz, D. C., & Decker, S. H. (2020). Head injury in prison: Gang membership and the role of prison violence. *Journal of Criminal Justice, 67*, 1–11. https://doi.org/10.1016/j.crimjus.2020.101658.

Fellner, J, Vinck, P. (2012). Old behind bars: The aging prison population in the United States. Human Rights Watch, January. URL (accessed 2 February 2021): https://www.hrw.org/sites/default/files/reports/usprisons0112_brochure_web.pdf

Franklin, T., Franklin, C., & Pratt, T. (2006). Examining the empirical relationship between prison crowding and inmate misconduct: A meta-analysis of conflicting research results. *Journal of Criminal Justice, 34*(4), 401–412.

Froman, J. (2012). Racial critiques of mass incarceration beyond the new Jim Crow. *New York University Law Review, 87*, 21–69.

Ghandnoosh, N. (2020). U.S. prison population trends: Massive build up, modest decline. *The Sentencing Project.* Washington D.C. https://www.sentencingproject.org/publications/u-s-prison-population-trends-massive-buildup-and-modest-decline/

Gilmore, R. W. (2007). *Golden gulag: Prisons, surplus, crisis, an opposition in globalizing California.* University of California Press.

Hart, C. L., Csete, J., & Habibi, D. (2014). Methamphetamine: Fact vs. fiction and lessons from the crack hysteria. https://www.opensocietyfoundations.org/sites/default/files/methamphetamine-dangers-exaggerated-20140218.pdf.

Hyder, A. A., Wunderlich, C. A., Puvanachandra, P., Gururaj, G., & Kobusingye, O. C. (2007). The impact of traumatic brain injuries: A global perspective. *NeuroRehabilitation, 22*, 341–353.

Ice Cube. (1998). Ghetto Vet [Recorded by Ice Cube]. *I Got the Hook Up.* No Limit Records.

Jain, N. B., Ayers, G. D., Peterson, E. N., et al. (2015). Traumatic spinal cord injury in the United States, 1993–2012. *JAMA, 313*(22), 2236–2243.

James, D. J., & Glaze, L. E. (2006). *Mental health problems of prison and jail inmates.* US Department of Justice.

Lasry, O., Liu, E. Y., Powell, G. A., Ruel-Laliberte, J. Marcoux, J., & Buckeridge, D. L. (2017). Epidemiology of recurrent traumatic brain injury in general population. *Neurology, 89*(21), 2198–2209.

Mauer, M. (2006). *Race to incarcerate.* The New Press.

McMahon, B. T., West, S. L., Lewis, A. N., Armstrong, A. J., & Conway, J. P. (2004). Hate crimes and disability in America. *Rehabilitation Counseling Bulletin, 47*(2), 66–75.

Miller, W. B. (1992). *Crime by youth gangs and groups in the United States.* US Department of Justice, Office of Justice Programs, Office of Juvenile Justice and Delinquency Prevention. (Revised from 1982)

Morgan, J. (2017). *Caged in: Solitary confinement's devastating harm on prisoners with physical disabilities.* American Civil Liberties Union.

Mustard, D. B. (2001). Racial, ethnic, and gender disparities in sentencing: Evidence from the U.S. federal courts. *Journal of Law and Economics, 44*, 285–314.

National Research Council. (2014). *The Growth of Incarceration in the United States: Exploring Causes and Consequences.* Washington, DC: The National Academies Press. https://doi.org/10.17226/18613.

National Academies of Sciences, Engineering, and Medicine. (2020). *Decarcerating correctional facilities during COVID-19: Advancing health, equity, and safety.* The National Academies Press.

Okoro CA, Hollis ND, Cyrus AC, Griffin-Blake S. Prevalence of Disabilities and Health Care Access by Disability Status and Type Among Adults — United States, 2016. MMWR Morb Mortal Wkly Rep 2018;67:882–887. DOI: http://dx.doi.org/10.15585/mmwr.mm6732a3exter nal icon.

Ostrander, R. N. (2008). When identities collide: Masculinity, disability and race. *Disability & Society*, 23(6), 585–597.

Penrice, K., Birch, P., & McAlpine, S. (2019). Exploring hate crimes amongst a cohort of Scottish prisoners: An exploratory study. *Journal of Criminological Research, Policy and Practice*, 5(1), 39–49.

Public Health England. (2020). Deaths of people identified as having learning disabilities with COVID-19 in England in the spring of 2020. https://assets.publishing.service.gov.uk/government/uploads/system/uploads/attachment_data/file/933612/COVID-19__learning _disabilities_mortality_report.pdf

Relia, K., Li, Z., Cook, S. H., & Chunara, R. (2019). Race, Ethnicity and National Origin-Based Discrimination in Social Media and Hate Crimes across 100 U.S. Cities. *Proceedings of the International AAAI Conference on Web and Social Media*, 13(01), 417-427. Retrieved from https://ojs.aaai.org/index.php/ICWSM/article/view/3354

Ritchie, A. (2017). *Invisible no more: Police violence against black women and women of color.* Beacon Press.

Schwartz, J. A. (2019). A longitudinal assessment of head injuries as a source of acquired neuropsychological deficits and the implications for criminal persistence. *Justice Quarterly*, 27, 1–28. http://doi.org/10-1080/07418825.2019.1599044.

Smith, P. S. (2006). The effects of solitary confinement on prison inmates: A brief history of the literature. *Crime & Justice*, 34(441), 476–81.

Spergel, I. A. (1995). *The youth gang problem*. Oxford University Press.

Turk, M. A., Landes, S. D., Formica, M. K., & Gross, K. D. (2020). Intellectual and developmental disability and COVID-19 case-fatality trends: TriNetX analysis. *Disability and Health Journal*, 13(3), 1–4. https://doi.org/10.1016/j.dhjo.2020.100942.

United Nations, 2020. United States: Prolonged solitary confinement amounts to psychological torture, says UN expert." https://www.ohchr.org/EN/NewsEvents/Pages/DisplayNews .aspx?NewsID=25633

Vallas, R. (2016). *Disabled behind bars: The mass incarceration of people with disabilities in America's jails and prisons.* Center for American Progress.

Walker, L. S., & Mezuk, B. (2018). Mandatory minimum sentencing policies and cocaine use in the U.S., 1985–2013. *BMC International Health and Human Rights*, 18(43), 1–10. https://doi .org/10.1186/s12914-018-0182-2

Wooldredge, J., Griffin, T., & Pratt, T. (2001). Considering hierarchical models for research on inmate behavior: Predicting misconduct with multilevel data. *Justice Quarterly*, 18, 203–231.

CHAPTER 35

BARRIERS TO ACCESS IN THE NORWEGIAN CRIMINAL JUSTICE SYSTEM

PATRICK KERMIT AND TERJE OLSEN

INTRODUCTION

THIS chapter discusses how public Norwegian Sign Language interpreter services provide a safety net for Deaf people facing the police or courts, either as accused of a crime, as a witness to a crime, or as a victim of a crime.[1] Working with an interpreter in itself does not simplify communication or proceedings when Deaf people face the Norwegian criminal justice system. On the contrary, because this judicial system fails to accommodate Deaf people in a reasonable manner, Deaf people facing this system are, generally, at risk of serious mutual misunderstanding and errors being made. Working with an interpreter increases the complexity of the process and also the general risk. Nevertheless, Norwegian Sign Language interpreters can, to a certain extent, compensate for some of the system's critical shortcomings, but not necessarily because their individual interpretations are always correct. Rather, interpreters reduce the risk of mistakes because they represent an independent public service able to bring about changes in the practices of the Norwegian police and courts that the police and courts would not themselves have initiated.

This chapter builds on studies conducted by the authors and their associates over a decade of researching disability in the context of the Norwegian criminal justice system. Our point of departure is our most recent study, which provides an updated general description of the Norwegian judicial system (Olsen et al., 2018; Søndenaa et al., 2019). When presenting the ways in which the interpreter service functions, we build mainly on our previously published work, but we also present empirical observation data hitherto not published.

Our research is conducted in the context of the Norwegian welfare state and its welfare policies, some of which are presented in the subsequent paragraphs. Norwegian disability policies and provisions might seem generous from an international perspective. However, the barriers to access we investigate and the measures we suggest for the partial removal of these barriers are not exceptional to the Norwegian or Nordic welfare models. On the contrary, both the barriers and the means to remove or soften them can be identified in many other countries outside Scandinavia, and as such, this topic requires further consideration.

The police, the public prosecutor, and the courts are the institutions responsible for legal security and the rule of law in Norway. Equality before the law is a legal principle stating that each citizen must be treated by the law in an equal manner and that all citizens are subjected to the same law and the same practices of justice. This principle is associated with questions about fairness, access, and due processes. The Universal Declaration of Human Rights (UDHR) states that "All are equal before the law and are entitled without any discrimination to equal protection of the law" (United Nations, 1966, Article 7). The UN Convention on the Rights of Persons with Disabilities (CRPD) has further developed this principle as a demand the state must observe: "States Parties shall ensure effective access to justice for persons with disabilities on an equal basis with others, including through the provision of procedural and age-appropriate accommodations, in order to facilitate their effective role as direct and indirect participants, including as witnesses, in all legal proceedings, including at investigative and other preliminary stages" (United Nations, 2006, Article 13).

We focus on one particular barrier to access—the barrier that Deaf people who have Norwegian Sign Language as their first language face in encounters with the Norwegian criminal justice system. This system bases its conduct on spoken languages only and no one within it, as far as we know, has advanced knowledge of Norwegian Sign Language. We also limit ourselves to addressing issues concerning the obtainment and use of Norwegian Sign Language interpreters. The questions we discuss are as follows: What role do sign language interpreters play in the Deaf peoples' encounters with the criminal justice system? How can the sign language interpreters' work be organized in ways that help to reduce communicative barriers and the risks of errors within a system without established critical, self-reflective practices related to disability? The case of sign language interpreting services represents a significant exception to the general bleak picture of inaccessibility and often exclusive practices that otherwise prevail in Norwegian judicial systems. This one example may thus also be applicable in other contexts where accessibility to an inaccessible system is obtained, not because of changes within the system itself, but because of an intervention originating outside the system.

BACKGROUND: RESEARCH ON DEAF PEOPLE'S ENCOUNTERS WITH THE POLICE AND COURTS

The international research on Deaf people's encounters with the criminal justice system is not comprehensive, but studies do exist. Most studies have been conducted in English-speaking contexts where the empirical data are often linked to the implementation of the British Disability Discrimination Act (DDA) and the Americans with Disabilities Act

(ADA). Common themes in this literature are shortcomings and problems occurring when Deaf citizens encounter a "phonocentric" hearing criminal justice system.[2] The thematic scopes in this literature address the lack of predictability, the need for accessibility, unclear norms for reasonable adjustments, and different variants of measures to remedy the situation. The existing research represents combinations of social science and forensic sociological studies, mainly dominated by case studies, studies of court processes, and interview studies.

Lack of predictability is a problem occurring where criminal justice systems base their practices on spoken languages only, making them unprepared for encounters with Deaf clients. Where routines or regulations for such adjustments are wanting, there is often a shortage of qualified interpreters or translators with legal training. Other people who know sign language but are not qualified interpreters will often be used to fill an interpreter's role in an ad hoc and improvised manner (Miller, 2001).[3] In legal processes, where linguistic nuances can be decisive to the outcome, this may make a critical and sometimes fatal difference (Brennan & Brown, 1997; Olsen & Kermit, 2015).

A closely related problem to the lack of predictability is the lack of accessibility. This is linked to how the criminal justice system itself establishes systems to safeguard disabled people. The principle of the right to due process is emphasized in the present research and reflects the framework set by the ADA, the DDA, the UN CRPD, and the measures taken to comply with statutory requirements (Elder & Schwartz, 2018; Kermit et al., 2011; MacDougall, 2001; Miller, 2001; Schwartz & Elder, 2018).

It is not always clear what "reasonable adjustment" means in the context of the criminal justice system. Most criminal laws entail regulations exacting demands and norms regarding adjustments, but the interpretations of such demands also depend on the knowledge and competence of those responsible for carrying them out (Elder & Schwartz, 2018; Søndenaa et al., 2019). Here, one explanation why interpreters are not routinely provided, is that professionals working in the court and the police do not critically question practices, but instead trust in their own and the legal system's ability to take the appropriate measures (Olsen et al., 2018).

The literature offers examples and documentation of various ways of providing interpretation, but simply recruiting a sign language interpreter might not fulfil the demand for adjustments. Among other things, sign languages are normally minority languages culturally dominated by spoken languages. As such, sign languages might not always have terminology for legal matters. This suggests that translation processes are often not straightforward for interpreting between established legal terminology in a spoken language and a sign language with few traditions for the use of such terms (MacDougall, 2001; Napier et al., 2007; Olsen & Kermit, 2015).

The Concept of Rechtssicherheit and the Nordic Welfare Model

Our research centers on a concept that is called "Rechtssicherheit" in German, and similarly, in Norwegian (and other Nordic languages), "rettssikkerhet." The term is associated with the concept in the rule of law that implies that individual citizens should be protected from discriminatory or arbitrary treatment by the government or other authorities (Echoff & Smith, 1997). Rechtssicherheit/rettssikkerhet also denotes a more positive right to be treated as an independent and competent subject, with a right to be informed about one's case and to have one's voice heard (European Convention on Human Rights and Fundamental Freedoms, 1950; United Nations, 1966; United Nations, 2006, Article 12–15). In practice, this implies that the police or the courts should avoid barring a citizen access to take part by the use of inaccessible language or unexplained procedures.

Built up in the aftermath of World War II, the Norwegian welfare society is based on the principles of universal welfare schemes, such as public health systems that include all citizens, disability pensions, general unemployment benefits, and sickness benefits (Esping-Andersen, 1990). Norway has a classic three-party power division structure, with a legislative power (the parliament), an executive power (the government), and a judicial power (the courts). Like the other Nordic countries, Norway has actively supported the United Nations and international conventions, such as the European Convention on Human Rights and Fundamental Freedoms (ECHR), the UN Convention on Human Rights, the Child Convention, the Women's Rights Convention, and CRPD. Norway ratified the CRPD in 2013, after Sweden (2008) and Denmark (2009), and before Finland and Iceland (2016).

In terms of disabled people's access to the criminal justice system, the historic situation in Norway is contradictory. On one hand, Norway is ranked at the top of international comparisons in terms of legal safety and due processes and has been so ranked for many years. This is reflected in indexes from the World Justice Project (worldjustice project.org) and Transparency International (trancparency.org). On the other hand, Norway also has one of the gravest examples of the miscarriage of justice known in postwar Europe. The victim in this case was a Deaf man.

In 1978 and 1981, Fritz Moen (1941–2005), a Norwegian citizen, was convicted twice and sentenced to the maximum penalty (21 years in prison) for two murders, but it was later proven he could not have committed them. Moen was the son of a German soldier and a Norwegian woman who gave him up to an orphanage. Moen was born deaf and grew up living more or less permanently in a Deaf boarding school. Here, he acquired Norwegian Sign Language as his first language. Troubles began for Moen in the late 1970s.

Moen was first convicted of killing a young woman in Trondheim, Norway, in 1978. In 1981, he was convicted again for the unsolved murder of another young girl killed in 1977 in the same town. The police maintained that Moen confessed to the first murder after days of heavy interrogations. The alleged confession was made during a recess when the acting interpreter—a police officer who had been called on as his parents were Deaf— was sent to fetch Moen something to eat. In retrospect, the evidence that there were several serious communication problems between Moen and the police investigators is overwhelming. There were also communicative problems during Moen's two court cases, but at least here some of the best qualified local sign language interpreters available were hired.[4] Moen maintained throughout his life that he was innocent. He served a total of 18 years under very severe conditions. In 2005 and 2007, he was acquitted of the two crimes. Unfortunately, Moen died in December 2005 and never got to experience the final acquittal.

Since this case, several system changes have been made to the way that police interrogations are carried out, and a public investigation in its aftermath resulted in improved procedural regulations for the police and for court professionals. However, the public investigation largely neglected to consider questions related to communication and accessibility. An understanding of the complexities involved when working with an interpreter was thus only established to a limited degree by these investigations. The grave errors of justice to which Fritz Moen fell victim were partly a result of the failures and shortcomings of a system where security mainly depends on the individual law professional's ability to establish critical, self-reflective practices, and this situation still prevails. Making reasonable adjustments for people who sign is still very much an individual responsibility within the framework of the criminal justice system.

This is the background for the primary topic of our discussion. If systems such as criminal justice make errors because too much depends on a criminal justice professional's ability to understand situations correctly and act accordingly, new security mechanisms may have to be built into the systems themselves. Disability studies have a long tradition of analyzing social injustice in this fashion. The development of an organization for sign language interpretation in Norway—and its systematic use by professionals working within the criminal justice system—can perhaps serve as an example of how to address barriers that are difficult to remove by moral appeals to the ones who are in charge.

In 2018, we (Olsen et al., 2018; Søndenaa et al., 2019) surveyed the Norwegian police, the public prosecutors, and the courts (n = 388), and conducted a series of focus group interviews with experienced professionals working within these institutions (n = 20). The aim of this study was to research encounters between people with learning disabilities (not Deaf people) and the criminal justice system. We make this study our point of departure because many of the results contribute to establishing a more general understanding of how the judicial system behaves when confronted with disability. When asked about routines or the use of established tools to assess if a client had a learning difficulty, 2% of respondents reported that they routinely followed a written procedure, 5% reported that they followed an established practice, 39% answered "no," and 20% answered that it was an individual responsibility to make an assessment. We also asked three questions about how confident the respondent was that the judicial system acted adequately when dealing with people with disabilities in general, and people with learning difficulties in particular. To these questions, between one-half and two-thirds (46–66%) of respondents answered "to a high degree" or "adequately." This seeming discrepancy between trust in the system that the respondents served and the actual tools and routines providing grounds for such trust became a topic in focus group interviews conducted parallel to the survey.

In these interviews, informants repeatedly voiced doubts that any servant of the judicial system was able to deal adequately with issues of disability. At the same time, informants were confident that they themselves had never been brought up short when facing clients with a disability. We interpret this as a result backing the notion that the Norwegian judicial system relies on the individual competence of its employees instead of on universally established routines in the context of disability. There is a high expectancy that the individual police officer, prosecutor, or judge knows how to act appropriately when faced with a disabled client, but there are almost no established practices that could render it plausible that there are grounds for such expectations and the corresponding confidence in the system.

There are some exceptions to this picture. One important exception is the special procedures for interrogations of people with intellectual disabilities and particularly vulnerable persons. This scheme was originally established to protect underage victims of sexual abuse from having to testify in an open court. Today, the scheme applies to both obtaining information in the investigation and securing evidence in a subsequent court case. In Norway, adults with intellectual disabilities are included in this scheme, which is implemented by the Children's House (Barnehus). The Children's House is an institution inspired by the Children's Advocacy Center in the United States and the Icelandic model of children's houses (Bakketeig et al., 2012).

The national routines for police interrogations of particularly vulnerable witnesses were revised in 2015. These routines are meant to be applied in all cases where the police have encounters with a person whom they may consider vulnerable. Special routines are established to secure the client's right to access information and access to preparation or guardianship during the process. In our interviews, actors in the criminal justice system expressed a solid trust in the system's capacity to make the right decisions. However, special procedures, such as using sign language interpreters or using alternative communication, were only to some degree known to our respondents. This again indicates that the system relies on personal competence and individualized responsibility for the results of criminal court cases.

The implications of this situation are immense. A Deaf person encountering the criminal justice system might be lucky and come across a police officer, prosecutor, or judge who—for individual reasons—is able to take appropriate measures, for example, providing an interpreter. However, the opposite is just as likely, if not more likely. The Deaf person might encounter someone who has no knowledge of Deafness and must make decisions on what to do based on whatever they can come up with there and then. Without a critical and self-reflective attitude toward practices, the judicial system will struggle to identify and correct shortcomings by means of self-initiated processes.

In the following, we propose that sign language interpreter services exert a kind of correctional power that compensates for some of the criminal justice system's shortcomings when dealing with Deaf people. This ability to induce improvement in practices is something we have not identified anywhere else while studying disability in the context of criminal justice, and we thus find it might be well worthwhile to elaborate on this case.

SIGN LANGUAGE INTERPRETING IN NORWAY

Over the last 35 years, Deaf people in Norway have gradually obtained extensive legal rights to sign language interpreting. There are different rights under many laws, and they define and divide the responsibility for funding interpretation. The finer details of the legislation on sign language interpreting are complex, but for all practical purposes, and on paper at least, Deaf people's access to interpreters is fairly unrestricted today in Norway (Bergh, 2004; Hjort, 2008).

As the rights to interpreters became more extensive, so did the demand for a functional and effective national interpreter service. By the mid-1990s, public interpreter services were established by the Norwegian government in all counties. The rights to an interpreter secured funding for the Norwegian sign language interpreting service. More importantly, they made it possible for the interpreter service to monopolize sign language interpreting because only interpreters employed through the service could receive publicly funded payments.

The practical implications of these regulations have been that interpreters are employed as civil servants in tenured positions with a pension scheme and all the work-related benefits of the Norwegian welfare system, such as maternity leave, sick leave, and sick pensions. Further, the interpreters usually share an office space together. The head of a sign language interpreting service in a county is normally an interpreter. The service handles all kinds of requests for interpreting and employs administrative staff responsible for handling the booking system and ensuring that demands are met to the highest degree possible. This administrative business is not entirely about exploiting the maximum work capacity of each employed interpreter. Over the years, interpreter quality control guidelines developed. These guidelines (Mjøen et al., 2004) also specify that for assignments considered especially demanding, multiple interpreters should be provided in order to secure the quality of the interpretation.

Parallel to the development of the public Norwegian sign language interpreting service, education and professional organizations have also expanded. Sign language interpreter education has increased from merely courses given by the National Deaf Association over a few weeks, as was the case from the late 1970s, to a three-year bachelor's university degree (beginning in 1998) offered at three universities across the country. Norwegian sign language interpreters also founded their own professional body at the end of the 1970s. This organization supports the interpreters' code of ethics, which is similar to other codes of ethics for interpreters around the world. The basic principles for professional conduct are interpreter–client confidentiality, neutrality/impartiality, and accuracy and completeness regarding interpretations (Phelan et al., 2020; Woll, 1999).

In total, professional development illustrated here shares many classic features with that of other professions. In classic sociological research on professions, the hallmarks of the formation of a profession are often designated as the obtaining of a public mandate that allows the profession to monopolize its services, a publicly financed and organized service, an independent professional body deciding the profession's code of ethics, and finally, a specialized education that increases in length (Eriksen & Molander, 2008). Based on these criteria, Norwegian Sign Language interpreters managed to establish themselves as a profession in the period from the late 1970s to the early years of the new millennium.

The forerunners working to improve interpreter education, extend rights to interpreters, and set up a professional body were interpreters like the aforementioned interpreters for Fritz Moen. Some were children of Deaf parents, while others knew sign language because they worked with Deaf people in other capacities. They had strong personal ties to the Norwegian Deaf community and to Deaf culture and sign language, and their efforts were carried out partly in cooperation with the Norwegian Deaf Association (NDF). The interpreters were, however, not Deaf. This term is usually reserved for people who share the full lived experience of being a member of a signing community, including, for example, the experience of having attended a Deaf school. The interpreters were, in other words, closely allied with the Deaf community, but were also "hearing" people. This has not changed. Even though a few Deaf people have obtained interpreter education in Norway during the last 5 or 6 years, to our knowledge, no Deaf person has been permanently employed by the public interpreting service.

Sign language interpretation within the Norwegian criminal justice system was a central topic in our earliest work on Deafness and criminal justice (Kermit et al., 2011; Olsen et al., 2011). Here, we reviewed criminal court cases involving Deaf and hearing-impaired people in the period between 2000 and 2010. We found that d/Deaf people were underrepresented within court cases compared to the general population. Of the total number of criminal cases in the Norwegian appeal courts registered in 2000–2010, we found 46 cases that included people described explicitly as deaf or hearing-impaired. This equaled two per thousand of the total number of cases, while the proportion of the deaf or hearing-impaired makes up just over 10% of the total population. This result can be interpreted in different ways, but it cannot be ruled out that Deaf and hearing-impaired people appear in the criminal courts less frequently than other people (either as victims or as accused of crimes) due to access barriers in the Norwegian criminal justice system.

We also conducted qualitative in-depth interviews with interpreters and other professionals working within the Norwegian criminal justice system. The interpreters consistently reported that their general working conditions as independent civil servants impacted their ability to do their job in a proper manner. Other informants expressed great confidence in sign language interpreters, stating that they were much more professional than "other" (spoken language) interpreters. In Norway, spoken language interpreters are still mostly private contractors that the police or courts hire and pay directly. Subsequent qualitative in-depth interviews with Deaf people who had experienced the Norwegian criminal justice system either as victims or suspects of crimes identified several barriers to equal access (Olsen & Kermit, 2015). However, also in this study, the Deaf informants expressed an almost unreserved trust in their interpreters.

Bringing these three sets of perspectives together—Deaf people interacting with the criminal justice system, interpreters, and other professionals—shows that interpreters are considered important to both Deaf people and hearing professionals, but not for the same reasons. From the hearing professionals' point of view, the high professional standard of the police and court systems guaranteed a high standard of legal matters and due processes. In their view, professional interpreters contributed to this high standard, but in instances where fewer professional interpreters were recruited, their lacking professionalism did not threaten the standard of the systems as such.

The Deaf informants saw the quality of the interpretation as the one crucial factor that decided the degree to which they could participate and obtain "Rechtssicherheit." As clients of the systems, they had a higher awareness of the risks involved because they were the ones who must suffer the consequences if mistakes were made. The trust our informants expressed in their interpreters, however, superseded that which was concerned with a mere calculation of the risks. The Deaf informants saw the interpreter service as something close to an ally, although they did not at all expect the interpreters to intervene actively on their behalf.

Correspondingly, the interpreters we interviewed stated clearly that impartiality was a keystone in their professional ethics. At the same time, they were conscious that even though the hearing professional and Deaf clients both shared the same role as the interpreters' clients, the relation between the hearing professional and the Deaf person was also a relation where the latter was—normally in the context of criminal law—the client of the former. The added vulnerability that could result from this double clientship of the Deaf person was something the interpreters were keenly aware of. Even though it was never said explicitly, the interpreters clearly indicated that improving social—and here, criminal—justice for Deaf people was a tacit ambition built into their formal ethical code of conduct.

WHAT INDEPENDENT AND PROFESSIONAL INTERPRETERS CAN DO: PRACTICAL EXAMPLES

We interviewed several Deaf informants while they were involved in active cases either with the police or in the courts. Learning about this through the interviews, we asked for and obtained consent to observe some of these encounters.[5] The participant observation sites comprised two criminal court cases, one remand hearing, and one police interrogation—all in all, around 20 hours of observation.[6] In the following paragraphs, we mobilize these hitherto unpublished observations in order to propose possible answers to the questions asked in the introduction:

1. What role do sign language interpreters play in Deaf people's encounters with the criminal justice system?
2. How can the sign language interpreters' work be organized in ways that help to reduce not only communicative barriers but also the risks of other errors that can occur in the judicial system?

Proceedings of the kind we observed are sensitive, and being convicted or suspected is associated with stigma. The details, especially concerning the Deaf persons who consented to participate in these studies, are masked in order not to disclose identifiable information. A Deaf person's individual dealings with the Norwegian criminal justice system are, in themselves, not important to this study, as the focus is on the conduct of the interpreters, regardless of the content of the dialogues they interpret.

Most of the observed interactions had the unmistakable character of routine; all participants knew well how to "play their part of the game." In saying this, we do not only imply that the police, judges, lawyers, and interpreters were professional. Many of the suspected or accused Deaf partakers and most of the Deaf witnesses had prior experiences with the police and the criminal courts. As "reappearing clients," many had considerable practical knowledge about the Norwegian criminal justice system, and they mobilized this competence in order to gain advantages in any way they could. It is thus important to state that the general character of the observations might have been different if the proceedings observed had included fewer "professionalized" Deaf clients.

Overall, findings support the notion of the sign language interpreters as autonomous and independent professionals, which communicates well with our main theoretical argument that the interpreter service's status as an independent and professionalized public service is a key aspect in the context of Deaf peoples' "Rechtssicherheit." However, the interpreters did not establish themselves as autonomous and independent so much through their words as through their actions, so in the following paragraphs we describe some of these actions in detail. These are actions showing that the interpreters (1) exerted professional power over both their hearing and their Deaf clients, and that they (2) had developed a professional conduct suited for a responsible handling and management of this kind of dominion.

Reporting the actions of the sign language interpreters, it must be stated that they (of course) did interpret. The interpreters worked according to a professional standard, and they observed certain rules regulating their conduct. However, they did not make statements about their code of ethics or inform the present clients (both the deaf and hearing ones) about things like impartiality, confidentiality, or accuracy and completeness regarding interpretations. This is, in itself, significant. Literature on interpreters' professional conduct normally emphasizes that an interpreter must clarify their role and give information instructing the clients about their roles, and what they can and cannot expect the interpreter to handle. Such literature is more often than not written by and for interpreters who mainly have experience as independent contractors. The interpreters we observed worked for the public sign language interpreting service, and they did not explain their role or their expectations about how their clients should act.

Several aspects of their behavior were notable. First, they worked in pairs and not alone, and as such, they took charge of the organizing of the available physical space in order to promote access for all participants and secure optimal working conditions. Second, as representatives of an independent service, the interpreters took responsibility for tasks designed to increase the quality of their service, such as preparation and planning. Finally, the interpreters worked in a manner where they would constantly adjust to different situations in order to promote optimal conditions for all kinds of communication.

Working in Pairs

Interpreters always came in pairs to the police or to the court, and all interpreting was carried out as a paired activity where the interpreters cooperated and supported each other. This cooperation was evident in how interpreters divided tasks and positioned themselves within the rooms. Working in pairs also limited the need for breaks and recesses, and it helped to provide continuity across cases.

Working in pairs is significant because the police and the courts would be billed by the interpreting service accordingly. As far as we know, there have been few protests or complaints about having to pay for two interpreters instead of one. If ever such questions were raised, qualified guesswork on our behalf suggests that the likely response from the administrative person handling requests for interpreters at the interpreting service would be to explain that the two interpreters working in a pair was a necessity given the task's complexity and severity. As the police and courts would not have any other service to turn to, that would probably settle the matter. The public service has a de facto monopoly on sign language interpreting services, so there would not be any other organization to turn to.

Working in pairs is described in other publications on interpreting (see, e.g., Hauland et al., 2018). However, we find it appropriate to describe in more detail how this particular cooperation between the interpreters was carried out, as such descriptions are seldom made in the context of Norwegian Sign Language interpreting.

The interpreters positioned themselves to maximize visual accessibility for the Deaf client but also to allow eye contact between the interpreters and the other hearing clients, to the extent that that was possible. They did this without much fuss and without asking permission. Only once, when the proceedings took place in a rather cramped space, did an interpreter comment that "it is best if we can sit in this fashion." This was, however, not a request for permission, but rather a polite informing about how things would have to be. No one ever opposed the interpreters' choices of positioning, though in one of the court cases, a Deaf spectator asked if the interpreters could turn a little in order to also secure their visual access to the interpreters. The interpreters complied with this request.

Depending on how the interpreters positioned or seated themselves, they would use one of two main types of cooperation which each other. In some situations, one interpreter would do all the interpreting, translating back and forth between spoken and signed Norwegian. The other interpreter would observe their colleague and offer support if necessary. Such support would typically be to offer a certain sign as a translation of a spoken word that the first interpreter might have missed, or, when translating from sign language, offer a whispered version of the signed uttering if the colleague seemed uncertain. Such visible and audible support activities seldom occurred. The most frequent observable supports were tiny nods from the observing interpreter, who continuously offered approval of the colleague's choices regarding the interpreting. When working like this, the two interpreters would typically switch the task of being the active interpreter every 10 or 15 minutes. The switches were done seamlessly. The interpreters would switch in the short breaks between speaking/signing turns, and it was normally the observing interpreter who kept track of the time intervals and gave small visual cues telling the other that it was time to switch at the next convenient stop. Sometimes, this switching included switching seats, but in cases where the interpreters sat next to one another, no movements were necessitated.

The other type of pair cooperation consisted of dividing the interpretation so that one interpreter did all the interpretation from spoken to signed language, and the other interpreter did all the interpretation from signed to spoken language. Here, the interpreters would also observe one another and be ready to lend support if necessary. The benefit of this latter routine, compared to the former, was that it allowed instant translations when different clients spoke or signed out of turn.

The interpreters varied routines according to contextual demands and possibilities. In one of the court cases, for example, all attending persons had to reposition themselves for a short while in order to view a video recording. Here, the interpreters swiftly repositioned themselves and switched their routine from the second one described earlier to the first, as it was more practical that only one interpreter stood beside the screen showing the video recording.

Cooperation in pairs presumably enhanced the quality of the interpreting because there were two pairs of eyes and ears present—one to do the actual interpreting and the other to secure accuracy and quality. The cooperation in pairs also allowed for longer work periods than one would recommend for a single interpreter working on their own. There were no observations of interpreters demanding a break before the other suggested it. The hearing clients, however, would often suggest a recess, saying things like "We must observe the interpreters' need for a break." In some of these instances, one of the interpreters would reply politely that such consideration was appreciated.

Another observable trait concerning the cooperation in pairs has to do with continuity. Some of the observed proceedings lasted for more than 1 day, and some involved moving proceedings from the police station to the court. Here, the interpreters would tell the responsible professional to remember to book interpreters at the sign language interpreting service, but they would also state that they themselves had noted the time and date of the next meeting (when this was known), and thus the demand for more interpreting. When interpreters showed up on occasions related to the same case, they would either be the same two prior interpreters, or one of the two might be replaced by another interpreter. This meant that in the different observed cases stretching over several meetings, at least one interpreter was continuously following this particular case.

Responsibility and the Quality of the Interpretation

In addition to the benefits of working in pairs, we also observed how interpreters took responsibility for preparation tasks to ensure the quality of interpretation. As mentioned earlier, observing without making video and audio recordings is not a favorable approach if the goal is to analyze and evaluate the quality of the interpretation itself. Having stated this reservation, we can nevertheless report the absence of observed situations where communication broke down completely. On the contrary, the communication between hearing and Deaf people generally flowed smoothly. The interpreters would, from time to time, halt proceedings and ask for clarifications or repetitions. This was done in a straightforward manner causing little disruption.

Interpreters would also expand their interpretations in order to clear up minor problems in understanding. This would typically include repetitions of numbers, names, titles, or other details of interest, and the interpreter would repeat or add something to what they had recently said or signed. On these occasions, the other interpreter would often make a short explanatory remark to the clients who did not receive the expanded interpretation, typically phrased "The interpreter just had to repeat the number/name/ similar details." Otherwise, the interpreters would translate requests for clarification in a manner that left the responsibility for providing an answer directed at one of the other participants.

The general impression here is that interpreters made quick decisions about the nature of these different requests. If the ambiguity—in the interpreter's opinion—concerned minor details, they could choose to handle it themselves. Otherwise, a request would be phrased so that the other participant (be it a hearing or a Deaf person) would provide the answer. This kind of decision-making on behalf of those who use the interpreters' services might seem like a dangerous business, where interpreters could run the risk of taking too much responsibility in the task of making the clients understand each other. However, there were no observations of decision-making openly backfiring and causing uncertainties. These small actions highlight the importance of having well-trained interpreters working in pairs.

Adjusting Behavior to Different Situations

Interpreters adapted to the circumstances of each case. Most of the topics deliberated during the observed proceeding were of a rather grave nature. However, none of the hearing professionals (police officers, lawyers, or judges) acted in verbally aggressive manners. Rather, the general tone was politely somber. This mode of communicating was generally mirrored by the Deaf persons interacting with them; there was little aggressiveness and generally a polite, though distant tone. However, there were some interesting exceptions.

During one of the court's recesses, the interpreters translated a comment made by the Deaf defendant about an upcoming football match. This was picked up by that hearing prosecutor, who declared her support for the same team as the defendant. This made for a short but pleasant social conversation. That such mutual identification of common interests in sport came about at all was due to the interpreters, who did not lay down their work during a recess but also chose to interpret social small talk.

The interpreters would generally show the same kind of somber politeness as most of the hearing and Deaf clients while interpreting proceedings, and they would not themselves invite small talk during breaks. Nevertheless, in the described situation, they added the task of interpreting small talk to their assignment quite automatically and without commenting on it. When interpreting the excitement associated with the sport events discussed, they also let go of the expressions they wore in court and mirrored the enthusiasm that the prosecutor and the Deaf defendant were showing.

In sum, all the actions of the interpreters were important, but not only as actions designed to facilitate interaction and communication between the participants. The interpreters' actions also signaled the professionalism of an independent service exacting demands on the practices of the police and the court.

WHAT WE OBSERVED AND WHAT WE DID NOT OBSERVE: ANALYTICAL POINTS

Because the observed proceedings took place between either professional or "professionalized" clients, the apparent absence of severe problems associated with interpreting is the most significant result of these empirical observations. To interpret the observations correctly is, however, a question of considering unobserved factors that still influenced the observed situation. As these factors are related to the aforementioned structure and organization of the Norwegian sign language interpreting service, we offer the following analysis.

The two interpreters were not a random pair showing up for an assignment that they otherwise knew little about. They were colleagues who had been working together on similar assignments. They shared an office space and were part of a collegium that would discuss the meaning of professional conduct and specific challenges related to different types of assessments. The interpreters were picked for the assignments because the administration and management handling the requests for interpretation judged that these assignments demanded skilled interpreters with prior experience from similar interpreting. To obtain the particular interpretation skills, the interpreters had probably at one point earlier in their careers been assigned for the first time to a police interrogation or a criminal court and had been paired up with an experienced colleague. By organizing the service in this manner, the service made sure that important qualifications were passed on to new members of the collegium.

Further, at some point between the booking of interpreters and the actual proceedings, the interpreters or the interpreting service requested available written material and general information relevant to the case. Expenses for preparation were billed to the police or the courts. Because many of the Deaf clients in the observed cases were known to the police and court, it is likely that the interpreters we observed had worked together with some of the police officers, lawyers, and judges as well as with some of the Deaf clients on prior occasions. This is probably the main reason why the interpreters did not deem it necessary to offer information about their conduct at the beginning of the proceedings. They knew their Deaf clients, and several of the hearing clients as well.

As far as we have been able to, information about the interpreters and the administrative routines at the interpretation service has been verified. This verification does not, however, account for the observed fluency of the cooperation between the interpreters working in pairs, nor for their ability to blend in and take on a professional task in mutual interaction with several other persons who all had in common that they some way or another relied on the job done by the interpreters.

As for the cooperation between the interpreters, the coordination they displayed was the result of knowing one another as colleagues, working together, and developing together. This would not have been so seemingly easy had they not been colleagues in tenured positions. All in all, their cooperation and the way they adjusted their behavior to match different demands at different times signifies the kind of expertise described by Dreyfus (2004), in which decisions are made not only as the results of analytical processes but also as the results of intuitive decision-making.

"Rechtssicherheit" and Interpreting

Our observations support the notion that independent and professional interpreters representing not only themselves, but a public service, have both the means and opportunity to exact demands for reasonable adjustments favoring both Deaf and hearing participants in the criminal justice system. The obvious benefit for the police and the court consists of their being able to perform their duties much in their usual manner, but at the same time tacitly directed by interpreters who have both the will and the power to exact demands for adjustments. This effectiveness of the service provided by the sign language interpreters can, however, have the adverse effect of removing incentives for changes of practice within the police and the court, since the professionals of these institutions are not confronted by the shortcomings of their routines as long as the interpreters are there to make corrections. If this is the case, the implications, for example, for other lingual minorities in Norway who do not have a professionalized interpreter service, is that their "Rechtssicherheit" continues to be at risk.

The observable benefit for Deaf clients, defendants, and witnesses would seem to consist primarily of lingual access to participation in the proceedings. We have not, however, suggested the naïve idea that the interpreters, simply by alleviating some of the communicative barriers, bring about a situation where Deaf people can participate on the same terms as any other defendent or witness. On the contrary, how the police and court operate very much clings to the outdated idea that proceedings should be uniformly designed to suit the imagined typical—here, hearing—client. Consequently, the criminal justice system in Norway is intrinsically inaccessible to people falling outside the system's normative idea about the average client.

This confirms that Deaf people's legal safety—"Rechtssicherheit"—is at risk when they face the Norwegian criminal justice system. The system does not recognize something already apparent to Lev Vygotski when he noted that being Deaf is not simply being a typical or "hearing" person who cannot hear (Vygotsky, 1929). As long as Deaf people fall outside the normative idea of the average client, chances are that Deaf people are systematically discriminated against because of mechanisms built into the judicial system.

Discrimination falls into two main categories. First, the lack of preparedness to recognize and accommodate for Deafness as a cultural and lingual status means that Deaf people are discriminated against as a cultural and lingual minority in much the same way as other lingual and cultural minorities facing the criminal justice system in Norway. It is true that the provision of interpreters must be understood as a recognition of Deaf people's right to access proceedings in a language they know, and such provision of access would seem to be the interpreters' main responsibility. However, merely calling for interpreters does not mean that any of the professionals in the police or the courts must reflect on what it means to be Deaf and how Deafness is a way of being in the world different from that of a member of the typical majority community. This latter point suggests that even if Deaf people are nominally recognized as a lingual and cultural minority, this does not preclude the fact that Deaf people are also disabled by the criminal justice system in the sense laid down by protagonists of social approaches to disability. Though such approaches vary, they generally maintain that disability is (often or most often) the result of discrimination and socially created barriers. This would imply that even though the criminal justice system in Norway provides interpreters, the system still places Deaf people in disadvantageous positions behind disabling barriers.

This implies a problem, and a risk to Deaf people's "Rechtssicherheit," that can only be solved permanently by a reformation of the system itself. The focus of this text, however, is not to analyze how such fundamental changes can be brought about, but to discuss under which circumstances interpreters can contribute to the safeguarding of Deaf people's "Rechtssicherheit," at least to some degree, while working within an imperfect system.

The interpreters do not make any promises about such contributions. On the contrary, the interpreter service's stated purpose is to offer interpreting and nothing else, and it has been so since the service was founded. The interpreters observe a code of ethics emphasizing a profound respect for clients' autonomy, be the client Deaf or "hearing." Impartiality and neutrality are important principles of this code, along with the principle that the interpreters have no professional responsibility other than to interpret faithfully. In short, neither the interpreter service nor the interpreters have ever suggested that they play any other role than interpreters when it comes to seeing criminal justice be done where Deaf people are involved. Moreover, suggesting that interpreters should have a formal responsibility for Deaf people's legal safety would be highly problematic both because it would contradict the interpreters' ethical code, which promote the clients' autonomy, and because it would be inadmissibly paternalistic.

The absence of a formal aspect of interpreting that can be said to strengthen Deaf people's legal safety is thus not an issue here. If the interpreters contribute to greater safety, this contribution is found in the *manner* the interpreters carry out their given task of interpreting. Here, our studies and the observations suggest several aspects of the manner the interpreters' work is organized—some are quite practical, and others are more theoretical. Our main theoretical argument is that the interpreter service's status as an independent and professionalized public service is a key aspect.

An independent civil service commands a type of respect for its employees that an interpreter employed directly by the police, for example, cannot automatically expect. This aspect of independence is of great importance regarding the discussion about legal safety. The interpreters are not the interpreters of the police or the courts, even if these institutions must cover their expenses, nor are they the Deaf clients' interpreters either. The impartiality principle that defines all attending parties as the interpreters' clients does not automatically give any benefits to the hearing professionals. More important, though, is the interpreter service's independence when it comes to defining its services.

The interpreting service itself sets the standard for the level of competence an interpreter must have before they can interpret for the police and the courts. The de facto monopoly that the service has as a publicly funded service also prevents these standards from being lowered due to competition in a market where cheap services are sought. Within general economic limits set by public budgets and salaries, the interpreter service has managed to obtain the processes of both collective professionalization and the development of a functional organization. As for the latter, the booking and management systems mentioned earlier exist not only to answer calls but also to make decisions on what qualifications are needed for individual assignments.

The processes of professionalization have allowed for the development of services with a general ambition of improving Deaf people's access to all kinds of societal practices, including the criminal justice system. The development and application of the system where two interpreters work as a pair constitutes a practical example of a professional development that would have been difficult to achieve had the interpreters not had the opportunity to cooperate as colleagues.

ORGANIZATION TRUMPS INDIVIDUAL SKILLS

In the context of disability studies, public services are often criticized and accused of practices that can be patriarchal and limiting to the autonomy of those receiving services. The Norwegian interpreting service is not flawless in this respect. Even though Deaf people in Norway have strong formal rights, there are frequent reports of the service failing to provide enough interpreters to meet demand. To our knowledge, however, there have been no reported incidents where Deaf people have been denied interpreters when facing the criminal justice system. This should not come as a surprise. The interpreter service's organization is set up to prioritize between assignments when it must, and along with critical health service interpreting, interpreting for the police and courts is routinely given priority.

This reliability might partly explain why our Deaf informants (Kermit et al., 2011; Olsen & Kermit, 2015) expressed such a high degree of trust in their interpreters. What they trusted was not so much the skill of individual interpreters. They trusted that the organization set up by the interpreting service would provide them with interpreters that were up to the task of delivering quality work at the police station or in the courtroom. Given that the interpreters are still exclusively non-Deaf persons, this might also attest to something more. The original alliance between the forerunning interpreters working for the establishment of interpreting services would not have succeeded had it not been for the cooperation of and alliances with the Norwegian Deaf community. As mentioned, this commitment to work for increased social justice together with the Deaf community suggests an element of professional ethics that precedes the code of ethics stating, for example, the principle of impartiality. The mutual recognition might still exist, albeit in the form of a mere tacit promise, that the interpreting service still strives for increased accessibility when it works to improve the quality of Deaf peoples' rights.

NOTES

1. Even though the distinction is far from clear, we follow the custom of differentiating between the medical condition of being deaf (which is written with a lowercase "d") and being a member of a signing community (in which case Deaf is written with a capital "D"). (See,

e.g., Markowicz & Woodward, 1978; Padden & Humphries, 1988; and Woodward, 1972. For an analysis of the different notions of d/Deafness, see Kermit, 2009.)

2. The term "phonocentric" is highly political and normally used in an activist context. Nevertheless, it pinpoints what we want to highlight as characteristic of the Norwegian criminal justice system: that it is a system for hearing people with very little reflection on or routines for how to deal with people who are (medically) deaf and who sign (are Deaf).

3. This is also likely to happen for Deaf people trying to access social services and government systems more broadly.

4. These interpreters, however, worked as freelancers and did not have any collegial network, nor could they make a living from interpreting full-time. Some were children of Deaf parents, while others knew sign language because they worked with Deaf people in other capacities.

5. We also obtained approval from the National Ethics Board to extend our work to observations.

6. We conducted the court case and police interrogation observations in order to form a broader understanding of the data from our previous interviews, not to do in-depth research of the translational activities of sign language interpreters. Since the hypothesis developed during our preceding work concerned structural and organizational aspects of interpreting, it made sense to examine (positive or negative) aspects of professionalism and professional conduct. Designing the study in this fashion, we did not prioritize the detection of possible errors or particularly good formulations in the translations themselves.

References

Bakketeig, E., Berg, M., Myklebust, T., & Stefansen, K. (2012). *Barnehusevalueringen 2012, delrapport 1: Barnehusmodellens implikasjoner for politiets arbeid med fokus på dommeravhør og rettsmedisinsk undersøkelse*. PHS Forskning.

Bergh, G. (2004). *Norsk tegnspråk som offisielt språk*. ABM-utvikling.

Brennan, M., & Brown, R. (1997). *Equality before the law: Deaf people's access to justice*. University of Durham.

Dreyfus, S. E. (2004). The five-stage model of adult skill acquisition. *Bulletin of Science, Technology & Society*, 24(3), 177–181. https://doi.org/10.1177/0270467604264992

Echoff, T., & Smith, E. (1997). *Forvaltningsrett* [Administrative legislation]. Oslo: Aschehoug.

Elder, B. C., & Schwartz, M. A. (2018). Effective Deaf access to justice. *Journal of Deaf Studies and Deaf Education*, 23(4): 331–340. https://doi.org/10.1093/deafed/eny023

Eriksen, E. O., & Molander, A. (2008). Profesjon, rett og politikk. In A. Molander & L. I. Terum (Eds.), *Profesjonsstudier* (pp. 161–176). Universitetsforlaget.

Esping-Andersen, G. (1990). *The three worlds of welfare capitalism*. Princeton University Press.

European Convention on Human Rights and Fundamental Freedoms. (1950). Adopted on November 4, 1950. Council of Europe, [not dated.] https://www.echr.coe.int/documents/convention_eng.pdf.

Hauland, H., Nilson, A-L., & Raanes, E. (2018). *Tolking—språkarbeid og profesjonsutøvelse*. Gyldendal Akademisk.

Hjort, P. (2008). *Tolkeutredningen 2008: Framtidens tolke—og kommunikasjonstjenester for døve, døvblinde og hørselshemmede*. NAV.

Kermit, P. (2009). Deaf or deaf? Questioning alleged antinomies in the bioethical discourses on cochlear implantation and suggesting an alternative approach to d/Deafness. *Scandinavian Journal of Disability Research*, 11(2), 159–174.

Kermit, P., Mjøen, O. M., & Olsen, T. (2011). Safe in the hands of the interpreter? A qualitative study investigating the legal protection of Deaf people facing the criminal justice system in Norway. *Disability Studies Quarterly*, 31(4). http://dx.doi.org/10.18061/dsq .v31i4.1714

Markowicz, H., & Woodward, J. C. (1982). Language and the maintenance of ethnic boundaries in the Deaf community. In J. C. Woodward (Ed.), *How you gonna get to heaven if you can't talk with Jesus: On depathologizing deafness* (pp. 3–9). TJ. (Original work published 1978).

MacDougall, J. C. (2001). Access to justice for Deaf Inuit in Nunavut: The role of "Inuit Sign Language." *Canadian Psychology/Psychologie Canadienne*, 42(1), 61–73.

Miller, K. R. (2001). Access to sign language interpreters in the criminal justice system. *American Annals of the Deaf*, 146(4), 328–330.

Mjøen, O.-M., Kermit, P. S., Midtbø, M., Aars, R., Urgård, S., Valestrand, K. L., & Sund, T. (2004). *Nasjonal standard for tolketjenesten*. Rikstrygdeverket.

Napier, J., Spencer, D. & Sabolcec, J. (2007). *Deaf jurors' access to court proceedings via sign language interpreting: An investigation*. Research report 14. A project funded by the NSW Law Reform Commission and the Macquarie University External Collaborative Grant Scheme.

Olsen, T., & Kermit, P. (2015). Sign language, translation and rule of law—Deaf people's experiences from encounters with the Norwegian criminal justice system. *Scandinavian Journal of Disability Research*, 17(S1), 23–41. http://dx.doi.org/10.1080/15017419 .2014.972448

Olsen, T., Kermit, P. S., Søndenaa, E., Dahl, N., & Envik, R. (2018). *Rettssikkerhet—likeverd og likeverdig behandling. Mennesker med kognitive funksjonsnedsettelser i møte med strafferettspleien*. Nordlandsforskning.

Olsen, T., Mjøen, O. M., Rønning, H., & Kermit, P. (2011). *Tegn, tillit og troverdighet—om rettssikkerheten for døve og hørselshemmede*. Bodø.

Padden, C., & Humphries, T. (1988). *Deaf in America: Voices from a culture*. Harvard University Press.

Phelan, M., Rudvin, M., Skaaden, H., & Kermit, P. S. (2020). *Ethics in public service interpreting*. Routledge.

Schwartz, M. A., & Elder, B. C. (2018). Deaf access to justice in Northern Ireland: Rethinking "reasonable adjustment" in the Disability Discrimination Act. *Disability & Society*, 33(7), 1003–1024. https://doi.org/10.1080/09687599.2018.1478801

Søndenaa, E., Olsen, T., Kermit Patrick, S., Dahl Nina, C., & Envik, R. (2019). Intellectual disabilities and offending behaviour: The awareness and concerns of the police, district attorneys and judges. *Journal of Intellectual Disabilities and Offending Behaviour*, 10(2), 34–42. https://doi.org/10.1108/JIDOB-04-2019-0007

United Nations. (1966). *International covenant on civil and political rights*. Adopted on December 19, 1966. United Nations. http://www.ohchr.org/Documents/ProfessionalInter est/ccpr.pdf.

United Nations. (2006). *Convention on the rights of persons with disabilities*. Adopted on December 13, 2006. United Nations. http://www.un.org/disabilities/convention/convent ionfull.shtml.

Vygotsky, L. (1929[1993]). *The fundamental problems of defectology*. Collected Works of L. S. Vygotsky. Vol. 2. New York: Plenum Press. https://www.marxists.org/archive/vygotsky/works/1929/defectology/index.htm

Woll, Heidi (1999). *Historien om tolkeyrkets fremvekst: hvordan døvetolker og døvblindetolker ble en egen yrkesgruppe i Norge*. Døves forlag.

Woodward, J. C., Jr. (1972). Implications for sociolinguistic research among the deaf. *Sign Language Studies*, 1, 1–7.

PART XI

Efforts toward Inclusion

CHAPTER 36

ACTIVISM, INCLUSION, AND SOCIAL JUSTICE

MICHAEL PRINCE

INTRODUCTION

OBSTACLES to the rightful inclusion of disabled citizens include their misrepresentation and nonrecognition as full persons in prevailing cultural value patterns; the maldistribution of resources in income, employment, housing, and other material resources; and their marginal voice and presence in elections, public policy development, and decision-making processes. Social justice priorities of disability activists in North America and elsewhere hence embrace a mixture of symbolic, material, and participatory concerns. Conceptions of social justice have widened considerably in recent decades, both in theoretical and practical terms, to include "a concern with respect and recognition, with addressing difference and identity politics, with the distribution of resources, with human capabilities, with voice and representation" (Craig, 2018, p. 1). More than mere philosophical notions, these concerns encapsulate well the actual interests of disability movements and the activities they undertake in mobilizing for social change and influencing policymaking and practice. Disability activists struggle against cultural, economic, and political exclusions and marginalization. Analytically these struggles for social justice correspond broadly to distinct institutional domains: a politics of recognition to the cultural-symbolic order of society, a politics of redistribution to the market economy and welfare state, and a politics of representation to the political system and civil society. While disability activists and theorists are attentive to discursive aspects of the formation and meaning of disability in popular culture, they similarly emphasize material resources and democratic dimensions of social justice.

This chapter considers disability as a contested human identity and complex assemblage of collective actions. It examines how disability intersects with politics and advances the argument that disability itself is a political phenomenon. Disabled people are actors involved in numerous civic sites within and across state and societal institutions and processes.[1] The focal point is on surveying various forms of activism practiced by disabled citizens in advancing goals of inclusion and social justice. The chapter examines the official public sphere of state politics as well as the cultural and material dimensions of politics to capture a wide array of activist practices and issues. To this end, the chapter is presented in two main sections. The first considers the relations between disability and the political in contemporary societies. This includes a discussion of possibilities of human agency and social movement capacities in the disability field. The analysis discusses several models of disability, which are evident in theory, movement advocacy, and public policy. These are the personal tragedy and worthy poor model, the biomedical model, the social model, the human rights model, and the psychoemotional model of disability. In turn, I examine activism as a repertoire of activities and roles, taking place in various jurisdictional spaces and territorial scales of mobilization. The second section considers three forms of social injustices and advocacy strategies pursued by disability rights movements: activism centered on recognition, redistribution, and representation. Concluding observations call on the need to examine disability and the struggle for social justice in relation to a politics of cultural recognition and identity, a politics of socioeconomic redistribution of material goods and services, and a politics of democratic representation that combines conventional and alternative modes of decision-making.

DISABILITY ACTIVISM AND THE POLITICAL

Disability movements pursue an expansive understanding of "the political"—one that includes not only governments, public service bureaucracies, legislatures, and the courts but also families and social networks, voluntary and charitable sectors, mainstream and marginal economies, health sciences, and cultural practices. This means that power relationships throughout the whole of society are amendable to disability activism; normative and empirical debates are ongoing about the respective responsibilities of the state, the market economy, and social enterprises, as well as innumerable kinds of communities and households.

Advocates, informal and formal groups, and various coalitions are contributing to politicization and deepening of citizenship. Disability communities understand that developing rights and responsibilities involves creating new choices, engaging in debates, building consensus, and changing policies. Disability activism expresses a multidimensional discourse on citizenship, addressing civil, legal, political, economic, and social elements in a broad agenda for policy action (Prince, 2009). The story of citizenship for people with disabilities, as for other oppressed groups on the margins of society (Glenn, 2011), differs from conventional accounts in liberal democracies. This is not a simple story of the continual and steady extension of rights and responsibilities over many decades or centuries. The status of full citizenship is a relatively recent struggle for people with disabilities; it is a struggle mixed with considerable rhetoric, setbacks and frequent delays, a few major successes, and many incremental gains. International developments have influenced the turn to citizenship in disability politics. Following on the civil rights movement for Blacks, the women's liberation movement and the disability rights campaign in the United States (Little, 2010; Shapiro, 1994; Switzer, 2003), and paralleling similar movements for Indigenous peoples in Canada,[2] disability advocates embrace the concepts and tactics of rights-seeking minority groups.

Matters of impairments, handicaps, mental health, and physical and developmental limitations are among the central issues of the human condition. Much of disability politics—that is, what makes disability political—is about choices made in power relations over whether the priority in policy should be to issues relating to body structures and functions, daily activities and social activities, or environmental and cultural factors requiring transformation. Disability activism embraces values of equality, diversity, dignity, inclusion, and independence plus the principles of rights and responsibilities, empowerment and participation. At a rhetorical level at least, these are dominant ideas in disability policy and politics. These dominant ideas concern individual liberty (self-determination and competence), stability in social relations (the critical issue of managing stable transitions across life stages), equality and inclusion (citizenship), and equity and fairness (reasonable accommodation, among other practices).

Possibilities of Human Agency and Social Movement Capacities

In an important paper on embodied citizenship, Bacchi and Beasley (2002) contend there are two types of citizens or political subjects. First, are people they call full citizens; people deemed to be in control over their body and mind. They are active and autonomous persons, enjoying civil liberties and a degree of distance from direct government supervision. They are the able, functional, and socially empowered members of the political community. Bodily matters, Bacchi and Beasley contend, are largely absent from everyday discourse for the full citizen, who is taken for granted to be a healthy consumer or producer. The second type of political subject is the lesser citizen; people presumably controlled by their body. They are passive and dependent individuals who tend to be more under government surveillance than full citizens are and certainly are objects of medical scrutiny. These lesser citizens are disabled people, those with dysfunctional bodies and/or minds, the biologically disempowered. For disabled members of political communities, bodily matters are present in their social identities and interactions. Taken to be limited and abnormal in some manner, prominent roles are often as patients, public clients, and recipients of charity.

Within these two types of citizens delineated by Bacchi and Beasley are multiple kinds of political subjects with different bodies and minds, varied lifeworlds, and particular social experiences. More than victims or passive clients, however, people with disabilities, as is discussed throughout this volume, exercise resistance and enact creative human agency in their interactions with others.

People with disabilities are active participants in both constituting and claiming social rights of citizenship as workers, contributors to social insurance programs, as applicants and recipients, and possibly as appellants of negative decisions on their entitlement claims. Disability, like other social identities, is a series of actions and performances: a doing and undoing, contemplation and preparation, a producing and reworking, accommodation and self- advocacy, achievements and setbacks, all within networks of relationships in state and societal structures. Activism and struggles for social justice involve the interaction of human agency and social structures, whether at the personal level of everyday life, public- or private-sector programs, medical knowledge and bureaucratic administration, labor markets or insurance firms, or general cultural beliefs and attitudes on normalcy and disability. People with disabilities, individually and in various collectivities (families, advocacy groups, service agencies, coalitions, and so forth), are political beings. They exercise human agency through advancing claims for fuller citizenship and making decisions about services and governance. Independent living models of service with self-managed care are politically significant as spaces for autonomy and self-determination. So, too, can be consultation exercises and advisory councils with meaningful representation. Political agency occurs through advocacy efforts of organizations and in partnerships with other community groups, government agencies, labor unions or business firms. Beside participation in formal organizations, political agency also takes place through individual decisions and informal actions. In short, the disabled subject exercises her or his rights through human agency in a structural context of many pathways, sites, and scales.

Disability justice and radical accessibility are two streams of the disability movement that use principles of *intersectionality*. Central principles of intersectionality include understanding the experience of lived realities as a set of connections across multiple categories of differences; linking individual experience to wider social, political, cultural, and economic processes; and refusing a preconfigured experience along any axis of power (Moss & Prince, 2020). Disability justice involves picking at, undoing, and dismantling ableism as a system of oppression in concert with other forms of oppression such as racism and sexism. Radical accessibility, an intersectionalist political strategy, challenges all forms of oppression. It seeks to go beyond the inclusion of disabled people and to create communities where difference is not an organizing principle of social order. Access is as much about wheelchair ramps as it is about shedding light on the privilege arising from one's social positionings in society (Withers, 2012).

Disabled people exercise human agency in claiming, managing, and defending social rights of citizenship. The sheer human agency of persons with disabilities when demanding rights to public services is evident in their interacting and negotiating with programs and wider cultural, medical, and economic institutions (Church et al., 2007; Moss et al., 2016; Orsini, 2012; Reeve, 2002). Agency arises from individuals learning about their changing bodies and minds, and in their managing impressions around impairments. Agency is likewise exercised through gathering and exchanging information as people acquire the status of disabled worker, who may or may not disclose their disability status (Prince, 2017), clients or patients engaged with health and social care systems (Moss & Teghtsoonian, 2008), veterans and families struggling with government bureaucracies for resources (Moss et al., 2016), voters and political candidates for elected offices (Prince, 2014), parents of a disabled child (Carey et al., 2020; Trainor, 2010), or self-advocates (Llewellyn & Northway, 2008), and then as rights claimants and possibly litigants (Stienstra, 2020). The image of activist citizen that emerges is of disabled bodies as multiple politicized bodies.

Capacity requires the wherewithal of staff, time, information, and support to disabled activists to participate in consultations, respond to public issues and governmental proposals, and initiate desired solutions. Broadly speaking, these efforts have yielded mixed results across countries and policy areas and by disability types and times (Barnartt & Scotch, 2001; Carey et al., 2020; Pettinicchio, 2019; Prince, 2016). Enhancing the capacity of the disability community as a social movement involves augmenting such activities as consciousness raising of people in the movement and wider society. It involves communicating in a positive manner the varied experiences and identities of persons with disabilities, and challenging the ableist attitudes and actions in society; in short, striving to institute progressive changes that tackle exclusion, cultural prejudice, and discrimination. A major concern of capacity building is the recruitment and preparation of a new generation of leaders and members for disability movements (Little, 2010; Oliver & Barnes, 2012).

Models of Disability and Statuses of Bodies

In varying approaches and degrees of emphases, several models of disability appear in advocacy debates in disability activism. Among these are the personal tragedy and worthy poor model, the biomedical model, the social model, the human rights model, and the psychoemotional model of disability (Robertson & Larson, 2016). Models of disability are similar to what social movement scholars call frames in that they are symbolic processes, which give meaning and legitimacy to particular activities and events, shape policy agendas and interactions, and may even attract (or discourage) individuals to participate in certain domains. Indeed, connections to the social movement literature with respect to frames and framing in disability activism (Barnartt & Scotch, 2001; Carey et al., 2020; Little, 2010). Different models of disability have distinctive ways of thinking about how people are identified as disabled or able and thus structuring ability/disability relationships. The models also express distinctive vocabularies or ways of talking about and discursively framing people with physical or mental disabilities with implications for social acceptance and stigma. Furthermore, the models imply different assessments as to the possibility of human agency by disabled individuals to influence the social world. Each is briefly noted.[3]

The *personal tragedy* or *worthy poor perspective* was historically and is still today a double-edged sword for people with disabilities (Charlton, 1998; Dunn & Langdon, 2016; Withers, 2012). Under this long-established approach, people with disabilities are the object of charity with an assigned status of deservingness, but often at the cost of basic citizenship rights. Considered unfortunate, helpless, and incompetent to function in society, authorities established systems of segregation for people with disabilities, such as asylums, special schools, and sheltered workshops. Disability is an individual impairment of pathology and personal calamity; persons with disabilities are unlucky and unemployable. Many people still hold this outlook on disability as passivity and inherent dependency (Anspach, 1979; Oliver & Barnes, 2012).

Attention to a version of the *biomedical model of disability* corresponds to three dimensions (Hughes, 2009; Oliver & Barnes, 2012; Stienstra, 2020). One is that the medical condition of a person (a disease or disturbance in body/mind function, organ, or system) is the main explanation for difficulties in the performance of everyday activities. A person's status is primarily on diagnosing and then classifying and, if possible, treating the person's body and mind, curing or fixing their pathologies. Professionals treat persons with disabilities as sick, abnormal, functionally limited, possibly rehabilitative, yet frequently unemployable and therefore dependent. Second, public programs and health services enact the medical model through a focus in eligibility rules on the degree of severity of disabilities as diagnosed by health science professionals. Third, the impact of the medical model works through attention (and inattention) to the need for aids, assistive devices, human supports, treatments and prescription medications. State laws define disability in terms of a range of impairments: physical, sensory, neurological, learning, intellectual or developmental, psychiatric or mental disorder. In this context, disability is a thing—whether temporary or permanent, stable or episodic, mild or severe—that is in the person. Patient groups and related biosocial communities of people with shared conditions feature in this perspective (Hughes, 2009).

In the evolution of thinking on disability, the postwar welfare state corresponded to a period of medicalization, among other social processes (Pettinicchio, 2019; Prince, 2016). The overall policy orientation to disabled persons was framed within the knowledge, discourse, and power of biomedical science. Physicians and related health professionals are not the only groups that generate medical control or medicalization. Other institutions, including life insurance companies and government health programs, are routinely engaged in these processes. Even self-advocates as well as family members may adopt medical discourse and accept medical practices to obtain a diagnosis and recognized identity in order to advance a claim. This is the status of the individually impaired body/mind or biological citizen.

The *social model of disability* highlights the significance of environmental and societal factors such as unsafe and unhealthy environments, discrimination, and the lack of accessibility (Barnes, 2007; Hanes, 2016; Oliver & Barnes, 2012; Prince, 2016). The disability creation process is when attitudinal, environmental, technological, and social factors affect the impairment or underlying medical condition(s) of an individual. Disability occurs when a person with impairment encounters barriers to performing everyday activities of living, barriers to participating in the societal mainstream, and barriers to exercising his or her human rights and fundamental freedoms. Disability here is a societal process more than some individual condition. Society is handicapping and disabling. In the social model, the status is of the communally embedded person.

A significant disjuncture exists between this perspective and much of Canadian public policy and service provision. Many programs, benefits, and delivery systems embody aspects of other perspectives on disability, especially a biomedical, charitable, or worthy poor welfare viewpoint.

The *human rights model of disability* (Charlton, 1998; Stienstra, 2020; Withers, 2012) receives explicit expression in movement activism and state policy with respect to national and subnational laws on anti-discrimination, for example, and the United Nations Convention on the Rights of Persons with Disabilities (CRPD), which Canada and other countries have signed and ratified, but not the United Sates. A range of guiding principles and aspirational commitments in the CRPD cover adequate standards of living, health, personal mobility, work and employment, education, safe and healthy working conditions, and women and disabilities. In turn, these commitments imply obligations on state parties (in the Canadian context, obligations on the federal, provincial, and territorial governments) to advance rights to full and equal participation in society by people with disabilities on an equal basis with others. Beside the CRPD, other foundational legal commitments are in the Charter of Rights and Freedoms, provincial and federal human rights laws, and other statutes (on accessibility and education, as examples). The image is of the person with disabilities as a rights holder, the equal citizen recognized and belonging to a political community (Glenn, 2011).

The *psychoemotional model of disability* draws attention to cultural and firsthand experiential facets of living with disabilities (Reeve, 2002). The focus is on personal emotions and feelings, individual and social perceptions, stereotypes, and self-images that arise from an individual's interactions and experiences of discrimination, denial, and disadvantage in social encounters within mainstream settings like a school or workplace. Dominant attitudes and practices in the labor market and in the education system challenge the emotional well-being of people with disabilities. Adults with severe disabilities experience disability as a negative status through reported feelings of discomfort, fear of rejection and reprisals, lack of confidence, and personal stress. Students with disabilities report unmet needs for accommodations in school and experiences at school of avoidance and bullying by other students. Survey research in Canada indicates that about one third of students with milder disabilities and fully one half of those with more severe disabilities say they have had such negative social experiences at school (Brisebois et al., 2018). Working-age adults with less apparent or so-called invisible disabilities, even severe ones, worry that disclosing their condition to a prospective or actual employer can have numerous potential disadvantages along with any advantages of workplace accommodation. Many disabled people therefore engage in the emotional labor of managing impression and hiding their conditions from customers or clients, colleagues, supervisors, and employers (Prince, 2017). This image is the person with disabilities as experiential actor negotiating and coping in an imperfect ableist world.

Models of disability are working paradigms, which shape the meaning of disability discourses, public policies, and everyday practices. A central feature of contemporary disability politics is an ongoing dispute over the conceptualization and implementation of disability. Just as notions of ability and disability are cultural conceptions, so, too, disability programs are historical constructs, their meanings varying over time and within a given period and given political context. Elements of the disabled state and the disability policy field are comparatively old, predating modern welfare regimes, while other parts are recent (Prince, 2016). Accordingly, the personal tragedy and deserving charity models of disability influence policy in particular ways that differ from a model of disablement based on medical rehabilitation or a model based on principles of human rights. In brief, the personal tragedy approach leads to public programs that are discretionary and exclusionary, placing considerable onus on families to meet the needs of personal care and activities of everyday living. The deserving charity model relies upon community interventions by nonprofits, foundations, and fundraisers. The medical model of disability involves a central role by various professionals in the assessment, provision, administration, and evaluation of public and private health services and therapeutic treatments. By comparison, the human rights model is associated with anti-discrimination laws, equity measures like affirmative action, reasonable accommodations, and procedural rights of informed consent and administrative fairness.

A Repertoire of Activities and Roles

In public commentary and right-wing political ideologies, there is frequent mention that "rights talk" diminishes the idea of obligations and responsibility talk. What such remarks typically ignore is the work involved in expressing and pursuing a right, the work in presenting a claim, the work in managing a benefit, and the work in defending rights attained. Exercising social citizenship is an endless commitment not some brief activity (Glenn, 2011; Moss et al., 2016; Orsini & Smith, 2010). Claiming a right to education, health care, social service, or income support involves a series of legal and moral expectations and transactions. Exercising a right to disability insurance, for example, can involve the risk of lengthy procedures and intense investigations, which, in turn, have the risk of adverse consequences to one's health. Concerning income programs, the effort of social citizenship ties closely to labor force participation and employment status. It links also to the labor performed in other public and private realms of life. There is considerable emotional and material labor with bodily effects expended by disabled citizens associated with claiming an income benefit or doing their job (Church et al., 2007; Erkulwater, 2006; Prince, 2016).

Employing notions of human rights and independent living, disability groups advocate for greater choice and control over decisions around assessing and addressing their needs. In so doing, they challenge traditional ways of governments, charities, and experts in organizing services and allocating resources to individuals and families (Moss & Teghtsoonian, 2008; Trainor, 2010). Decision-making powers, forms of service provision, and the structure of working conditions are issues all under scrutiny, whether the area is segregated classrooms, reforms to tax laws, community supports, or sheltered workshops versus supported regular employment.

Mobilization by disabled people and their allies takes many forms. "There is not a singular disability movement in Canada, but multiple, complex, and at times conflicting disability movements" (Kelly, 2013, 19). The same applies to disability activism across countries. The disability activist is no single role but many parts on many stages. In contemporary societies, we should speak of disability activisms to acknowledge the presence of different and often clashing perspectives on the significance of impairment for understanding lived experiences and the place of health sciences in advancing agendas of desired personal and social change (Hughes, 2009). There is, too, the presence of different geographical or spatial scales in where political mobilization can and perhaps cannot easily happen (Kitchin & Wilton, 2003); temporal dimensions to social life and activism (Bartlett, 2014); and the presence of different group voices on a range of topics (Shakespeare, 2019).

We can identify an ensemble of disability activists with varied political orientations and tactics, specific social locations, self-conceptions, and life histories. These include academic activists and engaged scholars (Shakespeare, 2019), artistic and creative activists (Kelly, 2013), autistic self-advocates (Orsini & Smith, 2010), dementia activists (Bartlett, 2014), dissenting bodies (Moss et al., 2016), embodied subjects (Bacchi & Beasley, 2002), equality seekers (Stienstra, 2020), and legal guardians for adults with intellectual disabilities as accountant, advocate, or surrogate family member (Giertz, 2018). Still others include Mad movement activists (LeFrançois et al., 2013), mothers who become accidental activists (Panitch, 2008), neurodiversity advocates (Orsini, 2012), parent activists (Carey, Block and Scotch, 2020), phenomenological warriors (Anspach, 1979), politicized and politicizing parents (Carter, 2016), psychiatric consumer/survivor organizers (Reville & Church, 2012), political reformists (Prince, 2009), radical progressives and anti-capitalists (Withers, 2012), social liberals (Prince, 2012), and virtual activists (Meekosha, 2001). Through different claims of experiences and types of knowledge, disability is ontologically constructed, administratively negotiated, and politically contested. Far from being a monolithic entity, disability is a multidimensional set of differential life experiences ignored or responded to in particular contexts and stages over the life course.

Spaces and Scales of Disability Activism

Disability politics involve debates and decisions over what actions to take, when, how, and for whom. Actions encompass potential and actual measures of public persuasion, research and knowledge transfer, direct expenditures, tax relief, service provisions, laws, and regulatory activities by state and/or societal organizations. The social spaces and geographical scales of disability activism occur at local, regional, provincial, national, and international levels (Kitchin & Wilton, 2003), in and through both the "official public sphere" of economics and politics as well as the "community sphere" of politics, covering a wide-ranging span of mobilization practices and issues.

A fundamental institutional framework in which disability activism occurs is market capitalism (Oliver & Barnes, 2012). The market economy represents and expresses values of individualism and self-interest, competition, a work ethic, the profit motive, private property, and personal responsibility. It shapes how private troubles and public issues of impairment and human need are recognized, if at all, and then defined. Market capitalism, moreover, commercializes and privatizes certain forms of social provision; creates, reformulates, and eliminates jobs through processes of creative destruction; structures identities and social statuses; and creates sentiments of isolation or connection (Church et al., 2007; Fraser, 1989). Ongoing tensions and interplay between market forces and democratic politics are the main source of delineating the scope and character of welfare states. Other institutions caught up in this interplay include family and gender relations, civil society structures, and social movements. Within the political realm itself, structures and actors such as parties, elections, federalism, interest groups, organized labor, parliamentary governments, public bureaucracies, and cabinet ministers are agents of change and inertia that influence social justice developments.

Disability movements in Europe, North America, the United Kingdom, and elsewhere regularly look to the state as the legitimate promoter of access and inclusion and the core source of citizenship (Barnes, 2007; Charlton, 1998; Craig, 2018; Erkulwater, 2006; Stienstra, 2020). The state comprises different orders of sovereign powers (federal, provincial/state, and, in some nations, Indigenous or Tribal governments) and other levels of public authority (health authorities, city governments and school boards) with myriad power relationships and practices of inclusion and exclusion. Disability activism vis-à-vis the modern state takes numerous forms: advisory councils and office attached to governments; electoral outreach measures; public funding to national and local organizations; knowledge creation and interpretation; litigation for claiming and defending rights; scrutinizing political parties and candidates; and participating in parliament and legislative assemblies, occasionally as elected members but more commonly as witnesses before committees. Political citizenship includes rights to vote, to stand for and hold elected office, and to participate in social activities supported by the fundamental freedoms of expression, association, and assembly (Prince, 2014). People with disabilities are political actors through participating in electoral systems as voters, organizers, candidates, and elected representatives.

Disability rights organizations engage in associational politics by forging networks and coalitions across groups, social movements, and sectors of the economy and society. There are risks to disability activists and movement organizations in engaging closely with governments and other state institutions. The dangers for disability activism, as expressed by British disability scholars are that "To get too close to the Government is to risk incorporation and end up carrying out their proposals rather than ours. To move too far way is to risk marginalization and eventual demise. To collaborate too eagerly with the organizations for people [in contrast to user-led organizations of and by disabled people] risk having our agendas taken over by them and having them presented to us and to politicians as theirs. To remain aloof risks appearing unrealistic and/or unreasonable and denies possible access to much needed resources" (Barnes & Oliver, 1995, p. 115). This complex set of risky relationships persists as challenges today with no simple or single answer.

Litigation, the advocacy of interests through judicial means, is a strategic tool for seeking to advance the rights of citizenship of people with disabilities (Orsini & Smith, 2010). Court-based activism can be a constitutional reform process understood as affirming or altering fundamental legal norms of the country. Into the 21st century, laws in Canada and the United States contained the terms "imbecile" and "lunatic" or "retarded" to describe people with cognitive or mental health conditions. Law reforms can modernize language as well as legislation of concern to people with disabilities. Such reforms represent a reordering of the symbolic fabric of citizenship. As well, there are the legal struggles by disabled workers who negotiate relationships and identities with social security programs, and by clients navigating systems of services and redress to realize their social rights to income support and a modicum of economic welfare.

SOCIAL INJUSTICES AND ADVOCACY STRATEGIES

From a critical perspective, disability is an assemblage of socioeconomic, cultural, and political disadvantages resulting from an individual's exclusion by society. Claims making for social justice express many ideas: compensation and restitution, needs, equality, diversity and difference, merit and deservingness, and contractual entitlements grounded in social insurance. All this makes social justice, as a concept and set of discourses, highly relevant and hotly contested in social policy and governing (Craig, 2018; Prince, 2018).

Contemporary disability politics in Canada has not marked a shift from a politics of socioeconomic redistribution toward a politics of cultural recognition displacing redistribution as a major ambition of political struggle (Danermark & Gellerstedt, 2004; Fraser, 1989, 2005). Other commentators describe a long-term shift in political values from materialist concerns of economic security and personal safety to postmaterialist concerns of identity, belonging, esteem, and dignity. This proposition is too simplistic an interpretation of disability movements in contemporary politics. Even though disability theorists and activists understand disability as an identity in group terms, they conceptualize disability as a social construction, a concept more nuanced in content and wider in scope than a cultural construction of identity. For understanding the matrix of oppressions and opportunities, the social construction approach by design forges close linkages to political and economic structures. While attentive to discursive aspects of disability, activists also emphasize material dimensions of struggles for justice such as employment, personal supports, and income benefits.

We can distinguish three different forms of disability activism that aim to foster positive change in raising the citizenship claims of persons with disabilities. Disability politics play out through struggles over absences and actions constituted by cultural, economic, and political structures. The main contours of disability activism concern the pursuit of respectful inclusion, adequate social security, and an authentic democratic voice.

Recognition Activism

American sociologist Evelyn Nakano Glenn (2011) connects the politics of recognition, citizenship, and social justice as follows: "Citizenship is not just a matter of formal legal status; it is a matter of *belonging*, which requires *recognition* by other members of the community. Community members participate in drawing the boundaries of citizenship and defining who is entitled to civil, political, and social rights by granting or withholding recognition" (Glenn, 2011, p. 3). A critically significant aspect of disability activism involves the challenging of prevailing problematic recognitions or misrecognitions of people with disabilities. Related aspects of recognition activism by disabled advocates involve the retrieval of forgotten or subjugated histories, by psychiatric survivors for example, and the creation and celebration of alternative identifications, by disability pride events for example (Kelly, 2013).

Everyday language, terminology in legislation, and the conceptual underpinnings of public policy receive considerable attention by disability advocates, their organizations, and government decision makers. An image of people with disabilities still common today is of a person who suffers from an affliction, accidental or biological, thus to be pitied or feared. Framing disability issues as matters of citizenship can be an effective strategy for disability movement organizations and coalitions. It challenges old images and stereotypical beliefs about disability, calling for the re-examination of medical definitions and approaches, in consultation with disability groups.

Disability is part of the fabric of society, something that all individuals experience in one way or another and from which potentially everyone can learn. Attention focuses especially on attitudes, beliefs, body identities, and social values as well as to issues of prejudice and stigma. Discourse points to the rhetorical and symbolic nature of much of our "policy talk" these days, and to the growing prominence of this language in advocacy work, government vision statements, and service agency strategic plans. Popular culture and the mass media are other important institutions for the discursive side of citizenship. Disability organizations are projecting a diverse mix of private and public images of persons with disabilities: roles as learners and teachers, workers and managers, family members, caregivers as well as care recipients, taxpayers and consumers, voters and political candidates, athletes and artists, and so forth. This deepens our conceptions of membership in society. This modernization is toward an enabling and more inclusive status, refashioning citizenship as rights and participation for the diverse lived experiences of persons with disabilities in towns or cities, Indigenous communities, or metropolitan centers.

Resembling many social movements, public cultures are under critique, with disability activists testing customary social practices along with established professional and administrative practices. Disability organizations are contributing to a broad range of economic and social policy debates, challenging certain beliefs, shaping the knowledge base of decision-making, and influencing the mode of service provision. Their most important contributions, however, are more than additions to existing ways of thinking; they are inserting previously ignored life experiences into valid knowledge about persons with disabilities, their families, and the effects of policies and programs on people.

Redistribution Activism

Income security programs, the tax system, and gainful employment are concrete expressions of citizenship and the politics of redistribution. Social citizenship more broadly is associated with programs and benefits in education, equalization and other transfer payments, health care, housing, income security, social services, and tax assistance. Citizenship as economic integration refers to participation and mobility within the paid labor market. For people with disabilities, fiscal and social benefits are especially critical for overcoming obstacles in achieving membership and participation within all segments of society.

For people with disabilities, social assistance as a deep-rooted residual policy sector, involves the distribution of a double stigma: a subordinate status as an individual who is dependent on state aid, like others on welfare, and a further stigma in the form of a spoiled identity as a person with an abnormal body or mind. Redistributive activism in this policy area involves advancing a reform agenda to modernize and include income assistance programs for individuals and families living with disability. This agenda of reforms includes raising basic rates and, where applicable, shelter components, to provide more adequate and dignified standards of living. Other reforms include indexing benefits automatically to the annual cost of living to ensure a degree of stability; increasing asset limits to allow clients to maintain and accumulate some savings; and investing further in supports for transition to employment such as allowing a short-term extension of extended health-related benefits.

Personal income tax systems contain several major disability-related programs that deal with income support and tax relief, as well as promoting independent community living, education, employment, family support, and caregiving. Tax assistance for persons with disabilities possesses advantages and disadvantages. Tax relief is a relatively straightforward policy instrument for a government to select on many disability issues, though it is not necessarily the most beneficial reform for individuals and families. Substantively, tax supports serve a welfare function of recognizing human needs and influencing in a positive manner the income, goods, and services available to persons with disabilities and their families. Symbolically, tax assistance is a way for government to respond visibly to group claims and to connect directly with citizens with disabilities across the country. Simultaneously, increasing use of the tax system for delivering disability benefits adds complexity, possible inequities, and information challenges to clients in accessing the system.

Employment is one of the building blocks for achieving full citizenship. Attention to employment by governments, advocates, and others is understandable considering changing ideas about the capacities of people with disability and the fact that the unemployment rate among disabled persons in many countries can be double the national average (Morris et al., 2018). Employment-related reforms advocated by disability activists include removing work disincentives from income support programs, such as enhancing earnings exemptions consequently lowering the tax-back rate on employment earnings; expanding access to the job training and skills development programs available to other citizens; increasing the availability of employment assistance and work-related supports; encouraging employers in all sectors to make appropriate job/workplace accommodations; and promoting work experience opportunities for youth and adults with disabilities.

Representation Activism

A fundamental measure of the quality of citizenship rights is the capacity to shape one's social standing by having a voice in decision-making systems. Claims making by disability movements includes a politics of representation that encompasses traditional concerns of citizen participation and voting and, more recently, the practices of deliberative democracy and community dialogue. "Disability issues" is a phrase full of diverse ideas, and activists are expanding public thinking on what it constitutes. Traditionally, and still today at times, disability issues are conceived narrowly as special concerns related to a group of individuals with a particular impairment or disease. Common misconceptions of disability issues are that they entail a narrow set of concerns, for instance, rehabilitation or ramps, and that they do not involve people without disabilities. Such misconceptions risk the further marginalization of people with disabilities, limiting the political profile of issues and narrowing policy responses. Often underlying this outlook is a biomedical and individual pathology approach. Disability issues are those issues that disability organizations and their political allies identify and develop as positions for social justice and social change. A still broader perspective is that disability issues include any issue that affects the values, interests, resources, and identities of persons with disabilities, whether in a positive or negative manner, and whether in a material, symbolic, or structural fashion. The idea of mainstreaming disability asserts that disability issues are not a narrow and separate field of activity, but instead a perspective that relates to all agendas, policies, and processes of the state.

The slogan "nothing about us without us" (Charlton, 1998) is not simply a rallying cry for the disability rights movement; it is a legitimate claim on other individuals and institutions to be democratically accessible and participatory in their conduct. Indeed, some disability leaders now speak of "nothing without us"—a shorter yet profoundly more ambitious statement on human capabilities and representational rights of political voice. This is a claim for the right to have democratic rights, to be heard, and to share in state governance and civil society decision-making authorities. In an age of general disparagement and cynicism toward governments and alienation from political systems, disabled activists and their allies are expressing strong claims for full membership in political communities.

Conclusion

Fundamental obstacles to full participation by people with disabilities include their nonrecognition as full persons in prevailing cultural value patterns; the maldistribution of resources in income, education, employment, housing, and other material goods and services; and their misrepresentation or marginal voice in elections, state policy development, and governmental and civil society decision-making processes. Fair access to existing services, programs, benefits, and policy processes is crucial, yet only a partial solution, to realizing full membership of people with disabilities. Many state and community services and programs need reviewing and altering to ensure they do not reproduce systemic biases. Social justice for persons with disabilities requires a robust agenda of both equity and equality measures. It means addressing differences without unwanted segregation, within a mix of general and specific measures that are accessible, affordable, and accountable.

Encounters between persons with disabilities and the modern state are numerous, complex, and often contested. People with disabilities and disability organizations participate politically as clients and consumers of programs; as social groups or intentional communities; as neighbors and strangers in cities; as experts advising on policy developments, budgets, or program evaluations; as voters or candidates in elections; and as activists, litigants, rights-bearers, and equality seekers. These manners of participation differ by level of public prominence and legitimacy and, therefore, acceptability or controversy by state authorities and societal interests. Canadian disability groups interact with various state institutions and tend to employ conventional tools of research, consultations, lobbying, and litigation. While some groups pursue nonconventional politics of radical protests, most frame social justice issues as obstacles, inclusion, equality rights, and citizenship, rather than oppression and domination, a language more common in British disability politics or the language of minority group and civil rights in American disability politics.

State policymaking and the allocation of public resources deeply matter to disability activists and movement organizations. With their authoritative allocation of resources and values, government budgets are central to supporting or threatening the principles and material circumstances of equity, inclusion, and full citizenship. Legislative reforms are decisive developments in state politics for persons with disabilities. Over the decades, these include human rights codes and employment equity laws and, more recently, accessibility laws enacted by provincial and the federal government for the removal of barriers in the private and public sectors. To define and enforce these rights to dignity and nondiscrimination and equality, litigation has become an important strategy of individuals with disabilities and organizations representing their interests. This raises the profile of the judiciary in the disability field and wider public policy domains. Disability advocates, families, and community groups have learned that judicial victories are not necessarily a case of winner take all. A rights-based approach to seeking equality through litigation can be lengthy, financially expensive, and emotionally stressful for individuals involved, and risks fragmenting wider campaigns for obtaining services or supports for all groups. In addition to court rulings against disability claims, even victories can result in further delays due to appeals, discretion of public agencies in interpreting decisions, and then the frustratingly gradual, partial implementation of changes.

Empirically the models of disability may be shifting toward greater attention to the capacities and employability of many disabled people, yet this move takes place within a long-standing cultural context of ideas about biomedical deficit, personal tragedy, and family responsibility. Furthering the status of persons with disabilities as full and equal members requires a decline in the tragedy/charity model, a careful definition of the role of the medical model, and a vigorous expansion of the citizenship model of disability politics and policymaking.

Disability activism is about multiplicities in social identities, biomedical conditions, and life circumstances. In this chapter I have argued the need to examine disability politics and the struggle for social justice in relation to three strategic modes of activism: a politics of cultural recognition and identity, a politics of socioeconomic redistribution of material goods and services, and a politics of democratic representation that combines conventional and alternative modes of decision-making. Any given advocate or activist movement can be committed to and function in one or other of these strategic modes and not in others. Over time, the mix may shift at the level of the individual or family, the agency or movement organization, or the national and international sectors more generally. This gives disability activism and the struggle for social justice dynamic qualities enacted through symbolic, materialist, and political concerns in interaction with public and private authorities.

Notes

1. I use both "disabled people" and "people with disabilities," recognizing that some authors, advocates, and disability-related movements prefer one or the other, such that both are in use. Orsini and Smith (2010, p. 49) explain with respect to autism activism: "Some autistic self advocates . . . eschew the person-first language that has become synonymous with the liberal-democratic response to dealing with marginalized identities, much of this sparked by the AIDS movement's insistence on person living with AIDS or person with AIDS to distinguish the virus from the person living with the virus. Autistic advocates prefer autistic child, autistic persons or simply autistic, over person-first language."
2. In Canada "Indigenous peoples" refers to members of three groups collectively, the Inuit, Métis, and First Nations. Inuit are the circumpolar peoples whose homelands in Canada spread over four jurisdictions: Labrador, Quebec, Nunavut, and the Northwest Territories. Métis are a distinct people, with a distinct culture, descended from the early marriages between Indigenous nations and European settlers. First Nations is the term generally used now to refer to members of many different nations, such as Haida, Dene, and Cree, among others. There are in the order of 40–60 historic Indigenous societies in Canada; some of these are now fragmented. Members of First Nations live in over 600, generally small, reserve-based communities created by federal administration of the Indian Act.
3. Other disability models in a large and growing literature are beyond the scope of this chapter (Hanes, 2016; Hughes, 2009; Withers, 2012).

References

Anspach, R. R. (1979). From stigma to identity politics: Political activism among the physically disabled and former mental patients. *Social Science and Medicine*, *13A*, 765–773. https://doi .org/10.1016/0271-7123(79)90123-8

Bacchi, C. L., & Beasley, C. (2002). Citizen bodies: Is embodied citizenship a contradiction in terms? *Critical Social Policy*, 22(2), 324–352. https://doi.org/10.1177/02610183020220020801

Barnes, C. (2007). Disability activism and the struggle for change: Disability, policy and politics in the UK. *Education, Citizenship and Social Justice*, 2(3), 203–221. https://doi.org/ 10.1177%2F1746197907081259

Barnes, C., & Oliver, M. (1995). Disability rights: Rhetoric and reality in the UK. *Disability and Society*, *10*(1), 111–116. https://doi.org/10.1080/09687599550023769

Barnartt, S., & Scotch, R. K. (2001). *Disability protests: Contentious politics 1970–1999*. Gallaudet Press.

Bartlett, R. (2014). The emergent modes of dementia activism. *Ageing and Society*, 34(4), 623–644. https://doi.org/10.1017/S0144686X12001158

Brisebois, L. Fawcett, G., & Hughes, J. with Kornelsen, E., Paulenko, J., Telake, D., & Yeung, S. (2018). *Profile of adults with severe disabilities*. Strategic and Service Policy Branch, Employment and Social Development Canada.

Carey, A. C., Block, P., & Scotch, R. K. (2020). *Allies and obstacles: Disability activism and parents of children with disabilities*. Temple University Press.

Carter, I. (2016). Empowering strategies for change: Advocacy by and for people with disabilities. In J. Robertson and G. Larson (Eds.), *Disability and social change: A progressive Canadian approach* (pp. 205–226). Fernwood.

Charlton, J. I. (1998). *Nothing about us without us: Disability, oppression and empowerment.* University of California Press.

Church, K., Frazee, C., Panitch, M., Luciani, T., & Bowman, V. (2007). *Doing disability at the bank: Discovering the work of learning/teaching done by disabled bank employees.* RBC Foundation Institute for Disability Studies, Ryerson University.

Craig, G. (2018). Introduction. In G. Craig (Ed.), *Handbook on global social justice* (pp. 1–16). Edward Elgar.

Danermark, B., & Gellerstedt, L. C. (2004). Social justice: Redistribution and recognition—A non-reductionist perspective on disability. *Disability and Society, 19*(4), 339–353. https://doi .org/10.1080/09687590410001689458

Dunn, P., & Langdon, T.-L. (2016). Looking back, rethinking historical perspectives and reflecting upon emerging trends. In J. Robertson and G. Larson (Eds.), *Disability and social change: A progressive Canadian approach* (pp. 27–44). Fernwood.

Erkulwater, J. L. (2006). *Disability rights and the American safety net.* Cornell University Press.

Fraser, N. (1989). *Unruly practices: Power, discourse and gender in contemporary social theory.* University of Minneapolis Press.

Fraser, N. (2005). Reframing justice in a globalizing world. *New Left Review, 36,* 69–88. https:// newleftreview.org/issues/II36/articles/nancy-fraser-reframing-justice-in-a-globalizing -world.pdf

Giertz, L. (2018). Guardianship for adults with intellectual disabilities: Accountant, advocate or "family" member. *Scandinavian Journal of Disability Research, 20*(1), 256–265. https://doi .org.10.16993/sjdr.40

Glenn, E. N. (2011). Constructing citizenship: Exclusion, subordination, and resistance. *American Sociological Review, 76*(1), 1–24. https://doi.org/10.1177%2F0003122411398443

Hanes, R. (2016). Critical disability theory: Developing a post-social model of disability. In J. Robertson & G. Larson (Eds.), *Disability and social change: A progressive Canadian approach* (pp. 65–79). Fernwood.

Hughes, B. (2009). Disability activisms: Social model stalwarts and biological citizens. *Disability and Society, 24*(6), 677–688. https://doi.org/10.1080/09687590903160118

Kelly, C. (2013). Towards renewed descriptions of Canadian disability movements: Disability outside of the non-profit sector. *Canadian Journal of Disability Studies, 2*(1), 1–27. doi:10.15353/cjds.v2i1.68

Kitchin, R., & Wilton, R. (2003). Disability activism and the politics of scale. *Canadian Geographer, 47*(2), 97–115. https://doi.org/10.1111/1541-0064.00005

LeFrançois, B., Menzies, R., & Reaume, G. (Eds.) (2013). *Mad matters: A critical reader in Canadian mad studies.* Canadian Scholars' Press.

Little, D. L. (2010). Identity, efficacy, and disability rights movement recruitment. *Disability Studies Quarterly, 30*(1). https://dsq-sds.org/article/view/1013/1226

Llewellyn, P., & Northway, R. (2008). The views and experiences of people with intellectual disabilities concerning advocacy: A focus study. *Journal of Intellectual Disabilities, 12*(3), 213–228. https://doi.org/10.1177%2F1744629508095726

Meekosha, H. (2001). Virtual activists? Women and the making of identities of disability. *Hypatia: Journal of Feminist Philosophy, 17*(3), 67–88. https://doi.org/10.1111/j.1527 -2001.2002.tb00942.x

Morris, S., Fawcett, G., Brisebois, L., & Hughes, J. (2018). *A demographic, employment and income profile of Canadians with disabilities aged 15 years and over, 2017.* Catalogue no. 89-654 -X2018002. Statistics Canada.

Moss, P., & Prince, M. J. (2020). Nomadic positionings: a call for critical approaches to disability policy in Canada. In S. M. Hall and R. Hiteva (Eds.), *Engaging with Policy, Practice and Publics: Intersectionality and Impact* (pp. 121–134). Policy Press.

Moss, P., Prince, M. J., De Volder, B., & Johnson, C. (2016). Placing disability politics: Uneven sitings of dissenting bodies. In W. K. Carroll & K. Sarker (Eds.), *A world to win: Contemporary social movements and counter-hegemony* (pp. 195–208). Arbeiter Ring.

Moss, P., & Teghtsoonian, K. (Eds.) (2008). *Contesting illness: Processes and practices.* University of Toronto Press.

Oliver, M., & Barnes, C. (2012). *The new politics of disablement.* Palgrave Macmillan.

Orsini, M. (2012). Autism, neurodiversity and the welfare state: The challenge of accommodating neurological difference. *Canadian Journal of Political Science, 45*(4), 805–827. https://doi.org/10.1017/S000842391200100X

Orsini, M., & Smith, M. (2010). Social movements, knowledge and public policy: The case of autism activism in Canada and the US. *Critical Policy Studies, 4*(1), 38–57. https://doi.org/10.1080/19460171003714989

Panitch, M. (2008). *Disability, mothers, and organization: Accidental activists.* Routledge.

Pettinicchio, D. (2019). *Politics of empowerment: Disability rights and the cycle of American policy reform.* Stanford University Press.

Prince, M. J. (2009). *Absent citizens: Disability politics and policy in Canada.* University of Toronto Press.

Prince, M. J. (2012). Canadian disability activism and political ideas: In and between neoliberalism and social liberalism. *Canadian Journal of Disability Studies, 1*(1), 1–34. https://doi.org/10.15353/cjds.v1i1.16

Prince, M. J. (2014). Enabling the voter participation of Canadians with disabilities: Reforming Canada's electoral systems. *Canadian Journal of Disability Studies, 3*(2), 94–120. https://doi.org/10.15353/cjds.v3i2.158

Prince, M. J. (2016). *Struggling for social citizenship: Disabled Canadians, income security, and prime ministerial eras.* McGill-Queens University Press.

Prince, M. J. (2017). Persons with invisible disabilities and workplace accommodation: Findings from a scoping literature review. *Journal of Vocational Rehabilitation, 46*(1), 75–86. http://dx.doi.org/10.3233/JVR-160844

Prince, M. J. (2018). Canada: Social justice and social policy in a liberal welfare state. In G. Craig (Ed.), *Handbook on global social justice* (pp. 93–104). Edward Elgar.

Reeve, D. (2002). Negotiating psycho-emotional dimensions of disability and their influence on identity constructions. *Disability & Society, 17*(5), 493–508. https://www.tandfonline.com/doi/abs/10.1080/09687590220148487

Reville, D., & Church, K. (2012). Mad activism enters its fifth decade: Psychiatric survivor organizing in Toronto. In A. Choudry, J. Hanley, & E. Shragge (Eds.), *Organize! Building from the local for global justice* (pp. 189–201). PM Press.

Robertson, J., & Larson, G. (Eds.) (2016). *Disability and social change: A progressive Canadian approach.* Fernwood.

Shakespeare, T. (2019). When the political becomes personal: Reflecting on disability bioethics. *Bioethics, 58*(3–4), 914–921. https://doi.org/10.1111/bioe.12668

Shapiro, J. P. (1994). *No pity: People with disabilities forging a new civil rights movement.* New York Times Books.

Stienstra, D. (2020). *Disability rights* (2nd ed.). Fernwood.

Switzer, J. V. (2003). *Disability rights: American disability policy and the fight for equality.* Georgetown University Press.

Trainor, A. (2010). Diverse approaches to parent advocacy during special education home-school interactions: Identification and use of cultural and social capital. *Remedial and Special Education, 31*(1), 34–47. https://doi.org/10.1177/0741932508324401

Withers, A. J. (2012). *Disability politics and theory.* Fernwood.

CHAPTER 37

....

DISABILITY AND SOCIAL
PARTICIPATION

....

CARRIE SHANDRA

INTRODUCTION

....

PARTICIPATION is considered a key component of many disability frameworks (Jette, 2006; Nagi, 1991; World Health Organization, 2001), yet the concept of *social partici- pation* remains amorphous and contested (Levasseur et al., 2010; Piškur et al., 2014; Whiteneck & Dijkers, 2009). Further, definitions that focus broadly on participation as the fulfillment of *roles* in particular types of *environments* fail to consider how people with disabilities are often excluded from many activities and contexts. As the physical and social environments where activities take place are key for understanding how people with disabilities experience everyday life, this chapter adds to the literature on disability and social participation by evaluating the what, where, and with whom of daily activities for a nationally representative sample of people with disabilities.

This chapter begins by reviewing how four disability frameworks—functional assessments (Lawton & Brody, 1969), Nagi's (1965) disablement model, Verbrugge and Jette's (1994) disablement process, and the World Health Organization's (2001) International Classification of Functioning, Disability, and Health—conceptualize how *activities*, *roles*, and *environments* relate to participation. These frameworks use varying terminology and originate from different disciplinary roots, but they share the focus of conceptualizing the lived experience of disability.[1]

I next discuss challenges to measuring (social) participation through the elements of activities, roles, and environments (Cobigo et al., 2012; Hammel et al., 2008) and de- scribe how time diary data can be used to understand daily life with disability. Finally, I present results from analyses of the nationally representative 2008–2018 American Time Use Surveys that compare how individuals with and without disabilities spend time in 15 activity categories, across six physical locations and eight types of social interactions.

Results indicate that people with disabilities spend less time working, less time in education, and more time obtaining services and in passive and active leisure. When considering the *where* of daily activities, people with disabilities spend more time at home, less time in public places, and less time in transportation than people without disabilities. When considering *with whom*, they spend more time alone and have less contact with others. However, these results depend upon activity type, illustrating the importance of social and environmental contexts in empirical and theoretical models of participation differences by disability status. Directions for future research are discussed.

WHAT IS PARTICIPATION? DIFFERENCES IN DISABILITY MODELS

Functional Assessments, Activities of Daily Living, and Instrumental Activities of Daily Living

Common social scientific models of disability have roots in the rehabilitation sciences, which typically conceptualize disability as deviation from function. Although these include many types of global and specific functional assessments, activities of daily living (ADLs) and instrumental activities of daily living (IADLs) are perhaps best known. ADLs include bathing, dressing, toileting, ambulation, grooming, and feeding. IADLs include telephone usage, shopping, food preparation, housekeeping, independent transportation, self-medication, and financial management. These instruments were introduced in the mid-1900s (Nagi, 1991) and remain widely used in clinical practice today (National Academies of Sciences, 2019; Wales et al., 2016).

Early theorizing by psychologist M. Powell Lawton—who is credited with developing IADLs and clarifying the theoretical framework of functional assessment (Katz, 1983)—considered ADLs and IADLs to be only two of seven "stages of competence" (Lawton & Brody, 1969; Lawton, 1972). From lowest to highest, these ranged from functional health, perception and cognition, ADLs, IADLs, effectance, and the performance of social roles. To Lawson, *roles* and *activities* were arranged along a continuum. Parenthood, altruism, and interpersonal contact were considered more complex than housekeeping, eating, and breathing. Competence in these roles and activities could be promoted or constrained by characteristics of a person's social and physical environment, which included living space and interactions with others (Lawton, 1970).

This theorizing was foundational to subsequent disability frameworks. Although many more recent studies focus exclusively on IDLs or IADLs, Lawton and contemporaries acknowledged that the contexts of *where* and *with whom*—in addition to the *what* of daily activities—were also salient for understanding life with disability.

Nagi and the Disablement Model

Nagi's disablement model (1965), in contrast, distinguished between the concepts of functional limitation and disability. Functional limitations represent restrictions in a person's performance of physical or cognitive actions, occurring at the level of the *organism*. Disability represents the expression of a limitation in a social context, occurring at the level of *society*. More specifically, disability is a

> limitation in performing socially defined roles and tasks expected of an individual within a sociocultural and physical environment. These roles and tasks are organized in spheres of life activities such as those of the family or other interpersonal relations; work, employment, and other economic pursuits; and education, recreation, and self-care.
>
> (Nagi, 1991, p. 315)

Roles and tasks are key to understanding social participation in this model. Nagi (1991), drawing from Parsons (1958), considered *roles* like parent or worker to be "organized systems" by which individuals participated in society. *Tasks* like driving or dressing were activities through which individuals enacted roles. Some tasks are role-specific, while other tasks are common to many roles. Roles are made up of many tasks, and singular tasks did not constitute roles. Disability in one role does not necessarily equate to disability in another (Nagi, 1976).[2]

Multiple contextual factors affect the dimensions and severity of disability in Nagi's model. People like family, friends, coworkers, and service providers react to, and have expectations about, others' disability status. Environments present varying degrees of physical or sociocultural barriers. In this way, disability is a relational concept not solely dependent on an individual but shaped by places and other people. Disability is also a fundamentally social concept, as an individual's performance of an activity is both indicative of their role in society and situated in a broader physical and social environment. Here, too, the *what* of daily life is inseparable from the *where* and *who* of participation.

The Disablement Process

Verbrugge and Jette's (1994, p. 1) disablement process similarly distinguished between functional limitation and disability, defining the latter as "difficulty doing activities in any domain of life (from hygiene to hobbies, errands to sleep) due to a health or physical problem." They, along with earlier work by Verbrugge (1990), extended Nagi's model in part by broadening the scope of activity domains and elaborating on the personal and environmental factors that reduced or increased disablement.

Verbrugge and Jette (1994; Verbrugge, 1990) critiqued the tendency of many studies to focus exclusively on ADLs, IADLs, and paid employment. These, they argued, were overly narrow and neglected other key life domains such as housework, shopping and errands, sleep, care work, leisure, recreation, religious activities, public service, social-ization, and transportation. They considered this more expansive perspective on ac-tivity categories to be more "democratic," with no category more important than others. Additionally, by including all activity domains in the conceptualization of participation, they intended to give the concept of disability "new sociological heft" (Verbrugge & Jette, 1994, p. 12).

Here, disability was conceptualized as a gap between a person and their environment—a gap that could be narrowed or widened either by a person's own capa-bility or an activity's demand. These demands could be reduced in part by accommo-dating an activity's "what, how, how long, and how often" (Verbrugge & Jette, 1994, p. 9). Built, physical, and social environments could be modified. And psychosocial coping and external support could reduce activity demands. Thus, the *characteristics* of activi-ties played a crucial role in determining person-environment fit.

The ICF and Distinctions between Participation and Social Participation

Finally, the World Health Organization's ([WHO] 2001) International Classification of Functioning, Disability, and Health (ICF) considered disability to be an umbrella term that included impairments, activity limitations, and participation restrictions. These terms refer, respectively, to body structures or functions, individual difficulties executing activities, and a person's involvement in society. Notably, the WHO chose the terminology of "participation restriction" to replace the term "handicap" used in their previous model, the International Classification of Impairments, Disabilities, and Handicaps.

The ICF (WHO, 2001, p. 14) included a list of activity and participation domains in-tended to cover "the full range of life areas," including communication, mobility and transportation, self-care, domestic life, interpersonal interactions, "major life areas" such as education and employment, and community/social/civic life. A person's perfor-mance in these domains is situated within an environment that included settings like the home, work, or school—as well as the presence of others, including family, peers, and acquaintances. The ICF was intended to be a flexible framework that could be applied in a variety of settings by myriad stakeholders. However, as others have noted, there is con-siderable conceptual ambiguity between the terms "activities" at the individual level and "participation" at the societal level (Hammel et al., 2008; Whiteneck & Dijkers, 2009).

Subsequent research provides nuance to the ICF model by evaluating the distinctive-ness of activity and participation concepts. Jette and colleagues' (2003) factor analysis suggested three underlying dimensions. Mobility activities included vigorous physical actions like hiking, running, and active recreation—corresponding to the ICF's mo-bility domain. Daily activities included basic and instrumental activities like lifting, dressing, and reaching—corresponding to the ICF's self-care and domestic life domain.

And social participation included "complex" behaviors like going out to public places, visiting friends and families, helping others, and volunteering—corresponding with the ICF's interpersonal interactions domain. Alternatively, Badley (2008) suggested dividing activities and participation into acts, tasks, and societal involvement. Later work by Jette and colleagues (2007) suggested five conceptual subdomains: daily activities, applied cognitive, role participation, mobility, and social participation.

Finally, another stream of research evaluates the distinction between concepts of *participation* and *social participation*. Piškur and colleagues' (2014) review of the literature emphasizes that clear definitions do not exist, and it argues that current ICF guidelines do not sufficiently capture societal involvement. They recommend, following Nagi (1991), that defining participation relative to a person's social roles would provide clarity. Levasseur and colleagues (2010) likewise note the difficulty of researching social participation when there is no agreement on what the term entails. They address this ambiguity by proposing a taxonomy of social participation's underlying dimensions via a content analysis of definitions of social participation in the aging literature. Their taxonomy is based on level of involvement with others as well as the goal of activities—from activities that prepare for connecting with others (Level 1), being with others (Level 2), interacting with others (Level 3), doing activities with others (Level 4), helping others (Level 5), and contributing to society through civic activities (Level 6). Notably, the authors analyzed results along who, how, what, where, with whom, when, and why dimensions.

MEASUREMENT CHALLENGES

Activities, environments, and roles are key to understanding (social) participation in contemporary disability frameworks; however, as previous research points out, there is no consensus about how to define or measure these terms. This ambiguity presents a challenge for research and clinical application (e.g., Nordenfelt, 2003; Verbrugge & Jette, 1994; Whiteneck & Dijkers, 2009). This is compounded by the multitude of disability measurements, with implications for the identification of disabled populations and for participation outcomes within and between disabled populations (e.g., Altman, 2014; Amilon et al., 2021; Pettinicchio & Maroto, 2021).

Further, studies that center people with disabilities' perspectives by asking what participation means to them emphasize that there is no "gold standard"; no singular set of activities can define the concept. Focus groups (Hammel et al., 2008) of people with diverse disabilities indicate that participation has components that are both social and personal, public and private, and that different people endorse different aspects. Conventional approaches that measure participation as performance of a standard set of roles or activities are unable to account for this variation.

Similar concerns are made about *social inclusion*—a related term that is also conceptually opaque. A synthesis review (Cobigo et al., 2012) of the social inclusion literature for people with intellectual and developmental disabilities identifies multiple critiques of conventional approaches. First, inclusion is traditionally defined as the achievement of dominant social lifestyles, including the valorization of some roles over others. Second, inclusion is often focused on productivity and independent living, neither of which may be relevant for many people with disabilities. And third, inclusion is often limited to participation in community-based activities and cannot account for other meaningful interactions. The authors instead recommend a definition of inclusion that centers social roles of one's choosing, access to public goods, recognition of competence, and mutually supportive social networks.

In sum, there is no standardized or universal approach to measure social participation among people with disabilities. And although social science research, more broadly, often includes a wide swath of activities under the umbrella of participation—economic, political, civic, religious, altruistic (e.g., Putnam, 2000)—many studies do not consider, much less account for, the implications these domains might have for people with disabilities.

TIME DIARIES AS DAILY LIVED EXPERIENCE

The current chapter evaluates daily life with a disability using time diaries—detailed records of a person's daily life as recorded (in the current analysis) over a 24-hour period. Although this approach cannot identify the domains that people with disabilities consider most important for social participation, it can leverage self-reports of time spent in a spectrum of activities without imposing assumptions about which are more salient for daily life. It also allows for the identification of where and with whom each of these activities occurs, and thus the physical and social environments in which activities take place.

Time dairies have other conceptual and methodological advantages. Time is a bounded resource where time spent in one activity carries opportunity costs of not engaging in other activities (Williams et al., 2016). Additionally, because time diaries require respondents to account for all minutes of the day, estimates of daily time use may be less prone to recall bias, aggregation bias, and social desirability bias than other data collection techniques (Bolger et al., 2003; Robinson & Godbey, 2010).

A growing literature utilizes time diary data to document differences in daily activities between adults with and without disabilities (Anand & Ben-Shalom, 2014; Freedman et al., 2017; Pagán, 2013; Shandra, 2018; Verbrugge & Liu, 2014). However, there is relatively less scholarly attention to the contextual components of daily activities for people with disabilities—where and with whom a person is with—than the amount of time spent in those activities.

This chapter adds to the literature on disability and social participation by evaluating the what, where, and with whom of daily activities for a nationally representative sample of people with disabilities. Identifying the physical and social environments in which activities take place is another way to understand how people with disabilities experience the context of everyday life.

DATA AND METHODS

The American Time Use Survey (Hofferth et al., 2020) is a nationally representative survey sponsored by the US Bureau of Labor Statistics that collects information on daily time use. Respondents aged 15 and over were chosen randomly from households that had undergone their final interview for the Current Population Survey (CPS), with the ATUS collected 2–5 months after the final CPS interview. The sample was randomized by day such that half the respondents reported on a weekday and half reported on a weekend day. Computer-assisted telephone interviewing was used to ask respondents to provide demographic information, as well as a detailed account of their activities during a 24-hour period beginning at 4:00 am. The "diary day" is the day about which the respondent reports, with pooled data from all available years (2003–2018) resulting in an initial sample size of 201,151 diary days.

Although the ATUS includes detailed information on time use and sociodemographic characteristics for every year, information on disability is available more sporadically. Detailed disability data were introduced in mid-2008, reducing the sample size to 119,716 diary days. Of the respondents with disability data, an additional 555 are excluded here due to interviewer-reported data quality problems. No other eligibility exclusions were made, leaving a total analytic sample of 119,161 respondents aged 15 and older between the years 2008 and 2018. All analyses are weighted using the ATUS person weights and Stata's (StataCorp, 2015) subpopulation command.

Measures

Disability status in the ATUS was measured in the CPS interview and designed to correspond to "four basic areas of functioning (vision, hearing, mobility, and cognitive functioning) that identified the largest component of the population of people with disabilities . . . [and] two key elements that could be used for monitoring independent living and the need for services" (Brault et al., 2007, p. 4). Analyses use a dichotomous indicator that includes any of these disabilities (N = 14,378, or 12.1% of the overall sample).

The ATUS includes 17 major categories in its activity lexicon (Shelley, 2005), and, in order to be as inclusive as possible, all original ATUS-defined domains are preserved. One additional refinement is made. Given the amount of time spent in leisure, and documented differences in health-promoting leisure types by people with and without disabilities (Pagán-Rodríguez, 2014; Shandra, 2021), I refine the original "Socializing, Relaxing, and Leisure" category into "passive" and "active" forms. Passive includes relaxing, drug use, television, radio, and computer use for leisure. Active includes playing games, hobbies, and reading and writing for personal interest. The categories of telephone calls and traveling are not shown; otherwise, no further revisions are made.

For the location where an activity takes place, the ATUS collects data on 15 different places and 11 modes of transportation. These are collapsed to designate the respondent's home or yard, the respondent's workplace, someone else's home, a public place (restaurant or bar, place of worship, store, library, bank, gym, or post office), other place (outdoors, other, unspecified, unknown), or in a mode of transportation. Location categories are mutually exclusive; a respondent cannot report being in more than one place during an activity.

For other people who are present during an activity, the ATUS collects data on 24 different types of relationships to the respondent. These are collapsed here to designate time spent in activities alone, with a household spouse or unmarried partner, household children (own household child, grandchild, or foster child), other household family (parent, sibling, other related person), household nonrelative[3] (roommate, boarder, other nonrelative), non-household children under age 18 (own child, other non-household family, other non-household children), non-household adult family (parents, other non-household family over age 18), non-household friends, neighbors, or acquaintances, and non-household other adults (coworkers, bosses or managers, other non-household adults). With whom categories are not mutually exclusive; respondents (except those reporting time "alone") can report being with more than one person at a time. In that instance, time spent is recorded across all relevant categories of people.

Where and with whom information is available for all activity categories except for the sleeping, grooming, and sexual activity subcategories of personal care. This means that only the personal care subcategories of health-related self-care, personal care emergencies, and personal care not elsewhere classified have valid where and with whom information. As a result, most personal care minutes are defined in the "other" location in where analyses and are not recorded in with whom analyses.

Methods

This chapter analyses the what, who, and where of activities domains for people with and without disabilities. I first present the distribution of overall time use by disability status across activity domains in Table 37.1 I differentiate between total mean minutes (including those who do and do not report the activity on diary day) and the mean minutes for those who report any minutes of the activity.[4] Table 37.2 and Table 37.3 take a similar approach for the where and with whom analyses, respectively. Specifically, I present the total mean minutes of an activity in a specific location or with a specific person, including those who do and do not report the activity on diary day. Then, I present the mean minutes for those who report any minutes of the activity in that location or with that person.

I evaluate bivariate differences in the mean or percentage of each outcome by disability status, with hypothesis tests calculated from adjusted Wald tests. Some of the cell

Table 37.1 Time Spent in Daily Activities, by Disability Status

	No Disability	Disability	
Personal care			
Mean minutes	572	622	*
Mean minutes | minutes > 0	573	622	*
Household activities			
Mean minutes	120	118	
Mean minutes | minutes > 0	150	148	
Caring for and helping household members			
Mean minutes	35	12	*
Mean minutes | minutes > 0	115	109	
Caring for and helping non-household members			
Mean minutes	9	9	
Mean minutes | minutes > 0	72	84	*
Work and work-related activities			
% minutes > 0	172	45	*
Mean minutes | minutes > 0	421	385	*
Education			
Mean minutes	17	5	*
Mean minutes | minutes > 0	287	243	*
Consumer purchases			
Mean minutes	25	18	*
Mean minutes | minutes > 0	59	58	
Professional and personal care services			
Mean minutes	4	8	*
Mean minutes | minutes > 0	60	86	*
Household services			
Mean minutes	1	1	
Mean minutes | minutes > 0	42	58	*
Eating and drinking			
Mean minutes	67	64	*
Mean minutes | minutes > 0	71	67	*

(continued)

Table 37.1 Continued

	No Disability	Disability	
Active leisure			
Mean minutes	86	99	*
Mean minutes | minutes > 0	151	171	*
Passive leisure			
Mean minutes	196	331	*
Mean minutes | minutes > 0	226	356	*
Sports, exercise, and recreation			
Mean minutes	21	11	*
Mean minutes | minutes > 0	105	87	*
Religious and spiritual activities			
Mean minutes	13	18	*
Mean minutes | minutes > 0	105	112	*
Volunteer activities			
Mean minutes	10	8	*
Mean minutes | minutes > 0	139	146	

Data are weighted.

* $p < .05$; tests difference between individuals with and without disabilities.

Source: American Time Use Survey, 2008–2018.

sizes in Table 37.2 and Table 37.3 are notably small; therefore, results are only presented for domains with at least 100 respondents reporting positive minutes in a specific place or with a specific person. Categories are not further collapsed in order to preserve the broadest possible array of activity domains, without assuming the primacy of some categories over others.

RESULTS

Total Time Use

Table 37.1 indicates significant differences in daily time use between people with and without disabilities. Those with disabilities spend more time in personal care (including

Table 37.2 Time Spent in Daily Activities, by Location of Activity and Disability Status

	Home		Work		Other's Home		Public Place		Other		Transportation	
	No Dis.	Dis.	No Dis.	Dis.	No Dis.	Dis.	No Dis.	Dis.	No Dis.	Dis.	No Dis.	Dis.
Total time use												
Mean minutes	462	614 *	151	37 *	46	37 *	78	51 *	628	653 *	75	48 *
Mean minutes | minutes = 0 in location	477	625 *	489	451 *	176	184 *	126	113 *	628	654 *	87	76 *
Personal care[a]												
Mean minutes	4	16 *	—	—	—	—	—	—	569	606 *	—	—
Mean minutes | minutes = 0 in location	72	73	—	—	—	—	—	—	569	606 *	—	—
Household activities												
Mean minutes	111	111	0	0	3	3 *	1	0	4	3 *	0	0
Mean minutes | minutes = 0 in location	145	143	22	38	70	76	19	17	53	49	35	34
Caring for and helping household members												
Mean minutes	28	10 *	0	0 *	1	0 *	2	1 *	5	2 *	0	0
Mean minutes | minutes = 0 in location	105	106	26	21	31	32	31	32	54	55	36	51
Caring for and helping non-household members												
Mean minutes	3	4 *	0	0 *	4	4	1	1	1	1	0	0 *
Mean minutes | minutes = 0 in location	101	110	41	30	58	66	36	37	39	48	34	16

(continued)

Table 37.2 Continued

	Home		Work		Other's Home		Public Place		Other		Transportation	
	No Dis.	Dis.	No Dis.	Dis.	No Dis.	Dis.	No Dis.	Dis.	No Dis.	Dis.	No Dis.	Dis.
Work and work-related activities												
Mean minutes	21	7 *	142	35 *	2	1 *	2	1 *	3	1 *	1	1 *
Mean minutes | minutes = 0 in location	168	180	469	444 *	189	185	135	138	190	183	183	220
Education												
Mean minutes	7	2 *	–	–	0	0 *	9	2 *	1	0 *	–	–
Mean minutes | minutes = 0 in location	166	161	–	–	130	254	320	302	202	155 *	–	–
Consumer purchases												
Mean minutes	1	1 *	0	0 *	0	0	23	17 *	1	1 *	0	0
Mean minutes | minutes = 0 in location	41	52 *	16	12	41	41	58	56 *	30	33	41	37
Professional and personal care services												
Mean minutes	0	1 *	–	–	0	0	1	1	3	7 *	–	–
Mean minutes | minutes = 0 in location	49	61 *	–	–	58	72	23	27	76	102 *	–	–
Household services												
Mean minutes	0	1 *	–	–	–	–	0	0 *	0	0	–	–
Mean minutes | minutes = 0 in location	63	82	–	–	–	–	32	35	33	43	–	–
Eating and drinking												
Mean minutes	41	49 *	5	1 *	4	3 *	15	9 *	2	2 *	0	0
Mean minutes | minutes = 0 in location	51	56 *	35	35	53	52	67	64 *	51	53	29	34

	Home		Work		Other's Home		Public Place		Other		Transportation	
	No Dis.	Dis.	No Dis.	Dis.	No Dis.	Dis.	No Dis.	Dis.	No Dis.	Dis.	No Dis.	Dis.
Active leisure												
Mean minutes	45	68 *	1	0 *	22	17 *	5	4 *	13	10 *	0	0
Mean minutes | minutes = 0 in location	116	152 *	33	37	146	140	73	66 *	145	144	66	68
Passive leisure												
Mean minutes	183	320 *	1	0 *	7	7	1	1	2	2	0	0
Mean minutes | minutes = 0 in location	223	353 *	28	28	158	189 *	74	68	110	133 *	58	98 *
Sports, exercise, and recreation												
Mean minutes	3	2 *	0	0 *	1	0 *	4	2 *	12	7 *	0	0
Mean minutes | minutes = 0 in location	59	49 *	32	24 *	117	102	94	97	117	98 *	118	170 *
Religious and spiritual activities												
Mean minutes	2	5 *	—	—	0	0	9	12 *	1	1	—	—
Mean minutes | minutes = 0 in location	51	65 *	—	—	86	117	121	135 *	95	82	—	—
Volunteer activities												
Mean minutes	2	3 *	0	0 *	0	0	4	2 *	3	2 *	0	0 *
Mean minutes | minutes = 0 in location	90	125 *	74	50	106	116	123	118	175	172	81	69

Data are weighted.

* $p < .05$; tests difference between individuals with and without disabilities. "Dis." abbreviates disability. Location categories are mutually exclusive.

a Not all subcategories of personal care include where information; see details in text

— Results not shown due to small cell size; see details in text.

Source: American Time Use Survey, 2008–2018.

Table 37.3 Time Spent in Daily Activities, by Presence of Others during Activity and Disability Status

| | Householders | | | | | | | | Non-householders | | | | | | | |
| | Alone | | Partner | | Child | | Adult Family | | Child | | Adult Family | | Friend | | Other adult | |
	No Dis.	Dis.	No Dis.	Dis.	No Dis.	Dis.	No Dis.	Dis.	No Dis.	Dis.	No Dis.	Dis.	No Dis.	Dis.	No Dis.	Dis.
Total time use																
Mean minutes	334	488 *	183	118 *	153	62 *	29	17 *	41	35 *	58	65 *	62	53 *	137	55 *
Mean minutes | minutes = 0 with whom	360	518 *	370	423 *	389	365 *	274	314 *	233	245 *	238	246 *	235	213 *	356	249 *
Personal care[a]																
Mean minutes	3	13 *	1	2 *	0	1 *	0	0	—	—	0	1 *	—	—	0	0 *
Mean minutes | minutes = 0 with whom	63	68	89	67 *	120	71 *	38	27	—	—	104	69	—	—	52	57
Household activities																
Mean minutes	74	90 *	23	12 *	21	8 *	3	2 *	2	2	4	4	3	2	1	2
Mean minutes | minutes = 0 with whom	116	127 *	88	91	93	92	81	79	74	67	81	75	74	76	62	72
Caring for and helping household members																
Mean minutes	1	1 *	10	3 *	32	10 *	1	1 *	2	1 *	1	0 *	1	0 *	1	0 *
Mean minutes | minutes = 0 with whom	26	27	76	71	117	118	70	92	67	82	61	60	69	78	53	63

| | Householders | | | | | | | | Non-householders | | | | | | | |
| | Alone | | Partner | | Child | | Adult Family | | Child | | Adult Family | | Friend | | Other adult | |
	No Dis.	Dis.	No Dis.	Dis.	No Dis.	Dis.	No Dis.	Dis.	No Dis.	Dis.	No Dis.	Dis.	No Dis.	Dis.	No dis.	Dis.
Caring for and helping non-household members																
Mean minutes	1	1	2	1 *	1	0 *	0	0	4	5 *	3	3	1	1	1	1
Mean minutes | minutes = 0 with whom	46	39	79	89	39	49	42	46	88	117 *	72	78	45	56	43	47
Work and work-related activities																
Mean minutes	39	12 *	3	1 *	2	1 *	1	0 *	3	1 *	1	1	2	1 *	102	24 *
Mean minutes | minutes = 0 with whom	256	246	130	197	131	136	193	142	311	294	208	201	221	167 *	451	424 *
Education																
Mean minutes	7	2 *	1	0 *	1	0 *	1	0 *	0	0 *	0	0 *	1	0 *	2	1 *
Mean minutes | minutes = 0 with whom	175	168	148	159	141	157	116	71	143	181	118	116	167	163	197	209
Consumer purchases																
Mean minutes	10	8 *	7	3 *	6	2 *	1	1 *	1	1	2	3 *	2	2	1	1
Mean minutes | minutes = 0 with whom	43	45 *	69	70	64	63	69	76	60	61	76	70	60	59	41	50 *
Professional and personal care services																

(continued)

Table 37.3 Continued

	Householders								Non-householders							
	Alone		Partner		Child		Adult Family		Child		Adult Family		Friend		Other adult	
	No Dis.	Dis.	No Dis.	Dis.	No Dis.	Dis.	No Dis.	Dis.	No Dis.	Dis.	No Dis.	Dis.	No Dis.	Dis.	No Dis.	Dis.
Mean minutes	2	3 *	1	1 *	0	0 *	0	0	0	0	0	1 *	0	0 *	1	3 *
Mean minutes | minutes = 0 with whom	47	74 *	66	96 *	48	56	60	82	45	60	76	80	65	73	66	78 *
Household services																
Mean minutes	0	0 *	0	0 *	0	0 *	–	–	–	–	0	0	0	0	0	0
Mean minutes | minutes = 0 with whom	34	40	44	44	36	50	–	–	–	–	43	98	56	31 *	49	67 *
Eating and drinking																
Mean minutes	18	29 *	26	15 *	19	7 *	4	2 *	4	3 *	7	7	8	7 *	6	4 *
Mean minutes | minutes = 0 with whom	39	47 *	63	64	58	52 *	50	52	56	52 *	63	59 *	71	67 *	46	53 *
Active leisure																
Mean minutes	22	42 *	26	15 *	16	6 *	4	2 *	11	9 *	21	23 *	20	19 *	8	7 *
Mean minutes | minutes = 0 with whom	106	141 *	121	125	123	118	121	123	147	140	144	139	139	124 *	100	106
Passive leisure																
Mean minutes	101	237 *	57	51 *	30	18 *	9	6 *	4	6 *	6	11 *	7	7	3	5 *

	Householders								Non-householders							
	Alone		Partner		Child		Adult Family		Child		Adult Family		Friend		Other adult	
	No Dis.	Dis.	No Dis.	Dis.	No Dis.	Dis.	No Dis.	Dis.	No Dis.	Dis.	No Dis.	Dis.	No Dis.	Dis.	No Dis.	Dis.
Mean minutes | minutes = 0 with whom	190	320 *	168	243 *	144	190 *	165	205 *	142	171 *	149	193 *	163	180 *	79	145 *
Sports, exercise, and recreation																
Mean minutes	7	5 *	4	1 *	4	1 *	1	0 *	2	1 *	2	1 *	6	2 *	2	1 *
Mean minutes | minutes = 0 with whom	68	64 *	110	98 *	116	114	128	109	137	134	150	133	150	139	117	98
Religious and spiritual activities																
Mean minutes	3	7 *	4	3 *	3	1 *	1	1 *	1	2 *	1	2 *	3	4 *	2	2 *
Mean minutes | minutes = 0 with whom	71	81 *	102	104	102	109	112	130	115	136 *	112	120	122	127	116	124
Volunteer activities																
Mean minutes	3	3 *	2	1 *	2	0 *	0	0 *	2	1 *	1	0	2	2 *	3	2 *
Mean minutes | minutes = 0 with whom	92	118 *	121	117	125	109	124	188	138	151	136	162	144	139	151	153

Data are weighted.

* p < .05; tests difference between individuals with and without disabilities. "Dis." abbreviates disability. With whom categories (with the exception of "alone", versus all others) are not mutually exclusive.

a Not all subcategories include with whom information; see details in text.

— Results not shown due to small cell size; see details in text

Source: American Time Use Survey, 2008–2018.

sleep) than those without disabilities. No differences are observed in household activities. Although those with disabilities spend less time caring for household members, they are also less likely to report any minutes in this activity[5] (11% of people with disabilities versus 31% of people without disabilities). There are no differences, by disability status, in time spent caring for householders among those reporting any minutes. There are also no differences in the total minutes spent caring for non-householders, and—among those reporting any minutes—people with disabilities spend more time than people without disabilities.

Those with disabilities spend less time in work-related activities and in education. They spend less time in consumer purchases, are less likely to report any time (32% versus 43%), but report no less time when they do. They spend more time in professional and personal care services, as well as in household services, if reporting any minutes. They spend more time in active leisure, passive leisure, and religious activities, and less time in sports and recreation. Although they report fewer total volunteer minutes, there is no difference among those reporting any volunteer time by disability status.

Location of Time Use

Table 37.2 indicates that people with disabilities distribute their time in different places than people without disabilities. They spend 2.5 more hours per day, on average, at home. They spend less time at work, less time in public places, and less time in transportation. Although they report fewer minutes in another person's home, they are less likely to report time there (20% versus 26%), and spend more time when they do.

There is variation in home-based time use by type of activity. Among those who report any minutes in the activity at home, people with disabilities spend significantly more time than those without disabilities in consumer purchases, professional and personal care services, eating and drinking, active leisure, passive leisure, religious activities, and volunteer activities. They spend less time in sports and recreation. Notably, there are no significant differences by disability status in time spent at home in work-related activities when any time is reported.

Overall, this means that people with disabilities spend less time outside the home than people without disabilities. They are less likely to report minutes of any activity at work (8% versus 31%)—including work-related time (8% versus 30%) as well as eating and drinking (3% versus 15%), active leisure (1% versus 3%), and passive leisure (2% versus 5%). People with disabilities spend fewer minutes working when any time is reported at work. Although people with disabilities are less likely than those without disabilities to report any time in others' homes (26% versus 20%), they report more time in some activities when any is reported—including total time use, caring for and helping non-householders, and passive leisure. People with disabilities are less likely to report any time in public places (46% versus 62%)—and spend less time when they do—overall, and in eating and drinking, consumer purchases, and active leisure. They report more time in religious activities in public places than those without disabilities.

Transportation patterns also vary by disability status, as people with disabilities are less likely to report any time (63% versus 86%) and report less time when they do.

Presence of Others During Time Use

Lastly, Table 37.3 presents time spent in daily activities by the presence of others. People with disabilities spend substantially more total time alone—2.5 hours—than people without disabilities. Among those reporting any time in specific activities, more time is spent alone in household activities, professional and personal care services, eating and drinking, active and passive leisure, religious activities, and volunteering. Less time is spent alone in sports and recreation.

Reports of total time with household others depend on household composition; therefore, I focus on interpreting time spent among those reporting any positive minutes in an activity with another person. Those with disabilities spend more total time—nearly an hour—with a household spouse or partner than those without disabilities and more time with a partner in work-related activities, professional and personal care services, and passive leisure. They spend less time in personal care. Among other householders, people with disabilities spend less total time with household children—but report no differences in care-related time. More time is spent in the presence of household children in passive leisure, and less time eating. People with disabilities spend 40 more minutes, overall, with other household adult family, including more time caring for householders, more time in passive leisure, and less time in education.

People with disabilities reporting any time with non-householders spend more total time with non-household children and non-household adult family—but less time with non-household friends or neighbors and non-household other adults. When time is reported with non-household children, people with disabilities spend significantly more time caring for and helping non-householders, in passive leisure, and in religious activities, compared to those without disabilities. They spend less time eating and drinking and more time in passive leisure when any time is reported with non-household adult family and non-household friends. People with disabilities spend less total time with other types of non-household adults, including (if they spend any time) in work and sports and recreation. If they report any minutes with non-household other adults, they spend more time in consumer purchases, professional and personal care services, household services, eating and drinking, and in passive leisure.

DISCUSSION

People with disabilities report different experiences of daily life than people without disabilities. Although a growing literature describes these differences using time diary data (Anand & Ben-Shalom, 2014; Pagán, 2013; Shandra, 2018), most studies focus on the *quantity* of time spent in certain activities.[6] Yet major disability models emphasize that the *context* in which daily activities take place is also important for understanding social participation. The results presented in this chapter offer evidence into how this context—measured by where and with whom activities take place—differs by disability status and by type of activity.

When evaluating *where* activities take place, people with disabilities spend a greater amount of daily total time at home (2.5 hours) and less total time in public places (27 minutes) and in transportation (27 minutes) than people without disabilities. They spend more time at home volunteering, in religious or spiritual activities, in passive forms of leisure such as watching television and relaxing, and in active forms of leisure such as hobbies and games. In public places, they are less likely to report any time spent in activities like consumer purchasing (29% versus 40% of people without disabilities) and eating and drinking (14% versus 22%). They are also less likely to report any time in transportation on diary day (64% versus 86%).

People with disabilities face multiple types of barriers to accessing public space. Attitudinal barriers such as stigma and negative labeling by other people may deter or prevent engagement in activities like community-based recreation (Bedini, 2000) and organization-based volunteering (Lindsay, 2016). Physical barriers in the built environment can make spaces such as fitness facilities, parks, and community centers unusable (Rimmer et al., 2017). And inadequate transportation and other transit barriers can make activities outside the home inaccessible (Bascom & Christensen, 2017) and further impact time use (Myers & Ravesloot, 2016).

The current analyses quantify how people with disabilities spend time in different physical places than people without disabilities. They also illustrate how activities that may be assumed public—like shopping or volunteering—can also happen outside of public spaces. The patterns observed for working from home are particularly notable and worthy of further research. Although people with disabilities report fewer minutes of overall work, there are no significant differences by disability status in time spent working from home among those who report any time. For some people with disabilities, remote ways to engage in daily activities may make participation more accessible (Baruch et al., 2016; Childers & Kaufman-Scarborough, 2009), particularly for individuals with Web-use skills and broadband connections. However, the opposite may be true for other people with disabilities, as many Web platforms are inaccessible and many people with disabilities experience disparities in Internet access (Dobransky & Hargittai, 2016; Jaeger, 2012).

When evaluating *with whom* activities take place, people with disabilities spend a greater amount of daily total time alone (2.5 hours) than people without disabilities. They are also less likely to report any time with a household partner (28% versus 50%), household child (17% versus 40%), other household adult family (5% versus 11%), or non-household other adult (22% versus 39%). When they do report time with these people, they spend 53 more minutes with household partners, and 40 more minutes with other household adult family—but 107 minutes less with non-household other adults. In sum, the likelihood and amount of time spent with householders and non-householders differ substantially by disability status.

The type of activities spent in the presence of family and nonfamily social connections also varies—particularly for the activities that take up most of peoples' time. Eating and drinking, an activity that people spend over 1 hour in each day, is more likely to be spent alone (62% versus 46%) and for more time among people with disabilities. The same is true for household activities like cooking and cleaning, which average 2 hours per day, and passive leisure, which averages over 3 hours per day.

These types of access disparities to other people and to spaces outside the home may become even more pronounced as a result of the COVID-19 pandemic. People with disabilities disproportionately report underlying health conditions and inequitable access to healthcare relative to those without disabilities (e.g., Krahn et al., 2015). These factors place them at higher risk for severe COVID infection and, subsequently, with greater need for distancing and quarantining behaviors. Evidence of people with disabilities' greater social isolation as a result of the pandemic—including increased loneliness and decreased belonging (Pettinicchio et al., 2021)—has major ramifications for mental health. And although the shift to remote forms of working, shopping, and social engagement may facilitate new forms of participation for some with disabilities, access to the Internet, ADA-compliant platforms, and telework opportunities may exacerbate participation disparities for others (Krahn et al., 2015; Schur et al., 2020). The full impact of the pandemic on social participation among people with disabilities remains to be seen.

These results lend nuance to existing studies that find lower levels or alternate forms of social participation, by disability status. Brucker (2015) found that those with disabilities in the United States Current Population Survey were less likely than those without disabilities to eat dinner with other householders, but they were more likely to talk with neighbors a few times per week in a typical month. Mithen and colleagues' (2015) analysis of Australian General Social Survey data found that people with disabilities were less likely to have face-to-face contact with family or friends at least once a week; however, these differences were explained by demographic and socioeconomic covariates. It may be that people with disabilities report fewer social interactions than those without disabilities; however, the current results suggest that differences are dependent upon type of activity and type of social connection. Future research should evaluate these trends in tandem with variations in household composition, as people with disabilities are more likely than those without disabilities to live alone and less likely to marry and to live with coresident children (Altman & Bernstein, 2008; Clarke & McKay, 2014; Schur et al., 2013).

Implications for Disability Models and Measurement

These results illustrate the importance of accounting for multiple activity contexts when measuring social participation among people with disabilities. Many services have shifted to online or remote platforms, allowing for activities such as shopping or financial management to be performed at home.[7] Yet traditional functional assessments use language that implies instrumental activities are completed outside the home (Lawton & Brody, 1969).

Analyses also complicate the relationship between activities and roles. For example, the ATUS defines volunteer activities as unpaid work through formal organizations. Table 37.1 indicates that people with disabilities report fewer overall volunteering minutes and are less likely to report volunteering on diary day. However, there are no significant time differences among those who volunteer—and people with disabilities report *more time* in helping behaviors outside the household. Other studies of volunteering and disability indicate similarly: People with disabilities are less likely than those without disabilities to report volunteering in an organization, but no less likely to report informal helping behaviors (Shandra, 2017). Many disability models consider activities to be a subset of roles. However, the measurement of concepts like altruism or caretaking (Shandra & Penner, 2017) or work (Shandra, 2016) may exclude people with disabilities because they assume related types of activities take place in narrowly defined contexts that are themselves inaccessible.

Future Directions and Limitations

This chapter takes an expansive view on social participation by providing a broad description of where and with whom daily activities take place. These patterns suggest multiple avenues for further research on disability. This includes the overlap between where and with whom categories, following previous analyses that have used the ATUS data to evaluate "socially isolated" time spent at home, alone (Passias et al., 2017). It is also possible to evaluate the timing and temporaral patterning of different types of activities across the day (Flood et al., 2018). Finally, the ATUS data can also be used to estimate experienced well-being and reports of happiness, fatigue, and stress during activities, in specific places, or among certain types of other people (Flood & Genadek, 2016).

People with disabilities are a heterogeneous group, and those with physical, sensory, and cognitive functional limitations report different time use (Shandra, 2018) and sociodemographic characteristics (Brault, 2012). Likewise, differences in time use by disability status have also been observed by gender (Shandra & Penner, 2017) and by stage in the life course (Shandra, 2021). The small cell sizes in many where and with whom analyses presented here precluded further disaggregation by gender, age, and type of disability; however, future research on commonly occurring activity domains could evaluate these differences.

Disability models suggest several limitations that cannot be accounted for in these data. It is not possible to differentiate between what Verbrugge and Jette (1994, p. 5) described as "can do" versus "do do"—a person's capabilities versus their behaviors. Nor can the ATUS address variation in peoples' subjective assessments of their individual participation needs and goals (Hammel et al., 2008). Further, it not possible to evaluate how an individual's social contacts may set expectations about disability, how a location might present physical or sociocultural barriers, or how the context where an activity takes place might narrow or widen the gap between a person and their environment (Nagi, 1991; Verbrugge & Jette, 1994).

Nonetheless, the ATUS provides researchers with the opportunity to explore multiple contexts of the what, where, and with whom of social participation (Levasseur et al., 2010) across a "comprehensive and more democratic" swath of activity domains (Verbrugge & Jette 1994, p. 5). The study of disability as a social category has been largely peripheral to many social science disciplines (Arneil & Hirschmann, 2016; Green & Gerschick, 2016) and omitted from one of the most often-cited tomes on social participation in the United States (Putnam, 2000). The results presented here suggest more inclusive ways to measure and conceptualize the characteristics of daily life with disability.

Notes

1. See Green and Barnartt (2016), Jette and Keysor (2003), Masala and Petretto (2008), and Rimmerman (2013) for more comprehensive discussions and comparisons between models.
2. See Altman (2016) for a comprehensive overview of Nagi's contributions.
3. This category is omitted from Table 37.3 due to small cell sizes. Among those reporting any time with household non-family adults, people with disabilities report spending 37 more total minutes than people without disabilities. Most of these differences can be attributed to passive time use.
4. When relevant, I also report the percentage of respondents who report any minutes of the activity on diary day in the text of this chapter but omit these values from the tables for brevity.
5. Results for the percentage of people with and without disabilities spending *any* time on diary day in an activity are reported in the text, only—not in the tables.
6. See Carr et al. (2017) for a notable exception using data from older adults in the United States.
7. Although divides in digital access, by disability status, persist (Dobransky & Hargittai, 2016; Parker et al., 2018).

References

Altman, B. M. (2014). Definitions, concepts, and measures of disability. *Annals of Epidemiology*, 24(1), 2–7. doi:10.1016/j.annepidem.2013.05.018

Altman, B., & Bernstein, A. (2008). *Disability and health in the United States, 2001–2005*. U.S. Department of Health and Human Services; Centers for Disease Control. https://stacks.cdc.gov/view/cdc/6983

Altman, B. M. (2016). Conceptual issues in disability: Saad Nagi's contribution to the disability knowledge base. In S. E. Green & S. N. Barnartt (Eds.), *Sociology looking at disability: What did we know and when did we know it* (Vol. 9) (pp. 57–95). Emerald.

Amilon, A., Hansen, K. M., Kjær, A. A., & Steffensen, T. (2021). Estimating disability prevalence and disability-related inequalities: Does the choice of measure matter? *Social Science & Medicine*, 272. doi:10.1016/j.socscimed.2021.113740

Anand, P., & Ben-Shalom, Y. (2014). How do working-age people with disabilities spend their time? New evidence from the American Time Use Survey. *Demography, 51*(6), 1977–1998. doi:10.1007/s13524-014-0336-3

Arneil, B., & Hirschmann, N. J. (2016). *Disability and political theory*. Cambridge University Press. doi:10.1017/9781316694053

Badley, E. M. (2008). Enhancing the conceptual clarity of the activity and participation components of the International Classification of Functioning, Disability, and Health. *Social Science & Medicine, 66*(11), 2335–2345. doi:10.1016/j.socscimed.2008.01.026

Baruch, A., May, A., & Yu, D. (2016). The motivations, enablers and barriers for voluntary participation in an online crowdsourcing platform. *Computers in Human Behavior, 64*, 923–931. doi:10.1016/j.chb.2016.07.039

Bascom, G. W., & Christensen, K. M. (2017). The impacts of limited transportation access on persons with disabilities' social participation. *Journal of Transport & Health, 7*, 227–234. doi:10.1016/j.jth.2017.10.002

Bedini, L. A. (2000). "Just sit down so we can talk": Perceived stigma and community recreation pursuits of people with disabilities. *Therapeutic Recreation Journal, 34*(1), 55–68.

Bolger, N., Davis, A., & Rafaeli, E. (2003). Diary methods: Capturing life as it is lived. *Annual Review of Psychology, 54*(1), 579–616. doi:10.1146/annurev.psych.54.101601.145030

Brault, M. (2012). *Americans with disabilities: 2010*. U.S. Department of Commerce.

Brault, M., Stern, S., & Raglin, D. (2007). *Evaluation report covering disability*. U.S. Census Bureau.

Brucker, D. L. (2015). Social capital, employment and labor force participation among persons with disabilities. *Journal of Vocational Rehabilitation, 43*(1), 17–31. doi:10.3233/JVR-150751

Carr, D., Cornman, J. C., & Freedman, V. A. (2017). Disability and activity-related emotion in later life: Are effects buffered by intimate relationship support and strain? *Journal of Health and Social Behavior, 58*(3), 387–403. doi:10.1177/0022146517713551

Childers, T. L., & Kaufman-Scarborough, C. (2009). Expanding opportunities for online shoppers with disabilities. *Journal of Business Research, 62*(5), 572–578. doi:10.1016/j.jbusres.2008.06.017

Clarke, H., & McKay, S. (2014). Disability, partnership and parenting. *Disability & Society, 29*(4), 543–555. doi:10.1080/09687599.2013.831745

Cobigo, V., Ouellette-Kuntz, H., Lysaght, R., & Martin, L. (2012). Shifting our conceptualization of social inclusion. *Stigma Research and Action, 2*(2), 75–84.

Dobransky, K., & Hargittai, E. (2016). Unrealized potential: Exploring the digital disability divide. *Poetics, 58*, 18–28. doi:10.1016/j.poetic.2016.08.003

Flood, S. M., & Genadek, K. R. (2016). Time for each other: Work and family constraints among couples. *Journal of Marriage and Family, 78*(1), 142–164. doi:10.1111/jomf.12255

Flood, S. M., Hill, R., & Genadek, K. R. (2018). Daily temporal pathways: A latent class approach to time diary data. *Social Indicators Research, 135*(1), 117–142. doi:/10.1007/s11205-016-1469-0

Freedman, V. A., Carr, D., Cornman, J. C., & Lucas, R. E. (2017). Impairment severity and evaluative and experienced well-being among older adults: Assessing the role of daily activities. *Innovation in Aging, 1*(1). doi:10.1093/geroni/igx010

Green, S., & Gerschick, T. (2016). Sections collaborate to explore disability as an overlooked axis of intersectionality and inequality. *Footnotes, 44*(7), 5–7.

Green, Sara, and Sharon N. Barnartt. 2016. Sociology Looking at Disability: What Did We Know and When Did We Know It? West Yorkshire, UK: Emerald Group Publishing.

Hammel, J., Magasi, S., Heinemann, A., Whiteneck, G., Bogner, J., & Rodriguez, E. (2008). What does participation mean? An insider perspective from people with disabilities. *Disability and Rehabilitation, 30*(19), 1445–1460. doi:10.1080/09638280701625534.

Hofferth, S. L., Flood, S., Sobek, M., & Backman, D. (2020). *American Time Use Survey Data Extract Builder: Version 2.8 [dataset]*. University of Maryland/IPUMS. https://doi.org/10.18128/D060.V2.8

Jaeger, P. T. (2012). *Disability and the Internet: Confronting a digital divide*: Lynne Rienner.

Jette, A. M. (2006). Toward a common language for function, disability, and health. *Physical Therapy, 86*(5), 726–734. doi:10.1093/ptj/86.5.726

Jette, A. M., Haley, S. M., & Kooyoomjian, J. T. (2003). Are the ICF activity and participation dimensions distinct? *Journal of Rehabilitation Medicine, 35*(3), 145–149. doi:10.1080/16501970310010501

Jette, A. M., & Keysor, J. J. (2003). Disability models: implications for arthritis exercise and physical activity interventions. *Arthritis Care & Research: Official Journal of the American College of Rheumatology, 49*(1), 114–120.

Jette, A. M., Tao, W., Haley, S. M., Jette, A. M., Tao, W., & Haley, S. M. (2007). Blending activity and participation sub-domains of the ICF. *Disability and Rehabilitation, 29*(22), 1742–1750. doi:10.1080/09638280601164790

Katz, S. (1983). Assessing self-maintenance: Activities of daily living, mobility, and instrumental activities of daily living. *Journal of the American Geriatrics Society, 31*(12), 721–727. doi:10.1111/j.1532-5415.1983.tb03391.x.

Krahn, G. L., Walker, D. K., & Correa-De-Araujo, R. (2015). Persons with disabilities as an unrecognized health disparity population. *American Journal of Public Health, 105*(S2), S198–S206. doi:10.2105/AJPH.2014.302182

Lawton, M. P. (1970). Assessment, integration, and environments for older people. *The Gerontologist, 10*(1), 38–46. doi:10.1093/geront/10.1_Part_1.38

Lawton, M. P. (1972). Assessing the competence of older people. In D. P. Kent, R. Kastenbaum, & S. Sherwood (Eds.), *Research planning and action for the elderly: The power and potential of social science* (pp. 122–143). Human Sciences Press.

Lawton, M. P., & Brody, E. M. (1969). Assessment of older people: self-maintaining and instrumental activities of daily living. *The Gerontologist, 9*(3), 179–186. doi:10.1093/geront/9.3_Part_1.179

Levasseur, M., Richard, L., Gauvin, L., & Raymond, É. (2010). Inventory and analysis of definitions of social participation found in the aging literature: Proposed taxonomy of social activities. *Social Science & Medicine, 71*(12), 2141–2149. doi:10.1016/j.socscimed.2010.09.041

Lindsay, S. (2016). A scoping review of the experiences, benefits, and challenges involved in volunteer work among youth and young adults with a disability. *Disability and Rehabilitation, 38*(16), 1533–1546. doi:10.3109/09638288.2015.1107634

Masala, C., & Petretto, D. R. (2008). From disablement to enablement: conceptual models of disability in the 20th century. *Disability and Rehabilitation, 30*(17), 1233–1244.

Mithen, J., Aitken, Z., Ziersch, A., & Kavanagh, A. M. (2015). Inequalities in social capital and health between people with and without disabilities. *Social Science & Medicine, 126*, 26–35. doi:10.1016/j.socscimed.2014.12.009

Myers, A., & Ravesloot, C. (2016). Navigating time and space: How Americans with disabilities use time and transportation. *Community Development, 47*(1), 75–90. doi:10.1080/15575330.2015.1111399

Nagi, S. Z. (1965). Some conceptual issues in disability and rehabilitation. In M. Sussman (Ed.), *Sociology and rehabilitation* (pp. 100–113). American Sociological Association.

Nagi, S. Z. (1976). An epidemiology of disability among adults in the United States. *The Milbank Memorial Fund Quarterly. Health and Society, 54*(4), 439–467.

Nagi, S. Z. (1991). Disability concepts revisited; implications for prevention. In Committee on a National Agenda for the Prevention of Disabilities, Institute of Medicine (Ed.), *Disability in America: Toward a national agenda for prevention* (pp. 309–327). National Academy Press. doi:10.17226/1579.

National Academies of Sciences, Engineering, and Medicine. (2019). *Functional assessment for adults with disabilities.* National Academies Press. doi:10.17226/25376

Nordenfelt, L. (2003). Action theory, disability and ICF. *Disability and Rehabilitation, 25*(18), 1075–1079. doi:10.1080/0963828031000137748

Pagán, R. (2013). Time allocation of disabled individuals. *Social Science & Medicine, 84*, 80–93. doi:10.1016/j.socscimed.2013.02.014

Pagán-Rodríguez, R. (2014). How do disabled individuals spend their leisure time? *Disability and Health Journal, 7*(2), 196–205. doi:10.1016/j.dhjo.2014.01.001

Parker, K., Horowitz, J., Brown, A., Fry, R., Cohn, D., & Igielnik, R. (2018). *What unites and divides urban, suburban and rural communities.* Pew Research Center.

Parsons, T. (1958). Definitions of health and illness in light of American values and social structure. In E. G. Jaco (Ed.), *Patients, physicians and illness* (pp. 120–144). Free Press.

Passias, E. J., Sayer, L., & Pepin, J. R. (2017). Who experiences leisure deficits? Mothers' marital status and leisure time. *Journal of Marriage and Family, 79*(4), 1001–1022. doi:10.1111/jomf.12365

Pettinicchio, D., & Maroto, M. (2021). Who counts? Measuring disability cross-nationally in census data. *Journal of Survey Statistics and Methodology, 9*(2), 257–284. doi:10.1093/jssam/smaa046

Pettinicchio, D., Maroto, M., Chai, L., & Lukk, M. (2021). Findings from an online survey on the mental health effects of COVID-19 on Canadians with disabilities and chronic health conditions. *Disability and Health Journal, 14*(3). doi:10.1016/j.dhjo.2021.101085

Piškur, B., Daniëls, R., Jongmans, M. J., Ketelaar, M., Smeets, R. J., Norton, M., & Beurskens, A. J. (2014). Participation and social participation: are they distinct concepts? *Clinical Rehabilitation, 28*(3), 211–220. doi:10.1177/0269215513499029

Putnam, R. D. (2000). *Bowling alone: The collapse and revival of American community.* Simon and Schuster. doi:10.1145/358916.361990

Rimmer, J. H., Padalabalanarayanan, S., Malone, L. A., & Mehta, T. (2017). Fitness facilities still lack accessibility for people with disabilities. *Disability and Health Journal, 10*(2), 214–221. doi:10.1016/j.dhjo.2016.12.011

Rimmerman, A. (2013). *Social inclusion of people with disabilities: National and international perspectives.* Cambridge University Press.

Robinson, J., & Godbey, G. (2010). *Time for life: The surprising ways Americans use their time.* Penn State Press.

Schur, L., Ameri, M., & Kruse, D. (2020). Telework after COVID: A "silver lining" for workers with disabilities? *Journal of Occupational Rehabilitation, 30*(4), 521–536. doi:10.1007/s10926-020-09936-5

Schur, L., Kruse, D., & Blanck, P. (2013). *People with disabilities: Sidelined or mainstreamed?* Cambridge University Press. doi:10.1017/CBO9780511843693

Shandra, C. L. (2016). Nonmarket work among working-age disability beneficiaries: Evidence from the American Time Use Survey. *Journal of Disability Policy Studies, 27*(2), 76–85. doi:10.1177/1044207315587569

Shandra, C. L. (2017). Disability and social participation: The case of formal and informal volunteering. *Social Science Research, 68*, 195–213. doi:10.1016/j.ssresearch.2017.02.006

Shandra, C. L. (2018). Disability as inequality: Social disparities, health disparities, and participation in daily activities. *Social Forces, 97*(1), 157–192. doi: 10.1093/sf/soy031

Shandra, C. L. (2021). Disability and patterns of leisure participation across the life course. *The Journals of Gerontology Series B: Psychological Sciences and Social Sciences, 76*(4), 801–809. doi:10.1093/geronb/gbaa065

Shandra, C. L., & Penner, A. (2017). Benefactors and beneficiaries? Disability and care to others. *Journal of Marriage and Family, 79*(4), 1160–1185. doi:10.1111/jomf.12401

Shelley, K. J. (2005). Developing the American time use survey activity classification system. *Monthly Labor Review, 128*, 3.

StataCorp. (2015). Stata Statistical Software: Release 14. StataCorp LP.

Verbrugge, L. M. (1990). *The iceberg of disability*. In S. M. Stahl (Ed.), *The legacy of longevity: Health and health care in later life* (pp. 55–75). SAGE Publications.

Verbrugge, L. M., & Jette, A. M. (1994). The disablement process. *Social Science & Medicine, 38*(1), 1–14. doi:10.1016/0277-9536(94)90294-1

Verbrugge, L. M., & Liu, X. (2014). Midlife trends in activities and disability. *Journal of Aging and Health, 26*(2), 178–206. doi:10.1177/0898264313508189

Wales, K., Clemson, L., Lannin, N., & Cameron, I. (2016). Functional assessments used by occupational therapists with older adults at risk of activity and participation limitations: A systematic review. *PloS One, 11*(2). doi:10.1371/journal.pone.0147980

Whiteneck, G., & Dijkers, M. P. (2009). Difficult to measure constructs: Conceptual and methodological issues concerning participation and environmental factors. *Archives of Physical Medicine and Rehabilitation, 90*(11), S22–S35. doi:10.1016/j.apmr.2009.06.009

Williams, J. R., Masuda, Y. J., & Tallis, H. (2016). A measure whose time has come: Formalizing time poverty. *Social Indicators Research, 128*(1), 265–283. doi:10.1007/s11205-015-1029-z

World Health Organization. (2001). *International Classification of Functioning, Disability and Health: ICF*. World Health Organization.

CHAPTER 38

THE DISABILITY RIGHTS MOVEMENT

RICHARD SCOTCH AND KARA SUTTON

INTRODUCTION

IN the past half-century, the disability rights movement (DRM) has made a significant impact in the United States and societies around the globe. Accessibility issues for people with disabilities have entered public consciousness and policy discourse, and while many significant barriers remain, many others have come down or at least been reduced. In the United States and a number of other societies, formal mandates have been enacted about architectural access and accessible technologies; in many others, governments have symbolically affirmed rights of access through the adoption of anti-discrimination statements. The achievements of the DRM have been both significant and modest, bringing many people with disabilities into mainstream economic, political, and social institutions, although many barriers to participation persist. Stigmatization and marginalization associated with disability remain embedded in institutional structures and practices to a significant extent; nevertheless, people with disabilities have become more visible and accepted participants in cultural, political, and social life.

In this chapter, we provide an overview of the social movement advocating for disability rights, including its origins, goals, strategies, and impact. We focus primarily on the DRM in the United States, with some consideration of developments in other nations. The chapter begins by reviewing the historical origins of the DRM. We then address the strategic political goals of the DRM and the conceptual models underlying those goals, followed by an overview of some of the major components of the movement and a review of the activities in which the DRM has engaged. We conclude with some thoughts on the significance of the DRM.

Origin and Context for the Disability Rights Movement

While the DRM, per se, has only been active since the 1960s, there is a long history of social and political activism from previous eras on behalf of people with disabilities in the United States and many other countries (Barnartt et al., 2001; Pelka, 1997). With the advent of urban capitalist industrial society in Western societies in the 19th century, people with disabilities who had been largely integrated into their families and communities became increasingly subject to identification, separation, and marginalization (Nielsen, 2012; Rose, 2017). In emerging market economies, where work shifted from households into discrete workplaces, where the value of people's social contributions became equated with the economic value they added to market processes, and where the standardization of commodities became associated with social and cultural normalization, anyone with physical or mental differences came to be seen in terms of the costs associated with their support. As Western societies sought to exclude and marginalize those who had disabilities, resistance was exercised by people with disabilities, the members of their families, and other allies. In some cases, such resistance was expressed by a lack of cooperation with exclusionary processes. In other cases, resistance manifested itself in individual acts of defiance. But in other instances, collective resistance occurred, with people joining together to remain in the larger community and to reject the stigma attributed to difference (Nielsen, 2012).

Early political activity to advance the position of people with disabilities often was focused on specific categories of impairment or by those affected by common circumstances (Barnartt & Scotch, 2001; Nielsen, 2012; Rose, 2017). Examples of the former included collective action by people who were deaf, blind, or experiencing medical conditions, while the latter included disabled military veterans, industrial workers who had experienced disabling occupational injuries, people restricted to lives in public or private facilities, or those excluded from participation in various institutional spheres such as schools or public benefit systems.

In many instances, advocacy organizations emerged more or less organically from informal networks among individuals or their family members whose disabled status brought them together, whether in rehabilitation facilities or other typically segregated spaces. Shared experiences helped to form shared identities based in part on their impairments but also on their shared exclusion from social participation. While such networks often began as mechanisms for mutual support and socialization, in some cases energetic leaders and/or triggering events fostered the initiation of collective behavior and activism on behalf of their members. When informal persuasion was unsuccessful in securing results, members might adopt more confrontational tactics to express their grievances and seek to influence the general public and policy makers (Carey et al., 2020, pp. 183–198).

In the middle decades of the 20th century, in the United States and elsewhere, a new form of disability advocacy organization developed, with new goals. The new form was cross-disability in nature, with the emergence of informal groups and formal organizations that incorporated people with varying types of impairments and conditions (Barnartt & Scotch, 2001; Scotch, 1984). In many US communities in the 1960s, disability activists with diverse impairments came together to seek expanded access to public and private facilities and services. Similar groups formed in many other societies at the local level, and local groups joined in coalitions at the regional, national, and global levels (Barnartt et al., 2001; Charlton, 1998). National bodies formed, such as the American Coalition of Citizens with Disabilities (ACCD) in the United States and the Union of the Physically Impaired Against Segregation (UPIAS) in the United Kingdom (Union of the Physically Impaired Against Segregation, 1975), and, ultimately, global coalitions such as Disabled Peoples International (DPI) were established to share information and coordinate activities cross-nationally (Driedger, 1989).

The new goals went beyond demands for specific types of services or benefits to a more generalized grievance concerning exclusion from or segregation within public and private social institutions and social life, and with challenging the stigma too often associated with impairment. Activism to attain such broad goals was expressed in the discourse of human rights, or in the United States, civil rights, and the advocates for those rights came to call themselves the DRM. The DRM sought acceptance of people with disabilities in all spheres of public and private life, as well as opportunities for full social participation in every sector of society (Pelka, 1997; Scotch, 1984).

For many, these goals resonated with and were informed by other social movements that were active in the 1960s and 1970s, including the second wave of the feminist movement, the movements by African Americans and other racial minorities for equal access and equal justice, and other efforts to challenge oppressive institutions, seek social justice, and promote equity and social equality (Scotch, 1984). Many of the goals were expressed in terms of human rights, such as the right to equal access to a public education, as with the black civil rights movement, the right to procedural guarantees of due process, as applied to those arbitrarily incarcerated, the right to privacy, as accorded to women and sexual minorities, and the right to self-determination, as claimed by other oppressed and excluded minorities. And while disability activists previously had engaged in protests and other acts of expression, in the 1960s and 1970s, the rhetoric and tactics of the DRM drew on the models of other social movements of that era (Barnartt & Scotch, 2001; Scotch, 1984).

To some extent, organizations focused on the rights of racial minorities initially resisted identification or alliance with disability rights groups, fearing that a broadened focus on various forms of oppression might undermine the influence of Black advocates and their allies (Scotch, 1984). However, by the late 1970s, with the growing conservative opposition to civil rights in the United States, advocates for civil rights based on race, gender, and other attributes joined cause to preserve policy protections affecting all marginalized groups through such alliances as the Leadership Conference on

Civil Rights (Scotch, 1984). These coalitions were to continue, with racial and gender advocates endorsing passage of the Americans with Disabilities Act (ADA) and a number of generic civil rights policies. This unity among a broad array of advocacy groups has enhanced their influence on many issues of public policy.

THEORETICAL AND POLITICAL PERSPECTIVES FOR THE DISABILITY RIGHTS MOVEMENT

The fundamental theoretical perspective which has guided the DRM for the past half-century has been what has come to be called the social model of disability (Barnes, 2012). This model has its origins in several formulations, including the organizing tenets of the key British group UPIAS in the 1970s (Union of the Physically Impaired Against Segregation, 1975) that refer to the social model; in the United States and elsewhere as the minority group model (Bickenbach, 1999; Scotch, 2000, 2002; Scotch & Schriner, 1997); and in other works as the sociopolitical model (Barton, 1992; Hahn, 1985). All versions shared a set of conceptual assumptions that disability was (at least) jointly determined by the environment as well as the impairment and that people with disabilities constituted a minority group that was politically and socially oppressed. Associated with this perspective was the conviction that most problems associated with disability could best be addressed through self-advocacy and the removal of disabling environmental barriers, such as cultural beliefs that stigmatized, public policies that provided perverse incentives that made it difficult to live independently, and technology and physical structures that effectively excluded people with disabilities. Since this approach has come to be referred to generally as the social model, we utilize that term here.

The social model has been advanced by the founders of the DRM in contrast to the traditional medical model of disability. The medical model, which has dominated public life and biomedical, policy, and cultural institutions since the 19th century, characterizes disability as the direct product of physical and/or mental impairment. Within this framework, impairment prevents the person from functioning effectively in social life and requires an intervention by medical and/or rehabilitation professionals to be overcome. If professional treatment fails, the model suggests that the disabled person may be rendered unable to function on her own and must be financially and socially supported by family members, by community service providers, or by specialized social welfare policies that compensate for the inability to function.

In contrast, the social model of disability reflects the perspective that while people do experience physical and mental impairments, any problems they may face with functioning are the result of a social and physical environment that does not accommodate their particular difference (Barnes, 2012; Scotch, 2000). Someone who uses a wheelchair is disabled in an environment without curb cuts, elevators, and accessible restrooms, and someone who is blind becomes disabled when encountering materials or technology that rely on vision, but is not functionally impaired when information is provided in an aural or tactile manner, as in recorded or Braille books. While the focus of the medical model is on interventions that repair those persons who are perceived to be damaged, the focus of the social model is on interventions that remove barriers and result in a more accessible environment. Within the context of the social model, barriers may be physical, such as stairs that are closed to wheelchair users, or messages only provided visually or aurally, reflecting assumptions that people are only a certain height, or have a certain amount of upper body strength. Barriers may also be the result of disabling assumptions about which people are capable of performing different kinds of tasks, leading to a focus on how work must be done rather than on whether an individual is capable of completing the work in some alternative manner. The social model characterizes disabling barriers as discriminatory, as constraints that are socially constructed resulting from prejudice and stereotypes that can be removed by more inclusive practices that reflect the capabilities of individuals with disabilities (Barnes, 2012).

Disability activist James I. Charlton has described the perspective of the DRM based on this social model:

> A growing number of people with disabilities have developed a consciousness that transforms the notion and concept of disability from a medical condition to a social and political condition. . . . [that] requires people with disabilities to recognize their need to control and take responsibility for their own lives . . . experiential knowledge is pivotal in making decisions that affect their lives.
>
> (Charlton, 1998, p. 17)

The difference between the medical and social models leads to very different responses to someone with an impairment, and to different strategies for empowering them (Scotch, 2000). The medical model has resulted in the creation of systems and institutions for rehabilitation, while the social model has led to campaigns to reconstruct the physical and social environment. The fundamental exclusion of people with disabilities from society results from barriers which prevent them from participating in societal institutions and processes and from the social construction of disability as a status reflecting incapacity and the inability to contribute to society. People with disabilities have been systematically excluded from participation in public schooling, employment, transportation, and many other public accommodations, services, and facilities. People with disabilities have routinely been incarcerated in the name of treatment and rehabilitation, and they have been made subject to social control based on disabling assumptions of dependence and incapacity. Inaccessible buildings, housing, transit systems, workplaces, and telecommunication systems establish a self-fulfilling prophecy of making participation difficult or impossible, which is then used to justify further exclusion and marginalization.

The DRM has concentrated on changing how buildings and communication and transportation technologies are designed and built, and on how social and organizational processes can intrinsically include people with differing characteristics rather than excluding them, mobilizing its constituencies to redesign buildings, technology, workplaces, transportation networks, and social benefit systems (Barnartt & Scotch, 2001; Scotch, 1984). The movement also has sought to reframe disability within popular culture, to challenge stereotypes that associate disability with incapacity and depict lives of people with disabilities as either tragic and inherently dependent and sad, or in instances when disabled people are successful, as exceptionally heroic and inspiring (Barnartt & Scotch, 2001; Charlton, 1998). The dilemmas of disabled people identified by the medical model can be addressed by individual efforts and generosity from philanthropy or a welfare state. The dilemmas identified within the social model demand transformative institutional change brought about by a social movement of mobilized advocates.

Major Disability Rights Movement Constituent Groups and Social Movement Organizations: Early Years

Many members of the DRM make the distinction between organizations *for* people *with* disabilities and organizations *of* people with disabilities (Carey et al., 2019, 2020; Scotch, 1984). While the former may take a number of forms, most advocates who themselves have disabilities contend that their own organizations are likely to take more rights-oriented positions that support autonomy for people with disabilities, while the positions taken by organizations led or comprised largely by those without disabilities tend to be more focused on improving access to services and objectives in which professionals, family members, and other caregivers may be able to define the best interests of those with disabilities. The discussion here will largely address organizations *of* people with disabilities whose goals include the advancement of rights.

Some of the earliest activism directed toward human or civil rights for people with disabilities has been by people with communication impairments, notably the blind and the deaf (Barnartt & Scotch, 2001). Paul Longmore (2009) notes that the earliest disability movements were among graduates of schools for the deaf in 19th-century Europe and the United States. School alumni formed groups at the local level; in the United States, ASL users established newspapers, churches, and social clubs, and in 1880, they formed the National Association of the Deaf. The organizations of the deaf were active in promoting the use of American Sign Language (ASL) and in opposing oralism, the belief, more common among hearing people, that deaf people would be better off communicating through lip reading and spoken language. Deaf advocates also acted to oppose discriminatory restrictions on deaf people, such as restrictions on driver's licenses in the 1910s and public employment in New Deal work relief programs in the 1930s (Burch, 2002). Later in the 20th century, deaf activists campaigned for the acceptance of ASL as a language, and to promote its use in schools. In 1988, deaf students at Gallaudet University, a federally chartered college in Washington, DC, conducted protests to successfully challenge the appointment of a hearing president in the Deaf President Now campaign (Christiansen & Barnartt, 2003).

Among the blind in the United States, rights-focused organizations began to be formed in the 1890s, also among graduates of special schools for the blind found in many American states. A national organization, the American Blind People's Higher Education and General Improvement Association, was formed in 1896, which published a magazine, *The Problem*, to promote the status of blind people, and a number of local groups were formed in the 20th century (Barnartt & Scotch, 2001). Several organizations of providers serving blind people formed in the 1920s and lobbied for expanded benefits and other opportunities in education and transportation, but these typically did not include blind people themselves (Barnartt & Scotch, 2001). The National Federation of the Blind (NFB) was established in 1940 by Jacobus tenBroek, a law professor at the University of California (Matson, 1990), and another national organization of blind people, the American Council of the Blind, formed in 1961. Both groups, but particularly NFB, favored autonomy for blind people and spoke out against the dominance of rehabilitation professionals over services and benefits for the blind. Blind activists opposed sheltered workshops that provided work training in controlled settings at subminimum wages, and promoted "white cane" and "guide dog" laws that guaranteed access to public places to blind people using white canes or service dogs to assist their mobility (Matson, 1990). Blind advocacy groups also formed in several European countries, including Portugal, Greece, and the United Kingdom (Longmore, 2009). In Spain, graduates of the Madrid School for the Blind formed a group in 1894, the Centro Protectivo e Instructor de Ciegos, to protest segregation and forced reliance on begging, and in South Africa the South African Union of the Blind organized in 1987 (Barnartt et al., 2001).

Organizations advocating for disabled military veterans also formed in the 20th century, although these groups did not always find common cause with other disability advocates (Barnartt & Scotch, 2001; Gerber, 2009). One of the earliest organizations in the United States was the Disabled American Veterans (DAV) founded by World War I veterans in 1920 and chartered by the US Congress in 1932. Still an active group, DAV provides a diverse array of services to disabled veterans and is an active advocate for their interests in public policy (Pelka 1997, p. 101). A series of groups advocating for disabled veterans were formed after many American military conflicts, either as separate organizations such the Paralyzed Veterans of America (PVA) founded in 1947 by World War II veterans (Jennings, 2016), or as part of broader veteran groups such as the Vietnam Veterans of America. PVA notably worked for greater accessibility, supporting the enactment of the Architectural Barriers Act of 1968 and the creation of a federal Architectural and Transportation Barriers Compliance Board to require that federally funded construction be designed to be accessible (Pelka, 1997, pp. 236–237). The Architectural Barriers Act was the first national legislation in the United States that addressed buildings that could not be used by wheelchair users and people with other mobility impairments (Scotch, 1984, pp. 29–31).

Another group of disability self-advocates that formed in the 20th century was comprised of individuals with mental disabilities who had been released from state treatment facilities. Such institutions were challenged by former patients and their allies as overly restrictive and abusive, and as primarily exerting social control over residents rather than providing them with beneficial treatment. One early effort, in 1946, occurred when former patients at New York City's Rockland State Hospital created a self-help group, We Are Not Alone, to publicize the conditions within the facility, helping to launch the deinstitutionalization movement. By the 1960s, many local activist groups of people with psychiatric diagnoses had joined together for self-advocacy, establishing groups with names such as the Insane Liberation Front, the Mental Patients Liberation Front, and the Network Against Psychiatric Assault (Hatfield, 1981; McLean, 2010; Tomes, 2006). Challenging the professional role of psychiatry and other "helping" professions, these self-styled psychiatric survivors spoke out against professional beliefs about mental illnesses and the prejudice and discrimination in employment, health care, and society at large experienced by people characterized as mentally ill. These organizations made statements to the media, filed lawsuits challenging involuntary commitment and harsh psychiatric treatments, argued for the closure of large custodial mental institutions, and successfully advocated the passage of legislation diverting people with mental illness from large residential facilities to smaller community based mental health agencies (Carey et al., 2020, pp. 67–70).

A parallel disability rights initiative challenged facilities for people with intellectual impairments, although this movement was largely led by parents of individuals with cognitive disabilities rather than by disabled people themselves (Carey, 2009). While there have been increasing instances of self-advocacy by people with intellectual disabilities in recent decades, since World War II, movement activity on their behalf has been largely conducted by parent-dominated groups. Since public schools were established in the United States, children with intellectual and other mental disabilities had been routinely excluded from public schools or relegated to programs that provided few educational benefits. Parents with children who had more acute cognitive impairments were strongly encouraged to place them into state residential "schools," which provided minimal educational or training services and functioned largely as custodial institutions.

Beginning in the 1940s, parent groups formed in many American communities to lobby local school systems and state governments to open regular public schools to their children (Carey, 2009; Carey et al., 2020). Among the leaders in this political activity was The Arc, founded as The Association for Retarded Children in Pennsylvania and several other states. Faced with resistance or token compliance, The Arc and other parents turned to the courts, filing lawsuits that demanded that children be given access to public education regardless of their disabilities. Parent groups also engaged in legal action in the 1960s and 1970s, challenging conditions at state residential facilities for people with intellectual disabilities. These cases were filed in federal courts and successfully asserted that the US Constitution provisions for due process and equal protection forbade institutionalization without the provision of appropriate treatment. The resulting court rulings placed important restrictions on state institutions and helped to pave the way for the enactment of a federal law, ultimately called the Individuals with Disabilities Education Act (IDEA), which guaranteed the right to a free and appropriate public education and related services to anyone regardless of their disability. In the early 1970s, parent advocates were joined by self-advocates with intellectual disabilities in local chapters of People First, following a model established in Sweden in the preceding decade (Carey, 2009; Carey et al., 2020).

Major Disability Rights Movement Cross-Disability Groups

In the late 1960s, a new form of disability rights organization, the independent living center (ILC), was created in many US communities, and spread around the globe (Barnartt & Scotch, 2001; Dejong, 1979; Fleischer & Zames, 2001). One of the first was founded in Berkeley, California, to promote self-help for people with disabilities as they left the University of California to live on their own in the wider community (Fleischer & Zames, 2001; Scotch, 1984). ILCs offered peer counseling, information on accessible housing and employment, and help with hiring and training personal assistance providers, as well as supporting civil rights advocacy by their members. ILCs included individuals with a variety of disabling conditions to promote greater accessibility for all disabled people through sharing information and peer support.

In addition to the self-help provided by ILCs, cross-disability groups formed to pursue policy objectives of equal access to public transportation, public services, employment, and voting. An early example, the League of the Physically Handicapped, formed in the 1930s in New York City. The League argued for greater participation of people with a variety of disabling conditions in New Deal work relief programs available only to able-bodied individuals, and their protests led to the hiring of more than 1,500 people with disabilities. A national organization, the American Federation of the Physically Handicapped, was formed in 1940 to promote nondiscrimination in employment (Longmore, 2009).

In the 1960s, in part following models established by other 1960s-era social movements to advance rights for racial minorities and women, these groups combined protests, grassroots organizing, and political lobbying to advance the rights of people with disabilities. One of the first such groups was Disabled in Action in New York City, formed by a diverse collection of people with different disabilities and different social circumstances, which engaged in protests calling for accessibility in public transportation, overcoming discriminatory barriers in education and employment, and enactment of local ordinances and national legislation helping disabled people participate more equally in community life (Fleischer & Zames, 2001; Scotch, 1984). Other local cross-disability groups advocating for accessibility and against disability discrimination formed in Boston, Chicago, the San Francisco Bay Area, and numerous other American cities and college towns. In the United Kingdom, the Union of the Physically Impaired Against Segregation (UPIAS) and other cross-disability coalitions were formed to seek political changes to end the oppression of people with disabilities.

In the 1970s, such national coalitions of disability rights groups became established as local groups joined together, in part based on contacts established through mutual participation in federal policymaking of such agencies as the President's Committee for the Employment of the Handicapped (PCEH), which sponsored periodic national conferences (Scotch, 1984). The most prominent coalition was the American Coalition of Citizens with Disabilities (ACCD), established in 1974 by representatives of 19 groups representing the blind, the deaf, other physical disabilities, the independent living movement, and cross-disability activists (Fleischer & Zames, 2001; Scotch, 1984). ACCD became a vocal advocate for federal civil rights measures protecting people with disabilities, lobbying federal agencies, and seeking to mobilize local activists in support of strengthening new anti-discrimination laws. Other coalitions formed around specific disability policy issues to better coordinate lawsuits, lobbying, and protest activities. In the United Kingdom, the British Council of Disabled People (BCODP) formed in 1981 to represent 80 organizations that included 200,000 Britons with disabilities and the Direct Action Network developed a registry of over 1,000 activists willing to engage in civil disobedience. In Canada, the Coalition of Provincial Organizations of the Handicapped (COPOH) was established in 1976 with affiliates from most Canadian provinces, and the Coalition, subsequently renamed as the Council of Canadians with Disabilities, coordinated national protests in 1981 to advocate for a human rights amendment protecting disabled Canadians. In Denmark, de samivirkende Invalideorganisationer (DSI) has actively promoted the integration of Danes with disabilities into Danish society (Barnartt et al., 2001).

Groups promoting independent living and engaging in cross-disability advocacy also were formed in many other countries in the developed and lesser developed world. Longmore (2009) mentions the organization of such associations in Finland (the Threshold, established in 1975), Sri Lanka (the United Front of the Handicapped established in 1977), Scotland (the National Forum for Disabled People established in 1978), Jamaica (the Combined Disabilities Association established in 1981), Costa Rica (the Congress on the Rights of People with Disabilities established in 1982), and New Zealand (the Disabled Persons Assembly established in 1982), as well as coalitions in the Netherlands (1977), Brazil (1981), and Zambia (1983) (Barnartt et al., 2001). Multinational disability advocacy groups formed among blind people, deaf people, and people with psychiatric conditions by representatives from many national groups, and in 1981, Disability Peoples' International was organized to bring together disability advocates from around the globe, including most parts of the developing world (Driedger, 1989).

DISABILITY RIGHTS MOVEMENT STRATEGIES

Legal Advocacy

One particularly effective component of DRM activism in the United States has been legal strategies seeking protection through the courts, particularly in the 1970s when federal judges were open to extending procedural rights such as due process and equal protection to include people with disabilities (Scotch, 1984). Legal advocates from such organizations as the Disability Rights Education and Legal Defense Fund in Berkeley, California; the Public Interest Law Center of Philadelphia; the National Center for Law and the Handicapped in South Bend, Indiana; the Western Center on Law and the Handicapped in Los Angeles; and the Bazelon Center for Mental Health Law in Washington, DC, have successfully filed suit on behalf of individual disabled plaintiffs as well as instituting class action suits which sought to establish more general guarantees of legal rights (Scotch, 1984).

Legislative Advocacy

Another DRM strategy was legislative advocacy. An important focal point for DRM activity in the 1970s was the reauthorization of the federal Rehabilitation Act, the basic legislation for the national vocational rehabilitation system. The 50-year-old Rehabilitation Act was to be reauthorized by Congress in 1973, and provisions were added to the legislation prohibiting discrimination on the basis of disability by recipients of federal financial assistance, federal agencies, and federal contractors. These anti-discrimination provisions, contained in Title V of the revised law, were enacted but required clarifying regulations in order to be implemented. The regulations were drafted by the Office of Civil Rights staff from the Department of Health, Education, and Welfare (HEW) in consultation with ACCD representatives, and therefore reflected the perspective of the DRM. The draft regulations for Section 504, which applied to federally funded programs and activities such as local government agencies, schools and universities, hospitals and doctor offices, and many community nonprofits, created new standards for nondiscrimination, requiring "reasonable" accommodations to disabilities of staff and members of the public. The administration of President Gerald Ford was unwilling to release these regulations, and when the new administration of President Jimmy Carter took office in early 1977, further reluctance was expressed by incoming HEW Secretary Joseph Califano about issuing the regulations until well-publicized protests by disabled activists led him to issue the anti-discrimination rules (Scotch, 1984).

As discussed earlier, the enactment of Section 504 created protections from discrimination on the basis of disability in several institutional spheres that receive federal financial assistance, but left virtually untouched many other aspects of public life, including private employment. Accordingly, disability rights activists sought to broaden policy protections from discrimination in the 1980s. Their efforts were bolstered by a study conducted by the federal National Council on the Handicapped, subsequently renamed as the National Council on Disability (NCD), which, for the first time, surveyed people with disabilities about what barriers they faced in their lives (Louis Harris and Associates, 1986). While NCD was an appointed body whose members were chosen by conservative president Ronald Reagan, they included in their membership and staff a number of persons who identified with the DRM and were strongly committed to disability rights. Respondents to the NCD survey reported that the major challenge they faced in their lives was not their impairments, but rather the prejudices of other people.

The survey and pressure from the DRM led NCD to recommend the drafting of new legislation that would extend federal disability anti-discrimination law to cover private employment and other realms, including state and local government and telecommunications (National Council on the Handicapped, 1986). The proposal, named the Americans with Disabilities Act (ADA), built on Section 504's definitions, that included protection for those perceived as disabled and those with a history of disability, and regulatory approaches, that required "reasonable" accommodations unless they would impose an "undue burden" on businesses and other regulated entities (Davis, 2015).

While the proposed law received wide bipartisan support, there was opposition from some libertarian conservatives in Congress and the Republican administration of President George H. W. Bush and outside of government from representatives of business sectors most resistant to mandates for increased access (Davis, 2015). DRM activists sought to apply pressure both through lobbying potential allies in Congress and the Administration and by conducting protests to publicize their concerns. ADAPT conducted a series of demonstrations in Washington, DC, and around the nation. After Congressional debate that centered on who should be considered disabled for the purposes of the law and whether some types of businesses should be exempted from coverage, the legislation passed both houses of Congress by wide majorities, and it was signed into law by President Bush on July 26, 1990 (Davis, 2015).

The impact of the ADA, however, was to be limited by a series of federal court decisions that narrowed the definition of who qualified as disabled for the purposes of the law as well as less than proactive enforcement by federal agencies and recalcitrance by some employers and private entities (Krieger, 2003). Thanks to persistent efforts by DRM advocates in the 2000s, in 2008, Congress passed the ADA Restoration Amendments to reenact ADA's main provisions with more explicit language about who would be covered (Pettinicchio, 2019). It was anticipated that the new Act would make it easier to receive relief from disability discrimination.

A recent focal point for the DRM in the 21st century has been the United Nations Convention on the Rights of Persons with Disabilities (CRPD), an attempt to codify disability rights into international law that is loosely based on the ADA. CRPD was passed by the United Nations General Assembly in 2006 and referred to UN members for ratification. DRM groups across the globe have lobbied their national governments to ratify CRPD, and as of 2020, 181 nations had ratified CRPD (United Nations, n.d.). Notably absent from the ratifying nations was the United States, whose increasingly conservative Congress refused to approve the measure due to concerns expressed for the loss of sovereignty and a general mistrust by Republican legislators with any international agreements, even though the convention was consistent with existing American law (National Council on Disability, n.d.).

Protests

When legislative advocacy stalled, some DRM groups turned to protests (Barnartt & Scotch, 2001). In 1977, DRM leaders called for a national set of demonstrations in response, protesting at federal HEW regional offices around the United States. Protesters sat in at federal offices around the country to demand that the draft regulations be immediately put into effect. While most protests lasted a single day, the San Francisco sit-in lasted for 28 days, receiving considerable attention from the media, and giving national prominence to the DRM for the first time. Statements of support for the protesters came from elected officials, community leaders, and nondisabled protest groups such as the Black Panthers, an African American activist group. The Section 504 protests culminated in a commitment from the Carter administration officials to implement the regulations, which were put into effect shortly afterward. By highlighting the problems of discrimination faced by Americans with disabilities, and showing them to the nation as determined and successful political actors, the protests over the Section 504 regulations helped to further the growth of the DRM, which spread to communities across the United States (Scotch, 1984).

One place where DRM protests played an important role was in Denver, Colorado, where disability activists affiliated with an independent living center known as the Atlantis Community had been frustrated by the lack of accessible public transportation. Many people with disabilities rely heavily on public transit systems to get around, due to the combination of their often limited incomes and mobility impairments that may constrain their access to work, shop, or community activities. Denver's public bus system did not feature accessible vehicles, despite persistent community requests for them, and the legal mandate of Section 504, which applied to federally assisted local transit systems. Atlantis Community members formed a protest group, American Disabled for Public Transportation, or ADAPT, and engaged in demonstrations to draw attention to the inaccessible transit in their community. The ADAPT protesters, many of whom were wheelchair users, physically blocked Denver buses from operating and received a great deal of media attention for their cause. After a series of such demonstrations, ADAPT was successful in obtaining a commitment from the Denver public transit system to convert to accessible buses (Barnartt & Scotch, 2001; Fleischer & Zames, 2001; Johnson & Shaw, 2001).

This successful model of grassroots political protest spread, with numerous local chapters of ADAPT forming in many American cities to protest inaccessible local transportation. ADAPT extended their activities nationally, demonstrating at national conferences of public transit authorities to demand that all local public transportation be made accessible and that federal transportation funding only support accessible systems. The network of ADAPT activists formed a loosely knit national organization that worked to more generally promote the rights of people with disabilities. As is addressed later, in the late 1980s, ADAPT became a leading advocate for passage of the ADA, engaging in protests and lobbying until its passage in 1990 (Barnartt & Scotch, 2001; Fleischer & Zames, 2001; Johnson & Shaw, 2001).

With the enactment of ADA in 1990, federal mandates for accessible transportation were strengthened, and ADAPT members redirected their protest activities from accessible transportation to the nursing home industry (Scotch 2009). The impairments of many people with disabilities mean that they need assistance with a variety of activities of daily living. Individuals with sufficient resources, or with adequate insurance benefits, are able to live on their own in accessible homes, with assistive technology and/ or personal assistance aides, who may be family members or paid helpers. For others, who lack needed supports and financial resources, living in the community is difficult or impossible. In many instances, individuals with disabilities who do not have medical needs for skilled nursing care must nevertheless reside in nursing homes or assisted living facilities. For some who rely on Medicaid, they may be eligible for support only in an institutional setting, and not in their own homes, and they experience a forced dependence on institutional support. Life in such institutions is typically regimented, with residents lacking control over many aspects of their lives and dependent on personal assistance staff they do not hire, supervise, or control. For some frail elderly people with degenerative health conditions, a nursing home may be an appropriate setting, but for many others, particularly nonelderly adults with physical but not mental impairments, nursing home care is essentially incarceration (Ben-Moshe et al. 2014). While the federal Medicaid program offers states an alternative stream of funding for home and community-based services which would allow more people with disabilities to live outside of institutions, in many states Medicaid programs favor placement in nursing homes over community settings. This is in part attributable to the political influence of the nursing home industry, and in part to a cultural approach that prioritizes life in medically controlled settings over greater independence and autonomy (Scotch, 2009).

Since 1990, ADAPT has focused its advocacy efforts on changing state and federal policies to promote noninstitutional alternatives to nursing home care. In these efforts, they have retained the combination of confrontational public protests against corporate leaders with political lobbying campaigns that was successful for them in the struggles for accessible transit and passage of the ADA (Pettinicchio, 2019). ADAPT activists converge on corporate meetings or at targeted institutions to demand shifts away from reliance on nursing homes to support disabled people. These persistent and visible protests have helped to generate public discussion about public policies on long-term care, but they have had only limited impact on policies themselves.

Having reviewed the various components of the DRM and the strategies it has undertaken, we now turn to a brief consideration of its significance.

THE SIGNIFICANCE OF THE DISABILITY RIGHTS MOVEMENT

Unfortunately, neither laws nor aspirational statements have been reliable guarantees of access; they typically have required some combination of vigorous enforcement and voluntary compliance that are not always forthcoming, particularly in the absence of proactive advocacy by DRM members.

On another front, the proliferation of restrictive segregated facilities confining many people with disabilities has been reduced, but again, not eliminated. Many more people are able to live inclusively in communities, but many others remain in coercive residential placements, even if those may be less massive and removed from society than was the case in the mid-20th century. Many more children with disabilities are being educated in regular classrooms, although not always in appropriate ways.

Overall, the benefits of enhanced accessibility are probably experienced more by people from middle-class families than by those from lower SES backgrounds, by whites more than people of color, by those who are heteronormative compared to people who identify as LGBTQ, and by individuals with better access to high-quality education than by those lacking such access. Disability is related intersectionally to other dimensions of social inequality, and the ability to take advantage of improved access is more available to those with other societal advantages and less so to those in otherwise marginalized communities.

If the economic, political, and social status of people with disabilities is assessed more holistically, large structural disadvantages persist and may have actually grown worse. By measures of poverty, employment status, and income, people with disabilities may on average be no better off than they were before the rise of the DRM, and many may have experienced greater difficulties with changes in the postindustrial economy (Maroto & Pettinicchio, 2015). However, there are some offsetting changes that have improved the status of people with disabilities. Technological improvements in telecommunications, prosthetic aids, pharmaceutical treatments, and medical devices have allowed many people with disabilities greater opportunities for societal participation and afforded them better quality of life.

Finally, beyond measures of economic and social status, the DRM has had a lasting effect on the development of an active and rich disability culture that includes many, if not all, persons with disabilities. That culture has emphasized self-worth, self-help, and peer support, and rejected associations of inferiority, incapacity, and dependence. The DRM has enhanced a positive sense of common identity and purpose among people with disabilities, in contrast to the stigma traditionally associated with impairment and disability. Pride movements have spread among people who are culturally deaf, among wheelchair users, among the neurodiverse, and many other segments of the disability community. And that evolving disability culture and community may serve as the basis for sustaining the DRM and its goals in the future.

REFERENCES

Barnartt, S., & Scotch, R. (2001). *Disability protests: Contentious politics 1970–1999*. Gallaudet University Press.

Barnartt, S., Schriner, K., & Scotch, R. (2001). Advocacy and political action. In G. Albrecht, K. D. Seelman, & M. Bury (Eds.), *Handbook of disability studies* (pp. 430–449). SAGE Publications.

Barnes, C. (2012). Understanding the social model of disability: Past, present, and future. In N. Watson, A. Roulstone, & C. Thomas (Eds.), *Routledge handbook of disability studies* (pp. 12–29). Routledge.

Barton, L. (1992). Disability and the necessity for a socio-political perspective. In *Monograph 51: Disability and the necessity for a socio-political perspective* (pp. 1–14). World Rehabilitation Fund.

Ben-Moshe, L., Chapman, C., & Carey, A. C. (Eds.). (2014). *Disability incarcerated: Imprisonment and disability in the United States and Canada*. Palgrave Macmillan.

Bickenbach, J. E. (1999). Minority rights or university participation; the politics of disablement. In M. Jones & L. A. P. Marks (Eds.), *Disability, divers-ability and legal change* (pp. 101–115). Kluwer Law International.

Burch, S. (2002). *Signs of resistance: American deaf cultural history, 1900 to World War II*. NYU Press.

Carey, A. C. (2009) *On the margins of citizenship: Intellectual disability and civil rights in twentieth-century America*. Temple University Press.

Carey, A. C., Block, P., & Scotch, R. K. (2019). Parent-led organizations and social movement framing. *Disability Studies Quarterly, 39*(1). doi:http://dx.doi.org/10.18061/dsq.v39i1

Carey, A. C., Block, P., & Scotch, R. K. (2020). *Allies and obstacles: Disability activism and parents of children with disabilities*. Temple University Press.

Charlton, J. I. (1998). *Nothing about us without us: Disability oppression and empowerment*. University of California Press.

Christiansen, J. B., & Barnartt, S. N. (2003). *Deaf president now! The 1988 revolution at Gallaudet University*. Gallaudet University Press.

Davis, L. J. (2015). *Enabling acts: The hidden story of how the Americans with Disabilities Act gave the largest US minority its rights*. Beacon Press.

Dejong, G. (1979). Independent living: From social movement to analytic paradigm. *Archives of Physical Medicine and Rehabilitation, 60*, 435–446.

Driedger, D. (1989). *The last civil rights movement: Disabled peoples' international*. St. Martin's Press.

Fleischer, D. Z., & Zames, F. (2001). *The disability rights movement: From charity to confrontation*. Temple University Press.

Gerber, D. A. (2009). Veterans. In S. Burch (Ed.), *Encyclopedia of American disability history* (pp. 926–928). Facts on File.

Hahn, H. (1985). Toward a politics of disability: Definitions, disciplines, and policies. *The Social Science Journal, 22*(4), 87–105.

Hatfield, A. B. (1981). Self-help groups for families of the mentally ill. *Social Work, 26*(5), 408–413.

Jennings, A. (2016). *Out of the horrors of war: Disability politics in World War II America.* University of Pennsylvania Press.

Johnson, M., & Shaw, B. (2001). *To ride the public's buses: The fight that built a movement.* The Advocado Press.

Krieger, L. H. (Ed.) (2003). *Backlash against the ADA: Reinterpreting disability rights.* University of Michigan Press.

Longmore, P. K. (2009). Disability rights movement. In S. Burch (Ed.), *Encyclopedia of American disability history* (pp. 280–285). Facts on File.

Louis Harris and Associates. (1986). *The ICD survey of disabled Americans: Bringing disabled Americans into the mainstream: A nationwide survey of 1,000 disabled people.* International Center for the Disabled.

Maroto, M., & Pettinicchio, D. (2015). Twenty-five years after the ADA: Situating disability in America's system of stratification. *Disability Studies Quarterly, 35*(3). doi:http://dx.doi.org/10.18061/dsq.v35i3

Matson, F. (1990). *Walking alone and marching together: A history of the organized blind movement.* National Federation of the Blind.

McLean, A. (2010). The mental health consumers/survivors movement in the United States. In T.L. Scheid & T. N. Brown (Eds.), *A handbook for the study of mental health: Social contacts, theories, and systems* (2nd ed., pp. 461–477). Cambridge University Press.

National Council on Disability. (n.d.). *NCD statement on failed CRPD ratification vote in the Senate.* National Council on Disability, Washington DC. https://ncd.gov/newsroom/2012/120512.

National Council on the Handicapped. (1986). *Toward independence: An assessment of federal laws and programs affecting persons with disabilities—with legislative recommendations.* National Council on the Handicapped.

Nielsen, K. (2012). *A disability history of the United States.* Beacon Press.

Pelka, F. (1997). *The ABC-CLIO Companion to the disability rights movement.* ABC-CLIO.

Pettinicchio, D. (2019). *Politics of empowerment: Disability rights and the cycle of American policy reform.* Stanford University Press.

Rose, S. F. (2017). *No right to be idle: The invention of disability, 1840s–1930s.* University of North Carolina Press.

Scotch, R. K. (1984). *From good will to civil rights: Transforming federal disability policy.* Temple University Press.

Scotch, R. K. (2000). Models of disability and the response to the Americans with Disabilities Act. *Berkeley Journal of Employment and Labor Law, 21*(1), 213–222.

Scotch, R. K. (2002). Paradigms of American social research on disability: What's new? *Disability Studies Quarterly, 22*(2), 23–34.

Scotch, R.K. (2009). Medicaid. In S. Burch (Ed.), *Encyclopedia of American disability history* (pp. 601–602). Facts on File.

Scotch, R. K., & Schriner, K. (1997). Disability as human variation: Implications for policy. *Annals of the American Academy of Political and Social Science, 549*, 148–159.

Tomes, N. (2006). The patient as a policy factor: A historical case study of the consumer/survivor movement in mental health. *Health Affairs, 25*(3), 720–729.

Union of the Physically Impaired Against Segregation. (1975). *Fundamental principles of disability.* https://disability-studies.leeds.ac.uk/wp-content/uploads/sites/40/library/UPIAS-fundamental-principles.pdf.

United Nations. (n.d.). *Convention of the rights of persons with disabilities.* https://www.un.org/development/desa/disabilities/convention-on-the-rights-of-persons-with-disabilities.html.

INDEX

Tables, figures, and boxes are indicated by *t*, *f*, and *b* following the page number